OPERATING SYSTEMS:

DESIGN AND IMPLEMENTATION

Second Edition

OPERATING SYSTEMS:
Design and Implementation

Second Edition

Andrew S. Tanenbaum

Vrije Universiteit
Amsterdam, The Netherlands

Albert S. Woodhull
Hampshire College
Amherst, Massachusetts

PRENTICE HALL, Upper Saddle River, New Jersey 07458

Library of Congress Cataloging-in-Publication Data
Tanenbaum, Andrew S.
    Operating systems : design and implementation / Andrew S. Tanenbaum,
    Albert S. Woodhull. — 2nd ed.
        p. cm.
    Includes bibliological references and index.
    ISBN: 0-13-638677-6
    1. Operating systems (Computers). I. Woodhull, Albert
    II. Title.
    QA76.76.063T36 1997
    005.4'32--dc21   96-37153
                                                        CIP

Acquisitions editor: ALAN APT
Developmental editor: SONDRA CHAVEZ
Production editor: ROSE KERNAN
Editor-in-chief: MARCIA HORTON
Copy editor: MARTHA WILLIAMS
Cover designer: BRUCE KENSELAAR
Director of production and manufacturing: DAVID W. RICCARDI
Managing editor: BAYANI MENDOZA DE LEON
Manufacturing buyer: DONNA SULLIVAN
Interior designer/Compositor: ANDREW S. TANENBAUM
Cover cartoon: JOS COLLIGNON

©1997, 1987 by Prentice-Hall, Inc.
Simon & Schuster/ A Viacom Company
Upper Saddle River , New Jersey 07458

The author and publisher of this book have used their best efforts in preparing this book. These efforts include the development, research, and testing of the theories and programs to determine their effectiveness. The author and publisher make no warranty of any kind, expressed or implied, with regard to these programs or the documentation contained in this book. The author and publisher shall not be liable in any event for incidental or consequential damages in connection with, or arising out of, the furnishing, performance, or use of these programs.

Printed in the United States of America

10 9 8 7 6 5 4 3 2

ISBN 0-13-638677-6

Prentice-Hall International (UK) Limited, London
Prentice-Hall of Australia Pty. Limited, Sydney
Prentice-Hall Canada Inc., Toronto
Prentice-Hall Hispanoamericana, S.A., Mexico
Prentice-Hall of India Private Limited, New Delhi
Prentice-Hall of Japan, Inc., Tokyo
Simon & Schuster Asia Pte. Ltd., Singapore
Editora Prentice-Hall do Brasil, Ltda., Rio de Janeiro

To Suzanne, Barbara, Marvin, and Little Bram

- AST

To Barbara and Gordon

- ASW

CONTENTS

2 PROCESSES   47

4 MEMORY MANAGEMENT 309

APPENDICES

PREFACE

Most books on operating systems are strong on theory and weak on practice. This one aims to provide a better balance between the two. It covers all the fundamental principles in great detail, including processes, interprocess communication, semaphores, monitors, message passing, scheduling algorithms, input/output, deadlocks, device drivers, memory management, paging algorithms, file system design, security, and protection mechanisms. But it also discusses one particular system—MINIX, a UNIX-compatible operating system—in detail, and even provides a complete source code listing for study. This arrangement allows the reader not only to learn the principles, but also to see how they are applied in a real operating system.

When the first edition of this book appeared in 1987, it caused something of a small revolution in the way operating systems courses were taught. Until then, most courses just covered theory. With the appearance of MINIX, many schools began to have laboratory courses in which students examined a real operating system to see how it worked inside. We consider this trend highly desirable and hope this second edition strengthens it.

It its first 10 years, MINIX has undergone many changes. The original code was designed for a 256K 8088-based IBM PC with two diskette drives and no hard disk. It was also based on Version 7 of UNIX. As time went on, MINIX evolved in many ways. For example, the current version will now run on anything from the original PC (in 16-bit real mode) to large Pentiums with massive hard disks (in 32-bit protected mode). It also changed from being based on Version 7, to being based on the international POSIX standard (IEEE 1003.1 and ISO 9945-1). Finally, many features were added, perhaps too many in our view, but too few in the view of some other people, which led to the creation of LINUX. In addition, MINIX was ported to many other platforms, including the Macintosh, Amiga, Atari, and SPARC. This book covers only MINIX 2.0, which so far runs only on computers with an 80x86 CPU, on systems which can emulate such a CPU, or on the SPARC.

This second edition of the book has many changes throughout. Nearly all of the material on principles has been revised, and considerable new material has been added. However, the main change is the discussion of the new, POSIX-based MINIX, and the inclusion of the new code in this book. Also new is the inclusion of a CD-ROM in each book containing the full MINIX source code plus instructions for installing MINIX on a PC (see the file README.TXT in the main CD-ROM directory).

Setting up MINIX on an 80x86 PC, whether for individual use or for a laboratory is straightforward. A disk partition of at least 30 MB must be made for it, then it can be installed by just following the instructions in the *README.TXT* file on the CD-ROM. To print the *README.TXT* file on a PC, first start MS-DOS, if it is not already running (from WINDOWS, click on the MS-DOS) icon. Then type

```
copy readme.txt prn
```

to make the printout. The file can also be examined in *edit*, *wordpad*, *notepad*, or any other text editor that can handle flat ASCII text.

For schools (or individuals) that do not have PCs available, two other options are now available. Two simulators are included on the CD-ROM. One, written by Paul Ashton, runs on SPARCs. It runs MINIX as a user program on top of Solaris. As a consequence, MINIX is compiled into a SPARC binary and runs at full speed. In this mode, MINIX is no longer an operating system, but a user program, so some changes to the low-level code were necessary.

The other simulator was written by Kevin P. Lawton of Bochs Software Company. This simulator interprets the Intel 80386 instruction set and enough I/O gear that MINIX can run on the simulator. Of course running on top of an interpreter costs some performance, but it makes debugging much easier for students. This simulator has the advantage that it will run on any computer that supports the M.I.T. X Window System. For more information about both simulators, please see the CD-ROM.

The development of MINIX is an ongoing proposition. The contents of this book and its CD-ROM are merely a snapshot of the system as of the time of publication. For the current state of affairs, please see the MINIX home page on the World Wide Wide, *http://www.cs.vu.nl/~ast/minix.html*. In addition, MINIX has its own USENET newsgroup: *comp.os.minix*, to which readers can subscribe to find out what is going on in the MINIX world. For those with e-mail, but without newsgroup access, there is also a mailing list. Write to *listserv@listserv.nodak.edu* with "subscribe minix-l <your full name>" as the first and only line in the body of the message. You will receive more information by return e-mail.

For classroom use, a problem solutions manual is available, to instructors only, from Prentice Hall. PostScript files containing all the figures in the book, suitable for making overhead sheets, can be found by following the link marked "Software and supplementary material" from *http://www.cs.vu.nl/~ast/*.

We have been extremely fortunate in having the help of many people during the course of this project. First and foremost, we would like to thank Kees Bot for doing the lion's share of the work in making MINIX conform to the standard and for managing the distribution. Without his enormous help, we would never have made it. He wrote large chunks of code himself (e.g. the POSIX terminal I/O), cleaned up other sections, and repaired numerous bugs that had crept in over the years. Thank you for a job well done.

Bruce Evans, Philip Homburg, Will Rose, and Michael Temari have all contributed to the development of MINIX over the years. Hundreds of other people have contributed to MINIX via the newsgroup. There were so many of them and their contributions have been so varied that we cannot even begin to list them all here, so the best we can do is a generic thank you to all of them.

Several people read parts of the manuscript and made suggestions. We would like to give our special thanks to John Casey, Dale Grit, and Frans Kaashoek.

A number of students at the Vrije Universiteit tested the beta version of the CD-ROM. These were: Ahmed Batou, Goran Dokic, Peter Gijzel, Thomer Gil, Dennis Grimbergen, Roderick Groesbeek, Wouter Haring, Guido Kollerie, Mark Lassche, Raymond Ris, Frans ter Borg, Alex van Ballegooy, Ries van der Velden, Alexander Wels, and Thomas Zeeman. We would like to thank all of them for their careful work and detailed reports.

ASW would also like to thank several of his former students, particularly Peter W. Young of Hampshire College and Maria Isabel Sanchez and William Puddy Vargas of the Universidad Nacional Autonoma de Nicaragua for the part their interest in MINIX played in sustaining his efforts.

Finally, we would like to thank our families. Suzanne has been through this ten times now. Barbara has been through it nine times now. Marvin has been through it eight times now. Even Little Bram has been through it four times. It's kind of getting to be routine, but the love and support is still much appreciated. (ast)

As for Al's Barbara, this is the first time she has been through this. It would not have been possible without her support, patience, and good humor. It has been Gordon's good fortune to have been away at college through most of this. But it is a delight to have a son who understands and cares about the same things that fascinate me. (asw)

Andrew S. Tanenbaum
Albert S. Woodhull

ABOUT THE AUTHORS

Andrew S. Tanenbaum has an S.B. degree from M.I.T. and a Ph.D. from the University of California at Berkeley. He is currently a Professor of Computer Science at the Vrije Universiteit in Amsterdam, The Netherlands, where he heads the Computer Systems Group. He is also Dean of the Advanced School for Computing and Imaging, an inter-university graduate school doing research on advanced parallel, distributed, and imaging systems. Nevertheless, he is trying very hard to avoid turning into a bureaucrat.

In the past, he has done research on compilers, operating systems, networking, and local-area distributed systems. His current research focuses primarily on the design of wide-area distributed systems that scale to millions of users. These research projects have led to over 70 refereed papers in journals and conference proceedings, and five books.

Prof. Tanenbaum has also produced a considerable volume of software. He was the principal architect of the Amsterdam Compiler Kit, a widely-used toolkit for writing portable compilers, as well as of MINIX. Together with his Ph.D. students and programmers, he helped design the Amoeba distributed operating system, a high-performance microkernel-based distributed operating system. MINIX and Amoeba are now available for free for education and research via the Internet.

His Ph.D. students have gone on to greater glory after getting their degrees. He is very proud of them. In this respect he resembles a mother hen.

Prof. Tanenbaum is a Fellow of the ACM, a Senior Member of the IEEE, a member of the Royal Netherlands Academy of Arts and Sciences, winner of the 1994 ACM Karl V. Karlstrom Outstanding Educator Award, and winner of the 1997 ACM/SIGCSE Award for Outstanding Contributions to Computer Science Education. He is also listed in *Who's Who in the World*. His home page on the World Wide Web can be found at URL *http://www.cs.vu.nl/~ast/* .

Albert S. Woodhull has an S.B. degree from M.I.T. and a Ph.D. from the University of Washington. He entered M.I.T. intending to become an electrical engineer, but he emerged as a biologist. He has been associated with the School of Natural Science of Hampshire College in Amherst, Massachusetts, since 1973. As a biologist using electronic instrumentation, he started working with microcomputers when they became readily available. His instrumentation courses for science students evolved into courses in computer interfacing and real-time programming.

Dr. Woodhull has always had strong interests in teaching and in the role of science and technology in development. Before entering graduate school he taught high school science for two years in Nigeria. More recently he spent several sabbaticals teaching computer science at Nicaragua's Universidad Nacional de Ingenieria and the Universidad Nacional Autonoma de Nicaragua.

He is interested in computers as electronic systems, and in interactions of computers with other electronic systems. He particularly enjoys teaching in the areas of computer architecture, assembly language programming, operating systems, and computer communications. He has also worked as a consultant in the development of electronic instrumentation and related software.

He has many nonacademic interests as well, including various outdoor sports, amateur radio, and reading. He enjoys travelling and trying to make himself understood in languages other than his native English. His World Wide Web home page is located on a system running MINIX, at URL *http://minix1.hampshire.edu/asw/* .

OPERATING SYSTEMS:

DESIGN AND IMPLEMENTATION

Second Edition

1

INTRODUCTION

Without its software, a computer is basically a useless lump of metal. With its software, a computer can store, process, and retrieve information; display multimedia documents; search the Internet; and engage in many other valuable activities to earn its keep. Computer software can be divided roughly into two kinds: system programs, which manage the operation of the computer itself, and application programs, which perform the actual work the user wants. The most fundamental system program is the **operating system**, which controls all the computer's resources and provides the base upon which the application programs can be written.

A modern computer system consists of one or more processors, some main memory (often known as RAM—Random Access Memory), disks, printers, network interfaces, and other input/output devices. All in all, a complex system. Writing programs that keep track of all these components and use them correctly, let alone optimally, is an extremely difficult job. If every programmer had to be concerned with how disk drives work, and with all the dozens of things that could go wrong when reading a disk block, it is unlikely that many programs could be written at all.

Many years ago it became abundantly clear that some way had to be found to shield programmers from the complexity of the hardware. The way that has evolved gradually is to put a layer of software on top of the bare hardware, to manage all parts of the system, and present the user with an interface or **virtual**

machine that is easier to understand and program. This layer of software is the operating system and forms the subject of this book.

The situation is shown in Fig. 1-1. At the bottom is the hardware, which, in many cases, is itself composed of two or more layers. The lowest layer contains physical devices, consisting of integrated circuit chips, wires, power supplies, cathode ray tubes, and similar physical devices. How these are constructed and how they work is the province of the electrical engineer.

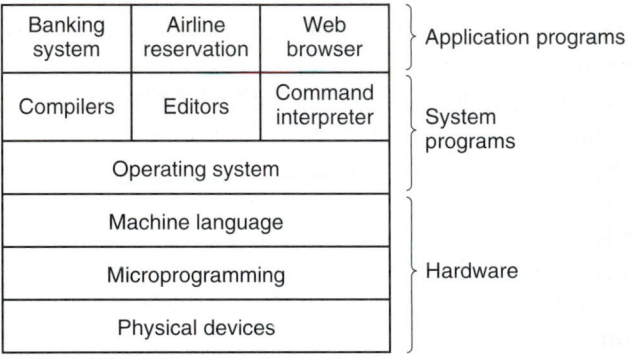

Figure 1-1. A computer system consists of hardware, system programs, and application programs.

Next (on some machines) comes a layer of primitive software that directly controls these devices and provides a cleaner interface to the next layer. This software, called the **microprogram**, is usually located in read-only memory. It is actually an interpreter, fetching the machine language instructions such as ADD, MOVE, and JUMP, and carrying them out as a series of little steps. To carry out an ADD instruction, for example, the microprogram must determine where the numbers to be added are located, fetch them, add them, and store the result somewhere. The set of instructions that the microprogram interprets defines the **machine language**, which is not really part of the hard machine at all, but computer manufacturers always describe it in their manuals as such, so many people think of it as being the real "machine."

Some computers, called **RISC** (**Reduced Instruction Set Computers**) machines, do not have a microprogramming level. On these machines, the hardware executes the machine language instructions directly. As examples, the Motorola 680x0 has a microprogramming level, but the IBM PowerPC does not.

The machine language typically has between 50 and 300 instructions, mostly for moving data around the machine, doing arithmetic, and comparing values. In this layer, the input/output devices are controlled by loading values into special **device registers**. For example, a disk can be commanded to read by loading the values of the disk address, main memory address, byte count, and direction (READ or WRITE) into its registers. In practice, many more parameters are needed, and the status returned by the drive after an operation is highly complex. Furthermore, for many I/O devices, timing plays an important role in the programming.

A major function of the operating system is to hide all this complexity and give the programmer a more convenient set of instructions to work with. For example, READ BLOCK FROM FILE is conceptually simpler than having to worry about the details of moving disk heads, waiting for them to settle down, and so on.

On top of the operating system is the rest of the system software. Here we find the command interpreter (shell), window systems, compilers, editors, and similar application-independent programs. It is important to realize that these programs are definitely not part of the operating system, even though they are typically supplied by the computer manufacturer. This is a crucial, but subtle, point. The operating system is that portion of the software that runs in **kernel mode** or **supervisor mode**. It is protected from user tampering by the hardware (ignoring for the moment some of the older microprocessors that do not have hardware protection at all). Compilers and editors run in **user mode**. If a user does not like a particular compiler, he† is free to write his own if he so chooses; he is not free to write his own disk interrupt handler, which is part of the operating system and is normally protected by hardware against attempts by users to modify it.

Finally, above the system programs come the application programs. These programs are purchased or written by the users to solve their particular problems, such as word processing, spreadsheets, engineering calculations, or game playing.

1.1 WHAT IS AN OPERATING SYSTEM?

Most computer users have had some experience with an operating system, but it is difficult to pin down precisely what an operating system is. Part of the problem is that operating systems perform two basically unrelated functions, and depending on who is doing the talking, you hear mostly about one function or the other. Let us now look at both.

1.1.1 The Operating System as an Extended Machine

As mentioned earlier, the **architecture** (instruction set, memory organization, I/O, and bus structure) of most computers at the machine language level is primitive and awkward to program, especially for input/output. To make this point more concrete, let us briefly look at how floppy disk I/O is done using the NEC PD765 (or equivalent) controller chip, which is used on most personal computers. (Throughout this book we will use the terms "floppy disk" and "diskette"

---

† "He" should be read as "he or she" throughout the book.

interchangeably.) The PD765 has 16 commands, each specified by loading between 1 and 9 bytes into a device register. These commands are for reading and writing data, moving the disk arm, and formatting tracks, as well as initializing, sensing, resetting, and recalibrating the controller and the drives.

The most basic commands are READ and WRITE, each of which requires 13 parameters, packed into 9 bytes. These parameters specify such items as the address of the disk block to be read, the number of sectors per track, the recording mode used on the physical medium, the intersector gap spacing, and what to do with a deleted-data-address-mark. If you do not understand this mumbo jumbo, do not worry; that is precisely the point—it is rather esoteric. When the operation is completed, the controller chip returns 23 status and error fields packed into 7 bytes. As if this were not enough, the floppy disk programmer must also be constantly aware of whether the motor is on or off. If the motor is off, it must be turned on (with a long startup delay) before data can be read or written. The motor cannot be left on too long, however, or the floppy disk will wear out. The programmer is thus forced to deal with the trade-off between long startup delays versus wearing out floppy disks (and losing the data on them).

Without going into the *real* details, it should be clear that the average programmer probably does not want to get too intimately involved with the programming of floppy disks (or hard disks, which are just as complex and quite different). Instead, what the programmer wants is a simple, high-level abstraction to deal with. In the case of disks, a typical abstraction would be that the disk contains a collection of named files. Each file can be opened for reading or writing, then read or written, and finally closed. Details such as whether or not recording should use modified frequency modulation and what the current state of the motor is should not appear in the abstraction presented to the user.

The program that hides the truth about the hardware from the programmer and presents a nice, simple view of named files that can be read and written is, of course, the operating system. Just as the operating system shields the programmer from the disk hardware and presents a simple file-oriented interface, it also conceals a lot of unpleasant business concerning interrupts, timers, memory management, and other low-level features. In each case, the abstraction offered by the operating system is simpler and easier to use than the underlying hardware.

In this view, the function of the operating system is to present the user with the equivalent of an **extended machine** or **virtual machine** that is easier to program than the underlying hardware. How the operating system achieves this goal is a long story, which we will study in detail throughout this book.

1.1.2 The Operating System as a Resource Manager

The concept of the operating system as primarily providing its users with a convenient interface is a top-down view. An alternative, bottom-up, view holds that the operating system is there to manage all the pieces of a complex system.

Modern computers consist of processors, memories, timers, disks, mice, network interfaces, laser printers, and a wide variety of other devices. In the alternative view, the job of the operating system is to provide for an orderly and controlled allocation of the processors, memories, and I/O devices among the various programs competing for them.

Imagine what would happen if three programs running on some computer all tried to print their output simultaneously on the same printer. The first few lines of printout might be from program 1, the next few from program 2, then some from program 3, and so forth. The result would be chaos. The operating system can bring order to the potential chaos by buffering all the output destined for the printer on the disk. When one program is finished, the operating system can then copy its output from the disk file where it has been stored to the printer, while at the same time the other program can continue generating more output, oblivious to the fact that the output is not really going to the printer (yet).

When a computer (or network) has multiple users, the need for managing and protecting the memory, I/O devices, and other resources is even greater, since the users might otherwise interfere with one another. In addition, users often need to share not only hardware, but information (files, data bases, etc.) as well. In short, this view of the operating system holds that its primary task is to keep track of who is using which resource, to grant resource requests, to account for usage, and to mediate conflicting requests from different programs and users.

1.2 HISTORY OF OPERATING SYSTEMS

Operating systems have been evolving through the years. In the following sections we will briefly look at this development. Since operating systems historically have been closely tied to the architecture of the computers on which they run, we will look at successive generations of computers to see what their operating systems were like. This mapping of operating system generations to computer generations is crude, but it does provide some structure where there would otherwise be none.

The first true digital computer was designed by the English mathematician Charles Babbage (1792–1871). Although Babbage spent most of his life and fortune trying to build his "analytical engine," he never got it working properly because it was purely mechanical, and the technology of his day could not produce the required wheels, gears, and cogs to the high precision that he needed. Needless to say, the analytical engine did not have an operating system.

As an interesting historical aside, Babbage realized that he would need software for his analytical engine, so he hired a young woman, named Ada Lovelace, who was the daughter of the famed British poet, Lord Byron, as the world's first programmer. The programming language Ada[®] is named after her.

1.2.1 The First Generation (1945–55) Vacuum Tubes and Plugboards

After Babbage's unsuccessful efforts, little progress was made in constructing digital computers until World War II. Around the mid-1940s, Howard Aiken at Harvard, John von Neumann at the Institute for Advanced Study in Princeton, J. Presper Eckert and William Mauchley at the University of Pennsylvania, and Konrad Zuse in Germany, among others, all succeeded in building calculating engines using vacuum tubes. These machines were enormous, filling up entire rooms with tens of thousands of vacuum tubes, but were much slower than even the cheapest personal computer available today.

In these early days, a single group of people designed, built, programmed, operated, and maintained each machine. All programming was done in absolute machine language, often by wiring up plugboards to control the machine's basic functions. Programming languages were unknown (not even assembly language). Operating systems were unheard of. The usual mode of operation was for the programmer to sign up for a block of time on the signup sheet on the wall, then come down to the machine room, insert his or her plugboard into the computer, and spend the next few hours hoping that none of the 20,000 or so vacuum tubes would burn out during the run. Virtually all the problems were straightforward numerical calculations, such as grinding out tables of sines and cosines.

By the early 1950s, the routine had improved somewhat with the introduction of punched cards. It was now possible to write programs on cards and read them in, instead of using plugboards; otherwise the procedure was the same.

1.2.2 The Second Generation (1955–65) Transistors and Batch Systems

The introduction of the transistor in the mid-1950s changed the picture radically. Computers became reliable enough that they could be manufactured and sold to paying customers with the expectation that they would continue to function long enough to get some useful work done. For the first time, there was a clear separation between designers, builders, operators, programmers, and maintenance personnel.

These machines were locked away in specially air conditioned computer rooms, with staffs of professional operators to run them. Only big corporations, or major government agencies or universities could afford the multimillion dollar price tag. To run a **job** (i.e., a program or set of programs), a programmer would first write the program on paper (in FORTRAN or assembler), then punch it on cards. He would then bring the card deck down to the input room and hand it to one of the operators.

When the computer finished whatever job it was currently running, an operator would go over to the printer and tear off the output and carry it over to the output room, so that the programmer could collect it later. Then he would take one of the card decks that had been brought from the input room and read it in. If the

FORTRAN compiler was needed, the operator would have to get it from a file cabinet and read it in. Much computer time was wasted while operators were walking around the machine room.

Given the high cost of the equipment, it is not surprising that people quickly looked for ways to reduce the wasted time. The solution generally adopted was the **batch system.** The idea behind it was to collect a tray full of jobs in the input room and then read them onto a magnetic tape using a small, (relatively) inexpensive computer, such as the IBM 1401, which was very good at reading cards, copying tapes, and printing output, but not at all good at numerical calculations. Other, much more expensive machines, such as the IBM 7094, were used for the real computing. This situation is shown in Fig. 1-2.

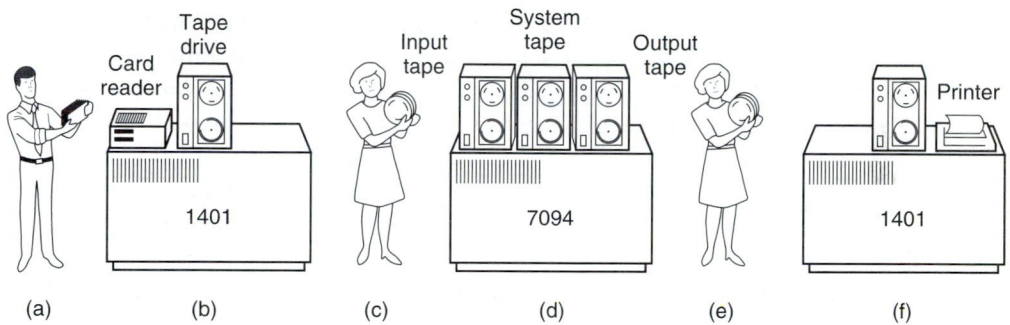

Figure 1-2. An early batch system. (a) Programmers bring cards to 1401. (b) 1401 reads batch of jobs onto tape. (c) Operator carries input tape to 7094. (d) 7094 does computing. (e) Operator carries output tape to 1401. (f) 1401 prints output.

After about an hour of collecting a batch of jobs, the tape was rewound and brought into the machine room, where it was mounted on a tape drive. The operator then loaded a special program (the ancestor of today's operating system), which read the first job from tape and ran it. The output was written onto a second tape, instead of being printed. After each job finished, the operating system automatically read the next job from the tape and began running it. When the whole batch was done, the operator removed the input and output tapes, replaced the input tape with the next batch, and brought the output tape to a 1401 for printing **off line** (i.e., not connected to the main computer).

The structure of a typical input job is shown in Fig. 1-3. It started out with a $JOB card, specifying the maximum run time in minutes, the account number to be charged, and the programmer's name. Then came a $FORTRAN card, telling the operating system to load the FORTRAN compiler from the system tape. It was followed by the program to be compiled, and then a $LOAD card, directing the operating system to load the object program just compiled. (Compiled programs were often written on scratch tapes and had to be loaded explicitly.) Next came the $RUN card, telling the operating system to run the program with the data following it. Finally, the $END card marked the end of the job. These primitive control cards were the forerunners of modern job control languages and command interpreters.

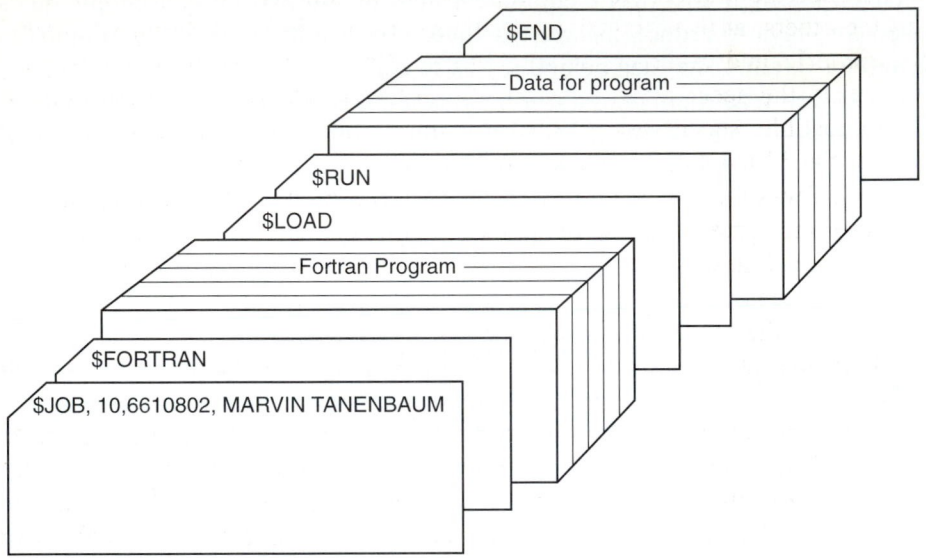

Figure 1-3. Structure of a typical FMS job.

Large second-generation computers were used mostly for scientific and engineering calculations, such as solving partial differential equations. They were largely programmed in FORTRAN and assembly language. Typical operating systems were FMS (the Fortran Monitor System) and IBSYS, IBM's operating system for the 7094.

1.2.3 The Third Generation (1965–1980): ICs and Multiprogramming

By the early 1960s, most computer manufacturers had two distinct, and totally incompatible, product lines. On the one hand there were the word-oriented, large-scale scientific computers, such as the 7094, which were used for numerical calculations in science and engineering. On the other hand, there were the character-oriented, commercial computers, such as the 1401, which were widely used for tape sorting and printing by banks and insurance companies.

Developing and maintaining two completely different product lines was an expensive proposition for the manufacturers. In addition, many new computer customers initially needed a small machine but later outgrew it and wanted a bigger machine that would run all their old programs, but faster.

IBM attempted to solve both of these problems at a single stroke by introducing the System/360. The 360 was a series of software-compatible machines ranging from 1401-sized to much more powerful than the 7094. The machines differed only in price and performance (maximum memory, processor speed, number of I/O devices permitted, and so forth.). Since all the machines had the same architecture and instruction set, programs written for one machine could run on all the others, at least in theory. Furthermore, the 360 was designed to handle both scientific and commercial computing. Thus a single family of machines could satisfy the needs of all customers. In subsequent years, IBM has come out with compatible successors to the 360 line, using more modern technology, known as the 370, 4300, 3080, and 3090 series.

The 360 was the first major computer line to use (small-scale) Integrated Circuits (ICs), thus providing a major price/performance advantage over the second-generation machines, which were built up from individual transistors. It was an immediate success, and the idea of a family of compatible computers was soon adopted by all the other major manufacturers. The descendants of these machines are still in use at scattered computer centers today, but their use is declining rapidly.

The greatest strength of the "one family" idea was simultaneously its greatest weakness. The intention was that all software, including the operating system, had to work on all models. It had to run on small systems, which often just replaced 1401s for copying cards to tape, and on very large systems, which often replaced 7094s for doing weather forecasting and other heavy computing. It had to be good on systems with few peripherals and on systems with many peripherals. It had to work in commercial environments and in scientific environments. Above all, it had to be efficient for all of these different uses.

There was no way that IBM (or anybody else) could write a piece of software to meet all those conflicting requirements. The result was an enormous and extraordinarily complex operating system, probably two to three orders of magnitude larger than FMS. It consisted of millions of lines of assembly language written by thousands of programmers, and contained thousands upon thousands of bugs, which necessitated a continuous stream of new releases in an attempt to correct them. Each new release fixed some bugs and introduced new ones, so the number of bugs probably remained constant in time.

One of the designers of OS/360, Fred Brooks, subsequently wrote a witty and incisive book (Brooks, 1975) describing his experiences with OS/360. While it would be impossible to summarize the book here, suffice it to say that the cover shows a herd of prehistoric beasts stuck in a tar pit. The cover of Silberschatz and Galvin's book (1994) makes a similar point.

Despite its enormous size and problems, OS/360 and the similar third-generation operating systems produced by other computer manufacturers actually satisfied most of their customers reasonably well. They also popularized several key techniques absent in second-generation operating systems. Probably the most important of these was **multiprogramming**. On the 7094, when the current job paused to wait for a tape or other I/O operation to complete, the CPU simply sat idle until the I/O finished. With heavily CPU-bound scientific calculations, I/O is infrequent, so this wasted time is not significant. With commercial data processing, the I/O wait time can often be 80 or 90 percent of the total time, so something had to be done to avoid having the CPU be idle so much.

The solution that evolved was to partition memory into several pieces, with a different job in each partition, as shown in Fig. 1-4. While one job was waiting for I/O to complete, another job could be using the CPU. If enough jobs could be held in main memory at once, the CPU could be kept busy nearly 100 percent of the time. Having multiple jobs in memory at once requires special hardware to protect each job against snooping and mischief by the other ones, but the 360 and other third-generation systems were equipped with this hardware.

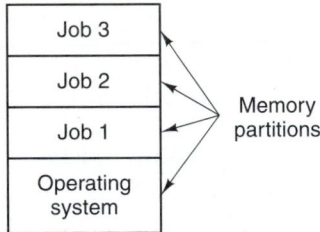

Figure 1-4. A multiprogramming system with three jobs in memory.

Another major feature present in third-generation operating systems was the ability to read jobs from cards onto the disk as soon as they were brought to the computer room. Then, whenever a running job finished, the operating system could load a new job from the disk into the now-empty partition and run it. This technique is called **spooling** (from Simultaneous Peripheral Operation On Line) and was also used for output. With spooling, the 1401s were no longer needed, and much carrying of tapes disappeared.

Although third-generation operating systems were well-suited for big scientific calculations and massive commercial data processing runs, they were still basically batch systems. Many programmers pined for the first-generation days when they had the machine all to themselves for a few hours, so they could debug their programs quickly. With third-generation systems, the time between submitting a job and getting back the output was often several hours, so a single misplaced comma could cause a compilation to fail, and the programmer to waste half a day.

This desire for quick response time paved the way for **timesharing**, a variant of multiprogramming, in which each user has an on-line terminal. In a timesharing system, if 20 users are logged in and 17 of them are thinking or talking or drinking coffee, the CPU can be allocated in turn to the three jobs that want service. Since people debugging programs usually issue short commands (e.g., compile a five-page procedure) rather than long ones (e.g., sort a million-record file), the computer can provide fast, interactive service to a number of users and perhaps also work on big batch jobs in the background when the CPU is otherwise idle. Although the first serious timesharing system (CTSS) was developed at M.I.T. on a specially modified 7094 (Corbato et al., 1962), timesharing did not really become popular until the necessary protection hardware became widespread during the third generation.

After the success of the CTSS system, MIT, Bell Labs, and General Electric (then a major computer manufacturer) decided to embark on the development of a "computer utility," a machine that would support hundreds of simultaneous timesharing users. Their model was the electricity distribution system—when you need electric power, you just stick a plug in the wall, and within reason, as much power as you need will be there. The designers of this system, known as **MULTICS** (MULTiplexed Information and Computing Service), envisioned one huge machine providing computing power for everyone in Boston. The idea that machines far more powerful than their GE-645 would be sold as personal computers for a few thousand dollars only 30 years later was pure science fiction at the time.

To make a long story short, MULTICS introduced many seminal ideas into the computer literature, but building it was a lot harder than anyone had expected. Bell Labs dropped out of the project, and General Electric quit the computer business altogether. Eventually, MULTICS ran well enough to be used in a production environment at MIT and dozens of sites elsewhere, but the concept of a computer utility fizzled out as computer prices plummeted. Still, MULTICS had an enormous influence on subsequent systems. It is described in (Corbato et al., 1972; Corbato and Vyssotsky, 1965; Daley and Dennis, 1968; Organick, 1972; Saltzer, 1974).

Another major development during the third generation was the phenomenal growth of minicomputers, starting with the DEC PDP-1 in 1961. The PDP-1 had only 4K of 18-bit words, but at $120,000 per machine (less than 5 percent of the price of a 7094), they sold like hotcakes. For certain kinds of nonnumerical work, it was almost as fast as the 7094, and gave birth to a whole new industry. It was quickly followed by a series of other PDPs (unlike IBM's family, all incompatible) culminating in the PDP-11.

One of the computer scientists at Bell Labs who had worked on the MULTICS project, Ken Thompson, subsequently found a small PDP-7 minicomputer that no one was using and set out to write a stripped-down, one-user version of MULTICS. This work later developed into the UNIX® operating system, which became popular in the academic world, with government agencies, and with many companies.

The history of UNIX has been told elsewhere (e.g., Salus, 1994). Suffice it to say, that because the source code was widely available, various organizations developed their own (incompatible) versions, which led to chaos. To make it possible to write programs that could run on any UNIX system, IEEE developed a standard for UNIX, called **POSIX**, that most versions of UNIX now support. POSIX defines a minimal sytem call interface that conformant UNIX systems must support. In fact, some other operating systems now also support the POSIX interface.

1.2.4 The Fourth Generation (1980–Present): Personal Computers

With the development of LSI (Large Scale Integration) circuits, chips containing thousands of transistors on a square centimeter of silicon, the age of the personal computer dawned. In terms of architecture, personal computers were not that different from minicomputers of the PDP-11 class, but in terms of price they certainly were different. Where the minicomputer made it possible for a department in a company or university to have its own computer, the microprocessor chip made it possible for a single individual to have his or her own personal computer. The most powerful personal computers used by businesses, universities, and government installations are usually called **workstations**, but they are really just large personal computers. Usually, they are connected together by a network.

The widespread availability of computing power, especially highly interactive computing power usually with excellent graphics, led to the growth of a major industry producing software for personal computers. Much of this software was **user**friendly meaning that it was intended for users who not only knew nothing about computers but furthermore had absolutely no intention whatsoever of learning. This was certainly a major change from OS/360, whose job control language, JCL, was so arcane that entire books were written about it (e.g., Cadow, 1970).

Two operating systems initially dominated the personal computer and workstation scene: Microsoft's MS-DOS and UNIX. MS-DOS was widely used on the IBM PC and other machines using the Intel 8088 CPU and its successors, the 80286, 80386, and 80486 (which we will refer to henceforth as the 286, 386, and 486, respectively), and later the Pentium and Pentium Pro. Although the initial version of MS-DOS was relatively primitive, subsequent versions have included more advanced features, including many taken from UNIX. Microsoft's successor to MS-DOS, WINDOWS, originally ran on top of MS-DOS (i.e., it was more like a shell than a true operating system), but starting in 1995 a freestanding version of WINDOWS, WINDOWS 95®, was released, so MS-DOS is no longer needed to support it. Another Microsoft operating system is WINDOWS NT, which is compatible with WINDOWS 95 at a certain level, but a complete rewrite from scratch internally.

The other major contender is UNIX, which is dominant on workstations and other high-end computers, such as network servers. It is especially popular on machines powered by high-performance RISC chips. These machines usually have the computing power of a minicomputer, even though they are dedicated to a single user, so it is logical that they are equipped with an operating system originally designed for minicomputers, namely UNIX.

An interesting development that began taking place during the mid-1980s is the growth of networks of personal computers running **network operating systems** and **distributed operating systems** (Tanenbaum, 1995). In a network operating system, the users are aware of the existence of multiple computers and can log in to remote machines and copy files from one machine to another. Each machine runs its own local operating system and has its own local user (or users).

Network operating systems are not fundamentally different from single-processor operating systems. They obviously need a network interface controller and some low-level software to drive it, as well as programs to achieve remote login and remote file access, but these additions do not change the essential structure of the operating system.

A distributed operating system, in contrast, is one that appears to its users as a traditional uniprocessor system, even though it is actually composed of multiple processors. The users should not be aware of where their programs are being run or where their files are located; that should all be handled automatically and efficiently by the operating system.

True distributed operating systems require more than just adding a little code to a uniprocessor operating system, because distributed and centralized systems differ in critical ways. Distributed systems, for example, often allow applications to run on several processors at the same time, thus requiring more complex processor scheduling algorithms in order to optimize the amount of parallelism.

Communication delays within the network often mean that these (and other) algorithms must run with incomplete, outdated, or even incorrect information. This situation is radically different from a single-processor system in which the operating system has complete information about the system state.

1.2.5 History of MINIX

When UNIX was young (Version 6), the source code was widely available, under AT&T license, and frequently studied. John Lions, of the University of New South Wales in Australia, even wrote a little booklet describing its operation, line by line (Lions, 1996). This booklet was used (with permission of AT&T) as a text in many university operating system courses.

When AT&T released Version 7, it began to realize that UNIX was a valuable commercial product, so it issued Version 7 with a license that prohibited the source code from being studied in courses, in order to avoid endangering its status as a trade secret. Many universities complied by simply dropping the study of UNIX and teaching only theory.

Unfortunately, teaching only theory leaves the student with a lopsided view of what an operating system is really like. The theoretical topics that are usually covered in great detail in courses and books on operating systems, such as scheduling algorithms, are in practice not really that important. Subjects that really are important, such as I/O and file systems, are generally neglected because there is little theory about them.

To remedy this situation, one of the authors of this book (Tanenbaum) decided to write a new operating system from scratch that would be compatible with UNIX from the user's point of view, but completely different on the inside. By not using even one line of AT&T code, this system avoids the licensing restrictions, so it can be used for class or individual study. In this manner, readers can dissect a real operating system to see what is inside, just as biology students dissect frogs. The name MINIX stands for mini-UNIX because it is small enough that even a nonguru can understand how it works.

In addition to the advantage of eliminating the legal problems, MINIX has another advantage over UNIX. It was written a decade after UNIX and has been structured in a more modular way. The MINIX file system, for example, is not part of the operating system at all but runs as a user program. Another difference is that UNIX was designed to be efficient; MINIX was designed to be readable (inasmuch as one can speak of any program hundreds of pages long as being readable). The MINIX code, for example, has thousands of comments in it.

MINIX was originally designed for compatibility with Version 7 (V7) UNIX. Version 7 was used as the model because of its simplicity and elegance. It is sometimes said that Version 7 was not only an improvement over all its predecessors, but also over all its successors. With the advent of POSIX, MINIX began evolving toward the new standard, while maintaining backward compatibility with existing programs. This kind of evolution is common in the computer industry, as no vendor wants to introduce a new system that none of its existing customers can use without great upheaval. The version of MINIX described in this book is based on the POSIX standard (unlike the version described in the First Edition, which was V7 based).

Like UNIX, MINIX was written in the C programming language and was intended to be easy to port to various computers. The initial implementation was for the IBM PC, because this computer is in widespread use. It was subsequently ported to the Atari, Amiga, Macintosh, and SPARC computers. In keeping with the "Small is Beautiful" philosophy, MINIX originally did not even require a hard disk to run, thus bringing it within range of many students' budgets (amazing as it may seem now, in the mid-1980s when MINIX first saw the light of day, hard disks were still an expensive novelty). As MINIX grew in functionality and size, it eventually got to the point that a hard disk is needed, but in keeping with the MINIX philosophy, a 30-megabyte partition is sufficient. In contrast, some commercial UNIX systems now recommend at least a 200-MB disk partition as the bare minimum.

To the average user sitting at an IBM PC, running MINIX is similar to running UNIX. Many of the basic programs, such as *cat*, *grep*, *ls*, *make*, and the shell are present and perform the same functions as their UNIX counterparts. Like the operating system itself, all these utility programs have been rewritten completely from scratch by the author, his students, and some other dedicated people.

Throughout this book MINIX will be used as an example. Most of the comments about MINIX, however, except those about the actual code, also apply to UNIX. Many of them also apply to other systems as well. This remark should be kept in mind when reading the text.

As an aside, a few words about LINUX and its relationship to MINIX may be of interest to some readers. Shortly after MINIX was released, a USENET newsgroup was formed to discuss it. Within weeks, it had 40,000 subscribers, most of whom wanted to add vast numbers of new features to MINIX to make it bigger and better (well, at least bigger). Every day, several hundred of them offered suggestions, ideas, and snippets of code. The author of MINIX successfully resisted this onslaught for several years, in order to keep MINIX small enough and clean enough for students to understand. Ever so gradually, it began to become clear that he really meant it. At that point, a Finnish student, Linus Torvalds, decided to write a MINIX clone intended to be a feature-heavy production system, rather than an educational tool. Thus was LINUX born.

1.3 OPERATING SYSTEM CONCEPTS

The interface between the operating system and the user programs is defined by the set of "extended instructions" that the operating system provides. These extended instructions have been traditionally known as **system calls**, although they can be implemented in several ways now. To really understand what operating systems do, we must examine this interface closely. The calls available in the interface vary from operating system to operating system (although the underlying concepts tend to be similar).

We are thus forced to make a choice between (1) vague generalities ("operating systems have system calls for reading files") and (2) some specific system ("MINIX has a READ system call with three parameters: one to specify the file, one to tell where the data are to be put, and one to tell how many bytes to read").

We have chosen the latter approach. It's more work that way, but it gives more insight into what operating systems really do. In Sec. 1.4 we will look closely at the system calls present in both UNIX and MINIX. For simplicity's sake, we will refer only to MINIX, but the corresponding UNIX system calls are based on POSIX in most cases. Before we look at the actual system calls, however, it is worth taking a bird's-eye view of MINIX, to get a general feel for what an operating system is all about. This overview applies equally well to UNIX.

The MINIX system calls fall roughly in two broad categories: those dealing with processes and those dealing with the file system. We will now examine each of these in turn.

1.3.1 Processes

A key concept in MINIX, and in all operating systems, is the **process**. A process is basically a program in execution. Associated with each process is its **address space**, a list of memory locations from some minimum (usually 0) to some maximum, which the process can read and write. The address space contains the executable program, the program's data, and its stack. Also associated with each process is some set of registers, including the program counter, stack pointer, and other hardware registers, and all the other information needed to run the program.

We will come back to the process concept in much more detail in Chap. 2, but for the time being, the easiest way to get a good intuitive feel for a process is to think about timesharing systems. Periodically, the operating system decides to stop running one process and start running another, for example, because the first one has had more than its share of CPU time in the past second.

When a process is suspended temporarily like this, it must later be restarted in exactly the same state it had when it was stopped. This means that all information about the process must be explicitly saved somewhere during the suspension. For example, the process may have several files open for reading. Associated with each of these files is a pointer giving the current position (i.e., the number of the byte or record to be read next). When a process is temporarily suspended, all these pointers must be saved so that a READ call executed after the process is restarted will read the proper data. In many operating systems, all the information about each process, other than the contents of its own address space, is stored in an operating system table called the **process table**, which is an array (or linked list) of structures, one for each process currently in existence.

Thus, a (suspended) process consists of its address space, usually called the **core image** (in honor of the magnetic core memories used in days of yore), and its process table entry, which contains its registers, among other things.

The key process management system calls are those dealing with the creation and termination of processes. Consider a typical example. A process called the **command interpreter** or **shell** reads commands from a terminal. The user has just typed a command requesting that a program be compiled. The shell must now create a new process that will run the compiler. When that process has finished the compilation, it executes a system call to terminate itself.

If a process can create one or more other processes (referred to as **child processes**) and these processes in turn can create child processes, we quickly arrive at the process tree structure of Fig. 1-5. Related processes that are cooperating to get some job done often need to communicate with one another and synchronize their activities. This communication is called **interprocess communication**, and will be addressed in detail in Chap. 2.

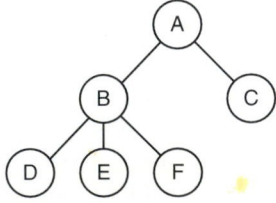

Figure 1-5. A process tree. Process *A* created two child processes, *B* and *C*. Process *B* created three child processes, *D*, *E*, and *F*.

Other process system calls are available to request more memory (or release unused memory), wait for a child process to terminate, and overlay its program with a different one.

Occasionally, there is a need to convey information to a running process that is not sitting around waiting for it. For example, a process that is communicating with another process on a different computer does so by sending messages over a network. To guard against the possibility that a message or its reply is lost, the sender may request that its own operating system notify it after a specified number of seconds, so that it can retransmit the message if no acknowledgement has been received yet. After setting this timer, the program may continue doing other work.

When the specified number of seconds has elapsed, the operating system sends a **signal** to the process. The signal causes the process to temporarily suspend whatever it was doing, save its registers on the stack, and start running a special signal handling procedure, for example, to retransmit a presumably lost message. When the signal handler is done, the running process is restarted in the state it was in just before the signal. Signals are the software analog of hardware interrupts and can be generated by a variety of causes in addition to timers expiring. Many traps detected by hardware, such as executing an illegal instruction or using an invalid address, are also converted into signals to the guilty process.

Each person authorized to use MINIX is assigned a **uid** (user identification) by the system administrator. Every process started in MINIX has the uid of the person who started it. A child process has the same uid as its parent. One uid, called the **super-user**, has special power, and may violate many of the protection rules. In large installations, only the system administrator knows the password needed to become super-user, but many of the ordinary users (especially students) devote considerable effort to trying to find flaws in the system that allow them to become super-user without the password.

1.3.2 Files

The other broad category of system calls relates to the file system. As noted before, a major function of the operating system is to hide the peculiarities of the disks and other I/O devices and present the programmer with a nice, clean abstract model of device-independent files. System calls are obviously needed to create files, remove files, read files, and write files. Before a file can be read, it must be opened, and after it has been read it should be closed, so calls are provided to do these things.

To provide a place to keep files, MINIX has the concept of a **directory** as a way of grouping files together. A student, for example, might have one directory for each course he was taking (for the programs needed for that course), another directory for his electronic mail, and still another directory for his World Wide Web home page. System calls are then needed to create and remove directories.

Calls are also provided to put an existing file in a directory, and to remove a file from a directory. Directory entries may be either files or other directories. This model also gives rise to a hierarchy—the file system—as shown in Fig. 1-6.

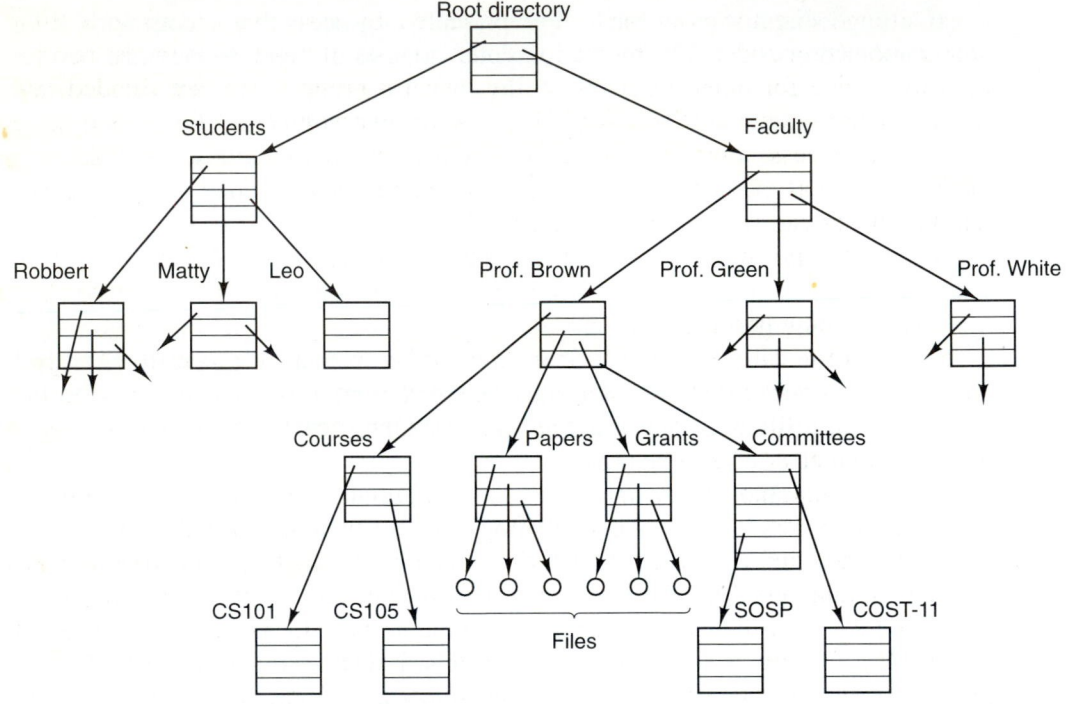

Figure 1-6. A file system for a university department.

The process and file hierarchies both are organized as trees, but the similarity stops there. Process hierarchies usually are not very deep (more than three levels is unusual), whereas file hierarchies are commonly four, five, or even more levels deep. Process hierarchies are typically short-lived, generally a few minutes at most, whereas the directory hierarchy may exist for years. Ownership and protection also differ for processes and files. Typically, only a parent process may control or even access a child process, but mechanisms nearly always exist to allow files and directories to be read by a wider group than just the owner.

Every file within the directory hierarchy can be specified by giving its **path name** from the top of the directory hierarchy, the **root directory**. Such absolute path names consist of the list of directories that must be traversed from the root directory to get to the file, with slashes separating the components. In Fig. 1-6, the path for file *CS101* is */Faculty/Prof.Brown/Courses/CS101*. The leading slash indicates that the path is absolute, that is, starting at the root directory.

At every instant, each process has a current **working directory**, in which path names not beginning with a slash are looked for. As an example, in Fig. 1-6, if

/Faculty/Prof.Brown were the working directory, then use of the path name *Courses/CS101* would yield the same file as the absolute path name given above. Processes can change their working directory by issuing a system call specifying the new working directory.

Files and directories in MINIX are protected by assigning each one a 9-bit binary protection code. The protection code consists of three 3-bit fields, one for the owner, one for other members of the owner's group (users are divided into groups by the system administrator), and one for everyone else. Each field has a bit for read access, a bit for write access, and a bit for execute access. These 3 bits are known as the **rwx bits**. For example, the protection code *rwxr-x--x* means that the owner can read, write, or execute the file, other group members can read or execute (but not write) the file, and everyone else can execute (but not read or write) the file. For a directory, *x* indicates search permission. A dash means that the corresponding permission is absent.

Before a file can be read or written, it must be opened, at which time the permissions are checked. If the access is permitted, the system returns a small integer called a **file descriptor** to use in subsequent operations. If the access is prohibited, an error code is returned.

Another important concept in MINIX is the mounted file system. Nearly all personal computers have one or more floppy disk drives into which floppy disks can be inserted and removed. To provide a clean way to deal with these removable media (and also CD-ROMs, which are also removable), MINIX allows the file system on a floppy disk to be attached to the main tree. Consider the situation of Fig. 1-7(a). Before the MOUNT call, the RAM disk (simulated disk in main memory) contains the primary, or **root file system**, and drive 0 contains a floppy disk containing another file system.

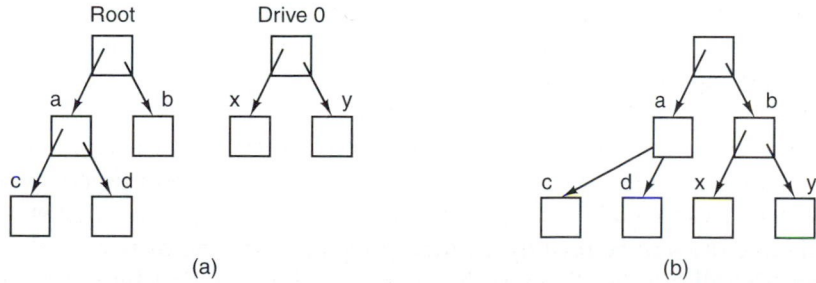

(a) (b)

Figure 1-7. (a) Before mounting, the files on drive 0 are not accessible. (b) After mounting, they are part of the file hierarchy.

However, the file system on drive 0 cannot be used, because there is no way to specify path names on it. MINIX does not allow path names to be prefixed by a drive name or number; that would be precisely the kind of device dependence that operating systems ought to eliminate. Instead, the MOUNT system call allows the file system on drive 0 to be attached to the root file system wherever the program wants it to be. In Fig. 1-7(b) the file system on drive 0 has been mounted on directory *b*, thus allowing access to files */b/x* and */b/y*. If directory *b* had contained any files they would not be accessible while drive 0 was mounted, since */b* would refer to the root directory of drive 0. (Not being able to access these files is not as serious as it at first seems: file systems are nearly always mounted on empty directories.)

Another important concept in MINIX is the **special file**. Special files are provided in order to make I/O devices look like files. That way, they can be read and written using the same system calls as are used for reading and writing files. Two kinds of special files exist: **block special files** and **character special files**. Block special files are used to model devices that consist of a collection of randomly addressable blocks, such as disks. By opening a block special file and reading, say, block 4, a program can directly access the fourth block on the device, without regard to the structure of the file system contained on it. Similarly, character special files are used to model printers, modems, and other devices that accept or output a character stream.

The last feature we will discuss in this overview is one that relates to both processes and files: pipes. A **pipe** is a sort of pseudofile that can be used to connect two processes together, as shown in Fig. 1-8. When process *A* wants to send data to process *B*, it writes on the pipe as though it were an output file. Process *B* can read the data by reading from the pipe as though it were an input file. Thus, communication between processes in MINIX looks very much like ordinary file reads and writes. Stronger yet, the only way a process can discover that the output file it is writing on is not really a file, but a pipe, is by making a special system call.

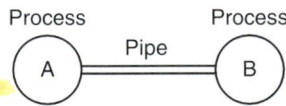

Figure 1-8. Two processes connected by a pipe.

1.3.3 The Shell

The MINIX operating system is the code that carries out the system calls. Editors, compilers, assemblers, linkers, and command interpreters definitely are not part of the operating system, even though they are important and useful. At the risk of confusing things somewhat, in this section we will look briefly at the MINIX command interpreter, called the **shell**, which, although not part of the operating system, makes heavy use of many operating system features and thus serves as a good example of how the system calls can be used. It is also the primary interface between a user sitting at his terminal and the operating system.

When any user logs in, a shell is started up. The shell has the terminal as standard input and standard output. It starts out by typing the **prompt**, a character such as a dollar sign, which tells the user that the shell is waiting to accept a command. If the user now types

```
date
```

for example, the shell creates a child process and runs the *date* program as the child. While the child process is running, the shell waits for it to terminate. When the child finishes, the shell types the prompt again and tries to read the next input line.

The user can specify that standard output be redirected to a file, for example,

```
date >file
```

Similarly, standard input can be redirected, as in

```
sort <file1 >file2
```

which invokes the sort program with input taken from *file1* and output sent to *file2*.

The output of one program can be used as the input for another program by connecting them with a pipe. Thus

```
cat file1 file2 file3 | sort >/dev/lp
```

invokes the *cat* program to concatenate three files and send the output to *sort* to arrange all the lines in alphabetical order. The output of *sort* is redirected to the file */dev/lp*, which is a typical name for the special character file for the printer. (By convention, all the special files are kept in the directory */dev*.)

If a user puts an ampersand after a command, the shell does not wait for it to complete. Instead it just gives a prompt immediately. Consequently,

```
cat file1 file2 file3 | sort >/dev/lp &
```

starts up the sort as a background job, allowing the user to continue working normally while the sort is going on. The shell has a number of other interesting features that we do not have space to discuss here. See any of the suggested references on UNIX for more information about the shell.

1.4 SYSTEM CALLS

Armed with our general knowledge of how MINIX deals with processes and files, we can now begin to look at the interface between the operating system and its application programs, that is, the set of system calls. Although this discussion specifically refers to POSIX (International Standard 9945-1), hence also to MINIX, most other modern operating systems have system calls that perform the same functions, even if the details differ. Since the actual mechanics of issuing a system call are highly machine dependent, and often must be expressed in assembly code, a procedure library is provided to make it possible to make system calls from C programs.

To make the system call mechanism clearer, let us take a quick look at READ. It has three parameters: the first one specifying the file, the second one specifying the buffer, and the third one specifying the number of bytes to read. A call to READ from a C program might look like this:

```
count = read(file, buffer, nbytes);
```

The system call (and the library procedure) return the number of bytes actually read in *count*. This value is normally the same as *nbytes*, but may be smaller, if, for example, end-of-file is encountered while reading.

If the system call cannot be carried out, either due to an invalid parameter or a disk error, *count* is set to −1, and the error number is put in a global variable, *errno*. Programs should always check the results of a system call to see if an error occurred.

MINIX has a total of 53 system calls These are listed in Fig. 1-9, grouped for convenience in six categories. In the following sections we will briefly examine each call to see what it does. To a large extent, the services offered by these calls determine most of what the operating system has to do, since the resource management on personal computers is minimal (at least compared to big machines with many users).

As an aside, it is worth pointing out that what constitutes a system call is open to some interpretation. The POSIX standard specifies a number of procedures that a conformant system must supply, but it does not specify whether they are system calls, library calls, or something else. In some cases, the POSIX procedures are supported as library routines in MINIX. In others, several required procedures are only minor variations of one another, and one system call handles all of them.

1.4.1 System Calls for Process Management

The first group of calls deals with process management. FORK is a good place to start the discussion. FORK is the only way to create a new process. It creates an exact duplicate of the original process, including all the file descriptors, registers—everything. After the FORK, the original process and the copy (the parent and child) go their separate ways. All the variables have identical values at the time of the FORK, but since the parent's data are copied to create the child, subsequent changes in one of them do not affect the other one. (The text, which is unchangeable, is shared between parent and child.) The FORK call returns a value, which is zero in the child, and equal to the child's process identifier or **pid** in the

Process management		
	pid = fork()	Create a child process identical to the parent
	pid = waitpid(pid, &statloc, opts)	Wait for a child to terminate
	s = wait(&status)	Old version of waitpid
	s = execve(name, argv, envp)	Replace a process core image
	exit(status)	Terminate process execution and return status
	size = brk(addr)	Set the size of the data segment
	pid = getpid()	Return the caller's process id
	pid = getpgrp()	Return the id of the caller's process group
	pid = setsid()	Create a new session and return its process group id
	l = ptrace(req, pid, addr, data)	Used for debugging
Signals		
	s = sigaction(sig, &act, &oldact)	Define action to take on signals
	s = sigreturn(&context)	Return from a signal
	s = sigprocmask(how, &set, &old)	Examine or change the signal mask
	s = sigpending(set)	Get the set of blocked signals
	s = sigsuspend(sigmask)	Replace the signal mask and suspend the process
	s = kill(pid, sig)	Send a signal to a process
	residual = alarm(seconds)	Set the alarm clock
	s = pause()	Suspend the caller until the next signal
File Management		
	fd = creat(name, mode)	Obsolete way to create a new file
	fd = mknod(name, mode, addr)	Create a regular, special, or directory i-node
	fd = open(file, how, ...)	Open a file for reading, writing or both
	s = close(fd)	Close an open file
	n = read(fd, buffer, nbytes)	Read data from a file into a buffer
	n = write(fd, buffer, nbytes)	Write data from a buffer into a file
	pos = lseek(fd, offset, whence)	Move the file pointer
	s = stat(name, &buf)	Get a file's status information
	s = fstat(fd, &buf)	Get a file's status information
	fd = dup(fd)	Allocate a new file descriptor for an open file
	s = pipe(&fd[0])	Create a pipe
	s = ioctl(fd, request, argp)	Perform special operations on a file
	s = access(name, amode)	Check a file's accessibility
	s = rename(old, new)	Give a file a new name
	s = fcntl(fd, cmd, ...)	File locking and other operations
Directory & File System Management		
	s = mkdir(name, mode)	Create a new directory
	s = rmdir(name)	Remove an empty directory
	s = link(name1, name2)	Create a new entry, name2, pointing to name1
	s = unlink(name)	Remove a directory entry
	s = mount(special, name, flag)	Mount a file system
	s = umount(special)	Unmount a file system
	s = sync()	Flush all cached blocks to the disk
	s = chdir(dirname)	Change the working directory
	s = chroot(dirname)	Change the root directory
Protection		
	s = chmod(name, mode)	Change a file's protection bits
	uid = getuid()	Get the caller's uid
	gid = getgid()	Get the caller's gid
	s = setuid(uid)	Set the caller's uid
	s = setgid(gid)	Set the caller's gid
	s = chown(name, owner, group)	Change a file's owner and group
	oldmask = umask(complmode)	Change the mode mask
Time Management		
	seconds = time(&seconds)	Get the elapsed time since Jan. 1, 1970
	s = stime(tp)	Set the elapsed time since Jan. 1, 1970
	s = utime(file, timep)	Set a file's "last access" time
	s = times(buffer)	Get the user and system times used so far

Figure 1-9. The MINIX system calls. The return code s is −1 if an error has occurred; *fd* is a file descriptor; and *n* is a byte count. The other return codes are what the name suggests. *core that C library is built on*

parent. Using the returned pid, the two processes can see which one is the parent process and which one is the child process.

In most cases, after a FORK, the child will need to execute different code from the parent. Consider the case of the shell. It reads a command from the terminal, forks off a child process, waits for the child to execute the command, and then reads the next command when the child terminates. To wait for the child to finish, the parent executes a WAITPID system call, which just waits until the child terminates (any child if more than one exists). WAITPID can wait for a specific child, or for any old child by setting the first parameter to −1. When WAITPID completes, the address pointed to by the second parameter will be set to the child's exit status (normal or abnormal termination and exit value). Various options are also provided. The WAITPID call replaces the previous WAIT call, which is now obsolete but is provided for reasons of backward compatibility.

Now consider how FORK is used by the shell. When a command is typed, the shell forks off a new process. This child process must execute the user command. It does this by using the EXEC system call, which causes its entire core image to be replaced by the file named in its first parameter. A highly simplified shell illustrating the use of FORK, WAITPID, and EXEC is shown in Fig. 1-10.

```
while (TRUE) {                            /* repeat forever */
    read_command(command, parameters);    /* read input from terminal */

    if (fork() != 0) {                    /* fork off child process */
        /* Parent code. */
        waitpid(−1, &status, 0);          /* wait for child to exit */
    } else {
        /* Child code. */
        execve(command, parameters, 0);   /* execute command */
    }
}
```

Figure 1-10. A stripped-down shell. Throughout this book, *TRUE* is assumed to be defined as 1.

In the most general case, EXEC has three parameters: the name of the file to be executed, a pointer to the argument array, and a pointer to the environment array. These will be described shortly. Various library routines, including *execl*, *execv*, *execle*, and *execve* are provided to allow the parameters to be omitted or specified in various ways. Throughout this book we will use the name EXEC to represent the system call invoked by all of these.

Let us consider the case of a command such as

cp file1 file2

used to copy *file1* to *file2*. After the shell has forked, the child process locates and executes the file *cp* and passes to it the names of the source and target files.

The main program of *cp* (and main program of most other programs) contains the declaration

```
main(argc, argv, envp)
```

where *argc* is a count of the number of items on the command line, including the program name. For the example above, *argc* is 3.

The second parameter, *argv*, is a pointer to an array. Element *i* of that array is a pointer to the *i*-th string on the command line. In our example, *argv*[0] would point to the string "cp." (As an aside, the string pointed to contains *two* characters, a "c" and a "p," although, if you look closely at the previous sentence you will also see a period inside the quotes. The period ends the sentence, but the rules of English punctuation require most punctuation marks to be *inside* the quotes, even though this is totally illogical. Hopefully, this will not cause any confusion.) Similarly, *argv*[1] would point to the 5-character string "file1" and *argv*[2] would point to the 5-character string "file2."

The third parameter of *main*, *envp*, is a pointer to the environment, an array of strings containing assignments of the form *name = value* used to pass information such as the terminal type and home directory name to a program. In Fig. 1-10, no environment is passed to the child, so the third parameter of *execve* is a zero.

If EXEC seems complicated, do not despair; it is the most complex system call. All the rest are much simpler. As an example of a simple one, consider EXIT, which processes should use when they are finished executing. It has one parameter, the exit status (0 to 255), which is returned to the parent in the variable *status* of the WAIT or WAITPID system call. The low-order byte of *status* contains the termination status, with 0 being normal termination and the other values being various error conditions. The high-order byte contains the child's exit status (0 to 255). For example, if a parent process executes the statement

```
n = waitpid(−1, &status, options);
```

it will be suspended until some child process terminates. If the child exits with, say, 4 as the parameter to *exit*, the parent will be awakened with *n* set to the child's pid and *status* set to 0x0400 (the C convention of prefixing hexadecimal constants with 0x will be used throughout this book).

Processes in MINIX have their memory divided up into three segments: the **text segment** (i.e., the program code), the **data segment** (i.e., the variables), and the **stack segment**. The data segment grows upward and the stack grows downward, as shown in Fig. 1-11. Between them is a gap of unused address space. The stack grows into the gap automatically, as needed, but expansion of the data segment is done explicitly by using the BRK system call. It has one parameter, which gives the address where the data segment is to end. This address may be more than the current value (data segment is growing) or less than the current value (data segment is shrinking). The parameter must, of course, be less than the stack pointer or the data and stack segments would overlap, which is forbidden.

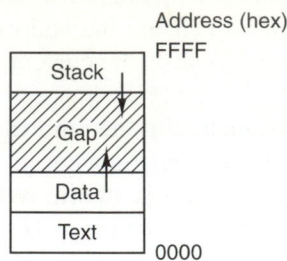

Figure 1-11. Processes have three segments: text, data, and stack. In this example, all three are in one address space, but separate instruction and data space is also supported.

As a convenience to the programmer, a library routine *sbrk* is provided that also changes the size of the data segment, only its parameter is the number of bytes to add to the data segment (negative parameters make the data segment smaller). It works by keeping track of the current size of the data segment, which is the value returned by BRK, computing the new size, and making a call asking for that number of bytes. BRK and SBRK were considered too implementation dependent and are not part of POSIX.

The next process system call is also the simplest, GETPID. It just returns the caller's pid. Remember that in FORK, only the parent was given the child's pid. If the child wants to find out its own pid, it must use GETPID. The GETPGRP call returns the pid of the caller's process group. SETSID creates a new session and sets the process group's pid to the caller's. Sessions are related to an optional feature of POSIX called **job control**, which is not supported by MINIX and which will not concern us further.

The last process management system call, PTRACE, is used by debugging programs to control the program being debugged. It allows the debugger to read and write the controlled process' memory and manage it in other ways.

1.4.2 System Calls for Signaling

Although most forms of interprocess communication are planned, situations exist in which unexpected communication is needed. For example, if a user accidently tells a text editor to list the entire contents of a very long file, and then realizes the error, some way is needed to interrupt the editor. In MINIX, the user can hit the DEL key on the keyboard, which sends a signal to the editor. The editor catches the signal and stops the print-out. Signals can also be used to report certain traps detected by the hardware, such as illegal instruction or floating point overflow. Timeouts are also implemented as signals.

When a signal is sent to a process that has not announced its willingness to accept that signal, the process is simply killed without further ado. To avoid this fate, a process can use the SIGACTION system call to announce that it is prepared to accept some signal type, and to provide the address of the signal handling procedure and a place to store the address of the current one. After a SIGACTION call, if a signal of the relevant type (e.g., the DEL key) is generated, the state of the process is pushed onto its own stack, and then the signal handler is called. It may run for as long as it wants to and perform any system calls it wants to. In practice, though, signal handlers are usually fairly short. When the signal handling procedure is done, it calls SIGRETURN to continue where it left off before the signal. The SIGACTION call replaces the older SIGNAL call, which is now provided as a library procedure, however, for backward compatibility.

Signals can be blocked in MINIX. A blocked signal is held pending until it is unblocked. It is not delivered, but also not lost. The SIGPROCMASK call allows a process to define the set of blocked signals by presenting the kernel with a bit map. It is also possible for a process to ask for the set of signals currently pending but not allowed to be delivered due to their being blocked. The SIGPENDING call returns this set as a bit map. Finally, the SIGSUSPEND call allows a process to atomically set the bit map of blocked signals and suspend itself.

Instead of providing a function to catch a signal, the program may also specify the constant SIG_IGN to have all subsequent signals of the specified type ignored, or SIG_DFL to restore the default action of the signal when it occurs. The default action is either to kill the process or ignore the signal, depending upon the signal. As an example of how SIG_IGN is used, consider what happens when the shell forks off a background process as a result of

command &

It would be undesirable for a DEL signal from the keyboard to affect the background process, so after the FORK but before the EXEC, the shell does

sigaction(SIGINT, SIG_IGN, NULL);

and

sigaction(SIGQUIT, SIG_IGN, NULL);

to disable the DEL and quit signals. (The quit signal is generated by CTRL-\; it is the same as DEL except that if it is not caught or ignored, it makes a core dump of the process killed.) For foreground processes (no ampersand), these signals are not ignored.

Hitting the DEL key is not the only way to send a signal. The KILL system call allows a process to signal another process (provided they have the same uid—unrelated processes cannot signal each other). Getting back to the example of background processes used above, suppose a background process is started up, but later it is decided that the process should be terminated. SIGINT and SIGQUIT have been disabled, so something else is needed. The solution is to use the *kill* program, which uses the KILL system call to send a signal to any process.

By sending signal 9 (SIGKILL), to a background process, that process can be killed. SIGKILL cannot be caught or ignored.

For many real-time applications, a process needs to be interrupted after a specific time interval to do something, such as to retransmit a potentially lost packet over an unreliable communication line. To handle this situation, the ALARM system call has been provided. The parameter specifies an interval, in seconds, after which a SIGALRM signal is sent to the process. A process may only have one alarm outstanding at any instant. If an ALARM call is made with a parameter of 10 seconds, and then 3 seconds later another ALARM call is made with a parameter of 20 seconds, only one signal will be generated, 20 seconds after the second call. The first signal is canceled by the second call to ALARM. If the parameter to ALARM is zero, any pending alarm signal is canceled. If an alarm signal is not caught, the default action is taken and the signaled process is killed.

It sometimes occurs that a process has nothing to do until a signal arrives. For example, consider a computer-aided-instruction program that is testing reading speed and comprehension. It displays some text on the screen and then calls ALARM to signal it after 30 seconds. While the student is reading the text, the program has nothing to do. It could sit in a tight loop doing nothing, but that would waste CPU time that another process or user might need. A better idea is to use PAUSE, which tells MINIX to suspend the process until the next signal.

1.4.3 System Calls for File Management

Many system calls relate to the file system. In this section we will look at calls that operate on individual files; in the next one we will examine those that involve directories or the file system as a whole. To create a new file, the CREAT call is used (why the call is CREAT and not CREATE has been lost in the mists of time). Its parameters provide the name of the file and the protection mode. Thus

```
fd = creat("abc", 0751);
```

creates a file called *abc* with mode 0751 octal (in C, a leading zero means that a constant is in octal). The low-order 9 bits of 0751 specify the *rwx* bits for the owner (7 means read-write-execute permission), his group (5 means read-execute), and others (1 means execute only).

CREAT not only creates a new file but also opens it for writing, regardless of the file's mode. The file descriptor returned, *fd*, can be used to write the file. If a CREAT is done on an existing file, that file is truncated to length 0, provided, of course, that the permissions are all right. The CREAT call is obsolete, as OPEN can now create new files, but it has been included for backward compatibility.

Special files are created using MKNOD rather than CREAT. A typical call is

```
fd = mknod("/dev/ttyc2", 020744, 0x0402);
```

which creates a file named */dev/ttyc2* (the usual name for console 2) and gives it mode 020744 octal (a character special file with protection bits *rwxr--r--*). The third parameter contains the major device (4) in the high-order byte and the minor device (2) in the low-order byte. The major device could have been anything, but a file named */dev/ttyc2* ought to be minor device 2. Calls to MKNOD fail unless the caller is the super-user.

To read or write an existing file, the file must first be opened using OPEN. This call specifies the file name to be opened, either as an absolute path name or relative to the working directory, and a code of *O_RDONLY*, *O_WRONLY*, or *O_RDWR*, meaning open for reading, writing, or both. The file descriptor returned can then be used for reading or writing. Afterward, the file can be closed by CLOSE, which makes the file descriptor available for reuse on a subsequent CREAT or OPEN.

The most heavily used calls are undoubtedly READ and WRITE. We saw READ earlier. WRITE has the same parameters.

Although most programs read and write files sequentially, for some applications programs need to be able to access any part of a file at random. Associated with each file is a pointer that indicates the current position in the file. When reading (writing) sequentially, it normally points to the next byte to be read (written). The LSEEK call changes the value of the position pointer, so that subsequent calls to READ or WRITE can begin anywhere in the file, or even beyond the end.

LSEEK has three parameters: the first is the file descriptor for the file, the second is a file position, and the third tells whether the file position is relative to the beginning of the file, the current position, or the end of the file. The value returned by LSEEK is the absolute position in the file after changing the pointer.

For each file, MINIX keeps track of the file mode (regular file, special file, directory, and so on), size, time of last modification, and other information. Programs can ask to see this information via the STAT and FSTAT system calls. These differ only in that the former specifies the file by name, whereas the latter takes a file descriptor, making it useful for open files, especially standard input and standard output, whose names may not be known. Both calls provide as the second parameter a pointer to a structure where the information is to be put. The structure is shown in Fig. 1-12.

When manipulating file descriptors, the DUP call is occasionally helpful. Consider, for example, a program that needs to close standard output (file descriptor 1), substitute another file as standard output, call a function that writes some output onto standard output, and then restore the original situation. Just closing file descriptor 1 and then opening a new file will make the new file standard output (assuming standard input, file descriptor 0, is in use), but it will be impossible to restore the original situation later.

The solution is first to execute the statement

```
fd = dup(1);
```

which uses the DUP system call to allocate a new file descriptor, *fd*, and arrange for it to correspond to the same file as standard output. Then standard output can

```
struct stat {
    short st_dev;                   /* device where i-node belongs */
    unsigned short st_ino;          /* i-node number */
    unsigned short st_mode;         /* mode word */
    short st_nlink;                 /* number of links */
    short st_uid;                   /* user id */
    short st_gid;                   /* group id */
    short st_rdev;                  /* major/minor device for special files */
    long st_size;                   /* file size */
    long st_atime;                  /* time of last access */
    long st_mtime;                  /* time of last modification */
    long st_ctime;                  /* time of last change to i-node */
};
```

Figure 1-12. The structure used to return information for the STAT and FSTAT system calls. In the actual code, symbolic names are used for some of the types.

be closed and a new file opened and used. When it is time to restore the original situation, file descriptor 1 can be closed, and then

n = dup(fd);

executed to assign the lowest file descriptor, namely, 1, to the same file as *fd*. Finally, *fd* can be closed and we are back where we started.

The DUP call has a variant that allows an arbitrary unassigned file descriptor to be made to refer to a given open file. It is called by

dup2(fd, fd2);

where *fd* refers to an open file and *fd2* is the unassigned file descriptor that is to be made to refer to the same file as *fd*. Thus if *fd* refers to standard input (file descriptor 0) and *fd2* is 4, after the call, file descriptors 0 and 4 will both refer to standard input.

Interprocess communication in MINIX uses pipes, as described earlier. When a user types

cat file1 file2 | sort

the shell creates a pipe and arranges for standard output of the first process to write to the pipe, so standard input of the second process can read from it. The PIPE system call creates a pipe and returns two file descriptors, one for writing and one for reading. The call is

pipe(&fd[0]);

where *fd* is an array of two integers and *fd*[0] is the file descriptor for reading and *fd*[1] is the one for writing. Typically, a FORK comes next, and the parent closes the file descriptor for reading and the child closes the file descriptor for writing (or vice versa), so when they are done, one process can read the pipe and the other can write on it.

Figure 1-13 depicts a skeleton procedure that creates two processes, with the output of the first one piped into the second one. (A more realistic example would do error checking and handle arguments.) First a pipe is created, and then the procedure forks, with the parent eventually becoming the first process in the pipeline and the child process becoming the second one. Since the files to be executed, *process1* and *process2*, do not know that they are part of a pipeline, it is essential that the file descriptors be manipulated so that the first process' standard output be the pipe and the second one's standard input be the pipe. The parent first closes off the file descriptor for reading from the pipe. Then it closes standard output and does a DUP call that allows file descriptor 1 to write on the pipe. It is important to realize that DUP always returns the lowest available file descriptor, in this case, 1. Then the program closes the other pipe file descriptor.

After the EXEC call, the process started will have file descriptors 0 and 2 be unchanged, and file descriptor 1 for writing on the pipe. The child code is analogous. The parameter to *execl* is repeated because the first one is the file to be executed and the second one is the first parameter, which most programs expect to be the file name.

The next system call, IOCTL, is potentially applicable to all special files. It is, for instance, used by block device drivers like the SCSI driver to control tape and CD-ROM devices. Its main use, however, is with special character files, primarily terminals. POSIX defines a number of functions which the library translates into IOCTL calls. The *tcgetattr* and *tcsetattr* library functions use IOCTL to change the characters used for correcting typing errors on the terminal, changing the terminal mode, and so forth.

Cooked mode is the normal terminal mode, in which the erase and kill characters work normally, CTRL-S and CTRL-Q can be used for stopping and starting terminal output, CTRL-D means end of file, DEL generates an interrupt signal, and CTRL-\ generates a quit signal to force a core dump.

In **raw mode**, all of these functions are disabled; every character is passed directly to the program with no special processing. Furthermore, in raw mode, a read from the terminal will give the program any characters that have been typed, even a partial line, rather than waiting for a complete line to be typed, as in cooked mode.

Cbreak mode is in between. The erase and kill characters for editing are disabled, as is CTRL-D, but CTRL-S, CTRL-Q, DEL, and CTRL-\ are enabled. Like raw mode, partial lines can be returned to programs (if intraline editing is turned off there is no need to wait until a whole line has been received—the user cannot change his mind and delete it, as he can in cooked mode).

POSIX does not use the terms cooked, raw, and cbreak. In POSIX terminology **canonical mode** corresponds to cooked mode. In this mode there are eleven special characters defined, and input is by lines. In **noncanonical mode** a minimum

```
#define STD_INPUT 0              /* file descriptor for standard input */
#define STD_OUTPUT 1             /* file descriptor for standard output */

pipeline(process1, process2)
char *process1, *process2;       /* pointers to program names */
{
  int fd[2];

  pipe(&fd[0]);                  /* create a pipe */
  if (fork() != 0) {
     /* The parent process executes these statements. */
     close(fd[0]);               /* process 1 does not need to read from pipe */
     close(STD_OUTPUT);          /* prepare for new standard output */
     dup(fd[1]);                 /* set standard output to fd[1] */
     close(fd[1]);               /* this file descriptor not needed any more */
     execl(process1, process1, 0);
  } else {
     /* The child process executes these statements. */
     close(fd[1]);               /* process 2 does not need to write to pipe */
     close(STD_INPUT);           /* prepare for new standard input */
     dup(fd[0]);                 /* set standard input to fd[0] */
     close(fd[0]);               /* this file descriptor not needed any more */
     execl(process2, process2, 0);
  }
}
```

Figure 1-13. A skeleton for setting up a two-process pipeline.

number of characters to accept and a time, specified in units of 1/10th of a second, determine how a read will be satisfied. Under POSIX there is a great deal of flexibility, and various flags can be set to make noncanonical mode behave like either cbreak or raw mode. The older terms are more descriptive, and we will continue to use them informally.

IOCTL has three parameters, for example a call to *tcsetattr* to set terminal parameters will result in

ioctl(fd, TCSETS, &termios);

The first parameter specifies a file, the second one specifies an operation, and the third one is the address of the POSIX structure that contains flags and the array of control characters. Other operation codes can postpone the changes until all output has been sent, cause unread input to be discarded, and return the current values.

The ACCESS system call is used to determine whether a certain file access is permitted by the protection system. It is needed because some programs can run using a different user's uid. This SETUID mechanism will be described later.

The RENAME system call is used to give a file a new name. The parameters specific the old and new names.

Finally, the FCNTL call is used to control files, somewhat analogous to IOCTL (i.e., both of them are horrible hacks). It has several options, the most important of which is for advisory file locking. Using FCNTL, it is possible for a process to lock and unlock parts of files and test part of a file to see if it is locked. The call does not enforce any lock semantics. Programs must do this themselves.

1.4.4 System Calls for Directory Management

In this section we will look at some system calls that relate more to directories or the file system as a whole, rather than just to one specific file as in the previous section. The first two calls, MKDIR and RMDIR, create and remove empty directories, respectively. The next call is LINK. Its purpose is to allow the same file to appear under two or more names, often in different directories. A typical use is to allow several members of the same programming team to share a common file, with each of them having the file appear in his own directory, possibly under different names. Sharing a file is not the same as giving every team member a private copy, because having a shared file means that changes that any member of the team makes are instantly visible to the other members—there is only one file. When copies are made of a file, subsequent changes made to one copy do not affect the other ones.

To see how LINK works, consider the situation of Fig. 1-14(a). Here are two users, *ast* and *jim*, each having their own directories with some files. If *ast* now executes a program containing the system call

link("/usr/jim/memo", "/usr/ast/note");

the file *memo* in *jim*'s directory is now entered into *ast*'s directory under the name *note*. Thereafter, */usr/jim/memo* and */usr/ast/note* refer to the same file.

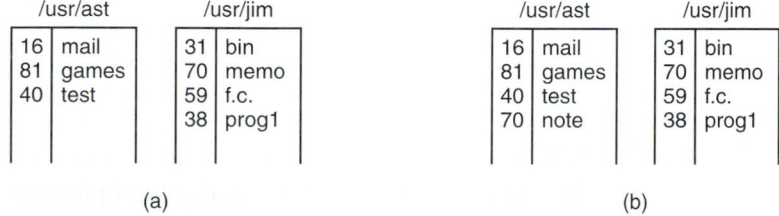

Figure 1-14. (a) Two directories before linking */usr/jim/memo* to ast's directory. (b) The same directories after linking.

Understanding how LINK works will probably make it clearer what it does. Every file in MINIX has a unique number, its i-number, that identifies it. This i-number is an index into a table of **i-nodes**, one per file, telling who owns the file, where its disk blocks are, and so on. A directory is simply a file containing a set of (i-number, ASCII name) pairs. In Fig. 1-14, *mail* has i-number 16, and so on. What LINK does is simply create a new directory entry with a (possibly new) name, using the i-number of an existing file. In Fig. 1-14(b), two entries have the same i-number (70), and thus refer to the same file. If either one is later removed, using the UNLINK system call, the other one remains. If both are removed, MINIX sees that no entries to the file exist (a field in the i-node keeps track of the number of directory entries pointing to the file), so the file is removed from the disk.

As we have mentioned earlier, the MOUNT system call allows two file systems to be merged into one. A common situation is to have the **root file system**, containing the binary (executable) versions of the common commands and other heavily used files, on the RAM disk. The user can then insert a floppy disk, for example, containing user programs, into drive 0.

By executing the MOUNT system call, the drive 0 file system can be attached to the root file system, as shown in Fig. 1-15. A typical statement in C to perform the mount is

```
mount("/dev/fd0", "/mnt", 0);
```

where the first parameter is the name of a block special file for drive 0 and the second parameter is the place in the tree where it is to be mounted.

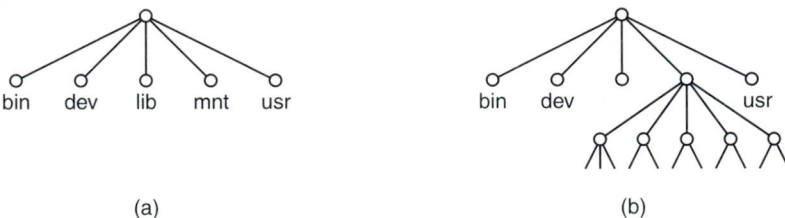

(a)   (b)

Figure 1-15. (a) File system before the mount. (b) File system after the mount.

After the MOUNT call, a file on drive 0 can be accessed by just using its path from the root directory or the working directory, without regard to which drive it is on. In fact, second, third, and fourth drives can also be mounted anywhere in the tree. The MOUNT command makes it possible to integrate removable media into a single integrated file hierarchy, without having to worry about which device a file is on. Although this example involves floppy disks, hard disks or portions of hard disks (often called **partitions** or **minor devices**) can also be mounted this way. When a file system is no longer needed, it can be unmounted with the UMOUNT system call.

MINIX maintains a cache of recently used blocks in main memory to avoid having to read them from the disk if they are used again quickly. If a block in the cache is modified (by a WRITE on a file) and the system crashes before the modified block is written out to disk, the file system will be damaged. To limit the potential damage, it is important to flush the cache periodically, so that the amount of data lost by a crash will be small. The system call SYNC tells MINIX to write out all the cache blocks that have been modified since being read in. When MINIX is started up, a program called *update* is started as a background process to do a SYNC every 30 seconds, to keep flushing the cache.

Two other calls that relate to directories are CHDIR and CHROOT. The former changes the working directory and the latter changes the root directory. After the call

```
chdir("/usr/ast/test");
```

an open on the file *xyz* will open */usr/ast/test/xyz*. CHROOT works in an analogous way. Once a process has told the system to change its root directory, all absolute path names (path names beginning with a "/") will start at the new root. Only super-users may execute CHROOT, and even super-users do not do it very often.

1.4.5 System Calls for Protection

In MINIX every file has an 11-bit mode used for protection. Nine of these bits are the read-write-execute bits for the owner, group, and others. The CHMOD system call makes it possible to change the mode of a file. For example, to make a file read-only by everyone except the owner, one could execute

```
chmod("file", 0644);
```

The other two protection bits, 02000 and 04000, are the SETGID (set-group-id) and SETUID (set-user-id) bits, respectively. When any user executes a program with the SETUID bit on, for the duration of that process the user's effective uid is changed to that of the file's owner. This feature is heavily used to allow users to execute programs that perform super-user only functions, such as creating directories. Creating a directory uses MKNOD, which is for the super-user only. By arranging for the *mkdir* program to be owned by the super-user and have mode 04755, ordinary users can be given the power to execute MKNOD but in a highly restricted way.

When a process executes a file that has the SETUID or SETGID bit on in its mode, it acquires an effective uid or gid different from its real uid or gid. It is sometimes important for a process to find out what its real and effective uid or gid is. The system calls GETUID and GETGID have been provided to supply this information. Each call returns both the real and effective uid or gid, so four library routines are needed to extract the proper information: *getuid*, *getgid*, *geteuid*, and *getegid*. The first two get the real uid/gid, and the last two the effective ones.

Ordinary users cannot change their uid, except by executing programs with the SETUID bit on, but the super-user has another possibility: the SETUID system call, which sets both the effective and real uids. SETGID sets both gids. The super-user can also change the owner of a file with the CHOWN system call. In short, the super-user has plenty of opportunity for violating all the protection rules, which explains why so many students devote so much of their time to trying to become super-user.

The last two system calls in this category can be executed by ordinary user processes. The first one, UMASK, sets an internal bit mask within the system, which is used to mask off mode bits when a file is created. After the call

```
umask(022);
```

the mode supplied by CREAT and MKNOD will have the 022 bits masked off before being used. Thus the call

```
creat("file", 0777);
```

will set the mode to 0755 rather than 0777. Since the bit mask is inherited by child processes, if the shell does a UMASK just after login, none of the user's processes in that session will accidently create files that other people can write on.

When a program owned by the root has the SETUID bit on, it can access any file, because its effective uid is the super-user. Frequently it is useful for the program to know if the person who called the program has permission to access a given file. If the program just tries the access, it will always succeed, and thus learn nothing.

What is needed is a way to see if the access is permitted for the real uid. The ACCESS system call provides a way to find out. The *mode* parameter is 4 to check for read access, 2 for write access, and 1 for execute access. Combinations are also allowed, for example, with *mode* equal to 6, the call returns 0 if both read and write access are allowed for the real uid; otherwise −1 is returned. With *mode* equal to 0, a check is made to see if the file exists and the directories leading up to it can be searched.

1.4.6 System Calls for Time Management

MINIX has four system calls that involve the time-of-day clock. TIME just returns the current time in seconds, with 0 corresponding to Jan. 1, 1970 at midnight (just as the day was starting, not ending). Of course, the system clock must be set at some point in order to allow it to be read later, so STIME has been provided to let the clock be set (by the super-user). The third time call is UTIME, which allows the owner of a file (or the super-user) to change the time stored in a file's i-node. Application of this system call is fairly limited, but a few programs need it, for example, *touch*, which sets the file's time to the current time.

Finally, we have TIMES, which returns the accounting information to a process, so it can see how much CPU time it has used directly, and how much CPU time the system itself has expended on its behalf (handling its system calls). The total user and system times used by all of its children combined are also returned.

1.5 OPERATING SYSTEM STRUCTURE

Now that we have seen what operating systems look like on the outside (i.e, the programmer's interface), it is time to take a look inside. In the following sections, we will examine four different structures that have been tried, in order to get some idea of the spectrum of possibilities. These are by no means exhaustive, but they give an idea of some designs that have been tried in practice. The four designs are monolithic systems, layered systems, virtual machines, and client-server systems.

1.5.1 Monolithic Systems

By far the most common organization, this approach might well be subtitled "The Big Mess." The structure is that there is no structure. The operating system is written as a collection of procedures, each of which can call any of the other ones whenever it needs to. When this technique is used, each procedure in the system has a well-defined interface in terms of parameters and results, and each one is free to call any other one, if the latter provides some useful computation that the former needs.

To construct the actual object program of the operating system when this approach is used, one first compiles all the individual procedures, or files containing the procedures, and then binds them all together into a single object file using the system linker. In terms of information hiding, there is essentially none—every procedure is visible to every other procedure (as opposed to a structure containing modules or packages, in which much of the information is hidden away inside modules, and only the officially designated entry points can be called from outside the module).

Even in monolithic systems, however, it is possible to have at least a little structure. The services (system calls) provided by the operating system are requested by putting the parameters in well-defined places, such as in registers or on the stack, and then executing a special trap instruction known as a **kernel call** or **supervisor call**.

This instruction switches the machine from user mode to kernel mode and transfers control to the operating system, shown as event (1) in Fig. 1-16. (Most CPUs have two modes: kernel mode, for the operating system, in which all instructions are allowed; and user mode, for user programs, in which I/O and certain other instructions are not allowed.)

The operating system then examines the parameters of the call to determine which system call is to be carried out, shown as (2) in Fig. 1-16. Next, the operating system indexes into a table that contains in slot k a pointer to the procedure that carries out system call k. This operation, shown as (3) in Fig. 1-16, identifies the service procedure, which is then called. When the work has been completed

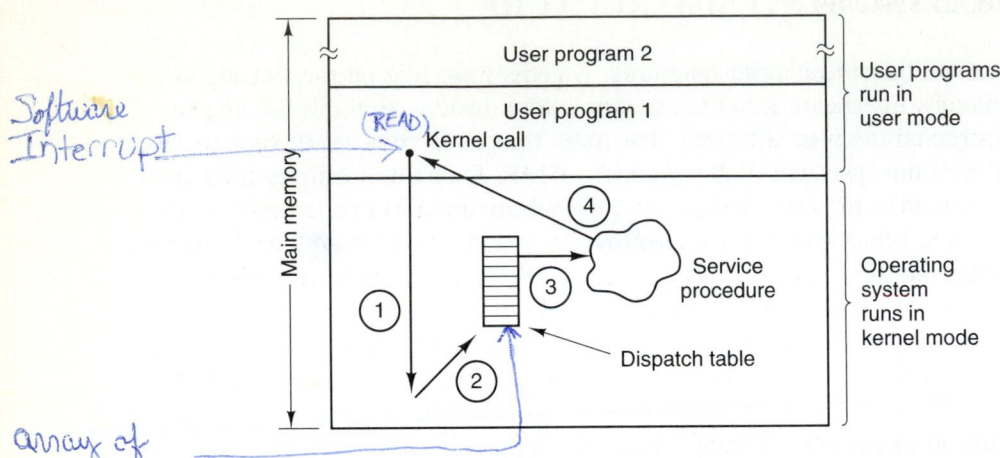

Software Interrupt

array of pointers

Figure 1-16. How a system call can be made: (1) User program traps to the kernel. (2) Operating system determines service number required. (3) Operating system calls service procedure. (4) Control is returned to user program.

and the system call is finished, control is given back to the user program (step 4), so it can continue execution with the statement following the system call.

This organization suggests a basic structure for the operating system:

1. A main program that invokes the requested service procedure.

2. A set of service procedures that carry out the system calls.

3. A set of utility procedures that help the service procedures.

In this model, for each system call there is one service procedure that takes care of it. The utility procedures do things that are needed by several service procedures, such as fetching data from user programs. This division of the procedures into three layers is shown in Fig. 1-17.

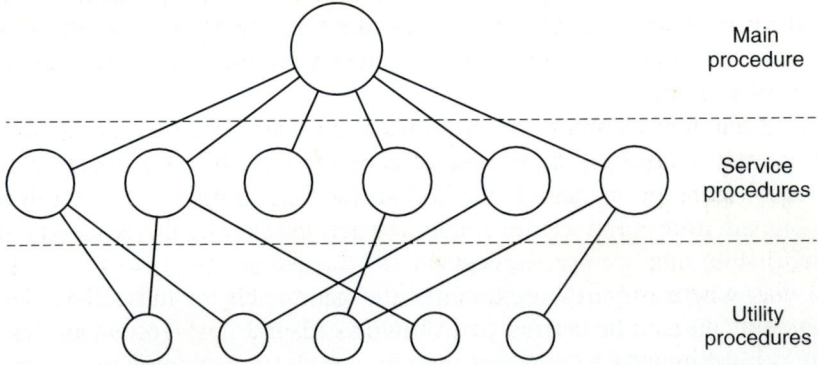

Figure 1-17. A simple structuring model for a monolithic system.

1.5.2 Layered Systems

A generalization of the approach of Fig. 1-17 is to organize the operating system as a hierarchy of layers, each one constructed upon the one below it. The first system constructed in this way was the THE system built at the Technische Hogeschool Eindhoven in the Netherlands by E. W. Dijkstra (1968) and his students. The THE system was a simple batch system for a Dutch computer, the Electrologica X8, which had 32K of 27-bit words (bits were expensive back then).

The system had 6 layers, as shown in Fig. 1-18. Layer 0 dealt with allocation of the processor, switching between processes when interrupts occurred or timers expired. Above layer 0, the system consisted of sequential processes, each of which could be programmed without having to worry about the fact that multiple processes were running on a single processor. In other words, layer 0 provided the basic multiprogramming of the CPU.

Layer	Function
5	The operator
4	User programs
3	Input/output management
2	Operator-process communication
1	Memory and drum management
0	Processor allocation and multiprogramming

Figure 1-18. Structure of the THE operating system.

Layer 1 did the memory management. It allocated space for processes in main memory and on a 512K word drum used for holding parts of processes (pages) for which there was no room in main memory. Above layer 1, processes did not have to worry about whether they were in memory or on the drum; the layer 1 software took care of making sure pages were brought into memory whenever they were needed.

Layer 2 handled communication between each process and the operator console. Above this layer each process effectively had its own operator console. Layer 3 took care of managing the I/O devices and buffering the information streams to and from them. Above layer 3 each process could deal with abstract I/O devices with nice properties, instead of real devices with many peculiarities. Layer 4 was where the user programs were found. They did not have to worry about process, memory, console, or I/O management. The system operator process was located in layer 5.

A further generalization of the layering concept was present in the MULTICS system. Instead of layers, MULTICS was organized as a series of concentric rings, with the inner ones being more privileged than the outer ones. When a procedure in an outer ring wanted to call a procedure in an inner ring, it had to make the equivalent of a system call, that is, a TRAP instruction whose parameters were carefully checked for validity before allowing the call to proceed. Although the entire operating system was part of the address space of each user process in MULTICS, the hardware made it possible to designate individual procedures (memory segments, actually) as protected against reading, writing, or executing.

Whereas the THE layering scheme was really only a design aid, because all the parts of the system were ultimately linked together into a single object program, in MULTICS, the ring mechanism was very much present at run time and enforced by the hardware. The advantage of the ring mechanism is that it can easily be extended to structure user subsystems. For example, a professor could write a program to test and grade student programs and run this program in ring n, with the student programs running in ring $n + 1$ so that they could not change their grades.

1.5.3 Virtual Machines

The initial releases of OS/360 were strictly batch systems. Nevertheless, many 360 users wanted to have timesharing, so various groups, both inside and outside IBM decided to write timesharing systems for it. The official IBM timesharing system, TSS/360, was delivered late, and when it finally arrived it was so big and slow that few sites converted over to it. It was eventually abandoned after its development had consumed some $50 million (Graham, 1970). But a group at IBM's Scientific Center in Cambridge, Massachusetts, produced a radically different system that IBM eventually accepted as a product, and which is now widely used on its remaining mainframes.

This system, originally called CP/CMS and later renamed VM/370 (Seawright and MacKinnon, 1979), was based on an astute observation: a timesharing system provides (1) multiprogramming and (2) an extended machine with a more convenient interface than the bare hardware. The essence of VM/370 is to completely separate these two functions.

The heart of the system, known as the **virtual machine monitor**, runs on the bare hardware and does the multiprogramming, providing not one, but several virtual machines to the next layer up, as shown in Fig. 1-19. However, unlike all other operating systems, these virtual machines are not extended machines, with files and other nice features. Instead, they are *exact* copies of the bare hardware, including kernel/user mode, I/O, interrupts, and everything else the real machine has.

Because each virtual machine is identical to the true hardware, each one can run any operating system that will run directly on the bare hardware. Different virtual machines can, and frequently do, run different operating systems. Some run one of the descendants of OS/360 for batch or transaction processing, while

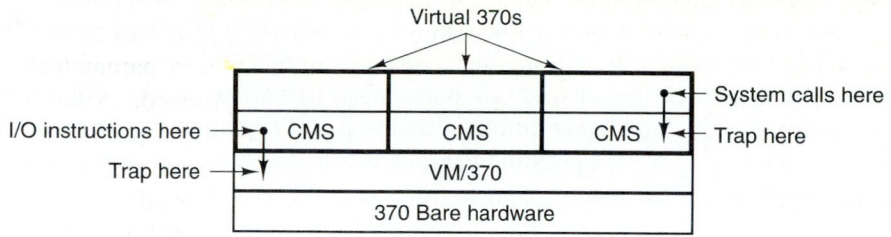

Figure 1-19. The structure of VM/370 with CMS.

other ones run a single-user, interactive system called **CMS** (Conversational Monitor System) for timesharing users.

When a CMS program executes a system call, the call is trapped to the operating system in its own virtual machine, not to VM/370, just as it would if it were running on a real machine instead of a virtual one. CMS then issues the normal hardware I/O instructions for reading its virtual disk or whatever is needed to carry out the call. These I/O instructions are trapped by VM/370, which then performs them as part of its simulation of the real hardware. By making a complete separation of the functions of multiprogramming and providing an extended machine, each of the pieces can be much simpler, more flexible, and easier to maintain.

The idea of a virtual machine is heavily used nowadays in a different context: running old MS-DOS programs on a Pentium (or other 32-bit Intel CPU). When designing the Pentium and its software, both Intel and Microsoft realized that there would be a big demand for running old software on new hardware. For this reason, Intel provided a virtual 8086 mode on the Pentium. In this mode, the machine acts like an 8086 (which is identical to an 8088 from a software point of view), including 16-bit addressing with a 1-MB limit.

This mode is used by WINDOWS, OS/2, and other operating systems for running MS-DOS programs. These programs are started up in virtual 8086 mode. As long as they execute normal instructions, they run on the bare hardware. However, when a program tries to trap to the operating system to make a system call, or tries to do protected I/O directly, a trap to the virtual machine monitor occurs.

Two variants on this design are possible. In the first one, MS-DOS itself is loaded into the virtual 8086's address space, so the virtual machine monitor just reflects the trap back to MS-DOS, just as would happen on a real 8086. When MS-DOS later tries to do the I/O itself, that operation is caught and carried out by the virtual machine monitor.

In the other variant, the virtual machine monitor just catches the first trap and does the I/O itself, since it knows what all the MS-DOS system calls are and thus knows what each trap is supposed to do. This variant is less pure than the first one, since it only emulates MS-DOS correctly, and not other operating systems, as the first one does. On the other hand, it is much faster, since it saves the trouble of starting up MS-DOS to do the I/O. A further disadvantage of actually running MS-DOS in virtual 8086 mode is that MS-DOS fiddles around with the interrupt enable/disable bit quite a lot, all of which must be emulated at considerable cost.

It is worth noting that neither of these approaches are really the same as VM/370, since the machine being emulated is not a full Pentium, but only an 8086. With the VM/370 system, it is possible to run VM/370, itself, in the virtual machine. With the Pentium, it is not possible to run, say, WINDOWS in the virtual 8086 because no version of WINDOWS runs on an 8086; a 286 is the minimum for even the oldest version, and 286 emulation is not provided (let alone Pentium emulation).

With VM/370, each user process gets an exact copy of the actual computer. With virtual 8086 mode on the Pentium, each user process gets an exact copy of a different computer. Going one step further, researchers at M.I.T. have built a system that gives each user a clone of the actual computer, but with a subset of the resources (Engler et al., 1995). Thus one virtual machine might get disk blocks 0 to 1023, the next one might get blocks 1024 to 2047, and so on.

At the bottom layer, running in kernel mode, is a program called the **exokernel**. Its job is to allocate resources to virtual machines and then check attempts to use them to make sure no machine is trying to use somebody else's resources. Each user-level virtual machine can run its own operating system, as on VM/370 and the Pentium virtual 8086s, except that each one is restricted to using only the resources it has asked for and been allocated.

The advantage of the exokernel scheme is that it saves a layer of mapping. In the other designs, each virtual machine thinks it has its own disk, with blocks running from 0 to some maximum, so the virtual machine monitor must maintain tables to remap disk addresses (and all other resources). With the exokernel, this remapping is not needed. The exokernel need only keep track of which virtual machine has been assigned which resource. This method still has the advantage of separating the multiprogramming (in the exokernel) from the user operating system code (in user space), but with less overhead, since all the exokernel has to do is keep the virtual machines out of each other's hair.

1.5.4 Client-Server Model

VM/370 gains much in simplicity by moving a large part of the traditional operating system code (implementing the extended machine) into a higher layer, CMS. Nevertheless, VM/370 itself is still a complex program because simulating a number of virtual 370s is not *that* simple (especially if you want to do it reasonably efficiently).

A trend in modern operating systems is to take this idea of moving code up into higher layers even further and remove as much as possible from the operating system, leaving a minimal **kernel**. The usual approach is to implement most of the operating system functions in user processes. To request a service, such as reading a block of a file, a user process (now known as the **client process**) sends the request to a **server process**, which then does the work and sends back the answer.

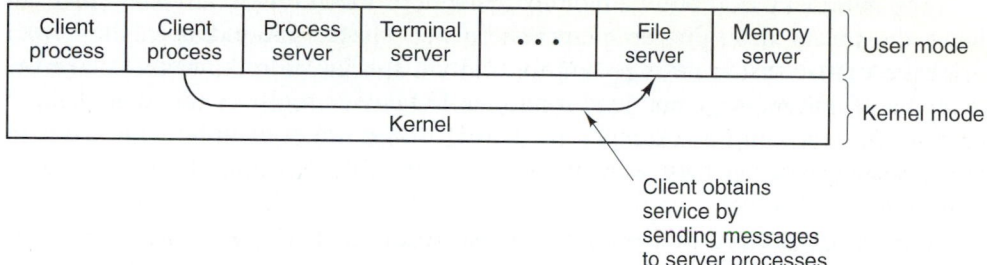

Figure 1-20. The client-server model.

In this model, shown in Fig. 1-20, all the kernel does is handle the communication between clients and servers. By splitting the operating system up into parts, each of which only handles one facet of the system, such as file service, process service, terminal service, or memory service, each part becomes small and manageable. Furthermore, because all the servers run as user-mode processes, and not in kernel mode, they do not have direct access to the hardware. As a consequence, if a bug in the file server is triggered, the file service may crash, but this will not usually bring the whole machine down.

Another advantage of the client-server model is its adaptability to use in distributed systems (see Fig. 1-21). If a client communicates with a server by sending it messages, the client need not know whether the message is handled locally in its own machine, or whether it was sent across a network to a server on a remote machine. As far as the client is concerned, the same thing happens in both cases: a request was sent and a reply came back.

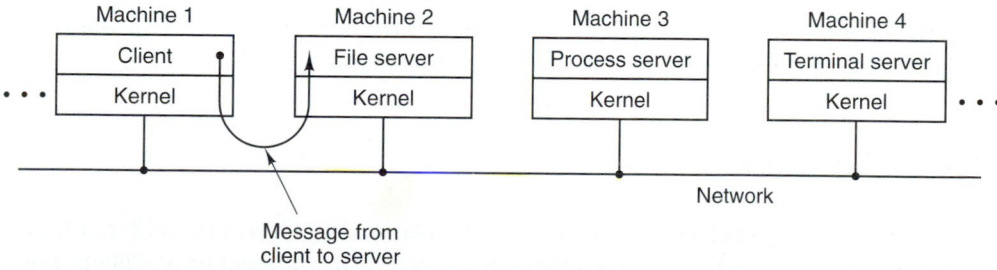

Figure 1-21. The client-server model in a distributed system.

The picture painted above of a kernel that handles only the transport of messages from clients to servers and back is not completely realistic. Some operating system functions (such as loading commands into the physical I/O device registers) are difficult, if not impossible, to do from user-space programs. There are two ways of dealing with this problem. One way is to have some critical server processes (e.g., I/O device drivers) actually run in kernel mode, with complete access to all the hardware, but still communicate with other processes using the normal message mechanism.

The other way is to build a minimal amount of **mechanism** into the kernel but leave the **policy** decisions up to servers in user space. For example, the kernel might recognize that a message sent to a certain special address means to take the contents of that message and load it into the I/O device registers for some disk, to start a disk read. In this example, the kernel would not even inspect the bytes in the message to see if they were valid or meaningful; it would just blindly copy them into the disk's device registers. (Obviously, some scheme for limiting such messages to authorized processes only must be used.) The split between mechanism and policy is an important concept; it occurs again and again in operating systems in various contexts.

1.6 OUTLINE OF THE REST OF THIS BOOK

Operating systems typically have four major components: process management, I/O device management, memory management, and file management. MINIX is also divided into these four parts. The next four chapters deal with these four topics, one topic per chapter. Chapter 6 is a list of suggested readings and a bibliography.

The chapters on processes, I/O, memory management, and file systems have the same general structure. First the general principles of the subject are laid out. Then comes an overview of the corresponding area of MINIX (which also applies to UNIX). Finally, the MINIX implementation is discussed in detail. The implementation section may be skimmed or skipped without loss of continuity by readers just interested in the principles of operating systems and not interested in the MINIX code. Readers who *are* interested in finding out how a real operating system (MINIX) works should read all the sections.

1.7 SUMMARY

Operating systems can be viewed from two viewpoints: resource managers and extended machines. In the resource manager view, the operating system's job is to efficiently manage the different parts of the system. In the extended machine view, the job of the system is to provide the users with a virtual machine that is more convenient to use than the actual machine.

Operating systems have a long history, starting from the days when they replaced the operator, to modern multiprogramming systems.

The heart of any operating system is the set of system calls that it can handle. These tell what the operating system really does. For MINIX, these calls can be divided into six groups. The first group of system calls relates to process creation and termination. The second group handles signals. The third group is for reading and writing files. A fourth group is for directory management. The fifth group protects information, and the sixth group is about keeping track of time.

Operating systems can be structured in several ways. The most common ones are as a monolithic system, as a hierarchy of layers, as a virtual machine system and using the client-server model.

PROBLEMS

1. What are the two main functions of an operating system?

2. What is multiprogramming?

3. What is spooling? Do you think that advanced personal computers will have spooling as a standard feature in the future?

4. On early computers, every byte of data read or written was directly handled by the CPU (i.e., there was no DMA—Direct Memory Access). What implications does this organization have for multiprogramming?

5. Why was timesharing not widespread on second-generation computers?

6. Which of the following instructions should be allowed only in kernel mode?

(a) Disable all interrupts.
(b) Read the time-of-day clock.
(c) Set the time-of-day clock.
(d) Change the memory map.

7. List some differences between personal computer operating systems and mainframe operating systems.

8. A MINIX file whose owner has uid = 12 and gid = 1 has mode *rwxr-x---*. Another user with uid = 6, gid = 1 tries to execute the file. What will happen?

9. In view of the fact that the mere existence of a super-user can lead to all kinds of security problems, why does such a concept exist?

10. The client-server model is popular in distributed systems. Can it also be used in a single-computer system?

11. Why is the process table needed in a timesharing system? Is it also needed in personal computer systems in which only one process exists, that process taking over the entire machine until it is finished?

12. What is the essential difference between a block special file and a character special file?

13. In MINIX, if user 2 links to a file owned by user 1, then user 1 removes the file, what happens when user 2 tries to read the file?

14. Why is the CHROOT system call limited to the super-user? (Hint: Think about protection problems.)

15. Why does MINIX have the program *update* running in the background all the time?

16. Does it ever make any sense to ignore the SIGALRM signal?

17. Write a program (or series of programs) to test all the MINIX system calls. For each call, try various sets of parameters, including some incorrect ones, to see if they are detected.

18. Write a shell that is similar to Fig. 1-10 but contains enough code that it actually works so you can test it. You might also add some features such as redirection of input and output, pipes, and background jobs.

2

PROCESSES

We are now about to embark on a detailed study of how operating systems, in general, and MINIX, in particular, are designed and constructed. The most central concept in any operating system is the *process*: an abstraction of a running program. Everything else hinges on this concept, and it is important that the operating system designer (and student) know what a process is as early as possible.

2.1 INTRODUCTION TO PROCESSES

All modern computers can do several things at the same time. While running a user program, a computer can also be reading from a disk and outputting text to a screen or printer. In a multiprogramming system, the CPU also switches from program to program, running each for tens or hundreds of milliseconds. While, strictly speaking, at any instant of time, the CPU is running only one program, in the course of 1 second, it may work on several programs, thus giving the users the illusion of parallelism. Sometimes people speak of **pseudoparallelism** to mean this rapid switching back and forth of the CPU between programs, to contrast it with the true hardware parallelism of **multiprocessor** systems (which have two or more CPUs sharing the same physical memory). Keeping track of multiple, parallel activities is hard for people to do. Therefore, operating system designers over the years have evolved a model (sequential processes) that makes parallelism easier to deal with. That model and its uses are the subject of this chapter.

2.1.1 The Process Model

In this model, all the runnable software on the computer, often including the operating system, is organized into a number of **sequential processes**, or just **processes** for short. A process is just an executing program, including the current values of the program counter, registers, and variables. Conceptually, each process has its own virtual CPU. In reality, of course, the real CPU switches back and forth from process to process, but to understand the system, it is much easier to think about a collection of processes running in (pseudo) parallel, than to try to keep track of how the CPU switches from program to program. This rapid switching back and forth is called **multiprogramming**, as we saw in the previous chapter.

In Fig. 2-1(a) we see a computer multiprogramming four programs in memory. In Fig. 2-1(b) we see four processes, each with its own flow of control (i.e., its own program counter), and each one running independently of the other ones. In Fig. 2-1(c) we see that viewed over a long enough time interval, all the processes have made progress, but at any given instant only one process is actually running.

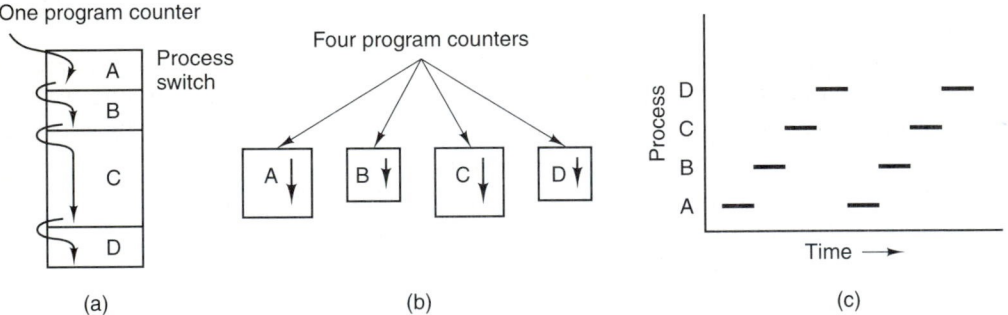

Figure 2-1. (a) Multiprogramming of four programs. (b) Conceptual model of four independent, sequential processes. (c) Only one program is active at any instant.

With the CPU switching back and forth among the processes, the rate at which a process performs its computation will not be uniform, and probably not even reproducible if the same processes are run again. Thus, processes must not be programmed with built-in assumptions about timing. Consider, for example, an I/O process that starts a streamer tape to restore backed up files, executes an idle loop 10,000 times to let it get up to speed, and then issues a command to read the first record. If the CPU decides to switch to another process during the idle loop, the tape process might not run again until after the first record was already past the read head. When a process has critical real-time requirements like this, that is, particular events *must* occur within a specified number of milliseconds, special measures must be taken to ensure that they do occur. Normally, however, most processes are not affected by the underlying multiprogramming of the CPU or the relative speeds of different processes.

The difference between a process and a program is subtle, but crucial. An analogy may help make this point clearer. Consider a culinary-minded computer scientist who is baking a birthday cake for his daughter. He has a birthday cake recipe and a kitchen well-stocked with the necessary input: flour, eggs, sugar, extract of vanilla, and so on. In this analogy, the recipe is the program (i.e., an algorithm expressed in some suitable notation), the computer scientist is the processor (CPU), and the cake ingredients are the input data. The process is the activity consisting of our baker reading the recipe, fetching the ingredients, and baking the cake.

Now imagine that the computer scientist's son comes running in crying, saying that he has been stung by a bee. The computer scientist records where he was in the recipe (the state of the current process is saved), gets out a first aid book, and begins following the directions in it. Here we see the processor being switched from one process (baking) to a higher priority process (administering medical care), each having a different program (recipe vs. first aid book). When the bee sting has been taken care of, the computer scientist goes back to his cake, continuing at the point where he left off.

The key idea here is that a process is an activity of some kind. It has a program, input, output, and a state. A single processor may be shared among several processes, with some scheduling algorithm being used to determine when to stop work on one process and service a different one.

Process Hierarchies

Operating systems that support the process concept must provide some way to create all the processes needed. In very simple systems, or in systems designed for running only a single application (e.g., controlling a device in real time), it may be possible to have all the processes that will ever be needed be present when the system comes up. In most systems, however, some way is needed to create and destroy processes as needed during operation. In MINIX, processes are created by the FORK system call, which creates an identical copy of the calling process. The child process can also execute FORK, so it is possible to get a whole tree of processes. In other operating systems, system calls exist to create a process, load its memory, and start it running. Whatever the exact nature of the system call, processes need a way to create other processes. Note that each process has one parent but zero, one, two, or more children.

As a simple example of how process trees are used, let us look at how MINIX initializes itself when it is started. A special process, called *init*, is present in the boot image. When it starts running, it reads a file telling how many terminals there are. Then it forks off one new process per terminal. These processes wait for someone to log in. If a login is successful, the login process executes a shell to accept commands. These commands may start up more processes, and so forth. Thus, all the processes in the whole system belong to a single tree, with *init* at the root. (The code for *init* is not listed in the book; neither is the shell. The line had to be drawn somewhere.)

Process States

Although each process is an independent entity, with its own program counter and internal state, processes often need to interact with other processes. One process may generate some output that another process uses as input. In the shell command

cat chapter1 chapter2 chapter3 | grep tree

the first process, running *cat*, concatenates and outputs three files. The second process, running *grep*, selects all lines containing the word "tree." Depending on the relative speeds of the two processes (which depends on both the relative complexity of the programs and how much CPU time each one has had), it may happen that *grep* is ready to run, but there is no input waiting for it. It must then **block** until some input is available.

When a process blocks, it does so because logically it cannot continue, typically because it is waiting for input that is not yet available. It is also possible for a process that is conceptually ready and able to run to be stopped because the operating system has decided to allocate the CPU to another process for a while. These two conditions are completely different. In the first case, the suspension is inherent in the problem (you cannot process the user's command line until it has been typed). In the second case, it is a technicality of the system (not enough CPUs to give each process its own private processor). In Fig. 2-2 we see a state diagram showing the three states a process may be in:

1. Running (actually using the CPU at that instant).

2. Ready (runnable; temporarily stopped to let another process run).

3. Blocked (unable to run until some external event happens).

Logically, the first two states are similar. In both cases the process is willing to run, only in the second one, there is temporarily no CPU available for it. The third state is different from the first two in that the process cannot run, even if the CPU has nothing else to do.

Four transitions are possible among these three states, as shown. Transition 1 occurs when a process discovers that it cannot continue. In some systems the process must execute a system call, BLOCK, to get into blocked state. In other systems, including MINIX, when a process reads from a pipe or special file (e.g., a terminal) and there is no input available, the process is automatically blocked.

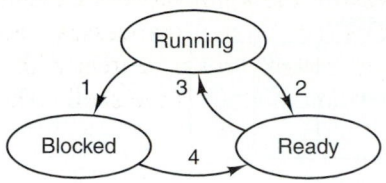

1. Process blocks for input
2. Scheduler picks another process
3. Scheduler picks this process
4. Input becomes available

Figure 2-2. A process can be in running, blocked, or ready state. Transitions between these states are as shown.

Transitions 2 and 3 are caused by the process scheduler, a part of the operating system, without the process even knowing about them. Transition 2 occurs when the scheduler decides that the running process has run long enough, and it is time to let another process have some CPU time. Transition 3 occurs when all the other processes have had their fair share and it is time for the first process to get the CPU to run again. The subject of scheduling, that is, deciding which process should run when and for how long, is an important one; we will look at it later in this chapter. Many algorithms have been devised to try to balance the competing demands of efficiency for the system as a whole and fairness to individual processes.

Transition 4 occurs when the external event for which a process was waiting (such as the arrival of some input) happens. If no other process is running at that instant, transition 3 will be triggered immediately, and the process will start running. Otherwise it may have to wait in *ready* state for a little while until the CPU is available.

Using the process model, it becomes much easier to think about what is going on inside the system. Some of the processes run programs that carry out commands typed in by a user. Other processes are part of the system and handle tasks such as carrying out requests for file services or managing the details of running a disk or a tape drive. When a disk interrupt occurs, the system makes a decision to stop running the current process and run the disk process, which was blocked waiting for that interrupt. Thus, instead of thinking about interrupts, we can think about user processes, disk processes, terminal processes, and so on, which block when they are waiting for something to happen. When the disk block has been read or the character typed, the process waiting for it is unblocked and is eligible to run again.

This view gives rise to the model shown in Fig. 2-3. Here the lowest level of the operating system is the scheduler, with a variety of processes on top of it. All the interrupt handling and details of actually starting and stopping processes are hidden away in the scheduler, which is actually quite small. The rest of the operating system is nicely structured in process form. The model of Fig. 2-3 is used in MINIX, with the understanding that "scheduler" really means not just process scheduling, but also interrupt handling and all the interprocess communication. Nevertheless, to a first approximation, it does show the basic structure.

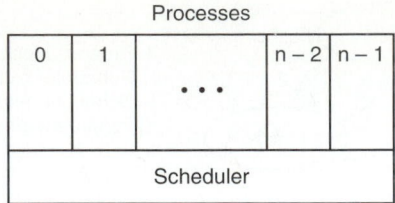

Figure 2-3. The lowest layer of a process-structured operating system handles interrupts and scheduling. Above that layer are sequential processes.

2.1.2 Implementation of Processes

To implement the process model, the operating system maintains a table (an array of structures), called the **process table**, with one entry per process. This entry contains information about the process' state, its program counter, stack pointer, memory allocation, the status of its open files, its accounting and scheduling information, and everything else about the process that must be saved when the process is switched from *running* to *ready* state so that it can be restarted later as if it had never been stopped.

In MINIX the process management, memory management, and file management are each handled by separate modules within the system, so the process table is partitioned, with each module maintaining the fields that it needs. Figure 2-4 shows some of the more important fields. The fields in the first column are the only ones relevant to this chapter. The other two columns are provided just to give an idea of what information is needed elsewhere in the system.

Now that we have looked at the process table, it is possible to explain a little more about how the illusion of multiple sequential processes is maintained on a machine with one CPU and many I/O devices. What follows is technically a description of how the "scheduler" of Fig. 2-3 works in MINIX but most modern operating systems work essentially the same way. Associated with each I/O device class (e.g., floppy disks, hard disks, timers, terminals) is a location near the bottom of memory called the **interrupt vector**. It contains the address of the interrupt service procedure. Suppose that user process 3 is running when a disk interrupt occurs. The program counter, program status word, and possibly one or more registers are pushed onto the (current) stack by the interrupt hardware. The computer then jumps to the address specified in the disk interrupt vector. That is all the hardware does. From here on, it is up to the software.

The interrupt service procedure starts out by saving all the registers in the process table entry for the current process. The current process number and a pointer to its entry are kept in global variables so they can be found quickly. Then the information deposited by the interrupt is removed from the stack, and the stack pointer is set to a temporary stack used by the process handler. Actions such as saving the registers and setting the stack pointer cannot even be expressed in C, so

Process management	Memory management	File management
Registers	Pointer to text segment	UMASK mask
Program counter	Pointer to data segment	Root directory
Program status word	Pointer to bss segment	Working directory
Stack pointer	Exit status	File descriptors
Process state	Signal status	Effective uid
Time when process started	Process id	Effective gid
CPU time used	Parent process	System call parameters
Children's CPU time	Process group	Various flag bits
Time of next alarm	Real uid	
Message queue pointers	Effective	
Pending signal bits	Real gid	
Process id	Effective gid	
Various flag bits	Bit maps for signals	
	Various flag bits	

Figure 2-4. Some of the fields of the MINIX process table.

they are performed by a small assembly language routine. When this routine is finished, it calls a C procedure to do the rest of the work.

Interprocess communication in MINIX is via messages, so the next step is to build a message to be sent to the disk process, which will be blocked waiting for it. The message says that an interrupt occurred, to distinguish it from messages from user processes requesting disk blocks to be read and things like that. The state of the disk process is now changed from *blocked* to *ready* and the scheduler is called. In MINIX, different processes have different priorities, to give better service to I/O device handlers than to user processes. If the disk process is now the highest priority runnable process, it will be scheduled to run. If the process that was interrupted is just as important or more so, then it will be scheduled to run again, and the disk process will have to wait a little while.

Either way, the C procedure called by the assembly language interrupt code now returns, and the assembly language code loads up the registers and memory map for the now-current process and starts it running. Interrupt handling and scheduling are summarized in Fig. 2-5. It is worth noting that the details vary slightly from system to system.

2.1.3 Threads

In a traditional process, of the type we have just studied, there is a single thread of control and a single program counter in each process. However, in some modern operating systems, support is provided for multiple threads of control

1. Hardware stacks program counter, etc.
2. Hardware loads new program counter from interrupt vector.
3. Assembly language procedure saves registers.
4. Assembly language procedure sets up new stack.
5. C interrupt service runs (typically reads and buffers input).
6. Scheduler marks waiting task as ready.
7. Scheduler decides which process is to run next.
8. C procedure returns to the assembly code.
9. Assembly language procedure starts up new current process.

Figure 2-5. Skeleton of what the lowest level of the operating system does when an interrupt occurs.

within a process. These threads of control are usually just called **threads**, or occasionally **lightweight processes**.

In Fig. 2-6(a) we see three traditional processes. Each process has its own address space and a single thread of control. In contrast, in Fig. 2-6(b) we see a single process with three threads of control. Although in both cases we have three threads, in Fig. 2-6(a) each of them operates in a different address space, whereas in Fig. 2-6(b) all three of them share the same address space.

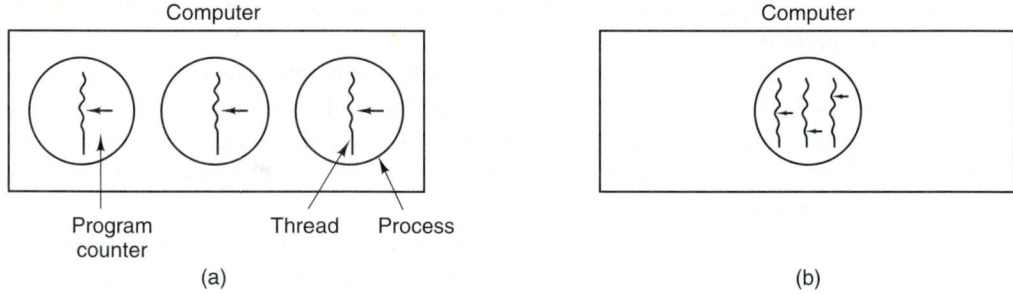

Figure 2-6. (a) Three processes each with one thread. (b) One process with three threads.

As an example of where multiple threads might be used, consider a file server process. It receives requests to read and write files and sends back the requested data or accepts updated data. To improve performance, the server maintains a cache of recently used files in memory, reading from the cache and writing to the cache when possible.

This situation lends itself well to the model of Fig. 2-6(b). When a request comes in, it is handed to a thread for processing. If that thread blocks part way through waiting for a disk transfer, other threads are still able to run, so the server can keep processing new requests even while disk I/O is taking place. The model of Fig. 2-6(a) is not suitable, because it is essential that all file server threads access the same cache, and the three threads of Fig. 2-6(a) do not share the same address space and thus cannot share the same memory cache.

Another example of where threads are useful is in browsers for the World Wide Web, such as Netscape and Mosaic. Many Web pages contain multiple small images. For each image on a Web page, the browser must set up a separate connection to the page's home site and request the image. A great deal of time is wasted establishing and releasing all these connections. By having multiple threads within the browser, many images can be requested at the same time, greatly speeding up performance in most cases, since with small images, the set-up time is the limiting factor, not the speed of the transmission line.

When multiple threads are present in the same address space, a few of the fields of Fig. 2-4 are not per process, but per thread, so a separate thread table is needed, with one entry per thread. Among the per-thread items are the program counter, registers, and state. The program counter is needed because threads, like processes, can be suspended and resumed. The registers are needed because when threads are suspended, their registers must be saved. Finally, threads, like processes, can be in *running*, *ready*, or *blocked* state.

In some systems, the operating system is not aware of the threads. In other words, they are managed entirely in user space. When a thread is about to block, for example, it chooses and starts its successor before stopping. Several user-level threads packages are in common use, including the POSIX **P-threads** and Mach **C-threads** packages.

In other systems, the operating system is aware of the existence of multiple threads per process, so when a thread blocks, the operating system chooses the next one to run, either from the same process or a different one. To do scheduling, the kernel must have a thread table that lists all the threads in the system, analogous to the process table.

Although these two alternatives may seem equivalent, they differ considerably in performance. Switching threads is much faster when thread management is done in user space than when a kernel call is needed. This fact argues strongly for doing thread management in user space. On the other hand, when threads are managed entirely in user space and one thread blocks (e.g., waiting for I/O or a page fault to be handled), the kernel blocks the entire process, since it is not even aware that other threads exist. This fact argues strongly for doing thread management in the kernel. As a consequence, both systems are in use, and various hybrid schemes have been proposed as well (Anderson et al., 1992).

No matter whether threads are managed by the kernel or in user space, they introduce a raft of problems that must be solved and which change the programming model appreciably. To start with, consider the effects of the FORK system call. If the parent process has multiple threads, should the child also have them? If not, the process may not function properly, since all of them may be essential.

However, if the child process gets as many threads as the parent, what happens if a thread was blocked on a READ call, say, from the keyboard. Are two threads now blocked on the keyboard? When a line is typed, do both threads get a copy of it? Only the parent? Only the child? The same problem exists with open network connections.

Another class of problems is related to the fact that threads share many data structures. What happens if one thread closes a file while another one is still reading from it? Suppose that one thread notices that there is too little memory and starts allocating more memory. Then, part way through, a thread switch occurs, and the new thread also notices that there is too little memory and also starts allocating more memory. Does the allocation happen once or twice? In nearly all systems that were not designed with threads in mind, the libraries (such as the memory allocation procedure) are not reentrant, and will crash if a second call is made while the first one is still active.

Another problem relates to error reporting. In UNIX, after a system call, the status of the call is put into a global variable, *errno*. What happens if a thread makes a system call, and before it is able to read *errno*, another thread makes a system call, wiping out the original value?

Next, consider signals. Some signals are logically thread specific, whereas others are not. For example, if a thread calls ALARM, it makes sense for the resulting signal to go to the thread that made the call. When the kernel is aware of threads, it can usually make sure the right thread gets the signal. When the kernel is not aware of threads, somehow the threads package must keep track of alarms. An additional complication for user-level threads exists when (as in UNIX) a process may only have one alarm at a time pending and several threads call ALARM independently.

Other signals, such as keyboard interrupt, are not thread specific. Who should catch them? One designated thread? All the threads? A newly created thread? All these solutions have problems. Furthermore, what happens if one thread changes the signal handlers without telling other threads?

One last problem introduced by threads is stack management. In many systems, when stack overflow occurs, the kernel just provides more stack, automatically. When a process has multiple threads, it must also have multiple stacks. If the kernel is not aware of all these stacks, it cannot grow them automatically upon stack fault. In fact, it may not even realize that a memory fault is related to stack growth.

These problems are certainly not insurmountable, but they do show that just introducing threads into an existing system without a fairly substantial system redesign is not going to work at all. The semantics of system calls have to be redefined and libraries have to be rewritten, at the very least. And all of these things must be done in such a way as to remain backward compatible with existing programs for the limiting case of a process with only one thread. For additional information about threads, see (Hauser et al., 1993; and Marsh et al., 1991).

2.2 INTERPROCESS COMMUNICATION

Processes frequently need to communicate with other processes. For example, in a shell pipeline, the output of the first process must be passed to the second process, and so on down the line. Thus there is a need for communication between processes, preferably in a well-structured way not using interrupts. In the following sections we will look at some of the issues related to this **InterProcess Communication** or **IPC**.

Very briefly, there are three issues here. The first was alluded to above: how one process can pass information to another. The second has to do with making sure two or more processes do not get into each other's way when engaging in critical activities (suppose two processes each try to grab the last 100K of memory). The third concerns proper sequencing when dependencies are present: if process A produces data and process B prints it, B has to wait until A has produced some data before starting to print. We will examine all three of these issues starting in the next section.

2.2.1 Race Conditions

In some operating systems, processes that are working together may share some common storage that each one can read and write. The shared storage may be in main memory or it may be a shared file; the location of the shared memory does not change the nature of the communication or the problems that arise. To see how interprocess communication works in practice, let us consider a simple but common example, a print spooler. When a process wants to print a file, it enters the file name in a special **spooler directory**. Another process, the **printer daemon**, periodically checks to see if there are any files to be printed, and if there are it prints them and then removes their names from the directory.

Imagine that our spooler directory has a large (potentially infinite) number of slots, numbered 0, 1, 2, ..., each one capable of holding a file name. Also imagine that there are two shared variables, *out*, which points to the next file to be printed, and *in*, which points to the next free slot in the directory. These two variables might well be kept on a two-word file available to all processes. At a certain instant, slots 0 to 3 are empty (the files have already been printed) and slots 4 to 6 are full (with the names of files queued for printing). More or less simultaneously, processes A and B decide they want to queue a file for printing. This situation is shown in Fig. 2-7.

In jurisdictions where Murphy's law† is applicable, the following might happen. Process A reads *in* and stores the value, 7, in a local variable called *next_free_slot*. Just then a clock interrupt occurs and the CPU decides that process A has run long enough, so it switches to process B. Process B also reads *in*,

---

† If something can go wrong, it will.

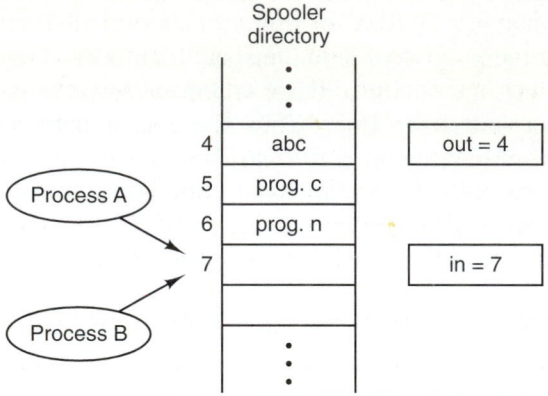

Figure 2-7. Two processes want to access shared memory at the same time.

and also gets a 7, so it stores the name of its file in slot 7 and updates *in* to be an 8. Then it goes off and does other things.

Eventually, process *A* runs again, starting from the place it left off. It looks at *next_free_slot*, finds a 7 there, and writes its file name in slot 7, erasing the name that process *B* just put there. Then it computes *next_free_slot* + 1, which is 8, and sets *in* to 8. The spooler directory is now internally consistent, so the printer daemon will not notice anything wrong, but process *B* will never get any output. Situations like this, where two or more processes are reading or writing some shared data and the final result depends on who runs precisely when, are called **race conditions.** Debugging programs containing race conditions is no fun at all. The results of most test runs are fine, but once in a rare while something weird and unexplained happens.

2.2.2 Critical Sections

How do we avoid race conditions? The key to preventing trouble here and in many other situations involving shared memory, shared files, and shared everything else is to find some way to prohibit more than one process from reading and writing the shared data at the same time. Put in other words, what we need is **mutual exclusion**—some way of making sure that if one process is using a shared variable or file, the other processes will be excluded from doing the same thing. The difficulty above occurred because process *B* started using one of the shared variables before process *A* was finished with it. The choice of appropriate primitive operations for achieving mutual exclusion is a major design issue in any operating system, and a subject that we will examine in great detail in the following sections.

The problem of avoiding race conditions can also be formulated in an abstract way. Part of the time, a process is busy doing internal computations and other things that do not lead to race conditions. However, sometimes a process may be accessing shared memory or files, or doing other critical things that can lead to races. That part of the program where the shared memory is accessed is called the **critical region** or **critical section**. If we could arrange matters such that no two processes were ever in their critical regions at the same time, we could avoid race conditions.

Although this requirement avoids race conditions, this is not sufficient for having parallel processes cooperate correctly and efficiently using shared data. We need four conditions to hold to have a good solution:

1. No two processes may be simultaneously inside their critical regions.

2. No assumptions may be made about speeds or the number of CPUs.

3. No process running outside its critical region may block other processes.

4. No process should have to wait forever to enter its critical region.

2.2.3 Mutual Exclusion with Busy Waiting

In this section we will examine various proposals for achieving mutual exclusion, so that while one process is busy updating shared memory in its critical region, no other process will enter *its* critical region and cause trouble.

Disabling Interrupts

The simplest solution is to have each process disable all interrupts just after entering its critical region and re-enable them just before leaving it. With interrupts disabled, no clock interrupts can occur. The CPU is only switched from process to process as a result of clock or other interrupts, after all, and with interrupts turned off the CPU will not be switched to another process. Thus, once a process has disabled interrupts, it can examine and update the shared memory without fear that any other process will intervene.

This approach is generally unattractive because it is unwise to give user processes the power to turn off interrupts. Suppose that one of them did it, and never turned them on again? That could be the end of the system. Furthermore, if the system is a multiprocessor, with two or more CPUs, disabling interrupts affects only the CPU that executed the disable instruction. The other ones will continue running and can access the shared memory.

On the other hand, it is frequently convenient for the kernel itself to disable interrupts for a few instructions while it is updating variables or lists. If an interrupt occurred while the list of ready processes, for example, was in an inconsistent state, race conditions could occur. The conclusion is: disabling interrupts is often a useful technique within the operating system itself but is not appropriate as a general mutual exclusion mechanism for user processes.

Lock Variables

As a second attempt, let us look for a software solution. Consider having a single, shared, (lock) variable, initially 0. When a process wants to enter its critical region, it first tests the lock. If the lock is 0, the process sets it to 1 and enters the critical region. If the lock is already 1, the process just waits until it becomes 0. Thus, a 0 means that no process is in its critical region, and a 1 means that some process is in its critical region.

Unfortunately, this idea contains exactly the same fatal flaw that we saw in the spooler directory. Suppose that one process reads the lock and sees that it is 0. Before it can set the lock to 1, another process is scheduled, runs, and sets the lock to 1. When the first process runs again, it will also set the lock to 1, and two processes will be in their critical regions at the same time.

Now you might think that we could get around this problem by first reading out the lock value, then checking it again just before storing into it, but that really does not help. The race now occurs if the second process modifies the lock just after the first process has finished its second check.

Strict Alternation

A third approach to the mutual exclusion problem is shown in Fig. 2-8. This program fragment, like nearly all the others in this book, is written in C. C was chosen here because real operating systems are commonly written in C (or occasionally C++), but hardly ever in languages like Modula 2 or Pascal.

```
while (TRUE) {                          while (TRUE) {
  while (turn != 0)  /* wait */ ;         while (turn != 1) /* wait */ ;
  critical_region();                      critical_region();
  turn = 1;                               turn = 0;
  noncritical_region();                   noncritical_region();
}                                       }

        (a)                                      (b)
```

Figure 2-8. A proposed solution to the critical region problem.

In Fig. 2-8, the integer variable *turn*, initially 0, keeps track of whose turn it is to enter the critical region and examine or update the shared memory. Initially, process 0 inspects *turn*, finds it to be 0, and enters its critical region. Process 1 also finds it to be 0 and therefore sits in a tight loop continually testing *turn* to see when it becomes 1. Continuously testing a variable until some value appears is called **busy waiting**. It should usually be avoided, since it wastes CPU time. Only when there is a reasonable expectation that the wait will be short is busy waiting used.

When process 0 leaves the critical region, it sets *turn* to 1, to allow process 1 to enter its critical region. Suppose that process 1 finishes its critical region quickly, so both processes are in their noncritical regions, with *turn* set to 0. Now process 0 executes its whole loop quickly, coming back to its noncritical region with *turn* set to 1. At this point, process 0 finishes its noncritical region and goes back to the top of its loop. Unfortunately, it is not permitted to enter its critical region now, because *turn* is 1 and process 1 is busy with its noncritical region. Put differently, taking turns is not a good idea when one of the processes is much slower than the other.

This situation violates condition 3 set out above: process 0 is being blocked by a process not in its critical region. Going back to the spooler directory discussed above, if we now associate the critical region with reading and writing the spooler directory, process 0 would not be allowed to print another file because process 1 was doing something else.

In fact, this solution requires that the two processes strictly alternate in entering their critical regions, for example, in spooling files. Neither one would be permitted to spool two in a row. While this algorithm does avoid all races, it is not really a serious candidate as a solution because it violates condition 3.

Peterson's Solution

By combining the idea of taking turns with the idea of lock variables and warning variables, a Dutch mathematician, T. Dekker, was the first one to devise a software solution to the mutual exclusion problem that does not require strict alternation. For a discussion of Dekker's algorithm, see (Dijkstra, 1965).

In 1981, G.L. Peterson discovered a much simpler way to achieve mutual exclusion, thus rendering Dekker's solution obsolete. Peterson's algorithm is shown in Fig. 2-9. This algorithm consists of two procedures written in ANSI C, which means that function prototypes should be supplied for all the functions defined and used. However, to save space, we will not show the prototypes in this or subsequent examples.

Before using the shared variables (i.e., before entering its critical region), each process calls *enter_region* with its own process number, 0 or 1, as parameter. This call will cause it to wait, if need be, until it is safe to enter. After it has finished with the shared variables, the process calls *leave_region* to indicate that it is done and to allow the other process to enter, if it so desires.

Let us see how this solution works. Initially neither process is in its critical region. Now process 0 calls *enter_region*. It indicates its interest by setting its array element and sets *turn* to 0. Since process 1 is not interested, *enter_region* returns immediately. If process 1 now calls *enter_region*, it will hang there until

```
#define FALSE     0
#define TRUE      1
#define N         2                    /* number of processes */

int turn;                              /* whose turn is it? */
int interested[N];                     /* all values initially 0 (FALSE) */

void enter_region(int process);        /* process is 0 or 1 */
{
  int other;                           /* number of the other process */

  other = 1 − process;                 /* the opposite of process */
  interested[process] = TRUE;          /* show that you are interested */
  turn = process;                      /* set flag */
  while (turn == process && interested[other] == TRUE) /* null statement */ ;
}

void leave_region(int process)         /* process: who is leaving */
{
  interested[process] = FALSE;         /* indicate departure from critical region */
}
```

Figure 2-9. Peterson's solution for achieving mutual exclusion.

interested [0] goes to *FALSE*, an event that only happens when process 0 calls *leave_region* to exit the critical region.

Now consider the case that both processes call *enter_region* almost simultaneously. Both will store their process number in *turn*. Whichever store is done last is the one that counts; the first one is lost. Suppose that process 1 stores last, so *turn* is 1. When both processes come to the while statement, process 0 executes it zero times and enters its critical region. Process 1 loops and does not enter its critical region.

The TSL Instruction

Now let us look at a proposal that requires a little help from the hardware. Many computers, especially those designed with multiple processors in mind, have an instruction TEST AND SET LOCK (TSL) that works as follows. It reads the contents of the memory word into a register and then stores a nonzero value at that memory address. The operations of reading the word and storing into it are guaranteed to be indivisible—no other processor can access the memory word until the instruction is finished. The CPU executing the TSL instruction locks the memory bus to prohibit other CPUs from accessing memory until it is done.

To use the TSL instruction, we will use a shared variable, *lock*, to coordinate access to shared memory. When *lock* is 0, any process may set it to 1 using the TSL instruction and then read or write the shared memory. When it is done, the process sets *lock* back to 0 using an ordinary MOVE instruction.

How can this instruction be used to prevent two processes from simultaneously entering their critical regions? The solution is given in Fig. 2-10. There a four-instruction subroutine in a fictitious (but typical) assembly language is shown. The first instruction copies the old value of *lock* to the register and then sets *lock* to 1. Then the old value is compared with 0. If it is nonzero, the lock was already set, so the program just goes back to the beginning and tests it again. Sooner or later it will become 0 (when the process currently in its critical region is done with its critical region), and the subroutine returns, with the lock set. Clearing the lock is simple. The program just stores a 0 in *lock*. No special instructions are needed.

```
enter_region:
        tsl register,lock          | copy lock to register and set lock to 1
        cmp register,#0            | was lock zero?
        jne enter_region          | if it was non zero, lock was set, so loop
        ret                        | return to caller; critical region entered


leave_region:
        move lock,#0              | store a 0 in lock
        ret                        | return to caller
```

Figure 2-10. Setting and clearing locks using TSL.

One solution to the critical region problem is now straightforward. Before entering its critical region, a process calls *enter_region*, which does busy waiting until the lock is free; then it acquires the lock and returns. After the critical region the process calls *leave_region*, which stores a 0 in *lock*. As with all solutions based on critical regions, the processes must call *enter_region* and *leave_region* at the correct times for the method to work. If a process cheats, the mutual exclusion will fail.

2.2.4 Sleep and Wakeup

Both Peterson's solution and the solution using TSL are correct, but both have the defect of requiring busy waiting. In essence, what these solutions do is this: when a process wants to enter its critical region, it checks to see if the entry is allowed. If it is not, the process just sits in a tight loop waiting until it is.

Not only does this approach waste CPU time, but it can also have unexpected effects. Consider a computer with two processes, H, with high priority and L, with low priority. The scheduling rules are such that H is run whenever it is in ready state. At a certain moment, with L in its critical region, H becomes ready to run (e.g., an I/O operation completes). H now begins busy waiting, but since L is never scheduled while H is running, L never gets the chance to leave its critical region, so H loops forever. This situation is sometimes referred to as the **priority inversion problem**.

Now let us look at some interprocess communication primitives that block instead of wasting CPU time when they are not allowed to enter their critical regions. One of the simplest is the pair SLEEP and WAKEUP. SLEEP is a system call that causes the caller to block, that is, be suspended until another process wakes it up. The WAKEUP call has one parameter, the process to be awakened. Alternatively, both SLEEP and WAKEUP each have one parameter, a memory address used to match up SLEEPs with WAKEUPs.

The Producer-Consumer Problem

As an example of how these primitives can be used, let us consider the **producer-consumer** problem (also known as the **bounded buffer** problem). Two processes share a common, fixed-size buffer. One of them, the producer, puts information into the buffer, and the other one, the consumer, takes it out. (It is also possible to generalize the problem to have m producers and n consumers, but we will only consider the case of one producer and one consumer because this assumption simplifies the solutions).

Trouble arises when the producer wants to put a new item in the buffer, but it is already full. The solution is for the producer to go to sleep, to be awakened when the consumer has removed one or more items. Similarly, if the consumer wants to remove an item from the buffer and sees that the buffer is empty, it goes to sleep until the producer puts something in the buffer and wakes it up.

This approach sounds simple enough, but it leads to the same kinds of race conditions we saw earlier with the spooler directory. To keep track of the number of items in the buffer, we will need a variable, *count*. If the maximum number of items the buffer can hold is N, the producer's code will first test to see if *count* is N. If it is, the producer will go to sleep; if it is not, the producer will add an item and increment *count*.

The consumer's code is similar: first test *count* to see if it is 0. If it is, go to sleep; if it is nonzero, remove an item and decrement the counter. Each of the processes also tests to see if the other should be sleeping, and if not, wakes it up. The code for both producer and consumer is shown in Fig. 2-11.

To express system calls such as SLEEP and WAKEUP in C, we will show them as calls to library routines. They are not part of the standard C library but presumably would be available on any system that actually had these system calls. The procedures *enter_item* and *remove_item*, which are not shown, handle the book-keeping of putting items into the buffer and taking items out of the buffer.

```
#define N  100                                /* number of slots in the buffer */
int count = 0;                               /* number of items in the buffer */

void producer(void)
{
  while (TRUE) {                             /* repeat forever */
        produce_item();                      /* generate next item */
        if (count == N) sleep();             /* if buffer is full, go to sleep */
        enter_item();                        /* put item in buffer */
        count = count + 1;                   /* increment count of items in buffer */
        if (count == 1) wakeup(consumer);    /* was buffer empty? */
  }
}


void consumer(void)
{
  while (TRUE) {                             /* repeat forever */
        if (count == 0) sleep();             /* if buffer is empty, got to sleep */
        remove_item();                       /* take item out of buffer */
        count = count - 1;                   /* decrement count of items in buffer */
        if (count == N-1) wakeup(producer);  /* was buffer full? */
        consume_item();                      /* print item */
  }
}
```

Figure 2-11. The producer-consumer problem with a fatal race condition.

Now let us get back to the race condition. It can occur because access to *count* is unconstrained. The following situation could possibly occur. The buffer is empty and the consumer has just read *count* to see if it is 0. At that instant, the scheduler decides to stop running the consumer temporarily and start running the producer. The producer enters an item in the buffer, increments *count*, and notices that it is now 1. Reasoning that *count* was just 0, and thus the consumer must be sleeping, the producer calls *wakeup* to wake the consumer up.

Unfortunately, the consumer is not yet logically asleep, so the wakeup signal is lost. When the consumer next runs, it will test the value of *count* it previously read, find it to be 0, and go to sleep. Sooner or later the producer will fill up the buffer and also go to sleep. Both will sleep forever.

The essence of the problem here is that a wakeup sent to a process that is not (yet) sleeping is lost. If it were not lost, everything would work. A quick fix is to modify the rules to add a **wakeup waiting bit** to the picture. When a wakeup is sent to a process that is still awake, this bit is set. Later, when the process tries to go to sleep, if the wakeup waiting bit is on, it will be turned off, but the process will stay awake. The wakeup waiting bit is a piggy bank for wakeup signals.

While the wakeup waiting bit saves the day in this simple example, it is easy to construct examples with three or more processes in which one wakeup waiting bit is insufficient. We could make another patch, and add a second wakeup waiting bit, or maybe 8 or 32 of them, but in principle the problem is still there.

2.2.5 Semaphores

This was the situation in 1965, when E. W. Dijkstra (1965) suggested using an integer variable to count the number of wakeups saved for future use. In his proposal, a new variable type, called a **semaphore**, was introduced. A semaphore could have the value 0, indicating that no wakeups were saved, or some positive value if one or more wakeups were pending.

Dijkstra proposed having two operations, DOWN and UP (generalizations of SLEEP and WAKEUP, respectively). The DOWN operation on a semaphore checks to see if the value is greater than 0. If so, it decrements the value (i.e., uses up one stored wakeup) and just continues. If the value is 0, the process is put to sleep without completing the DOWN for the moment. Checking the value, changing it, and possibly going to sleep is all done as a single, indivisible, **atomic action**. It is guaranteed that once a semaphore operation has started, no other process can access the semaphore until the operation has completed or blocked. This atomicity is absolutely essential to solving synchronization problems and avoiding race conditions.

The UP operation increments the value of the semaphore addressed. If one or more processes were sleeping on that semaphore, unable to complete an earlier DOWN operation, one of them is chosen by the system (e.g., at random) and is allowed to complete its DOWN. Thus, after an UP on a semaphore with processes sleeping on it, the semaphore will still be 0, but there will be one fewer process sleeping on it. The operation of incrementing the semaphore and waking up one process is also indivisible. No process ever blocks doing an UP, just as no process ever blocks doing a WAKEUP in the earlier model.

As an aside, in Dijkstra's original paper, he used the names P and V instead of DOWN and UP, respectively, but since these have no mnemonic significance to people who do not speak Dutch (and only marginal significance to those who do), we will use the terms DOWN and UP instead. These were first introduced in Algol 68.

Solving the Producer-Consumer Problem using Semaphores

Semaphores solve the lost-wakeup problem, as shown in Fig. 2-12. It is essential that they be implemented in an indivisible way. The normal way is to implement UP and DOWN as system calls, with the operating system briefly disabling all interrupts while it is testing the semaphore, updating it, and putting the process to sleep, if necessary. As all of these actions take only a few instructions, no harm is done in disabling interrupts. If multiple CPUs are being used, each semaphore should be protected by a lock variable, with the TSL instruction used to make sure that only one CPU at a time examines the semaphore. Be sure you understand that using TSL to prevent several CPUs from accessing the semaphore at the same time is quite different from busy waiting by the producer or consumer waiting for the other to empty or fill the buffer. The semaphore operation will only take a few microseconds, whereas the producer or consumer might take arbitrarily long.

```
#define N 100                      /* number of slots in the buffer */
typedef int semaphore;            /* semaphores are a special kind of int */
semaphore mutex = 1;              /* controls access to critical region */
semaphore empty = N;             /* counts empty buffer slots */
semaphore full = 0;               /* counts full buffer slots */

void producer(void)
{
  int item;

  while (TRUE) {                   /* TRUE is the constant 1 */
        produce_item(&item);      /* generate something to put in buffer */
        down(&empty);             /* decrement empty count */
        down(&mutex);             /* enter critical region */
        enter_item(item);         /* put new item in buffer */
        up(&mutex);               /* leave critical region */
        up(&full);                /* increment count of full slots */
  }
}


void consumer(void)
{
  int item;

  while (TRUE) {                   /* infinite loop */
        down(&full);              /* decrement full count */
        down(&mutex);             /* enter critical region */
        remove_item(&item);       /* take item from buffer */
        up(&mutex);               /* leave critical region */
        up(&empty);               /* increment count of empty slots */
        consume_item(item);       /* do something with the item */
  }
}
```

Figure 2-12. The producer-consumer problem using semaphores.

This solution uses three semaphores: one called *full* for counting the number of slots that are full, one called *empty* for counting the number of slots that are empty, and one called *mutex* to make sure the producer and consumer do not access the buffer at the same time. *Full* is initially 0, *empty* is initially equal to the number of slots in the buffer, and *mutex* is initially 1. Semaphores that are initialized to 1 and used by two or more processes to ensure that only one of them can enter its critical region at the same time are called **binary semaphores**. If each process does a DOWN just before entering its critical region and an UP just after leaving it, mutual exclusion is guaranteed.

Now that we have a good interprocess communication primitive at our disposal, let us go back and look at the interrupt sequence of Fig. 2-5 again. In a system using semaphores, the natural way to hide interrupts is to have a semaphore, initially set to 0, associated with each I/O device. Just after starting an I/O device, the managing process does a DOWN on the associated semaphore, thus blocking immediately. When the interrupt comes in, the interrupt handler then does an UP on the associated semaphore, which makes the relevant process ready to run again. In this model, step 6 in Fig. 2-5 consists of doing an UP on the device's semaphore, so that in step 7 the scheduler will be able to run the device manager. Of course, if several processes are now ready, the scheduler may choose to run an even more important process next. We will look at how scheduling is done later in this chapter.

In the example of Fig. 2-12, we have actually used semaphores in two different ways. This difference is important enough to make explicit. The *mutex* semaphore is used for mutual exclusion. It is designed to guarantee that only one process at a time will be reading or writing the buffer and the associated variables. This mutual exclusion is required to prevent chaos.

The other use of semaphores is for **synchronization**. The *full* and *empty* semaphores are needed to guarantee that certain event sequences do or do not occur. In this case, they ensure that the producer stops running when the buffer is full, and the consumer stops running when it is empty. This use is different from mutual exclusion.

Although semaphores have been around for more than a quarter of a century, people are still doing research about their use. As an example, see (Tai and Carver, 1996).

2.2.6 Monitors

With semaphores interprocess communication looks easy, right? Forget it. Look closely at the order of the DOWNs before entering or removing items from the buffer in Fig. 2-12. Suppose that the two DOWNs in the producer's code were reversed in order, so *mutex* was decremented before *empty* instead of after it. If the buffer were completely full, the producer would block, with *mutex* set to 0. Consequently, the next time the consumer tried to access the buffer, it would do a

DOWN on *mutex*, now 0, and block too. Both processes would stay blocked forever and no more work would ever be done. This unfortunate situation is called a **deadlock**. We will study deadlocks in detail in Chap. 3.

This problem is pointed out to show how careful you must be when using semaphores. One subtle error and everything comes to a grinding halt. It is like programming in assembly language, only worse, because the errors are race conditions, deadlocks, and other forms of unpredictable and irreproducible behavior.

To make it easier to write correct programs, Hoare (1974) and Brinch Hansen (1975) proposed a higher level synchronization primitive called a **monitor**. Their proposals differed slightly, as described below. A monitor is a collection of procedures, variables, and data structures that are all grouped together in a special kind of module or package. Processes may call the procedures in a monitor whenever they want to, but they cannot directly access the monitor's internal data structures from procedures declared outside the monitor. Figure 2-13 illustrates a monitor written in an imaginary language, pidgin Pascal.

```
monitor example
    integer i;
    condition c;

    procedure producer(x);
    .
    .
    .
    end;

    procedure consumer(x);
    .
    .
    .
    end;
end monitor;
```

Figure 2-13. A monitor.

Monitors have an important property that makes them useful for achieving mutual exclusion: only one process can be active in a monitor at any instant. Monitors are a programming language construct, so the compiler knows they are special and can handle calls to monitor procedures differently from other procedure calls. Typically, when a process calls a monitor procedure, the first few instructions of the procedure will check to see if any other process is currently active within the monitor. If so, the calling process will be suspended until the other process has left the monitor. If no other process is using the monitor, the calling process may enter.

It is up to the compiler to implement the mutual exclusion on monitor entries, but a common way is to use a binary semaphore. Because the compiler, not the programmer, is arranging for the mutual exclusion, it is much less likely that something will go wrong. In any event, the person writing the monitor does not have to be aware of how the compiler arranges for mutual exclusion. It is sufficient to know that by turning all the critical regions into monitor procedures, no two processes will ever execute their critical regions at the same time.

Although monitors provide an easy way to achieve mutual exclusion, as we have seen above, that is not enough. We also need a way for processes to block when they cannot proceed. In the producer-consumer problem, it is easy enough to put all the tests for buffer-full and buffer-empty in monitor procedures, but how should the producer block when it finds the buffer full?

The solution lies in the introduction of **condition variables**, along with two operations on them, WAIT and SIGNAL. When a monitor procedure discovers that it cannot continue (e.g., the producer finds the buffer full), it does a WAIT on some condition variable, say, *full*. This action causes the calling process to block. It also allows another process that had been previously prohibited from entering the monitor to enter now.

This other process, for example, the consumer, can wake up its sleeping partner by doing a SIGNAL on the condition variable that its partner is waiting on. To avoid having two active processes in the monitor at the same time, we need a rule telling what happens after a SIGNAL. Hoare proposed letting the newly awakened process run, suspending the other one. Brinch Hansen proposed finessing the problem by requiring that a process doing a SIGNAL *must* exit the monitor immediately. In other words, a SIGNAL statement may appear only as the final statement in a monitor procedure. We will use Brinch Hansen's proposal because it is conceptually simpler and is also easier to implement. If a SIGNAL is done on a condition variable on which several processes are waiting, only one of them, determined by the system scheduler, is revived.

Condition variables are not counters. They do not accumulate signals for later use the way semaphores do. Thus if a condition variable is signaled with no one waiting on it, the signal is lost. The WAIT must come before the SIGNAL. This rule makes the implementation much simpler. In practice it is not a problem because it is easy to keep track of the state of each process with variables, if need be. A process that might otherwise do a SIGNAL can see that this operation is not necessary by looking at the variables.

A skeleton of the producer-consumer problem with monitors is given in Fig. 2-14 in pidgin Pascal.

You may be thinking that the operations WAIT and SIGNAL look similar to SLEEP and WAKEUP, which we saw earlier had fatal race conditions. They *are* very similar, but with one crucial difference: SLEEP and WAKEUP failed because while one process was trying to go to sleep, the other one was trying to wake it up. With monitors, that cannot happen. The automatic mutual exclusion on monitor procedures guarantees that if, say, the producer inside a monitor procedure discovers that the buffer is full, it will be able to complete the WAIT operation

```
monitor ProducerConsumer
  condition full, empty;
  integer count;

  procedure enter;
  begin
    if count = N then wait(full);
    enter_item;
    count := count + 1;
    if count = 1 then signal(empty)
  end;


  procedure remove;
  begin
    if count = 0 then wait(empty);
    remove_item;
    count := count − 1;
    if count = N − 1 then signal(full)
  end;

  count := 0;
end monitor;


procedure producer;
begin
  while true do
  begin
    produce_item;
    ProducerConsumer.enter
  end
end;


procedure consumer;
begin
  while true do
  begin
    ProducerConsumer.remove;
    consume_item
  end
end;
```

Figure 2-14. An outline of the producer-consumer problem with monitors. Only one monitor procedure at a time is active. The buffer has N slots.

without having to worry about the possibility that the scheduler may switch to the consumer just before the WAIT completes. The consumer will not even be let into the monitor at all until the WAIT is finished and the producer has been marked as no longer runnable.

By making the mutual exclusion of critical regions automatic, monitors make parallel programming much less error-prone than with semaphores. Still, they too have some drawbacks. It is not for nothing that Fig. 2-14 is written in a strange kind of pidgin Pascal rather than in C, as are the other examples in this book. As we said earlier, monitors are a programming language concept. The compiler must recognize them and arrange for the mutual exclusion somehow. C, Pascal, and most other languages do not have monitors, so it is unreasonable to expect their compilers to enforce any mutual exclusion rules. In fact, how could the compiler even know which procedures were in monitors and which were not?

These same languages do not have semaphores either, but adding semaphores is easy: All you need to do is add two short assembly code routines to the library to issue the UP and DOWN system calls. The compilers do not even have to know that they exist. Of course, the operating systems have to know about the semaphores, but at least if you have a semaphore-based operating system, you can still write the user programs for it in C or C++ (or even BASIC if you are masochistic enough). With monitors, you need a language that has them built in. A few languages, such as Concurrent Euclid (Holt, 1983) have them, but they are rare.

Another problem with monitors, and also with semaphores, is that they were designed for solving the mutual exclusion problem on one or more CPUs that all have access to a common memory. By putting the semaphores in the shared memory and protecting them with TSL instructions, we can avoid races. When we go to a distributed system consisting of multiple CPUs, each with its own private memory, connected by a local area network, these primitives become inapplicable. The conclusion is that semaphores are too low level and monitors are not usable except in a few programming languages. Also, none of the primitives provide for information exchange between machines. Something else is needed.

2.2.7 Message Passing

That something else is **message passing**. This method of interprocess communication uses two primitives SEND and RECEIVE, which, like semaphores and unlike monitors, are system calls rather than language constructs. As such, they can easily be put into library procedures, such as

send(destination, &message);

and

receive(source, &message);

The former call sends a message to a given destination and the latter one receives a message from a given source (or from *ANY*, if the receiver does not care). If no message is available, the receiver could block until one arrives. Alternatively, it could return immediately with an error code.

Design Issues for Message Passing Systems

Message passing systems have many challenging problems and design issues that do not arise with semaphores or monitors, especially if the communicating processes are on different machines connected by a network. For example, messages can be lost by the network. To guard against lost messages, the sender and receiver can agree that as soon as a message has been received, the receiver will send back a special **acknowledgement** message. If the sender has not received the acknowledgement within a certain time interval, it retransmits the message.

Now consider what happens if the message itself is received correctly, but the acknowledgement is lost. The sender will retransmit the message, so the receiver will get it twice. It is essential that the receiver can distinguish a new message from the retransmission of an old one. Usually, this problem is solved by putting consecutive sequence numbers in each original message. If the receiver gets a message bearing the same sequence number as the previous message, it knows that the message is a duplicate that can be ignored.

Message systems also have to deal with the question of how processes are named, so that the process specified in a SEND or RECEIVE call is unambiguous. **Authentication** is also an issue in message systems: how can the client tell that he is communicating with the real file server, and not with an imposter?

At the other end of the spectrum, there are also design issues that are important when the sender and receiver are on the same machine. One of these is performance. Copying messages from one process to another is always slower than doing a semaphore operation or entering a monitor. Much work has gone into making message passing efficient. Cheriton (1984), for example, has suggested limiting message size to what will fit in the machine's registers, and then doing message passing using the registers.

The Producer-Consumer Problem with Message Passing

Now let us see how the producer-consumer problem can be solved with message passing and no shared memory. A solution is given in Fig. 2-15. We assume that all messages are the same size and that messages sent but not yet received are buffered automatically by the operating system. In this solution, a total of N messages is used, analogous to the N slots in a shared memory buffer. The consumer starts out by sending N empty messages to the producer. Whenever the producer has an item to give to the consumer, it takes an empty message and sends back a full one. In this way, the total number of messages in the system remains constant in time, so they can be stored in a given amount of memory known in advance.

If the producer works faster than the consumer, all the messages will end up full, waiting for the consumer; the producer will be blocked, waiting for an empty to come back. If the consumer works faster, then the reverse happens: all the messages will be empties waiting for the producer to fill them up; the consumer will be blocked, waiting for a full message.

```
#define N 100                          /* number of slots in the buffer */

void producer(void)
{
  int item;
  message m;                           /* message buffer */

  while (TRUE) {
        produce_item(&item);           /* generate something to put in buffer */
        receive(consumer, &m);         /* wait for an empty to arrive */
        build_message(&m, item);       /* construct a message to send */
        send(consumer, &m);            /* send item to consumer */
  }
}

void consumer(void)
{
  int item, i;
  message m;

  for (i = 0; i < N; i++) send(producer, &m); /* send N empties */
  while (TRUE) {
        receive(producer, &m);         /* get message containing item */
        extract_item(&m, &item);       /* extract item from message */
        send(producer, &m);            /* send back empty reply */
        consume_item(item);            /* do something with the item */
  }
}
```

Figure 2-15. The producer-consumer problem with N messages.

Many variants are possible with message passing. For starters, let us look at how messages are addressed. One way is to assign each process a unique address and have messages be addressed to processes. A different way is to invent a new data structure, called a **mailbox**. A mailbox is a place to buffer a certain number of messages, typically specified when the mailbox is created. When mailboxes are used, the address parameters in the SEND and RECEIVE calls are mailboxes, not processes. When a process tries to send to a mailbox that is full, it is suspended until a message is removed from that mailbox, making room for a new one.

For the producer-consumer problem, both the producer and consumer would create mailboxes large enough to hold N messages. The producer would send messages containing data to the consumer's mailbox, and the consumer would send empty messages to the producer's mailbox. When mailboxes are used, the buffering mechanism is clear: the destination mailbox holds messages that have been sent to the destination process but have not yet been accepted.

The other extreme from having mailboxes is to eliminate all buffering. When this approach is followed, if the SEND is done before the RECEIVE, the sending process is blocked until the RECEIVE happens, at which time the message can be copied directly from the sender to the receiver, with no intermediate buffering. Similarly, if the RECEIVE is done first, the receiver is blocked until a SEND happens. This strategy is often known as a **rendezvous**. It is easier to implement than a buffered message scheme but is less flexible since the sender and receiver are forced to run in lockstep.

The interprocess communication between user processes in MINIX (and UNIX) is via pipes, which are effectively mailboxes. The only real difference between a message system with mailboxes and the pipe mechanism is that pipes do not preserve message boundaries. In other words, if one process writes 10 messages of 100 bytes to a pipe and another process reads 1000 bytes from that pipe, the reader will get all 10 messages at once. With a true message system, each READ should return only one message. Of course, if the processes agree always to read and write fixed-size messages from the pipe, or to end each message with a special character (e.g., linefeed), no problems arise. The processes that make up the MINIX operating system itself use a true message scheme with fixed size messages for communication among themselves.

2.3 CLASSICAL IPC PROBLEMS

The operating systems literature is full of interesting problems that have been widely discussed and analyzed. In the following sections we will examine three of the better-known problems.

2.3.1 The Dining Philosophers Problem

In 1965, Dijkstra posed and solved a synchronization problem he called the **dining philosophers problem.** Since that time, everyone inventing yet another synchronization primitive has felt obligated to demonstrate how wonderful the new primitive is by showing how elegantly it solves the dining philosophers problem. The problem can be stated quite simply as follows. Five philosophers are seated around a circular table. Each philosopher has a plate of spaghetti. The spaghetti is so slippery that a philosopher needs two forks to eat it. Between each pair of plates is one fork. The layout of the table is illustrated in Fig. 2-16.

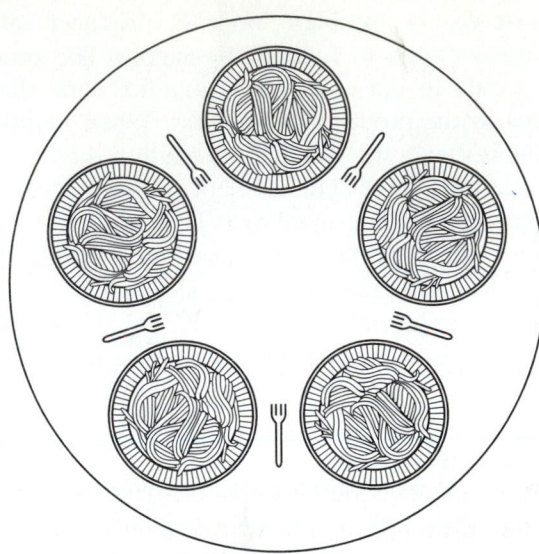

Figure 2-16. Lunch time in the Philosophy Department.

The life of a philosopher consists of alternate periods of eating and thinking. (This is something of an abstraction, even for philosophers, but the other activities are irrelevant here.) When a philosopher gets hungry, she tries to acquire her left and right fork, one at a time, in either order. If successful in acquiring two forks, she eats for a while, then puts down the forks and continues to think. The key question is: Can you write a program for each philosopher that does what it is supposed to do and never gets stuck? (It has been pointed out that the two-fork requirement is somewhat artificial; perhaps we should switch from Italian to Chinese food, substituting rice for spaghetti and chopsticks for forks.)

Figure 2-17 shows the obvious solution. The procedure *take_fork* waits until the specified fork is available and then seizes it. Unfortunately, the obvious solution is wrong. Suppose that all five philosophers take their left forks simultaneously. None will be able to take their right forks, and there will be a deadlock.

We could modify the program so that after taking the left fork, the program checks to see if the right fork is available. If it is not, the philosopher puts down the left one, waits for some time, and then repeats the whole process. This proposal too, fails, although for a different reason. With a little bit of bad luck, all the philosophers could start the algorithm simultaneously, picking up their left forks, seeing that their right forks were not available, putting down their left forks, waiting, picking up their left forks again simultaneously, and so on, forever. A situation like this, in which all the programs continue to run indefinitely but fail to make any progress is called **starvation**. (It is called starvation even when the problem does not occur in an Italian or a Chinese restaurant.)

Now you might think, "If the philosophers would just wait a random time instead of the same time after failing to acquire the right-hand fork, the chance

```
#define N 5                            /* number of philosophers */

void philosopher(int i)                /* i: philosopher number, from 0 to 4 */
{
  while (TRUE) {
        think();                       /* philosopher is thinking */
        take_fork(i);                  /* take left fork */
        take_fork((i+1) % N);          /* take right fork; % is modulo operator */
        eat();                         /* yum-yum, spaghetti */
        put_fork(i);                   /* put left fork back on the table */
        put_fork((i+1) % N);           /* put right fork back on the table */
  }
}
```

Figure 2-17. A nonsolution to the dining philosophers problem.

that everything would continue in lockstep for even an hour is very small.'' This observation is true, but in some applications one would prefer a solution that always works and cannot fail due to an unlikely series of random numbers. (Think about safety control in a nuclear power plant.)

One improvement to Fig. 2-17 that has no deadlock and no starvation is to protect the five statements following the call to *think* by a binary semaphore. Before starting to acquire forks, a philosopher would do a DOWN on *mutex*. After replacing the forks, she would do an UP on *mutex*. From a theoretical viewpoint, this solution is adequate. From a practical one, it has a performance bug: only one philosopher can be eating at any instant. With five forks available, we should be able to allow two philosophers to eat at the same time.

The solution presented in Fig. 2-18 is correct and also allows the maximum parallelism for an arbitrary number of philosophers. It uses an array, *state*, to keep track of whether a philosopher is eating, thinking, or hungry (trying to acquire forks). A philosopher may move only into eating state if neither neighbor is eating. Philosopher i's neighbors are defined by the macros *LEFT* and *RIGHT*. In other words, if i is 2, *LEFT* is 1 and *RIGHT* is 3.

The program uses an array of semaphores, one per philosopher, so hungry philosophers can block if the needed forks are busy. Note that each process runs the procedure *philosopher* as its main code, but the other procedures, *take_forks*, *put_forks*, and *test* are ordinary procedures and not separate processes.

2.3.2 The Readers and Writers Problem

The dining philosophers problem is useful for modeling processes that are competing for exclusive access to a limited number of resources, such as I/O devices. Another famous problem is the readers and writers problem (Courtois et al., 1971), which models access to a data base. Imagine, for example, an airline

```
#define N           5            /* number of philosophers */
#define LEFT    (i-1)%N          /* number of i's left neighbor */
#define RIGHT (i+1)%N            /* number of i's right neighbor */
#define THINKING    0            /* philosopher is thinking */
#define HUNGRY      1            /* philosopher is trying to get forks */
#define EATING      2            /* philosopher is eating */

typedef int semaphore;          /* semaphores are a special kind of int */
int state[N];                   /* array to keep track of everyone's state */
semaphore mutex = 1;            /* mutual exclusion for critical regions */
semaphore s[N];                 /* one semaphore per philosopher */

void philosopher(int i)         /* i: philosopher number, from 0 to N-1 */
{
  while (TRUE) {                /* repeat forever */
        think();               /* philosopher is thinking */
        take_forks(i);         /* acquire two forks or block */
        eat();                 /* yum-yum, spaghetti */
        put_forks(i);          /* put both forks back on table */
  }
}

void take_forks(int i)          /* i: philosopher number, from 0 to N-1 */
{
  down(&mutex);                /* enter critical region */
  state[i] = HUNGRY;           /* record fact that philosopher i is hungry */
  test(i);                     /* try to acquire 2 forks */
  up(&mutex);                  /* exit critical region */
  down(&s[i]);                 /* block if forks were not acquired */
}

void put_forks(i)               /* i: philosopher number, from 0 to N-1 */
{
  down(&mutex);                /* enter critical region */
  state[i] = THINKING;         /* philosopher has finished eating */
  test(LEFT);                  /* see if left neighbor can now eat */
  test(RIGHT);                 /* see if right neighbor can now eat */
  up(&mutex);                  /* exit critical region */
}

void test(i)                    /* i: philosopher number, from 0 to N-1 */
{
  if (state[i] == HUNGRY && state[LEFT] != EATING && state[RIGHT] != EATING) {
        state[i] = EATING;
        up(&s[i]);
  }
}
```

Figure 2-18. A solution to the dining philosopher's problem.

reservation system, with many competing processes wishing to read and write it. It is acceptable to have multiple processes reading the data base at the same time, but if one process is updating (writing) the data base, no other processes may have access to the data base, not even readers. The question is how do you program the readers and the writers? One solution is shown in Fig. 2-19.

```
typedef int semaphore;              /* use your imagination */
semaphore mutex = 1;                /* controls access to 'rc' */
semaphore db = 1;                   /* controls access to the data base */
int rc = 0;                         /* # of processes reading or wanting to */

void reader(void)
{
  while (TRUE) {                    /* repeat forever */
        down(&mutex);               /* get exclusive access to 'rc' */
        rc = rc + 1;                /* one reader more now */
        if (rc == 1) down(&db);     /* if this is the first reader ... */
        up(&mutex);                 /* release exclusive access to 'rc' */
        read_data_base();           /* access the data */
        down(&mutex);               /* get exclusive access to 'rc' */
        rc = rc - 1;                /* one reader fewer now */
        if (rc == 0) up(&db);       /* if this is the last reader ... */
        up(&mutex);                 /* release exclusive access to 'rc' */
        use_data_read();            /* noncritical region */
  }
}


void writer(void)
{
  while (TRUE) {                    /* repeat forever */
        think_up_data();            /* noncritical region */
        down(&db);                  /* get exclusive access */
        write_data_base();          /* update the data */
        up(&db);                    /* release exclusive access */
  }
}
```

Figure 2-19. A solution to the readers and writers problem.

In this solution, the first reader to get access to the data base does a DOWN on the semaphore *db*. Subsequent readers merely increment a counter, *rc*. As readers leave, they decrement the counter and the last one out does an UP on the semaphore, allowing a blocked writer, if there is one, to get in.

The solution presented here implicitly contains a subtle decision that is worth commenting on. Suppose that while a reader is using the data base, another reader comes along. Since having two readers at the same time is not a problem, the second reader is admitted. A third and subsequent readers can also be admitted if they come along.

Now suppose that a writer comes along. The writer cannot be admitted to the data base, since writers must have exclusive access, so the writer is suspended. Later, additional readers show up. As long as at least one reader is still active, subsequent readers are admitted. As a consequence of this strategy, as long as there is a steady supply of readers, they will all get in as soon as they arrive. The writer will be kept suspended until no reader is present. If a new reader arrives, say, every 2 seconds, and each reader takes 5 seconds to do its work, the writer will never get in.

To prevent this situation, the program could be written slightly differently: when a reader arrives and a writer is waiting, the reader is suspended behind the writer instead of being admitted immediately. In this way, a writer has to wait for readers that were active when it arrived to finish but does not have to wait for readers that came along after it. The disadvantage of this solution is that it achieves less concurrency and thus lower performance. Courtois et al. present a solution that gives priority to writers. For details, we refer you to the paper.

2.3.3 The Sleeping Barber Problem

Another classical IPC problem takes place in a barber shop. The barber shop has one barber, one barber chair, and n chairs for waiting customers, if any, to sit on. If there are no customers present, the barber sits down in the barber chair and falls asleep, as illustrated in Fig. 2-20. When a customer arrives, he has to wake up the sleeping barber. If additional customers arrive while the barber is cutting a customer's hair, they either sit down (if there are empty chairs) or leave the shop (if all chairs are full). The problem is to program the barber and the customers without getting into race conditions.

Our solution uses three semaphores: *customers*, which counts waiting customers (excluding the customer in the barber chair, who is not waiting), *barbers*, the number of barbers who are idle, waiting for customers (0 or 1), and *mutex*, which is used for mutual exclusion. We also need a variable, *waiting*, which also counts the waiting customers. It is essentially a copy of *customers*. The reason for having *waiting* is that there is no way to read the current value of a semaphore. In this solution, a customer entering the shop has to count the number of waiting customers. If it is less than the number of chairs, he stays; otherwise, he leaves.

Our solution is shown in Fig. 2-21. When the barber shows up for work in the morning, he executes the procedure *barber*, causing him to block on the semaphore *customers* until somebody arrives. He then goes to sleep as shown in Fig. 2-20.

When a customer arrives, he executes *customer*, starting by acquiring *mutex* to enter a critical region. If another customer enters shortly thereafter, the second

Figure 2-20. The sleeping barber.

one will not be able to do anything until the first one has released *mutex*. The customer then checks to see if the number of waiting customers is less than the number of chairs. If not, he releases *mutex* and leaves without a haircut.

If there is an available chair, the customer increments the integer variable, *waiting*. Then he does an UP on the semaphore *customers*, thus waking up the barber. At this point, the customer and barber are both awake. When the customer releases *mutex*, the barber grabs it, does some housekeeping, and begins the haircut.

When the haircut is over, the customer exits the procedure and leaves the shop. Unlike our earlier examples, there is no loop for the customer because each one gets only one haircut. The barber loops, however, to try to get the next customer. If one is present, another haircut is given. If not, the barber goes to sleep.

As an aside, it is worth pointing out that although the readers and writers and sleeping barber problems do not involve data transfer, they are still belong to the area of IPC because they involve synchronization between multiple processes.

```
#define CHAIRS 5                        /* # chairs for waiting customers */

typedef int semaphore;                  /* use your imagination */

semaphore customers = 0;                /* # of customers waiting for service */
semaphore barbers = 0;                  /* # of barbers waiting for customers */
semaphore mutex = 1;                    /* for mutual exclusion */
int waiting = 0;                        /* customers are waiting (not being cut) */

void barber(void)
{
  while (TRUE) {
        down(customers);                /* go to sleep if # of customers is 0 */
        down(mutex);                    /* acquire access to 'waiting' */
        waiting = waiting - 1;          /* decrement count of waiting customers */
        up(barbers);                    /* one barber is now ready to cut hair */
        up(mutex);                      /* release 'waiting' */
        cut_hair();                     /* cut hair (outside critical region) */
  }
}


void customer(void)
{
  down(mutex);                          /* enter critical region */
  if (waiting < CHAIRS) {               /* if there are no free chairs, leave */
        waiting = waiting + 1;          /* increment count of waiting customers */
        up(customers);                  /* wake up barber if necessary */
        up(mutex);                      /* release access to 'waiting' */
        down(barbers);                  /* go to sleep if # of free barbers is 0 */
        get_haircut();                  /* be seated and be serviced */
  } else {
        up(mutex);                      /* shop is full; do not wait */
  }
}
```

Figure 2-21. A solution to the sleeping barber problem.

2.4 PROCESS SCHEDULING

In the examples of the previous sections, we have often had situations in which two or more processes (e.g., producer and consumer) were logically runnable. When more than one process is runnable, the operating system must decide which one to run first. The part of the operating system that makes this decision is called the **scheduler**; the algorithm it uses is called the **scheduling algorithm**.

Back in the old days of batch systems with input in the form of card images on a magnetic tape, the scheduling algorithm was simple: just run the next job on the tape. With timesharing systems, the scheduling algorithm is more complex, as there are often multiple users waiting for service, and there may be one or more batch streams as well (e.g., at an insurance company, for processing claims). Even on personal computers, there may be several user-initiated processes competing for the CPU, not to mention background jobs, such as network or electronic mail daemons sending or receiving e-mail.

Before looking at specific scheduling algorithms, we should think about what the scheduler is trying to achieve. After all, the scheduler is concerned with deciding on policy, not providing a mechanism. Various criteria come to mind as to what constitutes a good scheduling algorithm. Some of the possibilities include:

1. Fairness—make sure each process gets its fair share of the CPU.

2. Efficiency—keep the CPU busy 100 percent of the time.

3. Response time—minimize response time for interactive users.

4. Turnaround—minimize the time batch users must wait for output.

5. Throughput—maximize the number of jobs processed per hour.

A little thought will show that some of these goals are contradictory. To minimize response time for interactive users, the scheduler should not run any batch jobs at all (except maybe between 3 A.M. and 6 A.M., when all the interactive users are snug in their beds). The batch users probably will not like this algorithm, however; it violates criterion 4. It can be shown (Kleinrock, 1975) that any scheduling algorithm that favors some class of jobs hurts another class of jobs. The amount of CPU time available is finite, after all. To give one user more you have to give another user less. Such is life.

A complication that schedulers have to deal with is that every process is unique and unpredictable. Some spend a lot of time waiting for file I/O, while others would use the CPU for hours at a time if given the chance. When the scheduler starts running some process, it never knows for sure how long it will be until that process blocks, either for I/O, or on a semaphore, or for some other reason. To make sure that no process runs too long, nearly all computers have an electronic timer or clock built in, which causes an interrupt periodically. A frequency of 50 or 60 times a second (called 50 or 60 **Hertz** and abbreviated **Hz**) is common, but on many computers the operating system can set the timer frequency to anything it wants. At each clock interrupt, the operating system gets to run and decide whether the currently running process should be allowed to continue, or whether it has had enough CPU time for the moment and should be suspended to give another process the CPU.

The strategy of allowing processes that are logically runnable to be temporarily suspended is called **preemptive scheduling**, and is in contrast to the **run**

to completion method of the early batch systems. Run to completion is also called **nonpreemptive scheduling**. As we have seen throughout this chapter, a process can be suspended at an arbitrary instant, without warning, so another process can be run. This leads to race conditions and necessitates semaphores, monitors, messages, or some other sophisticated method for preventing them. On the other hand, a policy of letting a process run as long as it wanted to would mean that some process computing π to a billion places could deny service to all other processes indefinitely.

Thus although nonpreemptive scheduling algorithms are simple and easy to implement, they are usually not suitable for general-purpose systems with multiple competing users. On the other hand, for a dedicated system, such as a data base server, it may well be reasonable for the master process to start a child process working on a request and let it run until it completes or blocks. The difference from the general-purpose system is that all processes in the data base system are under the control of a single master, which knows what each child is going to do and about how long it will take.

2.4.1 Round Robin Scheduling

Now let us look at some specific scheduling algorithms. One of the oldest, simplest, fairest, and most widely used algorithms is **round robin**. Each process is assigned a time interval, called its **quantum**, which it is allowed to run. If the process is still running at the end of the quantum, the CPU is preempted and given to another process. If the process has blocked or finished before the quantum has elapsed, the CPU switching is done when the process blocks, of course. Round robin is easy to implement. All the scheduler needs to do is maintain a list of runnable processes, as shown in Fig. 2-22(a). When the process uses up its quantum, it is put on the end of the list, as shown in Fig. 2-22(b).

(a)   (b)

Figure 2-22. Round robin scheduling. (a) The list of runnable processes. (b) The list of runnable processes after *B* uses up its quantum.

The only interesting issue with round robin is the length of the quantum. Switching from one process to another requires a certain amount of time for doing the administration—saving and loading registers and memory maps, updating various tables and lists, etc. Suppose that this **process switch** or **context switch**, as it is sometimes called, takes 5 msec. Also suppose that the quantum is set at 20 msec. With these parameters, after doing 20 msec of useful work, the CPU will have to spend 5 msec on process switching. Twenty percent of the CPU time will be wasted on administrative overhead.

To improve the CPU efficiency, we could set the quantum to, say, 500 msec. Now the wasted time is less than 1 percent. But consider what happens on a timesharing system if ten interactive users hit the carriage return key at roughly the same time. Ten processes will be put on the list of runnable processes. If the CPU is idle, the first one will start immediately, the second one may not start until about 1/2 sec later, and so on. The unlucky last one may have to wait 5 sec before getting a chance, assuming all the others use their full quanta. Most users will perceive a 5-sec response to a short command as terrible. The same problem can occur on a personal computer that supports multiprogramming.

The conclusion can be formulated as follows: setting the quantum too short causes too many process switches and lowers the CPU efficiency, but setting it too long may cause poor response to short interactive requests. A quantum around 100 msec is often a reasonable compromise.

2.4.2 Priority Scheduling

Round robin scheduling makes the implicit assumption that all processes are equally important. Frequently, the people who own and operate multiuser computers have different ideas on that subject. At a university, the pecking order may be deans first, then professors, secretaries, janitors, and finally students. The need to take external factors into account leads to **priority scheduling**. The basic idea is straightforward: each process is assigned a priority, and the runnable process with the highest priority is allowed to run.

Even on a PC with a single owner, there may be multiple processes, some more important than others. For example, a daemon process sending electronic mail in the background should be assigned a lower priority than a process displaying a video film on the screen in real time.

To prevent high-priority processes from running indefinitely, the scheduler may decrease the priority of the currently running process at each clock tick (i.e., at each clock interrupt). If this action causes its priority to drop below that of the next highest process, a process switch occurs. Alternatively, each process may be assigned a maximum quantum that it is allowed to hold the CPU continuously. When this quantum is used up, the next highest priority process is given a chance to run.

Priorities can be assigned to processes statically or dynamically. On a military computer, processes started by generals might begin at priority 100, processes started by colonels at 90, majors at 80, captains at 70, lieutenants at 60, and so on. Alternatively, at a commercial computer center, high-priority jobs might cost 100 dollars an hour, medium priority 75 dollars an hour, and low priority 50 dollars an hour. The UNIX system has a command, *nice*, which allows a user to voluntarily reduce the priority of his process, in order to be nice to the other users. Nobody ever uses it.

Priorities can also be assigned dynamically by the system to achieve certain system goals. For example, some processes are highly I/O bound and spend most of their time waiting for I/O to complete. Whenever such a process wants the CPU, it should be given the CPU immediately, to let it start its next I/O request, which can then proceed in parallel with another process actually computing. Making the I/O bound process wait a long time for the CPU will just mean having it around occupying memory for an unnecessarily long time. A simple algorithm for giving good service to I/O bound processes is to set the priority to $1/f$, where f is the fraction of the last quantum that a process used. A process that used only 2 msec of its 100 msec quantum would get priority 50, while a process that ran 50 msec before blocking would get priority 2, and a process that used the whole quantum would get priority 1.

It is often convenient to group processes into priority classes and use priority scheduling among the classes but round-robin scheduling within each class. Figure 2-23 shows a system with four priority classes. The scheduling algorithm is as follows: as long as there are runnable processes in priority class 4, just run each one for one quantum, round-robin fashion, and never bother with lower priority classes. If priority class 4 is empty, then run the class 3 processes round robin. If classes 4 and 3 are both empty, then run class 2 round robin, and so on. If priorities are not adjusted occasionally, lower priority classes may all starve to death.

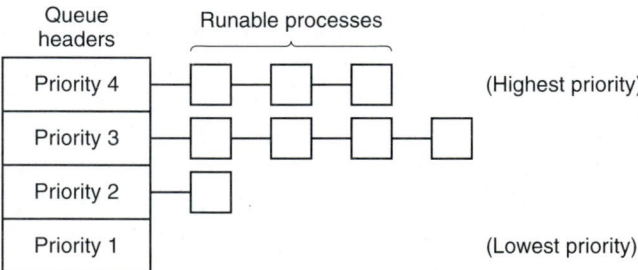

Figure 2-23. A scheduling algorithm with four priority classes.

2.4.3 Multiple Queues

One of the earliest priority schedulers was in CTSS (Corbato et al., 1962). CTSS had the problem that process switching was very slow because the 7094 could hold only one process in memory. Each switch meant swapping the current process to disk and reading in a new one from disk. The CTSS designers quickly realized that it was more efficient to give CPU-bound processes a large quantum once in a while, rather than giving them small quanta frequently (to reduce swapping). On the other hand, giving all processes a large quantum would mean poor response time, as we have already seen. Their solution was to set up priority classes. Processes in the highest class were run for one quantum. Processes in the next highest class were run for two quanta. Processes in the next class were run for four quanta, and so on. Whenever a process used up all the quanta allocated to it, it was moved down one class.

As an example, consider a process that needed to compute continuously for 100 quanta. It would initially be given one quantum, then swapped out. Next time it would get two quanta before being swapped out. On succeeding runs it would get 4, 8, 16, 32, and 64 quanta, although it would have used only 37 of the final 64 quanta to complete its work. Only 7 swaps would be needed (including the initial load) instead of 100 with a pure round-robin algorithm. Furthermore, as the process sank deeper and deeper into the priority queues, it would be run less and less frequently, saving the CPU for short, interactive processes.

The following policy was adopted to prevent a process that needed to run for a long time when it first started but became interactive later, from being punished forever. Whenever a carriage return was typed at a terminal, the process belonging to that terminal was moved to the highest priority class, on the assumption that it was about to become interactive. One fine day some user with a heavily CPU-bound process discovered that just sitting at the terminal and typing carriage returns at random every few seconds did wonders for his response time. He told all his friends. Moral of the story: getting it right in practice is much harder than getting it right in principle.

Many other algorithms have been used for assigning processes to priority classes. For example, the influential XDS 940 system (Lampson, 1968), built at Berkeley, had four priority classes, called terminal, I/O, short quantum, and long quantum. When a process that was waiting for terminal input was finally awakened, it went into the highest priority class (terminal). When a process waiting for a disk block became ready, it went into the second class. When a process was still running when its quantum ran out, it was initially placed in the third class. However, if a process used up its quantum too many times in a row without blocking for terminal or other I/O, it was moved down to the bottom queue. Many other systems use something similar to favor interactive users and processes over background ones.

2.4.4 Shortest Job First

Most of the above algorithms were designed for interactive systems. Now let us look at one that is especially appropriate for batch jobs for which the run times are known in advance. In an insurance company, for example, people can predict quite accurately how long it will take to run a batch of 1000 claims, since similar work is done every day. When several equally important jobs are sitting in the input queue waiting to be started, the scheduler should use **shortest job first**. Look at Fig. 2-24. Here we find four jobs A, B, C, and D with run times of 8, 4, 4, and 4 minutes, respectively. By running them in that order, the turnaround time for A is 8 minutes, for B is 12 minutes, for C is 16 minutes, and for D is 20 minutes for an average of 14 minutes.

Figure 2-24. An example of shortest job first scheduling.

Now let us consider running these four jobs using shortest job first, as shown in Fig. 2-24(b). The turnaround times are now 4, 8, 12, and 20 minutes for an average of 11 minutes. Shortest job first is provably optimal. Consider the case of four jobs, with run times of a, b, c, and d, respectively. The first job finishes at time a, the second finishes at time $a + b$, and so on. The mean turnaround time is $(4a + 3b + 2c + d)/4$. It is clear that a contributes more to the average than the other times, so it should be the shortest job, with b next, then c and finally d as the longest as it affects only its own turnaround time. The same argument applies equally well to any number of jobs.

Because shortest job first always produces the minimum average response time, it would be nice if it could be used for interactive processes as well. To a certain extent, it can be. Interactive processes generally follow the pattern of wait for command, execute command, wait for command, execute command, and so on. If we regard the execution of each command as a separate "job," then we could minimize overall response time by running the shortest one first. The only problem is figuring out which of the currently runnable processes is the shortest one.

One approach is to make estimates based on past behavior and run the process with the shortest estimated running time. Suppose that the estimated time per command for some terminal is T_0. Now suppose its next run is measured to be T_1. We could update our estimate by taking a weighted sum of these two numbers, that is, $aT_0 + (1 - a)T_1$. Through the choice of a we can decide to have the estimation process forget old runs quickly, or remember them for a long time. With $a = 1/2$, we get successive estimates of

$$T_0, \quad T_0/2 + T_1/2, \quad T_0/4 + T_1/4 + T_2/2, \quad T_0/8 + T_1/8 + T_2/4 + T_3/2$$

After three new runs, the weight of T_0 in the new estimate has dropped to 1/8.

The technique of estimating the next value in a series by taking the weighted average of the current measured value and the previous estimate is sometimes called **aging**. It is applicable to many situations where a prediction must be made based on previous values. Aging is especially easy to implement when $a = 1/2$. All that is needed is to add the new value to the current estimate and divide the sum by 2 (by shifting it right 1 bit).

It is worth pointing out that the shortest job first algorithm is only optimal when all the jobs are available simultaneously. As a counterexample, consider five jobs, *A* through *E*, with run times of 2, 4, 1, 1, and 1, respectively. Their arrival times are 0, 0, 3, 3, and 3.

Initially, only *A* or *B* can be chosen, since the other three jobs have not arrived yet. Using shortest job first we will run the jobs in the order *A, B, C, D, E*, for an average wait of 4.6. However, running them in the order *B, C, D, E, A* has an average wait of 4.4.

2.4.5 Guaranteed Scheduling

A completely different approach to scheduling is to make real promises to the user about performance and then live up to them. One promise that is realistic to make and easy to live up to is this: If there are *n* users logged in while you are working, you will receive about $1/n$ of the CPU power. Similarly, on a single-user system with *n* processes running, all things being equal, each one should get $1/n$ of the CPU cycles.

To make good on this promise, the system must keep track of how much CPU each process has had since its creation. It then computes the amount of CPU each one is entitled to, namely the time since creation divided by *n*. Since the amount of CPU time each process has actually had is also known, it is straightforward to compute the ratio of actual CPU had to CPU time entitled. A ratio of 0.5 means that a process has only had half of what it should have had, and a ratio of 2.0 means that a process has had twice as much as it was entitled to. The algorithm is then to run the process with the lowest ratio until its ratio has moved above its closest competitor.

2.4.6 Lottery Scheduling

While making promises to the users and then living up to them is a fine idea, it is difficult to implement. However, another algorithm can be used to give similarly predictable results with a much simpler implementation. It is called **lottery scheduling** (Waldspurger and Weihl, 1994).

The basic idea is to give processes lottery tickets for various system resources, such as CPU time. Whenever a scheduling decision has to be made, a lottery ticket is chosen at random, and the process holding that ticket gets the resource. When applied to CPU scheduling, the system might hold a lottery 50 times a second, with each winner getting 20 msec of CPU time as a prize.

To paraphrase George Orwell: "All processes are equal, but some processes are more equal." More important processes can be given extra tickets, to increase their odds of winning. If there are 100 tickets outstanding, and one process holds 20 of them, it will have a 20 percent chance of winning each lottery. In the long run, it will get about 20 percent of the CPU. In contrast to a priority scheduler, where it is very hard to state what having a priority of 40 actually means, here the rule is clear: a process holding a fraction f of the tickets will get about a fraction f of the resource in question.

Lottery scheduling has several interesting properties. For example, if a new process shows up and is granted some tickets, at the very next lottery it will have a chance of winning in proportion to the number of tickets it holds. In other words, lottery scheduling is highly responsive.

Cooperating processes may exchange tickets if they wish. For example, when a client process sends a message to a server process and then blocks, it may give all of its tickets to the server, to increase the chance of the server running next. When the server is finished, it returns the tickets so the client can run again. In fact, in the absence of clients, servers need no tickets at all.

Lottery scheduling can be used to solve problems that are difficult to handle with other methods. One example is a video server in which several processes are feeding video streams to their clients, but at different frame rates. Suppose that the processes need frames at 10, 20, and 25 frames/sec. By allocating these processes 10, 20, and 25 tickets, respectively, they will automatically divide the CPU in the correct proportion.

2.4.7 Real-Time Scheduling

A **real-time** system is one in which time plays an essential role. Typically, one or more physical devices external to the computer generate stimuli, and the computer must react appropriately to them within a fixed amount of time. For example, the computer in a compact disc player gets the bits as they come off the drive and must convert them into music within a very tight time interval. If the calculation takes too long, the music will sound peculiar. Other real-time systems are patient monitoring in a hospital intensive-care unit, the autopilot in an aircraft, and safety control in a nuclear reactor. In all these cases, having the right answer but having it too late is often just as bad as not having it at all.

Real-time systems are generally categorized as **hard real time**, meaning there are absolute deadlines that must be met, or else, and **soft real time**, meaning that missing an occasional deadline is tolerable. In both cases, real-time behavior is achieved by dividing the program into a number of processes, each of whose behavior is predictable and known in advance. These processes are generally short lived and can run to completion in under a second. When an external event is detected, it is the job of the scheduler to schedule the processes in such a way as that all deadlines are met.

The events that a real-time system may have to respond to can be further categorized as **periodic** (occurring at regular intervals) or **aperiodic** (occurring unpredictably). A system may have to respond to multiple periodic event streams. Depending on how much time each event requires for processing, it may not even be possible to handle them all. For example, if there are m periodic events and event i occurs with period P_i and requires C_i seconds of CPU time to handle each event, then the load can only be handled if

$$\sum_{i=1}^{m} \frac{C_i}{P_i} \leq 1$$

A real-time system that meets this criteria is said to be **schedulable**.

As an example, consider a soft real-time system with three periodic events, with periods of 100, 200, and 500 msec, respectively. If these events require 50, 30, and 100 msec of CPU time per event, respectively, the system is schedulable because $0.5 + 0.15 + 0.2 < 1$. If a fourth event with a period of 1 sec is added, the system will remain schedulable as long as this event does not need more than 150 msec of CPU time per event. Implicit in this calculation is the assumption that the context-switching overhead is so small that it can be ignored.

Real-time scheduling algorithms can be dynamic or static. The former make their scheduling decisions at run time; the latter make them before the system starts running. Let us briefly consider a few of the dynamic real-time scheduling algorithms. The classic algorithm is the **rate monotonic algorithm** (Liu and Layland, 1973). In advance, it assigns to each process a priority proportional to the frequency of occurrence of its triggering event. For example, a process to run every 20 msec gets priority 50 and a process to run every 100 msec gets priority 10. At run time, the scheduler always runs the highest priority ready process, preempting the running process if need be. Liu and Layland proved that this algorithm is optimal.

Another popular real-time scheduling algorithm is **earliest deadline first**. Whenever an event is detected, its process is added to the list of ready processes. The list is kept sorted by deadline, which for a periodic event is the next occurrence of the event. The algorithm runs the first process on the list, the one with the closest deadline.

A third algorithm first computes for each process the amount of time it has to spare, called its **laxity**. If a process requires 200 msec and must be finished in 250 msec, its laxity is 50 msec. The algorithm, called **least laxity**, choses the process with the smallest amount of time to spare.

While in theory it is possible to turn a general-purpose operating system into a real-time system by using one of these scheduling algorithms, in practice the context-switching overhead of general-purpose systems is so large that real-time performance can only be achieved for applications with easy time constraints. As a consequence, most real-time work uses special real-time operating systems that have certain important properties. Typically these include a small size, fast interrupt time, rapid context switch, short interval during which interrupts are disabled, and the ability to manage multiple timers in the millisecond or microsecond range.

2.4.8 Two-level Scheduling

Up until now we have more or less assumed that all runnable processes are in main memory. If insufficient main memory is available, some of the runnable processes will have to be kept on the disk, in whole or in part. This situation has major implications for scheduling, since the process switching time to bring in and run a process from disk is orders of magnitude more than switching to a process already in main memory.

A more practical way of dealing with swapped out processes is to use a two-level scheduler. Some subset of the runnable processes is first loaded into main memory, as shown in Fig. 2-25(a). The scheduler then restricts itself to only choosing processes from this subset for a while. Periodically, a higher-level scheduler is invoked to remove processes that have been in memory long enough and to load processes that have been on disk too long. Once the change has been made, as in Fig. 2-25(b), the lower-level scheduler again restricts itself to only running processes that are actually in memory. Thus, the lower-level scheduler is concerned with making a choice among the runnable processes that are in memory at that moment, while the higher-level scheduler is concerned with shuttling processes back and forth between memory and disk.

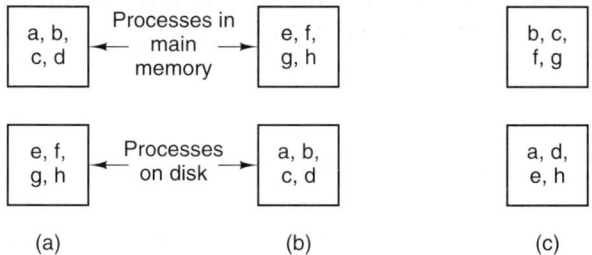

Figure 2-25. A two-level scheduler must move processes between disk and memory and also choose processes to run from among those in memory. Three different instants of time are represented by (a), (b), and (c).

Among the criteria that the higher-level scheduler could use to make its decisions are the following ones:

1. How long has it been since the process was swapped in or out?

2. How much CPU time has the process had recently?

3. How big is the process? (Small ones do not get in the way.)

4. How high is the priority of the process?

Again here we could use round-robin, priority scheduling, or any of various other methods. The two schedulers may or may not use the same algorithm.

2.4.9 Policy versus Mechanism

Up until now, we have tacitly assumed that all the processes in the system belong to different users and are thus competing for the CPU. While this is often true, sometimes it happens that one process has many children running under its control. For example, a data base management system process may have many children. Each child might be working on a different request, or each one might have some specific function to perform (query parsing, disk access, etc.). It is entirely possible that the main process has an excellent idea of which of its children are the most important (or time critical) and which the least. Unfortunately, none of the schedulers discussed above accept any input from user processes about scheduling decisions. As a result, the scheduler rarely makes the best choice.

The solution to this problem is to separate the **scheduling mechanism** from the **scheduling policy**. What this means is that the scheduling algorithm is parameterized in some way, but the parameters can be filled in by user processes. Let us consider the data base example again. Suppose that the kernel uses a priority scheduling algorithm but provides a system call by which a process can set (and change) the priorities of its children. In this way the parent can control in detail how its children are scheduled, even though it itself does not do the scheduling. Here the mechanism is in the kernel but the policy is set by a user process.

2.5 OVERVIEW OF PROCESSES IN MINIX

Having completed our study of the principles of process management, interprocess communication, and scheduling, we can now take a look at how they are applied in MINIX. Unlike UNIX, whose kernel is a monolithic program not split up into modules, MINIX itself is a collection of processes that communicate with each other and with user processes using a single interprocess communication primitive—message passing. This design gives a more modular and flexible structure, making it easy, for example, to replace the entire file system by a completely different one, without having even to recompile the kernel.

2.5.1 The Internal Structure of MINIX

Let us begin our study of MINIX by taking a bird's-eye view of the system. MINIX is structured in four layers, with each layer performing a well-defined function. The four layers are illustrated in Fig. 2-26

The bottom layer catches all interrupts and traps, does scheduling, and provides higher layers with a model of independent sequential processes that communicate using messages. The code in this layer has two major functions. The

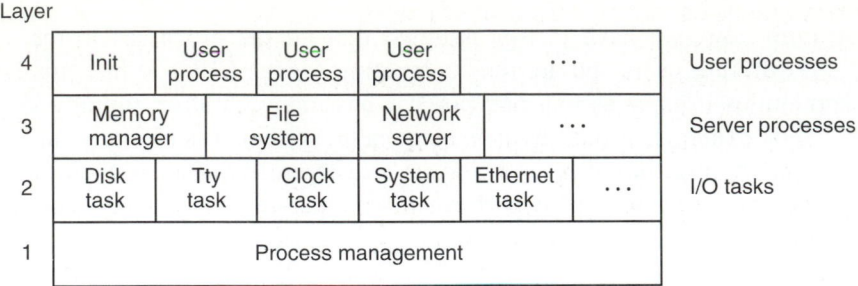

Figure 2-26. MINIX is structured in four layers.

first is catching the traps and interrupts, saving and restoring registers, scheduling, and the general nuts and bolts of actually making the process abstraction provided to the higher layers work. The second is handling the mechanics of messages; checking for legal destinations, locating send and receive buffers in physical memory, and copying bytes from sender to receiver. That part of the layer dealing with the lowest level of interrupt handling is written in assembly language. The rest of the layer and all of the higher layers, are written in C.

Layer 2 contains the I/O processes, one per device type. To distinguish them from ordinary user processes, we will call them **tasks**, but the differences between tasks and processes are minimal. In many systems the I/O tasks are called **device drivers**; we will use the terms "task" and "device driver" interchangeably. A task is needed for each device type, including disks, printers, terminals, network interfaces, and clocks. If other I/O devices are present, a task is needed for each one of those, too. One task, the system task, is a little different, since it does not correspond to any I/O device. We will discuss the tasks in the next chapter.

All of the tasks in layer 2 and all the code in layer 1 are linked together into a single binary program called the **kernel**. Some of the tasks share common subroutines, but otherwise they are independent from one another, are scheduled independently, and communicate using messages. Intel processors starting with the 286 assign one of four levels of privilege to each process. Although the tasks and the kernel are compiled together, when the kernel and the interrupt handlers are executing, they are accorded more privileges than the tasks. Thus the true kernel code can access any part of memory and any processor register—essentially, the kernel can execute any instruction using data from anywhere in the system. Tasks cannot execute all machine level instructions, nor can they access all CPU registers or all parts of memory. They can, however, access memory regions belonging to less-privileged processes, in order to perform I/O for them. One task, the system task, does not do I/O in the normal sense but exists in order to provide services, such as copying between different memory regions, for processes which are not allowed to do such things for themselves. On machines which do not provide different privilege levels, such as older Intel processors, these restrictions cannot be enforced, of course.

Layer 3 contains processes that provide useful services to the user processes. These server processes run at a less privileged level than the kernel and tasks and cannot access I/O ports directly. They also cannot access memory outside the segments allotted to them. The **memory manager** (MM) carries out all the MINIX system calls that involve memory management, such as FORK, EXEC, and BRK. The **file system** (FS) carries out all the file system calls, such as READ, MOUNT, and CHDIR.

As we noted at the start of Chap. 1, operating systems do two things: manage resources and provide an extended machine by implementing system calls. In MINIX the resource management is largely in the kernel (layers 1 and 2), and system call interpretation is in layer 3. The file system has been designed as a file "server" and can be moved to a remote machine with almost no changes. This also holds for the memory manager, although remote memory servers are not as useful as remote file servers.

Additional servers may also exist in layer 3. Figure 2-26 shows a network server there. Although MINIX as described in this book does not include the network server, its source code is part of the standard MINIX distribution. The system can easily be recompiled to include it.

This is a good place to note that although the servers are independent processes, they differ from user processes in that they are started when the system is started, and they never terminate while the system is active. Additionally, although they run at the same privilege level as the user processes in terms of the machine instructions they are allowed to execute, they receive higher execution priority than user processes. To accommodate a new server the kernel must be recompiled. The kernel startup code installs the servers in privileged slots in the process table before any user processes are allowed to run.

Finally, layer 4 contains all the user processes—shells, editors, compilers, and user-written *a.out* programs. A running system usually has some processes that are started when the system is booted and which run forever. For example, a **daemon** is a background process that executes periodically or always waits for some event, such as a packet arrival from the network. In a sense a daemon is a server that is started independently and runs as a user process. However, unlike true servers installed in privileged slots, such programs can not get the special treatment from the kernel that the memory and file server processes receive.

2.5.2 Process Management in MINIX

Processes in MINIX follow the general process model described at some length earlier in this chapter. Processes can create subprocesses, which in turn can create more subprocesses, yielding a tree of processes. In fact, all the user processes in the whole system are part of a single tree with *init* (see Fig. 2-26) at the root.

How does this situation come about? When the computer is turned on, the hardware reads the first sector of the first track of the boot disk into memory and executes the code it finds there. The details vary depending upon whether the boot disk is a diskette or a hard disk. On a diskette this sector contains the **bootstrap** program. It is very small, since it has to fit in one sector. The MINIX bootstrap loads a larger program, *boot*, which then loads the operating system itself.

In contrast, hard disks require an intermediate step. A hard disk is divided into **partitions**, and the first sector of a hard disk contains a small program and the disk's **partition table.** Collectively these are called the **master boot record**. The program part is executed to read the partition table and to select the **active** partition. The active partition has a bootstrap on its first sector, which is then loaded and executed to find and start a copy of *boot* in the partition, exactly as is done when booting from a diskette.

In either case, *boot* looks for a multipart file on the diskette or partition and loads the individual parts into memory at the proper locations. The parts include the kernel, the memory manager, the file system, and *init*, the first user process. This startup process is not a trivial operation. Operations that are in the realms of the disk task and the file system must be performed by boot before these parts of the system are active. In a later section we will return to the subject of how MINIX is started. For now suffice it to say that once the loading operation is complete the kernel starts running.

During its initialization phase, the kernel starts the tasks, and then the memory manager, the file system, and any other servers that run in layer 3. When all these have run and initialized themselves, they will block, waiting for something to do. When all tasks and servers are blocked, *init*, the first user process, will be executed. It is already in memory, but it could, of course, have been loaded from the disk as a separate program since everything else is working by the time it is started. However, since *init* is started only this one time and is never reloaded from the disk, it is easiest just to include it in the system image file with the kernel, tasks, and servers.

Init starts out by reading the file */etc/ttytab*, which lists all potential terminal devices. Those devices that can be used as login terminals (in the standard distribution, just the console) have an entry in the *getty* field of */etc/ttytab*, and *init* forks off a child process for each such terminal. Normally, each child executes */usr/bin/getty* which prints a message, then waits for a name to be typed. Then */usr/bin/login* is called with the name as its argument. If a particular terminal requires special treatment (e.g., a dial-up line) */etc/ttytab* can specify a command (such as */usr/bin/stty*) to be executed to initialize the line before running *getty*.

After a successful login, */bin/login* executes the user's shell (specified in the */etc/passwd* file, and normally */bin/sh* or */usr/bin/ash*). The shell waits for commands to be typed and then forks off a new process for each command. In this way, the shells are the children of *init*, the user processes are the grandchildren of *init*, and all the user processes in the system are part of a single tree.

The two principal MINIX system calls for process management are FORK and EXEC. FORK is the only way to create a new process. EXEC allows a process to execute a specified program. When a program is executed, it is allocated a portion of memory whose size is specified in the program file's header. It keeps this amount of memory throughout its execution, although the distribution among data segment, stack segment, and unused can vary as the process runs.

All the information about a process is kept in the process table, which is divided up among the kernel, memory manager, and file system, with each one having those fields that it needs. When a new process comes into existence (by FORK), or an old process terminates (by EXIT or a signal), the memory manager first updates its part of the process table and then sends messages to the file system and kernel telling them to do likewise.

2.5.3 Interprocess Communication in MINIX

Three primitives are provided for sending and receiving messages. They are called by the C library procedures

send(dest, &message);

to send a message to process *dest*,

receive(source, &message);

to receive a message from process *source* (or *ANY*), and

send_rec(src_dst, &message);

to send a message and wait for a reply from the same process. The second parameter in each call is the local address of the message data. The message passing mechanism in the kernel copies the message from the sender to the receiver. The reply (for *send_rec*) overwrites the original message. In principle this kernel mechanism could be replaced by a function which copies messages over a network to a corresponding function on another machine, to implement a distributed system. In practice this would be complicated somewhat by the fact that message contents are sometimes pointers to large data structures, and a distributed system would also have to provide for copying the data itself over the network.

Each process or task can send and receive messages from processes and tasks in its own layer, and from those in the layer directly below it. User processes may not communicate directly with the I/O tasks. The system enforces this restriction.

When a process (which also includes the tasks as a special case) sends a message to a process that is not currently waiting for a message, the sender blocks until the destination does a RECEIVE. In other words, MINIX uses the rendezvous method to avoid the problems of buffering sent, but not yet received, messages. Although less flexible than a scheme with buffering, it turns out to be adequate for this system, and much simpler because no buffer management is needed.

2.5.4 Process Scheduling in MINIX

The interrupt system is what keeps a multiprogramming operating system going. Processes block when they make requests for input, allowing other processes to execute. When input becomes available, the current running process is interrupted by the disk, keyboard, or other hardware. The clock also generates interrupts that are used to make sure a running user process that has not requested input eventually relinquishes the CPU, to give other processes their chance to run. It is the job of the lowest layer of MINIX to hide these interrupts by turning them into messages. As far as processes (and tasks) are concerned, when an I/O device completes an operation it sends a message to some process, waking it up and making it runnable.

Each time a process is interrupted, whether from a conventional I/O device or from the clock, there is an opportunity to redetermine which process is most deserving of an opportunity to run. Of course, this must be done whenever a process terminates, as well, but in a system like MINIX interruptions due to I/O operations or the clock occur more frequently than process termination. The MINIX scheduler uses a multilevel queueing system with three levels, corresponding to layers 2, 3, and 4 in Fig. 2-26. Within the task and server levels processes run until they block, but user processes are scheduled using round robin. Tasks have the highest priority, the memory manager and file server are next, and user processes are last.

When picking a process to run, the scheduler checks to see if any tasks are ready. If one or more are ready, the one at the head of the queue is run. If no tasks are ready, a server (MM or FS) is chosen, if possible; otherwise a user is run. If no process is ready, the *IDLE* process is chosen. This is a loop that executes until the next interrupt occurs.

At each clock tick, a check is made to see if the current process is a user process that has run more than 100 msec. If it is, the scheduler is called to see if another user process is waiting for the CPU. If one is found, the current process is moved to the end of its scheduling queue, and the process now at the head is run. Tasks, the memory manager, and the file system are never preempted by the clock, no matter how long they have been running.

2.6 IMPLEMENTATION OF PROCESSES IN MINIX

We are now moving closer to looking at the actual code, so a few words about the notation we will use are in order. The terms "procedure," "function," and "routine" will be used interchangeably. Names of variables, procedures, and files will be written in italics, as in *rw_flag*. When a variable, procedure, or file name starts a sentence, it will be capitalized, but the actual names all begin with lower case letters. System calls will be in small caps, for example, READ.

The book and the software, both of which are continuously evolving, did not "go to press" on the same day, so there may be minor discrepancies between the references to the code, the printed listing, and the CD-ROM version. Such differences generally only affect a line or two, however. The source code printed in the book has also been simplified by eliminating code used to compile options that are not discussed in the book.

2.6.1 Organization of the MINIX Source Code

Logically, the source code is organized as two directories. The full paths to these directories on a standard MINIX system are */usr/include/* and */usr/src/* (a trailing "/" in a path name indicates that it refers to a directory). The actual location of the directories may vary from system to system, but normally the structure of the directories below the topmost level will be the same on any system. We will refer to these directories as *include/* and *src/* in this text.

The *include/* directory contains a number of POSIX standard header files. In addition, it has three subdirectories:

1. *sys/*   – this subdirectory contains additional POSIX headers.

2. *minix/*   – includes header files used by the operating system.

3. *ibm/*   – includes header files with IBM PC-specific definitions.

To support extensions to MINIX and programs that run in the MINIX environment, other files and subdirectories are also present in *include/* as provided on the CD-ROM or over the Internet. For instance, the *include/net/* directory and its subdirectory *include/net/gen/* support network extensions. However, in this text only the files needed to compile the basic MINIX system are printed and discussed.

The *src/* directory contains three important subdirectories containing the operating system source code:

1. *kernel/*   – layers 1 and 2 (processes, messages, and drivers).

2. *mm/*   – the code for the memory manager.

3. *fs/*   – the code for the file system.

There are three other source code directories that are not printed or discussed in the text, but which are essential to producing a working system:

1. *src/lib/*   – source code for library procedures (e.g., open, read).

2. *src/tools/* – source code for the init program, used to start MINIX.

3. *src/boot/* – the code for booting and installing MINIX.

The standard distribution of MINIX includes several more source directories. An operating system exists, of course, to support commands (programs) that will run on it, so there is a large *src/commands/* directory with source code for the utility programs (e.g., *cat*, *cp*, *date*, *ls*, *pwd*). Since MINIX is an educational operating system, meant to be modified, there is a *src/test/* directory with programs designed to test thoroughly a newly compiled MINIX system. Finally, the */src/inet/* directory includes source code for recompiling MINIX with network support.

For convenience we will usually refer to simple file names when it will be clear from the context what the complete path name is. It should be noted, however, that some file names appear in more than one directory. For instance, there are several files named *const.h* in which constants relevant to a particular part of the system are defined. The files in a particular directory will be discussed together, so there should not be any confusion. The files are listed in Appendix A in the order they are discussed in the text, to make it easier to follow along. Acquisition of a couple of bookmarks might be of use at this point.

Also worth noting is that Appendix B contains an alphabetical list of all files described in Appendix A, and Appendix C contains a list of where to find the definitions of macros, global variables, and procedures used in MINIX.

The code for layers 1 and 2 is contained in the directory *src/kernel/*. In this chapter we will study the files in this directory which support process management, the lowest layer of the MINIX structure we saw in Fig. 2-26. This layer includes functions which handle system initialization, interrupts, message passing and process scheduling. In Chap. 3, we will look at the rest of the files in this directory, which support the various tasks, the second layer in Fig. 2-26. In Chap. 4, we will look at the memory manager files in *src/mm/*, and in Chap. 5, we will study the file system, whose source files are located in *src/fs/*.

When MINIX is compiled, all the source code files in *src/kernel/*, *src/mm/*, and *src/fs/* are compiled to object files. All the object files in *src/kernel/* are linked to form a single executable program, *kernel*. The object files in *src/mm/* are also linked together to form a single executable program, *mm*. The same holds for *fs*. Extensions can be added by adding additional servers, for instance network support is added by modifying *include/minix/config.h* to enable compilation of the files in *src/inet/* to form *inet*. Another executable program, *init*, is built in *src/tools/*. The program *installboot* (whose source is in *src/boot/*) adds names to each of these programs, pads each one out so that its length is a multiple of the disk sector size (to make it easier to load the parts independently), and concatenates them onto a single file. This new file is the binary of the operating system and can be copied onto the root directory or the */minix/* directory of a floppy disk or hard disk partition. Later, the boot monitor program can load and execute the operating system. Figure 2-27 shows the layout of memory after the concatenated programs are separated and loaded. Details, of course, depend upon the system configuration. The example in the figure is for a MINIX system configured to take advantage of a computer equipped with several megabytes of memory. This makes it possible to allocate a large number of file system buffers, but the resulting large file system does not fit in the lower range of memory, below 640K. If the number of buffers is reduced drastically it is possible to make the entire system fit into less than 640K of memory, with room for a few user processes as well.

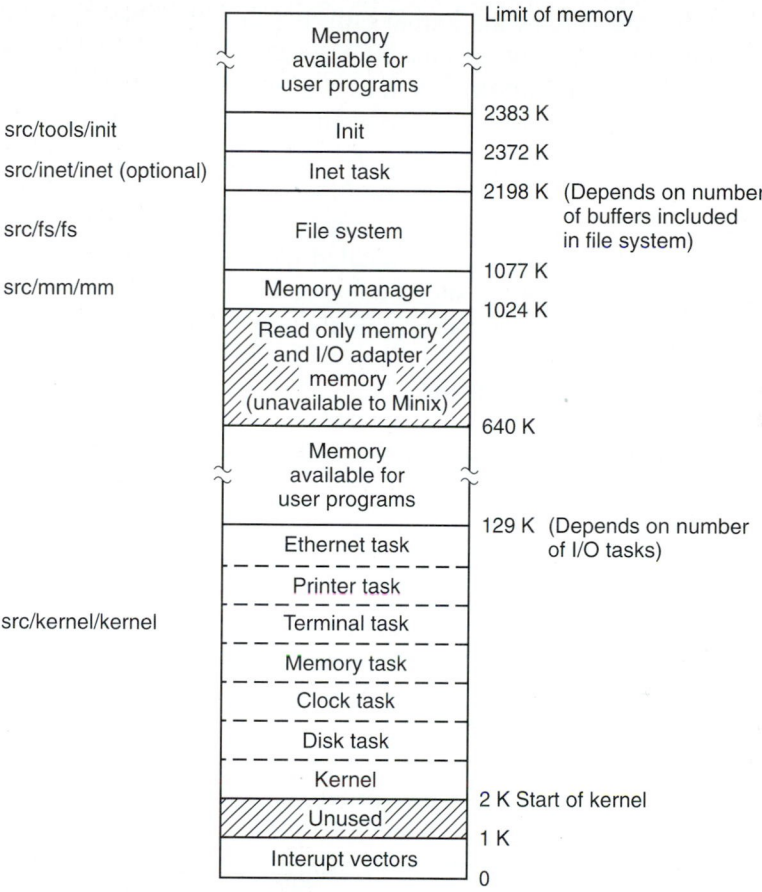

Figure 2-27. Memory layout after MINIX has been loaded from the disk into memory. The four (or five, with network support) independently compiled and linked parts are clearly distinct. The sizes are approximate, depending on the configuration.

It is important to realize that MINIX consists of three or more totally independent programs that communicate only by passing messages. A procedure called *panic* in *src/fs/* does not conflict with a procedure called *panic* in *src/mm/* because they ultimately are linked into different executable files. The only procedures that the three pieces of the operating system have in common are a few of the library routines in *lib/*. This modular structure makes it very easy to modify, say, the file system, without having these changes affect the memory manager. It also makes it straightforward to remove the file system altogether and to put it on a different machine as a file server, communicating with user machines by sending messages over a network.

As another example of the modularity of MINIX, compiling the system with or without network support makes absolutely no difference to the memory manager or the file system and affects the kernel only because the Ethernet task is compiled there, along with support for other I/O devices. When enabled, the network server is integrated into the MINIX system as a server with the same level of priority as the memory manager or the file server. Its operation can involve the transfer of large quantities of data very rapidly, and this requires higher priority than a user process would receive. Except for the Ethernet task, however, network functions could be performed by user level processes. Network functions are not traditional operating system functions, and detailed discussion of the network code is beyond the scope of this book. In succeeding sections and chapters the discussion will be based on a MINIX system compiled without network support.

2.6.2 The Common Header Files

The directory *include/* and its subdirectories contain a collection of files defining constants, macros, and types. The POSIX standard requires many of these definitions and specifies in which files of the main *include/* directory and its subdirectory *include/sys/* each required definition is to be found. The files in these directories are **header** or **include files**, identified by the suffix *.h*, and used by means of #include statements in C source files. These statements are a feature of the C language. Include files make maintenance of a large system easier.

Headers likely to be needed for compiling user programs are found in *include/* whereas *include/sys/* traditionally is used for files that are used primarily for compiling system programs and utilities. The distinction is not terribly important, and a typical compilation, whether of a user program or part of the operating system, will include files from both of these directories. We will discuss here the files that are needed to compile the standard MINIX system, first treating those in *include/* and then those in *include/sys/*. In the next section we will discuss all the files in the *include/minix/* and *include/ibm/* directories, which, as the directory names indicate, are unique to MINIX and its implementation on IBM-type computers.

The first headers to be considered are truly general purpose ones, so much so that they are not referenced directly by any of the C language source files for the MINIX system. Rather, they are themselves included in other header files, the master headers *src/kernel/kernel.h*, *src/mm/mm.h*, and *src/fs/fs.h* for each of the three main parts of the MINIX system, which in turn are included in every compilation. Each master header is tailored to the needs of the corresponding part of the MINIX system, but each one starts with a section like the one shown in Fig. 2-28. The master headers will be discussed again in other sections of the book. This preview is to emphasize that headers from several directories are used together. In this section and the next one we will mention each of the files referenced in Fig. 2-28.

```
#include <minix/config.h>        /* MUST be first */
#include <ansi.h>                /* MUST be second */
#include <sys/types.h>
#include <minix/const.h>
#include <minix/type.h>
#include <limits.h>
#include <errno.h>
#include <minix/syslib.h>
```

Figure 2-28. Part of a master header which ensures inclusion of header files needed by all C source files.

Let us start with the first header in *include/*, *ansi.h* (line 0000). This is the second header that is processed whenever any part of the MINIX system is compiled; only *include/minix/config.h* is processed earlier. The purpose of *ansi.h* is to test whether the compiler meets the requirements of Standard C, as defined by the International Organization for Standards. Standard C is also called ANSI C, since the standard was originally developed by the American National Standards Institute before gaining international recognition. A Standard C compiler defines several macros that can then be tested in programs being compiled. $\_\_STDC\_\_$ is such a macro, and it is defined by a standard compiler to have a value of 1, just as if the C preprocessor had read a line like

```
#define __STDC__ 1
```

The compiler distributed with current versions of MINIX conforms to Standard C, but older versions of MINIX were developed before the adoption of the standard, and it is still possible to compile MINIX with a classic (Kernighan & Ritchie) C compiler. It is intended that MINIX should be easy to port to new machines, and allowing older compilers is part of this. At lines 0023 to 0025 the statement

```
#define _ANSI
```

is processed if a Standard C compiler is in use. *Ansi.h* defines several macros in different ways, depending upon whether the *_ANSI* macro is defined.

The most important macro in this file is *_PROTOTYPE*. This macro allows us to write function prototypes in the form

```
_PROTOTYPE (return-type function-name, (argument-type argument, ... ) )
```

and have this transformed by the C preprocessor into

```
return-type function-name(argument-type, argument, ...)
```

if the compiler is an ANSI Standard C compiler, or

```
return-type function-name()
```

if the compiler is an old-fashioned (i.e., Kernighan & Ritchie) compiler.

Before we leave *ansi.h* let us mention one more feature. The entire file is enclosed between lines that read

#ifndef _ANSI_H

and

#endif

On the line immediately following the #ifndef *_ANSI_H* itself is defined. A header file should be included only once in a compilation; this construction ensures that the contents of the file will be ignored if it is included multiple times. We will see this technique used in all the header files in the *include/* directory.

The second file in *include/* that is indirectly included in every MINIX source file is the *limits.h* header (line 0100). This file defines many basic sizes, both language types such as the number of bits in an integer, as well as operating system limits such as the length of a file name. *Errno.h* (line 0200), is also included by all the master headers. It contains the error numbers that are returned to user programs in the global variable *errno* when a system call fails. *Errno* is also used to identify some internal errors, such as trying to send a message to a nonexistent task. The error numbers are negative to mark them as error codes within the MINIX system, but they must be made positive before being returned to user programs. The trick that is used is that each error code is defined in a line like

#define EPERM   (_SIGN 1)

(line 0236). The master header for each part of the operating system defines the macro *_SYSTEM*, but *_SYSTEM* is never defined when a user program is compiled. If *_SYSTEM* is defined, then *_SIGN* is defined as "–"; otherwise it is given a null definition.

The next group of files to be considered are not included in all the master headers, but are nevertheless used in many source files in all parts of the MINIX system. The most important is *unistd.h* (line 0400). This header defines many constants, most of which are required by POSIX. In addition, it includes prototypes for many C functions, including all those used to access MINIX system calls. Another widely used file is *string.h* (line 0600), which provides prototypes for many C functions used for string manipulation. The header *signal.h* (line 0700) defines the standard signal names. It also contains prototypes for some signal-related functions. As we will see later, signal handling involves all parts of MINIX.

Fcntl.h (line 0900) symbolically defines many parameters used in file control operations. For instance, it allows one to use the macro *O_RDONLY* instead of the numeric value 0 as a parameter to a *open* call. Although this file is referenced most by the file system, its definitions are also needed in a number of places in the kernel and the memory manager.

The remaining files in *include/* are not as widely used as the ones already mentioned. *Stdlib.h* (line 1000) defines types, macros, and function prototypes that are likely to be needed in the compilation of all but the most simple of C programs. It is one of the most frequently used headers in compiling user programs, although within the MINIX system source it is referenced by only a few files in the kernel.

As we will see when we look at the tasks layer in Chap. 3, the console and terminal interface of an operating system is complex, because many different types of hardware have to interact with the operating system and user programs in a standardized way. The *termios.h* (line 1100) header defines constants, macros, and function prototypes used for control of terminal-type I/O devices. The most important structure is the *termios* structure. It contains flags to signal various modes of operation, variables to set input and output transmission speeds, and an array to hold special characters, such as the *INTR* and *KILL* characters. This structure is required by POSIX, as are many of the macros and function prototypes defined in this file.

However, as all-encompassing as the POSIX standard is meant to be, it does not provide everything one might want, and the last part of the file, from line 1241 onward, provides extensions to POSIX. Some of these are of obvious value, such as extensions to define standard baud rates of 57,600 baud and higher, and support for terminal display screen windows. The POSIX standard does not forbid extensions, as no reasonable standard can ever be all-inclusive. But when writing a program in the MINIX environment which is intended to be portable to other environments, some caution is required to avoid the use of definitions specific to MINIX. This is easy to do. In this file and other files that define MINIX-specific extensions the use of the extensions is controlled by an

```
#ifdef _MINIX
```

statement. If *_MINIX* is not defined, the compiler will not even see the MINIX extensions.

The last file we will consider in *include/* is *a.out.h* (line 1400), a header which defines the format of the files in which executable programs are stored on disk, including the header structure used to start a file executing and the symbol table structure produced by the compiler. It is referenced only by the file system.

Now let us go on to the subdirectory *include/sys/*. As shown in Fig. 2-28, the master headers for the main parts of the MINIX system all include *sys/types.h* (line 1600) immediately after reading *ansi.h*. This header defines many data types used by MINIX. Errors that could arise from misunderstanding which fundamental data types are used in a particular situation can be avoided by using the definitions provided here. Fig. 2-29 shows the way the sizes, in bits, of a few types defined in this file differ when compiled for 16-bit or 32-bit processors. Note that all type names end with "_t". This is not just a convention; it is a requirement of the POSIX standard. This is an an example of a **reserved suffix**, and it should not be used as a suffix of any name which is *not* a type name.

Type	16-Bit MINIX	32-Bit MINIX
gid_t	8	8
dev_t	16	16
pid_t	16	32
ino_t	16	32

Figure 2-29. The size, in bits, of some types on 16-bit and 32-bit systems.

Although it is not so widely used that it is included in the master headers for each section, *sys/ioctl.h* (line 1800) defines many macros used for device control operations. It also contains the prototype for the IOCTL system call. This call is not directly invoked by programmers in many cases, since the POSIX-defined functions prototyped in *include/termios.h* have replaced many uses of the old *ioctl* library function for dealing with terminals, consoles, and similar devices. Nevertheless, it is still necessary. In fact, the POSIX functions for control of terminal devices are converted into IOCTL system calls by the library. Also, there are an ever-increasing number of devices, all of which need various kinds of control, which can be interfaced with a modern computer system. For instance, near the end of this file there are several operation codes defined that begin with *DSPIO*, for controlling a digital signal processor. Indeed, the main difference between MINIX as described in this book and other versions is that for purposes of the book we describe a MINIX with relatively few input/output devices. Many others, such as network interfaces, CD-ROM drives, and sound cards, can be added; control codes for all of these are defined as macros in this file.

Several other files in this directory are widely used in the MINIX system. The file *sys/sigcontext.h* (line 2000) defines structures used to preserve and restore normal system operation before and after execution of a signal handling routine and is used both in the kernel and the memory manager. There is support in MINIX for tracing executables and analyzing core dumps with a debugger program, and *sys/ptrace.h* (line 2200) defines the various operations possible with the PTRACE system call. *Sys/stat.h* (line 2300) defines the structure which we saw in Fig. 1-12, returned by the STAT and FSTAT system calls, as well as the prototypes of the functions *stat* and *fstat* and other functions used to manipulate file properties. It is referenced in several parts of the file system and the memory manager.

The last two files we will discuss in this section are not as widely referenced as the ones discussed above. *Sys/dir.h* (line 2400) defines the structure of a MINIX directory entry. It is only referenced directly once, but this reference includes it in another header that is widely used in the file system. It is important because, among other things, it tells how many characters a file name may contain. Finally, the *sys/wait.h* (line 2500) header defines macros used by the WAIT and WAITPID system calls, which are implemented in the memory manager.

2.6.3 The MINIX Header Files

The subdirectories *include/minix/* and *include/ibm/* contain header files specific to MINIX. Files in *include/minix/* are needed for an implementation of MINIX on any platform, although there are platform-specific alternative definitions within some of them. The files in *include/ibm/* define structures and macros that are specific to MINIX as implemented on IBM-type machines.

We will start with the *minix/* directory. In the previous section, it was noted that *config.h* (line 2600) is included in the master headers for all parts of the MINIX system, and is thus the first file actually processed by the compiler. On many occasions, when differences in hardware or the way the operating system is intended to be used require changes in the configuration of MINIX, editing this file and recompiling the system is all that must be done. The user-settable parameters are all in the first part of the file. The first of these is the *MACHINE* parameter, which can take values such as *IBM_PC*, *SUN_4*, *MACINTOSH*, or other values, depending on the type of machine for which MINIX is being compiled. Most of the code for MINIX is independent of the type of machine, but an operating system always has some system-dependent code. In the few places in this book where we discuss code that is written differently for different systems we will use as our examples code for IBM PC-type machines with advanced processor chips (80386, 80486, Pentium, Pentium Pro) that use 32-bit words. We will refer to all of these as Intel 32-bit processors. MINIX can also be compiled for older IBM PCs with a 16-bit word size, and the machine-dependent parts of MINIX must be coded differently for these machines. On a PC, the compiler itself determines the machine type for which MINIX will be compiled. The standard PC MINIX compiler is the Amsterdam Compiler Kit (ACK) compiler. It identifies itself by defining, in addition to the *__STDC__* macro, the *__ACK__* macro. It also defines a macro *_EM_WSIZE* which is the word size (in bytes) for its target machine. In lines 2626 to 2628 a macro *_WORD_SIZE* is assigned the value of *_EM_WSIZE*. Further along in the file and at various places in the other MINIX source files these definitions are used. For example, lines 2647 to 2650 begin with the test

```
#if (MACHINE == IBM_PC && _WORD_SIZE == 4)
```

and define a size for the file system's buffer cache on 32-bit systems.

Other definitions in *config.h* allow customization for other needs in a particular installation. For instance, there is a section that allows various types of device drivers to be included when the MINIX kernel is compiled. This is likely to be the most often edited part of the MINIX source code. This section starts out with:

```
#define ENABLE_NETWORKING 0
#define ENABLE_AT_WINI 1
#define ENABLE_BIOS_WINI 0
```

By changing the 0 in the first line to 1 we can compile a MINIX kernel for a machine that needs network support. By defining *ENABLE_AT_WINI* as 0 and *ENABLE_BIOS_WINI* as 1, we can eliminate the AT-type (i.e., IDE) hard disk driver code and use the PC BIOS for hard disk support.

The next file is *const.h* (line 2900), which illustrates another common use of header files. Here we find a variety of constant definitions that are not likely to be changed when compiling a new kernel but that are used in a number of places. Defining them here helps to prevent errors that could be hard to track down if inconsistent definitions were made in multiple places. There are other files named *const.h* in the MINIX source tree, but they are for more limited use. Definitions that are used only in the kernel are included in *src/kernel/const.h*. Definitions that are used only in the file system are included in *src/fs/const.h*. The memory manager uses *src/mm/const.h* for its local definitions. Only those definitions that are used in more than one part of the MINIX system are included in *include/minix/const.h*.

A few of the definitions in *const.h* are noteworthy. *EXTERN* is defined as a macro expanding into *extern* (line 2906). Global variables that are declared in header files and included in two or more files are declared *EXTERN*, as in

EXTERN int who;

If the variable were declared just as

int who;

and included in two or more files, some linkers would complain about a multiply defined variable. Furthermore, the C reference manual (Kernighan and Ritchie, 1988) explicitly forbids this construction.

To avoid this problem, it is necessary to have the declaration read

extern int who;

in all places but one. Using *EXTERN* prevents this problem by having it expand into *extern* everywhere that *const.h* is included, except following an explicit redefinition of *EXTERN* as the null string. This is done in each part of MINIX by putting global definitions in a special file called *glo.h*, for instance, *src/kernel/glo.h*, which is indirectly included in every compilation. Within each *glo.h* there is a sequence

```
#ifdef _TABLE
#undef EXTERN
#define EXTERN
#endif
```
and in the *table.c* files of each part of MINIX there is a line

```
#define _TABLE
```

preceding the #include section. Thus when the header files are included and expanded as part of the compilation of *table.c*, *extern* is not inserted anywhere (because *EXTERN* is defined as the null string within *table.c*) and storage for the global variables is reserved only in one place, in the object file *table.o*.

If you are new to C programming and do not quite understand what is going on here, fear not; the details are really not important. Multiple inclusion of header files can cause problems for some linkers because it can lead to multiple declarations for included variables. The *EXTERN* business is simply a way to make MINIX more portable so it can be linked on machines whose linkers do not accept multiply defined variables.

PRIVATE is defined as a synonym for *static*. Procedures and data that are not referenced outside the file in which they are declared are always declared as *PRIVATE* to prevent their names from being visible outside the file in which they are declared. As a general rule, all variables and procedures should be declared with as local a scope as possible. *PUBLIC* is defined as the null string. Thus, the declaration

PUBLIC void free_zone(Dev_t dev, zone_t numb)

comes out of the C preprocessor as

void free_zone(Dev_t dev, zone_t numb)

which, according to the C scope rules, means that the name *free_zone* is exported from the file and can be used in other files. *PRIVATE* and *PUBLIC* are not necessary but are attempts to undo the damage caused by the C scope rules (the default is that names are exported outside the file; it should be just the reverse).

The rest of *const.h* defines numerical constants used throughout the system. A section of *const.h* is devoted to machine or configuration-dependent definitions. For instance, throughout the source code the basic unit of memory size is the click. The size of a click depends upon the processor architecture, and alternatives for Intel, Motorola 68000, and Sun SPARC architectures are defined on lines 2957 to 2965. This file also contains the macros *MAX* and *MIN*, so we can say

z = MAX(x, y);

to assign the larger of x and y to z.

Type.h (line 3100) is another file that is included in every compilation by means of the master headers. It contains a number of key type definitions, along with related numerical values. The most important definition in this file is *message* on lines 3135 to 3146. While we could have defined *message* to be an array of some number of bytes, it is better programming practice to have it be a structure containing a union of the various message types that are possible. Six message formats, *mess_1* through *mess_6*, are defined. A message is a structure containing a field *m_source*, telling who sent the message, a field *m_type*, telling what the message type is (e.g., GET_TIME to the clock task) and the data fields. The six message types are shown in Fig. 2-30. In the figure the first and second message types seem identical, as do the fourth and sixth types. This is true for

MINIX as implemented on an Intel CPU with a 32-bit word size, but would not be the case on a machine where *int*s, *long*s and pointers were different sizes. Defining six distinct formats makes it easier to recompile for a different architecture.

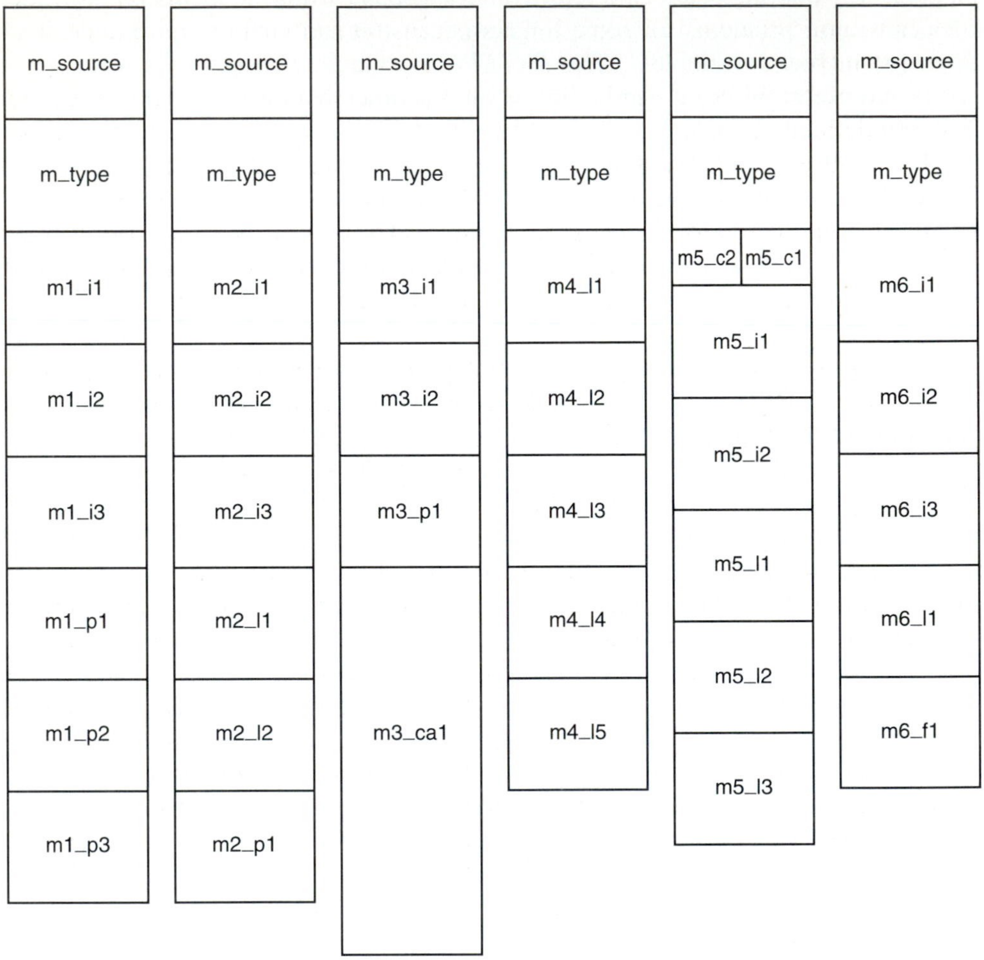

m_source	m_source	m_source	m_source	m_source	m_source
m_type	m_type	m_type	m_type	m_type	m_type
m1_i1	m2_i1	m3_i1	m4_l1	m5_c2 m5_c1	m6_i1
				m5_i1	
m1_i2	m2_i2	m3_i2	m4_l2	m5_i2	m6_i2
m1_i3	m2_i3	m3_p1	m4_l3	m5_l1	m6_i3
m1_p1	m2_l1		m4_l4	m5_l2	m6_l1
m1_p2	m2_l2	m3_ca1	m4_l5	m5_l3	m6_f1
m1_p3	m2_p1				

Figure 2-30. The six messages types used in MINIX. The sizes of message elements will vary, depending upon the architecture of the machine; this diagram illustrates sizes on a machine with 32-bit pointers, such as the Pentium (Pro).

When it is necessary to send a message containing, say, three integers and three pointers (or three integers and two pointers), then the first format in Fig. 2-30 is the one to use. The same applies to the other formats. How does one assign a value to the first integer in the first format? Suppose that the message is called *x*. Then *x.m_u* refers to the union portion of the message struct. To refer to the first of the six alternatives in the union, we use *x.m_u.m_m1*. Finally, to get at the first integer in this struct we say *x.m_u.m_m1.m1i1*. This is quite a mouthful, so somewhat shorter field names are defined as macros after the definition of message itself. Thus *x.m1_i1* can be used instead of *x.m_u.m_m1.m1i1*. The short names all have the form of the letter m, the format number, an underscore, one or two letters indicating whether the field is an integer, pointer, long, character, character array, or function, and a sequence number to distinguish multiple instances of the same type within a message.

As an aside, while discussing message formats, this is a good place to note that an operating system and its compiler often have an "understanding" about things like the layout of structures, and this can make the implementor's life easier. In MINIX the *int* fields in messages are sometimes used to hold *unsigned* data types. In some cases this could cause overflow, but the code was written using the knowledge that the MINIX compiler copies *unsigned* types to *int*s and *vice versa* without changing the data or generating code to detect overflow. A more compulsive approach would be to replace each *int* field with a *union* of an *int* and an *unsigned*. The same applies to the *long* fields in the messages; some of them may be used to pass *unsigned long* data. Are we cheating here? Perhaps, one might say, but if you wish to port MINIX to a new platform, quite clearly the exact format of the messages is something to which you must pay a great deal of attention, and now you have been alerted that the behavior of the compiler is another factor that needs attention.

There is one other file in *include/minix* that is universally used, by means of inclusion in the master headers. This is *syslib.h* (line 3300), which contains prototypes for C library functions called from within the operating system to access other operating system services. The C libraries are not discussed in detail in this text, but many of them are standard and will be available for any C compiler. However, the C functions referenced by *syslib.h* are of course quite specific to MINIX and a port of MINIX to a new system with a different compiler requires porting these library functions. Fortunately this is not difficult, since these functions simply extract the parameters of the function call and insert them into a message structure, then send the message and extract the results from the reply message. Many of these library functions are defined in a dozen or fewer lines of C code.

When a process needs to execute a MINIX system call, it sends a message to the memory manager (MM for short) or the file system (FS for short). Each message contains the number of the system call desired. These numbers are defined in the next file, *callnr.h* (line 3400).

The file *com.h* (line 3500) mostly contains common definitions used in messages from MM and FS to the I/O tasks. The task numbers are also defined. To distinguish them from process numbers, task numbers are negative. This header also defines the message types (function codes) that can be sent to each task. For example, the clock task accepts codes *SET_ALARM* (which is used to set a timer), *CLOCK_TICK* (when a clock interrupt has occurred), *GET_TIME* (request for the real time), and *SET_TIME* (to set the current time of day). The value *REAL_TIME* is the message type for the reply to the *GET_TIME* request.

Finally, *include/minix/* contains several more specialized headers. Among these are *boot.h* (line 3700), which is used by both the kernel and file system to define devices and to access parameters passed to the system by the *boot* program. Another example is *keymap.h* (line 3800), which defines the structures used to implement specialized keyboard layouts for the character sets needed for different languages. It is also needed by programs which generate and load these tables. Some files here, like *partition.h* (line 4000), are used only by the kernel, and not by the file system or the memory manager. In an implementation with support for additional I/O devices there are more header files like this, supporting other devices. Their placement in this directory needs explanation. Ideally all user programs would access devices only through the operating system, and files like this would be placed in *src/kernel/*. However, the realities of system management require that there be some user commands that access system-level structures, such as commands to make disk partitions. It is to support such utility programs that such specialized header files are placed in the *include/* directory tree.

The last specialized header directory we will consider, *include/ibm/*, contains two files which provide definitions related to the IBM PC family of computers. One of these is *diskparm.h*, which is needed by the floppy disk task. Although this task is included in the standard version of MINIX, its source code is not discussed in detail in this text, since it is so similar to the hard disk task. The other file in this directory is *partition.h* (line 4100), which defines disk partition tables and related constants as used on IBM compatible systems. These are placed here to facilitate porting MINIX to another hardware platform. For different hardware *include/ibm/partition.h* would have to be replaced, presumably with a *partition.h* in another appropriately named directory, but the structure defined in the file *include/minix/partition.h* is internal to MINIX and should remain unchanged in a MINIX hosted on a different hardware platform.

2.6.4 Process Data Structures and Header Files

Now let us dive in and see what the code in *src/kernel/* looks like. In the previous two sections we structured our discussion around an excerpt from a typical master header; we will look first at the real master header for the kernel, *kernel.h* (line 4200). It begins by defining three macros. The first, *_POSIX_SOURCE* is a **feature test macro** defined by the POSIX standard itself. All such macros are required to begin with the underscore character, "_". The effect of defining the *_POSIX_SOURCE* macro is to ensure that all symbols required by the standard and any that are explicitly permitted, but not required, will be visible, while hiding any additional symbols that are unofficial extensions to POSIX. We have already mentioned the next two definitions: the *_MINIX* macro overrides the effect of *_POSIX_SOURCE* for extensions defined by MINIX, and *_SYSTEM* can be tested wherever it is important to do something differently when compiling system code, as opposed to user code, such as changing the sign of error codes.

Kernel.h then includes other header files from *include/* and its subdirectories *include/sys/* and *include/minix/*, including all those referred to in Fig. 2-28. We have discussed all of these files in the previous two sections. Finally, four more headers from the local directory, *src/kernel/*, are included.

This is a good place to point out for newcomers to the C language how file names are quoted in a #include statement. Every C compiler has a default directory in which it looks for include files. Usually, this is */usr/include/*, as it is in a standard MINIX system. When the name of a file to be included is quoted between less-than and greater-than symbols ("< ... >") the compiler searches for the file in the default include directory or in a specified subdirectory of the default directory. When the name is quoted between ordinary quote characters (" ″ ... ″") the file is searched for first in the current directory (or a specified subdirectory) and then, if not found there, in the default directory.

Kernel.h makes it possible to guarantee that all source files share a large number of important definitions by writing the single line

```
#include "kernel.h"
```

in each of the other kernel source files. Since the order of inclusion of header files is sometimes important, *kernel.h* also ensures that this ordering is done correctly, once and forever. This carries to a higher level the "get it right once, then forget the details" technique embodied in the header file concept. There are similar master headers in the source directories for the file system and the memory manager.

Now let us proceed to look at the four local header files included in *kernel.h* Just as we have files *const.h* and *type.h* in the common header directory *include/minix/*, we also have files *const.h.* and *type.h* in the kernel source directory, *src/kernel/*. The files in *include/minix/* are placed there because they are needed by many parts of the system, including programs that run under the control of the system. The files in *src/kernel/* provide definitions needed only for compilation of the kernel. The FS and MM source directories also contain *const.h* and *type.h* files to define constants and types needed only for those parts of the system. The other two files included in the master header, *proto.h* and *glo.h*, have no counterparts in the main *include/* directories, but we will find that they, too, have counterparts used in compiling the file system and the memory manager.

Const.h (line 4300) contains a number of machine-dependent values, that is, values that apply to the Intel CPU chips, but that are likely to be different when MINIX is compiled for different hardware. These values are enclosed between

```
#if (CHIP == INTEL)
```

and

```
#endif
```

statements (lines 4302 to 4396) to bracket them.

When compiling MINIX for one of the Intel chips the macros *CHIP* and *INTEL* are defined and set equal in *include/minix/config.h* (line 2768), and thus the machine-dependent code will be compiled. When MINIX was ported to a system based on the Motorola 68000, the people doing the port added sections of code bracketed by

#if (CHIP == M68000)

and

#endif

and made appropriate changes in *include/minix/config.h* so a line reading

#define CHIP M68000

would be effective. In this way, MINIX can deal with constants and code that are specific to one system. This construction does not especially enhance readability, so it should be used as little as possible. In fact, in the interest of readability, we have removed many sections of machine-dependent code for 68000 and other processors from the version of the code printed in this text. The code distributed on the CD-ROM and via the Internet retains the code for other platforms.

A few of the definitions in *const.h* deserve special mention. Some of these are machine dependent, such as important interrupt vectors and field values used for resetting the interrupt controller chip after each interrupt. Each task within the kernel has its own stack, but while handling interrupts a special stack of size *K_STACK_BYTES*, defined here on line 4304, is used. This is also defined within the machine-dependent section, since a different architecture could require more or less stack space.

Other definitions are machine-independent, but needed by many parts of the kernel code. For instance, the MINIX scheduler has *NQ* (3) priority queues, named *TASK_Q* (highest priority), *SERVER_Q* (middle priority), and *USER_Q* (lowest priority). The names are used to make the source code understandable, but the numeric values defined by these macros are actually compiled into the executable program. Finally, the last line of *const.h* defines *printf* as a macro which will evaluate as *printk*. This allows the kernel to print messages, such as error messages, on the console using a procedure defined within the kernel. This bypasses the usual mechanism, which requires passing messages from the kernel to the file system, and then from the file system to the printer task. During a system failure this might not work. We will see calls to *printf*, alias *printk*, in a kernel procedure called *panic*, which, as you might expect, is invoked when fatal errors are detected.

The file *type.h* (line 4500) defines several prototypes and structures used in any implementation of MINIX. The *tasktab* structure defines the structure of an element of the *tasktab* array and the *memory* structure (lines 4513 to 4516) defines the two quantities that uniquely specify an area of memory. This is a good place to mention some concepts used in referring to memory. A *click* is the basic unit of measurement of memory; in MINIX for Intel processors a click is 256 bytes. Memory is measured as *phys_clicks*, which can be used by the kernel to access any memory element anywhere in the system, or as *vir_clicks*, used by processes other than the kernel. A *vir_clicks* memory reference is always with respect to the base of a segment of memory assigned to a particular process, and the kernel often has to make translations between the two. The inconvenience of this is offset by the fact that a process can do all its own memory references in *vir_clicks*. One might suppose that the same unit could be used to specify the size of either type of memory, but there is an advantage to using *vir_clicks* to specify the size of a unit of memory allocated to a process, since when this unit is used a check is done to be sure that no memory is accessed outside of what has been specifically assigned to the current process. This is a major feature of the **protected mode** of modern Intel processors, such as the Pentium and Pentium Pro. Its absence in the early 8086 and 8088 processors caused some headaches in the design of earlier versions of MINIX.

Type.h also contains several machine-dependent type definitions, such as the *port_t segm_t*, and *reg_t* types (lines 4525 to 4527) used on Intel processors, used, respectively, to address I/O ports, memory segments, and CPU registers.

Structures, too, may be machine-dependent. On lines 4537 to 4558 the *stackframe_s* structure, which defines how the machine registers are saved on the stack, is defined for Intel processors. This structure is extremely important—it is used to save and restore the internal state of the CPU whenever a process is put into or taken out of the "running" state of Fig. 2-2. Defining it in a form that can be efficiently read or written by assembly language code reduces the time required for a context switch. *Segdesc_s* is another structure related to the architecture of Intel processors. It is part of the protection mechanism that keeps processes from accessing memory regions outside those assigned to them.

To illustrate differences between platforms a few definitions for the Motorola 68000 family of processors were retained in this file. The Intel processor family includes some models with 16-bit registers and others with 32-bit registers, so the basic *reg_t* type is *unsigned* for the Intel architecture. For Motorola processors *reg_t* is defined as the *u32_t* type. These processors also need a *stackframe_s* structure (lines 4583 to 4603), but the layout is different, to make the assembly code operations that use it as fast as possible. The Motorola architecture has no need at all for the *port_t* and *segm_t* types, or for the *segdesc_s* structure. There are also several structures defined for the Motorola architecture that have no Intel counterparts.

The next file, *proto.h* (line 4700), is the longest header file we will see. Prototypes of all functions that must be known outside of the file in which they are defined are in this file. All are written using the *_PROTOTYPE* macro discussed in the previous section, and thus the MINIX kernel can be compiled either with a classic C (Kernighan and Ritchie) compiler, such as the original MINIX C compiler, or a modern ANSI Standard C compiler, such as the one which is part of the MINIX Version 2 distribution. A number of these prototypes are system-dependent, including interrupt and exception handlers and functions that are written in assembly language. Prototypes of functions needed by drivers not discussed in this text are not shown. Conditional code for Motorola processors has also been deleted from this and the remaining files we will discuss.

The last of the kernel headers included in the master header is *glo.h* (line 5000) Here we find the kernel's global variables. The purpose of the macro *EXTERN* was described in the discussion of *include/minix/const.h*. It normally expands into *extern*. Note that many definitions in *glo.h* are preceded by this macro. *EXTERN* is forced to be undefined when this file is included in *table.c*, where the macro *_TABLE* is defined. Including *glo.h* in other C source files makes the variables in *table.c* known to the other modules in the kernel. *Held_head* and *held_tail* (lines 5013 and 5014) are pointers to a queue of pending interrupts. *Proc_ptr* (line 5018) points to the process table entry for the current process. When a system call or interrupt occurs, it tells where to store the registers and processor state. *Sig_procs* (line 5021) counts the number of processes that have signals pending that have not yet been sent to the memory manager for processing. A few items in *glo.h* are defined with *extern* instead of *EXTERN*. These include *sizes*, an array filled in by the boot monitor, the task table, *tasktab*, and the task stack, *t_stack*. The last two are **initialized variables**, a feature of the C language. The use of the *EXTERN* macro is not compatible with C-style initialization, since a variable can only be initialized once.

Each task has its own stack within *t_stack*. During interrupt handling, the kernel uses a separate stack, but it is not declared here, since it is only accessed by the assembly language level routine that handles interrupt processing, and does not need to be known globally.

There are two more kernel header files that are widely used, although not so much that they are included in *kernel.h*. The first of these is *proc.h* (line 5100), which defines a process table entry as a struct *proc* (lines 5110 to 5148). Later on in the same file, it defines the process table itself as an array of such structs, *proc[NR_TASKS + NR_PROCS]* (line 5186). In the C language this reuse of a name is permitted. The macro *NR_TASKS* is defined in *include/minix/const.h* (line 2953) and *NR_PROCS* is defined in *include/minix/config.h* (line 2639). Together these set the size of the process table. *NR_PROCS* can be changed to create a system capable of handling a larger number of users. Because the process table is accessed frequently, and calculating an address in an array requires slow multiplication operations, an array of pointers to the process table elements, *pproc_addr* (line 5187), is used to allow speedy access.

Each table entry contains storage for the process' registers, stack pointer, state, memory map, stack limit, process id, accounting, alarm time, and message information. The first part of each process table entry is a *stackframe_s* structure. A process is put into execution by loading its stack pointer with the address of its process table entry and popping all the CPU registers from this structure. When a process cannot complete a SEND because the destination is not waiting, the sender is put onto a queue pointed to by the destination's *p_callerq* field (line 5137). That way, when the destination finally does a RECEIVE, it is easy to find all the processes wanting to send to it. The *p_sendlink* field (line 5138) is used to link the members of the queue together.

When a process does a RECEIVE and there is no message waiting for it, it blocks and the number of the process it wants to RECEIVE from is stored in *p_getfrom*. The address of the message buffer is stored in *p_messbuf*. The last three fields in each process table slot are *p_nextready*, *p_pending*, and *p_pendcount* (lines 5143 to 5145). The first is of these used to link processes together on the scheduler queues, and the second is a bit map used to keep track of signals that have not yet been passed to the memory manager (because the memory manager is not waiting for a message). The last field is a count of these signals.

The flag bits in *p_flags* define the state of each table entry. If any of the bits is set, the process cannot be run. The various flags are defined and described on lines 5154 to 5160. If the slot is not in use, *P_SLOT_FREE* is set. After a FORK, *NO_MAP* is set to prevent the child process from running until its memory map has been set up. *SENDING* and *RECEIVING* indicate that the process is blocked trying to send or receive a message. *PENDING* and *SIG_PENDING* indicate that signals have been received, and *P_STOP* provides support for tracing, during debugging.

The macro *proc_addr* (line 5179) is provided because it is not possible to have negative subscripts in C. Logically, the array *proc* should go from −*NR_TASKS* to +*NR_PROCS*. Unfortunately, in C it must start at 0, so *proc*[0] refers to the most negative task, and so forth. To make it easier to keep track of which slot goes with which process, we can write

```
rp = proc_addr(n);
```

to assign to *rp* the address of the process slot for process n, either positive or negative.

Bill_ptr (line 5191) points to the process being charged for the CPU. When a user process calls the file system, and the file system is running, *proc_ptr* (in *glo.h*) points to the file system process. However, *bill_ptr* will point to the user making the call, since CPU time used by the file system is charged as system time to the caller.

The two arrays *rdy_head* and *rdy_tail* are used to maintain the scheduling queues. The first process on, for example, the task queue is pointed to by *rdy_head*[*TASK_Q*].

Another header that is included in a number of different source files is *protect.h* (line 5200). Almost everything in this file deals with architecture details of the Intel processors that support protected mode (the 80286, 80386, 80486,

Pentium, and Pentium Pro). A detailed description of these chips is beyond the scope of this book. Suffice it to say that they contain internal registers that point to **descriptor tables** in memory. Descriptor tables define how system resources are used and prevent processes from accessing memory assigned to other processes. In addition the processor architecture provides for four **privilege levels**, of which MINIX takes advantage of three. These are defined symbolically on lines 5243 to 5245. The most central parts of the kernel, the parts that run during interrupts and that switch processes, run with *INTR_PRIVILEGE*. There is no part of memory or register in the CPU that cannot be accessed by a process with this privilege level. The tasks run at *TASK_PRIVILEGE* level, which allows them to access I/O but not to use instructions that modify special registers, like those that point to descriptor tables. Servers and user processes run at *USER_PRIVILEGE* level. Processes executing at this level are unable to execute certain instructions, for instance those that access I/O ports, change memory assignments, or change privilege levels themselves. The concept of privilege levels will be familiar to those who are familiar with the architecture of modern CPUs, but those who have learned computer architecture through study of the assembly language of low-end microprocessors may not have encountered such restrictions.

There are several other header files in the kernel directory, but we will mention only two more here. First, there is *sconst.h* (line 5400), which contains constants used by assembler code. These are all offsets into the *stackframe_s* structure portion of a process table entry, expressed in a form usable by the assembler. Since assembler code is not processed by the C compiler, it is simpler to have such definitions in a separate file. Also, since these definitions are all machine dependent, isolating them here simplifies the process of porting MINIX to another processor which will need a different version of *sconst.h*. Note that many offsets are expressed as the previous value plus *W*, which is set equal to the word size at line 5401. This allows the same file to serve for compiling a 16-bit or 32-bit version of MINIX.

There is a potential problem here. Header files are supposed to allow one to provide a single correct set of definitions and then proceed to use them in many places without devoting a lot of further attention to the details. Obviously, duplicate definitions, like those in *sconst.h*, violate that principle. This is a special case, of course, but as such, special attention is required if changes are made either to this file or to *proc.h*, to ensure the two files are consistent.

The final header we will mention here is *assert.h* (line 5500). The POSIX standard requires the availability of an *assert* function, which can be used to make a run-time test and abort a program, printing a message. In fact, POSIX requires that an *assert.h* header be provided in the *include/* directory, and one is provided there. So why is there another version here? The answer is that when something goes wrong in a user process, the operating system can be counted upon to provide services such as printing a message to the console. But if something goes wrong in the kernel itself, the normal system resources cannot be counted upon. The kernel thus provides its own routines to handle *assert* and print messages, independently of the versions in the normal system library.

There are a few header files in *kernel/* we have not discussed yet. They support the I/O tasks and will be described in the next chapter where they are relevant. Before passing on to the executable code, however, let us look at *table.c* (line 5600), whose compiled object file will contain all the kernel data structures. We have already seen many of these data structures defined, in *glo.h* and *proc.h*. On line 5625 the macro _TABLE is defined, immediately before the #include statements. As explained earlier, this definition causes *EXTERN* to become defined as the null string, and storage space to be allocated for all the data declarations preceded by *EXTERN*. In addition to the structures in *glo.h* and *proc.h*, storage for a few global variables used by the terminal task, defined in *tty.h*, is also allocated here.

In addition to the variables declared in header files there are two other places where global data storage is allocated. Some definitions are made directly in *table.c*. On lines 5639 to 5674 stack space is allocated for each task. For each optional task the corresponding *ENABLE_XXX* macro (defined in the file *include/minix/config.h*) is used to calculate the stack size. Thus no space is allocated for a task that is not enabled. Following this, the various *ENABLE_XXX* macros are used to determine whether each optional task will be represented in the *tasktab* array, composed of *tasktab* structures, as declared earlier in *src/kernel/type.h* (lines 5699 to 5731). There is an element for each process that is started during system initialization, whether task, server, or user process (i.e., *init*). The array index implicitly maps between task numbers and the associated startup procedures. *Tasktab* also specifies the stack space needed for each process and provides an identification string for each process. It has been put here rather than in a header file because the trick with *EXTERN* used to prevent multiple declarations does not work with initialized variables; that is, you may not say

```
extern int x = 3;
```

anywhere. The previous definitions of stack size also permit allocation of stack space for all of the tasks on line 5734.

Despite trying to isolate all user-settable configuration information in *include/minix/config.h*, an error is possible in matching the size of the *tasktab* array to *NR_TASKS*. At the end of *table.c* a test is made for this error, using a little trick. The array *dummy_tasktab* is declared here in such a way that its size will be impossible and will trigger a compiler error if a mistake has been made. Since the dummy array is declared as *extern*, no space is allocated for it here (or anywhere). Since it is not referenced anywhere else in the code, this will not bother the compiler.

The other place where global storage is allocated is at the end of the assembly language file *mpx386.s* (line 6483). This allocation, at the label _sizes, puts a magic number (to identify a valid MINIX kernel) at the very beginning of the kernel's data segment. Additional space is allocated here by the .space pseudoinstruction. Reservation of storage in this way by the assembly language program makes it possible to force the _sizes array to be physically located at the beginning of the kernel's data segment, making it easy to program *boot* to put the data in the right place. The boot monitor reads the magic number and, if it is correct, overwrites it to initialize the _sizes array with the sizes of different parts of the MINIX system. The kernel uses these data during initialization. At startup time, as far as the kernel is concerned, this is an initialized data area. However, the data the kernel eventually finds there are not available at compilation time. They are patched in by the boot monitor just before the kernel is started. This is all somewhat unusual normally one does not need to write programs that know about the internal structure of other programs. But the period of time after power is applied, but before the operating system is running, is nothing if not unusual and requires unusual techniques.

2.6.5 Bootstrapping MINIX

It is almost time to start looking at the executable code. But before we do that let us take a few moments to understand how MINIX is loaded into memory. It is, of course, loaded from a disk. Figure 2-31 shows how diskettes and partitioned disks are laid out.

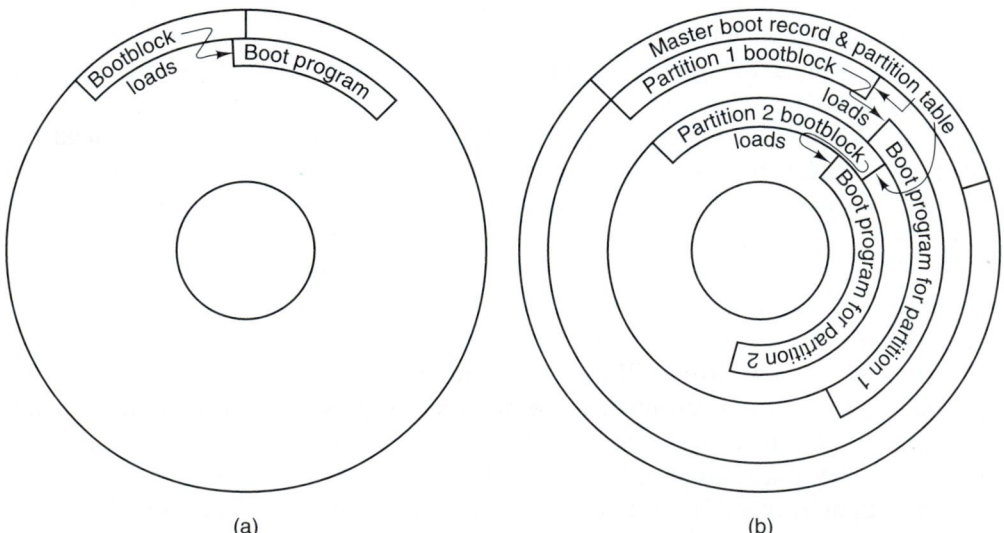

(a)   (b)

Figure 2-31. Disk structures used for bootstrapping. (a) Unpartitioned disk. The first sector is the bootblock. (b) Partitioned disk. The first sector is the master boot record.

When the system is started, the hardware (actually, a program in ROM) reads the first sector of the boot disk and executes the code found there. On an unpartitioned MINIX diskette the first sector is a bootblock which loads the boot program, as in Fig. 2-31(a). Hard disks are partitioned, and the program on the first sector reads the partition table, which is also in the first sector, and loads and executes the first sector of the active partition, as shown in Fig. 2-31(b). (Normally one and only one partition is marked active). A MINIX partition has the same structure as an unpartitioned MINIX diskette, with a bootblock that loads the boot program.

The actual situation can be a little more complicated than the figure shows, because a partition may contain subpartitions. In this case the first sector of the partition will be another master boot record containing the partition table for the subpartitions. Eventually, however, control will be passed to a boot sector, the first sector on a device that is not further subdivided. On a diskette the first sector is always a boot sector. MINIX does allow a form of partitioning of a diskette, but only the first partition may be booted; there is no separate master boot record, and subpartitions are not possible. This makes it possible for partitioned and nonpartitioned diskettes to be mounted in exactly the same way. The main use for a partitioned floppy disk is that it provides a convenient way to divide an installation disk into a root image to be copied to a RAM disk and a mounted portion that can be dismounted when no longer needed, in order to free the diskette drive for continuing the installation process.

The MINIX boot sector is modified at the time it is written to the disk by patching in the sector numbers needed to find a program called *boot* on its partition or subpartition. This patching is necessary because previous to loading the operating system there is no way to use the directory and file names to find a file. A special program called *installboot* is used to do the patching and writing of the boot sector. *Boot* is the secondary loader for MINIX. It can do more than just load the operating system however, as it is a **monitor program** that allows the user to change, set, and save various parameters. *Boot* looks in the second sector of its partition to find a set of parameters to use. MINIX, like standard UNIX, reserves the first 1K block of every disk device as a **bootblock**, but only one 512-byte sector is loaded by the ROM boot loader or the master boot sector, so 512 bytes are available for saving settings. These control the boot operation, and are also passed to the operating system itself. The default settings present a menu with one choice, to start MINIX, but the settings can be modified to present a more complex menu allowing other operating systems to be started (by loading and executing boot sectors from other partitions), or to start MINIX with various options. The default settings can also be modified to bypass the menu and start MINIX immediately.

Boot is not a part of the operating system, but it is smart enough to use the file system data structures to find the actual operating system image. By default, *boot* looks for a file called */minix*, or, if there is a */minix/* directory, for the newest file within it, but the boot parameters can be changed to look for a file with any name. This degree of flexibility is unusual, and most operating systems have a predefined file name for the system image. But, MINIX is an unusual operating system that encourages users to modify it and create experimental new versions. Prudence demands that users who do this should have a way to select multiple versions, in order to be able to return to the last version that worked correctly when an experiment fails.

The MINIX image loaded by *boot* is nothing more than a concatenation of the individual files produced by the compiler when the kernel, memory manager, file system, and *init* programs are compiled. Each of these includes a short header of the type defined in *include/a.out.h*, and from the information in the header of each part, *boot* determines how much space to reserve for uninitialized data after loading the executable code and the initialized data for each part, so the next part can be loaded at the proper address. The *_sizes* array mentioned in the previous section also receives a copy of this information so the kernel itself can have access to the locations and sizes of all the modules loaded by *boot*. The regions of memory available for loading the bootsector, *boot* itself, and MINIX will depend upon the hardware. Also, some machine architectures may require adjustment of internal addresses within executable code to correct them for the actual address where a program is loaded. The segmented architecture of Intel processors makes this unnecessary. Since details of the loading process differ with machine type, and *boot* is not itself part of the operating system, we will not discuss it further here. The important thing is that by one means or another the operating system is loaded into memory. Once the loading is complete, control passes to the executable code of the kernel.

As an aside, we should mention that operating systems are not universally loaded from local disks. **Diskless workstations** may load their operating systems from a remote disk, over a network connection. This requires network software in ROM, of course. Although details vary from what we have described here, the elements of the process are likely to be similar. The ROM code must be just smart enough to get an executable file over the net that can then obtain the complete operating system. If MINIX were loaded this way, very little would need to be changed in the initialization process that occurs once the operating system code is loaded into memory. It would, of course, need a network server and a modified file system that could access files via the network.

2.6.6 System Initialization

MINIX for IBM PC-type machines can be compiled in 16-bit mode if compatibility with older processor chips is required, or in 32-bit mode for better performance on 80386+ processors. The same C source code is used and the compiler generates the appropriate output depending upon whether the compiler itself is the 16-bit or 32-bit version of the compiler. A macro defined by the compiler itself determines the definition of the *_WORD_SIZE* macro in *include/minix/config.h*. The first part of MINIX to execute is written in assembly language, and different source code files must be used for the 16-bit or 32-bit compiler. The 32-bit version of the initialization code is in *mpx386.s*. The alternative, for 16-bit systems, is in *mpx88.s*. Both of these also include assembly language support for other low-level kernel operations. The selection is made automatically in *mpx.s*. This file is so short that the entire file can be presented in Fig. 2-32.

```
#include <minix/config.h>
#if _WORD_SIZE == 2
#include "mpx88.s"
#else
#include "mpx386.s"
#endif
```

Figure 2-32. How alternative assembly language source files are selected.

Mpx.s shows an unusual use of the C preprocessor #include statement. Customarily #include is used to include header files, but it can also be used to select an alternate section of source code. Using #if statements to do this would require putting all the code in both of the large files *mpx88.s* and *mpx386.s* into a single file. Not only would this be unwieldy; it would also be wasteful of disk space, since in a particular installation it is likely that one or the other of these two files will not be used at all and can be archived or deleted. In the following discussion we will use the 32-bit *mpx386.s* as our example.

Since this is our first look at executable code, let us start with a few words about how we will do this throughout the book. The multiple source files used in compiling a large C program can be hard to follow. In general, we will keep discussions confined to a single file at a time, and we will go in order through the files. We will start with the entry point for each part of the MINIX system, and we will follow the main line of execution. When a call to a supporting function is encountered, we will say a few words about the purpose of the call, but normally we will not go into a detailed description of the internals of the function at that point, leaving that until we arrive at the definition of the called function. Important subordinate functions are usually defined in the same file in which they are called, following the higher-level calling functions, but small or general-purpose functions are sometimes collected in separate files. Also, an attempt has been made to put machine-dependent code in separate files from machine-independent code to facilitate portability to other platforms. A substantial amount of effort has been made to organize the code, and, in fact, many files were rewritten in the course of writing this text in order to organize them better for the reader. But a large program has many branches, and sometimes understanding a main function requires reading the functions it calls, so having a few slips of paper to use as bookmarks and deviating from our order of discussion to look at things in a different order may be helpful at times.

Having laid out our intended way of organizing the discussion of the code, we must start off by immediately justifying a major exception. The startup of MINIX involves several transfers of control between the assembly language routines in *mpx386.s* and routines written in C and found in the files *start.c* and *main.c*. We will describe these routines in the order that they are executed, even though that involves jumping from one file to another.

Once the bootstrap process has loaded the operating system into memory, control is transferred to the label *MINIX* (in *mpx386.s*, line 6051). The first instruction is a jump over a few bytes of data; this includes the boot monitor flags (line 6054), used by the boot monitor to identify various characteristics of the kernel, most importantly, whether it is a 16-bit or 32-bit system. The boot monitor always starts in 16-bit mode, but switches the CPU to 32-bit mode if necessary. This happens before control passes to *MINIX*. The monitor also sets up a stack. There is a substantial amount of work to be done by the assembly language code, setting up a stack frame to provide the proper environment for code compiled by the C compiler, copying tables used by the processor to define memory segments, and setting up various processor registers. As soon as this work is complete, the initialization process continues by calling (at line 6109) the C function *cstart*. Note that it is referred to as *_cstart* in the assembly language code. This is because all functions compiled by the C compiler have an underscore prepended to their names in the symbol tables, and the linker looks for such names when separately compiled modules are linked. Since the assembler does not add underscores, the writer of an assembly language program must explicitly add one in order for the linker to be able to find a corresponding name in the object file compiled by the C compiler. *Cstart* calls another routine to initialize the **Global Descriptor Table**, the central data structure used by Intel 32-bit processors to oversee memory protection, and the **Interrupt Descriptor Table**, used to select the code to be executed for each possible interrupt type. Upon returning from *cstart* the lgdt and lidt instructions (lines 6115 and 6116) make these tables effective by loading the dedicated registers by which they are addressed. The following instruction,

jmpf CS_SELECTOR:csinit

looks at first glance like a no-operation, since it transfers control to exactly where control would be if there were a series of nop instructions in its place. But this is an important part of the initialization process. This jump forces use of the structures just initialized. After some more manipulation of the processor registers, *MINIX* terminates with a jump (not a call) at line 6131 to the kernel's *main* entry point (in *main.c*). At this point the initialization code in *mpx386.s* is complete. The rest of the file contains code to start or restart a task or process, interrupt handlers, and other support routines that had to be written in assembly language for efficiency. We will return to these in the next section.

We will now look at the top-level C initialization functions. The general strategy is to do as much as possible using high-level C code. There are already two versions of the *mpx* code, as we have seen, and anything that can be off-loaded to

C code eliminates two chunks of assembler code. Almost the first thing done by *cstart* (in *start.c*, line 6524) is to set up the CPU's protection mechanisms and the interrupt tables, by calling *prot_init*. Then it does such things as copying the boot parameters to the kernel's part of memory and converting them into numeric values. It also determines the type of video display, size of memory, machine type, processor operating mode (real or protected), and whether a return to the boot monitor is possible. All information is stored in appropriate global variables, for access when needed by any part of the kernel code.

Main (in *main.c*, line 6721), completes initialization and then starts normal execution of the system. It configures the interrupt control hardware by calling *intr_init*. This is done here because it can not be done until the machine type is known, and the procedure is in a separate file because it is so dependent upon the hardware. The parameter (1) in the call tells *intr_init* that it is initializing for MINIX. With a parameter (0) it can be called to reinitialize the hardware to the original state. The call to *intr_init* also takes two steps to insure that any interrupts that occur before initialization is complete have no effect. First a byte is written to each interrupt controller chip that inhibits response to external input. Then all entries in the table used to access device-specific interrupt handlers are filled in with the address of a routine that will harmlessly print a message if a spurious interrupt is received. Later these table entries will be replaced, one by one, with pointers to the handler routines, as each of the I/O tasks runs its own initialization routine. Each task then will reset a bit in the interrupt controller chip to enable its own interrupt input.

Mem_init is called next. It initializes an array that defines the location and size of each chunk of memory available in the system. As with the initialization of the interrupt hardware, the details are hardware-dependent and isolation of *mem_init* as a function in a separate file keeps *main* itself free of code that is not portable to different hardware.

The largest part of *main*'s code is devoted to setup of the process table, so that when the first tasks and processes are scheduled, their memory maps and registers will be set correctly. All slots in the process table are marked as free, and the *pproc_addr* array that speeds access to the process table is initialized by the loop on lines 6745 to 6749. The code on line 6748,

```
(pproc_addr + NR_TASKS)[t] = rp;
```

could just as well have been defined as

```
pproc_addr[t + NR_TASKS] = rp;
```

because in the C language $a[i]$ is just another way of writing $*(a+i)$. So it does not make much difference if you add a constant to a or to i. Some C compilers generate slightly better code if you add a constant to the array instead of the index.

The largest part of *main*, the long loop on lines 6762 to 6815, initializes the process table with the necessary information to run the tasks, servers, and *init*. All of these processes must be present at startup time and none of them will terminate during normal operation. At the start of the loop, *rp* is assigned the address of a process table entry (line 6763). Since *rp* is a pointer to a structure, the elements of the structure can be accessed using notation like *rp−>p_name*, as is done on line 6765. This notation is used extensively in the MINIX source code.

The tasks, of course, are all compiled into the same file as the kernel, and the information about their stack requirements is in the *tasktab* array defined in *table.c*. Since tasks are compiled into the kernel and can call code and access data located anywhere in the kernel's space, the size of an individual task is not meaningful, and the size field for each of them is filled with the sizes for the kernel itself. The array *sizes* contains the text and data sizes in clicks of the kernel, memory manager, file system, and *init*. This information is patched into the kernel's data area by *boot* before the kernel starts executing and appears to the kernel as if the compiler had provided it. The first two elements of *sizes* are the kernel's text and data sizes; the next two are the memory manager's, and so on. If any of the four programs does not use separate I and D space, the text size is 0 and the text and data are lumped together as data. Assigning *sizeindex* a value of zero (line 6775) for each of the tasks assures that the zeroth element of *sizes* at lines 6783 and 6784 will be accessed for all of the tasks. The assignment to *sizeindex* at line 6778 gives each of the servers and *init* its own index into *sizes*.

The design of the original IBM PC placed read-only memory at the top of the usable range of memory, which is limited to 1 MB on an 8088 CPU. Modern PC-compatible machines always have more memory than the original PC, but for compatibility they still have read-only memory at the same addresses as the older machines. Thus, the read-write memory is discontinuous, with a block of ROM between the lower 640 KB and the upper range above 1 MB. The boot monitor loads the servers and *init* into the memory range above the ROM if possible. This is primarily for the benefit of the file system, so a very large block cache can be used without bumping into the read-only memory. The conditional code at lines 6804 to 6810 ensures that this use of the high memory area is recorded in the process table.

Two entries in the process table correspond to processes that do not need to be scheduled in the ordinary way. These are the *IDLE* and *HARDWARE* processes. *IDLE* is a do-nothing loop that is executed when there is nothing else ready to run, and the *HARDWARE* process exists for bookkeeping purposes—it is credited with the time used while servicing an interrupt. All other processes are put on the appropriate queues by the code in line 6811. The function called, *lock_ready*, sets a lock variable, *switching*, before modifying the queues and then removes the lock when the queue has been modified. The locking and unlocking are not required at this point, when nothing is running yet, but this is the standard method, and there is no point in creating extra code to be used just once.

The last step in initializing each slot in the process table is to call *alloc_segments*. This procedure is part of the system task, but of course no tasks are running yet, and it is called as an ordinary procedure at line 6814. It is a machine-dependent routine that sets into the proper fields the locations, sizes, and permission levels for the memory segments used by each process. For older Intel processors that do not support protected mode, it defines only the segment locations. It would have to be rewritten to handle a processor type with a different method of allocating memory.

Once the process table is initialized for all the tasks, the servers, and *init*, the system is almost ready to roll. The variable *bill_ptr* tells which process gets billed for processor time; it needs to have an initial value set at line 6818, and *IDLE* is an appropriate choice. Later on it may be changed by the next function called, *lock_pick_proc*. All of the tasks are now ready to run and *bill_ptr* will be changed when a user process runs. *Lock_pick_proc*'s other job is to make the variable *proc_ptr* point to the entry in the process table for the next process to be run. This selection is made by examining the task, server, and user process queues, in that order. In this case, the result is to point *proc_ptr* to the entry point for the console task, which is always the first one to be started.

Finally, *main* has run its course. In many C programs *main* is a loop, but in the MINIX kernel its job is done once the initialization is complete. The call to *restart* on line 6822 starts the first task. Control will never return to *main*.

_Restart is an assembly language routine in *mpx386.s*. In fact, *_restart* is not a complete function; it is an intermediate entry point in a larger procedure. We will discuss it in detail in the next section; for now we will just say that *_restart* causes a context switch, so the process pointed to by *proc_ptr* will run. When *_restart* has executed for the first time we can say that MINIX is running—it is executing a process. *_Restart* is executed again and again as tasks, servers, and user processes are given their opportunities to run and then are suspended, either to wait for input or to give other processes their turns.

The task queued first (the one using slot 0 of the process table, that is, the one with the most negative number) is always the console task, so other tasks can use it to report progress or problems as they start. It runs until it blocks trying to receive a message. Then the next task will run until it, too, blocks trying to receive a message. Eventually, all the tasks will be blocked, so the memory manager and file system can run. Upon running for the first time, each of these will do some initialization, but both of them will eventually block, also. Finally *init* will fork off a *getty* process for each terminal. These processes will block until input is typed at some terminal, at which point the first user can log in.

We have now traced the startup of MINIX through three files, two written in C and one in assembly language. The assembly language file, *mpx386.s*, contains additional code used in handling interrupts, which we will look at in the next section. However, before we go on let us wrap up with a brief description of the remaining routines in the two C files. The other procedures in *start.c* are *k_atoi* (line 6594), which converts a string to an integer, and *k_getenv* (line 6606), which is used to find entries in the kernel's environment, which is a copy of the boot parameters. These are both simplified versions of standard library functions which are rewritten here in order to keep the kernel simple. The only remaining procedure in *main.c* is *panic* (line 6829). It is called when the system has discovered a condition that makes it impossible to continue. Typical panic conditions are a critical disk block being unreadable, an inconsistent internal state being detected, or one part of the system calling another part with invalid parameters. The calls to *printf* here are actually calls to the kernel routine *printk*, so the kernel can print on the console even if normal interprocess communication is disrupted.

2.6.7 Interrupt Handling in MINIX

The details of interrupt hardware are system dependent, but any system must have elements functionally equivalent to those to be described for systems with 32-bit Intel CPUs. Interrupts generated by hardware devices are electrical signals and are handled in the first place by an interrupt controller, an integrated circuit that can sense a number of such signals and for each one generate a unique data pattern on the processor's data bus. This is necessary because the processor itself has only one input for sensing all these devices, and thus cannot differentiate which device needs service. PCs using Intel 32-bit processors are normally equipped with two such controller chips. Each can handle eight inputs, but one is a slave which feeds its output to one of the inputs of the master, so fifteen distinct external devices can be sensed by the combination, as shown in Fig. 2-33.

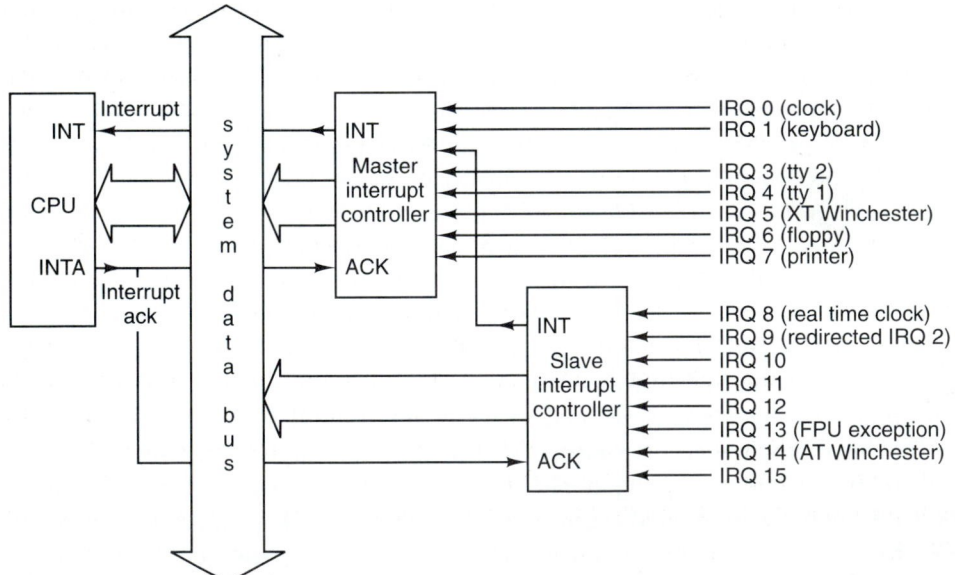

Figure 2-33. Interrupt processing hardware on a 32-bit Intel PC.

In the figure, interrupt signals arrive on the various *IRQ n* lines shown at the right. The connection to the CPU's INT pin tells the processor that an interrupt has occurred. The INTA (interrupt acknowledge) signal from the CPU causes the controller responsible for the interrupt to put data on the system data bus telling the processor which service routine to execute. The interrupt controller chips are programmed during system initialization, when *main* calls *intr_init*. The programming determines the output sent to the CPU for a signal received on each of the input lines, as well as various other parameters of the controller's operation. The data put on the bus is an 8-bit number, used to index into a table of up to 256 elements. The MINIX table has 56 elements. Of these, 35 are actually used; the others are reserved for use with future Intel processors or for future enhancements to MINIX. On 32-bit Intel processors this table contains interrupt gate descriptors, each of which is an 8-byte structure with several fields.

There are several possible modes of response to interrupts; in the one used by MINIX the fields of most concern to us in each of the interrupt gate descriptors point to the service routine's executable code segment and the starting address within it. The CPU executes the code pointed to by the selected descriptor. The result is exactly the same as execution of an

```
int     <nnn>
```

assembly language instruction. The only difference is that in the case of a hardware interrupt the *<nnn>* originates from a register in the interrupt controller chip, rather than from an instruction in program memory.

The task-switching mechanism of a 32-bit Intel processor that is called into play in response to an interrupt is complex, and changing the program counter to execute another function is only a part of it. When the CPU receives an interrupt while running a process it sets up a new stack for use during the interrupt service. The location of this stack is determined by an entry in the **Task State Segment** (TSS). There is one such structure for the entire system, initialized by *cstart*'s call to *prot_init*, and modified as each process is started. The effect is that the new stack created by an interrupt always starts at the end of the *stackframe_s* structure within the process table entry of the interrupted process. The CPU automatically pushes several key registers onto this new stack, including those necessary to reinstate the interrupted process' own stack and restore its program counter. When the interrupt handler code starts running, it uses this area in the process table as its stack, and much of the information needed to return to the interrupted process will have already been stored. The interrupt handler pushes the contents of additional registers, filling the stackframe, and then switches to a stack provided by the kernel while it does whatever must be done to service the interrupt.

Termination of an interrupt service routine is done by switching the stack from the kernel stack back to a stackframe in the process table (but not necessarily the same one that was created by the last interrupt), explicitly popping the additional registers, and executing an iretd (return from interrupt) instruction. Iretd restores the state that existed before an interrupt, restoring the registers that were pushed by the hardware and switching back to a stack that was in use before an interrupt. Thus an interrupt stops a process, and completion of the interrupt service restarts a process, possibly a different one from the one that was most recently stopped. Unlike the simpler interrupt mechanisms that are the usual subject of assembly language programming texts, nothing is stored on the interrupted process' working stack during an interrupt. Furthermore, because the stack is created anew in a known location (determined by the TSS) after an interrupt, control of multiple processes is simplified. To start a different process all that is necessary is to point the stack pointer to another process' stackframe, pop the registers that were explicitly pushed, and execute an iretd instruction.

The CPU disables all interrupts when it receives an interrupt. This guarantees that nothing can occur to cause the stackframe within a process table entry to overflow. This is automatic, but assembly-level instructions exist to disable and enable interrupts, as well. The interrupt handler reenables interrupts after switching to the kernel stack, located outside the process table. It must disable all interrupts again before it switches back to a stack within the process table, of course, but while it is handling an interrupt other interrupts can occur and be processed. The CPU keeps track of nested interrupts, and employs a simpler method of switching to an interrupt service routine and returning from one when an interrupt handler is interrupted. When a new interrupt is received while a handler (or other kernel code) is executing, a new stack is not created. Instead, the CPU pushes the essential registers needed for resumption of the interrupted code onto the existing stack. When an iretd is encountered while executing kernel code, a simpler return mechanism is used, too. The processor can determine how to handle the iretd by examining the code segment selector that is popped from the stack as part of the iretd's action.

The privilege levels mentioned earlier control the different responses to interrupts received while a process is running and while kernel code (including interrupt service routines) is executing. The simpler mechanism is used when the privilege level of the interrupted code is the same as the privilege level of the code to be executed in response to the interrupt. It is only when the interrupted code is less privileged than the interrupt service code that the more elaborate mechanism, using the TSS and a new stack, is employed. The privilege level of a code segment is recorded in the code segment selector, and as this is one of the items stacked during an interrupt, it can be examined upon return from the interrupt to determine what the iretd instruction must do. Another service is provided by the hardware when a new stack is created to use while servicing an interrupt. The hardware checks to make sure the new stack is big enough for at least the minimum quantity of information that must be placed on it. This protects the more privileged kernel code from being accidentally (or maliciously) crashed by a user process making a system call with an inadequate stack. These mechanisms are built into the processor specifically for use in the implementation of operating systems that support multiple processes.

This behavior may be confusing if you are unfamiliar with the internal working of 32-bit Intel CPUs. Ordinarily we try to avoid describing such details, but understanding what happens when an interrupt occurs and when an iretd instruction is executed is essential to understanding how the kernel controls the transitions to and from the "running" state of Fig. 2-2. The fact that the hardware handles much of the work makes life much easier for the programmer, and presumably makes the resulting system more efficient. All this help from the hardware does, however, make it hard to understand what is happening just by reading the software.

Only a tiny part of the MINIX kernel actually sees hardware interrupts. This code is in *mpx386.s*. There is an entry point for each interrupt. The source code at each entry point, *_hwint00* to *_hwint07*, (lines 6164 to 6193) looks like a call to *hwint_master* (line 6143), and the entry points *_hwint08* to *_hwint15* (lines 6222 to 6251) look like calls to *hwint_slave* (line 6199). Each entry point appears to pass a parameter in the call, indicating which device needs service. In fact, these are really not calls, but macros, and eight separate copies of the code defined by the macro definition of *hwint_master* are assembled, with only the *irq* parameter different. Similarly, eight copies of the *hwint_slave* macro are assembled. This may seem extravagant, but assembled code is very compact. The object code for each expanded macro occupies less than 40 bytes. In servicing an interrupt, speed is important, and doing it this way eliminates the overhead of executing code to load a parameter, call a subroutine, and retrieve the parameter.

We will continue the discussion of *hwint_master* as if it really were a single function, rather than a macro that is expanded in eight different places. Recall that before *hwint_master* begins to execute, the CPU has created a new stack in the interrupted process' *stackframe_s*, within its process table slot, and that several key registers have already been saved there. The first action of *hwint_master* is to call *save* (line 6144). This subroutine pushes all the other registers necessary to restart the interrupted process. *Save* could have been written inline as part of the macro to increase speed, but this would have more than doubled the size of the macro, and in any case *save* is needed for calls by other functions. As we shall see, *save* plays tricks with the stack. Upon returning to *hwint_master*, the kernel stack, not a stackframe in the process table, is in use. The next step is to manipulate the interrupt controller, to prevent it from receiving another interrupt from the source that generated the current interrupt (lines 6145 to 6147). This operation masks the ability of the controller chip to respond to a particular input; the CPU's ability to respond to all interrupts is inhibited internally when it first receives the interrupt signal and has not yet been restored at this point.

The code on lines 6148 to 6150 resets the interrupt controller and then enables the CPU to again receive interrupts from other sources. Next, the number of the interrupt being serviced is used by the indirect call instruction on line 6152 to index into a table of addresses of the device-specific low-level routines. We call these low-level routines, but they are written in C, and they typically perform operations like servicing an input device and transferring the data to a buffer where it can be accessed when the corresponding task has its next chance to run. A substantial amount of processing may happen before the return from this call.

We will see examples of low-level driver code in the next chapter. However, in order to understand what is happening here in *hwint_master*, we now mention that the low-level code may call *interrupt* (in *proc.c*, which we will discuss in the next section), and that *interrupt* transforms the interrupt into a message to the task that services the device that caused the interrupt. Furthermore, a call to *interrupt* invokes the scheduler and may select this task to run next. Upon returning from the call to the device-specific code, the processor's ability to respond to all interrupts is again disabled, by the cli instruction on line 6154, and the interrupt controller is prepared to be able to respond to the particular device that caused the current interrupt when all interrupts are next reenabled (lines 6157 to 6159). Then *hwint_master* terminates with a ret instruction (line 6160). It is not obvious that something tricky happens here. If a process was interrupted, the stack in use at this point is the kernel stack, and not the stack within a process table that was set up by the hardware before *hwint_master* was started. In this case, manipulation of the stack by *save* will have left the address of _restart on the kernel stack. This results in a task, server, or user process once again executing. It may not be, and in fact is unlikely to be, the same process as was executing originally. This depends upon whether the processing of the message created by the device-specific interrupt service routine caused a change in the process scheduling queues. This, then, is the heart of the mechanism which creates the illusion of multiple processes executing simultaneously.

To be complete, let us mention that when an interrupt occurs while kernel code is executing, the kernel stack is already in use, and *save* leaves the address of *restart1* on the kernel stack. In this case, whatever the kernel was doing previously continues after the ret at the end of *hwint_master*. Thus interrupts may be nested, but when all the low-level service routines are complete _restart will finally execute, and a process different from the one that was interrupted may be put into execution.

Hwint_slave (line 6199) is very similar to *hwint_master*, except that it must reenable both the master and slave controllers, since both of them are disabled by receipt of an interrupt by the slave. There are a few subtle aspects of assembly language to be seen here. First, on line 6206 there is a line

```
jmp    .+2
```

which specifies a jump whose target address is the immediately following instruction. This instruction is placed here solely to add a small delay. The authors of the original **IBM PC BIOS** considered a delay necessary between consecutive I/O instructions, and we are following their example, although it may not be necessary on all current IBM PC-compatible computers. This kind of fine tuning is one reason why programming hardware devices is considered an esoteric craft by some. On line 6214 there is a conditional jump to an instruction with a numeric label,

```
0:     ret
```

to be found on line 6218. Note that the line

```
jz 0f
```

does not specify a number of bytes to jump over, as in the previous example. The *0f* here is not a hexadecimal number. This is the way the assembler used by the MINIX compiler specifies a **local label**; the *0f* means a jump **forward** to the next numeric label 0. Ordinary label names are not permitted to begin with numeric characters. Another interesting and possibly confusing point is that the same label occurs elsewhere in the same file, on line 6160 in *hwint_master*. The situation is even more complicated than it looks at first glance since these labels are within macros and the macros are expanded before the assembler sees this code. Thus there are actually sixteen 0: labels in the code seen by the assembler. The possible proliferation of labels declared within macros is, indeed, the reason why the assembly language provides local labels; when resolving a local label the assembler uses the nearest one that matches in the specified direction, and additional occurrences of a local label are ignored.

Now let us move on to look at *save* (line 6261), which we have already mentioned several times. Its name describes one of its functions, which is to save the context of the interrupted process on the stack provided by the CPU, which is a stackframe within the process table. *Save* uses the variable *_k_reenter* to count and determine the level of nesting of interrupts. If a process was executing when the current interrupt occurred, the

```
mov    esp, k_stktop
```

instruction on line 6274 switches to the kernel stack, and the following instruction pushes the address of *_restart* (line 6275). Otherwise, the kernel stack is already in use, and the address of *restart1* is pushed instead (line 6281). In either case, with a possibly different stack in use from the one that was in effect upon entry, and with the return address in the routine that called it buried beneath the registers that have just been pushed, an ordinary return instruction is not adequate for returning to the caller. The

```
jmp    RETADR-P_STACKBASE(eax)
```

instructions that terminate the two exit points of *save*, at line 6277 and line 6282, use the address that was pushed when *save* was called.

The next procedure in *mpx386.s* is *_s_call*, which begins on line 6288. Before looking at its internal details, look at how it ends. There is no ret or jmp at its end. After disabling interrupts with the cli on line 6315, execution continues at *_restart*. *_S_call* is the system call counterpart of the interrupt handling mechanism. Control arrives at *_s_call* following a software interrupt, that is, execution of an int *nnn* instruction. Software interrupts are treated like hardware interrupts, except of course the index into the Interrupt Descriptor Table is encoded into the *nnn* part of an int *nnn* instruction, rather than being supplied by an interrupt controller chip. Thus, when *_s_call* is entered, the CPU has already switched to a stack inside the process table (supplied by the Task State Segment), and several registers have already been pushed onto this stack. By falling through to *_restart*, the call to *_s_call* ultimately terminates with an iretd instruction, and, just as with a hardware interrupt, this instruction will start whatever process is pointed to by *proc_ptr* at that point. Figure 2-34 compares the handling of a hardware interrupt and a system call using the software interrupt mechanism.

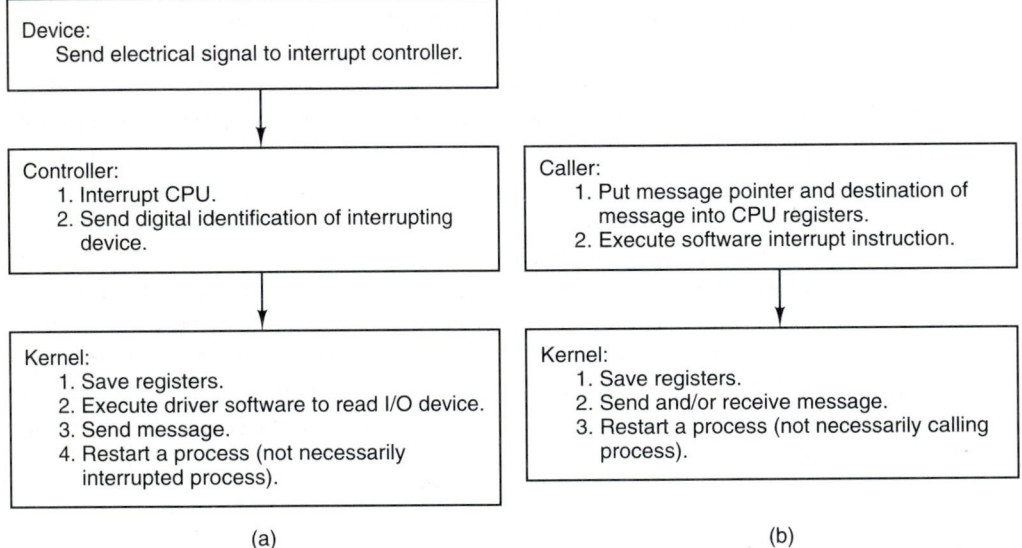

Figure 2-34. (a) How a hardware interrupt is processed. (b) How a system call is made.

Let us now look at some details of *_s_call*. The alternate label, *_p_s_call*, is a vestige of the 16-bit version of MINIX, which has separate routines for protected mode and real mode operation. In the 32-bit version all calls to either label end up here. A programmer invoking a MINIX system call writes a function call in C that looks like any other function call, whether to a locally defined function or to a routine in the C library. The library code supporting a system call sets up a message, loads the address of the message and the process id of the destination into CPU registers, and then invokes an int *SYS386_VECTOR* instruction. As described above, the result is that control passes to the start of *_s_call*, and several registers have already been pushed onto a stack inside the process table.

The first part of the _s_call code resembles an inline expansion of *save* and saves the additional registers that must be preserved. Just as in *save*, a

```
mov   esp, k_stktop
```

instruction then switches to the kernel stack, and interrupts are reenabled. (The similarity of a software interrupt to a hardware interrupt extends to both disabling all interrupts). Following this comes a call to _sys_call, which we will discuss in the next section. For now we just say that it causes a message to be delivered, and that this in turn causes the scheduler to run. Thus, when _sys_call returns, it is probable that *proc_ptr* will be pointing to a different process from the one that inititated the system call. Before execution falls through to *restart*, a cli instruction disables interrupts to protect the stackframe of the process that is about to be restarted.

We have seen that _restart (line 6322) is reached in several ways:

1. By a call from *main* when the system starts.

2. By a jump from *hwint_master* or *hwint_slave* after a hardware interrupt.

3. By falling through from _s_call after a system call.

In every case interrupts are disabled at this point. _Restart calls *unhold* if it detects that any unserviced interrupts have been held up because they arrived while other interrupts were being processed. This allows the other interrupts to be converted into messages before any process is restarted. This temporarily reenables interrupts, but they are disabled again before *unhold* returns. By line 6333 the next process to run has been definitively chosen, and with interrupts disabled it cannot be changed. The process table was carefully constructed so it begins with a stack frame, and the instruction on this line,

```
mov   esp, (_proc_ptr)
```

points the CPU's stack pointer register at the stack frame. The

```
lldt   P_LDT_SEL(esp)
```

instruction then loads the processor's local descriptor table register from the stack frame. This prepares the processor to use the memory segments belonging to the next process to be run. The following instruction loads the address in the next process' process table entry that where the stack for the next interrupt will be set up, and the following instruction stores this address into the TSS. The first part of _restart is not necessary after an interrupt that occurs when kernel code, (including interrupt service code) is executing, since the kernel stack will be in use and termination of the interrupt service should allow the kernel code to continue. The label *restart1* (line 6337) marks the point where execution resumes in this case. At this point *k_reenter* is decremented to record that one level of possibly nested interrupts has been disposed of, and the remaining instructions restore the processor to the state it was in when the next process executed last. The penultimate instruction modifies the stack pointer so the return address that was pushed when *save* was called is ignored. If the last interrupt occurred when a process was executing, the final instruction, iretd, completes the return to execution of whatever process is being allowed to run next, restoring its remaining registers, including its stack segment and stack pointer. If, however, this encounter with the iretd came via *restart1*, the kernel stack in use is not a stackframe, but the kernel stack, and this is not a return to an interrupted process, but the completion of an interrupt that occurred while kernel code was executing. The CPU detects this when the code segment descriptor is popped from the stack during execution of the iretd, and the complete action of the iretd in this case is to retain the kernel stack in use.

There are a few more things to discuss in *mpx386.s*. In addition to hardware and software interrupts, various error conditions internal to the CPU can cause the initiation of an **exception**. Exceptions are not always bad. They can be used to stimulate the operating system to provide a service, such as providing more memory for a process to use, or swapping in a currently swapped-out memory page, although such services are not implemented in standard MINIX. But, when an exception occurs, it should not be ignored. Exceptions are handled by the same mechanism as interrupts, using descriptors in the interrupt descriptor table. These entries in the table point to the sixteen exception handler entry points, beginning with *_divide_error* and ending with *_copr_error*, found near the end of *mpx386.s*, on lines 6350 to 6412. These all jump to *exception* (line 6420) or *errexception* (line 6431) depending upon whether the condition pushes an error code onto the stack or not. The handling here in the assembly code is similar to that we have already seen, registers are pushed and the C routine *_exception* (note the underscore) is called to handle the event. The consequences of exceptions vary. Some are ignored, some cause panics, and some result in sending signals to processes. We will examine *_exception* in a later section.

There is one other entry point that is handled like an interrupt, *_level0_call* (line 6458). Its function will be discussed in the next section, when we discuss the code to which it jumps, *_level0_func*. The entry point is here in *mpx386.s* with the interrupt and exception entry points because it too is invoked by execution of an int instruction. Like the exception routines, it calls *save*, and thus eventually the code that is jumped to here will terminate by a ret that leads to *_restart*. The last executable function in *mpx386.s* is *_idle_task* (line 6465). This is a do-nothing loop that is executed whenever there is no other process ready to run.

Finally, some data storage space is reserved at the end of the assembly language file. There are two different data segments defined here. The

.sect .rom

declaration at line 6478 ensures that this storage space is allocated at the very beginning of the kernel's data segment. The compiler puts a magic number here so *boot* can verify that the file it loads is a valid kernel image. *Boot* then overwrites the magic number and subsequent space with the _sizes_ array data, as described in the discussion of kernel data structures. Enough space is reserved here for a _sizes_ array with a total of sixteen entries, in case additional servers are added to MINIX. The other data storage area defined at the

```
.sect .bss
```

(line 6483) declaration reserves space in the kernel's normal uninitialized variable area for the kernel stack and for variables used by the exception handlers. Servers and ordinary processes have stack space reserved when an executable file is linked and depend upon the kernel to properly set the stack segment descriptor and the stack pointer when they are executed. The kernel has to do this for itself.

2.6.8 Interprocess Communication in MINIX

Processes in MINIX communicate by messages, using the rendezvous principle. When a process does a SEND, the lowest layer of the kernel checks to see if the destination is waiting for a message from the sender (or from ANY sender). If so, the message is copied from the sender's buffer to the receiver's buffer, and both processes are marked as runnable. If the destination is not waiting for a message from the sender, the sender is marked as blocked and put onto a queue of processes waiting to send to the receiver.

When a process does a RECEIVE, the kernel checks to see if any process is queued trying to send to it. If so, the message is copied from the blocked sender to the receiver, and both are marked as runnable. If no process is queued trying to send to it, the receiver blocks until a message arrives.

The high-level code for interprocess communication is found in _proc.c_. The kernel's job is to translate either a hardware interrupt or a software interrupt into a message. The former are generated by hardware and the latter are the way a request for system services, that is, a system call, is communicated to the kernel. These cases are similar enough that they could have been handled by a single function, but it was more efficient to create two specialized functions.

First we will look at _interrupt_ (line 6938). It is called by the low-level interrupt service routine for a device after receipt of a hardware interrupt. _Interrupt_'s function is to convert the interrupt into a message for the task that handles the interrupting device, and typically very little processing is done before calling _interrupt_. For example, the entire low-level interrupt handler for the hard disk driver consists of just these three lines:

```
w_status = in_byte(w_wn->base + REG_STATUS); /* acknowledge interrupt */
interrupt(WINCHESTER);
return 1;
```

If it were not necessary to read an I/O port on the hard disk controller to obtain the status, the call to _interrupt_ could have been in _mpx386.s_ instead of _at_wini.c_. The first thing *interrupt* does is check if an interrupt was already being serviced when the current interrupt was received, by looking at the variable *k_reenter* (line 6962). In this case the current interrupt is queued and *interrupt* returns. The current interrupt will be serviced later, when *unhold* is called. The next action is to check whether the task is waiting for an interrupt (lines 6978 to 6981). If the task is not ready to receive, its *p_int_blocked* flag is set—we will see later that this makes it possible to recover the lost interrupt—and no message is sent. If this test is passed, the message is sent. Sending a message from *HARDWARE* to a task is simple, because the tasks and the kernel are compiled into the same file and can access the same data areas. The code on lines 6989 to 6992 sends the message, by filling in the destination task's message buffer source and type fields, resetting the destination's *RECEIVING* flag, and unblocking the task. Once the message is ready the destination task is scheduled to run. We will discuss scheduling in more detail in the next section, but the code in *interrupt* on lines 6997 to 7003 provides a preview of what we will see—this is an inline substitute for the *ready* procedure that is called to queue a process. It is simple here, since messages originating from interrupts go only to tasks, and thus there is no need to determine which of the three process queues needs to be changed.

The next function in *proc.c* is *sys_call*. It has a similar function to *interrupt*: it converts a software interrupt (the int *SYS386_VECTOR* instruction by which a system call is initiated) into a message. But since there are a wider range of possible sources and destinations in this case, and since the call may require either sending or receiving or both sending and receiving a message, *sys_call* has more work to do. As is often the case, this means the code for *sys_call* is short and simple, since it does most of its work by calling other procedures. The first such call is to *isoksrc_dest*, a macro defined in *proc.h* (line 5172), which incorporates yet another macro, *isokprocn*, also defined in *proc.h* (line 5171). The effect is to check to make sure the process specified as the source or destination of the message is valid. At line 7026 a similar test, *isuserp* (also a macro defined in *proc.h*), is performed to make sure that if the call is from a user process it is asking to send a message and then receive a reply, the only kind of call permitted to user processes. Such errors are unlikely, but the tests are easily done, as ultimately they compile into code to perform comparisons of small integers. At this most basic level of the operating system testing for even the most unlikely errors is advisable. This code is likely to be executed many times each second during every second that the computer system on which it runs is active.

Finally, if the call requires sending a message, *mini_send* is called (line 7031), and if receiving a message is required, *mini_rec* is called (line 7039). These functions are the heart of the normal message passing mechanism of MINIX and deserve careful study.

Mini_send (line 7045) has three parameters: the caller, the process to be sent to, and a pointer to the buffer where the message is. It performs a number of tests. First, it makes sure that user processes try to send messages only to FS or MM. In line 7060 the parameter *caller_ptr* is tested with the macro *isuserp* to determine if the caller is a user process, and the parameter *dest* is tested with a similar function, *issysentn*, to determine if it is FS or MM. If the combination is not permitted *mini_send* terminates with an error.

Next a check is made to be sure the destination of the message is an active process, not an empty slot in the process table (line 7062). On lines 7068 to 7073 *mini_send* checks to see if the message falls entirely within the user's data segment, code segment, or the gap between them. If not, an error code is returned.

The next test is to check for a possible deadlock. On line 7079 is a test to make sure the destination of the message is not trying to send a message back to the caller.

The key test in *mini_send* is on lines 7088 to 7090. Here a check is made to see if the destination is blocked on a RECEIVE, as shown by the *RECEIVING* bit in the *p_flags* field of its process table entry. If it is waiting, then the next question is: "Who is it waiting for?" If it is waiting for the sender, or for ANY, *CopyMess* is executed to copy the message and the receiver is unblocked by resetting its *RECEIVING* bit. *CopyMess* is defined as a macro on line 6932. It calls the assembly language routine *cp_mess* in *klib386.s*.

If, on the other hand, the receiver is not blocked, or is blocked but waiting for a message from someone else, the code on lines 7098 to 7111 is executed to block and queue the sender. All processes wanting to send to a given destination are strung together on a linked list, with the destination's *p_callerq* field pointing to the process table entry of the process at the head of the queue. The example of Fig. 2-35(a) shows what happens when process 3 is unable to send to process 0. If process 4 is subsequently also unable to send to process 0, we get the situation of Fig. 2-35(b).

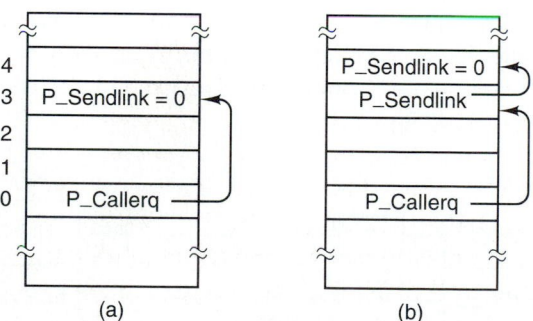

(a)   (b)

Figure 2-35. Queueing of processes trying to send to process 0.

Mini_rec (line 6119) is called by *sys_call* when its *function* parameter is *RECEIVE* or *BOTH*. The loop on lines 7137 to 7151 searches through all the processes queued waiting to send to the receiver to see if any are acceptable. If one is found, the message is copied from sender to receiver; then the sender is unblocked, made ready to run, and removed from the queue of processes trying to send to the receiver.

If no suitable sender is found, a check is made to see if the receiving process' $p\_int\_blocked$ flag indicates that an interrupt for this destination was previously blocked (line 7154). If so a message is constructed at this point—since messages from *HARDWARE* have no content other than *HARDWARE* in the source field and *HARD_INT* in the type field there is no need to call *CopyMess* in this case.

If a blocked interrupt is not found the process' source and buffer address are saved in its process table entry, and it is marked as blocked with its *RECEIVING* bit set. The call to *unready* on line 7165 removes the receiver from the scheduler's queue of runnable processes. The call is conditional to avoid blocking the process just yet if there is another bit set in its p_flags; a signal may be pending, and the process should have another chance to run soon to deal with the signal.

The penultimate statement in $mini\_rec$ (lines 7171 and 7172) has to do with how the kernel-generated signals *SIGINT*, *SIGQUIT*, and *SIGALRM* are handled. When one of these occurs, a message is sent to the memory manager, if it is waiting for a message from ANY. If not, the signal is remembered in the kernel until the memory manager finally tries to receive from ANY. That is tested here, and, if necessary, *inform* is called to informed it of the pending signals.

2.6.9 Scheduling in MINIX

MINIX uses a multilevel scheduling algorithm that closely follows the structure shown in Fig. 2-26. In that figure we see I/O tasks in layer 2, server processes in layer 3, and user processes in layer 4. The scheduler maintains three queues of runnable processes, one for each layer, as shown in Fig. 2-36. The array rdy_head has one entry for each queue, with that entry pointing to the process at the head of the queue. Similarly, rdy_tail is an array whose entries point to the last process on each queue. Both of these arrays are defined with the *EXTERN* macro in *proc.h* (lines 5192 and 5193).

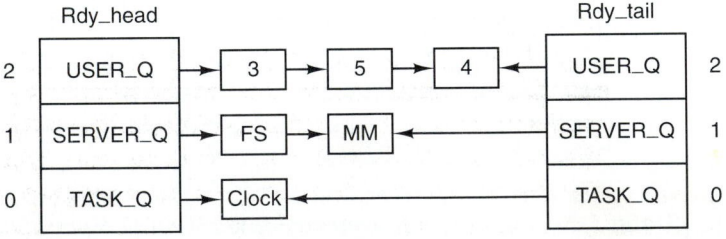

Figure 2-36. The scheduler maintains three queues, one per priority level.

Whenever a blocked process is awakened, it is appended to the end of its queue. The existence of the array rdy_tail makes adding a process to the end of a queue efficient. Whenever a running process becomes blocked, or a runnable process is killed by a signal, that process is removed from the scheduler's queues. Only runnable processes are queued.

Given the queue structures just described, the scheduling algorithm is simple: find the highest priority queue that is not empty and pick the process at the head of that queue. If all the queues are empty, the idle routine is run. In Fig. 2-36 *TASK_Q* has the highest priority. The scheduling code is in *proc.c*. The queue is chosen in *pick_proc* (line 7179). This function's major job is to set *proc_ptr*. Any change to the queues that might affect the choice of which process to run next requires *pick_proc* to be called again. Whenever the current process blocks, *pick_proc* is called to reschedule the CPU.

Pick_proc is simple. There is a test for each queue. *TASK_Q* is tested first, and if a process on this queue is ready, *pick_proc* sets *proc_ptr* and returns immediately. Next, *SERVER_Q* is tested, and, again, if a process is ready *pick_proc* sets *proc_ptr* and returns. If there is a ready process on the *USER_Q* queue, *bill_ptr* is changed to charge the user process for the CPU time it is about to be given (line 7198). This assures that the last user process to run is charged for work done on its behalf by the system. If none of the queues have a ready task line 7204 transfers billing to the *IDLE* process and schedules it. The process chosen to run is not removed from its queue merely because it has been selected.

The procedures *ready* (line 7210) and *unready* (line 7258) are called to enter a runnable process on its queue and remove a no-longer runnable process from its queue, respectively. *Ready* is called from both *mini_send* and *mini_rec*, as we have seen. It could also have been called from *interrupt,* but in the interest of speeding up interrupt processing its functional equivalent was written into *interrupt* as inline code. *Ready* manipulates one of the three process queues. It straightforwardly adds the process to the tail of the appropriate queue.

Unready also manipulates the queues. Normally, the process it removes is at the head of its queue, since a process must be running in order to block. In such a case *unready* calls *pick_proc* before returning, as, for example, in line 7293. A user process that is not running can also become unready if it is sent a signal, and if the process is not found at the head of one of the queues, a search is made through the *USER_Q* for it, and it is removed if found.

Although most scheduling decisions are made when a process blocks or unblocks, scheduling must also be done when the clock task notices that the current user process has exceeded its quantum. In this case the clock task calls *sched* (line 7311) to move the process at the head of *USER_Q* to the end of that queue. This algorithm results in running user processes in a straight round-robin fashion. The file system, memory manager, and I/O tasks are never put on the end of their queues because they have been running too long. They are trusted to work properly, and to block after having finished their work.

There are a few more routines in *proc.c* that support process scheduling. Five of these, *lock_mini_send*, *lock_pick_proc*, *lock_ready*, *lock_unready*, and *lock_sched*, set a lock, using the variable *switching* before calling the corresponding function and then release the lock upon completion. The last function in this file, *unhold* (line 7400), was mentioned in our discussion of *_restart* in *mpx386.s*. It loops through the queue of held-up interrupts, calling *interrupt* for each one, in order to get all pending interrupts converted to messages before another process is allowed to run.

In summary, the scheduling algorithm maintains three priority queues, one for the I/O tasks, one for the server processes, and one for the user processes. The first process on the highest priority queue is always run next. Tasks and servers are always allowed to run until they block, but the clock task monitors the time used by user processes. If a user process uses up its quantum, it is put at the end of its queue, thus achieving a simple round-robin scheduling among the competing user processes.

2.6.10 Hardware-Dependent Kernel Support

There are several C functions that are very dependent upon the hardware. To facilitate porting MINIX to other systems these functions are segregated in the files to be discussed in this section, *exception.c*, *i8259.c*, and *protect.c*, rather than being included in the same files with the higher-level code they support.

Exception.c contains the exception handler, *exception* (line 7512), which is called (as *_exception*) by the assembly language part of the exception handling code in *mpx386.s*. Exceptions originating from user processes are converted to signals. Users are expected to make mistakes in their own programs, but an exception originating in the operating system indicates something is seriously wrong and causes a panic. The array *ex_data* (lines 7522 to 7540) determines the error message to be printed in case of panic, or the signal to be sent to a user process for each exception. Earlier Intel processors do not generate all the exceptions, and the third field in each entry indicates the minimum processor model that is capable of generating each one. This array provides an interesting summary of the evolution of the Intel family of processors upon which MINIX has been implemented. On line 7563 an alternate message is printed if a panic results from an interrupt that would not be expected from the processor in use.

The three functions in *i8259.c* are used during system initialization to initialize the Intel 8259 interrupt controller chips. *Intr_init* (line 7621) initializes the controllers. It writes data to several port locations. On a few lines a variable derived from the boot parameters is tested, for instance, the first port writes on line 7637, to accommodate different computer models. On line 7638, and again on line 7644, the parameter *mine* is tested, and a value appropriate either for MINIX or for the BIOS ROM is written to the port. When leaving MINIX *intr_init* can be called to restore the BIOS vectors, allowing a graceful exit back to the boot monitor. *Mine* selects the mode to use. Fully understanding what is going on here would require study of the documentation for the 8259 integrated circuit, and thus we will not dwell on the details. We will point out that the *out_byte* call on line 7642 makes the master controller unresponsive to any input except from the slave, and the similar operation on line 7648 inhibits the response of the slave to all of its inputs. Also, the final line of the function preloads the address of *spurious_irq*, the next function in the file (line 7657), into each slot in *irq_table*. This ensures that any interrupt generated before the real handlers are installed will do no harm.

The last function in *i8259.c* is *put_irq_handler* (line 7673). At initialization each task that must respond to an interrupt calls this to put its own handler address into the interrupt table, overwriting the address of *spurious_irq*.

Protect.c contains routines related to protected mode operation of Intel processors. The **Global Descriptor Table** (GDT), **Local Descriptor Tables** (LDTs), and the **Interrupt Descriptor Table**, all located in memory, provide protected access to system resources. The GDT and IDT are pointed to by special registers within the CPU, and GDT entries point to LDTs. The GDT is available to all processes and holds segment descriptors for memory regions used by the operating system. There is normally one LDT for each process, holding segment descriptors for the memory regions used by the process. Descriptors are 8-byte structures with a number of components, but the most important parts of a segment descriptor are the fields that describe the base address and the limit of a memory region. The IDT is also composed of 8-byte descriptors, with the most important part being the address of the code to be executed when the corresponding interrupt is activated.

Prot_init (line 7767) is called by *start.c* to set up the GDT on lines 7828 to 7845. The IBM PC BIOS requires that it be ordered in a certain way, and all the indices into it are defined in *protect.h*. Space for an LDT for each process is allocated in the process table. Each contains two descriptors, for a code segment and a data segment—recall we are discussing here segments as defined by the hardware; these are not the same as the segments managed by the operating system, which considers the hardware-defined data segment to be further divided into data and stack segments. On lines 7851 to 7857 descriptors for each LDT are built in the GDT. The functions *init_dataseg* and *init_codeseg* actually build these descriptors. The entries in the LDTs themselves are initialized when a process' memory map is changed (i.e., when an EXEC system call is made).

Another processor data structure that needs initialization is the **Task State Segment** (TSS). The structure is defined at the start of this file (lines 7725 to 7753) and provides space for storage of processor registers and other information that must be saved when a task switch is made. MINIX uses only the fields that define where a new stack is to be built when an interrupt occurs. The call to *init_dataseg* on line 7867 ensures that it can be located using the GDT.

To understand how MINIX works at the lowest level, perhaps the most important thing is to understand how exceptions, hardware interrupts, or int *<nnn>* instructions lead to the execution of the various pieces of code that has been written to service them. This is accomplished by means of the interrupt gate descriptor table. The array *gate_table* (lines 7786 to 7818), is initialized by the compiler with the addresses of the routines that handle exceptions and hardware interrupts and then is used in the loop at lines 7873 to 7877 to initialize a large part of this table, using calls to the *int_gate* function. The remaining vectors, *SYS_VECTOR*, *SYS386_VECTOR*, and *LEVEL0_VECTOR*, require different privilege levels and are initialized following the loop.

There are good reasons for the way the data are structured in the descriptors, based on details of the hardware and the need to maintain compatibility between advanced processors and the 16-bit 286 processor. Fortunately, we can normally leave these details to Intel's processor designers. For the most part the C language allows us to avoid the details. However, in implementing a real operating system the details must be faced at some point. Figure 2-37 shows the internal structure of one kind of segment descriptor. Note that the base address, which C programs can refer to as a simple 32-bit unsigned integer, is split into three parts, two of which are separated by a number of 1-, 2-, and 4-bit quantities. The limit is a 20-bit quantity stored as separate 16-bit and 4-bit chunks. The limit is interpreted as either a number of bytes or a number of 4096-byte pages, based on the value of the *G* (granularity) bit. Other descriptors, such as those used to specify how interrupts are handled, have different, but equally complex structures. We discuss these structures in more detail in Chapter 4.

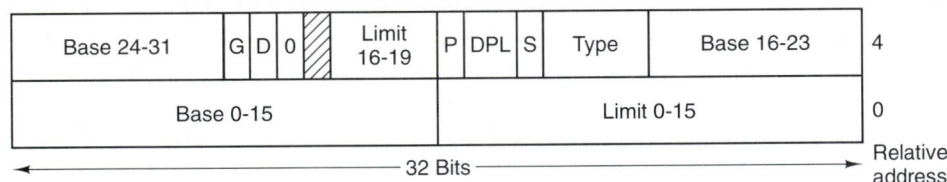

Figure 2-37. The format of an Intel segment descriptor.

Most of the other functions defined in *protect.c* are devoted to converting between variables used in C programs and the rather ugly forms these data take in the machine readable descriptors such as the one in Fig. 2-37. *Init_codeseg* (line 7889) and *init_dataseg* (line 7906) are similar in operation and are used to convert the parameters passed to them into segment descriptors. They each, in turn, call the next function, *sdesc* (line 7922), to complete the job. This is where the messy details of the structure shown in Fig. 2-37 are dealt with. *Init_codeseg* and *init_data_seg* are not used just at system initialization. In addition, they are also called by the system task whenever a new process is started up, in order to allocate the proper memory segments for the process to use. *Seg2phys* (line 7947), called only from *start.c*, performs an operation which is the inverse of that of *sdesc*, extracting the base address of a segment from a segment descriptor. *Int_gate* (line 7969) performs a similar function to *init_codeseg* and *init_dataseg* in building entries for the interrupt descriptor table.

The final function in *protect.c*, *enable_iop* (line 7988) performs a dirty trick. We have pointed out in several places that one function of an operating system is to protect system resources, and one way MINIX does so is by using privilege levels to make certain kinds of instructions off limits to user programs. However, MINIX is also intended to be run on small systems, which are likely to have only one user or perhaps just a few trusted users. On such a system a user could very well want to write an application program that accesses I/O ports, for instance, for use in scientific data acquisition. The file system has a little secret built into it— when the files */dev/mem* or */dev/kmem* are opened, the memory task calls *enable_iop*, which changes the privilege level for I/O operations, allowing the current process to execute instructions which read and write I/O ports. The description of the purpose of the function is more complicated than the function itself, which just sets two bits in the word in the stack frame entry of the calling process that will be loaded into the CPU status register when the process is next executed. There is no need for another function to undo this, as it will apply only to the calling process.

2.6.11 Utilities and the Kernel Library

Finally, the kernel has a library of support functions written in assembly language that are included by compiling *klib.s* and a few utility programs, written in C, in the file *misc.c*. Let us first look at the assembly language files. *Klib.s* (line 8000), is a short file similar to *mpx.s*, which selects the appropriate machine-specific version based upon the definition of *WORD_SIZE*. The code we will discuss is in *klib386.s* (line 8100). This contains about two dozen utility routines that are in assembly code, either for efficiency or because they cannot be written in C at all.

_Monitor (line 8166) makes it possible to return to the boot monitor. From the point of view of the boot monitor all of MINIX is just a subroutine, and when MINIX is started, a return address to the monitor is left on the monitor's stack. *_Monitor* just has to restore the various segment selectors and the stack pointer that was saved when MINIX was started, and then return as from any other subroutine.

The next function, *_check_mem* (line 8198), is used at startup time to determine the size of a block of memory. It performs a simple test on every sixteenth byte, using two patterns which test every bit with both "0" and "1" values.

Although *_phys_copy* (see below) could have been used for copying messages, *_cp_mess* (line 8243), a faster specialized procedure, has been provided for that purpose. It is called by

```
cp_mess(source, src_clicks, src_offset, dest_clicks, dest_offset);
```

where *source* is the sender's process number, which is copied into the *m_source* field of the receiver's buffer. Both the source and destination addresses are specified by giving a click number, typically the base of the segment containing the buffer, and an offset from that click. This form of specifying the source and destination is more efficient than the 32-bit addresses used by _phys_copy.

_Exit, __exit, and ___exit (lines 8283 to 8285) are defined because some library routines that might be used in compiling MINIX make calls to the standard C function exit. An exit from the kernel is not a meaningful concept; there is nowhere to go. The solution here is to enable interrupts and enter an endless loop. Eventually, an I/O operation or the clock will cause an interrupt and normal system operation will resume. The entry point for ___main (line 8289) is another attempt to deal with a compiler action which, while it might make sense while compiling a user program, does not have any purpose in the kernel. It points to an assembly language ret (return from subroutine) instruction.

_In_byte (line 8300), _in_word (line 8314), _out_byte (line 8328), and _out_word (line 8342) provide access to I/O ports, which on Intel hardware occupy a separate address space from memory and use different instructions from memory reads and writes. _Port_read (line 8359), _port_read_byte (line 8386), _port_write (line 8412), and _port_write_byte (line 8439) handle transfers of blocks of data between I/O ports and memory; they are used primarily for transfers to and from the disk which must be done more rapidly than is possible with the other I/O calls. The byte versions read 8 bits rather than 16 bits in each operation to accommodate older 8-bit peripheral devices.

Occasionally, it is necessary for a task to disable all CPU interrupts temporarily. It does this by calling _lock (line 8462). When interrupts can be reenabled, the task can call _unlock (line 8474) to enable interrupts. A single machine instruction performs each one of these operations. In contrast, the code for _Enable_irq (line 8488) and _disable_irq (line 8521) is more complicated. They work at the level of the interrupt controller chips to enable and disable individual hardware interrupts.

_Phys_copy (line 8564) is called in C by

phys_copy(source_address, destination_address, bytes);

and copies a block of data from anywhere in physical memory to anywhere else. Both addresses are absolute, that is, address 0 really means the first byte in the entire address space, and all three parameters are unsigned longs.

The next two short functions are very specific to Intel processors. _Mem_rdw (line 8608) returns a 16-bit word from anywhere in memory. The result is zero-extended into the 32-bit eax register. The _reset function (line 8623) resets the processor. It does this by loading the processor's interrupt descriptor table register with a null pointer and then executing a software interrupt. This has the same effect as a hardware reset.

The next two routines support the video display and are used by the console task. _Mem_vid_copy (line 8643) copies a string of words containing alternate character and attribute bytes from the kernel's memory region to the video display memory. _Vid_vid_copy (line 8696) copies a block within the video memory itself. This is somewhat more complicated, since the destination block may overlap the source block, and the direction of the move is important.

The last function in this file is _level0 (line 8773) It allows tasks to have the most privileged permission level, level zero, when necessary. It is used for such things as resetting the CPU or accessing the PC's ROM BIOS routines.

The C language utilities in misc.c are specialized. Mem_init (line 8820) is called only by main, when MINIX is first started. There can be two or three disjoint regions of memory on an IBM-PC compatible computer. The size of the lowest range, known to PC users as "ordinary" memory, and of the memory range that starts above the PC ROM area ("extended" memory) are reported by the BIOS to the boot monitor, which in turn passes the values as boot parameters, which are interpreted by cstart and written to low_memsize and ext_memsize at boot time. The third region is "shadow" memory, into which the BIOS ROM may be copied to provide an improvement in performance, since ROM memory is usually slower than writeable memory. Since MINIX does not normally use the BIOS, mem_init attempts to locate this memory and add it to the pool of memory available for its use. It does this by calling check_mem to test the memory region where this memory may sometimes be found.

The next routine, env_parse (line 8865) is also used at startup time. The boot monitor can pass arbitrary strings like "DPETH0=300:10" to MINIX in the boot parameters. Env_parse tries to find a string whose first field matches its first argument, env, and then to extract the requested field. The comments in the code explain the use of the function. It is provided primarily to aid the user who wants to add new drivers which may need to be provided with parameters. The example "DPETH0" is used to pass configuration information to an Ethernet adapter when networking support is compiled into MINIX.

The last two routines we will discuss in this chapter are bad_assertion (line 8935) and bad_compare (line 8947). They are compiled only if the macro DEBUG is defined as TRUE. They support the macros in assert.h. Although they are not referenced in any of the code discussed in this text, they may be useful for debugging to the reader who wants to create a modified version of MINIX.

2.7 SUMMARY

To hide the effects of interrupts, operating systems provide a conceptual model consisting of sequential processes running in parallel. Processes can communicate with each other using interprocess communication primitives, such as semaphores, monitors, or messages. These primitives are used to ensure that no two processes are ever in their critical sections at the same time. A process can be running, runnable, or blocked and can change state when it or another process executes one of the interprocess communication primitives.

Interprocess communication primitives can be used to solve such problems as the producer-consumer, dining philosophers, reader-writer, and sleeping barber. Even with these primitives, care has to be taken to avoid errors and deadlocks. Many scheduling algorithms are known, including round-robin, priority scheduling, multilevel queues, and policy-driven schedulers.

MINIX supports the process concept and provides messages for interprocess communication. Messages are not buffered, so a SEND succeeds only when the receiver is waiting for it. Similarly, a RECEIVE succeeds only when a message is already available. If either operation does not succeed, the caller is blocked.

When an interrupt occurs, the lowest level of the kernel creates and sends a message to the task associated with the interrupting device. For example, the disk task calls *receive* and is blocked after writing a command to the disk controller hardware requesting it to read a block of data. The controller hardware causes an interrupt to occur when the data are ready. The low-level software then builds a message for the disk task and marks it as runnable. When the scheduler chooses the disk task to run, it gets and processes the message. It is also possible for the interrupt handler to do some work directly, such as a clock interrupt updating the time.

Task switching may follow an interrupt. When a process is interrupted, a stack is created within the process table entry of the process, and all the information needed to restart it is put on the new stack. Any process can be restarted by setting the stack pointer to point to its process table entry and initiating a sequence of instructions to restore the CPU registers, culminating with an iretd instruction. The scheduler decides which process table entry to put into the stack pointer.

Interrupts also occur when the kernel itself is running. The CPU detects this, and the kernel stack, rather a stack within the process table, is used. Thus nested interrupts can occur, and when a later interrupt service routine terminates, the one below it can complete. When all interrupts have been serviced, a process is restarted.

The MINIX scheduling algorithm uses three priority queues, the highest one for tasks, the next one for the file system, memory manager, and other servers, if any, and the lowest one for user processes. User processes are run round robin for one quantum at a time. All the others are run until they block or are preempted.

PROBLEMS

1. Suppose that you were to design an advanced computer architecture that did process switching in hardware, instead of having interrupts. What information would the CPU need? Describe how the hardware process switching might work.

2. On all current computers, at least part of the interrupt handlers are written in assembly language. Why?

3. In the text it was stated that the model of Fig. 2-6(a) was not suited to a file server using a cache in memory. Why not? Could each process have its own cache?

4. In a system with threads, is there one stack per thread or one stack per process? Explain.

5. What is a race condition?

6. Write a shell script that produces a file of sequential numbers by reading the last number in the file, adding 1 to it, and then appending to the file. Run one instance of the script in the background and one in the foreground, each accessing the same file. How long does it take before a race condition manifests itself? What is the critical section? Modify the script to prevent the race (hint: use

   ln file file.lock

   to lock the data file).

7. Is a statement like

   ln file file.lock

   an effective locking mechanism for a user program like the scripts used in the previous problem? Why (or why not)?

8. Does the busy waiting solution using the *turn* variable (Fig. 2-8) work when the two processes are running on a shared-memory multiprocessor, that is, two CPUs, sharing a common memory?

9. Consider a computer that does not have a TEST AND SET LOCK instruction but does have an instruction to swap the contents of a register and a memory word in a single indivisible action. Can that be used to write a routine *enter_region* such as the one found in Fig. 2-10?

10. Give a sketch of how an operating system that can disable interrupts could implement semaphores.

11. Show how counting semaphores (i.e., semaphores that can hold an arbitrarily large value) can be implemented using only binary semaphores and ordinary machine instructions.

12. In Sec. 2.2.4, a situation with a high-priority process, H, and a low-priority process, L, was described, which led to H looping forever. Does the same problem occur if round-robin scheduling is used instead of priority scheduling? Discuss.

13. Synchronization within monitors uses condition variables and two special operations, WAIT and SIGNAL. A more general form of synchronization would be to have a single primitive, WAITUNTIL that had an arbitrary Boolean predicate as parameter. Thus, one could say, for example,

   WAITUNTIL $x < 0$ **or** $y + z < n$

   The SIGNAL primitive would no longer be needed. This scheme is clearly more general than that of Hoare or Brinch Hansen, but it is not used. Why not? (Hint: think about the implementation.)

14. A fast food restaurant has four kinds of employees: (1) order takers, who take customer's orders; (2) cooks, who prepare the food; (3) packaging specialists, who stuff the food into bags; and (4) cashiers, who give the bags to customers and take their money. Each employee can be regarded as a communicating sequential process. What form of interprocess communication do they use? Relate this model to processes in MINIX.

15. Suppose that we have a message-passing system using mailboxes. When sending to a full mailbox or trying to receive from an empty one, a process does not block. Instead, it gets an error code back. The process responds to the error code by just trying again, over and over, until it succeeds. Does this scheme lead to race conditions?

16. In the solution to the dining philosophers problem (Fig. 2-20), why is the state variable set to *HUNGRY* in the procedure *take_forks*?

17. Consider the procedure *put_forks* in Fig. 2-20. Suppose that the variable *state*[*i*] was set to *THINKING after* the two calls to *test*, rather than *before*. How would this change affect the solution for the case of 3 philosophers? For 100 philosophers?

18. The readers and writers problem can be formulated in several ways with regard to which category of processes can be started when. Carefully describe three different variations of the problem, each one favoring (or not favoring) some category of processes. For each variation, specify what happens when a reader or a writer becomes ready to access the data base, and what happens when a process is finished using the data base.

19. The CDC 6600 computers could handle up to 10 I/O processes simultaneously using an interesting form of round-robin scheduling called **processor sharing**. A process switch occurred after each instruction, so instruction 1 came from process 1, instruction 2 came from process 2, etc. The process switching was done by special hardware, and the overhead was zero. If a process needed T sec to complete in the absence of competition, how much time would it need if processor sharing was used with n processes?

20. Round robin schedulers normally maintain a list of all runnable processes, with each process occurring exactly once in the list. What would happen if a process occurred twice in the list? Can you think of any reason for allowing this?

21. Measurements of a certain system have shown that the average process runs for a time T before blocking on I/O. A process switch requires a time S, which is effectively wasted (overhead). For round-robin scheduling with quantum Q, give a formula for the CPU efficiency for each of the following.

   (a) $Q = \infty$
   (b) $Q > T$
   (c) $S < Q < T$
   (d) $Q = S$
   (e) Q nearly 0

22. Five jobs are waiting to be run. Their expected run times are 9, 6, 3, 5, and X. In what order should they be run to minimize average response time? (Your answer will depend on X.)

23. Five batch jobs *A* through *E*, arrive at a computer center at almost the same time. They have estimated running times of 10, 6, 2, 4, and 8 minutes. Their (externally determined) priorities are 3, 5, 2, 1, and 4, respectively, with 5 being the highest priority. For each of the following scheduling algorithms, determine the mean process turnaround time. Ignore process switching overhead.

(a) Round robin.
(b) Priority scheduling.
(c) First-come, first-served (run in order 10, 6, 2, 4, 8).
(d) Shortest job first.

For (a), assume that the system is multiprogrammed, and that each job gets its fair share of the CPU. For (b) through (d) assume that only one job at a time runs, until it finishes. All jobs are completely CPU bound.

24. A process running on CTSS needs 30 quanta to complete. How many times must it be swapped in, including the very first time (before it has run at all)?

25. The aging algorithm with $a = 1/2$ is being used to predict run times. The previous four runs, from oldest to most recent, are 40, 20, 40, and 15 msec. What is the prediction of the next time?

26. A soft real-time system has four periodic events with periods of 50, 100, 200, and 250 msec each. Suppose that the four events require 35, 20, 10, and x msec of CPU time, respectively. What is the largest value of x for which the system is schedulable?

27. Explain why two-level scheduling is commonly used.

28. During execution, MINIX maintains a variable *proc_ptr* that points to the process table entry for the current process. Why?

29. MINIX does not buffer messages. Explain how this design decision causes problems with clock and keyboard interrupts.

30. When a message is sent to a sleeping process in MINIX, the procedure *ready* is called to put that process on the proper scheduling queue. This procedure starts out by disabling interrupts. Explain.

31. The MINIX procedure *mini_rec* contains a loop. Explain what it is for.

32. MINIX essentially uses the scheduling method in Fig. 2-23, with different priorities for classes. The lowest class (user processes) has round-robin scheduling, but the tasks and servers always are allowed to run until they block. Is it possible for processes in the lowest class to starve? Why (or why not)?

33. Is MINIX suitable for real-time applications, such as data logging? If not, what could be done to make it so?

34. Assume that you have an operating system that provides semaphores. Implement a message system. Write the procedures for sending and receiving messages.

35. A student majoring in anthropology and minoring in computer science has embarked on a research project to see if African baboons can be taught about deadlocks. He locates a deep canyon and fastens a rope across it, so the baboons can cross hand-over-hand. Several baboons can cross at the same time, provided that they are all going in the same direction. If eastward moving and westward moving baboons ever get onto the rope at the same time, a deadlock will result (the baboons will get stuck in the middle) because it is impossible for one baboon to climb over another one while suspended over the canyon. If a baboon wants to cross the canyon, he must check to see that no other baboon is currently crossing in the opposite direction. Write a program using semaphores that avoids deadlock. Do not worry about a series of eastward moving baboons holding up the westward moving baboons indefinitely.

36. Repeat the previous problem, but now avoid starvation. When a baboon that wants to cross to the east arrives at the rope and finds baboons crossing to the west, he waits until the rope is empty, but no more westward moving baboons are allowed to start until at least one baboon has crossed the other way.

37. Solve the dining philosophers problem using monitors instead of semaphores.

38. Add code to the MINIX kernel to keep track of the number of messages sent from process (or task) i to process (or task) j. Print this matrix when the F4 key is hit.

39. Modify the MINIX scheduler to keep track of how much CPU time each user process has had recently. When no task or server wants to run, pick the user process that has had the smallest share of the CPU.

40. Redesign MINIX so each process has a priority level field in its process table that can be used to give higher or lower priorities to individual processes.

41. Modify the *hwint_master* and *hwint_slave* macros in *mpx386.s* so the operations now performed by the *save* function are performed inline. What is the cost in code size? Can you measure an increase in performance?

3

INPUT/OUTPUT

One of the main functions of an operating system is to control all the computer's I/O (Input/Output) devices. It must issue commands to the devices, catch interrupts, and handle errors. It should also provide an interface between the devices and the rest of the system that is simple and easy to use. To the extent possible, the interface should be the same for all devices (device independence). The I/O code represents a significant fraction of the total operating system. How the operating system manages I/O is the subject of this chapter.

An outline of the chapter is as follows. First we will look briefly at some of the principles of I/O hardware, and then we will look at I/O software in general. I/O software can be structured in layers, with each layer having a well-defined task to perform. We will look at these layers to see what they do and how they fit together.

After that comes a section on deadlocks. We will define deadlocks precisely, show how they are caused, give two models for analyzing them, and discuss some algorithms for preventing their occurrence.

Then we will take a bird's-eye view of I/O in MINIX. Following that introduction, we will look at four I/O devices in detail—the RAM disk, the hard disk, the clock, and the terminal. For each device we will look at its hardware, software, and implementation in MINIX. Finally, the chapter closes with a short discussion of a little piece of MINIX that is located in the same layer as the I/O tasks but is itself not an I/O task. It provides some services to the memory manager and file system, such as fetching blocks of data from a user process.

3.1 PRINCIPLES OF I/O HARDWARE

Different people look at I/O hardware in different ways. Electrical engineers look at it in terms of chips, wires, power supplies, motors, and all the other physical components that make up the hardware. Programmers look at the interface presented to the software—the commands the hardware accepts, the functions it carries out, and the errors that can be reported back. In this book we are concerned with programming I/O devices, not designing, building, or maintaining them, so our interest will be restricted to how the hardware is programmed, not how it works inside. Nevertheless, the programming of many I/O devices is often intimately connected with their internal operation. In the next three sections we will provide a little general background on I/O hardware as it relates to programming.

3.1.1 I/O Devices

I/O devices can be roughly divided into two categories: **block devices** and **character devices**. A block device is one that stores information in fixed-size blocks, each one with its own address. Common block sizes range from 512 bytes to 32,768 bytes. The essential property of a block device is that it is possible to read or write each block independently of all the other ones. Disks are the most common block devices.

If you look closely, the boundary between devices that are block addressable and those that are not is not well defined. Everyone agrees that a disk is a block addressable device because no matter where the arm currently is, it is always possible to seek to another cylinder and then wait for the required block to rotate under the head. Now consider an 8mm or DAT tape drive used for making disk backups. Its tapes generally contain fixed-size blocks. If the tape drive is given a command to read block N, it can always rewind the tape and go forward until it comes to block N. This operation is analogous to a disk doing a seek, except that it takes much longer. Also, it may or may not be possible to rewrite one block in the middle of a tape. Even if it were possible to use tapes as random access block devices, that is stretching the point somewhat: they are normally not used that way.

The other type of I/O device is the character device. A character device delivers or accepts a stream of characters, without regard to any block structure. It is not addressable and does not have any seek operation. Printers, network interfaces, mice (for pointing), rats (for psychology lab experiments), and most other devices that are not disk-like can be seen as character devices.

This classification scheme is not perfect. Some devices just do not fit in. Clocks, for example, are not block addressable. Nor do they generate or accept character streams. All they do is cause interrupts at well-defined intervals. Memory-mapped screens do not fit the model well either. Still, the model of block and character devices is general enough that it can be used as a basis for making some of the operating system software dealing with I/O device independent. The file system, for example, deals just with abstract block devices and leaves the device-dependent part to lower-level software called **device drivers**.

3.1.2 Device Controllers

I/O units typically consist of a mechanical component and an electronic component. It is often possible to separate the two portions to provide a more modular and general design. The electronic component is called the **device controller** or **adapter**. On personal computers, it often takes the form of a printed circuit card that can be inserted into a slot on the computer's **parentboard** (previously incorrectly called a motherboard). The mechanical component is the device itself.

The controller card usually has a connector on it, into which a cable leading to the device itself can be plugged. Many controllers can handle two, four, or even eight identical devices. If the interface between the controller and device is a standard interface, either an official standard such as ANSI, IEEE, or ISO, or a de facto one, then companies can make controllers or devices that fit that interface. Many companies, for example, make disk drives that match the IDE (Integrated Drive Electronics) or SCSI (Small Computer System Interface) disk controller interfaces.

We mention this distinction between controller and device because the operating system nearly always deals with the controller, not the device. Most small computers use the single bus model of Fig. 3-1 for communication between the CPU and the controllers. Large mainframes often use a different model, with multiple buses and specialized I/O computers called **I/O channels** taking some of the load off the main CPU.

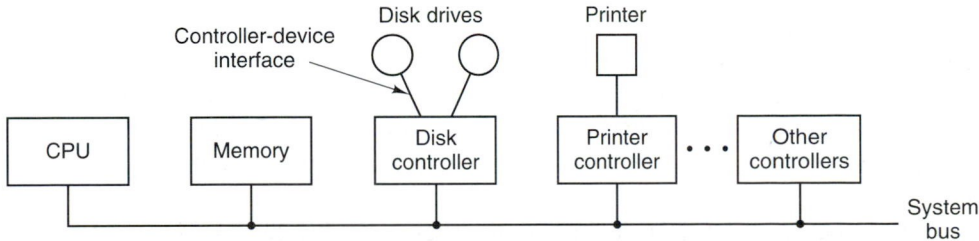

Figure 3-1. A model for connecting the CPU, memory, controllers, and I/O devices.

The interface between the controller and the device is often a very low-level interface. A disk, for example, might be formatted with 16 sectors of 512 bytes per track. What actually comes off the drive, however, is a serial bit stream, starting with a **preamble**, then the 4096 bits in a sector, and finally a checksum, also called an **Error-Correcting Code (ECC)**. The preamble is written when the disk is formatted and contains the cylinder and sector number, the sector size, and similar data, as well as synchronization information.

The controller's job is to convert the serial bit stream into a block of bytes and perform any error correction necessary. The block of bytes is typically first assembled, bit by bit, in a buffer inside the controller. After its checksum has been verified and the block declared to be error free, it can then be copied to main memory.

The controller for a CRT terminal also works as a bit serial device at an equally low level. It reads bytes containing the characters to be displayed from memory and generates the signals used to modulate the CRT beam to cause it to write on the screen. The controller also generates the signals for making the CRT beam do a horizontal retrace after it has finished a scan line, as well as the signals for making it do a vertical retrace after the entire screen has been scanned. If it were not for the CRT controller, the operating system programmer would have to explicitly program the analog scanning of the tube. With the controller, the operating system initializes the controller with a few parameters, such as the number of characters per line and number of lines per screen, and lets the controller take care of actually driving the beam.

Each controller has a few registers that are used for communicating with the CPU. On some computers, these registers are part of the regular memory address space. This scheme is called **memory-mapped I/O**. The 680x0, for example, uses this method. Other computers use a special address space for I/O, with each controller allocated a certain portion of it. The assignment of I/O addresses to devices is made by bus decoding logic associated with the controller. Some manufacturers of so-called IBM PC compatibles use different I/O addresses from those IBM uses. In addition to I/O ports, many controllers use interrupts to tell the CPU when they are ready to have their registers read or written. An interrupt is, in the first place, an electrical event. A hardware Interrupt ReQuest line (IRQ) is a physical input to the interrupt controller chip. The number of such inputs is limited; Pentium-class PCs have only 15 available for I/O devices. Some controllers are hard-wired onto the system parentboard, as is, for instance, the keyboard controller of an IBM PC. In the case of a controller that plugs into the backplane, switches or wire jumpers on the device controller sometimes can be used to select which IRQ the device will use, in order to avoid conflicts (although with some boards, such as Plug 'n Play, the IRQs can be set in software). The interrupt controller chip maps each IRQ input to an interrupt vector, which locates the corresponding interrupt service software. Figure 3-2 shows the I/O addresses, hardware interrupts, and interrupt vectors allocated to some of the controllers on an IBM PC, as an example. MINIX uses the same hardware interrupts, but the MINIX interrupt vectors are different from those shown here for MS-DOS.

The operating system performs I/O by writing commands into the controller's registers. The IBM PC floppy disk controller, for example, accepts 15 different commands, such as READ, WRITE, SEEK, FORMAT, and RECALIBRATE. Many of the

I/O controller	I/O address	Hardware IRQ	Interrupt vector
Clock	040 – 043	0	8
Keyboard	060 – 063	1	9
Hard disk	1F0 – 1F7	14	118
Secondary RS232	2F8 – 2FF	3	11
Printer	378 – 37F	7	15
Floppy disk	3F0 – 3F7	6	14
Primary RS232	3F8 – 3FF	4	12

Figure 3-2. Some examples of controllers, their I/O addresses, their hardware interrupt lines, and their interrupt vectors on a typical PC running MS-DOS.

commands have parameters, which are also loaded into the controller's registers. When a command has been accepted, the CPU can leave the controller alone and go off to do other work. When the command has been completed, the controller causes an interrupt in order to allow the operating system to gain control of the CPU and test the results of the operation. The CPU gets the results and device status by reading one or more bytes of information from the controller's registers.

3.1.3 Direct Memory Access (DMA)

Many controllers, especially those for block devices, support **Direct Memory Access** or **DMA**. To explain how DMA works, let us first look at how disk reads occur when DMA is not used. First the controller reads the block (one or more sectors) from the drive serially, bit by bit, until the entire block is in the controller's internal buffer. Next, it computes the checksum to verify that no read errors have occurred. Then the controller causes an interrupt. When the operating system starts running, it can read the disk block from the controller's buffer a byte or a word at a time by executing a loop, with each iteration reading one byte or word from a controller device register and storing it in memory.

Naturally, a programmed CPU loop to read the bytes one at a time from the controller wastes CPU time. DMA was invented to free the CPU from this low-level work. When it is used, the CPU gives the controller two items of information, in addition to the disk address of the block: the memory address where the block is to go, and the number of bytes to transfer, as shown in Fig. 3-3.

After the controller has read the entire block from the device into its buffer and verified the checksum, it copies the first byte or word into the main memory at the address specified by the DMA memory address. Then it increments the DMA address and decrements the DMA count by the number of bytes just transferred. This process is repeated until the DMA count becomes zero, at which time

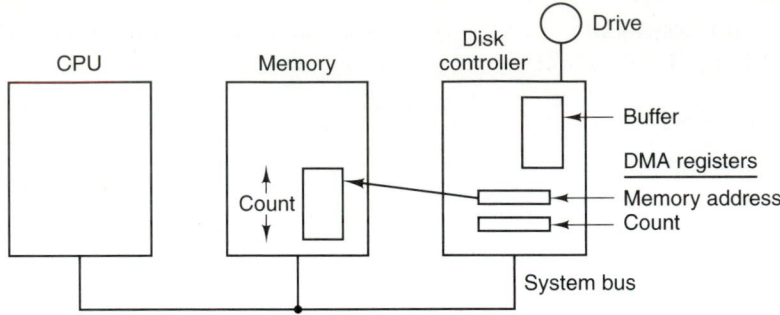

Figure 3-3. A DMA transfer is done entirely by the controller.

the controller causes an interrupt. When the operating system starts up, it does not have to copy the block to memory; it is already there.

You may be wondering why the controller does not just store the bytes in main memory as soon as it gets them from the disk. In other words, why does it need an internal buffer? The reason is that once a disk transfer has started, the bits keep arriving from the disk at a constant rate, whether the controller is ready for them or not. If the controller tried to write data directly to memory, it would have to go over the system bus for each word transferred. If the bus were busy due to some other device using it, the controller would have to wait. If the next disk word arrived before the previous one had been stored, the controller would have to store it somewhere. If the bus were very busy, the controller might end up storing quite a few words and having a lot of administration to do as well. When the block is buffered internally, the bus is not needed until the DMA begins, so the design of the controller is much simpler because the DMA transfer to memory is not time critical. (Some older controllers did, in fact, go directly to memory with only a small amount of internal buffering, but when the bus was very busy, a transfer might have had to be terminated with an overrun error.)

The two-step buffering process described above has important implications for I/O performance. While the data are being transferred from the controller to the memory, either by the CPU or by the controller, the next sector will be passing under the disk head and the bits arriving in the controller. Simple controllers just cannot cope with doing input and output at the same time, so while a memory transfer is taking place, the sector passing under the disk head is lost.

As a result, the controller will be able to read only every other block. Reading a complete track will then require two full rotations, one for the even blocks and one for the odd blocks. If the time to transfer a block from the controller to memory over the bus is longer than the time to read a block from the disk, it may be necessary to read one block and then skip two (or more) blocks.

Skipping blocks to give the controller time to transfer data to memory is called **interleaving**. When the disk is formatted, the blocks are numbered to take account of the interleave factor. In Fig. 3-4(a) we see a disk with 8 blocks per track and no interleaving. In Fig. 3-4(b) we see the same disk with single interleaving. In Fig. 3-4(c) double interleaving is shown.

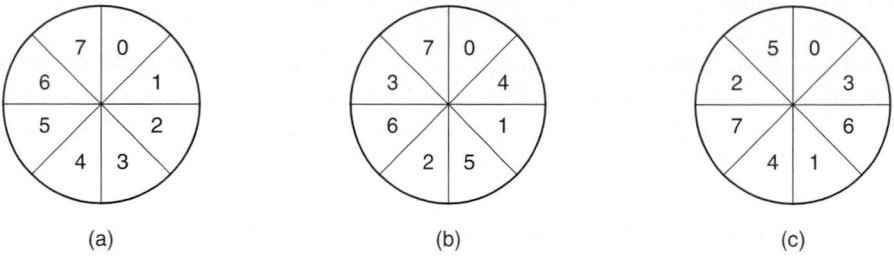

(a)   (b)   (c)

Figure 3-4. (a) No interleaving. (b) Single interleaving. (c) Double interleaving.

The idea of numbering the blocks this way is to allow the operating system to read consecutively numbered blocks and still achieve the maximum speed of which the hardware is capable. If the blocks were numbered as in Fig. 3-4(a) but the controller could read only alternate blocks, an operating system that allocated an 8-block file in consecutive disk blocks would require eight disk rotations to read blocks 0 through 7 in order. (Of course, if the operating system knew about the problem and allocated its blocks differently, it could solve the problem in software, but it is better to have the controller worry about the interleaving.)

Not all computers use DMA. The argument against it is that the main CPU is often far faster than the DMA controller and can do the job much faster (when the limiting factor is not the speed of the I/O device). If there is no other work for it to do, having the (fast) CPU wait for the (slow) DMA controller to finish is pointless. Also, getting rid of the DMA controller and having the CPU do all the work in software saves some money.

3.2 PRINCIPLES OF I/O SOFTWARE

Let us turn away from the hardware and now look at how the I/O software is structured. The general goals of the I/O software are easy to state. The basic idea is to organize the software as a series of layers, with the lower ones concerned with hiding the peculiarities of the hardware from the upper ones, and the upper ones concerned with presenting a nice, clean, regular interface to the users. In the following sections we will look at these goals and how they are achieved.

3.2.1 Goals of the I/O Software

A key concept in the design of I/O software is known as **device independence**. What it means is that it should be possible to write programs that can read files on a floppy disk, on a hard disk, or on a CD-ROM, without having to modify the programs for each different device type. One should be able to type a command such as

sort <input >output

and have it work with input coming from a floppy disk, a hard disk, or the keyboard, and the output going to the floppy disk, the hard disk, or even the screen. It is up to the operating system to take care of the problems caused by the fact that these devices really are different and require very different device drivers to actually write the data to the output device.

Closely related to device independence is the goal of **uniform naming**. The name of a file or a device should simply be a string or an integer and not depend on the device in any way. In UNIX, all disks can be integrated together in the file system hierarchy in arbitrary ways so the user need not be aware of which name corresponds to which device. For example, a floppy disk can be **mounted** on top of the directory */usr/ast/backup* so that copying a file to */usr/ast/backup/monday* copies the file to the floppy disk. In this way, all files and devices are addressed the same way: by a path name.

Another important issue for I/O software is error handling. In general, errors should be handled as close to the hardware as possible. If the controller discovers a read error, it should try to correct the error itself if it can. If it cannot, then the device driver should handle it, perhaps by just trying to read the block again. Many errors are transient, such as read errors caused by specks of dust on the read head, and will go away if the operation is repeated. Only if the lower layers are not able to deal with the problem should the upper layers be told about it. In many cases, error recovery can be done transparently at a low level without the upper levels even knowing about the error.

Still another key issue is synchronous (blocking) versus asynchronous (interrupt-driven) transfers. Most physical I/O is asynchronous—the CPU starts the transfer and goes off to do something else until the interrupt arrives. User programs are much easier to write if the I/O operations are blocking—after a READ command the program is automatically suspended until the data are available in the buffer. It is up to the operating system to make operations that are actually interrupt-driven look blocking to the user programs.

The final concept that we will deal with here is sharable versus dedicated devices. Some I/O devices, such as disks, can be used by many users at the same time. No problems are caused by multiple users having open files on the same disk at the same time. Other devices, such as tape drives, have to be dedicated to a single user until that user is finished. Then another user can have the tape drive. Having two or more users writing blocks intermixed at random to the same tape will definitely not work. Introducing dedicated (unshared) devices also introduces a variety of problems. Again, the operating system must be able to handle both shared and dedicated devices in a way that avoids problems.

These goals can be achieved in a comprehensible and efficient way by structuring the I/O software in four layers:

1. Interrupt handlers (bottom).

2. Device drivers.

3. Device-independent operating system software.

4. User-level software (top).

These four layers are (not accidently) the same four layers that we saw in Fig. 2-26. In the following sections we will look at each one in turn, starting at the bottom. The emphasis in this chapter is on the device drivers (layer 2), but we will summarize the rest of the I/O software to show how the various pieces of the I/O system fit together.

3.2.2 Interrupt Handlers

Interrupts are an unpleasant fact of life. They should be hidden away, deep in the bowels of the operating system, so that as little of the system as possible knows about them. The best way to hide them is to have every process starting an I/O operation block until the I/O has completed and the interrupt occurs. The process can block itself by doing a DOWN on a semaphore, a WAIT on a condition variable, or a RECEIVE on a message, for example.

When the interrupt happens, the interrupt procedure does whatever it has to in order to unblock the process that started it. In some systems it will do an UP on a semaphore. In others it will do a SIGNAL on a condition variable in a monitor. In still others, it will send a message to the blocked process. In all cases the net effect of the interrupt will be that a process that was previously blocked will now be able to run.

3.2.3 Device Drivers

All the device-dependent code goes in the device drivers. Each device driver handles one device type, or at most, one class of closely related devices. For example, it would probably be a good idea to have a single terminal driver, even if the system supported several different brands of terminals, all slightly different. On the other hand, a dumb, mechanical hardcopy terminal and an intelligent bit-map graphics terminal with a mouse are so different that different drivers should be used.

Earlier in this chapter we looked at what device controllers do. We saw that each controller has one or more device registers used to give it commands. The device drivers issue these commands and check that they are carried out properly. Thus, the disk driver is the only part of the operating system that knows how many registers that disk controller has and what they are used for. It alone knows about sectors, tracks, cylinders, heads, arm motion, interleave factors, motor drives, head settling times, and all the other mechanics of making the disk work properly.

In general terms, the job of a device driver is to accept abstract requests from the device-independent software above it and see to it that the request is executed. A typical request is to read block *n*. If the driver is idle at the time a request comes in, it starts carrying out the request immediately. If, however, it is already busy with a request, it will normally enter the new request into a queue of pending requests to be dealt with as soon as possible.

The first step in actually carrying out an I/O request, say, for a disk, is to translate it from abstract to concrete terms. For a disk driver, this means figuring out where on the disk the requested block actually is, checking to see if the drive's motor is running, determining if the arm is positioned on the proper cylinder, and so on. In short, it must decide which controller operations are required and in what sequence.

Once it has determined which commands to issue to the controller, it starts issuing them by writing into the controller's device registers. Some controllers can handle only one command at a time. Other controllers are willing to accept a linked list of commands, which they then carry out by themselves without further help from the operating system.

After the command or commands have been issued, one of two situations will apply. In many cases the device driver must wait until the controller does some work for it, so it blocks itself until the interrupt comes in to unblock it. In other cases, however, the operation finishes without delay, so the driver need not block. As an example of the latter situation, scrolling the screen on some terminals requires just writing a few bytes into the controller's registers. No mechanical motion is needed, so the entire operation can be completed in a few microseconds.

In the former case, the blocked driver will be awakened by the interrupt. In the latter case, it will never go to sleep. Either way, after the operation has been completed, it must check for errors. If everything is all right, the driver may have data to pass to the device-independent software (e.g., a block just read). Finally, it returns some status information for error reporting back to its caller. If any other requests are queued, one of them can now be selected and started. If nothing is queued, the driver blocks waiting for the next request.

3.2.4 Device-Independent I/O Software

Although some of the I/O software is device specific, a large fraction of it is device independent. The exact boundary between the drivers and the device-independent software is system dependent, because some functions that could be done in a device-independent way may actually be done in the drivers, for efficiency or other reasons. The functions shown in Fig. 3-5 are typically done in the device-independent software. In MINIX, most of the device-independent software is part of the file system, in layer 3 (Fig. 2-26). Although we will study the file system in Chap. 5, we will take a quick look at the device-independent software here, to provide some perspective on I/O and show better where the drivers fit in.

Uniform interfacing for device drivers
Device naming
Device protection
Providing a device-independent block size
Buffering
Storage allocation on block devices
Allocating and releasing dedicated devices
Error reporting

Figure 3-5. Functions of the device-independent I/O software.

The basic function of the device-independent software is to perform the I/O functions that are common to all devices and to provide a uniform interface to the user-level software.

A major issue in an operating system is how objects such as files and I/O devices are named. The device-independent software takes care of mapping symbolic device names onto the proper driver. In UNIX a device name, such as */dev/tty00*, uniquely specifies the i-node for a special file, and this i-node contains the **major device number**, which is used to locate the appropriate driver. The i-node also contains the **minor device number**, which is passed as a parameter to the driver to specify the unit to be read or written.

Closely related to naming is protection. How does the system prevent users from accessing devices that they are not entitled to access? In most personal computer systems, there is no protection at all. Any process can do anything it wants to. In most mainframe systems, access to I/O devices by user processes is completely forbidden. In UNIX, a more flexible scheme is used. The special files corresponding to I/O devices are protected by the usual *rwx* bits. The system administrator can then set the proper permissions for each device.

Different disks may have different sector sizes. It is up to the device-independent software to hide this fact and provide a uniform block size to higher layers, for example, by treating several sectors as a single logical block. In this way, the higher layers only deal with abstract devices that all use the same logical block size, independent of the physical sector size. Similarly, some character devices deliver their data one byte at a time (e.g., modems), while others deliver theirs in larger units (e.g., network interfaces). These differences must also be hidden.

Buffering is also an issue, both for block and character devices. For block devices, the hardware generally insists upon reading and writing entire blocks at once, but user processes are free to read and write in arbitrary units. If a user process writes half a block, the operating system will normally keep the data around internally until the rest of the data are written, at which time the block can go out to the disk. For character devices, users can write data to the system faster than it can be output, necessitating buffering. Keyboard input that arrives before it is needed also requires buffering.

When a file is created and filled with data, new disk blocks have to be allocated to the file. To perform this allocation, the operating system needs a list or bit map of free blocks per disk, but the algorithm for locating a free block is device independent and can be done above the level of the driver.

Some devices, such as CD-ROM recorders, can be used only by a single process at any given moment. It is up to the operating system to examine requests for device usage and accept or reject them, depending on whether the requested device is available or not. A simple way to handle these requests is to require processes to perform OPENs on the special files for devices directly. If the device is unavailable, the OPEN will fail. Closing such a dedicated device would then release it.

Error handling, by and large, is done by the drivers. Most errors are highly device dependent, so only the driver knows what to do (e.g., retry, ignore it, panic). A typical error is caused by a disk block that has been damaged and cannot be read any more. After the driver has tried to read the block a certain number of times, it gives up and informs the device-independent software. How the error is treated from here on is device independent. If the error occurred while reading a user file, it may be sufficient to report the error back to the caller. However, if it occurred while reading a critical system data structure, such as the block containing the bit map showing which blocks are free, the operating system may have no choice but to print an error message and terminate.

3.2.5 User-Space I/O Software

Although most of the I/O software is within the operating system, a small portion of it consists of libraries linked together with user programs, and even whole programs running outside the kernel. System calls, including the I/O system calls, are normally made by library procedures. When a C program contains the call

count = write(fd, buffer, nbytes);

the library procedure *write* will be linked with the program and contained in the binary program present in memory at run time. The collection of all these library procedures is clearly part of the I/O system.

While these procedures do little more than put their parameters in the appropriate place for the system call, there are other I/O procedures that actually do real work. In particular, formatting of input and output is done by library procedures. One example from C is *printf*, which takes a format string and possibly some variables as input, builds an ASCII string, and then calls WRITE to output the string. An example of a similar procedure for input is *scanf* which reads input and stores it into variables described in a format string using the same syntax as *printf*. The standard I/O library contains a number of procedures that involve I/O and all run as part of user programs.

Not all user-level I/O software consists of library procedures. Another important category is the spooling system. **Spooling** is a way of dealing with dedicated I/O devices in a multiprogramming system. Consider a typical spooled device: a printer. Although it would be technically easy to let any user process open the character special file for the printer, suppose a process opened it and then did nothing for hours. No other process could print anything.

Instead what is done is to create a special process, called a **daemon**, and a special directory, called a **spooling directory**. To print a file, a process first generates the entire file to be printed and puts it in the spooling directory. It is up to the daemon, which is the only process having permission to use the printer's special file, to print the files in the directory. By protecting the special file against direct use by users, the problem of having someone keeping it open unnecessarily long is eliminated.

Spooling is not only used for printers. It is also used in other situations. For example, file transfer over a network often uses a network daemon. To send a file somewhere, a user puts it in a network spooling directory. Later on, the network daemon takes it out and transmits it. One particular use of spooled file transmission is the Internet electronic mail system. This network consists of millions of machines around the world communicating using many computer networks. To send mail to someone, you call a program such as *send*, which accepts the letter to be sent and then deposits it in a spooling directory for transmission later. The entire mail system runs outside the operating system.

Figure 3-6 summarizes the I/O system, showing all the layers and the principal functions of each layer. Starting at the bottom, the layers are the hardware, interrupt handlers, device drivers, device-independent software, and finally the user processes.

The arrows in Fig. 3-6 show the flow of control. When a user program tries to read a block from a file, for example, the operating system is invoked to carry out the call. The device-independent software looks in the block cache, for example. If the needed block is not there, it calls the device driver to issue the request to the hardware. The process is then blocked until the disk operation has been completed.

When the disk is finished, the hardware generates an interrupt. The interrupt handler is run to discover what has happened, that is, which device wants attention right now. It then extracts the status from the device and wakes up the sleeping process to finish off the I/O request and let the user process continue.

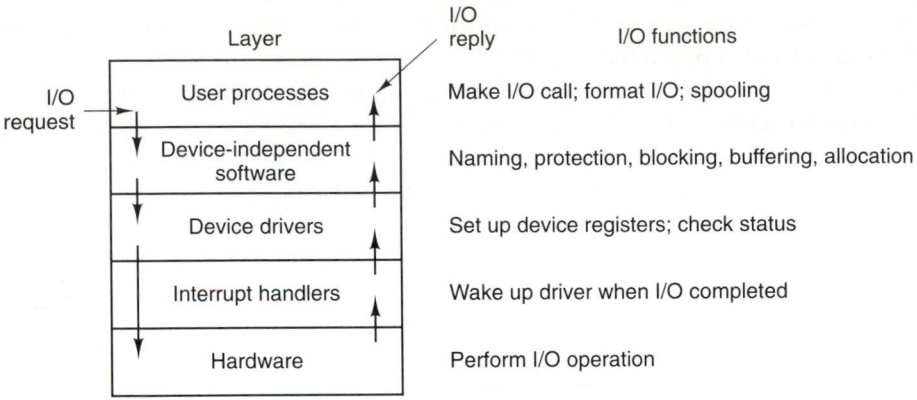

Figure 3-6. Layers of the I/O system and the main functions of each layer.

3.3 DEADLOCKS

Computer systems are full of resources that can only be used by one process at a time. Common examples include flatbed plotters, CD-ROM readers, CD-ROM recorders, 8mm DAT tape drive backup systems, imagesetters, and slots in the system's process table. Having two processes simultaneously writing to the printer leads to gibberish. Having two processes using the same slot in the process table will probably lead to a system crash. Consequently, all operating systems have the ability to (temporarily) grant a process exclusive access to certain resources.

For many applications, a process needs exclusive access to not one resource, but several. Consider, for example, a marketing company that specializes in making large, detailed demographic maps of the United States on a 1-meter wide flatbed plotter. The demographic information comes from CD-ROMs containing census and other data. Suppose that process *A* asks for the CD-ROM drive and gets it. A moment later, process *B* asks for the flatbed plotter and gets it, too. Now process *A* asks for the plotter and blocks waiting for it. Finally, process *B* asks for the CD-ROM drive and also blocks. At this point both processes are blocked and will remain so forever. This situation is called a **deadlock**. Deadlocks are not a good thing to have in your system.

Deadlocks can occur in many situations besides requesting dedicated I/O devices. In a data base system, for example, a program may have to lock several records it is using, to avoid race conditions. If process *A* locks record *R1* and process *B* locks record *R2*, and then each process tries to lock the other one's record, we also have a deadlock. Thus deadlocks can occur on hardware resources or on software resources.

In this section we will examine deadlocks more closely to see how they arise and how they can be prevented or avoided. As examples, we will talk about acquiring physical devices such as tape drives, CD-ROM drives, and plotters, because these are easy to visualize, but the principles and algorithms hold equally well for other kinds of deadlocks.

3.3.1 Resources

Deadlocks can occur when processes have been granted exclusive access to devices, files, and so forth. To make the discussion of deadlocks as general as possible, we will refer to the objects granted as **resources**. A resource can be a hardware device (e.g., a tape drive) or a piece of information (e.g., a locked record in a data base). A computer will normally have many different resources that can be acquired. For some resources, several identical instances may be available, such as three tape drives. When several copies of a resource are available, any one of them can be used to satisfy any request for the resource. In short, a resource is anything that can only be used by a single process at any instant.

Resources come in two types: preemptable and nonpreemptable. A **preemptable resource** is one that can be taken away from the process owning it with no ill effects. Memory is an example of a preemptable resource. Consider, for example, a system with 512K of user memory, one printer, and two 512K processes that each want to print something. Process A requests and gets the printer, then starts to compute the values to print. Before it has finished with the computation, it exceeds its time quantum and is swapped out.

Process B now runs and tries, unsuccessfully, to acquire the printer. Potentially, we now have a deadlock situation, because A has the printer and B has the memory, and neither can proceed without the resource held by the other. Fortunately, it is possible to preempt (take away) the memory from B by swapping it out and swapping A in. Now A can run, do its printing, and then release the printer. No deadlock occurs.

A **nonpreemptable resource**, in contrast, is one that cannot be taken away from its current owner without causing the computation to fail. If a process has begun to print output, taking the printer away from it and giving it to another process will result in garbled output. Printers are not preemptable.

In general, deadlocks involve nonpreemptable resources. Potential deadlocks that involve preemptable ones can usually be resolved by reallocating resources from one process to another. Thus our treatment will focus on nonpreemptable resources.

The sequence of events required to use a resource is:

1. Request the resource.

2. Use the resource.

3. Release the resource.

If the resource is not available when it is requested, the requesting process is forced to wait. In some operating systems, the process is automatically blocked when a resource request fails and awakened when it becomes available. In other systems, the request fails with an error code, and it is up to the calling process to wait a little while and try again.

3.3.2 Principles of Deadlock

Deadlock can be defined formally as follows:

A set of processes is deadlocked if each process in the set is waiting for an event that only another process in the set can cause.

Because all the processes are waiting, none of them will ever cause any of the events that could wake up any of the other members of the set, and all the processes continue to wait forever.

In most cases, the event that each process is waiting for is the release of some resource currently possessed by another member of the set. In other words, each member of the set of deadlocked processes is waiting for a resource that is owned by a deadlocked process. None of the processes can run, none of them can release any resources, and none of them can be awakened. The number of processes and the number and kind of resources possessed and requested are unimportant.

Conditions for Deadlock

Coffman et al. (1971) showed that four conditions must hold for there to be a deadlock:

1. Mutual exclusion condition. Each resource is either currently assigned to exactly one process or is available.

2. Hold and wait condition. Processes currently holding resources granted earlier can request new resources.

3. No preemption condition. Resources previously granted cannot be forcibly taken away from a process. They must be explicitly released by the process holding them.

4. Circular wait condition. There must be a circular chain of two or more processes, each of which is waiting for a resource held by the next member of the chain.

All four of these conditions must be present for a deadlock to occur. If one or more of these conditions is absent, no deadlock is possible.

Deadlock Modeling

Holt (1972) showed how these four conditions can be modeled using directed graphs. The graphs have two kinds of nodes: processes, shown as circles, and resources, shown as squares. An arc from a resource node (square) to a process node (circle) means that the resource previously has been requested by, granted to, and is currently held by that process. In Fig. 3-7(a), resource R is currently assigned to process A.

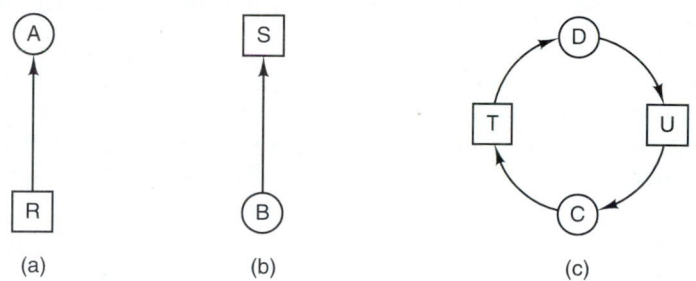

Figure 3-7. Resource allocation graphs. (a) Holding a resource. (b) Requesting a resource. (c) Deadlock.

An arc from a process to a resource means that the process is currently blocked waiting for that resource. In Fig. 3-7(b) process B is waiting for resource S. In Fig. 3-7(c) we see a deadlock: process C is waiting for resource T, which is currently held by process D. Process D is not about to release resource T because it is waiting for resource U, held by C. Both processes will wait forever. A cycle in the graph means that there is a deadlock involving the processes and resources in the cycle. In this example, the cycle is C–T–D–U–C.

Now let us look at an example of how resource graphs can be used. Imagine that we have three processes, A, B, and C, and three resources, R, S, and T. The requests and releases of the three processes are given in Fig. 3-8(a)-(c). The operating system is free to run any unblocked process at any instant, so it could decide to run A until A finished all its work, then run B to completion, and finally run C.

This ordering does not lead to any deadlocks (because there is no competition for resources) but it also has no parallelism at all. In addition to requesting and releasing resources, processes compute and do I/O. When the processes are run sequentially, there is no possibility that while one process is waiting for I/O, another can use the CPU. Thus running the processes strictly sequentially may not be optimal. On the other hand, if none of the processes do any I/O at all, shortest job first is better than round robin, so under some circumstances running all processes sequentially may be the best way.

Let us now suppose that the processes do both I/O and computing, so that round robin is a reasonable scheduling algorithm. The resource requests might occur in the order of Fig. 3-8(d). If these six requests are carried out in that order, the six resulting resource graphs are shown in Fig. 3-8(e)-(j). After request 4 has been made, A blocks waiting for S, as shown in Fig. 3-8(h). In the next two steps B and C also block, ultimately leading to a cycle and the deadlock of Fig. 3-8(j).

However, as we have already mentioned, the operating system is not required to run the processes in any special order. In particular, if granting a particular request might lead to deadlock, the operating system can simply suspend the process without granting the request (i.e., just not schedule the process) until it is safe. In Fig. 3-8, if the operating system knew about the impending deadlock, it could suspend B instead of granting it S. By running only A and C, we would get the requests and releases of Fig. 3-8(k) instead of Fig. 3-8(d). This sequence leads to the resource graphs of Fig. 3-8(l)-(q), which do not lead to deadlock.

After step (q), process B can be granted S because A is finished and C has everything it needs. Even if B should eventually block when requesting T, no deadlock can occur. B will just wait until C is finished.

Later in this chapter we will study a detailed algorithm for making allocation decisions that do not lead to deadlock. The point to understand now is that resource graphs are a tool that let us see if a given request/release sequence leads to deadlock. We just carry out the requests and releases step by step, and after every step check the graph to see if it contains any cycles. If so, we have a deadlock; if not, there is no deadlock. Although our treatment of resource graphs has been for the case of a single resource of each type, resource graphs can also be generalized to handle multiple resources of the same type (Holt, 1972).

In general, four strategies are used for dealing with deadlocks.

1. Just ignore the problem altogether.

2. Detection and recovery.

3. Dynamic avoidance by careful resource allocation.

4. Prevention, by structurally negating one of the four required conditions.

We will examine each of these methods in turn in the next four sections.

3.3.3 The Ostrich Algorithm

The simplest approach is the ostrich algorithm: stick your head in the sand and pretend there is no problem at all. Different people react to this strategy in different ways. Mathematicians find it totally unacceptable and say that deadlocks must be prevented at all costs. Engineers ask how often the problem is expected, how often the system crashes for other reasons, and how serious a deadlock is. If deadlocks occur on the average once every 50 years, but system crashes due to hardware failures, compiler errors, and operating system bugs occur once a month, most engineers would not be willing to pay a large penalty in performance or convenience to eliminate deadlocks.

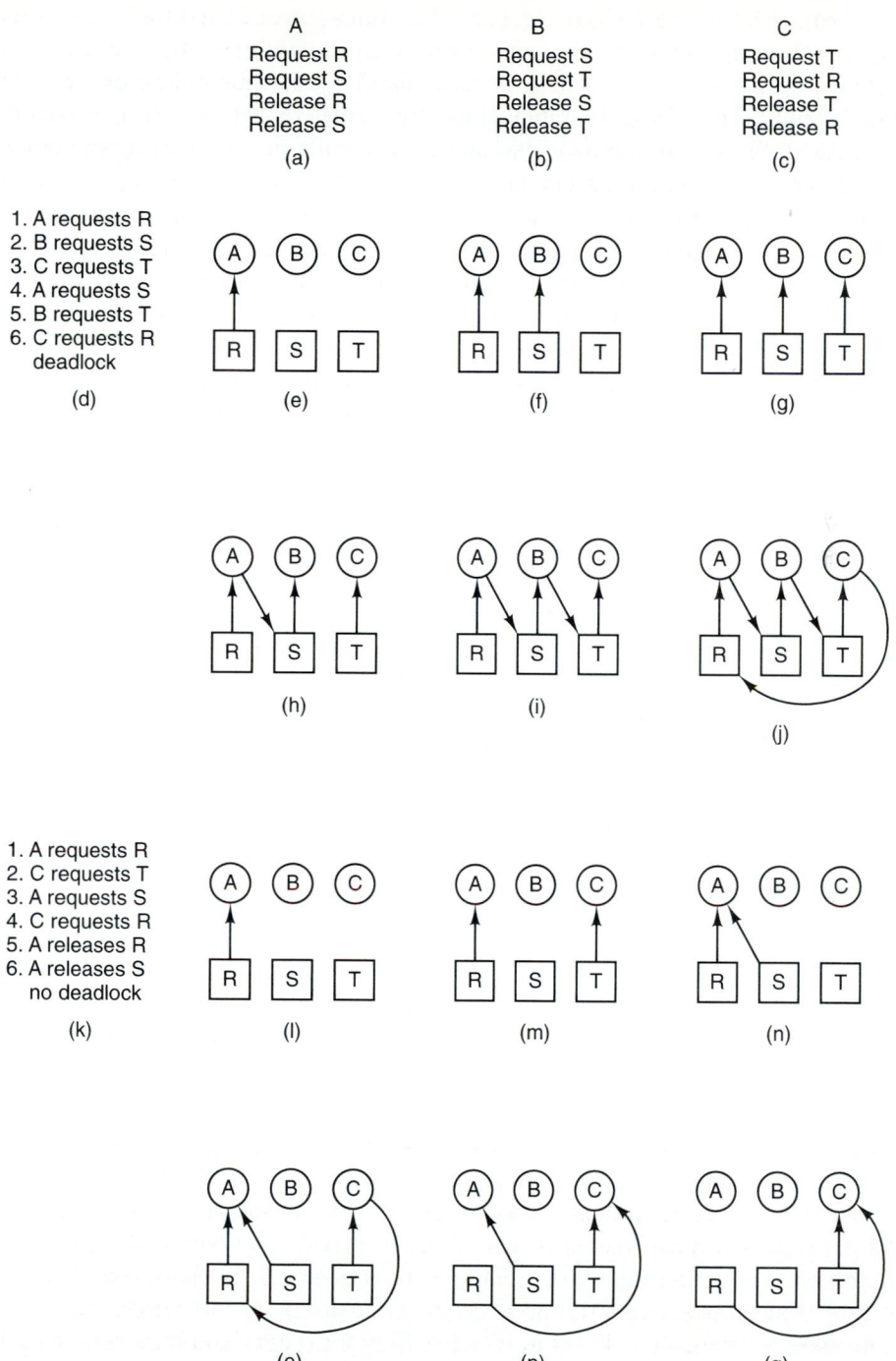

Figure 3-8. An example of how deadlock occurs and how it can be avoided.

To make this contrast more specific, UNIX (and MINIX) potentially suffer from deadlocks that are not even detected, let alone automatically broken. The total number of processes in the system is determined by the number of entries in the process table. Thus process table slots are finite resources. If a FORK fails because the table is full, a reasonable approach for the program doing the FORK is to wait a random time and try again.

Now suppose that a UNIX system has 100 process slots. Ten programs are running, each of which needs to create 12 (sub)processes. After each process has created 9 processes, the 10 original processes and the 90 new processes have exhausted the table. Each of the 10 original processes now sits in an endless loop forking and failing—a deadlock. The probability of this happening is minuscule, but it *could* happen. Should we abandon processes and the FORK call to eliminate the problem?

The maximum number of open files is similarly restricted by the size of the i-node table, so a similar problem occurs when it fills up. Swap space on the disk is another limited resource. In fact, almost every table in the operating system represents a finite resource. Should we abolish all of these because it might happen that a collection of n processes might each claim $1/n$ of the total, and then each try to claim another one?

The UNIX approach is just to ignore the problem on the assumption that most users would prefer an occasional deadlock to a rule restricting all users to one process, one open file, and one of everything. If deadlocks could be eliminated for free, there would not be much discussion. The problem is that the price is high, mostly in terms of putting inconvenient restrictions on processes, as we will see shortly. Thus we are faced with an unpleasant trade-off between convenience and correctness, and a great deal of discussion about which is more important.

3.3.4 Detection and Recovery

A second technique is detection and recovery. When this technique is used, the system does not do anything except monitor the requests and releases of resources. Every time a resource is requested or released, the resource graph is updated, and a check is made to see if any cycles exist. If a cycle exists, one of the processes in the cycle is killed. If this does not break the deadlock, another process is killed, and so on until the cycle is broken.

A somewhat cruder method is to not even maintain the resource graph but instead periodically check to see if there are any processes that have been continuously blocked for more than say, 1 hour. Such processes are then killed.

Detection and recovery is the strategy often used on large mainframe computers, especially batch systems in which killing a process and then restarting it is usually acceptable. Care must be taken to restore any modified files to their original state, however, and undo any other side effects that may have occurred.

3.3.5 Deadlock Prevention

The third deadlock strategy is to impose suitable restrictions on processes so that deadlocks are structurally impossible. The four conditions stated by Coffman et al. (1971) provide a clue to some possible solutions. If we can ensure that at least one of these conditions is never satisfied, then deadlocks will be impossible (Havender, 1968).

First let us attack the mutual exclusion condition. If no resource were ever assigned exclusively to a single process, we would never have deadlocks. However, it is equally clear that allowing two processes to write on the printer at the same time will lead to chaos. By spooling printer output, several processes can generate output at the same time. In this model, the only process that actually requests the physical printer is the printer daemon. Since the daemon never requests any other resources, we can eliminate deadlock for the printer.

Unfortunately, not all devices can be spooled (the process table does not lend itself well to being spooled). Furthermore, competition for disk space for spooling can itself lead to deadlock. What would happen if two processes each filled up half of the available spooling space with output and neither was finished? If the daemon were programmed to begin printing even before all the output were spooled, the printer might lie idle if an output process decided to wait several hours after the first burst of output. For this reason, daemons are normally programmed to print only after the complete output file is available. Neither process will ever finish, so we have a deadlock on the disk.

The second of the conditions stated by Coffman et al. looks more promising. If we can prevent processes that hold resources from waiting for more resources, we can eliminate deadlocks. One way to achieve this goal is to require all processes to request all their resources before starting execution. If everything were available, the process would be allocated whatever it needed and could run to completion. If one or more resources were busy, nothing would be allocated and the process would just wait.

An immediate problem with this approach is that many processes do not know how many resources they will need until they have started running. Another problem is that resources will not be used optimally with this approach. Take, as an example, a process that reads data from an input tape, analyzes it for an hour, and then writes an output tape as well as plots the results. If all resources must be requested in advance, the process will tie up the output tape drive and the plotter for an hour.

A slightly different way to break the hold-and-wait condition is to require a process requesting a resource to first temporarily release all the resources it currently holds. Only if the request is successful can it get the original resources back.

Attacking the third condition (no preemption) is even less promising than attacking the second one. If a process has been assigned the printer and is in the middle of printing its output, forcibly taking away the printer because a needed plotter is not available will lead to a mess.

Only one condition is left. The circular wait can be eliminated in several ways. One way is simply to have a rule saying that a process is entitled only to a single resource at any moment. If it needs a second one, it must release the first one. For a process that needs to copy a huge file from a tape to a printer, this restriction is unacceptable.

Another way to avoid the circular wait is to provide a global numbering of all the resources, as shown in Fig. 3-9(a). Now the rule is this: processes can request resources whenever they want to, but all requests must be made in numerical order. A process may request first a printer and then a tape drive, but it may not request first a plotter and then a printer.

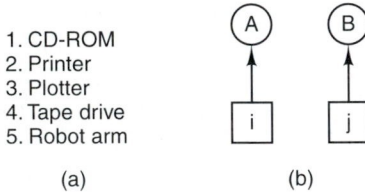

1. CD-ROM
2. Printer
3. Plotter
4. Tape drive
5. Robot arm

(a) (b)

Figure 3-9. (a) Numerically ordered resources. (b) A resource graph.

With this rule, the resource allocation graph can never have cycles. Let us see why this is true for the case of two processes, in Fig. 3-9(b). We can get a deadlock only if A requests resource j and B requests resource i. Assuming i and j are distinct resources, they will have different numbers. If $i > j$, then A is not allowed to request j. If $i < j$, then B is not allowed to request i. Either way, deadlock is impossible.

With multiple processes the same logic holds. At every instant, one of the assigned resources will be highest. The process holding that resource will never ask for a resource already assigned. It will either finish, or at worst, request even higher numbered resources, all of which are available. Eventually, it will finish and free its resources. At this point, some other process will hold the highest resource and can also finish. In short, there exists a scenario in which all processes finish, so no deadlock is present.

A minor variation of this algorithm is to drop the requirement that resources be acquired in strictly increasing sequence and merely insist that no process request a resource lower than what it is already holding. If a process initially requests 9 and 10, and then releases both of them, it is effectively starting all over, so there is no reason to prohibit it from now requesting resource 1.

Although numerically ordering the resources eliminates the problem of deadlocks, it may be impossible to find an ordering that satisfies everyone. When the resources include process table slots, disk spooler space, locked data base records, and other abstract resources, the number of potential resources and different uses may be so large that no ordering could possibly work.

The various approaches to deadlock prevention are summarized in Fig. 3-10.

Condition	Approach
Mutual exclusion	Spool everything
Hold and wait	Request all resources initially
No preemption	Take resources away
Circular wait	Order resources numerically

Figure 3-10. Summary of approaches to deadlock prevention.

3.3.6 Deadlock Avoidance

In Fig. 3-8 we saw that deadlock was avoided not by imposing arbitrary rules on processes but by carefully analyzing each resource request to see if it could be safely granted. The question arises: is there an algorithm that can always avoid deadlock by making the right choice all the time? The answer is a qualified yes—we can avoid deadlocks, but only if certain information is available in advance. In this section we examine ways to avoid deadlock by careful resource allocation.

The Banker's Algorithm for a Single Resource

A scheduling algorithm that can avoid deadlocks is due to Dijkstra (1965) and is known as the **banker's algorithm**. It is modeled on the way a small-town banker might deal with a group of customers to whom he has granted lines of credit. In Fig. 3-11(a) we see four customers, each of whom has been granted a certain number of credit units (e.g., 1 unit is 1K dollars). The banker knows that not all customers will need their maximum credit immediately, so he has only reserved 10 units rather than 22 to service them. (In this analogy, customers are processes, units are, say, tape drives, and the banker is the operating system.)

The customers go about their respective businesses, making loan requests from time to time. At a certain moment, the situation is as shown in Fig. 3-11(b). A list of customers showing the money already loaned (tape drives already assigned) and the maximum credit available (maximum number of tape drives needed at once later) is called the **state** of the system with respect to resource allocation.

A state is said to be a **safe** state if there exists a sequence of other states that leads to all the customers getting loans up to their credit limits (all the processes getting all their resources and terminating). The state of Fig. 3-11(b) is safe

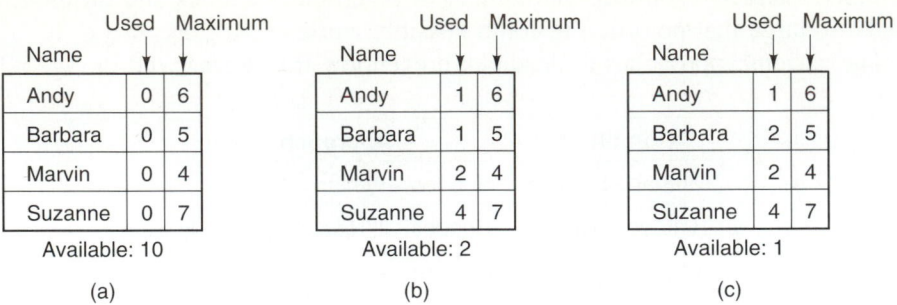

Figure 3-11. Three resource allocation states: (a) Safe. (b) Safe. (c) Unsafe.

because with two units left, the banker can delay any requests except Marvin's, thus letting Marvin finish and release all four of his resources. With four units in hand, the banker can let either Suzanne or Barbara have the necessary units, etc.

Consider what would happen if a request from Barbara for one more unit were granted in Fig. 3-11(b). We would have the situation of Fig. 3-11(c), which is unsafe. If all the customers suddenly asked for their maximum loans, the banker could not satisfy any of them, and we would have a deadlock. An unsafe state does not *have* to lead to deadlock, since a customer might not need the entire credit line available, but the banker cannot count on this behavior.

The banker's algorithm is thus to consider each request as it occurs and see if granting it leads to a safe state. If it does, the request is granted; otherwise, it is postponed until later. To see if a state is safe, the banker checks to see if he has enough resources to satisfy the customer closest to his or her maximum. If so, those loans are assumed to be repaid, and the customer now closest to his or her limit is checked, and so on. If all loans can eventually be repaid, the state is safe and the initial request can be granted.

Resource Trajectories

The above algorithm was described in terms of a single resource class (e.g., only tape drives or only printers, but not some of each). In Fig. 3-12 we see a model for dealing with two processes and two resources, for example, a printer and a plotter. The horizontal axis represents the number of instructions executed by process A. The vertical axis represents the number of instructions executed by process B. At I_1 A requests a printer; at I_2 it needs a plotter. The printer and plotter are released at I_3 and I_4, respectively. Process B needs the plotter from I_5 to I_7 and the printer from I_6 to I_8.

Every point in the diagram represents a joint state of the two processes. Initially, the state is at p, with neither process having executed any instructions. If the scheduler chooses to run A first, we get to the point q, in which A has executed some number of instructions, but B has executed none. At point q the trajectory

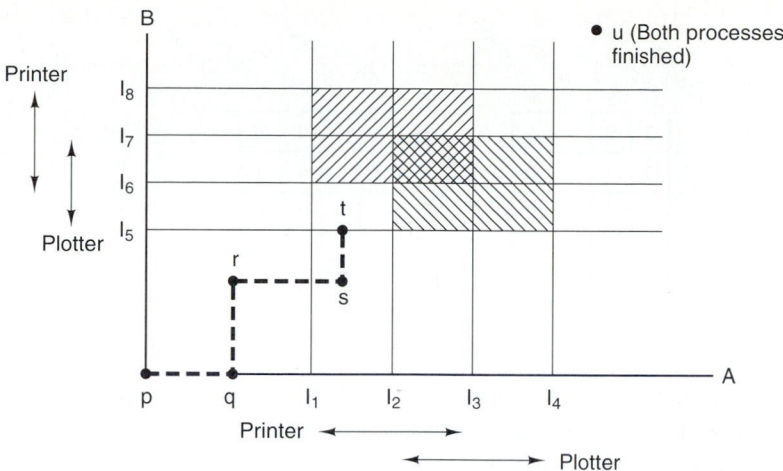

Figure 3-12. Two process resource trajectories.

becomes vertical, indicating that the scheduler has chosen to run B. With a single processor, all paths must be horizontal or vertical, never diagonal. Furthermore, motion is always to the north or east, never to the south or west (processes cannot run backward).

When A crosses the I_1 line on the path from r to s, it requests and is granted the printer. When B reaches point t, it requests the plotter.

The regions that are shaded are especially interesting. The region with lines slanting from southwest to northeast represents both processes having the printer. The mutual exclusion rule makes it impossible to enter this region. Similarly, the region shaded the other way represents both processes having the plotter and is equally impossible.

If the system ever enters the box bounded by I_1 and I_2 on the sides and I_5 and I_6 top and bottom, it will eventually deadlock when it gets to the intersection of I_2 and I_6. At this point, A is requesting the plotter and B is requesting the printer, and both are already assigned. The entire box is unsafe and must not be entered. At point t the only safe thing to do is run process A until it gets to I_4. Beyond that, any trajectory to u will do.

The Banker's Algorithm for Multiple Resources

This graphical model is difficult to apply to the general case of an arbitrary number of processes and an arbitrary number of resource classes, each with multiple instances (e.g., two plotters, three tape drives). However, the banker's algorithm can be generalized to do the job. Figure 3-13 shows how it works.

In Fig. 3-13 we see two matrices. The one on the left shows how many of each resource is currently assigned to each of the five processes. The matrix on

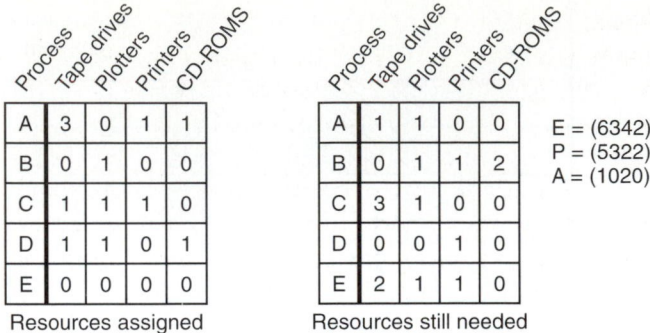

Figure 3-13. The banker's algorithm with multiple resources.

the right shows how many resources each process still needs in order to complete. As in the single resource case, processes must state their total resource needs before executing, so that the system can compute the right-hand matrix at each step.

The three vectors at the right of the figure show the existing resources, E, the possessed resources, P, and the available resources, A, respectively. From E we see that the system has six tape drives, three plotters, four printers, and two CD-ROMs. Of these, five tape drives, three plotters, two printers, and two CD-ROMs are currently assigned. This fact can be seen by adding up the four resource columns in the left-hand matrix. The available resource vector is simply the difference between what the system has and what is currently in use.

The algorithm for checking to see if a state is safe can now be stated.

1. Look for a row, R, whose unmet resource needs are all smaller than or equal to A. If no such row exists, the system will eventually deadlock since no process can run to completion.

2. Assume the process of the row chosen requests all the resources it needs (which is guaranteed to be possible) and finishes. Mark that process as terminated and add all its resources to the A vector.

3. Repeat steps 1 and 2 until either all processes are marked terminated, in which case the initial state was safe, or until a deadlock occurs, in which case it was not.

If several processes are eligible to be chosen in step 1, it does not matter which one is selected: the resource pool either gets larger, or at worst, stays the same.

Now let us get back to the example of Fig. 3-13. The current state is safe. Suppose that process B now requests a printer. This request can be granted because the resulting state is still safe (process D can finish, and then processes A or E, followed by the rest).

Now imagine that after giving B one of the two remaining printers, E wants to have the last printer. Granting that request would reduce the vector of available resources to (1 0 0 0), which leads to deadlock. Clearly E's request may not be satisfied immediately and must be deferred for a while.

This algorithm was first published by Dijkstra in 1965. Since that time, nearly every book on operating systems has described it in detail. Innumerable papers have been written about various aspects of it. Unfortunately, few authors have had the audacity to point out that although in theory the algorithm is wonderful, in practice it is essentially useless because processes rarely know what their maximum resource needs will be in advance. In addition, the number of processes is not fixed, but dynamically varying as new users log in and out. Furthermore, resources that were thought to be available can suddenly vanish (tape drives can break).

In summary, the schemes described earlier under the name "prevention" are overly restrictive, and the algorithm described here as "avoidance" requires information that is usually not available. If you can think of a general-purpose algorithm that does the job in practice as well as in theory, write it up and send it to your local computer science journal.

For specific applications, many excellent special-purpose algorithms are known. As an example, in many data base systems, an operation that occurs frequently is requesting locks on several records and then updating all the locked records. When multiple processes are running at the same time, there is a real danger of deadlock.

The approach often used is called **two-phase locking**. In the first phase, the process tries to lock all the records it needs, one at a time. If it succeeds, it performs its updates and releases the locks. If some record is already locked, it releases the locks it already has and just starts all over. In a certain sense, this approach is similar to requesting all the resources needed in advance, or at least before anything irreversible is done.

However, this strategy is not applicable in general. In real-time systems and process control systems, for example, it is not acceptable to just terminate a process partway through because a resource is not available and start all over again. Neither is it acceptable to start over if the process has read or written messages to the network, updated files, or anything else that cannot be safely repeated. The algorithm works only in those situations where the programmer has very carefully arranged things so that the program can be stopped at any point during the first phase and restarted. Unfortunately, not all applications can be structured in this way.

3.4 OVERVIEW OF I/O IN MINIX

MINIX I/O is structured as shown in Fig. 3-6. The top four layers of that figure correspond to the four-layered structure of MINIX shown in Fig. 2-26. In the following sections we will look briefly at each of the layers, with the emphasis on the device drivers. Interrupt handling was covered in the previous chapter, and the device-independent I/O will be discussed when we come to the file system, in Chap. 5.

3.4.1 Interrupt Handlers in MINIX

Many of the device drivers start some I/O device and then block, waiting for a message to arrive. That message is usually generated by the interrupt handler for the device. Other device drivers do not start any physical I/O (e.g., reading from RAM disk and writing to a memory-mapped display), do not use interrupts, and do not wait for a message from an I/O device. In the previous chapter the mechanism by which interrupts generate messages and cause task switches has been presented in great detail, and we will say no more about it here. But interrupt handlers may do more than just generate a message. Frequently they also do some work in processing input and output at the lowest level. We will discuss this in a general way here and then return to the details when we look at the code for various devices.

For disk devices, input and output is generally a matter of commanding a device to perform its operation, and then waiting until the operation is complete. The disk controller does most of the work, and very little is required of the interrupt handler. We saw that the entire interrupt handler for the hard disk task consists of just three lines of code, with the only I/O operation being the reading of a single byte to determine the status of the controller. Our lives would be simple indeed if all interrupts could be handled so easily.

However, there is sometimes more for the low-level handler to do. The message passing mechanism has a cost. When an interrupt may occur frequently but the amount of I/O handled per interrupt is small, it may pay to make the handler itself do somewhat more work and to postpone sending a message to the task until a subsequent interrupt, when there is more for the task to do. MINIX handles interrupts from the clock this way. On many clock ticks there is very little to be done, except for maintaining the time. This can be done without sending a message to the clock task itself. The clock handler increments a variable, appropriately named *pending_ticks*. The current time is the sum of the time recorded when the clock task itself last ran plus the value of *pending_ticks*. When the clock task receives a message and wakes up, it adds *pending_ticks* to its main timekeeping variable and then zeroes *pending_ticks*. The clock interrupt handler examines some other variables and sends a message to the clock task only when it detects the task has actual work to do, such as delivering an alarm or scheduling a new process to execute. It may also send a message to the terminal task.

In the terminal task we see another variation on the theme of interrupt handlers. This task handles several different kinds of hardware, including the keyboard and the RS-232 lines. These each have their own interrupt handler. The keyboard exactly fits the description of a device where there may be relatively little I/O to do in response to each interrupt. On a PC an interrupt occurs each time a key is pressed or released. This includes special keys like the SHIFT and CTRL keys, but if we ignore them for the moment, we can say that on the average half a character is received per interrupt. Since there is not much the terminal task can do with half a character, it makes sense to send it a message only when something worthwhile can be accomplished. We will examine the details later; for now we will just say that the keyboard interrupt handler does the low-level reading of data from the keyboard and then filters out events it can ignore, such as the release of an ordinary key. (The release of a special key, for instance, the SHIFT key, cannot be ignored.) Then codes representing all nonignored events are placed in a queue for later processing by the terminal task itself.

The keyboard interrupt handler differs from the simple paradigm we have presented of the interrupt handler that sends a message to its associated task, because the interrupt handler sends no message at all. Instead, when it adds a code to the queue, it modifies a variable, *tty_timeout*, that is read by the clock interrupt handler. When an interrupt does not change the queue, *tty_timeout* is not changed either. On the next clock tick the clock handler sends a message to the terminal task if there have been changes to the queue. Other terminal-type interrupt handlers, for instance those for the RS-232 lines, work the same way. A message to the terminal task will arrive soon after a character is received, but a message is not necessarily generated for each character when characters are arriving rapidly. Several characters may accumulate and then be processed in response to a single message. Moreover, all terminal devices are checked each time a message is received by the terminal task.

3.4.2 Device Drivers in MINIX

For each class of I/O device present in a MINIX system, a separate I/O task (device driver) is present. These drivers are full-fledged processes, each with its own state, registers, stack, and so on. Device drivers communicate with each other (where necessary) and with the file system using the standard message passing mechanism used by all MINIX processes. Simple device drivers are written as single source files, such as *clock.c*. For other drivers, such as the drivers for the RAM disk, the hard disk, and the floppy disk, there is a source file to support each type of device, as well as a set of common routines in *driver.c* to support all of the different hardware types. In a sense this divides the device driver level of Fig. 3-6 into two sublevels. This separation of the hardware-dependent and hardware-independent parts of the software makes for easy adaptation to a variety of different hardware configurations. Although some common source code is used, the driver for each disk type runs as a separate process, in order to support rapid data transfers.

The terminal driver source code is organized in a similar way, with hardware-independent code in *tty.c* and source code to support different devices, such as memory-mapped consoles, the keyboard, serial lines, and pseudo terminals in separate files. In this case, however, a single process supports all of the different device types.

For groups of devices such as disk devices and terminals, for which there are several source files, there are also header files. *Driver.h* supports all the block device drivers. *Tty.h* provides common definitions for all the terminal devices.

The main difference between device drivers and other processes is that the device drivers are linked together in the kernel, and thus all share a common address space. As a result, if several device drivers use a common procedure, only one copy will be linked into the MINIX binary.

This design is highly modular and moderately efficient. It is also one of the few places where MINIX differs from UNIX in an essential way. In MINIX a process reads a file by sending a message to the file system process. The file system, in turn, may send a message to the disk driver asking it to read the needed block. This sequence (slightly simplified from reality) is shown in Fig. 3-14(a). By making these interactions via the message mechanism, we force various parts of the system to interface in standard ways with other parts. Nevertheless, by putting all the device drivers in the kernel address space, they have easy access to the process table and other key data structures when needed.

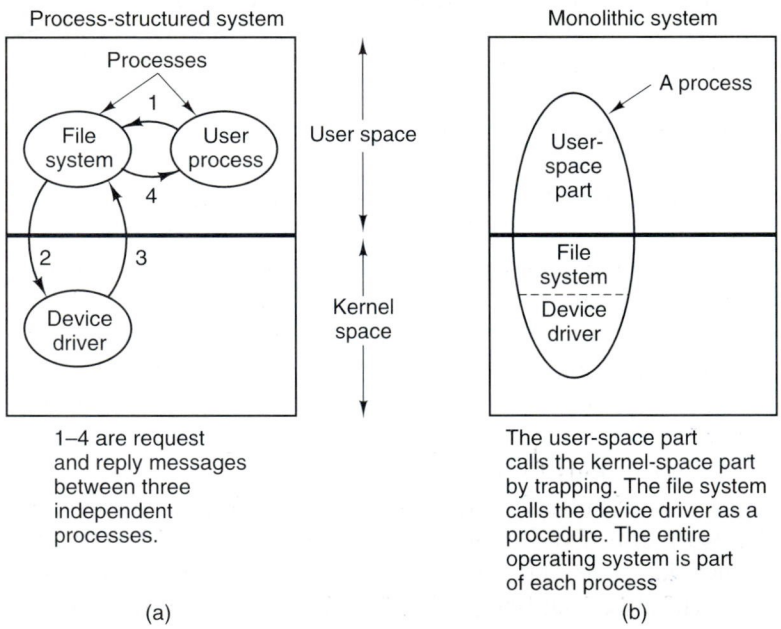

Figure 3-14. Two ways of structuring user-system communication.

In UNIX all processes have two parts: a user-space part and a kernel-space part, as shown in Fig. 3-14(b). When a system call is made, the operating system switches from the user-space part to the kernel-space part in a somewhat magical way. This structure is a remnant of the MULTICS design, in which the switch was just an ordinary procedure call, rather than a trap followed by saving the state of the user-part, as it is in UNIX.

Device drivers in UNIX are simply kernel procedures that are called by the kernel-space part of the process. When a driver needs to wait for an interrupt, it calls a kernel procedure that puts it to sleep until some interrupt handler wakes it up. Note that it is the user process itself that is being put to sleep here, because the kernel and user parts are really different parts of the same process.

Among operating system designers, arguments about the merits of monolithic systems, as in UNIX, versus process-structured systems, as in MINIX, are endless. The MINIX approach is better structured (more modular), has cleaner interfaces between the pieces, and extends easily to distributed systems in which the various processes run on different computers. The UNIX approach is more efficient, because procedure calls are much faster than sending messages. MINIX was split into many processes because we believe that with increasingly powerful personal computers available, cleaner software structure was worth making the system slightly slower. Be warned that many operating system designers do not share this belief.

In this chapter, drivers for RAM disk, hard disk, clock, and terminal are discussed. The standard MINIX configuration also includes drivers for floppy disk and printer, which are not discussed in detail. The MINIX software distribution contains source code for additional drivers for RS-232 serial lines, a SCSI interface, CD-ROM, Ethernet adapter, and sound card. These may be included by recompiling MINIX.

All of these tasks interface with other parts of the MINIX system in the same way: request messages are sent to the tasks. The messages contain a variety of fields used to hold the operation code (e.g., READ or WRITE) and its parameters. A task attempts to fulfill a request and returns a reply message.

For block devices, the fields of the request and reply messages are shown in Fig. 3-15. The request message includes the address of a buffer area containing data to be transmitted or in which received data are expected. The reply includes status information so the requesting process can verify that its request was properly carried out. The fields for the character devices are basically similar but can vary slightly from task to task. Messages to the clock task, for example, contain times, and messages to the terminal task can contain the address of a data structure which specifies all of the many configurable aspects of a terminal, such as the characters to use for the intraline editing functions erase-character and kill-line.

The function of each task is to accept requests from other processes, normally the file system, and carry them out. All the block device tasks have been written to get a message, carry it out, and send a reply. Among other things, this decision means that these tasks are strictly sequential and do not contain any internal multiprogramming, to keep them simple. When a hardware request has been

Requests		
Field	**Type**	**Meaning**
m.m_type	int	Operation requested
m.DEVICE	int	Minor device to use
m.PROC_NR	int	Process requesting the I/O
m.COUNT	int	Byte count or ioctl code
m.POSITION	long	Position on device
m.ADDRESS	char*	Address within requesting process

Replies		
Field	**Type**	**Meaning**
m.m_type	int	Always TASK_REPLY
m.REP_PROC_NR	int	Same as PROC_NR in request
m.REP_STATUS	int	Bytes transferred or error number

Figure 3-15. Fields of the messages sent by the file system to the block device drivers and fields of the replies sent back.

issued, the task does a RECEIVE operation specifying that it is interested only in accepting interrupt messages, not new requests for work. Any new request messages are just kept waiting until the current work has been done (rendezvous principle). The terminal task is slightly different, since a single task services several devices. Thus, it is possible to accept a new request for input from the keyboard while a request to read from a serial line is still being fulfilled. Nevertheless, for each device a request must be completed before beginning a new one.

The main program for each block device driver is structurally the same and is outlined in Fig. 3-16. When the system first comes up, each of the drivers is started up in turn to give each a chance to initialize internal tables and similar things. Then each driver task blocks by trying to get a message. When a message comes in, the identity of the caller is saved, and a procedure is called to carry out the work, with a different procedure invoked for each operation available. After the work has been finished, a reply is sent back to the caller, and the task then goes back to the top of the loop to wait for the next request.

Each of the *dev_xxx* procedures handles one of the operations of which the driver is capable. It returns a status code telling what happened. The status code, which is included in the reply message as the field *REP_STATUS*, is the count of bytes transferred (zero or positive) if all went well, or the error number (negative)

```
message mess;                          /* message buffer */

void io_task() {
    initialize();                      /* only done once, during system init. */
    while (TRUE) {
        receive(ANY, &mess);           /* wait for a request for work */
        caller = mess.source;          /* process from whom message came */
        switch(mess.type) {
            case READ:     rcode = dev_read(&mess); break;
            case WRITE:    rcode = dev_write(&mess); break;
            /* Other cases go here, including OPEN, CLOSE, and IOCTL */
             default:           rcode = ERROR;
        }
        mess.type = TASK_REPLY;
        mess.status = rcode;           /* result code */
        send(caller, &mess);           /* send reply message back to caller */
    }
}
```

Figure 3-16. Outline of the main procedure of an I/O task.

if something went wrong. This count may differ from the number of bytes requested. When the end of a file is reached, the number of bytes available may be less than number requested. On terminals at most one line is returned, even if the count requested is larger.

3.4.3 Device-Independent I/O Software in MINIX

In MINIX the file system process contains all the device-independent I/O code. The I/O system is so closely related to the file system that they were merged into one process. The functions performed by the file system are those shown in Fig. 3-5, except for requesting and releasing dedicated devices, which do not exist in MINIX as it is presently configured. They could, however, easily be added to the relevant device drivers should the need arise in the future.

In addition to handling the interface with the drivers, buffering, and block allocation, the file system also handles protection and the management of i-nodes, directories, and mounted file systems. It will be covered in detail in Chap. 5.

3.4.4 User-level I/O Software in MINIX

The general model outlined earlier in this chapter also applies here. Library procedures are available for making system calls and for all the C functions required by the POSIX standard, such as the formatted input and output functions *printf* and *scanf*. The standard MINIX configuration contains one spooler daemon, *lpd*, which spools and prints files passed to it by the *lp* command. The standard MINIX software distribution contains a number of daemons that support various network functions. Network operations require some operating system support that is not part of MINIX in the configuration described in this book, but MINIX can easily be recompiled to add the network server. It runs at the same priority as the memory manager and the file system, and like them, it runs as a user process.

3.4.5 Deadlock Handling in MINIX

True to its heritage, MINIX follows the same path as UNIX with respect to deadlocks: it just ignores the problem altogether. MINIX contains no dedicated I/O devices, although if someone wanted to hang an industry standard DAT tape drive on a PC, making the software for it would not pose any special problems. In short, the only place deadlocks can occur are with the implicit shared resources, such as process table slots, i-node table slots, and so on. None of the known deadlock algorithms can deal with resources like these that are not requested explicitly.

Actually, the above is not strictly true. Accepting the risk that user processes could deadlock is one thing, but within the operating system itself a few places do exist where considerable care has been taken to avoid problems. The main one is the interaction between the file system and the memory manager. The memory manager sends messages to the file system to read the binary file (executable program) during an EXEC system call, as well as in other contexts. If the file system is not idle when the memory manager is trying to send to it, the memory manager will be blocked. If the file system should then try to send a message to the memory manager, it too would discover that the rendezvous fails and would block, leading to a deadlock.

This problem has been avoided by constructing the system in such a way that the file system never sends *request* messages to the memory manager, just *replies*, with one minor exception. The exception is that upon starting up, the file system reports the size of the RAM disk to the memory manager, which is guaranteed to be waiting for the message.

It is possible to lock devices and files even without operating system support. A file name can serve as a truly global variable, whose presence or absence can be noted by all other processes. A special directory, */usr/spool/locks/*, is usually present on MINIX systems, as on most UNIX systems, where processes can create **lock files**, to mark any resources they are using. The MINIX file system also supports POSIX-style advisory file locking. But neither of these mechanisms is enforceable. They depend upon the good behavior of processes, and there is nothing to prevent a program from using a resource that is locked by another process. This is not exactly the same thing as preemption of the resource, because it does not prevent the first process from attempting to continue its use of the resource. In other words, there is no mutual exclusion. The result of such an action by an ill-behaved process is likely to be a mess, but no deadlock results.

3.5 BLOCK DEVICES IN MINIX

In the following sections we will return to the device drivers, the main topic of this chapter, and study several of them in detail. MINIX supports several different block devices, so we will begin by discussing common aspects of all block devices. Then we will discuss the RAM disk, the hard disk, and the floppy disk. Each of these is interesting for a different reason. The RAM disk is a good example to study because it has all the properties of block devices in general except the actual I/O—because the "disk" is actually just a portion of memory. This simplicity makes it a good place to start. The hard disk shows what a real disk driver looks like. One might expect the floppy disk to be easier to support than the hard disk, but, in fact, it is not. We will not discuss all the details of the floppy disk, but we will point out several of the complications to be found in the floppy disk driver.

Following the discussion of block drivers, we will discuss other driver classes. The clock is important because every system has one, and because it is completely different from all the other drivers. It is also of interest as an exception to the rule that all devices are either block or character devices, because it does not fit into either category. Finally, we will discuss the terminal driver, which is important on all systems, and, furthermore, is a good example of a character device driver.

Each of these sections describes the relevant hardware, the software principles behind the driver, an overview of the implementation, and the code itself. This structure makes the sections useful reading even for those readers who are not interested in the details of the code itself.

3.5.1 Overview of Block Device Drivers in MINIX

We mentioned earlier that the main procedures of all I/O tasks have a similar structure. MINIX always has at least three block device tasks (the RAM disk driver, the floppy disk driver, and one of several possible hard disk drivers) compiled into the system. In addition, a CD-ROM task and a SCSI (Small Computer Standard Interface) driver may be compiled in, if support for such devices is needed. Although the driver for each of these executes as an independent process, the fact that they are all compiled as part of the kernel executable makes it possible to share a considerable amount of the code, especially the utility procedures.

Each block device driver has to do some initialization, of course. The RAM disk driver has to reserve some memory, the hard disk driver has to determine the parameters of the hard disk hardware, and so on. All of the disk drivers are called individually for hardware-specific initialization, but after doing whatever may be necessary, each driver then calls the function containing the common main loop. This loop is executed forever; there is no return to the caller. Within the main loop a message is received, a function to perform the operation needed by each message is called, and then a reply message is generated.

The common main loop called by each disk driver task is not just a copy of a library function compiled into each driver. There is only one copy of the main loop code in the MINIX binary. The technique used is to have each of the individual drivers pass to the main loop a parameter consisting of a pointer to a table of the addresses of the functions that driver will use for each operation and then call these functions indirectly. This technique also makes it possible for drivers to share functions. Figure 3-17 shows an outline of the main loop, in a form similar to that of Fig. 3-16. Statements like

```
code = (*entry_points->dev_read)(&mess);
```

are indirect function calls. A different *dev_read* function is called by each driver, even though each driver is executing the same main loop. But some other operations, for example CLOSE, are simple enough that more than one device can call the same function.

```
message mess;                          /* message buffer */


void shared_io_task(struct driver_table *entry_points) {
/* initialization is done by each task before calling this */
  while (TRUE) {
      receive(ANY, &mess);
      caller = mess.source;
      switch(mess.type) {
          case READ:      rcode = (*entry_points->dev_read)(&mess); break;
          case WRITE:     rcode = (*entry_points->dev_write)(&mess); break;
          /* Other cases go here, including OPEN, CLOSE, and IOCTL */
          default:        rcode = ERROR;
      }
      mess.type = TASK_REPLY;
      mess.status = rcode;               /* result code */
      send(caller, &mess);
  }
}
```

Figure 3-17. A shared I/O task main procedure using indirect calls.

This use of a single copy of the loop is a good illustration of the process concept that we introduced in Chap. 1 and discussed at length in Chap 2. There is only one copy of the executable code in memory for the main loop of the block device drivers, but it is executed as the main loop of three or more distinct processes. Each of these processes is probably at a different point in the code at a given instant, and each is operating upon its own set of data and has its own stack.

There are six possible operations that can be requested of any device driver.

These correspond to the possible values that can be found in the m.m_type field of the message of Fig. 3-15. They are:

1. OPEN

2. CLOSE

3. READ

4. WRITE

5. IOCTL

6. SCATTERED_IO

Most of these operations are probably familiar to readers with programming experience. At the device driver level most operations are related to system calls with the same name. For instance, the meanings of *READ* and *WRITE* should be clear. For each of these operations, a block of data is transferred from the device to the memory of the process that initiated the call, or vice versa. A *READ* operation normally does not result in a return to the caller until the data transfer is complete, but an operating system may buffer data transferred during a *WRITE* for actual transfer to the destination at a later time, and return to the caller immediately. That is fine as far as the caller is concerned; it is then free to reuse the buffer from which the operating system has copied the data to write. *OPEN* and *CLOSE* for a device have similar meanings to the way the OPEN and CLOSE system calls apply to operations on files: an *OPEN* operation should verify that the device is accessible, or return an error message if not, and a *CLOSE* should guarantee that any buffered data that were written by the caller is completely transferred to their final destination on the device.

The *IOCTL* operation may not be so familiar. Many I/O devices have operational parameters which occasionally must be examined and perhaps changed. *IOCTL* operations do this. A familiar example is changing the speed of transmission or the parity of a communications line. For block devices, *IOCTL* operations are less common. Examining or changing the way a disk device is partitioned is done using an *IOCTL* operation in MINIX (although it could just as well have been done by reading and writing a block of data).

The *SCATTERED_IO* operation is no doubt the least familiar of these. Except with exceedingly fast disk devices (for example, the RAM disk), satisfactory disk I/O performance is difficult to obtain if all disk requests are for individual blocks, one at a time. A *SCATTERED_IO* request allows the file system to make a request to read or write multiple blocks. In the case of a *READ* operation, the additional blocks may not have been requested by the process on whose behalf the call is made; the operating system attempts to anticipate future requests for data. In such a request not all the transfers requested are necessarily honored by the device driver. The request for each block may be modified by a flag bit that tells the device driver that the request is optional. In effect the file system can say, "It would be nice to have all these data, but I do not really need them all right now." The device can do what is best for it. The floppy disk driver, for instance, will return all the data blocks it can read from a single track, effectively saying, "I will give you these, but it takes too long to move to another track; ask me again later for the rest."

When data must be written, there is no question of its being optional whether or not to write a particular block. Nevertheless, the operating system may buffer a number of write requests in the hope that writing multiple blocks can be done more efficiently than handling each request as it comes in. In a *SCATTERED_IO* request, whether for reading or writing, the list of blocks requested is sorted, and this makes the operation more efficient than handling the requests randomly. In addition, making only one call to the driver to transfer multiple blocks reduces the number of messages sent within MINIX.

3.5.2 Common Block Device Driver Software

Definitions that are needed by all the block device drivers are located in *driver.h*. The most important thing in this file is the *driver* structure, on lines 9010 to 9020, which is used by each driver to pass a list of the addresses of the functions it will use to perform each part of its job. Also defined here is the *device* structure (lines 9031 to 9034) which holds the most important information about partitions, the base address, and the size, in byte units. This format was chosen so no conversions are necessary when working with memory-based devices, maximizing speed of response. With real disks there are so many other factors delaying access that converting to sectors is not a significant inconvenience.

The main loop and shared functions of all the block driver tasks are in *driver.c*. After doing whatever hardware-specific initialization may be necessary, each driver calls *driver_task*, passing a *driver* structure as the argument to the call. After obtaining the address of a buffer to use for DMA operations the main loop (lines 9158 to 9199) is entered. This loop is executed forever; there is no return to the caller.

The file system is the only process that is supposed to send a message to a driver task. The switch on lines 9165 to 9175 checks for this. A leftover interrupt from the hardware is ignored, any other misdirected message results only in printing a warning on the screen. This seems innocuous enough, but of course the process that sent the erroneous message is probably permanently blocked waiting for a reply. In the switch in the main loop, the first three message types, *DEV_OPEN*, *DEV_CLOSE*, and *DEV_IOCTL*, result in indirect calls using addresses passed in the *driver* structure. The *DEV_READ*, *DEV_WRITE*, and *SCATTERED_IO* messages result in direct calls to *do_rdwt* or *do_vrdwt*. However, the *driver* structure is passed as an argument by all the calls from within the switch, whether direct or indirect, so all the called routines can make further use of it as needed.

After doing whatever is requested in the message, some sort of cleanup may be necessary, depending upon the nature of the device. For a floppy disk, for instance, this might involve starting a timer to turn off the disk drive motor if another request does not arrive soon. An indirect call is used for this as well. Following the cleanup, a reply message is constructed and sent to the caller (lines 9194 to 9198).

The first thing each task does after entering the main loop is to call *init_buffer* (line 9205), which assigns a buffer for use in DMA operations. The same buffer is used by all the driver tasks, if they use it all—some drivers do not use DMA. The initializations for each entry after the first are redundant but do no harm. It would be more cumbersome to code a test to see whether the initialization should be skipped.

That this initialization is even necessary at all is due to a quirk of the hardware of the original IBM PC, which requires that the DMA buffer not cross a 64K boundary. That is, a 1K DMA buffer may begin at 64510, but not at 64514 because a buffer starting at the latter address extends just beyond the 64K boundary at 65536.

This annoying rule occurs because the IBM PC used an old DMA chip, the Intel 8237A, which contains a 16-bit counter. A bigger counter is needed because DMA uses absolute addresses, not addresses relative to a segment register. On older machines that can address only 1M of memory, the low-order 16 bits of the DMA address are loaded into the 8237A, and the high-order 4 bits are loaded into a 4-bit latch. Newer machines use an 8-bit latch and can address 16M. When the 8237A goes from 0xFFFF to 0x0000, it does not generate a carry into the latch, so the DMA address suddenly jumps down by 64K in memory.

A portable C program cannot specify an absolute memory location for a data structure, so there is no way to prevent the compiler from placing the buffer in an unusable location. The solution is to allocate an array of bytes twice as large as necessary at *buffer* (line 9135) and to reserve a pointer *tmp_buf* (line 9136) to use for actually accessing this array. *Init_buffer* makes a trial setting of *tmp_buf* pointing to the beginning of *buffer*, then tests to see if that allows enough space before a 64K boundary is hit. If the trial setting does not provide enough space, *tmp_buf* is incremented by the number of bytes actually required. Thus some space is always wasted at one end or the other of the space allocated in *buffer*, but there is never a failure due to the buffer falling on a 64K boundary.

Newer computers of the IBM PC family have better DMA controllers, and this code could be simplified, and a small amount of memory reclaimed, if one could be sure that one's machine were immune to this problem. If you are considering this, however, consider how the bug will manifest itself if you are wrong. If a 1K DMA buffer is desired, the chance is 1 in 64 that there will be a problem on a machine with the old DMA chip. Every time the kernel source code is modified in a way that changes the size of the compiled kernel, there is the same probability that the problem will manifest itself. Most likely, when the failure occurs next month or next year, it will be attributed to the code that was last modified. Unexpected hardware "features" like this can cause weeks of time spent looking for exceedingly obscure bugs (all the more so when, like this one, the technical reference manual says nary a word about them).

Do_rdwt is the next function in *driver.c*. It, in turn, may call three device-dependent functions pointed to by the *dr_prepare*, *dr_schedule*, and *dr_finish* fields in the *driver* structure. In what follows we will use the C language notation **function_pointer* to indicate we are talking about the function pointed to by *function_pointer*.

After checking to see that the byte count in the request is positive, *do_rdwt* calls **dr_prepare*. This should succeed, since **dr_prepare* can fail only if an invalid device is specified in an OPEN operation. Next, a standard *iorequest_s* structure (defined on line 3194 in *include/minix/type.h*) is filled in. Then comes another indirect call, this time to **dr_schedule*. As we will see in the discussion of disk hardware in the next section, responding to disk requests in the order they are received can be inefficient, and this routine allows a particular device to handle requests in the way that is best for the device. The indirection here masks much possible variation in the way individual devices perform. For the RAM disk, *dr_schedule* points to a routine that actually performs the I/O, and the next indirect call, to **dr_finish*, is a do-nothing operation. For a real disk, *dr_finish* points to a routine that carries out all of the pending data transfers requested in all previous calls to **dr_schedule* since the last call to **dr_finish*. As we will see, however, in some circumstances the call to **dr_finish* may not result in a transfer of all the data requested.

In whichever call does an actual data transfer, the *io_nbytes* count in the *iorequest_s* structure is modified, returning a negative number if there was an error or a positive number indicating the difference between the number of bytes in the original request and the number successfully transferred. It is not necessarily an error if no bytes are transferred; this indicates that the end of the device has been reached. Upon returning to the main loop, the negative error code is returned in the reply message *REP_STATUS* field if there was an error. Otherwise the bytes remaining to be transferred are subtracted from the original request in the *COUNT* field of the message (line 9249), and the result (the number actually transferred) is returned in *REP_STATUS* in the reply message from *driver_task*.

The next function, *do_vrdwt*, handles all scattered I/O requests. A message that requests a scattered I/O request uses the *ADDRESS* field to point to an array of *iorequest_s* type structures, each of which specifies the information needed for one request: the address of the buffer, the offset on the device, the number of bytes, and whether the operation is a read or a write. All the operations in one request will be for either reading or writing, and they will be sorted into block order on the device. There is more work to do than for the simple read or write performed by *do_rdwt*, since the array of requests must be copied into the kernel's space, but once this has been done, the same three indirect calls to the device-dependent **dr_prepare*, **dr_schedule*, and **dr_finish* routines are made. The difference is that the middle call, to **dr_schedule*, is done in a loop, once for each request, or until an error occurs (lines 9288 to 9290). After termination of the loop, **dr_finish* is called once, and then the array of requests is copied back where it came from. The *io_nbytes* field of each element in the array will have been changed to reflect the number of bytes transferred, and although the total is not passed back directly in the reply message that *driver_task* constructs, the caller can extract the total from this array.

In a scattered I/O read request, not all the transfers requested in the call to **dr_schedule* are necessarily honored when the final call to **dr_finish* is made, as we discussed in the previous section. The *io_request* field in the *iorequest_s* structure contains a flag bit that tells the device driver if a request for that block is optional.

The next few routines in *driver.c* are for general support of the above operations. A **dr_name* call can be used to return the name of a device. For a device with no specific name the *no_name* function retrieves the device's name from the table of tasks. Some devices may not require a particular service, for instance, a RAM disk does not require that anything special be done upon a *DEV_CLOSE* request. The *do_nop* function fills in here, returning various codes depending upon the kind of request. The following functions, *nop_finish*, and *nop_cleanup*, are similar dummy routines for devices that need no **dr_finish* or **dr_cleanup* services.

Some disk device functions require delays, for example, to wait for a floppy disk motor to come up to speed. Thus *driver.c* is a good place for the next function, *clock_mess*, used to send messages to the clock task. It is called with the number of clock ticks to wait and the address of a function to call when the timeout period is complete.

Finally, *do_diocntl* (line 9364) carries out DEV_IOCTL requests for a block device. It is an error if any *DEV_IOCTL* operation other than reading *(DIOGETP)* or writing *(DIOSETP)* partition information is requested. *Do_diocntl* calls the device's **dr_prepare* function to verify the device is valid and to get a pointer to the *device* structure that describes the partition base and size in byte units. On a request to read, it calls the device's **dr_geometry* function to get the last cylinder, head, and sector information about the partition.

3.5.3 The Driver Library

The files *drvlib.h* and *drvlib.c* contain system-dependent code that supports disk partitions on IBM PC compatible computers.

Partitioning allows a single storage device to be divided up into subdevices. It is most commonly used with hard disks, but MINIX provides support for partitioning floppy disks, as well. Some reasons to partition a disk device are:

1. Disk capacity is cheaper per unit in large disks. If two or more operating systems with different file systems are used, it is more economical to partition a single large disk than to install multiple smaller disks for each operating system.

2. Operating systems may have limits to the device size they can handle. The version of MINIX discussed here can handle a 1-GB file system, but older versions are limited to 256 MB. Any disk space beyond that is wasted.

3. Two or more different file systems may be used by an operating system. For example, a standard file system may be used for ordinary files and a differently structured file system may be used for virtual memory swap space.

4. It may be convenient to put a portion of a system's files on a separate logical device. Putting the MINIX root file system on a small device makes it easy to back up and facilitates copying it to a RAM disk at boot time.

Support for disk partitions is platform specific. This specificity is not related to the hardware. Partition support is device independent. But if more than one operating system is to run on a particular set of hardware, all must agree on a format for the partition table. On IBM PCs the standard is set by the MS-DOS *fdisk* command, and other OSs, such as MINIX, OS/2, and Linux, use this format so they can coexist with MS-DOS. When MINIX is ported to another machine type, it makes sense to use a partition table format compatible with other operating systems used on the new hardware. Thus the MINIX source code to support partitions on IBM computers is put in *drvlib.c*, rather than being included in *driver.c*, to make it easier to port MINIX to different hardware.

The basic data structure inherited from the firmware designers is defined in *include/ibm/partition.h*, which is included by a #include statement in *drvlib.h*. This includes information on the cylinder-head-sector geometry of each partition, as well as codes identifying the type of file system on the partition and an active flag indicating if it is bootable. Most of this information is not needed by MINIX once the file system is verified.

The *partition* function (in *drvlib.c*, line 9521) is called when a block device is first opened. Its arguments include a *driver* structure, so it can call device-specific functions, an initial minor device number, and a parameter indicating whether the partitioning style is floppy disk, primary partition, or subpartition. It calls the device-specific **dr_prepare* function to verify the device is valid and to get the base address and the size into a *device* structure of the type mentioned in the previous section. Then it calls *get_part_table* to determine if a partition table is present and, if so, to read it. If there is no partition table, the work is done. Otherwise the minor device number of the first partition is computed, using the rules for numbering minor devices that apply to the style of partitioning specified in the original call. In the case of primary partitions the partition table is sorted so the order of the partitions is consistent with that used by other operating systems.

At this point another call is made to **dr_prepare*, this time using the newly calculated device number of the first partition. If the subdevice is valid, then a loop is made over all the entries in the table, checking that the values read from the table on the device are not out of the range obtained earlier for the base and size of the entire device. If there is a discrepancy, the table in memory is adjusted to conform. This may seem paranoid, but since partition tables may be written by different operating systems, a programmer using another system may have cleverly tried to use the partition table for something unexpected or there could be garbage in the table on disk for some other reason. We put the most trust in the numbers we calculate using MINIX. Better safe than sorry.

Still within the loop, for all partitions on the device, if the partition is identified as a MINIX partition, *partition* is called recursively to gather subpartition information. If a partition is identified as an extended partition, the next function in the file, *extpartition*, is called instead.

Extpartition (line 9593) really has nothing to do with the MINIX operating system, so we will not discuss its details. MS-DOS uses extended partitions, which are just another mechanism for creating subpartitions. In order to support MINIX commands that can read and write MS-DOS files, we need to know about these subpartitions.

Get_part_table (line 9642) calls *do_rdwt* to get the sector on a device (or subdevice) where a partition table is located. The offset argument is zero if it is called to get a primary partition or nonzero for a subpartition. It checks for the magic number (0xAA55) and returns true or false status to indicate whether a valid partition table was found. If a table is found, it copies it to the table address that was passed as an argument.

Finally, *sort* (line 9676) sorts the entries in a partition table by lowest sector. Entries that are marked as having no partition are excluded from the sort, so they come at the end, even though they may have a zero value in their low sector field. The sort is a simple bubble sort; there is no need to use a fancy algorithm to sort a list of four items.

3.6 RAM DISKS

Now we will get back to the individual block device drivers and study several of them in detail. The first one we will look at is the RAM disk driver. It can be used to provide access to any part of memory. Its primary use is to allow a part of memory to be reserved for use like an ordinary disk. This does not provide permanent storage, but once files have been copied to this area they can be accessed extremely quickly.

In a system such as MINIX, which was designed to work even on computers with only one floppy disk, the RAM disk has another advantage. By putting the root device on the RAM disk, the one floppy disk can be mounted and unmounted at will, allowing for removable media. Putting the root device on the floppy disk would make it impossible to save files on floppies, since the root device (the only floppy) cannot be unmounted. In addition, having the root device on the RAM disk makes the system highly flexible: any combination of floppy disks or hard disks can be mounted on it. Although most computers now have hard disks, except computers used in embedded systems, the RAM disk is useful during installation, before the hard disk is ready for use by MINIX, or when it is desired to use MINIX temporarily without doing a full installation.

3.6.1 RAM Disk Hardware and Software

The idea behind a RAM disk is simple. A block device is a storage medium with two commands: write a block and read a block. Normally these blocks are stored on rotating memories, such as floppy disks or hard disks. A RAM disk is simpler. It just uses a preallocated portion of the main memory for storing the blocks. A RAM disk has the advantage of having instant access (no seek or rotational delay), making it suitable for storing programs or data that are frequently accessed.

As an aside, it is worth briefly pointing out a difference between systems that support mounted file systems and those that do not (e.g., MS-DOS and WINDOWS). With mounted file systems, the root device is always present and in a fixed location, and removable file systems (i.e., disks) can be mounted in the file tree to form an integrated file system. Once everything has been mounted, the user need not worry at all about which device a file is on.

In contrast, with systems like MS-DOS, the user must specify the location of each file, either explicitly as in *B:\DIR\FILE* or using certain defaults (current device, current directory, and so on). With only one or two floppy disks, this burden is manageable, but on a large computer system, with dozens of disks, having to keep track of devices all the time would be unbearable. Remember that UNIX runs on systems ranging from an IBM PC, through workstations and supercomputers up to the Cray-2; MS-DOS runs only on small systems.

Figure 3-18 shows the idea behind a RAM disk. The RAM disk is split up into n blocks, depending on how much memory has been allocated for it. Each block is the same size as the block size used on the real disks. When the driver receives a message to read or write a block, it just computes where in the RAM disk memory the requested block lies and reads from it or writes to it, instead of from or to a floppy or hard disk. The transfer is done by calling an assembly language procedure that copies to or from the user program at the maximum speed of which the hardware is capable.

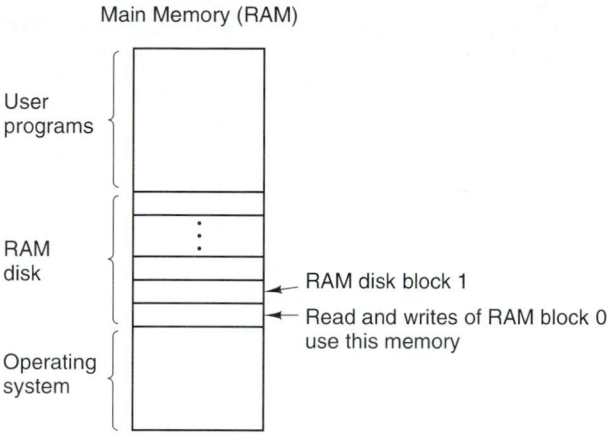

Figure 3-18. A RAM disk.

A RAM disk driver may support several areas of memory used as RAM disk, each distinguished by a different minor device number. Usually these areas are distinct, but in some situations it may be convenient to have them overlap, as we shall see in the next section.

3.6.2 Overview of the RAM Disk Driver in MINIX

The RAM disk driver is actually four closely related drivers in one. Each message to it specifies a minor device as follows:

0: /dev/ram   1: /dev/mem   2: /dev/kmem   3: /dev/null

The first special file listed above, */dev/ram*, is a true RAM disk. Neither its size nor its origin is built into the driver. They are determined by the file system when MINIX is booted. By default a RAM disk of the same size as the root file system image device is created, so the root file system can be copied to it. A boot parameter can be used to specify a RAM disk larger than the root file system, or if the root is not to be copied to the RAM, the specified size may be any value that fits in memory and leaves enough memory for system operation. Once the size is knownm a block of memory big enough is found and removed from the memory pool, even before the memory manager begins its work. This strategy makes it possible to increase or reduce the amount of RAM disk present without having to recompile the operating system.

The next two minor devices are used to read and write physical memory and kernel memory, respectively. When */dev/mem* is opened and read, it yields the contents of physical memory locations starting at absolute address zero (the real-mode interrupt vectors). Ordinary user programs never do this, but a system program concerned with debugging the system might need this facility. Opening */dev/mem* and writing on it will change the interrupt vectors. Needless to say, this should only be done with the greatest of caution by an experienced user who knows exactly what he is doing.

The special file */dev/kmem* is like */dev/mem*, except that byte 0 of this file is byte 0 of the kernel's data memory, a location whose absolute address varies, depending on the size of the MINIX kernel code. It too is used mostly for debugging and very special programs. Note that the RAM disk areas covered by these two minor devices overlap. If you know exactly how the kernel is placed in memory, you can open */dev/mem*, seek to the beginning of the kernel's data area, and see exactly the same thing as reading from the beginning of */dev/kmem*. But, if you recompile the kernel, changing its size, or if in a subsequent version of MINIX the kernel is moved somewhere else in memory, you will have to seek a different amount in */dev/mem* to see the same thing you see at the start of */dev/kmem*. Both of these special files should be protected to prevent everyone except the super-user from using them.

The last file in this group, */dev/null*, is a special file that accepts data and throws them away. It is commonly used in shell commands when the program being called generates output that is not needed. For example,

a.out >/dev/null

runs the program *a.out* but discards its output. The RAM disk driver effectively treats this minor device as having zero size, so no data are ever copied to or from it.

The code for handling */dev/ram*, */dev/mem*, and */dev/kmem* is identical. The only difference among them is that each one corresponds to a different portion of memory, indicated by the arrays *ram_origin* and *ram_limit*, each indexed by minor device number.

3.6.3 Implementation of the RAM Disk Driver in MINIX

As with other disk drivers the main loop of the RAM disk is in the file *driver.c*. The device-specific support for memory devices is in *memory.c*. The array *m_geom* (line 9721) holds the base and size of each of the four memory devices. The *driver* structure *m_dtab* on lines 9733 to 9743 defines the memory device calls that will be made from the main loop. Four of the entries in this table are do-little or do-nothing routines in *driver.c*, a sure clue that the operation of a RAM disk is not terribly complicated. The main procedure *mem_task* (line 9749) calls one function to do some local initialization. After that, it calls the main loop, which gets messages, dispatches to the appropriate procedure, and sends the replies. There is no return to *mem_task* upon completion.

On a read or write operation the main loop makes three calls: one to prepare a device, one to schedule the I/O operations, and one to finish the operation. For a memory device a call to *m_prepare* is the first of these. It checks that a valid minor device has been requested and then returns the address of the structure that holds the base address and size of the requested RAM area. The second call is for *m_schedule* (line 9774). This does all the work. For memory devices the name of this function is a misnomer; by definition, any location is as accessible as any other in random access memory, and thus there is no need to do any scheduling, as there would be with a disk having a moving arm.

The RAM disk's operation is so simple and fast there is never any reason to postpone a request, and the first thing done by this function is to clear the bit that may be set by a scattered I/O call to indicate completion of an operation is optional. The destination address passed in the message points to a location in the caller's memory space, and the code at lines 9792 to 9794 converts this into an absolute address in the system memory and then checks that it is a valid address. The actual data transfer takes place on line 9818 or line 9820 and is a straightforward copying of data from one place to another.

A memory device does not need a third step to finish a read or write operation, and the corresponding slot in *m_dtab* is a call to *nop_finish*.

Opening a memory device is done by *m_do_open* (line 9829). The main job is done by calling *m_prepare* to check that a valid device is being referenced. In the case of a reference to */dev/mem* or */dev/kmem*, a call to *enable_iop* (in the file *protect.c*) is made to change the CPU's current privilege level. This is not necessary to access memory. It is a trick to deal with another problem. Recall that Pentium-class CPUs implement four privilege levels. User programs are at the least privileged level. Intel processors also have an architectural feature that is not present in many other systems, a separate set of instructions to address I/O ports. On these processors I/O ports are treated separately from memory. Normally, an attempt by a user process to execute an instruction that addresses an I/O port causes a general protection exception. However, there are valid reasons for MINIX to allow users to write programs that can access ports, especially on small systems. Thus *enable_iop* changes the CPU's I/O Protection Level (IOPL) bits to permit this. The effect is to allow a process permitted to open */dev/mem* or */dev/kmem* the additional privilege of access to I/O ports. On an architecture where I/O devices are addressed as memory locations, the *rwx* bits for these devices automatically cover access to I/O. If this feature were hidden, it might be considered a security flaw, but now you know about it. If you plan to use MINIX to control a bank security system, you might want to recompile the kernel without this function.

The next function, *m_init* (line 9849), is called only once, when *mem_task* is called for the first time. It sets up the base address and size of */dev/kmem* and it also sets the size of */dev/mem* to 1 MB, 16 MB, or 4 GB−1, depending upon whether MINIX is running in 8088, 80286, or 80386 mode. These sizes are the maximum sizes supported by MINIX and do not have anything to do with how much RAM is installed in the machine.

The RAM disk supports several IOCTL operations in *m_ioctl* (line 9874). The *MIOCRAMSIZE* is a convenient way for the file system to set the RAM disk size. The *MIOCSPSINFO* operation is used by both the file system and the memory manager to set the addresses of their parts of the process table into the *psinfo* table, where the utility program *ps* can retrieve it using a *MIOCGPSINFO* operation. *Ps* is a standard UNIX program whose implementation is complicated by MINIX's microkernel structure, which puts the process table information needed by the program in several different places. The IOCTL system call is a convenient way to handle this problem. Otherwise a new version of *ps* would have to be compiled each time a new version of MINIX were compiled.

The last function in *memory.c* is *m_geometry* (line 9934). Memory devices do not have a geometry of cylinders, tracks, and sectors per track like mechanical disk drives, but in case the RAM disk is asked it will oblige by pretending it does.

3.7 DISKS

The RAM disk is a good introduction to disk drivers (because it is so simple), but real disks present a number of issues that we have not yet touched upon. In the following sections we will first say a few words about disk hardware and then take a look at disk drivers in general and the MINIX hard disk driver in particular. We will not examine the floppy disk driver in detail, but we will go over some of the ways a floppy disk driver differs from a hard disk driver.

3.7.1 Disk Hardware

All real disks are organized into cylinders, each one containing as many tracks as there are heads stacked vertically. The tracks are divided into sectors, with the number of sectors around the circumference typically being 8 to 32 on floppy disks, and up to several hundred on some hard disks. The simplest designs have the same number of sectors on each track. All sectors contain the same number of bytes, although a little thought will make it clear that sectors close to the outer rim of the disk will be physically longer than those close to the hub. The time to read or write each sector will be same, however. The data density is obviously higher on the innermost cylinders, and some disk designs require a change in the drive current to the read-write heads for the inner tracks. This is handled by the disk controller hardware and is not visible to the user (or the implementor of an operating system).

The difference in data density between inner and outer tracks means a sacrifice in capacity, and more sophisticated systems exist. Floppy disk designs that rotate at higher speeds when the heads are over the outer tracks have been tried.

This allows more sectors on those tracks, increasing disk capacity. Such disks are not supported by any system for which MINIX is currently available, however. Modern large hard drives also have more sectors per track on outer tracks than on inner tracks. These are **IDE (Integrated Drive Electronics)** drives, and the sophisticated processing done by the drive's built-in electronics masks the details. To the operating system they appear to have a simple geometry with the same number of sectors on each track.

The drive and controller electronics are as important as the mechanical hardware. The main element of the controller card that is plugged into the computer's backplane is a specialized integrated circuit, really a small microcomputer. For a hard disk the controller card circuitry may be simpler than for a floppy disk, but this is because the hard drive itself has a powerful electronic controller built in. A device feature that has important implications for the disk driver is the possibility of a controller doing seeks on two or more drives at the same time. These are known as **overlapped seeks**. While the controller and software are waiting for a seek to complete on one drive, the controller can initiate a seek on another drive. Many controllers can also read or write on one drive while seeking on one or more other drives, but a floppy disk controller cannot read or write on two drives at the same time. (Reading or writing requires the controller to move bits on a microsecond time scale, so one transfer uses up most of its computing power.) The situation is different for hard disks with integrated controllers, and in a system with more than one of these hard drives they can operate simultaneously, at least to the extent of transferring between the disk and the controller's buffer memory. Only one transfer between the controller and the system memory is possible at once, however. The ability to perform two or more operations at the same time can reduce the average access time considerably.

Figure 3-19 compares parameters of double-sided, double-density diskettes, the standard storage medium for the original IBM PC, with parameters of a typical medium-capacity hard drive such as might be found on a Pentium-based computer. MINIX uses 1K blocks, so with either of these disk formats the blocks used by the software consist of two consecutive sectors, which are always read or written together as a unit.

One thing to be aware of in looking at the specifications of modern hard disks is that the geometry specified, and used by the driver software, may be different than the physical format. The hard disk described in Fig. 3-19, for instance, is specified with "recommended setup parameters" of 1048 cylinders, 16 heads, and 63 sectors per track. The controller electronics mounted on the disk converts the logical head and sector parameters supplied by the operating system to the physical ones used by the disk. This is another example of a compromise designed to maintain compatibility with older systems, in this case old firmware. The designers of the original IBM PC only allotted a 6-bit field for the BIOS ROM's sector count, and a disk that has more than 63 physical sectors per track must work with an artificial set of logical disk parameters. In this case the vendor's

Parameter	IBM 360-KB floppy disk	WD 540-MB hard disk
Number of cylinders	40	1048
Tracks per cylinder	2	4
Sectors per track	9	252
Sectors per disk	720	1056384
Bytes per sector	512	512
Bytes per disk	368640	540868608
Seek time (adjacent cylinders)	6 msec	4 msec
Seek time (average case)	77 msec	11 msec
Rotation time	200 msec	13 msec
Motor stop/start time	250 msec	9 sec
Time to transfer 1 sector	22 msec	53 μsec

Figure 3-19. Disk parameters for the original IBM PC 360-KB floppy disk and a Western Digital WD AC2540 540-MB hard disk.

specifications state that there are really four heads, and thus it would appear that there are really 252 sectors per track, as indicated in the figure. This is an over-simplification, because disks like these have more sectors on the outermost tracks than on the inner tracks. The disk described in the figure does have four physical heads, but there are actually slightly over 3000 cylinders. The cylinders are grouped in a dozen zones which have from 57 sectors per track in the innermost zones to 105 cylinders per track on the outermost cylinders. These numbers are not to be found in the disk's specifications, and the translations done by the drive's electronics make it unnecessary for us to know such details.

3.7.2 Disk Software

In this section we will look at some issues related to disk drivers in general. First, consider how long it takes to read or write a disk block. The time required is determined by three factors:

1. The seek time (the time to move the arm to the proper cylinder).

2. The rotational delay (the time for the proper sector to rotate under the head).

3. The actual data transfer time.

For most disks, the seek time dominates the other two times, so reducing the mean seek time can improve system performance substantially.

Disk devices are prone to errors. Some kind of error check, a checksum or a cyclic redundancy check, is always recorded along with the data in each sector on a disk. Even the sector addresses recorded when the disk is formatted have check data. Floppy disk controller hardware can report when an error is detected, but the software must then decide what to do about it. Hard disk controllers often take on much of this burden.

Particularly with hard disks, the transfer time for consecutive sectors within a track can be very fast. Thus reading more data than is requested and caching them in memory can be very effective in speeding disk access.

Disk Arm Scheduling Algorithms

If the disk driver accepts requests one at a time and carries them out in that order, that is, First-Come, First-Served (FCFS), little can be done to optimize seek time. However, another strategy is possible when the disk is heavily loaded. It is likely that while the arm is seeking on behalf of one request, other disk requests may be generated by other processes. Many disk drivers maintain a table, indexed by cylinder number, with all the pending requests for each cylinder chained together in a linked list headed by the table entries.

Given this kind of data structure, we can improve upon the first-come, first-served scheduling algorithm. To see how, consider a disk with 40 cylinders. A request comes in to read a block on cylinder 11. While the seek to cylinder 11 is in progress, new requests come in for cylinders 1, 36, 16, 34, 9, and 12, in that order. They are entered into the table of pending requests, with a separate linked list for each cylinder. The requests are shown in Fig. 3-20.

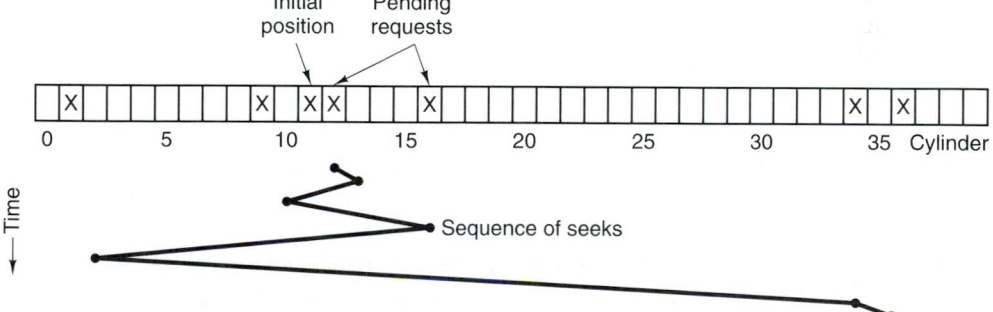

Figure 3-20. Shortest Seek First (SSF) disk scheduling algorithm.

When the current request (for cylinder 11) is finished, the disk driver has a choice of which request to handle next. Using FCFS, it would go next to cylinder 1, then to 36, and so on. This algorithm would require arm motions of 10, 35, 20, 18, 25, and 3, respectively, for a total of 111 cylinders.

Alternatively, it could always handle the closest request next, to minimize seek time. Given the requests of Fig. 3-20, the sequence is 12, 9, 16, 1, 34, and 36, as shown as the jagged line at the bottom of Fig. 3-20. With this sequence, the arm motions are 1, 3, 7, 15, 33, and 2, for a total of 61 cylinders. This algorithm, **Shortest Seek First** (SSF), cuts the total arm motion almost in half compared to FCFS.

Unfortunately, SSF has a problem. Suppose more requests keep coming in while the requests of Fig. 3-20 are being processed. For example, if, after going to cylinder 16, a new request for cylinder 8 is present, that request will have priority over cylinder 1. If a request for cylinder 13 then comes in, the arm will next go to 13, instead of 1. With a heavily loaded disk, the arm will tend to stay in the middle of the disk most of the time, so requests at either extreme will have to wait until a statistical fluctuation in the load causes there to be no requests near the middle. Requests far from the middle may get poor service. The goals of minimal response time and fairness are in conflict here.

Tall buildings also have to deal with this trade-off. The problem of scheduling an elevator in a tall building is similar to that of scheduling a disk arm. Requests come in continuously calling the elevator to floors (cylinders) at random. The microprocessor running the elevator could easily keep track of the sequence in which customers pushed the call button and service them using FCFS. It could also use SSF.

However, most elevators use a different algorithm to reconcile the conflicting goals of efficiency and fairness. They keep moving in the same direction until there are no more outstanding requests in that direction, then they switch directions. This algorithm, known both in the disk world and the elevator world as the **elevator algorithm**, requires the software to maintain 1 bit: the current direction bit, *UP* or *DOWN*. When a request finishes, the disk or elevator driver checks the bit. If it is *UP*, the arm or cabin is moved to the next highest pending request. If no requests are pending at higher positions, the direction bit is reversed. When the bit is set to *DOWN*, the move is to the next lowest requested position, if any.

Figure 3-21 shows the elevator algorithm using the same seven requests as Fig. 3-20, assuming the direction bit was initially *UP*. The order in which the cylinders are serviced is 12, 16, 34, 36, 9, and 1, which yields arm motions of 1, 4, 18, 2, 27, and 8, for a total of 60 cylinders. In this case the elevator algorithm is slightly better than SSF, although it is usually worse. One nice property that the elevator algorithm has is that given any collection of requests, the upper bound on the total motion is fixed: it is just twice the number of cylinders.

A slight modification of this algorithm that has a smaller variance in response times (Teory, 1972) is to always scan in the same direction. When the highest numbered cylinder with a pending request has been serviced, the arm goes to the lowest-numbered cylinder with a pending request and then continues moving in an upward direction. In effect, the lowest-numbered cylinder is thought of as being just above the highest-numbered cylinder.

Some disk controllers provide a way for the software to inspect the current sector number under the head. With such a controller, another optimization is

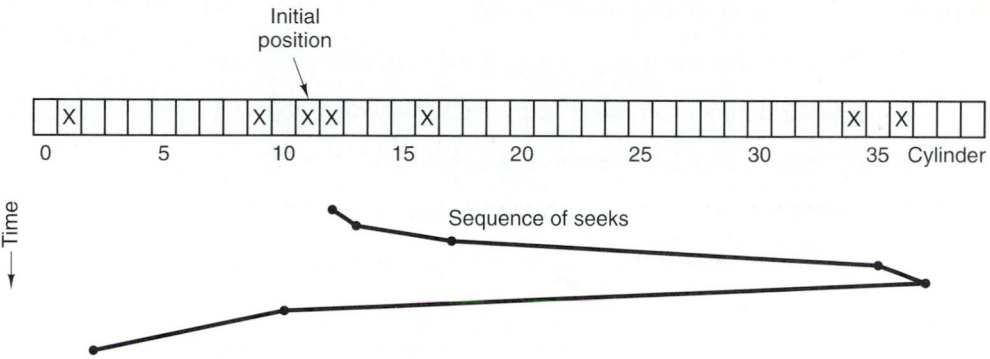

Figure 3-21. The elevator algorithm for scheduling disk requests.

possible. If two or more requests for the same cylinder are pending, the driver can issue a request for the sector that will pass under the head next. Note that when multiple tracks are present in a cylinder, consecutive requests can be for different tracks with no penalty. The controller can select any of its heads instantaneously, because head selection involves neither arm motion nor rotational delay.

With a modern hard disk, the data transfer rate is so much faster than that of a floppy disk that some kind of automatic caching is necessary. Typically any request to read a sector will cause that sector and up to the rest of the current track to be read, depending upon how much space is available in the controller's cache memory. The 540M disk described in Fig. 3-19 has a 64K or 128K cache. The use of the cache is determined dynamically by the controller. In its simplest mode, the cache is divided into two sections, one for reads and one for writes.

When several drives are present, a pending request table should be kept for each drive separately. Whenever any drive is idle, a seek should be issued to move its arm to the cylinder where it will be needed next (assuming the controller allows overlapped seeks). When the current transfer finishes, a check can be made to see if any drives are positioned on the correct cylinder. If one or more are, the next transfer can be started on a drive that is already on the right cylinder. If none of the arms is in the right place, the driver should issue a new seek on the drive that just completed a transfer and wait until the next interrupt to see which arm gets to its destination first.

Error Handling

RAM disks do not have to worry about seek or rotational optimization: at any instant all blocks can be read or written without any physical motion. Another area in which RAM disks are simpler than real disks is error handling. RAM disks always work; real ones do not always work. They are subject to a wide variety of errors. Some of the more common ones are:

1. Programming error (e.g., request for nonexistent sector).

2. Transient checksum error (e.g., caused by dust on the head).

3. Permanent checksum error (e.g., disk block physically damaged).

4. Seek error (e.g., the arm sent to cylinder 6 but it went to 7).

5. Controller error (e.g., controller refuses to accept commands).

It is up to the disk driver to handle each of these as best it can.

Programming errors occur when the driver tells the controller to seek to a nonexistent cylinder, read from a nonexistent sector, use a nonexistent head, or transfer to or from nonexistent memory. Most controllers check the parameters given to them and complain if they are invalid. In theory, these errors should never occur, but what should the driver do if the controller indicates that one has happened? For a home-grown system, the best thing to do is stop and print a message like ''Call the programmer'' so the error can be tracked down and fixed. For a commercial software product in use at thousands of sites around the world, this approach is less attractive. Probably the only thing to do is terminate the current disk request with an error and hope it will not recur too often.

Transient checksum errors are caused by specks of dust in the air that get between the head and the disk surface. Most of the time they can be eliminated by just repeating the operation a few times. If the error persists, the block has to be marked as a **bad block** and avoided.

One way to avoid bad blocks is to write a very special program that takes a list of bad blocks as input and carefully hand crafts a file containing all the bad blocks. Once this file has been made, the disk allocator will think these blocks are occupied and never allocate them. As long as no one ever tries to read the bad block file, no problems will occur.

Not reading the bad block file is easier said than done. Many disks are backed up by copying their contents a track at a time to a backup tape or disk drive. If this procedure is followed, the bad blocks will cause trouble. Backing up the disk one file at a time is slower but will solve the problem, provided that the backup program knows the name of the bad block file and refrains from copying it.

Another problem that cannot be solved with a bad block file is the problem of a bad block in a file system data structure that must be in a fixed location. Almost every file system has at least one data structure whose location is fixed, so it can be found easily. On a partitioned file system it may be possible to repartition and work around a bad track, but a permanent error in the first few sectors of either a floppy or hard disk generally means the disk is unusable.

''Intelligent'' controllers reserve a few tracks not normally available to user programs. When a disk drive is formatted, the controller determines which blocks are bad and automatically substitutes one of the spare tracks for the bad one. The table that maps bad tracks to spare tracks is kept in the controller's internal memory and on the disk. This substitution is transparent (invisible) to the driver, except that its carefully worked out elevator algorithm may perform poorly if the controller is secretly using cylinder 800 whenever cylinder 3 is requested. The technology of manufacturing disk recording surfaces is better than it used to be, but it is still not perfect. However, the technology of hiding the imperfections from the user has also improved. On hard disks such as the one described in Fig. 3-19, the controller also manages new errors that may develop with use, permanently assigning substitute blocks when it determines that an error is unrecoverable. With such disks the driver software rarely sees any indication that there any bad blocks.

Seek errors are caused by mechanical problems in the arm. The controller keeps track of the arm position internally. To perform a seek, it issues a series of pulses to the arm motor, one pulse per cylinder, to move the arm to the new cylinder. When the arm gets to its destination, the controller reads the actual cylinder number (written when the drive was formatted). If the arm is in the wrong place, a seek error has occurred.

Most hard disk controllers correct seek errors automatically, but many floppy controllers (including the IBM PCs) just set an error bit and leave the rest to the driver. The driver handles this error by issuing a RECALIBRATE command, to move the arm as far out as it will go and reset the controller's internal idea of the current cylinder to 0. Usually this solves the problem. If it does not, the drive must be repaired.

As we have seen, the controller is really a specialized little computer, complete with software, variables, buffers, and occasionally, bugs. Sometimes an unusual sequence of events such as an interrupt on one drive occurring simultaneously with a RECALIBRATE command for another drive will trigger a bug and cause the controller to go into a loop or lose track of what it was doing. Controller designers usually plan for the worst and provide a pin on the chip which, when asserted, forces the controller to forget whatever it was doing and reset itself. If all else fails, the disk driver can set a bit to invoke this signal and reset the controller. If that does not help, all the driver can do is print a message and give up.

Track-at-a-Time Caching

The time required to seek to a new cylinder is usually much more than the rotational delay, and always much more than the transfer time. In other words, once the driver has gone to the trouble of moving the arm somewhere, it hardly matters whether it reads one sector or a whole track. This effect is especially true if the controller provides rotational sensing, so the driver can see which sector is currently under the head and issue a request for the next sector, thereby making it possible to read a track in one rotation time. (Normally it takes half a rotation plus one sector time just to read a single sector, on the average.)

Some disk drivers take advantage of this property by maintaining a secret track-at-a-time cache, unknown to the device-independent software. If a sector that is in the cache is needed, no disk transfer is required. A disadvantage of track-at-a-time caching (in addition to the software complexity and buffer space needed) is that transfers from the cache to the calling program will have to be done by the CPU using a programmed loop, rather than letting the DMA hardware do the job.

Some controllers take this process a step further, and do track-at-a-time caching in their own internal memory, transparent to the driver, so that transfer between the controller and memory can use DMA. If the controller works this way, there is little point in having the disk driver do it as well. Note that both the controller and the driver are in a good position to read and write entire tracks in one command, but that the device-independent software cannot, because it regards a disk as a linear sequence of blocks, without regard to how they are divided up into tracks and cylinders.

3.7.3 Overview of the Hard Disk Driver in MINIX

The hard disk driver is the first part of MINIX we have looked at that has to deal with a wide range of different types of hardware. Before we discuss the details of the driver, we will briefly consider some of the problems hardware differences can cause. The "IBM PC" is really a family of different computers. Not only are different processors used in different members of the family, there are also some major differences in the basic hardware. The earliest members of the family, the original PC and the PC-XT, used an 8-bit bus, appropriate for the 8-bit external interface of the 8088 processor. The next generation, the PC-AT, used a 16-bit bus, which was cleverly designed so older 8-bit peripherals could still be used. Newer 16-bit peripherals generally cannot be used on older PC-XT systems, however. The AT bus was originally designed for systems using the 80286 processor, and many systems based on the 80386, 80486, and Pentium use the AT bus. However, since these newer processors have a 32-bit interface, there are now several different 32-bit bus systems available, such as Intel's PCI bus.

For every bus there is a different family of **I/O adapters**, which plug into the system parentboard. All the peripherals for a particular bus design must be compatible with the standards for that design but need not be compatible with older designs. In the IBM PC family, as in most other computer systems, each bus design also comes with firmware in the Basic I/O System Read-Only Memory (the BIOS ROM) which is designed to bridge the gap between the operating system and the peculiarities of the hardware. Some peripheral devices may provide extensions to the BIOS in ROM chips on the peripheral cards themselves. The difficulty faced by an operating system implementor is that the BIOS in IBM-type computers (certainly the early ones) was designed for an operating system, MS-DOS, that does not support multiprogramming and that runs in 16-bit real mode, the lowest common denominator of the various modes of operation available from the 80x86 family of CPUs.

The implementor of a new operating system for the IBM PC is thus faced with several choices. One is whether to use the driver support for peripherals in the BIOS or to write new drivers from scratch. This was not a hard choice in the original design of MINIX, since the BIOS was in many ways not suitable to the needs of MINIX. Of course, in order to get started, the MINIX boot monitor uses the BIOS to do the initial loading of the system, whether from hard disk or floppy disk—there is no practical alternative to doing it this way. Once we have loaded the system, including our own I/O drivers, we can do much better than the BIOS.

The second choice then must be faced: without the BIOS support how are we going to make our drivers adapt to the varied kinds of hardware on different systems? To make the discussion concrete, consider that there are at least four fundamentally different types of hard disk controllers that we might find on a system which is otherwise suitable for MINIX: the original 8-bit XT-type controller, the 16-bit AT-type controller, and two different controllers for two different types of IBM PS/2 series computers. There are several possible ways to deal with this:

1. Recompile a unique version of the operating system for each type of hard disk controller we need to accommodate.

2. Compile several different hard disk drivers into the kernel and have the kernel automatically determine at startup time which one to use.

3. Compile several different hard disk drivers into the kernel and provide a way for the user to determine which one to use.

As we shall see, these are not mutually exclusive.

The first way is really the best way in the long run. For use on a particular installation there is no need to use up disk and memory space with code for alternative drivers that will never be used. However, it is a nightmare for the distributor of the software. Supplying four different startup disks and advising users on how to use them is expensive and difficult. Thus, one of the other alternatives is advisable, at least for the initial installation.

The second method is to have the operating system probe the peripherals, by reading the ROM on each card or writing and reading I/O ports to identify each card. This is feasible on some systems but does not work well on IBM-type systems, because there are too many nonstandard I/O devices available. Probing I/O ports to identify one device may, in some cases, activate another device which seizes control and disables the system. This method complicates the startup code for each device, and yet still does not work very well. Operating systems that do use this method generally have to provide some kind of override, typically a mechanism such as we use with MINIX.

The third method, used in MINIX, is to allow compilation of several drivers, with one of them being the default. The MINIX boot monitor allows various **boot**

parameters to be read at startup time. These can be entered by hand, or stored permanently on the disk. At startup time, if a boot parameter of the form

hd = xt

is found, this forces use of the XT hard disk driver. If no hd boot parameter is found, the default driver is used.

There are two other things MINIX does to try to minimize problems with multiple hard disk drivers. One is that there is, after all, a driver that interfaces between MINIX and the ROM BIOS hard disk support. This driver is almost guaranteed to work on any system and can be selected by use of an

hd = bios

boot parameter. Generally, this should be a last resort, however. MINIX runs in protected mode on systems with an 80286 or better processor, but the BIOS code always runs in real (8086) mode. Switching out of protected mode and back again whenever a routine in the BIOS is called is very slow.

The other strategy MINIX uses in dealing with drivers is to postpone initialization until the last possible moment. Thus, if on some hardware configuration none of the hard disk drivers work, we can still start MINIX from a floppy disk and do some useful work. MINIX will have no problems as long as no attempt is made to access the hard disk. This may not seem like a major breakthrough in user friendliness, but consider this: if all the drivers try to initialize immediately on system startup, the system can be totally paralyzed by improper configuration of some device we do not need anyway. By postponing initialization of each driver until it is needed, the system can continue with whatever does work, while the user tries to resolve the problems.

As an aside, we learned this lesson the hard way: earlier versions of MINIX tried to initialize the hard disk as soon as the system was booted. If no hard disk was present, the system hung. This behavior was especially unfortunate because MINIX will run quite happily on a system without a hard disk, albeit with restricted storage capacity and reduced performance.

In the discussion in this section and the next, we will take as our model the AT-style hard disk driver, which is the default driver in the standard MINIX distribution. This is a versatile driver that handles hard disk controllers from the ones used in the earliest 80286 systems to modern **EIDE** (**Extended Integrated Drive Electronics**) controllers that handle gigabyte capacity hard disks. The general aspects of hard disk operation we discuss in this section apply to the other supported drivers as well.

The main loop of the hard disk task is the same shared code we have already discussed, and the standard six kinds of requests can be made. A *DEV_OPEN* request can entail a substantial amount of work, as there are always partitions and may be subpartitions on a hard disk. These must be read when a device is opened, (i.e., when it is first accessed). Some hard disk controllers can also support CD-ROM drives, which have removable media, and on a *DEV_OPEN* the presence of the medium must be verified. On a CD-ROM a *DEV_CLOSE* operation also has meaning: it requires that the door be unlocked and the CD-ROM ejected. There are other complications of removable media that are more applicable to floppy drives, so we will discuss these in a later section. For the hard disk, the *DEV_IOCTL* operation is used to set a flag to mark that the medium should be ejected upon a *DEV_CLOSE*. This feature is useful for CD-ROMs. It is also used to read and write partition tables, as we noted earlier.

The *DEV_READ*, *DEV_WRITE*, and *SCATTERED_IO* requests are each handled in three phases, prepare, schedule, and finish, as we saw previously. The hard disk, unlike the memory devices, makes a real distinction between the schedule and finish phases. The hard disk driver does not use SSF or the elevator algorithm, but it does do a more limited form of scheduling, gathering requests for consecutive sectors. Requests normally come from the MINIX file system and are for multiples of blocks of 1024 bytes, but the driver is able to handle requests for any multiple of a sector (512 bytes). As long as each request is for a starting sector immediately following the last sector requested, each request is appended to a list of requests. The list is maintained as an array, and when it is full, or when a nonconsecutive sector is requested, a call is made to the finish routine.

In a simple *DEV_READ* or *DEV_WRITE* request, more than a single block may be requested, but each call to the schedule routine is immediately followed by a call to the finish routine, which ensures the current request list is fulfilled. In the case of a *SCATTERED_IO* request, there may be multiple calls to the schedule routine before the finish routine is called. As long as they are for consecutive blocks of data, the list will be extended until the array becomes full. Recall that in a *SCATTERED_IO* request a flag can signify that a request for a particular block is optional. The hard disk driver, like the memory driver, ignores the *OPTIONAL* flag and delivers all data requested.

The rudimentary scheduling performed by the hard disk driver, postponing actual transfers while consecutive blocks are being requested, should be seen as the second step of a potential three-step process of scheduling. The file system itself, by using scattered I/O, can implement something similar to Teory's version of the elevator algorithm—recall that in a scattered I/O request the list of requests is sorted on the block number. The third step in scheduling takes place in the controller of a modern hard disk, like the one described in Fig. 3-19. Such controllers are "smart" and can buffer large quantities of data, using internally programmed algorithms to retrieve data is the most efficient order, irrespective of the order of receipt of the requests.

3.7.4 Implementation of the Hard Disk Driver in MINIX

Small hard disks used on microcomputers are sometimes called "winchester" disks. There are several different stories about the origin of the name. It was apparently an IBM code name for the project that developed the disk technology in which the read/write heads fly on a thin cushion of air and land on the recording medium when the disk stops spinning. One explanation of the name is that an early model had two data modules, a 30-Mbyte fixed and a 30-Mbyte removable one. Supposedly this reminded the developers of the Winchester 30-30 firearm which figures in many tales of the United States' western frontier. Whatever the origin of the name, the basic technology remains the same, although today's typical microcomputer disk is much smaller and the capacity is much larger than the 14-inch disks that were typical of the early 1970s when the winchester technology was developed.

The file *wini.c* has the job of hiding the actual hard disk driver used from the rest of the kernel. This allows us to follow the strategy discussed in the previous section, compiling several hard disk drivers into a single kernel image, and selecting the one to use at boot time. Later, a custom installation can be recompiled with only the one driver actually needed.

Wini.c contains one data definition, *hdmap* (line 10013), an array that associates a name with the address of a function. The array is initialized by the compiler with as many elements as are needed for the number of hard disk drivers enabled in *include/minix/config.h*. The array is used by the function *winchester_task*, which is the name entered in the *task_tab* table used when the kernel is first initialized. When *winchester_task* (line 10040) is called, it tries to find an *hd* environment variable, using a kernel function that works similarly to the mechanism used by ordinary C programs, reading the environment created by the MINIX boot monitor. If no *hd* value is defined, the first entry in the array is used; otherwise, the array is searched for a matching name. The corresponding function is then called indirectly. In the rest of this section we will discuss the *at_winchester_task*, which is the first entry in the *hdmap* array in the standard distribution of MINIX.

The AT-style driver is in *at_wini.c* (line 10100). This is a complicated driver for a sophisticated device, and there are several pages of macro definitions specifying controller registers, status bits and commands, dat a structures, and prototypes. As with other block device drivers, a *driver* structure, *w_dtab* (lines 10274 to 10284), is initialized with pointers to the functions that actually do the work. Most of them are defined in *at_wini.c*, but as the hard disk requires no special cleanup operation, its *dr_cleanup* entry points to the common *nop_cleanup* in *driver.c*, shared with other drivers that have no special cleanup requirement. The entry function, *at_winchester_task* (line 10294), calls a procedure that does hardware-specific initialization and then calls the main loop in *driver.c*. This runs forever, dispatching calls to the various functions pointed to by the *driver* table.

Since we are now dealing with real electromechanical storage devices, there is a substantial amount of work to be done to initialize the hard disk driver. Various parameters about the hard disks are kept in the *wini* array defined on lines 10214 to 10230. As part of the policy of postponing initialization steps that could fail until the first time they are truly necessary, *init_params* (line 10307), which is called during kernel initialization, does not do anything that requires accessing the disk device itself. The main thing it does is to copy some information about the hard disk logical configuration into the *wini* array. This is information that is retrieved by the ROM BIOS from the CMOS memory that Pentium-class computers use to preserve basic configuration data. The BIOS actions take place when the computer is first turned on, before the first part of the MINIX loading process begins. It is not necessarily fatal if this information cannot be retrieved; if the disk is a modern one, the information can be retrieved directly from the disk.

After the call to the common main loop, nothing may happen for a while until an attempt is made to access the hard disk. Then a message requesting a *DEV_OPEN* operation is received and *w_do_open* (line 10355) is indirectly called. In turn, *w_do_open* calls *w_prepare* to determine if the device requested is valid, and then *w_identify* to identify the type of device and initialize some more parameters in the *wini* array. Finally a counter in the *wini* array is used to test whether this is first time the device has been opened since MINIX was started. After being examined, the counter is incremented. If it is the first *DEV_OPEN* operation, the *partition* function (in *drvlib.c*) is called.

The next function, *w_prepare* (line 10388), accepts an integer argument, *device*, which is the minor device number of the drive or partition to be used, and returns a pointer to the *device* structure that indicates the base address and size of the device. In C the use of an identifier to name a structure does not preclude use of the same identifier to name a variable. Whether a device is a drive, a partition, or a subpartition can be determined from the minor device number. Once *w_prepare* has completed its job, none of the other functions used to read or write the disk need to concern themselves with partitioning. As we have seen, *w_prepare* is called when a *DEV_OPEN* request is made; it is also one phase of the prepare/schedule/finish cycle used by all data transfer requests. In that context its initialization of *w_count* to zero is important.

Software-compatible AT-type disks have been in use for quite a while, and *w_identify* (line 10415) has to distinguish between a number of different designs that have been introduced over the years. The first step is to see that a readable and writeable I/O port exists where one should exist on all disk controllers in this family (lines 10435 to 10437). If this condition is met, the address of the hard disk interrupt handler is installed in the interrupt descriptor table and the interrupt controller is enabled to respond to that interrupt. Then an *ATA_IDENTIFY* command is issued to the disk controller. If the result is *OK*, various pieces of information are retrieved, including a string that identifies the model of the disk, and the physical cylinder, head, and sector parameters for the device. (Note that the "physical" configuration reported may not be the true physical configuration, but we have no alternative to accepting what the disk drive claims.) The disk information also indicates whether or not the disk is capable of **Linear Block Addressing (LBA)**. If it is, the driver can ignore the cylinder, head, and sector parameters and can address the disk using absolute sector numbers, which is much simpler.

As we mentioned earlier, it is possible that *init_params* may not recover the logical disk configuration information from the BIOS tables. If that happens, the code at lines 10469 to 10477 tries to create an appropriate set of parameters based on what it reads from the drive itself. The idea is that the maximum cylinder, head, and sector numbers can be 1023, 255, and 63 respectively, due to the number of bits allowed for these fields in the original BIOS data structures.

If the *ATA_IDENTIFY* command fails, it may simply mean that the disk is an older model that does not support the command. In this case the logical configuration values previously read by *init_params* are all we have. If they are valid, they are copied to the physical parameter fields of *wini*; otherwise an error is returned and the disk is not usable.

Finally, MINIX uses a *u32_t* variable to count addresses in bytes. The size of device the driver can handle, expressed as a count of sectors, must be limited if the product of cylinders × heads × sectors is too large (line 10490). Although at the time of writing this code devices of 4-GB capacity were rarely found on machines that one might expect to be used for MINIX, experience has taught that software should be written to test for limits such as this, unnecessary as such tests may appear at the time the code is written. The base and size of the whole drive are then entered into the *wini* array, and *w_specify* is called, twice if necessary, to pass the parameters to be used back to the disk controller. Finally, the name of the device (determined by *w_name*) and the identification string found by *identify* (if it is an advanced device) or the cylinder head and sector parameters reported by the BIOS (if an old device) are printed on the console.

W_name (line 10511) returns a pointer to a string containing the device name, which will be either "at-hd0," "at-hd5," "at-hd10," or "at-hd15." *W_specify* (line 10531), in addition to passing the parameters to the controller, also recalibrates the drive (if it is an older model), by doing a seek to cylinder zero.

Now we are ready to discuss the functions called in satisfying a data transfer request. *W_prepare*, which we have already discussed, is called first. Its initialization of the variable *w_count* to zero is important here. The next function called during a transfer is *w_schedule* (line 10567). It sets up the basic parameters: where the data are to come from, where they are to go to, the count of bytes to transfer (which must be a multiple of the sector size, and is tested on line 10584), and whether the transfer is a read or write. The bit that may be present in a *SCATTERED_IO* request to indicate an optional transfer is reset in the operation code to be passed to the controller (line 10595), but note that it is retained in the *io_request* field of the *iorequest_s* structure. For the hard disk an attempt is made to honor all requests, but, as we will see, the driver may later decide not to do so if there have been errors. The last thing in the setup is to check that the request does not go beyond the last byte on the device and to reduce the request if it does. At this point the first sector to be read can be calculated.

On line 10602 the process of scheduling begins in earnest. If there are already requests pending (tested by seeing if *w_count* is greater than zero), and if the sector to read next is not consecutive with the last one requested, then *w_finish* is called to complete the previous requests. Otherwise, *w_nextblock*, which holds the sector number of the next sector, is updated, and the loop on lines 10611 to 10640 is entered to add new sector requests to the array of requests. Within maximum allowable number of requests has been reached (line 10614). The limit is kept in a variable, *max_count*, since, as we will see later, it is sometimes helpful to be able to adjust the limit. Here again, a call to *w_finish* may result.

As we have seen, there are two places within *w_prepare* where a call to *w_finish* may be made. Normally *w_prepare* terminates without calling *w_finish*, but whether or not it is called from within *w_prepare*, *w_finish* (line 10649) is always called eventually from the main loop in *driver.c*. If it has just been called, it may have no work, so there is a test on line 10659 to check this. If there are still requests in the request array, the main part of *w_finish* is entered.

As one might expect, since there may be a considerable number of requests queued, the main part of *w_finish* is a loop, on lines 10664 to 10761. Before entering the loop, the variable *r* is preset to a value signifying an error, to force reinitialization of the controller. If a call to *w_specify* succeeds the *command* structure, *cmd* is initialized to do a transfer. This structure is used to pass all the required parameters to the function that actually operates the disk controller. The *cmd.precomp* parameter is used by some drives to compensate for differences in the performance of the magnetic recording medium with differences in speed of passage of the medium under the disk heads as they move from outer to inner cylinders. It is always the same for a particular drive and is ignored by many drives. *Cmd.count* receives the number of sectors to transfer, masked to a quantity that fits in an 8-bit byte, since that is the size of all the command and status registers of the controller. The code on lines 10675 to 10689 specifies the first sector to transfer, either as a 28-bit logical block number (lines 10676 to 10679), or as cylinder, head, and sector parameters (lines 10681 to 10688). In either case the same fields in the *cmd* structure are used.

Finally, the command itself, read or write, is loaded and *com_out* is called at line 10692 to initiate the transfer. The call to *com_out* may fail if the controller is not ready or does not become ready within a preset timeout period. In this case the count of errors is incremented and the attempt is aborted if *MAX_ERRORS* is reached. Otherwise, the

continue;

statement on line 10697 causes the loop to start over again at line 10665.

If the controller accepts the command passed in the call to *com_out*, it may be a while before the data are available, so (assuming the command is *DEV_READ*) on line 10706 *w_intr_wait* is called. We will discuss this function in detail later, but for now just note that it calls *receive*, so at this point the disk task blocks.

Some time later, more or less, depending upon whether a seek was involved, the call to *w_intr_wait* will return. This driver does not use DMA, although some controllers support it. Instead, programmed I/O is used. If there is no error returned from *w_intr_wait*, the assembly language function *port_read* transfers *SECTOR_SIZE* bytes of data from the controller's data port to their final destination, which should be a buffer in the file system's block cache. Next, various addresses and counts are adjusted to account for the successful transfer. Finally, if the count of bytes in the current request goes to zero, the pointer to the array of requests is advanced to point to the next request (line 10714).

In the case of a *DEV_WRITE* command, the first part, setting up the command parameters and sending the command to the controller, is the same as for a read, except for the command operation code. The order of subsequent events is different for a write, however. First there is a wait for the controller to signal it is ready to receive data (line 10724). *Waitfor* is a macro, and normally will return very quickly. We will say more about it later; for now we will just note that the wait will time out eventually, but that long delays are expected to be extremely rare. Then the data are transferred from memory to the controller data port using *port_write* (line 10729), and at this point *w_intr_wait* is called and the disk task blocks. When the interrupt arrives and the disk task is awakened, the bookkeeping is done (lines 10736 to 10739).

Finally, if there have been errors in reading or writing, they must be dealt with. If the controller informs the driver that the error was due to a bad sector, there is no point in trying again, but other types of errors are worth a retry, at least up to a point. That point is determined by counting the errors and giving up if *MAX_ERRORS* is reached. When *MAX_ERRORS/2* is reached, *w_need_reset* is called to force reinitialization when the retry is made. However, if the request was originally an optional one (made by a *SCATTERED_IO* request), no retry is attempted.

Whether *w_finish* terminates without errors or because of an error, the variable *w_command* is always set to *CMD_IDLE*. This allows other functions to determine that the failure was not because of a mechanical or electrical malfunction of the disk itself causing failure to generate an interrupt following an attempted operation.

The disk controller is controlled through a set of registers, which could be memory mapped on some systems, but on an IBM compatible appear as I/O ports. The registers used by a standard IBM-AT class hard disk controller are shown in Fig. 3-22.

This is our first encounter with I/O hardware, and it may be helpful to mention some ways I/O ports may behave differently from memory addresses. In general, input and output registers that happen to have the same I/O port address are not the same register. Thus, the data written to a particular address cannot necessarily be retrieved by a subsequent read operation. For example, the last register address shown in Fig. 3-22 shows the status of the disk controller when read and is used to issue commands to the controller when written to. It is also common that the very act of reading or writing an I/O device register causes an action to

Register	Read Function	Write Function
0	Data	Data
1	Error	Write Precompensation
2	Sector Count	Sector Count
3	Sector Number (0-7)	Sector Number (0-7)
4	Cylinder Low (8-15)	Cylinder Low (8-15)
5	Cylinder High (16-23)	Cylinder High (16-23)
6	Select Drive/Head (24-27)	Select Drive/Head (24-27)
7	Status	Command

(a)

7	6	5	4	3	2	1	0
1	LBA	1	D	HS3	HS2	HS1	HS0

LBA: 0 = Cylinder/Head/Sector Mode
           1 = Logical Block Addressing Mode
D: 0 = master drive
           1 = slave drive
HSn: CHS mode: Head Select in CHS mode
           LBA mode: Block select bits 24 - 27

(b)

Figure 3-22. (a) The control registers of an IDE hard disk controller. The numbers in parentheses are the bits of the logical block address selected by each register in LBA mode. (b) The fields of the Select Drive/Head register.

occur, independently of the details of the data transferred. This is true of the command register on the AT disk controller. In use, data are written to the lower-numbered registers to select the disk address to be read from or written to, and then the command register is written last with an operation code. The act of writing the operation code into the command register starts the operation.

It is also the case that the use of some registers or fields in the registers may vary with different modes of operation. In the example given in the figure, writing a 0 or a 1 to the LBA bit, bit 6 of register 6, selects whether CHS (Cylinder-Head-Sector) or LBA (Linear Block Addressing) mode is used. The data written to or read from registers 3, 4, and 5, and the low four bits of register 6 are interpreted differently according to the setting of the LBA bit.

Now let us look at how a command is sent to the controller by calling *com_out* (line 10771). Before changing any registers, the status register is read to determine that the controller is not busy. This is done by testing the *STATUS_BSY* bit. Speed is important here, and normally the disk controller is ready or will be ready in a short time, so busy waiting is used. On line 10779 *waitfor* is called to test *STATUS_BSY*. To maximize the speed of response, *waitfor* is a macro, defined on line 10268. It makes the required test once, avoiding an expensive function call on most calls, when the disk is ready. On the rare occasions when a wait is necessary, it then calls *w_waitfor*, which executes the test in a loop until it is true or a predefined timeout period elapses. Thus the returned value will be true with the minimum possible delay if the controller is ready, true after a delay if it is temporarily unavailable, or false if it is not ready after the timeout period. We will have more to say about the timeout when we discuss *w_waitfor* itself.

A controller can handle more than one drive, so once it is determined that the controller is ready, a byte is written to select the drive, head, and mode of operation (line 10785) and then *waitfor* is called again. A disk drive sometimes fails to carry out a command or to properly return an error code—it is, after all, a mechanical device that can stick, jam, or break internally—and as insurance a message is sent to the clock task to schedule a call to a wakeup routine. Following this, the command is issued by first writing all the parameters to the various registers and finally writing the command code itself to the command register. The latter step and the subsequent modification of the *w_command* and *w_status* variables is a critical section, so the entire sequence is bracketed by calls to *lock* and *unlock* (lines 10801 to 10805) which disable and then reenable interrupts.

The next several functions are short. We noted that *w_need_reset* (line 10813) is called by *w_finish* when the failure count hits half of *MAX_ERRORS*. It is also called when timeouts occur while waiting for the disk to interrupt or become ready. The action of *w_need_reset* is just to mark the *state* variable for every drive in the *wini* array to force initialization on the next access.

W_do_close (line 10828) has very little to do for a conventional hard disk. When support is added for CD-ROMs or other removable devices, this routine will have to be extended to generate a command to unlock the door or eject the CD, depending upon what the hardware supports.

Com_simple is called to issue controller commands that terminate immediately without a data transfer phase. Commands that fall into this category include those that retrieve the disk identification, setting of some parameters, and recalibration.

When *com_out* calls the clock task to prepare for a possible rescue after a disk controller failure, it passes the address of *w_timeout* (line 10858) as the function for the clock task to awaken when the timeout period expires. Usually the disk completes the requested operation and when the timeout occurs, *w_command* will be found to have the value *CMD_IDLE*, meaning the disk completed its operation, and *w_timeout* can then terminate. If the command does not complete and the operation is a read or write, it may help to reduce the size of I/O requests. This is done in two steps, first reducing the maximum number of sectors that can be requested to 8, and then to 1. For all timeouts a message is printed, *w_need_reset* is called to force re-initialization of all drives on the next attempted access, and *interrupt* is called to deliver a message to the disk task and simulate the hardware-generated interrupt that should have occurred at the end of the disk operation.

When a reset is required, *w_reset* (line 10889) is called. This function makes use of a function provided by the clock driver, *milli_delay*. After an initial delay to give the drive time to recover from previous operations, a bit in the disk controller's control register is **strobed**—that is, brought to a logical 1 level for a definite period, then returned to the logical 0 level. Following this operation, *waitfor* is called to give the drive a reasonable period to signal it is ready. In case the reset does not succeed, a message is printed and an error status returned. It is left to the caller to decide what to do next.

Commands to the disk that involve data transfer normally terminate by generating an interrupt, which sends a message back to the disk task. In fact, an interrupt is generated for each sector read or written. Thus, after issuing such a command, *w_intr_wait* (line 10925) will always be called. In turn, *w_intr_wait* calls *receive* in a loop, ignoring the contents of each message, waiting for an interrupt that sets *w_status* to "not busy." Once such a message is received, the status of the request is checked. This is another critical section, so *lock* and *unlock* are used here to guarantee that a new interrupt will not occur and change *w_status* before the various steps involved are complete.

We have seen several places where the macro *waitfor* is called to do busy waiting on a bit in the disk controller status register. After the initial test, the *waitfor* macro calls *w_waitfor* (line 10955), which calls *milli_start* to begin a timer and then enters a loop that alternately checks the status register and the timer. If a timeout occurs, *w_need_reset* is called to set things up for a reset of the disk controller the next time its services are requested.

The *TIMEOUT* parameter used by *w_waitfor* is defined on line 10206 as 32 seconds. A similar parameter, *WAKEUP* (line 10193), used to schedule wakeups from the clock task, is set to 31 seconds. These are very long periods of time to spend busy waiting, when you consider that an ordinary process only gets 100 msec to run before it will be evicted. But, these numbers are based upon the published standard for interfacing disk devices to AT-class computers, which states that up to 31 seconds must be allowed for a disk to "spin up" to speed. The fact is, of course, that this is a worst-case specification, and that on most systems spin up will only occur at power-on time, or possibly after long periods of inactivity. MINIX is still being developed. It is possible that a new way of handling timeouts may be called for when support for CD-ROMs (or other devices which must spin up frequently) is added.

W_handler (line 10976) is the interrupt handler. The address of this function is put into the Interrupt Descriptor Table by *w_identify* when the hard disk task is first activated. When a disk interrupt occurs, the disk controller status register is copied to *w_status* and then the *interrupt* function in the kernel is called to reschedule the hard disk task. When this occurs, of course, the hard disk task is already blocked as a result of a previous call to *receive* from *w_intr_wait* after initiation of a disk operation.

The last function in *at_wini.c* is *w_geometry*. It returns the logical maximum cylinder, head, and sector values of the selected hard disk device. In this case the numbers are real ones, not made up as they were for the RAM disk driver.

3.7.5 Floppy Disk Handling

The floppy disk driver is longer and more complicated than the hard disk driver. This may seem paradoxical, since floppy disk mechanisms would appear to be simpler than those of hard disks, but the simpler mechanism has a simpler controller that requires more attention from the operating system, and the fact that the medium is removable adds some complications. In this section we will describe some of the things an implementor has to consider in dealing with floppy disks. However, we will not go into the details of the MINIX floppy disk driver code. The most important parts are similar to those for the hard disk.

One of the things we do not have to worry about with the floppy driver is the multiple types of controller to support that we had to deal with in the case of the hard disk driver. Although the high-density floppy disks currently used were not supported in the design of the original IBM PC, the floppy disk controllers of all computers in the IBM PC family are supported by a single software driver. The contrast with the hard disk situation is probably due to lack of pressure to increase floppy disk performance. Floppy disks are rarely used as working storage during operation of a computer system; their speed and data capacity are too limited compared to those of hard disks. Floppy disks remain important for distribution of new software and for backup, so almost all small computer systems are equipped with at least one floppy drive.

The floppy disk driver does not use the SSF or the elevator algorithm. It is strictly sequential, accepting a request and carrying it out before even accepting another request. In the original design of MINIX it was felt that, since MINIX was intended for use on personal computer, most of the time there would be only one process active, and the chance of a disk request arriving while another was being carried out was small. Thus there would be little to gain from the considerable increase in software complexity that would be required for queueing requests. It is even less worthwhile now, since floppy disks are rarely used for anything but transferring data into or out of a system with a hard disk.

That said, even though there is no support in the driver software for reordering requests, the floppy driver, like any other block driver, can handle a request for scattered I/O, and just like the hard disk driver, the floppy driver collects requests in an array and continues to collect such requests as long as sequential sectors are requested. However, in the case of the floppy driver the array of requests is smaller than for the hard disk, limited to the maximum number of sectors per track on a floppy diskette. In addition, the floppy driver pays attention to the *OPTIONAL* flag in scattered I/O requests and does not proceed to a new track if all current requests are optional.

The simplicity of the floppy disk hardware is responsible for some of the complications in floppy disk driver software. Cheap, slow, low-capacity floppy drives do not justify the sophisticated integrated controllers that are part of modern hard drives, so the driver software has to deal explicitly with aspects of disk operation that are hidden in the operation of a hard drive. As an example of a complication caused by the simplicity of floppy drives, consider positioning the read/write head to a particular track during a *SEEK* operation. No hard disk has ever required the driver software to explicitly call for a *SEEK*. For a hard disk the cylinder, head, and sector geometry visible to the programmer may not correspond to the physical geometry, and, in fact, the physical geometry may be quite complicated, with more sectors on outer cylinders than on inner ones. This is not visible to the user, however. Hard disks may accept Logical Block Addressing (LBA), addressing by the absolute sector number on the disk, as an alternative to cylinder, head, and sector addressing. Even if addressing is done by cylinder, head, and sector, any geometry that does not address nonexistent sectors may be used, since the integrated controller on the disk calculates where to move the read/write heads and does a seek operation when required.

For a floppy disk, however, explicit programming of *SEEK* operations is needed. In case a *SEEK* fails, it is necessary to provide a routine to perform a *RECALIBRATE* operation, which forces the heads to cylinder 0. This makes it possible for the controller to advance them to a desired track position by stepping the heads a known number of times. Similar operations are necessary for the hard drive, of course, but the drive controller handles them without detailed guidance from the device driver software.

Some characteristics of a floppy disk drive that complicate its driver are:

1. Removable media.

2. Multiple disk formats.

3. Motor control.

Some hard disk controllers provide for removable media, for instance, on a CD-ROM drive, but the drive controller is generally able to handle any complications without much support in the device driver software. With a floppy disk, however, the built-in support is not there, and yet it is needed more. Some of the most common uses for floppy disks—installing new software or backing up files—are likely to require switching of disks in and out of the drives. It can cause grief if data that were intended for one diskette are written onto another diskette. The device driver should do what it can to prevent this, although this is not always possible, as not all floppy drive hardware allows determination of whether the drive door has been opened since the last access. Another problem that can be caused by removable media is that a system can become hung up if an attempt is made to access a floppy drive that currently has no diskette inserted. This can be solved if an open door can be detected, but since this is not always possible some provision must be made for a timeout and an error return if an operation on a floppy disk does not terminate in a reasonable time.

Removable media can be replaced with other media, and in the case of floppy disks there are many different possible formats. MINIX hardware supports both 3.5-inch and 5.25-inch disk drives and the diskettes can be formatted in a variety of ways to hold from 360 KB up to 1.2 MB (on a 5.25-inch diskette) or 1.44 MB (on a 3.5-inch diskette). MINIX supports seven different floppy disk formats. There are two possible solutions to the problem this causes, and MINIX allows for both of them. One way is to refer to each possible format as a distinct drive and provide multiple minor devices. MINIX does this, and in the device directory you will find fourteen different devices defined, ranging from */dev/pc0*, a 360K 5.25-inch diskette in the first drive, to */dev/PS1*, a 1.44M 3.5-inch diskette in the second drive. Remembering the different combinations is cumbersome, and a second alternative is provided. When the first floppy disk drive is addressed as */dev/fd0*, or the second as */dev/fd1*, the floppy disk driver tests the diskette currently in the drive when it is accessed, in order to determine the format. Some formats have more cylinders, and others have more sectors per track than other formats. Determination of the format of a diskette is done by attempting to read the higher numbered sectors and tracks. By a process of elimination the format can be determined. This does, of course, take time, and a disk with bad sectors could be misidentified.

The final complication of the floppy disk driver is motor control. Diskettes cannot be read or written unless they are revolving. Hard disks are designed to run for thousands of hours on end without wearing out, but leaving the motors on all the time causes a floppy drive and diskette to wear out quickly. If the motor is not already on when a drive is accessed, it is necessary to issue a command to start the drive and then to wait about a half second before attempting to read or write data. Turning the motors on or off is slow, so MINIX leaves a drive motor on for a few seconds after a drive is used. If the drive is used again within this interval, the timer is extended for another few seconds. If the drive is not used in this interval, the motor is turned off.

3.8 CLOCKS

Clocks (also called **timers**) are essential to the operation of any timesharing system for a variety of reasons. They maintain the time of day and prevent one process from monopolizing the CPU, among other things. The clock software can take the form of a device driver, even though a clock is neither a block device, like a disk, nor a character device, like a terminal. Our examination of clocks will follow the same pattern as in the previous sections: first a look at clock hardware and software in general, and then a closer look at how these ideas are applied in MINIX.

3.8.1 Clock Hardware

Two types of clocks are commonly used in computers, and both are quite different from the clocks and watches used by people. The simpler clocks are tied to the 110- or 220-volt power line, and cause an interrupt on every voltage cycle, at 50 or 60 Hz.

The other kind of clock is built out of three components: a crystal oscillator, a counter, and a holding register, as shown in Fig. 3-23. When a piece of quartz crystal is properly cut and mounted under tension, it can be made to generate a periodic signal of very high accuracy, typically in the range of 5 to 100 MHz, depending on the crystal chosen. At least one such circuit is usually found in any computer, providing a synchronizing signal to the computer's various circuits. This signal is fed into the counter to make it count down to zero. When the counter gets to zero, it causes a CPU interrupt.

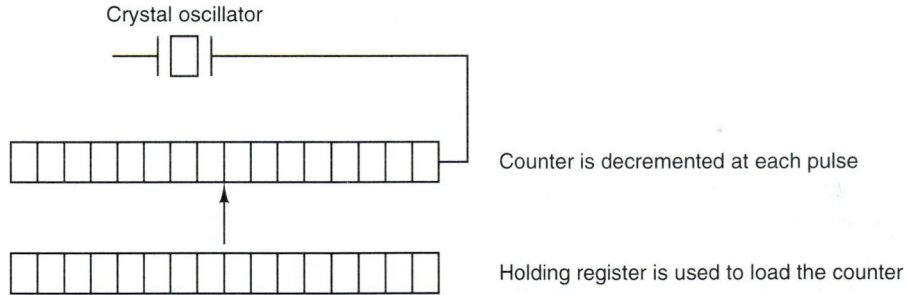

Figure 3-23. A programmable clock.

Programmable clocks typically have several modes of operation. In **one-shot mode**, when the clock is started, it copies the value of the holding register into the counter and then decrements the counter at each pulse from the crystal. When the counter gets to zero, it causes an interrupt and stops until it is explicitly started again by the software. In **square-wave mode**, after getting to zero and causing the interrupt, the holding register is automatically copied into the counter, and the whole process is repeated again indefinitely. These periodic interrupts are called **clock ticks**.

The advantage of the programmable clock is that its interrupt frequency can be controlled by software. If a 1-MHz crystal is used, then the counter is pulsed every microsecond. With 16-bit registers, interrupts can be programmed to occur at intervals from 1 microsecond to 65.536 milliseconds. Programmable clock chips usually contain two or three independently programmable clocks and have many other options as well (e.g., counting up instead of down, interrupts disabled, and more).

To prevent the current time from being lost when the computer's power is turned off, most computers have a battery-powered backup clock, implemented with the kind of low-power circuitry used in digital watches. The battery clock can be read at startup. If the backup clock is not present, the software may ask the user for the current date and time. There is also a standard protocol for a networked system to get the current time from a remote host. In any case the time is then translated into the number of clock ticks since 12 A.M. **Universal Coordinated Time (UTC)** (formerly known as Greenwich Mean Time) on Jan. 1, 1970, as UNIX and MINIX do, or since some other benchmark. At every clock tick, the real time is incremented by one count. Usually utility programs are provided to manually set the system clock and the backup clock and to synchronize the two clocks.

3.8.2 Clock Software

All the clock hardware does is generate interrupts at known intervals. Everything else involving time must be done by the software, the clock driver. The exact duties of the clock driver vary among operating systems, but usually include most of the following:

1. Maintaining the time of day.

2. Preventing processes from running longer than they are allowed to.

3. Accounting for CPU usage.

4. Handling the ALARM system call made by user processes.

5. Providing watchdog timers for parts of the system itself.

6. Doing profiling, monitoring, and statistics gathering.

The first clock function, maintaining the time of day (also called the **real time**) is not difficult. It just requires incrementing a counter at each clock tick, as mentioned before. The only thing to watch out for is the number of bits in the time-of-day counter. With a clock rate of 60 Hz, a 32-bit counter will overflow in just over 2 years. Clearly the system cannot store the real time as the number of ticks since Jan. 1, 1970 in 32 bits.

Three approaches can be taken to solve this problem. The first way is to use a 64-bit counter, although doing so makes maintaining the counter more expensive since it has to be done many times a second. The second way is to maintain the time of day in seconds, rather than in ticks, using a subsidiary counter to count ticks until a whole second has been accumulated. Because 2^{32} seconds is more than 136 years, this method will work until well into the twenty-second century.

The third approach is to count in ticks, but to do that relative to the time the system was booted, rather than relative to a fixed external moment. When the backup clock is read or the user types in the real time, the system boot time is calculated from the current time-of-day value and stored in memory in any convenient form. Later, when the time of day is requested, the stored time of day is added to the counter to get the current time of day. All three approaches are shown in Fig. 3-24.

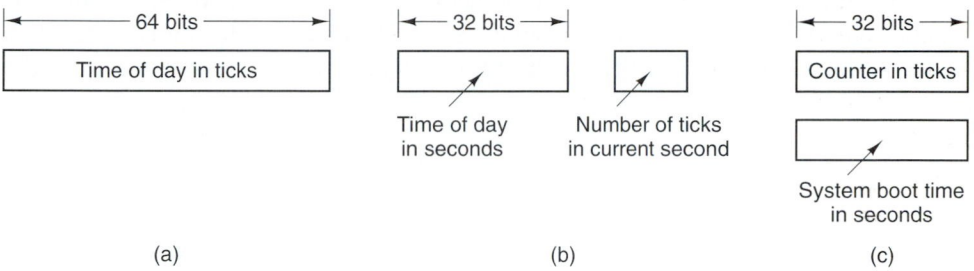

Figure 3-24. Three ways to maintain the time of day.

The second clock function is preventing processes from running too long. Whenever a process is started, the scheduler should initialize a counter to the value of that process' quantum in clock ticks. At every clock interrupt, the clock driver decrements the quantum counter by 1. When it gets to zero, the clock driver calls the scheduler to set up another process.

The third clock function is doing CPU accounting. The most accurate way to do it is to start a second timer, distinct from the main system timer, whenever a process is started. When that process is stopped, the timer can be read out to tell how long the process has run. To do things right, the second timer should be saved when an interrupt occurs and restored afterward.

A less accurate, but much simpler, way to do accounting is to maintain a pointer to the process table entry for the currently running process in a global variable. At every clock tick, a field in the current process' entry is incremented. In this way, every clock tick is "charged" to the process running at the time of the tick. A minor problem with this strategy is that if many interrupts occur during a process' run, it is still charged for a full tick, even though it did not get much work done. Properly accounting for the CPU during interrupts is too expensive and is never done.

In MINIX and many other systems, a process can request that the operating system give it a warning after a certain interval. The warning is usually a signal, interrupt, message, or something similar. One application requiring such warnings is networking, in which a packet not acknowledged within a certain time interval must be retransmitted. Another application is computer-aided instruction, where a student not providing a response within a certain time is told the answer.

If the clock driver had enough clocks, it could set a separate clock for each request. This not being the case, it must simulate multiple virtual clocks with a single physical clock. One way is to maintain a table in which the signal time for all pending timers is kept, as well as a variable giving the time of the next one. Whenever the time of day is updated, the driver checks to see if the closest signal has occurred. If it has, the table is searched for the next one to occur.

If many signals are expected, it is more efficient to simulate multiple clocks by chaining all the pending clock requests together, sorted on time, in a linked list, as shown in Fig. 3-25. Each entry on the list tells how many clock ticks following the previous one to wait before causing a signal. In this example, signals are pending for 4203, 4207, 4213, 4215, and 4216.

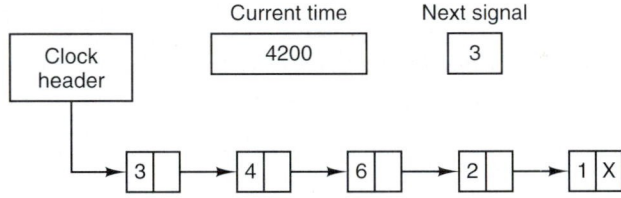

Figure 3-25. Simulating multiple timers with a single clock.

In Fig. 3-25, the next interrupt occurs in 3 ticks. On each tick, *Next signal* is decremented. When it gets to 0, the signal corresponding to the first item on the list is caused, and that item is removed from the list. Then *Next signal* is set to the value in the entry now at the head of the list, in this example, 4.

Note that during a clock interrupt, the clock driver has several things to do—increment the real time, decrement the quantum and check for 0, do CPU accounting, and decrement the alarm counter. However, each of these operations has been carefully arranged to be very fast because they have to be repeated many times a second.

Parts of the operating system also need to set timers. These are called **watchdog timers**. When studying the hard disk driver, we saw that a wakeup call is scheduled each time the disk controller is sent a command, so an attempt at recovery can be made if the command fails completely. We also mentioned that floppy disk drivers have to wait for the disk motor to get up to speed and must shut down the motor if no activity occurs for a while. Some printers with a movable print head can print at 120 characters/sec (8.3 msec/character) but cannot return the print head to the left margin in 8.3 msec, so the terminal driver must delay after typing a carriage return.

The mechanism used by the clock driver to handle watchdog timers is the same as for user signals. The only difference is that when a timer goes off, instead of causing a signal, the clock driver calls a procedure supplied by the caller. The procedure is part of the caller's code, but since all the drivers are in the same address space, the clock driver can call it anyway. The called procedure can do whatever is necessary, even causing an interrupt, although within the kernel interrupts are often inconvenient and signals do not exist. That is why the watchdog mechanism is provided.

The last thing in our list is profiling. Some operating systems provide a mechanism by which a user program can have the system build up a histogram of its program counter, so it can see where it is spending its time. When profiling is a possibility, at every tick the driver checks to see if the current process is being profiled, and if so, computes the bin number (a range of addresses) corresponding to the current program counter. It then increments that bin by one. This mechanism can also be used to profile the system itself.

3.8.3 Overview of the Clock Driver in MINIX

The MINIX clock driver is contained in the file *clock.c*. The clock task accepts these six message types, with the parameters shown:

1. HARD_INT
2. GET_UPTIME
3. GET_TIME
4. SET_TIME (new time in seconds)
5. SET_ALARM (process number, procedure to call, delay)
6. SET_SYN_AL (process number, delay)

HARD_INT is the message sent to the driver when a clock interrupt occurs and there is work to do, such as when an alarm must be sent or a process has run too long.

GET_UPTIME is used to get the time in ticks since boot time, *GET_TIME* returns the current real time as the number of seconds elapsed since Jan. 1, 1970 at 12:00 A.M., and *SET_TIME* sets the real time. It can only be invoked by the super-user.

Internal to the clock driver, the time is kept track of using the method of Fig. 3-24(c). When the time is set, the driver computes when the system was booted. It can make this computation because it has the current real time and it also knows how many ticks the system has been running. The system stores the real time of the boot in a variable. Later, when *GET_TIME* is called, it converts the current value of the tick counter to seconds and adds it to the stored boot time.

SET_ALARM allows a process to set a timer that goes off in a specified number of clock ticks. When a user process does an ALARM call, it sends a message to the memory manager, which then sends this message to the clock driver. When the alarm goes off, the clock driver sends a message back to the memory manager, which then takes care of making the signal happen.

SET_ALARM is also used by tasks that need to start a watchdog timer. When the timer goes off, the procedure provided is simply called. The clock driver has no knowledge of what the procedure does.

SET_SYN_AL is similar to *SET_ALARM*, but is used to set a **synchronous alarm**. A synchronous alarm sends a message to a process, rather than generating a signal or calling a procedure. The synchronous alarm task handles dispatching messages to the processes that require them. Synchronous alarms will be discussed in detail later.

The clock task uses no major data structures, but there are several variables used to keep track of time. Only one is a global variable, *lost_ticks*, defined in *glo.h* (line 5031). This variable is provided for the use of any driver that may be added to MINIX in the future that might disable interrupts long enough that one or more clock ticks could be lost. It currently is not used, but if such a driver were to be written the programmer could cause *lost_ticks* to be incremented to compensate for the time during which clock interrupts were inhibited.

Obviously, clock interrupts occur very frequently, and fast handling of the clock interrupt is important. MINIX achieves this by doing the bare minimum amount of processing on most clock interrupts. Upon receipt of an interrupt the handler sets a local variable, *ticks*, to *lost_ticks* + 1 and then uses this quantity to update accounting times and *pending_ticks* (line 11079) and resets *lost_ticks* to zero. *Pending_ticks* is a *PRIVATE* variable, declared outside of all function definitions, but known only to functions defined in *clock.c*. Another *PRIVATE* variable, *sched_ticks*, is decremented on each tick to keep track of execution time. The interrupt handler sends a message to the clock task only if an alarm is due or an execution quantum has been used. This scheme results in the interrupt handler returning almost immediately on most interrupts.

When the clock task receives any message, it adds *pending_ticks* to the variable *realtime* (line 11067) and then zeroes *pending_ticks*. *Realtime*, together with the variable *boot_time* (line 11068), allows the current time of day to be computed. These are both *PRIVATE* variables, so the only way for any other part of the system to get the time is by sending a message to the clock task. Although at any instant *realtime* may be inaccurate, this mechanism ensures it is always accurate when needed. If your watch is correct when you look at it, does it matter if it is incorrect when you are not looking?

To handle alarms, *next_alarm* records the time when the next signal or watchdog call may happen. The driver has to be careful here, because the process requesting the signal may exit or be killed before the signal happens. When it is time for the signal, a check is made to see if it is still needed. If it is not needed, it is not carried out.

Each user process is allowed to have only one outstanding alarm timer. Executing an ALARM call while the timer is still running cancels the first timer.

Therefore, a convenient way to store the timers is to reserve one word in the process table entry for each process for its timer, if any. For tasks, the function to be called must also be stored somewhere, so an array, *watch_dog*, has been provided for this purpose. A similar array, *syn_table*, stores flags to indicate for each process if it is due to receive a synchronous alarm.

The overall logic of the clock driver follows the same pattern as the disk drivers. The main program is an endless loop that gets messages, dispatches on the message type, and then sends a reply (except for *CLOCK_TICK*). Each message type is handled by a separate procedure, following our standard naming convention of naming all the procedures called from the main loop *do_xxx*, where *xxx* is different for each one, of course. As an aside, unfortunately, many linkers truncate procedure names to seven or eight characters, so the names *do_set_time* and *do_set_alarm* are potentially in conflict. The latter has been renamed *do_setalarm*. This problem occurs throughout MINIX and is usually solved by mangling one of the names.

The Synchronous Alarm Task

There is a second task to be discussed in this section, the **synchronous alarm task**. A synchronous alarm is similar to an alarm, but instead of sending a signal or calling a watchdog function when the timeout period expires, the synchronous alarm task sends a message. A signal may arrive or a watchdog task may be called without any relation to what part of a task is executing, so alarms of these types are **asynchronous**. In contrast, a message is received only when the receiver has executed a *receive* call.

The synchronous alarm mechanism was added to MINIX to support the network server, which, like the memory manager and the file server, runs as a separate process. Frequently there is a need to set a limit on the time a process may be blocked while waiting for input. For instance, in a network, failure to receive an acknowledgement of a data packet within a definite period is probably due to a failure of transmission. A network server can set a synchronous alarm before it tries to receive a message and blocks. Since the synchronous alarm is delivered as a message, it will unblock the server eventually if no message is received from the network. Upon receiving any message the server must first reset the alarm. Then by examining the type or origin of the message, it can determine a packet has arrived or if it has been unblocked by a timeout. If it is the latter, then the server can try to recover, usually by resending the last unacknowledged packet.

A synchronous alarm is faster than an alarm sent using a signal, which requires several messages and a considerable amount of processing. A watchdog function is fast, but is only useful for tasks compiled into the same address space as the clock task. When a process is waiting for a message, a synchronous alarm is more appropriate and simpler than either signals or watchdog functions, and it is easily handled with little additional processing.

The Clock Interrupt Handler

As described earlier, when a clock interrupt occurs, *realtime* is not updated immediately. The interrupt service routine maintains the *pending_ticks* counter and does simple jobs like charging the current tick to a process and decrementing the quantum timer. A message is sent to the clock task only when more complicated jobs must be done. This is something of a compromise with the ideal of MINIX tasks that communicate totally by messages, but it is a practical concession to the reality that servicing clock ticks consumes CPU time. On a slow machine it was found that doing it this way resulted in a 15% increase in system speed relative to an implementation that sent a message to the clock task on every clock interrupt.

Millisecond Timing

As another concession to reality, a few routines are provided in *clock.c* that provide millisecond resolution timing. Delays as short as a millisecond are needed by various I/O devices. There is no practical way to do this using alarms and the message passing interface. The functions here are meant to be called directly by tasks. The technique used is the oldest and simplest I/O technique: polling. The counter that is used for generating the clock interrupts is read directly, as rapidly as possible, and the count is converted to milliseconds. The caller does this repeatedly until the desired time has elapsed.

Summary of Clock Services

Figure 3-26 summarizes the various services provided by *clock.c*. There are several ways to access the clock, and several ways the request can be honored. Some services are available to any process, with results returned in a message.

Uptime can be obtained by a function call from the kernel or a task, avoiding the overhead of a message. An alarm can be requested by a user process, with the eventual result being a signal, or by a task, causing activation of a watchdog function. Neither of these mechanisms can be used by a server process, but a server can ask for a synchronous alarm. A task or the kernel can request a delay using the *milli_delay* function, or it can incorporate calls to *milli_elapsed* into a polling routine, for instance, while waiting for input from a port.

3.8.4 Implementation of the Clock Driver in MINIX

When MINIX starts up, all the drivers are called. Most of them just try to get a message and block. The clock driver, *clock_task* (line 11098), does that too, but first it calls *init_clock* to initialize the programmable clock frequency to 60 Hz. When any message is received, it adds *pending_ticks* to *realtime* and then resets

Service	Access	Response	Clients
Gettime	System call	Message	Any process
Uptime	System call	Message	Any process
Uptime	Function call	Function value	Kernel or task
Alarm	System call	Signal	Any process
Alarm	System call	Watchdog activation	Task
Synchronous alarm	System call	Message	Server process
Milli_delay	Function call	Busy wait	Kernel or task
Milli_elapsed	Function call	Function value	Kernel or task

Figure 3-26. The clock code supports a number of time-related services.

pending_ticks before doing anything else. This operation could potentially conflict with a clock interrupt, so calls to *lock* and *unlock* are used to prevent a race (lines 11115 to 11118). Otherwise the main loop of the clock driver is essentially the same as the other drivers: a message is received, a function to do the required work is called, and a reply message is sent.

Do_clocktick (line 11140) is not called on each tick of the clock, so its name is not an exact description of its function. It is called when the interrupt handler has determined there might be something important to do. First a check is made to see if a signal or watchdog timer has gone off. If one has, all the alarm entries in the process table are inspected. Because ticks are not processed individually, several alarms may go off in one pass over the table. It is also possible that the process that was to receive the next alarm has already exited. When a process is found whose alarm is less than the current time, but not zero, the slot in the *watch_dog* array corresponding to that process is checked. In the C programming language a numeric value also has a logical value, so the test on line 11161 returns *TRUE* if a valid address is stored in the *watch_dog* slot, and the corresponding function is called indirectly on line 11163. If a **null pointer** is found (represented in C by a value of zero), the test evaluates to *FALSE* and *cause_sig* is called to send a *SIGALRM* signal. The *watch_dog* slot is also used when a synchronous alarm is needed. In that case the address stored is the address of *cause_alarm*, rather than the address of a watchdog function belonging to a particular task. For sending a signal we could have stored the address of *cause_sig* but then we would have had to have written *cause_sig* differently, to expect no arguments and get the target process number from a global variable. Alternatively, we could have required all watchdog processes to expect an argument they do not need.

We will discuss *cause_sig* when we discuss the system task in a subsequent section. Its job is to send a message to the memory manager. This requires a check to see if the memory manager is currently waiting for a message. If so, it sends a message telling about the alarm. If the memory manager is busy, a note is made to inform it at the first opportunity.

While looping through the process table inspecting the *p_alarm* value for each process, *next_alarm* is updated. Before starting the loop it is set to a very large number (line 11151), and then, for each process whose alarm value is nonzero after sending alarms or signals, a comparison is made between the process' alarm and *next_alarm*, which is set to the smaller value (lines 11171 and 11172).

After processing alarms, *do_clocktick* goes on to see if it is time to schedule another process. The execution quantum is maintained in the *PRIVATE* variable *sched_ticks*, which is normally decremented by the clock interrupt handler on every clock tick. However, on those ticks when *do_clocktick* is activated, it is not decremented by the handler, allowing *do_clocktick* itself to do this and test for a zero result on line 11178. *Sched_ticks* is not reset whenever a new process is scheduled (because the file system and memory manager are allowed to run to completion). Instead it is reset after every *SCHED_RATE* ticks. The comparison on line 11179 is to make sure that the current process has actually run at least one full scheduler tick before taking the CPU away from it.

The next procedure, *do_getuptime* (line 11189), is just one line; it puts the current value of *realtime* (the number of ticks since boot) into the proper field in the message to be returned. Any process can find the elapsed time this way, but the message overhead is a big price to ask of tasks, so a related function, *get_uptime* (line 11200) is provided that can be called directly by tasks. Since it is not invoked via a message to the clock task, it has to add pending ticks to the current *realtime* itself. *Lock* and *unlock* are necessary here to prevent a clock interrupt occurring while *pending_ticks* is being accessed.

To get the current real time, *do_get_time* (line 11219) computes the current real time from *realtime* and *boot_time* (the system boot time in seconds). *Do_set_time* (line 11230) is its complement. It computes a new value for *boot_time* based on the given current real time and number of ticks since booting.

The procedures *do_setalarm* (line 11242) and *do_setsyn_alrm* (line 11269) are so similar we will discuss them together. Both extract the parameters that specify the process to be signaled and the time to wait from the message. *Do_setalarm* also extracts a function to call (line 11257), although a few lines farther on it replaces this value with a null pointer if the target process is a user process and not a task. We have already seen how this pointer is later tested in *do_clocktick* to determine whether the target should get a signal or a call to a watchdog. The time remaining to the alarm (in seconds) is also calculated by both functions and set into the return message. Both then call *common_setalarm* to finish up. In the case of the *do_setsyn_alarm* call, the function parameter passed to *common_setalarm* is always *cause_alarm*.

Common_setalarm (line 11291) finishes the work started by either of the two functions just discussed. Then it stores the alarm time in the process table and the pointer to the watchdog procedure (which may also be a pointer to *cause_alarm* or a null pointer) in the *watch_dog* array. Then it scans the entire process table to find the next alarm, just as is done by *do_clocktick*.

Cause_alarm (line 11318) is simple; it sets to *TRUE* an entry in the *syn_table* array corresponding to the target of the synchronous alarm. If the synchronous alarm task is not alive, it is sent a message to wake it up.

Implementation of the Synchronous Alarm Task

The synchronous alarm task, *syn_alarm_task* (line 11333), follows the basic model of all tasks. It initializes and then enters an endless loop in which it receives and sends messages. The initialization consists of declaring itself alive by setting the variable *syn_al_alive* to *TRUE* and then declaring that it has nothing to do by setting all the entries in *syn_table* to *FALSE*. There is a slot in *syn_table* for each slot in the process table. In begins its outer loop by declaring it has completed its work and then enters an inner loop where it checks all slots in *syn_table*. If it finds an entry indicating a synchronous alarm is expected, it resets the entry, sends a message of type *CLOCK_INT* to the appropriate process, and declares its work not complete. At the bottom of its outer loop it does not pause to wait for any new messages unless its *work_done* flag is set. A new message is not needed to tell it there is more work to do, since *cause_alarm* writes directly into *syn_table*. A message is needed only to wake it up after it has run out of work. The effect is that it cycles very rapidly as long as there are alarms to be delivered.

In fact, this task is not used by the distribution version of MINIX. If you recompile MINIX to add networking support, it will be used by the network server, however, which needs exactly this kind of mechanism to enforce rapid timeouts if packets are not received when expected. In addition to the need for speed, a server cannot be sent a signal, since servers must run forever, and the default action of most signals is to kill the target process.

Implementation of the Clock Interrupt Handler

The design of the clock interrupt handler is a compromise between doing very little (so the processing time will be minimized) and doing enough to make expensive activations of the clock task infrequent. It changes a few variables and tests a few others. *Clock_handler* (line 11374) starts off by doing system accounting. MINIX keeps track of both user time and system time. User time is charged against a process if it is running when the clock ticks. System time is charged if the file system or memory manager is running. The variable *bill_ptr* always points to the last user process scheduled (the two servers do not count). The billing is done on lines 11447 and 11448. After billing is finished, the most important variable maintained by *clock_handler*, *pending_ticks*, is incremented (line

11450). The real time must be known for testing whether *clock_handler* should wake up the tty or send a message to the clock task, but actually updating *realtime* itself is expensive, because this operation must be done using locks. To avoid this, the handler calculates its own version of the real time in the local variable *now*. There is a small chance that the result will be incorrect once in a while, but the consequences of such an error would not be serious.

The rest of the handler's work depends upon various tests. The terminal and the printer both need to be awakened from time to time. *Tty_timeout* is a global variable, maintained by the terminal task, which holds the next time the tty should be awakened. For the printer several variables which are *PRIVATE* within the printer module need to be checked, and they are tested in the call to *pr_restart*, which returns quickly even in the worst case of the printer being hung up. On lines 11455 to 11458 a test is made that activates the clock task if an alarm is due or if it is time to schedule another task. The latter test is complex, a logical AND of three simpler tests. The

```
interrupt(CLOCK);
```

code on line 11459 results in a *HARD_INT* message to the clock task.

In discussing *do_clocktick* we noted that it decrements *sched_ticks* and tests for zero to see if the execution quantum has expired. Testing whether *sched_ticks* is equal to one is part of the complex test we mentioned above; if the clock task is not activated, it is still necessary to decrement *sched_ticks* within the interrupt handler and, if it reaches zero, reset the quantum. If this occurs, it is also time to note that the current process was active at the start of the new quantum; this is done by the assignment of the current value of *bill_ptr* to *prev_ptr* on line 11466.

Time Utilities

Finally, *clock.c* contains some functions that provide various kinds of support. Many of these are hardware specific and will need to be replaced for a port of MINIX to non-Intel hardware. We will only describe the function of these, without going into details of their internals.

Init_clock (line 11474) is called by the timer task when it runs for the first time. It sets the mode and time delay of the timer chip to produce clock tick interrupts 60 times per second. Despite the fact that the "CPU speed" one sees in advertisements for PCs has increased from 4.77 Mhz for the original IBM PC to over 200 Mhz for modern systems, the constant *TIMER_COUNT*, used to initialize the timer, is the same no matter what PC model MINIX is run on. Every IBM compatible PC, no matter how fast its processor runs, provides a 14.3 Mhz signal for use by various devices that need a time reference. Serial communications lines and the video display also need such a timing reference.

The complement of *init_clock* is *clock_stop* (line 11489). It is not really necessary, but it is a concession to the fact that MINIX users may want to start another operating system at times. It simply resets the timer chip parameters to the default mode of operation that MS-DOS and other operating systems may expect the ROM BIOS to have provided when they first start.

Milli_delay (line 11502) is provided for use by any task that needs very short delays. It is written in C without any hardware-specific references, but it uses a technique one might expect to find only in a low-level assembly language routine. It initializes a counter to zero and then rapidly polls it until a desired value is reached. In Chapter 2 we said that this technique of busy waiting should generally be avoided, but the necessities of implementation can require exceptions to general rules. The initialization of the counter is done by the next function, *milli_start* (line 11516), which simply zeroes two variables. The polling is done by calling the last function, *milli_elapsed* (line 11529), which accesses the timer hardware. The counter that is examined is the same one used to count down clock ticks, and thus it can underflow and be reset to its maximum value before the desired delay is complete. *Milli_elapsed* corrects for this.

3.9 TERMINALS

Every general purpose computer has one or more terminals used to communicate with it. Terminals come in an extremely large number of different forms. It is up to the terminal driver to hide all these differences, so that the device-independent part of the operating system and the user programs do not have to be rewritten for each kind of terminal. In the following sections we will follow our now-standard approach of first discussing terminal hardware and software in general, and then discussing the MINIX software.

3.9.1 Terminal Hardware

From the operating system's point of view, terminals can be divided into three broad categories based on how the operating system communicates with them. The first category consists of memory-mapped terminals, which consist of a keyboard and a display, both of which are hardwired to the computer. The second category consists of terminals that interface via a serial communication line using the RS-232 standard, most frequently over a modem. The third category consists of terminals that are connected to the computer via a network. This taxonomy is shown in Fig. 3-27.

Memory-Mapped Terminals

The first broad category of terminals named in Fig. 3-27 consists of memory-mapped terminals. These are an integral part of the computers themselves. Memory-mapped terminals are interfaced via a special memory called a **video**

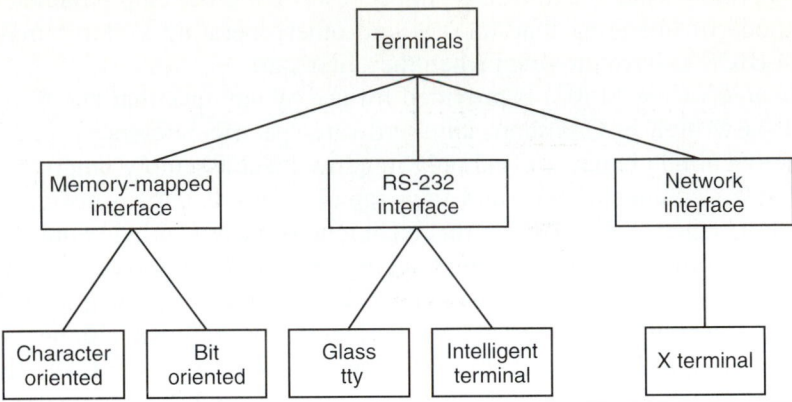

Figure 3-27. Terminal types.

RAM, which forms part of the computer's address space and is addressed by the CPU the same way as the rest of memory (see Fig. 3-28).

Also on the video RAM card is a chip called a **video controller**. This chip pulls character codes out of the video RAM and generates the video signal used to drive the display (monitor). The monitor generates a beam of electrons that scans horizontally across the screen, painting lines on it. Typically the screen has 480 to 1024 lines from top to bottom, with 640 to 1200 points per line. These points are called **pixels**. The video controller signal modulates the electron beam, determining whether a given pixel will be light or dark. Color monitors have three beams, for red, green, and blue, which are independently modulated.

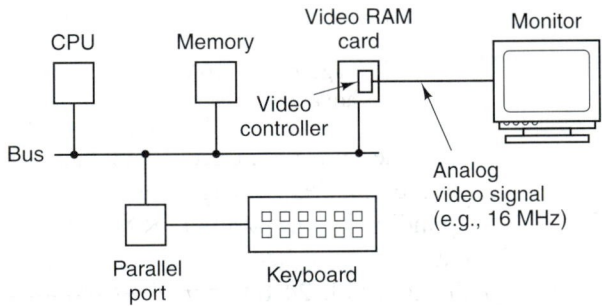

Figure 3-28. Memory-mapped terminals write directly into video RAM.

A simple monochrome display might fit each character in a box 9 pixels wide by 14 pixels high (including the space between characters), and have 25 lines of 80 characters. The display would then have 350 scan lines of 720 pixels each. Each of these frames is redrawn 45 to 70 times a second. The video controller could be designed to fetch the first 80 characters from the video RAM, generate 14 scan lines, fetch the next 80 characters from the video RAM, generate the following 14 scan lines, and so on. In fact, most fetch each character once per scan line to eliminate the need for buffering in the controller. The 9-by-14 bit patterns for the characters are kept in a ROM used by the video controller. (RAM may also be used to support custom fonts.) The ROM is addressed by a 12-bit address, 8 bits from the character code and 4 bits to specify a scan line. The 8 bits in each byte of the ROM control 8 pixels; the 9th pixel between characters is always blank. Thus $14 \times 80 = 1120$ memory references to the video RAM are needed per line of text on the screen. The same number of references are made to the character generator ROM.

The IBM PC has several modes for the screen. In the simplest one, it uses a character-mapped display for the console. In Fig. 3-29(a) we see a portion of the video RAM. Each character on the screen of Fig. 3-29(b) occupies two characters in the RAM. The low-order character is the ASCII code for the character to be displayed. The high-order character is the attribute byte, which is used to specify the color, reverse video, blinking, and so on. The full screen of 25 by 80 characters requires 4000 bytes of video RAM in this mode.

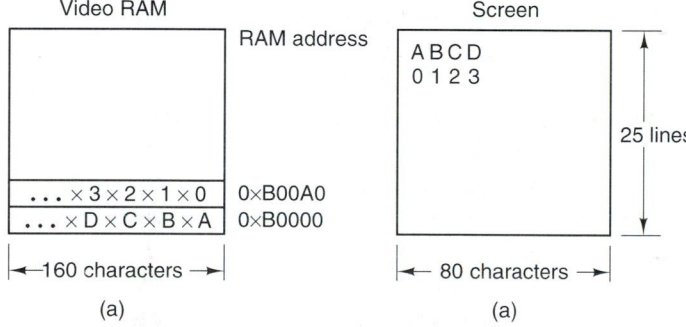

Figure 3-29. (a) A video RAM image for the IBM monochrome display. (b) The corresponding screen. The ×s are attribute bytes.

Bit-map terminals use the same principle, except that each pixel on the screen is individually controlled. In the simplest configuration, for a monochrome display, each pixel has a corresponding bit in the video RAM. At the other extreme, each pixel is represented by a 24-bit number, with 8 bits each for red, green, and blue. A 768×1024 color display with 24 bits per pixel requires 2 MB of RAM just to hold the image.

With a memory-mapped display, the keyboard is completely decoupled from the screen. It may be interfaced via a serial or parallel port. On every key action the CPU is interrupted, and the keyboard driver extracts the character typed by reading an I/O port.

On the IBM PC, the keyboard contains an embedded microprocessor which communicates through a specialized serial port with a controller chip on the motherboard. An interrupt is generated whenever a key is struck and also when one is released. Furthermore, all that the keyboard hardware provides is the key number, not the ASCII code. When the *A* key is struck, the key code (30) is put in an I/O register. It is up to the driver to determine whether it is lower case, upper case, CTRL-A, ALT-A, CTRL-ALT-A, or some other combination. Since the driver can tell which keys have been struck but not yet released (e.g., shift), it has enough information to do the job. Although this keyboard interface puts the full burden on the software, it is extremely flexible. For example, user programs may be interested in whether a digit just typed came from the top row of keys or the numeric key pad on the side. In principle, the driver can provide this information.

RS-232 Terminals

RS-232 terminals are devices containing a keyboard and a display that communicate using a serial interface, one bit at a time (see Fig. 3-30). These terminals use a 9-pin or 25-pin connector, of which one pin is used for transmitting data, one pin is for receiving data, and one pin is ground. The other pins are for various control functions, most of which are not used. To send a character to an RS-232 terminal, the computer must transmit it 1 bit at a time, prefixed by a start bit, and followed by 1 or 2 stop bits to delimit the character. A parity bit which provides rudimentary error detection may also be inserted preceding the stop bits, although this is commonly required only for communication with mainframe systems. Common transmission rates are 9600, 19,200, and 38,400 bps. RS-232 terminals are commonly used to communicate with a remote computer using a modem and a telephone line.

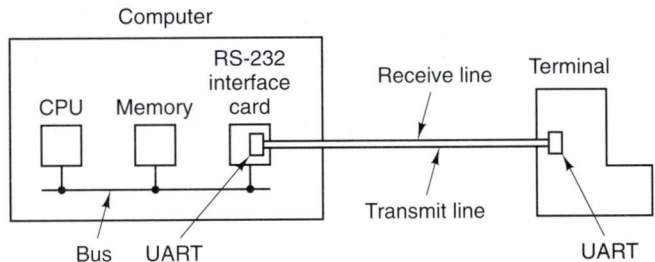

Figure 3-30. An RS-232 terminal communicates with a computer over a communication line, one bit at a time. The computer and the terminal are completely independent.

Since both computers and terminals work internally with whole characters but must communicate over a serial line a bit at a time, chips have been developed to do the character-to-serial and serial-to-character conversions. They are called **UART**s (Universal Asynchronous Receiver Transmitters). UARTs are attached to the computer by plugging RS-232 interface cards into the bus as illustrated in Fig. 3-31. RS-232 terminals are gradually dying off, being replaced by PCs and X terminals, but they are still encountered on older mainframe systems, especially in banking, airline reservation, and similar applications.

To print a character, the terminal driver writes the character to the interface card, where it is buffered and then shifted out over the serial line one bit at a time by the UART. Even at 38,400 bps, it takes just over 250 microsec to send a character. As a result of this slow transmission rate, the driver generally outputs a character to the RS-232 card and blocks, waiting for the interrupt generated by the interface when the character has been transmitted and the UART is able to accept another character. The UART can simultaneously send and receive characters, as its name implies. An interrupt is also generated when a character is received, and usually a small number of input characters can be buffered. The terminal driver must check a register when an interrupt is received to determine the cause of the interrupt. Some interface cards have a CPU and memory and can handle multiple lines, taking over much of the I/O load from the main CPU.

RS-232 terminals can be subdivided into categories, as mentioned above. The simplest ones were hardcopy (printing) terminals. Characters typed on the keyboard were transmitted to the computer. Characters sent by the computer were typed on the paper. These terminals are obsolete and rarely seen any more.

Dumb CRT terminals work the same way, only with a screen instead of paper. These are often called "glass ttys" because they are functionally the same as hardcopy ttys. (The term "tty" is an abbreviation for Teletype® a former company that pioneered in the computer terminal business; "tty" has come to mean any terminal.) Glass ttys are also obsolete.

Intelligent CRT terminals are in fact miniature, specialized computers. They have a CPU and memory and contain software, usually in ROM. From the operating system's viewpoint, the main difference between a glass tty and an intelligent terminal is that the latter understands certain escape sequences. For example, by sending the ASCII ESC character (033), followed by various other characters, it may be possible to move the cursor to any position on the screen, insert text in the middle of the screen, and so forth.

X Terminals

The ultimate in intelligent terminals is a terminal that contains a CPU as powerful as the main computer, along with megabytes of memory, a keyboard, and a mouse. One common terminal of this type is the **X terminal**, which runs M.I.T.'s X Window System. Usually, X terminals talk to the main computer over an Ethernet.

An X terminal is a computer that runs the X software. Some products are dedicated to running only X; others are general-purpose computers that simply run X as one program among many others. Either way, an X terminal has a large bit-mapped screen, usually 960×1200 or better resolution, in black and white, gray-scale, or color, a full keyboard, and a mouse, normally with three buttons.

The program inside the X terminal that collects input from the keyboard or mouse and accepts commands from a remote computer is called the **X server**. It communicates over the network with **X clients** running on some remote host. It may seem strange to have the X server inside the terminal and the clients on the remote host, but the X server's job is to display bits, so it makes sense to be near the user. The arrangement of client and server is shown in Fig. 3-31.

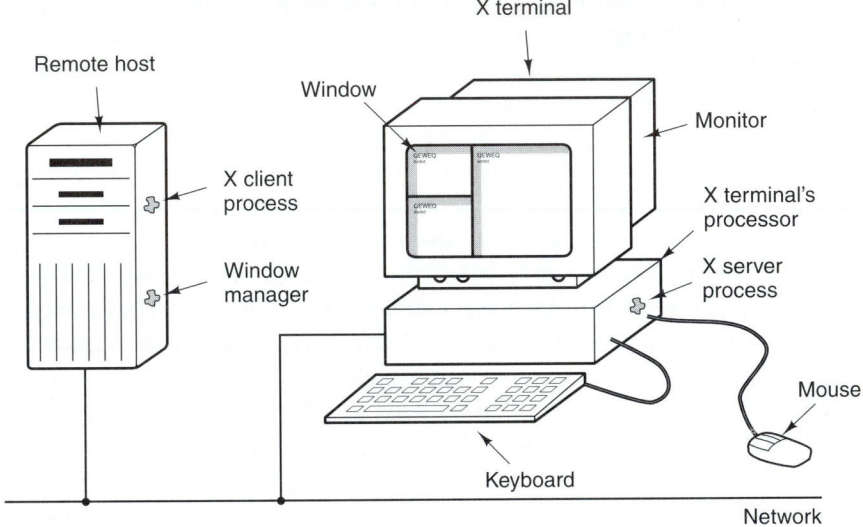

Figure 3-31. Clients and servers in the M.I.T. X Window System.

The screen of the X terminal contains some number of windows, each in the form of a rectangular grid of pixels. Each window usually has a title bar at the top, a scroll bar on the left, and a resizing box in the upper right-hand corner. One of the X clients is a program called a **window manager**. Its job is to control the creation, deletion, and movement of windows on the screen. To manage windows, it sends commands to the X server telling what to do. These commands include draw point, draw line, draw rectangle, draw polygon, fill rectangle, fill polygon, and so on.

The job of the X server is to coordinate input from the mouse, keyboard, and X clients and update the display accordingly. It has to keep track of which window is currently selected (where the mouse pointer is), so it knows which client to send any new keyboard input to.

3.9.2 Terminal Software

The keyboard and display are almost independent devices, so we will treat them separately here. (They are not quite independent, since typed characters must be displayed on the screen.) In MINIX the keyboard and screen drivers are part of the same task; in other systems they may be split into distinct drivers.

Input Software

The basic job of the keyboard driver is to collect input from the keyboard and pass it to user programs when they read from the terminal. Two possible philosophies can be adopted for the driver. In the first one, the driver's job is just to accept input and pass it upward unmodified. A program reading from the terminal gets a raw sequence of ASCII codes. (Giving user programs the key numbers is too primitive, as well as being highly machine dependent.)

This philosophy is well suited to the needs of sophisticated screen editors such as *emacs*, which allow the user to bind an arbitrary action to any character or sequence of characters. It does, however, mean that if the user types *dste* instead of *date* and then corrects the error by typing three backspaces and *ate*, followed by a carriage return, the user program will be given all 11 ASCII codes typed.

Most programs do not want this much detail. They just want the corrected input, not the exact sequence of how it was produced. This observation leads to the second philosophy: the driver handles all the intraline editing, and just delivers corrected lines to the user programs. The first philosophy is character-oriented; the second one is line-oriented. Originally they were referred to as **raw mode** and **cooked mode**, respectively. The POSIX standard uses the less-picturesque term **canonical mode** to describe line-oriented mode. On most systems canonical mode refers to a well-defined configuration. **Noncanonical mode** is equivalent to raw mode, although many details of terminal behavior can be changed. POSIX-compatible systems provide several library functions that support selecting either mode and changing many aspects of terminal configuration. In MINIX the IOCTL system call supports these functions.

The first task of the keyboard driver is to collect characters. If every keystroke causes an interrupt, the driver can acquire the character during the interrupt. If interrupts are turned into messages by the low-level software, it is possible to put the newly acquired character in the message. Alternatively, it can be put in a small buffer in memory and the message used to tell the driver that something has arrived. The latter approach is actually safer if a message can be sent only to a waiting process and there is some chance that the keyboard driver might still be busy with the previous character.

Once the driver has received the character, it must begin processing it. If the keyboard delivers key numbers rather than the character codes used by application software, then the driver must convert between the codes by using a table. Not all IBM "compatibles" use standard key numbering, so if the driver wants to support these machines, it must map different keyboards with different tables. A simple approach is to compile a table that maps between the codes provided by the keyboard and ASCII (American Standard Code for Information Interchange) codes into the keyboard driver, but this is unsatisfactory for users of languages other than English. Keyboards are arranged differently in different countries, and the ASCII character set is not adequate even for the majority of people in the Western

Hemisphere, where speakers of Spanish, Portuguese, and French need accented characters and punctuation marks not used in English. To respond to the need for flexibility of keyboard layouts to provide for different languages, many operating systems provide for loadable **keymaps** or **code pages**, which make it possible to choose the mapping between keyboard codes and codes delivered to the application, either when the system is booted or later.

If the terminal is in canonical (cooked) mode, characters must be stored until an entire line has been accumulated, because the user may subsequently decide to erase part of it. Even if the terminal is in raw mode, the program may not yet have requested input, so the characters must be buffered to allow type ahead. (System designers who do not allow users to type far ahead ought to be tarred and feathered, or worse yet, be forced to use their own system.)

Two approaches to character buffering are common. In the first one, the driver contains a central pool of buffers, each buffer holding perhaps 10 characters. Associated with each terminal is a data structure, which contains, among other items, a pointer to the chain of buffers for input collected from that terminal. As more characters are typed, more buffers are acquired and hung on the chain. When the characters are passed to a user program, the buffers are removed and put back in the central pool.

The other approach is to do the buffering directly in the terminal data structure itself, with no central pool of buffers. Since it is common for users to type a command that will take a little while (say, a compilation) and then type a few lines ahead, to be safe the driver should allocate something like 200 characters per terminal. In a large-scale timesharing system with 100 terminals, allocating 20K all the time for type ahead is clearly overkill, so a central buffer pool with space for perhaps 5K is probably enough. On the other hand, a dedicated buffer per terminal makes the driver simpler (no linked list management) and is to be preferred on personal computers with only one or two terminals. Figure 3-32 shows the difference between these two methods.

Although the keyboard and display are logically separate devices, many users have grown accustomed to seeing the characters they have just typed appear on the screen. Some (older) terminals oblige by automatically displaying (in hardware) whatever has just been typed, which is not only a nuisance when passwords are being entered but greatly limits the flexibility of sophisticated editors and other programs. Fortunately, most modern terminals display nothing when keys are typed. It is therefore up to the software to display the input. This process is called **echoing.**

Echoing is complicated by the fact that a program may be writing to the screen while the user is typing. At the very least, the keyboard driver has to figure out where to put the new input without it being overwritten by program output.

Echoing also gets complicated when more than 80-characters are typed on a terminal with 80-character lines. Depending on the application, wrapping around

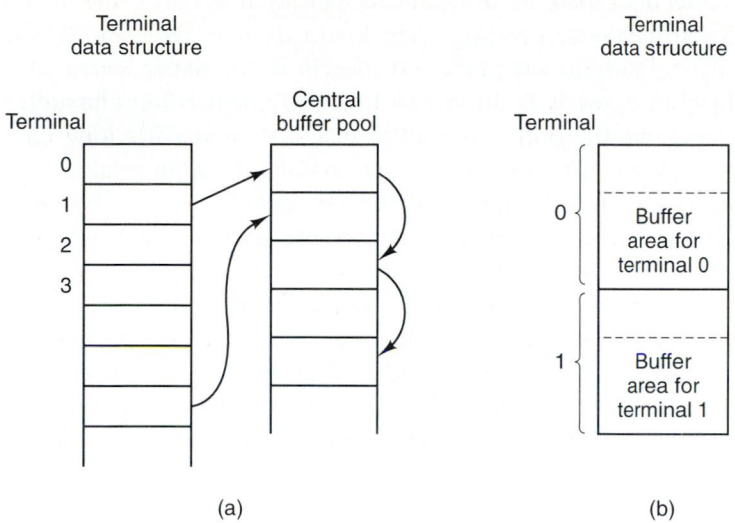

Figure 3-32. (a) Central buffer pool. (b) Dedicated buffer for each terminal.

to the next line may be appropriate. Some drivers just truncate lines to 80 characters by throwing away all characters beyond column 80.

Another problem is tab handling. Most terminals have a tab key, but few can handle tab on output. It is up to the driver to compute where the cursor is currently located, taking into account both output from programs and output from echoing, and compute the proper number of spaces to be echoed.

Now we come to the problem of device equivalence. Logically, at the end of a line of text, one wants a carriage return, to move the cursor back to column 1, and a linefeed, to advance to the next line. Requiring users to type both at the end of each line would not sell well (although some terminals have a key which generates both, with a 50 percent chance of doing so in the order that the software wants them). It is up to the driver to convert whatever comes in to the standard internal format used by the operating system.

If the standard form is just to store a linefeed (the MINIX convention), then carriage returns should be turned into linefeeds. If the internal format is to store both, then the driver should generate a linefeed when it gets a carriage return and a carriage return when it gets a linefeed. No matter what the internal convention, the terminal may require both a linefeed and a carriage return to be echoed in order to get the screen updated properly. Since a large computer may well have a wide variety of different terminals connected to it, it is up to the keyboard driver to get all the different carriage return/linefeed combinations converted to the internal system standard and arrange for all echoing to be done right.

A related problem is the timing of carriage return and linefeeds. On some terminals, it may take longer to display a carriage return or linefeed than a letter or number. If the microprocessor inside the terminal actually has to copy a large block of text to achieve scrolling, then linefeeds may be slow. If a mechanical print head has to be returned to the left margin of the paper, carriage returns may be slow. In both cases it is up to the driver to insert **filler characters** (dummy null characters) into the output stream or just stop outputting long enough for the terminal to catch up. The amount of time to delay is often related to the terminal speed, for example, at 4800 bps or slower, no delays may be, but at 9600 bps or higher one filler character might be required. Terminals with hardware tabs, especially hardcopy ones, may also require a delay after a tab.

When operating in canonical mode, a number of input characters have special meanings. Figure 3-33 shows all of the special characters required by POSIX and the additional ones recognized by MINIX. The defaults are all control characters that should not conflict with text input or codes used by programs, but all except the last two can be changed using the *stty* command, if desired. Older versions of UNIX used different defaults for many of these.

Character	POSIX name	Comment
CTRL-D	EOF	End of file
	EOL	End of line (undefined)
CTRL-H	ERASE	Backspace one character
DEL	INTR	Interrupt process (SIGINT)
CTRL-U	KILL	Erase entire line being typed
CTRL-\	QUIT	Force core dump (SIGQUIT)
CTRL-Z	SUSP	Suspend (ignored by MINIX)
CTRL-Q	START	Start output
CTRL-S	STOP	Stop output
CTRL-R	REPRINT	Redisplay input (MINIX extension)
CTRL-V	LNEXT	Literal next (MINIX extension)
CTRL-O	DISCARD	Discard output (MINIX extension)
CTRL-M	CR	Carriage return (unchangeable)
CTRL-J	NL	Linefeed (unchangeable)

Figure 3-33. Characters that are handled specially in canonical mode.

The *ERASE* character allows the user to rub out the character just typed. In MINIX it is the backspace (CTRL-H). It is not added to the character queue but instead removes the previous character from the queue. It should be echoed as a sequence of three characters, backspace, space, and backspace, in order to remove the previous character from the screen. If the previous character was a tab, erasing it requires keeping track of where the cursor was prior to the tab. In most systems, backspacing will only erase characters on the current line. It will not erase a carriage return and back up into the previous line.

When the user notices an error at the start of the line being typed in, it is often convenient to erase the entire line and start again. The *KILL* character (in MINIX CTRL-U) erases the entire line. MINIX makes the erased line vanish from the screen, but some systems echo it plus a carriage return and linefeed because some users like to see the old line. Consequently, how to echo *KILL* is a matter of taste. As with *ERASE* it is usually not possible to go further back than the current line. When a block of characters is killed, it may or may not be worth the trouble for the driver to return buffers to the pool, if one is used.

Sometimes the *ERASE* or *KILL* characters must be entered as ordinary data. The *LNEXT* character serves as an **escape character**. In MINIX CTRL-V is the default. As an example, older UNIX systems often used the @ sign for *KILL*, but the Internet mail system uses addresses of the form *linda@cs.washington.edu*. Someone who feels more comfortable with older conventions might redefine *KILL* as @, but then need to enter an @ sign literally to address e-mail. This can be done by typing CTRL-V @. The CTRL-V itself can be entered literally by typing CTRL-V CTRL-V. After seeing a CTRL-V, the driver sets a flag saying that the next character is exempt from special processing. The *LNEXT* character itself is not entered in the character queue.

To allow users to stop a screen image from scrolling out of view, control codes are provided to freeze the screen and restart it later. In MINIX these are *STOP*, (CTRL-S) and *START*, (CTRL-Q), respectively. They are not stored but are used to set and clear a flag in the terminal data structure. Whenever output is attempted, the flag is inspected. If it is set, no output occurs. Usually, echoing is also suppressed along with program output.

It is often necessary to kill a runaway program being debugged. The *INTR* (DEL) and *QUIT* (CTRL-\) characters can be used for this purpose. In MINIX, DEL sends the SIGINT signal to all the processes started up from the terminal. Implementing DEL can be quite tricky. The hard part is getting the information from the driver to the part of the system that handles signals, which, after all, has not asked for this information. CTRL-\ is similar to DEL, except that it sends the SIGQUIT signal, which forces a core dump if not caught or ignored. When either of these keys is struck, the driver should echo a carriage return and linefeed and discard all accumulated input to allow for a fresh start. The default value for *INTR* is often CTRL-C instead of DEL, since many programs use DEL interchangeably with the backspace for editing.

Another special character is *EOF* (CTRL-D), which in MINIX causes any pending read requests for the terminal to be satisfied with whatever is available in the buffer, even if the buffer is empty. Typing CTRL-D at the start of a line causes the program to get a read of 0 bytes, which is conventionally interpreted as

end-of-file and causes most programs to act the same way as they would upon
seeing end-of-file on an input file.

Some terminal drivers allow much fancier intraline editing than we have
sketched here. They have special control characters to erase a word, skip backward or forward characters or words, go to the beginning or end of the line being
typed, and so forth. Adding all these functions to the terminal driver makes it
much larger and, furthermore, is wasted when using fancy screen editors that
work in raw mode anyway.

To allow programs to control terminal parameters, POSIX requires that several
functions be available in the standard library, of which the most important are
tcgetattr and *tcsetattr*. *Tcgetattr* retrieves a copy of the structure shown in
Fig. 3-34, the *termios* structure, which contains all the information needed to
change special characters, set modes, and modify other characteristics of a terminal. A program can examine the current settings and modify them as desired.
Tcsetattr then writes the structure back to the terminal task.

```
struct termios {
  tcflag_t c_iflag;                     /* input modes */
  tcflag_t c_oflag;                     /* output modes */
  tcflag_t c_cflag;                     /* control modes */
  tcflag_t c_lflag;                     /* local modes */
  speed_t  c_ispeed;                    /* input speed */
  speed_t  c_ospeed;                    /* output speed */
  cc_t c_cc[NCCS];                      /* control characters */
};
```

Figure 3-34. The termios structure. In MINIX tc_flag_t is a short, speed_t is an
int, cc_t is a char.

POSIX does not specify whether its requirements should be implemented
through library functions or system calls. MINIX provides a system call, IOCTL,
called by

ioctl(file_descriptor, request, argp);

that is used to examine and modify the configurations of many I/O devices. This
call is used to implement the *tcgetattr* and *tcsetattr* functions. The variable *request* specifies whether the *termios* structure is to be read or written, and in the
latter case, whether the request is to take effect immediately or should be deferred
until all currently queued output is complete. The variable *argp* is a pointer to a
termios structure in the calling program. This particular choice of communication
between program and driver was chosen for its UNIX compatibility, rather than for
its inherent beauty.

A few notes about the termios structure are in order. The four flag words provide a great deal of flexibility. The individual bits in *c_iflag* control various ways

input is handled. For instance, the *ICRNL* bit causes *CR* characters to be converted into *NL* on input. This flag is set by default in MINIX. The *c_oflag* holds bits that affect output processing. For instance, the *OPOST* bit enables output processing. It and the *ONLCR* bit, which causes *NL* characters in the output to be converted into a *CR NL* sequence, are also set by default in MINIX. The *c_cflag* is the control flag. The default settings for MINIX enable a line to receive 8-bit characters and cause a modem to hang up if a user logs out on the line. The *c_lflag* is the *local mode* flags field. One bit, *ECHO*, enables echoing (this can be turned off during a login to provide security for entering a password). Its most important bit is the *ICANON* bit, which enables canonical mode. With *ICANON* off, several possibilities exist. If all other settings are left at their defaults, a mode identical to the traditional **cbreak mode** is entered. In this mode characters are passed to the program without waiting for a full line, but the *INTR*, *QUIT*, *START*, and *STOP* characters retain their effects. All of these can be disabled by resetting bits in the flags, however, to produce the equivalent of traditional raw mode.

The various special characters that can be changed, including those which are MINIX extensions, are held in the *c_cc* array. This array also holds two parameters which are used in noncanonical mode. The quantity *MIN*, stored in *c_cc[VMIN]*, specifies the minimum number of characters that must be received to satisfy a READ call. The quantity *TIME* in *c_cc[VTIME]* sets a time limit for such calls. *MIN* and *TIME* interact as shown in Fig. 3-35. A call that asks for *N* bytes is illustrated. With *TIME* = 0 and *MIN* = 1, the behavior is similar to the traditional raw mode.

	TIME = 0	TIME > 0
MIN = 0	Return immediately with whatever is available, 0 to N bytes	Timer starts immediately. Return with first byte entered or with 0 bytes after timeout
MIN > 0	Return with at least MIN and up to N bytes. Possible indefinite block.	Interbyte timer starts after first byte. Return N bytes if received by timeout, or at least 1 byte at timeout. Possible indefinite block

Figure 3-35. *MIN* and *TIME* determine when a call to read returns in noncanonical mode. *N* is the number of bytes requested.

Output Software

Output is simpler than input, but drivers for RS-232 terminals are radically different from drivers for memory-mapped terminals. The method that is commonly used for RS-232 terminals is to have output buffers associated with each terminal. The buffers can come from the same pool as the input buffers, or be dedicated, as with input. When programs write to the terminal, the output is first copied to the buffers. Similarly, output from echoing is also copied to the buffers. After all the output has been copied to the buffers (or the buffers are full), the first character is output, and the driver goes to sleep. When the interrupt comes in, the next character is output, and so on.

With memory-mapped terminals, a simpler scheme is possible. Characters to be printed are extracted one at a time from user space and put directly in the video RAM. With RS-232 terminals, each character to be output is just sent across the line to the terminal. With memory mapping, some characters require special treatment, among them, backspace, carriage return, linefeed, and the audible bell (CTRL-G). A driver for a memory-mapped terminal must keep track in software of the current position in the video RAM, so that printable characters can be put there and the current position advanced. Backspace, carriage return, and linefeed all require this position to be updated appropriately.

In particular, when a linefeed is output on the bottom line of the screen, the screen must be scrolled. To see how scrolling works, look at Fig. 3-29. If the video controller always began reading the RAM at 0xB0000, the only way to scroll the screen would be to copy 24×80 characters (each character requiring 2 bytes) from 0xB00A0 to 0xB0000, a time-consuming proposition.

Fortunately, the hardware usually provides some help here. Most video controllers contain a register that determines where in the video RAM to begin fetching bytes for the top line on the screen. By setting this register to point to 0xB00A0 instead of 0xB0000, the line that was previously number two moves to the top, and the whole screen scrolls up one line. The only other thing the driver must do is copy whatever is needed to the new bottom line. When the video controller gets to the top of the RAM, it just wraps around and continues fetching bytes starting at the lowest address.

Another issue that the driver must deal with on a memory-mapped terminal is cursor positioning. Again, the hardware usually provides some assistance in the form of a register that tells where the cursor is to go. Finally, there is the problem of the bell. It is sounded by outputting a sine or square wave to the loudspeaker, a part of the computer quite separate from the video RAM.

It is worth noting that many of the issues faced by the terminal driver for a memory-mapped display (scrolling, bell, and so on) are also faced by the microprocessor inside an RS-232 terminal. From the viewpoint of the microprocessor, it is the main processor in a system with a memory-mapped display.

Screen editors and many other sophisticated programs need to be able to update the screen in more complex ways than just scrolling text onto the bottom of the display. To accommodate them, many terminal drivers support a variety of escape sequences. Although some terminals support idiosyncratic escape sequence sets, it is advantageous to have a standard to facilitate adapting software from one system to another. The American National Standards Institute (ANSI) has defined a set of standard escape sequences, and MINIX supports a subset of the ANSI sequences, shown in Fig. 3-36, that is adequate for many common operations. When the driver sees the character that starts the escape sequences, it sets a flag and waits until the rest of the escape sequence comes in. When everything has arrived, the driver must carry it out in software. Inserting and deleting text require moving blocks of characters around the video RAM. The hardware is of no help with anything except scrolling and displaying the cursor.

Escape sequence	Meaning
ESC [n A	Move up n lines
ESC [n B	Move down n lines
ESC [n C	Move right n spaces
ESC [n D	Move left n spaces
ESC [m ; n H	Move cursor to (m,n)
ESC [s J	Clear screen from cursor (0 to end, 1 from start, 2 all)
ESC [s K	Clear line from cursor (0 to end, 1 from start, 2 all)
ESC [n L	Insert n lines at cursor
ESC [n M	Delete n lines at cursor
ESC [n P	Delete n chars at cursor
ESC [n @	Insert n chars at cursor
ESC [n m	Enable rendition n (0=normal, 4=bold, 5=blinking, 7=reverse)
ESC M	Scroll the screen backward if the cursor is on the top line

Figure 3-36. The ANSI escape sequences accepted by the terminal driver on output. ESC denotes the ASCII escape character (0x1B), and n, m, and s are optional numeric parameters.

3.9.3 Overview of the Terminal Driver in MINIX

The terminal driver is contained in four C files (six if RS-232 and pseudo terminal support are enabled) and together they far and away constitute the largest driver in MINIX. The size of the terminal driver is partly explained by the observation that the driver handles both the keyboard and the display, each of which is a complicated device in its own right, as well as two other optional types of terminals. Still, it comes as a surprise to most people to learn that terminal I/O requires thirty times as much code as the scheduler. (This feeling is reinforced by looking at the numerous books on operating systems that devote thirty times as much space to scheduling as to all I/O combined.)

The terminal driver accepts seven message types:

1. Read from the terminal (from FS on behalf of a user process).

2. Write to the terminal (from FS on behalf of a user process).

3. Set terminal parameters for IOCTL (from FS on behalf of a user process).

4. I/O occurred during last clock tick (from the clock interrupt).

5. Cancel previous request (from the file system when a signal occurs).

6. Open a device.

7. Close a device.

The messages for reading and writing have the same format as shown in Fig. 3-15, except that no *POSITION* field is needed. With a disk, the program has to specify which block it wants to read. With a terminal, there is no choice: the program always gets the next character typed in. Terminals do not support seeks.

The POSIX functions *tcgetattr* and *tcgetattr*, used to examine and modify terminal attributes (properties), are supported by the IOCTL system call. Good programming practice is to use these functions and others in *include/termios.h* and leave it to the C library to convert library calls to IOCTL system calls. There are, however, some control operations needed by MINIX that are not provided for in POSIX, for example, loading an alternate keymap, and for these the programmer must use IOCTL explicitly.

The message sent to the driver by an IOCTL system call contains a function request code and a pointer. For the *tcsetattr* function, an IOCTL call is made with a *TCSETS*, *TCSETSW*, or *TCSETSF* request type, and a pointer to a *termios* structure like the one shown in Fig. 3-34. All such calls replace the current set of attributes with a new set, the differences being that a *TCSETS* request takes effect immediately, a *TCSETSW* request does not take effect until all output has been transmitted, and a *TCSETSF* waits for output to finish and discards all input that has not yet been read. *Tcgetattr* is translated into an IOCTL call with a *TCGETS* request type and returns a filled in *termios* structure to the caller, so the current state of a device can be examined. IOCTL calls that do not correspond to functions defined by POSIX, like the *KIOCSMAP* request used to load a new keymap, pass pointers to other kinds of structures, in this case to a *keymap_t* which is a 1536-byte structure (16-bit codes for 128 keys × 6 modifiers). Figure 3-43 summarizes how standard POSIX calls are converted into IOCTL system calls.

The terminal driver uses one main data structure, *tty_table*, which is an array of *tty* structures, one per terminal. A standard PC has only one keyboard and display, but MINIX can support up to eight virtual terminals, depending upon the amount of memory on the display adapter card. This permits the person at the console to log on multiple times, switching the display output and keyboard input from one "user" to another. With two virtual consoles, pressing ALT-F2 selects the second one and ALT-F1 returns to the first. ALT plus the arrow keys also can be used. In addition, serial lines can support two users at remote locations, connected by RS-232 cable or modem, and **pseudo terminals** can support users connected through a network. The driver has been written to make it easy to add additional terminals. The standard configuration illustrated in the source code in this text has two virtual consoles, with serial lines and pseudo terminals disabled.

Each *tty* structure in *tty_table* keeps track of both input and output. For input, it holds a queue of all characters that have been typed but not yet read by the program, information about requests to read characters that have not yet been received, and timeout information, so input can be requested without the task blocking permanently if no character is typed. For output, it holds the parameters of write requests that are not yet finished. Other fields hold various general variables, such as the *termios* structure discussed above, which affects many properties of both input and output. There is also a field in the *tty* structure to point to information which is needed for a particular class of devices but is not needed in the *tty_table* entry for every device. For instance, the hardware-dependent part of the console driver needs the current position on the screen and in the video RAM, and the current attribute byte for the display, but this information is not needed to support an RS-232 line. The private data structures for each device type are also where the buffers that receive input from the interrupt service routines are located. Slow devices, such as the keyboard, do not need buffers as large as those needed by fast devices.

Terminal Input

To better understand how the driver works, let us first look at how characters typed in on the terminal work their way through the system to the program that wants them.

When a user logs in on the system console, a shell is created for him with */dev/console* as standard input, standard output, and standard error. The shell starts up and tries to read from standard input by calling the library procedure *read*. This procedure sends a message that contains the file descriptor, buffer address, and count to the file system. This message is shown as (1) in Fig. 3-37. After sending the message, the shell blocks, waiting for the reply. (User processes execute only the SEND_REC primitive, which combines a SEND with a RECEIVE from the process sent to.)

The file system gets the message and locates the i-node corresponding to the specified file descriptor. This i-node is for the character special file */dev/console* and contains the major and minor device numbers for the terminal. The major device type for terminals is 4; for the console the minor device number is 0.

The file system indexes into its device map, *dmap*, to find the number of the terminal task. Then it sends a message to the terminal task, shown as (2) in Fig. 3-37. Normally, the user will not have typed anything yet, so the terminal driver will be unable to satisfy the request. It sends a reply back immediately to unblock the file system and report that no characters are available, shown as (3). The file system records the fact that a process is waiting for terminal input in the console's structure in *tty_table* and then goes off to get the next request for work. The user's shell remains blocked until the requested characters arrive, of course.

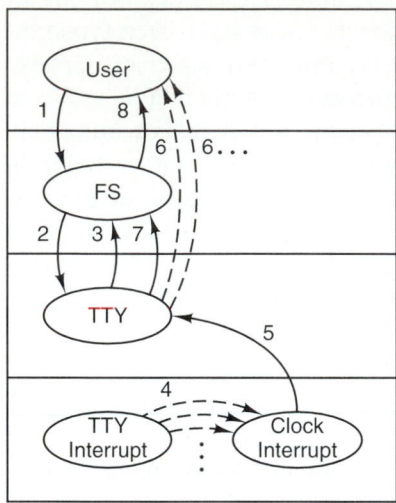

Figure 3-37. Read request from terminal when no characters are pending. FS is the file system. TTY is the terminal task. The interrupt handler for the terminal queues characters as they are entered, but it is the clock interrupt handler that awakens TTY.

When a character is finally typed on the keyboard, it causes two interrupts, one when the key is depressed and one when it is released. This rule also applies to modifier keys such as CTRL and SHIFT, which do not transmit any data by themselves but still cause two interrupts per key. The keyboard interrupt is IRQ 1, and _hwint01 in the assembly code file *mpx386.s* activates *kbd_hw_int* (line 13123), which in turn calls *scan_keyboard* (line 13432) to extract the key code from the keyboard hardware. If the code is for an ordinary character, it is put into the keyboard input queue, *ibuf*, if the interrupt was generated by a key being depressed, but it is ignored if the interrupt was generated by the release of a key. Codes for modifier keys like CTRL and SHIFT are put into the queue for both types of interrupt but can be distinguished later by a bit that is set only when a key is released. Note that at this point the codes received and stored in *ibuf* are not ASCII codes; they are simply the scan codes produced by the IBM keyboard. *Kbd_hw_int* then sets a flag, *tty_events* (part of the keyboard's section of the *tty_table*), calls *force_timeout*, and returns.

Unlike some other interrupt service routines, *kbd_hw_int* does not send a message to wake up the terminal task. The call to *force_timeout* is indicated by the dashed lines marked (4) in the figure. These are not messages. They set the *tty_timeout* variable in the address space common to the interrupt service routines. On the next clock interrupt *clock_handler* finds that *tty_timeout* indicates it is time for a call to *tty_wakeup* (line 11452) which then sends a message (5) to the terminal task. Note that although the source code for *tty_wakeup* is in the file *tty.c*, it runs in response to the clock interrupt, and thus we say the clock interrupt sends the message to the terminal task. If input is arriving rapidly, a number of character codes may be queued this way, which is why multiple calls to *force_timeout* (4) are shown in the figure.

Upon receiving the wakeup message the terminal task inspects the *tty_events* flag for each terminal device, and, for each device which has the flag set, calls *handle_events* (line 12256). The *tty_events* flag can signal various kinds of activity (although input is the most likely), so *handle_events* always calls the device-specific functions for both input and output. For input from the keyboard this results in a call to *kb_read* (line 13165), which keeps track of keyboard codes that indicate pressing or releasing of the CTRL, SHIFT, and ALT keys and converts keyboard codes into ASCII codes. *Kb_read* in turn calls *in_process* (line 12367), which processes the ASCII codes, taking into account special characters and different flags that may be set, including whether or not canonical mode is in effect. The effect is normally to add characters to the console's input queue in *tty_table*, although some codes, for instance BACKSPACE, have other effects. Normally, also, *in_process* initiates echoing of the ASCII codes to the display.

When enough characters have come in, the terminal task calls the assembly language procedure *phys_copy* to copy the data to the address requested by the shell. This operation also is not message passing and for that reason is shown by dashed lines (6) in Fig. 3-37. There is more than one such line shown because there may be more than one such operation before the user's request has been completely fulfilled. When the operation is finally complete, the terminal driver sends a message to the file system telling it that the work has been done (7), and the file system reacts to this message by sending a message back to the shell to unblock it (8).

The definition of when enough characters have come in depends upon the terminal mode. In canonical mode a request is complete when a linefeed, end-of-line, or end-of-file code is received, and, in order for proper input processing to be done, a line of input cannot exceed the size of the input queue. In noncanonical mode a read can request a much larger number of characters, and *in_process* may have to transfer characters more than once before a message is returned to the file system to indicate the operation is complete.

Note that the terminal driver copies the actual characters directly from its own address space to that of the shell. It does not first go through the file system. With block I/O, data do pass through the file system to allow it to maintain a buffer cache of the most recently used blocks. If a requested block happens to be in the cache, the request can be satisfied directly by the file system, without doing any disk I/O.

For terminal I/O, a cache makes no sense. Furthermore, a request from the file system to a disk driver can always be satisfied in at most a few hundred milliseconds, so there is no real harm in having the file system just wait. Terminal I/O may take hours to complete, or may never be complete (in canonical mode the terminal task waits for a complete line, and it may also wait a long time in non-canonical mode, depending upon the settings of *MIN* and *TIME*). Thus, it is unacceptable to have the file system block until a terminal input request is satisfied.

Later on, it may happen that the user has typed ahead, and that characters are available before they have been requested, from previous occurrences of events 4 and 5. In that case, events 1, 2, 6, 7, and 8 all happen in quick succession after the read request; 3 does not occur at all.

If the terminal task happens to be running at the time of a clock interrupt, no message can be sent to it because it will not be waiting for one. However, in order to keep input and output flowing smoothly when the terminal task is busy, the *tty_events* flags for all terminal devices are inspected at several other times, for instance, immediately after processing and replying to a message. Thus, it is possible for characters to be added to the console queue without the aid of a wakeup message from the clock. If two or more clock interrupts occur before the terminal driver finishes what it is doing, all the characters are stored in *ibuf*, and *tty_flags* is repeatedly set. Ultimately, the terminal task gets one message; the rest are lost. But since all the characters are safely stored in the buffer, no typed input is lost. It is even possible that by the time a message is received by the terminal task the input is complete and a reply has already been sent to the user process.

The problem of what to do in an unbuffered message system (rendezvous principle) when an interrupt routine wants to send a message to a process that is busy is inherent in this kind of design. For most devices, such as disks, interrupts occur only in response to commands issued by the driver, so only one interrupt can be pending at any instant. The only devices that generate interrupts on their own are the clock and terminals (and when enabled, the network). The clock is handled by counting pending ticks, so if the clock task does not receive a message from the clock interrupt, it can compensate later. Terminals are handled by having the interrupt routine accumulate the characters in a buffer and raising a flag to indicate characters have been received. If the terminal task is running, it checks all of these flags before it goes to sleep and postpones going to sleep if there is more work it can do.

The terminal task is not awakened directly by terminal interrupts due to the excessive overhead doing so would entail. The clock sends an interrupt to the terminal task on the next tick following each terminal interrupt. At 100 words per minute a typist enters fewer than 10 characters per second. Even with a fast typist the terminal task will probably be sent an interrupt message for each character typed at the keyboard, although some of these messages may be lost. If the buffer should fill before being emptied, excess characters are discarded, but experience shows that, for the keyboard, a 32-character buffer is adequate. In the case of other input devices higher data rates are probable—rates 1000 or more times faster than those of a typist are possible from a serial port connected to a 28,800-bps modem. At that speed approximately 48 characters may be received between clock ticks by the modem, but to allow for data compression on the modem link the serial port connected to the modem must be able to handle at least twice as many. For serial lines, MINIX provides a buffer of 1024 characters.

We have some regrets that the terminal task cannot be implemented without some compromise of our general design principles, but the method we use does the job without too much additional software complexity and no loss in performance. The obvious alternative, to throw away the rendezvous principle and have the system buffer all messages sent to destinations not waiting for them, is much more complicated and also slower.

Real system designers are often faced with a trade-off between using the general case, which is elegant all the time but somewhat slow, and using simpler techniques, which are usually fast but in one or two cases require a trick to make them work properly. Experience is really the only guide to which approach is better under given circumstances. A considerable amount of experience on designing operating systems is summarized by Lampson (1984) and Brooks (1975). While old, these references are still classics.

We will complete our overview of terminal input by summarizing the events that occur when the terminal task is first activated by a read request and when it is reactivated after receipt of keyboard input (see Fig. 3-38). In the first case, when a message comes in to the terminal task requesting characters from the keyboard, the main procedure, *tty_task* (line 11817) calls *do_read* (line 11891) to handle the request. *Do_read* stores the parameters of the call in the keyboard's entry in *tty_table*, in case there are insufficient characters buffered to satisfy the request.

Then it calls *in_transfer* (line 12303) to get any input already waiting, and then *handle_events* (line 12256) which in turn calls *kb_read* (line 13165) and then *in_transfer* once again, in order to try to milk the input stream for a few more characters. *Kb_read* calls several other procedures not shown in Fig. 3-38 to accomplish its work. The result is that whatever is immediately available is copied to the user. If nothing is available, nothing is copied. If the read is completed by *in_transfer* or by *handle_events*, a message is sent to the file system when all characters have been transferred, so the file system can unblock the caller. If the read was not completed (no characters, or not enough characters) *do_read* reports back to the file system, telling it whether it should suspend the original caller, or, if a nonblocking read was requested, cancel the read.

The right side of Fig. 3-38 summarizes the events that occur when the terminal task is awakened subsequent to an interrupt from the keyboard. When a character is typed, the interrupt procedure *kb_hw_int* (line 13123) puts the character code received into the keyboard buffer, sets a flag to identify that the console device has experienced an event, and then arranges for a timeout to occur on the next clock tick. The clock task sends a message to the terminal task telling it something has happened. Upon receiving this message, *tty_task* checks the event flags of all terminal devices and calls *handle_event* for each device with a raised flag. In the case of the keyboard, *handle_event* calls *kb_read* and *in_transfer*, just as was done on receipt of the original read request. The events shown on the

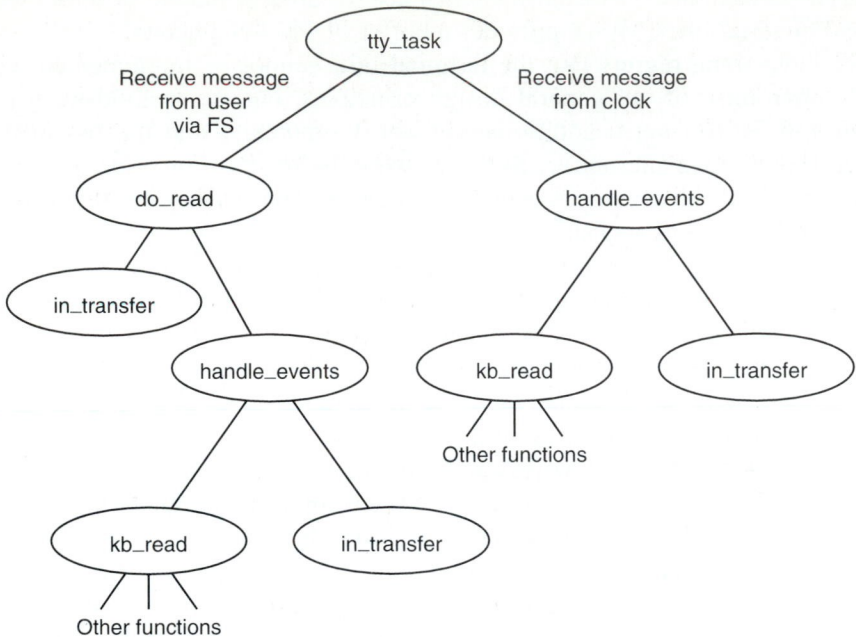

Figure 3-38. Input handling in the terminal driver. The left branch of the tree is taken to process a request to read characters. The right branch is taken when a character-has-been-typed message is sent to the driver.

right side of the figure may occur several times, until enough characters are received to fulfill the request accepted by *do_read* after the first message from the FS. If the FS tries to initiate a request for more characters from the same device before the first request is complete, an error is returned. Of course, each device is independent; a read request on behalf of a user at a remote terminal is processed separately from one for a user at the console.

The functions not shown in Fig. 3-38 that are called by *kb_read* include *map_key*, which converts the key codes (scan codes) generated by the hardware into ASCII codes, *make_break*, which keeps track of the state of modifier keys such as the SHIFT key, and *in_process*, which handles complications such as attempts by the user to backspace over input entered by mistake, other special characters, and options available in different input modes. *In_process* also calls *echo* (line 12531), so the typed characters will be displayed on the screen.

Terminal Output

In general, console output is simpler than terminal input, because the operating system is in control and does not need to be concerned with requests for output arriving at inconvenient times. Also, because the MINIX console is a memory-mapped display, output to the console is particularly simple. No interrupts are needed; the basic operation is to copy data from one memory region to another. On the other hand, all the details of managing the display, including handling escape sequences, must be handled by the driver software. As we did with keyboard input in the previous section we will trace through the steps involved in sending characters to the console display. We will assume in this example that the active display is being written; minor complications caused by virtual consoles will be discussed later.

When a process wants to print something, it generally calls *printf*. *Printf* calls WRITE to send a message to the file system. The message contains a pointer to the characters to be printed (not the characters themselves). The file system then sends a message to the terminal driver, which fetches them and copies them to the video RAM. Figure 3-39 shows the main procedures involved in output.

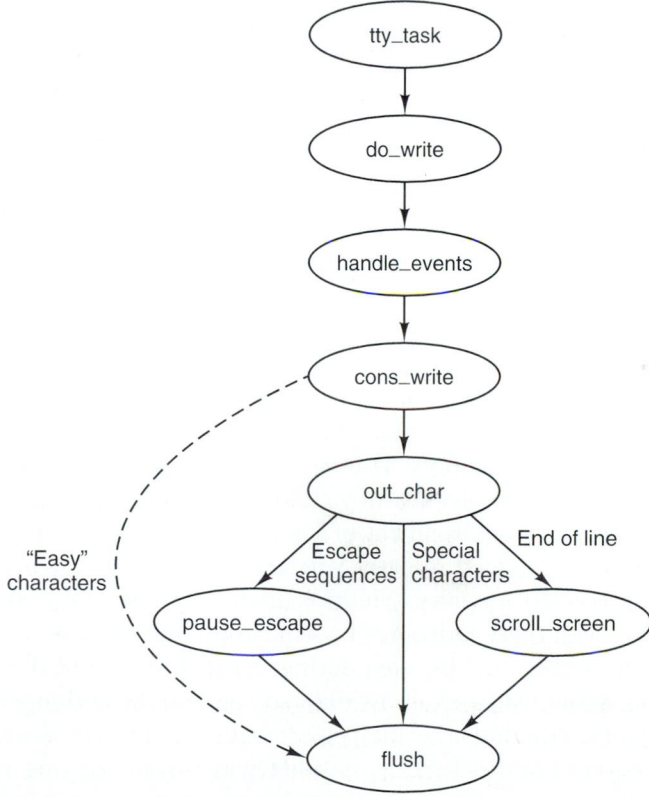

Figure 3-39. Major procedures used on terminal output. The dashed line indicates characters copied directly to *ramqueue* by *cons_write*.

When a message comes in to the terminal task requesting it to write on the screen, *do_write* (line 11964) is called to store the parameters in the console's *tty* struct in the *tty_table*. Then *handle_events* (the same function called whenever the *tty_events* flag is found set) is called. On every call this function calls both the input and output routines for the device selected in its argument. In the case of the console display this means that any keyboard input that is waiting is processed first. If there is input waiting, characters to be echoed are added to whatever characters are already awaiting output. Then a call is made to *cons_write* (line 13729), the output procedure for memory-mapped displays. This procedure uses *phys_copy* to copy blocks of characters from the user process to a local buffer, possibly repeating this and the following steps a number of times, since the local buffer holds only 64 bytes. When the local buffer is full, each 8-bit byte is transferred to another buffer, *ramqueue*. This is an array of 16-bit words. Alternate bytes are filled in with the current value of the screen attribute byte, which determines foreground and background colors and other attributes. When possible, characters are transferred directly into *ramqueue*, but certain characters, such as control characters or characters that are parts of escape sequences, need special handling. Special handling is also required when a character's screen position would exceed the width of the screen, or when *ramqueue* becomes full. In these cases *out_char* (line 13809) is called to transfer the characters and take whatever additional action is called for. For instance, *scroll_screen* (line 13896) is called when a linefeed is received while addressing the last line of the screen, and *parse_escape* handles characters during an escape sequence. Usually *out_char* calls *flush* (line 13951) which copies the contents of *ramqueue* to the video display memory, using the assembly language routine *mem_vid_copy*. *Flush* is also called after the last character is transferred into *ramqueue* to be sure all output is displayed. The final result of *flush* is to command the 6845 video controller chip to display the cursor in the correct position.

Logically, the bytes fetched from the user process could be written into the video RAM one per loop iteration. However, accumulating the characters in *ramqueue* and then copying the block with a call to *mem_vid_copy* are more efficient in the protected memory environment of Pentium-class processors. Interestingly, this technique was introduced in early versions of MINIX that ran on older processors without protected memory. The precursor of *mem_vid_copy* dealt with a timing problem—with older video displays the copy into the video memory had to be done when the screen was blanked during vertical retrace of the CRT beam to avoid generating visual garbage all over the screen. MINIX no longer provides this support for obsolete equipment as the performance penalty is too great. However, the modern version of MINIX benefits in other ways from copying *ramqueue* as a block.

The video RAM available to a console is delimited in the *console* structure by the fields *c_start* and *c_limit*. The current cursor position is stored in the *c_column* and *c_row* fields. The coordinate $(0, 0)$ is in the upper left corner of the screen, which is where the hardware starts to fill the screen. Each video scan begins at the address given by *c_org* and continues for 80×25 characters (4000 bytes). In other words, the 6845 chip pulls the word at offset c_org from the video RAM and displays the character byte in the upper left-hand corner, using the attribute byte to control color, blinking, and so forth. Then it fetches the next word and displays the character at $(1, 0)$. This process continues until it gets to $(79, 0)$, at which time it begins the second line on the screen, at coordinate $(0, 1)$.

When the computer is first started, the screen is cleared, output is written into the video RAM starting at location c_start, and c_org is assigned the same value as c_start. Thus the first line appears on the top line of the screen. When output must go to a new line, either because the first line is full or because a newline character is detected by out_char, output is written into the location given by c_start plus 80. Eventually all 25 lines are filled, and **scrolling** of the screen is required. Some programs, editors, for example, require scrolling in the downward direction too, when the cursor is on the top line and further movement upward within the text is required.

There are two ways scrolling the screen can be managed. In **software scrolling** the character to be displayed at position $(0, 0)$ is always in the first location in video memory, word 0 relative to the position pointed to by c_start, and the video controller chip is commanded to display this location first by keeping the same address in c_org. When the screen is to be scrolled, the contents of relative location 80 in the video RAM, the beginning of the second line on the screen, is copied to relative location 0, word 81 is copied to relative location 1, and so on. The scan sequence is unchanged, putting the data at location 0 in the memory at screen position $(0, 0)$ and the image on the screen appears to have moved up one line. The cost is that the CPU has moved $80 \times 24 = 1920$ words. In **hardware scrolling** the data are not moved in the memory; instead the video controller chip is instructed to start the display at a different point, for instance, with the data at word 80. The bookkeeping is done by adding 80 to the contents of c_org, saving it for future reference, and writing this value into the correct register of the video controller chip. This requires either that the controller be smart enough to wrap around the video RAM, taking data from the beginning of the RAM (the address in c_start) when it reaches the end (the address in c_limit), or that the video RAM have more capacity than just the 80×2000 words necessary to store a single screen of display. Older display adapters generally have smaller memory but are able to wrap around and do hardware scrolling. Newer adapters generally have much more memory than needed to display a single screen of text, but the controllers are not able to wrap. Thus an adapter with 32768 bytes of display memory can hold 204 complete lines of 160 bytes each, and can do hardware scrolling 179 times before the inability to wrap becomes a problem. But, eventually a memory copy operation will be needed to move the data for the last 24 lines back to location 0 in the video memory. Whichever method is used, a row of blanks is copied to the video RAM to ensure that the new line at the bottom of the screen is empty.

When virtual consoles are configured, the available memory within a video adapter is divided equally between the number of consoles desired by properly initializing the *c_start* and *c_limit* fields for each console. This has an effect upon scrolling. On any adapter large enough to support virtual consoles, software scrolling takes place every so often, even though hardware scrolling is nominally in effect. The smaller the amount of memory available to each console display, the more frequently software scrolling must be used. The limit is reached when the maximum possible number of consoles is configured. Then every scroll operation will be a software scroll operation.

The position of the cursor relative to the start of the video RAM can be derived from *c_column* and *c_row*, but it is faster to store it explicitly (in *c_cur*). When a character is to be printed, it is put into the video RAM at location *c_cur*, which is then updated, as is *c_column*. Figure 3-40 summarizes the fields of the *console* structure that affect the current position and the display origin.

Field	Meaning
c_start	Start of video memory for this console
c_limit	Limit of video memory for this console
c_column	Current column (0-79) with 0 at left
c_row	Current row (0-24) with 0 at top
c_cur	Offset into video RAM for cursor
c_org	Location in RAM pointed to by 6845 base register

Figure 3-40. Fields of the console structure that relate to the current screen position.

The characters that affect the cursor position (e.g., linefeed, backspace) are handled by adjusting the values of *c_column*, *c_row*, and *c_cur*. This work is done at the end of *flush* by a call to *set_6845* which sets the registers in the video controller chip.

The terminal driver supports escape sequences to allow screen editors and other interactive programs to update the screen in a flexible way. The sequences supported are a subset of an ANSI standard and should be adequate to allow many programs written for other hardware and other operating systems to be easily ported to MINIX. There are two categories of escape sequences: those that never contain a variable parameter, and those that may contain parameters. In the first category the only representative supported by MINIX is ESC M, which reverse indexes the screen, moving the cursor up one line and scrolling the screen downward if the cursor is already on the first line. The other category can have one or two numeric parameters. Sequences in this group all begin with ESC [. The "[" is the **control sequence introducer**. A table of escape sequences defined by the ANSI standard and recognized by MINIX was shown in Fig. 3-36.

Parsing escape sequences is not trivial. Valid escape sequences in MINIX can be as short as two characters, as in ESC M, or up to 8 characters long in the case of a sequence that accepts two numeric parameters that each can have a two-digit values as in ESC [20;60H, which moves the cursor to line 20, column 60. In a sequence that accepts a parameter, the parameter may be omitted, and in a sequence that accepts two parameters either or both may be omitted. When a parameter is omitted or one that is outside the valid range is used, a default is substituted. The default is the lowest valid value.

Consider the following ways one could construct a sequence to move to the upper-left corner of the screen:

1. ESC [H is acceptable, because if no parameters are entered the lowest valid parameters are assumed.

2. ESC [1;1H will correctly send the cursor to row 1 and column 1 (with ANSI, the row and column numbers start at 1).

3. Both ESC [1;H and ESC [;1H have an omitted parameter, which defaults to 1 as in the first example.

4. ESC [0;0H will do the same, since each parameter is less than the minimum valid value the minimum is substituted.

These examples are presented not to suggest one should deliberately use invalid parameters but to show that the code that parses such sequences is nontrivial.

MINIX implements a finite state automaton to do this parsing. The variable *c_esc_state* in the console structure normally has a value of 0. When *out_char* detects an ESC character, it changes *c_esc_state* to 1, and subsequent characters are processed by *parse_escape* (line 13986). If the next character is the control sequence introducer, state 2 is entered; otherwise the sequence is considered complete, and *do_escape* (line 14045) is called. In state 2, as long as incoming characters are numeric, a parameter is calculated by multiplying the previous value of the parameter (initially 0) by 10 and adding the numeric value of the current character. The parameter values are kept in an array and when a semicolon is detected the processing shifts to the next cell in the array. (The array in MINIX has only two elements, but the principle is the same). When a nonnumeric character that is not a semicolon is encountered the sequence is considered complete, and again *do_escape* is called. The current character on entry to *do_escape* then is used to select exactly what action to take and how to interpret the parameters, either the defaults or those entered in the character stream. This is illustrated in Fig. 3-48.

Loadable Keymaps

The IBM PC keyboard does not generate ASCII codes directly. The keys are each identified with a number, starting with the keys that are located in the upper left of the original PC keyboard—1 for the "ESC" key, 2 for the "1", and so on. Each key is assigned a number, including modifier keys like the left SHIFT and right SHIFT keys, numbers 42 and 54. When a key is pressed, MINIX receives the key number as a scan code. A scan code is also generated when a key is released, but the code generated upon release has the most significant bit set (equivalent to adding 128 to the key number). Thus a key press and a key release can be distinguished. By keeping track of which modifier keys have been pressed and not yet released, a large number of combinations are possible. For ordinary purposes, of course, two-finger combinations, such as SHIFT-A or CTRL-D, are most manageable for two-handed typists, but for special occasions three-key (or more) combinations are possible, for instance, CTRL-SHIFT-A, or the well-known CTRL-ALT-DEL combination that PC users recognize as the way to reset and reboot the system.

The complexity of the PC keyboard allows for a great deal of flexibility in how it used. A standard keyboard has 47 ordinary character keys defined (26 alphabetic, 10 numeric, and 11 punctuation). If we are willing to use three-fingered modifier key combinations, such as CTRL-ALT-SHIFT, we can support a character set of 376 (8×47) members. This is by no means the limit of what is possible, but for now let us assume we do not want to distinguish between the left- and right-hand modifier keys, or use any of the numeric keypad or function keys. Indeed, we are not limited to using just the CTRL, ALT, and SHIFT keys as modifiers; we could retire some keys from the set of ordinary keys and use them as modifiers if we desired to write a driver that supported such a system.

Operating systems that use such keyboards use a **keymap** to determine what character code to pass to a program based upon the key being pressed and the modifiers in effect. The MINIX keymap logically is an array of 128 rows, representing possible scan code values (this size was chosen to accommodate Japanese keyboards; U.S. and European keyboards do not have this many keys) and 6 columns. The columns represent no modifier, the SHIFT key, the Control key, the left ALT key, the right ALT key, and a combination of either ALT key plus the SHIFT key. There are thus 720 (($128 - 6) \times 6$) character codes that can be generated by this scheme, given an adequate keyboard. This requires that each entry in the table be a 16-bit quantity. For U.S. keyboards the ALT and ALT2 columns are identical. ALT2 is named ALTGR on keyboards for other languages, and many of these keymaps support keys with three symbols by using this key as a modifier.

A standard keymap (determined by the line

```
#include keymaps/us-std.src
```

in *keyboard.c*) is compiled into the MINIX kernel at compilation time, but an

```
ioctl(0, KIOCSMAP, keymap)
```

call can be used to load a different map into the kernel at address *keymap*. A full keymap occupies 1536 bytes ($128 \times 6 \times 2$). Extra keymaps are stored in compressed form. A program called *genmap* is used to make a new compressed keymap. When compiled, *genmap* includes the *keymap.src* code for a particular keymap, so the map is compiled within *genmap*. Normally, *genmap* is executed immediately after being compiled, at which time it outputs the compressed version to a file, and then the *genmap* binary is deleted. The command *loadkeys* reads a compressed keymap, expands it internally, and then calls IOCTL to transfer the keymap into the kernel memory. MINIX can execute *loadkeys* automatically upon starting, and the program can also be invoked by the user at any time.

Scan code	Character	Regular	SHIFT	ALT1	ALT2	ALT+SHIFT	CTRL
00	none	0	0	0	0	0	0
01	ESC	C('[')	C('[')	CA('[')	CA('[')	CA('[')	C('[')
02	'1'	'1'	'!'	A('1')	A('1')	A('!')	C('A')
13	'='	'='	'+'	A('=')	A('=')	A('+')	C('@')
16	'q'	L('q')	'Q'	A('q')	A('q')	A('Q')	C('Q')
28	CR/LF	C('M')	C('M')	CA('M')	CA('M')	CA('M')	C('J')
29	CTRL	CTRL	CTRL	CTRL	CTRL	CTRL	CTRL
59	F1	F1	SF1	AF1	AF1	ASF1	CF1
127	???	0	0	0	0	0	0

Figure 3-41. A few entries from a keymap source file.

The source code for a keymap defines a large initialized array, and in the interest of saving space a keymap file is not printed with the source code. Figure 3-41 shows in tabular form the contents of a few lines of *src/kernel/keymaps/us-std.src* which illustrate several aspects of keymaps. There is no key on the IBM-PC keyboard that generates a scan code of 0. The entry for code 1, the ESC key, shows that the value returned is unchanged when the SHIFT key or CTRL key are pressed, but that a different code is returned when an ALT key is pressed simultaneously with the ESC key. The values compiled into the various columns are determined by macros defined in *include/minix/keymap.h*:

```
#define C(c)    ((c) & 0x1F)         /* Map to control code */
#define A(c)    ((c) | 0x80)         /* Set eight bit (ALT) */
#define CA(c)   A(C(c))              /* CTRL-ALT */
#define L(c)    ((c) | HASCAPS)      /* Add "Caps Lock has effect" attribute */
```

The first three of these macros manipulate bits in the code for the quoted character to produce the necessary code to be returned to the application. The last one sets the HASCAPS bit in the high byte of the 16-bit value. This is a flag that indicates that the state of the capslock variable has to be checked and the code possibly modified before being returned. In the figure, the entries for scan codes 2, 13, and

16 show how typical numeric, punctuation, and alphabetic keys are handled. For code 28 a special feature is seen—normally the ENTER key produces a CR (0x0D) code, represented here as C('M'). Because the newline character in UNIX files is the LF (0x0A) code, and it is sometimes necessary to enter this directly, this keyboard map provides for a CTRL-ENTER combination, which produces this code, C('J').

Scan code 29 is one of the modifier codes and must be recognized no matter what other key is pressed, so the CTRL value is returned regardless of any other key that may be pressed. The function keys do not return ordinary ASCII values, and the row for scan code 59 shows symbolically the values (defined in *include/minix/keymap.h*) that are returned for the F1 key in combination with other modifiers. These values are F1: 0x0110, SF1: 0x1010, AF1: 0x0810, ASF1: 0x0C10, and CF1: 0x0210. The last entry shown in the figure, for scan code 127, is typical of many entries near the end of the array. For many keyboards, certainly most of those used in Europe and the Americas, there are not enough keys to generate all the possible codes, and these entries in the table are filled with zeroes.

Loadable Fonts

Early PCs had the patterns for generating characters on a video screen stored only in ROM, but the displays used on modern systems provide RAM on the video display adapters into which custom character generator patterns can be loaded. This is supported by MINIX with a

ioctl(0, TIOCSFON, font)

IOCTL operation. MINIX supports an 80 lines × 25 rows video mode, and font files contain 4096 bytes. Each byte represents a line of 8 pixels that are illuminated if the bit value is 1, and 16 such lines are needed to map each character. However the video display adapter uses 32 bytes to map each character, to provide higher resolution in modes not currently supported by MINIX. The *loadfont* command is provided to convert these files into the 8192-byte *font* structure referenced by the IOCTL call and to use that call to load the font. As with the keymaps, a font can be loaded at startup time, or at any time during normal operation. However, every video adapter has a standard font built into its ROM that is available by default. There is no need to compile a font into MINIX itself, and the only font support necessary in the kernel is the code to carry out the *TIOCSFON* IOCTL operation.

3.9.4 Implementation of the Device-Independent Terminal Driver

In this section we will begin to look at the source code of the terminal driver in detail. We saw when we studied the block devices that multiple tasks supporting several different devices could share a common base of software. The case with the terminal devices is similar, but with the difference that there is one terminal task that supports several different kinds of terminal device. Here we will start with the device-independent code. In later sections we will look at the device-dependent code for the keyboard and the memory-mapped console display.

Terminal Task Data Structures

The file *tty.h* contains definitions used by the C files which implement the terminal drivers. Most of the variables declared in this file are identified by the prefix *tty_*. There is also one such variable declared in *glo.h* as *EXTERN*. This is *tty_timeout*, which is used by both the clock and terminal interrupt handlers.

Within *tty.h*, the definitions of the *O_NOCTTY* and *O_NONBLOCK* flags (which are optional arguments to the OPEN call) are duplicates of definitions in *include/fcntl.h* but they are repeated here so as not to require including another file. The *devfun_t* and *devfunarg_t* types (lines 11611 and 11612) are used to define pointers to functions, in order to provide for indirect calls using a mechanism similar to what we saw in the code for the main loop of the disk drivers.

The most important definition in *tty.h* is the *tty* structure (lines 11614 to 11668). There is one such structure for each terminal device (the console display and keyboard together count as a single terminal). The first variable in the *tty* structure, *tty_events*, is the flag that is set when an interrupt causes a change that requires the terminal task to attend to the device. When this flag is raised, the global variable *tty_timeout* is also manipulated to tell the clock interrupt handler to awaken the terminal task on the next clock tick.

The rest of the *tty* structure is organized to group together variables that deal with input, output, status, and information about incomplete operations. In the input section, *tty_inhead* and *tty_intail* define the queue where received characters are buffered. *Tty_incount* counts the number of characters in this queue, and *tty_eotct* counts lines or characters, as explained below. All device-specific calls are done indirectly, with the exception of the routines that initialize the terminals, which are called to set up the pointers used for the indirect calls. The *tty_devread* and *tty_icancel* fields hold pointers to device-specific code to perform the read and input cancel operations. *Tty_min* is used in comparisons with *tty_eotct*. When the latter becomes equal to the former, a read operation is complete. During canonical input, *tty_min* is set to 1 and *tty_eotct* counts lines entered. During noncanonical input, *tty_eotct* counts characters and *tty_min* is set from the *MIN* field of the *termios* structure. The comparison of the two variables thus tells when a line is ready or when the minimum character count is reached, depending upon the mode.

Tty_time holds the timer value that determines when the terminal task should be awakened by the clock interrupt handler, and *tty_timenext* is a pointer used to chain the active *tty_time* fields together in a linked list. The list is sorted whenever a timer is set, so the clock interrupt handler only has to look at the first entry. MINIX can support many remote terminals, of which only a few may have timers set at any time. The list of active timers makes the job of the clock handler easier than it would be if it had to check each entry in *tty_table*.

Since queueing of output is handled by the device-specific code, the output section of *tty* declares no variables and consists entirely of pointers to device-specific functions that write, echo, send a break signal, and cancel output. In the status section the flags *tty_reprint*, *tty_escaped*, and *tty_inhibited* indicate that the last character seen has a special meaning; for instance, when a CTRL-V (LNEXT) character is seen, *tty_escaped* is set to 1 to indicate that any special meaning of the next character is to be ignored.

The next part of the structure holds data about *DEV_READ*, *DEV_WRITE*, and *DEV_IOCTL* operations in progress. There are two processes involved in each of these operations. The server managing the system call (normally FS) is identified in *tty_incaller* (line 11644). The server calls the tty task on behalf of another process that needs to do an I/O operation, and this client is identified in *tty_inproc* (line 11645). As described in Fig. 3-37, during a READ, characters are transferred directly from the terminal task to a buffer within the memory space of the original caller. *Tty_inproc* and *tty_in_vir* locate this buffer. The next two variables, *tty_inleft* and *tty_incum*, count the characters still needed and those already transferred. Similar sets of variables are needed for a WRITE system call. For IOCTL there may be an immediate transfer of data between the requesting process and the task, so a virtual address is needed, but there is no need for variables to mark the progress of an operation. An IOCTL request may be postponed, for instance, until current output is complete, but when the time is right the request is carried out in a single operation. Finally, the *tty* structure includes some variables that fall into no other category, including pointers to the functions to handle the *DEV_IOCTL* and *DEV_CLOSE* operations at the device level, a POSIX-style *termios* structure, and a *winsize* structure that provides support for window-oriented screen displays. The last part of the structure provides storage for the input queue itself in the array *tty_inbuf*. Note that this is an array of *u16_t*, not of 8-bit *char* characters. Although applications and devices use 8-bit codes for characters, the C language requires the input function *getchar* to work with a larger data type so it can return a symbolic *EOF* value in addition to all 256 possible byte values.

The *tty_table*, an array of *tty* structures, is declared using the *EXTERN* macro (line 11670). There is one element for each terminal enabled by the *NR_CONS*, *NR_RS_LINES*, and *NR_PTYS* definitions in *include/minix/config.h*. For the configuration discussed in this book, two consoles are enabled, but MINIX may be recompiled to add up to 2 serial lines, and up to 64 pseudo terminals.

There is one other *EXTERN* definition in *tty.h*. *Tty_timelist* (line 11690) is a pointer used by the timer to hold the head of the linked list of *tty_time* fields. The *tty.h* header file is included in many files and storage for *tty_table* and *tty_timelist* is allocated during compilation of *table.c*, in the same way as the *EXTERN* variables that are defined in the *glo.h* header file.

At the end of *tty.h* two macros, *buflen* and *bufend*, are defined. These are used frequently in the terminal task code, which does much copying of data into and out of buffers.

The Device-Independent Terminal Driver

The main terminal task and the device-independent supporting functions are all in *tty.c*. Since the task supports many different devices, the minor device numbers must be used to distinguish which device is being supported on a particular call, and they are defined on lines 11760 to 11764. Following this there are a number of macro definitions. If a device is not initialized, the pointers to that device's device-specific functions will contain zeroes put there by the C compiler. This makes it possible to define the *tty_active* macro (line 11774) which returns *FALSE* if a null pointer is found. Of course, the initialization code for a device cannot be accessed indirectly if part of its job is to initialize the pointers that make indirect access possible. On lines 11777 to 11783 are conditional macro definitions to equate initialization calls for RS-232 or pseudo terminal devices to calls to a null function when these devices are not configured. *Do_pty* may be similarly disabled in this section. This makes it possible to omit the code for these devices entirely if it is not needed.

Since there are so many configurable parameters for each terminal, and there may be quite a few terminals on a networked system, a *termios_defaults* structure is declared and initialized with default values (all of which are defined in *include/termios.h*) on lines 11803 to 11810. This structure is copied into the *tty_table* entry for a terminal whenever it is necessary to initialize or reinitialize it. The defaults for the special characters were shown in Fig. 3-33. Figure 3-42 shows the default values for the various flags. On the following line the *winsize_defaults* structure is similarly declared. It is left to be initialized to all zeroes by the C compiler. This is the proper default action; it means "window size is unknown, use */etc/termcap*."

Field	Default values
c_iflag	BRKINT ICRNL IXON IXANY
c_oflag	OPOST ONLCR
c_cflag	CREAD CS8 HUPCL
c_lflag	ISIG IEXTEN ICANON ECHO ECHOE

Figure 3-42. Default termios flag values.

The entry point for the terminal task is *tty_task* (line 11817). Before entering the main loop, a call is made to *tty_init* for each configured terminal (in the loop on line 11826), and then the MINIX startup message is displayed (lines 11829 to

11831). Although the source code shows a call to *printf*, when this code is compiled the macro that converts calls to the *printf* library routine into calls to *printk* is in effect. *Printk* uses a routine called *putk* within the console driver, so the FS is not involved. This message goes only to the primary console display and cannot be redirected.

The main loop on lines 11833 to 11884 is, in principle, like the main loop of any task—it receives a message, executes a switch on the message type to call the appropriate function, and then generates a return message. However, there are some complications. First, much work is done by low-level interrupt routines, especially in handling terminal input. In the previous section we saw that individual characters from the keyboard are accepted and buffered without sending a message to the terminal task for each character. Thus, before attempting to receive a message, the main loop always sweeps through the entire *tty_table*, inspecting each terminal's *tp->tty_events* flag and calling *handle_events* as necessary (lines 11835 to 11837), to take care of unfinished business. Only when there is nothing demanding immediate attention is a call made to receive. If the message received is from the hardware a continue statement short-circuits the loop, and the check for events is repeated.

Second, this task services several devices. If a received message is from a hardware interrupt, the device or devices that need service are identified by checking the *tp->tty_events* flags. If the interrupt is not a hardware interrupt the *TTY_LINE* field in the message is used to determine which device should respond to the message. The minor device number is decoded by a series of comparisons, by means of which *tp* is pointed to the correct entry in the *tty_table* (lines 11845 to 11864). If the device is a pseudo terminal, *do_pty* (in *pty.c*) is called and the main loop is restarted. In this case *do_pty* generates the reply message. Of course, if pseudo terminals are not enabled, the call to *do_pty* uses the dummy macro defined earlier. One would hope that attempts to access nonexistent devices would not occur, but it is always easier to add another check than to verify that there are no errors elsewhere in the system. In case the device does not exist or is not configured, a reply message with an *ENXIO* error message is generated and, again, control returns to the top of the loop.

The rest of the task resembles what we have seen in the main loop of other tasks, a switch on the message type (lines 11874 to 11883). The appropriate function for the type of request, *do_read*, *do_write*, and so on, is called. In each case the called function generates the reply message, rather than pass the information needed to construct the message back to the main loop. A reply message is generated at the end of the main loop only if a valid message type was not received, in which case an *EINVAL* error message is sent. Because reply messages are sent from many different places within the terminal task a common routine, *tty_reply*, is called to handle the details of constructing reply messages.

If the message received by *tty_task* is a valid message type, not the result of an interrupt, and does not come from a pseudo terminal, the switch at the end of the main loop will dispatch to one of the functions *do_read*, *do_write*, *do_ioctl*, *do_open*, *do_close*, or *do_cancel*. The arguments to each of these calls are *tp*, a pointer to a *tty* structure, and the address of the message. Before looking at each of them, we will mention a few general considerations. Since *tty_task* may service multiple terminal devices, these functions must return quickly so the main loop can continue. However, *do_read*, *do_write*, and *do_ioctl* may not be able to complete immediately all the requested work. In order to allow FS to service other calls, an immediate reply is required. If the request cannot be completed immediately, the *SUSPEND* code is returned in the status field of the reply message. This corresponds to the message marked (3) in Fig. 3-37 and suspends the process that initiated the call, while unblocking the FS. Messages corresponding to (7) and (8) in the figure will be sent later when the operation can be completed. If the request can be fully satisfied, or an error occurs, either the count of bytes transferred or the error code is returned in the status field of the return message to the FS. In this case a message will be sent immediately from the FS back to the process that made the original call, to wake it up.

Reading from a terminal is fundamentally different from reading from a disk device. The disk driver issues a command to the disk hardware and eventually data will be returned, barring a mechanical or electrical failure. The computer can display a prompt upon the screen, but there is no way for it to force a person sitting at the keyboard to start typing. For that matter, there is no guarantee that anybody will be sitting there at all. In order to make the speedy return that is required, *do_read* (line 11891) starts by storing information that will enable the request to be completed later, when and if input arrives. There are a few error checks to be made first. It is an error if the device is still expecting input to fulfill a previous request, or if the parameters in the message are invalid (lines 11901 to 11908). If these tests are passed, information about the request is copied into the proper fields in the device's *tp->tty_table* entry on lines 11911 to 11915. The last step, setting *tp->tty_inleft* to the number of characters requested, is important. This variable is used to determine when the read request is satisfied. In canonical mode *tp->tty_inleft* is decremented by one for each character returned, until an end of line is received, at which point it is suddenly reduced to zero. In noncanonical mode it is handled differently, but in any case it is reset to zero whenever the call is satisfied, whether by a timeout or by receiving at least the minimum number of bytes requested. When *tp->tty_inleft* reaches zero, a reply message is sent. As we will see, reply messages can be generated in several places. It is sometimes necessary to check whether a reading process still expects a reply; a nonzero value of *tp->tty_inleft* serves as a flag for that purpose.

In canonical mode a terminal device waits for input until either the number of characters asked for in the call has been received, or the end of a line or the end of the file is reached. The *ICANON* bit in the *termios* structure is tested on line 11917 to see if canonical mode is in effect for the terminal. If it is not set, the *termios MIN* and *TIME* values are checked to determine what action to take.

In Fig. 3-35 we saw how *MIN* and *TIME* interact to provide different ways a read call can behave. *TIME* is tested on line 11918. A value of zero corresponds to the left-hand column in Fig. 3-35, and in this case no further tests are needed at this point. If *TIME* is nonzero, then *MIN* is tested. If it is zero, *settimer* is called on to start the timer that will terminate the *DEV_READ* request after a delay, even if no bytes have been received. *Tp−>tty_min* is set to 1 here, so the call will terminate immediately if one or more bytes are received before the timeout. At this point no check for possible input has yet been made, so more than one character may already be waiting to satisfy the request. In that case, as many characters as are ready, up to the number specified in the READ call, will be returned as soon as the input is found. If both *TIME* and *MIN* are nonzero, the timer has a different meaning. The timer is used as an inter-character timer in this case. It is started only after the first character is received and is restarted after each successive character. *Tp−>tty_eotct* counts characters in noncanonical mode, and if it is zero at line 11931, no characters have been received yet and the inter-byte timer is inhibited. *Lock* and *unlock* are used to protect both of these calls to *settimer*, to prevent clock interrupts when *settimer* is running.

In any case, at line 11941, *in_transfer* is called to transfer any bytes already in the input queue directly to the reading process. Next there is a call to *handle_events*, which may put more data into the input queue and which calls *in_transfer* again. This apparent duplication of calls requires some explanation. Although the discussion so far has been in terms of keyboard input, *do_read* is in the device-independent part of the code and also services input from remote terminals connected by serial lines. It is possible that previous input has filled the RS-232 input buffer to the point where input has been inhibited. The first call to *in_transfer* does not start the flow again, but the call to *handle_events* can have this effect. The fact that it then causes a second call to *in_transfer* is just a bonus. The important thing is to be sure the remote terminal is allowed to send again. Either of these calls may result in satisfaction of the request and sending of the reply message to the FS. *Tp−>tty_inleft* is used as a flag to see if the reply has been sent; if it is still nonzero at line 11944, *do_read* generates and sends the reply message itself. This is done on lines 11949 to 11957. If the original request specified a nonblocking read, the FS is told to pass an *EAGAIN* error code back to original caller. If the call is an ordinary blocking read, the FS receives a *SUSPEND* code, unblocking it but telling it to leave the original caller blocked. In this case the terminal's *tp−>tty_inrepcode* field is set to *REVIVE*. When and if the READ is later satisfied, this code will be placed in the reply message to the FS to indicate that the original caller was put to sleep and needs to be revived.

Do_write (line 11964) is similar to *do_read*, but simpler, because there are fewer options to be concerned about in handling a WRITE system call. Checks similar to those made by *do_read* are made to see that a previous write is not still in progress and that the message parameters are valid, and then the parameters of the request are copied into the *tty* structure. *Handle_events* is then called, and *tp−>tty_outleft* is checked to see if the work was done (lines 11991 and 11992). If so, a reply message already has been sent by *handle_events* and there is nothing left to do. If not, a reply message is generated. with the message parameters depending upon whether or not the original WRITE call was called in nonblocking mode.

POSIX function	POSIX operation	IOCTL type	IOCTL parameter
tcdrain	(none)	TCDRAIN	(none)
tcflow	TCOOFF	TCFLOW	int=TCOOFF
tcflow	TCOON	TCFLOW	int=TCOON
tcflow	TCIOFF	TCFLOW	int=TCIOFF
tcflow	TCION	TCFLOW	int=TCION
tcflush	TCIFLUSH	TCFLSH	int=TCIFLUSH
tcflush	TCOFLUSH	TCFLSH	int=TCOFLUSH
tcflush	TCIOFLUSH	TCFLSH	int=TCIOFLUSH
tcgetattr	(none)	TCGETS	termios
tcsetattr	TCSANOW	TCSETS	termios
tcsetattr	TCSADRAIN	TCSETSW	termios
tcsetattr	TCSAFLUSH	TCSETSF	termios
tcsendbreak	(none)	TCSBRK	int=duration

Figure 3-43. POSIX calls and IOCTL operations.

The next function, *do_ioctl* (line 12012), is a long one, but not difficult to understand. The body of *do_ioctl* is two switch statements. The first determines the size of the parameter pointed to by the pointer in the request message (lines 12033 to 12064). If the size is not zero, the parameter's validity is tested. The contents cannot be tested here, but what can be tested is whether a structure of the required size beginning at the specified address fits within the segment it is specified to be in. The rest of the function is another switch on the type of IOCTL operation requested (lines 12075 to 12161). Unfortunately, supporting the POSIX-required operations with the IOCTL call meant that names for IOCTL operations had to be invented that suggest, but do not duplicate, names required by POSIX. Figure 3-43 shows the relationship between the POSIX request names and the names used by the MINIX IOCTL call. A *TCGETS* operation services a *tcgetattr* call by the user and simply returns a copy of the terminal device's *tp−>tty_termios* structure. The next four request types share code. The *TCSETSW*, *TCSETSF*, and *TCSETS* request types correspond to user calls to the POSIX-defined function *tcsetattr*, and all have the basic action of copying a new *termios* structure into a terminal's *tty* structure. The copying is done immediately for *TCSETS* calls and may be done for *TCSETSW* and *TCSETSF* calls if output is complete, by a *phys_copy* call to get the data from the user, followed by a call to *setattr*, on lines 12098 and 12099. If *tcsetattr* was called with a modifier requesting postponement of the action until completion of current output, the parameters for the request are placed in the terminal's *tty* structure for later processing if the test of $tp{-}{>}tty\_outleft$ on line 12084 reveals output is not complete. *Tcdrain* suspends a program until output is complete and is translated into an IOCTL call of type *TCDRAIN*. If output is already complete, it has nothing more to do. If not, it also must leave information in the *tty* structure.

The POSIX *tcflush* function discards unread input and/or unsent output data, according to its argument, and the IOCTL translation is straightforward, consisting of a call to the *tty_icancel* function that services all terminals, and/or the device-specific function pointed to by $tp{-}{>}tty\_ocancel$ (lines 12102 to 12109). *Tcflow* is similarly translated in a straightforward way into an IOCTL call. To suspend or restart output, it sets a *TRUE* or *FALSE* value into $tp{-}{>}tty\_inhibited$ and then sets the $tp{-}{>}tty\_events$ flag. To suspend or restart input, it sends the appropriate *STOP* (normally CTRL-S) or *START* (CTRL-Q) code to the remote terminal, using the device-specific echo routine pointed to by $tp{-}{>}tty\_echo$ (lines 12120 to 12125).

Most of the rest of the operations handled by *do_ioctl* are handled in one line of code, by calling an appropriate function. In the cases of the *KIOCSMAP* (load keymap) and *TIOCSFON* (load font) operations, a test is made to be sure the device really is a console, since these operations do not apply to other terminals. If virtual terminals are in use the same keymap and font apply to all consoles, the hardware does not permit any easy way of doing otherwise. The window size operations copy a *winsize* structure between the user process and the terminal task. Note, however, the comment under the code for the *TIOCSWINSZ* operation. When a process changes its window size, the kernel is expected to send a *SIGWINCH* signal to the process group under some versions of UNIX. The signal is not required by the POSIX standard. But, anyone thinking of using these structures should consider adding code here to initiate this signal.

The last two cases in *do_ioctl* support the POSIX required *tcgetpgrp* and *tcsetpgrp* functions. There is no action associated with these cases, and they always return an error. There is nothing wrong with this. These functions support **job control**, the ability to suspend and restart a process from the keyboard. Job control is not required by POSIX and is not supported by MINIX. However, POSIX requires these functions, even when job control is not supported, to ensure portability of programs.

Do_open (line 12171) has a simple basic action to perform—it increments the variable $tp{-}{>}tty\_openct$ for the device so it can be verified that it is open. However, there are some tests to be done first. POSIX specifies that for ordinary terminals the first process to open a terminal is the **session leader**, and when a session leader dies, access to the terminal is revoked from other processes in its group. Daemons need to be able to write error messages, and if their error output is not redirected to a file, it should go to a display that cannot be closed. For this purpose a device called */dev/log* exists in MINIX. Physically it is the same device as */dev/console*, but it is addressed by a separate minor device number and is treated differently. It is a write-only device, and thus *do_open* returns an *EACCESS* error if an attempt is made to open it for reading (line 12183). The other test done by *do_open* is to test the *O_NOCTTY* flag. If it is not set and the device is not */dev/log*, the terminal becomes the controlling terminal for a process group. This is done by putting the process number of the caller into the *tp->tty_pgrp* field of the *tty_table* entry. Following this, the *tp->tty_openct* variable is incremented and the reply message is sent.

A terminal device may be opened more than once, and the next function, *do_close* (line 12198), has nothing to do except decrement *tp->tty_openct*. The test on line 12204 foils an attempt to close the device if it happens to be */dev/log*. If this operation is the last close, input is canceled by calling *tp->tty_icancel*. Device-specific routines pointed to by *tp->tty_ocancel* and *tp->tty_close* are also called. Then various fields in the *tty* structure for the device are set back to their default values and the reply message is sent.

The last message type handler is *do_cancel* (line 12220). This is invoked when a signal is received for a process that is blocked trying to read or write. There are three states that must be checked:

1. The process may have been reading when killed.

2. The process may have been writing when killed.

3. The process may have been suspended by *tcdrain* until its output was complete.

A test is made for each case, and the general *tp->tty_icancel*, or the device-specific routine pointed to by *tp->tty_ocancel*, is called as necessary. In the last case the only action required is to reset the flag *tp->tty_ioreq*, to indicate the IOCTL operation is now complete. Finally, the *tp->tty_events* flag is set and a reply message is sent.

Terminal Driver Support Code

Now that we have looked at the top-level functions called in the main loop of *tty_task*, it is time to look at the code that supports them. We will start with *handle_events* (line 12256). As mentioned earlier, on each pass through the main loop of the terminal task, the *tp->tty_events* flag for each terminal device is checked and *handle_events* is called if it shows that attention is required for a particular terminal. *Do_read* and *do_write* also call *handle_events*. This routine must work fast. It resets the *tp->tty_events* flag and then calls device-specific

routines to read and write, using the pointers to the functions *tp−>tty_devread*
and *tp−>tty_devwrite* (lines 12279 to 12282). These are called unconditionally,
because there is no way to test whether a read or a write caused the raising of the
flag—a design choice was made here, that checking two flags for each device
would be more expensive than making two calls each time a device was active.
Also, most of the time a character received from a terminal must be echoed, so
both calls will be necessary. As noted in the discussion of the handling of
tcsetattr calls by *do_ioctl*, POSIX may postpone control operations on devices until
current output is complete, so immediately after calling the device-specific
tty_devwrite function is a good time take care of ioctl operations. This is done on
line 12285, where *dev_ioctl* is called if there is a pending control request.

Since the *tp−>tty_events* flag is raised by interrupts, and characters may
arrive in a rapid stream from a fast device, there is a chance that by the time the
calls to the device-specific read and write routines and *dev_ioctl* are completed,
another interrupt will have raised the flag again. A high priority is placed on getting input moved along from the buffer where the interrupt routine places it initially. Thus *handle_events* repeats the calls to the device-specific routines as long
as the *tp−>tty_events* flag is found raised at the end of the loop (line 12286).
When the flow of input stops (it also could be output, but input is more likely to
make such repeated demands), *in_transfer* is called to transfer characters from the
input queue to the buffer within the process that called for a read operation.
In_transfer itself sends a reply message if the transfer completes the request,
either by transferring the maximum number of characters requested or by reaching
the end of a line (in canonical mode). If it does so, *tp−>tty_left* will be zero upon
the return to *handle_events*. Here a further test is made and a reply message is
sent if the number of characters transferred has reached the minimum number requested. Testing *tp−>tty_inleft* prevents sending a duplicate message.

Next we will look at *in_transfer* (line 12303), which is responsible for moving data from the input queue in the task's memory space to the buffer of the user
process that requested the input. However, a straightforward block copy is not
possible. The input queue is a circular buffer and characters have to be checked
to see that the end of the file has not been reached, or, if canonical mode is in
effect, that the transfer only continues up through the end of a line. Also, the
input queue is a queue of 16-bit quantities, but the recipient's buffer is an array of
8-bit characters. Thus an intermediate local buffer is used. Characters are
checked one by one as they are placed in the local buffer, and when it fills up or
when the input queue has been emptied, *phys_copy* is called to move the contents
of the local buffer to the receiving process' buffer (lines 12319 to 12345).

Three variables in the *tty* structure, *tp−>tty_inleft*, *tp−>tty_eotct*, and
tp−>tty_min, are used to decide whether *in_transfer* has any work to do, and the
first two of these control its main loop. As mentioned earlier, *tp−>tty_inleft* is set
initially to the number of characters requested by a READ call. Normally, it is
decremented by one whenever a character is transferred but it may be abruptly

decreased to zero when a condition signaling the end of input is reached. Whenever it becomes zero, a reply message to the reader is generated, so it also serves as a flag to indicate whether or not a message has been sent. Thus in the test on line 12314, finding that $tp->tty\_inleft$ is already zero is a sufficient reason to abort execution of $in\_transfer$ without sending a reply.

In the next part of the test, $tp->tty\_eotct$ and $tp->tty\_min$ are compared. In canonical mode both of these variables refer to complete lines of input, and in noncanonical mode they refer to characters. $Tp->tty\_eotct$ is incremented whenever a "line break" or a byte is placed in the input queue and is decremented by $in\_transfer$ whenever a line or byte is removed from the queue. Thus it counts the number of lines or bytes that have been received by the terminal task but not yet passed on to a reader. $Tp->tty\_min$ indicates the minimum number of lines (in canonical mode) or characters (in noncanonical mode) that must be transferred to complete a read request. Its value is always 1 in canonical mode and may be any value from 0 up to MAX_INPUT (255 in MINIX) in noncanonical mode. The second half of the test on line 12314 causes $in\_transfer$ to return immediately in canonical mode if a full line has not yet been received. The transfer is not done until a line is complete so the queue contents can be modified if, for instance, an ERASE or KILL character is subsequently typed in by the user before the ENTER key is pressed. In noncanonical mode an immediate return occurs if the minimum number of characters is not yet available.

A few lines later, $tp->tty\_inleft$ and $tp->tty\_eotct$ are used to control the main loop of $in\_transfer$. In canonical mode the transfer continues until there is no longer a complete line left in the queue. In noncanonical mode $tp->tty\_eotct$ is a count of pending characters. $Tp->tty\_min$ controls whether the loop is entered but is not used in determining when to stop. Once the loop is entered, either all available characters or the number of characters requested in the original call will be transferred, whichever is smaller.

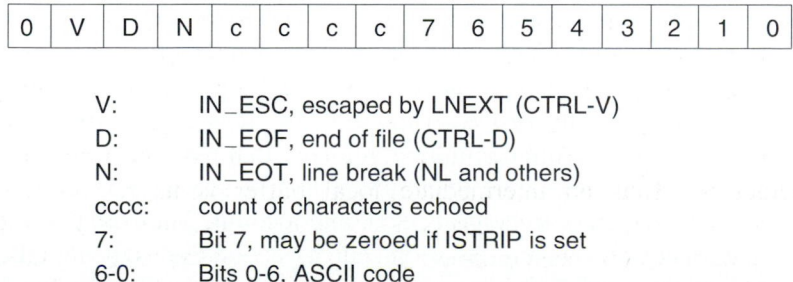

0	V	D	N	c	c	c	c	7	6	5	4	3	2	1	0

V:	IN_ESC, escaped by LNEXT (CTRL-V)
D:	IN_EOF, end of file (CTRL-D)
N:	IN_EOT, line break (NL and others)
cccc:	count of characters echoed
7:	Bit 7, may be zeroed if ISTRIP is set
6-0:	Bits 0-6, ASCII code

Figure 3-44. The fields in a character code as it is placed into the input queue.

Characters are 16-bit quantities in the input queue. The actual character code to be transferred to the user process is in the low 8 bits. Fig. 3-44 shows how the high bits are used. Three are used to flag whether the character is being escaped (by CTRL-V), whether it signifies end-of-file, or whether it represents one of several codes that signify a line is complete. Four bits are used for a count to show how much screen space is used when the character is echoed. The test on line 12322 checks whether the *IN_EOF* bit (*D* in the figure) is set. This is tested at the top of the inner loop because an end-of-file (CTRL-D) is not itself transferred to a reader, nor is it counted in the character count. As each character is transferred, a mask is applied to zero the upper 8 bits, and only the ASCII value in the low 8 bits is transferred into the local buffer (line 12324).

There is more than one way to signal the end of input, but the device-specific input routine is expected to determine whether a character received is a linefeed, CTRL-D, or other such character and to mark each such character. *In_transfer* only needs to test for this mark, the *IN_EOT* bit (*N* in Fig. 3-44), on line 12340. If this is detected, *tp−>tty_eotct* is decremented. In noncanonical mode every character is counted this way as it is put into the input queue, and every character is also marked with the *IN_EOT* bit at that time, so *tp−>tty_eotct* counts characters not yet removed from the queue. The only difference in the operation of the main loop of *in_transfer* in the two different modes is found on line 12343. Here *tp−>tty_inleft* is zeroed in response to finding a character marked as a line break, but only if canonical mode is in effect. Thus when control returns to the top of the loop, the loop terminates properly after a line break in canonical mode, but in noncanonical line breaks are ignored.

When the loop terminates there is usually a partially full local buffer to be transferred (lines 12347 to 12353). Then a reply message is sent if *tp−>tty_inleft* has reached zero. This is always the case in canonical mode, but if noncanonical mode is in effect and the number of characters transferred is less than the full request, the reply is not sent. This may be puzzling if you have a good enough memory for details to remember that where we have seen calls to *in_transfer* (in *do_read* and *handle_events*), the code following the call to *in_transfer* sends a reply message if *in_transfer* returns having transferred more than the amount specified in *tp−>tty_min*, which will certainly be the case here. The reason why a reply is not made unconditionally from *in_transfer* will be seen when we discuss the next function, which calls *in_transfer* under a different set of circumstances.

That next function is *in_process* (line 12367). It is called from the device-specific software to handle the common processing that must be done on all input. Its parameters are a pointer to the *tty* structure for the source device, a pointer to the array of 8-bit characters to be processed, and a count. The count is returned to the caller. *In_process* is a long function, but its actions are not complicated. It adds 16-bit characters to the input queue that is later processed by *in_transfer*.

There are several categories of treatment provided by *in_transfer*.

1. Normal characters are added to the input queue, extended to 16 bits.

2. Characters which affect later processing modify flags to signal the effect but are not placed in the queue.

3. Characters which control echoing are acted upon immediately without being placed in the queue.

4. Characters with special significance have codes such as the *EOT* bit added to their high byte as they are placed in the input queue.

Let us look first at a completely normal situation, an ordinary character, such as "x" (ASCII code 0x78), typed in the middle of a short line, with no escape sequence in effect, on a terminal that is set up with the standard MINIX default properties. As received from the input device this character occupies bits 0 through 7 in Fig. 3-44. On line 12385 it would have its most significant bit, bit 7, reset to zero if the *ISTRIP* bit were set, but the default in MINIX is not to strip the bit, allowing full 8-bit codes to be entered. This would not affect our "x" anyway. The MINIX default is to allow extended processing of input, so the test of the *IEX-TEN* bit in *tp−>tty_termios.c_lflag* (line 12388) passes, but the succeeding tests fail under the conditions we postulate: no character escape is in effect (line 12391), this input is not itself the character escape character (line 12397), and this input is not the *REPRINT* character (line 12405).

Tests on the next several lines find that the input character is not the special *_POSIX_VDISABLE* character, nor is it a *CR* or an *NL*. Finally, a positive result: canonical mode is in effect, this is the normal default (line 12424). However our "x" is not the *ERASE* character, nor is it any of the *KILL, EOF* (CTRL-D), *NL*, or *EOL* characters, so by line 12457 still nothing will have happened to it. Here it is found that the *IXON* bit is set, by default, allowing use of the *STOP* (CTRL-S) and *START* (CTRL-Q) characters, but in the ensuing tests for these no match is found. On line 12478 it is found that the *ISIG* bit, enabling the use of the *INTR* and *QUIT* characters, is set by default, but again no match is found.

In fact, the first interesting thing that might happen to an ordinary character occurs on line 12491, where a test is made to see if the input queue is already full. If this were the case, the character would be discarded at this point, since canonical mode is in effect, and the user would not see it echoed on the screen. (The continue statement discards the character, since it causes the outer loop to restart). However, since we postulate completely normal conditions for this illustration, let us assume the buffer is not full yet. The next test, to see if special noncanonical mode processing is needed (line 12497), fails, causing a jump forward to line 12512. Here *echo* is called to display the character to the user, since the *ECHO* bit in *tp−>tty_termios.c_lflag* is set by default.

Finally, on lines 12515 to 12519 the character is disposed of by being put into the input queue. At this time *tp−>tty_incount* is incremented, but since this is an ordinary character, not marked by the *EOT* bit, *tp−>tty_eotct* is not changed.

The last line in the loop calls *in_transfer* if the character just transferred into the queue fills it. However, under the ordinary conditions we postulate for this example, *in_transfer* would do nothing, even if called, since (assuming the queue has been serviced normally and previous input was accepted when the previous line of input was complete) *tp->tty_eotct* is zero, *tp->tty_min* is one, and the test at the start of *in_transfer* (line 12314) causes an immediate return.

Having passed through *in_process* with an ordinary character under ordinary conditions, let us now go back to the start of *in_process* and look at what happens in less ordinary circumstances. First, we will look at the character escape, which allows a character which ordinarily has a special effect to be passed on to the user process. If a character escape is in effect, the *tp->tty_escaped* flag is set, and when this is detected (on line 12391) the flag is reset immediately and the *IN_ESC* bit, bit V in Fig. 3-44, is added to the current character. This causes special processing when the character is echoed—escaped control characters are displayed as "^" plus the character to make them visible. The *IN_ESC* bit also prevents the character from being recognized by tests for special characters. The next few lines process the escape character itself, the *LNEXT* character (CTRL-V by default). When the *LNEXT* code is detected the *tp->tty_escaped* flag is set, and *rawecho* is called twice to output a "^" followed by a backspace. This reminds the user at the keyboard that an escape is in effect, and when the following character is echoed, it overwrites the "^". The *LNEXT* character is an example of one that affects later characters (in this case, only the very next character). It is not placed in the queue, and the loop restarts after the two calls to *rawecho*. The order of these two tests is important, making it possible to enter the *LNEXT* character itself twice in a row, in order to pass the second copy on to a process.

The next special character processed by *in_process* is the *REPRINT* character (CTRL-R). When it is found a call to *reprint* ensues (line 12406), causing the current echoed output to be redisplayed. The *REPRINT* itself is then discarded with no effect upon the input queue.

Going into detail on the handling of every special character would be tedious, and the source code of *in_process* is straightforward. We will mention just a few more points. One is that the use of special bits in the high byte of the 16-bit value placed in the input queue makes it easy to identify a class of characters that have similar effects. Thus, *EOT* (CTRL-D), *LF*, and the alternate *EOL* character (undefined by default) are all marked by the *EOT* bit, bit D in Fig. 3-44 (lines 12447 to 12453), making later recognition easy. Finally, we will justify the peculiar behavior of *in_transfer* noted earlier. A reply is not generated each time it terminates, although in the calls to *in_transfer* we have seen previously, it seemed that a reply would always be generated upon return. Recall that the call to *in_transfer* made by *in_process* when the input queue is full (line 12522) has no effect when canonical mode is in effect. But if noncanonical processing is desired, every character is marked with the *EOT* bit on line 12499, and thus every character is counted by *tp->tty_eotct* on line 12519. In turn, this causes entry into the main loop of *in_transfer* when it is called because of a full input queue in noncanonical mode. On such occasions no message should be sent at the termination of *in_transfer*, because there are likely to be more characters read after returning to *in_process*. Indeed, although in canonical mode input to a single READ is limited by the size of the input queue (255 characters in MINIX), in noncanonical mode a READ call must be able to deliver the POSIX-required _POSIX_SSIZE_MAX number of characters. Its value in MINIX is 32767.

The next few functions in *tty.c* support character input. *Echo* (line 12531) treats a few characters in a special way, but most just get displayed on the output side of the same device being used for input. Output from a process may be going to a device at the same time input is being echoed, which makes things messy if the user at the keyboard tries to backspace. To deal with this, the *tp−>tty_reprint* flag is always set to *TRUE* by the device-specific output routines when normal output is produced, so the function called to handle a backspace can tell that mixed output has been produced. Since *echo* also uses the device-output routines, the current value of *tp−>tty_reprint* is preserved while echoing, using the local variable *rp* (lines 12552 to 12585). However, if a new line of input has just begun, *rp* is set to *FALSE* instead of taking on the old value, thus assuring that *tp−>tty_reprint* will be reset when *echo* terminates.

You may have noticed that *echo* returns a value, for instance, in the call on line 12512 in *in_process*:

```
ch = echo(tp, ch)
```

The value returned by *echo* contains the number of spaces used on the screen for the echo display, which may be up to eight if the character is a *TAB*. This count is placed in the *cccc* field in Fig. 3-44. Ordinary characters occupy one space on the screen, but if a control character (other than *TAB*, *NL*, or *CR* or a *DEL* (0x7F) is echoed, it is displayed as a ""^"" plus a printable ASCII character and occupies two positions on the screen. On the other hand an *NL* or *CR* occupies zero spaces. The actual echoing must be done by a device-specific routine, of course, and whenever a character must be passed to the device, an indirect call is made using *tp−>tty_echo*, as, for instance, on line 12580, for ordinary characters.

The next function, *rawecho*, is used to bypass the special handling done by *echo*. It checks to see if the *ECHO* flag is set, and if it is, sends the character along to the device-specific *tp−>tty_echo* routine without any special processing. A local variable *rp* is used here to prevent *rawecho*'s own call to the output routine from changing the value of *tp−>tty_reprint*.

When a backspace is found by *in_process*, the next function, *backover* (line 12607), is called. It manipulates the input queue to remove the previous head of the queue if backing up is possible—if the queue is empty or if the last character is a line break, then backing up is not possible. Here the *tp−>tty_reprint* flag mentioned in the discussions of *echo* and *rawecho* is tested. If it is *TRUE*, then *reprint* is called (line 12618) to put a clean copy of the output line on the screen. Then the *len* field of the last character displayed (the *cccc* field of Fig. 3-44) is consulted to find out how many characters have to be deleted on the display, and for each character a sequence of backspace-space-backspace characters is sent through *rawecho* to remove the unwanted character from the screen.

Reprint is the next function. In addition to being called by *backover*, it may be invoked by the user pressing the *REPRINT* key (CTRL-R). The loop on lines 12651 to 12656 searches backward through the input queue for the last line break. If it is found in the last position filled, there is nothing to do and *reprint* returns. Otherwise, it echos the CTRL-R, which appears on the display as the two character sequence "^R", and then moves to the next line and redisplays the queue from the last line break to the end.

Now we have arrived at *out_process* (line 12677). Like *in_process*, it is called by device-specific output routines, but it is simpler. It is called by the RS-232 and pseudo terminal device-specific output routines, but not by the console routine. *Out_process* works upon a circular buffer of bytes but does not remove them from the buffer. The only change it makes to the array is to insert a *CR* character ahead of an *NL* character in the buffer if the *OPOST* (enable output processing) and *ONLCR* (map NL to CR-NL) bits in *tp->tty_termios.oflag* are set. Both bits are set by default in MINIX. Its job is to keep the *tp->tty_position* variable in the device's *tty* structure up to date. Tabs and backspaces complicate life.

The next routine is *dev_ioctl* (line 12763). It supports *do_ioctl* in carrying out the *tcdrain* function and the *tcsetattr* function when it is called with either the *TCSADRAIN* or *TCSAFLUSH* options. In these cases, *do_ioctl* cannot complete the action immediately if output is incomplete, so information about the request is stored in the parts of the *tty* structure reserved for delayed IOCTL operations. Whenever *handle_events* runs, it checks the *tp->tty_ioreq* field after calling the device-specific output routine and calls *dev_ioctl* if an operation is pending. *Dev_ioctl* tests *tp->tty_outleft* to see if output is complete, and if so, carries out the same actions that *do_ioctl* would have carried out immediately if there had been no delay. To service *tcdrain*, the only action is to reset the *tp->tty_ioreq* field and send the reply message to the FS, telling it to wake up the process that made the original call. The *TCSAFLUSH* variant of *tcsetattr* calls *tty_icancel* to cancel input. For both variants of *tcsetattr*, the *termios* structure whose address was passed in the original call to IOCTL is copied to the device's *tp->tty_termios* structure. *Setattr* is then called, followed, as with *tcdrain*, by sending a reply message to wake up the blocked original caller.

Setattr (line 12789) is the next procedure. As we have seen, it is called by *do_ioctl* or *dev_ioctl* to change the attributes of a terminal device, and by *do_close* to reset the attributes back to the default settings. *Setattr* is always called after copying a new *termios* structure into a device's *tty* structure, because merely copying the parameters is not enough. If the device being controlled is now in noncanonical mode, the first action is to mark all characters currently in the input queue with the *IN_EOT* bit, as would have been done when these characters were originally entered in the queue if noncanonical mode had been in effect then. It is easier just to go ahead and do this (lines 12803 to 12809) than to test whether the characters already have the bit set. There is no way to know which attributes have just been changed and which still retain their old values.

The next action is to check the *MIN* and *TIME* values. In canonical mode *tp->tty_min* is always 1; that is set on line 12818. In noncanonical mode the combination of the two values allows for four different modes of operation, as we saw in Fig. 3-35. On lines 12823 to 12825 *tp->tty_min* is first set up with the value passed in *tp->tty_termiso.cc[VMIN]*, which is then modified if it is zero and *tp->tty_termiso.cc[VTIME]* is not zero.

Finally, *setattr* makes sure output is not stopped if XON/XOFF control is disabled, sends a *SIGHUP* signal if the output speed is set to zero, and makes an indirect call to the device-specific routine pointed to by *tp->tty_ioctl* to do what can only be done at the device level.

The next function, *tty_reply* (line 12845) has been mentioned many times in the preceding discussion. Its action is entirely straightforward, constructing a message and sending it. If for some reason the reply fails, a panic ensues. The following functions are equally simple. *Sigchar* (line 12866) asks MM to send a signal. If the *NOFLSH* flag is not set, queued input is removed—the count of characters or lines received is zeroed and the pointers to the tail and head of the queue are equated. This is the default action. When a *SIGHUP* signal is to be caught, *NOFLSH* can be set, to allow input and output to resume after catching the signal. *Tty_icancel* (line 12891) unconditionally discards pending input in the way described for *sigchar*, and in addition calls the device-specific function pointed to by *tp->tty_icancel*, to cancel input that may exist in the device itself or be buffered in the low-level code.

Tty_init (line 12905) is called once for each device when *tty_task* first starts. It sets up defaults. Initially a pointer to *tty_devnop*, a dummy function that does nothing, is set into the *tp->tty_icancel*, *tp->tty_ocancel*, *tp->tty_ioctl*, and *tp->tty_close* variables. *Tty_init* then calls a device-specific initialization functions for the appropriate category of terminal (console, serial line, or pseudo terminal). These set up the real pointers to indirectly called device-specific functions. Recall that if there are no devices at all configured in a particular category, a macro that returns immediately is created, so no part of the code for a nonconfigured device need be compiled. The call to *scr_init* initializes the console driver and also calls the initialization routine for the keyboard.

Tty_wakeup (line 12929), although short, is extremely important in the functioning of the terminal task. Whenever the clock interrupt handler runs, that is to say, for every tick of the clock, the global variable *tty_timeout* (defined in *glo.h* on line 5032), is checked to see if it contains a value less than the present time. If so *tty_wakeup* is called. *Tty_timeout* is set to zero by the interrupt service routines for terminal drivers, so wakeup is forced to run at the next clock tick after any terminal device interrupt. *Tty_timeout* is also altered by *settimer* when a terminal device is servicing a READ call in noncanonical mode and needs to set a timeout, as we will see shortly. When *tty_wakeup* runs, it first disables the next wakeup by assigning *TIME_NEVER*, a value very far in the future, to *tty_timeout*. Then it scans the linked list of timer values, which is sorted with the earliest scheduled wakeups first, until it comes to one that is later than the current time. This is the next wakeup, and it is then put into *tty_timeout*. *Tty_wakeup* also sets *tp−>tty_min* for that device to 0, which ensures that the next read will succeed even if no bytes have been received, sets the *tp−>tty_events* flag for the device to ensure it gets attention when the terminal task runs next, and removes the device from the timer list. Finally, it calls *interrupt* to send the wakeup message to the task. As mentioned in the discussion of the clock task, *tty_wakeup* is logically part of the clock interrupt service code, since it is called only from there.

The next function, *settimer* (line 12958), sets timers for determining when to return from a READ call in noncanonical mode. It is called with parameters of *tp*, a pointer to a *tty* structure, and *on*, an integer which represents *TRUE* or *FALSE*. First the linked list of *tty* structures pointed to by *timelist* is scanned, searching for an existing entry that matches the *tp* parameter. If one is found, it is removed from the list (lines 12968 to 12973). If *settimer* is called to unset a timer, this is all it must do. If it is called to set a timer, the *tp−>tty_time* element in the *tty* structure of the device is set to the current time plus the increment in tenths of a second specified in the *TIME* value in the device's *termios* structure. Then the entry is put into the list, which is maintained in sorted order. Finally, the timeout just entered on the list is compared with the value in the global *tty_timeout*, and the latter is replaced if the new timeout is due sooner.

Finally, the last definition in *tty.c* is *tty_devnop* (line 12992), a "no-operation" function to be indirectly addressed where a device does not require a service. We have seen *tty_devnop* used in *tty_init* as the default value entered into various function pointers before calling the initialization routine for a device.

3.9.5 Implementation of the Keyboard Driver

Now we turn to the device-dependent code that supports the MINIX console, which consists of an IBM PC keyboard and a memory-mapped display. The physical devices that support these are entirely separate: on a standard desktop system the display uses an adapter card (of which there are at least a half-dozen basic types) plugged into the backplane, while the keyboard is supported by circuitry built into the parentboard which interfaces with an 8-bit single-chip computer inside the keyboard unit. The two subdevices require entirely separate software support, which is found in the files *keyboard.c* and *console.c*.

The operating system sees the keyboard and console as parts of the same device, */dev/console*. If there is enough memory available on the display adapter, **virtual console** support may be compiled, and in addition to */dev/console* there may be additional logical devices, */dev/ttyc1*, */dev/ttyc2*, and so on. Output from only one goes to the display at any given time, and there is only one keyboard to use for input to whichever console is active. Logically the keyboard is subservient to the console, but this is manifested in only two relatively minor ways. First, *tty_table* contains a *tty* structure for the console, and where separate fields are provided for input and output, for instance, the *tty_devread* and *tty_devwrite* fields, pointers to functions in *keyboard.c* and *console.c* are filled in at startup time. However, there is only one *tty_priv* field, and this points to the console's data structures only. Second, before entering its main loop, *tty_task* calls each logical device once to initialize it. The routine called for */dev/console* is in *console.c*, and the initialization code for the keyboard is called from there. The implied hierarchy could just as well have been reversed, however. We have always looked at input before output in dealing with I/O devices and we will continue that pattern, discussing *keyboard.c* in this section and leaving the discussion of *console.c* for the following section.

Keyboard.c begins, like most source files we have seen, with several #include statements. One of these is unusual, however. The file *keymaps/us-std.src* (included on line 13014) is not an ordinary header; it is a C source file that results in compilation of the default keymap within *keyboard.o* as an initialized array. The keymap source file is not included in the listings at the end of the book because of its size, but some representative entries are illustrated in Fig. 3-41. Following the #includes are macros to define various constants. The first group are used in low-level interaction with the keyboard controller. Many of these are I/O port addresses or bit combinations that have meaning in these interactions. The next group includes symbolic names for special keys. The macro *kb_addr* (line 13041) always returns a pointer to the first element of the *kb_lines* array, since the IBM hardware supports only one keyboard. On the next line the size of the keyboard input buffer is symbolically defined as *KB_IN_BYTES*, with a value of 32. The next 11 variables are used to hold various states that must be remembered to properly interpret a key press. They are used in different ways. For instance, the value of the *capslock* flag (line 13046) is toggled between *TRUE* and *FALSE* each time the Caps Lock key is pressed. The *shift* flag (line 13054) is set to *TRUE* when the Shift key is pressed and to *FALSE* when the Shift key is released. The *esc* variable is set when a scan code escape is received. It is always reset upon receipt of the following character.

The *kb_s* structure on lines 13060 to 13065 is used to keep track of scan codes as they are entered. Within this structure the codes are held in a circular buffer, in the array *ibuf*, of size *KB_IN_BYTES*. An array *kb_lines[NR_CONS]* of these structures is declared, one per console, but in fact only the first one is used, since the *kbaddr* macro is always used to determine the address of the current *kb_s*. However, we usually refer to variables within *kb_lines[0]* using a pointer to the structure, for example, *kb->ihead*, for consistency with the way we treat other devices and to make the references in the text consistent with those in the source code listing. A small amount of memory is wasted because of the unused array elements, of course. However, if someone manufactures a PC with hardware support for multiple keyboards, MINIX is ready; only a modification of the *kbaddr* macro is required.

Map_key0 (line 13084) is defined as a macro. It returns the ASCII code that corresponds to a scan code, ignoring modifiers. This is equivalent to the first column (unshifted) in the keymap array. Its big brother is *map_key* (line 13091), which performs the complete mapping of a scan code to an ASCII code, including accounting for (multiple) modifier keys that are depressed at the same time as ordinary keys.

The keyboard interrupt service routine is *kbd_hw_int* (line 13123), called whenever a key is pressed or released. It calls *scan_keyboard* to get the scan code from the keyboard controller chip. The most significant bit of the scan code is set when a key release causes the interrupt, and in this case the key is ignored unless it is one of the modifier keys. If the interrupt is caused by a press of any key, or the release of a modifier key, the raw scan code is placed in the circular buffer if there is space, the *tp−>tty_events* flag for the current console is raised (line 13154), and then *force_timeout* is called to make sure the clock task will start the terminal task on the next clock tick. Figure 3-45 shows scan codes in the buffer for a short line of input that contains two upper case characters, each preceded by the scan code for depression of a shift key and followed by the code for the release of the shift key.

42	35	170	18	38	38	24	57	54	17	182	24	19	38	32	28
L+	h	L-	e	l	l	o	SP	R+	w	R-	o	r	l	d	CR

Figure 3-45. Scan codes in the input buffer, with corresponding key presses below, for a line of text entered at the keyboard. L+, L-, R+, and R- represent, respectively, pressing and releasing the left and right Shift keys. The code for a key release is 128 more than the code for a press of the same key.

When the clock interrupt occurs, the terminal task itself runs, and upon finding the *tp−>tty_events* flag for the console device set, it calls *kb_read* (line 13165), the device-specific routine, using the pointer in the *tp−>tty_devread* field of the console's *tty* structure. *Kb_read* takes scan codes from the keyboard's circular buffer and places ASCII codes in its local buffer, which is large enough to hold the escape sequences that must be generated in response to some scan codes from the numeric keypad. Then it calls *in_process* in the hardware-independent code to put the characters into the input queue. On lines 13181 to 13183 *lock* and *unlock* are used to protect the decrement of *kb−>icount* from a possible keyboard interrupt arriving at the same time. The call to *make_break* returns the ASCII code as an integer. Special keys, such as keypad and function keys, have values greater than 0xFF at this point. Codes in the range from *HOME* to *INSRT* (0x101 to 0x10C, defined in *include/minix/keymap.h*) result from pressing the numeric keypad, and are converted into 3-character escape sequences shown in Fig. 3-46 using the *numpad_map* array. The sequences are then passed to *in_process* (lines 13196 to 13201). Higher codes are not passed on to *in_process*, but a check is made for the codes for ALT-LEFT-ARROW, ALT-RIGHT-ARROW, or ALT-F1 through ALT-F12, and if one of these is found, *select_console* is called to switch virtual consoles.

Key	Scan code	"ASCII"	Escape sequence
Home	71	0x101	ESC [H
Up Arrow	72	0x103	ESC [A
Pg Up	73	0x107	ESC [V
–	74	0x10A	ESC [S
Left Arrow	75	0x105	ESC [D
5	76	0x109	ESC [G
Right Arrow	77	0x106	ESC [C
+	78	0x10B	ESC [T
End	79	0x102	ESC [Y
Down Arrow	80	0x104	ESC [B
Pg Dn	81	0x108	ESC [U
Ins	82	0x10C	ESC [@

Figure 3-46. Escape codes generated by the numeric keypad. When scan codes for ordinary keys are translated into ASCII codes the special keys are assigned "pseudo ASCII" codes with values greater than 0xFF.

Make_break (line 13222) converts scan codes into ASCII and then updates the variables that keep track of the state of modifier keys. First, however, it checks for the magic CTRL-ALT-DEL combination that PC users all know as the way to force a reboot under MS-DOS. An orderly shutdown is desirable, however, so rather than try to start the PC BIOS routines, a *SIGABRT* signal is sent to *init*, the parent process of all other processes. *Init* is expected to catch this signal and interpret it as a command to begin an orderly process of shutting down, prior to causing a return to the boot monitor, from which a full restart of the system or a reboot of MINIX can be commanded. Of course, it is not realistic to expect this to work every time. Most users understand the dangers of an abrupt shutdown and do not press CTRL-ALT-DEL until something is really going wrong and normal control of the system has become impossible. At this point it is likely that the system may be so disrupted that an orderly sending of a signal to another process may be impossible. This is why there is a *static* variable *CAD_count* in *make_break*. Most system crashes leave the interrupt system still functioning, so keyboard input can still be received and the clock task can keep the terminal task running. Here MINIX takes advantage of the expected behavior of computer users, who are likely to bang on the keys repeatedly when something does not seem to work correctly. If the attempt to send the *SIGABRT* to *init* fails and the user presses

CTRL-ALT-DEL twice more, a call to *wreboot* is made directly, causing a return to the monitor without going through the call to *init*.

The main part of *make_break* is not hard to follow. The variable *make* records whether the scan code was generated by a key press or a key release, and then the call to *map_key* returns the ASCII code to *ch*. Next is a switch on *ch* (lines 13248 to 13294). Let us consider two cases, an ordinary key and a special key. For an ordinary key, none of the cases match, and nothing should happen in the default case either (line 13292), since ordinary keys codes are supposed to be accepted only on the make (press) phase of a key press and release. If somehow an ordinary key code is accepted at key release, a value of −1 is substituted here, and this is ignored by the caller, *kb_read*. A special key, for example *CTRL*, is identified at the appropriate place in the switch, in this case on line 13249. The corresponding variable, in this case *control*, records the state of *make*, and −1 is substituted for the character code to be returned (and ignored). The handling of the *ALT*, *CALOCK*, *NLOCK*, and *SLOCK* keys is more complicated, but for all of these special keys the effect is similar: a variable records either the current state (for keys that are only effective while pressed) or toggles the previous state (for the lock keys).

There is one more case to consider, that of the *EXTKEY* code and the *esc* variable. This is not to be confused with the ESC key on the keyboard, which returns the ASCII code 0x1B. There is no way to generate the *EXTKEY* code alone by pressing any key or combination of keys; it is the PC keyboard's **extended key prefix**, the first byte of a 2-byte scan code that signifies that a key that was not part of the original PC's complement of keys but that has the same scan code, has been pressed. In many cases software treats the two keys identically. For instance, this is almost always the case for the normal "/" key and the gray "/" key on the numeric keyboard. In other cases, one would like to distinguish between such keys. For instance, many keyboard layouts for languages other than English treat the left and right ALT keys differently, to support keys that must generate three different character codes. Both ALT keys generate the same scan code (56), but the *EXTKEY* code precedes this when the right-hand ALT is pressed. When the *EXTKEY* code is returned, the *esc* flag is set. In this case, *make_break* returns from within the switch, thus bypassing the last step before a normal return, which sets *esc* to zero in every other case (line 13295). This has the effect of making the *esc* effective only for the very next code received. If you are familiar with the intricacies of the PC keyboard as it is ordinarily used, this will be both familiar and yet a little strange, because the PC BIOS does not allow one to read the scan code for an ALT key and returns a different value for the extended code than does MINIX.

Set_leds (line 13303) turns on and off the lights that indicate whether the Num Lock, Caps Lock, or Scroll Lock keys on a PC keyboard have been pressed. A control byte, *LED_CODE*, is written to an output port to instruct the keyboard that the next byte written to that port is for control of the lights, and the status of the three lights is encoded in 3 bits of that next byte. The next two functions support this operation. *Kb_wait* (line 13327) is called to determine that the keyboard is ready to receive a command sequence, and *kb_ack* (line 13343) is called to verify that the command has been acknowledged. Both of these commands use busy waiting, continually reading until a desired code is seen. This is not a recommended technique for handling most I/O operations, but turning lights on and off on the keyboard is not going to be done very often and doing it inefficiently does not waste much time. Note also that both *kb_wait* and *kb_ack* could fail, and one can determine from the return code if this happens. But setting the light on the keyboard is not important enough to merit checking the value returned by either call, and *set_leds* just proceeds blindly.

Since the keyboard is part of the console, its initialization routine, *kb_init* (line 13359), is called from *scr_init* in *console.c*, not directly from *tty_init* in *tty.c*. If virtual consoles are enabled, (i.e., *NR_CONS* in *include/minix/config.h* is greater than 1), *kb_init* is called once for each logical console. After the first time the only part of *kb_init* that is essential for additional consoles is setting the address of *kb_read* into *tp−>tty_devread* (line 13367), but no harm is done by repeating the rest of the function. The rest of *kb_init* initializes some variables, sets the lights on the keyboard, and scans the keyboard to be sure no leftover keystroke is read. When all is ready, it calls *put_irq_handler* and then *enable_irq*, so *kbd_hw_int* will be executed whenever a key is pressed or released.

The next three functions are all rather simple. *Kbd_loadmap* (line 13392) is almost trivial. It is called by *do_ioctl* in *tty.c* to do the copying of a keymap from user space to overwrite the default keymap compiled by the inclusion of a keymap source file at the start of *keyboard.c*.

Func_key (line 13405) is called from *kb_read* to see if a special key meant for local processing has been pressed. Figure 3-47 summarizes these keys and their effects. The code called is found in several files. The *F1* and *F2* codes activate code in *dmp.c*, which we will discuss in the next section. The *F3* code activates *toggle_scroll*, which is in *console.c*, also to be discussed in the next section. The *CF7*, *CF8*, and *CF9* codes cause calls to *sigchar*, in *tty.c*. When networking is added to MINIX, an additional case, to detect the *F5* code, is added to display Ethernet statistics. A large number of other scan codes are available that could be used to trigger other debugging messages or special events from the console.

Scan_keyboard (line 13432) works at the hardware interface level, by reading and writing bytes from I/O ports. The keyboard controller is informed that a character has been read by the sequence on lines 13440 to 13442, which reads a byte, writes it again with the most significant bit set to 1, and then rewrites it with the same bit rest to 0. This prevents the same data from being read on a subsequent read. There is no status checking in reading the keyboard, but there should be no problems in any case, since *scan_keyboard* is only called in response to an interrupt, with the exception of the call from *kb_init* to clear out any garbage.

Key	Purpose
F1	Display process table
F2	Display details of process memory use
F3	Toggle between hardware and software scrolling
F5	Show Ethernet statistics (if network support compiled)
CF7	Send SIGQUIT, same effect as CTRL-\
CF8	Send SIGINT, same effect as DEL
CF9	Send SIGKILL, same effect as CTRL-U

Figure 3-47. The function keys detected by *func_key( )*.

The last function in *keyboard.c* is *wreboot* (line 13450). If invoked as a result of a system panic, it provides an opportunity for the user to use the function keys to display debugging information. The loop on lines 13478 to 13487 is another example of busy waiting. The keyboard is read repeatedly until an ESC is typed. Certainly no one can claim that a more efficient technique is needed after a crash, while awaiting a command to reboot. Within the loop, *func_key* is called to provide a possibility of obtaining information that might help analyze the cause of a crash. We will not discuss further details of the return to the monitor. The details are very hardware-specific and do not have a lot to do with the operating system.

3.9.6 Implementation of the Display Driver

The IBM PC display may be configured as several virtual terminals, if sufficient memory is available. We will examine the console's device-dependent code in this section. We will also look at the debug dump routines that use low-level services of the keyboard and display. These provide support for limited interaction with the user at the console, even when other parts of the MINIX system are not functioning and can provide useful information even following a near-total system crash.

Hardware-specific support for console output to the PC memory-mapped screen is in *console.c*. The *console* structure is defined on lines 13677 to 13693. In a sense this structure is an extension of the *tty* structure defined in *tty.c*. At initialization the *tp−>tty_priv* field of a console's *tty* structure is assigned a pointer to its own *console* structure. The first item in the *console* structure is a pointer back to the corresponding *tty* structure. The components of a *console* structure are what one would expect for a video display: variables to record the row and column of the cursor location, the memory addresses of the start and limit of memory used for the display, the memory address pointed to by the controller chip's base pointer, and the current address of the cursor. Other variables are used for managing escape sequences. Since characters are initially received as 8-bit bytes and must be combined with attribute bytes and transferred as 16-bit words to video memory, a block to be transferred is built up in *c_ramqueue*, an array big enough to hold an entire 80-column row of 16-bit character-attribute pairs. Each virtual console needs one *console* structure, and the storage is allocated in the array *cons_table* (line 13696). As we did with the *tty* and kb_s structures, we will usually refer to the elements of a *console* structure using a pointer, for example, *cons->c_tty*.

The function whose address is stored in each console's *tp->tty_devwrite* entry is *cons_write* (line 13729). It is called from only one place, *handle_events* in *tty.c*. Most of the other functions in *console.c* exist to support this function. When it is called for the first time after a client process makes a WRITE call, the data to be output are in the client's buffer, which can be found using the *tp->tty_outproc* and *tp->out_vir* fields in the *tty* structure. The *tp->tty_outleft* field tells how many characters are to be transferred, and the *tp->tty_outcum* field is initially zero, indicating none have yet been transferred. This is the usual situation upon entry to *cons_write*, because normally, once called, it transfers all the data requested in the original call. However, if the user wants to slow the process in order to review the data on the screen, he may enter a *STOP* (CTRL-S) character at the keyboard, resulting in raising of the *tp->tty_inhibited* flag. *Cons_write* returns immediately when this flag is raised, even though the WRITE has not been completed. In such a case *handle_events* will continue to call *cons_write*, and when *tp->tty_inhibited* is finally reset, by the user entering a *START* (CTRL-Q) character, *cons_write* continues with the interrupted transfer.

Cons_write's sole argument is a pointer to the particular console's *tty* structure, so the first thing that must be done is to initialize *cons*, the pointer to this console's *console* structure (line 13741). Then, because *handle_events* calls *cons_write* whenever it runs, the first action is a test to see if there really is work to be done. A quick return is made if not (line 13746). Following this the main loop on lines 13751 to 13778 is entered. This loop is very similar in structure to the main loop of *in_transfer* in *tty.c*. A local buffer that can hold 64 characters is filled by calling *phys_copy* to get the data from the client's buffer, the pointer to the source and the counts are updated, and then each character in the local buffer is transferred to the *cons->c_ramqueue* array, along with an attribute byte, for later transfer to the screen by *flush*. There is more than one way to do this transfer, as we saw in Fig. 3-39. *Out_char* can be called to do this for each character, but it is predictable that none of the special services of *out_char* will be needed if the character is a visible character, an escape sequence is not in progress, the screen width has not been exceeded, and *cons->c_ramqueue* is not full. If the full service of *out_char* is not needed, the character is placed directly into *cons->c_ramqueue*, along with the attribute byte (retrieved from *cons->c_attr*), and *cons->c_rwords* (the index into the queue), *cons->c_column* (which keeps track of the column on the screen), and *tbuf*, the pointer into the buffer, are all incremented. This direct placement of characters into *cons->c_ramqueue* corresponds to the dashed line on the left side of Fig. 3-39. If needed, *out_char* is called (lines 13766 to 13777). It does all of the bookkeeping, and additionally calls *flush*, which does the final transfer to screen memory, when necessary. The transfer from the user buffer to the local buffer to the queue is repeated as long as *tp->tty_outleft* indicates there are still characters to be transferred and the flag *tp->tty_inhibited* has not been raised. When the transfer stops, whether because the WRITE operation is complete or because *tp->tty_inhibited* has been raised, *flush* is called again to transfer the last characters in the queue to screen memory. If the operation is complete (tested by seeing if *tp->tty_outleft* is zero), a reply message is sent by calling *tty_reply* (lines 13784 and 13785).

In addition to calls to *cons_write* from *handle_events,* characters to be displayed are also sent to the console by *echo* and *rawecho* in the hardware-independent part of the terminal task. If the console is the current output device, calls via the *tp->tty_echo* pointer are directed to the next function, *cons_echo* (line 13794). *Cons_echo* does all of its work by calling *out_char* and then *flush*. Input from the keyboard arrives character by character and the person doing the typing wants to see the echo with no perceptible delay, so putting characters into the output queue would be unsatisfactory.

Now we arrive at *out_char* (line 13809). It does a test to see if an escape sequence is in progress, calling *parse_escape* and then returning immediately if so (lines 13814 to 13816). Otherwise, a switch is entered to check for special cases: null, backspace, the bell character, and so on. The handling of most of these is easy to follow. The linefeed and the tab are the most complicated, since they involve complicated changes to the position of the cursor on the screen and may require scrolling as well. The last test is for the *ESC* code. If it is found, the *cons->c_esc_state* flag is set (line 13871), and future calls to *out_char* are diverted to *parse_escape* until the sequence is complete. At the end, the default is taken for printable characters. If the screen width has been exceeded, the screen may need to be scrolled, and *flush* is called. Before a character is placed in the output queue a test is made to see that the queue is not full, and *flush* is called if it is. Putting a character into the queue requires the same bookkeeping we saw earlier in *cons_write*.

The next function is *scroll_screen* (line 13896). *Scroll_screen* handles both scrolling up, the normal situation that must be dealt with whenever the bottom line on the screen is full, and scrolling down, which occurs when cursor positioning commands attempt to move the cursor beyond the top line of the screen. For each direction of scroll there are three possible methods. These are required to support different kinds of video cards.

We will look at the scrolling up case. To begin, *chars* is assigned the size of the screen minus one line. Softscrolling is accomplished by a single call to *vid_vid_copy* to move *chars* characters lower in memory, the size of the move being the number of characters in a line. *Vid_vid_copy* can wrap, that is, if asked to move a block of memory that overflows the upper end of the block assigned to the video display, it fetches the overflow portion from the low end of the memory block and moves it to an address higher than the part that is moved lower, treating the entire block as a circular array. The simplicity of the call hides a fairly slow operation. Even though *vid_vid_copy* is an assembly language routine defined in *klib386.s*, this call requires the CPU to move 3840 bytes, which is a large job even in assembly language.

The softscroll method is never the default; the operator is supposed to select it only if hardware scrolling does not work or is not desired for some reason. One such reason might be a desire to use the *screendump* command to save the screen memory in a file. When hardware scrolling is in effect, *screendump* is likely to give unexpected results, because the start of the screen memory is likely not to coincide with the start of the visible display.

On line 13917 the *wrap* variable is tested as the first part of a compound test. *Wrap* is true for older displays that can support hardware scrolling, and if the test fails, simple hardware scrolling occurs on line 13921, where the origin pointer used by the video controller chip, *cons−>c_org*, is updated to point to the first character to be displayed at the upper-left corner of the display. If *wrap* is *FALSE*, the compound test continues with a test of whether the block to be moved up in the scroll operation overflows the bounds of the memory block designated for this console. If this is so, *vid_vid_copy* is called again to make a wrapped move of the block to the start of the console's allocated memory, and the origin pointer is updated. If there is no overlap, control passes to the simple hardware scrolling method always used by older video controllers. This consists of adjusting *cons−>c_org* and then putting the new origin in the correct register of the controller chip. The call to do this is done later, as is a call to blank the bottom line on the screen.

The code for scrolling down is very similar to that for scrolling up. Finally, *mem_vid_copy* is called to blank out the line at the bottom (or top) addressed by *new_line*. Then *set_6845* is called to write the new origin from *cons−>c_org* into the appropriate registers, and *flush* makes sure all changes become visible on the screen.

We have mentioned *flush* (line 13951) several times. It transfers the characters in the queue to the video memory using *mem_vid_copy*, updates some variables, and then makes sure the row and column numbers are reasonable, adjusting them if, for instance, an escape sequence has tried to move the cursor to a negative column position. Finally a calculation of where the cursor ought to be is made and is compared with *cons−>c_cur*. If they do not agree, and if the video memory that is currently being handled belongs to the current virtual console, a call to *set_6845* is made to set the correct value in the controller's cursor register.

Figure 3-48 shows how escape sequence handling can be represented as a finite state machine. This is implemented by *parse_escape* (line 13986) which is called at the start of *out_char* if *cons−>c_esc_state* is nonzero. An ESC itself is

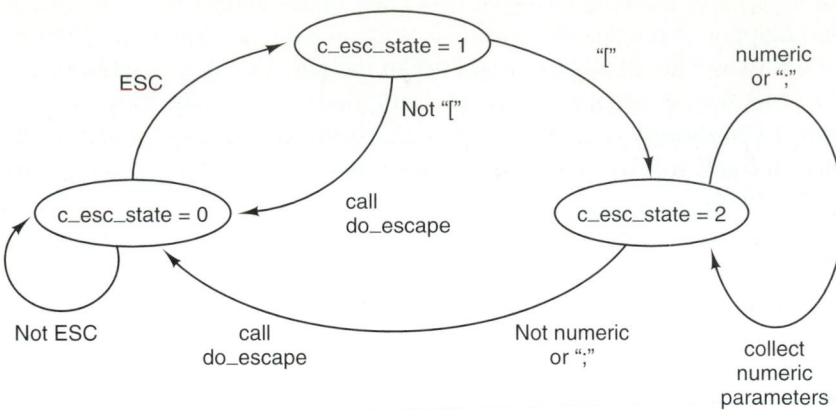

Figure 3-48. Finite state machine for processing escape sequences.

detected by *out_char* and makes *cons->c_esc_state* equal to 1. When the next character is received, *parse_escape* prepares for further processing by putting a '\0' in *cons->c_esc_intro*, a pointer to the start of the array of parameters, *cons->c_esc_parmv*[0] into *cons->c_esc_parmp*, and zeroes into the parameter array itself. Then the first character following the ESC is examined—valid values are either "[" or "M". In the first case the "[" is copied to *cons->c_esc_intro* and the state is advanced to 2. In the second case, *do_escape* is called to carry out the action, and the escape state is reset to zero. If the first character after the ESC is not one of the valid ones, it is ignored and succeeding characters are once again displayed normally.

When an ESC [sequence has been seen, the next character entered is processed by the escape state 2 code. There are three possibilities at this point. If the character is a numeric character, its value is extracted and added to 10 times the existing value in the position currently pointed to by *cons->c_esc_parmp*, initially *cons->c_esc_parmv*[0] (which was initialized to zero). The escape state does not change. This makes it possible to enter a series of decimal digits and accumulate a large numeric parameter, although the maximum value currently recognized by MINIX is 80, used by the sequence that moves the cursor to an arbitrary position (lines 14027 to 14029). If the character is a semicolon, the pointer to the parameter string is advanced, so succeeding numeric values can be accumulated in the second parameter (lines 14031 to 14033). If *MAX_ESC_PARMS* were to be changed to allocate a larger array for the parameters, this code would not have to be altered to accumulate additional numeric values after entry of additional parameters. Finally, if the character is neither a numeric digit nor a semicolon, *do_escape* is called.

Do_escape (line 14045) is one of the longer functions in the MINIX system source code, even though MINIX's complement of recognized escape sequences is relatively modest. For all its length, however, the code should be easy to follow.

After an initial call to *flush* to make sure the video display is fully updated, there is a simple if choice, depending upon whether the character immediately following the ESC character was a special control sequence introducer or not. If not, there is only one valid action, moving the cursor up one line if the sequence was ESC M. Note that the test for the "M" is done within a switch with a default action, as a validity check and in anticipation of addition of other sequences that do not use the ESC [format. The action is typical of many escape sequences: the *cons->c_row* variable is inspected to determine if scrolling is required. If the cursor is already on row 0, a *SCROLL_DOWN* call is made to *scroll_screen*; otherwise the cursor is moved up one line. The latter is accomplished just by decrementing *cons->c_row* and then calling *flush*. If a control sequence introducer is found, the code following the else on line 14069 is taken. A test is made for "[", the only control sequence introducer currently recognized by MINIX. If the sequence is valid, the first parameter found in the escape sequence, or zero if no numeric parameter was entered, is assigned to *value* (line 14072). If the sequence is invalid, nothing happens except that the large switch that ensues (lines 14073 to 14272) is skipped and the escape state is reset to zero before returning from *do_escape*. In the more interesting case that the sequence is valid, the switch is entered. We will not discuss all the cases; we will just note several that are representative of the types of actions governed by escape sequences.

The first five sequences are generated, with no numeric arguments, by the four "arrow" keys and the Home key on the IBM PC keyboard. The first two, ESC [A and ESC [B, are similar to ESC M, except they can accept a numeric parameter and move up and down by more than one line, and they do not scroll the screen if the parameter specifies a move that exceeds the bounds of the screen. In such cases, *flush* catches requests to move out of bounds and limits the move to the last row or the first row, as appropriate. The next two sequences, ESC [C and ESC [D, which move the cursor right and left, are similarly limited by *flush*. When generated by the "arrow" keys there is no numeric argument, and thus the default movement of one line or column occurs.

The next sequence, ESC [H, can take two numeric parameters, for instance, ESC [20;60H. The parameters specify an absolute position rather than one relative to the current position and are converted from 1-based numbers to 0-based numbers for proper interpretation. The Home key generates the default (no parameters) sequence which moves the cursor to position (1, 1).

The next two sequences, ESC [*s*J and ESC [*s*K, clear a part of either the entire screen or the current line, depending upon the parameter that is entered. In each case a count of characters is calculated. For instance, for ESC [1J, *count* gets the number of characters from the start of the screen to the cursor position, and the count and a position parameter, *dst*, which may be the start of the screen, *cons->c_org*, or the current cursor position, *cons->c_cur*, are used as parameters to a call to *mem_vid_copy*. This procedure is called with a parameter that causes it to fill the specified region with the current background color.

The next four sequences insert and delete lines and spaces at the cursor position, and their actions do not require detailed explanation. The last case, ESC [*nm* (note the *n* represents a numeric parameter, but the "m" is a literal character) has its effect upon *cons−>c_attr*, the attribute byte that is interleaved between the character codes when they are written to video memory.

The next function, *set_6845* (line 14280), is used whenever it is necessary to update the video controller chip. The 6845 has internal 16-bit registers that are programmed 8 bits at a time, and writing a single register requires four I/O port write operations. *Lock* and *unlock* calls are used to disable interrupts, which can cause problems if allowed to disrupt the sequence. Some of the registers of the 6845 video controller chip are shown in Fig. 3-49

Registers	Function
10 − 11	Cursor size
12 − 13	Start address for drawing screen
14 − 15	Cursor position

Figure 3-49. Some of the 6845's registers.

The *beep* function (line 14300) is called when a CTRL-G character must be output. It takes advantage of the built-in support provided by the PC for making sounds by sending a square wave to the speaker. The sound is initiated by more of the kind of magic manipulation of I/O ports that only assembly language programmers can love, again with some concern that a critical part of the process should be protected from interrupts. The more interesting part of the code is the use of the clock task's capability to set an alarm, which can be used to initiate a function. The next routine, *stop_beep* (line 14329), is the one whose address is put into the message to the clock task. It stops the beep after the designated time has elapsed and also resets the *beeping* flag which is used to prevent superfluous calls to the beep routine from having any effect.

Scr_init (line 14343) is called by *tty_init NR_CONS* times. Each time its argument is a pointer to a *tty* structure, one element of the *tty_table*. On lines 14354 and 14355 *line*, to be used as the index into the *cons_table* array, is calculated, tested for validity, and, if valid, used to initialize *cons*, the pointer to the current console table entry. At this point the *cons−>c_tty* field can be initialized with the pointer to the main *tty* structure for the device, and, in turn, *tp−>tty_priv* can be pointed to this device's *console_t* structure. Next, *kb_init* is called to initialize the keyboard, and then the pointers to device specific routines are set up, *tp−>tty_devwrite* pointing to *cons_write* and *tp−>tty_echo* pointing to *cons_echo*. The I/O address of the base register of the CRT controller is fetched and the address and size of the video memory are determined on lines 14368 to 14378, and the *wrap* flag (used to determine how to scroll) is set according to the class of video controller in use. On lines 14382 to 14384 the segment descriptor for the video memory is initialized in the global descriptor table.

Next comes the initialization of virtual consoles. Each time *scr_init* is called, the argument is a different value of *tp*, and thus a different *line* and *cons* are used on lines 14393 to 14396 to provide each virtual console with its own share of the available video memory. Each screen is then blanked, ready to start, and finally console 0 is selected to be the first active one.

The remaining routines in *console.c* are short and simple and we will review them quickly. *Putk* (line 14408) has been mentioned earlier. It prints a character on behalf of any code linked into the kernel image that needs the service, without going through the FS. *Toggle_scroll* (line 14429) does what its name says, it toggles the flag that determines whether hardware or software scrolling is used. It also displays a message at the current cursor position to identify the selected mode. *Cons_stop* (line 14442) reinitializes the console to the state that the boot monitor expects, prior to a shutdown or reboot. *Cons_org0* (line 14456) is used only when a change of scrolling mode is forced by the F3 key, or when preparing to shut down. *Select_console* (line 14482) selects a virtual console. It is called with the new index and calls *set_6845* twice to get the video controller to display the proper part of the video memory.

The last two routines are highly hardware-specific. *Con_loadfont* (line 14497) loads a font into a graphics adapter, in support of the IOCTL *TIOCSFON* operation. It calls *ga_program* (line 14540) to do a series of magical writes to an I/O port that cause the video adapter's font memory, which is normally not addressable by the CPU, to be visible. Then *phys_copy* is called to copy the font data to this area of memory, and another magic sequence is invoked to return the graphics adapter to its normal mode of operation.

Debugging Dumps

The final group of procedures we will discuss in the terminal task were originally intended only for temporary use when debugging MINIX. They can be removed when this assistance is no longer needed, but many users find them useful and leave them in place. They are particularly helpful when modifying MINIX.

As we have seen, *func_key* is called at the start of *kb_read* to detect scan codes used for control and debugging. The dump routines called when the F1 and F2 keys are detected are in *dmp.c*. The first, *p_dmp* (line 14613) displays basic process information for all processes, including some information on memory use, when the F1 key is pressed. The second, *map_dmp* (line 14660), provides more detailed information on memory use in response to F2. *Proc_name* (line 14690) supports *p_dmp* by looking up process names.

Since this code is completely contained within the kernel binary itself and does not run as a user process or task, it frequently continues to function correctly, even after a major system crash. Of course, these routines are accessible only from the console. The information provided by the dump routines cannot be redirected to a file or to any other device, so hardcopy or use over a network connection are not options.

We suggest that the first step in trying to add any improvement to MINIX might very well be to extend the dumping routines to provide more information on the aspect of the system you wish to improve.

3.10 THE SYSTEM TASK IN MINIX

One consequence of making the file system and memory manager server processes outside the kernel is that occasionally they have some piece of information that the kernel needs. This structure, however, forbids them from just writing it into a kernel table. For example, the FORK system call is handled by the memory manager. When a new process is created, the kernel must know about it, in order to schedule it. How can the memory manager tell the kernel?

The solution to this problem is to have a kernel task that communicates with the file system and memory manager via the standard message mechanism and which also has access to all the kernel tables. This task, called the **system task**, is in layer 2 in Fig. 2-26, and functions like the other tasks we have studied in this chapter. The only difference is that it does not control any I/O device. But, like I/O tasks, it implements an interface, in this case not to the external world, but to the most internal part of the system. It has the same privileges as the I/O tasks and is compiled with them into the kernel image, and it makes more sense to study it here than in any other chapter.

The system task accepts 19 kinds of messages, shown in Fig. 3-50. The main program of the system task, *sys_task* (line 14837), is structured like other tasks. It gets a message, dispatches to the appropriate service procedure, and then sends a reply. We will now look at each of these messages and its service procedure.

The *SYS_FORK* message is used by the memory manager to tell the kernel that a new process has come into existence. The kernel needs to know this in order to schedule it. The message contains the slot numbers within the process table corresponding to the parent and child. The memory manager and file system also have process tables, with entry k referring to the same process in all three. In this manner, the memory manager can specify just the parent and child slot numbers, and the kernel will know which processes are meant.

The procedure *do_fork* (line 14877) first makes a check (line 14886) to see if the memory manager is feeding the kernel garbage. The test uses a macro, *isoksusern*, defined in *proc.h*, to test that the process table entries of the parent and child are valid. Similar tests are made by most of the service procedures in *system.c*. This is pure paranoia, but a little internal consistency checking does no

Message type	From	Meaning
SYS_FORK	MM	A process has forked
SYS_NEWMAP	MM	Install memory map for a new process
SYS_GETMAP	MM	MM wants memory map of a process
SYS_EXEC	MM	Set stack pointer after EXEC call
SYS_XIT	MM	A process has exited
SYS_GETSP	MM	MM wants a process' stack pointer
SYS_TIMES	FS	FS wants a process' execution times
SYS_ABORT	Both	Panic: MINIX is unable to continue
SYS_SENDSIG	MM	Send a signal to a process
SYS_SIGRETURN	MM	Cleanup after completion of a signal.
SYS_KILL	FS	Send signal to a process after KILL call
SYS_ENDSIG	MM	Cleanup after a signal from the kernel
SYS_COPY	Both	Copy data between processes
SYS_VCOPY	Both	Copy multiple blocks of data between processes
SYS_GBOOT	FS	Get boot parameters
SYS_MEM	MM	MM wants next free chunk of physical memory
SYS_UMAP	FS	Convert virtual address to physical address
SYS_TRACE	MM	Carry out an operation of the PTRACE call

Figure 3-50. The message types accepted by the system task.

harm. Then *do_fork* copies the parent's process table entry to the child's slot. Some things need adjustment here. The child is freed from any pending signals for the parent, and the child does not inherit the parent's trace status. And, of course, all the child's accounting information is set to zero.

After a FORK, the memory manager allocates memory for the child. The kernel must know where the child is located in memory so it can set up the segment registers properly when running the child. The *SYS_NEWMAP* message allows the memory manager to give the kernel any process' memory map. This message can also be used after a BRK system call changes the map.

The message is handled by *do_newmap* (line 14921), which must first copy the new map from the memory manager's address space. The map is not contained in the message itself because it is too big. In theory, the memory manager could tell the kernel that the map is at address *m*, where *m* is an illegal address. The memory manager is not supposed to do this, but the kernel checks anyway. The map is copied directly into the *p_map* field of the process table entry for the process getting the new map. The call to *alloc_segments* extracts information from the map and loads it into the *p_reg* fields that hold the segment registers. This is not complicated, but the details are processor dependent and are segregated in a separate function for this reason.

The *SYS_NEWMAP* message is much used in the normal operation of a MINIX system. A similar message, *SYS_GETMAP*, is used only when the file system initially starts up. This message requests a transfer of the process map information in the opposite direction, from the kernel to the memory manager. It is carried out by *do_getmap* (line 14957). The code of the two functions is similar, differing mainly in the swapping of the source and destination arguments of the call to *phys_copy* used by each function.

When a process does an EXEC system call, the memory manager sets up a new stack for it containing the arguments and environment. It passes the resulting stack pointer to the kernel using *SYS_EXEC*, which is handled by *do_exec* (line 14990). After the usual check for a valid process, there is a test of the *PROC2* field in the message. This field is used here as a flag to indicate whether the process is being traced and has nothing to do with identifying a process. If tracing is in force, *cause_sig* is called to send a *SIGTRAP* signal to the process. This does not have the usual consequences of this signal, which would normally terminate a process and cause a core dump. In the memory manager all signals to a traced process except for *SIGKILL* are intercepted and cause the signaled process to stop so a debugging program can then control its further execution.

The EXEC call causes a slight anomaly. The process invoking the call sends a message to the memory manager and blocks. With other system calls, the resulting reply unblocks it. With EXEC there is no reply, because the newly loaded core image is not expecting a reply. Therefore, *do_exec* unblocks the process itself on line 15009. The next line makes the new image ready to run, using the *lock_ready* function that protects against a possible race condition. Finally, the command string is saved so the process can be identified when the user presses the F1 function key to display the status of all processes.

Processes can exit in MINIX either by doing an EXIT system call, which sends a message to the memory manager, or by being killed by a signal. In both cases, the memory manager tells the kernel by the *SYS_XIT* message. The work is done by *do_xit* (line 15027), which is more complicated than you might expect. Taking care of the accounting information is straightforward. The alarm timer, if any, is killed by storing a zero on top of it. It is for this reason that the clock task always checks when a timer has run out to see if anybody is still interested. The tricky part of *do_xit* is that the process might have been queued trying to send or receive at the time it was killed. The code on lines 15056 to 15076 checks for this possibility. If the exiting process is found on any other process' message queue, it is carefully removed.

In contrast to the previous message, which is slightly complicated, *SYS_GETSP* is completely trivial. It is used by the memory manager to find out the value of the current stack pointer for some process. This value is needed for the BRK and SBRK system calls to see if the data segment and stack segment have collided. The code is in *do_getsp* (line 15089).

Now we come to one of the few message types used exclusively by the file system, *SYS_TIMES*. It is needed to implement the TIMES system call, which returns the accounting times to the caller. All *do_times* (line 15106) does is put the requested times into the reply message. Calls to *lock* and *unlock* are used to protect against a possible race while accessing the time counters.

It can happen that either the memory manager or the file system discovers an error that makes it impossible to continue operation. For example, if upon first starting up the file system sees that the super-block on the root device has been fatally corrupted, it panics and sends a *SYS_ABORT* message to the kernel. It is also possible for the super-user to force a return to the boot monitor and/or a reboot, using the *reboot* command, which in turn calls the REBOOT system call. In any of these cases, the system task executes *do_abort* (line 15131), which copies instructions to the monitor, if necessary, and then calls *wreboot* to complete the process.

Most of the work of signal handling is done by the memory manager, which checks to see if the process to be signaled is enabled to catch or ignore the signal, if the sender of the signal is entitled to do so, and so on. However, the memory manager cannot actually cause the signal, which requires pushing some information onto the stack of the signaled process.

Signal handling previous to POSIX was problematic, because catching a signal restored the default response to signals. If continued special handling of subsequent signals were required, the programmer could not guarantee reliability. Signals are asynchronous, and a second signal could very well arrive before the handling were reenabled. POSIX-style signal handling solves this problem, but the price is a more complicated mechanism. Old-style signal handling could be implemented by the operating system pushing some information onto the signaled process' stack, similar to the information pushed by an interrupt. The programmer would then write a handler that ended with a return instruction, popping the information needed to resume execution. POSIX saves more information when a signal is received than can be conveniently handled this way. There is additional work to do afterward, before the signaled process can resume what it was doing. The memory manager thus has to send two messages to the system task to process a signal. The payoff for this effort is more reliable handling of signals.

When a signal is to be sent to a process, the *SYS_SENDSIG* message is sent to the system task. It is handled by *do_sendsig* (line 15157). The information needed to handle POSIX-style signals is in a *sigcontext* structure, which contains the processor register contents, and a *sigframe* structure, which contains information about how signals are to be handled by the process. Both of these structures need some initialization, but the basic work of *do_sendsig* is just to put the required information on the signaled process' stack, and adjust the signaled process' program counter and stack pointer so the signal handling code will be executed the next time the scheduler allows the process to execute.

When a POSIX-style signal handler completes its work, it does not pop the address where execution of the interrupted process resumes, as is the case with old-style signals. The programmer writing the handler writes a *return* instruction (or the high-level language equivalent), but the manipulation of the stack by the SENDSIG call causes the *return* to execute a SIGRETURN system call. The memory manager then sends the system task a *SYS_SIGRETURN* message. This is handled by *do_sigreturn* (line 15221), which copies the sigcontext structure back into the kernel's space and then restores the signaled process' registers. The interrupted process will resume execution at the point where it was interrupted the next time the scheduler allows it to run, retaining any special signal handling that was previously set up.

The SIGRETURN system call, unlike most of the others discussed in this section, is not required by POSIX. It is a MINIX invention, a convenient way to initiate the processing needed when a signal handler is complete. Programmers should not use this call; it will not be recognized by other operating systems, and in any case there is no need to refer to it explicitly.

Some signals come from within the kernel image, or are handled by the kernel before they go to the memory manager. These include signals originating from tasks, such as alarms from the clock task, or signal-causing key presses detected by the terminal task, as well as signals caused by exceptions (such as division by zero or illegal instructions) detected by the CPU. Signals originating from the file system are also handled first by the kernel. The *SYS_KILL* message is used by the file system to request that such a signal be generated. The name is perhaps a bit misleading. This has nothing to do with handling of the KILL system call, used by ordinary processes to send signals. This message is handled by *do_kill* (line 15276), which makes the usual check for a valid origin of the message, and then calls *cause_sig* to actually pass the signal on to the process. Signals originating in the kernel are also passed on by a call to this function, which initiates signals by sending a *KSIG* message to the memory manager.

Whenever the memory manager has finished with one of these *KSIG*-type signals, it sends a *SYS_ENDSIG* message back to the system task. This message is handled by *do_endsig* (line 15294), which decrements the count of pending signals, and, if it reaches zero, resets the *SIG_PENDING* bit for the signaled process. If there are no other flags set indicating reasons the process should not be runnable, *lock_ready* is then called to allow the process to run again.

The *SYS_COPY* message is the most heavily used one. It is needed to allow the file system and memory manager to copy information to and from user processes.

When a user does a READ call, the file system checks its cache to see if it has the block needed. If not, it sends a message to the appropriate disk task to load it into the cache. Then the file system sends a message to the system task telling it to copy the block to the user process. In the worst case, seven messages are needed to read a block; in the best case, four messages are needed. Both cases are shown in Fig. 3-51. These messages are a significant source of overhead in MINIX and are the price paid for the highly modular design.

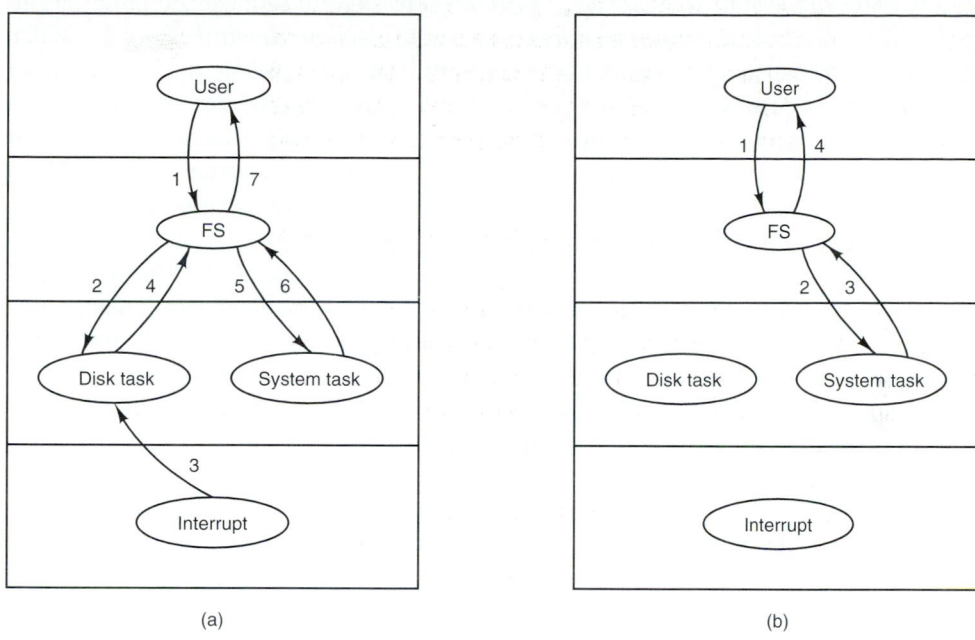

(a) (b)

Figure 3-51. (a) Worst case for reading a block requires seven messages. (b) Best case for reading a block requires four messages.

As an aside, on the 8088, which had no protection, it would have been easy enough to cheat and let the file system copy the data to the caller's address space, but this would have violated the design principle. Anyone with access to such an antique machine who is interested in improving the performance of MINIX should look carefully at this mechanism to see how much improper behavior one can tolerate for how much gain in performance. Of course, this means of improvement is not available on Pentium-class machines with protection mechanisms.

Handling a *SYS_COPY* request is straightforward. It is done by *do_copy* (line 15316) and consists of little more than extracting the message parameters and calling *phys_copy*.

One way to deal with some of the inefficiency of the message passing mechanism is to pack multiple requests into a message. The *SYS_VCOPY* message does this. The content of this message is a pointer to a vector specifying multiple blocks to be copied between memory locations. The function *do_vcopy* (line 15364) executes a loop, extracting source and destination addresses and block lengths and calling *phys_copy* repeatedly until all the copies are complete. This is similar to the capability of disk devices to handle multiple transfers based on a single request.

There are several more message types received by the system task, most of which are fairly simple. Two of these are normally used only during system startup. The file system sends a *SYS_GBOOT* message to request the boot parameters. This is a structure, *bparam_s*, declared in *include/minix/boot.h*, which allows various aspects of system configuration to be specified by the boot monitor program before MINIX is started. The *do_gboot* (line 15403) function carries out this operation, which is just a copy from one part of memory to another. Also at startup time, the memory manager sends the system task a series of *SYS_MEM* messages to request the base and size of the available chunks of memory. *Do_mem* (line 15424) handles this request.

The *SYS_UMAP* message is used by a nonkernel process to request calculation of the physical memory address for a given virtual address. *Do_umap* (line 15445) carries this out by calling *umap*, which is the function called from within the kernel to handle this conversion.

The last message type we will discuss is *SYS_TRACE*, which supports the PTRACE system call, used for debugging. Debugging is not a fundamental operating system function, but operating system support can make it easier. With help from the operating system, a debugger can examine and modify the memory used by a process under test, as well as the contents of the processor registers that are stored in the process table whenever the debugged program is not running.

Normally, a process runs until it blocks to wait for I/O or uses up a time quantum. Most CPU designs also provide means by which a process can be limited to executing just a single instruction, or can be made to execute only until a particular instruction is reached, by setting a **breakpoint**. Taking advantage of such facilities makes possible detailed analysis of a program.

There are eleven operations that can be carried out using PTRACE. A few are carried out totally by the memory manager, but for most of them the memory manager sends a *SYS_TRACE* message to the system task, which then calls *do_trace* (line 15467). This function implements a switch on the trace operation code. The operations are generally simple. A *P_STOP* bit in the process table is used by MINIX to recognize that debugging is in progress and is set by the command to stop the process (case *T_STOP*) or reset to restart it (case *T_RESUME*). Debugging depends upon hardware support, and on Intel processors is controlled by a bit in the CPU's flag register. When the bit is set, the processor executes just one instruction, then generates a *SIGTRAP* exception. As mentioned earlier, the memory manager stops a program being traced when a signal is sent to it. This *TRACEBIT* is manipulated by the *T_STOP* and *T_STEP* commands. Breakpoints can be set in two ways: either by using the *T_SETINS* command to replace an instruction with a special code that generates a *SIGTRAP*, or by using the *T_SETUSER* command to modify special breakpoint registers. On any kind of system to which MINIX may be ported, it will probably be possible to implement a debugger using similar techniques, but porting these functions will require study of the particular hardware.

Most of the commands carried out by *dotrace* either return or modify values in the traced process' text or data space, or in its process table entry, and the code is straightforward. Altering certain registers and certain bits of the CPU flags is too dangerous to allow, so there are many checks in the code that handle the *T_SETUSER* command to prevent such operations.

At the end of *system.c* are several utility procedures used in various places throughout the kernel. When a task needs to cause a signal (e.g., the clock task needs to cause a SIGALRM signal, or the terminal task needs to cause a SIGINT signal), it calls *cause_sig* (line 15586). This procedure sets a bit in the *p_pending* field of the process table entry for the process to be signaled and then checks to see if the memory manager is currently waiting for a message from *ANY*, that is, if it is idle and waiting for the next request to process. If it is idle, *inform* is called to tell the memory manager to handle the signal.

Inform (line 15627) is called only after a check that the memory manager is not busy, as described above. In addition to the call from *cause_sig*, it is called from *mini_rec* (in *proc.c*), whenever the memory manager blocks and there are kernel signals pending. *Inform* builds a message of type *KSIG* and sends it to the memory manager. The task or process calling *cause_sig* continues running as soon as the message has been copied into the memory manager's receive buffer. It does not wait for the memory manager to run, as would be the case if the normal send mechanism, which causes the sender to block, were to be used. Before it returns, however, *inform* calls *lock_pick_proc*, which schedules the memory manager to run. Since tasks have a higher priority than servers, the memory manager will not run until all tasks are satisfied. When the signaling task finishes, the scheduler will be entered. If the memory manager is the highest priority runnable process, it will run and process the signal.

The procedure *umap* (line 15658) is a generally useful procedure that maps a virtual address onto a physical address. As we have noted, it is called by *do_umap*, which services the *SYS_UMAP* message. Its parameters are a pointer to the process table entry for the process or task whose virtual address space is to be mapped, a flag specifying the text, data, or stack segment, the virtual address itself, and a byte count. The byte count is useful because *umap* checks to make sure that the entire buffer starting at the virtual address is within the process' address space. To do this, it must know the buffer's size. The byte count is not used for the mapping itself, just this check. All the tasks that copy data to or from user space compute the physical address of the buffer using *umap*. For device drivers it is convenient to be able to get the services of *umap* starting with the process number instead of a pointer to a process table entry. *Numap* (line 15697) does this. It calls *proc_addr* to convert its first argument and then calls *umap*.

The last function defined in *system.c* is *alloc_segments* (line 15715). It is called by *do_newmap*. It is also called by the *main* routine of the kernel during initialization. This definition is very hardware dependent. It takes the segment assignments that are recorded in a process table entry and manipulates the registers and descriptors the Pentium processor uses to support protected segments at the hardware level.

3.11 SUMMARY

Input/output is an often neglected, but important, topic. A substantial fraction of any operating system is concerned with I/O. We started out by looking at I/O hardware, and the relation of I/O devices to I/O controllers, which are what the software has to deal with. Then we looked at the four levels of I/O software: the interrupt routines, the device drivers, the device-independent I/O software, and the I/O libraries and spoolers that run in user space.

Next we studied the problem of deadlock and how it can be tackled. Deadlock occurs when a group of processes each have been granted exclusive access to some resources, and each one wants yet another resource that belongs to another process in the group. All of them are blocked and none will ever run again. Deadlock can be prevented by structuring the system so it can never occur, for example, by allowing a process to hold only one resource at any instant. It can also be avoided by examining each resource request to see if it leads to a situation in which deadlock is possible (an unsafe state) and denying or delaying those that lead to trouble.

Device drivers in MINIX are implemented as processes embedded in the kernel. We have looked at the RAM disk driver, hard disk driver, clock driver, and terminal driver. The synchronous alarm task and the system task are not device drivers but are structurally very similar to one. Each of these tasks has a main loop that gets requests and processes them, eventually sending back replies to report on what happened. All the tasks are located in the same address space. The RAM disk, hard disk, and floppy disk driver tasks all use a single copy of the same main loop and also share common functions. Nevertheless, each one is an independent process. Several different terminals, using the system console, the serial lines, and network connections are all supported by a single terminal task.

Device drivers have varying relationships to the interrupt system. Devices which can complete their work rapidly, such as the RAM disk and the memory-mapped display, do not use interrupts at all. The hard disk driver task does most of its work in the task code itself, and the interrupt handlers just return status information. The clock interrupt handler does a number of bookkeeping operations itself and only sends a message to the clock task when there is some work that cannot be taken care of by the handler. The keyboard interrupt handler buffers input and never sends a message to its task. Instead it changes a variable inspected by the clock interrupt handler; the latter sends a message to the terminal task.

PROBLEMS

1. Imagine that advances in chip technology make it possible to put an entire controller, including all the bus access logic, on an inexpensive chip. How will that affect the model of Fig. 3-1?

2. If a disk controller writes the bytes it receives from the disk to memory as fast as it receives them, with no internal buffering, is interleaving conceivably useful? Discuss.

3. Based on the rotation speed and geometry of the disks, what are the bit rates for transfers between the disk itself and the controller's buffer for a floppy disk and a hard disk? How does this compare with other forms of I/O (serial lines and networks)?

4. A disk is double interleaved, as in Fig. 3-4(c). It has eight sectors of 512 bytes per track, and a rotation rate of 300 rpm. How long does it take to read all the sectors of a track in order, assuming the arm is already correctly positioned, and 1/2 rotation is needed to get sector 0 under the head? What is the data rate? Now repeat the problem for a noninterleaved disk with the same characteristics. How much does the data rate degrade due to interleaving?

5. The DM-11 terminal multiplexer, which was used on the PDP-11 many, many years ago, sampled each (half-duplex) terminal line at seven times the baud rate to see if the incoming bit was a 0 or a 1. Sampling the line took 5.7 microsec. How many 1200-baud lines could the DM-11 support?

6. A local area network is used as follows. The user issues a system call to write data packets to the network. The operating system then copies the data to a kernel buffer. Then it copies the data to the network controller board. When all the bytes are safely inside the controller, they are sent over the network at a rate of 10 megabits/sec. The receiving network controller stores each bit a microsecond after it is sent. When the last bit arrives, the destination CPU is interrupted, and the kernel copies the newly arrived packet to a kernel buffer to inspect it. Once it has figured out which user the packet is for, the kernel copies the data to the user space. If we assume that each interrupt and its associated processing takes 1 msec, that packets are 1024 bytes (ignore the headers), and that copying a byte takes 1 microsec, what is the maximum rate at which one process can pump data to another? Assume that the sender is blocked until the work is finished at the receiving side and an acknowledgement comes back. For simplicity, assume that the time to get the acknowledgement back is so small it can be ignored.

7. What is "device independence?"

8. In which of the four I/O software layers is each of the following done.

   (a) Computing the track, sector, and head for a disk read.
   (b) Maintaining a cache of recently used blocks.
   (c) Writing commands to the device registers.
   (d) Checking to see if the user is permitted to use the device.
   (e) Converting binary integers to ASCII for printing.

9. Why are output files for the printer normally spooled on disk before being printed?

10. Consider Fig. 3-8. Suppose that in step (o) C requested S instead of requesting R. Would this lead to deadlock? Suppose that it requested both S and R?

11. Take a careful look at Fig. 3-11(b). If Suzanne asks for one more unit, does this lead to a safe state or an unsafe one? What if the request came from Marvin instead of Suzanne?

12. All the trajectories in Fig. 3-12 are horizontal or vertical. Can you envision any circumstances in which diagonal trajectories were also possible?

13. Suppose that process A in Fig. 3-13 requests the last tape drive. Does this action lead to a deadlock?

14. A computer has six tape drives, with n processes competing for them. Each process may need two drives. For which values of n is the system deadlock free?

15. Can a system be in a state that is neither deadlocked nor safe? If so, give an example. If not, prove that all states are either deadlocked or safe.

16. A distributed system using mailboxes has two IPC primitives, SEND and RECEIVE. The latter primitive specifies a process to receive from, and blocks if no message from that process is available, even though messages may be waiting from other processes. There are no shared resources, but processes need to communicate frequently about other matters. Is deadlock possible? Discuss.

17. In an electronic funds transfer system, there are hundreds of identical processes that work as follows. Each process reads an input line specifying an amount of money, the account to be credited, and the account to be debited. Then it locks both accounts and transfers the money, releasing the locks when done. With many processes running in parallel, there is a very real danger that having locked account x it will be unable to lock y because y has been locked by a process now waiting for x. Devise a scheme that avoids deadlocks. Do not release an account record until you have completed the transactions. (In other words, solutions that lock one account and then release it immediately if the other is locked are not allowed.)

18. The banker's algorithm is being run in a system with m resource classes and n processes. In the limit of large m and n, the number of operations that must be performed to check a state for safety is proportional to $m^a n^b$. What are the values of a and b?

19. Cinderella and the Prince are getting divorced. To divide their property, they have agreed on the following algorithm. Every morning, each one may send a letter to the other's lawyer requesting one item of property. Since it takes a day for letters to be delivered, they have agreed that if both discover that they have requested the same item on the same day, the next day they will send a letter canceling the request. Among their property is their dog, Woofer, Woofer's doghouse, their canary, Tweeter, and Tweeter's cage. The animals love their houses, so it has been agreed that any division of property separating an animal from its house is invalid, requiring the whole division to start over from scratch. Both Cinderella and the Prince desperately want Woofer. So they can go on (separate) vacations, each spouse has programmed a personal computer to handle the negotiation. When they come back from vacation, the computers are still negotiating. Why? Is deadlock possible? Is starvation (waiting forever) possible? Discuss.

20. The message format of Fig. 3-15 is used for sending request messages to drivers for block devices. Which fields, if any, could be omitted for messages to character devices?

21. Disk requests come in to the disk driver for cylinders 10, 22, 20, 2, 40, 6, and 38, in that order. A seek takes 6 msec per cylinder moved. How much seek time is needed for

    (a) First-come, first served.
    (b) Closest cylinder next.
    (c) Elevator algorithm (initially moving upward).

    In all cases, the arm is initially at cylinder 20.

22. A personal computer salesman visiting a university in South-West Amsterdam remarked during his sales pitch that his company had devoted substantial effort to making their version of UNIX very fast. As an example, he noted that their disk driver used the elevator algorithm and also queued multiple requests within a cylinder in sector order. A student, Harry Hacker, was impressed and bought one. He took it home and wrote a program to randomly read 10,000 blocks spread across the disk. To his amazement, the performance that he measured was identical to what would be expected from first-come, first-served. Was the salesman lying?

23. A UNIX process has two parts—the user part and the kernel part. Is the kernel part like a subroutine or a coroutine?

24. The clock interrupt handler on a certain computer requires 2 msec (including process switching overhead) per clock tick. The clock runs at 60 Hz. What fraction of the CPU is devoted to the clock?

25. Two examples of watchdog timers were given in the text: timing the startup of the floppy disk motor and allowing for carriage return on hardcopy terminals. Give a third example.

26. Why are RS232 terminals interrupt driven, but memory-mapped terminals not interrupt driven?

27. Consider how a terminal works. The driver outputs one character and then blocks. When the character has been printed, an interrupt occurs and a message is sent to the blocked driver, which outputs the next character and then blocks again. If the time to pass a message, output a character, and block is 4 msec, does this method work well on 110-baud lines? How about 4800-baud lines?

28. A bit-map terminal contains 1200 by 800 pixels. To scroll a window, the CPU (or controller) must move all the lines of text upward by copying their bits from one part of the video RAM to another. If a particular window is 66 lines high by 80 characters wide (5280 characters, total), and a character's box is 8 pixels wide by 12 pixels high, how long does it take to scroll the whole window at a copying rate of 500 nsec per byte? If all lines are 80 characters long, what is the equivalent baud rate of the terminal? Putting a character on the screen takes 50 microsec. Now compute the baud rate for the same terminal in color, with 4 bits/pixel. (Putting a character on the screen now takes 200 microsec.)

29. Why do operating systems provide escape characters, such as CTRL-V in MINIX?

30. After receiving a DEL (SIGINT) character, the MINIX driver discards all output currently queued for that terminal. Why?

31. Many RS232 terminals have escape sequences for deleting the current line and moving all the lines below it up one line. How do you think this feature is implemented inside the terminal?

32. On the original IBM PC's color display, writing to the video RAM at any time other than during the CRT beam's vertical retrace caused ugly spots to appear all over the screen. A screen image is 25 by 80 characters, each of which fits in a box 8 pixels by 8 pixels. Each row of 640 pixels is drawn on a single horizontal scan of the beam, which takes 63.6 microsec, including the horizontal retrace. The screen is redrawn 60 times a second, each of which requires a vertical retrace period to get the beam back to the top. What fraction of the time is the video RAM available for writing in?

33. Write a graphics driver for the IBM color display, or some other suitable bit-map display. The driver should accept commands to set and clear individual pixels, move rectangles around the screen, and any other features you think are interesting. User programs interface to the driver by opening */dev/graphics* and writing commands to it.

34. Modify the MINIX floppy disk driver to do track-at-a-time caching.

35. Implement a floppy disk driver that works as a character, rather than a block device, to bypass the file system's block cache. In this way, users can read large chunks of data from the disk, which are DMA'ed directly to user space, greatly improving performance. This driver would primarily be of interest to programs that need to read the raw bits on the disk, without regard to the file system. File system checkers fall into this category.

36. Implement the UNIX PROFIL system call, which is missing from MINIX.

37. Modify the terminal driver so that in addition to a having a special key to erase the previous character, there is a key to erase the previous word.

38. A new hard disk device with removable media has been added to a MINIX system. This device must spin up to speed every time the media are changed, and the spin up time is quite long. It is anticipated media changes will be made frequently while the system is running. Suddenly the *waitfor* routine in *at_wini.c* is unsatisfactory. Design a new *waitfor* routine in which, if the bit pattern being awaited is not found after 1 second of busy waiting, a phase will be entered in which the disk task will sleep for 1 second, test the port, and go back to sleep for another second until either the sought-for pattern is found or the preset *TIMEOUT* period expires.

4

MEMORY MANAGEMENT

Memory is an important resource that must be carefully managed. While the average home computer nowadays has fifty times as much memory as the IBM 7094, the largest computer in the world in the early 1960s, programs are getting bigger just as fast as memories. To paraphrase Parkinson's law, "Programs expand to fill the memory available to hold them." In this chapter we will study how operating systems manage their memory.

Ideally, what every programmer would like is an infinitely large, fast memory that is also nonvolatile, that is, does not lose its contents when the electric power fails. While we are at it, why not also ask for it to be inexpensive, too. Unfortunately technology does not provide such memories. Consequently, most computers have a **memory hierarchy**, with a small amount of very fast, expensive, volatile cache memory, some number of megabytes of medium-speed, medium-price, volatile main memory (RAM), and hundreds or thousands of megabytes of slow, cheap, nonvolatile disk storage. It is the job of the operating system to coordinate how these memories are used.

The part of the operating system that manages the memory hierarchy is called the **memory manager**. Its job is to keep track of which parts of memory are in use and which parts are not in use, to allocate memory to processes when they need it and deallocate it when they are done, and to manage swapping between main memory and disk when main memory is too small to hold all the processes.

In this chapter we will investigate a number of different memory management schemes, ranging from very simple to highly sophisticated. We will start at the beginning and look first at the simplest possible memory management system and then gradually progress to more and more elaborate ones.

4.1 BASIC MEMORY MANAGEMENT

Memory management systems can be divided into two classes: those that move processes back and forth between main memory and disk during execution (swapping and paging), and those that do not. The latter are simpler, so we will study them first. Later in the chapter we will examine swapping and paging. Throughout this chapter the reader should keep in mind that swapping and paging are largely artifacts caused by the lack of sufficient main memory to hold all the programs at once. As main memory gets cheaper, the arguments in favor of one kind of memory management scheme or another may become obsolete—unless programs get bigger faster than memory gets cheaper.

4.1.1 Monoprogramming without Swapping or Paging

The simplest possible memory management scheme is to run just one program at a time, sharing the memory between that program and the operating system. Three variations on this theme are shown in Fig. 4-1. The operating system may be at the bottom of memory in RAM (Random Access Memory), as shown in Fig. 4-1(a), or it may be in ROM (Read-Only Memory) at the top of memory, as shown in Fig. 4-1(b), or the device drivers may be at the top of memory in a ROM and the rest of the system in RAM down below, as shown in Fig. 4-1(c). The latter model is used by small MS-DOS systems, for example. On IBM PCs, the portion of the system in the ROM is called the **BIOS** (Basic Input Output System).

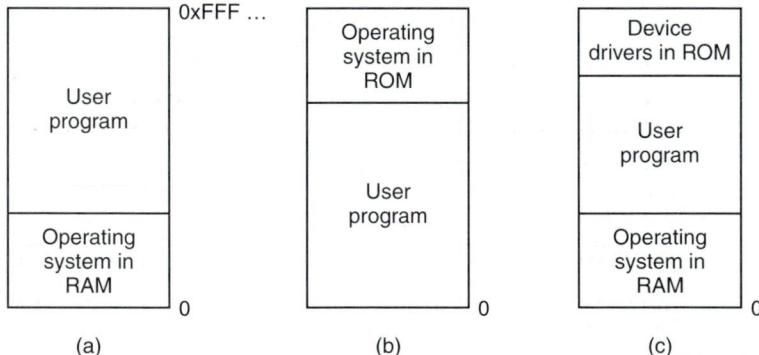

Figure 4-1. Three simple ways of organizing memory with an operating system and one user process. Other possibilities also exist.

When the system is organized in this way, only one process at a time can be running. As soon as the user types a command, the operating system copies the requested program from disk to memory and executes it. When the process finishes, the operating system displays a prompt character and waits for a new command. When it receives the command, it loads a new program into memory, overwriting the first one.

4.1.2 Multiprogramming with Fixed Partitions

Although monoprogramming is sometimes used on small computers with simple operating systems, often it is desirable to allow multiple processes to run at once. On timesharing systems, having multiple processes in memory at once means that when one process is blocked waiting for I/O to finish, another one can use the CPU. Thus multiprogramming increases the CPU utilization. However, even on personal computers it is often useful to be able to run two or more programs at once.

The easiest way to achieve multiprogramming is simply to divide memory up into n (possibly unequal) partitions. This partitioning can, for example, be done manually when the system is started up.

When a job arrives, it can be put into the input queue for the smallest partition large enough to hold it. Since the partitions are fixed in this scheme, any space in a partition not used by a job is lost. In Fig. 4-2(a) we see how this system of fixed partitions and separate input queues looks.

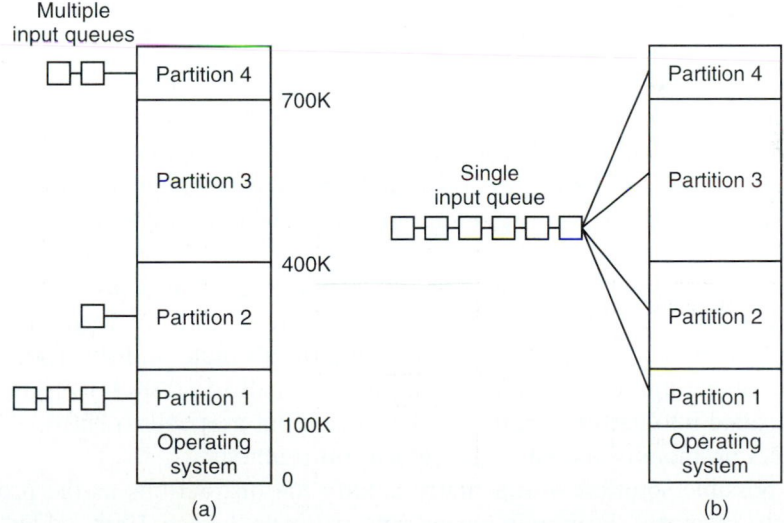

Figure 4-2. (a) Fixed memory partitions with separate input queues for each partition. (b) Fixed memory partitions with a single input queue.

The disadvantage of sorting the incoming jobs into separate queues becomes apparent when the queue for a large partition is empty but the queue for a small partition is full, as is the case for partitions 1 and 3 in Fig. 4-2(a). An alternative organization is to maintain a single queue as in Fig. 4-2(b). Whenever a partition becomes free, the job closest to the front of the queue that fits in it could be loaded into the empty partition and run. Since it is undesirable to waste a large partition on a small job, a different strategy is to search the whole input queue whenever a partition becomes free and pick the largest job that fits. Note that the latter algorithm discriminates against small jobs as being unworthy of having a whole partition, whereas usually it is desirable to give the smallest jobs (assumed to be interactive jobs) the best service, not the worst.

One way out is to have at least one small partition around. Such a partition will allow small jobs to run without having to allocate a large partition for them.

Another approach is to have a rule stating that a job that is eligible to run may not be skipped over more than k times. Each time it is skipped over, it gets one point. When it has acquired k points, it may not be skipped again.

This system, with fixed partitions set up by the operator in the morning and not changed thereafter, was used by OS/360 on large IBM mainframes for many years. It was called MFT (Multiprogramming with a Fixed number of Tasks or OS/MFT). It is simple to understand and equally simple to implement: incoming jobs are queued until a suitable partition is available, at which time the job is loaded into that partition and run until it terminates. Nowadays, few, if any, operating systems, support this model.

Relocation and Protection

Multiprogramming introduces two essential problems that must be solved— relocation and protection. Look at Fig. 4-2. From the figure it is clear that different jobs will be run at different addresses. When a program is linked (i.e., the main program, user-written procedures, and library procedures are combined into a single address space), the linker must know at what address the program will begin in memory.

For example, suppose that the first instruction is a call to a procedure at absolute address 100 within the binary file produced by the linker. If this program is loaded in partition 1, that instruction will jump to absolute address 100, which is inside the operating system. What is needed is a call to 100K + 100. If the program is loaded into partition 2, it must be carried out as a call to 200K + 100, and so on. This problem is known as the **relocation** problem.

One possible solution is to actually modify the instructions as the program is loaded into memory. Programs loaded into partition 1 have 100K added to each address, programs loaded into partition 2 have 200K added to addresses, and so forth. To perform relocation during loading like this, the linker must include in the binary program a list or bit map telling which program words are addresses to be relocated and which are opcodes, constants, or other items that must not be relocated. OS/MFT worked this way. Some microcomputers also work like this.

Relocation during loading does not solve the protection problem. A malicious program can always construct a new instruction and jump to it. Because programs in this system use absolute memory addresses rather than addresses relative to a register, there is no way to stop a program from building an instruction that reads or writes any word in memory. In multiuser systems, it is undesirable to let processes read and write memory belonging to other users.

The solution that IBM chose for protecting the 360 was to divide memory into blocks of 2K bytes and assign a 4-bit protection code to each block. The PSW contained a 4-bit key. The 360 hardware trapped any attempt by a running process to access memory whose protection code differed from the PSW key. Since only the operating system could change the protection codes and key, user processes were prevented from interfering with one another and with the operating system itself.

An alternative solution to both the relocation and protection problems is to equip the machine with two special hardware registers, called the **base** and **limit** registers. When a process is scheduled, the base register is loaded with the address of the start of its partition, and the limit register is loaded with the length of the partition. Every memory address generated automatically has the base register contents added to it before being sent to memory. Thus if the base register is 100K, a CALL 100 instruction is effectively turned into a CALL 100K + 100 instruction, without the instruction itself being modified. Addresses are also checked against the limit register to make sure that they do not attempt to address memory outside the current partition. The hardware protects the base and limit registers to prevent user programs from modifying them.

The CDC 6600—the world's first supercomputer—used this scheme. The Intel 8088 CPU used for the original IBM PC used a weaker version of this scheme—base registers, but no limit registers. Starting with the 286, a better scheme was adopted.

4.2 SWAPPING

With a batch system, organizing memory into fixed partitions is simple and effective. Each job is loaded into a partition when it gets to the head of the queue. It stays in memory until it has finished. As long as enough jobs can be kept in memory to keep the CPU busy all the time, there is no reason to use anything more complicated.

With timesharing systems or graphically oriented personal computers, the situation is different. Sometimes there is not enough main memory to hold all the currently active processes, so excess processes must be kept on disk and brought in to run dynamically.

Two general approaches to memory management can be used, depending (in part) on the available hardware. The simplest strategy, called **swapping**, consists of bringing in each process in its entirety, running it for a while, then putting it back on the disk. The other strategy, called **virtual memory**, allows programs to run even when they are only partially in main memory. Below we will studying swapping; in Sec. 4-3 we will examine virtual memory.

The operation of a swapping system is illustrated in Fig. 4-3. Initially only process *A* is in memory. Then processes *B* and *C* are created or swapped in from disk. In Fig. 4-3(d) *A* terminates or is swapped out to disk. Then *D* comes in and *B* goes out. Finally *E* comes in.

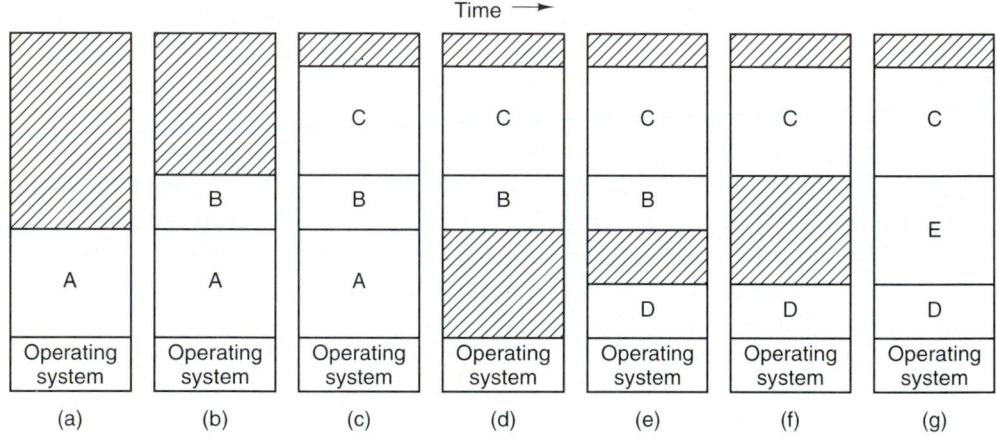

Figure 4-3. Memory allocation changes as processes come into memory and leave it. The shaded regions are unused memory.

The main difference between the fixed partitions of Fig. 4-2 and the variable partitions of Fig. 4-3 is that the number, location, and size of the partitions vary dynamically in the latter as processes come and go, whereas they are fixed in the former. The flexibility of not being tied to a fixed number of partitions that may be too large or too small improves memory utilization, but it also complicates allocating and deallocating memory, as well as keeping track of it.

When swapping creates multiple holes in memory, it is possible to combine them all into one big one by moving all the processes downward as far as possible. This technique is known as **memory compaction**. It is usually not done because it requires a lot of CPU time. For example, on a 32-MB machine that can copy 16 bytes per microsecond, it takes 2 sec to compact all of memory.

A point that is worth making concerns how much memory should be allocated for a process when it is created or swapped in. If processes are created with a fixed size that never changes, then the allocation is simple: you allocate exactly what is needed, no more and no less.

If, however, processes' data segments can grow, for example, by dynamically allocating memory from a heap, as in many programming languages, a problem occurs whenever a process tries to grow. If a hole is adjacent to the process, it can be allocated and the process allowed to grow into the hole. On the other hand, if the process is adjacent to another process, the growing process will either have to be moved to a hole in memory large enough for it, or one or more processes will have to be swapped out to create a large enough hole. If a process cannot grow in memory and the swap area on the disk is full, the process will have to wait or be killed.

If it is expected that most processes will grow as they run, it is probably a good idea to allocate a little extra memory whenever a process is swapped in or moved, to reduce the overhead associated with moving or swapping processes that no longer fit in their allocated memory. However, when swapping processes to disk, only the memory actually in use should be swapped; it is wasteful to swap the extra memory as well. In Fig. 4-4(a) we see a memory configuration in which space for growth has been allocated to two processes.

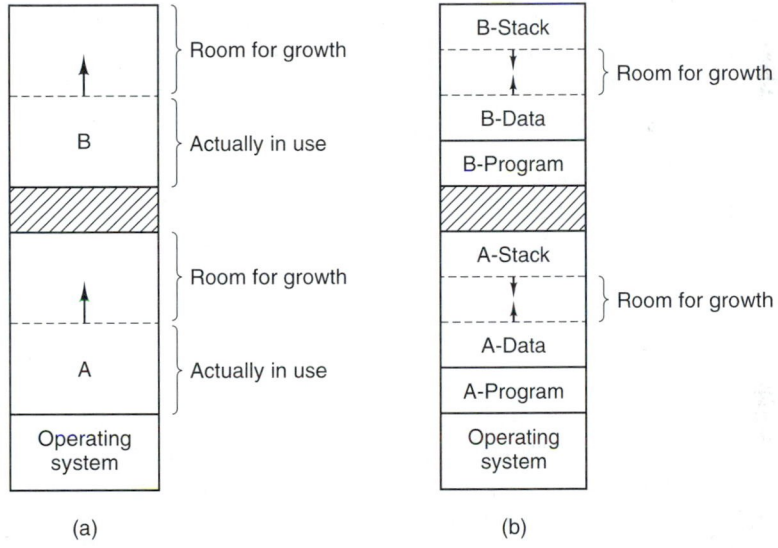

Figure 4-4. (a) Allocating space for a growing data segment. (b) Allocating space for a growing stack and a growing data segment.

If processes can have two growing segments, for example, the data segment being used as a heap for variables that are dynamically allocated and released and a stack segment for the normal local variables and return addresses, an alternative arrangement suggests itself, namely that of Fig. 4-4(b). In this figure we see that each process illustrated has a stack at the top of its allocated memory that is growing downward, and a data segment just beyond the program text that is growing upward. The memory between them can be used for either segment. If it runs out, either the process will have to be moved to a hole with enough space, swapped out of memory until a large enough hole can be created, or killed.

4.2.1 Memory Management with Bit Maps

When memory is assigned dynamically, the operating system must manage it. In general terms, there are two ways to keep track of memory usage: bit maps and free lists. In this section and the next one we will look at these two methods in turn.

With a bit map, memory is divided up into allocation units, perhaps as small as a few words and perhaps as large as several kilobytes. Corresponding to each allocation unit is a bit in the bit map, which is 0 if the unit is free and 1 if it is occupied (or vice versa). Figure 4-5 shows part of memory and the corresponding bit map.

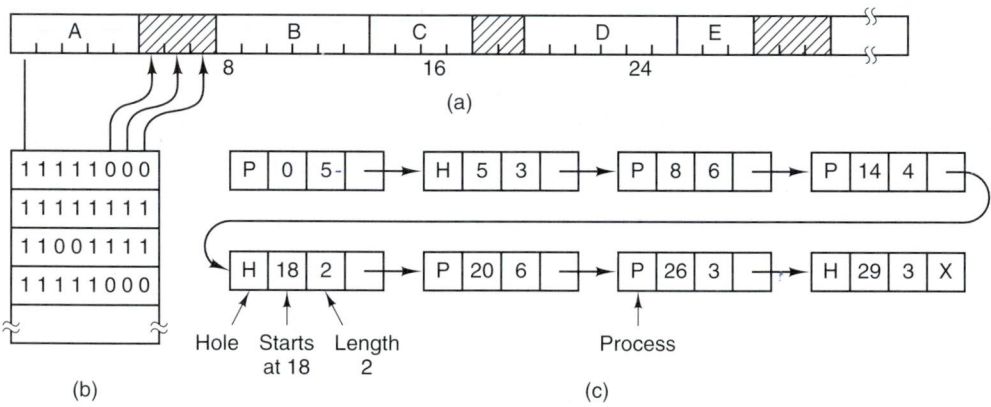

Figure 4-5. (a) A part of memory with five processes and three holes. The tick marks show the memory allocation units. The shaded regions (0 in the bit map) are free. (b) The corresponding bit map. (c) The same information as a list.

The size of the allocation unit is an important design issue. The smaller the allocation unit, the larger the bit map. However, even with an allocation unit as small as 4 bytes, 32 bits of memory will require only 1 bit of the map. A memory of $32n$ bits will use n map bits, so the bit map will take up only 1/33 of memory. If the allocation unit is chosen large, the bit map will be smaller, but appreciable memory may be wasted in the last unit if the process size is not an exact multiple of the allocation unit.

A bit map provides a simple way to keep track of memory words in a fixed amount of memory because the size of the bit map depends only on the size of memory and the size of the allocation unit. The main problem with it is that when it has been decided to bring a k unit process into memory, the memory manager must search the bit map to find a run of k consecutive 0 bits in the map. Searching a bit map for a run of a given length is a slow operation (because the run may straddle word boundaries in the map); this is an argument against bit maps.

4.2.2 Memory Management with Linked Lists

Another way of keeping track of memory is to maintain a linked list of allocated and free memory segments, where a segment is either a process or a hole between two processes. The memory of Fig. 4-5(a) is represented in Fig. 4-5(c) as a linked list of segments. Each entry in the list specifies a hole (H) or process (P), the address at which it starts, the length, and a pointer to the next entry.

In this example, the segment list is kept sorted by address. Sorting this way has the advantage that when a process terminates or is swapped out, updating the list is straightforward. A terminating process normally has two neighbors (except when it is at the very top or bottom of memory). These may be either processes or holes, leading to the four combinations of Fig. 4-6. In Fig. 4-6(a) updating the list requires replacing a P by an H. In Fig. 4-6(b) and Fig. 4-6(c), two entries are coalesced into one, and the list becomes one entry shorter. In Fig. 4-6(d), three entries are merged and two items are removed from the list. Since the process table slot for the terminating process will normally point to the list entry for the process itself, it may be more convenient to have the list as a double-linked list, rather than the single-linked list of Fig. 4-5(c). This structure makes it easier to find the previous entry and to see if a merge is possible.

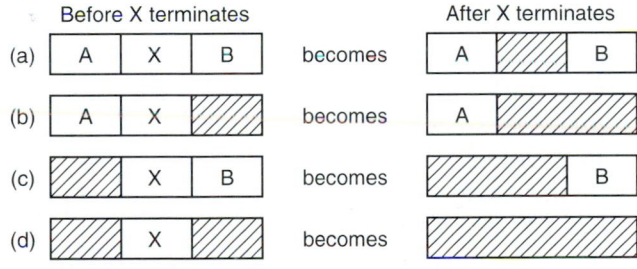

Figure 4-6. Four neighbor combinations for the terminating process, X.

When the processes and holes are kept on a list sorted by address, several algorithms can be used to allocate memory for a newly created or swapped in process. We assume that the memory manager knows how much memory to allocate. The simplest algorithm is **first fit**. The memory manager scans along the list of segments until it finds a hole that is big enough. The hole is then broken up into two pieces, one for the process and one for the unused memory, except in the unlikely case of an exact fit. First fit is a fast algorithm because it searches as little as possible.

A minor variation of first fit is **next fit**. It works the same way as first fit, except that it keeps track of where it is whenever it finds a suitable hole. The next time it is called to find a hole, it starts searching the list from the place where it left off last time. instead of always at the beginning, as first fit does. Simulations by Bays (1977) show that next fit gives slightly worse performance than first fit.

Another well-known algorithm is **best fit**. Best fit searches the entire list and takes the smallest hole that is adequate. Rather than breaking up a big hole that might be needed later, best fit tries to find a hole that is close to the actual size needed.

As an example of first fit and best fit, consider Fig. 4-5 again. If a block of size 2 is needed, first fit will allocate the hole at 5, but best fit will allocate the hole at 18.

Best fit is slower than first fit because it must search the entire list every time it is called. Somewhat surprisingly, it also results in more wasted memory than first fit or next fit because it tends to fill up memory with tiny, useless holes. First fit generates larger holes on the average.

To get around the problem of breaking up nearly exact matches into a process and a tiny hole, one could think about **worst fit**, that is, always take the largest available hole, so that the hole broken off will be big enough to be useful. Simulation has shown that worst fit is not a very good idea either.

All four algorithms can be speeded up by maintaining separate lists for processes and holes. In this way, all of them devote their full energy to inspecting holes, not processes. The inevitable price that is paid for this speedup on allocation is the additional complexity and slowdown when deallocating memory, since a freed segment has to be removed from the process list and inserted into the hole list.

If distinct lists are maintained for processes and holes, the hole list may be kept sorted on size, to make best fit faster. When best fit searches a list of holes from smallest to largest, as soon as it finds a hole that fits, it knows that the hole is the smallest one that will do the job, hence the best fit. No further searching is needed, as it is with the single list scheme. With a hole list sorted by size, first fit and best fit are equally fast, and next fit is pointless.

When the holes are kept on separate lists from the processes, a small optimization is possible. Instead of having a separate set of data structures for maintaining the hole list, as is done in Fig. 4-5(c), the holes themselves can be used. The first word of each hole could be the hole size, and the second word a pointer to the following entry. The nodes of the list of Fig. 4-5(c), which require three words and one bit (P/H), are no longer needed.

Yet another allocation algorithm is **quick fit**, which maintains separate lists for some of the more common sizes requested. For example, it might have a table with n entries, in which the first entry is a pointer to the head of a list of 4K holes, the second entry is a pointer to a list of 8K holes, the third entry a pointer to 12K holes, and so on. Holes of say, 21K, could either be put on the 20K list or on a special list of odd-sized holes. With quick fit, finding a hole of the required size is extremely fast, but it has the same disadvantage as all schemes that sort by hole size, namely, when a process terminates or is swapped out, finding its neighbors to see if a merge is possible is expensive. If merging is not done, memory will quickly fragment into a large number of small holes into which no processes fit.

4.3 VIRTUAL MEMORY

Many years ago people were first confronted with programs that were too big to fit in the available memory. The solution usually adopted was to split the program into pieces, called **overlays**. Overlay 0 would start running first. When it was done, it would call another overlay. Some overlay systems were highly complex, allowing multiple overlays in memory at once. The overlays were kept on the disk and swapped in and out of memory by the operating system, dynamically, as needed.

Although the actual work of swapping overlays in and out was done by the system, the work of splitting the program into pieces had to be done by the programmer. Splitting up large programs into small, modular pieces was time consuming and boring. It did not take long before someone thought of a way to turn the whole job over to the computer.

The method that was devised (Fotheringham, 1961) has come to be known as **virtual memory**. The basic idea behind virtual memory is that the combined size of the program, data, and stack may exceed the amount of physical memory available for it. The operating system keeps those parts of the program currently in use in main memory, and the rest on the disk. For example, a 16M program can run on a 4M machine by carefully choosing which 4M to keep in memory at each instant, with pieces of the program being swapped between disk and memory as needed.

Virtual memory can also work in a multiprogramming system, with bits and pieces of many programs in memory at once. While a program is waiting for part of itself to be brought in, it is waiting for I/O and cannot run, so the CPU can be given to another process, the same way as for any other multiprogramming system.

4.3.1 Paging

Most virtual memory systems use a technique called **paging**, which we will now describe. On any computer, there exists a set of memory addresses that programs can produce. When a program uses an instruction like

```
MOVE REG,1000
```

it is copying the contents of memory address 1000 to REG (or vice versa, depending on the computer). Addresses can be generated using indexing, base registers, segment registers, and other ways.

These program-generated addresses are called **virtual addresses** and form the **virtual address space**. On computers without virtual memory, the virtual address is put directly onto the memory bus and causes the physical memory word with the same address to be read or written. When virtual memory is used, the virtual addresses do not go directly to the memory bus. Instead, they go to a **Memory Management Unit** (MMU), a chip or collection of chips that maps the virtual addresses onto the physical memory addresses as illustrated in Fig. 4-7.

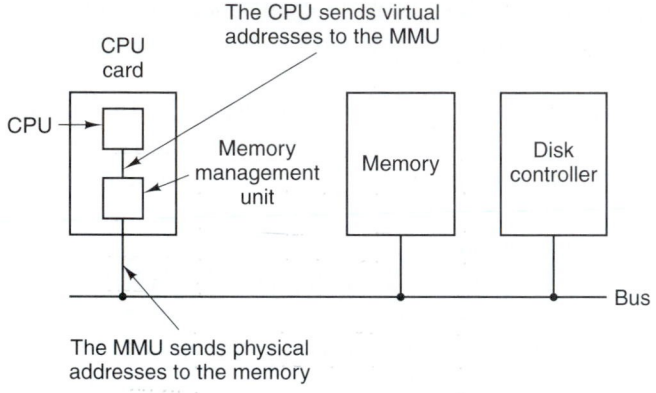

Figure 4-7. The position and function of the MMU.

A very simple example of how this mapping works is shown in Fig. 4-8. In this example, we have a computer that can generate 16-bit addresses, from 0 up to 64K. These are the virtual addresses. This computer, however, has only 32K of physical memory, so although 64K programs can be written, they cannot be loaded into memory in their entirety and run. A complete copy of a program's core image, up to 64K, must be present on the disk, however, so that pieces can be brought in as needed.

The virtual address space is divided up into units called **pages**. The corresponding units in the physical memory are called **page frames**. The pages and page frames are always exactly the same size. In this example they are 4K, but page sizes from 512 bytes to 64K are commonly used in existing systems. With 64K of virtual address space and 32K of physical memory, we have 16 virtual pages and 8 page frames. Transfers between memory and disk are always in units of a page.

When the program tries to access address 0, for example, using the instruction

MOVE REG,0

the virtual address 0 is sent to the MMU. The MMU sees that this virtual address falls in page 0 (0 to 4095), which according to its mapping is page frame 2 (8192 to 12287). It thus transforms the address to 8192 and outputs address 8192 onto the bus. The memory board knows nothing at all about the MMU and just sees a

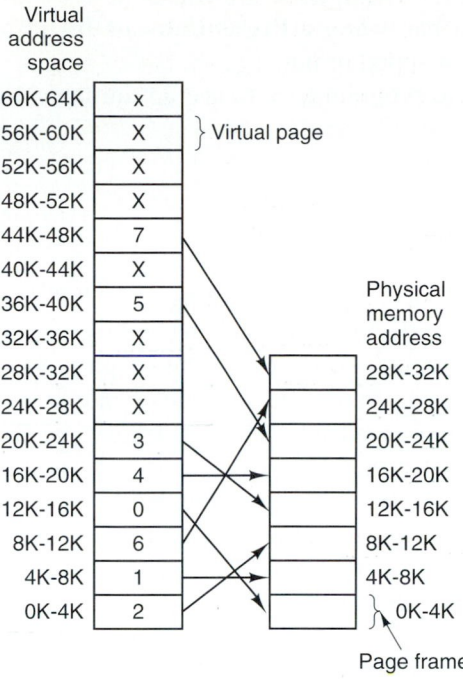

Figure 4-8. The relation between virtual addresses and physical memory addresses is given by the page table.

request for reading or writing address 8192, which it honors. Thus, the MMU has effectively mapped all virtual addresses between 0 and 4095 onto physical addresses 8192 to 12287.

Similarly, an instruction

MOVE REG,8192

is effectively transformed into

MOVE REG,24576

because virtual address 8192 is in virtual page 2 and this page is mapped onto physical page frame 6 (physical addresses 24576 to 28671). As a third example, virtual address 20500 is 20 bytes from the start of virtual page 5 (virtual addresses 20480 to 24575) and maps onto physical address 12288 + 20 = 12308.

By itself, this ability to map the 16 virtual pages onto any of the eight page frames by setting the MMU's map appropriately does not solve the problem that the virtual address space is larger than the physical memory. Since we have only eight physical page frames, only eight of the virtual pages in Fig. 4-8 are mapped onto physical memory. The others, shown as a cross in the figure, are not mapped. In the actual hardware, a **Present/absent bit** in each entry keeps track of whether the page is mapped or not.

What happens if the program tries to use an unmapped page, for example, by using the instruction

MOVE REG,32780

which is byte 12 within virtual page 8 (starting at 32768)? The MMU notices that the page is unmapped (indicated by a cross in the figure), and causes the CPU to trap to the operating system. This trap is called a **page fault**. The operating system picks a little-used page frame and writes its contents back to the disk. It then fetches the page just referenced into the page frame just freed, changes the map, and restarts the trapped instruction.

For example, if the operating system decided to evict page frame 1, it would load virtual page 8 at physical address 4K and make two changes to the MMU map. First, it would mark virtual page 1's entry as unmapped, to trap any future accesses to virtual addresses between 4K and 8K. Then it would replace the cross in virtual page 8's entry with a 1, so that when the trapped instruction is re-executed, it will map virtual address 32780 onto physical address 4108.

Now let us look inside the MMU to see how it works and why we have chosen to use a page size that is a power of 2. In Fig. 4-9 we see an example of a virtual address, 8196 (0010000000000100 in binary), being mapped using the MMU map of Fig. 4-8. The incoming 16-bit virtual address is split up into a 4-bit page number and a 12-bit offset. With 4 bits for the page number, we can represent 16 pages, and with 12 bits for the offset, we can address all 4096 bytes within a page.

The page number is used as an index into the **page table**, yielding the number of the page frame corresponding to that virtual page. If the *Present/absent* bit is 0, a trap to the operating system is caused. If the bit is 1, the page frame number found in the page table is copied to the high-order 3 bits of the output register, along with the 12-bit offset, which is copied unmodified from the incoming virtual address. Together they form a 15-bit physical address. The output register is then put onto the memory bus as the physical memory address.

4.3.2 Page Tables

In theory, the mapping of virtual addresses onto physical addresses is as we have just described it. The virtual address is split into a virtual page number (high-order bits) and an offset (low-order bits). The virtual page number is used as an index into the page table to find the entry for that virtual page. From the

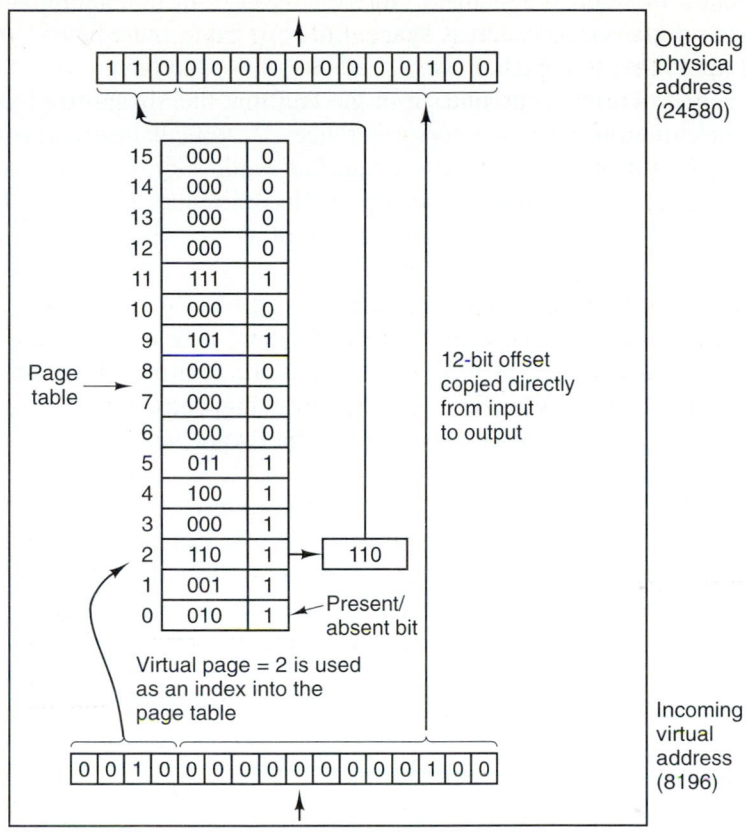

Figure 4-9. The internal operation of the MMU with 16 4K pages.

page table entry, the page frame number (if any) is found. The page frame number is attached to the high-order end of the offset, replacing the virtual page number, to form a physical address that can be sent to the memory.

The purpose of the page table is to map virtual pages onto page frames. Mathematically speaking, the page table is a function, with the virtual page number as argument and the physical frame number as result. Using the result of this function, the virtual page field in a virtual address can be replaced by a page frame field, thus forming a physical memory address.

Despite this simple description, two major issues must be faced:

1. The page table can be extremely large.

2. The mapping must be fast.

The first point follows from the fact that modern computers use virtual addresses of at least 32 bits. With, say, a 4K page size, a 32-bit address space has 1 million pages, and a 64-bit address space has more than you want to contemplate. With 1 million pages in the virtual address space, the page table must have 1 million entries. And remember that each process needs its own page table.

The second point is a consequence of the fact that the virtual-to-physical mapping must be done on every memory reference. A typical instruction has an instruction word, and often a memory operand as well. Consequently, it is necessary to make 1, 2, or sometimes more page table references per instruction. If an instruction takes, say, 10 nsec, the page table lookup must be done in a few nanoseconds to avoid becoming a major bottleneck.

The need for large, fast page mapping is a significant constraint on the way computers are built. Although the problem is most serious with top-of-the-line machines, it is also an issue at the low end as well, where cost and price/performance are critical. In this section and the following ones, we will look at page table design in detail and show a number of hardware solutions that have been used in actual computers.

The simplest design (at least conceptually) is to have a single page table consisting of an array of fast hardware registers, with one entry for each virtual page, indexed by virtual page number. When a process is started up, the operating system loads the registers with the process' page table, taken from a copy kept in main memory. During process execution, no more memory references are needed for the page table. The advantages of this method are that it is straightforward and requires no memory references during mapping. A disadvantage is that it is potentially expensive (if the page table is large). Having to load the page table at every context switch can also hurt performance.

At the other extreme, the page table can be entirely in main memory. All the hardware needs then is a single register that points to the start of the page table. This design allows the memory map to be changed at a context switch by reloading one register. Of course, it has the disadvantage of requiring one or more memory references to read page table entries during the execution of each instruction. For this reason, this approach is rarely used in its most pure form, but below we will study some variations that have much better performance.

Multilevel Page Tables

To get around the problem of having huge page tables in memory all the time, many computers use a multilevel page table. A simple example is shown in Fig. 4-10. In Fig. 4-10(a) we have a 32-bit virtual address that is partitioned into a 10-bit *PT1* field, a 10-bit *PT2* field, and a 12-bit *Offset* field. Since offsets are 12 bits, pages are 4K, and there are a total of 2^{20} of them.

The secret to the multilevel page table method is to avoid keeping all the page tables in memory all the time. In particular, those that are not needed should not be kept around. Suppose, for example, that a process needs 12 megabytes, the bottom 4 megabytes of memory for program text, the next 4 megabytes for data,

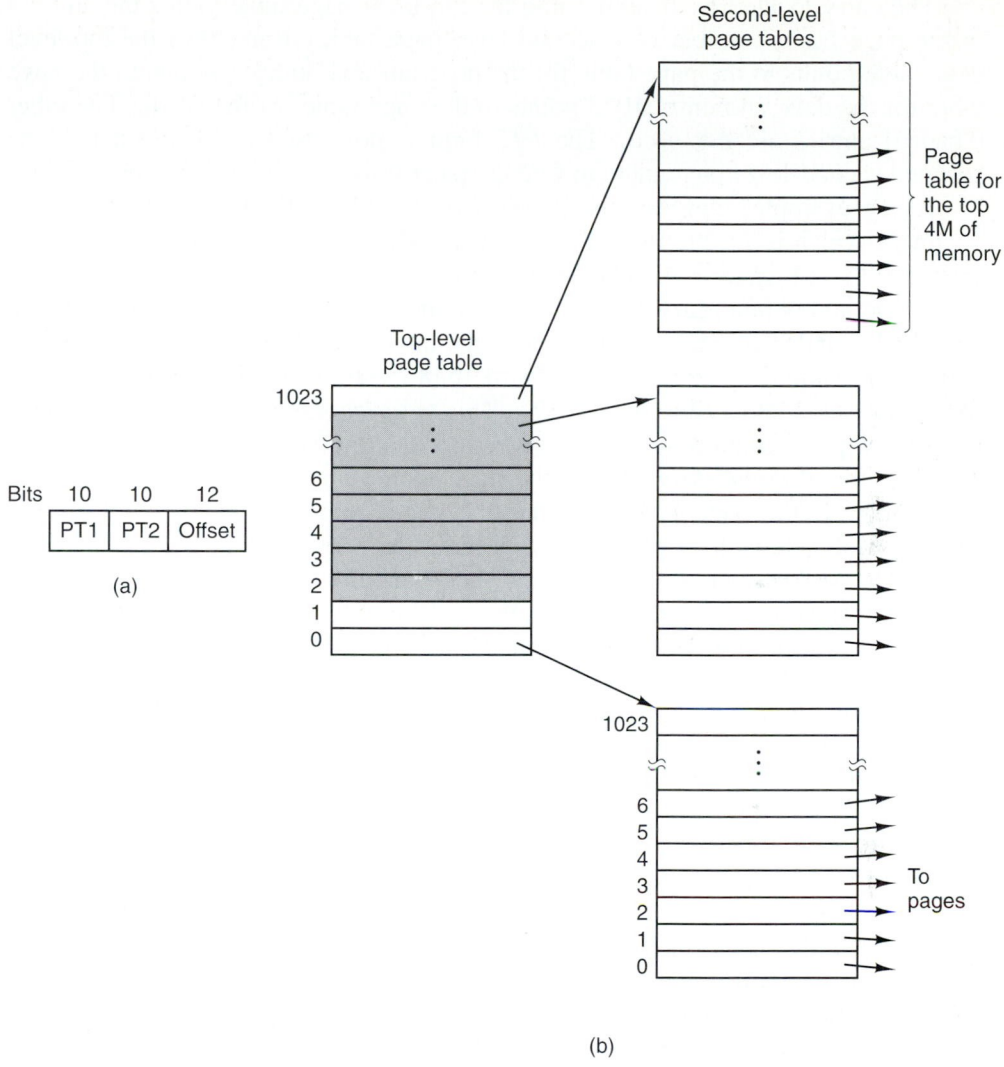

Figure 4-10. (a) A 32-bit address with two page table fields. (b) Two-level page tables.

and the top 4 megabytes for the stack. In between the top of the data and the bottom of the stack is a gigantic hole that is not used.

In Fig. 4-10(b) we see how the two-level page table works in this example. On the left we have the top-level page table, with 1024 entries, corresponding to the 10-bit *PT1* field. When a virtual address is presented to the MMU, it first extracts the *PT1* field and uses this value as an index into the top-level page table. Each of these 1024 entries represents 4M because the entire 4-gigabyte (i.e., 32-bit) virtual address space has been chopped into chunks of 1024 bytes.

The entry located by indexing into the top-level page table yields the address or the page frame number of a second-level page table. Entry 0 of the top-level page table points to the page table for the program text, entry 1 points to the page table for the data, and entry 1023 points to the page table for the stack. The other (shaded) entries are not used. The *PT2* field is now used as an index into the selected second-level page table to find the page frame number for the page itself.

As an example, consider the 32-bit virtual address 0x00403004 (4,206,596 decimal), which is 12,292 bytes into the data. This address corresponds to *PT1* = 1, *PT2* = 3, and *Offset* = 4. The MMU first uses *PT1* to index into the top-level page table and obtain entry 1, which corresponds to addresses 4M to 8M. It then uses *PT2* to index into the second-level page table just found and extract entry 3, which corresponds to addresses 12288 to 16383 within its 4M chunk (i.e., absolute addresses 4,206,592 to 4,210,687). This entry contains the page frame number of the page containing virtual address 0x00403004. If that page is not in memory, the *Present/absent* bit in the page table entry will be zero, causing a page fault. If the page is in memory, the page frame number taken from the second-level page table is combined with the offset (4) to construct a physical address. This address is put on the bus and sent to memory.

The interesting thing to note about Fig. 4-10 is that although the address space contains over a million pages, only four page tables are actually needed: the top-level table, and the second-level tables for 0 to 4M, 4M to 8M, and the top 4M. The *Present/absent* bits in 1021 entries of the top-level page table are set to 0, forcing a page fault if they are ever accessed. Should this occur, the operating system will notice that the process is trying to reference memory that it is not supposed to and will take appropriate action, such as sending it a signal or killing it. In this example we have chosen round numbers for the various sizes and have picked *PT1* equal to *PT2* but in actual practice other values are also possible, of course.

The two-level page table system of Fig. 4-10 can be expanded to three, four, or more levels. Additional levels give more flexibility, but it is doubtful that the additional complexity is worth it beyond three levels.

Let us now turn from the structure of the page tables in the large, to the details of a single page table entry. The exact layout of an entry is highly machine dependent, but the kind of information present is roughly the same from machine to machine. In Fig. 4-11 we give a sample page table entry. The size varies from computer to computer, but 32 bits is a common size. The most important field is the *Page frame number*. After all, the goal of the page mapping is to locate this value. Next to it we have the *Present/absent* bit. If this bit is 1, the entry is valid and can be used. If it is 0, the virtual page to which the entry belongs is not currently in memory. Accessing a page table entry with this bit set to 0 causes a page fault.

The *Protection* bits tell what kinds of access are permitted. In the simplest form, this field contains 1 bit, with 0 for read/write and 1 for read only. A more

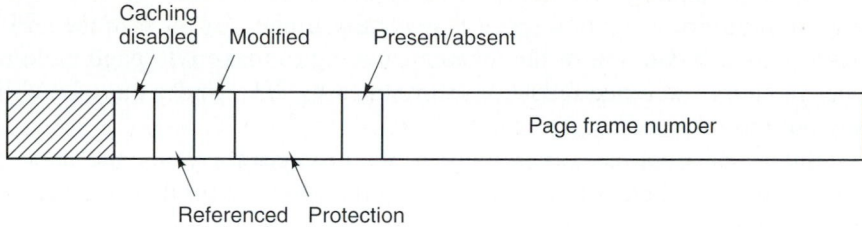

Figure 4-11. A typical page table entry.

sophisticated arrangement is having 3 bits, one bit each for enabling reading, writing, and executing the page.

The *Modified* and *Referenced* bits keep track of page usage. When a page is written to, the hardware automatically sets the *Modified* bit. This bit is of value when the operating system decides to reclaim a page frame. If the page in it has been modified (i.e., is "dirty"), it must be written back to the disk. If it has not been modified (i.e., is "clean"), it can just be abandoned, since the disk copy is still valid. The bit is sometimes called the **dirty bit**, since it reflects the page's state.

The *Referenced* bit is set whenever a page is referenced, either for reading or writing. Its value is to help the operating system choose a page to evict when a page fault occurs. Pages that are not being used are better candidates than pages that are, and this bit plays an important role in several of the page replacement algorithms that we will study later in this chapter.

Finally, the last bit allows caching to be disabled for the page. This feature is important for pages that map onto device registers rather than memory. If the operating system is sitting in a tight loop waiting for some I/O device to respond to a command it was just given, it is essential that the hardware keep fetching the word from the device, and not use an old cached copy. With this bit, caching can be turned off. Machines that have a separate I/O space and do not use memory mapped I/O do not need this bit.

Note that the disk address used to hold the page when it is not in memory is not part of the page table. The reason is simple. The page table holds only that information the hardware needs to translate a virtual address to a physical address. Information the operating system needs to handle page faults is kept in software tables inside the operating system.

4.3.3 TLBs—Translation Lookaside Buffers

In most paging schemes, the page tables are kept in memory, due to their large size. Potentially, this design has an enormous impact on performance. Consider, for example, an instruction that copies one register to another. In the absence of paging, this instruction makes only one memory reference, to fetch the instruction. With paging, additional memory references will be needed to access the page table. Since execution speed is generally limited by the rate the CPU can get instructions and data out of the memory, having to make two page table references per memory reference reduces performance by 2/3. Under these conditions, no one would use it.

Computer designers have known about this problem for years and have come up with a solution. Their solution is based on the observation that most programs tend to make a large number of references to a small number of pages, and not the other way around. Thus only a small fraction of the page table entries are heavily read; the rest are barely used at all.

The solution that has been devised is to equip computers with a small hardware device for mapping virtual addresses to physical addresses without going through the page table. The device, called a **TLB** (**Translation Lookaside Buffer**) or sometimes an **associative memory**, is illustrated in Fig. 4-12. It is usually inside the MMU and consists of a small number of entries, eight in this example, but rarely more than 64. Each entry contains information about one page, in particular, the virtual page number, a bit that is set when the page is modified, the protection code (read/write/execute permissions), and the physical page frame in which the page is located. These fields have a one-to-one correspondence with the fields in the page table. Another bit indicates whether the entry is valid (i.e., in use) or not.

Valid	Virtual page	Modified	Protection	Page frame
1	140	1	RW	31
1	20	0	R X	38
1	130	1	RW	29
1	129	1	RW	62
1	19	0	R X	50
1	21	0	R X	45
1	860	1	RW	14
1	861	1	RW	75

Figure 4-12. A TLB to speed up paging.

An example that might generate the TLB of Fig. 4-12 is a process in a loop that spans virtual pages 19, 20, and 21, so these TLB entries have protection codes for reading and executing. The main data currently being used (say, an array being processed) are on pages 129 and 130. Page 140 contains the indices used in the array calculations. Finally, the stack is on pages 860 and 861.

Let us now see how the TLB functions. When a virtual address is presented to the MMU for translation, the hardware first checks to see if its virtual page number is present in the TLB by comparing it to all the entries simultaneously (i.e., in parallel). If a valid match is found and the access does not violate the protection bits, the page frame is taken directly from the TLB, without going to the page table. If the virtual page number is present in the TLB but the instruction is trying to write on a read-only page, a protection fault is generated, the same way as it would be from the page table itself.

The interesting case is what happens when the virtual page number is not in the TLB. The MMU detects the miss and does an ordinary page table lookup. It then evicts one of the entries from the TLB and replaces it with the page table entry just looked up. Thus if that page is used again soon, the second time it will result in a hit rather than a miss. When an entry is purged from the TLB, the modified bit is copied back into the page table entry in memory. The other values are already there. When the TLB is loaded from the page table, all the fields are taken from memory.

Software TLB Management

Up until now, we have assumed that every machine with paged virtual memory has page tables recognized by the hardware, plus a TLB. In this design, TLB management and handling TLB faults are done entirely by the MMU hardware. Traps to the operating system occur only when a page is not in memory.

In the past, this assumption was true. However, some modern RISC machines, including the MIPS, Alpha, and HP PA, do nearly all of this page management in software. On these machines, the TLB entries are explicitly loaded by the operating system. When a TLB miss occurs, instead of the MMU just going to the page tables to find and fetch the needed page reference, it just generates a TLB fault and tosses the problem into the lap of the operating system. The system must find the page, remove an entry from the TLB, enter the new one, and restart the instruction that faulted. And, of course, all of this must be done in a handful of instructions because TLB misses occur much more frequently than page faults.

Surprisingly enough, if the TLB is reasonably large (say, 64 entries) to reduce the miss rate, software management of the TLB turns out to be quite efficient. The main gain here is a much simpler MMU, which frees up a considerable amount of area on the CPU chip for caches and other features that can improve performance. Software TLB management is discussed at length by Uhlig et al. (1994).

Various strategies have been developed to improve performance on machines that do TLB management in software. One approach attacks both reducing TLB misses and reducing the cost of a TLB miss when it does occur (Bala et al., 1994). To reduce TLB misses, sometimes the operating system can use its intuition to figure out which pages are likely to be used next and to preload entries for them in the TLB. For example, when a client process does an RPC to a server process on the same machine, it is very likely that the server will have to run soon. Knowing this, while processing the trap to do the RPC, the system can also check to see where the server's code, data, and stack pages are, and map them in before they can cause TLB faults.

The normal way to process a TLB miss, whether in hardware or in software, is to go to the page table and perform the indexing operations to locate the page referenced. The problem with doing this search in software is that the pages holding the page table may not be in the TLB, which will cause additional TLB faults during the processing. These faults can be reduced by maintaining a large (e.g., 4K) software cache of TLB entries in a fixed location whose page is always kept in the TLB. By first checking the software cache, the operating system can substantially reduce TLB misses.

4.3.4 Inverted Page Tables

Traditional page tables of the type described so far require one entry per virtual page, since they are indexed by virtual page number. If the address space consists of 2^{32} bytes, with 4096 bytes per page, then over 1 million page table entries are needed. As a bare minimum, the page table will have to be at least 4 megabytes. On larger systems, this size is probably doable.

However, as 64-bit computers become more common, the situation changes drastically. If the address space is now 2^{64} bytes, with 4K pages, we need over 10^{15} bytes for the page table. Tying up 1 million gigabytes just for the page table is not doable, not now and not for decades to come, if ever. Consequently, a different solution is needed for 64-bit paged virtual address spaces.

One such solution is the **inverted page table**. In this design, there is one entry per page frame in real memory, rather than one entry per page of virtual address space. For example, with 64-bit virtual addresses, a 4K page, and 32 MB of RAM, an inverted page table only requires 8192 entries. The entry keeps track of which (process, virtual page) is located in the page frame.

Although inverted page tables save vast amounts of space, at least when the virtual address space is much larger than the physical memory, they have a serious downside: virtual-to-physical translation becomes much harder. When process n references virtual page p, the hardware can no longer find the physical page by using p as an index into the page table. Instead, it must search the entire inverted page table for an entry (n, p). Furthermore, this search must be done on every memory reference, not just on page faults. Searching an 8K table on every memory reference is not the way to make your machine blindingly fast.

The way out of this dilemma is to use the TLB. If the TLB can hold all of the heavily used pages, translation can happen just as fast as with regular page tables. On a TLB miss, however, the inverted page table has to be searched. Using a hash table as an index into the inverted page table, this search can be made reasonably fast, however. Inverted page tables are currently used on some IBM and

Hewlett-Packard workstations and will become more common as 64-bit machines become widespread.

Other approaches to handling large virtual memories can be found in (Huck and Hays, 1993; Talluri and Hill, 1994; and Talluri et al., 1995).

4.4 PAGE REPLACEMENT ALGORITHMS

When a page fault occurs, the operating system has to choose a page to remove from memory to make room for the page that has to be brought in. If the page to be removed has been modified while in memory, it must be rewritten to the disk to bring the disk copy up to date. If, however, the page has not been changed (e.g., a page contains program text), the disk copy is already up to date, so no rewrite is needed. The page to be read in just overwrites the page being evicted.

While it would be possible to pick a random page to replace at each page fault, system performance is much better if a page that is not heavily used is chosen. If a heavily used page is removed, it will probably have to be brought back in quickly, resulting in extra overhead. Much work has been done on the subject of page replacement algorithms, both theoretical and experimental. Below we will describe some of the most important algorithms.

4.4.1 The Optimal Page Replacement Algorithm

The best possible page replacement algorithm is easy to describe but impossible to implement. It goes like this. At the moment that a page fault occurs, some set of pages is in memory. One of these pages will be referenced on the very next instruction (the page containing that instruction). Other pages may not be referenced until 10, 100, or perhaps 1000 instructions later. Each page can be labeled with the number of instructions that will be executed before that page is first referenced.

The optimal page algorithm simply says that the page with the highest label should be removed. If one page will not be used for 8 million instructions and another page will not be used for 6 million instructions, removing the former pushes the page fault that will fetch it back as far into the future as possible. Computers, like people, try to put off unpleasant events for as long as they can.

The only problem with this algorithm is that it is unrealizable. At the time of the page fault, the operating system has no way of knowing when each of the pages will be referenced next. (We saw a similar situation earlier with the shortest job first scheduling algorithm—how can the system tell which job is shortest?) Still, by running a program on a simulator and keeping track of all page references, it is possible to implement optimal page replacement on the *second* run by using the page reference information collected during the *first* run.

In this way it is possible to compare the performance of realizable algorithms with the best possible one. If an operating system achieves a performance of, say, only 1 percent worse than the optimal algorithm, effort spent in looking for a better algorithm will yield at most a 1 percent improvement.

To avoid any possible confusion, it should be made clear that this log of page references refers only to the one program just measured. The page replacement algorithm derived from it is thus specific to that one program. Although this method is useful for evaluating page replacement algorithms, it is of no use in practical systems. Below we will study algorithms that *are* useful on real systems.

4.4.2 The Not Recently Used Page Replacement Algorithm

In order to allow the operating system to collect useful statistics about which pages are being used and which ones are not, most computers with virtual memory have two status bits associated with each page. R is set whenever the page is referenced (read or written). M is set when the page is written to (i.e., modified). The bits are contained in each page table entry, as shown in Fig. 4-11. It is important to realize that these bits must be updated on every memory reference, so it is essential that they be set by the hardware. Once a bit has been set to 1, it stays 1 until the operating system resets it to 0 in software.

If the hardware does not have these bits, they can be simulated as follows. When a process is started up, all of its page table entries are marked as not in memory. As soon as any page is referenced, a page fault will occur. The operating system then sets the R bit (in its internal tables), changes the page table entry to point to the correct page, with mode READ ONLY, and restarts the instruction. If the page is subsequently written on, another page fault will occur, allowing the operating system to set the M bit and change the page's mode to READ/WRITE.

The R and M bits can be used to build a simple paging algorithm as follows. When a process is started up, both page bits for all its pages are set to 0 by the operating system. Periodically (e.g., on each clock interrupt), the R bit is cleared, to distinguish pages that have not been referenced recently from those that have been.

When a page fault occurs, the operating system inspects all the pages and divides them into four categories based on the current values of their R and M bits:

Class 0: not referenced, not modified.
Class 1: not referenced, modified.
Class 2: referenced, not modified.
Class 3: referenced, modified.

Although class 1 pages seem, at first glance, impossible, they occur when a class 3 page has its R bit cleared by a clock interrupt. Clock interrupts do not clear the

M bit because this information is needed to know whether the page has to be rewritten to disk or not.

The **NRU** (**Not Recently Used**) algorithm removes a page at random from the lowest numbered nonempty class. Implicit in this algorithm is that it is better to remove a modified page that has not been referenced in at least one clock tick (typically 20 msec) than a clean page that is in heavy use. The main attraction of NRU is that it is easy to understand, efficient to implement, and gives a performance that, while certainly not optimal, is often adequate.

4.4.3 The First-In, First-Out (FIFO) Page Replacement Algorithm

Another low-overhead paging algorithm is the **FIFO** (**First-In, First-Out**) algorithm. To illustrate how this works, consider a supermarket that has enough shelves to display exactly k different products. One day, some company introduces a new convenience food—instant, freeze-dried, organic yogurt that can be reconstituted in a microwave oven. It is an immediate success, so our finite supermarket has to get rid of one old product in order to stock it.

One possibility is to find the product that the supermarket has been stocking the longest (i.e., something it began selling 120 years ago) and get rid of it on the grounds that no one is interested any more. In effect, the supermarket maintains a linked list of all the products it currently sells in the order they were introduced. The new one goes on the back of the list; the one at the front of the list is dropped.

As a page replacement algorithm, the same idea is applicable. The operating system maintains a list of all pages currently in memory, with the page at the head of the list the oldest one and the page at the tail the most recent arrival. On a page fault, the page at the head is removed and the new page added to the tail of the list. When applied to stores, FIFO might remove mustache wax, but it might also remove flour, salt, or butter. When applied to computers the same problem arises. For this reason, FIFO in its pure form is rarely used.

4.4.4 The Second Chance Page Replacement Algorithm

A simple modification to FIFO that avoids the problem of throwing out a heavily used page is to inspect the R bit of the oldest page. If it is 0, the page is both old and unused, so it is replaced immediately. If the R bit is 1, the bit is cleared, the page is put onto the end of the list of pages, and its load time is updated as though it had just arrived in memory. Then the search continues.

The operation of this algorithm, called **second chance**, is shown in Fig. 4-13. In Fig. 4-13(a) we see pages A through H kept on a linked list and sorted by the time they arrived in memory.

Suppose that a page fault occurs at time 20. The oldest page is A, which arrived at time 0, when the process started. If A has the R bit cleared, it is evicted from memory, either by being written to the disk (if it is dirty), or just abandoned

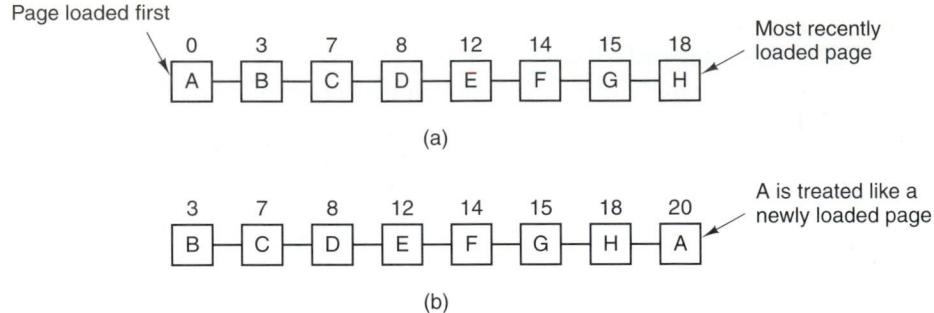

Figure 4-13. Operation of second chance. (a) Pages sorted in FIFO order. (b) Page list if a page fault occurs at time 20 and A has its R bit set.

(if it is clean). On the other hand, if the R bit is set, A is put onto the end of the list and its "load time" is reset to the current time (20). The R bit is also cleared. The search for a suitable page continues with B.

What second chance is doing is looking for an old page that has not been referenced in the previous clock interval. If all the pages have been referenced, second chance degenerates into pure FIFO. Specifically, imagine that all the pages in Fig. 4-13(a) have their R bits set. One by one, the operating system moves the pages to the end of the list, clearing the R bit each time it appends a page to the end of the list. Eventually, it comes back to page A, which now has its R bit cleared. At this point A is evicted. Thus the algorithm always terminates.

4.4.5 The Clock Page Replacement Algorithm

Although second chance is a reasonable algorithm, it is unnecessarily ineffi-cient because it is constantly moving pages around on its list. A better approach is to keep all the pages on a circular list in the form of a clock, as shown in Fig. 4-14. A hand points to the oldest page.

When a page fault occurs, the page being pointed to by the hand is inspected. If its R bit is 0, the page is evicted, the new page is inserted into the clock in its place, and the hand is advanced one position. If R is 1, it is cleared and the hand is advanced to the next page. This process is repeated until a page is found with $R = 0$. Not surprisingly, this algorithm is called **clock**. It differs from second chance only in the implementation.

4.4.6 The Least Recently Used (LRU) Page Replacement Algorithm

A good approximation to the optimal algorithm is based on the observation that pages that have been heavily used in the last few instructions will probably be heavily used again in the next few. Conversely, pages that have not been used for

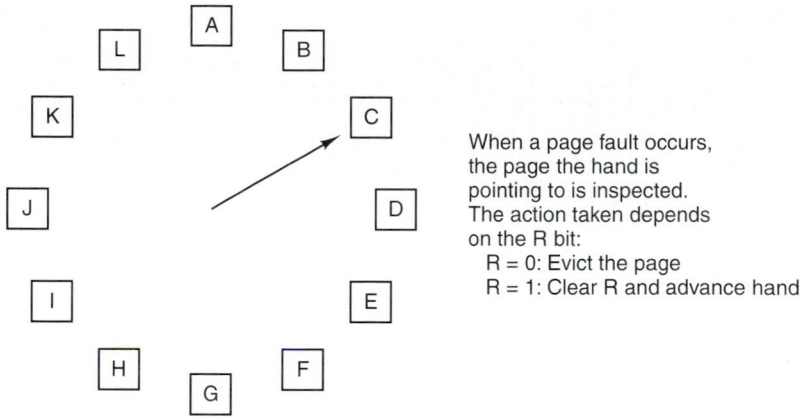

When a page fault occurs, the page the hand is pointing to is inspected. The action taken depends on the R bit:
R = 0: Evict the page
R = 1: Clear R and advance hand

Figure 4-14. The clock page replacement algorithm.

ages will probably remain unused for a long time. This idea suggests a realizable algorithm: when a page fault occurs, throw out the page that has been unused for the longest time. This strategy is called **LRU** (**Least Recently Used**) paging.

Although LRU is theoretically realizable, it is not cheap. To fully implement LRU, it is necessary to maintain a linked list of all pages in memory, with the most recently used page at the front and the least recently used page at the rear. The difficulty is that the list must be updated on every memory reference. Finding a page in the list, deleting it, and then moving it to the front is a very time consuming operation, even in hardware (assuming that such hardware could be built).

However, there are other ways to implement LRU with special hardware. Let us consider the simplest way first. This method requires equipping the hardware with a 64-bit counter, C, that is automatically incremented after each instruction. Furthermore, each page table entry must also have a field large enough to contain the counter. After each memory reference, the current value of C is stored in the page table entry for the page just referenced. When a page fault occurs, the operating system examines all the counters in the page table to find the lowest one. That page is the least recently used.

Now let us look at a second hardware LRU algorithm. For a machine with n page frames, the LRU hardware can maintain a matrix of $n \times n$ bits, initially all zero. Whenever page frame k is referenced, the hardware first sets all the bits of row k to 1, then sets all the bits of column k to 0. At any instant, the row whose binary value is lowest is the least recently used, the row whose value is next lowest is next least recently used, and so forth. The workings of this algorithm are given in Fig. 4-15 for four page frames and page references in the order

0 1 2 3 2 1 0 3 2 3

After page 0 is referenced we have the situation of Fig. 4-15(a), and so forth.

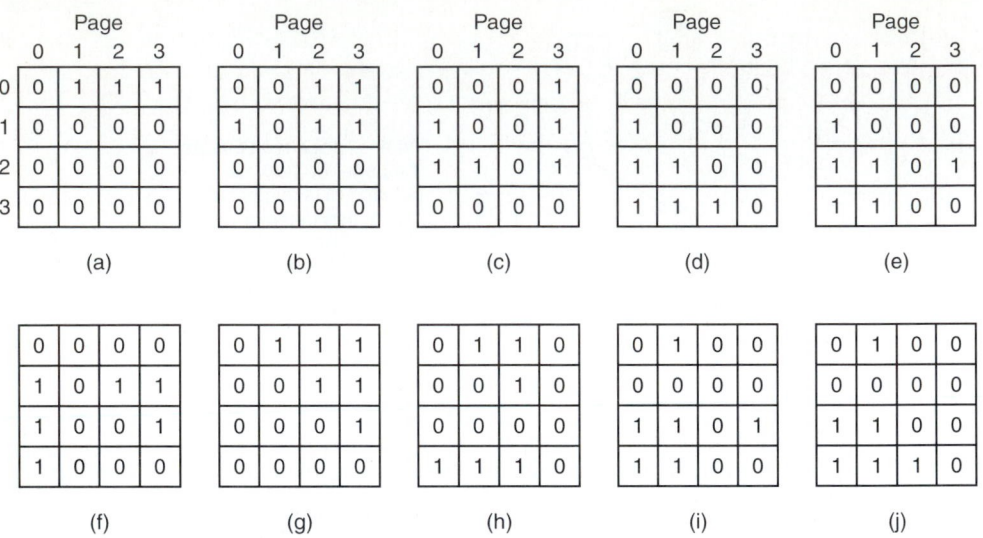

Figure 4-15. LRU using a matrix.

4.4.7 Simulating LRU in Software

Although both of the previous LRU algorithms are realizable in principle, few, if any, machines have this hardware, so they are of little use to the operating system designer who is making a system for a machine that does not have this hardware. Instead, a solution that can be implemented in software is needed. One possibility is called the **Not Frequently Used** or **NFU** algorithm. It requires a software counter associated with each page, initially zero. At each clock interrupt, the operating system scans all the pages in memory. For each page, the R bit, which is 0 or 1, is added to the counter. In effect, the counters are an attempt to keep track of how often each page has been referenced. When a page fault occurs, the page with the lowest counter is chosen for replacement.

The main problem with NFU is that it never forgets anything. For example, in a multipass compiler, pages that were heavily used during pass 1 may still have a high count well into later passes. In fact, if pass 1 happens to have the longest execution time of all the passes, the pages containing the code for subsequent passes may always have lower counts than the pass 1 pages. Consequently, the operating system will remove useful pages instead of pages no longer in use.

Fortunately, a small modification to NFU makes it able to simulate LRU quite well. The modification has two parts. First, the counters are each shifted right 1 bit before the R bit is added in. Second, the R bit is added to the leftmost, rather than the rightmost bit.

Figure 4-16 illustrates how the modified algorithm, known as **aging**, works. Suppose that after the first clock tick the R bits for pages 0 to 5 have the values 1,

0, 1, 0, 1, and 1 respectively (page 0 is 1, page 1 is 0, page 2 is 1, etc.). In other words, between tick 0 and tick 1, pages 0, 2, 4, and 5 were referenced, setting their R bits to 1, while the other ones remain 0. After the six corresponding counters have been shifted and the R bit inserted at the left, they have the values shown in Fig. 4-16(a). The four remaining columns show the six counters after the next four clock ticks.

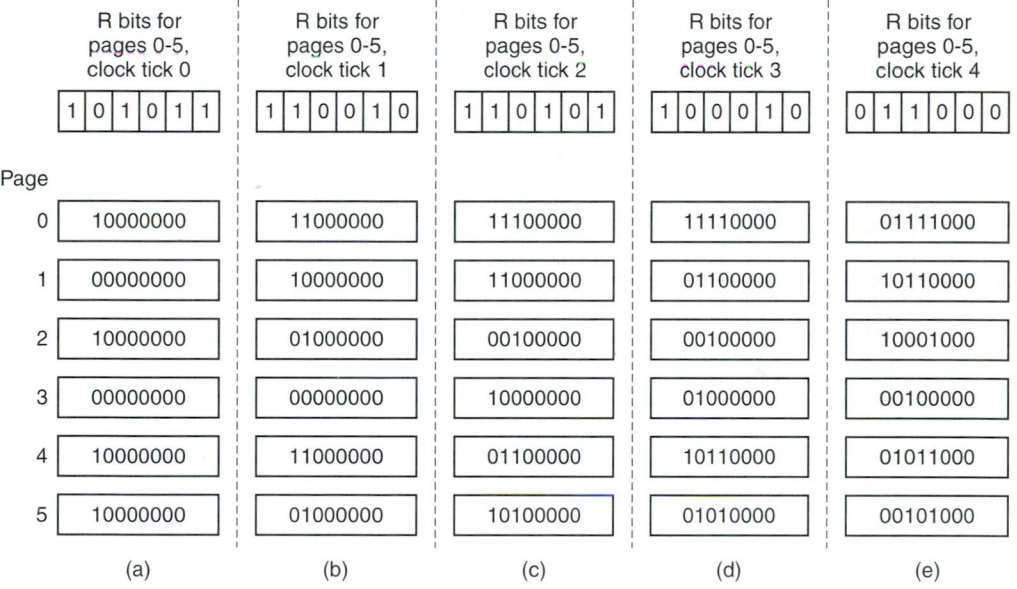

Figure 4-16. The aging algorithm simulates LRU in software. Shown are six pages for five clock ticks. The five clock ticks are represented by (a) to (e).

When a page fault occurs, the page whose counter is the lowest is removed. It is clear that a page that has not been referenced for, say, four clock ticks will have four leading zeroes in its counter, and thus will have a lower value than a counter that has not been referenced for three clock ticks.

This algorithm differs from LRU in two ways. Consider pages 3 and 5 in Fig. 4-16(e). Neither has been referenced for two clock ticks; both were referenced in the tick prior to that. According to LRU, if a page must be replaced, we should choose one of these two. The trouble is, we do not know which of these two was referenced last in the interval between tick 1 and tick 2. By recording only one bit per time interval, we have lost the ability to distinguish references early in the clock interval from those occurring later. All we can do is remove page 3, because page 5 was also referenced two ticks earlier and page 3 was not.

The second difference between LRU and aging is that in aging the counters have a finite number of bits, 8 bits in this example. Suppose that two pages each have a counter value of 0. All we can do is pick one of them at random. In reality, it may well be that one of the pages was last referenced 9 ticks ago and the other was last referenced 1000 ticks ago. We have no way of seeing that. In practice, however, 8 bits is generally enough if a clock tick is around 20 msec. If a page has not been referenced in 160 msec, it probably is not that important.

4.5 DESIGN ISSUES FOR PAGING SYSTEMS

In the previous sections we have explained how paging works and have given a few of the basic page replacement algorithms. But knowing the bare mechanics is not enough. To design a system, you have to know a lot more to make it work well. It is like the difference between knowing how to move the rook, knight, bishop, and other pieces in chess, and being a good player. In the following sections, we will look at other issues that operating system designers must consider carefully in order to get good performance from a paging system.

4.5.1 The Working Set Model

In the purest form of paging, processes are started up with none of their pages in memory. As soon as the CPU tries to fetch the first instruction, it gets a page fault, causing the operating system to bring in the page containing the first instruction. Other page faults for global variables and the stack usually follow quickly. After a while, the process has most of the pages it needs and settles down to run with relatively few page faults. This strategy is called **demand paging** because pages are loaded only on demand, not in advance.

Of course, it is easy enough to write a test program that systematically reads all the pages in a large address space, causing so many page faults that there is not enough memory to hold them all. Fortunately, most processes do not work this way. They exhibit a **locality of reference**, meaning that during any phase of execution, the process references only a relatively small fraction of its pages. Each pass of a multipass compiler, for example, references only a fraction of all the pages, and a different fraction at that.

The set of pages that a process is currently using is called its **working set** (Denning, 1968a; Denning, 1980). If the entire working set is in memory, the process will run without causing many faults until it moves into another execution phase (e.g., the next pass of the compiler). If the available memory is too small to hold the entire working set, the process will cause many page faults and run slowly since executing an instruction often takes a few nanoseconds and reading in a page from the disk typically takes tens of milliseconds. At a rate of one or two instructions per 20 milliseconds, it will take ages to finish. A program causing page faults every few instructions is said to be **thrashing** (Denning, 1968b).

In a timesharing system, processes are frequently moved to disk (i.e., all their pages are removed from memory) to let other processes have a turn at the CPU.

The question arises of what to do when a process is brought back in again. Technically, nothing need be done. The process will just cause page faults until its working set has been loaded. The problem is that having 20, 50, or even 100 page faults every time a process is loaded is slow, and it also wastes considerable CPU time, since it takes the operating system a few milliseconds of CPU time to process a page fault.

Therefore, many paging systems try to keep track of each process' working set and make sure that it is in memory before letting the process run. This approach is called the **working set model** (Denning, 1970). It is designed to greatly reduce the page fault rate. Loading the pages *before* letting processes run is also called **prepaging.**

To implement the working set model, it is necessary for the operating system to keep track of which pages are in the working set. One way to monitor this information is to use the aging algorithm discussed above. Any page containing a 1 bit among the high order n bits of the counter is considered to be a member of the working set. If a page has not been referenced in n consecutive clock ticks, it is dropped from the working set. The parameter n has to be determined experimentally for each system, but the system performance is usually not especially sensitive to the exact value.

Information about the working set can be used to improve the performance of the clock algorithm. Normally, when the hand points to a page whose R bit is 0, the page is evicted. The improvement is to check to see if that page is part of the working set of the current process. If it is, the page is spared. This algorithm is called **wsclock**.

4.5.2 Local versus Global Allocation Policies

In the preceding sections we have discussed several algorithms for choosing a page to replace when a fault occurs. A major issue associated with this choice (which we have carefully swept under the rug until now) is how memory should be allocated among the competing runnable processes.

Take a look at Fig. 4-17(a). In this figure, three processes, A, B, and C, make up the set of runnable processes. Suppose A gets a page fault. Should the page replacement algorithm try to find the least recently used page considering only the six pages currently allocated to A, or should it consider all the pages in memory? If it looks only at A's pages, the page with the lowest age value is $A5$, so we get the situation of Fig. 4-17(b).

On the other hand, if the page with the lowest age value is removed without regard to whose page it is, page $B3$ will be chosen and we will get the situation of Fig. 4-17(c). The algorithm of Fig. 4-17(b) is said to be a **local** page replacement algorithm, whereas Fig. 4-17(c) is said to be a **global** algorithm. Local algorithms effectively correspond to allocating every process a fixed fraction of the memory.

	Age				
A0	10		A0		A0
A1	7		A1		A1
A2	5		A2		A2
A3	4		A3		A3
A4	6		A4		A4
A5	3		(A6)		A5
B0	9		B0		B0
B1	4		B1		B1
B2	6		B2		B2
B3	2		B3		(A6)
B4	5		B4		B4
B5	6		B5		B5
B6	12		B6		B6
C1	3		C1		C1
C2	5		C2		C2
C3	6		C3		C3
(a)			(b)		(c)

Figure 4-17. Local versus global page replacement. (a) Original configuration. (b) Local page replacement. (c) Global page replacement.

Global algorithms dynamically allocate page frames among the runnable processes. Thus the number of page frames assigned to each process varies in time.

In general, global algorithms work better, especially when the working set size can vary over the lifetime of a process. If a local algorithm is used and the working set grows, thrashing will result, even if there are plenty of free page frames. If the working set shrinks, local algorithms waste memory. If a global algorithm is used, the system must continually decide how many page frames to assign to each process. One way is to monitor the working set size as indicated by the aging bits, but this approach does not necessarily prevent thrashing. The working set may change size in microseconds, whereas the aging bits are a crude measure spread over a number of clock ticks.

Another approach is to have an algorithm for allocating page frames to processes. One way is to periodically determine the number of running processes and allocate each process an equal share. Thus with 475 available (i.e., non-operating system) page frames and 10 processes, each process gets 47 frames. The remaining 5 go into a pool to be used when page faults occur.

Although this method seems fair, it makes little sense to give equal shares of the memory to a 10K process and a 300K process. Instead, pages can be allocated in proportion to each process' total size, with a 300K process getting 30 times the allotment of a 10K process. It is probably wise to give each process some minimum number, so it can run, no matter how small it is. On some machines, for example, a single instruction may need as many as six pages because the instruction itself, the source operand, and the destination operand may all straddle page boundaries. With an allocation of only five pages, programs containing such instructions cannot execute at all.

Neither the equal allocation nor the proportional allocation method directly deals with the thrashing problem. A more direct way to control it is to use the **Page Fault Frequency** or **PFF** allocation algorithm. For a large class of page replacement algorithms, including LRU, it is known that the fault rate decreases as more pages are assigned, as we discussed above. This property is illustrated in Fig. 4-18.

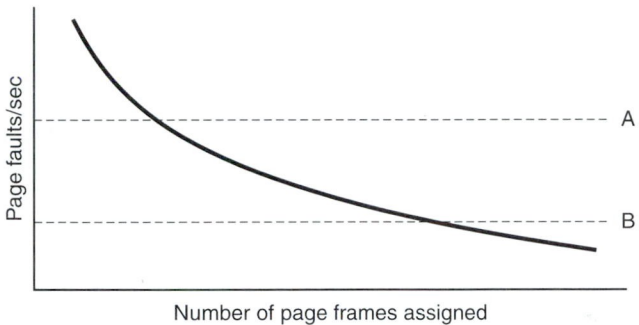

Figure 4-18. Page fault rate as a function of the number of page frames assigned.

The dashed line marked A corresponds to a page fault rate that is unacceptably high, so the faulting process is given more page frames to reduce the fault rate. The dashed line marked B corresponds to a page fault rate so low that it can be concluded that the process has too much memory. In this case page frames may be taken away from it. Thus, PFF tries to keep the paging rate within acceptable bounds.

If it discovers that there are so many processes in memory that it is not possible to keep all of them below A, then some process is removed from memory, and its page frames are divided up among the remaining processes or put into a pool of available pages that can be used on subsequent page faults. The decision to remove a process from memory is a form of load control. It shows that even with paging, swapping is still needed, only now swapping is used to reduce potential demand for memory, rather than to reclaim blocks of it for immediate use.

4.5.3 Page Size

The page size is often a parameter that can be chosen by the operating system. Even if the hardware has been designed with, for example, 512-byte pages, the operating system can easily regard pages 0 and 1, 2 and 3, 4 and 5, and so on, as 1K pages by always allocating two consecutive 512-byte page frames for them.

Determining the optimum page size requires balancing several competing factors. To start with, a randomly chosen text, data, or stack segment will not fill an integral number of pages. On the average, half of the final page will be empty. The extra space in that page is wasted This wastage is called **internal fragmentation**. With n segments in memory and a page size of p bytes, $np/2$ bytes will be wasted on internal fragmentation. This reasoning argues for a small page size.

Another argument for a small page size becomes apparent if we think about a program consisting of eight sequential phases of 4K each. With a 32K page size, the program must be allocated 32K all the time. With a 16K page size, it needs only 16K. With a page size of 4K or smaller, it requires only 4K at any instant. In general, a large page size will cause more unused program to be in memory than a small page size.

On the other hand, small pages mean that programs will need many pages, hence a large page table. A 32K program needs only four 8K pages, but 64 512-byte pages. Transfers to and from the disk are generally a page at a time, with most of the time being for the seek and rotational delay, so that transferring a small page takes almost as much time as transferring a large page. It might take 64×15 msec to load 64 512-byte pages, but only 4×25 msec to load four 8K pages.

On some machines, the page table must be loaded into hardware registers every time the CPU switches from one process to another. On these machines having a small page size means that the time required to load the page registers gets longer as the page size gets smaller. Furthermore, the space occupied by the page table increases as the page size decreases.

This last point can be analyzed mathematically. Let the average process size be s bytes and the page size be p bytes. Furthermore, assume that each page entry requires e bytes. The approximate number of pages needed per process is then s/p, occupying se/p bytes of page table space. The wasted memory in the last page of the process due to internal fragmentation is $p/2$. Thus, the total overhead due to the page table and the internal fragmentation loss is given by

$$overhead = se/p + p/2$$

The first term (page table size) is large when the page size is small. The second term (internal fragmentation) is large when the page size is large. The optimum must lie somewhere in between. By taking the first derivative with respect to p and equating it to zero, we get the equation

$$-se/p^2 + 1/2 = 0$$

From this equation we can derive a formula that gives the optimum page size (considering only memory wasted in fragmentation and page table size). The result is:

$$p = \sqrt{2se}$$

For $s = 128K$ and $e = 8$ bytes per page table entry, the optimum page size is 1448 bytes. In practice 1K or 2K would be used, depending on the other factors (e.g., disk speed). Most commercially available computers use page sizes ranging from 512 bytes to 64K.

4.5.4 Virtual Memory Interface

Up until now, our whole discussion has assumed that virtual memory is transparent to processes and programmers, that is, all they see is a large virtual address space on a computer with a small(er) physical memory. With many systems, that is true, but in some advanced systems, programmers have some control over the memory map and can use it in nontraditional ways. In this section, we will briefly look at a few of these.

One reason for giving programmers control over their memory map is to allow two or more processes to share the same memory. If programmers can name regions of their memory, it may be possible for one process to give another process the name of a memory region so that process can also map it in. With two (or more) processes sharing the same pages, high bandwidth sharing becomes possible—one process writes into the shared memory and another one reads from it.

Sharing of pages can also be used to implement a high-performance message-passing system. Normally, when messages are passed, the data are copied from one address space to another, at considerable cost. If processes can control their page map, a message can be passed by having the sending process unmap the page(s) containing the message, and the receiving process mapping them in. Here only the page names have to be copied, instead of all the data.

Yet another advanced memory management technique is **distributed shared memory** (Feeley et al., 1995; Li and Hudak, 1989; Zekauskas et al., 1994). The idea here is to allow multiple processes over a network to share a set of pages, possibly, but not necessarily, as a single shared linear address space. When a process references a page that is not currently mapped in, it gets a page fault. The page fault handler, which may be in the kernel or in user space, then locates the machine holding the page and sends it a message asking it to unmap the page and send it over the network. When the page arrives, it is mapped in and the faulting instruction is restarted.

4.6 SEGMENTATION

The virtual memory discussed so far is one-dimensional because the virtual addresses go from 0 to some maximum address, one address after another. For many problems, having two or more separate virtual address spaces may be much better than having only one. For example, a compiler has many tables that are built up as compilation proceeds, possibly including

1. The source text being saved for the printed listing (on batch systems).

2. The symbol table, containing the names and attributes of variables.

3. The table containing all the integer and floating-point constants used.

4. The parse tree, containing the syntactic analysis of the program.

5. The stack used for procedure calls within the compiler.

Each of the first four tables grows continuously as compilation proceeds. The last one grows and shrinks in unpredictable ways during compilation. In a one-dimensional memory, these five tables would have to be allocated contiguous chunks of virtual address space, as in Fig. 4-19.

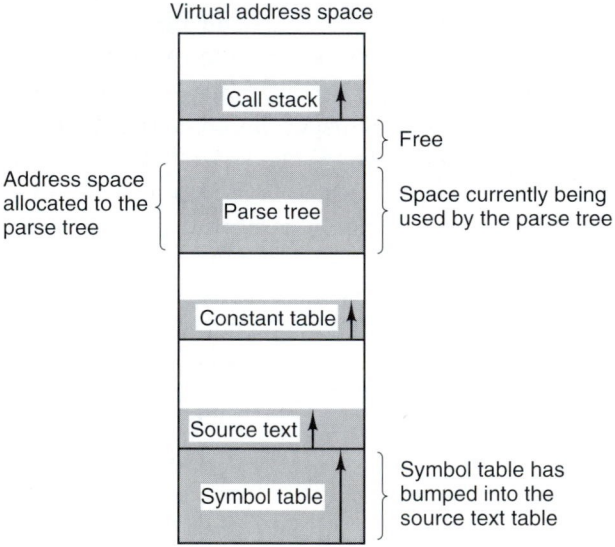

Figure 4-19. In a one-dimensional address space with growing tables, one table may bump into another.

Consider what happens if a program has an exceptionally large number of variables. The chunk of address space allocated for the symbol table may fill up, but there may be lots of room in the other tables. The compiler could, of course, simply issue a message saying that the compilation cannot continue due to too many variables, but doing so does not seem very sporting when unused space is left in the other tables.

Another possibility is to play Robin Hood, taking space from the tables with an excess of room and giving it to the tables with little room. This shuffling can be done, but it is analogous to managing one's own overlays—a nuisance at best and a great deal of tedious, unrewarding work at worst.

What is really needed is a way of freeing the programmer from having to manage the expanding and contracting tables, in the same way that virtual memory eliminates the worry of organizing the program into overlays.

A straightforward and extremely general solution is to provide the machine with many completely independent address spaces, called **segments**. Each segment consists of a linear sequence of addresses, from 0 to some maximum. The length of each segment may be anything from 0 to the maximum allowed. Different segments may, and usually do, have different lengths. Moreover, segment lengths may change during execution. The length of a stack segment may be increased whenever something is pushed onto the stack and decreased whenever something is popped off the stack.

Because each segment constitutes a separate address space, different segments can grow or shrink independently, without affecting each other. If a stack in a certain segment needs more address space to grow, it can have it, because there is nothing else in its address space to bump into. Of course, a segment can fill up but segments are usually very large, so this occurrence is rare. To specify an address in this segmented or two-dimensional memory, the program must supply a two-part address, a segment number, and an address within the segment. Figure 4-20 illustrates a segmented memory being used for the compiler tables discussed earlier.

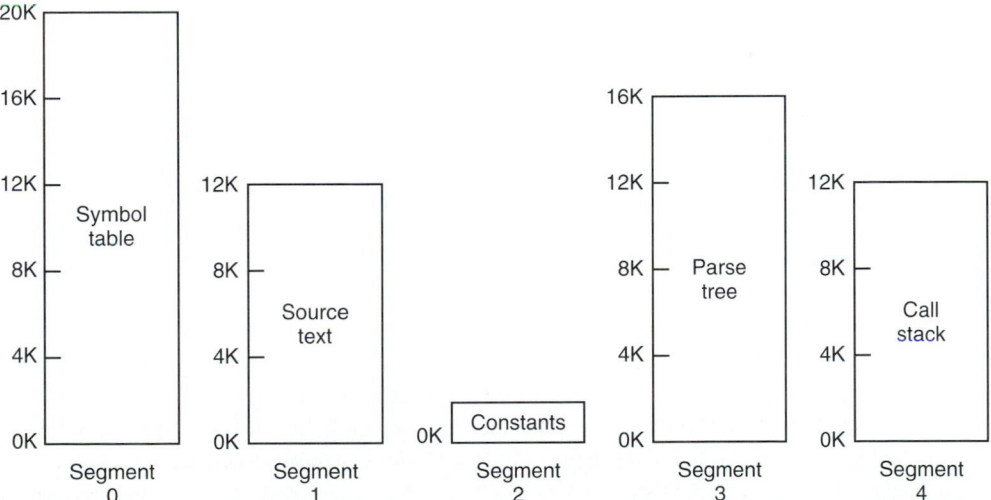

Figure 4-20. A segmented memory allows each table to grow or shrink independently of the other tables.

We emphasize that a segment is a logical entity, which the programmer is aware of and uses as a logical entity. A segment might contain a procedure, or an array, or a stack, or a collection of scalar variables, but usually it does not contain a mixture of different types.

A segmented memory has other advantages besides simplifying the handling of data structures that are growing or shrinking. If each procedure occupies a separate segment, with address 0 as its starting address, the linking up of procedures compiled separately is greatly simplified. After all the procedures that constitute a program have been compiled and linked up, a procedure call to the procedure in segment n will use the two-part address $(n, 0)$ to address word 0 (the entry point).

If the procedure in segment n is subsequently modified and recompiled, no other procedures need be changed (because no starting addresses have been modified), even if the new version is larger than the old one. With a one-dimensional memory, the procedures are packed tightly next to each other, with no address space between them. Consequently, changing one procedure's size can affect the starting address of other, unrelated procedures. This, in turn, requires modifying all procedures that call any of the moved procedures, in order to incorporate their new starting addresses. If a program contains hundreds of procedures, this process can be costly.

Segmentation also facilitates sharing procedures or data between several processes. A common example is the **shared library**. Modern workstations that run advanced window systems often have extremely large graphical libraries compiled into nearly every program. In a segmented system, the graphical library can be put in a segment and shared by multiple processes, eliminating the need for having it in every process' address space. While it is also possible to have shared libraries in pure paging systems, it is much more complicated. In effect, these systems do it by simulating segmentation.

Because each segment forms a logical entity of which the programmer is aware, such as a procedure, or an array, or a stack, different segments can have different kinds of protection. A procedure segment can be specified as execute only, prohibiting attempts to read from it or store into it. A floating-point array can be specified as read/write but not execute, and attempts to jump to it will be caught. Such protection is helpful in catching programming errors.

You should try to understand why protection makes sense in a segmented memory but not in a one-dimensional paged memory. In a segmented memory the user is aware of what is in each segment. Normally, a segment would not contain a procedure and a stack, for example, but one or the other. Since each segment contains only one type of object, the segment can have the protection appropriate for that particular type. Paging and segmentation are compared in Fig. 4-21.

The contents of a page are, in a sense, accidental. The programmer is unaware of the fact that paging is even occurring. Although putting a few bits in each entry of the page table to specify the access allowed would be possible, to utilize this feature the programmer would have to keep track of where in his address space the page boundaries were. That is precisely the sort of administration

Consideration	Paging	Segmentation
Need the programmer be aware that this technique is being used?	No	Yes
How many linear address spaces are there?	1	Many
Can the total address space exceed the size of physical memory?	Yes	Yes
Can procedures and data be distinguished and separately protected?	No	Yes
Can tables whose size fluctuates be accommodated easily?	No	Yes
Is sharing of procedures between users facilitated?	No	Yes
Why was this technique invented?	To get a large linear address space without having to buy more physical memory	To allow programs and data to be broken up into logically independent address spaces and to aid sharing and protection

Figure 4-21. Comparison of paging and segmentation.

that paging was invented to eliminate. Because the user of a segmented memory has the illusion that all segments are in main memory all the time—that is, he can address them as though they were—he can protect each segment separately, without having to be concerned with the administration of overlaying them.

4.6.1 Implementation of Pure Segmentation

The implementation of segmentation differs from paging in an essential way: pages are fixed size and segments are not. Figure 4-22(a) shows an example of physical memory initially containing five segments. Now consider what happens if segment 1 is evicted and segment 7, which is smaller, is put in its place. We arrive at the memory configuration of Fig. 4-22(b). Between segment 7 and segment 2 is an unused area—that is, a hole. Then segment 4 is replaced by segment 5, as in Fig. 4-22(c), and segment 3 is replaced by segment 6, as in Fig. 4-22(d). After the system has been running for a while, memory will be divided up into a number of chunks, some containing segments and some containing holes. This phenomenon, called **checkerboarding** or **external fragmentation**, wastes memory in the holes. It can be dealt with by compaction, as shown in Fig. 4-22(e).

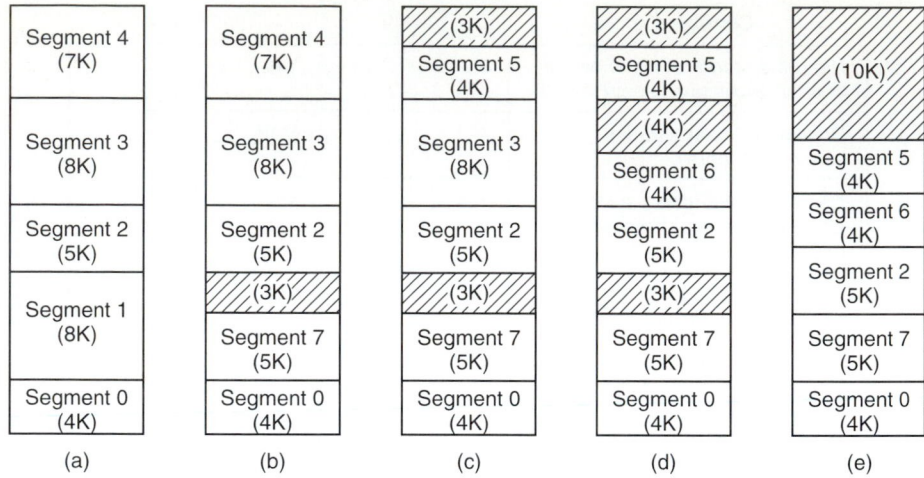

Figure 4-22. (a)-(d) Development of checkerboarding. (e) Removal of the checkerboarding by compaction.

4.6.2 Segmentation with Paging: MULTICS

If the segments are large, it may be inconvenient, or even impossible, to keep them in main memory in their entirety. This leads to the idea of paging them, so that only those pages that are actually needed have to be around. Several significant systems have supported paged segments. In this section we will describe the first one: MULTICS. In the next one we will discuss a more recent one: the Intel Pentium.

MULTICS ran on the Honeywell 6000 machines and their descendants and provided each program with a virtual memory of up to 2^{18} segments (more than 250,000), each of which could be up to 65,536 (36-bit) words long. To implement this, the MULTICS designers chose to treat each segment as a virtual memory and to page it, combining the advantages of paging (uniform page size and not having to keep the whole segment in memory if only part of it is being used) with the advantages of segmentation (ease of programming, modularity, protection, and sharing).

Each MULTICS program has a segment table, with one descriptor per segment. Since there are potentially more than a quarter of a million entries in the table, the segment table is itself a segment and is paged. A segment descriptor contains an indication of whether the segment is in main memory or not. If any part of the segment is in memory, the segment is considered to be in memory, and its page table will be in memory. If the segment is in memory, its descriptor contains an 18-bit pointer to its page table [see Fig. 4-23(a)]. Because physical addresses are 24 bits and pages are aligned on 64-byte boundaries (implying that the low-order 6 bits of page addresses are 000000), only 18 bits are needed in the descriptor to store a page table address. The descriptor also contains the segment size, the protection bits, and a few other items. Figure 4-23(b) illustrates a MULTICS segment descriptor. The address of the segment in secondary memory is not in the segment descriptor but in another table used by the segment fault handler.

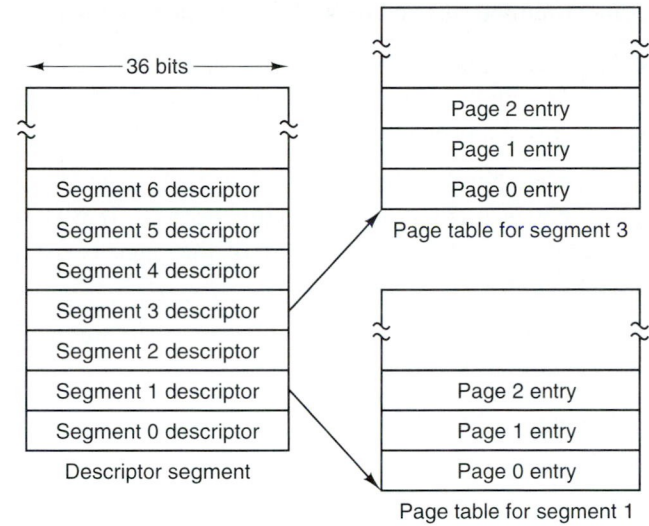

(a)

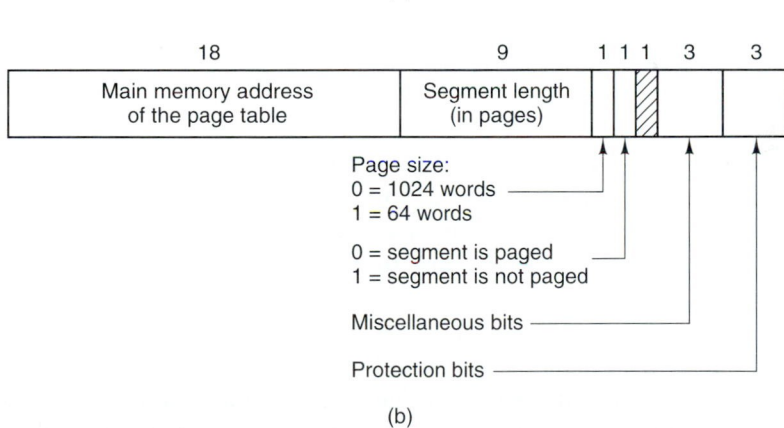

(b)

Figure 4-23. The MULTICS virtual memory. (a) The descriptor segment points to the page tables. (b) A segment descriptor. The numbers are the field lengths.

Each segment is an ordinary virtual address space and is paged in the same way as the nonsegmented paged memory described earlier in this chapter. The normal page size is 1024 words (although a few small segments used by MULTICS itself are not paged or are paged in units of 64 words to save physical memory).

An address in MULTICS consists of two parts: the segment and the address within the segment. The address within the segment is further divided into a page number and a word within the page, as shown in Fig. 4-24. When a memory reference occurs, the following algorithm is carried out.

1. The segment number is used to find the segment descriptor.

2. A check is made to see if the segment's page table is in memory. If the page table is in memory, it is located. If it is not, a segment fault occurs. If there is a protection violation, a fault (trap) occurs.

3. The page table entry for the requested virtual page is examined. If the page is not in memory, a page fault occurs. If it is in memory, the main memory address of the start of the page is extracted from the page table entry.

4. The offset is added to the page origin to give the main memory address where the word is located.

5. The read or store finally takes place.

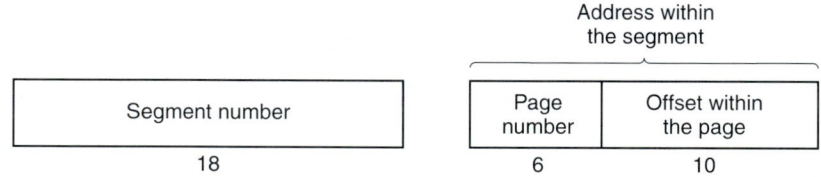

Figure 4-24. A 34-bit MULTICS virtual address.

This process is illustrated in Fig. 4-25. For simplicity, the fact that the descriptor segment is itself paged has been omitted. What really happens is that a register (the descriptor base register), is used to locate the descriptor segment's page table, which, in turn, points to the pages of the descriptor segment. Once the descriptor for the needed segment has been found, the addressing proceeds as shown in Fig. 4-25.

As you have no doubt guessed by now, if the preceding algorithm were actually carried out by the operating system on every instruction, programs would not run very fast. In reality, the MULTICS hardware contains a 16-word high-speed TLB that can search all its entries in parallel for a given key. It is illustrated in Fig. 4-26. When an address is presented to the computer, the addressing hardware first checks to see if the virtual address is in the TLB. If so, it gets the page frame number directly from the TLB and forms the actual address of the referenced word without having to look in the descriptor segment or page table.

The addresses of the 16 most recently referenced pages are kept in the TLB. Programs whose working set is smaller than the TLB size will come to equilibrium with the addresses of the entire working set in the TLB and therefore will

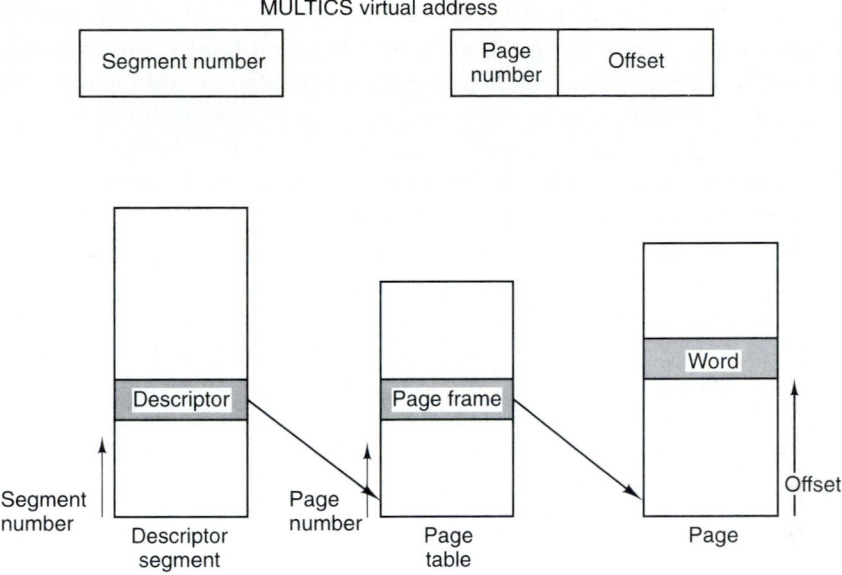

Figure 4-25. Conversion of a two-part MULTICS address into a main memory address.

Segment number	Virtual page	Page frame	Protection	Age	Is this entry used?
4	1	7	Read/write	13	1
6	0	2	Read only	10	1
12	3	1	Read/write	2	1
					0
2	1	0	Execute only	7	1
2	2	12	Execute only	9	1

(Comparison field spans Segment number and Virtual page columns)

Figure 4-26. A simplified version of the MULTICS TLB. The existence of two page sizes makes the actual TLB more complicated.

run efficiently. If the page is not in the TLB, the descriptor and page tables are actually referenced to find the page frame address, and the TLB is updated to include this page, the least recently used page being thrown out. The age field keeps track of which entry is the least recently used. The reason that a TLB is used is for comparing the segment and page number of all the entries in parallel.

4.6.3 Segmentation with Paging: The Intel Pentium

In many ways, the virtual memory on the Pentium (and Pentium Pro) resembles MULTICS, including the presence of both segmentation and paging. Whereas MULTICS has 256K independent segments, each up to 64K 36-bit words, the Pentium has 16K independent segments, each holding up to 1 billion 32-bit words. Although there are fewer segments, the larger segment size is far more important, as few programs need more than 1000 segments, but many programs need segments holding megabytes.

The heart of the Pentium virtual memory consists of two tables, the **LDT** (**Local Descriptor Table**) and the **GDT** (**Global Descriptor Table**). Each program has its own LDT, but there is a single GDT, shared by all the programs on the computer. The LDT describes segments local to each program, including its code, data, stack, and so on, whereas the GDT describes system segments, including the operating system itself.

To access a segment, a Pentium program first loads a selector for that segment into one of the machine's six segment registers. During execution, the CS register holds the selector for the code segment and the DS register holds the selector for the data segment. The other segment registers are less important. Each selector is a 16-bit number, as shown in Fig. 4-27.

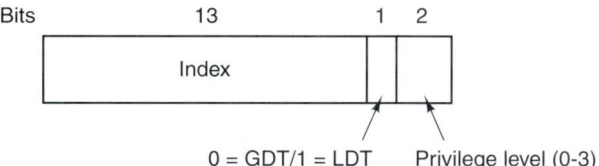

Figure 4-27. A Pentium selector.

One of the selector bits tells whether the segment is local or global (i.e., whether it is in the LDT or GDT). Thirteen other bits specify the LDT or GDT entry number, so these tables are each restricted to holding 8K segment descriptors. The other 2 bits relate to protection, and will be described later. Descriptor 0 is forbidden. It may be safely loaded into a segment register to indicate that the segment register is not currently available. It causes a trap if used.

At the time a selector is loaded into a segment register, the corresponding descriptor is fetched from the LDT or GDT and stored in microprogram registers, so it can be accessed quickly. A descriptor consists of 8 bytes, including the segment's base address, size, and other information, as depicted in Fig. 4-28.

The format of the selector has been cleverly chosen to make locating the descriptor easy. First either the LDT or GDT is selected, based on selector bit 2. Then the selector is copied to an internal scratch register, and the 3 low-order bits set to 0. Finally, the address of either the LDT or GDT table is added to it, to give

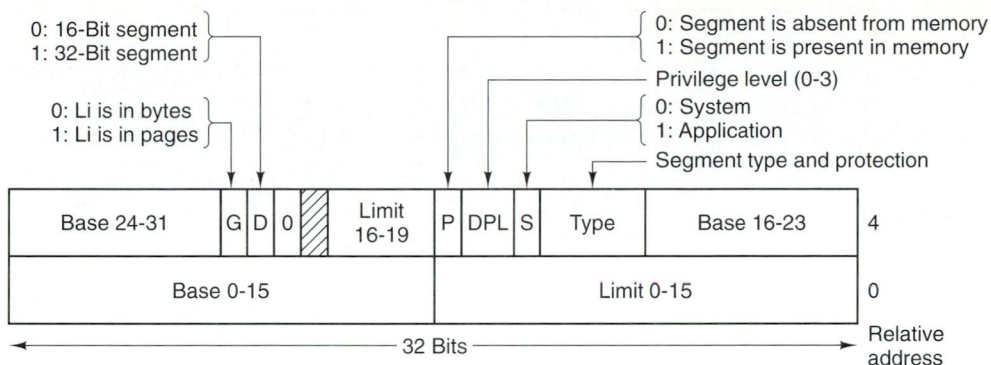

Figure 4-28. Pentium code segment descriptor. Data segments differ slightly.

a direct pointer to the descriptor. For example, selector 72 refers to entry 9 in the GDT, which is located at address GDT + 72.

Let us trace the steps by which a (selector, offset) pair is converted to a physical address. As soon as the microprogram knows which segment register is being used, it can find the complete descriptor corresponding to that selector in its internal registers. If the segment does not exist (selector 0), or is currently paged out, a trap occurs.

It then checks to see if the offset is beyond the end of the segment, in which case a trap also occurs. Logically, there should simply be a 32-bit field in the descriptor giving the size of the segment, but there are only 20 bits available, so a different scheme is used. If the *Gbit* (Granularity) field is 0, the *Limit* field is the exact segment size, up to 1 MB. If it is 1, the *Limit* field gives the segment size in pages instead of bytes. The Pentium page size is fixed at 4K bytes, so 20 bits are enough for segments up to 2^{32} bytes.

Assuming that the segment is in memory and the offset is in range, the Pentium then adds the 32-bit *Base* field in the descriptor to the offset to form what is called a **linear address**, as shown in Fig. 4-29. The *Base* field is broken up into three pieces and spread all over the descriptor for compatibility with the 286, in which the *Base* is only 24 bits. In effect, the *Base* field allows each segment to start at an arbitrary place within the 32-bit linear address space.

If paging is disabled (by a bit in a global control register), the linear address is interpreted as the physical address and sent to the memory for the read or write. Thus with paging disabled, we have a pure segmentation scheme, with each segment's base address given in its descriptor. Segments are permitted to overlap, incidentally, probably because it would be too much trouble and take too much time to verify that they were all disjoint.

On the other hand, if paging is enabled, the linear address is interpreted as a virtual address and mapped onto the physical address using page tables, pretty much as in our earlier examples. The only real complication is that with a 32-bit

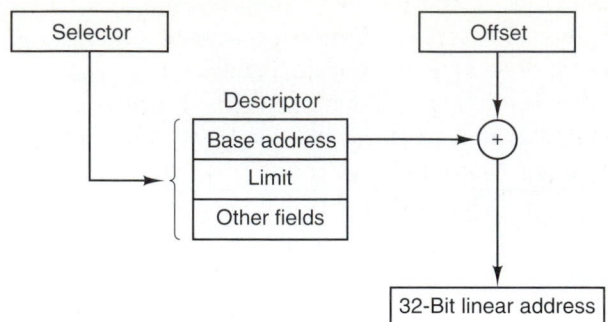

Figure 4-29. Conversion of a (selector, offset) pair to a linear address.

virtual address and a 4K page, a segment might contain 1 million pages, so a two-level mapping is used to reduce the page table size for small segments.

Each running program has a **page directory** consisting of 1024 32-bit entries. It is located at an address pointed to by a global register. Each entry in this directory points to a page table also containing 1024 32-bit entries. The page table entries point to page frames. The scheme is shown in Fig. 4-30.

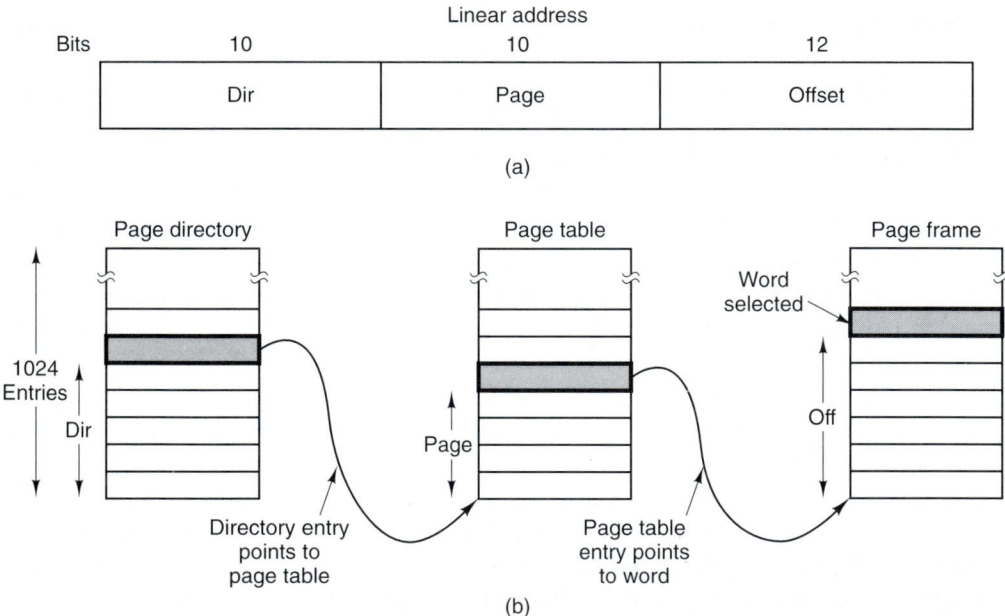

Figure 4-30. Mapping of a linear address onto a physical address.

In Fig. 4-30(a) we see a linear address divided into three fields, *Dir*, *Page*, and *Off*. The *Dir* field is used to index into the page directory to locate a pointer to the proper page table. Then the *Page* field is used as an index into the page table to find the physical address of the page frame. Finally, *Off* is added to the address of the page frame to get the physical address of the byte or word needed.

The page table entries are 32 bits each, 20 of which contain a page frame number. The remaining bits contain access and dirty bits, set by the hardware for the benefit of the operating system, protection bits, and other utility bits.

Each page table has entries for 1024 4K page frames, so a single page table handles 4 megabytes of memory. A segment shorter than 4M will have a page directory with a single entry, a pointer to its one and only page table. In this way, the overhead for short segments is only two pages, instead of the million pages that would be needed in a one-level page table.

To avoid making repeated references to memory, the Pentium, like MULTICS, has a small TLB that directly maps the most recently used *Dir–Page* combinations onto the physical address of the page frame. Only when the current combination is not present in the TLB is the mechanism of Fig. 4-30 actually carried out and the TLB updated.

A little thought will reveal the fact that when paging is used, there is really no point in having the *Base* field in the descriptor be nonzero. All that *Base* does is cause a small offset to use an entry in the middle of the page directory, instead of at the beginning. The real reason for including *Base* at all is to allow pure (non-paged) segmentation, and for compatibility with the 286, which always has paging disabled (i.e., the 286 has only pure segmentation, but not paging).

It is also worth noting that if some application does not need segmentation but is content with a single, paged, 32-bit address space, that model is possible. All the segment registers can be set up with the same selector, whose descriptor has *Base* = 0 and *Limit* set to the maximum. The instruction offset will then be the linear address, with only a single address space used—in effect, normal paging.

All in all, one has to give credit to the Pentium designers. Given the conflicting goals of implementing pure paging, pure segmentation, and paged segments, while at the same time being compatible with the 286, and doing all of this efficiently, the resulting design is surprisingly simple and clean.

Although we have covered the complete architecture of the Pentium virtual memory, albeit briefly, it is worth saying a few words about protection, since this subject is intimately related to the virtual memory. Just as the virtual memory scheme is closely modeled on MULTICS, so is the protection system. The Pentium supports four protection levels with level 0 being the most privileged and level 3 the least. These are shown in Fig. 4-31. At each instant, a running program is at a certain level, indicated by a 2-bit field in its PSW. Each segment in the system also has a level.

As long as a program restricts itself to using segments at its own level, everything works fine. Attempts to access data at a higher level are permitted. Attempts to access data at a lower level are illegal and cause traps. Attempts to call procedures at a different level (higher or lower) are allowed, but in a carefully

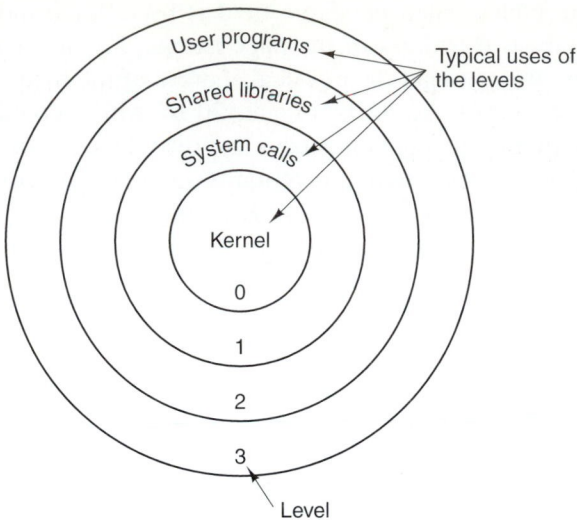

Figure 4-31. Protection on the Pentium.

controlled way. To make an interlevel call, the CALL instruction must contain a selector instead of an address. This selector designates a descriptor called a **call gate**, which gives the address of the procedure to be called. Thus it is not possible to jump into the middle of an arbitrary code segment at a different level. Only official entry points may be used. The concepts of protection levels and call gates were pioneered in MULTICS, where they were viewed as **protection rings**.

A typical use for this mechanism is suggested in Fig. 4-31. At level 0, we find the kernel of the operating system, which handles I/O, memory management, and other critical matters. At level 1, the system call handler is present. User programs may call procedures here to have system calls carried out, but only a specific and protected list of procedures may be called. Level 2 contains library procedures, possibly shared among many running programs. User programs may call these procedures and read their data, but they may not modify them. Finally, user programs run at level 3, which has the least protection.

Traps and interrupts use a mechanism similar to the call gates. They, too, reference descriptors, rather than absolute addresses, and these descriptors point to specific procedures to be executed. The *Type* field in Fig. 4-28 distinguishes between code segments, data segments, and the various kinds of gates.

4.7 OVERVIEW OF MEMORY MANAGEMENT IN MINIX

Memory management in MINIX is simple: neither paging nor swapping is used. The memory manager maintains a list of holes sorted in memory address order. When memory is needed, either due to a FORK or an EXEC system call, the hole list is searched using first fit for a hole that is big enough. Once a process has been placed in memory, it remains in exactly the same place until it terminates. It is never swapped out and also never moved to another place in memory. Nor does the allocated area ever grow or shrink.

This strategy deserves some explanation. It derives from three factors: (1) the idea that MINIX is for personal computers, rather than for large timesharing systems, (2) the desire to have MINIX work on all IBM PCs, and (3) a desire to make the system straightforward to implement on other small computers.

The first factor means that, on the average, the number of running processes will be small, so that typically enough memory will be available to hold all the processes with room left over. Swapping will not be needed then. Since it adds complexity to the system, not swapping leads to simpler code.

The desire to have MINIX run on all IBM PC-compatible computers also had substantial impact on the memory management design. The simplest systems in this family use the 8088 processor, whose memory management architecture is very primitive. It does not support virtual memory in any form and does not even detect stack overflow, a defect that has major implications for the way processes are laid out in memory. These limitations do not exist in later designs which use the 80386, 80486, or Pentium processors. However, taking advantage of these features would make MINIX incompatible with many low-end machines that are still serviceable and in use.

The portability issue argues for as simple a memory management scheme as possible. If MINIX used paging or segmentation, it would be difficult, if not impossible, to port it to machines not having these features. By making a minimal number of assumptions about what the hardware can do, the number of machines to which MINIX can be ported is increased.

Another unusual aspect of MINIX is the way the memory management is implemented. It is not part of the kernel. Instead, it is handled by the memory manager process, which runs in user space and communicates with the kernel by the standard message mechanism. The position of the memory manager in the server level is shown in Fig. 2-26.

Moving the memory manager out of the kernel is an example of the separation of **policy** and **mechanism**. The decisions about which process will be placed where in memory (policy) are made by the memory manager. The actual setting of memory maps for processes (mechanism) is done by the system task within the kernel. This split makes it relatively easy to change the memory management policy (algorithms, etc.) without having to modify the lowest layers of the operating system.

Most of the memory manager code is devoted to handling the MINIX system calls that involve memory management, primarily FORK and EXEC, rather than just manipulating lists of processes and holes. In the next section we will look at the memory layout, and in subsequent sections we will take a bird's-eye view of how the memory management system calls are processed by the memory manager.

4.7.1 Memory Layout

Simple MINIX processes use combined I and D space, in which all parts of the process (text, data, and stack) share a block of memory which is allocated and released as one block. Processes can also be compiled to use separate I and D space. For clarity, allocation of memory for the simpler model will be discussed first. Processes using separate I and D space can use memory more efficiently, but taking advantage of this feature complicates things. We will discuss the complications after the simple case has been outlined.

Memory is allocated in MINIX on two occasions. First, when a process forks, the amount of memory needed by the child is allocated. Second, when a process changes its memory image via the EXEC system call, the old image is returned to the free list as a hole, and memory is allocated for the new image. The new image may be in a part of memory different from the released memory. Its location will depend upon where an adequate hole is found. Memory is also released whenever a process terminates, either by exiting or by being killed by a signal.

Figure 4-32 shows both ways of allocating memory. In Fig. 4-32(a) we see two processes, A and B, in memory. If A forks, we get the situation of Fig. 4-32(b). The child is an exact copy of A. If the child now executes the file C, the memory looks like Fig. 4-32(c). The child's image is replaced by C.

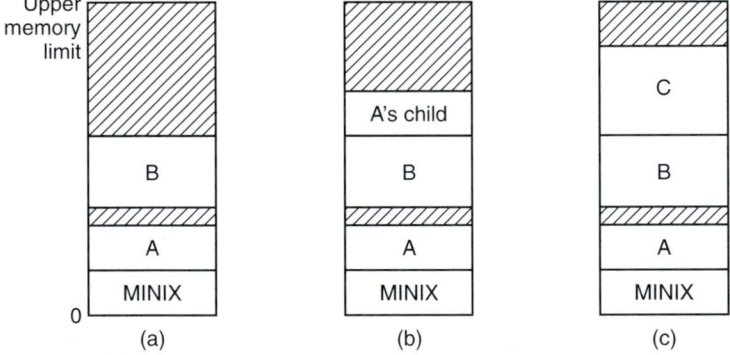

Figure 4-32. Memory allocation. (a) Originally. (b) After a SY FORK. (c) After the child does an EXEC . The shaded regions are unused memory. The process is a common I&D one.

Note that the old memory for the child is released before the new memory for C is allocated, so that C can use the child's memory. In this way, a series of FORK and EXEC pairs (such as the shell setting up a pipeline) results in all the processes being adjacent, with no holes between them, as would have been the case had the new memory been allocated before the old memory had been released.

When memory is allocated, either by the FORK or EXEC system calls, a certain amount of it is taken for the new process. In the former case, the amount taken is identical to what the parent process has. In the latter case, the memory manager takes the amount specified in the header of the file executed. Once this allocation has been made, under no conditions is the process ever allocated any more total memory.

What has been said so far applies to programs that have been compiled with combined I and D space. Programs with separate I and D space take advantage of an enhanced mode of memory management called **shared text**. When such a process does a FORK, only the amount of memory needed for a copy of the new process' data and stack is allocated. Both the parent and the child share the executable code already in use by the parent. When such a process does an EXEC, a search is made of the process table to see if another process already is using the executable code needed. If one is found, new memory is allocated only for the data and stack, and the text already in memory is shared. Shared text complicates termination of a process. When a process terminates it always releases the memory occupied by its data and stack. But it only releases the memory occupied by its text segment after a search of the process table reveals that no other current process is sharing that memory. Thus a process may be allocated more memory when it starts than it releases when it terminates, if it loaded its own text when it started but that text is being shared by one or more other processes when the first process terminates.

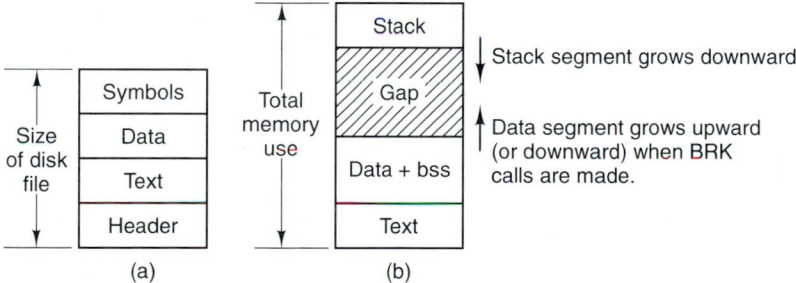

Figure 4-33. (a) A program as stored in a disk file. (b) Internal memory layout for a single process. In both parts of the figure the lowest disk or memory address is at the bottom and the highest address is at the top.

Figure 4-33 shows how a program is stored as a disk file and how this is transferred to the internal memory layout of a MINIX process. The header on the disk file contains information about the sizes of the different parts of the image, as well as the total size. In the header of a program with common I and D space, a field specifies the total size of the text and data parts; these parts are copied directly to the memory image. The data part in the image is enlarged by the amount specified in the *bss* field in the header. This area is cleared to contain all zeroes and is used for uninitialized static data. The total amount of memory to be allocated is specified by the *total* field in the header. If, for example, a program

has 4K of text, 2K of data plus bss, and 1K of stack, and the header says to allocate 40K total, the gap of unused memory between the data segment and the stack
segment will be 33K. A program file on the disk may also contain a symbol table.
This is for use in debugging and is not copied into memory.

If the programmer knows that the total memory needed for the combined
growth of the data and stack segments for the file *a.out* is at most 10K, he can
give the command

chmem =10240 a.out

which changes the header field so that upon EXEC the memory manager allocates
a space 10240 bytes more than the sum of the initial text and data segments. For
the above example, a total of 16K will be allocated on all subsequent EXECs of the
file. Of this amount, the topmost 1K will be used for the stack, and 9K will be in
the gap, where it can be used by growth of the stack, the data area, or both.

For a program using separate I and D space (indicated by a bit in the header
that is set by the linker), the total field in the header applies to the combined data
and stack space only. A program with 4K of text, 2K of data, 1K of stack, and a
total size of 64K will be allocated 68K (4K instruction space, 64K data space),
leaving 61K for the data segment and stack to consume during execution. The
boundary of the data segment can be moved only by the BRK system call. All BRK
does is check to see if the new data segment bumps into the current stack pointer,
and if not, notes the change in some internal tables. This is entirely internal to the
memory originally allocated to the process; no additional memory is allocated by
the operating system. If the new data segment bumps into the stack, the call fails.

This strategy was chosen to make it possible to run MINIX on an IBM PC with
an 8088 processor, which does not check for stack overflow in hardware. A user
program can push as many words as it wants onto the stack without the operating
system being aware of it. On computers with more sophisticated memory management hardware, the stack is allocated a certain amount of memory initially. If
it attempts to grow beyond this amount, a trap to the operating system occurs, and
the system allocates another piece of memory to the stack, if possible. This trap
does not exist on the 8088, making it dangerous to have the stack adjacent to anything except a large chunk of unused memory, since the stack can grow quickly
and without warning. MINIX has been designed so that when it is implemented on
a computer with better memory management, it is straightforward to change the
MINIX memory manager.

This is a good place to mention a possible semantic difficulty. When we use
the word "segment," we refer to an area of memory defined by the operating system. The Intel 80x86 processors have a set of internal "segment registers" and
(in the more advanced processors) "segment descriptor tables" which provide
hardware support for "segments." The Intel hardware designers' concept of a segment is similar to, but not always the same as, the segments used and defined by
MINIX. All references to segments in this text should be interpreted as references

to memory areas delineated by MINIX data structures. We will refer explicitly to segment registers or segment descriptors when talking about the hardware.

This warning can be generalized. Hardware designers often try to provide support for the operating systems that they expect to be used on their machines, and the terminology used to describe registers and other aspects of a processor's architecture usually reflects an idea of how the features will be used. Such features are often useful to the implementor of an operating system, but they may not be used in the same way the hardware designer foresaw. This can lead to misunderstandings when the same word has different meanings when used to describe an aspect of an operating system or of the underlying hardware.

4.7.2 Message Handling

Like all the other components of MINIX, the memory manager is message driven. After the system has been initialized, the memory manager enters its main loop, which consists of waiting for a message, carrying out the request contained in the message, and sending a reply. Figure 4-34 gives the list of legal message types, their input parameters, and the value sent back in the reply message.

FORK, EXIT, WAIT, WAITPID, BRK, and EXEC are clearly closely related to memory allocation and deallocation. The calls KILL, ALARM, and PAUSE are all related to signals, as are SIGACTION, SIGSUSPEND, SIGPENDING, SIGMASK, and SIGRETURN. These also can affect what is in memory, because when a signal kills a process the process' memory is deallocated. REBOOT has effects throughout the operating system, but its first job is to send signals to terminate all processes in a controlled way, so the memory manager is a good place for it. The seven GET/SET calls have nothing to do with memory management at all. They also have nothing to do with the file system. But they had to go either in the file system or the memory manager, since each system call is handled by one or the other. They were put here simply because the file system was large enough already. PTRACE, which is used in debugging, is here for the same reason.

The final message, KSIG, is not a system call. KSIG is the message type used by the kernel to inform the memory manager of a signal originating in the kernel, such as SIGINT, SIGQUIT, or SIGALRM.

Although there is a library routine *sbrk*, there is no system call SBRK. The library routine computes the amount of memory needed by adding the increment or decrement specified as parameter to the current size and makes a BRK call to set the size. Similarly, there are no separate system calls for *geteuid* and *getegid*. The calls GETUID and GETGID return both the effective and real identifiers. In like manner, GETPID returns the pid of both the calling process and its parent.

A key data structure used for message processing is the table *call_vec* declared in *table.c* (line 16515). It contains pointers to the procedures that handle the various message types. When a message comes in to the memory manager,

Message type	Input parameters	Reply value
FORK	(none)	Child's pid, (to child: 0)
EXIT	Exit status	(No reply if successful)
WAIT	(none)	Status
WAITPID	(none)	Status
BRK	New size	New size
EXEC	Pointer to initial stack	(No reply if successful)
KILL	Process identifier and signal	Status
ALARM	Number of seconds to wait	Residual time
PAUSE	(none)	(No reply if successful)
SIGACTION	Sig. number, action, old action	Status
SIGSUSPEND	Signal mask	(No reply if successful)
SIGPENDING	(none)	Status
SIGMASK	How, set, old set	Status
SIGRETURN	Context	Status
GETUID	(none)	Uid, effective uid
GETGID	(none)	Gid, effective gid
GETPID	(none)	Pid, parent pid
SETUID	New uid	Status
SETGID	New gid	Status
SETSID	New sid	Process group
GETPGRP	New gid	Process group
PTRACE	Request, pid, address, data	Status
REBOOT	How (halt, reboot, or panic)	(No reply if successful)
KSIG	Process slot and signals	(No reply)

Figure 4-34. The message types, input parameters, and reply values used for communicating with the memory manager.

the main loop extracts the message type and puts it in the global variable *mm_call*. This value is then used to index into *callvec* to find the pointer to the procedure that handles the newly arrived message. That procedure is then called to execute the system call. The value that it returns is sent back to the caller in the reply message to report on the success or failure of the call. This mechanism is similar to that of Fig. 1-16, only in user space rather than in the kernel.

4.7.3 Memory Manager Data Structures and Algorithms

The memory manager has two key data structures: the process table and the hole table. We will now look at each of these in turn.

In Fig. 2-4 we saw that some process table fields are needed for process management, others for memory management, and yet others for the file system. In MINIX, each of these three pieces of the operating system has its own process table, containing just those fields that it needs. The entries correspond exactly, to keep things simple. Thus, slot k of the memory manager's table refers to the same process as slot k of the file system's table. When a process is created or destroyed, all three parts update their tables to reflect the new situation, in order to keep them synchronized.

The memory manager's process table is called *mproc*; its definition is in */usr/src/mm/mproc.h*. It contains all the fields related to a process' memory allocation, as well as some additional items. The most important field is the array *mp_seg*, which has three entries, for the text, data, and stack segments, respectively. Each entry is a structure containing the virtual address, physical address, and length of the segment, all measured in clicks rather than in bytes. The size of a click is implementation dependent; for standard MINIX it is 256 bytes. All segments must start on a click boundary and occupy an integral number of clicks.

The method used for recording memory allocation is shown in Fig. 4-35. In this figure we have a process with 3K of text, 4K of data, a gap of 1K, and then a 2K stack, for a total memory allocation of 10K. In Fig. 4-35(b) we see what the virtual, physical, and length fields for each of the three segments are, assuming that the process does not have separate I and D space. In this model, the text segment is always empty, and the data segment contains both text and data. When a process references virtual address 0, either to jump to it or to read it (i.e., as instruction space or as data space), physical address 0x32000 (in decimal, 200K) will be used. This address is at click 0x320.

Note that the virtual address at which the stack begins depends initially on the total amount of memory allocated to the process. If the *chmem* command were used to modify the file header to provide a larger dynamic allocation area (bigger gap between data and stack segments), the next time the file was executed, the stack would start at a higher virtual address. If the stack grows longer by one click, the stack entry *should* change from the triple (0x20, 0x340, 0x8) to the triple (0x1F, 0x33F, 0x9).

The 8088 hardware does not have a stack limit trap, and MINIX defines the stack in a way that will not trigger the trap on 32-bit processors until the stack has already overwritten the data segment. Thus, this change will not be made until the next BRK system call, at which point the operating system explicitly reads SP and recomputes the segment entries. On a machine with a stack trap, the stack segment's entry could be updated as soon as the stack outgrew its segment. This is not done by MINIX on 32-bit Intel processors, for reasons we will now discuss.

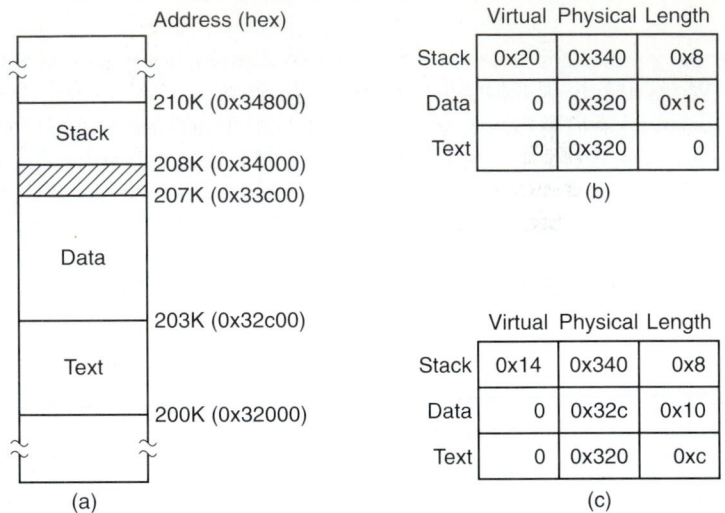

Figure 4-35. (a) A process in memory. (b) Its memory representation for nonseparate I and D space. (c) Its memory representation for separate I and D space.

We mentioned previously that the efforts of hardware designers may not always produce exactly what the software designer needs. Even in protected mode on a Pentium, MINIX does not trap when the stack outgrows its segment. Although in protected mode the Intel hardware detects attempted access to memory outside a segment (as defined by a segment descriptor such as the one in Fig. 4-28), in MINIX the data segment descriptor and the stack segment descriptor are always identical. The MINIX-defined data and stack each use part of this space, and thus either or both can expand into the gap between them. However, only MINIX can manage this. The CPU has no way to detect errors involving the gap, since as far as the hardware is concerned the gap is a valid part of both the data area and the stack area. Of course, the hardware can detect a very large error, such as an attempt to access memory outside the combined data-gap-stack area. This will protect one process from another process' mistakes but is not enough to protect a process from itself.

A design decision was made here. We recognize an argument can be made for abandoning the shared hardware-defined segment that allows MINIX to dynamically reallocate the gap area. The alternative, using the hardware to define nonoverlapping stack and data segments, would offer somewhat more security from certain errors but would make MINIX more memory-hungry. The source code is available to anybody who wants to evaluate the other approach.

Fig. 4-35(c) shows the segment entries for the memory layout of Fig. 4-35(a) for separate I and D space. Here both the text and data segments are nonzero in length. The *mp_seg* array shown in Fig. 4-35(b) or (c) is primarily used to map virtual addresses onto physical memory addresses. Given a virtual address and the space to which it belongs, it is a simple matter to see whether the virtual address is legal or not (i.e., falls inside a segment), and if legal, what the corresponding physical address is. The kernel procedure *umap* performs this mapping for the I/O tasks and for copying to and from user space, for example.

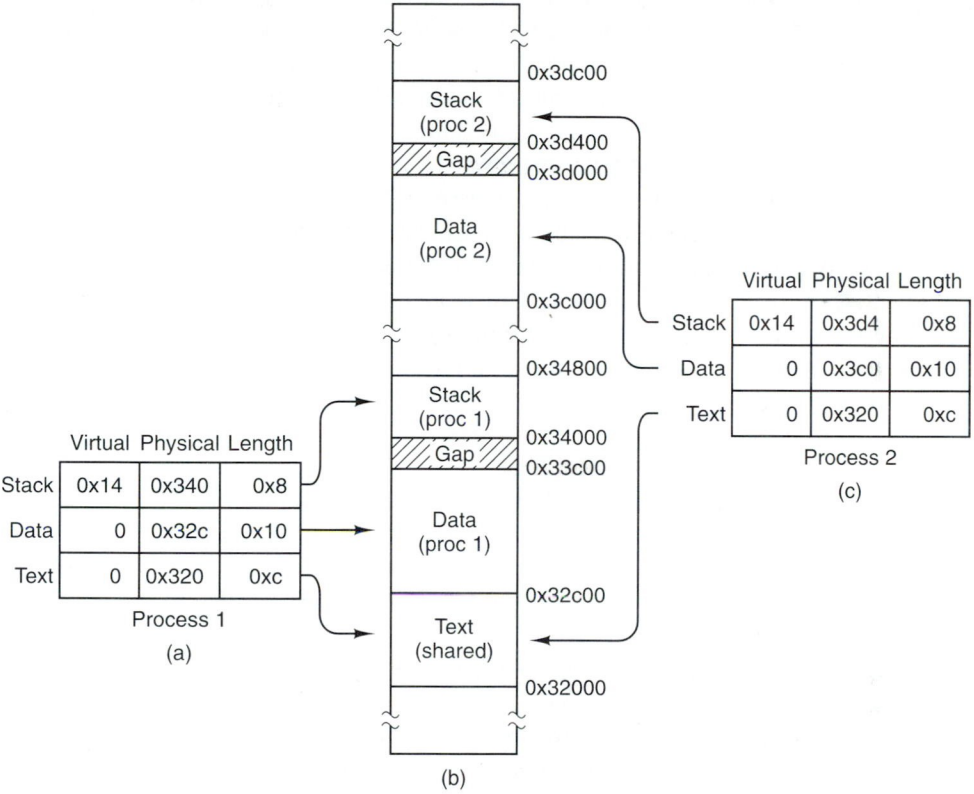

Figure 4-36. (a) The memory map of a separate I and D space process, as in the previous figure. (b) The layout in memory after a second process starts, executing the same program image with shared text. (c) The memory map of the second process.

The contents of the data and stack areas belonging to a process may change as the process executes, but the text does not change. It is common for several processes to be executing copies of the same program, for instance several users may be executing the same shell. Memory efficiency is improved by using shared text. When EXEC is about to load a process, it opens the file holding the disk image of the program to be loaded and reads the file header. If the process uses separate I and D space, a search of the *mp_dev*, *mp_ino*, and *mp_ctime* fields in each slot of *mproc* is made. These hold the device and i-node numbers and changed-status times of the images being executed by other processes. If a process already loaded is found to be executing the same program that is about to be loaded, there is no need to allocate memory for another copy of the text. Instead the *mp_seg*[*T*] portion of the new process' memory map is initialized to point to the same place where the text segment is already loaded, and only the data and stack portions are set up in a new memory allocation. This is shown in Fig. 4-36. If the program uses combined I and D space or no match is found, memory is allocated as shown in Fig. 4-35 and the text and data for the new process are copied in from the disk.

In addition to the segment information, *mproc* also holds the process ID (pid) of the process itself and of its parent, the uids and gids (both real and effective), information about signals, and the exit status, if the process has already terminated but its parent has not yet done a WAIT for it.

The other major memory manager table is the hole table, *hole*, defined in *alloc.c*, which lists every hole in memory in order of increasing memory address. The gaps between the data and stack segments are not considered holes; they have already been allocated to processes. Consequently, they are not contained in the free hole list. Each hole list entry has three fields: the base address of the hole, in clicks; the length of the hole, in clicks; and a pointer to the next entry on the list. The list is singly linked, so it is easy to find the next hole starting from any given hole, but to find the previous hole, you have to search the entire list from the beginning until you come to the given hole.

The reason for recording everything about segments and holes in clicks rather than bytes is simple: it is much more efficient. In 16-bit mode, 16-bit integers are used for recording memory addresses, so with 256-bit clicks, up to 16 MB of memory can be supported. In 32-bit mode, address fields can refer to up to 2^{40} bytes, which is 1024 gigabytes.

The principal operations on the hole list are allocating a piece of memory of a given size and returning an existing allocation. To allocate memory, the hole list is searched, starting at the hole with the lowest address, until a hole that is large enough is found (first fit). The segment is then allocated by reducing the hole by the amount needed for the segment, or in the rare case of an exact fit, removing the hole from the list. This scheme is fast and simple but suffers from both a small amount of internal fragmentation (up to 255 bytes may be wasted in the final click, since an integral number of clicks is always taken) and external fragmentation.

When a process terminates and is cleaned up, its data and stack memory are returned to the free list. If it uses common I and D, this releases all its memory, since such programs never have a separate allocation of memory for text. If the program uses separate I and D and a search of the process table reveals no other process is sharing the text, the text allocation will also be returned. Since with shared text the text and data regions are not necessarily contiguous, two regions of memory may be returned. For each region returned, if either or both of the region's neighbors are holes, they are merged, so adjacent holes never occur. In this way, the number, location, and sizes of the holes vary continuously during system operation. Whenever all user processes have terminated, all of available memory is once again ready for allocation. This isn't necessarily a single hole, however, since physical memory may be interrupted by regions unusable by the operating system, as in IBM compatible systems where read-only memory (ROM) and memory reserved for I/O transfers separate usable memory below address 640K from memory above 1M.

4.7.4 The FORK, EXIT, and WAIT System Calls

When processes are created or destroyed, memory must be allocated or deallocated. Also, the process table must be updated, including the parts held by the kernel and FS. The memory manager coordinates all this activity. Process creation is done by FORK, and carried out in the series of steps shown in Fig. 4-37.

1. Check to see if process table is full.
2. Try to allocate memory for the child's data and stack.
3. Copy the parent's data and stack to the child's memory.
4. Find a free process slot and copy parent's slot to it.
5. Enter child's memory map in process table.
6. Choose a pid for the child.
7. Tell kernel and file system about child.
8. Report child's memory map to kernel.
9. Send reply messages to parent and child.

Figure 4-37. The steps required to carry out the FORK system call.

It is difficult and inconvenient to stop a FORK call part way through, so the memory manager maintains a count at all times of the number of processes currently in existence in order to see easily if a process table slot is available. If the table is not full, an attempt is made to allocate memory for the child. If the program is one with separate I and D space, only enough memory for new data and stack allocations is requested. If this step also succeeds, the FORK is guaranteed to work. The newly allocated memory is then filled in, a process slot is located and filled in, a pid is chosen, and the other parts of the system are informed that a new process has been created.

A process fully terminates when two events have both happened: (1) the process itself has exited (or has been killed by a signal), and (2) its parent has executed a WAIT system call to find out what happened. A process that has exited or has been killed, but whose parent has not (yet) done a WAIT for it, enters a kind of suspended animation, sometimes known as **zombie state**. It is prevented from being scheduled and has its alarm timer turned off (if it was on), but it is not removed from the process table. Its memory is freed. Zombie state is temporary and rarely lasts long. When the parent finally does the WAIT, the process table slot is freed, and the file system and kernel are informed.

A problem arises if the parent of an exiting process is itself already dead. If no special action were taken, the exiting process would remain a zombie forever. Instead, the tables are changed to make it a child of the *init* process. When the system comes up, *init* reads the */etc/ttytab* file to get a list of all terminals, and then forks off a login process to handle each one. It then blocks, waiting for processes to terminate. In this way, orphan zombies are cleaned up quickly.

4.7.5 The EXEC System Call

When a command is typed at the terminal, the shell forks off a new process, which then executes the command requested. It would have been possible to have a single system call to do both FORK and EXEC at once, but they were provided as two distinct calls for a very good reason: to make it easy to implement I/O redirection. When the shell forks, if standard input is redirected, the child closes standard input and then opens the new standard input before executing the command. In this way the newly started process inherits the redirected standard input. Standard output is handled the same way.

EXEC is the most complex system call in MINIX. It must replace the current memory image with a new one, including setting up a new stack. It carries out its job in a series of steps, as shown in Fig. 4-38.

1. Check permissions—is the file executable?
2. Read the header to get the segment and total sizes.
3. Fetch the arguments and environment from the caller.
4. Allocate new memory and release unneeded old memory.
5. Copy stack to new memory image.
6. Copy data (and possibly text) segment to new memory image.
7. Check for and handle setuid, setgid bits.
8. Fix up process table entry.
9. Tell kernel that process is now runnable.

Figure 4-38. The steps required to carry out the EXEC system call.

Each step consists, in turn, of yet smaller steps, some of which can fail. For example, there might be insufficient memory available. The order in which the tests are made has been carefully chosen to make sure the old memory image is not released until it is certain that the EXEC will succeed, to avoid the embarrassing situation of not being able to set up a new memory image, but not having the old one to go back to, either. Normally EXEC does not return, but if it fails, the calling process must get control again, with an error indication.

There are a few steps in Fig. 4-38 that deserve some more comment. First is the question of whether or not there is enough room or not. After determining how much memory is needed, which requires determining if the text memory of another process can be shared, the hole list is searched to check whether there is sufficient physical memory *before* freeing the old memory—if the old memory were freed first and there were insufficient memory, it would be hard to get the old image back again.

However, this test is overly strict. It sometimes rejects EXEC calls that, in fact, could succeed. Suppose, for example, the process doing the EXEC call occupies 20K and its text is not shared by any other process. Further suppose that there is a 30K hole available and that the new image requires 50K. By testing before releasing, we will discover that only 30K is available and reject the call. If we had released first, we might have succeeded, depending on whether or not the new 20K hole were adjacent to, and thus now merged with, the 30K hole. A more sophisticated implementation could handle this situation a little better.

Another possible improvement would be to search for two holes, one for the text segment and one for the data segment, if the process to be EXECed uses separate I and D space. There is no need for the segments to be contiguous.

A more subtle issue is whether the executable file fits in the *virtual* address space. The problem is that memory is allocated not in bytes, but in 256-byte clicks. Each click must belong to a single segment, and may not be, for example, half data, half stack, because the entire memory administration is in clicks.

To see how this restriction can give trouble, note that the address space on 16-bit systems (8088 and 80286) is limited to 64K, which can be divided into 256 clicks. Suppose that a separate I and D space program has 40,000 bytes of text, 32,770 bytes of data, and 32,760 bytes of stack. The data segment occupies 129 clicks, of which the last one is only partially used; still, the whole click is part of the data segment. The stack segment is 128 clicks. Together they exceed 256 clicks, and thus cannot co-exist, even though the number of *bytes* needed fits in the virtual address space (barely). In theory this problem exists on all machines whose click size is larger than 1 byte, but in practice it rarely occurs on Pentium-class processors, since they permit large (4-GB) segments.

Another important issue is how the initial stack is set up. The library call normally used to invoke EXEC with arguments and an environment is

execve(name, argv, envp);

where *name* is a pointer to the name of the file to be executed, *argv* is a pointer to an array of pointers, each one pointing to an argument, and *envp* is a pointer to an array of pointers, each one pointing to an environment string.

It would be easy enough to implement EXEC by just putting the three pointers in the message to the memory manager and letting it fetch the file name and two arrays by itself. Then it would have to fetch each argument and each string one at a time. Doing it this way requires at least one message to the system task per argument or string and probably more, since the memory manager has no way of knowing how big each one is in advance.

To avoid the overhead of multiple messages to read all these pieces, a completely different strategy has been chosen. The *execve* library procedure builds the entire initial stack inside itself and passes its base address and size to the memory manager. Building the new stack within the user space is highly efficient, because references to the arguments and strings are just local memory references, not references to a different address space.

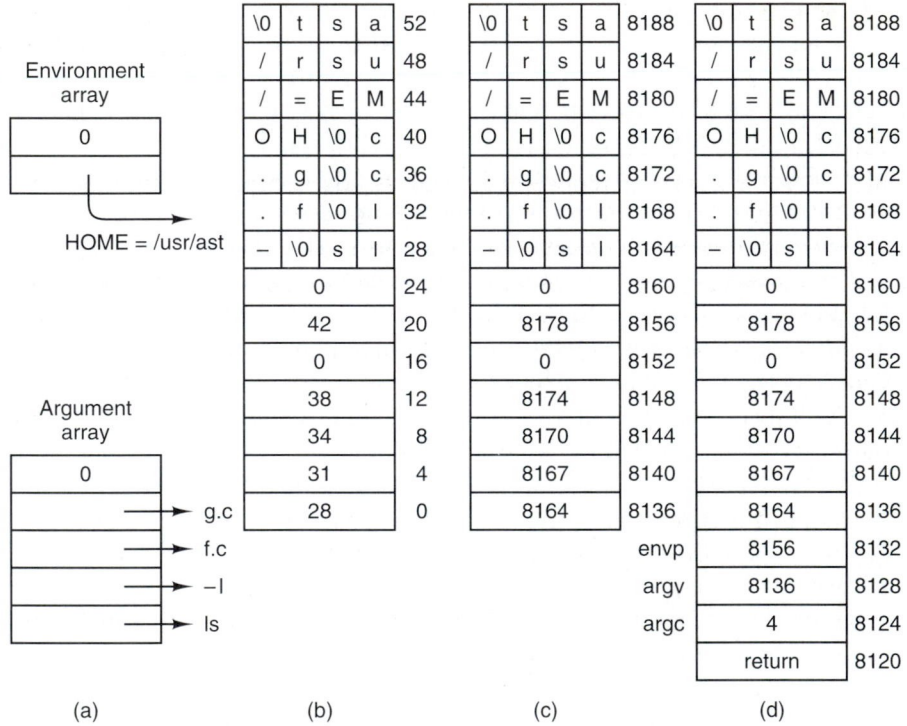

Figure 4-39. (a) The arrays passed to *execve*. (b) The stack built by *execve*. (c) The stack after relocation by the memory manager. (d) The stack as it appears to *main* at the start of execution.

To make this mechanism clearer, consider an example. When a user types

ls –l f.c g.c

to the shell, the shell interprets it and then makes the call

execve("/bin/ls", argv, envp);

to the library procedure. The contents of the two pointer arrays are shown in Fig. 4-39(a). The procedure *execve*, within the shell's address space, now builds the initial stack, as shown in Fig. 4-39(b). This stack is eventually copied intact to the memory manager during the processing of the EXEC call.

When the stack is finally copied to the user process, it will not be put at virtual address 0. Instead, it will be put at the end of the memory allocation, as determined by the total memory size field in the executable file's header. As an example, let us arbitrarily assume that the total size is 8192 bytes, so the last byte available to the program is at address 8191. It is up to the memory manager to relocate the pointers within the stack so that when deposited into the new address, the stack looks like Fig. 4-39(c).

When the EXEC call completes and the program starts running, the stack will indeed look exactly like Fig. 4-39(c), with the stack pointer having the value 8136. However, another problem is yet to be dealt with. The main program of the executed file is probably declared something like this:

```
main(argc, argv, envp);
```

As far as the C compiler is concerned, *main* is just another function. It does not know that *main* is special, so it compiles code to access the three parameters on the assumption that they will be passed according to the standard C calling convention, last parameter first. With one integer and two pointers, the three parameters are expected to occupy the three words just before the return address. Of course, the stack of Fig. 4-39(c) does not look like that at all.

The solution is that programs do not begin with *main*. Instead, a small, assembly language routine called the C run-time, start-off procedure, *crtso*, is always linked in at text address 0 so it gets control first. Its job is to push three more words onto the stack and then to call *main* using the standard call instruction. This results in the stack of Fig. 4-39(d) at the time that *main* starts executing. Thus, *main* is tricked into thinking it was called in the usual way (actually, it is not really a trick; it *is* called that way).

If the programmer neglects to call *exit* at the end of *main*, control will pass back to the C run-time, start-off routine when main is finished. Again, the compiler just sees *main* as an ordinary procedure and generates the usual code to return from it after the last statement. Thus *main* returns to its caller, the C run-time, start-off routine which then calls *exit* itself. Most of the code of 32-bit *crtso* is shown in Fig. 4-40. The comments should make its operation clear. All that has been left out is the code that loads the registers that are pushed and a few lines that set a flag that indicates if a floating point coprocessor is present or not.

4.7.6 The BRK System Call

The library procedures *brk* and *sbrk* are used to adjust the upper bound of the data segment. The former takes an absolute size (in bytes) and calls BRK. The latter takes a positive or negative increment to the current size, computes the new data segment size, and then calls BRK. There is no actual SBRK system call.

```
push  ecx                    ! push environ
push  edx                    ! push argv
push  eax                    ! push argc
call  _main                  ! main(argc, argv, envp)
push  eax                    ! push exit status
call  _exit
hlt                          ! force a trap if exit fails
```

Figure 4-40. The key part of the C run-time, start-off routine.

An interesting question is: "How does *sbrk* keep track of the current size, so it can compute the new size?" The answer is that a variable, *brksize*, always holds the current size so *sbrk* can find it. This variable is initialized to a compiler generated symbol giving the initial size of text plus data (nonseparate I and D) or just data (separate I and D). The name, and, in fact, very existence of such a symbol is compiler dependent, and thus it will not be found defined in any header file in the source file directories. It is defined in the library, in the file *brksize.s*. Exactly where it will be found depends on the system, but it will be in the same directory as *crtso.s*.

Carrying out BRK is easy for the memory manager. All that must be done is to check to see that everything still fits in the address space, adjust the tables, and tell the kernel.

4.7.7 Signal Handling

In Chap. 1 signals were described as a mechanism to convey information to a process that is not necessarily waiting for input. There is a defined set of signals, and each signal has a default action—either kill the process to which it is directed, or ignore the signal. Signal processing would be easy to understand and to implement if these were the only alternatives. However, processes can use system calls that alter these responses. A process can request that any signal (except for the special SIGKILL signal) be ignored. Furthermore, a process can prepare to **catch** a signal by requesting that a **signal handler** procedure internal to the process be activated instead of the default action for any signal (except, again, for SIGKILL). Thus to the programmer it appears that there are two distinct times when the operating system deals with signals: a preparation phase when a process may modify its response to a future signal, and a response phase when a signal is generated and acted upon. The action can be execution of a custom-written signal handler. There is actually a third phase. When a user-written handler terminates, a special system call cleans up and restores normal operation of the signaled process. The programmer does not need to know about this third phase. He writes a signal handler just like any other function. The operating system takes care of the details of invoking and terminating the handler and managing the stack.

In the preparation phase there are several system calls that a process can execute at any time to change its response to a signal. The most general of these is SIGACTION, which can specify that the process ignore some signal, catch some signal (replacing the default action with execution of user-defined signal-handling code within the process), or restore the default response to some signal. Another system call, SIGPROCMASK, can block a signal, causing it to be queued and to be acted upon only when and if the process unblocks that particular signal at a later time. These calls may be made at any time, even from within a signal catching function. In MINIX the preparation phase of signal processing is handled entirely by the memory manager, since the necessary data structures are all in the memory manager's part of the process table. For each process there are several $sigset\_t$ variables, in which each possible signal is represented by a bit. One such variable defines a set of signals to be ignored, another defines a set to be caught, and so on. For each process there is also an array of $sigaction$ structures, one for each signal. Each element of the $sigaction$ structure contains a variable to hold the address of a custom handler for that signal and an additional $sigset\_t$ variable to map signals to be blocked while that handler is executing. The field used for the address of the handler can instead hold special values signifying that the signal is to be ignored or is to be handled in the default way defined for that signal.

When a signal is generated, multiple parts of the MINIX system may become involved. The response begins in the memory manager, which figures out which processes should get the signal using the data structures just mentioned. If the signal is to be caught, it must be delivered to the target process. This requires saving information about the state of the process, so normal execution can be resumed. The information is stored on the signaled process' stack, and a check must be made to determine that there is sufficient stack space. The memory manager does this checking, since this is within its realm, and then calls the system task in the kernel to put the information on the stack. The system task also manipulates the process' program counter, so the process can execute the handler code. When the handler terminates, a SIGRETURN system call is made. Through this call, both the memory manager and the kernel participate in restoring the process' signal context and registers so it can resume normal execution. If the signal is not caught, the default action is taken, which may involve calling the file system to produce a **core dump** (writing the process' image to a file that may be examined with a debugger), as well as killing the process, which involves all of the memory manager, file system, and kernel. Finally, the memory manager may direct one or more repetitions of these actions, since a single signal may need to be delivered to a group of processes.

The signals known to MINIX are defined in */usr/include/signal.h*, a file required by the POSIX standard. They are listed in Fig. 4-41. All of the POSIX-required signals are defined in MINIX, but not all of them are currently supported. For instance, POSIX requires several signals related to job control, the ability to put a running program into the background and bring it back. MINIX does not support job control, but programs that might generate these signals can be ported to MINIX. These signals will be ignored if generated. MINIX also defines some non-POSIX signals and some synonyms for POSIX names for compatibility with older source code.

Signal	Description	Generated by
SIGHUP	Hangup	KILL system call
SIGINT	Interrupt	Kernel
SIGQUIT	Quit	Kernel
SIGILL	Illegal instruction	Kernel (*)
SIGTRAP	Trace trap	Kernel (M)
SIGABRT	Abnormal termination	Kernel
SIGFPE	Floating point exception	Kernel (*)
SIGKILL	Kill (cannot be caught or ignored)	KILL system call
SIGUSR1	User-defined signal # 1	Not supported
SIGSEGV	Segmentation violation	Kernel (*)
SIGUSR2	User defined signal # 2	Not supported
SIGPIPE	Write on a pipe with no one to read it	Kernel
SIGALRM	Alarm clock, timeout	Kernel
SIGTERM	Software termination signal from kill	KILL system call
SIGCHLD	Child process terminated or stopped	Not supported
SIGCONT	Continue if stopped	Not supported
SIGSTOP	Stop signal	Not supported
SIGTSTP	Interactive stop signal	Not supported
SIGTTIN	Background process wants to read	Not supported
SIGTTOU	Background process wants to write	Not supported

Figure 4-41. Signals defined by POSIX and MINIX. Signals indicated by (*) depend upon hardware support. Signals marked (M) are not defined by POSIX, but are defined by MINIX for compatibility with older programs. Several obsolete names and synonyms are not listed here.

Signals can be generated in two ways: by the KILL system call, and by the kernel. The signals generated by the MINIX kernel always include SIGINT, SIGQUIT, and SIGALRM. Other kernel signals depend upon hardware support. For instance, the 8086 and 8088 processors do not support detection of illegal instruction operation codes, but this capability is available on the 286 and above, which trap on an attempt to execute an illegal opcode. This service is provided by the hardware.

The implementor of the operating system must provide code to generate a signal in response to the trap. We saw in Chap. 2 that *kernel/exception.c* contains code to do just this for a number of different conditions. Thus a SIGILL signal can be generated in response to an illegal instruction when MINIX runs on a 286 or higher processor, but this signal will never be seen when MINIX runs on an 8088.

Just because the hardware can trap on a certain condition does not mean the capability can be used fully by the operating system implementor. For instance, several kinds of violations of memory integrity result in exceptions on all Intel processors beginning with the 286. Code in *kernel/exception.c* translates these exceptions into SIGSEGV signals. There are separate exceptions generated for violations of the limits of the hardware-defined stack segment and for other segments, since these might need to be treated differently. However, because of the way MINIX uses memory, the hardware cannot detect all the errors that might occur. The hardware defines a base and a limit for each segment. The hardware-defined data segment base is the same as the MINIX data segment base, but the hardware-defined data segment limit is higher than the limit that MINIX enforces in software. In other words, the hardware defines the data segment as the maximum amount of memory that MINIX could possibly use for data, if somehow the stack could shrink to nothing. Similarly the hardware defines the stack as the maximum amount of memory the MINIX stack could use if the data area could shrink to nothing. Although certain violations can be detected by the hardware, the hardware cannot detect the most probable stack violation, growth of the stack into the data area, since as far as the hardware registers and descriptor tables are concerned the data area and the stack area overlap.

Conceivably some code could be added to the kernel that would check each process' registers after each time the process gets a chance to run and generate a SIGSEGV signal upon detection of a violation of the integrity of the MINIX-defined data or stack areas. Whether this would be worthwhile is unclear; hardware traps can catch a violation immediately. A software check might not get a chance to do its work until many thousands of additional instructions had been executed, and at that point there might be very little a signal handler could do to try to recover.

Whatever their origin, the memory manager processes all signals the same way. For each process to be signaled, a variety of checks are made to see if the signal is feasible. One process can signal another if the signaler is the super-user or if the real or effective uid of the signaler is equal to either the real or effective uid of the signaled process. But there are several conditions that can prevent a signal being sent. Zombies cannot be signaled, for example. A process cannot be signaled if it has explicitly called SIGACTION to ignore the signal or SIGPROCMASK to block it. Blocking a signal is distinct from ignoring it; receipt of a blocked signal is remembered, and it is delivered when and if the signaled process removes the block. Finally, if its stack space is not adequate the signaled process is killed.

If all the conditions are met, the signal can be sent. If the process has not arranged for the signal to be caught, no information needs to be passed to the process. In this case the memory manager executes the default action for the signal, which is usually to kill the process, possibly also producing a core dump. For a few signals the default action is to ignore the signal. The signals marked "Not supported" in Fig. 4-41 are required to be defined by POSIX but are ignored by MINIX.

Catching a signal means executing the process' custom signal-handling code, the address of which is stored in a *sigaction* structure in the process table. In Chap. 2 we saw how a process' stackframe within its process table entry receives the information needed to restart the process when it is interrupted. By modifying the stackframe of a process to be signaled, it can be arranged that when the process next is allowed to execute the signal handler will run. By modifying the process' own stack in user space, it can be arranged that when the signal handler terminates the SIGRETURN system call will be made. This system call is never invoked by user-written code. It is executed after the kernel puts its address on the stack in such a way that its address becomes the return address popped from the stack when a signal handler terminates. SIGRETURN restores the original stackframe of the signaled process, so it can resume execution at the point where it was interrupted by the signal.

Although the final stage of sending a signal is done by the system task, this is a good place to summarize how it is done, since the data used are passed to the kernel from the memory manager. Catching a signal requires something much like the context switch that occurs when one process is taken out of execution and another process is put into execution, since when the handler terminates the process ought to be able to continue as if nothing had happened. However, there is only one place in the process table to store the contents of all the CPU registers that are needed to restore the process to its original state. The solution to this problem is shown in Fig. 4-42. Part (a) of the figure is a simplified view of the stack of a process and part of its process table entry just after it has been taken out of execution following an interrupt. At the time of suspension the contents of all of the CPU registers are copied into the stackframe structure in the process' process table entry in the kernel's part of the process table. This will be the situation at the moment a signal is generated, since a signal is generated by a process or task different from the intended recipient.

In preparation for handling the signal, the stackframe from the process table is copied onto the process' own stack as a *sigcontext* structure, thus preserving it. Then a *sigframe* structure is placed on the stack. This structure contains information to be used by SIGRETURN after the handler finishes. It also contains the address of the library procedure that invokes SIGRETURN itself, *ret addr1*, and another return address, *ret addr2*, which is the address where execution of the interrupted program will resume. As will be seen, however, the latter address is not used during normal execution.

Although the handler is written as an ordinary procedure by the programmer, it is not called by a call instruction. The instruction pointer (program counter)

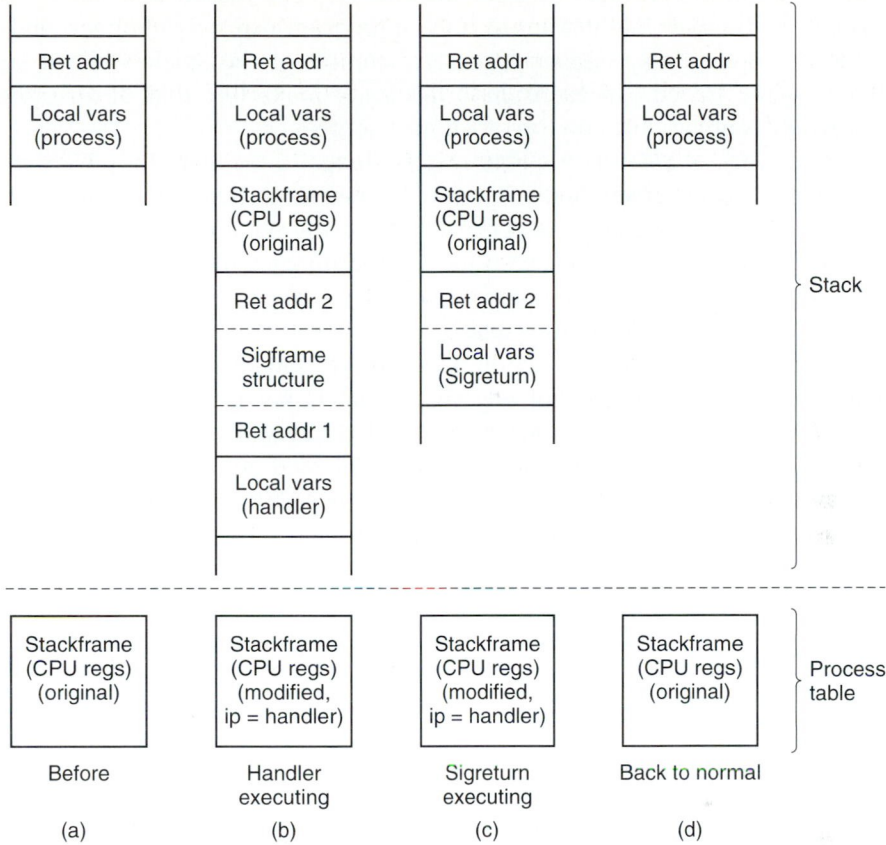

Figure 4-42. A process' stack (above) and its stackframe in the process table (below) corresponding to phases in handling a signal. (a) State as process is taken out of execution. (b) State as handler begins execution. (c) State while SIGRETURN is executing. (d) State after SIGRETURN completes execution.

field in the stackframe in the process table is altered to cause the signal handler to begin executing when *restart* puts the signaled process back into execution. Figure 4-42(b) shows the situation after this preparation has been completed and as the signal handler executes. Recall that the signal handler is an ordinary procedure, so when it terminates, *ret addr1* is popped and SIGRETURN executes.

Part (c) shows the situation while SIGRETURN is executing. The rest of the sigframe structure is now SIGRETURN's local variables. Part of SIGRETURN's action is to adjust its own stack pointer so that if it were to terminate like an ordinary function, it would use *ret addr2* as its return address. However, SIGRETURN does not actually terminate this way. It terminates like other system calls, allowing the scheduler in the kernel to decide which process to restart. Eventually, the signaled process will be rescheduled and will restart at this address, because the address is also in the process' original stackframe. The reason this address is on the stack is that a user might want to trace a program using a debugger, and this fools the debugger into a reasonable interpretation of the stack while a signal handler is being traced. In each phase the stack looks like that of an ordinary process, with local variables on top of a return address.

The real work of SIGRETURN is to restore things to the state they were in before the signal was received, and to clean up. Most importantly, the stackframe in the process table is restored to its original state, using the copy that was saved on the signaled process' stack. When SIGRETURN terminates, the situation will be as in Fig. 4-42(d), which shows the process waiting to be put back into execution in the same state it was in when interrupted.

For most signals the default action is to kill the signaled process. The memory manager takes care of this for any signal that is not ignored by default, and which the recipient process has not been enabled to handle, block, or ignore. If the parent is waiting for it, the killed process is cleaned up and removed from the process table. If the parent is not waiting, it becomes a zombie. For certain signal numbers (e.g., SIGQUIT), the memory manager also writes a core dump of the process to the current directory.

It can easily happen that a signal is sent to a process that is currently blocked waiting for a READ on a terminal for which no input is available. If the process has not specified that the signal is to be caught, it is just killed in the usual way. If, however, the signal is caught, the issue arises of what to do after the signal interrupt has been processed. Should the process go back to waiting, or should it continue with the next statement?

What MINIX does is this: the system call is terminated in such a way as to return the error code *EINTR*, so the process can see that the call was broken off by a signal. Determining that a signaled process was blocked on a system call is not entirely trivial. The memory manager must ask the file system to check for it.

This behavior is suggested, but not required, by POSIX, which also allows a READ to return the number of bytes read so far at the time of receipt of the signal. Returning *EINTR* makes it possible to set an alarm and to catch SIGALRM. This is an easy way to implement a timeout, for instance to terminate *login* and hang up a modem line if a user does not respond within a certain period. The synchronous clock task can be used to do the same thing with less overhead, but it is a MINIX invention and not as portable as using signals. Also, it is available only to server processes, and not to ordinary user processes.

4.7.8 Other System Calls

The memory manager handles a few more simple system calls. The library functions *getuid* and *geteuid* both invoke the GETUID system call, which returns both values in its return message. Similarly, the GETGID system call also returns real and effective values for use by the *getgid* and *getegid* functions. GETPID works the same way to return both the process ID and the ID of the parent process, and SETUID and SETGID can each set both real and effective values in one call. There are two additional system calls in this group, GETPGRP and SETSID. The former returns the process group ID, and the latter sets it to the current pid value. These seven calls are the simplest MINIX system calls.

The PTRACE and REBOOT system calls are also handled by the memory manager. The former supports debugging of programs. The latter affects many aspects of the system. It is appropriate to place it in the memory manager because its first action is to send signals to kill all processes except init. After that it calls upon the file system and the system task to complete its work.

4.8 IMPLEMENTATION OF MEMORY MANAGEMENT IN MINIX

Armed with a general overview of how the memory manager works, let us now turn to the code itself. The memory manager is written entirely in C, is straightforward, and contains a substantial amount of commentary in the code itself, so our treatment of most parts need not be long or involved. We will first look briefly at the header files, then the main program, and finally the files for the various system call groups discussed previously.

4.8.1 The Header Files and Data Structures

Several header files in the memory manager source directory have the same names as files in the kernel directory, and these names will be seen again in the file system. These files have similar functions in their own contexts. The parallel structure is designed to make it easier to understand the organization of the whole MINIX system. The memory manager also has a number of headers with unique names. As in other parts of the system, storage for global variables is reserved when the memory manager's version of *table.c* is compiled. In this section we will look at all of the header files, as well as *table.c*.

As with the other major parts of MINIX, the memory manager has a master header file, *mm.h* (line 15800). It is included in every compilation, and it in turn includes all the system-wide header files from */usr/include* and its subdirectories that are needed by every object module. Most of the files that are included in *kernel/kernel.h* are also included here. The memory manager also needs definitions in *include/fcntl.h* and *include/unistd.h*. The memory manager's own versions of *const.h*, *type.h*, *proto.h*, and *glo.h* also are included.

Const.h (line 15900) defines a some constants used by the memory manager, especially when compiled for 16-bit machines. The line

```
#define printf printk
```

is contained here so that calls to *printf* will be compiled as calls to the *printk* function. The function is similar to the one we saw in the kernel, and is defined for a similar reason, so the memory manager can display error and debugging messages without calling on the file system for help.

Type.h is currently unused and exists in skeletal form just so the memory manager files will have the same organization as the other parts of MINIX. *Proto.h* (line 16100) collects in one place function prototypes needed throughout the memory manager.

The memory manager's global variables are declared in *glo.h* (line 16200). The same trick used in the kernel with *EXTERN* is used here, namely, *EXTERN* is normally a macro that expands to *extern*, except in the file *table.c*. There it becomes the null string so storage can be reserved for the variables declared as *EXTERN*.

The first of these variables, *mp*, is a pointer to an *mproc* structure, the MM part of the process table for the process whose system call is being processed. The second variable, *dont_reply*, is initialized to *FALSE* when each new request arrives but can be set to *TRUE* during the call if it is discovered that no reply message should be sent. No replies are sent for a successful EXEC, for example. The third variable, *procs_in_use*, keeps track of how many process slots are currently in use, making it easy to see if a FORK call is feasible.

The message buffers *mm_in* and *mm_out* are for the request and reply messages, respectively. *Who* is the index of the current process; it is related to *mp* by

```
mp = &mproc[who];
```

When a message comes in, the system call number is extracted from it and put in *mm_call*.

The three variables *err_code*, *result2*, and *res_ptr* are used to hold values returned to the caller in the reply message. The most important of these variables is *err_code*, which is set to *OK* if the call is completed without error. The last two variables are used when a problem develops. MINIX writes an image of a process to a core file when a process terminates abnormally. *Core_name* defines the name this file will have, and *core_sset* is a bit map which defines which signals should produce core dumps.

The memory manager's part of the process table is in the next file, *mproc.h* (line 16300). Most of the fields are adequately described by their comments. Several fields deal with signal handling. *Mp_ignore*, *mp_catch*, *mp_sigmask*, *mp_sigmask2*, and *mp_sigpending* are bit maps, in which each bit represents one of the signals that can be sent to a process. The type *sigset_t* is a 32-bit integer, so MINIX could easily support up to 32 signals, but currently only 16 signals are defined, with signal 1 being the least significant (rightmost) bit. In any case, POSIX requires standard functions to add or delete members of the signal sets represented by these bit maps, so all necessary manipulations can be done without the programmer being aware of these details. The array *mp_sigact* is important for handling signals. There is an element for each signal type, and each element is a *sigaction* structure (defined in *include/signal.h*). Each *sigaction* structure consists of three fields:

1. The *sa_handler* field defines whether the signal is to be handled in the default way, ignored, or handled by a special handler.

2. The *sa_mask* field is a *sigset_t* that defines which signals are to be blocked when the signal is being handled by a custom handler.

3. The *sa_flags* field is a set of flags that apply to the signal.

This array makes possible a great deal of flexibility in handling signals.

The *mp_flags* field is used to hold a miscellaneous collection of bits, as indicated at the end of the file. This field is an unsigned integer, 16 bits on low-end CPUs or 32 bits on a 386 and up. There is plenty of room for expansion here, even on an 8088, as only 9 bits are used.

The last field in the process table is *mp_procargs*. When a new process is started, a stack like the one shown in Fig. 4-39 is built, and a pointer to the start of the new process' *argv* array is stored here. This is used by the *ps* command. For instance, for the example of Fig. 4-39, the value 8164 would be stored here, making it possible for *ps* to display the command line,

ls −l f.c g.c

if executed while the *ls* command is active.

The next file is *param.h* (line 16400), which contains macros for many of the system call parameters contained in the request message. It also contains four macros for fields in the reply message. When the statement

k = pid;

appears in any file in which *param.h* is included, the preprocessor converts it to

k = mm_in.m1_i1;

before feeding it to the compiler proper.

Before we continue with the executable code, let us look at *table.c* (line 16500). Its compilation reserves storage for the various *EXTERN* variables and structures we have seen in *glo.h* and *mproc.h*. The statement

#define _TABLE

causes *EXTERN* to become the null string. This is the same mechanism that we saw in the kernel code.

The other major feature of *table.c* is the array *call_vec* (line 16515). When a request message arrives, the system call number is extracted from it and used as an index into *call_vec* to locate the procedure that carries out that system call. System call numbers that are not valid calls all invoke *no_sys*, which just returns an error code. Note that although the *_PROTOTYPE* macro is used in defining *call_vec*, this is not a declaration of a prototype; it is definition of an initialized array. However, it is an array of functions, and use of *_PROTOTYPE* is the easiest way to do this that is compatible with both classic (Kernighan & Ritchie) C and Standard C.

4.8.2 The Main Program

The memory manager is compiled and linked independently from the kernel and the file system. Consequently, it has its own main program, which is started up after the kernel has finished initializing itself. The main program is in *main.c*, at line 16627. After doing its own initialization by calling *mm_init*, the memory manager enters its loop on line 16636. In this loop, it calls *get_work* to wait for an incoming request message. Then it calls one of its *do_XXX* procedures via the *call_vec* table to carry out the request, and finally sends a reply, if needed. This construction should be familiar by now: it is the same one used by the I/O tasks.

The procedures *get_work* (line 16663) and *reply* (line 16676) handle the actual receiving and sending, respectively.

The last procedure in this file is *mm_init*, which initializes the memory manager. It is not used after the system has started running. The call to *sys_getmap* on line 16730 gets information about the kernel's memory use. The loop on lines 16734 to 16741 initializes all the process table entries for tasks and servers, and the following lines prepare *init*'s process table entry. On line 16749 MM waits for FS to send it a message. As mentioned in the discussion of deadlock handling in MINIX, this is the only time the file system ever sends a request message to the file system. The message tells how much memory is being used for the RAM disk. The call to *mem_init* on line 16755 initializes the hole list by calling the system task. After this, normal memory management can begin. This call also fills in the *total_clicks* and *free_clicks* variables, completing the information *mm_init* needs to print a message showing total memory, kernel memory use, RAM disk size, and free memory. After printing the message a reply is sent to FS (line 16764), allowing it to continue. Finally, the memory task is given the address of MM's part of the process table, for the benefit of the *ps* command.

4.8.3 Implementation of FORK, EXIT, and WAIT

The FORK, EXIT, and WAIT system calls are implemented by the procedures *do_fork*, *do_mm_exit*, and *do_wait* in the file *forkexit.c*. The procedure *do_fork* (line 16832) follows the steps shown in Fig. 4-37. Notice that the second call to *procs_in_use* (line 16847) reserves the last few process table slots for the superuser. In computing how much memory the child needs, the gap between the data and stack segments is included, but the text segment is not. Either the parent's text is shared, or, if the process has common I and D space, its text segment is of zero length. After doing the computation, a call is made to *alloc_mem* to get the memory. If this is successful, the base addresses of child and parent are converted from clicks into absolute bytes, and *sys_copy* is called to send a message to the system task to get the copying done.

Now a slot is found in the process table. The test involving *procs_in_use* earlier guarantees that one will exist. After the slot has been found, it is filled in, first by copying the parent's slot there, and then updating the fields *mp_parent*, *mp_flags*, *mp_seg*, *mp_exitstatus*, and *mp_sigstatus*. Some of these fields need special handling. The *TRACED* bit in the *mp_flags* field is zeroed, since a child does not inherit trace status. The *mp_seg* field is an array containing elements for the text, data, and stack segments, and the text portion is left pointing to the parent's text segment if the flags indicate this is a separate I and D program that can share text.

The next step is assigning a pid to the child. The variable *next_pid* keeps track of the next pid to be assigned. However, the following problem could conceivably occur. After assigning, say, pid 20 to a very long-lived process, 30,000 more processes might be created and destroyed, and *next_pid* might come back to 20 again. Assigning a pid that was still in use would be a disaster (suppose someone later tried to signal process 20), so we search the whole process table to make sure that the pid to be assigned is not already in use.

The calls to *sys_fork* and *tell_fs* inform the kernel and file system, respectively, that a new process has been created, so they can update their process tables. (All the procedures beginning with *sys_* are library routines that send a message to the system task in the kernel to request one of the services of Fig. 3-50.) Process creation and destruction are always initiated by the memory manager and then propagated to the kernel and file system when completed.

The reply message to the child is sent explicitly at the end of *do_fork*. The reply to the parent, containing the child's pid, is sent by the loop in *main*, as the normal reply to a request.

The next system call handled by the memory manager is EXIT. The procedure *do_mm_exit* (line 16912) accepts the call, but most of the work is done by the call to *mm_exit*, a few lines further down. The reason for this division of labor is that *mm_exit* is also called to take care of processes terminated by a signal. The work is the same, but the parameters are different, so it is convenient to split things up this way.

The first thing *mm_exit* does is to stop the timer, if the process has one running. Next, the kernel and file system are notified that the process is no longer runnable (lines 16949 and 16950). The call to the library procedure *sys_xit* sends a message to the system task telling it to mark the process as no longer runnable, so it will not be scheduled any more. Next the memory is released. A call to *find_share* determines whether the text segment is being shared by another process, and if not the text segment is released by a call to *free_mem*. This is followed by another call to the same procedure to release the data and stack. It is not worth the trouble to decide whether all the memory could be released in one call to *free_mem*. If the parent is waiting, *cleanup* is called to release the process table slot. If the parent is not waiting, the process becomes a zombie, indicated by the *HANGING* bit in the *mp_flags* word. Whether the process is completely eliminated or made into a zombie, the final action of *mm_exit* is to loop through the process table and look for children of the process it has just terminated (lines 16975 to 16982). If any are found, they are disinherited and become children of *init*. If *init* is waiting and a child is hanging, *cleanup* is then called for that child. This deals with situations such as the one shown in Fig. 4-43(a). In this figure we see that process 12 is about to exit, and that its parent, 7, is waiting for it. *Cleanup* will be called to get rid of 12, so 52 and 53 are turned into children of *init*, as shown in Fig. 4-43(b). Now we have the situation that 53, which has already exited, is the child of a process doing a WAIT. Consequently, it can also be cleaned up.

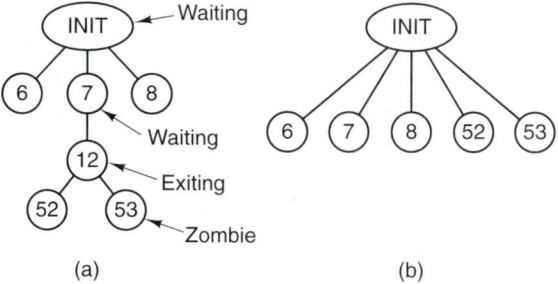

(a)   (b)

Figure 4-43. (a) The situation as process 12 is about to exit. (b) The situation after it has exited.

When the parent process does a WAIT or a WAITPID, control comes to procedure *do_waitpid* on line 16992. The parameters supplied by the two calls are different, and the actions expected are also different, but the setup done in lines 17009 to 17011 prepares internal variables so *do_waitpid* can perform the actions of either call. The loop on lines 17019 to 17041 scans the entire process table to see if the process has any children at all, and if so, checks to see if any are zombies that can now be cleaned up. If a zombie is found (line 17026), it is cleaned up and *do_waitpid* returns. The flag *dont_reply* is set because the reply to the parent is sent from inside *cleanup*, not from the loop in *main*. If a traced child is found, a reply is sent indicating the process is stopped, and *do_waitpid* returns. *Dont_reply* is also set true to prevent a second reply being sent by *main*.

If the process doing the WAIT has no children, it simply gets an error return (line 17053). If it has children, but none are zombies or are being traced, a test is made to see if *do_waitpid* was called with a bit set indicating the parent didn't want to wait. If not (the usual case), then a bit is set on line 17047 to indicate that it is waiting, and the parent is suspended until a child terminates.

When a process has exited and its parent is waiting for it, in whichever order these events occur, the procedure *cleanup* (line 17061) is called to perform the last rites. There is not much to do by this point. The parent is awakened from its WAIT or WAITPID call and is given the pid of the terminated child, as well as its exit and signal status. The file system has already released the child's memory, and the kernel has already suspended scheduling, so all the kernel now has to do is free up the child's slot in the process table.

4.8.4 Implementation of EXEC

The code for EXEC follows the outline of Fig. 4-38. It is contained in the procedure *do_exec* (line 17140). After making a few simple validity checks, the memory manager fetches the name of the file to be executed from user space. On line 17172 it sends a special message to the file system, to switch to the user's directory, so that the path just fetched will be interpreted relative to the user's, rather than to MM's, working directory.

If the file is present and executable, the memory manager reads the header to extract the segment sizes. Then it fetches the stack from user space (lines 17188 and 17189), checks to see if the new process can share text with a process that is already running (line 17196), allocates memory for the new image (line 17199), patches up the pointers [see the differences between Fig. 4-39(b) and (c)], and reads in the text segment (if needed) and the data segment (lines 17221 to 17226). Finally, it processes the setuid and setgid bits, updates the process table entry, and tells the kernel that it is finished, so that the process can be scheduled again.

Although the control of all the steps is in *do_exec*, many of the details are carried out by subsidiary procedures within *exec.c*. *Read_header* (line 17272), for example, not only reads the header and returns the segment sizes, it also verifies that the file is a valid MINIX executable for the same CPU type as the operating system is compiled for. This is done by conditional compilation of the appropriate test at the time the memory manager is compiled (lines 17322 to 17327). *Read_header* also verifies that all the segments fit in the virtual address space.

Procedure *new_mem* (line 17366) checks to see if sufficient memory is available for the new memory image. It searches for a hole big enough for just the data and stack if the text is being shared; otherwise it searches for a single hole big enough for the combined text, data, and stack. A possible improvement here would be to search for two separate holes, one for the text and one for the data and stack, since there is no need for these areas to be contiguous. In earlier versions of MINIX this was required. If sufficient memory is found, the old memory is released and the new memory acquired. If insufficient memory is available, the EXEC call fails. After the new memory is allocated, *new_mem* updates the memory map (in *mp_seg*) and reports it to the kernel by calling the library procedure *sys_newmap*.

The remainder of *new_mem* is concerned with zeroing the bss segment, gap, and stack segment. (The bss segment is that part of the data segment that contains all the uninitialized global variables.) Many compilers generate explicit code to zero the bss segment, but doing it here allows MINIX to work even with compilers that do not. The gap between data and stack segments is also zeroed, so that when the data segment is extended by BRK, the newly acquired memory will contain zeroes. This is not only a convenience for the programmer, who can count on new variables having an initial value of zero, it is also a security feature on a multiuser operating system, where a process previously using this memory may have been using data that should not be seen by other processes.

The next procedure is *patch_ptr* (line 17465), which does the job of relocating the pointers of Fig. 4-39(b) to the form of Fig. 4-39(c). The work is simple: examine the stack to find all the pointers and add the base address to each one.

The procedure *load_seg* (line 17498) is called once or twice per EXEC, possibly to load the text segment and always to load the data segment. Rather than just reading the file block by block and then copying the blocks to the user, a trick is used to allow the file system to load the entire segment directly to the user space. In effect, the call is decoded by the file system in a slightly special way so that it appears to be a read of the entire segment by the user process itself. Only a few lines at the beginning of the file system's read routine know that some monkey business is going on here. Loading is appreciably speeded up by this maneuver.

The final procedure in *exec.c* is *find_share* (line 17535). It searches for a process that can share text by comparing the i-node, device, and modification times of the file to be executed with those of existing processes. This is just a straightforward search of the appropriate fields in *mproc*. Of course, it must ignore the process on behalf of which the search is being made.

4.8.5 Implementation of BRK

As we have just seen, the memory model used by MINIX is quite simple: each process is given a single contiguous allocation for its data and stack when it is created. It is never moved around in memory, it is never swapped out of memory, it never grows, and it never shrinks. All that can happen is that the data segment can eat away at the gap from the low end, and the stack can eat away at it from the high end. Under these circumstances, the implementation of the BRK call in *break.c* is especially easy. It consists of verifying that the new sizes are feasible and then updating the tables to reflect them.

The top-level procedure is *do_brk* (line 17628), but most of the work is done in *adjust* (line 17661). The latter checks to see if the stack and data segments have collided. If they have, the BRK call cannot be carried out, but the process is not killed immediately. A safety factor, *SAFETY_BYTES*, is added to the top of the data segment before making the test, so (hopefully) the decision that the stack has grown too far can be made while there is still enough room on the stack for the process to continue for a short while. It gets control back (with an error message), so it can print appropriate messages and shut down gracefully.

Note that *SAFETY_BYTES* is defined using a #define statement in the middle of the procedure (line 17693). This use is rather unusual; normally such definitions appear at the beginning of files, or in separate header files. The associated comment reveals that the programmer found deciding upon the size of the safety factor to be difficult. There is no doubt that this definition was done in this way to attract attention and, perhaps, to stimulate additional experimentation.

The base of the data segment is constant, so if *adjust* has to adjust the data segment, all it does is update the length field. The stack grows downward from a fixed end point, so if *adjust* also notices that the stack pointer, which is given to it as a parameter, has grown beyond the stack segment (to a lower address), both the origin and length are updated.

The last procedure in this file, *size_ok* (line 17736) makes a test to see if the segment sizes fit within the address space, in clicks as well as in bytes. The conditional code for 16-bit machines has been retained in the listing in order to show why this is written as a separate function. There would be little point in having this as a separate function for 32-bit MINIX. It is called in only two places, and substituting line 17765 in place of the calls would result in more compact code, since the calls pass several arguments that are not used in the 32-bit implementation.

4.8.6 Implementation of Signal Handling

There are eight system calls relating to signals. They are summarized in Fig. 4-44. These system calls, as well as the signals themselves, are processed in the file *signal.c*. An additional system call, REBOOT, is also handled by this file, since it uses signals to terminate all processes.

System call	Purpose
SIGACTION	Modify response to future signal
SIGPROCMASK	Change set of blocked signals
KILL	Send signal to another process
ALARM	Send ALRM signal to self after delay
PAUSE	Suspend self until future signal
SIGSUSPEND	Change set of blocked signals, then PAUSE
SIGPENDING	Examine set of pending (blocked) signals
SIGRETURN	Clean up after signal handler

Figure 4-44. System calls relating to signals.

The SIGACTION call supports the *sigaction* and *signal* functions, which allow a process to alter how it will respond to signals. *Sigaction* is required by POSIX and is the preferred call for most purposes, but the *signal* library function is required by Standard C, and programs that must be portable to non-POSIX systems should be written using it. The code for *do_sigaction* (line 17845) begins with checks for a valid signal number and verification that the call is not an attempt to change the response to a SIGKILL signal (lines 17851 and 17852). (It is not permitted to ignore, catch, or block SIGKILL. SIGKILL is the ultimate means by which a user can control his processes and a system manager can control his users.) SIGACTION is called with pointers to a *sigaction* structure, *sig_osa*, that receives the old signal attributes that were in effect before the call, and another such structure, *sig_nsa*, containing a new set of attributes.

The first step is to call the system task to copy the current attributes into the structure pointed to by *sig_osa*. SIGACTION can be called with a *NULL* pointer in *sig_nsa* to examine the old signal attributes without changing them. In this case *do_sigaction* returns immediately (line 17860). If *sig_nsa* is not *NULL*, the structure defining the new signal action is copied to the memory manager's space. The code in lines 17867 to 17877 modifies the *mp_catch*, *mp_ignore*, and *mp_sigpending* bit maps according to whether the new action is to be to ignore the signal, to use the default handler, or to catch the signal. The library functions *sigaddset* and *sigdelset* are used, although the actions are straightforward bit manipulation operations that could have been implemented with simple macros. However, these functions are required by the POSIX standard in order to make programs that use them easily portable, even to systems in which the number of signals exceeds the number of bits available in an integer. Using the library functions helps to make MINIX itself easily portable to different architectures.

Finally, the other signal-related fields in the memory manager's part of the process table are filled in. For each potential signal there is bit map, the *sa_mask*, which defines which signals are to be blocked while a handler for that signal is executing. For each signal there is also a pointer, *sa_handler*. It can contain a pointer to the handler function, or special values to indicate the signal is to be ignored or handled in the default way. The address of the library routine that invokes SIGRETURN when the handler terminates is stored in *mp_sigreturn*. This address is one of the fields in the message received by the memory manager.

POSIX allows a process to manipulate its own signal handling, even while within a signal handler. This can be used to change signal response to subsequent signals while a signal is being processed, and then to restore the normal set of responses. The next group of system calls support these signal-manipulation features. SIGPENDING is handled by *do_sigpending* (line 17889), which returns the *mp_sigpending* bit map, so a process can determine if it has pending signals. SIGPROCMASK, handled by *do_sigprocmask*, returns the set of signals that are currently blocked, and can also be used to change the state of a single signal in the set, or to replace the entire set with a new one. The moment that a signal is unblocked is an appropriate time to check for pending signals, and this is done by calls to *check_pending* on line 17927 and line 17933. *Do_sigsuspend* (line

17949) carries out the SIGSUSPEND system call. This call suspends a process until a signal is received. Like the other functions we have discussed here, it manipulates bit maps. It also sets the SIGSUSPENDED bit in *mp_flags*, which is all it takes to prevent execution of the process. Again, this is a good time to make a call to *check_pending*. Finally, *do_sigreturn* handles SIGRETURN, which is used to return from a custom handler. It restores the signal context that existed when the handler was entered, and it also calls *check_pending* on line 17980.

Some signals, such as SIGINT, originate in the kernel itself. Such signals are handled in a way that is similar to signals generated by a user process calling KILL. The two procedures, *do_kill* (line 17983) and *do_ksig* (line 17994), are conceptually similar. Both cause the memory manager to send a signal. A single call to KILL may require delivery of signals to a group of processes, and *do_kill* just calls *check_sig*, which checks the entire process table for eligible recipients. *Do_ksig* is called when a message arrives from the kernel. The message contains a bit map, allowing the kernel to generate multiple signals with one message. As with KILL, each of these may need to be delivered to a group of processes. The bit map is processed one bit at a time by the loop on lines 18026 to 18048. Some kernel signals need special attention: the process ID is changed in some cases to cause the signal to be delivered to a group of processes (lines 18030 to 18033), and a SIGALRM is ignored if it hasn't been requested. With that exception, each bit set results in a call to *check_sig*, just as in *do_kill*.

The ALARM system call is controlled by *do_alarm* (line 18056). It calls the next function, *set_alarm*, which sends a message to the clock task telling it to start the timer. *Set_alarm* (line 18067) is a separate function because it is also used to turn the timer off when a process exits with the timer still on. When the timer runs out, the kernel announces the fact by sending the memory manager a message of type KSIG, which causes *do_ksig* to run, as discussed above. The default action of the SIGALRM signal is to kill the process if it is not caught. If the SIGALRM is to be caught, a handler must be installed by SIGACTION. The complete sequence of events for a SIGALRM signal with a custom handler is shown in Fig. 4-45. There are three sequences of messages here. In messages (1), (2), and (3) the user does an ALARM call via a message to the memory manager, the manager sends a request to the clock, and the clock acknowledges. In messages (4), (5), and (6), the clock task sends the alarm to the memory manager, the memory manager calls the system task to prepare the user process' stack for execution of the signal handler (as in Fig. 4-42(b)), and the system task replies. Message (7) is the call to SIGRETURN that occurs when the handler completes execution. In response the memory manager sends message (8) to the system task to have it complete the cleanup, and the system task replies with message (9). Message (6) does not itself cause the handler to execute, but the sequence will be maintained, because the system task, as a task, will be allowed to complete its work due to the priority scheduling algorithm used in MINIX. The handler is part of the user process and will execute only after the system task has completed its work.

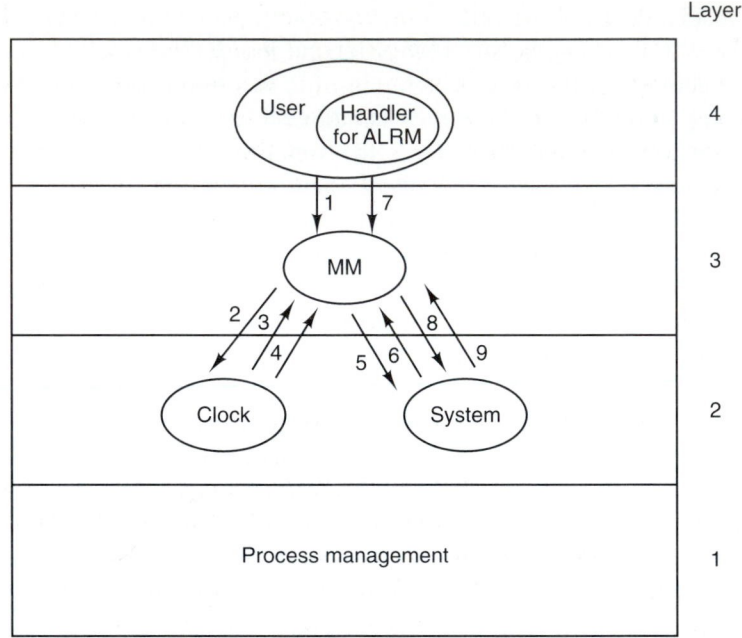

Figure 4-45. Messages for an alarm. The most important are: (1) User does ALARM. (4) After the set time has elapsed, the signal arrives. (7) Handler terminates with call to SIGRETURN. See text for details.

Do_pause takes care of the PAUSE system call (line 18115). All that is necessary is to set a bit and refrain from replying, thus keeping the caller blocked. The kernel need not even be informed, since it knows that the caller is blocked.

The final system call handled in *signal.c* is REBOOT (line 18128). This call is used only by specialized programs executable by the super-user, but it serves an important function. It ensures that all processes are terminated in an orderly way and that the file system is synched before the system task in the kernel is called to shut down. The termination of processes is done using *check_sig* to send a SIG-KILL to all processes except *init*. This is why REBOOT is included in this file.

Several support functions in *signal.c* have been mentioned in passing. We will now look at them in more detail. By far the most important is *sig_proc* (line 18168), which actually sends a signal. First a number of tests are made. Attempts to send to dead (lines 18190 to 18192) or hanging (lines 18194 to 18196) processes are serious problems that cause a system panic. A process that is currently being traced is stopped when signaled (lines 18198 to 18202). If the signal is to be ignored, *sig_proc*'s work is complete on line 18204. This is the default action for some signals, for instance, those signals that are required by POSIX but are not supported by MINIX. If the signal is blocked, the only action that needs to be taken is to set a bit in that process' *mp_sigpending* bit map. The key test (line

18213) is to distinguish processes that have been enabled to catch signals from those that have not. By this point all other special considerations have been eliminated, and a process that cannot catch the signal will be terminated.

Signals that are eligible to be caught are processed on lines 18214 to 18249. A message is constructed to be sent to the kernel, some parts of which are copies of information in the memory manager's part of the process table. If the process to be signaled was previously suspended by SIGSUSPEND, the signal mask that was saved at the time of suspension is included in the message; otherwise the current signal mask is included (lines 18213 to 18217). Other items included in the message are several addresses in the space of the signaled process space: the signal handler, the address of the *sigreturn* library routine to be called on completion of the handler, and the current stack pointer.

Next, space is allocated on the process' stack. Figure 4-46 shows the structure that is put on the stack. The *sigcontext* portion is put on the stack to preserve it for later restoration, since the corresponding structure in the process table itself is altered in preparation for execution of the signal handler. The *sigframe* part provides a return address for the signal handler and data needed by SIGRETURN to complete restoration of the process' state when the handler is done. The return address and frame pointer are not actually used by any part of MINIX. They are there to fool a debugger if anyone should ever try to trace execution of a signal handler.

The structure to be put on the signaled process' stack is fairly large. The code in lines 18225 and 18226 reserves space for it, following which a call to *adjust* tests to see whether there is enough room on the process' stack. If there is not enough stack space, the process is killed by jumping to the label *doterminate* using the seldom-used C goto (lines 18228 and 18229).

There is a potential problem with the call to *adjust*. Recall from our discussion of the implementation of BRK that *adjust* returns an error if the stack is within *SAFETY_BYTES* of running into the data segment. The extra margin of error is provided because the validity of the stack can only be checked occasionally by software. This margin of error is probably excessive in the present instance, since it is known exactly how much space is needed on the stack for the signal, and additional space is needed only for the signal handler, presumably a relatively simple function. It is possible that some processes may be terminated unnecessarily because the call to *adjust* fails. This is certainly better than having programs fail mysteriously at other times, but finer tuning of these tests may be possible.

If there is enough room on the stack, two more flags are checked. The *SA_NODEFER* flag indicates if the signaled process is to block further signals of the same type while handling a signal. The *SA_RESETHAND* flag tells if the signal handler is to be reset upon receiving this signal. (This provides faithful emulation of the old *signal* call. Although this "feature" is often considered a fault in the old call, support of old features requires supporting their faults as well.) The kernel is then notified, using the library routine *sys_sendsig* (line 18242). Finally,

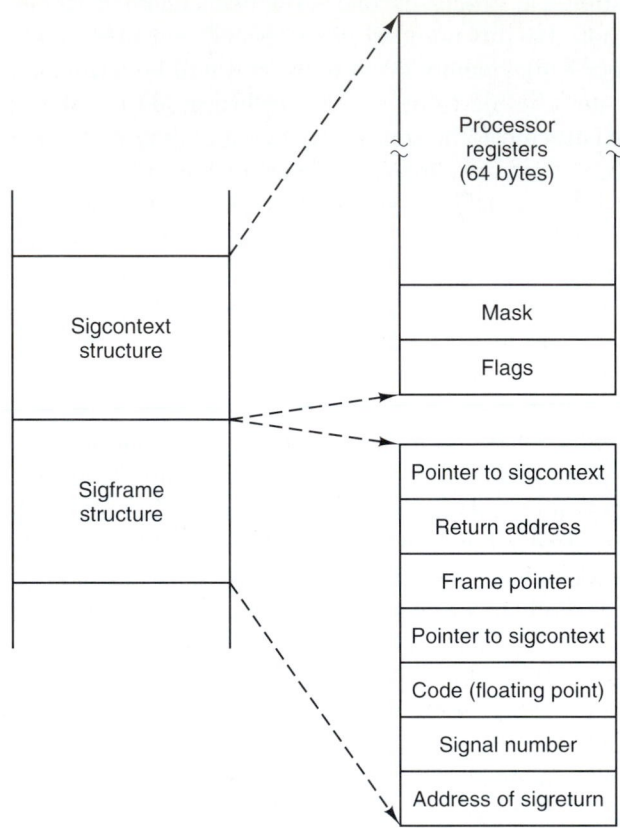

Figure 4-46. The sigcontext and sigframe structures pushed on the stack to prepare for a signal handler. The processor registers are a copy of the stack-frame used during a context switch.

the bit indicating a signal is pending is cleared, and *unpause* is called to terminate any system call on which the process may be hanging. When the signaled process next executes, the signal handler will run.

Now let us look at the termination code, marked by the label *doterminate* (line 18250). The label and a goto are the easiest way to handle the possible failure of the call to *adjust*. Here signals are processed that for one reason or another cannot or should not be caught. The action may include a core dump, if that is appropriate to the signal, and always ends with termination of the process as if it had exited, through a call to *mm_exit* (line 18258).

Check_sig (line 18265) is where the memory manager checks to see if a signal can be sent. The call

kill(0, sig);

causes the indicated signal to be sent to all the processes in the caller's group (i.e., all the processes started from the same terminal). Signals originating in the kernel and REBOOT also may affect multiple processes. For this reason, *check_sig* loops on lines 18288 to 18318 to scan through the process table to find all the processes to which a signal should be sent. The loop contains a large number of tests. Only if all of them are passed is the signal sent, by calling *sig_proc* on line 18315.

Check_pending (line 18330) is another function called several times in the code we have just reviewed. It loops through all the bits in the *mp_sigpending* bit map for the process referred to by *do_sigmask*, *do_sigreturn*, or *do_sigsuspend*, to see if any blocked signal has become unblocked. It calls *sig_proc* to send the first unblocked pending signal it finds. Since all signal handlers eventually cause execution of *do_sigreturn*, this suffices eventually to deliver all pending unmasked signals.

The procedure *unpause* (line 18359) has to do with signals that are sent to processes suspended on PAUSE, WAIT, READ, WRITE, or SIGSUSPEND calls. PAUSE, WAIT, and SIGSUSPEND can be checked by consulting the memory manager's part of the process table, but if none of these are found, the file system must be asked to use its own *do_unpause* function to check for a possible hangup on READ or WRITE. In every case the action is the same: an error reply is sent to the waiting call and the flag bit that corresponds to the cause of the wait is reset so the process may resume execution and process the signal.

The final procedure in this file is *dump_core* (line 18402), which writes core dumps to the disk. A core dump consists of a header with information about the size of the segments occupied by a process, a copy of all the process' state information, obtained by copying the kernel process table information for the process, and the memory image of each of the segments. A debugger can interpret this information to help the programmer determine what went wrong during execution of the process. The code to write the file is straightforward. The potential problem mentioned in the previous section again raises its head, but in a somewhat different form. To be sure the stack segment to be recorded in the core dump is up to date, *adjust* is called on line 18428. This call may fail because of the safety margin built into it. The success of the call is not checked by *dump_core*, so the core dump will be written in any case, but within the file the information about the stack may be incorrect.

4.8.7 Implementation of the Other System Calls

The file *getset.c* contains one procedure, *do_getset* (line 18515), which carries out the seven remaining memory manager calls. They are shown in Fig. 4-47. They are all so simple that they are not worth an entire procedure each. The GETUID and GETGID calls both return the real and effective uid or gid.

Setting the uid or gid is slightly more complex than just reading it. A check has to be made to see if the caller is authorized to set the uid or gid. If the caller passes the test, the file system must be informed of the new uid or gid, since file

System Call	Description
GETUID	Return real and effective uid
GETGID	Return real and effective gid
GETPID	Return pids of process and its parent
SETUID	Set caller's real and effective uid
SETGID	Set caller's real and effective gid
SETSID	Create new session, return pid
GETPGRP	Return ID of process group

Figure 4-47. The system calls supported in *mm/getset.c*.

protection depends on it. The SETSID call creates a new session, and a process which is already a process group leader is not allowed to do this. The test on line 18561 checks this. The file system completes the job of making a process into a session leader with no controlling terminal.

Minimal debugging support, by means of the PTRACE system call, is in the file *trace.c*. There are eleven commands that can be given as a parameter to the PTRACE system call. They are shown in Fig. 4-48. In the memory manager *do_trace* processes four of them: enable, exit, resume, step. Requests to enable or exit tracing are completed here. All other commands are passed on to the system task, which has access to the kernel's part of the process table. This is done by the call to the *sys_trace* library function on line 18669. Two support functions for tracing are provided at the end of *trace.c*. *Stop_proc* is used to stop a traced process when it is signaled, and *findproc* supports *do_trace* by searching the process table for the process to be traced.

4.8.8 Memory Manager Utilities

The remaining files contain utility routines and tables. The file *alloc.c* is where the system keeps track of which parts of memory are in use and which are free. It has four entry points:

1. *alloc_mem* – request a block of memory of a given size.

2. *free_mem* – return memory that is no longer needed.

3. *max_hole* – compute the size of the largest available hole.

4. *mem_init* – initialize the free list when the memory manager starts running.

As we have said before, *alloc_mem* (line 18840) just uses first fit on a list of holes sorted by memory address. If it finds a piece that is too big, it takes what it

Command	Description
T_STOP	Stop the process
T_OK	Enable tracing by parent for this process
T_GETINS	Return value from text (instruction) space
T_GETDATA	Return value from data space
T_GETUSER	Return value from user process table
T_SETINS	Set value in instruction space
T_SETDATA	Set value in data space
T_SETUSER	Set value in user process table
T_RESUME	Resume execution
T_EXIT	Exit
T_STEP	Set trace bit

Figure 4-48. Debugging commands supported by *mm/trace.c*.

needs and leaves the rest on the free list, but reduced in size by the amount taken. If an entire hole is needed, *del_slot* (line 18926) is called to remove the entry from the free list.

Free_mem's job is to check if a newly released piece of memory can be merged with holes on either side. If it can, *merge* (line 18949) is called to join the holes and update the lists.

Max_hole (line 18985) scans the hole list and returns the largest item it finds. *Mem_init* (line 19005) builds the initial free list, consisting of all available memory.

The next file is *utility.c*, which holds a few miscellaneous procedures used in various places in the memory manager. The procedure *allowed* (line 19120) checks to see if a given access is allowed to a file. For example, *do_exec* needs to know if a file is executable.

The procedure *no_sys* (line 19161) should never be called. It is provided just in case a user ever calls the memory manager with a system call number that is invalid or is not handled by the memory manager.

Panic (line 19172) is called only when the memory manager has detected an error from which it cannot recover. It reports the error to the system task, which then brings MINIX to a screeching halt. It is not called lightly.

The last function in *utility.c* is *tell_fs*, which constructs a message and sends it to the file system when the latter needs to be informed of events handled by the memory manager.

The two procedures in the file *putk.c* are also utilities, although of quite a different character from the previous ones. From time to time, calls to *printf* are inserted into the memory manager, mostly for debugging. Also, *panic* calls *printf*. As mentioned earlier, the name *printf* is actually a macro defined as *printk*, so that calls to *printf* do not use the standard I/O library procedure that sends messages to the file system. *Printk* calls *putk* to communicate directly with the terminal task, something that is forbidden to ordinary users. We saw a routine of the same name in the kernel code.

4.9 SUMMARY

In this chapter we have examined memory management, both in general and in MINIX. We saw that the simplest systems do not swap or page at all. Once a program is loaded into memory, it remains there until it finishes. Some operating systems allow only one process at a time in memory, while others support multiprogramming.

The next step up is swapping. When swapping is used, the system can handle more processes than it has room for in memory. Processes for which there is no room are swapped out to the disk. Free space in memory and on disk can be kept track of with a bit map or a hole list.

More advanced computers often have some form of virtual memory. In the simplest form, each process' address space is divided up into uniform sized blocks called pages, which can be placed into any available page frame in memory. There are many page replacement algorithms, two of the better known ones being second chance and aging. To make paging systems work well, choosing an algorithm is not enough; attention to issues such as determining the working set, memory allocation policy, and page size are required.

Segmentation helps in handling data structures that change size during execution and simplifies linking and sharing. It also facilitates providing different protection for different segments. Sometimes segmentation and paging are combined to provide a two-dimensional virtual memory. The MULTICS system and the Intel Pentium support segmentation and paging.

Memory management in MINIX is simple. Memory is allocated when a process executes a FORK or EXEC system call. The memory so allocated is never increased or decreased as long as the process lives. On Intel processors there are two memory models used by MINIX. Small programs can have instructions and data in the same memory segment. Larger programs use separate instruction and data space (separate I and D). Processes with separate I and D space can share the text portion of their memory, so only data and stack memory must be allocated during a FORK. This may also be true during an EXEC if another process already is using the text needed by the new program.

Most of the work of the memory manager is concerned not with keeping track of free memory, which it does using a hole list and the first fit algorithm, but rather with carrying out the system calls relating to memory management. A number of system calls support POSIX-style signals, and since the default action of most signals is to terminate the signaled process, it is appropriate to handle them in the memory manager, which initiates termination of all processes. Several system calls not directly related to memory are also handled by the memory manager, mainly because it is smaller than the file system, and thus it was most convenient to put them here.

PROBLEMS

1. A computer system has enough room to hold four programs in its main memory. These programs are idle waiting for I/O half the time. What fraction of the CPU time is wasted?

2. Consider a swapping system in which memory consists of the following hole sizes in memory order: 10K, 4K, 20K, 18K, 7K, 9K, 12K, and 15K. Which hole is taken for successive segment requests of

   (a) 12K
   (b) 10K
   (c) 9K

   for first fit? Now repeat the question for best fit, worst fit, and next fit.

3. What is the difference between a physical address and a virtual address?

4. Using the page table of Fig. 4-8, give the physical address corresponding to each of the following virtual addresses:

   (a) 20
   (b) 4100
   (c) 8300

5. The Intel 8086 processor does not support virtual memory. Nevertheless, some companies previously sold systems that contained an unmodified 8086 CPU and do paging. Make an educated guess as to how they did it. (Hint: think about the logical location of the MMU.)

6. If an instruction takes 1 microsec and a page fault takes an additional n microsec, give a formula for the effective instruction time if page faults occur every k instructions.

7. A machine has a 32-bit address space and an 8K page. The page table is entirely in hardware, with one 32-bit word per entry. When a process starts, the page table is copied to the hardware from memory, at one word every 100 nsec. If each process runs for 100 msec (including the time to load the page table), what fraction of the CPU time is devoted to loading the page tables?

8. A computer with a 32-bit address uses a two-level page table. Virtual addresses are split into a 9-bit top-level page table field, an 11-bit second-level page table field, and an offset. How large are the pages and how many are there in the address space?

9. Below is the listing of a short assembly language program for a computer with 512-byte pages. The program is located at address 1020, and its stack pointer is at 8192 (the stack grows toward 0). Give the page reference string generated by this program. Each instruction occupies 4 bytes (1 word), and both instruction and data references count in the reference string.

   Load word 6144 into register 0
   Push register 0 onto the stack
   Call a procedure at 5120, stacking the return address
   Subtract the immediate constant 16 from the stack pointer
   Compare the actual parameter to the immediate constant 4
   Jump if equal to 5152

10. Suppose that a 32-bit virtual address is broken up into four fields, a, b, c, and d. The first three are used for a three-level page table system. The fourth field, d, is the offset. Does the number of pages depend on the sizes of all four fields? If not, which ones matter and which ones do not?

11. A computer whose processes have 1024 pages in their address spaces keeps its page tables in memory. The overhead required for reading a word from the page table is 500 nsec. To reduce this overhead, the computer has a TLB, which holds 32 (virtual page, physical page frame) pairs, and can do a look up in 100 nsec. What hit rate is needed to reduce the mean overhead to 200 nsec?

12. The TLB on the VAX does not contain an R bit. Why?

13. A machine has 48-bit virtual addresses and 32-bit physical addresses. Pages are 8K. How many entries are needed for the page table?

14. A computer has four page frames. The time of loading, time of last access, and the R and M bits for each page are as shown below (the times are in clock ticks):

Page	Loaded	Last ref.	R	M
0	126	279	0	0
1	230	260	1	0
2	120	272	1	1
3	160	280	1	1

    (a) Which page will NRU replace?
    (b) Which page will FIFO replace?
    (c) Which page will LRU replace?
    (d) Which page will second chance replace?

15. If FIFO page replacement is used with four page frames and eight pages, how many page faults will occur with the reference string 0172327103 if the four frames are initially empty? Now repeat this problem for LRU.

16. A small computer has four page frames. At the first clock tick, the R bits are 0111 (page 0 is 0, the rest are 1). At subsequent clock ticks, the values are 1011, 1010, 1101, 0010, 1010, 1100, and 0001. If the aging algorithm is used with an 8-bit counter, give the values of the four counters after the last tick.

17. How long does it take to load a 64K program from a disk whose average seek time is 30 msec, whose rotation time is 20 msec, and whose tracks hold 32K

(a) for a 2K page size?
(b) for a 4K page size?

The pages are spread randomly around the disk.

18. One of the first timesharing machines, the PDP-1, had a memory of 4K 18-bit words. It held one process at a time in memory. When the scheduler decided to run another process, the process in memory was written to a paging drum, with 4K 18-bit words around the circumference of the drum. The drum could start writing (or reading) at any word, rather than only at word 0. Why do you suppose this drum was chosen?

19. A computer provides each process with 65,536 bytes of address space divided into pages of 4096 bytes. A particular program has a text size of 32,768 bytes, a data size of 16,386 bytes, and a stack size of 15,870 bytes. Will this program fit in the address space? If the page size were 512 bytes, would it fit? Remember that a page may not contain parts of two different segments.

20. It has been observed that the number of instructions executed between page faults is directly proportional to the number of page frames allocated to a program. If the available memory is doubled, the mean interval between page faults is also doubled. Suppose that a normal instruction takes 1 microsec, but if a page fault occurs, it takes 2001 microsec (i.e., 2 msec to handle the fault). If a program takes 60 sec to run, during which time it gets 15,000 page faults, how long would it take to run if twice as much memory were available?

21. A group of operating system designers for the Frugal Computer Company are thinking about ways of reducing the amount of backing store needed in their new operating system. The head guru has just suggested not bothering to save the program text in the swap area at all, but just page it in directly from the binary file whenever it is needed. Are there any problems with this approach?

22. Explain the difference between internal fragmentation and external fragmentation. Which one occurs in paging systems? Which one occurs in systems using pure segmentation?

23. When segmentation and paging are both being used, as in MULTICS, first the segment descriptor must be looked up, then the page descriptor. Does the TLB also work this way, with two levels of lookup?

24. Why does the MINIX memory management scheme make it necessary to have a program like *chmem*?

25. Modify MINIX to release a zombie's memory as soon as it enters the zombie state, rather than waiting until the parent waits for it.

26. In the current implementation of MINIX, when an EXEC system call is made, the memory manager checks to see if a hole large enough to contain the new memory image is currently available. If not, the call is rejected. A better algorithm would be to see if a sufficiently large hole would be available after the current memory image were released. Implement this algorithm.

27. When carrying out an EXEC system call, MINIX uses a trick to have the file system read in entire segments at once. Devise and implement a similar trick to allow core dumps to be written in a similar way.

28. Modify MINIX to do swapping.

29. In Sec. 4.7.5, it was pointed out that on an EXEC call, by testing for an adequate hole before releasing the current process' memory, a suboptimal implementation is achieved. Reprogram this algorithm to do better.

30. In Sec. 4.8.4, it was pointed out that it would be better to search for holes for the text and data segments separately. Implement this improvement.

31. Redesign *adjust* to avoid the problem of signaled processes being killed unnecessarily because of a too-strict test for stack space.

5

FILE SYSTEMS

All computer applications need to store and retrieve information. While a process is running, it can store a limited amount of information within its own address space. However, the storage capacity is restricted to the size of the virtual address space. For some applications this size is adequate, but for others, such as airline reservations, banking, or corporate record keeping, it is far too small.

A second problem with keeping information within a process' address space is that when the process terminates, the information is lost. For many applications, (e.g., for data bases), the information must be retained for weeks, months, or even forever. Having it vanish when the process using it terminates is unacceptable. Furthermore, it must not go away when a computer crash kills the process.

A third problem is that it is frequently necessary for multiple processes to access (parts of) the information at the same time. If we have an on-line telephone directory stored inside the address space of a single process, only that process can access it. The way to solve this problem is to make the information itself independent of any one process.

Thus we have three essential requirements for long-term information storage:

1. It must be possible to store a very large amount of information.

2. The information must survive the termination of the process using it.

3. Multiple processes must be able to access the information concurrently.

The usual solution to all these problems is to store information on disks and other external media in units called **files**. Processes can then read them and write new ones if need be. Information stored in files must be **persistent**, that is, not be affected by process creation and termination. A file should only disappear when its owner explicitly removes it.

Files are managed by the operating system. How they are structured, named, accessed, used, protected, and implemented are major topics in operating system design. As a whole, that part of the operating system dealing with files is known as the **file system** and is the subject of this chapter.

From the users' standpoint, the most important aspect of a file system is how it appears to them, that is, what constitutes a file, how files are named and protected, what operations are allowed on files, and so on. The details of whether linked lists or bit maps are used to keep track of free storage and how many sectors there are in a logical block are of less interest, although they are of great importance to the designers of the file system. For this reason, we have structured the chapter as several sections. The first two are concerned with the user interface to files and directories, respectively. Then comes a detailed discussion of how the file system is implemented. After that we will look at security and protection mechanisms in file systems. Finally we will look at the file system.

5.1 FILES

In this section we will look at files from the user's point of view, that is, how they are used and what properties they have.

5.1.1 File Naming

Files are an abstraction mechanism. They provide a way to store information on the disk and read it back later. This must be done in such a way as to shield the user from the details of how and where the information is stored, and how the disks actually work.

Probably the most important characteristic of any abstraction mechanism is the way the objects being managed are named, so we will start our examination of file systems with the subject of file naming. When a process creates a file, it gives the file a name. When the process terminates, the file continues to exist and can be accessed by other processes using its name.

The exact rules for file naming vary somewhat from system to system, but all operating systems allow strings of one to eight letters as legal file names. Thus *andrea*, *bruce*, and *cathy* are possible file names. Frequently digits and special characters are also permitted, so names like *2*, *urgent!*, and *Fig.2-14* are often valid as well. Many file systems support names as long as 255 characters.

Some file systems distinguish between upper case letters and lower case letters, whereas others do not. UNIX falls in the first category; MS-DOS falls in the second. Thus a UNIX system can have all of the following as distinct files: *barbara*, *Barbara*, *BARBARA*, *BARbara*, and *BarBaRa*. In MS-DOS they all designate the same file.

Many operating systems support two-part file names, with the two parts separated by a period, as in *prog.c*. The part following the period is called the **file extension** and usually indicates something about the file. In MS-DOS, for example, file names are 1 to 8 characters, plus an optional extension of 1 to 3 characters. In UNIX, the size of the extension, if any, is up to the user, and a file may even have two or more extensions, as in *prog.c.Z*, where *.Z* is commonly used to indicate that the file (*prog.c*) has been compressed using the Ziv-Lempel compression algorithm. Some of the more common file extensions and their meanings are shown in Fig. 5-1.

Extension	Meaning
file.bak	Backup file
file.c	C source program
file.f77	Fortran 77 program
file.gif	Compuserve Graphical Interchange Format image
file.hlp	Help file
file.html	World Wide Web HyperText Markup Language document
file.mpg	Movie encoded with the MPEG standard
file.o	Object file (compiler output, not yet linked)
file.ps	PostScript file
file.tex	Input for the TEX formatting program
file.txt	General text file
file.zip	Compressed archive

Figure 5-1. Some typical file extensions.

In some cases, the file extensions are just conventions and are not enforced in any way. A file named *file.txt* is probably some kind of text file, but that name is more to remind the owner than to convey any specific information to the computer. On the other hand, a C compiler may actually insist that the files it is to compile end in *.c*, and it may refuse to compile them if they do not.

Conventions like this are especially useful when the same program can handle several different kinds of files. The C compiler, for example, can be given a list of several files to compile and link together, some of them C files and some of them assembly language files. The extension then becomes essential for the compiler to tell which are C files, which are assembly files, and which are other files.

5.1.2 File Structure

Files can be structured in any of several ways. Three common possibilities are depicted in Fig. 5-2. The file in Fig. 5-2(a) is an unstructured sequence of bytes. In effect, the operating system does not know or care what is in the file. All it sees are bytes. Any meaning must be imposed by user-level programs. Both UNIX and MS-DOS use this approach. As an aside, WINDOWS 95 basically uses the MS-DOS file system, with a little syntactic sugar added (e.g., long file names), so nearly everything said in this chapter about MS-DOS also holds for WINDOWS 95. WINDOWS NT is completely different, however.

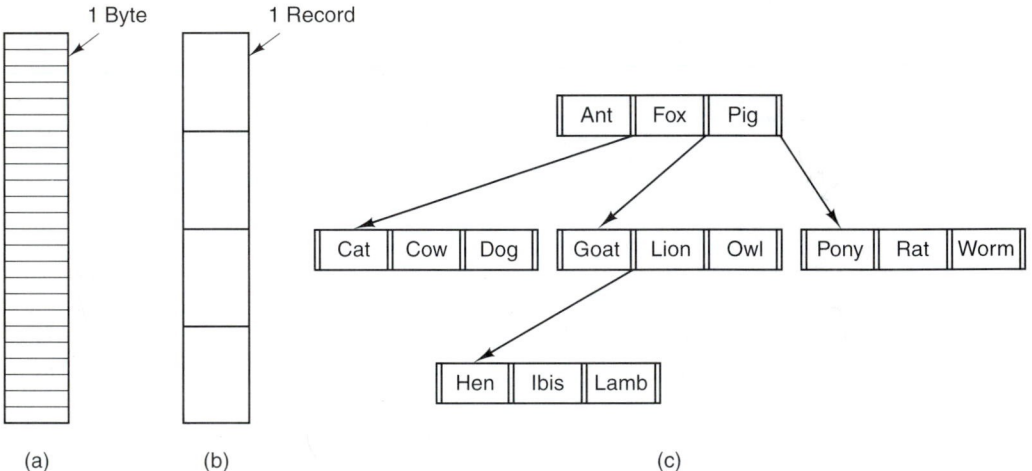

Figure 5-2. Three kinds of files. (a) Byte sequence. (b) Record sequence. (c) Tree.

Having the operating system regard files as nothing more than byte sequences provides the maximum flexibility. User programs can put anything they want in files and name them any way that is convenient. The operating system does not help, but it also does not get in the way. For users who want to do unusual things, the latter can be very important.

The first step up in structure is shown in Fig. 5-2(b). In this model, a file is a sequence of fixed-length records, each with some internal structure. Central to the idea of a file being a sequence of records is the idea that the read operation returns one record and the write operations overwrites or appends one record. In years gone by, when the 80-column punched card was king, many operating systems based their file systems on files consisting of 80-character records, in effect, card images. These systems also supported files of 132-character records, which were intended for the line printer (which in those days were big chain printers having 132 columns). Programs read input in units of 80 characters and wrote it in units of 132 characters, although the final 52 could be spaces, of course.

An (old) system that viewed files as sequences of fixed-length records was CP/M. It used a 128-character record. Nowadays, the idea of a file as a sequence of fixed length records is pretty much gone, although it was once the norm.

The third kind of file structure is shown in Fig. 5-2(c). In this organization, a file consists of a tree of records, not necessarily all the same length, each containing a **key** field in a fixed position in the record. The tree is sorted on the key field, to allow rapid searching for a particular key.

The basic operation here is not to get the "next" record, although that is also possible, but to get the record with a specific key. For the zoo file of Fig. 5-2(c), one could ask the system to get the record whose key is *pony*, for example, without worrying about its exact position in the file. Furthermore, new records can be added to the file, with the operating system, and not the user, deciding where to place them. This type of file is clearly quite different from the unstructured byte streams used in UNIX and MS-DOS but is widely used on the large mainframe computers still used in some commercial data processing.

5.1.3 File Types

Many operating systems support several types of files. UNIX and MS-DOS, for example, have regular files and directories. UNIX also has character and block special files. **Regular files** are the ones that contain user information. All the files of Fig. 5-2 are regular files. **Directories** are system files for maintaining the structure of the file system. We will study directories below. **Character special files** are related to input/output and used to model serial I/O devices such as terminals, printers, and networks. **Block special files** are used to model disks. In this chapter we will be primarily interested in regular files.

Regular files are generally either ASCII files or binary files. ASCII files consist of lines of text. In some systems each line is terminated by a carriage return character. In others, the line feed character is used. Occasionally, both are required. Lines need not all be of the same length.

The great advantage of ASCII files is that they can be displayed and printed as is, and they can be edited with an ordinary text editor. Furthermore, if large numbers of programs use ASCII files for input and output, it is easy to connect the output of one program to the input of another, as in shell pipelines. (The interprocess plumbing is not any easier, but interpreting the information certainly is if a standard convention, such as ASCII, is used for expressing it.)

Other files are binary files, which just means that they are not ASCII files. Listing them on the printer gives an incomprehensible listing full of what is apparently random junk. Usually, they have some internal structure.

For example, in Fig. 5-3(a) we see a simple executable binary file taken from an early version of UNIX. Although technically the file is just a sequence of bytes, the operating system will only execute a file if it has the proper format. It has five sections: header, text, data, relocation bits, and symbol table. The header starts with a so-called **magic number**, identifying the file as an executable file (to prevent the accidental execution of a file not in this format). Then come 16-bit integers giving the sizes of the various pieces of the file, the address at which execution starts, and some flag bits. Following the header are the text and data of the program itself. These are loaded into memory and relocated using the relocation bits. The symbol table is used for debugging.

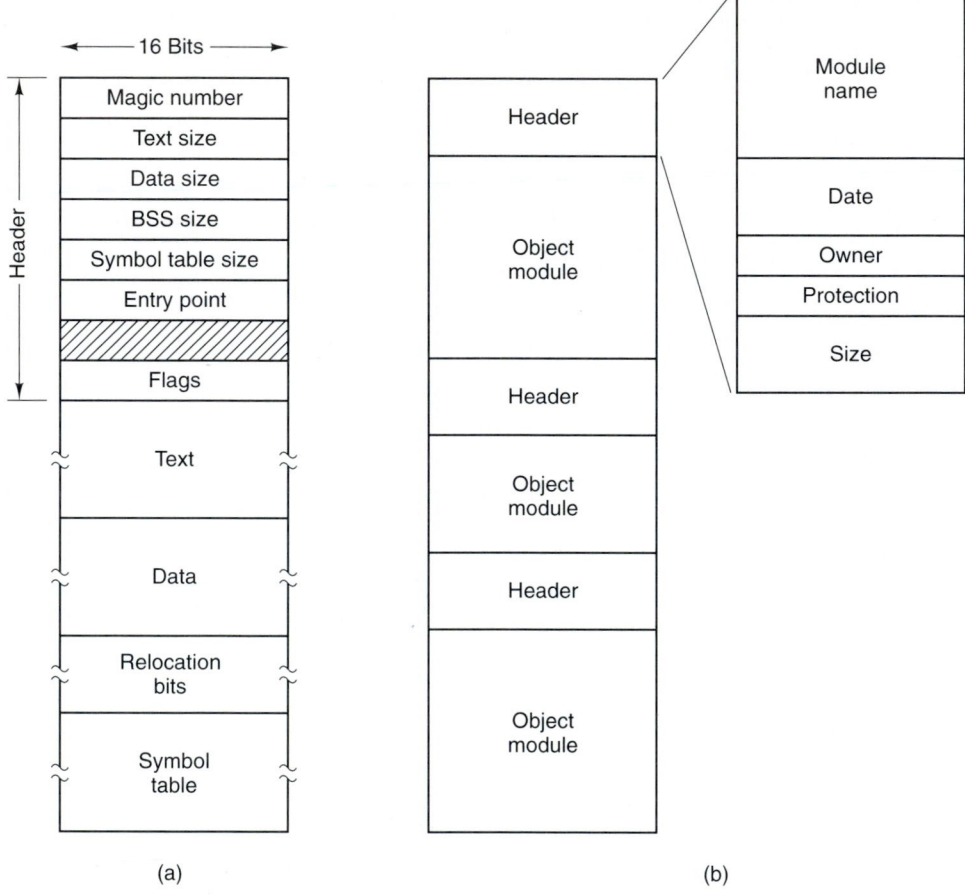

Figure 5-3. (a) An executable file. (b) An archive.

Our second example of a binary file is an archive, also from UNIX. It consists of a collection of library procedures (modules) compiled but not linked. Each one is prefaced by a header telling its name, creation date, owner, protection code, and size. Just as with the executable file, the module headers are full of binary numbers. Copying them to the printer would produce complete gibberish.

All operating systems must recognize one file type, their own executable file, but some recognize more. The old TOPS-20 system went so far as to examine the creation time of any file to be executed. Then it located the source file and saw if the source had been modified since the binary was made. If it had been, it automatically recompiled the source. In UNIX terms, the *make* program had been built into the shell. The file extensions were mandatory so the operating system could tell which binary program was derived from which source.

In a similar vein, when a WINDOWS user double clicks on a file name, an appropriate program is launched with the file as parameter. The operating system determines which program to run based on the file extension.

Having strongly typed files like this causes problems whenever the user does anything that the system designers did not expect. Consider, as an example, a system in which program output files have type *dat* (data files). If a user writes a program formatter that reads a *.pas* file, transforms it (e.g., by converting it to a standard indentation layout), and then writes the transformed file as output, the output file will be of type *.dat*. If the user tries to offer this to the Pascal compiler to compile it, the system will refuse because it has the wrong extension. Attempts to copy *file.dat* to *file.pas* will be rejected by the system as invalid (to protect the user against mistakes).

While this kind of "user friendliness" may help novices, it drives experienced users up the wall since they have to devote considerable effort to circumventing the operating system's idea of what is reasonable and what is not.

5.1.4 File Access

Early operating systems provided only one kind of file access: **sequential access**. In these systems, a process could read all the bytes or records in a file in order, starting at the beginning, but could not skip around and read them out of order. Sequential files can be rewound, however, so they can be read as often as needed. Sequential files are convenient when the storage medium is magnetic tape, rather than disk.

When disks came into use for storing files, it became possible to read the bytes or records of a file out of order, or to access records by key, rather than by position. Files whose bytes or records can be read in any order are called **random access files**.

Random access files are essential for many applications, for example, data base systems. If an airline customer calls up and wants to reserve a seat on a particular flight, the reservation program must be able to access the record for that flight without having to read the records for thousands of other flights first.

Two methods are used for specifying where to start reading. In the first one, every READ operation gives the position in the file to start reading at. In the second one, a special operation, SEEK, is provided to set the current position. After a SEEK, the file can be read sequentially from the now-current position.

In some older mainframe operating systems, files are classified as being either sequential or random access at the time they are created. This allows the system to use different storage techniques for the two classes. Modern operating systems do not make this distinction. All their files are automatically random access.

5.1.5 File Attributes

Every file has a name and its data. In addition, all operating systems associate other information with each file, for example, the date and time the file was created and the file's size. We will call these extra items the file's **attributes**. The list of attributes varies considerably from system to system. The table of Fig. 5-4 shows some of the possibilities, but other ones also exist. No existing system has all of these, but each one is present in some system.

Field	Meaning
Protection	Who can access the file and in what way
Password	Password needed to access the file
Creator	Id of the person who created the file
Owner	Current owner
Read-only flag	0 for read/write; 1 for read only
Hidden flag	0 for normal; 1 for do not display in listings
System flag	0 for normal files; 1 for system file
Archive flag	0 for has been backed up; 1 for needs to be backed up
ASCII/binary flag	0 for ASCII file; 1 for binary file
Random access flag	0 for sequential access only; 1 for random access
Temporary flag	0 for normal; 1 for delete file on process exit
Lock flags	0 for unlocked; nonzero for locked
Record length	Number of bytes in a record
Key position	Offset of the key within each record
Key length	Number of bytes in the key field
Creation time	Date and time the file was created
Time of last access	Date and time the file was last accessed
Time of last change	Date and time the file has last changed
Current size	Number of bytes in the file
Maximum size	Number of bytes the file may grow to

Figure 5-4. Some possible file attributes.

The first four attributes relate to the file's protection and tell who may access it and who may not. All kinds of schemes are possible, some of which we will study later. In some systems the user must present a password to access a file, in which case the password must be one of the attributes.

The flags are bits or short fields that control or enable some specific property. Hidden files, for example, do not appear in listings of all the files. The archive flag is a bit that keeps track of whether the file has been backed up. The backup program clears it, and the operating system sets it whenever a file is changed. In this way, the backup program can tell which files need backing up. The temporary flag allows a file to be marked for automatic deletion when the process that created it terminates.

The record length, key position, and key length fields are only present in files whose records can be looked up using a key. They provide the information required to find the keys.

The various times keep track of when the file was created, most recently accessed and most recently modified. These are useful for a variety of purposes. For example, a source file that has been modified after the creation of the corresponding object file needs to be recompiled. These fields provide the necessary information.

The current size tells how big the file is at present. Some mainframe operating systems require the maximum size to be specified when the file is created, to let the operating system reserve the maximum amount of storage in advance. Workstation and personal computer operating systems are clever enough to do without this feature.

5.1.6 File Operations

Files exist to store information and allow it to be retrieved later. Different systems provide different operations to allow storage and retrieval. Below is a discussion of the most common system calls relating to files.

1. **CREATE**. The file is created with no data. The purpose of the call is to announce that the file is coming and to set some of the attributes.

2. **DELETE**. When the file is no longer needed, it has to be deleted to free up disk space. There is always a system call for this purpose.

3. **OPEN**. Before using a file, a process must open it. The purpose of the OPEN call is to allow the system to fetch the attributes and list of disk addresses into main memory for rapid access on later calls.

4. **CLOSE**. When all the accesses are finished, the attributes and disk addresses are no longer needed, so the file should be closed to free up internal table space. Many systems encourage this by imposing a maximum number of open files on processes. A disk is written in blocks, and closing a file forces writing of the file's last block, even though that block may not be entirely full yet.

5. **READ**. Data are read from file. Usually, the bytes come from the current position. The caller must specify how much data are needed and must also provide a buffer to put them in.

6. **WRITE**. Data are written to the file, again, usually at the current position. If the current position is the end of the file, the file's size increases. If the current position is in the middle of the file, existing data are overwritten and lost forever.

7. **APPEND**. This call is a restricted form of WRITE. It can only add data to the end of the file. Systems that provide a minimal set of system calls do not generally have APPEND, but many systems provide multiple ways of doing the same thing, and these systems sometimes have APPEND.

8. **SEEK**. For random access files, a method is needed to specify from where to take the data. One common approach is a system call, SEEK, that repositions the pointer to the current position to a specific place in the file. After this call has completed, data can be read from, or written to, that position.

9. **GET ATTRIBUTES**. Processes often need to read file attributes to do their work. For example, the UNIX *make* program is commonly used to manage software development projects consisting of many source files. When *make* is called, it examines the modification times of all the source and object files and arranges for the minimum number of compilations required to bring everything up to date. To do its job, it must look at the attributes, namely, the modification times.

10. **SET ATTRIBUTES**. Some of the attributes are user settable and can be changed after the file has been created. This system call makes that possible. The protection mode information is an obvious example. Most of the flags also fall in this category.

11. **RENAME**. It frequently happens that a user needs to change the name of an existing file. This system call makes that possible. It is not always strictly necessary, because the file can usually be copied to a new file with the new name, and the old file then deleted.

5.2 DIRECTORIES

To keep track of files, file systems normally have **directories**, which, in many systems, are themselves files. In this section we will discuss directories, their organization, their properties, and the operations that can be performed on them.

5.2.1 Hierarchical Directory Systems

A directory typically contains a number of entries, one per file. One possibility is shown in Fig. 5-5(a), in which each entry contains the file name, the file attributes, and the disk addresses where the data are stored. Another possibility is shown in Fig. 5-5(b). Here a directory entry holds the file name and a pointer to another data structure where the attributes and disk addresses are found. Both of these systems are commonly used.

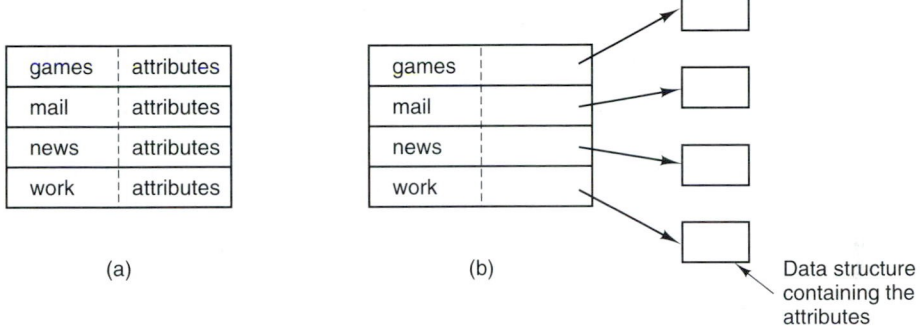

Figure 5-5. (a) Attributes in the directory entry. (b) Attributes elsewhere.

When a file is opened, the operating system searches its directory until it finds the name of the file to be opened. It then extracts the attributes and disk addresses, either directly from the directory entry or from the data structure pointed to, and puts them in a table in main memory. All subsequent references to the file use the information in main memory.

The number of directories varies from system to system. The simplest design is for the system to maintain a single directory containing all the files of all the users, as illustrated in Fig. 5-6(a). If there are many users, and they choose the same file names (e.g., *mail* and *games*), conflicts and confusion will quickly make the system unworkable. This system model was used by the first microcomputer operating systems but is rarely seen any more.

An improvement on the idea of having a single directory for all files in the entire system is to have one directory per user [see Fig. 5-6(b)]. This design eliminates name conflicts among users but is not satisfactory for users with a large number of files. It is quite common for users to want to group their files together in logical ways. A professor, for example, might have a collection of files that together form a book that he is writing for one course, a second collection of files containing student programs submitted for another course, a third group of files containing the code of an advanced compiler-writing system he is building, a fourth group of files containing grant proposals, as well as other files for electronic mail, minutes of meetings, papers he is writing, games, and so on. Some way is needed to group these files together in flexible ways chosen by the user.

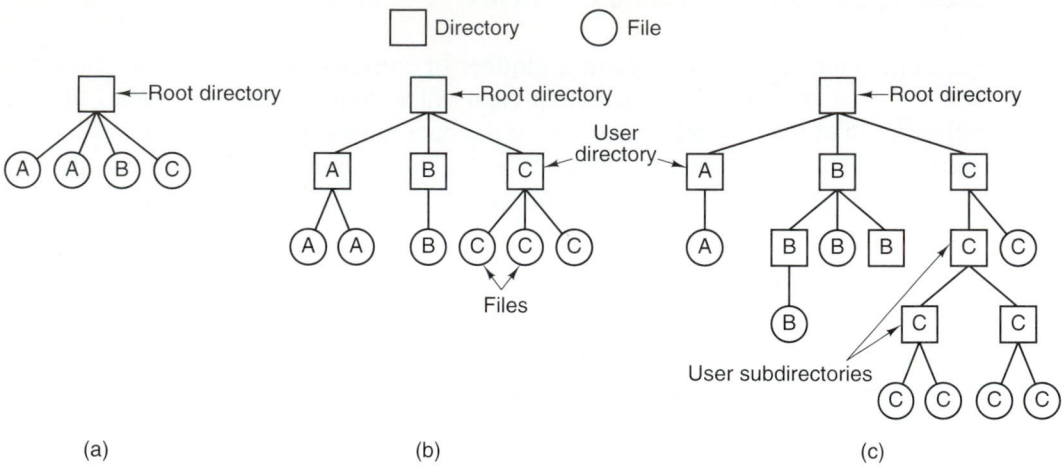

Figure 5-6. Three file system designs. (a) Single directory shared by all users. (b) One directory per user. (c) Arbitrary tree per user. The letters indicate the directory or file's owner.

What is needed is a general hierarchy (i.e., a tree of directories). With this approach, each user can have as many directories as are needed so that files can be grouped together in natural ways. This approach is shown in Fig. 5-6(c). Here, the directories *A*, *B*, and *C* contained in the root directory each belong to a different user, two of whom have created subdirectories for projects they are working on.

5.2.2 Path Names

When the file system is organized as a directory tree, some way is needed for specifying file names. Two different methods are commonly used. In the first method, each file is given an **absolute path name** consisting of the path from the root directory to the file. As an example, the path */usr/ast/mailbox* means that the root directory contains a subdirectory *usr*, which in turn contains a subdirectory *ast*, which contains the file *mailbox*. Absolute path names always start at the root directory and are unique. In UNIX the components of the path are separated by /. In MS-DOS the separator is \. In MULTICS it is >. No matter which character is used, if the first character of the path name is the separator, then the path is absolute.

The other kind of name is the **relative path name**. This is used in conjunction with the concept of the **working directory** (also called the **current directory**). A user can designate one directory as the current working directory, in which case all path names not beginning at the root directory are taken relative to the working directory. For example, if the current working directory is */usr/ast*, then the file whose absolute path is */usr/ast/mailbox* can be referenced simply as *mailbox*. In other words, the UNIX command

cp /usr/ast/mailbox /usr/ast/mailbox.bak

and the command

cp mailbox mailbox.bak

do exactly the same thing if the working directory is */usr/ast*. The relative form is often more convenient, but it does the same thing as the absolute form.

Some programs need to access a specific file without regard to what the working directory is. In that case, they should always use absolute path names. For example, a spelling checker might need to read */usr/lib/dictionary* to do its work. It should use the full, absolute path name in this case because it does not know what the working directory will be when it is called. The absolute path name will always work, no matter what the working directory is.

Of course, if the spelling checker needs a large number of files from */usr/lib*, an alternative approach is for it to issue a system call to change its working directory to */usr/lib*, and then use just *dictionary* as the first parameter to *open*. By explicitly changing the working directory, it knows for sure where it is in the directory tree, so it can then use relative paths.

In most systems, each process has its own working directory, so when a process changes its working directory and later exits, no other processes are affected and no traces of the change are left behind in the file system. In this way it is always perfectly safe for a process to change its working directory whenever that is convenient. On the other hand, if a library procedure changes the working directory and does not change back to where it was when it is finished, the rest of the program may not work since its assumption about where it is may now be invalid. For this reason, library procedures rarely change the working directory, and when they must, they always change it back again before returning.

Most operating systems that support a hierarchical directory system have two special entries in every directory, ".." and "..", generally pronounced "dot" and "dotdot." Dot refers to the current directory; dotdot refers to its parent. To see how these are used, consider the UNIX file tree of Fig. 5-7. A certain process has */usr/ast* as its working directory. It can use .. to go up the tree. For example, it can copy the file */usr/lib/dictionary* to its own directory using the shell command

cp ../lib/dictionary .

The first path instructs the system to go upward (to the *usr* directory), then to go down to the directory *lib* to find the file *dictionary*.

The second argument names the current directory. When the *cp* command gets a directory name (including dot) as its last argument, it copies all the files there. Of course, a more normal way to do the copy would be to type

cp /usr/lib/dictionary .

Here the use of dot saves the user the trouble of typing *dictionary* a second time.

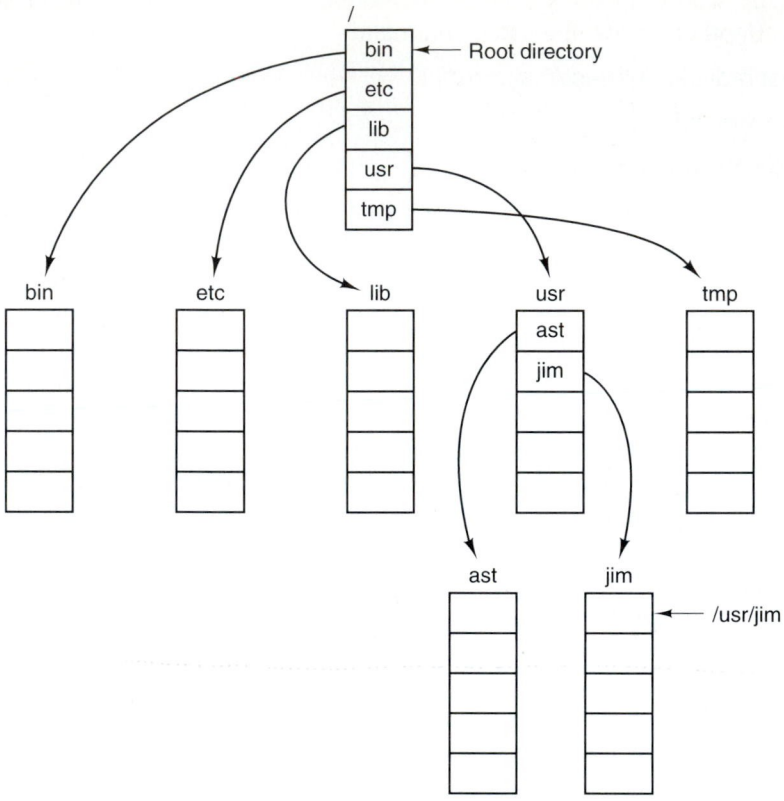

Figure 5-7. A UNIX directory tree.

5.2.3 Directory Operations

The allowed system calls for managing directories exhibit more variation from system to system than system calls for files. To give an impression of what they are and how they work, we will give a sample (taken from UNIX).

1. **CREATE**. A directory is created. It is empty except for dot and dot-dot, which are put there automatically by the system (or in a few cases, by the *mkdir* program).

2. **DELETE**. A directory is deleted. Only an empty directory can be deleted. A directory containing only dot and dotdot is considered empty as these usually cannot be deleted.

3. **OPENDIR**. Directories can be read. For example, to list all the files in a directory, a listing program opens the directory to read out the names of all the files it contains. Before a directory can be read, it must be opened, analogous to opening and reading a file.

4. **CLOSEDIR**. When a directory has been read, it should be closed to free up internal table space.

5. **READDIR**. This call returns the next entry in an open directory. Formerly, it was possible to read directories using the usual READ system call, but that approach has the disadvantage of forcing the programmer to know and deal with the internal structure of directories. In contrast, READDIR always returns one entry in a standard format, no matter which of the possible directory structures is being used.

6. **RENAME**. In many respects, directories are just like files and can be renamed the same way files can be.

7. **LINK**. Linking is a technique that allows a file to appear in more than one directory. This system call specifies an existing file and a path name, and creates a link from the existing file to the name specified by the path. In this way, the same file may appear in multiple directories.

8. **UNLINK**. A directory entry is removed. If the file being unlinked is only present in one directory (the normal case), it is removed from the file system. If it is present in multiple directories, only the path name specified is removed. The others remain. In UNIX, the system call for deleting files (discussed earlier) is, in fact, UNLINK.

The above list gives the most important calls, but there are a few others as well, for example, for managing the protection information associated with a directory.

5.3 FILE SYSTEM IMPLEMENTATION

Now it is time to turn from the user's view of the file system to the implementor's view. Users are concerned with how files are named, what operations are allowed on them, what the directory tree looks like, and similar interface issues. Implementors are interested in how files and directories are stored, how disk space is managed, and how to make everything work efficiently and reliably. In the following sections we will examine a number of these areas to see what the issues and trade-offs are.

5.3.1 Implementing Files

Probably the most important issue in implementing file storage is keeping track of which disk blocks go with which file. Various methods are used in different operating systems. In this section, we will examine a few of them.

Contiguous Allocation

The simplest allocation scheme is to store each file as a contiguous block of data on the disk. Thus on a disk with 1K blocks, a 50K file would be allocated 50 consecutive blocks. This scheme has two significant advantages. First, it is simple to implement because keeping track of where a file's blocks are is reduced to remembering one number, the disk address of the first block. Second, the performance is excellent because the entire file can be read from the disk in a single operation.

Unfortunately, contiguous allocation also has two equally significant drawbacks. First, it is not feasible unless the maximum file size is known at the time the file is created. Without this information, the operating system does not know how much disk space to reserve. In systems where files must be written in a single blow, it can be used to great advantage, however.

The second disadvantage is the fragmentation of the disk that results from this allocation policy. Space is wasted that might otherwise have been used. Compaction of the disk is usually prohibitively expensive, although it can conceivably be done late at night when the system is otherwise idle.

Linked List Allocation

The second method for storing files is to keep each one as a linked list of disk blocks, as shown in Fig. 5-8. The first word of each block is used as a pointer to the next one. The rest of the block is for data.

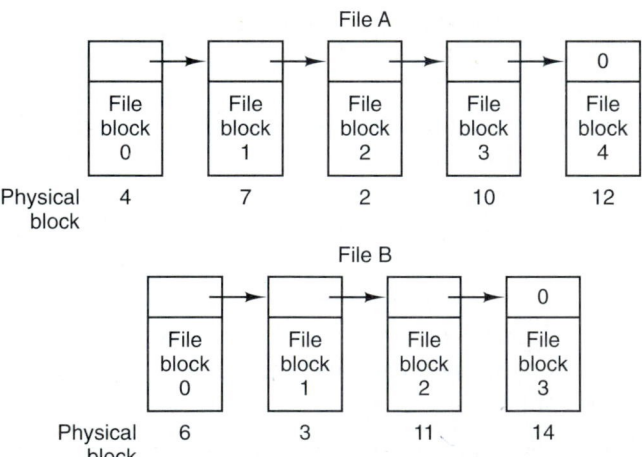

Figure 5-8. Storing a file as a linked list of disk blocks.

Unlike contiguous allocation, every disk block can be used in this method. No space is lost to disk fragmentation (except for internal fragmentation in the last block). Also, it is sufficient for the directory entry to merely store the disk address of the first block. The rest can be found starting there.

On the other hand, although reading a file sequentially is straightforward, random access is extremely slow. Also, the amount of data storage in a block is no longer a power of two because the pointer takes up a few bytes. While not fatal, having a peculiar size is less efficient because many programs read and write in blocks whose size is a power of two.

Linked List Allocation Using an Index

Both disadvantages of the linked list allocation can be eliminated by taking the pointer word from each disk block and putting it in a table or index in memory. Figure 5-9 shows what the table looks like for the example of Fig. 5-8. In both figures, we have two files. File *A* uses disk blocks 4, 7, 2, 10, and 12, in that order, and file *B* uses disk blocks 6, 3, 11, and 14, in that order. Using the table of Fig. 5-9, we can start with block 4 and follow the chain all the way to the end. The same can be done starting with block 6.

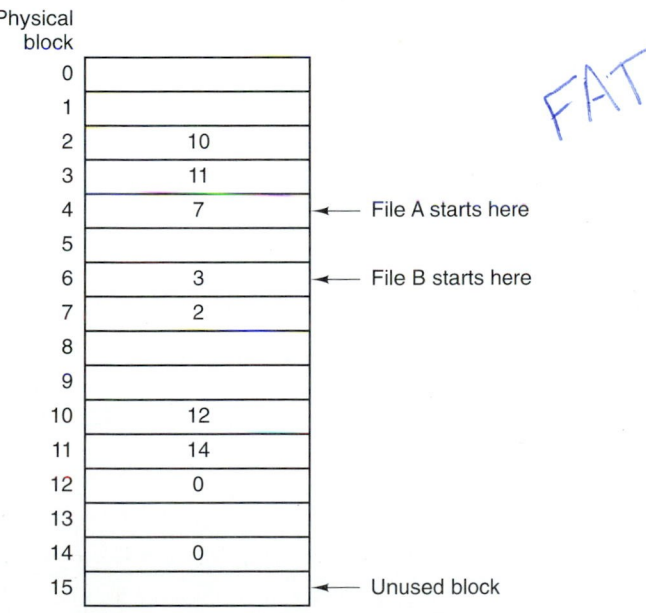

Figure 5-9. Linked list allocation using a table in main memory.

Using this organization, the entire block is available for data. Furthermore, random access is much easier. Although the chain must still be followed to find a given offset within the file, the chain is entirely in memory, so it can be followed without making any disk references. Like the previous method, it is sufficient for the directory entry to keep a single integer (the starting block number) and still be able to locate all the blocks, no matter how large the file is. MS-DOS uses this method for disk allocation.

The primary disadvantage of this method is that the entire table must be in memory all the time to make it work. With a large disk, say, 500,000 1K blocks (500M), the table will have 500,000 entries, each of which will have to be a minimum of 3 bytes. For speed in lookup, they should be 4 bytes. Thus the table will take up 1.5 or 2 megabytes all the time depending on whether the system is optimized for space or time. Although MS-DOS uses this mechanism, it avoids huge tables by using large blocks (up to 32K) on large disks.

I-nodes

Our last method for keeping track of which blocks belong to which file is to associate with each file a little table called an **i-node** (**index-node**), which lists the attributes and disk addresses of the file's blocks, as shown in Fig. 5-10.

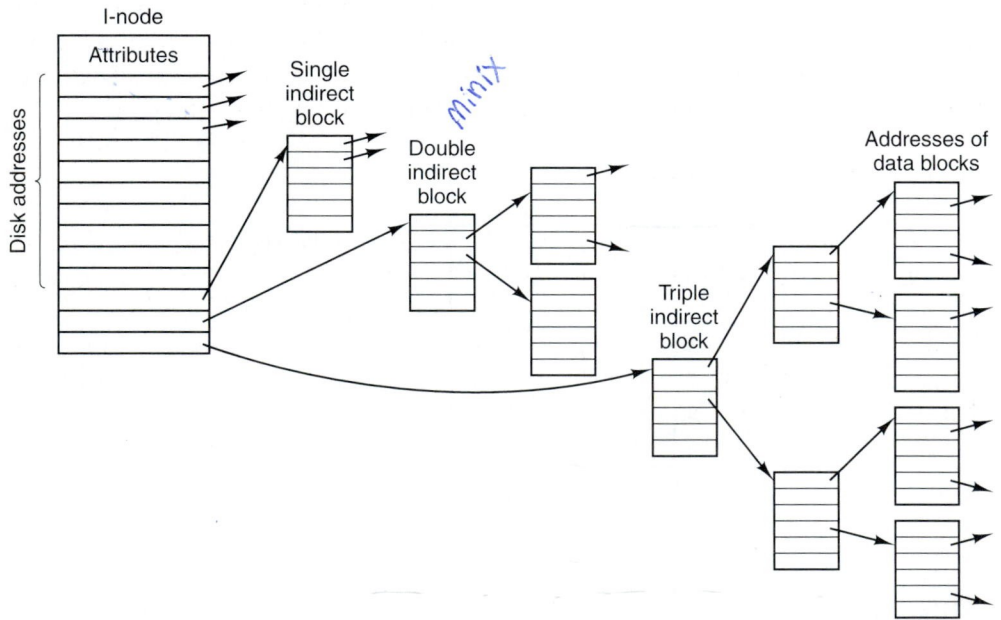

Figure 5-10. An i-node.

The first few disk addresses are stored in the i-node itself, so for small files, all the necessary information is right in the i-node, which is fetched from disk to main memory when the file is opened. For somewhat larger files, one of the addresses in the i-node is the address of a disk block called a **single indirect block**. This block contains additional disk addresses. If this still is not enough, another address in the i-node, called a **double indirect block**, contains the address of a block that contains a list of single indirect blocks. Each of these single indirect blocks points to a few hundred data blocks. If even this is not enough, a **triple indirect block** can also be used. UNIX uses this scheme.

5.3.2 Implementing Directories

Before a file can be read, it must be opened. When a file is opened, the operating system uses the path name supplied by the user to locate the directory entry. The directory entry provides the information needed to find the disk blocks. Depending on the system, this information may be the disk address of the entire file (contiguous allocation), the number of the first block (both linked list schemes), or the number of the i-node. In all cases, the main function of the directory system is to map the ASCII name of the file onto the information needed to locate the data.

A closely related issue is where the attributes should be stored. One obvious possibility is to store them directly in the directory entry. Many systems do precisely that. For systems that use i-nodes, another possibility is to store the attributes in the i-node, rather than in the directory entry. As we shall see later, this method has certain advantages over putting them in the directory entry.

Directories in CP/M

Let us start our study of directories with a particularly simple example, that of CP/M (Golden and Pechura, 1986), illustrated in Fig. 5-11. In this system, there is only one directory, so all the file system has to do to look up a file name is search the one and only directory. When it finds the entry, it also has the disk block numbers, since they are stored right in the directory entry, as are all the attributes. If the file uses more disk blocks than fit in one entry, the file is allocated additional directory entries.

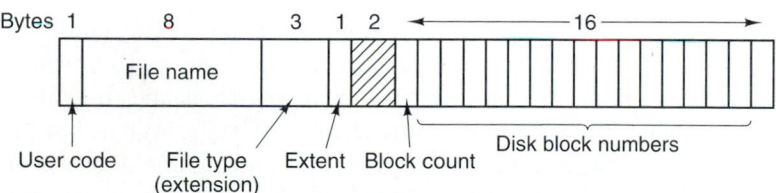

Figure 5-11. A directory entry that contains the disk block numbers for each file.

The fields in Fig. 5-11 have the following meanings. The *User code* field keeps track of which user owns the file. During a search, only those entries belonging to the currently logged-in user are checked. The next two fields give the name and extension of the file. The *Extent* field is needed because a file larger than 16 blocks occupies multiple directory entries. This field is used to tell which entry comes first, second, and so on. The *Block count* field tells how many of the 16 potential disk block entries are in use. The final 16 fields contain the disk block numbers themselves. The last block may not be full, so the system has no way to determine the exact size of a file down to the last byte (i.e., it keeps track of file sizes in blocks, not bytes).

Directories in MS-DOS

Now let us consider some examples of systems with hierarchical directory trees. Figure 5-12 shows an MS-DOS directory entry. It is 32 bytes long and contains the file name, attributes, and the number of the first disk block. The first block number is used as an index into a table of the type of Fig. 5-9. By following the chain, all the blocks can be found.

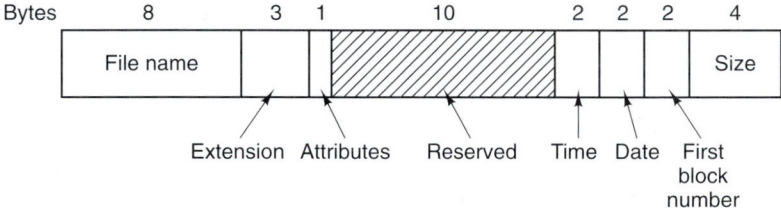

Figure 5-12. The MS-DOS directory entry.

In MS-DOS, directories may contain other directories, leading to a hierarchical file system. It is common in MS-DOS that different application programs each start out by creating a directory in the root directory and putting all their files there, so that different applications do not conflict.

Directories in UNIX

The directory structure traditionally used in UNIX is extremely simple, as shown in Fig. 5-13. Each entry contains just a file name and its i-node number. All the information about the type, size, times, ownership, and disk blocks is contained in the i-node. Some UNIX systems have a different layout, but in all cases, a directory entry ultimately contains only an ASCII string and an i-node number.

When a file is opened, the file system must take the file name supplied and locate its disk blocks. Let us consider how the path name */usr/ast/mbox* is looked up. We will use UNIX as an example, but the algorithm is basically the same for all hierarchical directory systems. First the file system locates the root directory. In UNIX its i-node is located at a fixed place on the disk.

Then it looks up the first component of the path, *usr*, in the root directory to find the i-node number of the file */usr*. Locating an i-node from its number is

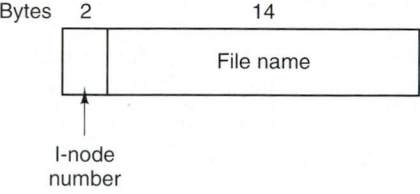

Figure 5-13. A UNIX directory entry.

straightforward, since each one has a fixed location on the disk. From this i-node, the system locates the directory for */usr* and looks up the next component, *ast*, in it. When it has found the entry for *ast*, it has the i-node for the directory */usr/ast*. From this i-node it can find the directory itself and look up *mbox*. The i-node for this file is then read into memory and kept there until the file is closed. The lookup process is illustrated in Fig. 5-14.

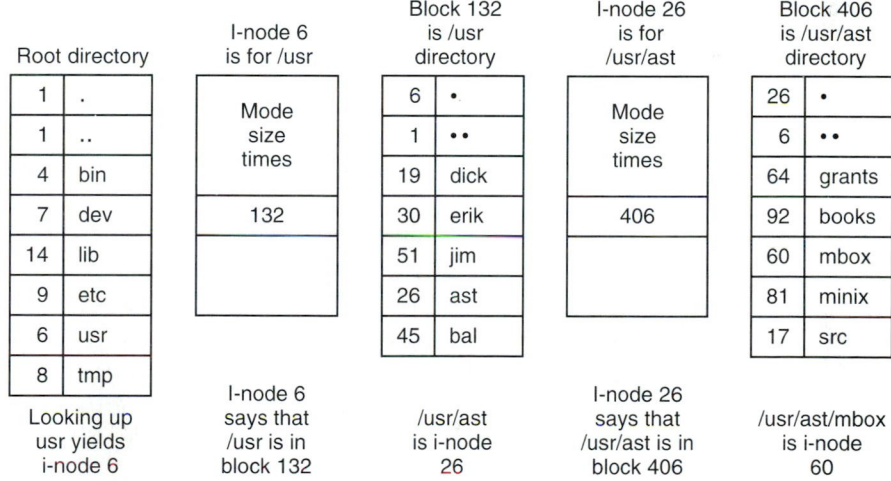

Figure 5-14. The steps in looking up */usr/ast/mbox*.

Relative path names are looked up the same way as absolute ones, only starting from the working directory instead of starting from the root directory. Every directory has entries for . and .. which are put there when the directory is created. The entry . has the i-node number for the current directory, and the entry for .. has the i-node number for the parent directory. Thus, a procedure looking up *../dick/prog.c* simply looks up .. in the working directory, finds the i-node number for the parent directory, and searches that directory for *dick*. No special mechanism is needed to handle these names. As far as the directory system is concerned, they are just ordinary ASCII strings, just the same as any other names.

5.3.3 Disk Space Management

Files are normally stored on disk, so management of disk space is a major concern to file system designers. Two general strategies are possible for storing an n byte file: n consecutive bytes of disk space are allocated, or the file is split up into a number of (not necessarily) contiguous blocks. The same trade-off is present in memory management systems between pure segmentation and paging.

Storing a file as a contiguous sequence of bytes has the obvious problem that if a file grows, it will probably have to be moved on the disk. The same problem holds for segments in memory, except that moving a segment in memory is a relatively fast operation compared to moving a file from one disk position to another. For this reason, nearly all file systems chop files up into fixed-size blocks that need not be adjacent.

Block Size

Once it has been decided to store files in fixed-size blocks, the question arises of how big the block should be. Given the way disks are organized, the sector, the track and the cylinder are obvious candidates for the unit of allocation. In a paging system, the page size is also a major contender.

Having a large allocation unit, such as a cylinder, means that every file, even a 1-byte file, ties up an entire cylinder. Studies (Mullender and Tanenbaum, 1984) have shown that the median file size in UNIX environments is about 1K, so allocating a 32K cylinder for each file would waste 31/32 or 97 percent of the total disk space. On the other hand, using a small allocation unit means that each file will consist of many blocks. Reading each block normally requires a seek and a rotational delay, so reading a file consisting of many small blocks will be slow.

As an example, consider a disk with 32,768 bytes per track, a rotation time of 16.67 msec, and an average seek time of 30 msec. The time in milliseconds to read a block of k bytes is then the sum of the seek, rotational delay, and transfer times:

$$30 + 8.3 + (k/32768) \times 16.67$$

The solid curve of Fig. 5-15 shows the data rate for such a disk as a function of block size. If we make the gross assumption that all files are 1K (the measured median size), the dashed curve of Fig. 5-15 gives the disk space efficiency. The bad news is that good space utilization (block size < 2K) means low data rates and vice versa. Time efficiency and space efficiency are inherently in conflict.

The usual compromise is to choose a block size of 512, 1K or 2K bytes. If a 1K block size is chosen on a disk with a 512-byte sector size, then the file system will always read or write two consecutive sectors and treat them as a single, indivisible unit. Whatever decision is made, it should probably be re-evaluated periodically, since, as with all aspects of computer technology, users take advantage

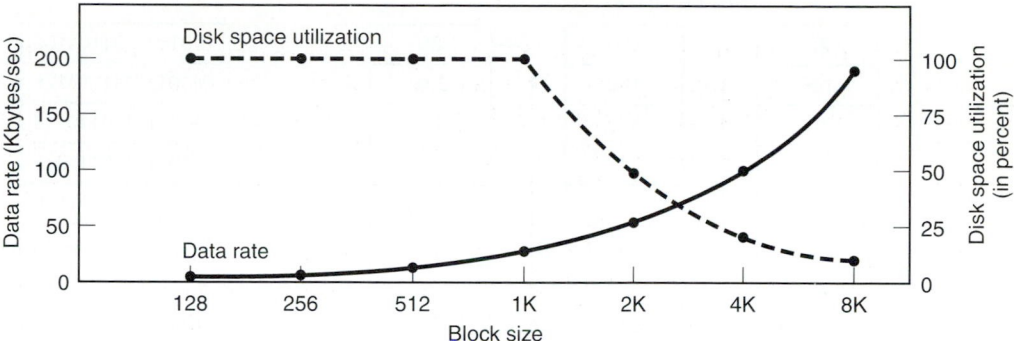

Figure 5-15. The solid curve (left-hand scale) gives the data rate of a disk. The dashed curve (right-hand scale) gives the disk space efficiency. All files are 1K.

of more abundant resources by demanding even more. One system manager reports that the average size of files in the university system he manages has increased slowly over the years, and that in 1997 the average size of files has grown to 12K for students and 15K for faculty.

Keeping Track of Free Blocks

Once a block size has been chosen, the next issue is how to keep track of free blocks. Two methods are widely used, as shown in Fig. 5-16. The first one consists of using a linked list of disk blocks, with each block holding as many free disk block numbers as will fit. With a 1K block and a 32-bit disk block number, each block on the free list holds the numbers of 255 free blocks. (One slot is needed for the pointer to the next block). A 200M disk needs a free list of maximum 804 blocks to hold all 200K disk block numbers. Often free blocks are used to hold the free list.

The other free space management technique is the bit map. A disk with n blocks requires a bit map with n bits. Free blocks are represented by 1s in the map, allocated blocks by 0s (or vice versa). A 200M disk requires 200K bits for the map, which requires only 25 blocks. It is not surprising that the bit map requires less space, since it uses 1 bit per block, versus 32 bits in the linked list model. Only if the disk is nearly full will the linked list scheme require fewer blocks than the bit map.

If there is enough main memory to hold the bit map, that method is generally preferable. If, however, only 1 block of memory can be spared for keeping track of free disk blocks, and the disk is nearly full, then the linked list may be better. With only 1 block of the bit map in memory, it may turn out that no free blocks can be found on it, causing disk accesses to read the rest of the bit map. When a fresh block of the linked list is loaded into memory, 255 disk blocks can be allocated before having to go to the disk to fetch the next block from the list.

Free disk blocks: 16, 17, 18

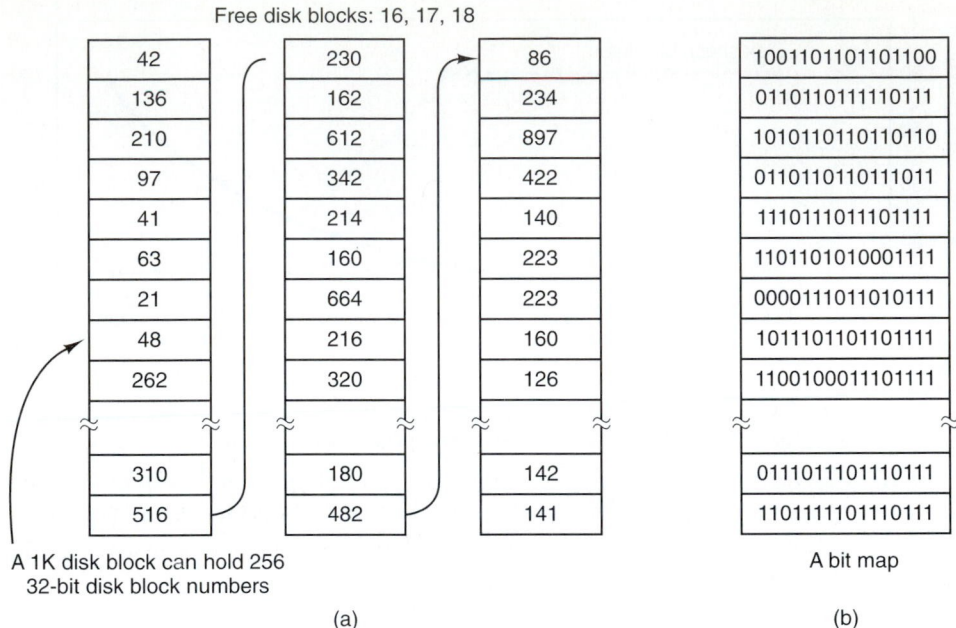

A 1K disk block can hold 256
32-bit disk block numbers

A bit map

(a)   (b)

Figure 5-16. (a) Storing the free list on a linked list. (b) A bit map.

5.3.4 File System Reliability

Destruction of a file system is often a far greater disaster than destruction of a computer. If a computer is destroyed by fire, lightning surges, or a cup of coffee poured onto the keyboard, it is annoying and will cost money, but generally a replacement can be purchased with a minimum of fuss. Inexpensive personal computers can even be replaced within a few hours by just going to the dealer (except at universities where issuing a purchase order takes three committees, five signatures, and 90 days).

If a computer's file system is irrevocably lost, whether due to hardware, software, or rats gnawing on the floppy disks, restoring all the information will be difficult, time consuming, and in many cases, impossible. For the people whose programs, documents, customer files, tax records, data bases, marketing plans, or other data are gone forever, the consequences can be catastrophic. While the file system cannot offer any protection against physical destruction of the equipment and media, it can help protect the information. In this section we will look at some of the issues involved in safeguarding the file system.

Disks may have bad blocks, as we pointed out in Chap. 3. Floppy disks are generally perfect when they leave the factory, but they can develop bad blocks during use. Winchester disks frequently have bad blocks right from the start: it is just too expensive to manufacture them completely free of all defects. In fact, older hard disks used to be supplied with a list of the bad blocks discovered by the manufacturer's tests. On such disks a sector is reserved for a bad block list. When the controller is first initialized, it reads the bad block list and picks a spare block (or track) to replace the defective ones, recording the mapping in the bad block list. Henceforth, all requests for the bad block will use the spare. When new errors are discovered this list is updated as part of a low-level format.

There has been a steady improvement in manufacturing techniques, so bad blocks are less common than they once were. However, they still occur. The controller on a modern disk drive is very sophisticated, as noted in Chap. 3. On these disks, tracks are at least one sector bigger than needed, so that at least one bad spot can be skipped by leaving it in a gap between two consecutive sectors. There are also a few spare sectors per cylinder so the controller can do automatic sector remapping if it notices that a sector needs more than a certain number of retries to be read or written. Thus the user is usually unaware of bad blocks or their management. Nevertheless, when a modern IDE or SCSI disk fails, it will usually fail horribly, because it has run out of spare sectors. SCSI disks provide a "recovered error" when they remap a block. If the driver notes this and prints a message on the keyboard the user will know it is time to buy a new disk when these messages begin to appear frequently.

There is a simple software solution to the bad block problem, suitable for use on older disks. This approach requires the user or file system to carefully construct a file containing all the bad blocks. This technique removes them from the free list, so they will never occur in data files. As long as the bad block file is never read or written, no problems will arise. Care has to be taken during disk backups to avoid reading this file.

Backups

Even with a clever strategy for dealing with bad blocks, it is important to back up the files frequently. After all, automatically switching to a spare track after a crucial data block has been ruined is somewhat akin to locking the barn door after the prize race horse has escaped.

File systems on floppy disk can be backed up by just copying the entire floppy disk to a blank one. File systems on small winchester disks can be backed up by dumping the entire disk to magnetic tape. Current technologies include 150M cartridge tapes, and 8G Exabyte or DAT tapes.

For large winchesters (e.g., 10 GB), backing up the entire drive on tape is awkward and time consuming. One strategy that is easy to implement but wastes half the storage is to provide each computer with two drives instead of one. Both drives are divided into two halves: data and backup. Each night the data portion of drive 0 is copied to the backup portion of drive 1, and vice versa, as shown in Fig. 5-17. In this way, if one drive is completely ruined, no information is lost.

An alternative to dumping the entire file system every day is to make **incremental dumps**. The simplest form of incremental dumping is to make a complete

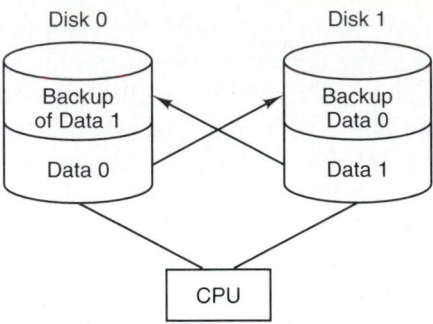

Figure 5-17. Backing up each drive on the other one wastes half the storage.

dump periodically, say weekly or monthly, and to make a daily dump of only those files that have been modified since the last full dump. A better scheme is to dump only those files that have changed since they were last dumped.

To implement this method, a list of the dump times for each file must be kept on disk. The dump program then checks each file on the disk. If it has been modified since it was last dumped, it is dumped again and its time-of-last-dump is changed to the current time. If done on a monthly cycle, this method requires 31 daily dump tapes, one per day, plus enough tapes to hold a full dump, made once a month. Other more complex schemes that use fewer tapes are also in use.

Automatic methods using multiple disks are also used. For example, **mirroring** uses two disks. Writes go to both disks, and reads come from one. The write to the mirror disk is delayed a bit, so it can be done when the system is idle. Such a system can continue to run in "degraded mode" when one disk fails, allowing a failed disk to be swapped and data to be recovered with no downtime.

File System Consistency

Another area where reliability is an issue is file system consistency. Many file systems read blocks, modify them, and write them out later. If the system crashes before all the modified blocks have been written out, the file system can be left in an inconsistent state. This problem is especially critical if some of the blocks that have not been written out are i-node blocks, directory blocks, or blocks containing the free list.

To deal with the problem of inconsistent file systems, most computers have a utility program that checks file system consistency. It can be run whenever the system is booted, especially after a crash. The description below tells how such a utility works in UNIX and MINIX; other systems have something similar. These file system checkers verify each file system (disk) independently of the other ones.

Two kinds of consistency checks can be made: blocks and files. To check for block consistency, the program builds two tables, each one containing a counter for each block, initially set to 0. The counters in the first table keep track of how many times each block is present in a file; the counters in the second table record how often each block is present in the free list (or the bit map of free blocks).

The program then reads all the i-nodes. Starting from an i-node, it is possible to build a list of all the block numbers used in the corresponding file. As each block number is read, its counter in the first table is incremented. The program then examines the free list or bit map, to find all the blocks that are not in use. Each occurrence of a block in the free list results in its counter in the second table being incremented.

If the file system is consistent, each block will have a 1 either in the first table or in the second table, as illustrated in Fig. 5-18(a). However, as a result of a crash, the tables might look like Fig. 5-18(b), in which block 2 does not occur in either table. It will be reported as being a **missing block**. While missing blocks do no real harm, they do waste space and thus reduce the capacity of the disk. The solution to missing blocks is straightforward: the file system checker just adds them to the free list.

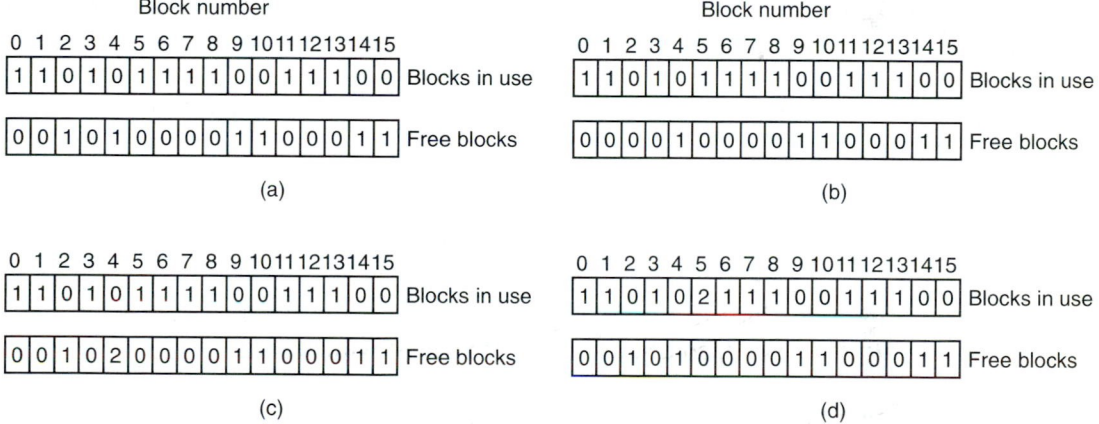

Figure 5-18. File system states. (a) Consistent. (b) Missing block. (c) Duplicate block in free list. (d) Duplicate data block.

Another situation that might occur is that of Fig. 5-18(c). Here we see a block, number 4, that occurs twice in the free list. (Duplicates can occur only if the free list is really a list; with a bit map it is impossible.) The solution here is also simple: rebuild the free list.

The worst thing that can happen is that the same data block is present in two or more files, as shown in Fig. 5-18(d) with block 5. If either of these files is removed, block 5 will be put on the free list, leading to a situation in which the same block is both in use and free at the same time. If both files are removed, the block will be put onto the free list twice.

The appropriate action for the file system checker to take is to allocate a free block, copy the contents of block 5 into it, and insert the copy into one of the files.

In this way, the information content of the files is unchanged (although almost assuredly garbled), but the file system structure is at least made consistent. The error should be reported, to allow the user to inspect the damage.

In addition to checking to see that each block is properly accounted for, the file system checker also checks the directory system. It too, uses a table of counters, but these are per file, rather than per block. It starts at the root directory and recursively descends the tree, inspecting each directory in the file system. For every file in every directory, it increments the counter for that file's i-node (see Fig. 5-13 for the layout of a directory entry).

When it is all done, it has a list, indexed by i-node number, telling how many directories point to that i-node. It then compares these numbers with the link counts stored in the i-nodes themselves. In a consistent file system, both counts will agree. However, two kinds of errors can occur: the link count in the i-node can be too high or it can be too low.

If the link count is higher than the number of directory entries, then even if all the files are removed from the directories, the count will still be nonzero and the i-node will not be removed. This error is not serious, but it wastes space on the disk with files that are not in any directory. It should be fixed by setting the link count in the i-node to the correct value.

The other error is potentially catastrophic. If two directory entries are linked to a file, but the i-node says that there is only one, when either directory entry is removed, the i-node count will go to zero. When an i-node count goes to zero, the file system marks it as unused and releases all of its blocks. This action will result in one of the directories now pointing to an unused i-node, whose blocks may soon be assigned to other files. Again, the solution is just to force the link count in the i-node to the actual number of directory entries.

These two operations, checking blocks and checking directories, are often integrated for efficiency reasons (i.e., only one pass over the i-nodes is required). Other heuristic checks are also possible. For example, directories have a definite format, with i-node numbers and ASCII names. If an i-node number is larger than the number of i-nodes on the disk, the directory has been damaged.

Furthermore, each i-node has a mode, some of which are legal but strange, such as 0007, which allows the owner and his group no access at all, but allows outsiders to read, write, and execute the file. It might be useful to at least report files that give outsiders more rights than the owner. Directories with more than, say, 1000 entries are also suspicious. Files located in user directories, but which are owned by the super-user and have the SETUID bit on, are potential security problems. With a little effort, one can put together a fairly long list of legal, but peculiar, situations that might be worth reporting.

The previous paragraphs have discussed the problem of protecting the user against crashes. Some file systems also worry about protecting the user against himself. If the user intends to type

rm *.o

to remove all the files ending with *.o* (compiler generated object files), but accidentally types

rm * .o

(note the space after the asterisk), *rm* will remove all the files in the current directory and then complain that it cannot find *.o*. In MS-DOS and some other systems, when a file is removed, all that happens is that a bit is set in the directory or i-node marking the file as removed. No disk blocks are returned to the free list until they are actually needed. Thus, if the user discovers the error immediately, it is possible to run a special utility program that "unremoves" (i.e., restores) the removed files. In WINDOWS 95, files that are removed are placed in a special *recycled* directory, from which they can later be retrieved if need be. Of course, no storage is reclaimed until they are actually deleted from this directory.

5.3.5 File System Performance

Access to disk is much slower than access to memory. Reading a memory word typically takes tens of nanoseconds. Reading a block from a hard disk may take fifty microseconds, a factor of four slower per 32-bit word, but to this must be added 10 to 20 milliseconds to seek to the track and then wait for the desired sector to arrive under the read head. If only a single word is needed, the memory access is of the order of 100,000 times as fast as disk access. As a result of this difference in access time, many file systems have been designed to reduce the number of disk accesses needed.

The most common technique used to reduce disk accesses is the **block cache** or **buffer cache**. (Cache is pronounced "cash," and is derived from the French *cacher*, meaning to hide.) In this context, a cache is a collection of blocks that logically belong on the disk but are being kept in memory for performance reasons.

Various algorithms can be used to manage the cache, but a common one is to check all read requests to see if the needed block is in the cache. If it is, the read request can be satisfied without a disk access. If the block is not in the cache, it is first read into the cache, and then copied to wherever it is needed. Subsequent requests for the same block can be satisfied from the cache.

When a block has to be loaded into a full cache, some block has to be removed and rewritten to the disk if it has been modified since being brought in. This situation is very much like paging, and all the usual paging algorithms described in Chap. 4, such as FIFO, second chance, and LRU, are applicable. One pleasant difference between paging and caching is that cache references are relatively infrequent, so that it is feasible to keep all the blocks in exact LRU order with linked lists.

Unfortunately, there is a catch. Now that we have a situation in which exact LRU is possible, it turns out that LRU is undesirable. The problem has to do with the crashes and file system consistency discussed in the previous section. If a critical block, such as an i-node block, is read into the cache and modified, but not rewritten to the disk, a crash will leave the file system in an inconsistent state. If the i-node block is put at the end of the LRU chain, it may be quite a while before it reaches the front and is rewritten to the disk.

Furthermore, some blocks, such as double indirect blocks, are rarely referenced two times within a short interval. These considerations lead to a modified LRU scheme, taking two factors into account:

1. Is the block likely to be needed again soon?

2. Is the block essential to the consistency of the file system?

For both questions, blocks can be divided into categories such as i-node blocks, indirect blocks, directory blocks, full data blocks, and partly full data blocks. Blocks that will probably not be needed again soon go on the front, rather than the rear of the LRU list, so their buffers will be reused quickly. Blocks that might be needed again soon, such as a partly full block that is being written, go on the end of the list, so they will stay around for a long time.

The second question is independent of the first one. If the block is essential to the file system consistency (basically, everything except data blocks), and it has been modified, it should be written to disk immediately, regardless of which end of the LRU list it is put on. By writing critical blocks quickly, we greatly reduce the probability that a crash will wreck the file system.

Even with this measure to keep the file system integrity intact, it is undesirable to keep data blocks in the cache too long before writing them out. Consider the plight of someone who is using a personal computer to write a book. Even if our writer periodically tells the editor to write the file being edited to the disk, there is a good chance that everything will still be in the cache and nothing on the disk. If the system crashes, the file system structure will not be corrupted, but a whole day's work will be lost.

This situation need not happen very often before we have a fairly unhappy user. Systems take two approaches to dealing with it. The UNIX way is to have a system call, SYNC, which forces all the modified blocks out onto the disk immediately. When the system is started up, a program, usually called *update*, is started up in the background to sit in an endless loop issuing SYNC calls, sleeping for 30 sec between calls. As a result, no more than 30 seconds of work is lost due to a crash.

The MS-DOS way is to write every modified block to disk as soon as it has been written. Caches in which all modified blocks are written back to the disk immediately are called **write-through caches**. They require much more disk I/O than nonwrite-through caches. The difference between these two approaches can be seen when a program writes a 1K block full, one character at a time. UNIX will collect all the characters in the cache and write the block out once every 30 seconds, or whenever the block is removed from the cache. MS-DOS will make a disk access for every character written. Of course, most programs do internal buffering, so they normally write not a character, but a line or a larger unit on each WRITE system call.

A consequence of this difference in caching strategy is that just removing a (floppy) disk from a UNIX system without doing a SYNC will almost always result in lost data, and frequently in a corrupted file system as well. With MS-DOS, no problem arises. These differing strategies were chosen because UNIX was developed in an environment in which all disks were hard disks and not removable, whereas MS-DOS started out in the floppy disk world. As hard disks become the norm, even on small microcomputers, the UNIX approach, with its better efficiency, will definitely be the way to go.

Caching is not the only way to increase the performance of a file system. Another important technique is to reduce the amount of disk arm motion by putting blocks that are likely to be accessed in sequence close to each other, preferably in the same cylinder. When an output file is written, the file system has to allocate the blocks one at a time, as they are needed. If the free blocks are recorded in a bit map, and the whole bit map is in main memory, it is easy enough to choose a free block as close as possible to the previous block. With a free list, part of which is on disk, it is much harder to allocate blocks close together.

However, even with a free list, some block clustering can be done. The trick is to keep track of disk storage not in blocks, but in groups of consecutive blocks. If a track consists of 64 sectors of 512 bytes, the system could use 1K blocks (2 sectors), but allocate disk storage in units of 2 blocks (4 sectors). This is not the same as having a 2K disk block, since the cache would still use 1K blocks and disk transfers would still be 1K but reading a file sequentially on an otherwise idle system would reduce the number of seeks by a factor of two, considerably improving performance.

A variation on the same theme is to take account of rotational positioning. When allocating blocks, the system attempts to place consecutive blocks in a file in the same cylinder, but interleaved for maximum throughput. Thus, if a disk has a rotation time of 16.67 msec and it takes about 4 msec for a user process to request and get a disk block, each block should be placed at least a quarter of the way around from its predecessor.

Another performance bottleneck in systems that use i-nodes or anything equivalent to i-nodes is that reading even a short file requires two disk accesses: one for the i-node and one for the block. The usual i-node placement is shown in Fig. 5-19(a). Here all the i-nodes are near the beginning of the disk, so the average distance between an i-node and its blocks will be about half the number of cylinders, requiring long seeks.

One easy performance improvement is to put the i-nodes in the middle of the disk, rather than at the start, thus reducing the average seek between the i-node and the first block by a factor of two. Another idea, shown in Fig. 5-19(b), is to

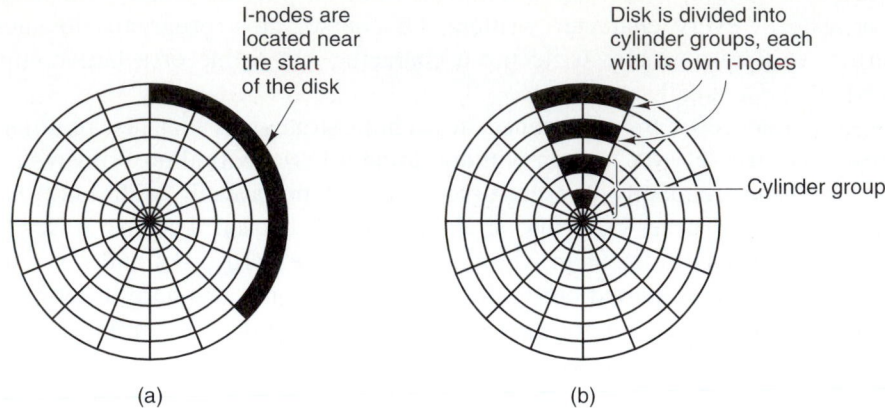

Figure 5-19. (a) I-nodes placed at the start of the disk. (b) Disk divided into cylinder groups, each with its own blocks and i-nodes.

divide the disk into cylinder groups, each with its own i-nodes, blocks, and free list (McKusick et al., 1984). When creating a new file, any i-node can be chosen, but an attempt is made to find a block in the same cylinder group as the i-node. If none is available, then a block in a nearby cylinder group is used.

5.3.6 Log-Structured File Systems

Changes in technology are putting pressure on current file systems. In particular, CPUs keep getting faster, disks are becoming much bigger and cheaper (but not much faster), and memories are growing exponentially in size. The one parameter that is not improving by leaps and bounds is disk seek time. The combination of these factors means that a performance bottleneck is arising in many file systems. Research done at Berkeley attempted to alleviate this problem by designing a completely new kind of file system, LFS (the **Log-structured File System**). In this section we will briefly describe how LFS works. For a more complete treatment, see (Rosenblum and Ousterhout, 1991).

The idea that drove the LFS design is that as CPUs get faster and RAM memories get larger, disk caches are increasingly rapidly. As a consequence, it is now possible to satisfy a very substantial fraction of all read requests directly from the file system cache, with no disk access needed. It follows from this observation, that in the future, most disk accesses will be writes, so the read-ahead mechanism used in some file systems to fetch blocks before they are needed no longer gains much performance.

To make matters worse, in most file systems, writes are done in very small chunks. Small writes are highly inefficient, since a 50-microsec disk write is typically preceded by a 10-msec seek and a 6-msec rotational delay. With these parameters, disk efficiency drops to a fraction of 1 percent.

To see where all the small writes come from, consider creating a new file on a UNIX system. To write this file, the i-node for the directory, the directory block, the i-node for the file, and the file itself must all be written. While these writes can be delayed, doing so exposes the file system to serious consistency problems if a crash occurs before the writes are done. For this reason, the i-node writes are generally done immediately.

From this reasoning, the LFS designers decided to re-implement the UNIX file system in such a way as to achieve the full bandwidth of the disk, even in the face of a workload consisting in large part of small random writes. The basic idea is to structure the entire disk as a log. Periodically, and when there is a special need for it, all the pending writes being buffered in memory are collected into a single segment and written to the disk as a single contiguous segment at the end of the log. A single segment may thus contain i-nodes, directory blocks, and data blocks, all mixed together. At the start of each segment is a segment summary, telling what can be found in the segment. If the average segment can be made to be about 1 MB, almost the full bandwidth of the disk can be utilized.

In this design, i-nodes still exist and have the same structure as in UNIX, but they are now scattered all over the log, instead of being at a fixed position on the disk. Nevertheless, when an i-node is located, locating the blocks is done in the usual way. Of course, finding an i-node is now much harder, since its address cannot simply be calculated from its i-number, as in UNIX. To make it possible to find i-nodes, an i-node map, indexed by i-number, is maintained. Entry i in this map points to i-node i on the disk. The map is kept on disk, but it is also cached, so the most heavily used parts will be in memory most of the time.

To summarize what we have said so far, all writes are initially buffered in memory, and periodically all the buffered writes are written to the disk in a single segment, at the end of the log. Opening a file now consists of using the map to locate the i-node for the file. Once the i-node has been located, the addresses of the blocks can be found from it. All of the blocks will themselves be in segments, somewhere in the log.

If disks were infinitely large, the above description would be the entire story. However, real disks are finite, so eventually the log will occupy the entire disk, at which time no new segments can be written to the log. Fortunately, many existing segments may have blocks that are no longer needed, for example, if a file is overwritten, its i-node will now point to the new blocks, but the old ones will still be occupying space in previously written segments.

To deal with both of these problems, LFS has a **cleaner** thread that spends its time scanning the log circularly to compact it. It starts out by reading the summary of the first segment in the log to see which i-nodes and files are there. It then checks the current i-node map to see if the i-nodes are still current and file blocks are still in use. If not, that information is discarded. The i-nodes and blocks that are still in use go into memory to be written out in the next segment. The orginal segment is then marked as free, so the log can use it for new data. In this manner, the cleaner moves along the log, removing old segments from the back and putting any live data into memory for rewriting in the next segment. Consequently, the disk is a big circular buffer, with the writer thread adding new segments to the front and the cleaner thread removing old ones from the back.

The bookkeeping here is nontrivial, since when a file block is written back to a new segment, the i-node of the file (somewhere in the log) must be located, updated, and put into memory to be written out in the next segment. The i-node map must then be updated to point to the new copy. Nevertheless, it is possible to do the administration, and the performance results show that all this complexity is worthwhile. Measurements given in the papers cited above show that LFS outperforms UNIX by an order of magnitude on small writes, while having a performance that is as good or better than UNIX for reads and large writes.

5.4 SECURITY

File systems often contain information that is highly valuable to their users. Protecting this information against unauthorized usage is therefore a major concern of all file systems. In the following sections we will look at a variety of issues concerned with security and protection. These issues apply equally well to timesharing systems as to networks of personal computers connected to shared servers via local area networks.

5.4.1 The Security Environment

The terms "security" and "protection" are often used interchangeably. Nevertheless, it is frequently useful to make a distinction between the general problems involved in making sure that files are not read or modified by unauthorized persons, which include technical, managerial, legal, and political issues on the one hand, and the specific operating system mechanisms used to provide security, on the other. To avoid confusion, we will use the term **security** to refer to the overall problem, and the term **protection mechanisms** to refer to the specific operating system mechanisms used to safeguard information in the computer. The boundary between them is not well defined, however. First we will look at security; later on in the chapter we will look at protection.

Security has many facets. Two of the more important ones are data loss and intruders. Some of the common causes of data loss are:

1. Acts of God: fires, floods, earthquakes, wars, riots, or rats gnawing tapes or floppy disks.

2. Hardware or software errors: CPU malfunctions, unreadable disks or tapes, telecommunication errors, program bugs.

3. Human errors: incorrect data entry, wrong tape or disk mounted, wrong program run, lost disk or tape, or some other mistake.

Most of these can be dealt with by maintaining adequate backups, preferably far away from the original data.

A more interesting problem is what to do about intruders. These come in two varieties. Passive intruders just want to read files they are not authorized to read. Active intruders are more malicious; they want to make unauthorized changes to data. When designing a system to be secure against intruders, it is important to keep in mind the kind of intruder one is trying to protect against. Some common categories are:

1. Casual prying by nontechnical users. Many people have terminals to timesharing systems or networked personal computers on their desks, and human nature being what it is, some of them will read other people's electronic mail and other files if no barriers are placed in the way. Most UNIX systems, for example, have the default that all files are publicly readable.

2. Snooping by insiders. Students, system programmers, operators, and other technical personnel often consider it to be a personal challenge to break the security of the local computer system. They often are highly skilled and are willing to devote a substantial amount of time to the effort.

3. Determined attempt to make money. Some bank programmers have attempted to break into a banking system to steal from the bank. Schemes have varied from changing the software to truncate rather than round interest, keeping the fraction of a cent for themselves, to siphoning off accounts not used in years, to blackmail ("Pay me or I will destroy all the bank's records.").

4. Commercial or military espionage. Espionage refers to a serious and well-funded attempt by a competitor or a foreign country to steal programs, trade secrets, patents, technology, circuit designs, marketing plans, and so forth. Often this attempt will involve wiretapping or even erecting antennas directed at the computer to pick up its electromagnetic radiation.

It should be clear that trying to keep a hostile foreign government from stealing military secrets is quite a different matter from trying to keep students from inserting a funny message-of-the-day into the system. The amount of effort that one puts into security and protection clearly depends on who the enemy is thought to be.

Another aspect of the security problem is **privacy**: protecting individuals from misuse of information about them. This quickly gets into many legal and moral issues. Should the government compile dossiers on everyone in order to catch X-cheaters, where X is "welfare" or "tax," depending on your politics? Should the police be able to look up anything on anyone in order to stop organized crime? Do employers and insurance companies have rights? What happens when these rights conflict with individual rights? All of these issues are extremely important but are beyond the scope of this book.

5.4.2 Famous Security Flaws

Just as the transportation industry has the *Titanic* and the *Hindenburg*, computer security experts have a few things they would rather forget about. In this section we will look at some interesting security problems that have occurred in three different operating systems: UNIX, TENEX, and OS/360.

The UNIX utility *lpr*, which prints a file on the line printer, has an option to remove the file after it has been printed. In early versions of UNIX it was possible for anyone to use *lpr* to print, and then have the system remove, the password file.

Another way to break into UNIX was to link a file called *core* in the working directory to the password file. The intruder then forced a core dump of a SETUID program, which the system wrote on the *core* file, that is, on top of the password file. In this way, a user could replace the password file with one containing a few strings of his own choosing (e.g., command arguments).

Yet another subtle flaw in UNIX involved the command

mkdir foo

Mkdir, which was a SETUID program owned by the root, first created the i-node for the directory *foo* with the system call MKNOD and then changed the owner of *foo* from its effective uid (i.e., root) to its real uid (the user's uid). When the system was slow, it was sometimes possible for the user to quickly remove the directory i-node and make a link to the password file under the name *foo* after the MKNOD but before the CHOWN. When *mkdir* did the CHOWN it made the user the owner of the password file. By putting the necessary commands in a shell script, they could be tried over and over until the trick worked.

The TENEX operating system used to be very popular on the DEC-10 computers. It is no longer used, but it will live on forever in the annals of computer security due to the following design error. TENEX supported paging. To allow users to monitor the behavior of their programs, it was possible to instruct the system to call a user function on each page fault.

TENEX also used passwords to protect files. To access a file, a program had to present the proper password. The operating system checked passwords one character at a time, stopping as soon as it saw that the password was wrong. To break into TENEX an intruder would carefully position a password as shown in Fig. 5-20(a), with the first character at the end of one page, and the rest at the start of the next page.

The next step was to make sure that the second page was not in memory, for example, by referencing so many other pages that the second page would surely

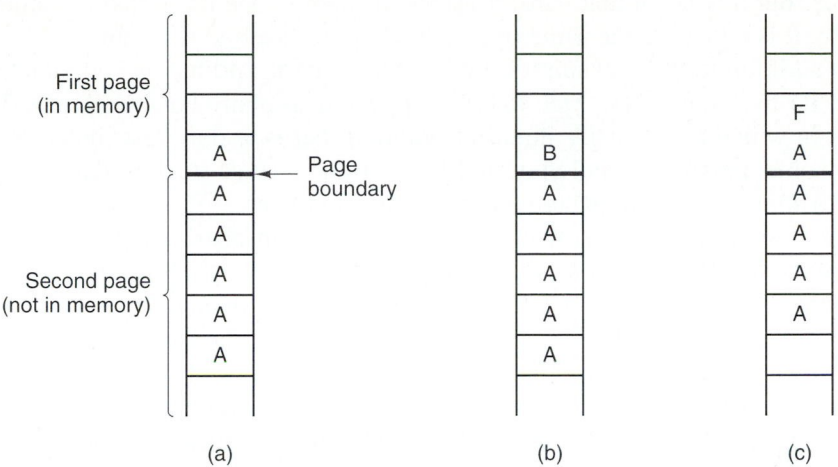

Figure 5-20. The TENEX password problem.

be evicted to make room for them. Now the program tried to open the victim's file, using the carefully aligned password. If the first character of the real password was anything but A, the system would stop checking at the first character and report back with ILLEGAL PASSWORD. If, however, the real password did begin with A, the system continued reading, and got a page fault, about which the intruder was informed.

If the password did not begin with A, the intruder changed the password to that of Fig. 5-20(b) and repeated the whole process to see if it began with B. It took at most 128 tries to go through the whole ASCII character set and thus determine the first character.

Suppose that the first character was an F. The memory layout of Fig. 5-20(c) allowed the intruder to test strings of the form FA, FB, and so on. Using this approach it took at most $128n$ tries to guess an n character ASCII password, instead of 128^n.

Our last flaw concerns OS/360. The description that follows is slightly simplified but preserves the essence of the flaw. In this system it was possible to start up a tape read and then continue computing while the tape drive was transferring data to the user space. The trick here was to carefully start up a tape read and then do a system call that required a user data structure, for example, a file to read and its password.

The operating system first verified that the password was indeed the correct one for the given file. Then it went back and read the file name again for the actual access (it could have saved the name internally, but it did not). Unfortunately, just before the system went to fetch the file name the second time, the file name was overwritten by the tape drive. The system then read the new file, for which no password had been presented. Getting the timing right took some practice, but it was not that hard. Besides, if there is one thing that computers are good at, it is repeating the same operation over and over ad nauseam .

In addition to these examples, many other security problems and attacks have turned up over the years. One that has appeared in many contexts is the **Trojan horse**, in which a seemingly innocent program that is widely distributed also performs some unexpected and undesirable function, such as stealing data and emailing it to some distant site where it can be collected later.

Another security problem in these times of job insecurity is the **logic bomb**. This device is a piece of code written by one of a company's (currently employed) programmers and secretly inserted into the production operating system. As long as the programmer feeds it its daily password, it does nothing. However, if the programmer is suddenly fired and physically removed from the premises without warning, the next day the logic bomb does not get its password, so it goes off.

Going off might involve clearing the disk, erasing files at random, carefully making hard-to-detect changes to key programs, or encrypting essential files. In the latter case, the company has a tough choice about whether to call the police (which may or may not result in a conviction many months later) or to give in to this blackmail and to rehire the ex-programmer as a "consultant" for an astronomical sum to fix the problem (and hope that he does not plant new logic bombs while doing so).

Probably the greatest computer security violation of all time began in the evening of Nov. 2, 1988 when a Cornell graduate student, Robert Tappan Morris, released a worm program into the Internet that eventually brought down thousands of machines all over the world.

The worm consisted of two programs, the bootstrap and the worm proper. The bootstrap was 99 lines of C called *ll.c*. It was compiled and executed on the system under attack. Once running, it connected to the machine from which it came, uploaded the main worm, and executed it. After going to some trouble to hide its existence, the worm then looked through its new host's routing tables to see what machines that host was connected to and attempted to spread the bootstrap to those machines.

Once established on a machine, the worm tried to break user passwords. Morris did not have to do much research on how to accomplish this. All he had to do was ask his father, a security expert at the National Security Agency, the U.S. government's top-secret code breaking agency, for a reprint of a classic paper on the subject that Morris Sr. and Ken Thompson had written a decade earlier at Bell Labs (Morris and Thompson, 1979). Each broken password allowed the worm to log in on any machines the password's owner had accounts on.

Morris was caught when one of his friends spoke with the *New York Times* computer reporter, John Markoff, and tried to convince Markoff that the incident was an accident, the worm was harmless, and the author was sorry. The next day the story was the lead on page one, even upstaging the presidential election three days later. Morris was tried and convicted in federal court. He was sentenced to a 10,000 dollar fine, 3 years probation, and 400 hours of community service. His legal costs probably exceeded 150,000 dollars.

This sentence generated a great deal of controversy. Many in the computer community felt that he was a bright graduate student whose harmless prank had gotten out of control. Nothing in the worm suggested that Morris was trying to steal or damage anything. Others felt he was a serious criminal and should have gone to jail.

One permanent effect of this incident was the establishment of **CERT** (**Computer Emergency Response Team**), which provides a central place to report break-in attempts, and a group of experts to analyze security problems and design fixes. While this action was certainly a step forward, it also has its downside. CERT collects information about system flaws that can be attacked and how to fix them. Of necessity, it circulates this information widely to thousands of system administrators on the Internet, which means that the bad guys may also be able to get it and exploit the loopholes in the hours (or even days) before they are closed.

5.4.3 Generic Security Attacks

The flaws described above have been fixed but the average operating system still leaks like a sieve. The usual way to test a system's security is to hire a group of experts, known as **tiger teams** or **penetration teams**, to see if they can break in. Hebbard et al. (1980) tried the same thing with graduate students. In the course of the years, these penetration teams have discovered a number of areas in which systems are likely to be weak. Below we have listed some of the more common attacks that are often successful. When designing a system, be sure it can withstand attacks like these.

1. Request memory pages, disk space, or tapes and just read them. Many systems do not erase them before allocating them, and they may be full of interesting information written by the previous owner.

2. Try illegal system calls, or legal system calls with illegal parameters, or even legal system calls with legal but unreasonable parameters. Many systems can easily be confused.

3. Start logging in and then hit DEL, RUBOUT or BREAK halfway through the login sequence. In some systems, the password checking program will be killed and the login considered successful.

4. Try modifying complex operating system structures kept in user space (if any). In some systems (especially on mainframes), to open a file, the program builds a large data structure containing the file name and many other parameters and passes it to the system. As the file is read and written, the system sometimes updates the structure itself. Changing these fields can wreak havoc with the security.

5. Spoof the user by writing a program that types "login:" on the screen and go away. Many users will walk up to the terminal and willingly tell it their login name and password, which the program carefully records for its evil master.

6. Look for manuals that say "Do not do *X*." Try as many variations of *X* as possible.

7. Convince a system programmer to change the system to skip certain vital security checks for any user with your login name. This attack is known as a **trapdoor**.

8. All else failing, the penetrator might find the computer center director's secretary and offer a large bribe. The secretary probably has easy access to all kinds of wonderful information, and is usually poorly paid. Do not underestimate problems caused by personnel.

These and other attacks are discussed by Linde (1975).

Viruses

A special category of attack is the computer virus, which has become a major problem for many computer users. A **virus** is a program fragment that is attached to a legitimate program with the intention of infecting other programs. It differs from a worm only in that a virus piggybacks on an existing program, whereas a worm is a complete program in itself. Viruses and worms both attempt to spread themselves and both can do severe damage.

A typical virus works as follows. The person writing the virus first produces a useful new program, often a game for MS-DOS. This program contains the virus code hidden away in it. The game is then uploaded to a public bulletin board system or offered for free or for a modest price on floppy disk. The program is then advertised, and people begin downloading and using it. Constructing a virus is not easy, so the people doing this are invariably quite bright, and the quality of the game or other program is often excellent.

When the program is started up, it immediately begins examining all the binary programs on the hard disk to see if they are already infected. When an uninfected program is found, it is infected by attaching the virus code to the end of the file, and replacing the first instruction with a jump to the virus. When the virus code is finished executing, it executes the instruction that had previously been first and then jumps to the second instruction. In this way, every time an infected program runs, it tries to infect more programs.

In addition to just infecting other programs, a virus can do other things, such as erasing, modifying, or encrypting files. One virus even displayed an extortion note on the screen, telling the user to send 500 dollars in cash to a post office box in Panama or face the permanent loss of his data and damage to the hardware.

It is also possible for a virus to infect the hard disk's boot sector, making it impossible to boot the computer. Such a virus may ask for a password, which the virus' writer may offer to supply in exchange for some small unmarked bills.

Virus problems are easier to prevent than to cure. The safest course is to buy only shrink-wrapped software from respectable stores. Uploading free software from bulletin boards or getting pirated copies on floppy disk is asking for trouble. Commercial antivirus packages exist, but some of these work by just looking for specific known viruses.

A more general approach is to first reformat the hard disk completely, including the boot sector. Next, install all the trusted software and compute a checksum for each file. The algorithm does not matter, as long as it has enough bits (at least 32). Store the list of (file, checksum) pairs in a safe place, either offline on a floppy disk, or online but encrypted. Starting at that point, whenever the system is booted, all the checksums should be recomputed and compared to the secure list of original checksums. Any file whose current checksum differs from the original one is immediately suspect. While this approach does not prevent infection, it at least allows early detection.

Infection can be made more difficult if the directory where binary programs reside is made unwritable for ordinary users. This technique makes it difficult for the virus to modify other binaries. Although it can be used in UNIX, it is not applicable to MS-DOS because the latter's directories cannot be made unwritable at all.

5.4.4 Design Principles for Security

Viruses mostly occur on desktop systems. On larger systems other problems occur and other methods are needed for dealing with them. Saltzer and Schroeder (1975) have identified several general principles that can be used as a guide to designing secure systems. A brief summary of their ideas (based on experience with MULTICS) is given below.

First, the system design should be public. Assuming that the intruder will not know how the system works serves only to delude the designers.

Second, the default should be no access. Errors in which legitimate access is refused will be reported much faster than errors in which unauthorized access is allowed.

Third, check for current authority. The system should not check for permission, determine that access is permitted, and then squirrel away this information for subsequent use. Many systems check for permission when a file is opened, and not afterward. This means that a user who opens a file, and keeps it open for weeks, will continue to have access, even if the owner has long since changed the file protection.

Fourth, give each process the least privilege possible. If an editor has only the authority to access the file to be edited (specified when the editor is invoked), editors with Trojan horses will not be able to do much damage. This principle implies a fine-grained protection scheme. We will discuss such schemes later in this chapter.

Fifth, the protection mechanism should be simple, uniform, and built into the lowest layers of the system. Trying to retrofit security to an existing insecure system is nearly impossible. Security, like correctness, is not an add-on feature.

Sixth, the scheme chosen must be psychologically acceptable. If users feel that protecting their files is too much work, they just will not do it. Nevertheless, they will complain loudly if something goes wrong. Replies of the form "It is your own fault" will generally not be well received.

5.4.5 User Authentication

Many protection schemes are based on the assumption that the system knows the identity of each user. The problem of identifying users when they log in is called **user authentication**. Most authentication methods are based on identifying something the user knows, something the user has, or something the user is.

Passwords

The most widely used form of authentication is to require the user to type a password. Password protection is easy to understand and easy to implement. In UNIX it works like this. The login program asks the user to type his name and password. The password is immediately encrypted. The login program then reads the password file, which is a series of ASCII lines, one per user, until it finds the line containing the user's login name. If the (encrypted) password contained in this line matches the encrypted password just computed, the login is permitted, otherwise it is refused.

Password authentication is easy to defeat. One frequently reads about groups of high school, or even junior high school students who, with the aid of their trusty home computers, have just broken into some top secret system owned by a giant corporation or government agency. Virtually all the time the break-in consists of guessing a user name and password combination.

Although more recent studies have been made (e.g., Klein, 1990) the classic work on password security remains the one done by Morris and Thompson (1979) on UNIX systems. They compiled a list of likely passwords: first and last names, street names, city names, words from a moderate-sized dictionary (also words spelled backward), license plate numbers, and short strings of random characters.

They then encrypted each of these using the known password encryption algorithm and checked to see if any of the encrypted passwords matched entries in their list. Over 86 percent of all passwords turned up in their list.

If all passwords consisted of 7 characters chosen at random from the 95 printable ASCII characters, the search space becomes 95^7, which is about 7×10^{13}.

At 1000 encryptions per second, it would take 2000 years to build the list to check the password file against. Furthermore, the list would fill 20 million magnetic tapes. Even requiring passwords to contain at least one lowercase character, one uppercase character, and one special character, and be at least seven or eight characters long would be a major improvement over unrestricted user-chosen passwords.

Even if it is considered politically impossible to require users to pick reasonable passwords, Morris and Thompson have described a technique that renders their own attack (encrypting a large number of passwords in advance) almost useless. Their idea is to associate an n-bit random number with each password. The random number is changed whenever the password is changed. The random number is stored in the password file in unencrypted form, so that everyone can read it. Instead of just storing the encrypted password in the password file, the password and the random number are first concatenated and then encrypted together. This encrypted result is stored in the password file.

Now consider the implications for an intruder who wants to build up a list of likely passwords, encrypt them, and save the results in a sorted file, f, so that any encrypted password can be looked up easily. If an intruder suspects that *Marilyn* might be a password, it is no longer sufficient just to encrypt *Marilyn* and put the result in f. He has to encrypt 2^n strings, such as *Marilyn0000*, *Marilyn0001*, *Marilyn0002*, and so forth and enter all of them in f. This technique increases the size of f by 2^n. UNIX uses this method with $n = 12$. It is known as **salting** the password file. Some versions of UNIX make the password file itself unreadable but provide a program to look up entries upon request, adding just enough delay to greatly slow down any attacker.

Although this method offers protection against intruders who try to precompute a large list of encrypted passwords, it does little to protect a user *David* whose password is also *David*. One way to encourage people to pick better passwords is to have the computer offer advice. Some computers have a program that generates random easy-to-pronounce nonsense words, such as *fotally*, *garbungy*, or *bipitty* that can be used as passwords (preferably with some upper case and special characters thrown in).

Other computers require users to change their passwords regularly, to limit the damage done if a password leaks out. The most extreme form of this approach is the **one-time password**. When one-time passwords are used, the user gets a book containing a list of passwords. Each login uses the next password in the list. If an intruder ever discovers a password, it will not do him any good, since next time a different password must be used. It is suggested that the user try to avoid losing the password book.

It goes almost without saying that while a password is being typed in, the computer should not display the typed characters, to keep them from prying eyes near the terminal. What is less obvious is that passwords should never be stored in the computer in unencrypted form. Furthermore, not even the computer center management should have unencrypted copies. Keeping unencrypted passwords anywhere is looking for trouble.

A variation on the password idea is to have each new user provide a long list of questions and answers that are then stored in the computer in encrypted form. The questions should be chosen so that the user does not need to write them down. Typical questions are:

1. Who is Marjolein's sister?

2. On what street was your elementary school?

3. What did Mrs. Woroboff teach?

At login, the computer asks one of them at random and checks the answer.

Another variation is **challenge-response**. When this is used, the user picks an algorithm when signing up as a user, for example x^2. When the user logs in, the computer types an argument, say 7, in which case the user types 49. The algorithm can be different in the morning and afternoon, on different days of the week, from different terminals, and so on.

Physical Identification

A completely different approach to authorization is to check to see if the user has some item, normally a plastic card with a magnetic stripe on it. The card is inserted into the terminal, which then checks to see whose card it is. This method can be combined with a password, so a user can only log in if he (1) has the card and (2) knows the password. Automated cash-dispensing machines usually work this way.

Yet another approach is to measure physical characteristics that are hard to forge. For example, a fingerprint or a voiceprint reader in the terminal could verify the user's identity. (It makes the search go faster if the user tells the computer who he is, rather than making the computer compare the given fingerprint to the entire data base.) Direct visual recognition is not yet feasible but may be one day.

Another technique is signature analysis. The user signs his name with a special pen connected to the terminal, and the computer compares it to a known specimen stored on line. Even better is not to compare the signature, but compare the pen motions made while writing it. A good forger may be able to copy the signature, but will not have a clue as to the exact order in which the strokes were made.

Finger length analysis is surprisingly practical. When this is used, each terminal has a device like the one of Fig. 5-21. The user inserts his hand into it, and the length of all his fingers is measured and checked against the data base.

We could go on and on with more examples, but two more will help make an important point. Cats and other animals mark off their territory by urinating around its perimeter. Apparently cats can identify each other this way. Suppose

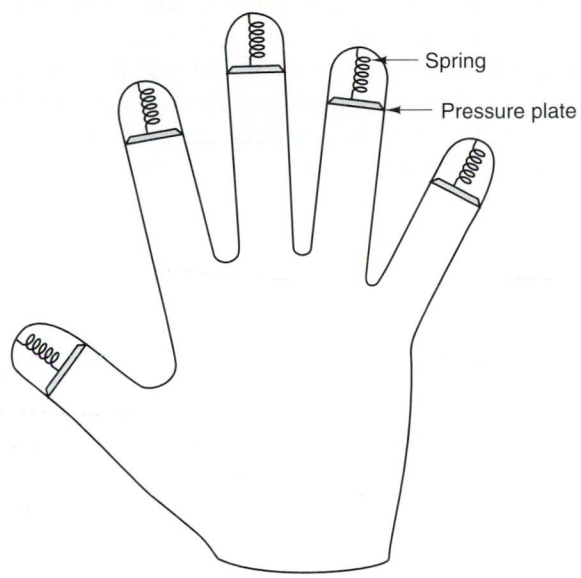

Spring

Pressure plate

Figure 5-21. A device for measuring finger length.

that someone comes up with a tiny device capable of doing an instant urinalysis, thereby providing a foolproof identification. Each terminal could be equipped with one of these devices, along with a discreet sign reading: "For login, please deposit sample here." This might be an absolutely unbreakable system, but it would probably have a fairly serious user acceptance problem.

The same could be said of a system consisting of a thumbtack and a small spectrograph. The user would be requested to press his thumb against the thumbtack, thus extracting a drop of blood for spectrographic analysis. The point is that any authentication scheme must be psychologically acceptable to the user community. Finger-length measurements probably will not cause any problem, but even something as nonintrusive as storing fingerprints on line may be unacceptable to many people.

Countermeasures

Computer installations that are really serious about security, something that frequently happens the day after an intruder has broken in and done major damage, often take steps to make unauthorized entry much harder. For example, each user could be allowed to log in only from a specific terminal, and only during certain days of the week and hours of the day.

Dial-up telephone lines could be made to work as follows. Anyone can dial up and log in, but after a successful login, the system immediately breaks the connection and calls the user back at an agreed upon number. This measure means than an intruder cannot just try breaking in from any phone line; only the user's (home) phone will do. In any event, with or without call back, the system should take at least 10 seconds to check any password typed in on a dial-up line, and should increase this time after several consecutive unsuccessful login attempts, in order to reduce the rate at which intruders can try. After three failed login attempts, the line should be disconnected for 10 minutes and security personnel notified.

All logins should be recorded. When a user logs in, the system should report the time and terminal of the previous login, so he can detect possible break ins.

The next step up is laying baited traps to catch intruders. A simple scheme is to have one special login name with an easy password (e.g., login name: guest, password: guest). Whenever anyone logs in using this name, the system security specialists are immediately notified. Other traps can be easy-to-find bugs in the operating system and similar things, designed for the purpose of catching intruders in the act. Stoll (1989) has written an entertaining account of the traps he set to track down a spy who broke into a university computer in search of military secrets.

5.5 PROTECTION MECHANISMS

In the previous sections we have looked at many potential problems, some of them technical and some of them not. In the following sections we will concentrate on some of the detailed technical ways that are used in operating systems to protect files and other things. All of these techniques make a clear distinction between policy (whose data are to be protected from whom) and mechanism (how the system enforces the policy). The separation of policy and mechanism is discussed in (Levin et al., 1975). Our emphasis will be on the mechanism, not the policy. For more advanced material, see (Sandhu, 1993).

In some systems, protection is enforced by a program called a **reference monitor**. Every time an access to a potentially protected resource is attempted, the system first asks the reference monitor to check its legality. The reference monitor then looks at its policy tables and makes a decision. Below we will describe the environment in which a reference monitor operates.

5.5.1 Protection Domains

A computer system contains many "objects" that need to be protected. These objects can be hardware (e.g., CPUs, memory segments, disk drives, or printers), or they can be software (e.g., processes, files, data bases, or semaphores).

Each object has a unique name by which it is referenced, and a finite set of operations that processes are allowed to carry out on it. READ and WRITE are operations appropriate to a file; UP and DOWN make sense on a semaphore.

It is obvious that a way is needed to prohibit processes from accessing objects that they are not authorized to access. Furthermore, this mechanism must also make it possible to restrict processes to a subset of the legal operations when that is needed. For example, process *A* may be entitled to read, but not write, file *F*.

In order to discuss different protection mechanisms, it is useful to introduce the concept of a domain. A **domain** is a set of (object, rights) pairs. Each pair specifies an object and some subset of the operations that can be performed on it. A **right** in this context means permission to perform one of the operations.

Figure 5-22 shows three domains, showing the objects in each domain and the rights [Read, Write, eXecute] available on each object. Note that *Printer1* is in two domains at the same time. Although not shown in this example, it is possible for the same object to be in multiple domains, with *different* rights in each one.

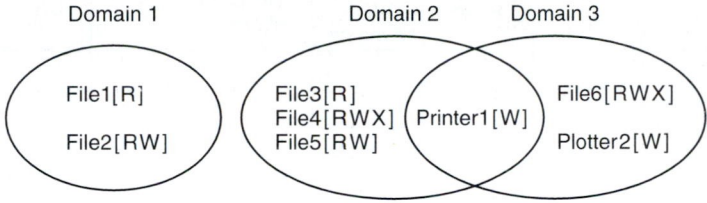

Figure 5-22. Three protection domains.

At every instant of time, each process runs in some protection domain. In other words, there is some collection of objects it can access, and for each object it has some set of rights. Processes can also switch from domain to domain during execution. The rules for domain switching are highly system dependent.

To make the idea of a protection domain more concrete, let us look at UNIX. In UNIX, the domain of a process is defined by its uid and gid. Given any (uid, gid) combination, it is possible to make a complete list of all objects (files, including I/O devices represented by special files, etc.) that can be accessed, and whether they can be accessed for reading, writing, or executing. Two processes with the same (uid, gid) combination will have access to exactly the same set of objects. Processes with different (uid, gid) values will have access to a different set of files, although there will be considerable overlap in most cases.

Furthermore, each process in UNIX has two halves: the user part and the kernel part. When the process does a system call, it switches from the user part to the kernel part. The kernel part has access to a different set of objects from the user part. For example, the kernel can access all the pages in physical memory, the entire disk, and all the other protected resources. Thus, a system call causes a domain switch.

When a process does an EXEC on a file with the SETUID or SETGID bit on, it acquires a new effective uid or gid. With a different (uid, gid) combination, it has a different set of files and operations available. Running a program with SETUID or SETGID is also a domain switch, since the rights available are now different.

An important question is how the system keeps track of which object belongs to which domain. Conceptually, at least, one can envision a large matrix, with the rows being the domains and the columns being the objects. Each box lists the rights, if any, that the domain contains for the object. The matrix for Fig. 5-22 is shown in Fig. 5-23. Given this matrix and the current domain number, the system can tell if an access to a given object in a particular way from a specified domain is allowed.

	File1	File2	File3	File4	File5	File6	Printer1	Plotter2
Domain 1	Read	Read Write						
2			Read	Read Write Execute	Read Write		Write	
3						Read Write Execute	Write	Write

Figure 5-23. A protection matrix.

Domain switching itself can be easily included in the matrix model by realizing that a domain is itself an object, with the operation ENTER. Figure 5-24 shows the matrix of Fig. 5-23 again, only now with the three domains as objects themselves. Processes in domain 1 can switch to domain 2, but once there, they cannot go back. This situation models executing a SETUID program in UNIX. No other domain switches are permitted in this example.

	File1	File2	File3	File4	File5	File6	Printer1	Plotter2	Domain1	Domain2	Domain3
Domain 1	Read	Read Write								Enter	
2			Read	Read Write Execute	Read Write		Write				
3						Read Write Execute	Write	Write			

Figure 5-24. A protection matrix with domains as objects.

5.5.2 Access Control Lists

In practice, actually storing the matrix of Fig. 5-24 is rarely done because it is large and sparse. Most domains have no access at all to most objects, so storing a very large, mostly empty, matrix is a waste of disk space. Two methods that are practical, however, are storing the matrix by rows or by columns, and then storing only the nonempty elements. The two approaches are surprisingly different. In this section we will look at storing it by column; in the next one we will study storing it by row.

The first technique consists of associating with each object an (ordered) list containing all the domains that may access the object, and how. This list is called the **Access Control List** or **ACL**. If it were to be implemented in UNIX, the easiest way would be to put the ACL for each file in a separate disk block and include the block number in the file's i-node. As only the nonempty entries of the matrix are stored, the total storage required for all the ACLs combined is much less than what would be needed for the whole matrix.

As an example of how ACLs work, let us continue to imagine that they were used in UNIX, where a domain is specified by a (uid, gid) pair. Actually, ACLs were used in UNIX' role model, MULTICS, more or less in the way we will describe, so the example is not so hypothetical.

Let us now assume that we have four users (i.e., uids) *Jan, Els, Jelle*, and *Maaike*, who belong to groups *system, staff, student*, and *student*, respectively. Suppose that some files have the following ACLs:

File0: (Jan, *, RWX)
File1: (Jan, system, RWX)
File2: (Jan, *, RW-), (Els, staff, RW-), (Maaike, *, RW-)
File3: (*, student, R−−)
File4: (Jelle, *, −−−), (*, student, R−−)

Each ACL entry, in parentheses, specifies a uid, a gid, and the allowed accesses (Read, Write, eXecute). An asterisk means all uids or gids. *File0* can be read, written, or executed by any process with uid = *Jan*, and any gid. *File1* can be accessed only by processes with uid = *Jan* and gid = *system*. A process that has uid = *Jan* and gid = *staff* can access *File0* but not *File1*. *File2* can be read or written by processes with uid = *Jan* and any gid, read by processes with uid = *Els* and gid = *staff*, or by processes with uid = *Maaike* and any gid. *File3* can be read by any student. *File4* is especially interesting. It says that anyone with uid = *Jelle*, in any group, has no access at all, but all other students can read it. By using ACLs it is possible to prohibit specific uids or gids from accessing an object, while allowing everyone else in the same class.

So much for what UNIX does not do. Now let us look at what it *does* do. It provides three bits, *rwx*, per file for the owner, the owner's group, and others. This scheme is just the ACL again, but compressed to 9 bits. It is a list associated with the object saying who may access it and how. While the 9-bit UNIX scheme is clearly less general than a full-blown ACL system, in practice it is adequate, and its implementation is much simpler and cheaper.

The owner of an object can change its ACL at any time, thus making it easy to prohibit accesses that were previously allowed. The only problem is that changing the ACL will most probably not affect any users who are currently using the object (e.g., currently have the file open).

5.5.3 Capabilities

The other way of slicing up the matrix of Fig. 5-24 is by rows. When this method is used, associated with each process is a list of objects that may be accessed, along with an indication of which operations are permitted on each, in other words, its domain. This list is called a **capability list**, and the individual items on it are called **capabilities** (Dennis and Van Horn, 1966; Fabry, 1974).

A typical capability list is shown in Fig. 5-25. Each capability has a *Type* field, which tells what kind of an object it is, a *Rights* field, which is a bit map indicating which of the legal operations on this type of object are permitted, and an *Object* field, which is a pointer to the object itself (e.g., its i-node number). Capability lists are themselves objects and may be pointed to from other capability lists, thus facilitating sharing of subdomains. Capabilities are often referred to by their position in the capability list. A process might say: "Read 1K from the file pointed to by capability 2." This form of addressing is similar to using file descriptors in UNIX.

#	Type	Rights	Object
0	File	R––	Pointer to File3
1	File	RWX	Pointer to File4
2	File	RW–	Pointer to File5
3	Pointer	–W–	Pointer to Printer1

Figure 5-25. The capability list for domain 2 in Fig. 5-23.

It is fairly obvious that capability lists, or **C-lists** as they are often called, must be protected from user tampering. Three methods have been proposed to protect them. The first way requires a **tagged architecture**, a hardware design in which each memory word has an extra (or tag) bit that tells whether the word contains a capability or not. The tag bit is not used by arithmetic, comparison, or similar ordinary instructions, and it can be modified only by programs running in kernel mode (i.e., the operating system).

The second way is to keep the C-list inside the operating system and just have processes refer to capabilities by their slot number, as mentioned above. Hydra (Wulf et al., 1974) worked this way.

The third way is to keep the C-list in user space, but encrypt each capability with a secret key unknown to the user. This approach is particularly suited to distributed systems, and is used extensively by Amoeba (Tanenbaum et al., 1990).

In addition to the specific object-dependent rights, such as read and execute, capabilities usually have **generic rights** which are applicable to all objects. Examples of generic rights are

1. Copy capability: create a new capability for the same object.

2. Copy object: create a duplicate object with a new capability.

3. Remove capability: delete an entry from the C-list; object unaffected.

4. Destroy object: permanently remove an object and a capability.

A last remark worth making about capability systems is that revoking access to an object is quite difficult. It is hard for the system to find all the outstanding capabilities for any object to take them back, since they may be stored in C-lists all over the disk. One approach is to have each capability point to an indirect object, rather than to the object itself. By having the indirect object point to the real object, the system can always break that connection, thus invalidating the capabilities. (When a capability to the indirect object is later presented to the system, the user will discover that the indirect object is now pointing to a null object.)

Another way to achieve revocation is the scheme used in Amoeba. Each object contains a long random number, which is also present in the capability. When a capability is presented for use, the two are compared. Only if they agree is the operation allowed. The owner of an object can request that the random number in the object be changed, thus invalidating existing capabilities. Neither scheme allows selective revocation, that is, taking back, say, John's permission, but nobody else's.

5.5.4 Covert Channels

Even with access control lists and capabilities, security leaks can occur. In this section we discuss one class of problem. These ideas are due to Lampson (1973).

Lampson's model involves three processes and is primarily applicable to large timesharing systems. The first process is the client, which wants some work performed by the second one, the server. The client and the server do not entirely trust each other. For example, the server's job is to help clients with filling out their tax forms. The clients are worried that the server will secretly record their financial data, for example, maintaining a secret list of who earns how much, and then selling the list. The server is worried that the clients will try to steal the valuable tax program.

The third process is the collaborator, which is conspiring with the server to indeed steal the client's confidential data. The collaborator and server are typically owned by the same person. These three processes are shown in Fig. 5-26.

The object of this exercise is to design a system in which it is impossible for the server to leak to the collaborator the information that it has legitimately received from the client. Lampson called this the **confinement problem**.

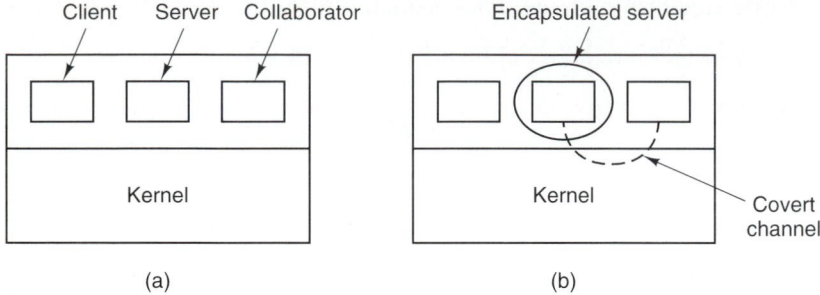

Figure 5-26. (a) The client, server, and collaborator processes. (b) The encapsulated server can still leak to the collaborator via covert channels.

From the system designer's point of view, the goal is to encapsulate or confine the server in such a way that it cannot pass information to the collaborator. Using a protection matrix scheme we can easily guarantee that the server cannot communicate with the collaborator by writing a file to which the collaborator has read access. We can probably also ensure that the server cannot communicate with the collaborator using the system's interprocess communication mechanism.

Unfortunately, more subtle communication channels may be available. For example, the server can try to communicate a binary bit stream as follows. To send a 1 bit, it computes as hard as it can for a fixed interval of time. To send a 0 bit, it goes to sleep for the same length of time.

The collaborator can try to detect the bit stream by carefully monitoring its response time. In general, it will get better response when the server is sending a 0 than when the server is sending a 1. This communication channel is known as a **covert channel**, and is illustrated in Fig. 5-26(b).

Of course, the covert channel is a noisy channel, containing a lot of extraneous information, but information can be reliably sent over a noisy channel by using an error-correcting code (e.g., a Hamming code, or even something more sophisticated). The use of an error-correcting code reduces the already low bandwidth of the covert channel even more, but it still may be enough to leak substantial information. It is fairly obvious that no protection model based on a matrix of objects and domains is going to prevent this kind of leakage.

Modulating the CPU usage is not the only covert channel. The paging rate can also be modulated (many page faults for a 1, no page faults for a 0). In fact, almost any way of degrading system performance in a clocked way is a candidate. If the system provides a way of locking files, then the server can lock some file to indicate a 1, and unlock it to indicate a 0. On some systems, it may be possible for a process to detect the status of a lock even on a file that it cannot access.

Acquiring and releasing dedicated resources (tape drives, plotters, etc.) can also be used for signaling. The server acquires the resource to send a 1 and releases it to send a 0. In UNIX, the server could create a file to indicate a 1 and remove it to indicate a 0; the collaborator could use the ACCESS system call to see if the file exists. This call works even though the collaborator has no permission to use the file. Unfortunately, many other covert channels exist.

Lampson also mentions a way of leaking information to the (human) owner of the server process. Presumably the server process will be entitled to tell its owner how much work it did on behalf of the client, so the client can be billed. If the actual computing bill is, say, 100 dollars and the client's income is 53K dollars, the server could report the bill as 100.53 to its owner.

Just finding all the covert channels, let alone blocking them, is extremely difficult. In practice, there is little that can be done. Introducing a process that causes page faults at random, or otherwise spends its time degrading system performance in order to reduce the bandwidth of the covert channels is not an attractive proposition.

5.6 OVERVIEW OF THE MINIX FILE SYSTEM

Like any file system, the MINIX file system must deal with all the issues we have just studied. It must allocate and deallocate space for files, keep track of disk blocks and free space, provide some way to protect files against unauthorized usage, and so on. In the remainder of this chapter we will look closely at MINIX to see how it accomplishes these goals.

In the first part of this chapter, we have repeatedly referred to UNIX rather than to MINIX for the sake of generality, although the external interface of the two is virtually identical. Now we will concentrate on the internal design of MINIX. For information about the UNIX internals, see Thompson (1978), Bach (1987), Lions (1996), and Vahalia (1996).

The MINIX file system is just a big C program that runs in user space (see Fig. 2-26). To read and write files, user processes send messages to the file system telling what they want done. The file system does the work and then sends back a reply. The file system is, in fact, a network file server that happens to be running on the same machine as the caller.

This design has some important implications. For one thing, the file system can be modified, experimented with, and tested almost completely independently of the rest of MINIX. For another, it is very easy to move the whole file system to any computer that has a C compiler, compile it there, and use it as a free-standing UNIX-like remote file server. The only changes that need to be made are in the area of how messages are sent and received, which differs from system to system.

In the following sections, we will present an overview of many of the key areas of the file system design. Specifically, we will look at messages, the file system layout, the bit maps, i-nodes, the block cache, directories and paths, file descriptors, file locking, and special files (plus pipes). After studying all of these topics, we will show a simple example of how the pieces fit together by tracing what happens when a user process executes the READ system call.

5.6.1 Messages

The file system accepts 39 types of messages requesting work. All but two are for MINIX system calls. The two exceptions are messages generated by other parts of MINIX. Of the system calls, 31 are accepted from user processes. Six system call messages are for system calls which are handled first by the memory manager, which then calls the file system to do a part of the work. Two other messages are also processed by the file system. The messages are shown in Fig. 5-27

The structure of the file system is basically the same as that of the memory manager and all the I/O tasks. It has a main loop that waits for a message to arrive. When a message arrives, its type is extracted and used as an index into a table containing pointers to the procedures within the file system that handle all the types. Then the appropriate procedure is called, it does its work and returns a status value. The file system then sends a reply back to the caller and goes back to the top of the loop to wait for the next message.

5.6.2 File System Layout

A MINIX file system is a logical, self-contained entity with i-nodes, directories, and data blocks. It can be stored on any block device, such as a floppy disk or a (portion of a) hard disk. In all cases, the layout of the file system has the same structure. Figure 5-28 shows this layout for a 360K floppy disk with 128 i-nodes and a 1K block size. Larger file systems, or those with more or fewer i-nodes or a different block size, will have the same six components in the same order, but their relative sizes may be different.

Each file system begins with a **boot block**. This contains executable code. When the computer is turned on, the hardware reads the boot block from the boot device into memory, jumps to it, and begins executing its code. The boot block code begins the process of loading the operating system itself. Once the system has been booted, the boot block is not used any more. Not every disk drive can be used as a boot device, but to keep the structure uniform, every block device has a block reserved for boot block code. At worst this strategy wastes one block. To prevent the hardware from trying to boot an unbootable device a **magic number** is placed at a known location in the boot block when and only when the executable code is written to the device. When booting from a device, the hardware

Messages from users	Input parameters	Reply value
ACCESS	File name, access mode	Status
CHDIR	Name of new working directory	Status
CHMOD	File name, new mode	Status
CHOWN	File name, new owner, group	Status
CHROOT	Name of new root directory	Status
CLOSE	File descriptor of file to close	Status
CREAT	Name of file to be created, mode	File descriptor
DUP	File descriptor (for dup2, two fds)	New file descriptor
FCNTL	File descriptor, function code, arg	Depends on function
FSTAT	Name of file, buffer	Status
IOCTL	File descriptor, function code, arg	Status
LINK	Name of file to link to, name of link	Status
LSEEK	File descriptor, offset, whence	New position
MKDIR	File name, mode	Status
MKNOD	Name of dir or special, mode, address	Status
MOUNT	Special file, where to mount, ro flag	Status
OPEN	Name of file to open, r/w flag	File descriptor
PIPE	Pointer to 2 file descriptors (modified)	Status
READ	File descriptor, buffer, how many bytes	# Bytes read
RENAME	File name, file name	Status
RMDIR	File name	Status
STAT	File name, status buffer	Status
STIME	Pointer to current time	Status
SYNC	(None)	Always OK
TIME	Pointer to place where current time goes	Status
TIMES	Pointer to buffer for process and child times	Status
UMASK	Complement of mode mask	Always OK
UMOUNT	Name of special file to unmount	Status
UNLINK	Name of file to unlink	Status
UTIME	File name, file times	Always OK
WRITE	File descriptor, buffer, how many bytes	# Bytes written
Messages from MM	**Input parameters**	**Reply value**
EXEC	Pid	Status
EXIT	Pid	Status
FORK	Parent pid, child pid	Status
SETGID	Pid, real and effective gid	Status
SETSID	Pid	Status
SETUID	Pid, real and effective uid	Status
Other messages	**Input parameters**	**Reply value**
REVIVE	Process to revive	(No reply)
UNPAUSE	Process to check	(See text)

Figure 5-27. File system messages. File name parameters are always pointers to the name. The code status as reply value means *OK* or *ERROR*.

(actually, the BIOS code) will refuse to attempt to load from a device lacking the magic number. Doing this prevents inadvertently using garbage as a boot program.

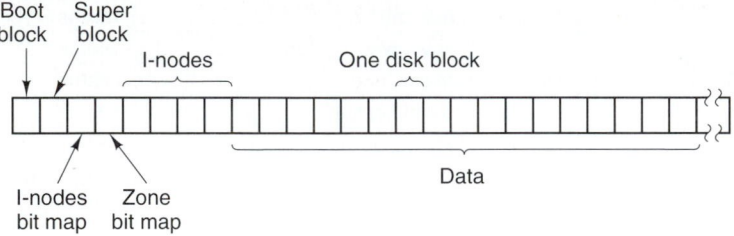

Figure 5-28. Disk layout for the simplest disk: a 360K floppy disk, with 128 i-nodes and a 1K block size (i.e., two consecutive 512-byte sectors are treated as a single block).

The **super-block** contains information describing the layout of the file system. It is illustrated in Fig. 5-29. The main function of the super-block is to tell the file system how big the various pieces of the file system are. Given the block size and the number of i-nodes, it is easy to calculate the size of the i-node bit map and the number of blocks of i-nodes. For example, for a 1K block, each block of the bit map has 1K bytes (8K bits), and thus can keep track of the status of up to 8192 i-nodes. (Actually the first block can handle only up to 8191 i-nodes, since there is no 0th inode, but it is given a bit in the bit map, anyway). For 10,000 i-nodes, two bit map blocks are needed. Since i-nodes each occupy 64 bytes, a 1K block holds up to 16 i-nodes. With 128 usable i-nodes, 8 disk blocks are needed to contain them all.

We will explain the difference between zones and blocks in detail later, but for the time being it is sufficient to say that disk storage can be allocated in units (zones) of 1, 2, 4, 8, or in general 2^n blocks. The zone bit map keeps track of free storage in zones, not blocks. For all standard floppy disks used by MINIX the zone and block sizes are the same (1K), so for a first approximation a zone is the same as a block on these devices. Until we come to the details of storage allocation later in the chapter, it is adequate to think "block" whenever you see "zone."

Note that the number of blocks per zone is not stored in the super-block, as it is never needed. All that is needed is the base 2 logarithm of the zone to block ratio, which is used as the shift count to convert zones to blocks and vice versa. For example, with 8 blocks per zone, $\log_2 8 = 3$, so to find the zone containing block 128 we shift 128 right 3 bits to get zone 16.

The zone bit map includes only the data zones (i.e., the blocks used for the bit maps and i-nodes are not in the map), with the first data zone designated zone 1 in the bit map. As with the i-node bit map, bit 0 in the map is unused, so the first block in the zone bit map can map 8191 zones and subsequent blocks can map 8192 zones each. If you examine the bit maps on a newly formatted disk, you will

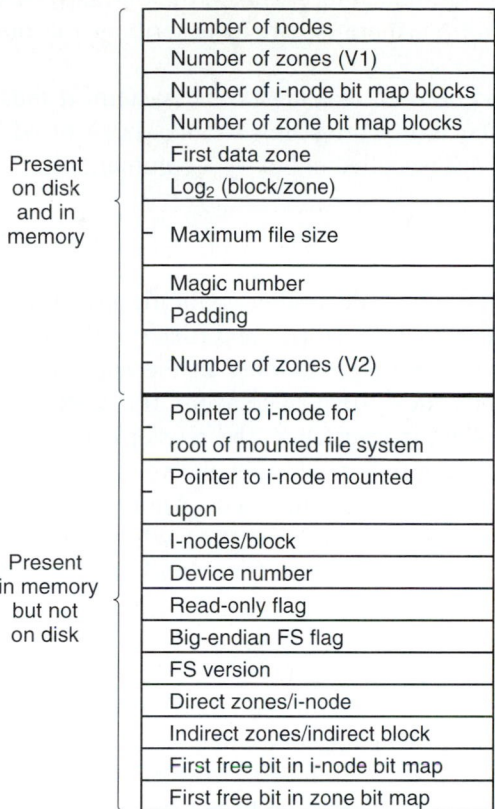

Figure 5-29. The MINIX super-block.

find that both the i-node and zone bit maps have 2 bits set to 1. One is for the nonexistent 0th i-node or zone; the other is for the i-node and zone used by the root directory on the device, which is placed there when the file system is created.

The information in the super-block is redundant because sometimes it is needed in one form and sometimes in another. With 1K devoted to the super-block, it makes sense to compute this information in all the forms it is needed, rather than having to recompute it frequently during execution. The zone number of the first data zone on the disk, for example, can be calculated from the block size, zone size, number of i-nodes, and number of zones, but it is faster just to keep it in the super-block. The rest of the super-block is wasted anyhow, so using up another word of it costs nothing.

When MINIX is booted, the super-block for the root device is read into a table in memory. Similarly, as other file systems are mounted, their super-blocks are also brought into memory. The super-block table holds a number of fields not present on the disk. These include flags that allow a device to be specified as read-only or as following a byte-order convention opposite to the standard, and fields to speed access by indicating points in the bit maps below which all bits are marked used. In addition, there is a field describing the device from which the super-block came.

Before a disk can be used as a MINIX file system, it must be given the structure of Fig. 5-28. The utility program *mkfs* has been provided to build file systems. This program can be called either by a command like

```
mkfs /dev/fd1 1440
```

to build an empty 1440 block file system on the floppy disk in drive 1, or it can be given a prototype file listing directories and files to include in the new file system. This command also puts a magic number in the super-block to identify the file system as a valid Minix file system. The Minix file system has evolved, and some aspects of the file system (for instance, the size of i-nodes) were different in earlier versions. The magic number identifies the version of *mkfs* that created the file system, so differences can be accomodated. Attempts to mount a file system not in MINIX format, such as an MS-DOS diskette, will be rejected by the MOUNT system call, which checks the super-block for a valid magic number and other things.

5.6.3 Bit Maps

MINIX keeps tracks of which i-nodes and zones are free by using two bit maps (see Fig. 5-29). When a file is removed, it is then a simple matter to calculate which block of the bit map contains the bit for the i-node being freed and to find it using the normal cache mechanism. Once the block is found, the bit corresponding to the freed i-node is set to 0. Zones are released from the zone bit map in the same way.

Logically, when a file is to be created, the file system must search through the bit-map blocks one at a time for the first free i-node. This i-node is then allocated for the new file. In fact, the in-memory copy of the super-block has a field which points to the first free i-node, so no search is necessary until after a node is used, when the pointer must be updated to point to the new next free i-node, which will often turn out to be the next one, or a close one. Similarly, when an i-node is freed, a check is made to see if the free i-node comes before the currently-pointed-to one, and the pointer is updated if necessary. If every i-node slot on the disk is full, the search routine returns a 0, which is why i-node 0 is not used (i.e., so it can be used to indicate the search failed). (When *mkfs* creates a new file system, it zeroes i-node 0 and sets the lowest bit in the bit map to 1, so the file system will never attempt to allocate it.) Everything that has been said here about the i-node bit maps also applies to the zone bit map; logically it is searched for the first free zone when space is needed, but a pointer to the first free zone is maintained to eliminate most of the need for sequential searches through the bit map.

With this background, we can now explain the difference between zones and blocks. The idea behind zones is to help ensure that disk blocks that belong to the same file are located on the same cylinder, to improve performance when the file is read sequentially. The approach chosen is to make it possible to allocate several blocks at a time. If, for example, the block size is 1K and the zone size is 4K, the zone bit map keeps track of zones, not blocks. A 20M disk has 5K zones of 4K, hence 5K bits in its zone map.

Most of the file system works with blocks. Disk transfers are always a block at a time, and the buffer cache also works with individual blocks. Only a few parts of the system that keep track of physical disk addresses (e.g., the zone bit map and the i-nodes) know about zones.

Some design decisions had to be made in developing the MINIX file system. In 1985, when MINIX was conceived, disk capacities were small, and it was expected that many users would have only floppy disks. A decision was made to restrict disk addresses to 16 bits in the V1 file system, primarily to be able to store many of them in the indirect blocks. With a 16-bit zone number and a 1K zone, only 64K zones can be addressed, limiting disks to 64M. This was an enormous amount of storage in those days, and it was thought that as disks got larger, it would be easy to switch to 2K or 4K zones, without changing the block size. The 16-bit zone numbers also made it easy to keep the i-node size to 32 bytes.

As MINIX developed, and larger disks became much more common, it was obvious that changes were desirable. Many files are smaller than 1K, so increasing the block size would mean wasting disk bandwidth, reading and writing mostly empty blocks and wasting precious main memory storing them in the buffer cache. The zone size could have been increased, but a larger zone size means more wasted disk space, and it was still desirable to retain efficient operation on small disks. Another reasonable alternative would have been to have different zone sizes on large and small devices.

In the end it was decided to increase the size of disk pointers to 32 bits. This makes it possible for the MINIX V2 file system to deal with device sizes up to 4 terabytes as 1K blocks and zones. In part this decision was driven by other decisions about what should be in the i-node, which made increasing the size of the i-node to 64 bytes reasonable.

Zones also introduce an unexpected problem, best illustrated by a simple example, again with 4K zones and 1K blocks. Suppose that a file is of length 1K, meaning that 1 zone has been allocated for it. The blocks between 1K and 4K contain garbage (residue from the previous owner), but no harm is done because the file size is clearly marked in the i-node as 1K. In fact, the blocks containing garbage will not be read into the block cache, since reads are done by blocks, not by zones. Reads beyond the end of a file always return a count of 0 and no data.

Now someone seeks to 32768 and writes 1 byte. The file size is now changed to 32769. Subsequent seeks to 1K followed by attempts to read the data will now be able to read the previous contents of the block, a major security breach.

The solution is to check for this situation when a write is done beyond the end of a file, and explicitly zero all the not-yet-allocated blocks in the zone that was previously the last one. Although this situation rarely occurs, the code has to deal with it, making the system slightly more complex.

5.6.4 I-nodes

The layout of the MINIX i-node is given in Fig. 5-30. It is almost the same as a standard UNIX i-node. The disk zone pointers are 32-bit pointers, and there are only 9 pointers, 7 direct and 2 indirect. The MINIX i-nodes occupy 64 bytes, the same as standard UNIX i-nodes, and there is space available for a 10th (triple indirect) pointer, although its use is not supported by the standard version of the FS. The MINIX i-node access, modification time and i-node change times are standard, as in UNIX. The last of these is updated for almost every file operation except a read of the file.

When a file is opened, its i-node is located and brought into the *inode* table in memory, where it remains until the file is closed. The *inode* table has a few additional fields not present on the disk, such as the i-node's device and number, so the file system knows where to rewrite it if it is modified while in memory. It also has a counter per i-node. If the same file is opened more than once, only one copy of the i-node is kept in memory, but the counter is incremented each time the file is opened and decremented each time the file is closed. Only when the counter finally reaches zero is the i-node removed from the table. If it has been modified since being loaded into memory, it is also rewritten to the disk.

The main function of a file's i-node is to tell where the data blocks are. The first seven zone numbers are given right in the i-node itself. For the standard distribution, with zones and blocks both 1K, files up to 7K do not need indirect blocks. Beyond 7K, indirect zones are needed, using the scheme of Fig. 5-10, except that only the single and double indirect blocks are used. With 1K blocks and zones and 32-bit zone numbers, a single indirect block holds 256 entries, representing a quarter megabyte of storage. The double indirect block points to 256 single indirect blocks, giving access to up to 64 megabytes. The maximum size of a MINIX file system is 1G, so modification to use the triple indirect block or larger zone sizes could both be useful if it were desirable to access very large files on a MINIX system.

The i-node also holds the mode information, which tells what kind of a file it is (regular, directory, block special, character special, or pipe), and gives the protection and SETUID and SETGID bits. The *link* field in the i-node records how many directory entries point to the i-node, so the file system knows when to release the file's storage. This field should not be confused with the counter (present only in the *inode* table in memory, not on the disk) that tells how many times the file is currently open, typically by different processes.

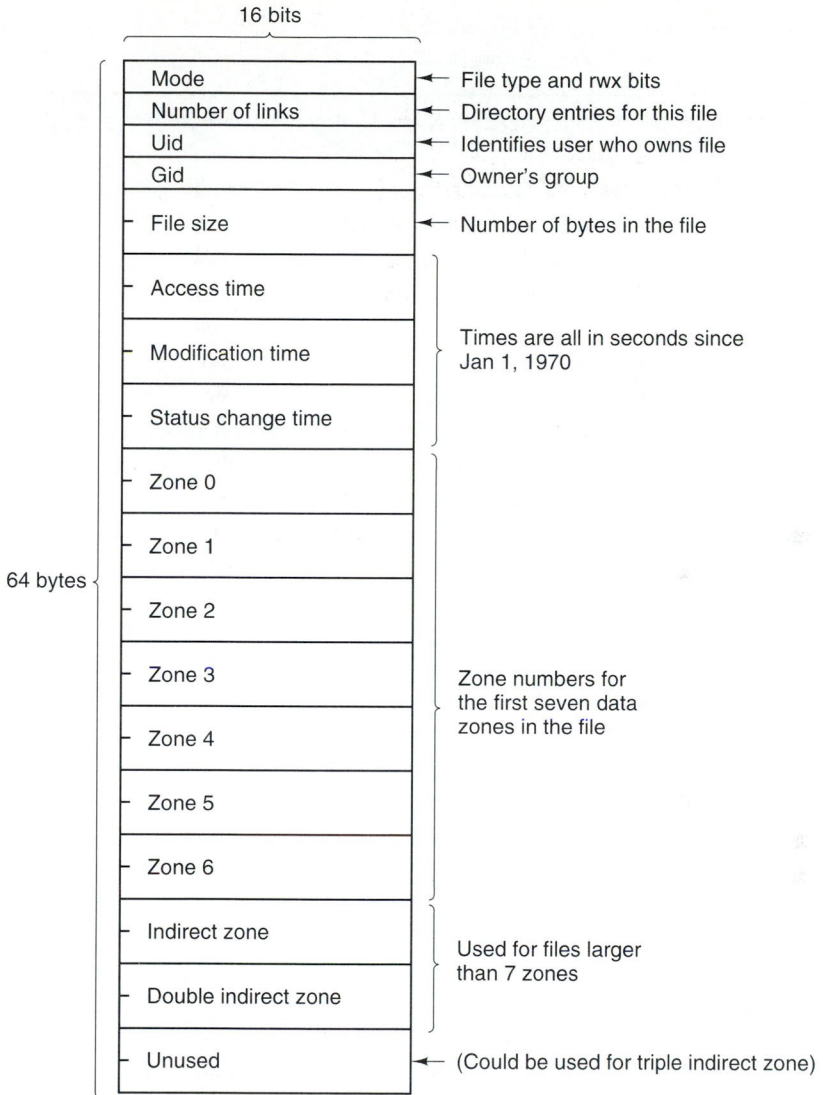

Figure 5-30. The MINIX i-node.

5.6.5 The Block Cache

MINIX uses a block cache to improve file system performance. The cache is implemented as an array of buffers, each consisting of a header containing pointers, counters, and flags, and a body with room for one disk block. All the buffers that are not in use are chained together in a double-linked list, from most recently used (MRU) to least recently used (LRU) as illustrated in Fig. 5-31.

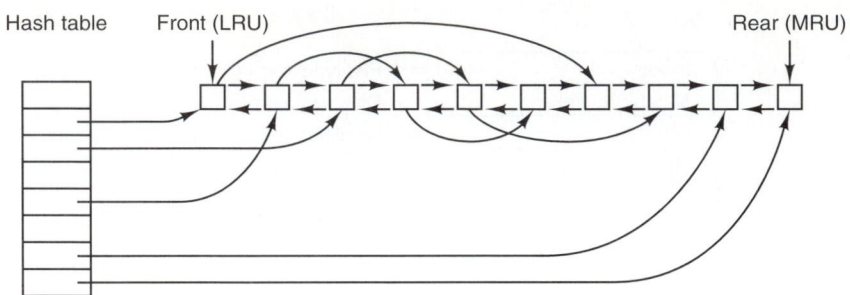

Figure 5-31. The linked lists used by the block cache.

In addition, to be able to quickly determine if a given block is in the cache or not, a hash table is used. All the buffers containing a block that has hash code k are linked together on a single-linked list pointed to by entry k in the hash table. The hash function just extracts the low-order n bits from the block number, so blocks from different devices appear on the same hash chain. Every buffer is on one of these chains. When the file system is initialized after MINIX is booted, all buffers are unused, of course, and all are in a single chain pointed to by the 0th hash table entry. At that time all the other hash table entries contain a null pointer, but once the system starts, buffers will be removed from the 0th chain and other chains will be built.

When the file system needs a block, it calls a procedure, *get_block*, which computes the hash code for that block and searches the appropriate list. *Get_block* is called with a device number as well as a block number, and the search compares both numbers with the corresponding fields in the buffer chain. If a buffer containing the block is found, a counter in the buffer header is incremented to show that the block is in use, and a pointer to it is returned. If a block is not found on the hash list, the first buffer on the LRU list can be used; it is guaranteed not to be still in use, and the block it contains may be evicted to free up the buffer.

Once a block has been chosen for eviction, another flag in its header is checked to see if the block has been modified since being read in. If so, it is rewritten to the disk. At this point the block needed is read in by sending a message to the disk task. The file system is suspended until the block arrives, at which time it continues and a pointer to the block is returned to the caller.

When the procedure that requested the block has completed its job, it calls another procedure, *put_block*, to free the block. Normally, a block will be used immediately and then released, but since it is possible that additional requests for a block will be made before it has been released, *put_block* decrements the use counter and puts the buffer back onto the LRU list only when the use counter has gone back to zero. While the counter is nonzero, the block remains in limbo.

One of the parameters to *put_block* tells what class of block (e.g., i-nodes, directory, data) is being freed. Depending on the class, two key decisions are made:

1. Whether to put the block on the front or rear of the LRU list.

2. Whether to write the block (if modified) to disk immediately or not.

Blocks that are not likely to be needed again soon, such as super-blocks, go on the front of the list so they will be claimed the next time a free buffer is needed. All other blocks go on the rear of the list in true LRU fashion.

A modified block is not rewritten until either one of two events occurs:

1. It reaches the front of the LRU chain and is evicted.

2. A SYNC system call is executed.

SYNC does not traverse the LRU chain but instead indexes through the array of buffers in the cache. Even if a buffer has not been released yet, if it has been modified, SYNC will find it and ensure that the copy on disk is updated.

There is an exception, however. A modified super-block is written to disk immediately. In an older version of MINIX a super-block was modified when a file system was mounted, and the purpose of the immediate write was to reduce the chance of corrupting the file system in the event of a crash. Super-blocks are not modified now, so the code to write them immediately is an anachronism. In the standard configuration, no other blocks are written immediately. However, by modifying the default definition of *ROBUST* in the system configuration file, *include/minix/config.h*, the file system can be compiled to mark i-node, directory, indirect, and bit-map blocks so they will be written immediately upon release. This is intended to make the file system more robust; the price paid is slower operation. Whether this will be effective is not clear. A power failure occurring when all blocks have not been yet been written is going to cause a headache whether it is an i-node or a data block that is lost.

Note that the header flag indicating that a block has been modified is set by the procedure within the file system that requested and used the block. The procedures *get_block* and *put_block* are concerned just with manipulating the linked lists. They have no idea which file system procedure wants which block or why.

5.6.6 Directories and Paths

Another important subsystem within the file system is the management of directories and path names. Many system calls, such as OPEN, have a file name as a parameter. What is really needed is the i-node for that file, so it is up to the file system to look up the file in the directory tree and locate its i-node.

A MINIX directory consists of a file containing 16-byte entries. The first 2 bytes form a 16-bit i-node number, and the remaining 14 bytes are the file name.

This is the same as the traditional UNIX directory entry we saw in Fig. 5-13. To look up the path */usr/ast/mbox*, the system first looks up *usr* in the root directory, then it looks up *ast* in */usr*, and finally it looks up *mbox* in */usr/ast*. The actual lookup proceeds one path component at a time, as illustrated in Fig. 5-14.

The only complication is what happens when a mounted file system is encountered. The usual configuration for MINIX and many other UNIX-like systems is to have a small root file system containing the files needed to start the system and to do basic system maintenance, and to have the majority of the files, including users' directories, on a separate device mounted on /usr. This is a good time to look at how mounting is done. When the user types the command

mount /dev/hd2c /usr

on the terminal, the file system contained on hard disk partition 2 is mounted on top of */usr* in the root file system. The file systems before and after mounting are shown in Fig. 5-32.

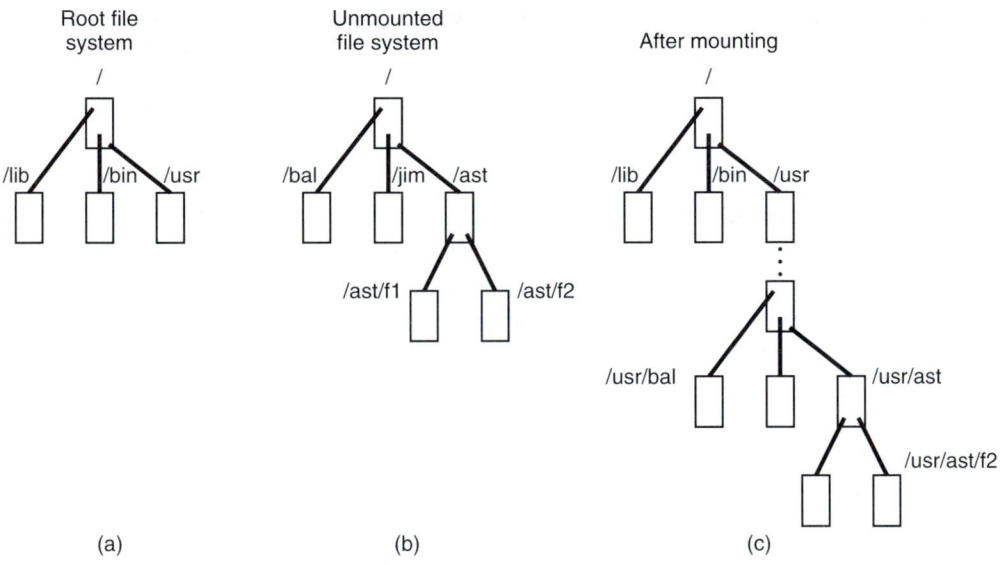

(a)   (b)   (c)

Figure 5-32. (a) Root file system. (b) An unmounted file system. (c) The result of mounting the file system of (b) on */usr*.

The key to the whole mount business is a flag set in the memory copy of the i-node of */usr* after a successful mount. This flag indicates that the i-node is mounted on. The MOUNT call also loads the super-block for the newly mounted file system into the *super_block* table and sets two pointers in it. Furthermore, it puts the root i-node of the mounted file system in the *inode* table.

In Fig. 5-29 we see that super-blocks in memory contain two fields related to mounted file systems. The first of these, the *i-node-of-the-mounted-file-system*, is set to point to the root i-node of the newly mounted file system. The second, the *i-node-mounted-on*, is set to point to the i-node mounted on, in this case, the i-node for */usr*. These two pointers serve to connect the mounted file system to the root and represent the "glue" that holds the mounted file system to the root [shown as the dots in Fig. 5-32(c)]. This glue is what makes mounted file systems work.

When a path such as */usr/ast/f2* is being looked up, the file system will see a flag in the i-node for */usr* and realize that it must continue searching at the root i-node of the file system mounted on */usr*. The question is: "How does it find this root i-node?"

The answer is straightforward. The system searches all the super-blocks in memory until it finds the one whose *i-node mounted on* field points to */usr*. This must be the super-block for the file system mounted on */usr*. Once it has the super-block, it is easy to follow the other pointer to find the root i-node for the mounted file system. Now the file system can continue searching. In this example, it looks for *ast* in the root directory of hard disk partition 2.

5.6.7 File Descriptors

Once a file has been opened, a file descriptor is returned to the user process for use in subsequent READ and WRITE calls. In this section we will look at how file descriptors are managed within the file system.

Like the kernel and the memory manager, the file system maintains part of the process table within its address space. Three of its fields are of particular interest. The first two are pointers to the i-nodes for the root directory and the working directory. Path searches, such as that of Fig. 5-14, always begin at one or the other, depending on whether the path is absolute or relative. These pointers are changed by the CHROOT and CHDIR system calls to point to the new root or new working directory, respectively.

The third interesting field in the process table is an array indexed by file descriptor number. It is used to locate the proper file when a file descriptor is presented. At first glance, it might seem sufficient to have the k-th entry in this array just point to the i-node for the file belonging to file descriptor k. After all, the i-node is fetched into memory when the file is opened and kept there until it is closed, so it is sure to be available.

Unfortunately, this simple plan fails because files can be shared in subtle ways in MINIX (as well as in UNIX). The trouble arises because associated with each file is a 32-bit number that indicates the next byte to be read or written. It is this number, called the **file position**, that is changed by the LSEEK system call. The problem can be stated easily: "Where should the file pointer be stored?"

The first possibility is to put it in the i-node. Unfortunately, if two or more processes have the same file open at the same time, they must all have their own file pointers, since it would hardly do to have an LSEEK by one process affect the next read of a different process. Conclusion: the file position cannot go in the i-node.

What about putting it in the process table? Why not have a second array, paralleling the file descriptor array, giving the current position of each file? This idea does not work either, but the reasoning is more subtle. Basically, the trouble comes from the semantics of the FORK system call. When a process forks, both the parent and the child are required to share a single pointer giving the current position of each open file.

To understand the problem better, consider the case of a shell script whose output has been redirected to a file. When the shell forks off the first program, its file position for standard output is 0. This position is then inherited by the child, which writes, say, 1K of output. When the child terminates, the shared file position must now be 1K.

Now the shell reads some more of the shell script and forks off another child. It is essential that the second child inherit a file position of 1K from the shell, so it will begin writing at the place where the first program left off. If the shell did not share the file position with its children, the second program would overwrite the output from the first one, instead of appending to it.

As a result, it is not possible to put the file position in the process table. It really must be shared. The solution used in MINIX is to introduce a new, shared table, *filp*, which contains all the file positions. Its use is illustrated in Fig. 5-33. By having the file position truly shared, the semantics of FORK can be implemented correctly, and shell scripts work properly.

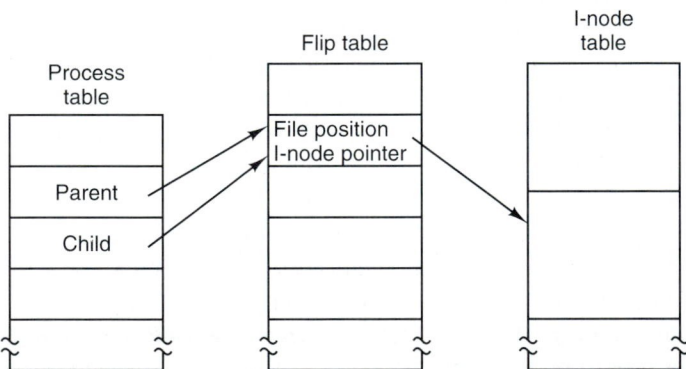

Figure 5-33. How file positions are shared between a parent and a child.

Although the only thing that the *filp* table really must contain is the shared file position, it is convenient to put the i-node pointer there, too. In this way, all that the file descriptor array in the process table contains is a pointer to a *filp* entry.

The *filp* entry also contains the file mode (permission bits), some flags indicating whether the file was opened in a special mode, and a count of the number of processes using it, so the file system can tell when the last process using the entry has terminated, in order to reclaim the slot.

5.6.8 File Locking

There is yet another aspect of file system management that requires a special table. This is file locking. MINIX supports the POSIX interprocess communication mechanism of **advisory file locking**. This permits any part, or multiple parts, of a file to be marked as locked. The operating system does not enforce locking, but processes are expected to be well behaved and to look for locks on a file before doing anything that would conflict with another process.

The reasons for providing a separate table for locks are similar to the justifications for the *filp* table discussed in the previous section. A single process can have more than one lock active, and different parts of a file may be locked by more than one process (although, of course, the locks cannot overlap), so neither the process table nor the *filp* table is a good place to record locks. Since a file may have more than one lock placed upon it, the i-node is not a good place either.

MINIX uses another table, the *file_lock* table, to record all locks. Each slot in this table has space for a lock type, indicating if the file is locked for reading or writing, the process ID holding the lock, a pointer to the i-node of the locked file, and the offsets of the first and last bytes of the locked region.

5.6.9 Pipes and Special Files

Pipes and special files differ from ordinary files in an important way. When a process tries to read or write from a disk file, it is certain that the operation will complete within a few hundred milliseconds at most. In the worst case, two or three disk accesses might be needed, not more. When reading from a pipe, the situation is different: if the pipe is empty, the reader will have to wait until some other process puts data in the pipe, which might take hours. Similarly, when reading from a terminal, a process will have to wait until somebody types something.

As a consequence, the file system's normal rule of handling a request until it is finished does not work. It is necessary to suspend these requests and restart them later. When a process tries to read or write from a pipe, the file system can check the state of the pipe immediately to see if the operation can be completed. If it can be, it is, but if it cannot be, the file system records the parameters of the system call in the process table, so it can restart the process when the time comes.

Note that the file system need not take any action to have the caller suspended. All it has to do is refrain from sending a reply, leaving the caller blocked waiting for the reply. Thus, after suspending a process, the file system goes back to its main loop to wait for the next system call. As soon as another process modifies the pipe's state so that the suspended process can complete, the file system sets a flag so that next time through the main loop it extracts the suspended process' parameters from the process table and executes the call.

The situation with terminals and other character special files is slightly different. The i-node for each special file contains two numbers, the major device and the minor device. The major device number indicates the device class (e.g., RAM disk, floppy disk, hard disk, terminal). It is used as an index into a file system table that maps it onto the number of the corresponding task (i.e., I/O driver). In effect, the major device determines which I/O driver to call. The minor device number is passed to the driver as a parameter. It specifies which device is to be used, for example, terminal 2 or drive 1.

In some cases, most notably terminal devices, the minor device number encodes some information about a category of devices handled by a task. For instance, the primary MINIX console, */dev/console*, is device 4, 0 (major, minor). Virtual consoles are handled by the same part of the driver software. These are devices */dev/ttyc1* (4,1), */dev/ttyc2* (4,2), and so on. Serial line terminals need different low-level software, and these devices, */dev/tty00*, and */dev/tty01* are assigned device numbers 4, 16 and 4, 17. Similarly, network terminals use pseudo-terminal drivers, and these also need different low-level software. In MINIX these devices, *ttyp0*, *ttyp1*, etc., are assigned device numbers such as 4, 128 and 4, 129. These pseudo devices each have an associated device, *ptyp0*, *ptyp1*, etc. The major, minor device number pairs for these are 4,192, 4,193, and so on. These numbers are chosen to make it easy for the driver task to call the low-level functions required for each group of devices. There is no expectation that anyone is going to equip a MINIX system with 192 or more terminals.

When a process reads from a special file, the file system extracts the major and minor device numbers from the file's i-node, and uses the major device number as an index into a file system table to map it onto the corresponding task number. Once it has the task number, the file system sends the task a message, including as parameters the minor device, the operation to be performed, the caller's process number and buffer address, and the number of bytes to be transferred. The format is the same as in Fig. 3-15, except that *POSITION* is not used.

If the driver is able to carry out the work immediately (e.g., a line of input has already been typed on the terminal), it copies the data from its own internal buffers to the user and sends the file system a reply message saying that the work is done. The file system then sends a reply message to the user, and the call is finished. Note that the driver does not copy the data to the file system. Data from block devices go through the block cache, but data from character special files do not.

On the other hand, if the driver is not able to carry out the work, it records the message parameters in its internal tables, and immediately sends a reply to the file system saying that the call could not be completed. At this point, the file system is in the same situation as having discovered that someone is trying to read from an empty pipe. It records the fact that the process is suspended and waits for the next message.

When the driver has acquired enough data to complete the call, it transfers them to the buffer of the still-blocked user and then sends the file system a message reporting what it has done. All the file system has to do is send a reply message to the user to unblock it and report the number of bytes transferred.

5.6.10 An Example: The READ System Call

As we shall see shortly, most of the code of the file system is devoted to carrying out system calls. Therefore, it is appropriate that we conclude this overview with a brief sketch of how the most important call, READ, works.

When a user program executes the statement

```
n = read(fd, buffer, nbytes);
```

to read an ordinary file, the library procedure *read* is called with three parameters. It builds a message containing these parameters, along with the code for READ as the message type, sends the message to the file system, and blocks waiting for the reply. When the message arrives, the file system uses the message type as an index into its tables to call the procedure that handles reading.

This procedure extracts the file descriptor from the message and uses it to locate the *filp* entry and then the i-node for the file to be read (see Fig. 5-33). The request is then broken up into pieces such that each piece fits within a block. For example, if the current file position is 600 and 1K bytes have been requested, the request is split into two parts, for 600 to 1023, and for 1024 to 1623 (assuming 1K blocks).

For each of these pieces in turn, a check is made to see if the relevant block is in the cache. If the block is not present, the file system picks the least recently used buffer not currently in use and claims it, sending a message to the disk task to rewrite it if it is dirty. Then the disk task is asked to fetch the block to be read.

Once the block is in the cache, the file system sends a message to the system task asking it to copy the data to the appropriate place in the user's buffer (i.e., bytes 600 to 1023 to the start of the buffer, and bytes 1024 to 1623 to offset 424 within the buffer). After the copy has been done, the file system sends a reply message to the user specifying how many bytes have been copied.

When the reply comes back to the user, the library function *read* extracts the reply code and returns it as the function value to the caller.

There is one extra step that is not really part of the READ call itself. After the file system completes a read and sends a reply, it then initiates a read of the next block, provided that the read is from a block device and certain other conditions are met. Since sequential file reads are common, it is reasonable to expect that the next block in a file will be requested in the next read request, and this makes it likely that the desired block will already be in the cache when it is needed.

5.7 IMPLEMENTATION OF THE MINIX FILE SYSTEM

The MINIX file system is relatively large (more than 100 pages of C) but quite straightforward. Requests to carry out system calls come in, are carried out, and replies are sent. In the following sections we will go through it a file at a time, pointing out the highlights. The code itself contains many comments to aid the reader.

In looking at the code for other parts of MINIX we have generally looked at the main loop of a process first and then looked at the routines that handle the different message types. We will organize our approach to the file system differently. First we will go through the major subsystems (cache management, i-node management, etc.). Then we will look at the main loop and the system calls that operate upon files. Next we will look at system call that operate upon directories. Finally, we will discuss the remaining system calls that fall into neither category.

5.7.1 Header Files and Global Data Structures

Like the kernel and memory manager, various data structures and tables used in the file system are defined in header files. Some of these data structures are placed in system-wide header files in *include/* and its subdirectories. For instance, *include/sys/stat.h* defines the format by which system calls can provide i-node information to other programs and the structure of a directory entry is defined in *include/sys/dir.h*. Both of these files are required by POSIX. The file system is affected by a number of definitions contained in the global configuration file *include/minix/config.h*, such as the *ROBUST* macro which defines whether important file system data structures will always be written immediately to the disk, and *NR_BUFS* and *NR_BUF_HASH*, which control the size of the block cache.

File System Headers

The file system's own header files are in the file system source directory *src/fs/*. Many file names will be familiar from studying other parts of the MINIX system. The FS master header file, *fs.h* (line 19400), is very similar to *src/kernel/kernel.h* and *src/mm/mm.h*. It includes other header files needed by all the C source files in the file system. As in the other parts of MINIX, the file system master header includes the file system's own *const.h*, *type.h*, *proto.h*, and *glo.h*. We will look at these next.

Const.h (line 19500) defines some constants, such as table sizes and flags, that are used throughout the file system. MINIX already has a history. An earlier version had a different file system, and for users who want to access files written by the earlier version, support is provided for both the old *V1* and the current *V2* file systems. The super-block of a file system contains a **magic number** so the operating system can identify the type; the constants *SUPER_MAGIC* and *SUPER_V2* define these numbers. Support of old versions is not something one reads about in theoretical texts, but it is always a concern for the implementor of a new version of any software. One must decide how much effort to devote to making life easier for users of the old version. We will see several places in the file system where support for the old version is an issue.

Type.h (line 19600) defines both the old V1 and new V2 i-node structures as they are laid out on the disk. The V2 i-node is twice as big as the old one, which was designed for compactness on systems with no hard drive and 360-KB diskettes. The new version provides space for the three time fields which UNIX systems provide. In the V1 i-node there was only one time field, but a STAT or FSTAT would "fake it" and return a *stat* structure containing all three fields. There is a minor difficulty in providing support for the two file system versions. This is flagged by the comment on line 19616. Older MINIX software expects the *gid_t* type to be an 8-bit quantity, so *d2_gid* must be declared as type *u16_t*.

Proto.h (line 19700) provides function prototypes in forms acceptable to either old K&R or newer ANSI Standard C compilers. It is a long file, but not of great interest. However, there is one point to note: because there are so many different system calls handled by the file system, and because of the way the file system is organized, the various *do_xxx* functions are scattered through a number of files. *Proto.h* is organized by file and is a handy way to find the file to consult when you want to see the code that handles a particular system call.

Finally, *glo.h* (line 19900) defines global variables. The message buffers for the incoming and reply messages are also here. The now-familiar trick with the *EXTERN* macro is used, so these variables can be accessed by all parts of the file system. As in the other parts of MINIX the storage space will be reserved when *table.c* is compiled.

The file system's part of the process table is contained in *fproc.h* (line 20000). The *fproc* array is declared with the *EXTERN* macro. It holds the mode mask, pointers to the i-nodes for the current root directory and working directory, the file descriptor array, uid, gid, and terminal number for each process. The process id and the process group id are also found here. These are duplicated in parts of the process table located in the kernel and the memory manager.

Several fields are used to store the parameters of system calls that may be suspended part way through, such as reads from an empty pipe. The fields *fp_suspended* and *fp_revived* actually require only single bits, but nearly all compilers generate better code for characters than bit fields. There is also a field for the *FD_CLOEXEC* bits called for by the POSIX standard. These are used to indicate that a file should be closed when an EXEC call is made.

Now we come to files that define other tables maintained by the file system. The first, *buf.h* (line 20100), defines the block cache. The structures here are all declared with *EXTERN*. The array *buf* holds all the buffers, each of which contains a data part, *b*, and a header full of pointers, flags, and counters. The data part is declared as a union of five types (line 20117) because sometimes it is convenient to refer to the block as a character array, sometimes as a directory, etc.

The proper way to refer to the data part of buffer 3 as a character array is *buf*[3].*b.b_ _data* because *buf*[3].*b* refers to the union as a whole, from which the *b_ _data* field is selected. Although this syntax is correct, it is cumbersome, so on line 20142 we define a macro *b_data*, which allows us to write *buf*[3].*b_data* instead. Note that *b_ _data* (the field of the union) contains two underscores, whereas *b_data* (the macro) contains just one, to distinguish them. Macros for other ways of accessing the block are defined on lines 20143 to 20148.

The buffer hash table, *buf_hash*, is defined on line 20150. Each entry points to a list of buffers. Originally all the lists are empty. The macros at the end of *buf.h* (lines 20160 to 20166) define different block types. When a block is returned to the buffer cache after use, one of these values is supplied to tell the cache manager whether to put the block on the front or rear of the LRU list, and whether to write it to disk immediately or not. The *WRITE_IMMED* bit signals that a block must be rewritten to the disk immediately if it is changed. The super-block is the only structure unconditionally marked with this. What about the other structures marked with *MAYBE_WRITE_IMMED*? This is defined in *include/minix/config.h* to be equal to *WRITE_IMMED* if *ROBUST* is true, or 0 otherwise. In the standard configuration of MINIX. *ROBUST* is defined as 0, and these blocks will be written when data blocks are written.

Finally, in the last line (line 20168) *HASH_MASK* is defined, based upon the value of *NR_BUF_HASH* configured in *include/minix/config.h*. *HASH_MASK* is ANDed with a block number to determine which entry in *buf_hash* to use as the starting point in a search for a block buffer.

The next file, *dev.h* (line 20200), defines the *dmap* table. The table itself is declared in *table.c* with initial values, so that version cannot be included in several files. This is why *dev.h* is needed. *Dmap* is declared here with *extern*, instead of *EXTERN*. The table provides the mapping between the major device number and the corresponding task.

File.h (line 20300) contains the intermediate table *filp* (declared as *EXTERN*), used to hold the current file position and i-node pointer (see Fig. 5-33). It also tells whether the file was opened for reading, writing, or both, and how many file descriptors are currently pointing to the entry.

The file locking table, *file_lock* (declared as *EXTERN*), is in *lock.h* (line 20400). The size of the array is determined by *NR_LOCKS*, which is defined as 8 in *const.h*. This number should be increased if it is desired to implement a multi-user data base on a MINIX system.

In *inode.h* (line 20500) the i-node table *inode* is declared (using *EXTERN*). It holds i-nodes that are currently in use. As we said earlier, when a file is opened its i-node is read into memory and kept there until the file is closed. The *inode* structure definition provides for information that is kept in memory, but not written to the disk i-node. Notice that there is only one version, and nothing is version-specific here. When the i-node is read in from the disk, differences between V1 and V2 file systems are handled. The rest of the file system does not need to know about the file system format on the disk, at least until the time comes to write back modified information.

Most of the fields should be self-explanatory at this point. However, *i_seek* deserves some comment. It was mentioned earlier that, as an optimization, when the file system notices that a file is being read sequentially, it tries to read blocks into the cache even before they are asked for. For randomly accessed files there is no read ahead. When an LSEEK call is made, the field *i_seek* is set to inhibit read ahead.

The file *param.h* (line 20600) is analogous to the file of the same name in the memory manager. It defines names for message fields containing parameters, so the code can refer to, for example, *buffer*, instead of *m.m1_p1*, which selects one of the fields of the message buffer *m*.

In *super.h* (line 20700), we have the declaration of the super-block table. When the system is booted, the super-block for the root device is loaded here. As file systems are mounted, their super-blocks go here as well. As with other tables, *super_block* is declared as *EXTERN*.

File System Storage Allocation

The last file we will discuss in this section is not a header. However, as we did when discussing the memory manager, it seems appropriate to discuss *table.c* immediately after reviewing the header files, since they are all included when *table.c* is compiled. Most of the data structures we have mentioned—the block cache, the *filp* table, and so on—are defined with the *EXTERN* macro, as are also the file system's global variables and the file system's part of the process table. In the same way we have seen in other parts of the MINIX system, the storage is actually reserved when *table.c* is compiled. This file also contains two major initialized arrays. *Call_vector* contains the pointer array used in the main loop for determining which procedure handles which system call number. We saw a similar table inside the memory manager.

Something new, however, is the table *dmap* on line 20914. This table has one row for each major device, starting at zero. When a device is opened, closed, read, or written, it is this table that provides the name of the procedure to call to handle the operation. All of these procedures are located in the file system's address space. Many of these procedures do nothing, but some call a task to actually request I/O. The task number corresponding to each major device is also provided by the table.

Whenever a new major device is added to MINIX, a line must be added to this table telling what action, if any, is to be taken when the device is opened, closed, read, or written. As a simple example, if a tape drive is added to MINIX, when its special file is opened, the procedure in the table could check to see if the tape drive is already in use. In order to spare users the effort of modifying this table when reconfiguring, a macro, *DT*, is defined to automate the process (line 20900).

There is a line in the table for each possible major device, and each line is written with the macro. Required devices have a 1 as the value of the *enable* argument to the macro. Some entries are not used, either because a planned driver is not yet ready or because an old driver has been removed. These entries are defined with a value of 0 for *enable*. Entries for devices that may be configured in *include/minix/config.h* use the enabling macro for the device, for instance, *ENABLE_WINI* on line 20920.

5.7.2 Table Management

Associated with each of the main tables—blocks, i-nodes, super-blocks, and so forth—is a file that contains procedures that manage the table. These procedures are heavily used by the rest of the file system and form the principal interface between tables and the file system. For this reason, it is appropriate to begin our study of the file system code with them.

Block Management

The block cache is managed by the procedures in the file *cache.c*. This file contains the nine procedures listed in Fig. 5-34. The first one, *get_block* (line 21027), is the standard way the file system gets data blocks. When a file system procedure needs to read a user data block, a directory block, a super-block, or any other kind of block, it calls *get_block*, specifying the device and block number.

Procedure	Function
get_block	Fetch a block for reading or writing
put_block	Return a block previously requested with get_block
alloc_zone	Allocate a new zone (to make a file longer)
free_zone	Release a zone (when a file is removed)
rw_block	Transfer a block between disk and cache
invalidate	Purge all the cache blocks for some device
flushall	Flush all dirty blocks for one device
rw_scattered	Read or write scattered data from or to a device
rm_lru	Remove a block from its LRU chain

Figure 5-34. Procedures used for block management.

When *get_block* is called, it first examines the block cache to see if the requested block is there. If so, it returns a pointer to it. Otherwise, it has to read the block in. The blocks in the cache are linked together on *NR_BUF_HASH* linked lists. *NR_BUF_HASH* is a tunable parameter, along with *NR_BUFS*, the size of the block cache. Both of these are set in *include/minix/config.h*. At the end of this section we will say a few words about optimizing the size of the block cache and the hash table. The *HASH_MASK* is *NR_BUF_HASH* − 1. With 256 hash lists, the mask is 255, so all the blocks on each list have block numbers that end with the same string of 8 bits, that is 00000000, 00000001, ..., or 11111111.

The first step is usually to search a hash chain for a block, although there is a special case, when a hole in a sparse file is being read, where this search is skipped. This its the reason for the test on line 21055. Otherwise, the next two lines set *bp* to point to the start of the list on which the requested block would be, if it were in the cache, applying *HASH_MASK* to the block number. The loop on the next line searches this list to see if the block can be found. If it is found and is not in use, it is removed from the LRU list. If it is already in use, it is not on the LRU list anyway. The pointer to the found block is returned to the caller on line 21063.

If the block is not on the hash list, it is not in the cache, so the least recently used block from the LRU list is taken. The buffer chosen is removed from its hash chain, since it is about to acquire a new block number and hence belongs on a different hash chain. If it is dirty, it is rewritten to the disk on line 21095. Doing this with a call to *flushall* rewrites any other dirty blocks for the same device. Blocks that are currently in use are never chosen for eviction, since they are not on the LRU chain. Blocks will hardly ever be found to be in use, however; normally a block is released by *put_block* immediately upon being used.

As soon as the buffer is available, all of the fields, including *b_dev*, are updated with the new parameters (lines 21099 to 21104), and the block may be read in from the disk. However, there are two occasions when it may not be necessary to read the block from the disk. *Get_block* is called with a parameter *only_search*. This may indicate that this is a prefetch. During a prefetch an available buffer is found, writing the old contents to the disk if necessary, and a new block number is assigned to the buffer, but the *b_dev* field is set to *NO_DEV* to signal there are as yet no valid data in this block. We will see how this is used when we discuss the *rw_scattered* function. *Only_search* can also be used to signal that the file system needs a block just to rewrite all of it. In this case it is wasteful to first read the old version in. In either of these cases the parameters are updated, but the actual disk read is omitted (lines 21107 to 21111). When the new block has been read in, *get_block* returns to its caller with a pointer to it.

Suppose that the file system needs a directory block temporarily, to look up a file name. It calls *get_block* to acquire the directory block. When it has looked up its file name, it calls *put_block* (line 21119) to return the block to the cache, thus making the buffer available in case it is needed later for a different block.

Put_block takes care of putting the newly returned block on the LRU list, and in some cases, rewriting it to the disk. At line 21144 a decision is made to put it on the front or rear of the LRU list, depending on *block_type*, a flag provided by the caller telling what kind of a block it is. Blocks that may be needed again soon go on the rear, so they will stay around for a while. Blocks that are not likely to be needed again soon are put on the front, where they will be reused quickly. Currently, only super-blocks are treated this way.

After the block has been repositioned on the LRU list, another check is made (lines 21172 and 21173) to see if the block should be rewritten to disk immediately. In the standard configuration only super-blocks are marked for immediate writing, but the only time a super-block is modified and needs to be written is when a RAM disk is resized at system initialization. In that case the write is to the RAM disk, and it is unlikely the super-block of a RAM disk will ever need to be read again. Thus, this capability is hardly used. However, the *ROBUST* macro in *include/minix/config.h* can be edited to mark for immediate writing i-nodes, directory blocks, and other blocks that are essential for the correct functioning of the file system itself.

As a file grows, from time to time a new zone must be allocated to hold the new data. The procedure *alloc_zone* (line 21180) takes care of allocating new zones. It does this by finding a free zone in the zone bit map. There is no need to search through the bit map if this is to be the first zone in a file; the *s_zsearch* field in the super-block, which always points to the first available zone on the device, is consulted. Otherwise an attempt is made to find a zone close to the last existing zone of the current file, in order to keep the zones of a file together. This is done by starting the search of the bit map at this last zone (line 21203). The mapping between the bit number in the bit map and the zone number is handled on line 21215, with bit 1 corresponding to the first data zone.

When a file is removed, its zones must be returned to the bit map. *Free_zone* (line 21222) is responsible for returning these zones. All it does is call *free_bit*, passing the zone map and the bit number as parameters. *Free_bit* is also used to return free i-nodes, but then with the i-node map as the first parameter, of course.

Managing the cache requires reading and writing blocks. To provide a simple disk interface, the procedure *rw_block* (line 21243) has been provided. It reads or writes one block. Analogously, *rw_inode* exists to read and write i-nodes.

The next procedure in the file is *invalidate* (line 21280). It is called when a disk is unmounted, for example, to remove from the cache all the blocks belonging to the file system just unmounted. If this were not done, then when the device were reused (with a different floppy disk), the file system might find the old blocks instead of the new ones.

Flushall (line 21295) is called by the SYNC system call to flush to disk all dirty buffers belonging to a specific device. It is called once for each mounted device. It treats the buffer cache as a linear array, so all dirty buffers are found, even ones that are currently in use and are not in the LRU list. All buffers in the cache are scanned, and those that belong to the device to be flushed and that need to be written are added to an array of pointers, *dirty*. This array is declared as *static* to keep it off the stack. It is then passed to *rw_scattered*.

Rw_scattered (line 21313) receives a device identifier, a pointer to an array of pointers to buffers, the size of the array, and a flag indicating whether to read or write. The first thing it does is sort the array it receives on the block numbers, so the actual read or write operation will be performed in an efficient order. It is called with the *WRITING* flag only from the *flushall* function described above. In this case the origin of these block numbers is easy to understand. They are buffers which contain data from blocks previously read but now modified. The only call to *rw_scattered* for a read operation is from *rahead* in *read.c*. At this point, we just need to know that before calling *rw_scattered*, *get_block* has been called repeatedly in prefetch mode, thus reserving a group of buffers. These buffers contain block numbers, but no valid device parameter. This is not a problem, since *rw_scattered* is called with a device parameter as one of its arguments.

There is an important difference in the way a device driver may respond to a read (as opposed to a write) request, from *rw_scattered*. A request to write a number of blocks *must* be honored completely, but a request to read a number of blocks may be handled differently by different drivers, depending upon what is most efficient for the particular driver. *Rahead* often calls *rw_scattered* with a request for a list of blocks that may not actually be needed, so the best response is to get as many blocks as can be gotten easily, but not to go wildly seeking all over a device that may have a substantial seek time. For instance, the floppy driver may stop at a track boundary, and many other drivers will read only consecutive blocks. When the read is complete, *rw_scattered* marks the blocks read by filling in the device number field in their block buffers.

The last function in Fig. 5-34 is *rm_lru* (line 21387). This function is used to remove a block from the LRU list. It is used only by *get_block* in this file, so it is declared *PRIVATE* instead of *PUBLIC* to hide it from procedures outside the file.

Before we leave the block cache, let us say a few words about fine-tuning it. *NR_BUF_HASH* must be a power of 2. If it is larger than *NR_BUFS*, the average length of a hash chain will be less than one. If there is enough memory for a large number of buffers, there is space for a large number of hash chains, so the usual choice is to make *NR_BUF_HASH* the next power of 2 greater than *NR_BUFS*. The listing in the text shows settings of 512 blocks and 1024 hash lists. The optimal size depends upon how the system is used, since that determines how much must be buffered. Empirically it was found that increasing the number of buffers beyond 1024 did not improve performance when recompiling the MINIX system, so apparently this is large enough to hold the binaries for all compiler passes. For some other kind of work a smaller size might be adequate or a larger size might improve performance.

The binary files for the MINIX system on the CD-ROM are compiled with a much smaller block cache. This is because the distribution binary is meant to run on as many machines as possible. It was desired to produce a distribution version of MINIX that could be installed in a system with only 2 MB of RAM memory. A system compiled with a 1024-block cache requires more than 2 MB of RAM. The distributed binary also includes every possible hard disk driver and other drivers that may not be useful in a particular installation. Most users will want to edit *include/minix/config.h* and recompile the system soon after installation, leaving out unnecessary drivers and enlarging the block cache as much as possible.

While on the subject of the block cache, we will point out that the 64 KB limit on memory segment size on 16-bit Intel processors makes a large cache impossible on these machines. It is possible to configure the file system to use the RAM disk as a secondary cache, to hold blocks that are pushed out of the primary cache. We do not discuss this here because it is not necessary on a 32-bit Intel system; when possible, a large primary cache will give the best performance. A secondary cache can be helpful, however, on a machine (such as a 286) that does not have room for a large primary cache within the file system's virtual address space. A secondary cache should perform better than a conventional RAM disk. A cache holds only data that is needed at least once, and if large enough can make a big improvement in system performance. "Large enough" cannot be defined in advance; it can only be measured by seeing if further increases in size result in further increases in performance. The *time* command, which measures the time used in running a program, is a useful tool when trying to optimize a system.

I-node Management

The block cache is not the only table that needs support procedures. The i-node table does, too. Many of the procedures are similar in function to the block management procedures. They are listed in Fig. 5-35.

Procedure	Function
get_inode	Fetch an i-node into memory
put_inode	Return an i-node that is no longer needed
alloc_inode	Allocate a new i-node (for a new file)
wipe_inode	Clear some fields in an i-node
free_inode	Release an i-node (when a file is removed)
update_times	Update time fields in an i-node
rw_inode	Transfer an i-node between memory and disk
old_icopy	Convert i-node contents to write to V1 disk i-node
new_icopy	Convert data read from V1 file system disk i-node
dup_inode	Indicate that someone else is using an i-node

Figure 5-35. Procedures used for i-node management.

The procedure *get_inode* (line 21534) is analogous to *get_block*. When any part of the file system needs an i-node, it calls *get_inode* to acquire it. *Get_inode* first searches the *inode* table to see if the i-node is already present. If so, it increments the usage counter and returns a pointer to it. This search is contained on lines 21546 to 21556. If the i-node is not present in memory, the i-node is loaded by calling *rw_inode*.

When the procedure that needed the i-node is finished with it, the i-node is returned by calling the procedure *put_inode* (line 21578), which decrements the usage count *i_count*. If the count is then zero, the file is no longer in use, and the i-node can be removed from the table. If it is dirty, it is rewritten to disk.

If the *i_link* field is zero, no directory entry is pointing to the file, so all its zones can be freed. Note that the usage count going to zero and the number of links going to zero are different events, with different causes and different consequences. If the i-node is for a pipe, all the zones must be released, even though the number of links may not be zero. This happens when a process reading from a pipe releases the pipe. There is no sense in having a pipe for one process.

When a new file is created, an i-node must be allocated by *alloc_inode* (line 21605). MINIX allows mounting of devices in read-only mode, so the super-block is checked to make sure the device is writable. Unlike zones, where an attempt is made to keep the zones of a file close together, any i-node will do. In order to save the time of searching the i-node bit map, advantage is taken of the field in the super-block where the first unused i-node is recorded.

After the i-node has been acquired, *get_inode* is called to fetch the i-node into the table in memory. Then its fields are initialized, partly in-line (lines 21641 to 21648) and partly using the procedure *wipe_inode* (line 21664). This particular division of labor has been chosen because *wipe_inode* is also needed elsewhere in the file system to clear certain i-node fields (but not all of them).

When a file is removed, its i-node is freed by calling *free_inode* (line 21684). All that happens here is that the corresponding bit in the i-node bit map is set to 0 and the super-block's record of the first unused i-node is updated.

The next function, *update_times* (line 21704), is called to get the time from the system clock and change the time fields that require updating. *Update_times* is also called by the STAT and FSTAT system calls, so it is declared *PUBLIC*.

The procedure *rw_inode* (line 21731) is analogous to *rw_block*. Its job is to fetch an i-node from the disk. It does its work by carrying out the following steps:

1. Calculate which block contains the required i-node.

2. Read in the block by calling *get_block*.

3. Extract the i-node and copy it to the *inode* table.

4. Return the block by calling *put_block*.

Rw_inode is a bit more complex than the basic outline given above, so some additional functions are needed. First, because getting the current time is expensive, any need for a change to the time fields in the i-node is only marked by setting bits in the i-node's *i_update* field while the i-node is in memory. If this field is nonzero when an i-node must be written, *update_times* is called.

Second, MINIX' history adds a complication: In the old *V1* version of the file system the i-nodes on the disk have a different structure from *V2*. Two functions, *old_icopy* (line 21774) and *new_icopy* (line 21821) take care of the conversions. The first converts between i-node information in memory and the format used by the *V1* filesystem. The second does the same conversion for *V2* filesystem disks. Both of these functions are called only from within this file, so they are declared *PRIVATE*. Each function handles conversions in both directions (disk to memory or memory to disk). MINIX has been implemented on systems which use a different byte order from Intel processors. Every implementation uses the native byte order on its disk; the *sp−>native* field in the super-block identifies which order is used. Both *old_icopy* and *new_icopy* call functions *conv2* and *conv4* to swap byte orders, if necessary.

The procedure *dup_inode* (line 21865) just increments the usage count of the i-node. It is called when an open file is opened again. On the second open, the i-node need not be fetched from disk again.

Super-block Management

The file *super.c* contains procedures that manage the super-block and the bit maps. There are five procedures in this file, listed in Fig. 5-36.

Procedure	Function
alloc_bit	Allocate a bit from the zone or i-node map
free_bit	Free a bit in the zone or i-node map
get_super	Search the super-block table for a device
mounted	Report whether given i-node is on a mounted (or root) f.s.
read_super	Read a super-block

Figure 5-36. Procedures used to manage the super-block and bit maps.

When an i-node or zone is needed, *alloc_inode* or *alloc_zone* is called, as we have seen above. Both of these call *alloc_bit* (line 21926) to actually search the relevant bit map. The search involves three nested loops, as follows:

1. The outer one loops on all the blocks of a bit map.

2. The middle one loops on all the words of a block.

3. The inner one loops on all the bits of a word.

The middle loop works by seeing if the current word is equal to the one's complement of zero, that is, a complete word full of 1s. If so, it has no free i-nodes or zones, so the next word is tried. When a word with a different value is found, it must have at least one 0 bit in it, so the inner loop is entered to find the free (i.e., 0) bit. If all the blocks have been tried without success, there are no free i-nodes or zones, so the code *NO_BIT* (0) is returned. Searches like this can consume a lot of processor time, but the use of the super-block fields that point to the first unused i-node and zone, passed to *alloc_bit* in *origin*, helps to keep these searches short.

Freeing a bit is simpler than allocating one, because no search is needed. *Free_bit* (line 22003) calculates which bit map block contains the bit to free and sets the proper bit to 0 by calling *get_block*, zeroing the bit in memory and then calling *put_block*.

The next procedure, *get_super* (line 22047), is used to search the super-block table for a specific device. For example, when a file system is to be mounted, it is necessary to check that it is not already mounted. This check can be performed by asking *get_super* to find the file system's device. If it does not find the device, then the file system is not mounted.

The next function, *mounted* (line 22067), is called only when a block device is closed. Normally, all cached data for a device are discarded when it is last closed. But, if the device happens to be mounted, this is not desirable. *Mounted* is called with a pointer to the i-node for a device. It just returns *TRUE* if the device is the root device, or if it is a mounted device.

Finally, we have *read_super* (line 22088). This is partially analogous to *rw_block* and *rw_inode*, but it is called only to read. Writing a super-block is not necessary in the normal operation of the system. *Read_super* checks the version of the file system from which it has just read and performs conversions, if necessary, so the copy of the super-block in memory will have the standard structure even when read from a disk with a different super-block structure.

File Descriptor Management

MINIX contains special procedures to manage file descriptors and the *filp* table (see Fig. 5-33). They are contained in the file *filedes.c*. When a file is created or opened, a free file descriptor and a free *filp* slot are needed. The procedure *get_fd* (line 22216) is used to find them. They are not marked as in use, however, because many checks must first be made before it is known for sure that the CREAT or OPEN will succeed.

Get_filp (line 22263) is used to see if a file descriptor is in range, and if so, returns its *filp* pointer.

The last procedure in this file is *find_filp* (line 22277). It is needed to find out when a process is writing on a broken pipe (i.e., a pipe not open for reading by any other process). It locates potential readers by a brute force search of the *filp* table. If it cannot find one, the pipe is broken and the write fails.

File Locking

The POSIX record locking functions are shown in Fig. 5-37. A part of a file can be locked for reading and writing, or for writing only, by an FCNTL call specifying a *F_SETLK* or *F_SETLKW* request. Whether a lock exists over a part of a file can be determined using the *F_GETLK* request.

Operation	Meaning
F_SETLK	Lock region for both reading and writing
F_SETLKW	Lock region for writing
F_GETLK	Report if region is locked

Figure 5-37. The POSIX advisory record locking operations. These operations are requested by using an FCNTL system call.

There are only two functions in the file *lock.c*. *Lock_op* (line 22319) is called by the FCNTL system call with a code for one of the operations shown in Fig. 5-37. It does some error checking to be sure the region specified is valid. When a lock is being set, it must not conflict with an existing lock, and when a lock is being cleared, an existing lock must not be split in two. When any lock is cleared, the other function in this file, *lock_revive* (line 22463), is called. It wakes up all the processes that are blocked waiting for locks. This strategy is a compromise; it would take extra code to figure out exactly which processes were waiting for a particular lock to be released. Those processes that are still waiting for a locked file will block again when they start. This strategy is based on an assumption that locking will be used infrequently. If a major multiuser data base were to built upon a MINIX system, it might be desirable to reimplement this.

Lock_revive is also called when a locked file is closed, as might happen, for instance, if a process is killed before it finishes using a locked file.

5.7.3 The Main Program

The main loop of the file system is contained in file *main.c*, starting at line 22537. Structurally, it is very similar to the main loop of the memory manager and the I/O tasks. The call to *get_work* waits for the next request message to arrive (unless a process previously suspended on a pipe or terminal can now be handled). It also sets a global variable, *who*, to the caller's process table slot number and another global variable, *fs_call*, to the number of the system call to be carried out.

Once back in the main loop, three flags are set: *fp* points to the caller's process table slot, *super_user* tells whether the caller is the super-user or not, and *dont_reply* is initialized to *FALSE*. Then comes the main attraction—the call to the procedure that carries out the system call. The procedure to call is selected by using *fs_call* as an index into the array of procedure pointers, *call_vector*.

When control comes back to the main loop, if *dont_reply* has been set, the reply is inhibited (e.g., a process has blocked trying to read from an empty pipe). Otherwise a reply is sent. The final statement in the main loop has been designed to detect that a file is being read sequentially and to load the next block into the cache before it is actually requested, to improve performance.

The procedure *get_work* (line 22572) checks to see if any previously blocked procedures have now been revived. If so, these have priority over new messages. Only if there is no internal work to do does the file system call the kernel to get a message, on line 22598.

After a system call has been completed, successfully or otherwise, a reply is sent back to the caller by *reply* (line 22608). The process may have been killed by a signal, so the status code returned by the kernel is ignored. In this case there is nothing to be done anyway.

Initialization Functions

The rest of *main.c* consists of functions that are used only at system startup. Before the file system enters its main loop, it initializes itself by calling *fs_init* (line 22625), which in turn calls several other functions to initialize the block cache, get the boot parameters, load the RAM disk if necessary, and load the root device super-block. The next step is to initialize the file system's part of the process table for all the tasks and servers, up through *init* (lines 22643 to 22654). Finally, tests are done on some important constants, to see if they make sense, and a message is sent to the memory task with the address of the file system's part of the process table, for use by the *ps* program.

The first function called by *fs_init* is *buf_pool* (line 22679), which builds the linked lists used by the block cache. Figure 5-31 shows the normal state of the block cache, in which all blocks are linked on both the LRU chain and a hash chain. It may be helpful to see how the situation of Fig. 5-31 comes about. Immediately after the cache is initialized by *buf_pool*, all the buffers will be on the LRU chain, and all will be linked into the 0th hash chain, as in Fig. 5-38(a). When a buffer is requested, and while it is in use, we have the situation of Fig. 5-38(b), in which we see that a block has been removed from the LRU chain and is now on a different hash chain. Normally, blocks are released and returned to the LRU chain immediately. Figure 5-38(c) shows the situation after the block has been returned to the LRU chain. Although it is no longer in use, it can be accessed again to provide the same data, if need be, and so it is retained on the hash chain. After the system has been in operation for awhile, almost all of the blocks can be expected to have been used and to be distributed among the different hash chains at random. Then the LRU chain will look like Fig. 5-31.

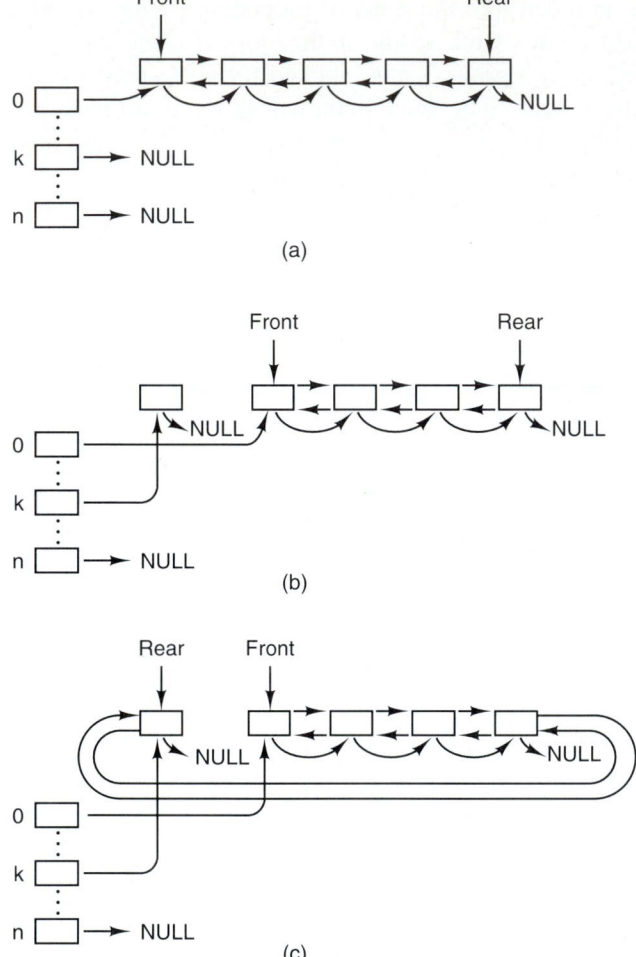

Figure 5-38. Block cache initialization. (a) Before any buffers have been used. (b) After one block has been requested. (c) After the block has been released.

The next function is *get_boot_parameters* (line 22706). It sends a message to the system task to ask it for a copy of the boot parameters. They are needed by the following function, *load_ram* (line 22722), which allocates space for a RAM disk. If the boot parameters specify

rootdev = ram

the root device file system is copied from the device named by *ramimagedev* to the RAM disk block by block, starting with the bootblock, with no interpretation of the various file system data structures. If the *ramsize* boot parameter is smaller than the size of the root device file system, the RAM disk is made large enough to hold it. If *ramsize* specifies a size larger than the boot device file system the specified size is allocated and the RAM disk file system is adjusted to use the full size specified (lines 22819 to 22825). The call to *put_block* on line 22825 is the only time that the file system ever writes a super-block.

Load_ram allocates space for an empty RAM disk if a nonzero *ramsize* is specified. In this case, since no file system structures are copied, the RAM device cannot be used as a file system until it has been initialized by the *mkfs* command. Alternatively, such a RAM disk can be used for a secondary cache if support for this is compiled into the file system.

The last function in *main.c* is *load_super* (line 22832). It initializes the super-block table and reads in the super-block of the root device.

5.7.4 Operations on Individual Files

In this section we will look at the system calls that operate on individual files one at a time (as opposed to, say, operations on directories). We will start with how files are created, opened, and closed. After that we will examine in some detail the mechanism by which files are read and written. After that we will look at how pipes and how operations on them differ from those on files.

Creating, Opening, and Closing Files

The file *open.c* contains the code for six system calls: CREAT, OPEN, MKNOD, MKDIR, CLOSE, and LSEEK. We will examine CREAT and OPEN together, and then look at each of the others.

In older versions of UNIX, the CREAT and OPEN calls had distinct purposes. Trying to open a file that did not exist was an error, and a new file had to be created with CREAT, which could also be used to truncate an existing file to zero length. The need for two distinct calls is no longer present in a POSIX system, however. Under POSIX, the OPEN call now allows creating a new file or truncating an old file, so the CREAT call now represents a subset of the possible uses of the OPEN call and is really only necessary for compatibility with older programs. The procedures that handle CREAT and OPEN are *do_creat* (line 22937) and *do_open* (line 22951). (As in the memory manager, the convention is used in the file system that system call XXX is performed by procedure *do_xxx*). Opening or creating a file involves three steps:

1. Finding the i-node (allocating and initializing if the file is new).

2. Finding or creating the directory entry.

3. Setting up and returning a file descriptor for the file.

Both the CREAT and the OPEN calls do two things: they fetch the name of a file and then they call *common_open* which takes care of tasks common to both calls.

Common_open (line 22975) starts by making sure that free file descriptor and *filp* table slots are available. If the calling function specified creation of a new file (by calling with the *O_CREAT* bit set), *new_node* is called on line 22998. *New_node* returns a pointer to an existing i-node if the directory entry already exists; otherwise it will create both a new directory entry and i-node. If the i-node cannot be created, *new_node* sets the global variable *err_code*. An error code does not always mean an error. If *new_node* finds an existing file, the error code returned will indicate that the file exists, but in this case that error is acceptable (line 23001). If the *O_CREAT* bit is not set, a search is made for the i-node using an alternative method, the *eat_path* function in *path.c*, which we will discuss further on. At this point, the important thing to understand is that if an i-node is not found or successfully created, *common_open* will terminate with an error before line 23010 is reached. Otherwise, execution continues here with assignment of a file descriptor and claiming of a slot in the *filp* table, Following this, if a new file has just been created, lines 23017 to 23094 are skipped.

If the file is not new, then the file system must test to see what kind of a file it is, what its mode is, and so on, to determine whether it can be opened. The call to *forbidden* on line 23018 first makes a general check of the *rwx* bits. If the file is a regular file and *common_open* was called with the *O_TRUNC* bit set, it is truncated to length zero and *forbidden* is called again (line 23024), this time to be sure the file may be written. If the permissions allow, *wipe_inode* and *rw_inode* are called to re-initialize the i-node and write it to the disk. Other file types (directories, special files, and named pipes) are subjected to appropriate tests. In the case of a device, a call is made on line 23053 (using the *dmap* structure) to the appropriate routine to open the device. In the case of a named pipe, a call is made to *pipe_open* (line 23060), and various tests relevant to pipes are made.

The code of *common_open*, as well as many other file system procedures, contains a large amount of code that checks for various errors and illegal combinations. While not glamorous, this code is essential to having an error-free, robust file system. If something is wrong, the file descriptor and *filp* slot previously allocated are deallocated and the i-node is released (lines 23098 to 23101). In this case the value returned by *common_open* will be a negative number, indicating an error. If there are no problems the file descriptor, a positive value, is returned.

This is a good place to discuss in more detail the operation of *new_node* (line 23111), which does the allocation of the i-node and the entering of the path name into the file system for CREAT and OPEN calls. It is also used for the MKNOD and MKDIR calls, yet to be discussed. The statement on line 23128 parses the path name (i.e., looks it up component by component) as far as the final directory; the call to *advance* three lines later tries to see if the final component can be opened.

For example, on the call

fd = creat("/usr/ast/foobar", 0755);

last_dir tries to load the i-node for */usr/ast* into the tables and return a pointer to it. If the file does not exist, we will need this i-node shortly in order to add *foobar* to the directory. All the other system calls that add or delete files also use *last_dir* to first open the final directory in the path.

If *new_node* discovers that the file does not exist, it calls *alloc_inode* on line 23134 to allocate and load a new i-node, returning a pointer to it. If no free i-nodes are left, *new_node* fails and returns *NIL_INODE*.

If an i-node can be allocated, the operation continues at line 23144, filling in some of the fields, writing it back to the disk, and entering the file name in the final directory (on line 23149). Again we see that the file system must constantly check for errors, and upon encountering one, carefully release all the resources, such as i-nodes and blocks that it is holding. If we were prepared to just let MINIX panic when we ran out of, say, i-nodes, rather than undoing all the effects of the current call and returning an error code to the caller, the file system would be appreciably simpler.

As mentioned above, pipes require special treatment. If there is not at least one reader/writer pair for a pipe, *pipe_open* (line 23176) suspends the caller. Otherwise, it calls *release*, which looks through the process table for processes that are blocked on the pipe. If it is successful, the processes are revived.

The MKNOD call is handled by *do_mknod* (line 23205). This procedure is similar to *do_creat*, except that it just creates the i-node and makes a directory entry for it. In fact, most of the work is done by the call to *new_node* on line 23217. If the i-node already exists, an error code will be returned. This is the same error code that was an acceptable result from *new_node* when it was called by *common_open*; in this case, however, the error code is passed back to the caller, which presumably will act accordingly. The case-by-case analysis we saw in *common_open* is not needed here.

The MKDIR call is handled by the function *do_mkdir* (line 23226). As with the other system calls we have discussed here, *new_node* plays an important part. Directories, unlike files, always have links and are never completely empty because every directory must contain two entries from the time of its creation: the "." and ".." entries that refer to the directory itself and to its parent directory. There is a limit to the number of links a file may have, *LINK_MAX* (defined in *include/limits.h* as 127 for the standard MINIX system). Since the reference to a parent directory in a child is a link to the parent, the first thing *do_mkdir* does is to see if it is possible to make another link in the parent directory (line 23240). Once this test has been passed, *new_node* is called. If *new_node* succeeds, then the directory entries for "." and ".." are made (lines 23261 and 23262). All of this is straightforward, but there could be failures (for instance, if the disk is full), and to avoid making a mess of things provision is made for undoing the initial stages of the process if it can not be completed.

Closing a file is easier than opening one. The work is done by *do_close* (line 23286). Pipes and special files need some attention, but for regular files, almost all that needs to be done is to decrement the *filp* counter and check to see if it is zero, in which case the i-node is returned with *put_inode*. The final step is to remove any locks and to revive any process that may have been suspended waiting for a lock on the file to be released.

Note that returning an i-node means that its counter in the *inode* table is decremented, so it can be removed from the table eventually. This operation has nothing to do with freeing the i-node (i.e., setting a bit in the bit map saying that it is available). The i-node is only freed when the file has been removed from all directories.

The final procedure in *open.c* is *do_lseek* (line 23367). When a seek is done, this procedure is called to set the file position to a new value. On line 23394 reading ahead is inhibited; an explicit attempt to seek to a position in a file is incompatible with sequential access.

Reading a File

Once a file has been opened, it can be read or written. Many functions are used during both reading and writing. These are found in the file *read.c*. We will discuss these first and then proceed to the following file, *write.c*, to look at code specifically used for writing. Reading and writing differ in a number of ways, but they have enough similarities that all that is required of *do_read* (line 23434) is to call the common procedure *read_write* with a flag set to *READING*. We will see in the next section that *do_write* is equally simple.

Read_write begins on line 23443. There is some special code on lines 23459 to 23462 that is used by the memory manager to have the file system load entire segments in user space for it. Normal calls are processed starting on line 23464. Some validity checks follow (e.g., reading from a file opened only for writing) and some variables are initialized. Reads from character special files do not go through the block cache, so they are filtered out on line 23498.

The tests on lines 23507 to 23518 apply only to writes and have to do with files that may get bigger than the device can hold, or writes that will create a hole in the file by writing *beyond* the end-of-file. As we discussed in the MINIX overview, the presence of multiple blocks per zone causes problems that must be dealt with explicitly. Pipes are also special and are checked for.

The heart of the read mechanism, at least for ordinary files, is the loop starting on line 23530. This loop breaks the request up into chunks, each of which fits in a single disk block. A chunk begins at the current position and extends until one of the following conditions is met:

1. All the bytes have been read.

2. A block boundary is encountered.

3. The end-of-file is hit.

These rules mean that a chunk never requires two disk blocks to satisfy it. Figure

5-39 shows three examples of how the chunk size is determined, for chunk sizes of 6, 2, and 1 bytes, respectively. The actual calculation is done on lines 23632 to 23641.

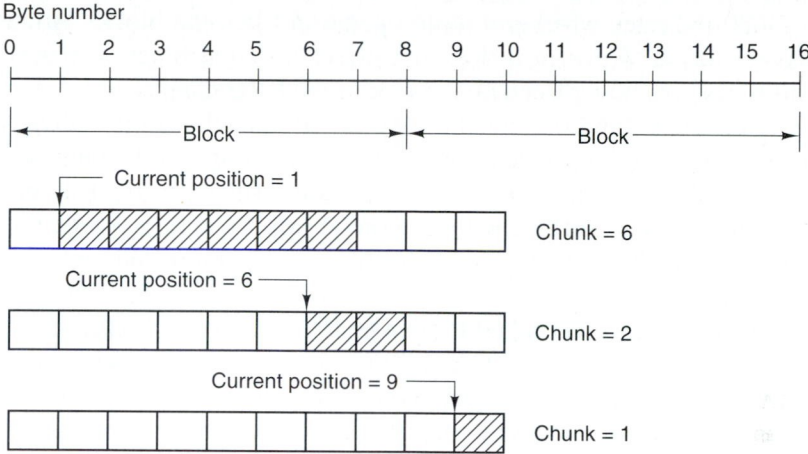

Figure 5-39. Three examples of how the first chunk size is determined for a 10-byte file. The block size is 8 bytes, and the number of bytes requested is 6. The chunk is shown shaded.

The actual reading of the chunk is done by *rw_chunk*. When control returns, various counters and pointers are incremented, and the next iteration begins. When the loop terminates, the file position and other variables may be updated (e.g., pipe pointers).

Finally, if read ahead is called for, the i-node to read from and the position to read from are stored in global variables, so that after the reply message is sent to the user, the file system can start working on getting the next block. In many cases the file system will block, waiting for the next disk block, during which time the user process will be able to work on the data it just received. This arrangement overlaps processing and I/O and can improve performance substantially.

The procedure *rw_chunk* (line 23613) is concerned with taking an i-node and a file position, converting them into a physical disk block number, and requesting the transfer of that block (or a portion of it) to the user space. The mapping of the relative file position to the physical disk address is done by *read_map*, which understands about i-nodes and indirect blocks. For an ordinary file, the variables *b* and *dev* on lines 23637 and 23638 contain the physical block number and device number, respectively. The call to *get_block* on line 23660 is where the cache handler is asked to find the block, reading it in if need be.

Once we have a pointer to the block, the call to *sys_copy* on line 23670 takes care of transferring the required portion of it to the user space. The block is then released by *put_block*, so that it can be evicted from the cache later, when the time comes. (After being acquired by *get_block*, it will not be in the LRU queue and it will not be returned there while the counter in the block's header shows that it is in use, so it will be exempt from eviction; *put_block* decrements the counter and returns the block to the LRU queue when the counter reaches zero.) The code on line 23680 indicates whether a write operation filled the block. However, the value passed to *put_block* in *n* does not affect how the block is placed on the queue; all blocks are now placed on the rear of the LRU chain.

Read_map (line 23689) converts a logical file position to the physical block number by inspecting the i-node. For blocks close enough to the beginning of the file that they fall within one of the first seven zones (the ones right in the i-node), a simple calculation is sufficient to determine which zone is needed, and then which block. For blocks further into the file, one or more indirect blocks may have to be read.

Rd_indir (line 23753) is called to read an indirect block. It is made a separate procedure because there are different formats the data may take on the disk, depending upon the version of the file system and the hardware on which the file system was written. The messy conversions are done here, if necessary, so the rest of the file system sees data in only one form.

Read_ahead (line 23786) converts the logical position to a physical block number, calls *get_block* to make sure the block is in the cache (or bring it in), and then returns the block immediately. It cannot do anything with the block, after all. It just wants to improve the chance that the block is around if it should be used soon.

Note that *read_ahead* is called only from the main loop in *main*. It is not called as part of the processing of the READ system call. It is important to realize that the call to *read_ahead* is performed *after* the reply is sent, so that the user will be able to continue running even if the file system has to wait for a disk block while reading ahead.

Read_ahead by itself is designed to ask for just one more block. It calls the last function in *read.c*, *rahead*, to actually get the job done. *Rahead* (line 23805) works according to the theory that if a little more is good, a lot more is better. Since disks and other storage devices often take a relatively long time to locate the first block requested but then can relatively quickly read in a number of adjacent blocks, it may be possible to get many more blocks read with little additional effort. A prefetch request is made to *get_block*, which prepares the block cache to receive a number of blocks at once. Then *rw_scattered* is called with a list of blocks. We have previously discussed this; recall that when the device drivers are actually called by *rw_scattered*, each one is free to answer only as much of the request as it can efficiently handle. This all sounds fairly complicated, but the complications make possible a significant speedup of applications which read large amounts of data from the disk.

Figure 5-40 shows the relations between some of the major procedures involved in reading a file, in particular, who calls whom.

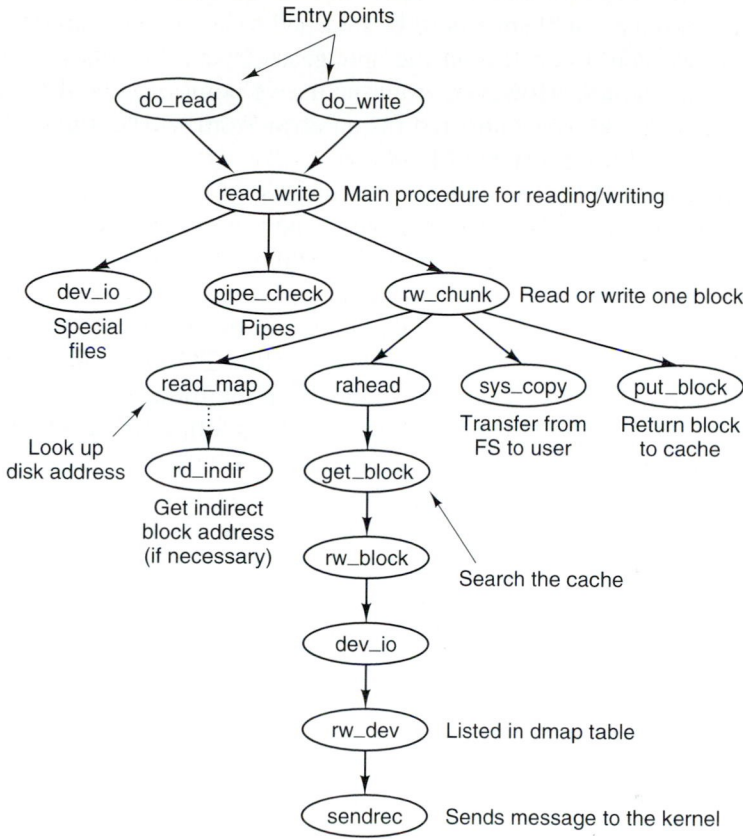

Figure 5-40. Some of the procedures involved in reading a file.

Writing a File

The code for writing to files is in *write.c*. Writing a file is similar to reading one, and *do_write* (line 24025) just calls *read_write* with the *WRITING* flag. A major difference between reading and writing is that writing requires allocating new disk blocks. *Write_map* (line 24036) is analogous to *read_map*, only instead of looking up physical block numbers in the i-node and its indirect blocks, it enters new ones there (to be precise, it enters zone numbers, not block numbers).

The code of *write_map* is long and detailed because it must deal with several cases. If the zone to be inserted is close to the beginning of the file, it is just inserted into the i-node on (line 24058).

The worst case is when a file exceeds the size that can be handled by a single-indirect block, so a double-indirect block is now required. Next, a single-indirect block must be allocated and its address put into the double-indirect block. As with reading, a separate procedure, *wr_indir*, is called. If the double-indirect block is acquired correctly, but the disk is full so the single-indirect block cannot be allocated, then the double one must be returned to avoid corrupting the bit map.

Again, if we could just toss in the sponge and panic at this point, the code would be much simpler. However, from the user's point of view it is much nicer that running out of disk space just returns an error from WRITE, rather than crashing the computer with a corrupted file system.

Wr_indir (line 24127) calls one of the conversion routines, *conv2* or *conv4* to do any necessary data conversion and puts a new zone number into an indirect block. Keep in mind that the name of this function, like the names of many other functions that involve reading and writing, is not literally true. The actual writing to the disk is handled by the functions that maintain the block cache.

The next procedure in *write.c* is *clear_zone* (line 24149), which takes care of the problem of erasing blocks that are suddenly in the middle of a file. This happens when a seek is done beyond the end of a file, followed by a write of some data. Fortunately, this situation does not occur very often.

New_block (line 24190) is called by *rw_chunk* whenever a new block is needed. Figure 5-41 shows six successive stages of the growth of a sequential file. The block size is 1K and the zone size is 2K in this example.

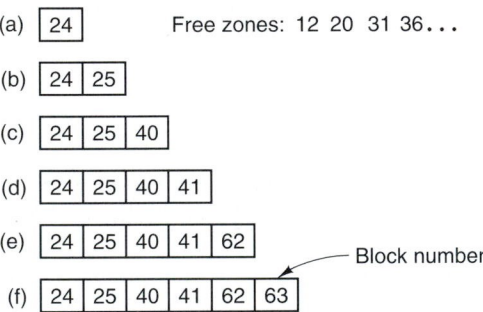

Figure 5-41. (a) - (f) The successive allocation of 1K blocks with a 2K zone.

The first time *new_block* is called, it allocates zone 12 (blocks 24 and 25). The next time it uses block 25, which has already been allocated but is not yet in use. On the third call, zone 20 (blocks 40 and 41) is allocated, and so on. *Zero_block* (line 24243) clears a block, erasing its previous contents. This description is considerably longer than the actual code.

Pipes

Pipes are similar to ordinary files in many respects. In this section we will focus on the differences. The code we will discuss is all in *pipe.c*.

First of all, pipes are created differently, by the PIPE call, rather than the CREAT call. The PIPE call is handled by *do_pipe* (line 24332). All *do_pipe* really does is allocate an i-node for the pipe and return two file descriptors for it. Pipes are owned by the system, not by the user, and are located on the designated pipe device (configured in *include/minix/config.h*), which could very well be a RAM disk, since pipe data do not have to be preserved permanently.

Reading and writing a pipe is slightly different from reading and writing a file, because a pipe has a finite capacity. An attempt to write to a pipe that is already full will cause the writer to be suspended. Similarly, reading from an empty pipe will suspend the reader. In effect, a pipe has two pointers, the current position (used by readers) and the size (used by writers), to determine where data come from or go to.

The various checks to see if an operation on a pipe is possible are carried out by *pipe_check* (line 24385). In addition to the above tests, which may lead to the caller being suspended, *pipe_check* calls *release* to see if a process previously suspended due to no data or too much data can now be revived. These revivals are done on line 24413 and line 24452, for sleeping writers and readers, respectively. Writing on a broken pipe (no readers) is also detected here.

The act of suspending a process is done by *suspend* (line 24463). All it does is save the parameters of the call in the process table and set the flag *dont_reply* to *TRUE*, to inhibit the file system's reply message.

The procedure *release* (line 24490) is called to check if a process that was suspended on a pipe can now be allowed to continue. If it finds one, it calls *revive* to set a flag so that the main loop will notice it later. This function is not a system call, but is listed in Fig. 5-27(c) because it uses the message passing mechanism.

The last procedure in *pipe.c* is *do_unpause* (line 24560). When the memory manager is trying to signal a process, it must find out if that process is hanging on a pipe or special file (in which case it must be awakened with an *EINTR* error). Since the memory manager knows nothing about pipes or special files, it sends a message to the file system to ask. That message is processed by *do_unpause*, which revives the process, if it is blocked. Like *revive*, *do_unpause* has some similarity to a system call, although it is not one.

5.7.5 Directories and Paths

We have now finished looking at how files are read and written. Our next task is to see how path names and directories are handled.

Converting a Path to an I-node

Many system calls (e.g., OPEN, UNLINK, and MOUNT) have path names (i.e., file names) as a parameter. Most of these calls must fetch the i-node for the named file before they can start working on the call itself. How a path name is converted to an i-node is a subject we will now look at in detail. We already saw the general outline in Fig. 5-14.

The parsing of path names is done in the file *path.c*. The first procedure, *eat_path* (line 24727), accepts a pointer to a path name, parses it, arranges for its i-node to be loaded into memory, and returns a pointer to the i-node. It does its work by calling *last_dir* to get the i-node to the final directory and then calling *advance* to get the final component of the path. If the search fails, for example, because one of the directories along the path does not exist, or exists but is protected against being searched, *NIL_INODE* is returned instead of a pointer to the i-node.

Path names may be absolute or relative and may have arbitrarily many components, separated by slashes. These issues are dealt with by *last_dir* (line 24754). It begins (line 24771) by examining the first character of the path name to see if it is an absolute path or a relative one. For absolute paths, *rip* is set to point to the root i-node; for relative ones, it is set to point to the i-node for the current working directory.

At this point, *last_dir* has the path name and a pointer to the i-node of the directory to look up the first component in. It enters a loop on line 24782 now, parsing the path name, component by component. When it gets to the end, it returns a pointer to the final directory.

Get_name (line 24813) is a utility procedure that extracts components from strings. More interesting is *advance* (line 24855), which takes as parameters a directory pointer and a string, and looks up the string in the directory. If it finds the string, *advance* returns a pointer to its i-node. The details of transferring across mounted file systems are handled here.

Although *advance* controls the string lookup, the actual comparison of the string against the directory entries is done in *search_dir* (line 24936), which is the only place in the file system where directory files are actually examined. It contains two nested loops, one to loop over the blocks in a directory, and one to loop over the entries in a block. *Search_dir* is also used to enter and delete names from directories. Figure 5-42 shows the relationships between some of the major procedures used in looking up path names.

Mounting File Systems

Two system calls that affect the file system as a whole are MOUNT and UMOUNT. They allow independent file systems on different minor devices to be "glued" together to form a single, seamless naming tree. Mounting, as we saw in Fig. 5-32, is effectively achieved by reading in the root i-node and super-block of the file system to be mounted and setting two pointers in its super-block. One of them points to the i-node mounted on, and the other points to the root i-node of the mounted file system. These pointers hook the file systems together.

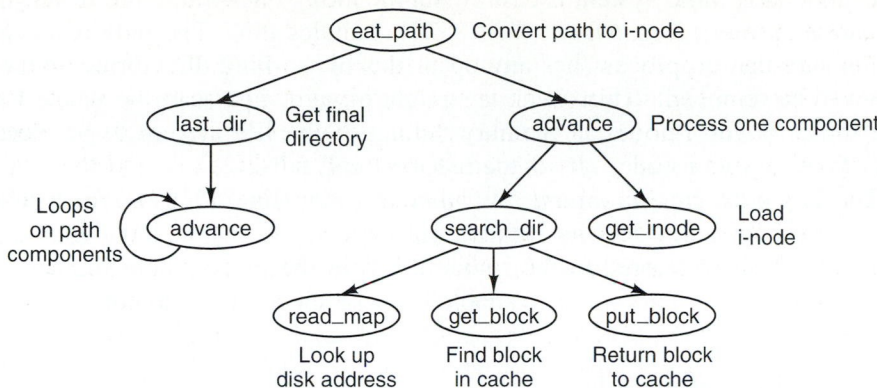

Figure 5-42. Some of the procedures used in looking up path names.

The setting of these pointers is done in the file *mount.c* by *do_mount* on lines 25231 and 25232. The two pages of code that precede setting the pointers are almost entirely concerned with checking for all the errors that can occur while mounting a file system, among them:

1. The special file given is not a block device.

2. The special file is a block device but is already mounted.

3. The file system to be mounted has a rotten magic number.

4. The file system to be mounted is invalid (e.g., no i-nodes).

5. The file to be mounted on does not exist or is a special file.

6. There is no room for the mounted file system's bit maps.

7. There is no room for the mounted file system's super-block.

8. There is no room for the mounted file system's root i-node.

Perhaps it seems inappropriate to keep harping on this point, but the reality of any practical operating system is that a substantial fraction of the code is devoted to doing minor chores that are not intellectually very exciting but are crucial to making a system usable. If a user attempts to mount the wrong floppy disk by accident, say, once a month, and this leads to a crash and a corrupted file system, the user will perceive the system as being unreliable and blame the designer, not himself.

Thomas Edison once made a remark that is relevant here. He said that "genius" is 1 percent inspiration and 99 percent perspiration. The difference between a good system and a mediocre one is not the brilliance of the former's scheduling algorithm, but its attention to getting all the details right.

Unmounting a file system is easier than mounting one—there are fewer things that can go wrong. *Do_umount* (line 25241) handles this. The only real issue is making sure that no process has any open files or working directories on the file system to be removed. This check is straightforward: just scan the whole i-node table to see if any i-nodes in memory belong to the file system to be removed (other than the root i-node). If so, the UMOUNT call fails.

The last procedure in *mount.c* is *name_to_dev* (line 25299), which takes a special file pathname, gets its i-node, and extracts its major and minor device numbers. These are stored in the i-node itself, in the place where the first zone would normally go. This slot is available because special files do not have zones.

Linking and Unlinking Files

The next file to consider is *link.c*, which deals with linking and unlinking files. The procedure *do_link* (line 25434) is very much like *do_mount* in that nearly all of the code is concerned with error checking. Some of the possible errors that can occur in the call

link(file_name, link_name);

are listed below:

1. *File_name* does not exist or cannot be accessed.

2. *File_name* already has the maximum number of links.

3. *File_name* is a directory (only super-user can link to it).

4. *Link_name* already exists.

5. *File_name* and *link_name* are on different devices.

If no errors are present, a new directory entry is made with the string *link_name* and the i-node number of *file_name*. In the code, *name1* corresponds to *file_name* and *name2* corresponds to *link_name*. The actual entry is made by *search_dir*, called from *do_link* on line 25485.

Files and directories are removed by unlinking them. The work of both the UNLINK and RMDIR system calls is done by *do_unlink* (line 25504). Again, a variety of checks must be made; testing that a file exists and that a directory is not a mount point are done by the common code in *do_unlink*, and then either *remove_dir* or *unlink_file* is called, depending upon the system call being supported. We will discuss these shortly.

The other system call supported in *link.c* is RENAME. UNIX users are familiar with the *mv* shell command which ultimately uses this call; its name reflects another aspect of the call. Not only can it change the name of a file within a directory, it can also effectively move the file from one directory to another, and it can do this atomically, which prevents certain race conditions. The work is done by *do_rename* (line 25563). There are many conditions that must be tested before this command can be completed, among which are:

1. The original file must exist (line 25578).

2. The old pathname must not be a directory above the new pathname in the directory tree (lines 25596 to 25613).

3. Neither . nor .. is acceptable as an old or new name (lines 25618 and 25619).

4. Both parent directories must be on the same device (line 25622).

5. Both parent directories must be writable, searchable, and on a writable device (lines 25625 and 25626).

6. Neither the old nor the new name may be a directory with a file system mounted upon it.

There are some other conditions that must be checked if the new name already exists, most importantly it must be possible to remove the existing file with the new name.

In the code for *do_rename* there are a few examples of design decisions that were taken to minimize the possibility of certain problems. Renaming a file to a name that already exists could fail on a full disk, even though in the end no additional space is used, if the old file were not removed first, and this is what is done at lines 25660 to 25666. The same logic is used at line 25680, removing the old file name before creating a new name in the same directory, to avoid the possibility that the directory might need to acquire an additional block. However, if the new file and the old file are to be in different directories, that concern is not relevant, and at line 25685 a new file name is created (in a different directory) before the old one is removed, because from a system integrity standpoint a crash that left two filenames pointing to an i-node would be much less serious than a crash that left an i-node not pointed to by any directory entry. The probability of running out of space during a rename operation is low, and that of a system crash even lower, but in these cases it costs nothing more to be prepared for the worst case.

The remaining functions in *link.c* support the ones that we have already discussed. In addition, the first of them, *truncate* (line 25717), is called from several other places in the file system. It steps through an i-node one zone at a time, freeing all the zones it finds, as well as the indirect blocks. *Remove_dir* (line 25777) carries out a number of additional tests to be sure the directory can be removed, and then it in turn calls *unlink_file* (line 25818). If no errors are found, the directory entry is cleared and the link count in the i-node is reduced by one.

5.7.6 Other System Calls

The last group of system calls is a mixed bag of things involving status, directories, protection, time, and other services.

Changing Directories and File Status

The file *stadir.c* contains the code for four system calls: CHDIR, CHROOT, STAT, and FSTAT. In studying *last_dir* we saw how path searches start out by looking at the first character of the path, to see if it is a slash or not. Depending on the result, a pointer is then set to the working directory or the root directory.

Changing from one working directory (or root directory) to another is just a matter of changing these two pointers within the caller's process table. These changes are made by *do_chdir* (line 25924) and *do_chroot* (line 25963). Both of them do the necessary checking and then call *change* (line 25978) to open the new directory and replace the old one.

In *do_chdir* the code on lines 25935 to 25951 is not executed on CHDIR calls made by user processes. It is specifically for calls made by the memory manager, to change to a user's directory for the purpose of handling EXEC calls. When a user tries to execute a file, say, *a.out* in his working directory, it is easier for the memory manager to change to that directory than to try to figure out where it is.

The remaining two system calls handled in this file, STAT and FSTAT, are basically the same, except for how the file is specified. The former gives a path name, whereas the latter provides the file descriptor of an open file. The top-level procedures, *do_stat* (line 26014) and *do_fstat* (line 26035), both call *stat_inode* to do the work. Before calling *stat_inode*, *do_stat* opens the file to get its i-node. In this way, both *do_stat* and *do_fstat* pass an i-node pointer to *stat_inode*.

All *stat_inode* (line 26051) does is to extract information from the i-node and copy it into a buffer. The buffer must be explicitly copied to user space by calling *sys_copy* on line 26088 because it is too large to fit in a message.

Protection

The MINIX protection mechanism uses the *rwx* bits. Three sets of bits are present for each file: for the owner, for his group, and for others. The bits are set by the CHMOD system call, which is carried out by *do_chmod*, in file *protect.c* (line 26124). After making a series of validity checks, the mode is changed on line 26150.

The CHOWN system call is similar to CHMOD in that both of them change an internal i-node field in some file. The implementation is also similar although *do_chown* (line 26163) can be used to change the owner only by the super-user. Ordinary users can use this call to change the group of their own files.

The UMASK system call allows the user to set a mask (stored in the process table), which then masks out bits in subsequent CREAT system calls. The complete implementation would be only one statement, line 26209, except that the call must return the old mask value as its result. This additional burden triples the number of lines of code required (lines 26208 to 26210).

The ACCESS system call makes it possible for a process to find out if it can access a file in a specified way (e.g., for reading). It is implemented by *do_access* (line 26217), which fetches the file's i-node and calls the internal procedure, *forbidden* (line 26242), to see if the access is forbidden. *Forbidden* checks the uid and gid, as well as the information in the i-node. Depending on what it finds, it selects one of the three *rwx* groups and checks to see if the access is permitted or forbidden.

Read_only (line 26304) is a little internal procedure that tells whether the file system on which its i-node parameter is located is mounted read only or read-write. It is needed to prevent writes on file systems mounted read only.

Time

MINIX has several system calls that involve time: UTIME, TIME, STIME, and TIMES. They are summarized in Fig. 5-43. Although most of them do not have anything to do with files, it makes sense to include them in the file system because time information is recorded in a file's i-node.

Call	Function
UTIME	Set a file's time of last modification
TIME	Set the current real time in seconds
STIME	Set the real time clock
TIMES	Get the process accounting times

Figure 5-43. The four system calls involving time.

Associated with each file are three 32-bit numbers. Two of these record the times when the file was last accessed and last modified. The third records when the status of the i-node itself was last changed. This time will change for almost every access to a file except a READ or EXEC. These times are kept in the i-node. With the UTIME system call, the access and modification times can be set by the owner of the file or the super-user. The procedure *do_utime* (line 26422) in file *time.c* performs the system call by fetching the i-node and storing the time in it. At line 26450 the flags that indicate a time update is required are reset, so the system will not make an expensive and redundant call to *clock_time*.

The real time is not maintained by the file system. It is maintained by the clock task within the kernel. Consequently, the only way to get or set the real time is to send a message to the clock task. This is, in fact, what *do_time* and *do_stime* both do. The real time is in seconds, since Jan 1, 1970.

The accounting information is also maintained by the kernel. At each clock tick it charges one tick to some process. This information can be retrieved by sending a message to the system task, which is what *do_tims* (line 26492) does. The procedure is not named *do_times* because most C compilers add an underscore to the front of all external symbols, and most linkers truncate symbols to eight characters, which would make *do_time* indistinguishable from *do_times*.

Leftovers

The file *misc.c* contains procedures for a few system calls that do not fit in anywhere else. The DUP system call duplicates a file descriptor. In other words, it creates a new file descriptor that points to the same file as its argument. The call has a variant DUP2. Both versions of the call are handled by *do_dup* (line 26632). This function is included in MINIX to support old binary programs. Both of these calls are obsolete. The current version of the MINIX C library will invoke the FCNTL system call when either of these are encountered in a C source file.

Operation	Meaning
F_DUPFD	Duplicate a file descriptor
F_GETFD	Get the close-on-exec flag
F_SETFD	Set the close-on-exec flag
F_GETFL	Get file status flags
F_SETFL	Set file status flags
F_GETLK	Get lock status of a file
F_SETLK	Set read/write lock on a file
F_SETLKW	Set write lock on a file

Figure 5-44. The POSIX request parameters for the FCNTL system call.

FCNTL, handled by *do_fcntl* (line 26670) is the preferred way to request operations on an open file. Services are requested using POSIX-defined flags described in Fig. 5-44. The call is invoked with a file descriptor, a request code, and additional arguments as necessary for the particular request. For instance, the equivalent of the old call

dup2(fd, fd2);

would be

fcntl(fd, F_DUPFD, fd2);

Several of these requests set or read a flag; the code consists of just a few lines.

For instance, the *F_SETFD* request sets a bit that forces closing of a file when its owner process does an EXEC. The *F_GETFD* request is used to determine whether a file must be closed when an EXEC call is made. The *F_SETFL* and *F_GETFL* requests permit setting flags to indicate a particular file is available in nonblocking mode or for append operations.

Do_fcntl handles file locking, also. A call with the *F_GETLK*, *F_SETLK*, or *F_SETLKW* command specified is translated into a call to *lock_op*, discussed in an earlier section.

The next system call is SYNC, which copies all blocks and i-nodes that have been modified since being loaded back to the disk. The call is processed by *do_sync* (line 26730). It simply searches through all the tables looking for dirty entries. The i-nodes must be processed first, since *rw_inode* leaves its results in the block cache. After all dirty i-nodes are written to the block cache, then all dirty blocks are written to the disk.

The system calls FORK, EXEC, EXIT, and SET are really memory manager calls, but the results have to be posted here as well. When a process forks, it is essential that the kernel, memory manager, and file system all know about it. These "system calls" do not come from user processes, but from the memory manager. *Do_fork*, *do_exit*, and *do_set* record the relevant information in the file system's part of the process table. *Do_exec* searches for and closes (using *do_close*) any files marked to be closed-on-exec.

The last function in this file is not really a system call but is handled like one. This is *do_revive* (line 26921). It is called when a task that was previously unable to complete work that the file system had requested, such as providing input data for a user process, has now completed the work. The file system then revives the process and sends it the reply message.

5.7.7 The I/O Device Interface

I/O in MINIX is done by sending messages to the tasks within the kernel. The file system's interface with these tasks is contained in the file *device.c*. When actual device I/O is needed, *dev_io* (line 27033) is called from *read_write* to handle character special files, and from *rw_block* for block special files. It builds a standard message (see Fig. 3-15) and sends it to the specified task. Tasks are called by the line

```
(*dmap[major].dmap_rw)(task, &dev_mess);
```

(line 27056). This calls functions via pointers in the *dmap* array defined in *table.c*. The functions that take care of this are all here in *device.c*. While *dev_io* is waiting for a reply from the task, the file system waits. It has no internal multiprogramming. Usually, these waits are quite short though (e.g., 50 msec).

Special files may need special processing when they are opened or closed. Exactly what must be done depends upon the type of device. The *dmap* table is also used to determine which functions are called for opening and closing each type of major device. The procedure *dev_opcl* (line 27071) is called for disk devices, whether floppy disks, hard disks, or memory-based devices. The line

```
mess_ptr->PROC_NR = fp – fproc;
```

(line 27081) calculates the process number of the caller. The actual work is done by passing the task number and a pointer to the message to *call_task*, to be discussed below. *Dev_opcl* is also used to close the same devices. In fact, the only difference in the open and close functions at the level of this function is in what happens after the return from *call_task*.

Other functions called via the *dmap* struct include *tty_open* and *tty_close*, which service the serial lines, and *ctty_open* and *ctty_close* which service the console. The last of these, *ctty_close*, is almost a dummy routine, as all it does is to return status *OK* unconditionally.

The SETSID system call requires some work by the file system, and this is performed by *do_setsid* (line 27164). One system call, IOCTL, is handled primarily in *device.c*. This call has been put here because it is closely tied to the task interface. When an IOCTL is done, *do_ioctl* is called to build a message and send it to the proper task.

To control terminal devices one of the functions declared in *include/termios.h* should be used in programs written to be POSIX compliant. The C library will translate such functions into IOCTL calls. For devices other than terminals IOCTL is used for many operations, many of which were described in Chap. 3.

The next function is the only *PRIVATE* function in this file. This is *find_dev* (line 27228), a little helper procedure that extracts the major and minor device numbers from a full device number.

The actual reading and writing of most devices goes through *call_task* (line 27245), which directs a message to the appropriate task in the kernel image, by calling *sendrec*. The attempt may fail if the task is trying to revive a process in response to an earlier request. It will likely be a different process from the one on behalf of which the current request is being made. *Call_task* will display a message on the console if an inappropriate message is received. These messages hopefully will not be seen during normal operation of MINIX but could appear during attempts to develop a new device driver.

The device */dev/tty* does not physically exist. It is a fiction to which any user on a multiuser system can refer, without a need to determine which of all possible real terminals is in use. When a message that refers to */dev/tty* must be sent, the next function, *call_ctty* (line 27311), finds the correct major and minor device and substitutes them into the message before passing the message on via *call_task*.

Finally, the last function in the file is *no_dev* (line 27337), which is called from slots in the table for which a device does not exist, for example when a network device is referenced on a machine with no network support. It returns an *ENODEV* status. It prevents crashes when nonexistent devices are accessed.

5.7.8 General Utilities

The file system contains a few general purpose utility procedures that are used in various places. They are collected together in the file *utility.c*.

The first procedure is *clock_time* (line 27428). It sends messages to the clock task to find out what the current real time is. The next procedure, *fetch_name* (line 27447), is needed because many system calls have a file name as parameter. If the file name is short, it is included in the message from the user to the file system. If it is long, a pointer to the name in user space is put in the message. *Fetch_name* checks for both cases, and either way, gets the name.

Two functions here handle general classes of errors. *No_sys* is the error handler that is called when the file system receives a system call that is not one of its calls. *Panic* prints a message and tells the kernel to throw in the towel when something catastrophic happens.

The last two functions, *conv2* and *conv4*, exist to help MINIX deal with the problem of different byte orders on Intel and Motorola processors. These routines are called when reading from or writing to a disk data structure, such as an i-node or bit map. The byte order in the system that created the disk is recorded in the super-block. If it is different from the order used by the local processor the order will be swapped. The rest of the file system does not need to know anything about the byte order on the disk.

The last file is *putk.c*. It contains two procedures, both of which have to do with printing messages. The standard library procedures cannot be used, because they send messages to the file system. These procedures send messages directly to the terminal task. We saw an almost identical pair of functions in the memory manager's version of this file.

5.8 SUMMARY

When seen from the outside, a file system is a collection of files and directories, plus operations on them. Files can be read and written, directories can be created and destroyed, and files can be moved from directory to directory. Most modern file systems support a hierarchical directory system, in which directories may have subdirectories ad infinitum.

When seen from the inside, a file system looks quite different. The file system designers have to be concerned with how storage is allocated, and how the system keeps track of which block goes with which file. We have also seen how different systems have different directory structures. File system reliability and performance are also important issues.

Security and protection are of vital concern to both the system users and designers. We discussed some security flaws in older systems, and generic problems that many systems have. We also looked at authentication, with and without passwords, access control lists, and capabilities, as well as a matrix model for thinking about protection.

Finally, we studied the MINIX file system in detail. It is large but not very complicated. It accepts requests for work from user processes, indexes into a table of procedure pointers, and calls that procedure to carry out the requested system call. Due to its modular structure and position outside the kernel, it can be removed from MINIX and used as a free-standing network file server with only minor modifications.

Internally, the MINIX buffers data in a block cache and attempts to read ahead when making sequential access to file. If the cache is made large enough, most program text will be found to be already in memory during operations that repeatedly access a particular set of programs, such as a compilation.

PROBLEMS

1. Give 5 different path names for the file */etc/passwd*. (Hint: think about the directory entries "." and "..".)

2. Systems that support sequential files always have an operation to rewind files. Do systems that support random access files need this too?

3. Some operating systems provide a system call RENAME to give a file a new name. Is there any difference at all between using this call to rename a file, and just copying the file to a new file with the new name, followed by deleting the old one?

4. Consider the directory tree of Fig. 5-7. If */usr/jim* is the working directory, what is the absolute path name for the file whose relative path name is *../ast/x*?

5. Contiguous allocation of files leads to disk fragmentation, as mentioned in the text. Is this internal fragmentation or external fragmentation? Make an analogy with something discussed in the previous chapter.

6. An operating system only supports a single directory but allows that directory to have arbitrarily many files with arbitrarily long file names. Can something approximating a hierarchical file system be simulated? How?

7. Free disk space can be kept track of using a free list or a bit map. Disk addresses require D bits. For a disk with B blocks, F of which are free, state the condition under which the free list uses less space than the bit map. For D having the value 16 bits, express your answer as a percentage of the disk space that must be free.

8. It has been suggested that the first part of each UNIX file be kept in the same disk block as its i-node. What good would this do?

9. The performance of a file system depends upon the cache hit rate (fraction of blocks found in the cache). If it takes 1 msec to satisfy a request from the cache, but 40 msec to satisfy a request if a disk read is needed, give a formula for the mean time required to satisfy a request if the hit rate is h. Plot this function for values of h from 0 to 1.0.

10. A floppy disk has 40 cylinders. A seek takes 6 msec per cylinder moved. If no attempt is made to put the blocks of a file close to each other, two blocks that are logically consecutive (i.e., follow one another in the file) will be about 13 cylinders apart, on the average. If, however, the operating system makes an attempt to cluster related blocks, the mean interblock distance can be reduced to 2 cylinders (for example). How long does it take to read a 100 block file in both cases, if the rotational latency is 100 msec and the transfer time is 25 msec per block?

11. Would compacting disk storage periodically be of any conceivable value? Explain.

12. How could TENEX be modified to avoid the password problem described in the text?

13. After getting your degree, you apply for a job as director of a large university computer center that has just put its ancient operating system out to pasture and switched over to UNIX. You get the job. Fifteen minutes after starting work, your assistant bursts into your office screaming: "Some students have discovered the algorithm we use for encrypting passwords and posted it on the bulletin board." What should you do?

14. The Morris-Thompson protection scheme with the *n*-bit random numbers was designed to make it difficult for an intruder to discover a large number of passwords by encrypting common strings in advance. Does the scheme also offer protection against a student user who is trying to guess the super-user password on his machine?

15. A computer science department has a large collection of UNIX machines on its local network. Users on any machine can issue a command of the form

    machine4 who

    and have it executed on *machine4*, without having the user log in on the remote machine. This feature is implemented by having the user's kernel send the command and his uid to the remote machine. Is this scheme secure if the kernels are all trustworthy (e.g., large timeshared minicomputers with protection hardware)? What if some of the machines are students' personal computers, with no protection hardware?

16. When a file is removed, its blocks are generally put back on the free list, but they are not erased. Do you think it would be a good idea to have the operating system erase each block before releasing it? Consider both security and performance factors in your answer, and explain the effect of each.

17. Three different protection mechanisms that we have discussed are capabilities, access control lists, and the UNIX *rwx* bits. For each of the following protection problems, tell which of these mechanisms can be used.

    (a) Ken wants his files readable by everyone except his office mate.
    (b) Mitch and Steve want to share some secret files.
    (c) Linda wants some of her files to be public.

    For UNIX, assume that groups are categories such as faculty, students, secretaries, etc.

18. Consider the following protection mechanism. Each object and each process is assigned a number. A process can only access an object if the object has a higher number than the process. Which of the schemes discussed in the text does this resemble? In what essential way does it differ from the scheme in the text?

19. Can the Trojan horse attack work in a system protected by capabilities?

20. Two computer science students, Carolyn and Elinor, are having a discussion about i-nodes. Carolyn maintains that memories have gotten so large and so cheap that when a file is opened, it is simpler and faster just to fetch a new copy of the i-node into the i-node table, rather than search the entire table to see if it is already there. Elinor disagrees. Who is right?

21. What is the difference between a virus and a worm? How do they each reproduce?

22. Symbolic links are files that point to other files or directories indirectly. Unlike ordinary links such as those currently implemented in MINIX, a symbolic link has its own i-node, which points to a data block. The data block contains the path to the file being linked to, and the i-node makes it possible for the link to have different ownership and permissions from the file linked to. A symbolic link and the file or directory to which it points can be located on different devices. Symbolic links are not part of the 1990 POSIX standard, but it is expected they will be added to POSIX in the future. Implement symbolic links for MINIX.

23. You find that the 64 MByte file size limit in MINIX is not enough for your needs. Extend the file system to use the unused space in the i-node for a triple-indirect block.

24. Show if setting ROBUST makes the file system more or less robust in the face of a crash. Whether this is the case in the current version of MINIX has not been researched, so it may be either way. Take a good look at what happens when a modified block is evicted from the cache. Take into account that a modified data block may be accompanied by a modified i-node and bit map.

25. The size of the *filp* table is currently defined as a constant, *NR_FILPS*, in *fs/const.h*. In order to accomodate more users on a networked system you want to increase *NR_PROCS* in *include/minix/config.h*. How should *NR_FILPS* be defined as a function of *NR_PROCS*?

26. Design a mechanism to add support for a "foreign" file system, so that one could, for instance, mount an MS-DOS file system on a directory in the MINIX file system.

27. Suppose that a technological breakthrough occurs, and that nonvolatile RAM, that retains its contents reliably following a power failure, becomes available with no price or performance disadvantage over conventional RAM. What aspects of file system design would be affected by this development?

6

READING LIST AND BIBLIOGRAPHY

In the previous five chapters we have touched upon a variety of topics. This chapter is intended as an aid to readers interested in pursuing their study of operating systems further. Section 6.1 is a list of suggested readings. Section 6.2 is an alphabetical bibliography of all books and articles cited in this book.

In addition to the references given below, the *Proceedings of the n-th ACM Symposium on Operating Systems Principles* (ACM) held every other year and the *Proceedings of the n-th International Conference on Distributed Computing Systems* (IEEE) held every year are good places to look for recent papers on operating systems. So is the USENIX *Symposium on Operating Systems Design and Implementation*. Furthermore, *ACM Transactions on Computer Systems* and *Operating Systems Review* are two journals that often have relevant articles.

6.1 SUGGESTIONS FOR FURTHER READING

6.1.1 Introduction and General Works

Brooks, *The Mythical Man-Month: Essays on Software Engineering*
 A witty, amusing, and informative book on how *not* to write an operating system by someone who learned the hard way. Full of good advice.

Comer, *Operating System Design. The Xinu Approach*

A book about the Xinu operating system, which runs on the LSI-11 computer. It contains a detailed exposition of the source code, including a complete listing in C.

Corbató, "On Building Systems That Will Fail"

In his Turing Award lecture, the father of timesharing addresses many of the same concerns that Brooks does in the *Mythical Man-Month*. His conclusion is that all complex systems will ultimately fail, and that to have any chance for success at all, it is absolutely essential to avoid complexity and strive for simplicity and elegance in design.

Deitel, *Operating Systems,* 2nd Ed.

A general textbook on operating systems. In addition to the standard material, it contains case studies of UNIX, MS-DOS, MVS, VM, OS/2, and the Macintosh operating system.

Finkel, *An Operating Systems Vade Mecum*

Another general text on operating systems. It is practically oriented and well written and covers many of the topics treated in this book, making it a good place to look for a different perspective on the same subject.

IEEE, *Information Technology—Portable Operating System Interface (POSIX), Part 1: System Application Program Interface (API) [C Language]*

This is the standard. Some parts are actually quite readable, especially Annex B, "Rationale and Notes," which often sheds light on why things are done as they are. One advantage of referring to the standard document is that, by definition, there are no errors. If a typographical error in a macro name makes it through the editing process it is no longer an error, it is official.

Lampson, "Hints for Computer System Design"

Butler Lampson, one of the world's leading designers of innovative operating systems, has collected many hints, suggestions, and guidelines from his years of experience and put them together in this entertaining and informative article. Like Brooks' book, this is required reading for every aspiring operating system designer.

Lewine, *POSIX Programmer's Guide*

This book describes the POSIX standard in a much more readable way than the standards document itself, and includes discussions on how to convert older programs to POSIX and how to develop new programs for the POSIX environment. There are numerous examples of code, including several complete programs. All POSIX-required library functions and header files are described.

Silberschatz and Galvin, *Operating System Concepts,* 4th Ed.

Another textbook on operating systems. It covers processes, storage management, files, and distributed systems. Two case studies are given: UNIX and Mach. The cover is full of dinosaurs. What, if anything, this has to do with operating systems in the 1990s is unclear.

Stallings, *Operating Systems,* 2nd Ed.

Still another textbook on operating systems. It covers all the usual topics, and also includes a small amount of material on distributed systems, plus an appendix on queueing theory.

Stevens, *Advanced Programming in the UNIX Environment*

This book tells how to write C programs that use the UNIX system call interface and the standard C library. Examples are based on the System V Release 4 and the 4.4BSD versions of UNIX. The relationship of these implementations to POSIX is described in detail.

Switzer, *Operating Systems, A Practical Approach,*

An approach similar to this text. Theoretical concepts are illustrated with pseudocode examples and a large part of the C source code for TUNIX, a model operating system. Unlike MINIX, TUNIX is not meant to run on a real machine, it runs on a virtual machine. It is not as realistic as MINIX in its treatment of device drivers, but it does go further than MINIX in other directions, such as implementation of virtual memory.

6.1.2 Processes

Andrews and Schneider, "Concepts and Notations for Concurrent Programming"

A tutorial and survey of processes and interprocess communication, including busy waiting, semaphores, monitors, message passing, and other techniques. The article also shows how these concepts are embedded in various programming languages.

Ben-Ari, *Principles of Concurrent Programming*

This little book is entirely devoted to the problems of interprocess communication. There are chapters on mutual exclusion, semaphores, monitors, and the dining philosophers problem, among others.

Dubois et al., "Synchronization, Coherence, and Event Ordering in Multiprocessors"

A tutorial on synchronization in shared-memory multiprocessor systems. However, some of the ideas are equally applicable to single processor and distributed memory systems as well.

Silberschatz and Galvin, *Operating System Concepts,* 4th Ed.

Chapters 4 through 6 cover processes and interprocess communication, including scheduling, critical sections, semaphores, monitors, and classical interprocess communication problems.

6.1.3 Input/Output

Chen et al., "RAID: High Performance Reliable Secondary Storage"

The use of multiple disk drives in parallel for fast I/O is a trend in high end systems. The authors discuss this idea and examine different organizations in terms of performance, cost, and reliability.

Coffman et al., "System Deadlocks"

A short introduction to deadlocks, what causes them, and how they can be prevented or detected.

Finkel, *An Operating Systems Vade Mecum.* 2nd Ed.

Chapter 5 discusses I/O hardware and device drivers, particularly for terminals and disks.

Geist and Daniel, "A Continuum of Disk Scheduling Algorithms"

A generalized disk arm scheduling algorithm is presented. Extensive simulation and experimental results are given.

Holt, "Some Deadlock Properties of Computer Systems"

A discussion of deadlocks. Holt introduces a directed graph model that can be used to analyze some deadlock situations.

IEEE *Computer* Magazine, March 1994

This issue of *Computer* contains eight articles on advanced I/O, and covers simulation, high performance storage, caching, I/O for parallel computers, and multimedia.

Isloor and Marsland, "The Deadlock Problem: An Overview"

A tutorial on deadlocks, with special emphasis on data base systems. A variety of models and algorithms are covered.

Stevens, "Heuristics for Disk Drive Positioning in 4.3BSD"

A detailed study of disk performance in Berkeley UNIX. As is often the case with computer systems, reality is more complicated than the theory predicts.

Wilkes et al., "The HP AutoRAID Hierarchical Storage System"

An important new development in high-performance disk systems is RAID

(Redundant Array of Inexpensive Disks), in which an array of small disks work together to produce a high-bandwidth system. In this paper, the authors describe in some detail the system they built at HP Labs.

6.1.4 Memory Management

Denning, "Virtual Memory"
A classic paper on many aspects of virtual memory. Denning was one of the pioneers in this field, and was the inventor of the working set concept.

Denning, "Working Sets Past and Present"
A good overview of numerous memory management and paging algorithms. A comprehensive bibliography is included.

Knuth, *The Art of Computer Programming* Vol. 1
First fit, best fit, and other memory management algorithms are discussed and compared in this book.

Silberschatz and Galvin, *Operating System Concepts,* 4th Ed.
Chapters 8 and 9 deal with memory management, including swapping, paging, and segmentation. A variety of paging algorithms are mentioned.

6.1.5 File Systems

Denning, "The United States vs. Craig Neidorf"
When a young hacker discovered and published information about how the telephone system works, he was indicted for computer fraud. This article describes the case, which involved many fundamental issues, including freedom of speech. The article is followed by some dissenting views and a rebuttal by Denning.

Hafner and Markoff, *Cyberpunk*
Three compelling tales of young hackers breaking into computers around the world are told here by the New York Times computer reporter who broke the Internet worm story and his journalist wife.

Harbron, *File Systems*
A book on file system design, applications, and performance. Both structure and algorithms are covered.

McKusick et al., "A Fast File System for UNIX"
The UNIX file system was completely reimplemented for 4.2 BSD. This paper describes the design of the new file system, with emphasis on its performance.

Silberschatz and Galvin *Operating System Concepts,* 4th Ed.
Chapters 10 and 11 are about file systems. They cover file operations, access methods, consistency semantics, directories, and protection, and implementation, among other topics.

Stallings, *Operating Systems,* 2nd Ed.
Chapter 14 contains a fair amount of material about the security environment especially about hackers, viruses and other threats.

6.2 ALPHABETICAL BIBLIOGRAPHY

ANDERSON, T.E., BERSHAD, B.N., LAZOWSKA, E.D., and LEVY, H.M.: "Scheduler Activations: Effective Kernel Support for the User-level Management of Parallelism," *ACM Trans. on Computer Systems*, vol. 10, pp. 53-79, Feb. 1992.

ANDREWS, G.R., and SCHNEIDER, F.B.: "Concepts and Notations for Concurrent Programming," *Computing Surveys*, vol. 15, pp. 3-43, March 1983.

BACH, M.J.: *The Design of the UNIX Operating System*, Englewood Cliffs, NJ: Prentice Hall, 1987.

BALA, K., KAASHOEK, M.F., WEIHL, W.: "Software Prefetching and Caching for Translation Lookaside Buffers," *Proc. First Symp. on Operating System Design and Implementation*, USENIX, pp. 243-254, 1994.

BAYS, C.: "A Comparison of Next-Fit, First-Fit, and Best-Fit," *Commun. of the ACM*, vol. 20, pp. 191-192, March 1977.

BEN-ARI, M: *Principles of Concurrent Programming*, Englewood Cliffs, NJ: Prentice Hall International, 1982.

BRINCH HANSEN, P.: "The Programming Language Concurrent Pascal," *IEEE Trans. on Software Engineering*, vol. SE-1, pp. 199-207, June 1975.

BROOKS, F. P., Jr.: *The Mythical Man-Month: Essays on Software Engineering*, Anniversary edition, Reading, MA: Addison-Wesley, 1996.

CADOW, H.: *OS/360 Job Control Language*, Englewood Cliffs, NJ: Prentice Hall, 1970.

CHEN, P.M., LEE, E.K., GIBSON, G.A., KATZ, R.H., and PATTERSON, D.A.: "RAID: High Performance Reliable Storage," *Computing Surveys*, vol. 26, pp. 145-185, June 1994.

CHERITON, D.R.: "An Experiment Using Registers for Fast Message-Based Interprocess Communication," *Operating Systems Review*, vol. 18, pp. 12-20, Oct. 1984.

COFFMAN, E.G., ELPHICK, M.J., and SHOSHANI, A.: "System Deadlocks," *Computing Surveys*, vol. 3, pp. 67-78, June 1971.

COMER, D.: *Operating System Design. The Xinu Approach*, Englewood Cliffs, N.J.: Prentice Hall, 1984.

CORBATO, F.J.: "On Building Systems That Will Fail," *Commun. of the ACM*, vol. 34, pp. 72-81, June 1991.

CORBATO, F.J., MERWIN-DAGGETT, M., and DALEY, R.C: "An Experimental Time-Sharing System," *Proc. AFIPS Fall Joint Computer Conf.*, AFIPS, pp. 335-344, 1962.

CORBATO, F.J., SALTZER, J.H., and CLINGEN, C.T.: "MULTICS—The First Seven Years," *Proc. AFIPS Spring Joint Computer Conf.*, AFIPS, pp. 571-583, 1972.

CORBATO, F.J., and VYSSOTSKY, V.A.: "Introduction and Overview of the MULTICS System," *Proc. AFIPS Fall Joint Computer Conf.*, AFIPS, pp. 185-196, 1965.

COURTOIS, P.J., HEYMANS, F., and PARNAS, D.L.: "Concurrent Control with Readers and Writers," *Commun. of the ACM*, vol. 10, pp. 667-668, Oct. 1971.

DALEY, R.C., and DENNIS, J.B.: "Virtual Memory, Process, and Sharing in MULTICS," *Commun. of the ACM*, vol. 11, pp. 306-312, May 1968.

DEITEL, H.M.: *Operating Systems,* 2nd Ed., Reading, MA: Addison-Wesley, 1990.

DENNING, D.: "The United states vs. Craig Neidorf," *Commun. of the ACM*, vol. 34, pp. 22-43, March 1991.

DENNING, P.J.: "The Working Set Model for Program Behavior," *Commun. of the ACM*, vol. 11, pp. 323-333, 1968a.

DENNING, P.J.: "Thrashing: Its Causes and Prevention," *Proc. AFIPS National Computer Conf.*, AFIPS, pp. 915-922, 1968b.

DENNING, P.J.: "Virtual Memory," *Computing Surveys*, vol. 2, pp. 153-189, Sept. 1970.

DENNING, P.J.: "Working Sets Past and Present," *IEEE Trans. on Software Engineering*, vol. SE-6, pp. 64-84, Jan. 1980.

DENNIS, J.B., and VAN HORN, E.C.: "Programming Semantics for Multiprogrammed Computations," *Commun. of the ACM*, vol. 9, pp. 143-155, March 1966.

DIJKSTRA, E.W.: "Co-operating Sequential Processes," in *Programming Languages*, Genuys, F. (Ed.), London: Academic Press, 1965.

DIJKSTRA, E.W.: "The Structure of THE Multiprogramming System," *Commun. of the ACM*, vol. 11, pp. 341-346, May 1968.

DUBOIS, M., SCHEURICH, C., and BRIGGS, F.A.: "Synchronization, Coherence, and Event Ordering in Multiprocessors," *IEEE Computer*, vol. 21, pp. 9-21, Feb. 1988.

ENGLER, D.R., KAASHOEK, M.F., and O'TOOLE, J. Jr.: "Exokernel: An Operating System Architecture for Application-Level Resource Management," *Proc. of the Fifteenth Symp. on Operating Systems Principles*, ACM, pp. 251-266, 1995.

FABRY, R.S.: "Capability-Based Addressing," *Commun. of the ACM*, vol. 17, pp. 403-412, July 1974.

FEELEY, M.J., MORGAN, W.E., PIGHIN, F.H., KARLIN, A.R., LEVY, H.M., and THEKKATH, C.A.: "Implementing Global Memory Management in a Workstation CLuster," *Proc. of the Fifteenth Symp. on Operating Systems Principles*, ACM, pp. 201-212, 1995.

FINKEL, R.A.: *An Operating Systems Vade Mecum,* 2nd Ed., Englewood Cliffs, NJ: Prentice Hall, 1988.

FOTHERINGHAM, J.: "Dynamic Storage Allocation in the Atlas Including an Automatic Use of a Backing Store," *Commun. of the ACM*, vol. 4, pp. 435-436, Oct. 1961.

GEIST, R., and DANIEL, S.: "A Continuum of Disk Scheduling Algorithms," *ACM Trans. on Computer Systems*, vol. 5, pp. 77-92, Feb. 1987.

GOLDEN, D., and PECHURA, M.: "The Structure of Microcomputer File Systems," *Commun. of the ACM*, vol. 29, pp. 222-230, March 1986.

GRAHAM, R.: "Use of High-Level Languages for System Programming," Project MAC Report TM-13, M.I.T., Sept. 1970.

HAFNER, K., and MARKOFF, J.: *Cyberpunk*, New York: Simon and Schuster, 1991.

HARBRON, T.R.: *File Systems*, Englewood Cliffs, NJ: Prentice Hall, 1988.

HAUSER, C., JACOBI, C., THEIMER, M., WELCH, B., and WEISER, M.: "Using Threads in Interactive Systems: A Case Study," *Proc. of the Fourteenth Symp. on Operating Systems Principles*, ACM, pp. 94-105, 1993.

HAVENDER, J.W.: "Avoiding Deadlock in Multitasking Systems," *IBM Systems Journal*, vol. 7, pp. 74-84, 1968.

HEBBARD, B. et al.: "A Penetration Analysis of the Michigan Terminal System," *Operating Systems Review*, vol. 14, pp. 7-20, Jan. 1980.

HOARE, C.A.R.: "Monitors, An Operating System Structuring Concept," *Commun. of the ACM*, vol. 17, pp. 549-557, Oct. 1974; Erratum in *Commun. of the ACM*, vol. 18, p. 95, Feb. 1975.

HOLT, R.C: "Some Deadlock Properties of Computer Systems," *Computing Surveys*, vol. 4, pp. 179-196, Sept. 1972.

HOLT, R.C: *Concurrent Euclid, The UNIX System, and TUNIS*, Reading, MA: Addison-Wesley, 1983.

HUCK, J., and HAYS, J.: "Architectural Support for Translation Table Management in Large Address Sapce Machines," *Proc. Twentieth Annual Int'l Symp. on Computer Arch.*, ACM, pp. 39-50, 1993.

IEEE: *Information technology—Portable Operating System Interface (POSIX), Part 1: System Application Program Interface (API) [C Language]*, New York: Institute of Electrical and Electronics Engineers, Inc., 1990

ISLOOR, S.S., and MARSLAND, T.A.: "The Deadlock Problem: An Overview," *IEEE Computer*, vol. 13, pp. 58-78, Sept. 1980.

KERNIGHAN, B.W., and RITCHIE, D.M.: *The C Programming Language,* 2nd Ed., Englewood Cliffs, NJ: Prentice Hall, 1988.

KLEIN, D.V.: "Foiling the Cracker: A Survey of, and Improvements to, Password Security," *Proc. UNIX Security Workshop II,* USENIX, Summer 1990.

KLEINROCK, L.: *Queueing Systems. Vol. 1,* New York: John Wiley, 1975.

KNUTH, D.E.: *The Art of Computer Programming, Volume 1: Fundamental Algorithms,* 2nd Ed., Reading, MA: Addison-Wesley, 1973.

LAMPSON, B.W.: "A Scheduling Philosophy for Multiprogramming Systems," *Commun. of the ACM,* vol. 11, pp. 347-360, May 1968.

LAMPSON, B.W.: "A Note on the Confinement Problem," *Commun. of the ACM,* vol. 10, pp. 613-615, Oct. 1973.

LAMPSON, B.W.: "Hints for Computer System Design," *IEEE Software,* vol. 1, pp. 11-28, Jan. 1984.

LEVIN, R., COHEN, E.S., CORWIN, W.M., POLLACK, F.J., and WULF, W.A.: "Policy/Mechanism Separation in Hydra," *Proc. of the Fifth Symp. on Operating Systems Principles,* ACM, pp. 132-140, 1975.

LEWINE, D.: *POSIX Programmer's Guide,* Sebastopol, CA: O'Reilly & Associates, 1991.

LI, K., and HUDAK, P.: "Memory Coherence in Shared Virtual Memory Systems," *ACM Trans. on Computer Systems,* vol. 7, pp. 321-359, Nov. 1989.

LINDE, R.R.: "Operating System Penetration," *Proc. AFIPS National Computer Conf.,* AFIPS, pp. 361-368, 1975.

LIONS, J.: *Lions' Commentary on Unix 6th Edition, with Source Code,* San Jose, CA: Peer-to-Peer Communications, 1996.

LIU, C.L., and LAYLAND, J.W.: "Scheduling Algorithms for Multiprogramming in a Hard Real-Time Environment," *Journal of the ACM,* vol. 20, pp. 46-61, Jan. 1973.

MARSH, B.D., SCOTT, M.L., LEBLANC, T.J., and MARKATOS, E.P.: "First-Class User-Level Threads," *Proc. of the Thirteenth Symp. on Operating Systems Principles,* ACM, pp. 110-121, 1991.

McKUSICK, M.J., JOY, W.N., LEFFLER, S.J., and FABRY, R.S.: "A Fast File System for UNIX," *ACM Trans. on Computer Systems,* vol. 2, pp. 181-197, Aug. 1984.

MORRIS, R., and THOMPSON, K.: "Password Security: A Case History," *Commun. of the ACM,* vol. 22, pp. 594-597, Nov. 1979.

MULLENDER, S.J., and TANENBAUM, A.S.: "Immediate Files," *Software—Practice and Experience,* vol. 14, pp. 365-368, April 1984.

ORGANICK, E.I.: *The Multics System,* Cambridge, MA: M.I.T. Press, 1972.

PETERSON, G.L.: "Myths about the Mutual Exclusion Problem," *Information Processing Letters,* vol. 12, pp. 115-116, June 1981.

ROSENBLUM, M., and OUSTERHOUT, J.K.: "The Design and Implementation of a Log-Structured File System," *Proc. Thirteenth Symp. on Operating System Principles*, ACM, pp. 1-15, 1991.

SALTZER, J.H.: "Protection and Control of Information Sharing in MULTICS," *Commun. of the ACM*, vol. 17, pp. 388-402, July 1974.

SALTZER, J.H., and SCHROEDER, M.D.: "The Protection of Information in Computer Systems," *Proc. IEEE*, vol. 63, pp. 1278-1308, Sept. 1975.

SALUS, P.H.: "UNIX At 25," *Byte*, vol. 19, pp. 75-82, Oct. 1994.

SANDHU, R.S.: "Lattice-Based Access Control Models," *Computer*, vol. 26, pp. 9-19, Nov. 1993.

SEAWRIGHT, L.H., and MACKINNON, R.A.: "VM/370—A Study of Multiplicity and Usefulness," *IBM Systems Journal*, vol. 18, pp. 4-17, 1979.

SILBERSCHATZ, A., and GALVIN, P.B.: *Operating System Concepts,* 4th Ed. Reading, MA: Addison-Wesley, 1994.

STALLINGS, W.: *Operating Systems,* 2nd Ed., Englewood Cliffs, NJ: Prentice Hall, 1995.

STEVENS, W.R.: *Advanced Programming in the UNIX Environment*, Reading, MA: Addison-Wesley, 1992.

STEVENS, W.R.: "Heuristics for Disk Drive Partitioning in 4.3BSD," *Computing Systems*, vol. 2, pp. 251-274, Summer 1989.

STOLL, C.: *The Cuckoo's Egg: Tracking a Spy through the Maze of Computer Espionage*, New York: Doubleday, 1989.

SWITZER, R.W.: *Operating Systems, A Practical Approach*, London: Prentice Hall Int'l, 1993.

TAI, K.C., and CARVER, R.H.: "VP: A New Operation for Semaphores," *Operating Systems Review*, vol. 30, pp. 5-11, July 1996.

TALLURI, M., and HILL, M.D.: "Surpassing the TLB Performance of Superpages with Less Operating System Support," *Proc. Sixth Int'l Conf. on Architectural Support for Progr. Lang. and Operating Systems*, ACM, pp. 171-182, 1994.

TALLURI, M., HILL, M.D., and KHALIDI, Y.A.: "A New Page Table for 64-bit Address Spaces," *Proc. of the Fifteenth Symp. on Operating Systems Principles*, ACM, pp. 184-200, 1995.

TANENBAUM, A.S.: *Distributed Operating Systems*, Englewood Cliffs, NJ: Prentice Hall, 1995.

TANENBAUM, A.S., VAN RENESSE, R., STAVEREN, H. VAN, SHARP, G.J., MULLENDER, S.J., JANSEN, J., and ROSSUM, G. VAN: "Experiences with the Amoeba Distributed Operating System," *Commun. of the ACM*, vol. 33, pp. 46-63, Dec. 1990.

TEORY, T.J.: "Properties of Disk Scheduling Policies in Multiprogrammed Computer Systems," *Proc. AFIPS Fall Joint Computer Conf.*, AFIPS, pp. 1-11, 1972.

THOMPSON, K.: "Unix Implementation," *Bell System Technical Journal*, vol. 57, pp. 1931-1946, July-Aug. 1978.

UHLIG, R., NAGLE, D., STANLEY, T, MUDGE, T., SECREST, S., and BROWN, R: "Design Trade-offs for Software-Managed TLBs," *ACM Trans. on Computer Systems*, vol. 12, pp. 175-205, AUg. 1994.

VAHALIA, U.: *UNIX Internals—The New Frontiers*, Upper Saddle River, NJ: Prentice Hall, 1996.

WALDSPURGER, C.A., and WEIHL, W.E.: "Lottery Scheduling: Flexible Proportional-Share Resource Management," *Proc. First Symp. on Operating System Design and Implementation*, USENIX, pp. 1-12, 1994.

WILKES, J., GOLDING, R., STAELIN, C, abd SULLIVAN, T.: "The HP AutoRAID Hierarchical Storage System," *ACM Trans. on Computer Systems*, vol. 14, pp. 108-136, Feb. 1996.

WULF, W.A., COHEN, E.S., CORWIN, W.M., JONES, A.K., LEVIN, R., PIERSON, C., and POLLACK, F.J.: "HYDRA: The Kernel of a Multiprocessor Operating System," *Commun. of the ACM*, vol. 17, pp. 337-345, June 1974.

ZEKAUSKAS, M.J., SAWDON, W.A., and BERSHAD, B.N.: "Software Write Detection for a Distributed Shared Memory," *Proc. First Symp. on Operating System Design and Implementation*, USENIX, pp. 87-100, 1994.

APPENDICES

APPENDIX A

THE MINIX SOURCE CODE

```
++++++++++++++++++++++++++++++++++++++++++++++++++++++++++++++++++++++++++++++++
                               include/ansi.h
++++++++++++++++++++++++++++++++++++++++++++++++++++++++++++++++++++++++++++++++
00000   /* The <ansi.h> header attempts to decide whether the compiler has enough
00001    * conformance to Standard C for Minix to take advantage of.  If so, the
00002    * symbol _ANSI is defined (as 31415).  Otherwise _ANSI is not defined
00003    * here, but it may be defined by applications that want to bend the rules.
00004    * The magic number in the definition is to inhibit unnecessary bending
00005    * of the rules.  (For consistency with the new '#ifdef _ANSI" tests in
00006    * the headers, _ANSI should really be defined as nothing, but that would
00007    * break many library routines that use "#if _ANSI".)
00008    *
00009    * If _ANSI ends up being defined, a macro
00010    *
00011    *      _PROTOTYPE(function, params)
00012    *
00013    * is defined.  This macro expands in different ways, generating either
00014    * ANSI Standard C prototypes or old-style K&R (Kernighan & Ritchie)
00015    * prototypes, as needed.  Finally, some programs use _CONST, _VOIDSTAR etc
00016    * in such a way that they are portable over both ANSI and K&R compilers.
00017    * The appropriate macros are defined here.
00018    */
00019
00020   #ifndef _ANSI_H
00021   #define _ANSI_H
00022
00023   #if __STDC__ == 1
00024   #define _ANSI            31459    /* compiler claims full ANSI conformance */
00025   #endif
00026
00027   #ifdef __GNUC__
00028   #define _ANSI            31459    /* gcc conforms enough even in non-ANSI mode */
00029   #endif
00030
00031   #ifdef _ANSI
00032
00033   /* Keep everything for ANSI prototypes. */
00034   #define _PROTOTYPE(function, params)    function params
00035   #define _ARGS(params)                   params
00036
00037   #define _VOIDSTAR      void *
00038   #define _VOID          void
00039   #define _CONST         const
00040   #define _VOLATILE      volatile
00041   #define _SIZET         size_t
00042
00043   #else
00044
00045   /* Throw away the parameters for K&R prototypes. */
00046   #define _PROTOTYPE(function, params)    function()
00047   #define _ARGS(params)                   ()
00048
00049   #define _VOIDSTAR      void *
00050   #define _VOID          void
00051   #define _CONST
00052   #define _VOLATILE
00053   #define _SIZET         int
00054
```

```
00055     #endif /* _ANSI */
00056
00057     #endif /* ANSI_H */


+++++++++++++++++++++++++++++++++++++++++++++++++++++++++++++++++++++++++++++++++
                              include/limits.h
+++++++++++++++++++++++++++++++++++++++++++++++++++++++++++++++++++++++++++++++++

00100     /* The <limits.h> header defines some basic sizes, both of the language types
00101      * (e.g., the number of bits in an integer), and of the operating system (e.g.
00102      * the number of characters in a file name.
00103      */
00104
00105     #ifndef _LIMITS_H
00106     #define _LIMITS_H
00107
00108     /* Definitions about chars (8 bits in MINIX, and signed). */
00109     #define CHAR_BIT          8      /* # bits in a char */
00110     #define CHAR_MIN       -128      /* minimum value of a char */
00111     #define CHAR_MAX        127      /* maximum value of a char */
00112     #define SCHAR_MIN      -128      /* minimum value of a signed char */
00113     #define SCHAR_MAX       127      /* maximum value of a signed char */
00114     #define UCHAR_MAX       255      /* maximum value of an unsigned char */
00115     #define MB_LEN_MAX        1      /* maximum length of a multibyte char */
00116
00117     /* Definitions about shorts (16 bits in MINIX). */
00118     #define SHRT_MIN   (-32767-1)    /* minimum value of a short */
00119     #define SHRT_MAX       32767     /* maximum value of a short */
00120     #define USHRT_MAX      0xFFFF    /* maximum value of unsigned short */
00121
00122     /* _EM_WSIZE is a compiler-generated symbol giving the word size in bytes. */
00123     #if _EM_WSIZE == 2
00124     #define INT_MIN    (-32767-1)    /* minimum value of a 16-bit int */
00125     #define INT_MAX        32767     /* maximum value of a 16-bit int */
00126     #define UINT_MAX       0xFFFF    /* maximum value of an unsigned 16-bit int */
00127     #endif
00128
00129     #if _EM_WSIZE == 4
00130     #define INT_MIN (-2147483647-1)  /* minimum value of a 32-bit int */
00131     #define INT_MAX    2147483647    /* maximum value of a 32-bit int */
00132     #define UINT_MAX  0xFFFFFFFF      /* maximum value of an unsigned 32-bit int */
00133     #endif
00134
00135     /*Definitions about longs (32 bits in MINIX). */
00136     #define LONG_MIN (-2147483647L-1)/* minimum value of a long */
00137     #define LONG_MAX  2147483647L    /* maximum value of a long */
00138     #define ULONG_MAX 0xFFFFFFFFL    /* maximum value of an unsigned long */
00139
00140     /* Minimum sizes required by the POSIX P1003.1 standard (Table 2-3). */
00141     #ifdef _POSIX_SOURCE             /* these are only visible for POSIX */
00142     #define _POSIX_ARG_MAX     4096  /* exec() may have 4K worth of args */
00143     #define _POSIX_CHILD_MAX      6  /* a process may have 6 children */
00144     #define _POSIX_LINK_MAX       8  /* a file may have 8 links */
00145     #define _POSIX_MAX_CANON    255  /* size of the canonical input queue */
00146     #define _POSIX_MAX_INPUT    255  /* you can type 255 chars ahead */
00147     #define _POSIX_NAME_MAX      14  /* a file name may have 14 chars */
00148     #define _POSIX_NGROUPS_MAX    0  /* supplementary group IDs are optional */
00149     #define _POSIX_OPEN_MAX      16  /* a process may have 16 files open */
```

```
00150    #define _POSIX_PATH_MAX     255  /* a pathname may contain 255 chars */
00151    #define _POSIX_PIPE_BUF     512  /* pipes writes of 512 bytes must be atomic */
00152    #define _POSIX_STREAM_MAX     8  /* at least 8 FILEs can be open at once */
00153    #define _POSIX_TZNAME_MAX     3  /* time zone names can be at least 3 chars */
00154    #define _POSIX_SSIZE_MAX  32767  /* read() must support 32767 byte reads */
00155
00156    /* Values actually implemented by MINIX (Tables 2-4, 2-5, 2-6, and 2-7). */
00157    /* Some of these old names had better be defined when not POSIX. */
00158    #define _NO_LIMIT           100  /* arbitrary number; limit not enforced */
00159
00160    #define NGROUPS_MAX           0  /* supplemental group IDs not available */
00161    #if _EM_WSIZE > 2
00162    #define ARG_MAX           16384  /* # bytes of args + environ for exec() */
00163    #else
00164    #define ARG_MAX            4096  /* args + environ on small machines */
00165    #endif
00166    #define CHILD_MAX     _NO_LIMIT  /* MINIX does not limit children */
00167    #define OPEN_MAX             20  /* # open files a process may have */
00168    #define LINK_MAX            127  /* # links a file may have */
00169    #define MAX_CANON           255  /* size of the canonical input queue */
00170    #define MAX_INPUT           255  /* size of the type-ahead buffer */
00171    #define NAME_MAX             14  /* # chars in a file name */
00172    #define PATH_MAX            255  /* # chars in a path name */
00173    #define PIPE_BUF           7168  /* # bytes in atomic write to a pipe */
00174    #define STREAM_MAX           20  /* must be the same as FOPEN_MAX in stdio.h */
00175    #define TZNAME_MAX            3  /* maximum bytes in a time zone name is 3 */
00176    #define SSIZE_MAX         32767  /* max defined byte count for read() */
00177
00178    #endif /* _POSIX_SOURCE */
00179
00180    #endif /* _LIMITS_H */
```

```
++++++++++++++++++++++++++++++++++++++++++++++++++++++++++++++++++++++++++++++++
                               include/errno.h
++++++++++++++++++++++++++++++++++++++++++++++++++++++++++++++++++++++++++++++++
```

```
00200    /* The <errno.h> header defines the numbers of the various errors that can
00201     * occur during program execution.  They are visible to user programs and
00202     * should be small positive integers.  However, they are also used within
00203     * MINIX, where they must be negative.  For example, the READ system call is
00204     * executed internally by calling do_read().  This function returns either a
00205     * (negative) error number or a (positive) number of bytes actually read.
00206     *
00207     * To solve the problem of having the error numbers be negative inside the
00208     * the system and positive outside, the following mechanism is used.  All the
00209     * definitions are are the form:
00210     *
00211     *        #define EPERM          (_SIGN 1)
00212     *
00213     * If the macro _SYSTEM is defined, then  _SIGN is set to "-", otherwise it is
00214     * set to "".  Thus when compiling the operating system, the  macro _SYSTEM
00215     * will be defined, setting EPERM to (- 1), whereas when when this
00216     * file is included in an ordinary user program, EPERM has the value ( 1).
00217     */
00218
00219    #ifndef _ERRNO_H                    /* check if <errno.h> is already included */
```

```
00220   #define _ERRNO_H                      /* it is not included; note that fact */
00221
00222   /* Now define _SIGN as "" or "-" depending on _SYSTEM. */
00223   #ifdef _SYSTEM
00224   #   define _SIGN          -
00225   #   define OK             0
00226   #else
00227   #   define _SIGN
00228   #endif
00229
00230   extern int errno;                     /* place where the error numbers go */
00231
00232   /* Here are the numerical values of the error numbers. */
00233   #define _NERROR              70  /* number of errors */
00234
00235   #define EGENERIC     (_SIGN 99)  /* generic error */
00236   #define EPERM        (_SIGN  1)  /* operation not permitted */
00237   #define ENOENT       (_SIGN  2)  /* no such file or directory */
00238   #define ESRCH        (_SIGN  3)  /* no such process */
00239   #define EINTR        (_SIGN  4)  /* interrupted function call */
00240   #define EIO          (_SIGN  5)  /* input/output error */
00241   #define ENXIO        (_SIGN  6)  /* no such device or address */
00242   #define E2BIG        (_SIGN  7)  /* arg list too long */
00243   #define ENOEXEC      (_SIGN  8)  /* exec format error */
00244   #define EBADF        (_SIGN  9)  /* bad file descriptor */
00245   #define ECHILD       (_SIGN 10)  /* no child process */
00246   #define EAGAIN       (_SIGN 11)  /* resource temporarily unavailable */
00247   #define ENOMEM       (_SIGN 12)  /* not enough space */
00248   #define EACCES       (_SIGN 13)  /* permission denied */
00249   #define EFAULT       (_SIGN 14)  /* bad address */
00250   #define ENOTBLK      (_SIGN 15)  /* Extension: not a block special file */
00251   #define EBUSY        (_SIGN 16)  /* resource busy */
00252   #define EEXIST       (_SIGN 17)  /* file exists */
00253   #define EXDEV        (_SIGN 18)  /* improper link */
00254   #define ENODEV       (_SIGN 19)  /* no such device */
00255   #define ENOTDIR      (_SIGN 20)  /* not a directory */
00256   #define EISDIR       (_SIGN 21)  /* is a directory */
00257   #define EINVAL       (_SIGN 22)  /* invalid argument */
00258   #define ENFILE       (_SIGN 23)  /* too many open files in system */
00259   #define EMFILE       (_SIGN 24)  /* too many open files */
00260   #define ENOTTY       (_SIGN 25)  /* inappropriate I/O control operation */
00261   #define ETXTBSY      (_SIGN 26)  /* no longer used */
00262   #define EFBIG        (_SIGN 27)  /* file too large */
00263   #define ENOSPC       (_SIGN 28)  /* no space left on device */
00264   #define ESPIPE       (_SIGN 29)  /* invalid seek */
00265   #define EROFS        (_SIGN 30)  /* read-only file system */
00266   #define EMLINK       (_SIGN 31)  /* too many links */
00267   #define EPIPE        (_SIGN 32)  /* broken pipe */
00268   #define EDOM         (_SIGN 33)  /* domain error       (from ANSI C std) */
00269   #define ERANGE       (_SIGN 34)  /* result too large   (from ANSI C std) */
00270   #define EDEADLK      (_SIGN 35)  /* resource deadlock avoided */
00271   #define ENAMETOOLONG (_SIGN 36)  /* file name too long */
00272   #define ENOLCK       (_SIGN 37)  /* no locks available */
00273   #define ENOSYS       (_SIGN 38)  /* function not implemented */
00274   #define ENOTEMPTY    (_SIGN 39)  /* directory not empty */
00275
00276   /* The following errors relate to networking. */
00277   #define EPACKSIZE    (_SIGN 50)  /* invalid packet size for some protocol */
00278   #define EOUTOFBUFS   (_SIGN 51)  /* not enough buffers left */
00279   #define EBADIOCTL    (_SIGN 52)  /* illegal ioctl for device */
```

```
00280    #define EBADMODE      (_SIGN 53)   /* badmode in ioctl */
00281    #define EWOULDBLOCK   (_SIGN 54)
00282    #define EBADDEST      (_SIGN 55)   /* not a valid destination address */
00283    #define EDSTNOTRCH    (_SIGN 56)   /* destination not reachable */
00284    #define EISCONN       (_SIGN 57)   /* all ready connected */
00285    #define EADDRINUSE    (_SIGN 58)   /* address in use */
00286    #define ECONNREFUSED  (_SIGN 59)   /* connection refused */
00287    #define ECONNRESET    (_SIGN 60)   /* connection reset */
00288    #define ETIMEDOUT     (_SIGN 61)   /* connection timed out */
00289    #define EURG          (_SIGN 62)   /* urgent data present */
00290    #define ENOURG        (_SIGN 63)   /* no urgent data present */
00291    #define ENOTCONN      (_SIGN 64)   /* no connection (yet or anymore) */
00292    #define ESHUTDOWN     (_SIGN 65)   /* a write call to a shutdown connection */
00293    #define ENOCONN       (_SIGN 66)   /* no such connection */
00294
00295    /* The following are not POSIX errors, but they can still happen. */
00296    #define ELOCKED     (_SIGN 101)  /* can't send message */
00297    #define EBADCALL    (_SIGN 102)  /* error on send/receive */
00298
00299    /* The following error codes are generated by the kernel itself. */
00300    #ifdef _SYSTEM
00301    #define E_BAD_DEST      -1001    /* destination address illegal */
00302    #define E_BAD_SRC       -1002    /* source address illegal */
00303    #define E_TRY_AGAIN     -1003    /* can't send-- tables full */
00304    #define E_OVERRUN       -1004    /* interrupt for task that is not waiting */
00305    #define E_BAD_BUF       -1005    /* message buf outside caller's addr space */
00306    #define E_TASK          -1006    /* can't send to task */
00307    #define E_NO_MESSAGE    -1007    /* RECEIVE failed: no message present */
00308    #define E_NO_PERM       -1008    /* ordinary users can't send to tasks */
00309    #define E_BAD_FCN       -1009    /* only valid fcns are SEND, RECEIVE, BOTH */
00310    #define E_BAD_ADDR      -1010    /* bad address given to utility routine */
00311    #define E_BAD_PROC      -1011    /* bad proc number given to utility */
00312    #endif /* _SYSTEM */
00313
00314    #endif /* _ERRNO_H */
```

```
++++++++++++++++++++++++++++++++++++++++++++++++++++++++++++++++++++++++++++++++
                              include/unistd.h
++++++++++++++++++++++++++++++++++++++++++++++++++++++++++++++++++++++++++++++++
```

```
00400    /* The <unistd.h> header contains a few miscellaneous manifest constants. */
00401
00402    #ifndef _UNISTD_H
00403    #define _UNISTD_H
00404
00405    /* POSIX requires size_t and ssize_t in <unistd.h> and elsewhere. */
00406    #ifndef _SIZE_T
00407    #define _SIZE_T
00408    typedef unsigned int size_t;
00409    #endif
00410
00411    #ifndef _SSIZE_T
00412    #define _SSIZE_T
00413    typedef int ssize_t;
00414    #endif
```

```
00415
00416   /* Values used by access().  POSIX Table 2-8. */
00417   #define F_OK              0     /* test if file exists */
00418   #define X_OK              1     /* test if file is executable */
00419   #define W_OK              2     /* test if file is writable */
00420   #define R_OK              4     /* test if file is readable */
00421
00422   /* Values used for whence in lseek(fd, offset, whence).  POSIX Table 2-9. */
00423   #define SEEK_SET          0     /* offset is absolute  */
00424   #define SEEK_CUR          1     /* offset is relative to current position */
00425   #define SEEK_END          2     /* offset is relative to end of file */
00426
00427   /* This value is required by POSIX Table 2-10. */
00428   #define _POSIX_VERSION 199009L  /* which standard is being conformed to */
00429
00430   /* These three definitions are required by POSIX Sec. 8.2.1.2. */
00431   #define STDIN_FILENO      0     /* file descriptor for stdin */
00432   #define STDOUT_FILENO     1     /* file descriptor for stdout */
00433   #define STDERR_FILENO     2     /* file descriptor for stderr */
00434
00435   #ifdef _MINIX
00436   /* How to exit the system. */
00437   #define RBT_HALT          0
00438   #define RBT_REBOOT        1
00439   #define RBT_PANIC         2     /* for servers */
00440   #define RBT_MONITOR       3     /* let the monitor do this */
00441   #define RBT_RESET         4     /* hard reset the system */
00442   #endif
00443
00444   /* NULL must be defined in <unistd.h> according to POSIX Sec. 2.7.1. */
00445   #define NULL    ((void *)0)
00446
00447   /* The following relate to configurable system variables. POSIX Table 4-2. */
00448   #define _SC_ARG_MAX            1
00449   #define _SC_CHILD_MAX          2
00450   #define _SC_CLOCKS_PER_SEC     3
00451   #define _SC_CLK_TCK            3
00452   #define _SC_NGROUPS_MAX        4
00453   #define _SC_OPEN_MAX           5
00454   #define _SC_JOB_CONTROL        6
00455   #define _SC_SAVED_IDS          7
00456   #define _SC_VERSION            8
00457   #define _SC_STREAM_MAX         9
00458   #define _SC_TZNAME_MAX        10
00459
00460   /* The following relate to configurable pathname variables. POSIX Table 5-2. */
00461   #define _PC_LINK_MAX           1     /* link count */
00462   #define _PC_MAX_CANON          2     /* size of the canonical input queue */
00463   #define _PC_MAX_INPUT          3     /* type-ahead buffer size */
00464   #define _PC_NAME_MAX           4     /* file name size */
00465   #define _PC_PATH_MAX           5     /* pathname size */
00466   #define _PC_PIPE_BUF           6     /* pipe size */
00467   #define _PC_NO_TRUNC           7     /* treatment of long name components */
00468   #define _PC_VDISABLE           8     /* tty disable */
00469   #define _PC_CHOWN_RESTRICTED   9     /* chown restricted or not */
00470
00471   /* POSIX defines several options that may be implemented or not, at the
00472    * implementer's whim.  This implementer has made the following choices:
00473    *
00474    * _POSIX_JOB_CONTROL       not defined:        no job control
```

```
00475      * _POSIX_SAVED_IDS        not defined:      no saved uid/gid
00476      * _POSIX_NO_TRUNC         defined as -1:    long path names are truncated
00477      * _POSIX_CHOWN_RESTRICTED  defined:         you can't give away files
00478      * _POSIX_VDISABLE         defined:          tty functions can be disabled
00479      */
00480     #define _POSIX_NO_TRUNC         (-1)
00481     #define _POSIX_CHOWN_RESTRICTED  1
00482
00483     /* Function Prototypes. */
00484     #ifndef _ANSI_H
00485     #include <ansi.h>
00486     #endif
00487
00488     _PROTOTYPE( void _exit, (int _status)                                    );
00489     _PROTOTYPE( int access, (const char *_path, int _amode)                  );
00490     _PROTOTYPE( unsigned int alarm, (unsigned int _seconds)                  );
00491     _PROTOTYPE( int chdir, (const char *_path)                               );
00492     _PROTOTYPE( int chown, (const char *_path, Uid_t _owner, Gid_t _group)   );
00493     _PROTOTYPE( int close, (int _fd)                                         );
00494     _PROTOTYPE( char *ctermid, (char *_s)                                    );
00495     _PROTOTYPE( char *cuserid, (char *_s)                                    );
00496     _PROTOTYPE( int dup, (int _fd)                                           );
00497     _PROTOTYPE( int dup2, (int _fd, int _fd2)                                );
00498     _PROTOTYPE( int execl, (const char *_path, const char *_arg, ...)        );
00499     _PROTOTYPE( int execle, (const char *_path, const char *_arg, ...)       );
00500     _PROTOTYPE( int execlp, (const char *_file, const char *arg, ...)        );
00501     _PROTOTYPE( int execv, (const char *_path, char *const _argv[])          );
00502     _PROTOTYPE( int execve, (const char *_path, char *const _argv[],
00503                                                 char *const _envp[])         );
00504     _PROTOTYPE( int execvp, (const char *_file, char *const _argv[])         );
00505     _PROTOTYPE( pid_t fork, (void)                                           );
00506     _PROTOTYPE( long fpathconf, (int _fd, int _name)                         );
00507     _PROTOTYPE( char *getcwd, (char *_buf, size_t _size)                     );
00508     _PROTOTYPE( gid_t getegid, (void)                                        );
00509     _PROTOTYPE( uid_t geteuid, (void)                                        );
00510     _PROTOTYPE( gid_t getgid, (void)                                         );
00511     _PROTOTYPE( int getgroups, (int _gidsetsize, gid_t _grouplist[])         );
00512     _PROTOTYPE( char *getlogin, (void)                                       );
00513     _PROTOTYPE( pid_t getpgrp, (void)                                        );
00514     _PROTOTYPE( pid_t getpid, (void)                                         );
00515     _PROTOTYPE( pid_t getppid, (void)                                        );
00516     _PROTOTYPE( uid_t getuid, (void)                                         );
00517     _PROTOTYPE( int isatty, (int _fd)                                        );
00518     _PROTOTYPE( int link, (const char *_existing, const char *_new)          );
00519     _PROTOTYPE( off_t lseek, (int _fd, off_t _offset, int _whence)           );
00520     _PROTOTYPE( long pathconf, (const char *_path, int _name)                );
00521     _PROTOTYPE( int pause, (void)                                            );
00522     _PROTOTYPE( int pipe, (int _fildes[2])                                   );
00523     _PROTOTYPE( ssize_t read, (int _fd, void *_buf, size_t _n)               );
00524     _PROTOTYPE( int rmdir, (const char *_path)                               );
00525     _PROTOTYPE( int setgid, (Gid_t _gid)                                     );
00526     _PROTOTYPE( int setpgid, (pid_t _pid, pid_t _pgid)                       );
00527     _PROTOTYPE( pid_t setsid, (void)                                         );
00528     _PROTOTYPE( int setuid, (Uid_t _uid)                                     );
00529     _PROTOTYPE( unsigned int sleep, (unsigned int _seconds)                  );
00530     _PROTOTYPE( long sysconf, (int _name)                                    );
00531     _PROTOTYPE( pid_t tcgetpgrp, (int _fd)                                   );
00532     _PROTOTYPE( int tcsetpgrp, (int _fd, pid_t _pgrp_id)                     );
00533     _PROTOTYPE( char *ttyname, (int _fd)                                     );
00534     _PROTOTYPE( int unlink, (const char *_path)                              );
```

```
00535    _PROTOTYPE( ssize_t write, (int _fd, const void *_buf, size_t _n)        );
00536
00537    #ifdef _MINIX
00538    _PROTOTYPE( int brk, (char *_addr)                                       );
00539    _PROTOTYPE( int chroot, (const char *_name)                              );
00540    _PROTOTYPE( int mknod, (const char *_name, Mode_t _mode, Dev_t _addr)    );
00541    _PROTOTYPE( int mknod4, (const char *_name, Mode_t _mode, Dev_t _addr,
00542               long _size)                                                   );
00543    _PROTOTYPE( char *mktemp, (char *_template)                              );
00544    _PROTOTYPE( int mount, (char *_spec, char *_name, int _flag)             );
00545    _PROTOTYPE( long ptrace, (int _req, pid_t _pid, long _addr, long _data)  );
00546    _PROTOTYPE( char *sbrk, (int _incr)                                      );
00547    _PROTOTYPE( int sync, (void)                                             );
00548    _PROTOTYPE( int umount, (const char *_name)                              );
00549    _PROTOTYPE( int reboot, (int _how, ...)                                  );
00550    _PROTOTYPE( int gethostname, (char *_hostname, size_t _len)              );
00551    _PROTOTYPE( int getdomainname, (char *_domain, size_t _len)              );
00552    _PROTOTYPE( int ttyslot, (void)                                          );
00553    _PROTOTYPE( int fttyslot, (int _fd)                                      );
00554    _PROTOTYPE( char *crypt, (const char *_key, const char *_salt)           );
00555    #endif
00556
00557    #endif /* _UNISTD_H */
```

```
++++++++++++++++++++++++++++++++++++++++++++++++++++++++++++++++++++++++++++++++
                               include/string.h
++++++++++++++++++++++++++++++++++++++++++++++++++++++++++++++++++++++++++++++++
```

```
00600    /* The <string.h> header contains prototypes for the string handling
00601     * functions.
00602     */
00603
00604    #ifndef _STRING_H
00605    #define _STRING_H
00606
00607    #define NULL     ((void *)0)
00608
00609    #ifndef _SIZE_T
00610    #define _SIZE_T
00611    typedef unsigned int size_t;     /* type returned by sizeof */
00612    #endif /*_SIZE_T */
00613
00614    /* Function Prototypes. */
00615    #ifndef _ANSI_H
00616    #include <ansi.h>
00617    #endif
00618
00619    _PROTOTYPE( void *memchr, (const void *_s, int _c, size_t _n)            );
00620    _PROTOTYPE( int memcmp, (const void *_s1, const void *_s2, size_t _n)    );
00621    _PROTOTYPE( void *memcpy, (void *_s1, const void *_s2, size_t _n)        );
00622    _PROTOTYPE( void *memmove, (void *_s1, const void *_s2, size_t _n)       );
00623    _PROTOTYPE( void *memset, (void *_s, int _c, size_t _n)                  );
00624    _PROTOTYPE( char *strcat, (char *_s1, const char *_s2)                   );
00625    _PROTOTYPE( char *strchr, (const char *_s, int _c)                       );
00626    _PROTOTYPE( int strncmp, (const char *_s1, const char *_s2, size_t _n)   );
00627    _PROTOTYPE( int strcmp, (const char *_s1, const char *_s2)               );
00628    _PROTOTYPE( int strcoll, (const char *_s1, const char *_s2)              );
00629    _PROTOTYPE( char *strcpy, (char *_s1, const char *_s2)                   );
```

```
00630    _PROTOTYPE( size_t strcspn, (const char *_s1, const char *_s2)          );
00631    _PROTOTYPE( char *strerror, (int _errnum)                               );
00632    _PROTOTYPE( size_t strlen, (const char *_s)                             );
00633    _PROTOTYPE( char *strncat, (char *_s1, const char *_s2, size_t _n)      );
00634    _PROTOTYPE( char *strncpy, (char *_s1, const char *_s2, size_t _n)      );
00635    _PROTOTYPE( char *strpbrk, (const char *_s1, const char *_s2)           );
00636    _PROTOTYPE( char *strrchr, (const char *_s, int _c)                     );
00637    _PROTOTYPE( size_t strspn, (const char *_s1, const char *_s2)           );
00638    _PROTOTYPE( char *strstr, (const char *_s1, const char *_s2)            );
00639    _PROTOTYPE( char *strtok, (char *_s1, const char *_s2)                  );
00640    _PROTOTYPE( size_t strxfrm, (char *_s1, const char *_s2, size_t _n)     );
00641
00642    #ifdef _MINIX
00643    /* For backward compatibility. */
00644    _PROTOTYPE( char *index, (const char *_s, int _charwanted)              );
00645    _PROTOTYPE( char *rindex, (const char *_s, int _charwanted)             );
00646    _PROTOTYPE( void bcopy, (const void *_src, void *_dst, size_t _length)  );
00647    _PROTOTYPE( int bcmp, (const void *_s1, const void *_s2, size_t _length));
00648    _PROTOTYPE( void bzero, (void *_dst, size_t _length)                    );
00649    _PROTOTYPE( void *memccpy, (char *_dst, const char *_src, int _ucharstop,
00650                                                    size_t _size)          );
00651    /* BSD functions */
00652    _PROTOTYPE( int strcasecmp, (const char *_s1, const char *_s2)          );
00653    #endif
00654
00655    #endif /* _STRING_H */
```

```
+++++++++++++++++++++++++++++++++++++++++++++++++++++++++++++++++++++++++++++++++
                              include/signal.h
+++++++++++++++++++++++++++++++++++++++++++++++++++++++++++++++++++++++++++++++++

00700    /* The <signal.h> header defines all the ANSI and POSIX signals.
00701     * MINIX supports all the signals required by POSIX. They are defined below.
00702     * Some additional signals are also supported.
00703     */
00704
00705    #ifndef _SIGNAL_H
00706    #define _SIGNAL_H
00707
00708    #ifndef _ANSI_H
00709    #include <ansi.h>
00710    #endif
00711
00712    /* Here are types that are closely associated with signal handling. */
00713    typedef int sig_atomic_t;
00714
00715    #ifdef _POSIX_SOURCE
00716    #ifndef _SIGSET_T
00717    #define _SIGSET_T
00718    typedef unsigned long sigset_t;
00719    #endif
00720    #endif
00721
00722    #define _NSIG            16     /* number of signals used */
00723
00724    #define SIGHUP            1     /* hangup */
```

```
00725  #define SIGINT              2       /* interrupt (DEL) */
00726  #define SIGQUIT             3       /* quit (ASCII FS) */
00727  #define SIGILL              4       /* illegal instruction */
00728  #define SIGTRAP             5       /* trace trap (not reset when caught) */
00729  #define SIGABRT             6       /* IOT instruction */
00730  #define SIGIOT              6       /* SIGABRT for people who speak PDP-11 */
00731  #define SIGUNUSED           7       /* spare code */
00732  #define SIGFPE              8       /* floating point exception */
00733  #define SIGKILL             9       /* kill (cannot be caught or ignored) */
00734  #define SIGUSR1            10       /* user defined signal # 1 */
00735  #define SIGSEGV            11       /* segmentation violation */
00736  #define SIGUSR2            12       /* user defined signal # 2 */
00737  #define SIGPIPE            13       /* write on a pipe with no one to read it */
00738  #define SIGALRM            14       /* alarm clock */
00739  #define SIGTERM            15       /* software termination signal from kill */
00740
00741  #define SIGEMT              7       /* obsolete */
00742  #define SIGBUS             10       /* obsolete */
00743
00744  /* POSIX requires the following signals to be defined, even if they are
00745   * not supported.  Here are the definitions, but they are not supported.
00746   */
00747  #define SIGCHLD            17       /* child process terminated or stopped */
00748  #define SIGCONT            18       /* continue if stopped */
00749  #define SIGSTOP            19       /* stop signal */
00750  #define SIGTSTP            20       /* interactive stop signal */
00751  #define SIGTTIN            21       /* background process wants to read */
00752  #define SIGTTOU            22       /* background process wants to write */
00753
00754  /* The sighandler_t type is not allowed unless _POSIX_SOURCE is defined. */
00755  #ifdef _POSIX_SOURCE
00756  #define __sighandler_t sighandler_t
00757  #else
00758  typedef void (*__sighandler_t) (int);
00759  #endif
00760
00761  /* Macros used as function pointers. */
00762  #define SIG_ERR    ((__sighandler_t) -1)        /* error return */
00763  #define SIG_DFL    ((__sighandler_t)  0)        /* default signal handling */
00764  #define SIG_IGN    ((__sighandler_t)  1)        /* ignore signal */
00765  #define SIG_HOLD   ((__sighandler_t)  2)        /* block signal */
00766  #define SIG_CATCH  ((__sighandler_t)  3)        /* catch signal */
00767
00768  #ifdef _POSIX_SOURCE
00769  struct sigaction {
00770    __sighandler_t sa_handler;      /* SIG_DFL, SIG_IGN, or pointer to function */
00771    sigset_t sa_mask;               /* signals to be blocked during handler */
00772    int sa_flags;                   /* special flags */
00773  };
00774
00775  /* Fields for sa_flags. */
00776  #define SA_ONSTACK    0x0001      /* deliver signal on alternate stack */
00777  #define SA_RESETHAND  0x0002      /* reset signal handler when signal caught */
00778  #define SA_NODEFER    0x0004      /* don't block signal while catching it */
00779  #define SA_RESTART    0x0008      /* automatic system call restart */
00780  #define SA_SIGINFO    0x0010      /* extended signal handling */
00781  #define SA_NOCLDWAIT  0x0020      /* don't create zombies */
00782  #define SA_NOCLDSTOP  0x0040      /* don't receive SIGCHLD when child stops */
00783
00784  /* POSIX requires these values for use with sigprocmask(2). */
```

```
00785   #define SIG_BLOCK        0    /* for blocking signals */
00786   #define SIG_UNBLOCK      1    /* for unblocking signals */
00787   #define SIG_SETMASK      2    /* for setting the signal mask */
00788   #define SIG_INQUIRE      4    /* for internal use only */
00789   #endif  /* _POSIX_SOURCE */
00790
00791   /* POSIX and ANSI function prototypes. */
00792   _PROTOTYPE( int raise, (int _sig)                                       );
00793   _PROTOTYPE( __sighandler_t signal, (int _sig, __sighandler_t _func)     );
00794
00795   #ifdef _POSIX_SOURCE
00796   _PROTOTYPE( int kill, (pid_t _pid, int _sig)                            );
00797   _PROTOTYPE( int sigaction,
00798       (int _sig, const struct sigaction *_act, struct sigaction *_oact)   );
00799   _PROTOTYPE( int sigaddset, (sigset_t *_set, int _sig)                   );
00800   _PROTOTYPE( int sigdelset, (sigset_t *_set, int _sig)                   );
00801   _PROTOTYPE( int sigemptyset, (sigset_t *_set)                           );
00802   _PROTOTYPE( int sigfillset, (sigset_t *_set)                            );
00803   _PROTOTYPE( int sigismember, (sigset_t *_set, int _sig)                 );
00804   _PROTOTYPE( int sigpending, (sigset_t *_set)                            );
00805   _PROTOTYPE( int sigprocmask,
00806           (int _how, const sigset_t *_set, sigset_t *_oset)               );
00807   _PROTOTYPE( int sigsuspend, (const sigset_t *_sigmask)                  );
00808   #endif
00809
00810   #endif /* _SIGNAL_H */
```

```
++++++++++++++++++++++++++++++++++++++++++++++++++++++++++++++++++++++++++++++++
                               include/fcntl.h
++++++++++++++++++++++++++++++++++++++++++++++++++++++++++++++++++++++++++++++++
```

```
00900   /* The <fcntl.h> header is needed by the open() and fcntl() system calls,
00901    * which  have a variety of parameters and flags.  They are described here.
00902    * The formats of the calls to each of these are:
00903    *
00904    *     open(path, oflag [,mode])      open a file
00905    *     fcntl(fd, cmd [,arg])          get or set file attributes
00906    *
00907    */
00908
00909   #ifndef _FCNTL_H
00910   #define _FCNTL_H
00911
00912   /* These values are used for cmd in fcntl().  POSIX Table 6-1.  */
00913   #define F_DUPFD          0    /* duplicate file descriptor */
00914   #define F_GETFD          1    /* get file descriptor flags */
00915   #define F_SETFD          2    /* set file descriptor flags */
00916   #define F_GETFL          3    /* get file status flags */
00917   #define F_SETFL          4    /* set file status flags */
00918   #define F_GETLK          5    /* get record locking information */
00919   #define F_SETLK          6    /* set record locking information */
00920   #define F_SETLKW         7    /* set record locking info; wait if blocked */
00921
00922   /* File descriptor flags used for fcntl().  POSIX Table 6-2. */
00923   #define FD_CLOEXEC       1    /* close on exec flag for third arg of fcntl */
00924
```

```
00925   /* L_type values for record locking with fcntl().  POSIX Table 6-3. */
00926   #define F_RDLCK           1   /* shared or read lock */
00927   #define F_WRLCK           2   /* exclusive or write lock */
00928   #define F_UNLCK           3   /* unlock */
00929
00930   /* Oflag values for open().  POSIX Table 6-4. */
00931   #define O_CREAT        00100   /* creat file if it doesn't exist */
00932   #define O_EXCL         00200   /* exclusive use flag */
00933   #define O_NOCTTY       00400   /* do not assign a controlling terminal */
00934   #define O_TRUNC        01000   /* truncate flag */
00935
00936   /* File status flags for open() and fcntl().  POSIX Table 6-5. */
00937   #define O_APPEND       02000   /* set append mode */
00938   #define O_NONBLOCK     04000   /* no delay */
00939
00940   /* File access modes for open() and fcntl().  POSIX Table 6-6. */
00941   #define O_RDONLY          0   /* open(name, O_RDONLY) opens read only */
00942   #define O_WRONLY          1   /* open(name, O_WRONLY) opens write only */
00943   #define O_RDWR            2   /* open(name, O_RDWR) opens read/write */
00944
00945   /* Mask for use with file access modes.  POSIX Table 6-7. */
00946   #define O_ACCMODE        03   /* mask for file access modes */
00947
00948   /* Struct used for locking.  POSIX Table 6-8. */
00949   struct flock {
00950     short l_type;                  /* type: F_RDLCK, F_WRLCK, or F_UNLCK */
00951     short l_whence;                /* flag for starting offset */
00952     off_t l_start;                 /* relative offset in bytes */
00953     off_t l_len;                   /* size; if 0, then until EOF */
00954     pid_t l_pid;                   /* process id of the locks' owner */
00955   };
00956
00957
00958   /* Function Prototypes. */
00959   #ifndef _ANSI_H
00960   #include <ansi.h>
00961   #endif
00962
00963   _PROTOTYPE( int creat, (const char *_path, Mode_t _mode)          );
00964   _PROTOTYPE( int fcntl, (int _filedes, int _cmd, ...)              );
00965   _PROTOTYPE( int open,  (const char *_path, int _oflag, ...)       );
00966
00967   #endif /* _FCNTL_H */
```

```
++++++++++++++++++++++++++++++++++++++++++++++++++++++++++++++++++++++++++++++++
                              include/stdlib.h
++++++++++++++++++++++++++++++++++++++++++++++++++++++++++++++++++++++++++++++++
```

```
01000   /* The <stdlib.h> header defines certain common macros, types, and functions.*/
01001
01002   #ifndef _STDLIB_H
01003   #define _STDLIB_H
01004
01005   /* The macros are NULL, EXIT_FAILURE, EXIT_SUCCESS, RAND_MAX, and MB_CUR_MAX.*/
01006   #define NULL     ((void *)0)
01007
01008   #define EXIT_FAILURE      1   /* standard error return using exit() */
01009   #define EXIT_SUCCESS      0   /* successful return using exit() */
```

```
01010    #define RAND_MAX     32767    /* largest value generated by rand() */
01011    #define MB_CUR_MAX       1    /* max value of multibyte character in MINIX */
01012
01013    typedef struct { int quot, rem; } div_t;
01014    typedef struct { long quot, rem; } ldiv_t;
01015
01016    /* The types are size_t, wchar_t, div_t, and ldiv_t. */
01017    #ifndef _SIZE_T
01018    #define _SIZE_T
01019    typedef unsigned int size_t;     /* type returned by sizeof */
01020    #endif
01021
01022    #ifndef _WCHAR_T
01023    #define _WCHAR_T
01024    typedef char wchar_t;             /* type expanded character set */
01025    #endif
01026
01027    /* Function Prototypes. */
01028    #ifndef _ANSI_H
01029    #include <ansi.h>
01030    #endif
01031
01032    _PROTOTYPE( void abort, (void)                                           );
01033    _PROTOTYPE( int abs, (int _j)                                            );
01034    _PROTOTYPE( int atexit, (void (*_func)(void))                            );
01035    _PROTOTYPE( double atof, (const char *_nptr)                             );
01036    _PROTOTYPE( int atoi, (const char *_nptr)                                );
01037    _PROTOTYPE( long atol, (const char *_nptr)                               );
01038    _PROTOTYPE( void *calloc, (size_t _nmemb, size_t _size)                  );
01039    _PROTOTYPE( div_t div, (int _numer, int _denom)                          );
01040    _PROTOTYPE( void exit, (int _status)                                     );
01041    _PROTOTYPE( void free, (void *_ptr)                                      );
01042    _PROTOTYPE( char *getenv, (const char *_name)                            );
01043    _PROTOTYPE( long labs, (long _j)                                         );
01044    _PROTOTYPE( ldiv_t ldiv, (long _numer, long _denom)                      );
01045    _PROTOTYPE( void *malloc, (size_t _size)                                 );
01046    _PROTOTYPE( int mblen, (const char *_s, size_t _n)                       );
01047    _PROTOTYPE( size_t mbstowcs, (wchar_t *_pwcs, const char *_s, size_t _n));
01048    _PROTOTYPE( int mbtowc, (wchar_t *_pwc, const char *_s, size_t _n)       );
01049    _PROTOTYPE( int rand, (void)                                             );
01050    _PROTOTYPE( void *realloc, (void *_ptr, size_t _size)                    );
01051    _PROTOTYPE( void srand, (unsigned int _seed)                             );
01052    _PROTOTYPE( double strtod, (const char *_nptr, char **_endptr)           );
01053    _PROTOTYPE( long strtol, (const char *_nptr, char **_endptr, int _base) );
01054    _PROTOTYPE( int system, (const char *_string)                            );
01055    _PROTOTYPE( size_t wcstombs, (char *_s, const wchar_t *_pwcs, size_t _n));
01056    _PROTOTYPE( int wctomb, (char *_s, wchar_t _wchar)                       );
01057    _PROTOTYPE( void *bsearch, (const void *_key, const void *_base,
01058            size_t _nmemb, size_t _size,
01059            int (*compar) (const void *, const void *))                     );
01060    _PROTOTYPE( void qsort, (void *_base, size_t _nmemb, size_t _size,
01061            int (*compar) (const void *, const void *))                     );
01062    _PROTOTYPE( unsigned long int strtoul,
01063                            (const char *_nptr, char **_endptr, int _base)  );
01064
01065    #ifdef _MINIX
01066    _PROTOTYPE( int putenv, (const char *_name)                              );
01067    _PROTOTYPE(int getopt, (int _argc, char **_argv, char *_opts));
01068    extern char *optarg;
01069    extern int optind, opterr, optopt;
```

```
01070     #endif /* _MINIX */
01071
01072     #endif /* STDLIB_H */



++++++++++++++++++++++++++++++++++++++++++++++++++++++++++++++++++++++++++++++++++
                                include/termios.h
++++++++++++++++++++++++++++++++++++++++++++++++++++++++++++++++++++++++++++++++++

01100     /* The <termios.h> header is used for controlling tty modes. */
01101
01102     #ifndef _TERMIOS_H
01103     #define _TERMIOS_H
01104
01105     typedef unsigned short tcflag_t;
01106     typedef unsigned char cc_t;
01107     typedef unsigned int speed_t;
01108
01109     #define NCCS          20      /* size of cc_c array, some extra space
01110                                    * for extensions. */
01111
01112     /* Primary terminal control structure. POSIX Table 7-1. */
01113     struct termios {
01114       tcflag_t c_iflag;                /* input modes */
01115       tcflag_t c_oflag;                /* output modes */
01116       tcflag_t c_cflag;                /* control modes */
01117       tcflag_t c_lflag;                /* local modes */
01118       speed_t  c_ispeed;               /* input speed */
01119       speed_t  c_ospeed;               /* output speed */
01120       cc_t c_cc[NCCS];                 /* control characters */
01121     };
01122
01123     /* Values for termios c_iflag bit map.  POSIX Table 7-2. */
01124     #define BRKINT          0x0001  /* signal interrupt on break */
01125     #define ICRNL           0x0002  /* map CR to NL on input */
01126     #define IGNBRK          0x0004  /* ignore break */
01127     #define IGNCR           0x0008  /* ignore CR */
01128     #define IGNPAR          0x0010  /* ignore characters with parity errors */
01129     #define INLCR           0x0020  /* map NL to CR on input */
01130     #define INPCK           0x0040  /* enable input parity check */
01131     #define ISTRIP          0x0080  /* mask off 8th bit */
01132     #define IXOFF           0x0100  /* enable start/stop input control */
01133     #define IXON            0x0200  /* enable start/stop output control */
01134     #define PARMRK          0x0400  /* mark parity errors in the input queue */
01135
01136     /* Values for termios c_oflag bit map.  POSIX Sec. 7.1.2.3. */
01137     #define OPOST           0x0001  /* perform output processing */
01138
01139     /* Values for termios c_cflag bit map.  POSIX Table 7-3. */
01140     #define CLOCAL          0x0001  /* ignore modem status lines */
01141     #define CREAD           0x0002  /* enable receiver */
01142     #define CSIZE           0x000C  /* number of bits per character */
01143     #define      CS5        0x0000  /* if CSIZE is CS5, characters are 5 bits */
01144     #define      CS6        0x0004  /* if CSIZE is CS6, characters are 6 bits */
01145     #define      CS7        0x0008  /* if CSIZE is CS7, characters are 7 bits */
01146     #define      CS8        0x000C  /* if CSIZE is CS8, characters are 8 bits */
01147     #define CSTOPB          0x0010  /* send 2 stop bits if set, else 1 */
01148     #define HUPCL           0x0020  /* hang up on last close */
01149     #define PARENB          0x0040  /* enable parity on output */
```

```
01150        #define PARODD            0x0080  /* use odd parity if set, else even */
01151
01152        /* Values for termios c_lflag bit map.  POSIX Table 7-4. */
01153        #define ECHO              0x0001  /* enable echoing of input characters */
01154        #define ECHOE             0x0002  /* echo ERASE as backspace */
01155        #define ECHOK             0x0004  /* echo KILL */
01156        #define ECHONL            0x0008  /* echo NL */
01157        #define ICANON            0x0010  /* canonical input (erase and kill enabled) */
01158        #define IEXTEN            0x0020  /* enable extended functions */
01159        #define ISIG              0x0040  /* enable signals */
01160        #define NOFLSH            0x0080  /* disable flush after interrupt or quit */
01161        #define TOSTOP            0x0100  /* send SIGTTOU (job control, not implemented*/
01162
01163        /* Indices into c_cc array.  Default values in parentheses. POSIX Table 7-5. */
01164        #define VEOF              0       /* cc_c[VEOF] = EOF char (^D) */
01165        #define VEOL              1       /* cc_c[VEOL] = EOL char (undef) */
01166        #define VERASE            2       /* cc_c[VERASE] = ERASE char (^H) */
01167        #define VINTR             3       /* cc_c[VINTR] = INTR char (DEL) */
01168        #define VKILL             4       /* cc_c[VKILL] = KILL char (^U) */
01169        #define VMIN              5       /* cc_c[VMIN] = MIN value for timer */
01170        #define VQUIT             6       /* cc_c[VQUIT] = QUIT char (^\) */
01171        #define VTIME             7       /* cc_c[VTIME] = TIME value for timer */
01172        #define VSUSP             8       /* cc_c[VSUSP] = SUSP (^Z, ignored) */
01173        #define VSTART            9       /* cc_c[VSTART] = START char (^S) */
01174        #define VSTOP             10      /* cc_c[VSTOP] = STOP char (^Q) */
01175
01176        #define _POSIX_VDISABLE   (cc_t)0xFF    /* You can't even generate this
01177                                               * character with 'normal' keyboards.
01178                                               * But some language specific keyboards
01179                                               * can generate 0xFF. It seems that all
01180                                               * 256 are used, so cc_t should be a
01181                                               * short...
01182                                               */
01183
01184        /* Values for the baud rate settings.  POSIX Table 7-6. */
01185        #define B0                0x0000  /* hang up the line */
01186        #define B50               0x1000  /* 50 baud */
01187        #define B75               0x2000  /* 75 baud */
01188        #define B110              0x3000  /* 110 baud */
01189        #define B134              0x4000  /* 134.5 baud */
01190        #define B150              0x5000  /* 150 baud */
01191        #define B200              0x6000  /* 200 baud */
01192        #define B300              0x7000  /* 300 baud */
01193        #define B600              0x8000  /* 600 baud */
01194        #define B1200             0x9000  /* 1200 baud */
01195        #define B1800             0xA000  /* 1800 baud */
01196        #define B2400             0xB000  /* 2400 baud */
01197        #define B4800             0xC000  /* 4800 baud */
01198        #define B9600             0xD000  /* 9600 baud */
01199        #define B19200            0xE000  /* 19200 baud */
01200        #define B38400            0xF000  /* 38400 baud */
01201
01202        /* Optional actions for tcsetattr().  POSIX Sec. 7.2.1.2. */
01203        #define TCSANOW           1       /* changes take effect immediately */
01204        #define TCSADRAIN         2       /* changes take effect after output is done */
01205        #define TCSAFLUSH         3       /* wait for output to finish and flush input */
01206
01207        /* Queue_selector values for tcflush().  POSIX Sec. 7.2.2.2. */
01208        #define TCIFLUSH          1       /* flush accumulated input data */
01209        #define TCOFLUSH          2       /* flush accumulated output data */
```

```
01210   #define TCIOFLUSH          3     /* flush accumulated input and output data */
01211
01212   /* Action values for tcflow().  POSIX Sec. 7.2.2.2. */
01213   #define TCOOFF             1     /* suspend output */
01214   #define TCOON              2     /* restart suspended output */
01215   #define TCIOFF             3     /* transmit a STOP character on the line */
01216   #define TCION              4     /* transmit a START character on the line */
01217
01218
01219   /* Function Prototypes. */
01220   #ifndef _ANSI_H
01221   #include <ansi.h>
01222   #endif
01223
01224   _PROTOTYPE( int tcsendbreak, (int _fildes, int _duration)                  );
01225   _PROTOTYPE( int tcdrain, (int _filedes)                                    );
01226   _PROTOTYPE( int tcflush, (int _filedes, int _queue_selector)               );
01227   _PROTOTYPE( int tcflow, (int _filedes, int _action)                        );
01228   _PROTOTYPE( speed_t cfgetispeed, (const struct termios *_termios_p)        );
01229   _PROTOTYPE( speed_t cfgetospeed, (const struct termios *_termios_p)        );
01230   _PROTOTYPE( int cfsetispeed, (struct termios *_termios_p, speed_t _speed)  );
01231   _PROTOTYPE( int cfsetospeed, (struct termios *_termios_p, speed_t _speed)  );
01232   _PROTOTYPE( int tcgetattr, (int _filedes, struct termios *_termios_p)      );
01233   _PROTOTYPE( int tcsetattr, \
01234           (int _filedes, int _opt_actions, const struct termios *_termios_p)   );
01235
01236   #define cfgetispeed(termios_p)          ((termios_p)->c_ispeed)
01237   #define cfgetospeed(termios_p)          ((termios_p)->c_ospeed)
01238   #define cfsetispeed(termios_p, speed)   ((termios_p)->c_ispeed = (speed), 0)
01239   #define cfsetospeed(termios_p, speed)   ((termios_p)->c_ospeed = (speed), 0)
01240
01241   #ifdef _MINIX
01242   /* Here are the local extensions to the POSIX standard for Minix. Posix
01243    * conforming programs are not able to access these, and therefore they are
01244    * only defined when a Minix program is compiled.
01245    */
01246
01247   /* Extensions to the termios c_iflag bit map.  */
01248   #define IXANY           0x0800  /* allow any key to continue ouptut */
01249
01250   /* Extensions to the termios c_oflag bit map. They are only active iff
01251    * OPOST is enabled. */
01252   #define ONLCR           0x0002  /* Map NL to CR-NL on output */
01253   #define XTABS           0x0004  /* Expand tabs to spaces */
01254   #define ONOEOT          0x0008  /* discard EOT's (^D) on output) */
01255
01256   /* Extensions to the termios c_lflag bit map.  */
01257   #define LFLUSHO         0x0200  /* Flush output. */
01258
01259   /* Extensions to the c_cc array. */
01260   #define VREPRINT           11     /* cc_c[VREPRINT] (^R) */
01261   #define VLNEXT             12     /* cc_c[VLNEXT] (^V) */
01262   #define VDISCARD           13     /* cc_c[VDISCARD] (^O) */
01263
01264   /* Extensions to baud rate settings. */
01265   #define B57600          0x0100  /* 57600 baud */
01266   #define B115200         0x0200  /* 115200 baud */
01267
01268   /* These are the default settings used by the kernel and by 'stty sane' */
01269
```

```
01270    #define TCTRL_DEF        (CREAD | CS8 | HUPCL)
01271    #define TINPUT_DEF       (BRKINT | ICRNL | IXON | IXANY)
01272    #define TOUTPUT_DEF      (OPOST | ONLCR)
01273    #define TLOCAL_DEF       (ISIG | IEXTEN | ICANON | ECHO | ECHOE)
01274    #define TSPEED_DEF       B9600
01275
01276    #define TEOF_DEF         '\4'     /* ^D */
01277    #define TEOL_DEF         _POSIX_VDISABLE
01278    #define TERASE_DEF       '\10'    /* ^H */
01279    #define TINTR_DEF        '\177'   /* ^? */
01280    #define TKILL_DEF        '\25'    /* ^U */
01281    #define TMIN_DEF         1
01282    #define TQUIT_DEF        '\34'    /* ^\ */
01283    #define TSTART_DEF       '\21'    /* ^Q */
01284    #define TSTOP_DEF        '\23'    /* ^S */
01285    #define TSUSP_DEF        '\32'    /* ^Z */
01286    #define TTIME_DEF        0
01287    #define TREPRINT_DEF     '\22'    /* ^R */
01288    #define TLNEXT_DEF       '\26'    /* ^V */
01289    #define TDISCARD_DEF     '\17'    /* ^O */
01290
01291    /* Window size. This information is stored in the TTY driver but not used.
01292     * This can be used for screen based applications in a window environment.
01293     * The ioctls TIOCGWINSZ and TIOCSWINSZ can be used to get and set this
01294     * information.
01295     */
01296
01297    struct winsize
01298    {
01299            unsigned short  ws_row;          /* rows, in characters */
01300            unsigned short  ws_col;          /* columns, in characters */
01301            unsigned short  ws_xpixel;       /* horizontal size, pixels */
01302            unsigned short  ws_ypixel;       /* vertical size, pixels */
01303    };
01304    #endif /* _MINIX */
01305
01306    #endif /* _TERMIOS_H */
```

```
++++++++++++++++++++++++++++++++++++++++++++++++++++++++++++++++++++++++++++++++
                               include/a.out.h
++++++++++++++++++++++++++++++++++++++++++++++++++++++++++++++++++++++++++++++++
```

```
01400    /* The <a.out> header file describes the format of executable files. */
01401
01402    #ifndef _AOUT_H
01403    #define _AOUT_H
01404
01405    struct  exec {                  /* a.out header */
01406      unsigned char a_magic[2];     /* magic number */
01407      unsigned char a_flags;        /* flags, see below */
01408      unsigned char a_cpu;          /* cpu id */
01409      unsigned char a_hdrlen;       /* length of header */
01410      unsigned char a_unused;       /* reserved for future use */
01411      unsigned short a_version;     /* version stamp (not used at present) */
01412      long          a_text;         /* size of text segement in bytes */
01413      long          a_data;         /* size of data segment in bytes */
01414      long          a_bss;          /* size of bss segment in bytes */
```

```
01415      long         a_entry;         /* entry point */
01416      long         a_total;         /* total memory allocated */
01417      long         a_syms;          /* size of symbol table */
01418
01419      /* SHORT FORM ENDS HERE */
01420      long         a_trsize;        /* text relocation size */
01421      long         a_drsize;        /* data relocation size */
01422      long         a_tbase;         /* text relocation base */
01423      long         a_dbase;         /* data relocation base */
01424   };
01425
01426   #define A_MAGIC0      (unsigned char) 0x01
01427   #define A_MAGIC1      (unsigned char) 0x03
01428   #define BADMAG(X)     ((X).a_magic[0] != A_MAGIC0 ||(X).a_magic[1] != A_MAGIC1)
01429
01430   /* CPU Id of TARGET machine (byte order coded in low order two bits) */
01431   #define A_NONE   0x00    /* unknown */
01432   #define A_I8086 0x04    /* intel i8086/8088 */
01433   #define A_M68K   0x0B    /* motorola m68000 */
01434   #define A_NS16K 0x0C    /* national semiconductor 16032 */
01435   #define A_I80386 0x10    /* intel i80386 */
01436   #define A_SPARC 0x17    /* Sun SPARC */
01437
01438   #define A_BLR(cputype)  ((cputype&0x01)!=0) /* TRUE if bytes left-to-right */
01439   #define A_WLR(cputype)  ((cputype&0x02)!=0) /* TRUE if words left-to-right */
01440
01441   /* Flags. */
01442   #define A_UZP    0x01    /* unmapped zero page (pages) */
01443   #define A_PAL    0x02    /* page aligned executable */
01444   #define A_NSYM   0x04    /* new style symbol table */
01445   #define A_EXEC   0x10    /* executable */
01446   #define A_SEP    0x20    /* separate I/D */
01447   #define A_PURE   0x40    /* pure text */         /* not used */
01448   #define A_TOVLY 0x80    /* text overlay */       /* not used */
01449
01450   /* Offsets of various things. */
01451   #define A_MINHDR          32
01452   #define A_TEXTPOS(X)      ((long)(X).a_hdrlen)
01453   #define A_DATAPOS(X)      (A_TEXTPOS(X) + (X).a_text)
01454   #define A_HASRELS(X)      ((X).a_hdrlen > (unsigned char) A_MINHDR)
01455   #define A_HASEXT(X)       ((X).a_hdrlen > (unsigned char) (A_MINHDR +  8))
01456   #define A_HASLNS(X)       ((X).a_hdrlen > (unsigned char) (A_MINHDR + 16))
01457   #define A_HASTOFF(X)      ((X).a_hdrlen > (unsigned char) (A_MINHDR + 24))
01458   #define A_TRELPOS(X)      (A_DATAPOS(X) + (X).a_data)
01459   #define A_DRELPOS(X)      (A_TRELPOS(X) + (X).a_trsize)
01460   #define A_SYMPOS(X)       (A_TRELPOS(X) + (A_HASRELS(X) ? \
01461                             ((X).a_trsize + (X).a_drsize) : 0))
01462
01463   struct reloc {
01464     long r_vaddr;                  /* virtual address of reference */
01465     unsigned short r_symndx;       /* internal segnum or extern symbol num */
01466     unsigned short r_type;         /* relocation type */
01467   };
01468
01469   /* r_tyep values: */
01470   #define R_ABBS            0
01471   #define R_RELLBYTE        2
01472   #define R_PCRBYTE         3
01473   #define R_RELWORD         4
01474   #define R_PCRWORD         5
```

```
01475      #define R_RELLONG        6
01476      #define R_PCRLONG        7
01477      #define R_REL3BYTE       8
01478      #define R_KBRANCHE       9
01479
01480      /* r_symndx for internal segments */
01481      #define S_ABS            ((unsigned short)-1)
01482      #define S_TEXT           ((unsigned short)-2)
01483      #define S_DATA           ((unsigned short)-3)
01484      #define S_BSS            ((unsigned short)-4)
01485
01486      struct nlist {                    /* symbol table entry */
01487        char n_name[8];                 /* symbol name */
01488        long n_value;                   /* value */
01489        unsigned char n_sclass;         /* storage class */
01490        unsigned char n_numaux;         /* number of auxiliary entries (not used) */
01491        unsigned short n_type;          /* language base and derived type (not used) */
01492      };
01493
01494      /* Low bits of storage class (section). */
01495      #define N_SECT           07        /* section mask */
01496      #define N_UNDF           00        /* undefined */
01497      #define N_ABS            01        /* absolute */
01498      #define N_TEXT           02        /* text */
01499      #define N_DATA           03        /* data */
01500      #define N_BSS            04        /* bss */
01501      #define N_COMM           05        /* (common) */
01502
01503      /* High bits of storage class. */
01504      #define N_CLASS          0370      /* storage class mask */
01505      #define C_NULL
01506      #define C_EXT            0020      /* external symbol */
01507      #define C_STAT           0030      /* static */
01508
01509      /* Function prototypes. */
01510      #ifndef _ANSI_H
01511      #include <ansi.h>
01512      #endif
01513
01514      _PROTOTYPE( int nlist, (char *_file, struct nlist *_nl)                );
01515
01516      #endif /* _AOUT_H */
```

```
++++++++++++++++++++++++++++++++++++++++++++++++++++++++++++++++++++++++++++++++
                               include/sys/types.h
++++++++++++++++++++++++++++++++++++++++++++++++++++++++++++++++++++++++++++++++
```

```
01600      /* The <sys/types.h> header contains important data type definitions.
01601       * It is considered good programming practice to use these definitions,
01602       * instead of the underlying base type.  By convention, all type names end
01603       * with _t.
01604       */
01605
01606      #ifndef _TYPES_H
01607      #define _TYPES_H
01608
01609      /* _ANSI is somehow used to determine whether or not the compiler is a
```

```
01610     * 16 bit compiler
01611     */
01612    #ifndef _ANSI
01613    #include <ansi.h>
01614    #endif
01615
01616    /* The type size_t holds all results of the sizeof operator.  At first glance,
01617     * it seems obvious that it should be an unsigned int, but this is not always
01618     * the case. For example, MINIX-ST (68000) has 32-bit pointers and 16-bit
01619     * integers. When one asks for the size of a 70K struct or array, the result
01620     * requires 17 bits to express, so size_t must be a long type.  The type
01621     * ssize_t is the signed version of size_t.
01622     */
01623    #ifndef _SIZE_T
01624    #define _SIZE_T
01625    typedef unsigned int size_t;
01626    #endif
01627
01628    #ifndef _SSIZE_T
01629    #define _SSIZE_T
01630    typedef int ssize_t;
01631    #endif
01632
01633    #ifndef _TIME_T
01634    #define _TIME_T
01635    typedef long time_t;                    /* time in sec since 1 Jan 1970 0000 GMT */
01636    #endif
01637
01638    #ifndef _CLOCK_T
01639    #define _CLOCK_T
01640    typedef long clock_t;                   /* unit for system accounting */
01641    #endif
01642
01643    #ifndef _SIGSET_T
01644    #define _SIGSET_T
01645    typedef unsigned long sigset_t;
01646    #endif
01647
01648    /* Types used in disk, inode, etc. data structures. */
01649    typedef short           dev_t;          /* holds (major|minor) device pair */
01650    typedef char            gid_t;          /* group id */
01651    typedef unsigned short ino_t;           /* i-node number */
01652    typedef unsigned short mode_t;          /* file type and permissions bits */
01653    typedef char            nlink_t;        /* number of links to a file */
01654    typedef unsigned long  off_t;           /* offset within a file */
01655    typedef int             pid_t;          /* process id (must be signed) */
01656    typedef short           uid_t;          /* user id */
01657    typedef unsigned long zone_t;           /* zone number */
01658    typedef unsigned long block_t;          /* block number */
01659    typedef unsigned long  bit_t;           /* bit number in a bit map */
01660    typedef unsigned short zone1_t;         /* zone number for V1 file systems */
01661    typedef unsigned short bitchunk_t;      /* collection of bits in a bitmap */
01662
01663    typedef unsigned char   u8_t;           /* 8 bit type */
01664    typedef unsigned short u16_t;           /* 16 bit type */
01665    typedef unsigned long  u32_t;           /* 32 bit type */
01666
01667    typedef char            i8_t;           /* 8 bit signed type */
01668    typedef short           i16_t;          /* 16 bit signed type */
01669    typedef long            i32_t;          /* 32 bit signed type */
```

```
01670
01671    /* The following types are needed because MINIX uses K&R style function
01672     * definitions (for maximum portability).  When a short, such as dev_t, is
01673     * passed to a function with a K&R definition, the compiler automatically
01674     * promotes it to an int.  The prototype must contain an int as the parameter,
01675     * not a short, because an int is what an old-style function definition
01676     * expects.  Thus using dev_t in a prototype would be incorrect.  It would be
01677     * sufficient to just use int instead of dev_t in the prototypes, but Dev_t
01678     * is clearer.
01679     */
01680    typedef int            Dev_t;
01681    typedef int            Gid_t;
01682    typedef int            Nlink_t;
01683    typedef int            Uid_t;
01684    typedef int            U8_t;
01685    typedef unsigned long  U32_t;
01686    typedef int            I8_t;
01687    typedef int            I16_t;
01688    typedef long           I32_t;
01689
01690    /* ANSI C makes writing down the promotion of unsigned types very messy.  When
01691     * sizeof(short) == sizeof(int), there is no promotion, so the type stays
01692     * unsigned.  When the compiler is not ANSI, there is usually no loss of
01693     * unsignedness, and there are usually no prototypes so the promoted type
01694     * doesn't matter.  The use of types like Ino_t is an attempt to use ints
01695     * (which are not promoted) while providing information to the reader.
01696     */
01697
01698    #ifndef _ANSI_H
01699    #include <ansi.h>
01700    #endif
01701
01702    #if _EM_WSIZE == 2 || !defined(_ANSI)
01703    typedef unsigned int    Ino_t;
01704    typedef unsigned int    Zone1_t;
01705    typedef unsigned int Bitchunk_t;
01706    typedef unsigned int    U16_t;
01707    typedef unsigned int  Mode_t;
01708
01709    #else /* _EM_WSIZE == 4, or _EM_WSIZE undefined, or _ANSI defined */
01710    typedef int            Ino_t;
01711    typedef int            Zone1_t;
01712    typedef int            Bitchunk_t;
01713    typedef int            U16_t;
01714    typedef int            Mode_t;
01715
01716    #endif /* _EM_WSIZE == 2, etc */
01717
01718    /* Signal handler type, e.g. SIG_IGN */
01719    #if defined(_ANSI)
01720    typedef void (*sighandler_t) (int);
01721    #else
01722    typedef void (*sighandler_t)();
01723    #endif
01724
01725    #endif /* _TYPES_H */
```

```
++++++++++++++++++++++++++++++++++++++++++++++++++++++++++++++++++++++++++++++++
                                include/sys/ioctl.h
++++++++++++++++++++++++++++++++++++++++++++++++++++++++++++++++++++++++++++++++
01800   /* The ioctl.h header declares device controlling operations. */
01801
01802   #ifndef _IOCTL_H
01803   #define _IOCTL_H
01804
01805   #if _EM_WSIZE >= 4
01806   /* Ioctls have the command encoded in the low-order word, and the size
01807    * of the parameter in the high-order word. The 3 high bits of the high-
01808    * order word are used to encode the in/out/void status of the parameter.
01809    */
01810
01811   #define _IOCPARM_MASK     0x1FFF
01812   #define _IOC_VOID         0x20000000
01813   #define _IOCTYPE_MASK     0xFFFF
01814   #define _IOC_IN           0x40000000
01815   #define _IOC_OUT          0x80000000
01816   #define _IOC_INOUT        (_IOC_IN | _IOC_OUT)
01817
01818   #define _IO(x,y)          ((x << 8) | y | _IOC_VOID)
01819   #define _IOR(x,y,t)       ((x << 8) | y | ((sizeof(t) & _IOCPARM_MASK) << 16) |\
01820                                 _IOC_OUT)
01821   #define _IOW(x,y,t)       ((x << 8) | y | ((sizeof(t) & _IOCPARM_MASK) << 16) |\
01822                                 _IOC_IN)
01823   #define _IORW(x,y,t)      ((x << 8) | y | ((sizeof(t) & _IOCPARM_MASK) << 16) |\
01824                                 _IOC_INOUT)
01825   #else
01826   /* No fancy encoding on a 16-bit machine. */
01827
01828   #define _IO(x,y)          ((x << 8) | y)
01829   #define _IOR(x,y,t)       _IO(x,y)
01830   #define _IOW(x,y,t)       _IO(x,y)
01831   #define _IORW(x,y,t)      _IO(x,y)
01832   #endif
01833
01834
01835   /* Terminal ioctls. */
01836   #define TCGETS            _IOR('T',  8, struct termios) /* tcgetattr */
01837   #define TCSETS            _IOW('T',  9, struct termios) /* tcsetattr, TCSANOW */
01838   #define TCSETSW           _IOW('T', 10, struct termios) /* tcsetattr, TCSADRAIN */
01839   #define TCSETSF           _IOW('T', 11, struct termios) /* tcsetattr, TCSAFLUSH */
01840   #define TCSBRK            _IOW('T', 12, int)            /* tcsendbreak */
01841   #define TCDRAIN           _IO ('T', 13)                 /* tcdrain */
01842   #define TCFLOW            _IOW('T', 14, int)            /* tcflow */
01843   #define TCFLSH            _IOW('T', 15, int)            /* tcflush */
01844   #define TIOCGWINSZ        _IOR('T', 16, struct winsize)
01845   #define TIOCSWINSZ        _IOW('T', 17, struct winsize)
01846   #define TIOCGPGRP         _IOW('T', 18, int)
01847   #define TIOCSPGRP         _IOW('T', 19, int)
01848   #define TIOCSFON          _IOW('T', 20, u8_t [8192])
01849
01850   #define TIOCGETP          _IOR('t',  1, struct sgttyb)
01851   #define TIOCSETP          _IOW('t',  2, struct sgttyb)
01852   #define TIOCGETC          _IOR('t',  3, struct tchars)
01853   #define TIOCSETC          _IOW('t',  4, struct tchars)
01854
```

```
01855
01856    /* Network ioctls. */
01857    #define NWIOSETHOPT      _IOW('n', 16, struct nwio_ethopt)
01858    #define NWIOGETHOPT      _IOR('n', 17, struct nwio_ethopt)
01859    #define NWIOGETHSTAT     _IOR('n', 18, struct nwio_ethstat)
01860
01861    #define NWIOSIPCONF      _IOW('n', 32, struct nwio_ipconf)
01862    #define NWIOGIPCONF      _IOR('n', 33, struct nwio_ipconf)
01863    #define NWIOSIPOPT       _IOW('n', 34, struct nwio_ipopt)
01864    #define NWIOGIPOPT       _IOR('n', 35, struct nwio_ipopt)
01865
01866    #define NWIOIPGROUTE     _IORW('n', 40, struct nwio_route)
01867    #define NWIOIPSROUTE     _IOW ('n', 41, struct nwio_route)
01868    #define NWIOIPDROUTE     _IOW ('n', 42, struct nwio_route)
01869
01870    #define NWIOSTCPCONF     _IOW('n', 48, struct nwio_tcpconf)
01871    #define NWIOGTCPCONF     _IOR('n', 49, struct nwio_tcpconf)
01872    #define NWIOTCPCONN      _IOW('n', 50, struct nwio_tcpcl)
01873    #define NWIOTCPLISTEN    _IOW('n', 51, struct nwio_tcpcl)
01874    #define NWIOTCPATTACH    _IOW('n', 52, struct nwio_tcpatt)
01875    #define NWIOTCPSHUTDOWN _IO ('n', 53)
01876    #define NWIOSTCPOPT      _IOW('n', 54, struct nwio_tcpopt)
01877    #define NWIOGTCPOPT      _IOR('n', 55, struct nwio_tcpopt)
01878
01879    #define NWIOSUDPOPT      _IOW('n', 64, struct nwio_udpopt)
01880    #define NWIOGUDPOPT      _IOR('n', 65, struct nwio_udpopt)
01881
01882    /* Disk ioctls. */
01883    #define DIOCEJECT        _IO ('d', 5)
01884    #define DIOCSETP         _IOW('d', 6, struct partition)
01885    #define DIOCGETP         _IOR('d', 7, struct partition)
01886
01887    /* Keyboard ioctls. */
01888    #define KIOCSMAP         _IOW('k', 3, keymap_t)
01889
01890    /* Memory ioctls. */
01891    #define MIOCRAMSIZE      _IOW('m', 3, u32_t)      /* Size of the ramdisk */
01892    #define MIOCSPSINFO      _IOW('m', 4, void *)
01893    #define MIOCGPSINFO      _IOR('m', 5, struct psinfo)
01894
01895    /* Magnetic tape ioctls. */
01896    #define MTIOCTOP         _IOW('M', 1, struct mtop)
01897    #define MTIOCGET         _IOR('M', 2, struct mtget)
01898
01899    /* SCSI command. */
01900    #define SCIOCCMD         _IOW('S', 1, struct scsicmd)
01901
01902    /* CD-ROM ioctls. */
01903    #define CDIOPLAYTI       _IOR('c', 1, struct cd_play_track)
01904    #define CDIOPLAYMSS      _IOR('c', 2, struct cd_play_mss)
01905    #define CDIOREADTOCHDR   _IOW('c', 3, struct cd_toc_entry)
01906    #define CDIOREADTOC      _IOW('c', 4, struct cd_toc_entry)
01907    #define CDIOREADSUBCH    _IOW('c', 5, struct cd_toc_entry)
01908    #define CDIOSTOP         _IO ('c', 10)
01909    #define CDIOPAUSE        _IO ('c', 11)
01910    #define CDIORESUME       _IO ('c', 12)
01911    #define CDIOEJECT        DIOCEJECT
01912
01913    /* Soundcard DSP ioctls. */
01914    #define DSPIORATE        _IOR('s', 1, unsigned int)
```

```
01915   #define DSPIOSTEREO       _IOR('s', 2, unsigned int)
01916   #define DSPIOSIZE         _IOR('s', 3, unsigned int)
01917   #define DSPIOBITS         _IOR('s', 4, unsigned int)
01918   #define DSPIOSIGN         _IOR('s', 5, unsigned int)
01919   #define DSPIOMAX          _IOW('s', 6, unsigned int)
01920   #define DSPIORESET        _IO ('s', 7)
01921
01922   /* Soundcard mixer ioctls. */
01923   #define MIXIOGETVOLUME        _IORW('s', 10, struct volume_level)
01924   #define MIXIOGETINPUTLEFT     _IORW('s', 11, struct inout_ctrl)
01925   #define MIXIOGETINPUTRIGHT    _IORW('s', 12, struct inout_ctrl)
01926   #define MIXIOGETOUTPUT        _IORW('s', 13, struct inout_ctrl)
01927   #define MIXIOSETVOLUME        _IORW('s', 20, struct volume_level)
01928   #define MIXIOSETINPUTLEFT     _IORW('s', 21, struct inout_ctrl)
01929   #define MIXIOSETINPUTRIGHT    _IORW('s', 22, struct inout_ctrl)
01930   #define MIXIOSETOUTPUT        _IORW('s', 23, struct inout_ctrl)
01931
01932   #ifndef _ANSI
01933   #include <ansi.h>
01934   #endif
01935
01936   _PROTOTYPE( int ioctl, (int _fd, int _request, void *_data)                  );
01937
01938   #endif /* _IOCTL_H */



++++++++++++++++++++++++++++++++++++++++++++++++++++++++++++++++++++++++++++++++
                              include/sys/sigcontext.h
++++++++++++++++++++++++++++++++++++++++++++++++++++++++++++++++++++++++++++++++

02000   #ifndef _SIGCONTEXT_H
02001   #define _SIGCONTEXT_H
02002
02003   /* The sigcontext structure is used by the sigreturn(2) system call.
02004    * sigreturn() is seldom called by user programs, but it is used internally
02005    * by the signal catching mechanism.
02006    */
02007
02008   #ifndef _ANSI_H
02009   #include <ansi.h>
02010   #endif
02011
02012   #ifndef _CONFIG_H
02013   #include <minix/config.h>
02014   #endif
02015
02016   #if !defined(CHIP)
02017   #include "error, configuration is not known"
02018   #endif
02019
02020   /* The following structure should match the stackframe_s structure used
02021    * by the kernel's context switching code.  Floating point registers should
02022    * be added in a different struct.
02023    */
02024   #if (CHIP == INTEL)
02025   struct sigregs {
02026   #if _WORD_SIZE == 4
02027     short sr_gs;
02028     short sr_fs;
02029   #endif /* _WORD_SIZE == 4 */
```

```
02030          short sr_es;
02031          short sr_ds;
02032          int sr_di;
02033          int sr_si;
02034          int sr_bp;
02035          int sr_st;                    /* stack top -- used in kernel */
02036          int sr_bx;
02037          int sr_dx;
02038          int sr_cx;
02039          int sr_retreg;
02040          int sr_retadr;                /* return address to caller of save -- used
02041                                         * in kernel */
02042          int sr_pc;
02043          int sr_cs;
02044          int sr_psw;
02045          int sr_sp;
02046          int sr_ss;
02047      };
02048
02049      struct sigframe {               /* stack frame created for signalled process */
02050          _PROTOTYPE( void (*sf_retadr), (void) );
02051          int sf_signo;
02052          int sf_code;
02053          struct sigcontext *sf_scp;
02054          int sf_fp;
02055          _PROTOTYPE( void (*sf_retadr2), (void) );
02056          struct sigcontext *sf_scpcopy;
02057      };
02058
02059      #else
02060      #if (CHIP == M68000)
02061      struct sigregs {
02062          long sr_retreg;                    /* d0 */
02063          long sr_d1;
02064          long sr_d2;
02065          long sr_d3;
02066          long sr_d4;
02067          long sr_d5;
02068          long sr_d6;
02069          long sr_d7;
02070          long sr_a0;
02071          long sr_a1;
02072          long sr_a2;
02073          long sr_a3;
02074          long sr_a4;
02075          long sr_a5;
02076          long sr_a6;
02077          long sr_sp;                    /* also known as a7 */
02078          long sr_pc;
02079          short sr_psw;
02080          short sr_dummy;                /* make size multiple of 4 for system.c */
02081      };
02082      #else
02083      #include "error, CHIP is not supported"
02084      #endif
02085      #endif /* CHIP == INTEL */
02086
02087      struct sigcontext {
02088          int sc_flags;                 /* sigstack state to restore */
02089          long sc_mask;                 /* signal mask to restore */
```

```
02090       struct sigregs sc_regs;           /* register set to restore */
02091   };
02092
02093   #if (CHIP == INTEL)
02094   #if _WORD_SIZE == 4
02095   #define sc_gs sc_regs.sr_gs
02096   #define sc_fs sc_regs.sr_fs
02097   #endif /* _WORD_SIZE == 4 */
02098   #define sc_es sc_regs.sr_es
02099   #define sc_ds sc_regs.sr_ds
02100   #define sc_di sc_regs.sr_di
02101   #define sc_si sc_regs.sr_si
02102   #define sc_fp sc_regs.sr_bp
02103   #define sc_st sc_regs.sr_st              /* stack top -- used in kernel */
02104   #define sc_bx sc_regs.sr_bx
02105   #define sc_dx sc_regs.sr_dx
02106   #define sc_cx sc_regs.sr_cx
02107   #define sc_retreg sc_regs.sr_retreg
02108   #define sc_retadr sc_regs.sr_retadr      /* return address to caller of
02109                                            save -- used in kernel */
02110   #define sc_pc sc_regs.sr_pc
02111   #define sc_cs sc_regs.sr_cs
02112   #define sc_psw sc_regs.sr_psw
02113   #define sc_sp sc_regs.sr_sp
02114   #define sc_ss sc_regs.sr_ss
02115   #endif /* CHIP == INTEL */
02116
02117   #if (CHIP == M68000)
02118   #define sc_retreg sc_regs.sr_retreg
02119   #define sc_d1 sc_regs.sr_d1
02120   #define sc_d2 sc_regs.sr_d2
02121   #define sc_d3 sc_regs.sr_d3
02122   #define sc_d4 sc_regs.sr_d4
02123   #define sc_d5 sc_regs.sr_d5
02124   #define sc_d6 sc_regs.sr_d6
02125   #define sc_d7 sc_regs.sr_d7
02126   #define sc_a0 sc_regs.sr_a0
02127   #define sc_a1 sc_regs.sr_a1
02128   #define sc_a2 sc_regs.sr_a2
02129   #define sc_a3 sc_regs.sr_a3
02130   #define sc_a4 sc_regs.sr_a4
02131   #define sc_a5 sc_regs.sr_a5
02132   #define sc_fp sc_regs.sr_a6
02133   #define sc_sp sc_regs.sr_sp
02134   #define sc_pc sc_regs.sr_pc
02135   #define sc_psw sc_regs.sr_psw
02136   #endif /* CHIP == M68000 */
02137
02138   /* Values for sc_flags.  Must agree with <minix/jmp_buf.h>. */
02139   #define SC_SIGCONTEXT    2        /* nonzero when signal context is included */
02140   #define SC_NOREGLOCALS   4        /* nonzero when registers are not to be
02141                                            saved and restored */
02142
02143   _PROTOTYPE( int sigreturn, (struct sigcontext *_scp)              );
02144
02145   #endif /* _SIGCONTEXT_H */
```

```
++++++++++++++++++++++++++++++++++++++++++++++++++++++++++++++++++++++++++++++++++
                                include/sys/ptrace.h
++++++++++++++++++++++++++++++++++++++++++++++++++++++++++++++++++++++++++++++++++

02200    /* <sys/ptrace.h>
02201     * definitions for ptrace(2)
02202     */
02203
02204    #ifndef _PTRACE_H
02205    #define _PTRACE_H
02206
02207    #define T_STOP          -1        /* stop the process */
02208    #define T_OK             0        /* enable tracing by parent for this process */
02209    #define T_GETINS         1        /* return value from instruction space */
02210    #define T_GETDATA        2        /* return value from data space */
02211    #define T_GETUSER        3        /* return value from user process table */
02212    #define T_SETINS         4        /* set value from instruction space */
02213    #define T_SETDATA        5        /* set value from data space */
02214    #define T_SETUSER        6        /* set value in user process table */
02215    #define T_RESUME         7        /* resume execution */
02216    #define T_EXIT           8        /* exit */
02217    #define T_STEP           9        /* set trace bit */
02218
02219    /* Function Prototypes. */
02220    #ifndef _ANSI_H
02221    #include <ansi.h>
02222    #endif
02223
02224    _PROTOTYPE( long ptrace, (int _req, pid_t _pid, long _addr, long _data) );
02225
02226    #endif /* _PTRACE_H */




++++++++++++++++++++++++++++++++++++++++++++++++++++++++++++++++++++++++++++++++++
                                include/sys/stat.h
++++++++++++++++++++++++++++++++++++++++++++++++++++++++++++++++++++++++++++++++++

02300    /* The <sys/stat.h> header defines a struct that is used in the stat() and
02301     * fstat functions.  The information in this struct comes from the i-node of
02302     * some file.  These calls are the only approved way to inspect i-nodes.
02303     */
02304
02305    #ifndef _STAT_H
02306    #define _STAT_H
02307
02308    struct stat {
02309      dev_t st_dev;                    /* major/minor device number */
02310      ino_t st_ino;                    /* i-node number */
02311      mode_t st_mode;                  /* file mode, protection bits, etc. */
02312      short int st_nlink;              /* # links; TEMPORARY HACK: should be nlink_t*/
02313      uid_t st_uid;                    /* uid of the file's owner */
02314      short int st_gid;                /* gid; TEMPORARY HACK: should be gid_t */
02315      dev_t st_rdev;
02316      off_t st_size;                   /* file size */
02317      time_t st_atime;                 /* time of last access */
02318      time_t st_mtime;                 /* time of last data modification */
02319      time_t st_ctime;                 /* time of last file status change */
```

```
02320     };
02321
02322     /* Traditional mask definitions for st_mode. */
02323     /* The ugly casts on only some of the definitions are to avoid suprising sign
02324      * extensions such as S_IFREG != (mode_t) S_IFREG when ints are 32 bits.
02325      */
02326     #define S_IFMT   ((mode_t) 0170000)      /* type of file */
02327     #define S_IFREG  ((mode_t) 0100000)      /* regular */
02328     #define S_IFBLK 0060000              /* block special */
02329     #define S_IFDIR 0040000              /* directory */
02330     #define S_IFCHR 0020000              /* character special */
02331     #define S_IFIFO 0010000              /* this is a FIFO */
02332     #define S_ISUID 0004000              /* set user id on execution */
02333     #define S_ISGID 0002000              /* set group id on execution */
02334                                          /* next is reserved for future use */
02335     #define S_ISVTX    01000             /* save swapped text even after use */
02336
02337     /* POSIX masks for st_mode. */
02338     #define S_IRWXU    00700             /* owner:  rwx------ */
02339     #define S_IRUSR    00400             /* owner:  r-------- */
02340     #define S_IWUSR    00200             /* owner:  -w------- */
02341     #define S_IXUSR    00100             /* owner:  --x------ */
02342
02343     #define S_IRWXG    00070             /* group:  ---rwx--- */
02344     #define S_IRGRP    00040             /* group:  ---r----- */
02345     #define S_IWGRP    00020             /* group:  ----w---- */
02346     #define S_IXGRP    00010             /* group:  -----x--- */
02347
02348     #define S_IRWXO    00007             /* others: ------rwx */
02349     #define S_IROTH    00004             /* others: ------r-- */
02350     #define S_IWOTH    00002             /* others: -------w- */
02351     #define S_IXOTH    00001             /* others: --------x */
02352
02353     /* The following macros test st_mode (from POSIX Sec. 5.6.1.1). */
02354     #define S_ISREG(m)     (((m) & S_IFMT) == S_IFREG)     /* is a reg file */
02355     #define S_ISDIR(m)     (((m) & S_IFMT) == S_IFDIR)     /* is a directory */
02356     #define S_ISCHR(m)     (((m) & S_IFMT) == S_IFCHR)     /* is a char spec */
02357     #define S_ISBLK(m)     (((m) & S_IFMT) == S_IFBLK)     /* is a block spec */
02358     #define S_ISFIFO(m)    (((m) & S_IFMT) == S_IFIFO)     /* is a pipe/FIFO */
02359
02360
02361     /* Function Prototypes. */
02362     #ifndef _ANSI_H
02363     #include <ansi.h>
02364     #endif
02365
02366     _PROTOTYPE( int chmod, (const char *_path, Mode_t _mode)          );
02367     _PROTOTYPE( int fstat, (int _fildes, struct stat *_buf)           );
02368     _PROTOTYPE( int mkdir, (const char *_path, Mode_t _mode)          );
02369     _PROTOTYPE( int mkfifo, (const char *_path, Mode_t _mode)         );
02370     _PROTOTYPE( int stat, (const char *_path, struct stat *_buf)      );
02371     _PROTOTYPE( mode_t umask, (Mode_t _cmask)                         );
02372
02373     #endif /* _STAT_H */
```

```
++++++++++++++++++++++++++++++++++++++++++++++++++++++++++++++++++++++++++++++++
                               include/sys/dir.h
++++++++++++++++++++++++++++++++++++++++++++++++++++++++++++++++++++++++++++++++

02400     /* The <dir.h> header gives the layout of a directory. */
02401
02402     #ifndef _DIR_H
02403     #define _DIR_H
02404
02405     #define DIRBLKSIZ        512      /* size of directory block */
02406
02407     #ifndef DIRSIZ
02408     #define DIRSIZ  14
02409     #endif
02410
02411     struct direct {
02412       ino_t d_ino;
02413       char d_name[DIRSIZ];
02414     };
02415
02416     #endif /* _DIR_H */




++++++++++++++++++++++++++++++++++++++++++++++++++++++++++++++++++++++++++++++++
                               include/sys/wait.h
++++++++++++++++++++++++++++++++++++++++++++++++++++++++++++++++++++++++++++++++

02500     /* The <sys/wait.h> header contains macros related to wait(). The value
02501      * returned by wait() and waitpid() depends on whether the process
02502      * terminated by an exit() call, was killed by a signal, or was stopped
02503      * due to job control, as follows:
02504      *
02505      *                                   High byte   Low byte
02506      *                                 +---------------------+
02507      *         exit(status)            |  status  |    0     |
02508      *                                 +---------------------+
02509      *         killed by signal        |    0     |  signal  |
02510      *                                 +---------------------+
02511      *         stopped (job control)   |  signal  |   0177   |
02512      *                                 +---------------------+
02513      */
02514
02515     #ifndef _WAIT_H
02516     #define _WAIT_H
02517
02518     #define _LOW(v)          ( (v) & 0377)
02519     #define _HIGH(v)         ( ((v) >> 8) & 0377)
02520
02521     #define WNOHANG          1        /* do not wait for child to exit */
02522     #define WUNTRACED        2        /* for job control; not implemented */
02523
02524     #define WIFEXITED(s)     (_LOW(s) == 0)                  /* normal exit */
02525     #define WEXITSTATUS(s)   (_HIGH(s))                      /* exit status */
02526     #define WTERMSIG(s)      (_LOW(s) & 0177)                /* sig value */
02527     #define WIFSIGNALED(s)   (((unsigned int)(s)-1 & 0xFFFF) < 0xFF) /* signaled */
02528     #define WIFSTOPPED(s)    (_LOW(s) == 0177)               /* stopped */
02529     #define WSTOPSIG(s)      (_HIGH(s) & 0377)               /* stop signal */
```

```
02530
02531     /* Function Prototypes. */
02532     #ifndef _ANSI_H
02533     #include <ansi.h>
02534     #endif
02535
02536     _PROTOTYPE( pid_t wait, (int *_stat_loc)                              );
02537     _PROTOTYPE( pid_t waitpid, (pid_t _pid, int *_stat_loc, int _options)  );
02538
02539     #endif /* _WAIT_H */
```

```
++++++++++++++++++++++++++++++++++++++++++++++++++++++++++++++++++++++++++++++
                            include/minix/config.h
++++++++++++++++++++++++++++++++++++++++++++++++++++++++++++++++++++++++++++++
```

```
02600     #ifndef _CONFIG_H
02601     #define _CONFIG_H
02602
02603     /* Minix release and version numbers. */
02604     #define OS_RELEASE "2.0"
02605     #define OS_VERSION "0"
02606
02607     /* This file sets configuration parameters for the MINIX kernel, FS, and MM.
02608      * It is divided up into two main sections.  The first section contains
02609      * user-settable parameters.  In the second section, various internal system
02610      * parameters are set based on the user-settable parameters.
02611      */
02612
02613     /*===========================================================================*
02614      *                This section contains user-settable parameters             *
02615      *===========================================================================*/
02616     #define MACHINE        IBM_PC     /* Must be one of the names listed below */
02617
02618     #define IBM_PC            1       /* any  8088 or 80x86-based system */
02619     #define SUN_4            40       /* any Sun SPARC-based system */
02620     #define SUN_4_60         40       /* Sun-4/60 (aka SparcStation 1 or Campus) */
02621     #define ATARI            60       /* ATARI ST/STe/TT (68000/68030) */
02622     #define AMIGA            61       /* Commodore Amiga (68000) */
02623     #define MACINTOSH        62       /* Apple Macintosh (68000) */
02624
02625     /* Word size in bytes (a constant equal to sizeof(int)). */
02626     #if __ACK__
02627     #define _WORD_SIZE       _EM_WSIZE
02628     #endif
02629
02630
02631     /* If ROBUST is set to 1, writes of i-node, directory, and indirect blocks
02632      * from the cache happen as soon as the blocks are modified.  This gives a more
02633      * robust, but slower, file system.  If it is set to 0, these blocks are not
02634      * given any special treatment, which may cause problems if the system crashes.
02635      */
02636     #define ROBUST           0       /* 0 for speed, 1 for robustness */
02637
02638     /* Number of slots in the process table for user processes. */
02639     #define NR_PROCS         32
```

```
02640
02641    /* The buffer cache should be made as large as you can afford. */
02642    #if (MACHINE == IBM_PC && _WORD_SIZE == 2)
02643    #define NR_BUFS          40      /* # blocks in the buffer cache */
02644    #define NR_BUF_HASH      64      /* size of buf hash table; MUST BE POWER OF 2*/
02645    #endif
02646
02647    #if (MACHINE == IBM_PC && _WORD_SIZE == 4)
02648    #define NR_BUFS          512     /* # blocks in the buffer cache */
02649    #define NR_BUF_HASH      1024    /* size of buf hash table; MUST BE POWER OF 2*/
02650    #endif
02651
02652    #if (MACHINE == SUN_4_60)
02653    #define NR_BUFS          512     /* # blocks in the buffer cache (<=1536) */
02654    #define NR_BUF_HASH      512     /* size of buf hash table; MUST BE POWER OF 2*/
02655    #endif
02656
02657    #if (MACHINE == ATARI)
02658    #define NR_BUFS          1536    /* # blocks in the buffer cache (<=1536) */
02659    #define NR_BUF_HASH      2048    /* size of buf hash table; MUST BE POWER OF 2*/
02660    #endif
02661
02662    /* Defines for kernel configuration. */
02663    #define AUTO_BIOS             0     /* xt_wini.c - use Western's autoconfig BIOS */
02664    #define LINEWRAP              1     /* console.c - wrap lines at column 80 */
02665    #define ALLOW_GAP_MESSAGES 1       /* proc.c - allow messages in the gap between
02666                                        * the end of bss and lowest stack address */
02667
02668    /* Enable or disable the second level file system cache on the RAM disk. */
02669    #define ENABLE_CACHE2      0
02670
02671    /* Include or exclude device drivers.  Set to 1 to include, 0 to exclude. */
02672    #define ENABLE_NETWORKING  0     /* enable TCP/IP code */
02673    #define ENABLE_AT_WINI     1     /* enable AT winchester driver */
02674    #define ENABLE_BIOS_WINI   0     /* enable BIOS winchester driver */
02675    #define ENABLE_ESDI_WINI   0     /* enable ESDI winchester driver */
02676    #define ENABLE_XT_WINI     0     /* enable XT winchester driver */
02677    #define ENABLE_ADAPTEC_SCSI 0    /* enable ADAPTEC SCSI driver */
02678    #define ENABLE_MITSUMI_CDROM 0   /* enable Mitsumi CD-ROM driver */
02679    #define ENABLE_SB_AUDIO    0     /* enable Soundblaster audio driver */
02680
02681    /* DMA_SECTORS may be increased to speed up DMA based drivers. */
02682    #define DMA_SECTORS        1     /* DMA buffer size (must be >= 1) */
02683
02684    /* Include or exclude backwards compatibility code. */
02685    #define ENABLE_BINCOMPAT   0     /* for binaries using obsolete calls */
02686    #define ENABLE_SRCCOMPAT   0     /* for sources using obsolete calls */
02687
02688    /* Determine which device to use for pipes. */
02689    #define PIPE_DEV      ROOT_DEV   /* put pipes on root device */
02690
02691    /* NR_CONS, NR_RS_LINES, and NR_PTYS determine the number of terminals the
02692     * system can handle.
02693     */
02694    #define NR_CONS            2     /* # system consoles (1 to 8) */
02695    #define NR_RS_LINES        0     /* # rs232 terminals (0, 1, or 2) */
02696    #define NR_PTYS            0     /* # pseudo terminals (0 to 64) */
02697
02698    #if (MACHINE == ATARI)
02699    /* The next define says if you have an ATARI ST or TT */
```

```
02700   #define ATARI_TYPE      TT
02701   #define ST              1       /* all ST's and Mega ST's */
02702   #define STE             2       /* all STe and Mega STe's */
02703   #define TT              3
02704
02705   /* if SCREEN is set to 1 graphical screen operations are possible */
02706   #define SCREEN          1
02707
02708   /* This define says whether the keyboard generates VT100 or IBM_PC escapes. */
02709   #define KEYBOARD        VT100   /* either VT100 or IBM_PC */
02710   #define VT100           100
02711
02712   /* The next define determines the kind of partitioning. */
02713   #define PARTITIONING    SUPRA   /* one of the following or ATARI */
02714   #define SUPRA           1       /*ICD, SUPRA and BMS are all the same */
02715   #define BMS             1
02716   #define ICD             1
02717   #define CBHD            2
02718   #define EICKMANN        3
02719
02720   /* Define the number of hard disk drives on your system. */
02721   #define NR_ACSI_DRIVES  3       /* typically 0 or 1 */
02722   #define NR_SCSI_DRIVES  1       /* typically 0 (ST, STe) or 1 (TT) */
02723
02724   /* Some systems need to have a little delay after each winchester
02725    * commands. These systems need FAST_DISK set to 0. Other disks do not
02726    * need this delay, and thus can have FAST_DISK set to 1 to avoid this delay.
02727    */
02728   #define FAST_DISK       1       /* 0 or 1 */
02729
02730   /* Note: if you want to make your kernel smaller, you can set NR_FD_DRIVES
02731    * to 0. You will still be able to boot minix.img from floppy. However, you
02732    * MUST fetch both the root and usr filesystem from a hard disk
02733    */
02734
02735   /* Define the number of floppy disk drives on your system. */
02736   #define NR_FD_DRIVES    1       /* 0, 1, 2 */
02737
02738   /* This configuration define controls parallel printer code. */
02739   #define PAR_PRINTER     1       /* disable (0) / enable (1) parallel printer */
02740
02741   /* This configuration define controls disk controller clock code. */
02742   #define HD_CLOCK        1       /* disable (0) / enable (1) hard disk clock */
02743
02744   #endif
02745
02746
02747   /*========================================================================*
02748    *         There are no user-settable parameters after this line          *
02749    *========================================================================*/
02750   /* Set the CHIP type based on the machine selected. The symbol CHIP is actually
02751    * indicative of more than just the CPU.  For example, machines for which
02752    * CHIP == INTEL are expected to have 8259A interrrupt controllers and the
02753    * other properties of IBM PC/XT/AT/386 types machines in general. */
02754   #define INTEL           1       /* CHIP type for PC, XT, AT, 386 and clones */
02755   #define M68000          2       /* CHIP type for Atari, Amiga, Macintosh    */
02756   #define SPARC           3       /* CHIP type for SUN-4 (e.g. SPARCstation)  */
02757
02758   /* Set the FP_FORMAT type based on the machine selected, either hw or sw   */
02759   #define FP_NONE         0       /* no floating point support               */
```

```
02760    #define FP_IEEE           1       /* conform IEEE floating point standard    */
02761
02762    #if (MACHINE == IBM_PC)
02763    #define CHIP              INTEL
02764    #define SHADOWING         0
02765    #define ENABLE_WINI       (ENABLE_AT_WINI || ENABLE_BIOS_WINI || \
02766                              ENABLE_ESDI_WINI || ENABLE_XT_WINI)
02767    #define ENABLE_SCSI       (ENABLE_ADAPTEC_SCSI)
02768    #define ENABLE_CDROM      (ENABLE_MITSUMI_CDROM)
02769    #define ENABLE_AUDIO      (ENABLE_SB_AUDIO)
02770    #endif
02771
02772    #if (MACHINE == ATARI) || (MACHINE == AMIGA) || (MACHINE == MACINTOSH)
02773    #define CHIP              M68000
02774    #define SHADOWING         1
02775    #endif
02776
02777    #if (MACHINE == SUN_4) || (MACHINE == SUN_4_60)
02778    #define CHIP              SPARC
02779    #define FP_FORMAT    FP_IEEE
02780    #define SHADOWING         0
02781    #endif
02782
02783    #if (MACHINE == ATARI) || (MACHINE == SUN_4)
02784    #define ASKDEV            1       /* ask for boot device */
02785    #define FASTLOAD          1       /* use multiple block transfers to init ram */
02786    #endif
02787
02788    #if (ATARI_TYPE == TT) /* and all other 68030's */
02789    #define FPP
02790    #undef SHADOWING
02791    #define SHADOWING 0
02792    #endif
02793
02794    #ifndef FP_FORMAT
02795    #define FP_FORMAT    FP_NONE
02796    #endif
02797
02798    /* The file buf.h uses MAYBE_WRITE_IMMED. */
02799    #if ROBUST
02800    #define MAYBE_WRITE_IMMED  WRITE_IMMED  /* slower but perhaps safer */
02801    #else
02802    #define MAYBE_WRITE_IMMED 0            /* faster */
02803    #endif
02804
02805    #ifndef MACHINE
02806    error "In <minix/config.h> please define MACHINE"
02807    #endif
02808
02809    #ifndef CHIP
02810    error "In <minix/config.h> please define MACHINE to have a legal value"
02811    #endif
02812
02813    #if (MACHINE == 0)
02814    error "MACHINE has incorrect value (0)"
02815    #endif
02816
02817    #endif /* _CONFIG_H */
```

```
+++++++++++++++++++++++++++++++++++++++++++++++++++++++++++++++++++++++++++++++++
                            include/minix/const.h
+++++++++++++++++++++++++++++++++++++++++++++++++++++++++++++++++++++++++++++++++
02900     /* Copyright (C) 1995 by Prentice-Hall, Inc.  Permission is hereby granted
02901      * to redistribute the binary and source programs of this system for
02902      * educational or research purposes.  For other use, written permission from
02903      * Prentice-Hall is required.
02904      */
02905
02906     #define EXTERN          extern      /* used in *.h files */
02907     #define PRIVATE         static      /* PRIVATE x limits the scope of x */
02908     #define PUBLIC                      /* PUBLIC is the opposite of PRIVATE */
02909     #define FORWARD         static      /* some compilers require this to be 'static'*/
02910
02911     #define TRUE               1        /* used for turning integers into Booleans */
02912     #define FALSE              0        /* used for turning integers into Booleans */
02913
02914     #define HZ                60        /* clock freq (software settable on IBM-PC) */
02915     #define BLOCK_SIZE      1024        /* # bytes in a disk block */
02916     #define SUPER_USER (uid_t) 0        /* uid_t of superuser */
02917
02918     #define MAJOR              8        /* major device = (dev>>MAJOR) & 0377 */
02919     #define MINOR              0        /* minor device = (dev>>MINOR) & 0377 */
02920
02921     #define NULL      ((void *)0)       /* null pointer */
02922     #define CPVEC_NR          16        /* max # of entries in a SYS_VCOPY request */
02923     #define NR_IOREQS       MIN(NR_BUFS, 64)
02924                                        /* maximum number of entries in an iorequest */
02925
02926     #define NR_SEGS            3        /* # segments per process */
02927     #define T                  0        /* proc[i].mem_map[T] is for text */
02928     #define D                  1        /* proc[i].mem_map[D] is for data */
02929     #define S                  2        /* proc[i].mem_map[S] is for stack */
02930
02931     /* Process numbers of some important processes. */
02932     #define MM_PROC_NR         0        /* process number of memory manager */
02933     #define FS_PROC_NR         1        /* process number of file system */
02934     #define INET_PROC_NR       2        /* process number of the TCP/IP server */
02935     #define INIT_PROC_NR    (INET_PROC_NR + ENABLE_NETWORKING)
02936                                        /* init -- the process that goes multiuser */
02937     #define LOW_USER        (INET_PROC_NR + ENABLE_NETWORKING)
02938                                        /* first user not part of operating system */
02939
02940     /* Miscellaneous */
02941     #define BYTE            0377        /* mask for 8 bits */
02942     #define READING            0        /* copy data to user */
02943     #define WRITING            1        /* copy data from user */
02944     #define NO_NUM        0x8000        /* used as numerical argument to panic() */
02945     #define NIL_PTR   (char *) 0        /* generally useful expression */
02946     #define HAVE_SCATTERED_IO 1         /* scattered I/O is now standard */
02947
02948     /* Macros. */
02949     #define MAX(a, b)   ((a) > (b) ? (a) : (b))
02950     #define MIN(a, b)   ((a) < (b) ? (a) : (b))
02951
02952     /* Number of tasks. */
02953     #define NR_TASKS          (9 + ENABLE_WINI + ENABLE_SCSI + ENABLE_CDROM \
02954                               + ENABLE_NETWORKING + 2 * ENABLE_AUDIO)
```

```
02955
02956    /* Memory is allocated in clicks. */
02957    #if (CHIP == INTEL)
02958    #define CLICK_SIZE        256     /* unit in which memory is allocated */
02959    #define CLICK_SHIFT         8     /* log2 of CLICK_SIZE */
02960    #endif
02961
02962    #if (CHIP == SPARC) || (CHIP == M68000)
02963    #define CLICK_SIZE       4096     /* unit in which memory is alocated */
02964    #define CLICK_SHIFT        12     /* 2log of CLICK_SIZE */
02965    #endif
02966
02967    #define click_to_round_k(n) \
02968            ((unsigned) ((((unsigned long) (n) << CLICK_SHIFT) + 512) / 1024))
02969    #if CLICK_SIZE < 1024
02970    #define k_to_click(n) ((n) * (1024 / CLICK_SIZE))
02971    #else
02972    #define k_to_click(n) ((n) / (CLICK_SIZE / 1024))
02973    #endif
02974
02975    #define ABS               -999     /* this process means absolute memory */
02976
02977    /* Flag bits for i_mode in the inode. */
02978    #define I_TYPE           0170000 /* this field gives inode type */
02979    #define I_REGULAR        0100000 /* regular file, not dir or special */
02980    #define I_BLOCK_SPECIAL  0060000 /* block special file */
02981    #define I_DIRECTORY      0040000 /* file is a directory */
02982    #define I_CHAR_SPECIAL   0020000 /* character special file */
02983    #define I_NAMED_PIPE     0010000 /* named pipe (FIFO) */
02984    #define I_SET_UID_BIT    0004000 /* set effective uid_t on exec */
02985    #define I_SET_GID_BIT    0002000 /* set effective gid_t on exec */
02986    #define ALL_MODES        0006777 /* all bits for user, group and others */
02987    #define RWX_MODES        0000777 /* mode bits for RWX only */
02988    #define R_BIT            0000004 /* Rwx protection bit */
02989    #define W_BIT            0000002 /* rWx protection bit */
02990    #define X_BIT            0000001 /* rwX protection bit */
02991    #define I_NOT_ALLOC      0000000 /* this inode is free */
02992
02993    /* Some limits. */
02994    #define MAX_BLOCK_NR  ((block_t) 077777777)       /* largest block number */
02995    #define HIGHEST_ZONE  ((zone_t) 077777777)        /* largest zone number */
02996    #define MAX_INODE_NR      ((ino_t) 0177777)       /* largest inode number */
02997    #define MAX_FILE_POS ((off_t) 037777777777)       /* largest legal file offset */
02998
02999    #define NO_BLOCK             ((block_t) 0)     /* absence of a block number */
03000    #define NO_ENTRY              ((ino_t) 0)     /* absence of a dir entry */
03001    #define NO_ZONE              ((zone_t) 0)     /* absence of a zone number */
03002    #define NO_DEV                ((dev_t) 0)     /* absence of a device numb */
```

```
++++++++++++++++++++++++++++++++++++++++++++++++++++++++++++++++++++++++++++++++
                              include/minix/type.h
++++++++++++++++++++++++++++++++++++++++++++++++++++++++++++++++++++++++++++++++
03100    #ifndef _TYPE_H
03101    #define _TYPE_H
03102    #ifndef _MINIX_TYPE_H
03103    #define _MINIX_TYPE_H
03104
03105    /* Type definitions. */
03106    typedef unsigned int vir_clicks; /* virtual  addresses and lengths in clicks */
03107    typedef unsigned long phys_bytes;/* physical addresses and lengths in bytes */
03108    typedef unsigned int phys_clicks;/* physical addresses and lengths in clicks */
03109
03110    #if (CHIP == INTEL)
03111    typedef unsigned int vir_bytes; /* virtual addresses and lengths in bytes */
03112    #endif
03113
03114    #if (CHIP == M68000)
03115    typedef unsigned long vir_bytes;/* virtual addresses and lengths in bytes */
03116    #endif
03117
03118    #if (CHIP == SPARC)
03119    typedef unsigned long vir_bytes;/* virtual addresses and lengths in bytes */
03120    #endif
03121
03122    /* Types relating to messages. */
03123    #define M1                  1
03124    #define M3                  3
03125    #define M4                  4
03126    #define M3_STRING          14
03127
03128    typedef struct {int m1i1, m1i2, m1i3; char *m1p1, *m1p2, *m1p3;} mess_1;
03129    typedef struct {int m2i1, m2i2, m2i3; long m2l1, m2l2; char *m2p1;} mess_2;
03130    typedef struct {int m3i1, m3i2; char *m3p1; char m3ca1[M3_STRING];} mess_3;
03131    typedef struct {long m4l1, m4l2, m4l3, m4l4, m4l5;} mess_4;
03132    typedef struct {char m5c1, m5c2; int m5i1, m5i2; long m5l1, m5l2, m5l3;}mess_5;
03133    typedef struct {int m6i1, m6i2, m6i3; long m6l1; sighandler_t m6f1;} mess_6;
03134
03135    typedef struct {
03136      int m_source;                     /* who sent the message */
03137      int m_type;                       /* what kind of message is it */
03138      union {
03139            mess_1 m_m1;
03140            mess_2 m_m2;
03141            mess_3 m_m3;
03142            mess_4 m_m4;
03143            mess_5 m_m5;
03144            mess_6 m_m6;
03145      } m_u;
03146    } message;
03147
03148    /* The following defines provide names for useful members. */
03149    #define m1_i1   m_u.m_m1.m1i1
03150    #define m1_i2   m_u.m_m1.m1i2
03151    #define m1_i3   m_u.m_m1.m1i3
03152    #define m1_p1   m_u.m_m1.m1p1
03153    #define m1_p2   m_u.m_m1.m1p2
03154    #define m1_p3   m_u.m_m1.m1p3
```

```
03155
03156    #define m2_i1  m_u.m_m2.m2i1
03157    #define m2_i2  m_u.m_m2.m2i2
03158    #define m2_i3  m_u.m_m2.m2i3
03159    #define m2_l1  m_u.m_m2.m2l1
03160    #define m2_l2  m_u.m_m2.m2l2
03161    #define m2_p1  m_u.m_m2.m2p1
03162
03163    #define m3_i1  m_u.m_m3.m3i1
03164    #define m3_i2  m_u.m_m3.m3i2
03165    #define m3_p1  m_u.m_m3.m3p1
03166    #define m3_ca1 m_u.m_m3.m3ca1
03167
03168    #define m4_l1  m_u.m_m4.m4l1
03169    #define m4_l2  m_u.m_m4.m4l2
03170    #define m4_l3  m_u.m_m4.m4l3
03171    #define m4_l4  m_u.m_m4.m4l4
03172    #define m4_l5  m_u.m_m4.m4l5
03173
03174    #define m5_c1  m_u.m_m5.m5c1
03175    #define m5_c2  m_u.m_m5.m5c2
03176    #define m5_i1  m_u.m_m5.m5i1
03177    #define m5_i2  m_u.m_m5.m5i2
03178    #define m5_l1  m_u.m_m5.m5l1
03179    #define m5_l2  m_u.m_m5.m5l2
03180    #define m5_l3  m_u.m_m5.m5l3
03181
03182    #define m6_i1  m_u.m_m6.m6i1
03183    #define m6_i2  m_u.m_m6.m6i2
03184    #define m6_i3  m_u.m_m6.m6i3
03185    #define m6_l1  m_u.m_m6.m6l1
03186    #define m6_f1  m_u.m_m6.m6f1
03187
03188    struct mem_map {
03189      vir_clicks mem_vir;             /* virtual address */
03190      phys_clicks mem_phys;           /* physical address */
03191      vir_clicks mem_len;             /* length */
03192    };
03193
03194    struct iorequest_s {
03195      long io_position;               /* position in device file (really off_t) */
03196      char *io_buf;                   /* buffer in user space */
03197      int io_nbytes;                  /* size of request */
03198      unsigned short io_request;      /* read, write (optionally) */
03199    };
03200    #endif /* _TYPE_H */
03201
03202    typedef struct {
03203      vir_bytes iov_addr;             /* address of an I/O buffer */
03204      vir_bytes iov_size;             /* sizeof an I/O buffer */
03205    } iovec_t;
03206
03207    typedef struct {
03208      vir_bytes cpv_src;              /* src address of data */
03209      vir_bytes cpv_dst;              /* dst address of data */
03210      vir_bytes cpv_size;             /* size of data */
03211    } cpvec_t;
03212
03213    /* MM passes the address of a structure of this type to KERNEL when
03214     * do_sendsig() is invoked as part of the signal catching mechanism.
```

```
03215       * The structure contain all the information that KERNEL needs to build
03216       * the signal stack.
03217       */
03218      struct sigmsg {
03219        int sm_signo;                   /* signal number being caught */
03220        unsigned long sm_mask;          /* mask to restore when handler returns */
03221        vir_bytes sm_sighandler;        /* address of handler */
03222        vir_bytes sm_sigreturn;         /* address of _sigreturn in C library */
03223        vir_bytes sm_stkptr;            /* user stack pointer */
03224      };
03225
03226      #define MESS_SIZE (sizeof(message))     /* might need usizeof from fs here */
03227      #define NIL_MESS ((message *) 0)
03228
03229      struct psinfo {            /* information for the ps(1) program */
03230        u16_t nr_tasks, nr_procs;       /* NR_TASKS and NR_PROCS constants. */
03231        vir_bytes proc, mproc, fproc; /* addresses of the main process tables. */
03232      };
03233
03234      #endif /* _MINIX_TYPE_H */
```

```
+++++++++++++++++++++++++++++++++++++++++++++++++++++++++++++++++++++++++++++++++
                              include/minix/syslib.h
+++++++++++++++++++++++++++++++++++++++++++++++++++++++++++++++++++++++++++++++++
```

```
03300      /* Prototypes for system library functions. */
03301
03302      #ifndef _SYSLIB_H
03303      #define _SYSLIB_H
03304
03305      /* Hide names to avoid name space pollution. */
03306      #define sendrec         _sendrec
03307      #define receive         _receive
03308      #define send            _send
03309
03310      /* Minix user+system library. */
03311      _PROTOTYPE( void printk, (char *_fmt, ...)                       );
03312      _PROTOTYPE( int sendrec, (int _src_dest, message *_m_ptr)        );
03313      _PROTOTYPE( int _taskcall, (int _who, int _syscallnr, message *_msgptr) );
03314
03315      /* Minix system library. */
03316      _PROTOTYPE( int receive, (int _src, message *_m_ptr)             );
03317      _PROTOTYPE( int send, (int _dest, message *_m_ptr)               );
03318
03319      _PROTOTYPE( int sys_abort, (int _how, ...)                       );
03320      _PROTOTYPE( int sys_adjmap, (int _proc, struct mem_map *_ptr,
03321                      vir_clicks _data_clicks, vir_clicks _sp)         );
03322      _PROTOTYPE( int sys_copy, (int _src_proc, int _src_seg, phys_bytes _src_vir,
03323              int _dst_proc, int _dst_seg, phys_bytes _dst_vir, phys_bytes _bytes));
03324      _PROTOTYPE( int sys_exec, (int _proc, char *_ptr, int _traced,
03325                          char *_aout, vir_bytes _initpc)              );
03326      _PROTOTYPE( int sys_execmap, (int _proc, struct mem_map *_ptr)   );
03327      _PROTOTYPE( int sys_fork, (int _parent, int _child, int _pid,
03328                          phys_clicks _shadow)                         );
03329      _PROTOTYPE( int sys_fresh, (int _proc, struct mem_map *_ptr,
```

```
03330                phys_clicks _dc, phys_clicks *_basep, phys_clicks *_sizep)      );
03331    _PROTOTYPE( int sys_getsp, (int _proc, vir_bytes *_newsp)                    );
03332    _PROTOTYPE( int sys_newmap, (int _proc, struct mem_map *_ptr)                );
03333    _PROTOTYPE( int sys_getmap, (int _proc, struct mem_map *_ptr)                );
03334    _PROTOTYPE( int sys_sendsig, (int _proc, struct sigmsg *_ptr)                );
03335    _PROTOTYPE( int sys_oldsig, (int _proc, int _sig, sighandler_t _sighandler));
03336    _PROTOTYPE( int sys_endsig, (int _proc)                                      );
03337    _PROTOTYPE( int sys_sigreturn, (int _proc, vir_bytes _scp, int _flags)  );
03338    _PROTOTYPE( int sys_trace, (int _req, int _procnr, long _addr, long *_data_p));
03339    _PROTOTYPE( int sys_xit, (int _parent, int _proc, phys_clicks *_basep,
03340                                                  phys_clicks *_sizep));
03341    _PROTOTYPE( int sys_kill, (int _proc, int _sig)                              );
03342    _PROTOTYPE( int sys_times, (int _proc, clock_t _ptr[5])                      );
03343
03344    #endif /* _SYSLIB_H */
```

```
++++++++++++++++++++++++++++++++++++++++++++++++++++++++++++++++++++++++++++++++++++
                               include/minix/callnr.h
++++++++++++++++++++++++++++++++++++++++++++++++++++++++++++++++++++++++++++++++++++

03400    #define NCALLS          77     /* number of system calls allowed */
03401
03402    #define EXIT             1
03403    #define FORK             2
03404    #define READ             3
03405    #define WRITE            4
03406    #define OPEN             5
03407    #define CLOSE            6
03408    #define WAIT             7
03409    #define CREAT            8
03410    #define LINK             9
03411    #define UNLINK          10
03412    #define WAITPID         11
03413    #define CHDIR           12
03414    #define TIME            13
03415    #define MKNOD           14
03416    #define CHMOD           15
03417    #define CHOWN           16
03418    #define BRK             17
03419    #define STAT            18
03420    #define LSEEK           19
03421    #define GETPID          20
03422    #define MOUNT           21
03423    #define UMOUNT          22
03424    #define SETUID          23
03425    #define GETUID          24
03426    #define STIME           25
03427    #define PTRACE          26
03428    #define ALARM           27
03429    #define FSTAT           28
03430    #define PAUSE           29
03431    #define UTIME           30
03432    #define ACCESS          33
03433    #define SYNC            36
03434    #define KILL            37
```

```
03435   #define RENAME              38
03436   #define MKDIR               39
03437   #define RMDIR               40
03438   #define DUP                 41
03439   #define PIPE                42
03440   #define TIMES               43
03441   #define SETGID              46
03442   #define GETGID              47
03443   #define SIGNAL              48
03444   #define IOCTL               54
03445   #define FCNTL               55
03446   #define EXEC                59
03447   #define UMASK               60
03448   #define CHROOT              61
03449   #define SETSID              62
03450   #define GETPGRP             63
03451
03452   /* The following are not system calls, but are processed like them. */
03453   #define KSIG                64      /* kernel detected a signal */
03454   #define UNPAUSE             65      /* to MM or FS: check for EINTR */
03455   #define REVIVE              67      /* to FS: revive a sleeping process */
03456   #define TASK_REPLY          68      /* to FS: reply code from tty task */
03457
03458   /* Posix signal handling. */
03459   #define SIGACTION           71
03460   #define SIGSUSPEND          72
03461   #define SIGPENDING          73
03462   #define SIGPROCMASK         74
03463   #define SIGRETURN           75
03464
03465   #define REBOOT              76
```

```
++++++++++++++++++++++++++++++++++++++++++++++++++++++++++++++++++++++++++++++++
                              include/minix/com.h
++++++++++++++++++++++++++++++++++++++++++++++++++++++++++++++++++++++++++++++++
```

```
03500   /* System calls. */
03501   #define SEND                1       /* function code for sending messages */
03502   #define RECEIVE             2       /* function code for receiving messages */
03503   #define BOTH                3       /* function code for SEND + RECEIVE */
03504   #define ANY     (NR_PROCS+100)      /* receive(ANY, buf) accepts from any source */
03505
03506   /* Task numbers, function codes and reply codes. */
03507
03508   /* The values of several task numbers depend on whether they or other tasks
03509    * are enabled.  They are defined as (PREVIOUS_TASK - ENABLE_TASK) in general.
03510    * ENABLE_TASK is either 0 or 1, so a task either gets a new number, or gets
03511    * the same number as the previous task and is further unused.
03512    * The TTY task must always have the most negative number so that it is
03513    * initialized first.  Many of the TTY function codes are shared with other
03514    * tasks.
03515    */
03516
03517   #define TTY                 (DL_ETH - 1)
03518                                       /* terminal I/O class */
03519   #       define CANCEL       0       /* general req to force a task to cancel */
```

```
03520   #       define HARD_INT     2     /* fcn code for all hardware interrupts */
03521   #       define DEV_READ     3     /* fcn code for reading from tty */
03522   #       define DEV_WRITE    4     /* fcn code for writing to tty */
03523   #       define DEV_IOCTL    5     /* fcn code for ioctl */
03524   #       define DEV_OPEN     6     /* fcn code for opening tty */
03525   #       define DEV_CLOSE    7     /* fcn code for closing tty */
03526   #       define SCATTERED_IO 8     /* fcn code for multiple reads/writes */
03527   #       define TTY_SETPGRP  9     /* fcn code for setpgroup */
03528   #       define TTY_EXIT     10    /* a process group leader has exited */
03529   #       define OPTIONAL_IO  16    /* modifier to DEV_* codes within vector */
03530   #       define SUSPEND      -998  /* used in interrupts when tty has no data */
03531
03532   #define DL_ETH          (CDROM - ENABLE_NETWORKING)
03533                                     /* networking task */
03534
03535   /* Message type for data link layer reqests. */
03536   #       define DL_WRITE        3
03537   #       define DL_WRITEV       4
03538   #       define DL_READ         5
03539   #       define DL_READV        6
03540   #       define DL_INIT         7
03541   #       define DL_STOP         8
03542   #       define DL_GETSTAT      9
03543
03544   /* Message type for data link layer replies. */
03545   #       define DL_INIT_REPLY   20
03546   #       define DL_TASK_REPLY   21
03547
03548   #       define DL_PORT         m2_i1
03549   #       define DL_PROC         m2_i2
03550   #       define DL_COUNT        m2_i3
03551   #       define DL_MODE         m2_l1
03552   #       define DL_CLCK         m2_l2
03553   #       define DL_ADDR         m2_p1
03554   #       define DL_STAT         m2_l1
03555
03556   /* Bits in 'DL_STAT' field of DL replies. */
03557   #       define DL_PACK_SEND    0x01
03558   #       define DL_PACK_RECV    0x02
03559   #       define DL_READ_IP      0x04
03560
03561   /* Bits in 'DL_MODE' field of DL requests. */
03562   #       define DL_NOMODE       0x0
03563   #       define DL_PROMISC_REQ  0x2
03564   #       define DL_MULTI_REQ    0x4
03565   #       define DL_BROAD_REQ    0x8
03566
03567   #       define NW_OPEN         DEV_OPEN
03568   #       define NW_CLOSE        DEV_CLOSE
03569   #       define NW_READ         DEV_READ
03570   #       define NW_WRITE        DEV_WRITE
03571   #       define NW_IOCTL        DEV_IOCTL
03572   #       define NW_CANCEL       CANCEL
03573
03574   #define CDROM           (AUDIO - ENABLE_CDROM)
03575                                     /* cd-rom device task */
03576
03577   #define AUDIO           (MIXER - ENABLE_AUDIO)
03578   #define MIXER           (SCSI - ENABLE_AUDIO)
03579                                     /* audio & mixer device tasks */
```

```
03580
03581  #define SCSI            (WINCHESTER - ENABLE_SCSI)
03582                          /* scsi device task */
03583
03584  #define WINCHESTER      (SYN_ALRM_TASK - ENABLE_WINI)
03585                          /* winchester (hard) disk class */
03586
03587  #define SYN_ALRM_TASK   -8   /* task to send CLOCK_INT messages */
03588
03589  #define IDLE            -7   /* task to run when there's nothing to run */
03590
03591  #define PRINTER         -6   /* printer I/O class */
03592
03593  #define FLOPPY          -5   /* floppy disk class */
03594
03595  #define MEM             -4   /* /dev/ram, /dev/(k)mem and /dev/null class */
03596  #       define NULL_MAJOR  1   /* major device for /dev/null */
03597  #       define RAM_DEV     0   /* minor device for /dev/ram */
03598  #       define MEM_DEV     1   /* minor device for /dev/mem */
03599  #       define KMEM_DEV    2   /* minor device for /dev/kmem */
03600  #       define NULL_DEV    3   /* minor device for /dev/null */
03601
03602  #define CLOCK           -3   /* clock class */
03603  #       define SET_ALARM   1   /* fcn code to CLOCK, set up alarm */
03604  #       define GET_TIME    3   /* fcn code to CLOCK, get real time */
03605  #       define SET_TIME    4   /* fcn code to CLOCK, set real time */
03606  #       define GET_UPTIME  5   /* fcn code to CLOCK, get uptime */
03607  #       define SET_SYNC_AL 6   /* fcn code to CLOCK, set up alarm which */
03608                          /* times out with a send */
03609  #       define REAL_TIME   1   /* reply from CLOCK: here is real time */
03610  #       define CLOCK_INT   HARD_INT
03611                          /* this code will only be sent by */
03612                          /* SYN_ALRM_TASK to a task that requested a */
03613                          /* synchronous alarm */
03614
03615  #define SYSTASK         -2   /* internal functions */
03616  #       define SYS_XIT     1 /* fcn code for sys_xit(parent, proc) */
03617  #       define SYS_GETSP   2 /* fcn code for sys_sp(proc, &new_sp) */
03618  #       define SYS_OLDSIG  3 /* fcn code for sys_oldsig(proc, sig) */
03619  #       define SYS_FORK    4 /* fcn code for sys_fork(parent, child) */
03620  #       define SYS_NEWMAP  5 /* fcn code for sys_newmap(procno, map_ptr) */
03621  #       define SYS_COPY    6 /* fcn code for sys_copy(ptr) */
03622  #       define SYS_EXEC    7 /* fcn code for sys_exec(procno, new_sp) */
03623  #       define SYS_TIMES   8 /* fcn code for sys_times(procno, bufptr) */
03624  #       define SYS_ABORT   9 /* fcn code for sys_abort() */
03625  #       define SYS_FRESH   10 /* fcn code for sys_fresh()  (Atari only) */
03626  #       define SYS_KILL    11 /* fcn code for sys_kill(proc, sig) */
03627  #       define SYS_GBOOT   12 /* fcn code for sys_gboot(procno, bootptr) */
03628  #       define SYS_UMAP    13 /* fcn code for sys_umap(procno, etc) */
03629  #       define SYS_MEM     14 /* fcn code for sys_mem() */
03630  #       define SYS_TRACE   15 /* fcn code for sys_trace(req,pid,addr,data) */
03631  #       define SYS_VCOPY   16 /* fnc code for sys_vcopy(src_proc, dest_proc, */
03632                          vcopy_s, vcopy_ptr) */
03633  #       define SYS_SENDSIG 17 /* fcn code for sys_sendsig(&sigmsg) */
03634  #       define SYS_SIGRETURN 18 /* fcn code for sys_sigreturn(&sigmsg) */
03635  #       define SYS_ENDSIG  19 /* fcn code for sys_endsig(procno) */
03636  #       define SYS_GETMAP  20 /* fcn code for sys_getmap(procno, map_ptr) */
03637
03638  #define HARDWARE        -1   /* used as source on interrupt generated msgs*/
03639
```

```
03640     /* Names of message fields for messages to CLOCK task. */
03641     #define DELTA_TICKS    m6_l1     /* alarm interval in clock ticks */
03642     #define FUNC_TO_CALL   m6_f1     /* pointer to function to call */
03643     #define NEW_TIME       m6_l1     /* value to set clock to (SET_TIME) */
03644     #define CLOCK_PROC_NR  m6_i1     /* which proc (or task) wants the alarm? */
03645     #define SECONDS_LEFT   m6_l1     /* how many seconds were remaining */
03646
03647     /* Names of message fields used for messages to block and character tasks. */
03648     #define DEVICE         m2_i1     /* major-minor device */
03649     #define PROC_NR        m2_i2     /* which (proc) wants I/O? */
03650     #define COUNT          m2_i3     /* how many bytes to transfer */
03651     #define REQUEST        m2_i3     /* ioctl request code */
03652     #define POSITION       m2_l1     /* file offset */
03653     #define ADDRESS        m2_p1     /* core buffer address */
03654
03655     /* Names of message fields for messages to TTY task. */
03656     #define TTY_LINE       DEVICE    /* message parameter: terminal line */
03657     #define TTY_REQUEST    COUNT     /* message parameter: ioctl request code */
03658     #define TTY_SPEK       POSITION  /* message parameter: ioctl speed, erasing */
03659     #define TTY_FLAGS      m2_l2     /* message parameter: ioctl tty mode */
03660     #define TTY_PGRP       m2_i3     /* message parameter: process group */
03661
03662     /* Names of the message fields for QIC 02 status reply from tape driver */
03663     #define TAPE_STAT0     m2_l1
03664     #define TAPE_STAT1     m2_l2
03665
03666     /* Names of messages fields used in reply messages from tasks. */
03667     #define REP_PROC_NR    m2_i1     /* # of proc on whose behalf I/O was done */
03668     #define REP_STATUS     m2_i2     /* bytes transferred or error number */
03669
03670     /* Names of fields for copy message to SYSTASK. */
03671     #define SRC_SPACE      m5_c1     /* T or D space (stack is also D) */
03672     #define SRC_PROC_NR    m5_i1     /* process to copy from */
03673     #define SRC_BUFFER     m5_l1     /* virtual address where data come from */
03674     #define DST_SPACE      m5_c2     /* T or D space (stack is also D) */
03675     #define DST_PROC_NR    m5_i2     /* process to copy to */
03676     #define DST_BUFFER     m5_l2     /* virtual address where data go to */
03677     #define COPY_BYTES     m5_l3     /* number of bytes to copy */
03678
03679     /* Field names for accounting, SYSTASK and miscellaneous. */
03680     #define USER_TIME      m4_l1     /* user time consumed by process */
03681     #define SYSTEM_TIME    m4_l2     /* system time consumed by process */
03682     #define CHILD_UTIME    m4_l3     /* user time consumed by process' children */
03683     #define CHILD_STIME    m4_l4     /* sys time consumed by process' children */
03684     #define BOOT_TICKS     m4_l5     /* number of clock ticks since boot time */
03685
03686     #define PROC1          m1_i1     /* indicates a process */
03687     #define PROC2          m1_i2     /* indicates a process */
03688     #define PID            m1_i3     /* process id passed from MM to kernel */
03689     #define STACK_PTR      m1_p1     /* used for stack ptr in sys_exec, sys_getsp */
03690     #define PR             m6_i1     /* process number for sys_sig */
03691     #define SIGNUM         m6_i2     /* signal number for sys_sig */
03692     #define FUNC           m6_f1     /* function pointer for sys_sig */
03693     #define MEM_PTR        m1_p1     /* tells where memory map is for sys_newmap */
03694     #define NAME_PTR       m1_p2     /* tells where program name is for dmp */
03695     #define IP_PTR         m1_p3     /* initial value for ip after exec */
03696     #define SIG_PROC       m2_i1     /* process number for inform */
03697     #define SIG_MAP        m2_l1     /* used by kernel for passing signal bit map */
03698     #define SIG_MSG_PTR    m1_i1     /* pointer to info to build sig catch stack */
03699     #define SIG_CTXT_PTR   m1_p1     /* pointer to info to restore signal context */
```

```
++++++++++++++++++++++++++++++++++++++++++++++++++++++++++++++++++++++++++++++++++
                            include/minix/boot.h
++++++++++++++++++++++++++++++++++++++++++++++++++++++++++++++++++++++++++++++++++
03700    /* boot.h */
03701
03702    #ifndef _BOOT_H
03703    #define _BOOT_H
03704
03705    /* Redefine root and root image devices as variables.
03706     * This keeps the diffs small but may cause future confusion.
03707     */
03708    #define ROOT_DEV    (boot_parameters.bp_rootdev)
03709    #define IMAGE_DEV   (boot_parameters.bp_ramimagedev)
03710
03711    /* Device numbers of RAM, floppy and hard disk devices.
03712     * h/com.h defines RAM_DEV but only as the minor number.
03713     */
03714    #define DEV_FD0    0x200
03715    #define DEV_HD0    0x300
03716    #define DEV_RAM    0x100
03717    #define DEV_SCSI   0x700 /* Atari TT only */
03718
03719    /* Structure to hold boot parameters. */
03720    struct bparam_s
03721    {
03722      dev_t bp_rootdev;
03723      dev_t bp_ramimagedev;
03724      unsigned short bp_ramsize;
03725      unsigned short bp_processor;
03726    };
03727
03728    extern struct bparam_s boot_parameters;
03729    #endif /* _BOOT_H */




++++++++++++++++++++++++++++++++++++++++++++++++++++++++++++++++++++++++++++++++++
                            include/minix/keymap.h
++++++++++++++++++++++++++++++++++++++++++++++++++++++++++++++++++++++++++++++++++
03800    /*     keymap.h - defines for keymapping           Author: Marcus Hampel
03801     */
03802    #ifndef _SYS__KEYMAP_H
03803    #define _SYS__KEYMAP_H
03804
03805    #define C(c)     ((c) & 0x1F)      /* Map to control code           */
03806    #define A(c)     ((c) | 0x80)      /* Set eight bit (ALT)           */
03807    #define CA(c)    A(C(c))           /* Control-Alt                   */
03808    #define L(c)     ((c) | HASCAPS) /* Add "Caps Lock has effect" attribute */
03809
03810    #define EXT      0x0100           /* Normal function keys          */
03811    #define CTRL     0x0200           /* Control key                   */
03812    #define SHIFT    0x0400           /* Shift key                     */
03813    #define ALT      0x0800           /* Alternate key                 */
03814    #define EXTKEY   0x1000           /* extended keycode              */
```

```
03815    #define HASCAPS 0x8000          /* Caps Lock has effect     */
03816
03817    /* Numeric keypad */
03818    #define HOME      (0x01 + EXT)
03819    #define END       (0x02 + EXT)
03820    #define UP        (0x03 + EXT)
03821    #define DOWN      (0x04 + EXT)
03822    #define LEFT      (0x05 + EXT)
03823    #define RIGHT     (0x06 + EXT)
03824    #define PGUP      (0x07 + EXT)
03825    #define PGDN      (0x08 + EXT)
03826    #define MID       (0x09 + EXT)
03827    #define NMIN      (0x0A + EXT)
03828    #define PLUS      (0x0B + EXT)
03829    #define INSRT     (0x0C + EXT)
03830
03831    /* Alt + Numeric keypad */
03832    #define AHOME     (0x01 + ALT)
03833    #define AEND      (0x02 + ALT)
03834    #define AUP       (0x03 + ALT)
03835    #define ADOWN     (0x04 + ALT)
03836    #define ALEFT     (0x05 + ALT)
03837    #define ARIGHT    (0x06 + ALT)
03838    #define APGUP     (0x07 + ALT)
03839    #define APGDN     (0x08 + ALT)
03840    #define AMID      (0x09 + ALT)
03841    #define ANMIN     (0x0A + ALT)
03842    #define APLUS     (0x0B + ALT)
03843    #define AINSRT    (0x0C + ALT)
03844
03845    /* Ctrl + Numeric keypad */
03846    #define CHOME     (0x01 + CTRL)
03847    #define CEND      (0x02 + CTRL)
03848    #define CUP       (0x03 + CTRL)
03849    #define CDOWN     (0x04 + CTRL)
03850    #define CLEFT     (0x05 + CTRL)
03851    #define CRIGHT    (0x06 + CTRL)
03852    #define CPGUP     (0x07 + CTRL)
03853    #define CPGDN     (0x08 + CTRL)
03854    #define CMID      (0x09 + CTRL)
03855    #define CNMIN     (0x0A + CTRL)
03856    #define CPLUS     (0x0B + CTRL)
03857    #define CINSRT    (0x0C + CTRL)
03858
03859    /* Lock keys */
03860    #define CALOCK    (0x0D + EXT)    /* caps lock     */
03861    #define NLOCK     (0x0E + EXT)    /* number lock   */
03862    #define SLOCK     (0x0F + EXT)    /* scroll lock   */
03863
03864    /* Function keys */
03865    #define F1        (0x10 + EXT)
03866    #define F2        (0x11 + EXT)
03867    #define F3        (0x12 + EXT)
03868    #define F4        (0x13 + EXT)
03869    #define F5        (0x14 + EXT)
03870    #define F6        (0x15 + EXT)
03871    #define F7        (0x16 + EXT)
03872    #define F8        (0x17 + EXT)
03873    #define F9        (0x18 + EXT)
03874    #define F10       (0x19 + EXT)
```

```
03875   #define F11        (0x1A + EXT)
03876   #define F12        (0x1B + EXT)
03877
03878   /* Alt+Fn */
03879   #define AF1        (0x10 + ALT)
03880   #define AF2        (0x11 + ALT)
03881   #define AF3        (0x12 + ALT)
03882   #define AF4        (0x13 + ALT)
03883   #define AF5        (0x14 + ALT)
03884   #define AF6        (0x15 + ALT)
03885   #define AF7        (0x16 + ALT)
03886   #define AF8        (0x17 + ALT)
03887   #define AF9        (0x18 + ALT)
03888   #define AF10       (0x19 + ALT)
03889   #define AF11       (0x1A + ALT)
03890   #define AF12       (0x1B + ALT)
03891
03892   /* Ctrl+Fn */
03893   #define CF1        (0x10 + CTRL)
03894   #define CF2        (0x11 + CTRL)
03895   #define CF3        (0x12 + CTRL)
03896   #define CF4        (0x13 + CTRL)
03897   #define CF5        (0x14 + CTRL)
03898   #define CF6        (0x15 + CTRL)
03899   #define CF7        (0x16 + CTRL)
03900   #define CF8        (0x17 + CTRL)
03901   #define CF9        (0x18 + CTRL)
03902   #define CF10       (0x19 + CTRL)
03903   #define CF11       (0x1A + CTRL)
03904   #define CF12       (0x1B + CTRL)
03905
03906   /* Shift+Fn */
03907   #define SF1        (0x10 + SHIFT)
03908   #define SF2        (0x11 + SHIFT)
03909   #define SF3        (0x12 + SHIFT)
03910   #define SF4        (0x13 + SHIFT)
03911   #define SF5        (0x14 + SHIFT)
03912   #define SF6        (0x15 + SHIFT)
03913   #define SF7        (0x16 + SHIFT)
03914   #define SF8        (0x17 + SHIFT)
03915   #define SF9        (0x18 + SHIFT)
03916   #define SF10       (0x19 + SHIFT)
03917   #define SF11       (0x1A + SHIFT)
03918   #define SF12       (0x1B + SHIFT)
03919
03920   /* Alt+Shift+Fn */
03921   #define ASF1       (0x10 + ALT + SHIFT)
03922   #define ASF2       (0x11 + ALT + SHIFT)
03923   #define ASF3       (0x12 + ALT + SHIFT)
03924   #define ASF4       (0x13 + ALT + SHIFT)
03925   #define ASF5       (0x14 + ALT + SHIFT)
03926   #define ASF6       (0x15 + ALT + SHIFT)
03927   #define ASF7       (0x16 + ALT + SHIFT)
03928   #define ASF8       (0x17 + ALT + SHIFT)
03929   #define ASF9       (0x18 + ALT + SHIFT)
03930   #define ASF10      (0x19 + ALT + SHIFT)
03931   #define ASF11      (0x1A + ALT + SHIFT)
03932   #define ASF12      (0x1B + ALT + SHIFT)
03933
03934   #define MAP_COLS        6       /* Number of columns in keymap */
```

```
03935     #define NR_SCAN_CODES    0x80      /* Number of scan codes (rows in keymap) */
03936
03937     typedef unsigned short keymap_t[NR_SCAN_CODES * MAP_COLS];
03938
03939     #define KEY_MAGIC        "KMAZ"   /* Magic number of keymap file */
03940
03941     #endif /* _SYS__KEYMAP_H */
```

```
++++++++++++++++++++++++++++++++++++++++++++++++++++++++++++++++++++++++++++++++
                              include/minix/partition.h
++++++++++++++++++++++++++++++++++++++++++++++++++++++++++++++++++++++++++++++++
```

```
04000     /*      minix/partition.h                          Author: Kees J. Bot
04001      *                                                          7 Dec 1995
04002      * Place of a partition on disk and the disk geometry,
04003      * for use with the DIOCGETP and DIOCSETP ioctl's.
04004      */
04005     #ifndef _MINIX__PARTITION_H
04006     #define _MINIX__PARTITION_H
04007
04008     struct partition {
04009       u32_t base;            /* byte offset to the partition start */
04010       u32_t size;            /* number of bytes in the partition */
04011       unsigned cylinders;    /* disk geometry */
04012       unsigned heads;
04013       unsigned sectors;
04014     };
04015     #endif /* _MINIX__PARTITION_H */
```

```
++++++++++++++++++++++++++++++++++++++++++++++++++++++++++++++++++++++++++++++++
                              include/ibm/partition.h
++++++++++++++++++++++++++++++++++++++++++++++++++++++++++++++++++++++++++++++++
```

```
04100     /* Description of entry in partition table.  */
04101     #ifndef _PARTITION_H
04102     #define _PARTITION_H
04103
04104     struct part_entry {
04105       unsigned char bootind;        /* boot indicator 0/ACTIVE_FLAG  */
04106       unsigned char start_head;     /* head value for first sector   */
04107       unsigned char start_sec;      /* sector value + cyl bits for first sector */
04108       unsigned char start_cyl;      /* track value for first sector  */
04109       unsigned char sysind;         /* system indicator              */
04110       unsigned char last_head;      /* head value for last sector    */
04111       unsigned char last_sec;       /* sector value + cyl bits for last sector */
04112       unsigned char last_cyl;       /* track value for last sector   */
04113       unsigned long lowsec;         /* logical first sector          */
04114       unsigned long size;           /* size of partition in sectors  */
04115     };
04116
04117     #define ACTIVE_FLAG      0x80    /* value for active in bootind field (hd0) */
04118     #define NR_PARTITIONS    4       /* number of entries in partition table */
04119     #define PART_TABLE_OFF   0x1BE   /* offset of partition table in boot sector */
```

```
04120
04121   /* Partition types. */
04122   #define MINIX_PART       0x81     /* Minix partition type */
04123   #define NO_PART          0x00     /* unused entry */
04124   #define OLD_MINIX_PART   0x80     /* created before 1.4b, obsolete */
04125   #define EXT_PART         0x05     /* extended partition */
04126
04127   #endif /* _PARTITION_H */
```

```
++++++++++++++++++++++++++++++++++++++++++++++++++++++++++++++++++++++++++++++
                            src/kernel/kernel.h
++++++++++++++++++++++++++++++++++++++++++++++++++++++++++++++++++++++++++++++
```

```
04200   /* This is the master header for the kernel.  It includes some other files
04201    * and defines the principal constants.
04202    */
04203   #define _POSIX_SOURCE      1     /* tell headers to include POSIX stuff */
04204   #define _MINIX             1     /* tell headers to include MINIX stuff */
04205   #define _SYSTEM            1     /* tell headers that this is the kernel */
04206
04207   /* The following are so basic, all the *.c files get them automatically. */
04208   #include <minix/config.h>      /* MUST be first */
04209   #include <ansi.h>             /* MUST be second */
04210   #include <sys/types.h>
04211   #include <minix/const.h>
04212   #include <minix/type.h>
04213   #include <minix/syslib.h>
04214
04215   #include <string.h>
04216   #include <limits.h>
04217   #include <errno.h>
04218
04219   #include "const.h"
04220   #include "type.h"
04221   #include "proto.h"
04222   #include "glo.h"
```

```
++++++++++++++++++++++++++++++++++++++++++++++++++++++++++++++++++++++++++++++
                            src/kernel/const.h
++++++++++++++++++++++++++++++++++++++++++++++++++++++++++++++++++++++++++++++
```

```
04300   /* General constants used by the kernel. */
04301
04302   #if (CHIP == INTEL)
04303
04304   #define K_STACK_BYTES    1024     /* how many bytes for the kernel stack */
04305
04306   #define INIT_PSW        0x0200    /* initial psw */
04307   #define INIT_TASK_PSW   0x1200    /* initial psw for tasks (with IOPL 1) */
04308   #define TRACEBIT        0x100     /* OR this with psw in proc[] for tracing */
04309   #define SETPSW(rp, new) /* permits only certain bits to be set */ \
04310           ((rp)->p_reg.psw = (rp)->p_reg.psw & ~0xCD5 | (new) & 0xCD5)
04311
04312   /* Initial sp for mm, fs and init.
04313    *      2 bytes for short jump
04314    *      2 bytes unused
```

```
04315          *       3 words for init_org[] used by fs only
04316          *       3 words for real mode debugger trap (actually needs 1 more)
04317          *       3 words for save and restart temporaries
04318          *       3 words for interrupt
04319          * Leave no margin, to flush bugs early.
04320          */
04321         #define INIT_SP (2 + 2 + 3 * 2 + 3 * 2 + 3 * 2 + 3 * 2)
04322
04323         #define HCLICK_SHIFT       4      /* log2 of HCLICK_SIZE */
04324         #define HCLICK_SIZE       16      /* hardware segment conversion magic */
04325         #if CLICK_SIZE >= HCLICK_SIZE
04326         #define click_to_hclick(n) ((n) << (CLICK_SHIFT - HCLICK_SHIFT))
04327         #else
04328         #define click_to_hclick(n) ((n) >> (HCLICK_SHIFT - CLICK_SHIFT))
04329         #endif
04330         #define hclick_to_physb(n) ((phys_bytes) (n) << HCLICK_SHIFT)
04331         #define physb_to_hclick(n) ((n) >> HCLICK_SHIFT)
04332
04333         /* Interrupt vectors defined/reserved by processor. */
04334         #define DIVIDE_VECTOR      0      /* divide error */
04335         #define DEBUG_VECTOR       1      /* single step (trace) */
04336         #define NMI_VECTOR         2      /* non-maskable interrupt */
04337         #define BREAKPOINT_VECTOR  3      /* software breakpoint */
04338         #define OVERFLOW_VECTOR    4      /* from INTO */
04339
04340         /* Fixed system call vector. */
04341         #define SYS_VECTOR        32      /* system calls are made with int SYSVEC */
04342         #define SYS386_VECTOR     33      /* except 386 system calls use this */
04343         #define LEVEL0_VECTOR     34      /* for execution of a function at level 0 */
04344
04345         /* Suitable irq bases for hardware interrupts.  Reprogram the 8259(s) from
04346          * the PC BIOS defaults since the BIOS doesn't respect all the processor's
04347          * reserved vectors (0 to 31).
04348          */
04349         #define BIOS_IRQ0_VEC    0x08      /* base of IRQ0-7 vectors used by BIOS */
04350         #define BIOS_IRQ8_VEC    0x70      /* base of IRQ8-15 vectors used by BIOS */
04351         #define IRQ0_VECTOR      0x28      /* more or less arbitrary, but > SYS_VECTOR */
04352         #define IRQ8_VECTOR      0x30      /* together for simplicity */
04353
04354         /* Hardware interrupt numbers. */
04355         #define NR_IRQ_VECTORS    16
04356         #define CLOCK_IRQ          0
04357         #define KEYBOARD_IRQ       1
04358         #define CASCADE_IRQ        2      /* cascade enable for 2nd AT controller */
04359         #define ETHER_IRQ          3      /* default ethernet interrupt vector */
04360         #define SECONDARY_IRQ      3      /* RS232 interrupt vector for port 2 */
04361         #define RS232_IRQ          4      /* RS232 interrupt vector for port 1 */
04362         #define XT_WINI_IRQ        5      /* xt winchester */
04363         #define FLOPPY_IRQ         6      /* floppy disk */
04364         #define PRINTER_IRQ        7
04365         #define AT_WINI_IRQ       14      /* at winchester */
04366
04367         /* Interrupt number to hardware vector. */
04368         #define BIOS_VECTOR(irq)                \
04369                 (((irq) < 8 ? BIOS_IRQ0_VEC : BIOS_IRQ8_VEC) + ((irq) & 0x07))
04370         #define VECTOR(irq)             \
04371                 (((irq) < 8 ? IRQ0_VECTOR : IRQ8_VECTOR) + ((irq) & 0x07))
04372
04373         /* BIOS hard disk parameter vectors. */
04374         #define WINI_0_PARM_VEC 0x41
```

```
04375  #define WINI_1_PARM_VEC 0x46
04376
04377  /* 8259A interrupt controller ports. */
04378  #define INT_CTL         0x20     /* I/O port for interrupt controller */
04379  #define INT_CTLMASK     0x21     /* setting bits in this port disables ints */
04380  #define INT2_CTL        0xA0     /* I/O port for second interrupt controller */
04381  #define INT2_CTLMASK    0xA1     /* setting bits in this port disables ints */
04382
04383  /* Magic numbers for interrupt controller. */
04384  #define ENABLE          0x20     /* code used to re-enable after an interrupt */
04385
04386  /* Sizes of memory tables. */
04387  #define NR_MEMS         3        /* number of chunks of memory */
04388
04389  /* Miscellaneous ports. */
04390  #define PCR             0x65     /* Planar Control Register */
04391  #define PORT_B          0x61     /* I/O port for 8255 port B (kbd, beeper...) */
04392  #define TIMER0          0x40     /* I/O port for timer channel 0 */
04393  #define TIMER2          0x42     /* I/O port for timer channel 2 */
04394  #define TIMER_MODE      0x43     /* I/O port for timer mode control */
04395
04396  #endif /* (CHIP == INTEL) */
04397
04398  #if (CHIP == M68000)
04399
04400  #define K_STACK_BYTES   1024     /* how many bytes for the kernel stack */
04401
04402  /* Sizes of memory tables. */
04403  #define NR_MEMS         2        /* number of chunks of memory */
04404
04405  /* p_reg contains: d0-d7, a0-a6,  in that order. */
04406  #define NR_REGS         15       /* number of general regs in each proc slot */
04407
04408  #define TRACEBIT        0x8000   /* or this with psw in proc[] for tracing */
04409  #define SETPSW(rp, new)          /* permits only certain bits to be set */ \
04410        ((rp)->p_reg.psw = (rp)->p_reg.psw & ~0xFF | (new) & 0xFF)
04411
04412  #define MEM_BYTES  0xffffffff    /* memory size for /dev/mem */
04413
04414  #ifdef __ACK__
04415  #define FSTRUCOPY
04416  #endif
04417
04418  #endif /* (CHIP == M68000) */
04419
04420  /* The following items pertain to the scheduling queues. */
04421  #define TASK_Q          0        /* ready tasks are scheduled via queue 0 */
04422  #define SERVER_Q        1        /* ready servers are scheduled via queue 1 */
04423  #define USER_Q          2        /* ready users are scheduled via queue 2 */
04424
04425  #if (MACHINE == ATARI)
04426  #define SHADOW_Q        3        /* runnable, but shadowed processes */
04427  #define NQ              4        /* # of scheduling queues */
04428  #else
04429  #define NQ              3        /* # of scheduling queues */
04430  #endif
04431
04432  /* Env_parse() return values. */
04433  #define EP_UNSET        0        /* variable not set */
04434  #define EP_OFF          1        /* var = off */
```

```
04435    #define EP_ON           2         /* var = on (or field left blank) */
04436    #define EP_SET          3         /* var = 1:2:3 (nonblank field) */
04437
04438    /* To translate an address in kernel space to a physical address.  This is
04439     * the same as umap(proc_ptr, D, vir, sizeof(*vir)), but a lot less costly.
04440     */
04441    #define vir2phys(vir)   (data_base + (vir_bytes) (vir))
04442
04443    #define printf          printk    /* the kernel really uses printk, not printf */
```

```
++++++++++++++++++++++++++++++++++++++++++++++++++++++++++++++++++++++++++++++
                              src/kernel/type.h
++++++++++++++++++++++++++++++++++++++++++++++++++++++++++++++++++++++++++++++
```

```
04500    #ifndef TYPE_H
04501    #define TYPE_H
04502
04503    typedef _PROTOTYPE( void task_t, (void) );
04504    typedef _PROTOTYPE( int (*rdwt_t), (message *m_ptr) );
04505    typedef _PROTOTYPE( void (*watchdog_t), (void) );
04506
04507    struct tasktab {
04508      task_t *initial_pc;
04509      int stksize;
04510      char name[8];
04511    };
04512
04513    struct memory {
04514      phys_clicks base;
04515      phys_clicks size;
04516    };
04517
04518    /* Administration for clock polling. */
04519    struct milli_state {
04520      unsigned long accum_count;    /* accumulated clock ticks */
04521      unsigned prev_count;          /* previous clock value */
04522    };
04523
04524    #if (CHIP == INTEL)
04525    typedef unsigned port_t;
04526    typedef unsigned segm_t;
04527    typedef unsigned reg_t;            /* machine register */
04528
04529    /* The stack frame layout is determined by the software, but for efficiency
04530     * it is laid out so the assembly code to use it is as simple as possible.
04531     * 80286 protected mode and all real modes use the same frame, built with
04532     * 16-bit registers.  Real mode lacks an automatic stack switch, so little
04533     * is lost by using the 286 frame for it.  The 386 frame differs only in
04534     * having 32-bit registers and more segment registers.  The same names are
04535     * used for the larger registers to avoid differences in the code.
04536     */
04537    struct stackframe_s {            /* proc_ptr points here */
04538    #if _WORD_SIZE == 4
04539      u16_t gs;                      /* last item pushed by save */
04540      u16_t fs;                      /*  ^ */
04541    #endif
04542      u16_t es;                      /*  | */
04543      u16_t ds;                      /*  | */
04544      reg_t di;                      /* di through cx are not accessed in C */
```

```
04545      reg_t si;                        /* order is to match pusha/popa */
04546      reg_t fp;                        /* bp */
04547      reg_t st;                        /* hole for another copy of sp */
04548      reg_t bx;                        /* | */
04549      reg_t dx;                        /* | */
04550      reg_t cx;                        /* | */
04551      reg_t retreg;                    /* ax and above are all pushed by save */
04552      reg_t retadr;                    /* return address for assembly code save() */
04553      reg_t pc;                        /* ^  last item pushed by interrupt */
04554      reg_t cs;                        /* | */
04555      reg_t psw;                       /* | */
04556      reg_t sp;                        /* | */
04557      reg_t ss;                        /* these are pushed by CPU during interrupt */
04558    };
04559
04560    struct segdesc_s {                 /* segment descriptor for protected mode */
04561      u16_t limit_low;
04562      u16_t base_low;
04563      u8_t base_middle;
04564      u8_t access;                     /* |P|DL|1|X|E|R|A| */
04565    #if _WORD_SIZE == 4
04566      u8_t granularity;                /* |G|X|0|A|LIMT| */
04567      u8_t base_high;
04568    #else
04569      u16_t reserved;
04570    #endif
04571    };
04572
04573    typedef _PROTOTYPE( int (*irq_handler_t), (int irq) );
04574
04575    #endif /* (CHIP == INTEL) */
04576
04577    #if (CHIP == M68000)
04578    typedef _PROTOTYPE( void (*dmaint_t), (void) );
04579
04580    typedef u32_t reg_t;               /* machine register */
04581
04582    /* The name and fields of this struct were chosen for PC compatibility. */
04583    struct stackframe_s {
04584      reg_t retreg;                    /* d0 */
04585      reg_t d1;
04586      reg_t d2;
04587      reg_t d3;
04588      reg_t d4;
04589      reg_t d5;
04590      reg_t d6;
04591      reg_t d7;
04592      reg_t a0;
04593      reg_t a1;
04594      reg_t a2;
04595      reg_t a3;
04596      reg_t a4;
04597      reg_t a5;
04598      reg_t fp;                        /* also known as a6 */
04599      reg_t sp;                        /* also known as a7 */
04600      reg_t pc;
04601      u16_t psw;
04602      u16_t dummy;                     /* make size multiple of reg_t for system.c */
04603    };
04604
```

```
04605    struct fsave {
04606      struct cpu_state {
04607            u16_t i_format;
04608            u32_t i_addr;
04609            u16_t i_state[4];
04610      } cpu_state;
04611      struct state_frame {
04612            u8_t frame_type;
04613            u8_t frame_size;
04614            u16_t reserved;
04615            u8_t frame[212];
04616      } state_frame;
04617      struct fpp_model {
04618            u32_t fpcr;
04619            u32_t fpsr;
04620            u32_t fpiar;
04621            struct fpN {
04622                    u32_t high;
04623                    u32_t low;
04624                    u32_t mid;
04625            } fpN[8];
04626      } fpp_model;
04627    };
04628    #endif /* (CHIP == M68000) */
04629
04630    #endif /* TYPE_H */
```

```
++++++++++++++++++++++++++++++++++++++++++++++++++++++++++++++++++++++++++++++++++
                            src/kernel/proto.h
++++++++++++++++++++++++++++++++++++++++++++++++++++++++++++++++++++++++++++++++++

04700    /* Function prototypes. */
04701
04702    #ifndef PROTO_H
04703    #define PROTO_H
04704
04705    /* Struct declarations. */
04706    struct proc;
04707    struct tty;
04708
04709    /* at_wini.c, wini.c */
04710    _PROTOTYPE( void winchester_task, (void)                            );
04711    _PROTOTYPE( void at_winchester_task, (void)                         );
04712
04713    /* clock.c */
04714    _PROTOTYPE( void clock_task, (void)                                 );
04715    _PROTOTYPE( void clock_stop, (void)                                 );
04716    _PROTOTYPE( clock_t get_uptime, (void)                              );
04717    _PROTOTYPE( void syn_alrm_task, (void)                              );
04718
04719    /* dmp.c */
04720    _PROTOTYPE( void map_dmp, (void)                                    );
04721    _PROTOTYPE( void p_dmp, (void)                                      );
04722    _PROTOTYPE( void reg_dmp, (struct proc *rp)                         );
04723
04724    /* dp8390.c */
```

```
04725   _PROTOTYPE( void dp8390_task, (void)                                );
04726   _PROTOTYPE( void dp_dump, (void)                                    );
04727   _PROTOTYPE( void dp8390_stop, (void)                                );
04728
04729   /* floppy.c, stfloppy.c */
04730   _PROTOTYPE( void floppy_task, (void)                                );
04731   _PROTOTYPE( void floppy_stop, (void)                                );
04732
04733   /* main.c, stmain.c */
04734   _PROTOTYPE( void main, (void)                                       );
04735   _PROTOTYPE( void panic, (const char *s, int n)                      );
04736
04737   /* memory.c */
04738   _PROTOTYPE( void mem_task, (void)                                   );
04739
04740   /* misc.c */
04741   _PROTOTYPE( int env_parse, (char *env, char *fmt, int field,
04742                       long *param, long min, long max)                );
04743
04744   /* printer.c, stprint.c */
04745   _PROTOTYPE( void printer_task, (void)                               );
04746
04747   /* proc.c */
04748   _PROTOTYPE( void interrupt, (int task)                              );
04749   _PROTOTYPE( int lock_mini_send, (struct proc *caller_ptr,
04750                       int dest, message *m_ptr)                        );
04751   _PROTOTYPE( void lock_pick_proc, (void)                             );
04752   _PROTOTYPE( void lock_ready, (struct proc *rp)                      );
04753   _PROTOTYPE( void lock_sched, (void)                                 );
04754   _PROTOTYPE( void lock_unready, (struct proc *rp)                    );
04755   _PROTOTYPE( int sys_call, (int function, int src_dest, message *m_ptr) );
04756   _PROTOTYPE( void unhold, (void)                                     );
04757
04758   /* rs232.c */
04759   _PROTOTYPE( void rs_init, (struct tty *tp)                          );
04760
04761   /* system.c */
04762   _PROTOTYPE( void cause_sig, (int proc_nr, int sig_nr)               );
04763   _PROTOTYPE( void inform, (void)                                     );
04764   _PROTOTYPE( phys_bytes numap, (int proc_nr, vir_bytes vir_addr,
04765                       vir_bytes bytes)                                 );
04766   _PROTOTYPE( void sys_task, (void)                                   );
04767   _PROTOTYPE( phys_bytes umap, (struct proc *rp, int seg, vir_bytes vir_addr,
04768                       vir_bytes bytes)                                 );
04769
04770   /* tty.c */
04771   _PROTOTYPE( void handle_events, (struct tty *tp)                    );
04772   _PROTOTYPE( void sigchar, (struct tty *tp, int sig)                 );
04773   _PROTOTYPE( void tty_task, (void)                                   );
04774   _PROTOTYPE( int in_process, (struct tty *tp, char *buf, int count)  );
04775   _PROTOTYPE( void out_process, (struct tty *tp, char *bstart, char *bpos,
04776                       char *bend, int *icount, int *ocount)            );
04777   _PROTOTYPE( void tty_wakeup, (clock_t now)                          );
04778   _PROTOTYPE( void tty_reply, (int code, int replyee, int proc_nr,
04779                                       int status)                      );
04780   _PROTOTYPE( void tty_devnop, (struct tty *tp)                       );
04781
04782   /* library */
04783   _PROTOTYPE( void *memcpy, (void *_s1, const void *_s2, size_t _n)    );
04784
```

```
04785    #if (CHIP == INTEL)
04786
04787    /* clock.c */
04788    _PROTOTYPE( void milli_start, (struct milli_state *msp)              );
04789    _PROTOTYPE( unsigned milli_elapsed, (struct milli_state *msp)        );
04790    _PROTOTYPE( void milli_delay, (unsigned millisec)                    );
04791
04792    /* console.c */
04793    _PROTOTYPE( void cons_stop, (void)                                   );
04794    _PROTOTYPE( void putk, (int c)                                       );
04795    _PROTOTYPE( void scr_init, (struct tty *tp)                          );
04796    _PROTOTYPE( void toggle_scroll, (void)                               );
04797    _PROTOTYPE( int con_loadfont, (phys_bytes user_phys)                 );
04798    _PROTOTYPE( void select_console, (int cons_line)                     );
04799
04800    /* cstart.c */
04801    _PROTOTYPE( void cstart, (U16_t cs, U16_t ds, U16_t mcs, U16_t mds,
04802                                    U16_t parmoff, U16_t parmsize)        );
04803    _PROTOTYPE( char *k_getenv, (char *name)                             );
04804
04805    /* exception.c */
04806    _PROTOTYPE( void exception, (unsigned vec_nr)                        );
04807
04808    /* i8259.c */
04809    _PROTOTYPE( irq_handler_t get_irq_handler, (int irq)                 );
04810    _PROTOTYPE( void put_irq_handler, (int irq, irq_handler_t handler)   );
04811    _PROTOTYPE( void intr_init, (int mine)                               );
04812
04813    /* keyboard.c */
04814    _PROTOTYPE( void kb_init, (struct tty *tp)                           );
04815    _PROTOTYPE( int kbd_loadmap, (phys_bytes user_phys)                  );
04816    _PROTOTYPE( void wreboot, (int how)                                  );
04817
04818    /* klib*.s */
04819    _PROTOTYPE( void bios13, (void)                                      );
04820    _PROTOTYPE( phys_bytes check_mem, (phys_bytes base, phys_bytes size) );
04821    _PROTOTYPE( void cp_mess, (int src,phys_clicks src_clicks,vir_bytes src_offset,
04822                    phys_clicks dst_clicks, vir_bytes dst_offset)        );
04823    _PROTOTYPE( int in_byte, (port_t port)                               );
04824    _PROTOTYPE( int in_word, (port_t port)                               );
04825    _PROTOTYPE( void lock, (void)                                        );
04826    _PROTOTYPE( void unlock, (void)                                      );
04827    _PROTOTYPE( void enable_irq, (unsigned irq)                          );
04828    _PROTOTYPE( int disable_irq, (unsigned irq)                          );
04829    _PROTOTYPE( u16_t mem_rdw, (segm_t segm, vir_bytes offset)           );
04830    _PROTOTYPE( void out_byte, (port_t port, int value)                  );
04831    _PROTOTYPE( void out_word, (port_t port, int value)                  );
04832    _PROTOTYPE( void phys_copy, (phys_bytes source, phys_bytes dest,
04833                    phys_bytes count)                                    );
04834    _PROTOTYPE( void port_read, (unsigned port, phys_bytes destination,
04835                    unsigned bytcount)                                   );
04836    _PROTOTYPE( void port_read_byte, (unsigned port, phys_bytes destination,
04837                    unsigned bytcount)                                   );
04838    _PROTOTYPE( void port_write, (unsigned port, phys_bytes source,
04839                    unsigned bytcount)                                   );
04840    _PROTOTYPE( void port_write_byte, (unsigned port, phys_bytes source,
04841                    unsigned bytcount)                                   );
04842    _PROTOTYPE( void reset, (void)                                       );
04843    _PROTOTYPE( void vid_vid_copy, (unsigned src, unsigned dst, unsigned count));
04844    _PROTOTYPE( void mem_vid_copy, (u16_t *src, unsigned dst, unsigned count));
```

```
04845   _PROTOTYPE( void level0, (void (*func)(void))                    );
04846   _PROTOTYPE( void monitor, (void)                                 );
04847
04848   /* misc.c */
04849   _PROTOTYPE( void mem_init, (void)                                );
04850
04851   /* mpx*.s */
04852   _PROTOTYPE( void idle_task, (void)                               );
04853   _PROTOTYPE( void restart, (void)                                 );
04854
04855   /* The following are never called from C (pure asm procs). */
04856
04857   /* Exception handlers (real or protected mode), in numerical order. */
04858   void _PROTOTYPE( int00, (void) ), _PROTOTYPE( divide_error, (void) );
04859   void _PROTOTYPE( int01, (void) ), _PROTOTYPE( single_step_exception, (void) );
04860   void _PROTOTYPE( int02, (void) ), _PROTOTYPE( nmi, (void) );
04861   void _PROTOTYPE( int03, (void) ), _PROTOTYPE( breakpoint_exception, (void) );
04862   void _PROTOTYPE( int04, (void) ), _PROTOTYPE( overflow, (void) );
04863   void _PROTOTYPE( int05, (void) ), _PROTOTYPE( bounds_check, (void) );
04864   void _PROTOTYPE( int06, (void) ), _PROTOTYPE( inval_opcode, (void) );
04865   void _PROTOTYPE( int07, (void) ), _PROTOTYPE( copr_not_available, (void) );
04866   void                              _PROTOTYPE( double_fault, (void) );
04867   void                              _PROTOTYPE( copr_seg_overrun, (void) );
04868   void                              _PROTOTYPE( inval_tss, (void) );
04869   void                              _PROTOTYPE( segment_not_present, (void) );
04870   void                              _PROTOTYPE( stack_exception, (void) );
04871   void                              _PROTOTYPE( general_protection, (void) );
04872   void                              _PROTOTYPE( page_fault, (void) );
04873   void                              _PROTOTYPE( copr_error, (void) );
04874
04875   /* Hardware interrupt handlers. */
04876   _PROTOTYPE( void hwint00, (void) );
04877   _PROTOTYPE( void hwint01, (void) );
04878   _PROTOTYPE( void hwint02, (void) );
04879   _PROTOTYPE( void hwint03, (void) );
04880   _PROTOTYPE( void hwint04, (void) );
04881   _PROTOTYPE( void hwint05, (void) );
04882   _PROTOTYPE( void hwint06, (void) );
04883   _PROTOTYPE( void hwint07, (void) );
04884   _PROTOTYPE( void hwint08, (void) );
04885   _PROTOTYPE( void hwint09, (void) );
04886   _PROTOTYPE( void hwint10, (void) );
04887   _PROTOTYPE( void hwint11, (void) );
04888   _PROTOTYPE( void hwint12, (void) );
04889   _PROTOTYPE( void hwint13, (void) );
04890   _PROTOTYPE( void hwint14, (void) );
04891   _PROTOTYPE( void hwint15, (void) );
04892
04893   /* Software interrupt handlers, in numerical order. */
04894   _PROTOTYPE( void trp, (void) );
04895   _PROTOTYPE( void s_call, (void) ), _PROTOTYPE( p_s_call, (void) );
04896   _PROTOTYPE( void level0_call, (void) );
04897
04898   /* printer.c */
04899   _PROTOTYPE( void pr_restart, (void)                              );
04900
04901   /* protect.c */
04902   _PROTOTYPE( void prot_init, (void)                               );
04903   _PROTOTYPE( void init_codeseg, (struct segdesc_s *segdp, phys_bytes base,
04904                   phys_bytes size, int privilege)                  );
```

```
04905    _PROTOTYPE( void init_dataseg, (struct segdesc_s *segdp, phys_bytes base,
04906                      phys_bytes size, int privilege)              );
04907    _PROTOTYPE( phys_bytes seg2phys, (U16_t seg)                   );
04908    _PROTOTYPE( void enable_iop, (struct proc *pp)                 );
04909
04910    /* pty.c */
04911    _PROTOTYPE( void do_pty, (struct tty *tp, message *m_ptr)      );
04912    _PROTOTYPE( void pty_init, (struct tty *tp)                    );
04913
04914    /* system.c */
04915    _PROTOTYPE( void alloc_segments, (struct proc *rp)             );
04916
04917    #endif /* (CHIP == INTEL) */
04918
04919    #endif /* PROTO_H */
```

```
++++++++++++++++++++++++++++++++++++++++++++++++++++++++++++++++++++++++++++++++
                              src/kernel/glo.h
++++++++++++++++++++++++++++++++++++++++++++++++++++++++++++++++++++++++++++++++
05000    /* Global variables used in the kernel. */
05001
05002    /* EXTERN is defined as extern except in table.c. */
05003    #ifdef _TABLE
05004    #undef EXTERN
05005    #define EXTERN
05006    #endif
05007
05008    /* Kernel memory. */
05009    EXTERN phys_bytes code_base;      /* base of kernel code */
05010    EXTERN phys_bytes data_base;      /* base of kernel data */
05011
05012    /* Low level interrupt communications. */
05013    EXTERN struct proc *held_head;  /* head of queue of held-up interrupts */
05014    EXTERN struct proc *held_tail;  /* tail of queue of held-up interrupts */
05015    EXTERN unsigned char k_reenter; /* kernel reentry count (entry count less 1)*/
05016
05017    /* Process table.  Here to stop too many things having to include proc.h. */
05018    EXTERN struct proc *proc_ptr;   /* pointer to currently running process */
05019
05020    /* Signals. */
05021    EXTERN int sig_procs;           /* number of procs with p_pending != 0 */
05022
05023    /* Memory sizes. */
05024    EXTERN struct memory mem[NR_MEMS];      /* base and size of chunks of memory */
05025    EXTERN phys_clicks tot_mem_size;        /* total system memory size */
05026
05027    /* Miscellaneous. */
05028    extern u16_t sizes[];           /* table filled in by boot monitor */
05029    extern struct tasktab tasktab[];/* initialized in table.c, so extern here */
05030    extern char *t_stack[];         /* initialized in table.c, so extern here */
05031    EXTERN unsigned lost_ticks;     /* clock ticks counted outside the clock task */
05032    EXTERN clock_t tty_timeout;     /* time to wake up the TTY task */
05033    EXTERN int current;             /* currently visible console */
05034
```

```
05035    #if (CHIP == INTEL)
05036
05037    /* Machine type. */
05038    EXTERN int pc_at;                /* PC-AT compatible hardware interface */
05039    EXTERN int ps_mca;               /* PS/2 with Micro Channel */
05040    EXTERN unsigned int processor;   /* 86, 186, 286, 386, ... */
05041    #if _WORD_SIZE == 2
05042    EXTERN int protected_mode;       /* nonzero if running in Intel protected mode*/
05043    #else
05044    #define protected_mode  1        /* 386 mode implies protected mode */
05045    #endif
05046
05047    /* Video card types. */
05048    EXTERN int ega;                  /* nonzero if console is EGA or VGA */
05049    EXTERN int vga;                  /* nonzero if console is VGA */
05050
05051    /* Memory sizes. */
05052    EXTERN unsigned ext_memsize;     /* initialized by assembler startup code */
05053    EXTERN unsigned low_memsize;
05054
05055    /* Miscellaneous. */
05056    EXTERN irq_handler_t irq_table[NR_IRQ_VECTORS];
05057    EXTERN int irq_use;              /* bit map of all in-use irq's */
05058    EXTERN reg_t mon_ss, mon_sp;     /* monitor stack */
05059    EXTERN int mon_return;           /* true if return to the monitor possible */
05060    EXTERN phys_bytes reboot_code;   /* program for the boot monitor */
05061
05062    /* Variables that are initialized elsewhere are just extern here. */
05063    extern struct segdesc_s gdt[];   /* global descriptor table for protected mode*/
05064
05065    EXTERN _PROTOTYPE( void (*level0_func), (void) );
05066    #endif /* (CHIP == INTEL) */
05067
05068    #if (CHIP == M68000)
05069    /* Variables that are initialized elsewhere are just extern here. */
05070    extern int keypad;               /* Flag for keypad mode */
05071    extern int app_mode;             /* Flag for arrow key application mode */
05072    extern int STdebKey;             /* nonzero if ctl-alt-Fx detected */
05073    extern struct tty *cur_cons;     /* virtual cons currently displayed */
05074    extern unsigned char font8[];    /* 8 pixel wide font table (initialized) */
05075    extern unsigned char font12[];   /* 12 pixel wide font table (initialized) */
05076    extern unsigned char font16[];   /* 16 pixel wide font table (initialized) */
05077    extern unsigned short resolution; /* screen res; ST_RES_LOW..TT_RES_HIGH */
05078    #endif
```

```
++++++++++++++++++++++++++++++++++++++++++++++++++++++++++++++++++++++++++++++++
                              src/kernel/proc.h
++++++++++++++++++++++++++++++++++++++++++++++++++++++++++++++++++++++++++++++++
```

```
05100    #ifndef PROC_H
05101    #define PROC_H
05102
05103    /* Here is the declaration of the process table.  It contains the process'
05104     * registers, memory map, accounting, and message send/receive information.
05105     * Many assembly code routines reference fields in it.  The offsets to these
05106     * fields are defined in the assembler include file sconst.h.  When changing
05107     * 'proc', be sure to change sconst.h to match.
05108     */
05109
```

```
05110    struct proc {
05111      struct stackframe_s p_reg;     /* process' registers saved in stack frame */
05112
05113    #if (CHIP == INTEL)
05114      reg_t p_ldt_sel;               /* selector in gdt giving ldt base and limit*/
05115      struct segdesc_s p_ldt[2];     /* local descriptors for code and data */
05116                                     /* 2 is LDT_SIZE - avoid include protect.h */
05117    #endif /* (CHIP == INTEL) */
05118
05119      reg_t *p_stguard;              /* stack guard word */
05120
05121      int p_nr;                      /* number of this process (for fast access) */
05122
05123      int p_int_blocked;             /* nonzero if int msg blocked by busy task */
05124      int p_int_held;                /* nonzero if int msg held by busy syscall */
05125      struct proc *p_nextheld;       /* next in chain of held-up int processes */
05126
05127      int p_flags;                   /* P_SLOT_FREE, SENDING, RECEIVING, etc. */
05128      struct mem_map p_map[NR_SEGS]; /* memory map */
05129      pid_t p_pid;                   /* process id passed in from MM */
05130
05131      clock_t user_time;             /* user time in ticks */
05132      clock_t sys_time;              /* sys time in ticks */
05133      clock_t child_utime;           /* cumulative user time of children */
05134      clock_t child_stime;           /* cumulative sys time of children */
05135      clock_t p_alarm;               /* time of next alarm in ticks, or 0 */
05136
05137      struct proc *p_callerq;        /* head of list of procs wishing to send */
05138      struct proc *p_sendlink;       /* link to next proc wishing to send */
05139      message *p_messbuf;            /* pointer to message buffer */
05140      int p_getfrom;                 /* from whom does process want to receive? */
05141      int p_sendto;
05142
05143      struct proc *p_nextready;      /* pointer to next ready process */
05144      sigset_t p_pending;            /* bit map for pending signals */
05145      unsigned p_pendcount;          /* count of pending and unfinished signals */
05146
05147      char p_name[16];               /* name of the process */
05148    };
05149
05150    /* Guard word for task stacks. */
05151    #define STACK_GUARD     ((reg_t) (sizeof(reg_t) == 2 ? 0xBEEF : 0xDEADBEEF))
05152
05153    /* Bits for p_flags in proc[].  A process is runnable iff p_flags == 0. */
05154    #define P_SLOT_FREE     001    /* set when slot is not in use */
05155    #define NO_MAP          002    /* keeps unmapped forked child from running */
05156    #define SENDING         004    /* set when process blocked trying to send */
05157    #define RECEIVING       010    /* set when process blocked trying to recv */
05158    #define PENDING         020    /* set when inform() of signal pending */
05159    #define SIG_PENDING     040    /* keeps to-be-signalled proc from running */
05160    #define P_STOP          0100   /* set when process is being traced */
05161
05162    /* Magic process table addresses. */
05163    #define BEG_PROC_ADDR (&proc[0])
05164    #define END_PROC_ADDR (&proc[NR_TASKS + NR_PROCS])
05165    #define END_TASK_ADDR (&proc[NR_TASKS])
05166    #define BEG_SERV_ADDR (&proc[NR_TASKS])
05167    #define BEG_USER_ADDR (&proc[NR_TASKS + LOW_USER])
05168
05169    #define NIL_PROC          ((struct proc *) 0)
```

```
05170    #define isidlehardware(n) ((n) == IDLE || (n) == HARDWARE)
05171    #define isokprocn(n)      ((unsigned) ((n) + NR_TASKS) < NR_PROCS + NR_TASKS)
05172    #define isoksrc_dest(n)   (isokprocn(n) || (n) == ANY)
05173    #define isoksusern(n)     ((unsigned) (n) < NR_PROCS)
05174    #define isokusern(n)      ((unsigned) ((n) - LOW_USER) < NR_PROCS - LOW_USER)
05175    #define isrxhardware(n)   ((n) == ANY || (n) == HARDWARE)
05176    #define issysentn(n)      ((n) == FS_PROC_NR || (n) == MM_PROC_NR)
05177    #define istaskp(p)        ((p) < END_TASK_ADDR && (p) != proc_addr(IDLE))
05178    #define isuserp(p)        ((p) >= BEG_USER_ADDR)
05179    #define proc_addr(n)      (pproc_addr + NR_TASKS)[(n)]
05180    #define cproc_addr(n)     (&(proc + NR_TASKS)[(n)])
05181    #define proc_number(p)    ((p)->p_nr)
05182    #define proc_vir2phys(p, vir) \
05183                            (((phys_bytes)(p)->p_map[D].mem_phys << CLICK_SHIFT) \
05184                                                    + (vir_bytes) (vir))
05185
05186    EXTERN struct proc proc[NR_TASKS + NR_PROCS];   /* process table */
05187    EXTERN struct proc *pproc_addr[NR_TASKS + NR_PROCS];
05188    /* ptrs to process table slots; fast because now a process entry can be found
05189       by indexing the pproc_addr array, while accessing an element i requires
05190       a multiplication with sizeof(struct proc) to determine the address */
05191    EXTERN struct proc *bill_ptr;   /* ptr to process to bill for clock ticks */
05192    EXTERN struct proc *rdy_head[NQ];      /* pointers to ready list headers */
05193    EXTERN struct proc *rdy_tail[NQ];      /* pointers to ready list tails */
05194
05195    #endif /* PROC_H */
```

```
++++++++++++++++++++++++++++++++++++++++++++++++++++++++++++++++++++++++++++++++
                            src/kernel/protect.h
++++++++++++++++++++++++++++++++++++++++++++++++++++++++++++++++++++++++++++++++
```

```
05200    /* Constants for protected mode. */
05201
05202    /* Table sizes. */
05203    #define GDT_SIZE (FIRST_LDT_INDEX + NR_TASKS + NR_PROCS) /* spec. and LDT's */
05204    #define IDT_SIZE (IRQ8_VECTOR + 8)      /* only up to the highest vector */
05205    #define LDT_SIZE       2       /* contains CS and DS only */
05206
05207    /* Fixed global descriptors.  1 to 7 are prescribed by the BIOS. */
05208    #define GDT_INDEX       1       /* GDT descriptor */
05209    #define IDT_INDEX       2       /* IDT descriptor */
05210    #define DS_INDEX        3       /* kernel DS */
05211    #define ES_INDEX        4       /* kernel ES (386: flag 4 Gb at startup) */
05212    #define SS_INDEX        5       /* kernel SS (386: monitor SS at startup) */
05213    #define CS_INDEX        6       /* kernel CS */
05214    #define MON_CS_INDEX    7       /* temp for BIOS (386: monitor CS at startup) */
05215    #define TSS_INDEX       8       /* kernel TSS */
05216    #define DS_286_INDEX    9       /* scratch 16-bit source segment */
05217    #define ES_286_INDEX   10       /* scratch 16-bit destination segment */
05218    #define VIDEO_INDEX    11       /* video memory segment */
05219    #define DP_ETH0_INDEX  12       /* Western Digital Etherplus buffer */
05220    #define DP_ETH1_INDEX  13       /* Western Digital Etherplus buffer */
05221    #define FIRST_LDT_INDEX 14      /* rest of descriptors are LDT's */
05222
05223    #define GDT_SELECTOR    0x08  /* (GDT_INDEX * DESC_SIZE) bad for asld */
05224    #define IDT_SELECTOR    0x10  /* (IDT_INDEX * DESC_SIZE) */
```

```
05225    #define DS_SELECTOR         0x18    /* (DS_INDEX * DESC_SIZE) */
05226    #define ES_SELECTOR         0x20    /* (ES_INDEX * DESC_SIZE) */
05227    #define FLAT_DS_SELECTOR    0x21    /* less privileged ES */
05228    #define SS_SELECTOR         0x28    /* (SS_INDEX * DESC_SIZE) */
05229    #define CS_SELECTOR         0x30    /* (CS_INDEX * DESC_SIZE) */
05230    #define MON_CS_SELECTOR     0x38    /* (MON_CS_INDEX * DESC_SIZE) */
05231    #define TSS_SELECTOR        0x40    /* (TSS_INDEX * DESC_SIZE) */
05232    #define DS_286_SELECTOR     0x49    /* (DS_286_INDEX * DESC_SIZE + 1) */
05233    #define ES_286_SELECTOR     0x51    /* (ES_286_INDEX * DESC_SIZE + 1) */
05234    #define VIDEO_SELECTOR      0x59    /* (VIDEO_INDEX * DESC_SIZE + 1) */
05235    #define DP_ETH0_SELECTOR    0x61    /* (DP_ETH0_INDEX * DESC_SIZE) */
05236    #define DP_ETH1_SELECTOR    0x69    /* (DP_ETH1_INDEX * DESC_SIZE) */
05237
05238    /* Fixed local descriptors. */
05239    #define CS_LDT_INDEX        0       /* process CS */
05240    #define DS_LDT_INDEX        1       /* process DS=ES=FS=GS=SS */
05241
05242    /* Privileges. */
05243    #define INTR_PRIVILEGE      0       /* kernel and interrupt handlers */
05244    #define TASK_PRIVILEGE      1
05245    #define USER_PRIVILEGE      3
05246
05247    /* 286 hardware constants. */
05248
05249    /* Exception vector numbers. */
05250    #define BOUNDS_VECTOR       5       /* bounds check failed */
05251    #define INVAL_OP_VECTOR     6       /* invalid opcode */
05252    #define COPROC_NOT_VECTOR   7       /* coprocessor not available */
05253    #define DOUBLE_FAULT_VECTOR 8
05254    #define COPROC_SEG_VECTOR   9       /* coprocessor segment overrun */
05255    #define INVAL_TSS_VECTOR    10      /* invalid TSS */
05256    #define SEG_NOT_VECTOR      11      /* segment not present */
05257    #define STACK_FAULT_VECTOR  12      /* stack exception */
05258    #define PROTECTION_VECTOR   13      /* general protection */
05259
05260    /* Selector bits. */
05261    #define TI                  0x04    /* table indicator */
05262    #define RPL                 0x03    /* requester privilege level */
05263
05264    /* Descriptor structure offsets. */
05265    #define DESC_BASE           2       /* to base_low */
05266    #define DESC_BASE_MIDDLE    4       /* to base_middle */
05267    #define DESC_ACCESS         5       /* to access byte */
05268    #define DESC_SIZE           8       /* sizeof (struct segdesc_s) */
05269
05270    /* Segment sizes. */
05271    #define MAX_286_SEG_SIZE 0x10000L
05272
05273    /* Base and limit sizes and shifts. */
05274    #define BASE_MIDDLE_SHIFT   16  /* shift for base --> base_middle */
05275
05276    /* Access-byte and type-byte bits. */
05277    #define PRESENT             0x80      /* set for descriptor present */
05278    #define DPL                 0x60      /* descriptor privilege level mask */
05279    #define DPL_SHIFT           5
05280    #define SEGMENT             0x10      /* set for segment-type descriptors */
05281
05282    /* Access-byte bits. */
05283    #define EXECUTABLE          0x08      /* set for executable segment */
05284    #define CONFORMING          0x04      /* set for conforming segment if executable */
```

```
05285   #define EXPAND_DOWN     0x04     /* set for expand-down segment if !executable*/
05286   #define READABLE        0x02     /* set for readable segment if executable */
05287   #define WRITEABLE       0x02     /* set for writeable segment if !executable */
05288   #define TSS_BUSY        0x02     /* set if TSS descriptor is busy */
05289   #define ACCESSED        0x01     /* set if segment accessed */
05290
05291   /* Special descriptor types. */
05292   #define AVL_286_TSS     1        /* available 286 TSS */
05293   #define LDT             2        /* local descriptor table */
05294   #define BUSY_286_TSS    3        /* set transparently to the software */
05295   #define CALL_286_GATE   4        /* not used */
05296   #define TASK_GATE       5        /* only used by debugger */
05297   #define INT_286_GATE    6        /* interrupt gate, used for all vectors */
05298   #define TRAP_286_GATE   7        /* not used */
05299
05300   /* Extra 386 hardware constants. */
05301
05302   /* Exception vector numbers. */
05303   #define PAGE_FAULT_VECTOR    14
05304   #define COPROC_ERR_VECTOR    16  /* coprocessor error */
05305
05306   /* Descriptor structure offsets. */
05307   #define DESC_GRANULARITY     6   /* to granularity byte */
05308   #define DESC_BASE_HIGH       7   /* to base_high */
05309
05310   /* Base and limit sizes and shifts. */
05311   #define BASE_HIGH_SHIFT      24  /* shift for base --> base_high */
05312   #define BYTE_GRAN_MAX        0xFFFFFL    /* maximum size for byte granular segment */
05313   #define GRANULARITY_SHIFT    16  /* shift for limit --> granularity */
05314   #define OFFSET_HIGH_SHIFT    16  /* shift for (gate) offset --> offset_high */
05315   #define PAGE_GRAN_SHIFT      12  /* extra shift for page granular limits */
05316
05317   /* Type-byte bits. */
05318   #define DESC_386_BIT    0x08     /* 386 types are obtained by ORing with this */
05319                                   /* LDT's and TASK_GATE's don't need it */
05320
05321   /* Granularity byte. */
05322   #define GRANULAR        0x80     /* set for 4K granularilty */
05323   #define DEFAULT         0x40     /* set for 32-bit defaults (executable seg) */
05324   #define BIG             0x40     /* set for "BIG" (expand-down seg) */
05325   #define AVL             0x10     /* 0 for available */
05326   #define LIMIT_HIGH      0x0F     /* mask for high bits of limit */
```

```
++++++++++++++++++++++++++++++++++++++++++++++++++++++++++++++++++++++++++++
                            src/kernel/sconst.h
++++++++++++++++++++++++++++++++++++++++++++++++++++++++++++++++++++++++++++
```

```
05400   ! Miscellaneous constants used in assembler code.
05401   W               =       _WORD_SIZE       ! Machine word size.
05402
05403   ! Offsets in struct proc. They MUST match proc.h.
05404   P_STACKBASE     =       0
05405   #if _WORD_SIZE == 2
05406   ESREG           =       P_STACKBASE
05407   #else
05408   GSREG           =       P_STACKBASE
05409   FSREG           =       GSREG + 2        ! 386 introduces FS and GS segments
```

```
05410    ESREG          =         FSREG + 2
05411    #endif
05412    DSREG          =         ESREG + 2
05413    DIREG          =         DSREG + 2
05414    SIREG          =         DIREG + W
05415    BPREG          =         SIREG + W
05416    STREG          =         BPREG + W        ! hole for another SP
05417    BXREG          =         STREG + W
05418    DXREG          =         BXREG + W
05419    CXREG          =         DXREG + W
05420    AXREG          =         CXREG + W
05421    RETADR         =         AXREG + W        ! return address for save() call
05422    PCREG          =         RETADR + W
05423    CSREG          =         PCREG + W
05424    PSWREG         =         CSREG + W
05425    SPREG          =         PSWREG + W
05426    SSREG          =         SPREG + W
05427    P_STACKTOP     =         SSREG + W
05428    P_LDT_SEL      =         P_STACKTOP
05429    P_LDT          =         P_LDT_SEL + W
05430
05431    #if _WORD_SIZE == 2
05432    Msize          =         12               ! size of a message in 16-bit words
05433    #else
05434    Msize          =         9                ! size of a message in 32-bit words
05435    #endif
```

```
++++++++++++++++++++++++++++++++++++++++++++++++++++++++++++++++++++++++++++++++++++
                              src/kernel/assert.h
++++++++++++++++++++++++++++++++++++++++++++++++++++++++++++++++++++++++++++++++++++
```

```
05500    /*
05501    assert.h
05502    */
05503    #ifndef ASSERT_H
05504    #define ASSERT_H
05505
05506    #if DEBUG
05507
05508    #define INIT_ASSERT     static char *assert_file= __FILE__;
05509
05510    void bad_assertion(char *file, int line, char *what);
05511    void bad_compare(char *file, int line, int lhs, char *what, int rhs);
05512
05513    #define assert(x)       (!(x) ? bad_assertion(assert_file, __LINE__, #x) \
05514                                                        : (void) 0)
05515    #define compare(a,t,b)  (!((a) t (b)) ? bad_compare(assert_file, __LINE__, \
05516                                    (a), #a " " #t " " #b, (b)) : (void) 0)
05517    #else /* !DEBUG */
05518
05519    #define INIT_ASSERT     /* nothing */
05520
05521    #define assert(x)       (void)0
05522    #define compare(a,t,b)  (void)0
05523
05524    #endif /* !DEBUG */
```

```
05525
05526   #endif /* ASSERT_H */



+++++++++++++++++++++++++++++++++++++++++++++++++++++++++++++++++++++++++++++++
                              src/kernel/table.c
+++++++++++++++++++++++++++++++++++++++++++++++++++++++++++++++++++++++++++++++

05600   /* The object file of "table.c" contains all the data.  In the *.h files,
05601    * declared variables appear with EXTERN in front of them, as in
05602    *
05603    *     EXTERN int x;
05604    *
05605    * Normally EXTERN is defined as extern, so when they are included in another
05606    * file, no storage is allocated.  If the EXTERN were not present, but just
05607    * say,
05608    *
05609    *     int x;
05610    *
05611    * then including this file in several source files would cause 'x' to be
05612    * declared several times.  While some linkers accept this, others do not,
05613    * so they are declared extern when included normally.  However, it must
05614    * be declared for real somewhere.  That is done here, by redefining
05615    * EXTERN as the null string, so the inclusion of all the *.h files in
05616    * table.c actually generates storage for them.  All the initialized
05617    * variables are also declared here, since
05618    *
05619    * extern int x = 4;
05620    *
05621    * is not allowed.  If such variables are shared, they must also be declared
05622    * in one of the *.h files without the initialization.
05623    */

05624
05625   #define _TABLE

05626
05627   #include "kernel.h"
05628   #include <termios.h>
05629   #include <minix/com.h>
05630   #include "proc.h"
05631   #include "tty.h"

05632
05633   /* The startup routine of each task is given below, from -NR_TASKS upwards.
05634    * The order of the names here MUST agree with the numerical values assigned to
05635    * the tasks in <minix/com.h>.
05636    */
05637   #define SMALL_STACK       (128 * sizeof(char *))

05638
05639   #define TTY_STACK         (3 * SMALL_STACK)
05640   #define SYN_ALRM_STACK    SMALL_STACK

05641
05642   #define DP8390_STACK      (SMALL_STACK * ENABLE_NETWORKING)

05643
05644   #if (CHIP == INTEL)
05645   #define IDLE_STACK        ((3+3+4) * sizeof(char *))   /* 3 intr, 3 temps, 4 db */
05646   #else
05647   #define IDLE_STACK        SMALL_STACK
05648   #endif
05649
```

```
05650    #define PRINTER_STACK    SMALL_STACK
05651
05652    #if (CHIP == INTEL)
05653    #define WINCH_STACK      (2 * SMALL_STACK * ENABLE_WINI)
05654    #else
05655    #define WINCH_STACK      (3 * SMALL_STACK * ENABLE_WINI)
05656    #endif
05657
05658    #if (MACHINE == ATARI)
05659    #define SCSI_STACK       (3 * SMALL_STACK)
05660    #endif
05661
05662    #if (MACHINE == IBM_PC)
05663    #define SCSI_STACK       (2 * SMALL_STACK * ENABLE_SCSI)
05664    #endif
05665
05666    #define CDROM_STACK      (4 * SMALL_STACK * ENABLE_CDROM)
05667    #define AUDIO_STACK      (4 * SMALL_STACK * ENABLE_AUDIO)
05668    #define MIXER_STACK      (4 * SMALL_STACK * ENABLE_AUDIO)
05669
05670    #define FLOP_STACK       (3 * SMALL_STACK)
05671    #define MEM_STACK        SMALL_STACK
05672    #define CLOCK_STACK      SMALL_STACK
05673    #define SYS_STACK        SMALL_STACK
05674    #define HARDWARE_STACK   0                  /* dummy task, uses kernel stack */
05675
05676
05677    #define TOT_STACK_SPACE          (TTY_STACK + DP8390_STACK + SCSI_STACK + \
05678            SYN_ALRM_STACK + IDLE_STACK + HARDWARE_STACK + PRINTER_STACK + \
05679            WINCH_STACK + FLOP_STACK + MEM_STACK + CLOCK_STACK + SYS_STACK + \
05680            CDROM_STACK + AUDIO_STACK + MIXER_STACK)
05681
05682
05683    /* SCSI, CDROM and AUDIO may in the future have different choices like
05684     * WINCHESTER, but for now the choice is fixed.
05685     */
05686    #define scsi_task        aha_scsi_task
05687    #define cdrom_task       mcd_task
05688    #define audio_task       dsp_task
05689
05690
05691    /*
05692     * Some notes about the following table:
05693     *  1) The tty_task should always be first so that other tasks can use printf
05694     *     if their initialisation has problems.
05695     *  2) If you add a new kernel task, add it before the printer task.
05696     *  3) The task name is used for the process name (p_name).
05697     */
05698
05699    PUBLIC struct tasktab tasktab[] = {
05700            { tty_task,             TTY_STACK,      "TTY"           },
05701    #if ENABLE_NETWORKING
05702            { dp8390_task,          DP8390_STACK,   "DP8390"        },
05703    #endif
05704    #if ENABLE_CDROM
05705            { cdrom_task,           CDROM_STACK,    "CDROM"         },
05706    #endif
05707    #if ENABLE_AUDIO
05708            { audio_task,           AUDIO_STACK,    "AUDIO"         },
05709            { mixer_task,           MIXER_STACK,    "MIXER"         },
```

```
05710    #endif
05711    #if ENABLE_SCSI
05712            { scsi_task,            SCSI_STACK,       "SCSI"            },
05713    #endif
05714    #if ENABLE_WINI
05715            { winchester_task,      WINCH_STACK,      "WINCH"           },
05716    #endif
05717            { syn_alrm_task,        SYN_ALRM_STACK,   "SYN_AL"          },
05718            { idle_task,            IDLE_STACK,       "IDLE"            },
05719            { printer_task,         PRINTER_STACK,    "PRINTER"         },
05720            { floppy_task,          FLOP_STACK,       "FLOPPY"          },
05721            { mem_task,             MEM_STACK,        "MEMORY"          },
05722            { clock_task,           CLOCK_STACK,      "CLOCK"           },
05723            { sys_task,             SYS_STACK,        "SYS"             },
05724            { 0,                    HARDWARE_STACK,   "HARDWAR"         },
05725            { 0,                    0,                "MM"              },
05726            { 0,                    0,                "FS"              },
05727    #if ENABLE_NETWORKING
05728            { 0,                    0,                "INET"            },
05729    #endif
05730            { 0,                    0,                "INIT"            },
05731    };
05732
05733    /* Stack space for all the task stacks.  (Declared as (char *) to align it.) */
05734    PUBLIC char *t_stack[TOT_STACK_SPACE / sizeof(char *)];
05735
05736    /*
05737     * The number of kernel tasks must be the same as NR_TASKS.
05738     * If NR_TASKS is not correct then you will get the compile error:
05739     *    "array size is negative"
05740     */
05741
05742    #define NKT (sizeof tasktab / sizeof (struct tasktab) - (INIT_PROC_NR + 1))
05743
05744    extern int dummy_tasktab_check[NR_TASKS == NKT ? 1 : -1];
```

```
++++++++++++++++++++++++++++++++++++++++++++++++++++++++++++++++++++++++++++++++++
                              src/kernel/mpx.s
++++++++++++++++++++++++++++++++++++++++++++++++++++++++++++++++++++++++++++++++++
```

```
05800    #
05801    ! Chooses between the 8086 and 386 versions of the Minix startup code.
05802
05803    #include <minix/config.h>
05804    #if _WORD_SIZE == 2
05805    #include "mpx88.s"
05806    #else
05807    #include "mpx386.s"
05808    #endif
```

```
++++++++++++++++++++++++++++++++++++++++++++++++++++++++++++++++++++++++++++++
                              src/kernel/mpx386.s
++++++++++++++++++++++++++++++++++++++++++++++++++++++++++++++++++++++++++++++
05900   #
05901   ! This file contains the assembler startup code for Minix and the 32-bit
05902   ! interrupt handlers.  It cooperates with start.c to set up a good
05903   ! environment for main().
05904
05905   ! This file is part of the lowest layer of the MINIX kernel.  The other part
05906   ! is "proc.c".  The lowest layer does process switching and message handling.
05907
05908   ! Every transition to the kernel goes through this file.  Transitions are
05909   ! caused by sending/receiving messages and by most interrupts.  (RS232
05910   ! interrupts may be handled in the file "rs2.s" and then they rarely enter
05911   ! the kernel.)
05912
05913   ! Transitions to the kernel may be nested.  The initial entry may be with a
05914   ! system call, exception or hardware interrupt; reentries may only be made
05915   ! by hardware interrupts.  The count of reentries is kept in "k_reenter".
05916   ! It is important for deciding whether to switch to the kernel stack and
05917   ! for protecting the message passing code in "proc.c".
05918
05919   ! For the message passing trap, most of the machine state is saved in the
05920   ! proc table.  (Some of the registers need not be saved.)  Then the stack is
05921   ! switched to "k_stack", and interrupts are reenabled.  Finally, the system
05922   ! call handler (in C) is called.  When it returns, interrupts are disabled
05923   ! again and the code falls into the restart routine, to finish off held-up
05924   ! interrupts and run the process or task whose pointer is in "proc_ptr".
05925
05926   ! Hardware interrupt handlers do the same, except  (1) The entire state must
05927   ! be saved.  (2) There are too many handlers to do this inline, so the save
05928   ! routine is called.  A few cycles are saved by pushing the address of the
05929   ! appropiate restart routine for a return later.  (3) A stack switch is
05930   ! avoided when the stack is already switched.  (4) The (master) 8259 interrupt
05931   ! controller is reenabled centrally in save().  (5) Each interrupt handler
05932   ! masks its interrupt line using the 8259 before enabling (other unmasked)
05933   ! interrupts, and unmasks it after servicing the interrupt.  This limits the
05934   ! nest level to the number of lines and protects the handler from itself.
05935
05936   ! For communication with the boot monitor at startup time some constant
05937   ! data are compiled into the beginning of the text segment. This facilitates
05938   ! reading the data at the start of the boot process, since only the first
05939   ! sector of the file needs to be read.
05940
05941   ! Some data storage is also allocated at the end of this file. This data
05942   ! will be at the start of the data segment of the kernel and will be read
05943   ! and modified by the boot monitor before the kernel starts.
05944
05945   ! sections
05946
05947   .sect .text
05948   begtext:
05949   .sect .rom
05950   begrom:
05951   .sect .data
05952   begdata:
05953   .sect .bss
05954   begbss:
```

```
05955
05956    #include <minix/config.h>
05957    #include <minix/const.h>
05958    #include <minix/com.h>
05959    #include "const.h"
05960    #include "protect.h"
05961    #include "sconst.h"
05962
05963    /* Selected 386 tss offsets. */
05964    #define TSS3_S_SP0      4
05965
05966    ! Exported functions
05967    ! Note: in assembly language the .define statement applied to a function name
05968    ! is loosely equivalent to a prototype in C code -- it makes it possible to
05969    ! link to an entity declared in the assembly code but does not create
05970    ! the entity.
05971
05972    .define _idle_task
05973    .define _restart
05974    .define save
05975
05976    .define _divide_error
05977    .define _single_step_exception
05978    .define _nmi
05979    .define _breakpoint_exception
05980    .define _overflow
05981    .define _bounds_check
05982    .define _inval_opcode
05983    .define _copr_not_available
05984    .define _double_fault
05985    .define _copr_seg_overrun
05986    .define _inval_tss
05987    .define _segment_not_present
05988    .define _stack_exception
05989    .define _general_protection
05990    .define _page_fault
05991    .define _copr_error
05992
05993    .define _hwint00           ! handlers for hardware interrupts
05994    .define _hwint01
05995    .define _hwint02
05996    .define _hwint03
05997    .define _hwint04
05998    .define _hwint05
05999    .define _hwint06
06000    .define _hwint07
06001    .define _hwint08
06002    .define _hwint09
06003    .define _hwint10
06004    .define _hwint11
06005    .define _hwint12
06006    .define _hwint13
06007    .define _hwint14
06008    .define _hwint15
06009
06010    .define _s_call
06011    .define _p_s_call
06012    .define _level0_call
06013
06014    ! Imported functions.
```

```
06015
06016     .extern _cstart
06017     .extern _main
06018     .extern _exception
06019     .extern _interrupt
06020     .extern _sys_call
06021     .extern _unhold
06022
06023     ! Exported variables.
06024     ! Note: when used with a variable the .define does not reserve storage,
06025     ! it makes the name externally visible so it may be linked to.
06026
06027     .define begbss
06028     .define begdata
06029     .define _sizes
06030
06031     ! Imported variables.
06032
06033     .extern _gdt
06034     .extern _code_base
06035     .extern _data_base
06036     .extern _held_head
06037     .extern _k_reenter
06038     .extern _pc_at
06039     .extern _proc_ptr
06040     .extern _ps_mca
06041     .extern _tss
06042     .extern _level0_func
06043     .extern _mon_sp
06044     .extern _mon_return
06045     .extern _reboot_code
06046
06047     .sect .text
06048     !*=====================================================================*
06049     !*                            MINIX                                    *
06050     !*=====================================================================*
06051     MINIX:                            ! this is the entry point for the MINIX kernel
06052             jmp     over_flags        ! skip over the next few bytes
06053             .data2  CLICK_SHIFT       ! for the monitor: memory granularity
06054     flags:
06055             .data2  0x002D            ! boot monitor flags:
06056                                       !       call in 386 mode, make stack,
06057                                       !       load high, will return
06058             nop                       ! extra byte to sync up disassembler
06059     over_flags:
06060
06061     ! Set up a C stack frame on the monitor stack.  (The monitor sets cs and ds
06062     ! right.  The ss descriptor still references the monitor data segment.)
06063             movzx   esp, sp           ! monitor stack is a 16 bit stack
06064             push    ebp
06065             mov     ebp, esp
06066             push    esi
06067             push    edi
06068             cmp     4(ebp), 0         ! nonzero if return possible
06069             jz      noret
06070             inc     (_mon_return)
06071     noret:  mov     (_mon_sp), esp  ! save stack pointer for later return
06072
06073     ! Copy the monitor global descriptor table to the address space of kernel and
06074     ! switch over to it.  Prot_init() can then update it with immediate effect.
```

```
06075
06076            sgdt    (_gdt+GDT_SELECTOR)                ! get the monitor gdtr
06077            mov     esi, (_gdt+GDT_SELECTOR+2)         ! absolute address of GDT
06078            mov     ebx, _gdt                          ! address of kernel GDT
06079            mov     ecx, 8*8                           ! copying eight descriptors
06080    copygdt:
06081      eseg  movb    al, (esi)
06082            movb    (ebx), al
06083            inc     esi
06084            inc     ebx
06085            loop    copygdt
06086            mov     eax, (_gdt+DS_SELECTOR+2)          ! base of kernel data
06087            and     eax, 0x00FFFFFF                    ! only 24 bits
06088            add     eax, _gdt                          ! eax = vir2phys(gdt)
06089            mov     (_gdt+GDT_SELECTOR+2), eax         ! set base of GDT
06090            lgdt    (_gdt+GDT_SELECTOR)                ! switch over to kernel GDT
06091
06092    ! Locate boot parameters, set up kernel segment registers and stack.
06093            mov     ebx, 8(ebp)     ! boot parameters offset
06094            mov     edx, 12(ebp)    ! boot parameters length
06095            mov     ax, ds          ! kernel data
06096            mov     es, ax
06097            mov     fs, ax
06098            mov     gs, ax
06099            mov     ss, ax
06100            mov     esp, k_stktop   ! set sp to point to the top of kernel stack
06101
06102    ! Call C startup code to set up a proper environment to run main().
06103            push    edx
06104            push    ebx
06105            push    SS_SELECTOR
06106            push    MON_CS_SELECTOR
06107            push    DS_SELECTOR
06108            push    CS_SELECTOR
06109            call    _cstart         ! cstart(cs, ds, mcs, mds, parmoff, parmlen)
06110            add     esp, 6*4
06111
06112    ! Reload gdtr, idtr and the segment registers to global descriptor table set
06113    ! up by prot_init().
06114
06115            lgdt    (_gdt+GDT_SELECTOR)
06116            lidt    (_gdt+IDT_SELECTOR)
06117
06118            jmpf    CS_SELECTOR:csinit
06119    csinit:
06120      o16 mov     ax, DS_SELECTOR
06121            mov     ds, ax
06122            mov     es, ax
06123            mov     fs, ax
06124            mov     gs, ax
06125            mov     ss, ax
06126      o16 mov     ax, TSS_SELECTOR          ! no other TSS is used
06127            ltr     ax
06128            push    0                        ! set flags to known good state
06129            popf                             ! esp, clear nested task and int enable
06130
06131            jmp     _main                    ! main()
06132
06133
06134    !*========================================================================*
```

```
06135   !*                              interrupt handlers                    *
06136   !*                  interrupt handlers for 386 32-bit protected mode   *
06137   !*========================================================================*
06138
06139   !*========================================================================*
06140   !*                              hwint00 - 07                            *
06141   !*========================================================================*
06142   ! Note this is a macro, it looks like a subroutine.
06143   #define hwint_master(irq)              \
06144           call    save                    /* save interrupted process state */;\
06145           inb     INT_CTLMASK                                           ;\
06146           orb     al, [1<<irq]                                          ;\
06147           outb    INT_CTLMASK             /* disable the irq            */;\
06148           movb    al, ENABLE                                            ;\
06149           outb    INT_CTL                 /* reenable master 8259       */;\
06150           sti                             /* enable interrupts          */;\
06151           push    irq                     /* irq                        */;\
06152           call    (_irq_table + 4*irq)    /* eax = (*irq_table[irq])(irq) */;\
06153           pop     ecx                                                   ;\
06154           cli                             /* disable interrupts         */;\
06155           test    eax, eax                /* need to reenable irq?      */;\
06156           jz      0f                                                    ;\
06157           inb     INT_CTLMASK                                           ;\
06158           andb    al, ~[1<<irq]                                         ;\
06159           outb    INT_CTLMASK             /* enable the irq             */;\
06160   0:      ret                             /* restart (another) process  */
06161
06162   ! Each of these entry points is an expansion of the hwint_master macro
06163           .align  16
06164   _hwint00:               ! Interrupt routine for irq 0 (the clock).
06165           hwint_master(0)
06166
06167           .align  16
06168   _hwint01:               ! Interrupt routine for irq 1 (keyboard)
06169           hwint_master(1)
06170
06171           .align  16
06172   _hwint02:               ! Interrupt routine for irq 2 (cascade!)
06173           hwint_master(2)
06174
06175           .align  16
06176   _hwint03:               ! Interrupt routine for irq 3 (second serial)
06177           hwint_master(3)
06178
06179           .align  16
06180   _hwint04:               ! Interrupt routine for irq 4 (first serial)
06181           hwint_master(4)
06182
06183           .align  16
06184   _hwint05:               ! Interrupt routine for irq 5 (XT winchester)
06185           hwint_master(5)
06186
06187           .align  16
06188   _hwint06:               ! Interrupt routine for irq 6 (floppy)
06189           hwint_master(6)
06190
06191           .align  16
06192   _hwint07:               ! Interrupt routine for irq 7 (printer)
06193           hwint_master(7)
06194
```

```
06195   !*===========================================================================*
06196   !*                              hwint08 - 15                                 *
06197   !*===========================================================================*
06198   ! Note this is a macro, it looks like a subroutine.
06199   #define hwint_slave(irq)          \
06200           call    save                    /* save interrupted process state */;\
06201           inb     INT2_CTLMASK                                                ;\
06202           orb     al, [1<<[irq-8]]                                            ;\
06203           outb    INT2_CTLMASK            /* disable the irq               */;\
06204           movb    al, ENABLE                                                  ;\
06205           outb    INT_CTL                 /* reenable master 8259          */;\
06206           jmp     .+2                     /* delay                         */;\
06207           outb    INT2_CTL                /* reenable slave 8259           */;\
06208           sti                             /* enable interrupts             */;\
06209           push    irq                     /* irq                           */;\
06210           call    (_irq_table + 4*irq)    /* eax = (*irq_table[irq])(irq)  */;\
06211           pop     ecx                                                         ;\
06212           cli                             /* disable interrupts            */;\
06213           test    eax, eax                /* need to reenable irq?         */;\
06214           jz      0f                                                          ;\
06215           inb     INT2_CTLMASK                                                ;\
06216           andb    al, ~[1<<[irq-8]]                                           ;\
06217           outb    INT2_CTLMASK            /* enable the irq                */;\
06218   0:      ret                             /* restart (another) process     */
06219
06220   ! Each of these entry points is an expansion of the hwint_slave macro
06221           .align  16
06222   _hwint08:                       ! Interrupt routine for irq 8 (realtime clock)
06223           hwint_slave(8)
06224
06225           .align  16
06226   _hwint09:                       ! Interrupt routine for irq 9 (irq 2 redirected)
06227           hwint_slave(9)
06228
06229           .align  16
06230   _hwint10:                       ! Interrupt routine for irq 10
06231           hwint_slave(10)
06232
06233           .align  16
06234   _hwint11:                       ! Interrupt routine for irq 11
06235           hwint_slave(11)
06236
06237           .align  16
06238   _hwint12:                       ! Interrupt routine for irq 12
06239           hwint_slave(12)
06240
06241           .align  16
06242   _hwint13:                       ! Interrupt routine for irq 13 (FPU exception)
06243           hwint_slave(13)
06244
06245           .align  16
06246   _hwint14:                       ! Interrupt routine for irq 14 (AT winchester)
06247           hwint_slave(14)
06248
06249           .align  16
06250   _hwint15:                       ! Interrupt routine for irq 15
06251           hwint_slave(15)
06252
06253   !*===========================================================================*
06254   !*                              save                                         *
```

```
06255       !*======================================================================*
06256       ! Save for protected mode.
06257       ! This is much simpler than for 8086 mode, because the stack already points
06258       ! into the process table, or has already been switched to the kernel stack.
06259
06260               .align  16
06261       save:
06262               cld                         ! set direction flag to a known value
06263               pushad                      ! save "general" registers
06264         o16 push    ds                  ! save ds
06265         o16 push    es                  ! save es
06266         o16 push    fs                  ! save fs
06267         o16 push    gs                  ! save gs
06268               mov     dx, ss              ! ss is kernel data segment
06269               mov     ds, dx              ! load rest of kernel segments
06270               mov     es, dx              ! kernel does not use fs, gs
06271               mov     eax, esp            ! prepare to return
06272               incb    (_k_reenter)        ! from -1 if not reentering
06273               jnz     set_restart1        ! stack is already kernel stack
06274               mov     esp, k_stktop
06275               push    _restart            ! build return address for int handler
06276               xor     ebp, ebp            ! for stacktrace
06277               jmp     RETADR-P_STACKBASE(eax)
06278
06279               .align  4
06280       set_restart1:
06281               push    restart1
06282               jmp     RETADR-P_STACKBASE(eax)
06283
06284       !*======================================================================*
06285       !*                              _s_call                                *
06286       !*======================================================================*
06287               .align  16
06288       _s_call:
06289       _p_s_call:
06290               cld                         ! set direction flag to a known value
06291               sub     esp, 6*4            ! skip RETADR, eax, ecx, edx, ebx, est
06292               push    ebp                 ! stack already points into proc table
06293               push    esi
06294               push    edi
06295         o16 push    ds
06296         o16 push    es
06297         o16 push    fs
06298         o16 push    gs
06299               mov     dx, ss
06300               mov     ds, dx
06301               mov     es, dx
06302               incb    (_k_reenter)
06303               mov     esi, esp            ! assumes P_STACKBASE == 0
06304               mov     esp, k_stktop
06305               xor     ebp, ebp            ! for stacktrace
06306                                           ! end of inline save
06307               sti                         ! allow SWITCHER to be interrupted
06308                                           ! now set up parameters for sys_call()
06309               push    ebx                 ! pointer to user message
06310               push    eax                 ! src/dest
06311               push    ecx                 ! SEND/RECEIVE/BOTH
06312               call    _sys_call           ! sys_call(function, src_dest, m_ptr)
06313                                           ! caller is now explicitly in proc_ptr
06314               mov     AXREG(esi), eax     ! sys_call MUST PRESERVE si
```

```
06315              cli                      ! disable interrupts
06316
06317    ! Fall into code to restart proc/task running.
06318
06319    !*========================================================================*
06320    !*                              restart                                   *
06321    !*========================================================================*
06322    _restart:
06323
06324    ! Flush any held-up interrupts.
06325    ! This reenables interrupts, so the current interrupt handler may reenter.
06326    ! This does not matter, because the current handler is about to exit and no
06327    ! other handlers can reenter since flushing is only done when k_reenter == 0.
06328
06329              cmp      (_held_head), 0 ! do fast test to usually avoid function call
06330              jz       over_call_unhold
06331              call     _unhold         ! this is rare so overhead acceptable
06332    over_call_unhold:
06333              mov      esp, (_proc_ptr)        ! will assume P_STACKBASE == 0
06334              lldt     P_LDT_SEL(esp)          ! enable segment descriptors for task
06335              lea      eax, P_STACKTOP(esp)    ! arrange for next interrupt
06336              mov      (_tss+TSS3_S_SP0), eax  ! to save state in process table
06337    restart1:
06338              decb     (_k_reenter)
06339        o16 pop      gs
06340        o16 pop      fs
06341        o16 pop      es
06342        o16 pop      ds
06343              popad
06344              add      esp, 4         ! skip return adr
06345              iretd                   ! continue process
06346
06347    !*========================================================================*
06348    !*                          exception handlers                            *
06349    !*========================================================================*
06350    _divide_error:
06351              push     DIVIDE_VECTOR
06352              jmp      exception
06353
06354    _single_step_exception:
06355              push     DEBUG_VECTOR
06356              jmp      exception
06357
06358    _nmi:
06359              push     NMI_VECTOR
06360              jmp      exception
06361
06362    _breakpoint_exception:
06363              push     BREAKPOINT_VECTOR
06364              jmp      exception
06365
06366    _overflow:
06367              push     OVERFLOW_VECTOR
06368              jmp      exception
06369
06370    _bounds_check:
06371              push     BOUNDS_VECTOR
06372              jmp      exception
06373
06374    _inval_opcode:
```

```
06375                   push      INVAL_OP_VECTOR
06376                   jmp       exception
06377
06378     _copr_not_available:
06379                   push      COPROC_NOT_VECTOR
06380                   jmp       exception
06381
06382     _double_fault:
06383                   push      DOUBLE_FAULT_VECTOR
06384                   jmp       errexception
06385
06386     _copr_seg_overrun:
06387                   push      COPROC_SEG_VECTOR
06388                   jmp       exception
06389
06390     _inval_tss:
06391                   push      INVAL_TSS_VECTOR
06392                   jmp       errexception
06393
06394     _segment_not_present:
06395                   push      SEG_NOT_VECTOR
06396                   jmp       errexception
06397
06398     _stack_exception:
06399                   push      STACK_FAULT_VECTOR
06400                   jmp       errexception
06401
06402     _general_protection:
06403                   push      PROTECTION_VECTOR
06404                   jmp       errexception
06405
06406     _page_fault:
06407                   push      PAGE_FAULT_VECTOR
06408                   jmp       errexception
06409
06410     _copr_error:
06411                   push      COPROC_ERR_VECTOR
06412                   jmp       exception
06413
06414     !*========================================================================*
06415     !*                              exception                                 *
06416     !*========================================================================*
06417     ! This is called for all exceptions which do not push an error code.
06418
06419                   .align    16
06420     exception:
06421      sseg   mov      (trap_errno), 0          ! clear trap_errno
06422      sseg   pop      (ex_number)
06423                   jmp       exception1
06424
06425     !*========================================================================*
06426     !*                              errexception                              *
06427     !*========================================================================*
06428     ! This is called for all exceptions which push an error code.
06429
06430                   .align    16
06431     errexception:
06432      sseg   pop      (ex_number)
06433      sseg   pop      (trap_errno)
06434     exception1:                                    ! Common for all exceptions.
```

```
06435              push    eax                        ! eax is scratch register
06436              mov     eax, 0+4(esp)              ! old eip
06437      sseg    mov     (old_eip), eax
06438              movzx   eax, 4+4(esp)              ! old cs
06439      sseg    mov     (old_cs), eax
06440              mov     eax, 8+4(esp)              ! old eflags
06441      sseg    mov     (old_eflags), eax
06442              pop     eax
06443              call    save
06444              push    (old_eflags)
06445              push    (old_cs)
06446              push    (old_eip)
06447              push    (trap_errno)
06448              push    (ex_number)
06449              call    _exception                 ! (ex_number, trap_errno, old_eip,
06450                                                 !      old_cs, old_eflags)
06451              add     esp, 5*4
06452              cli
06453              ret
06454
06455      !*===========================================================================*
06456      !*                              level0_call                                  *
06457      !*===========================================================================*
06458      _level0_call:
06459              call    save
06460              jmp     (_level0_func)
06461
06462      !*===========================================================================*
06463      !*                              idle_task                                    *
06464      !*===========================================================================*
06465      _idle_task:                                ! executed when there is no work
06466              jmp     _idle_task                 ! a "hlt" before this fails in protected mode
06467
06468      !*===========================================================================*
06469      !*                              data                                         *
06470      !*===========================================================================*
06471      ! These declarations assure that storage will be allocated at the very
06472      ! beginning of the kernel data section, so the boot monitor can be easily
06473      ! told how to patch these locations. Note that the magic number is put
06474      ! here by the compiler, but will be read by, and then overwritten by,
06475      ! the boot monitor. When the kernel starts the sizes array will be
06476      ! found here, as if it had been initialized by the compiler.
06477
06478      .sect .rom         ! Before the string table please
06479      _sizes:                                    ! sizes of kernel, mm, fs filled in by boot
06480              .data2  0x526F                     ! this must be the first data entry (magic #)
06481              .space  16*2*2-2                   ! monitor uses previous word and this space
06482                                                 ! extra space allows for additional servers
06483      .sect .bss
06484      k_stack:
06485              .space  K_STACK_BYTES      ! kernel stack
06486      k_stktop:                          ! top of kernel stack
06487              .comm   ex_number, 4
06488              .comm   trap_errno, 4
06489              .comm   old_eip, 4
06490              .comm   old_cs, 4
06491              .comm   old_eflags, 4
```

```
+++++++++++++++++++++++++++++++++++++++++++++++++++++++++++++++++++++++++++++++
                                src/kernel/start.c
+++++++++++++++++++++++++++++++++++++++++++++++++++++++++++++++++++++++++++++++
06500   /* This file contains the C startup code for Minix on Intel processors.
06501    * It cooperates with mpx.s to set up a good environment for main().
06502    *
06503    * This code runs in real mode for a 16 bit kernel and may have to switch
06504    * to protected mode for a 286.
06505    *
06506    * For a 32 bit kernel this already runs in protected mode, but the selectors
06507    * are still those given by the BIOS with interrupts disabled, so the
06508    * descriptors need to be reloaded and interrupt descriptors made.
06509    */
06510
06511   #include "kernel.h"
06512   #include <stdlib.h>
06513   #include <minix/boot.h>
06514   #include "protect.h"
06515
06516   PRIVATE char k_environ[256];     /* environment strings passed by loader */
06517
06518   FORWARD _PROTOTYPE( int k_atoi, (char *s) );
06519
06520
06521   /*===========================================================================*
06522    *                              cstart                                        *
06523    *===========================================================================*/
06524   PUBLIC void cstart(cs, ds, mcs, mds, parmoff, parmsize)
06525   U16_t cs, ds;                  /* Kernel code and data segment */
06526   U16_t mcs, mds;                /* Monitor code and data segment */
06527   U16_t parmoff, parmsize;       /* boot parameters offset and length */
06528   {
06529   /* Perform system initializations prior to calling main(). */
06530
06531     register char *envp;
06532     phys_bytes mcode_base, mdata_base;
06533     unsigned mon_start;
06534
06535     /* Record where the kernel and the monitor are. */
06536     code_base = seg2phys(cs);
06537     data_base = seg2phys(ds);
06538     mcode_base = seg2phys(mcs);
06539     mdata_base = seg2phys(mds);
06540
06541     /* Initialize protected mode descriptors. */
06542     prot_init();
06543
06544     /* Copy the boot parameters to kernel memory. */
06545     if (parmsize > sizeof k_environ - 2) parmsize = sizeof k_environ - 2;
06546     phys_copy(mdata_base + parmoff, vir2phys(k_environ), (phys_bytes) parmsize);
06547
06548     /* Convert important boot environment variables. */
06549     boot_parameters.bp_rootdev = k_atoi(k_getenv("rootdev"));
06550     boot_parameters.bp_ramimagedev = k_atoi(k_getenv("ramimagedev"));
06551     boot_parameters.bp_ramsize = k_atoi(k_getenv("ramsize"));
06552     boot_parameters.bp_processor = k_atoi(k_getenv("processor"));
06553
06554     /* Type of VDU: */
```

```
06555          envp = k_getenv("video");
06556          if (strcmp(envp, "ega") == 0) ega = TRUE;
06557          if (strcmp(envp, "vga") == 0) vga = ega = TRUE;
06558
06559          /* Memory sizes: */
06560          low_memsize = k_atoi(k_getenv("memsize"));
06561          ext_memsize = k_atoi(k_getenv("emssize"));
06562
06563          /* Processor? */
06564          processor = boot_parameters.bp_processor;     /* 86, 186, 286, 386, ... */
06565
06566          /* XT, AT or MCA bus? */
06567          envp = k_getenv("bus");
06568          if (envp == NIL_PTR || strcmp(envp, "at") == 0) {
06569                  pc_at = TRUE;
06570          } else
06571          if (strcmp(envp, "mca") == 0) {
06572                  pc_at = ps_mca = TRUE;
06573          }
06574
06575          /* Decide if mode is protected. */
06576  #if _WORD_SIZE == 2
06577          protected_mode = processor >= 286;
06578  #endif
06579
06580          /* Is there a monitor to return to?  If so then keep it safe. */
06581          if (!protected_mode) mon_return = 0;
06582          mon_start = mcode_base / 1024;
06583          if (mon_return && low_memsize > mon_start) low_memsize = mon_start;
06584
06585          /* Return to assembler code to switch to protected mode (if 286), reload
06586           * selectors and call main().
06587           */
06588  }


06591  /*===========================================================================*
06592   *                              k_atoi                                       *
06593   *===========================================================================*/
06594  PRIVATE int k_atoi(s)
06595  register char *s;
06596  {
06597  /* Convert string to integer. */
06598
06599          return strtol(s, (char **) NULL, 10);
06600  }


06603  /*===========================================================================*
06604   *                              k_getenv                                     *
06605   *===========================================================================*/
06606  PUBLIC char *k_getenv(name)
06607  char *name;
06608  {
06609  /* Get environment value - kernel version of getenv to avoid setting up the
06610   * usual environment array.
06611   */
06612
06613          register char *namep;
06614          register char *envp;
```

```
06615
06616        for (envp = k_environ; *envp != 0;) {
06617             for (namep = name; *namep != 0 && *namep == *envp; namep++, envp++)
06618                  ;
06619             if (*namep == '\0' && *envp == '=') return(envp + 1);
06620             while (*envp++ != 0)
06621                  ;
06622        }
06623        return(NIL_PTR);
06624   }
```

```
++++++++++++++++++++++++++++++++++++++++++++++++++++++++++++++++++++++++++++++++
                              src/kernel/main.c
++++++++++++++++++++++++++++++++++++++++++++++++++++++++++++++++++++++++++++++++
```

```
06700    /* This file contains the main program of MINIX.  The routine main()
06701     * initializes the system and starts the ball rolling by setting up the proc
06702     * table, interrupt vectors, and scheduling each task to run to initialize
06703     * itself.
06704     *
06705     * The entries into this file are:
06706     *   main:                MINIX main program
06707     *   panic:               abort MINIX due to a fatal error
06708     */
06709
06710    #include "kernel.h"
06711    #include <signal.h>
06712    #include <unistd.h>
06713    #include <minix/callnr.h>
06714    #include <minix/com.h>
06715    #include "proc.h"
06716
06717
06718    /*===========================================================================*
06719     *                                main                                        *
06720     *===========================================================================*/
06721    PUBLIC void main()
06722    {
06723    /* Start the ball rolling. */
06724
06725      register struct proc *rp;
06726      register int t;
06727      int sizeindex;
06728      phys_clicks text_base;
06729      vir_clicks text_clicks;
06730      vir_clicks data_clicks;
06731      phys_bytes phys_b;
06732      reg_t ktsb;                        /* kernel task stack base */
06733      struct memory *memp;
06734      struct tasktab *ttp;
06735
06736      /* Initialize the interrupt controller. */
06737      intr_init(1);
06738
06739      /* Interpret memory sizes. */
```

```
06740            mem_init();
06741
06742            /* Clear the process table.
06743             * Set up mappings for proc_addr() and proc_number() macros.
06744             */
06745            for (rp = BEG_PROC_ADDR, t = -NR_TASKS; rp < END_PROC_ADDR; ++rp, ++t) {
06746                    rp->p_flags = P_SLOT_FREE;
06747                    rp->p_nr = t;                 /* proc number from ptr */
06748                    (pproc_addr + NR_TASKS)[t] = rp;          /* proc ptr from number */
06749            }
06750
06751            /* Set up proc table entries for tasks and servers.  The stacks of the
06752             * kernel tasks are initialized to an array in data space.  The stacks
06753             * of the servers have been added to the data segment by the monitor, so
06754             * the stack pointer is set to the end of the data segment.  All the
06755             * processes are in low memory on the 8086.  On the 386 only the kernel
06756             * is in low memory, the rest if loaded in extended memory.
06757             */
06758
06759            /* Task stacks. */
06760            ktsb = (reg_t) t_stack;
06761
06762            for (t = -NR_TASKS; t <= LOW_USER; ++t) {
06763                    rp = proc_addr(t);                     /* t's process slot */
06764                    ttp = &tasktab[t + NR_TASKS];          /* t's task attributes */
06765                    strcpy(rp->p_name, ttp->name);
06766                    if (t < 0) {
06767                            if (ttp->stksize > 0) {
06768                                    rp->p_stguard = (reg_t *) ktsb;
06769                                    *rp->p_stguard = STACK_GUARD;
06770                            }
06771                            ktsb += ttp->stksize;
06772                            rp->p_reg.sp = ktsb;
06773                            text_base = code_base >> CLICK_SHIFT;
06774                                            /* tasks are all in the kernel */
06775                            sizeindex = 0;              /* and use the full kernel sizes */
06776                            memp = &mem[0];             /* remove from this memory chunk */
06777                    } else {
06778                            sizeindex = 2 * t + 2;   /* MM, FS, INIT have their own sizes */
06779                    }
06780                    rp->p_reg.pc = (reg_t) ttp->initial_pc;
06781                    rp->p_reg.psw = istaskp(rp) ? INIT_TASK_PSW : INIT_PSW;
06782
06783                    text_clicks = sizes[sizeindex];
06784                    data_clicks = sizes[sizeindex + 1];
06785                    rp->p_map[T].mem_phys = text_base;
06786                    rp->p_map[T].mem_len  = text_clicks;
06787                    rp->p_map[D].mem_phys = text_base + text_clicks;
06788                    rp->p_map[D].mem_len  = data_clicks;
06789                    rp->p_map[S].mem_phys = text_base + text_clicks + data_clicks;
06790                    rp->p_map[S].mem_vir  = data_clicks;    /* empty - stack is in data */
06791                    text_base += text_clicks + data_clicks; /* ready for next, if server */
06792                    memp->size -= (text_base - memp->base);
06793                    memp->base = text_base;                    /* memory no longer free */
06794
06795                    if (t >= 0) {
06796                            /* Initialize the server stack pointer.  Take it down one word
06797                             * to give crtso.s something to use as "argc".
06798                             */
06799                            rp->p_reg.sp = (rp->p_map[S].mem_vir +
```

```
06800                                          rp->p_map[S].mem_len) << CLICK_SHIFT;
06801                        rp->p_reg.sp -= sizeof(reg_t);
06802              }
06803
06804      #if _WORD_SIZE == 4
06805              /* Servers are loaded in extended memory if in 386 mode. */
06806              if (t < 0) {
06807                      memp = &mem[1];
06808                      text_base = 0x100000 >> CLICK_SHIFT;
06809              }
06810      #endif
06811              if (!isidlehardware(t)) lock_ready(rp); /* IDLE, HARDWARE neveready */
06812              rp->p_flags = 0;
06813
06814              alloc_segments(rp);
06815        }
06816
06817        proc[NR_TASKS+INIT_PROC_NR].p_pid = 1;/* INIT of course has pid 1 */
06818        bill_ptr = proc_addr(IDLE);            /* it has to point somewhere */
06819        lock_pick_proc();
06820
06821        /* Now go to the assembly code to start running the current process. */
06822        restart();
06823      }


06826      /*===========================================================================*
06827       *                                 panic                                     *
06828       *===========================================================================*/
06829      PUBLIC void panic(s,n)
06830      _CONST char *s;
06831      int n;
06832      {
06833      /* The system has run aground of a fatal error.  Terminate execution.
06834       * If the panic originated in MM or FS, the string will be empty and the
06835       * file system already syncked.  If the panic originates in the kernel, we are
06836       * kind of stuck.
06837       */
06838
06839        if (*s != 0) {
06840              printf("\nKernel panic: %s",s);
06841              if (n != NO_NUM) printf(" %d", n);
06842              printf("\n");
06843        }
06844        wreboot(RBT_PANIC);
06845      }
```

```
+++++++++++++++++++++++++++++++++++++++++++++++++++++++++++++++++++++++++++++++++
                              src/kernel/proc.c
+++++++++++++++++++++++++++++++++++++++++++++++++++++++++++++++++++++++++++++++++
06900    /* This file contains essentially all of the process and message handling.
06901     * It has two main entry points from the outside:
06902     *
06903     *   sys_call:   called when a process or task does SEND, RECEIVE or SENDREC
06904     *   interrupt: called by interrupt routines to send a message to task
06905     *
06906     * It also has several minor entry points:
06907     *
06908     *   lock_ready:     put a process on one of the ready queues so it can be run
06909     *   lock_unready:   remove a process from the ready queues
06910     *   lock_sched:     a process has run too long; schedule another one
06911     *   lock_mini_send: send a message (used by interrupt signals, etc.)
06912     *   lock_pick_proc: pick a process to run (used by system initialization)
06913     *   unhold:         repeat all held-up interrupts
06914     */
06915
06916    #include "kernel.h"
06917    #include <minix/callnr.h>
06918    #include <minix/com.h>
06919    #include "proc.h"
06920
06921    PRIVATE unsigned char switching;        /* nonzero to inhibit interrupt() */
06922
06923    FORWARD _PROTOTYPE( int mini_send, (struct proc *caller_ptr, int dest,
06924                    message *m_ptr) );
06925    FORWARD _PROTOTYPE( int mini_rec, (struct proc *caller_ptr, int src,
06926                    message *m_ptr) );
06927    FORWARD _PROTOTYPE( void ready, (struct proc *rp) );
06928    FORWARD _PROTOTYPE( void sched, (void) );
06929    FORWARD _PROTOTYPE( void unready, (struct proc *rp) );
06930    FORWARD _PROTOTYPE( void pick_proc, (void) );
06931
06932    #define CopyMess(s,sp,sm,dp,dm) \
06933            cp_mess(s, (sp)->p_map[D].mem_phys, (vir_bytes)sm, (dp)->p_map[D].mem_phys, (vir_byt
06934
06935    /*===========================================================================*
06936     *                              interrupt                                    *
06937     *===========================================================================*/
06938    PUBLIC void interrupt(task)
06939    int task;                       /* number of task to be started */
06940    {
06941    /* An interrupt has occurred.  Schedule the task that handles it. */
06942
06943      register struct proc *rp;       /* pointer to task's proc entry */
06944
06945      rp = proc_addr(task);
06946
06947      /* If this call would compete with other process-switching functions, put
06948       * it on the 'held' queue to be flushed at the next non-competing restart().
06949       * The competing conditions are:
06950       * (1) k_reenter == (typeof k_reenter) -1:
06951       *     Call from the task level, typically from an output interrupt
06952       *     routine.  An interrupt handler might reenter interrupt().  Rare,
06953       *     so not worth special treatment.
06954       * (2) k_reenter > 0:
```

```
06955        *        Call from a nested interrupt handler.  A previous interrupt handler
06956        *        might be inside interrupt() or sys_call().
06957        * (3) switching != 0:
06958        *        Some process-switching function other than interrupt() is being
06959        *        called from the task level, typically sched() from CLOCK.   An
06960        *        interrupt handler might call interrupt and pass the k_reenter test.
06961        */
06962       if (k_reenter != 0 || switching) {
06963             lock();
06964             if (!rp->p_int_held) {
06965                     rp->p_int_held = TRUE;
06966                     if (held_head != NIL_PROC)
06967                             held_tail->p_nextheld = rp;
06968                     else
06969                             held_head = rp;
06970                     held_tail = rp;
06971                     rp->p_nextheld = NIL_PROC;
06972             }
06973             unlock();
06974             return;
06975       }
06976
06977       /* If task is not waiting for an interrupt, record the blockage. */
06978       if ( (rp->p_flags & (RECEIVING | SENDING)) != RECEIVING ||
06979          !isrxhardware(rp->p_getfrom)) {
06980             rp->p_int_blocked = TRUE;
06981             return;
06982       }
06983
06984       /* Destination is waiting for an interrupt.
06985        * Send it a message with source HARDWARE and type HARD_INT.
06986        * No more information can be reliably provided since interrupt messages
06987        * are not queued.
06988        */
06989       rp->p_messbuf->m_source = HARDWARE;
06990       rp->p_messbuf->m_type = HARD_INT;
06991       rp->p_flags &= ~RECEIVING;
06992       rp->p_int_blocked = FALSE;
06993
06994        /* Make rp ready and run it unless a task is already running.  This is
06995         * ready(rp) in-line for speed.
06996         */
06997       if (rdy_head[TASK_Q] != NIL_PROC)
06998             rdy_tail[TASK_Q]->p_nextready = rp;
06999       else
07000             proc_ptr = rdy_head[TASK_Q] = rp;
07001       rdy_tail[TASK_Q] = rp;
07002       rp->p_nextready = NIL_PROC;
07003     }
07004
07005     /*===========================================================================*
07006      *                              sys_call                                     *
07007      *===========================================================================*/
07008     PUBLIC int sys_call(function, src_dest, m_ptr)
07009     int function;                    /* SEND, RECEIVE, or BOTH */
07010     int src_dest;                    /* source to receive from or dest to send to */
07011     message *m_ptr;                  /* pointer to message */
07012     {
07013     /* The only system calls that exist in MINIX are sending and receiving
07014      * messages.  These are done by trapping to the kernel with an INT instruction.
```

```
07015     * The trap is caught and sys_call() is called to send or receive a message
07016     * (or both). The caller is always given by proc_ptr.
07017     */
07018
07019     register struct proc *rp;
07020     int n;
07021
07022     /* Check for bad system call parameters. */
07023     if (!isoksrc_dest(src_dest)) return(E_BAD_SRC);
07024     rp = proc_ptr;
07025
07026     if (isuserp(rp) && function != BOTH) return(E_NO_PERM);
07027
07028     /* The parameters are ok. Do the call. */
07029     if (function & SEND) {
07030         /* Function = SEND or BOTH. */
07031         n = mini_send(rp, src_dest, m_ptr);
07032         if (function == SEND || n != OK)
07033             return(n);      /* done, or SEND failed */
07034     }
07035
07036     /* Function = RECEIVE or BOTH.
07037      * We have checked user calls are BOTH, and trust 'function' otherwise.
07038      */
07039     return(mini_rec(rp, src_dest, m_ptr));
07040 }

07042 /*===========================================================================*
07043  *                              mini_send                                    *
07044  *===========================================================================*/
07045 PRIVATE int mini_send(caller_ptr, dest, m_ptr)
07046 register struct proc *caller_ptr;       /* who is trying to send a message? */
07047 int dest;                               /* to whom is message being sent? */
07048 message *m_ptr;                         /* pointer to message buffer */
07049 {
07050 /* Send a message from 'caller_ptr' to 'dest'. If 'dest' is blocked waiting
07051  * for this message, copy the message to it and unblock 'dest'. If 'dest' is
07052  * not waiting at all, or is waiting for another source, queue 'caller_ptr'.
07053  */
07054
07055     register struct proc *dest_ptr, *next_ptr;
07056     vir_bytes vb;                       /* message buffer pointer as vir_bytes */
07057     vir_clicks vlo, vhi;                /* virtual clicks containing message to send */
07058
07059     /* User processes are only allowed to send to FS and MM.  Check for this. */
07060     if (isuserp(caller_ptr) && !issysentn(dest)) return(E_BAD_DEST);
07061     dest_ptr = proc_addr(dest);     /* pointer to destination's proc entry */
07062     if (dest_ptr->p_flags & P_SLOT_FREE) return(E_BAD_DEST);        /* dead dest */
07063
07064     /* This check allows a message to be anywhere in data or stack or gap.
07065      * It will have to be made more elaborate later for machines which
07066      * don't have the gap mapped.
07067      */
07068     vb = (vir_bytes) m_ptr;
07069     vlo = vb >> CLICK_SHIFT;        /* vir click for bottom of message */
07070     vhi = (vb + MESS_SIZE - 1) >> CLICK_SHIFT;    /* vir click for top of msg */
07071     if (vlo < caller_ptr->p_map[D].mem_vir || vlo > vhi ||
07072         vhi >= caller_ptr->p_map[S].mem_vir + caller_ptr->p_map[S].mem_len)
07073         return(EFAULT);
07074
```

```
07075        /* Check for deadlock by 'caller_ptr' and 'dest' sending to each other. */
07076        if (dest_ptr->p_flags & SENDING) {
07077                next_ptr = proc_addr(dest_ptr->p_sendto);
07078                while (TRUE) {
07079                        if (next_ptr == caller_ptr) return(ELOCKED);
07080                        if (next_ptr->p_flags & SENDING)
07081                                next_ptr = proc_addr(next_ptr->p_sendto);
07082                        else
07083                                break;
07084                }
07085        }
07086
07087        /* Check to see if 'dest' is blocked waiting for this message. */
07088        if ( (dest_ptr->p_flags & (RECEIVING | SENDING)) == RECEIVING &&
07089             (dest_ptr->p_getfrom == ANY ||
07090              dest_ptr->p_getfrom == proc_number(caller_ptr))) {
07091                /* Destination is indeed waiting for this message. */
07092                CopyMess(proc_number(caller_ptr), caller_ptr, m_ptr, dest_ptr,
07093                        dest_ptr->p_messbuf);
07094                dest_ptr->p_flags &= ~RECEIVING;        /* deblock destination */
07095                if (dest_ptr->p_flags == 0) ready(dest_ptr);
07096        } else {
07097                /* Destination is not waiting.  Block and queue caller. */
07098                caller_ptr->p_messbuf = m_ptr;
07099                if (caller_ptr->p_flags == 0) unready(caller_ptr);
07100                caller_ptr->p_flags |= SENDING;
07101                caller_ptr->p_sendto= dest;
07102
07103                /* Process is now blocked.  Put in on the destination's queue. */
07104                if ( (next_ptr = dest_ptr->p_callerq) == NIL_PROC)
07105                        dest_ptr->p_callerq = caller_ptr;
07106                else {
07107                        while (next_ptr->p_sendlink != NIL_PROC)
07108                                next_ptr = next_ptr->p_sendlink;
07109                        next_ptr->p_sendlink = caller_ptr;
07110                }
07111                caller_ptr->p_sendlink = NIL_PROC;
07112        }
07113        return(OK);
07114 }
07115
07116  /*===========================================================================*
07117   *                              mini_rec                                     *
07118   *===========================================================================*/
07119 PRIVATE int mini_rec(caller_ptr, src, m_ptr)
07120 register struct proc *caller_ptr;        /* process trying to get message */
07121 int src;                                 /* which message source is wanted (or ANY) */
07122 message *m_ptr;                          /* pointer to message buffer */
07123 {
07124 /* A process or task wants to get a message.  If one is already queued,
07125  * acquire it and deblock the sender.  If no message from the desired source
07126  * is available, block the caller.  No need to check parameters for validity.
07127  * Users calls are always sendrec(), and mini_send() has checked already.
07128  * Calls from the tasks, MM, and FS are trusted.
07129  */
07130
07131   register struct proc *sender_ptr;
07132   register struct proc *previous_ptr;
07133
07134        /* Check to see if a message from desired source is already available. */
```

```
07135          if (!(caller_ptr->p_flags & SENDING)) {
07136                  /* Check caller queue. */
07137            for (sender_ptr = caller_ptr->p_callerq; sender_ptr != NIL_PROC;
07138                  previous_ptr = sender_ptr, sender_ptr = sender_ptr->p_sendlink) {
07139                  if (src == ANY || src == proc_number(sender_ptr)) {
07140                          /* An acceptable message has been found. */
07141                          CopyMess(proc_number(sender_ptr), sender_ptr,
07142                                  sender_ptr->p_messbuf, caller_ptr, m_ptr);
07143                          if (sender_ptr == caller_ptr->p_callerq)
07144                                  caller_ptr->p_callerq = sender_ptr->p_sendlink;
07145                          else
07146                                  previous_ptr->p_sendlink = sender_ptr->p_sendlink;
07147                          if ((sender_ptr->p_flags &= ~SENDING) == 0)
07148                                  ready(sender_ptr);     /* deblock sender */
07149                          return(OK);
07150                  }
07151            }
07152
07153            /* Check for blocked interrupt. */
07154            if (caller_ptr->p_int_blocked && isrxhardware(src)) {
07155                  m_ptr->m_source = HARDWARE;
07156                  m_ptr->m_type = HARD_INT;
07157                  caller_ptr->p_int_blocked = FALSE;
07158                  return(OK);
07159            }
07160          }
07161
07162          /* No suitable message is available.  Block the process trying to receive. */
07163          caller_ptr->p_getfrom = src;
07164          caller_ptr->p_messbuf = m_ptr;
07165          if (caller_ptr->p_flags == 0) unready(caller_ptr);
07166          caller_ptr->p_flags |= RECEIVING;
07167
07168          /* If MM has just blocked and there are kernel signals pending, now is the
07169           * time to tell MM about them, since it will be able to accept the message.
07170           */
07171          if (sig_procs > 0 && proc_number(caller_ptr) == MM_PROC_NR && src == ANY)
07172                  inform();
07173          return(OK);
07174  }

07176  /*===========================================================================*
07177   *                              pick_proc                                    *
07178   *===========================================================================*/
07179  PRIVATE void pick_proc()
07180  {
07181  /* Decide who to run now.  A new process is selected by setting 'proc_ptr'.
07182   * When a fresh user (or idle) process is selected, record it in 'bill_ptr',
07183   * so the clock task can tell who to bill for system time.
07184   */
07185
07186    register struct proc *rp;     /* process to run */
07187
07188    if ( (rp = rdy_head[TASK_Q]) != NIL_PROC) {
07189          proc_ptr = rp;
07190          return;
07191    }
07192    if ( (rp = rdy_head[SERVER_Q]) != NIL_PROC) {
07193          proc_ptr = rp;
07194          return;
```

```
07195        }
07196        if ( (rp = rdy_head[USER_Q]) != NIL_PROC) {
07197                proc_ptr = rp;
07198                bill_ptr = rp;
07199                return;
07200        }
07201    /* No one is ready.  Run the idle task.  The idle task might be made an
07202     * always-ready user task to avoid this special case.
07203     */
07204    bill_ptr = proc_ptr = proc_addr(IDLE);
07205    }


07207    /*===========================================================================*
07208     *                              ready                                        *
07209     *===========================================================================*/
07210    PRIVATE void ready(rp)
07211    register struct proc *rp;        /* this process is now runnable */
07212    {
07213    /* Add 'rp' to the end of one of the queues of runnable processes. Three
07214     * queues are maintained:
07215     *    TASK_Q   - (highest priority) for runnable tasks
07216     *    SERVER_Q - (middle priority) for MM and FS only
07217     *    USER_Q   - (lowest priority) for user processes
07218     */
07219
07220      if (istaskp(rp)) {
07221            if (rdy_head[TASK_Q] != NIL_PROC)
07222                    /* Add to tail of nonempty queue. */
07223                    rdy_tail[TASK_Q]->p_nextready = rp;
07224            else {
07225                    proc_ptr =                  /* run fresh task next */
07226                    rdy_head[TASK_Q] = rp;  /* add to empty queue */
07227            }
07228            rdy_tail[TASK_Q] = rp;
07229            rp->p_nextready = NIL_PROC;        /* new entry has no successor */
07230            return;
07231      }
07232      if (!isuserp(rp)) {             /* others are similar */
07233            if (rdy_head[SERVER_Q] != NIL_PROC)
07234                    rdy_tail[SERVER_Q]->p_nextready = rp;
07235            else
07236                    rdy_head[SERVER_Q] = rp;
07237            rdy_tail[SERVER_Q] = rp;
07238            rp->p_nextready = NIL_PROC;
07239            return;
07240      }
07241      if (rdy_head[USER_Q] == NIL_PROC)
07242            rdy_tail[USER_Q] = rp;
07243      rp->p_nextready = rdy_head[USER_Q];
07244      rdy_head[USER_Q] = rp;
07245    /*
07246      if (rdy_head[USER_Q] != NIL_PROC)
07247            rdy_tail[USER_Q]->p_nextready = rp;
07248      else
07249            rdy_head[USER_Q] = rp;
07250      rdy_tail[USER_Q] = rp;
07251      rp->p_nextready = NIL_PROC;
07252    */
07253    }
```

```
07255   /*===========================================================================*
07256    *                              unready                                       *
07257    *===========================================================================*/
07258   PRIVATE void unready(rp)
07259   register struct proc *rp;          /* this process is no longer runnable */
07260   {
07261   /* A process has blocked. */
07262
07263     register struct proc *xp;
07264     register struct proc **qtail;   /* TASK_Q, SERVER_Q, or USER_Q rdy_tail */
07265
07266     if (istaskp(rp)) {
07267           /* task stack still ok? */
07268           if (*rp->p_stguard != STACK_GUARD)
07269                 panic("stack overrun by task", proc_number(rp));
07270
07271           if ( (xp = rdy_head[TASK_Q]) == NIL_PROC) return;
07272           if (xp == rp) {
07273                 /* Remove head of queue */
07274                 rdy_head[TASK_Q] = xp->p_nextready;
07275                 if (rp == proc_ptr) pick_proc();
07276                 return;
07277           }
07278           qtail = &rdy_tail[TASK_Q];
07279     }
07280     else if (!isuserp(rp)) {
07281           if ( (xp = rdy_head[SERVER_Q]) == NIL_PROC) return;
07282           if (xp == rp) {
07283                 rdy_head[SERVER_Q] = xp->p_nextready;
07284                 pick_proc();
07285                 return;
07286           }
07287           qtail = &rdy_tail[SERVER_Q];
07288     } else
07289     {
07290           if ( (xp = rdy_head[USER_Q]) == NIL_PROC) return;
07291           if (xp == rp) {
07292                 rdy_head[USER_Q] = xp->p_nextready;
07293                 pick_proc();
07294                 return;
07295           }
07296           qtail = &rdy_tail[USER_Q];
07297     }
07298
07299     /* Search body of queue.  A process can be made unready even if it is
07300      * not running by being sent a signal that kills it.
07301      */
07302     while (xp->p_nextready != rp)
07303           if ( (xp = xp->p_nextready) == NIL_PROC) return;
07304     xp->p_nextready = xp->p_nextready->p_nextready;
07305     if (*qtail == rp) *qtail = xp;
07306   }

07308   /*===========================================================================*
07309    *                              sched                                         *
07310    *===========================================================================*/
07311   PRIVATE void sched()
07312   {
07313   /* The current process has run too long.  If another low priority (user)
07314    * process is runnable, put the current process on the end of the user queue,
```

```
07315        * possibly promoting another user to head of the queue.
07316        */
07317
07318       if (rdy_head[USER_Q] == NIL_PROC) return;
07319
07320       /* One or more user processes queued. */
07321       rdy_tail[USER_Q]->p_nextready = rdy_head[USER_Q];
07322       rdy_tail[USER_Q] = rdy_head[USER_Q];
07323       rdy_head[USER_Q] = rdy_head[USER_Q]->p_nextready;
07324       rdy_tail[USER_Q]->p_nextready = NIL_PROC;
07325       pick_proc();
07326     }


07328     /*===========================================================================*
07329      *                              lock_mini_send                               *
07330      *===========================================================================*/
07331     PUBLIC int lock_mini_send(caller_ptr, dest, m_ptr)
07332     struct proc *caller_ptr;        /* who is trying to send a message? */
07333     int dest;                       /* to whom is message being sent? */
07334     message *m_ptr;                 /* pointer to message buffer */
07335     {
07336     /* Safe gateway to mini_send() for tasks. */
07337
07338       int result;
07339
07340       switching = TRUE;
07341       result = mini_send(caller_ptr, dest, m_ptr);
07342       switching = FALSE;
07343       return(result);
07344     }


07346     /*===========================================================================*
07347      *                              lock_pick_proc                                *
07348      *===========================================================================*/
07349     PUBLIC void lock_pick_proc()
07350     {
07351     /* Safe gateway to pick_proc() for tasks. */
07352
07353       switching = TRUE;
07354       pick_proc();
07355       switching = FALSE;
07356     }


07358     /*===========================================================================*
07359      *                              lock_ready                                    *
07360      *===========================================================================*/
07361     PUBLIC void lock_ready(rp)
07362     struct proc *rp;                /* this process is now runnable */
07363     {
07364     /* Safe gateway to ready() for tasks. */
07365
07366       switching = TRUE;
07367       ready(rp);
07368       switching = FALSE;
07369     }


07372     /*===========================================================================*
07373      *                              lock_unready                                  *
07374      *===========================================================================*/
```

```
07375   PUBLIC void lock_unready(rp)
07376   struct proc *rp;                /* this process is no longer runnable */
07377   {
07378   /* Safe gateway to unready() for tasks. */
07379
07380     switching = TRUE;
07381     unready(rp);
07382     switching = FALSE;
07383   }

07385   /*===========================================================================*
07386    *                              lock_sched                                   *
07387    *===========================================================================*/
07388   PUBLIC void lock_sched()
07389   {
07390   /* Safe gateway to sched() for tasks. */
07391
07392     switching = TRUE;
07393     sched();
07394     switching = FALSE;
07395   }

07397   /*===========================================================================*
07398    *                              unhold                                       *
07399    *===========================================================================*/
07400   PUBLIC void unhold()
07401   {
07402   /* Flush any held-up interrupts.  k_reenter must be 0.  held_head must not
07403    * be NIL_PROC.  Interrupts must be disabled.  They will be enabled but will
07404    * be disabled when this returns.
07405    */
07406
07407     register struct proc *rp;     /* current head of held queue */
07408
07409     if (switching) return;
07410     rp = held_head;
07411     do {
07412           if ( (held_head = rp->p_nextheld) == NIL_PROC) held_tail = NIL_PROC;
07413           rp->p_int_held = FALSE;
07414           unlock();                 /* reduce latency; held queue may change! */
07415           interrupt(proc_number(rp));
07416           lock();                   /* protect the held queue again */
07417     }
07418     while ( (rp = held_head) != NIL_PROC);
07419   }
```

```
++++++++++++++++++++++++++++++++++++++++++++++++++++++++++++++++++++++++++++++++
                              src/kernel/exception.c
++++++++++++++++++++++++++++++++++++++++++++++++++++++++++++++++++++++++++++++++
07500   /* This file contains a simple exception handler.  Exceptions in user
07501    * processes are converted to signals.  Exceptions in the kernel, MM and
07502    * FS cause a panic.
07503    */
07504
07505   #include "kernel.h"
07506   #include <signal.h>
07507   #include "proc.h"
07508
07509   /*===========================================================================*
07510    *                              exception                                     *
07511    *===========================================================================*/
07512   PUBLIC void exception(vec_nr)
07513   unsigned vec_nr;
07514   {
07515   /* An exception or unexpected interrupt has occurred. */
07516
07517     struct ex_s {
07518           char *msg;
07519           int signum;
07520           int minprocessor;
07521     };
07522     static struct ex_s ex_data[] = {
07523           "Divide error", SIGFPE, 86,
07524           "Debug exception", SIGTRAP, 86,
07525           "Nonmaskable interrupt", SIGBUS, 86,
07526           "Breakpoint", SIGEMT, 86,
07527           "Overflow", SIGFPE, 86,
07528           "Bounds check", SIGFPE, 186,
07529           "Invalid opcode", SIGILL, 186,
07530           "Coprocessor not available", SIGFPE, 186,
07531           "Double fault", SIGBUS, 286,
07532           "Copressor segment overrun", SIGSEGV, 286,
07533           "Invalid TSS", SIGSEGV, 286,
07534           "Segment not present", SIGSEGV, 286,
07535           "Stack exception", SIGSEGV, 286,          /* STACK_FAULT already used */
07536           "General protection", SIGSEGV, 286,
07537           "Page fault", SIGSEGV, 386,               /* not close */
07538           NIL_PTR, SIGILL, 0,                       /* probably software trap */
07539           "Coprocessor error", SIGFPE, 386,
07540     };
07541     register struct ex_s *ep;
07542     struct proc *saved_proc;
07543
07544     saved_proc= proc_ptr; /* Save proc_ptr, because it may be changed by debug
07545                            * statements.
07546                            */
07547
07548     ep = &ex_data[vec_nr];
07549
07550     if (vec_nr == 2) {             /* spurious NMI on some machines */
07551           printf("got spurious NMI\n");
07552           return;
07553     }
07554
```

```
07555          if (k_reenter == 0 && isuserp(saved_proc)) {
07556                  unlock();                /* this is protected like sys_call() */
07557                  cause_sig(proc_number(saved_proc), ep->signum);
07558                  return;
07559          }
07560
07561          /* This is not supposed to happen. */
07562          if (ep->msg == NIL_PTR || processor < ep->minprocessor)
07563                  printf("\nIntel-reserved exception %d\n", vec_nr);
07564          else
07565                  printf("\n%s\n", ep->msg);
07566          printf("process number %d, pc = 0x%04x:0x%08x\n",
07567                  proc_number(saved_proc),
07568                  (unsigned) saved_proc->p_reg.cs,
07569                  (unsigned) saved_proc->p_reg.pc);
07570          panic("exception in system code", NO_NUM);
07571  }
```

```
++++++++++++++++++++++++++++++++++++++++++++++++++++++++++++++++++++++++++++++++++
                               src/kernel/i8259.c
++++++++++++++++++++++++++++++++++++++++++++++++++++++++++++++++++++++++++++++++++
```

```
07600  /* This file contains routines for initializing the 8259 interrupt controller:
07601   *        get_irq_handler: address of handler for a given interrupt
07602   *        put_irq_handler: register an interrupt handler
07603   *        intr_init:       initialize the interrupt controller(s)
07604   */
07605
07606  #include "kernel.h"
07607
07608  #define ICW1_AT          0x11    /* edge triggered, cascade, need ICW4 */
07609  #define ICW1_PC          0x13    /* edge triggered, no cascade, need ICW4 */
07610  #define ICW1_PS          0x19    /* level triggered, cascade, need ICW4 */
07611  #define ICW4_AT          0x01    /* not SFNM, not buffered, normal EOI, 8086 */
07612  #define ICW4_PC          0x09    /* not SFNM, buffered, normal EOI, 8086 */
07613
07614  FORWARD _PROTOTYPE( int spurious_irq, (int irq) );
07615
07616  #define set_vec(nr, addr)        ((void)0) /* kluge for protected mode */
07617
07618  /*===========================================================================*
07619   *                              intr_init                                    *
07620   *===========================================================================*/
07621  PUBLIC void intr_init(mine)
07622  int mine;
07623  {
07624  /* Initialize the 8259s, finishing with all interrupts disabled.  This is
07625   * only done in protected mode, in real mode we don't touch the 8259s, but
07626   * use the BIOS locations instead.  The flag "mine" is set if the 8259s are
07627   * to be programmed for Minix, or to be reset to what the BIOS expects.
07628   */
07629
07630    int i;
07631
07632    lock();
07633    /* The AT and newer PS/2 have two interrupt controllers, one master,
07634     * one slaved at IRQ 2.  (We don't have to deal with the PC that
```

```
07635          * has just one controller, because it must run in real mode.)
07636          */
07637          out_byte(INT_CTL, ps_mca ? ICW1_PS : ICW1_AT);
07638          out_byte(INT_CTLMASK, mine ? IRQ0_VECTOR : BIOS_IRQ0_VEC);
07639                                                /* ICW2 for master */
07640          out_byte(INT_CTLMASK, (1 << CASCADE_IRQ));   /* ICW3 tells slaves */
07641          out_byte(INT_CTLMASK, ICW4_AT);
07642          out_byte(INT_CTLMASK, ~(1 << CASCADE_IRQ));   /* IRQ 0-7 mask */
07643          out_byte(INT2_CTL, ps_mca ? ICW1_PS : ICW1_AT);
07644          out_byte(INT2_CTLMASK, mine ? IRQ8_VECTOR : BIOS_IRQ8_VEC);
07645                                                /* ICW2 for slave */
07646          out_byte(INT2_CTLMASK, CASCADE_IRQ);          /* ICW3 is slave nr */
07647          out_byte(INT2_CTLMASK, ICW4_AT);
07648          out_byte(INT2_CTLMASK, ~0);                   /* IRQ 8-15 mask */
07649
07650          /* Initialize the table of interrupt handlers. */
07651          for (i = 0; i < NR_IRQ_VECTORS; i++) irq_table[i] = spurious_irq;
07652     }


07654     /*========================================================================*
07655      *                              spurious_irq                              *
07656      *========================================================================*/
07657     PRIVATE int spurious_irq(irq)
07658     int irq;
07659     {
07660     /* Default interrupt handler.  It complains a lot. */
07661
07662          if (irq < 0 || irq >= NR_IRQ_VECTORS)
07663               panic("invalid call to spurious_irq", irq);
07664
07665          printf("spurious irq %d\n", irq);
07666
07667          return 1;      /* Reenable interrupt */
07668     }


07670     /*========================================================================*
07671      *                              put_irq_handler                           *
07672      *========================================================================*/
07673     PUBLIC void put_irq_handler(irq, handler)
07674     int irq;
07675     irq_handler_t handler;
07676     {
07677     /* Register an interrupt handler. */
07678
07679          if (irq < 0 || irq >= NR_IRQ_VECTORS)
07680               panic("invalid call to put_irq_handler", irq);
07681
07682          if (irq_table[irq] == handler)
07683               return;         /* extra initialization */
07684
07685          if (irq_table[irq] != spurious_irq)
07686               panic("attempt to register second irq handler for irq", irq);
07687
07688          disable_irq(irq);
07689          if (!protected_mode) set_vec(BIOS_VECTOR(irq), irq_vec[irq]);
07690          irq_table[irq]= handler;
07691          irq_use |= 1 << irq;
07692     }
```

```
++++++++++++++++++++++++++++++++++++++++++++++++++++++++++++++++++++++++++++++++
                                src/kernel/protect.c
++++++++++++++++++++++++++++++++++++++++++++++++++++++++++++++++++++++++++++++++
07700   /* This file contains code for initialization of protected mode, to initialize
07701    * code and data segment descriptors, and to initialize global descriptors
07702    * for local descriptors in the process table.
07703    */
07704
07705   #include "kernel.h"
07706   #include "proc.h"
07707   #include "protect.h"
07708
07709   #define INT_GATE_TYPE   (INT_286_GATE | DESC_386_BIT)
07710   #define TSS_TYPE        (AVL_286_TSS  | DESC_386_BIT)
07711
07712   struct desctableptr_s {
07713     char limit[sizeof(u16_t)];
07714     char base[sizeof(u32_t)];              /* really u24_t + pad for 286 */
07715   };
07716
07717   struct gatedesc_s {
07718     u16_t offset_low;
07719     u16_t selector;
07720     u8_t pad;                              /* |000|XXXXX| ig & trpg, |XXXXXXXX| task g */
07721     u8_t p_dpl_type;                       /* |P|DL|0|TYPE| */
07722     u16_t offset_high;
07723   };
07724
07725   struct tss_s {
07726     reg_t backlink;
07727     reg_t sp0;                             /* stack pointer to use during interrupt */
07728     reg_t ss0;                             /*  "   segment  "   "       "      " */
07729     reg_t sp1;
07730     reg_t ss1;
07731     reg_t sp2;
07732     reg_t ss2;
07733     reg_t cr3;
07734     reg_t ip;
07735     reg_t flags;
07736     reg_t ax;
07737     reg_t cx;
07738     reg_t dx;
07739     reg_t bx;
07740     reg_t sp;
07741     reg_t bp;
07742     reg_t si;
07743     reg_t di;
07744     reg_t es;
07745     reg_t cs;
07746     reg_t ss;
07747     reg_t ds;
07748     reg_t fs;
07749     reg_t gs;
07750     reg_t ldt;
07751     u16_t trap;
07752     u16_t iobase;
07753   };
07754
```

```
07755    PUBLIC struct segdesc_s gdt[GDT_SIZE];
07756    PRIVATE struct gatedesc_s idt[IDT_SIZE];          /* zero-init so none present */
07757    PUBLIC struct tss_s tss;          /* zero init */
07758
07759    FORWARD _PROTOTYPE( void int_gate, (unsigned vec_nr, phys_bytes base,
07760                        unsigned dpl_type) );
07761    FORWARD _PROTOTYPE( void sdesc, (struct segdesc_s *segdp, phys_bytes base,
07762                        phys_bytes size) );
07763
07764    /*=======================================================================*
07765     *                              prot_init                                *
07766     *=======================================================================*/
07767    PUBLIC void prot_init()
07768    {
07769    /* Set up tables for protected mode.
07770     * All GDT slots are allocated at compile time.
07771     */
07772
07773      phys_bytes code_bytes;
07774      phys_bytes data_bytes;
07775      struct gate_table_s *gtp;
07776      struct desctableptr_s *dtp;
07777      unsigned ldt_selector;
07778      register struct proc *rp;
07779
07780      static struct gate_table_s {
07781            _PROTOTYPE( void (*gate), (void) );
07782            unsigned char vec_nr;
07783            unsigned char privilege;
07784      }
07785      gate_table[] = {
07786            divide_error, DIVIDE_VECTOR, INTR_PRIVILEGE,
07787            single_step_exception, DEBUG_VECTOR, INTR_PRIVILEGE,
07788            nmi, NMI_VECTOR, INTR_PRIVILEGE,
07789            breakpoint_exception, BREAKPOINT_VECTOR, USER_PRIVILEGE,
07790            overflow, OVERFLOW_VECTOR, USER_PRIVILEGE,
07791            bounds_check, BOUNDS_VECTOR, INTR_PRIVILEGE,
07792            inval_opcode, INVAL_OP_VECTOR, INTR_PRIVILEGE,
07793            copr_not_available, COPROC_NOT_VECTOR, INTR_PRIVILEGE,
07794            double_fault, DOUBLE_FAULT_VECTOR, INTR_PRIVILEGE,
07795            copr_seg_overrun, COPROC_SEG_VECTOR, INTR_PRIVILEGE,
07796            inval_tss, INVAL_TSS_VECTOR, INTR_PRIVILEGE,
07797            segment_not_present, SEG_NOT_VECTOR, INTR_PRIVILEGE,
07798            stack_exception, STACK_FAULT_VECTOR, INTR_PRIVILEGE,
07799            general_protection, PROTECTION_VECTOR, INTR_PRIVILEGE,
07800            page_fault, PAGE_FAULT_VECTOR, INTR_PRIVILEGE,
07801            copr_error, COPROC_ERR_VECTOR, INTR_PRIVILEGE,
07802            { hwint00, VECTOR( 0), INTR_PRIVILEGE },
07803            { hwint01, VECTOR( 1), INTR_PRIVILEGE },
07804            { hwint02, VECTOR( 2), INTR_PRIVILEGE },
07805            { hwint03, VECTOR( 3), INTR_PRIVILEGE },
07806            { hwint04, VECTOR( 4), INTR_PRIVILEGE },
07807            { hwint05, VECTOR( 5), INTR_PRIVILEGE },
07808            { hwint06, VECTOR( 6), INTR_PRIVILEGE },
07809            { hwint07, VECTOR( 7), INTR_PRIVILEGE },
07810            { hwint08, VECTOR( 8), INTR_PRIVILEGE },
07811            { hwint09, VECTOR( 9), INTR_PRIVILEGE },
07812            { hwint10, VECTOR(10), INTR_PRIVILEGE },
07813            { hwint11, VECTOR(11), INTR_PRIVILEGE },
07814            { hwint12, VECTOR(12), INTR_PRIVILEGE },
```

```
07815                    { hwint13, VECTOR(13), INTR_PRIVILEGE },
07816                    { hwint14, VECTOR(14), INTR_PRIVILEGE },
07817                    { hwint15, VECTOR(15), INTR_PRIVILEGE },
07818            };
07819
07820            /* This is called early and can't use tables set up by main(). */
07821            data_bytes = (phys_bytes) sizes[1] << CLICK_SHIFT;
07822            if (sizes[0] == 0)
07823                    code_bytes = data_bytes;            /* common I&D */
07824            else
07825                    code_bytes = (phys_bytes) sizes[0] << CLICK_SHIFT;
07826
07827            /* Build gdt and idt pointers in GDT where the BIOS expects them. */
07828            dtp= (struct desctableptr_s *) &gdt[GDT_INDEX];
07829            * (u16_t *) dtp->limit = (sizeof gdt) - 1;
07830            * (u32_t *) dtp->base = vir2phys(gdt);
07831
07832            dtp= (struct desctableptr_s *) &gdt[IDT_INDEX];
07833            * (u16_t *) dtp->limit = (sizeof idt) - 1;
07834            * (u32_t *) dtp->base = vir2phys(idt);
07835
07836            /* Build segment descriptors for tasks and interrupt handlers. */
07837            init_codeseg(&gdt[CS_INDEX], code_base, code_bytes, INTR_PRIVILEGE);
07838            init_dataseg(&gdt[DS_INDEX], data_base, data_bytes, INTR_PRIVILEGE);
07839            init_dataseg(&gdt[ES_INDEX], 0L, 0L, TASK_PRIVILEGE);
07840
07841            /* Build scratch descriptors for functions in klib88. */
07842            init_dataseg(&gdt[DS_286_INDEX], (phys_bytes) 0,
07843                        (phys_bytes) MAX_286_SEG_SIZE, TASK_PRIVILEGE);
07844            init_dataseg(&gdt[ES_286_INDEX], (phys_bytes) 0,
07845                        (phys_bytes) MAX_286_SEG_SIZE, TASK_PRIVILEGE);
07846
07847            /* Build local descriptors in GDT for LDT's in process table.
07848             * The LDT's are allocated at compile time in the process table, and
07849             * initialized whenever a process' map is initialized or changed.
07850             */
07851            for (rp = BEG_PROC_ADDR, ldt_selector = FIRST_LDT_INDEX * DESC_SIZE;
07852                rp < END_PROC_ADDR; ++rp, ldt_selector += DESC_SIZE) {
07853                init_dataseg(&gdt[ldt_selector / DESC_SIZE], vir2phys(rp->p_ldt),
07854                            (phys_bytes) sizeof rp->p_ldt, INTR_PRIVILEGE);
07855                gdt[ldt_selector / DESC_SIZE].access = PRESENT | LDT;
07856                rp->p_ldt_sel = ldt_selector;
07857            }
07858
07859            /* Build main TSS.
07860             * This is used only to record the stack pointer to be used after an
07861             * interrupt.
07862             * The pointer is set up so that an interrupt automatically saves the
07863             * current process's registers ip:cs:f:sp:ss in the correct slots in the
07864             * process table.
07865             */
07866            tss.ss0 = DS_SELECTOR;
07867            init_dataseg(&gdt[TSS_INDEX], vir2phys(&tss), (phys_bytes) sizeof tss,
07868                                                    INTR_PRIVILEGE);
07869            gdt[TSS_INDEX].access = PRESENT | (INTR_PRIVILEGE << DPL_SHIFT) | TSS_TYPE;
07870            tss.iobase = sizeof tss;      /* empty i/o permissions map */
07871
07872            /* Build descriptors for interrupt gates in IDT. */
07873            for (gtp = &gate_table[0];
07874                gtp < &gate_table[sizeof gate_table / sizeof gate_table[0]]; ++gtp) {
```

```
07875                 int_gate(gtp->vec_nr, (phys_bytes) (vir_bytes) gtp->gate,
07876                         PRESENT | INT_GATE_TYPE | (gtp->privilege << DPL_SHIFT));
07877         }
07878         int_gate(SYS_VECTOR, (phys_bytes) (vir_bytes) p_s_call,
07879                 PRESENT | (USER_PRIVILEGE << DPL_SHIFT) | INT_GATE_TYPE);
07880         int_gate(LEVEL0_VECTOR, (phys_bytes) (vir_bytes) level0_call,
07881                 PRESENT | (TASK_PRIVILEGE << DPL_SHIFT) | INT_GATE_TYPE);
07882         int_gate(SYS386_VECTOR, (phys_bytes) (vir_bytes) s_call,
07883                 PRESENT | (USER_PRIVILEGE << DPL_SHIFT) | INT_GATE_TYPE);
07884   }

07886   /*========================================================================*
07887    *                              init_codeseg                              *
07888    *========================================================================*/
07889   PUBLIC void init_codeseg(segdp, base, size, privilege)
07890   register struct segdesc_s *segdp;
07891   phys_bytes base;
07892   phys_bytes size;
07893   int privilege;
07894   {
07895   /* Build descriptor for a code segment. */
07896
07897     sdesc(segdp, base, size);
07898     segdp->access = (privilege << DPL_SHIFT)
07899                     | (PRESENT | SEGMENT | EXECUTABLE | READABLE);
07900                     /* CONFORMING = 0, ACCESSED = 0 */
07901   }

07903   /*========================================================================*
07904    *                              init_dataseg                              *
07905    *========================================================================*/
07906   PUBLIC void init_dataseg(segdp, base, size, privilege)
07907   register struct segdesc_s *segdp;
07908   phys_bytes base;
07909   phys_bytes size;
07910   int privilege;
07911   {
07912   /* Build descriptor for a data segment. */
07913
07914     sdesc(segdp, base, size);
07915     segdp->access = (privilege << DPL_SHIFT) | (PRESENT | SEGMENT | WRITEABLE);
07916                     /* EXECUTABLE = 0, EXPAND_DOWN = 0, ACCESSED = 0 */
07917   }

07919   /*========================================================================*
07920    *                                sdesc                                   *
07921    *========================================================================*/
07922   PRIVATE void sdesc(segdp, base, size)
07923   register struct segdesc_s *segdp;
07924   phys_bytes base;
07925   phys_bytes size;
07926   {
07927   /* Fill in the size fields (base, limit and granularity) of a descriptor. */
07928
07929     segdp->base_low = base;
07930     segdp->base_middle = base >> BASE_MIDDLE_SHIFT;
07931     segdp->base_high = base >> BASE_HIGH_SHIFT;
07932     --size;                         /* convert to a limit, 0 size means 4G */
07933     if (size > BYTE_GRAN_MAX) {
07934         segdp->limit_low = size >> PAGE_GRAN_SHIFT;
```

```
07935              segdp->granularity = GRANULAR | (size >>
07936                                  (PAGE_GRAN_SHIFT + GRANULARITY_SHIFT));
07937      } else {
07938              segdp->limit_low = size;
07939              segdp->granularity = size >> GRANULARITY_SHIFT;
07940      }
07941      segdp->granularity |= DEFAULT;          /* means BIG for data seg */
07942  }

07944  /*===========================================================================*
07945   *                              seg2phys                                     *
07946   *===========================================================================*/
07947  PUBLIC phys_bytes seg2phys(seg)
07948  U16_t seg;
07949  {
07950  /* Return the base address of a segment, with seg being either a 8086 segment
07951   * register, or a 286/386 segment selector.
07952   */
07953      phys_bytes base;
07954      struct segdesc_s *segdp;
07955
07956      if (!protected_mode) {
07957              base = hclick_to_physb(seg);
07958      } else {
07959              segdp = &gdt[seg >> 3];
07960              base = segdp->base_low | ((u32_t) segdp->base_middle << 16);
07961              base |= ((u32_t) segdp->base_high << 24);
07962      }
07963      return base;
07964  }

07966  /*===========================================================================*
07967   *                              int_gate                                     *
07968   *===========================================================================*/
07969  PRIVATE void int_gate(vec_nr, base, dpl_type)
07970  unsigned vec_nr;
07971  phys_bytes base;
07972  unsigned dpl_type;
07973  {
07974  /* Build descriptor for an interrupt gate. */
07975
07976      register struct gatedesc_s *idp;
07977
07978      idp = &idt[vec_nr];
07979      idp->offset_low = base;
07980      idp->selector = CS_SELECTOR;
07981      idp->p_dpl_type = dpl_type;
07982      idp->offset_high = base >> OFFSET_HIGH_SHIFT;
07983  }

07985  /*===========================================================================*
07986   *                              enable_iop                                   *
07987   *===========================================================================*/
07988  PUBLIC void enable_iop(pp)
07989  struct proc *pp;
07990  {
07991  /* Allow a user process to use I/O instructions.  Change the I/O Permission
07992   * Level bits in the psw. These specify least-privileged Current Permission
07993   * Level allowed to execute I/O instructions. Users and servers have CPL 3.
07994   * You can't have less privilege than that. Kernel has CPL 0, tasks CPL 1.
```

```
07995      */
07996        pp->p_reg.psw |= 0x3000;
07997      }
```

```
++++++++++++++++++++++++++++++++++++++++++++++++++++++++++++++++++++++++++++++++
                              src/kernel/klib.s
++++++++++++++++++++++++++++++++++++++++++++++++++++++++++++++++++++++++++++++++
```

```
08000      #
08001      ! Chooses between the 8086 and 386 versions of the low level kernel code.
08002
08003      #include <minix/config.h>
08004      #if _WORD_SIZE == 2
08005      #include "klib88.s"
08006      #else
08007      #include "klib386.s"
08008      #endif
```

```
++++++++++++++++++++++++++++++++++++++++++++++++++++++++++++++++++++++++++++++++
                             src/kernel/klib386.s
++++++++++++++++++++++++++++++++++++++++++++++++++++++++++++++++++++++++++++++++
```

```
08100      #
08101      ! sections
08102
08103      .sect .text; .sect .rom; .sect .data; .sect .bss
08104
08105      #include <minix/config.h>
08106      #include <minix/const.h>
08107      #include "const.h"
08108      #include "sconst.h"
08109      #include "protect.h"
08110
08111      ! This file contains a number of assembly code utility routines needed by the
08112      ! kernel.  They are:
08113
08114      .define _monitor          ! exit Minix and return to the monitor
08115      .define _check_mem        ! check a block of memory, return the valid size
08116      .define _cp_mess          ! copies messages from source to destination
08117      .define _exit             ! dummy for library routines
08118      .define __exit            ! dummy for library routines
08119      .define ___exit           ! dummy for library routines
08120      .define ___main           ! dummy for GCC
08121      .define _in_byte          ! read a byte from a port and return it
08122      .define _in_word          ! read a word from a port and return it
08123      .define _out_byte         ! write a byte to a port
08124      .define _out_word         ! write a word to a port
08125      .define _port_read        ! transfer data from (disk controller) port to memory
08126      .define _port_read_byte   ! likewise byte by byte
08127      .define _port_write       ! transfer data from memory to (disk controller) port
08128      .define _port_write_byte  ! likewise byte by byte
08129      .define _lock             ! disable interrupts
08130      .define _unlock           ! enable interrupts
08131      .define _enable_irq       ! enable an irq at the 8259 controller
08132      .define _disable_irq      ! disable an irq
08133      .define _phys_copy        ! copy data from anywhere to anywhere in memory
08134      .define _mem_rdw          ! copy one word from [segment:offset]
```

```
08135   .define _reset            ! reset the system
08136   .define _mem_vid_copy     ! copy data to video ram
08137   .define _vid_vid_copy     ! move data in video ram
08138   .define _level0           ! call a function at level 0
08139
08140   ! The routines only guarantee to preserve the registers the C compiler
08141   ! expects to be preserved (ebx, esi, edi, ebp, esp, segment registers, and
08142   ! direction bit in the flags).
08143
08144   ! imported variables
08145
08146   .sect .bss
08147   .extern _mon_return, _mon_sp
08148   .extern _irq_use
08149   .extern _blank_color
08150   .extern _ext_memsize
08151   .extern _gdt
08152   .extern _low_memsize
08153   .extern _sizes
08154   .extern _vid_seg
08155   .extern _vid_size
08156   .extern _vid_mask
08157   .extern _level0_func
08158
08159   .sect .text
08160   !*===========================================================================*
08161   !*                              monitor                                      *
08162   !*===========================================================================*
08163   ! PUBLIC void monitor();
08164   ! Return to the monitor.
08165
08166   _monitor:
08167           mov     eax, (_reboot_code)        ! address of new parameters
08168           mov     esp, (_mon_sp)             ! restore monitor stack pointer
08169       o16 mov     dx, SS_SELECTOR            ! monitor data segment
08170           mov     ds, dx
08171           mov     es, dx
08172           mov     fs, dx
08173           mov     gs, dx
08174           mov     ss, dx
08175           pop     edi
08176           pop     esi
08177           pop     ebp
08178       o16 retf                               ! return to the monitor
08179
08180
08181   !*===========================================================================*
08182   !*                              check_mem                                     *
08183   !*===========================================================================*
08184   ! PUBLIC phys_bytes check_mem(phys_bytes base, phys_bytes size);
08185   ! Check a block of memory, return the amount valid.
08186   ! Only every 16th byte is checked.
08187   ! An initial size of 0 means everything.
08188   ! This really should do some alias checks.
08189
08190   CM_DENSITY       =      16
08191   CM_LOG_DENSITY   =      4
08192   TEST1PATTERN     =      0x55        ! memory test pattern 1
08193   TEST2PATTERN     =      0xAA        ! memory test pattern 2
08194
```

```
08195    CHKM_ARGS        =          4 + 4 + 4        ! 4 + 4
08196    !                           ds ebx eip       base size
08197
08198    _check_mem:
08199            push     ebx
08200            push     ds
08201    o16 mov          ax, FLAT_DS_SELECTOR
08202            mov      ds, ax
08203            mov      eax, CHKM_ARGS(esp)
08204            mov      ebx, eax
08205            mov      ecx, CHKM_ARGS+4(esp)
08206            shr      ecx, CM_LOG_DENSITY
08207    cm_loop:
08208            movb     dl, TEST1PATTERN
08209            xchgb    dl, (eax)                    ! write test pattern, remember original
08210            xchgb    dl, (eax)                    ! restore original, read test pattern
08211            cmpb     dl, TEST1PATTERN             ! must agree if good real memory
08212            jnz      cm_exit                      ! if different, memory is unusable
08213            movb     dl, TEST2PATTERN
08214            xchgb    dl, (eax)
08215            xchgb    dl, (eax)
08216            add      eax, CM_DENSITY
08217            cmpb     dl, TEST2PATTERN
08218            loopz    cm_loop
08219    cm_exit:
08220            sub      eax, ebx
08221            pop      ds
08222            pop      ebx
08223            ret
08224
08225
08226    !*=======================================================================*
08227    !*                              cp_mess                                  *
08228    !*=======================================================================*
08229    ! PUBLIC void cp_mess(int src, phys_clicks src_clicks, vir_bytes src_offset,
08230    !                     phys_clicks dst_clicks, vir_bytes dst_offset);
08231    ! This routine makes a fast copy of a message from anywhere in the address
08232    ! space to anywhere else.  It also copies the source address provided as a
08233    ! parameter to the call into the first word of the destination message.
08234    !
08235    ! Note that the message size, "Msize" is in DWORDS (not bytes) and must be set
08236    ! correctly.  Changing the definition of message in the type file and not
08237    ! changing it here will lead to total disaster.
08238
08239    CM_ARGS =        4 + 4 + 4 + 4 + 4        ! 4 + 4 + 4 + 4 + 4
08240    !                es  ds edi esi eip       proc scl sof dcl dof
08241
08242            .align   16
08243    _cp_mess:
08244            cld
08245            push     esi
08246            push     edi
08247            push     ds
08248            push     es
08249
08250            mov      eax, FLAT_DS_SELECTOR
08251            mov      ds, ax
08252            mov      es, ax
08253
08254            mov      esi, CM_ARGS+4(esp)          ! src clicks
```

```
08255          shl     esi, CLICK_SHIFT
08256          add     esi, CM_ARGS+4+4(esp)              ! src offset
08257          mov     edi, CM_ARGS+4+4+4(esp)            ! dst clicks
08258          shl     edi, CLICK_SHIFT
08259          add     edi, CM_ARGS+4+4+4+4(esp)          ! dst offset
08260
08261          mov     eax, CM_ARGS(esp)         ! process number of sender
08262          stos                             ! copy number of sender to dest message
08263          add     esi, 4                   ! do not copy first word
08264          mov     ecx, Msize - 1           ! remember, first word does not count
08265          rep
08266          movs                             ! copy the message
08267
08268          pop     es
08269          pop     ds
08270          pop     edi
08271          pop     esi
08272          ret                              ! that is all folks!
08273
08274
08275   !*===========================================================================*
08276   !*                              exit                                         *
08277   !*===========================================================================*
08278   ! PUBLIC void exit();
08279   ! Some library routines use exit, so provide a dummy version.
08280   ! Actual calls to exit cannot occur in the kernel.
08281   ! GNU CC likes to call ___main from main() for nonobvious reasons.
08282
08283   _exit:
08284   __exit:
08285   ___exit:
08286          sti
08287          jmp     ___exit
08288
08289   ___main:
08290          ret
08291
08292
08293   !*===========================================================================*
08294   !*                              in_byte                                      *
08295   !*===========================================================================*
08296   ! PUBLIC unsigned in_byte(port_t port);
08297   ! Read an (unsigned) byte from the i/o port  port  and return it.
08298
08299          .align  16
08300   _in_byte:
08301          mov     edx, 4(esp)              ! port
08302          sub     eax, eax
08303          inb     dx                       ! read 1 byte
08304          ret
08305
08306
08307   !*===========================================================================*
08308   !*                              in_word                                      *
08309   !*===========================================================================*
08310   ! PUBLIC unsigned in_word(port_t port);
08311   ! Read an (unsigned) word from the i/o port  port  and return it.
08312
08313          .align  16
08314   _in_word:
```

```
08315            mov      edx, 4(esp)                 ! port
08316            sub      eax, eax
08317     o16 in          dx                          ! read 1 word
08318            ret
08319
08320
08321     !*===========================================================================*
08322     !*                              out_byte                                     *
08323     !*===========================================================================*
08324     ! PUBLIC void out_byte(port_t port, u8_t value);
08325     ! Write  value  (cast to a byte)  to the I/O port  port.
08326
08327            .align   16
08328     _out_byte:
08329            mov      edx, 4(esp)                 ! port
08330            movb     al, 4+4(esp)                ! value
08331            outb     dx                          ! output 1 byte
08332            ret
08333
08334
08335     !*===========================================================================*
08336     !*                              out_word                                     *
08337     !*===========================================================================*
08338     ! PUBLIC void out_word(Port_t port, U16_t value);
08339     ! Write  value  (cast to a word)  to the I/O port  port.
08340
08341            .align   16
08342     _out_word:
08343            mov      edx, 4(esp)                 ! port
08344            mov      eax, 4+4(esp)               ! value
08345     o16 out         dx                          ! output 1 word
08346            ret
08347
08348
08349     !*===========================================================================*
08350     !*                              port_read                                    *
08351     !*===========================================================================*
08352     ! PUBLIC void port_read(port_t port, phys_bytes destination, unsigned bytcount);
08353     ! Transfer data from (hard disk controller) port to memory.
08354
08355     PR_ARGS =       4 + 4 + 4                   ! 4 + 4 + 4
08356     !               es edi eip                  port dst len
08357
08358            .align   16
08359     _port_read:
08360            cld
08361            push     edi
08362            push     es
08363            mov      ecx, FLAT_DS_SELECTOR
08364            mov      es, cx
08365            mov      edx, PR_ARGS(esp)           ! port to read from
08366            mov      edi, PR_ARGS+4(esp)         ! destination addr
08367            mov      ecx, PR_ARGS+4+4(esp)       ! byte count
08368            shr      ecx, 1                      ! word count
08369            rep                                  ! (hardware cannot handle dwords)
08370     o16 ins                                     ! read everything
08371            pop      es
08372            pop      edi
08373            ret
08374
```

```
08375
08376   !*===========================================================================*
08377   !*                              port_read_byte                               *
08378   !*===========================================================================*
08379   ! PUBLIC void port_read_byte(port_t port, phys_bytes destination,
08380   !                                               unsigned bytcount);
08381   ! Transfer data from port to memory.
08382
08383   PR_ARGS_B =     4 + 4 + 4                   ! 4 + 4 + 4
08384   !               es edi eip                  port dst len
08385
08386   _port_read_byte:
08387           cld
08388           push    edi
08389           push    es
08390           mov     ecx, FLAT_DS_SELECTOR
08391           mov     es, cx
08392           mov     edx, PR_ARGS_B(esp)
08393           mov     edi, PR_ARGS_B+4(esp)
08394           mov     ecx, PR_ARGS_B+4+4(esp)
08395           rep
08396           insb
08397           pop     es
08398           pop     edi
08399           ret
08400
08401
08402   !*===========================================================================*
08403   !*                              port_write                                   *
08404   !*===========================================================================*
08405   ! PUBLIC void port_write(port_t port, phys_bytes source, unsigned bytcount);
08406   ! Transfer data from memory to (hard disk controller) port.
08407
08408   PW_ARGS =       4 + 4 + 4                   ! 4 + 4 + 4
08409   !               es edi eip                  port src len
08410
08411           .align  16
08412   _port_write:
08413           cld
08414           push    esi
08415           push    ds
08416           mov     ecx, FLAT_DS_SELECTOR
08417           mov     ds, cx
08418           mov     edx, PW_ARGS(esp)          ! port to write to
08419           mov     esi, PW_ARGS+4(esp)        ! source addr
08420           mov     ecx, PW_ARGS+4+4(esp)      ! byte count
08421           shr     ecx, 1                     ! word count
08422           rep                                ! (hardware cannot handle dwords)
08423       o16 outs                               ! write everything
08424           pop     ds
08425           pop     esi
08426           ret
08427
08428
08429   !*===========================================================================*
08430   !*                              port_write_byte                              *
08431   !*===========================================================================*
08432   ! PUBLIC void port_write_byte(port_t port, phys_bytes source,
08433   !                                               unsigned bytcount);
08434   ! Transfer data from memory to port.
```

```
08435
08436     PW_ARGS_B =        4 + 4 + 4                   ! 4 + 4 + 4
08437     !                  es edi eip                  port src len
08438
08439     _port_write_byte:
08440          cld
08441          push     esi
08442          push     ds
08443          mov      ecx, FLAT_DS_SELECTOR
08444          mov      ds, cx
08445          mov      edx, PW_ARGS_B(esp)
08446          mov      esi, PW_ARGS_B+4(esp)
08447          mov      ecx, PW_ARGS_B+4+4(esp)
08448          rep
08449          outsb
08450          pop      ds
08451          pop      esi
08452          ret
08453
08454
08455     !*===========================================================*
08456     !*                        lock                               *
08457     !*===========================================================*
08458     ! PUBLIC void lock();
08459     ! Disable CPU interrupts.
08460
08461          .align  16
08462     _lock:
08463          cli                                    ! disable interrupts
08464          ret
08465
08466
08467     !*===========================================================*
08468     !*                        unlock                             *
08469     !*===========================================================*
08470     ! PUBLIC void unlock();
08471     ! Enable CPU interrupts.
08472
08473          .align  16
08474     _unlock:
08475          sti
08476          ret
08477
08478
08479     !*===========================================================*
08480     !*                        enable_irq                         *
08481     !*===========================================================*/
08482     ! PUBLIC void enable_irq(unsigned irq)
08483     ! Enable an interrupt request line by clearing an 8259 bit.
08484     ! Equivalent code for irq < 8:
08485     !       out_byte(INT_CTLMASK, in_byte(INT_CTLMASK) & ~(1 << irq));
08486
08487          .align  16
08488     _enable_irq:
08489          mov      ecx, 4(esp)              ! irq
08490          pushf
08491          cli
08492          movb     ah, ~1
08493          rolb     ah, cl                   ! ah = ~(1 << (irq % 8))
08494          cmpb     cl, 8
```

```
08495          jae      enable_8                ! enable irq >= 8 at the slave 8259
08496  enable_0:
08497          inb      INT_CTLMASK
08498          andb     al, ah
08499          outb     INT_CTLMASK             ! clear bit at master 8259
08500          popf
08501          ret
08502          .align   4
08503  enable_8:
08504          inb      INT2_CTLMASK
08505          andb     al, ah
08506          outb     INT2_CTLMASK            ! clear bit at slave 8259
08507          popf
08508          ret
08509
08510
08511  !*===========================================================================*
08512  !*                              disable_irq                                  *
08513  !*===========================================================================*/
08514  ! PUBLIC int disable_irq(unsigned irq)
08515  ! Disable an interrupt request line by setting an 8259 bit.
08516  ! Equivalent code for irq < 8:
08517  !       out_byte(INT_CTLMASK, in_byte(INT_CTLMASK) | (1 << irq));
08518  ! Returns true iff the interrupt was not already disabled.
08519
08520          .align   16
08521  _disable_irq:
08522          mov      ecx, 4(esp)             ! irq
08523          pushf
08524          cli
08525          movb     ah, 1
08526          rolb     ah, cl                  ! ah = (1 << (irq % 8))
08527          cmpb     cl, 8
08528          jae      disable_8               ! disable irq >= 8 at the slave 8259
08529  disable_0:
08530          inb      INT_CTLMASK
08531          testb    al, ah
08532          jnz      dis_already             ! already disabled?
08533          orb      al, ah
08534          outb     INT_CTLMASK             ! set bit at master 8259
08535          popf
08536          mov      eax, 1                  ! disabled by this function
08537          ret
08538  disable_8:
08539          inb      INT2_CTLMASK
08540          testb    al, ah
08541          jnz      dis_already             ! already disabled?
08542          orb      al, ah
08543          outb     INT2_CTLMASK            ! set bit at slave 8259
08544          popf
08545          mov      eax, 1                  ! disabled by this function
08546          ret
08547  dis_already:
08548          popf
08549          xor      eax, eax                ! already disabled
08550          ret
08551
08552
08553  !*===========================================================================*
08554  !*                              phys_copy                                    *
```

```
08555      !*===========================================================================*
08556      ! PUBLIC void phys_copy(phys_bytes source, phys_bytes destination,
08557      !                       phys_bytes bytecount);
08558      ! Copy a block of physical memory.
08559
08560      PC_ARGS  =       4 + 4 + 4 + 4    ! 4 + 4 + 4
08561      !                es edi esi eip   src dst len
08562
08563              .align  16
08564      _phys_copy:
08565              cld
08566              push    esi
08567              push    edi
08568              push    es
08569
08570              mov     eax, FLAT_DS_SELECTOR
08571              mov     es, ax
08572
08573              mov     esi, PC_ARGS(esp)
08574              mov     edi, PC_ARGS+4(esp)
08575              mov     eax, PC_ARGS+4+4(esp)
08576
08577              cmp     eax, 10                  ! avoid align overhead for small counts
08578              jb      pc_small
08579              mov     ecx, esi                 ! align source, hope target is too
08580              neg     ecx
08581              and     ecx, 3                   ! count for alignment
08582              sub     eax, ecx
08583              rep
08584        eseg movsb
08585              mov     ecx, eax
08586              shr     ecx, 2                   ! count of dwords
08587              rep
08588        eseg movs
08589              and     eax, 3
08590      pc_small:
08591              xchg    ecx, eax                 ! remainder
08592              rep
08593        eseg movsb
08594
08595              pop     es
08596              pop     edi
08597              pop     esi
08598              ret
08599
08600
08601      !*===========================================================================*
08602      !*                              mem_rdw                                       *
08603      !*===========================================================================*
08604      ! PUBLIC u16_t mem_rdw(U16_t segment, u16_t *offset);
08605      ! Load and return word at far pointer segment:offset.
08606
08607              .align  16
08608      _mem_rdw:
08609              mov     cx, ds
08610              mov     ds, 4(esp)               ! segment
08611              mov     eax, 4+4(esp)            ! offset
08612              movzx   eax, (eax)               ! word to return
08613              mov     ds, cx
08614              ret
```

```
08615
08616
08617   !*===========================================================================*
08618   !*                              reset                                         *
08619   !*===========================================================================*
08620   ! PUBLIC void reset();
08621   ! Reset the system by loading IDT with offset 0 and interrupting.
08622
08623   _reset:
08624           lidt    (idt_zero)
08625           int     3                       ! anything goes, the 386 will not like it
08626   .sect .data
08627   idt_zero:       .data4  0, 0
08628   .sect .text
08629
08630
08631   !*===========================================================================*
08632   !*                              mem_vid_copy                                 *
08633   !*===========================================================================*
08634   ! PUBLIC void mem_vid_copy(u16 *src, unsigned dst, unsigned count);
08635   !
08636   ! Copy count characters from kernel memory to video memory.  Src, dst and
08637   ! count are character (word) based video offsets and counts.  If src is null
08638   ! then screen memory is blanked by filling it with blank_color.
08639
08640   MVC_ARGS        =       4 + 4 + 4 + 4     ! 4 + 4 + 4
08641   !                       es edi esi eip   src dst ct
08642
08643   _mem_vid_copy:
08644           push    esi
08645           push    edi
08646           push    es
08647           mov     esi, MVC_ARGS(esp)          ! source
08648           mov     edi, MVC_ARGS+4(esp)        ! destination
08649           mov     edx, MVC_ARGS+4+4(esp)      ! count
08650           mov     es, (_vid_seg)              ! destination is video segment
08651           cld                                 ! make sure direction is up
08652   mvc_loop:
08653           and     edi, (_vid_mask)            ! wrap address
08654           mov     ecx, edx                    ! one chunk to copy
08655           mov     eax, (_vid_size)
08656           sub     eax, edi
08657           cmp     ecx, eax
08658           jbe     0f
08659           mov     ecx, eax                    ! ecx = min(ecx, vid_size - edi)
08660   0:      sub     edx, ecx                    ! count -= ecx
08661           shl     edi, 1                      ! byte address
08662           test    esi, esi                    ! source == 0 means blank the screen
08663           jz      mvc_blank
08664   mvc_copy:
08665           rep                                 ! copy words to video memory
08666       o16 movs
08667           jmp     mvc_test
08668   mvc_blank:
08669           mov     eax, (_blank_color)         ! ax = blanking character
08670           rep
08671       o16 stos                                ! copy blanks to video memory
08672           !jmp    mvc_test
08673   mvc_test:
08674           shr     edi, 1                      ! word addresses
```

```
08675                   test    edx, edx
08676                   jnz     mvc_loop
08677           mvc_done:
08678                   pop     es
08679                   pop     edi
08680                   pop     esi
08681                   ret
08682
08683
08684           !*===========================================================================*
08685           !*                              vid_vid_copy                                 *
08686           !*===========================================================================*
08687           ! PUBLIC void vid_vid_copy(unsigned src, unsigned dst, unsigned count);
08688           !
08689           ! Copy count characters from video memory to video memory.  Handle overlap.
08690           ! Used for scrolling, line or character insertion and deletion.  Src, dst
08691           ! and count are character (word) based video offsets and counts.
08692
08693           VVC_ARGS        =       4 + 4 + 4 + 4   ! 4 + 4 + 4
08694           !                       es edi esi eip   src dst ct
08695
08696           _vid_vid_copy:
08697                   push    esi
08698                   push    edi
08699                   push    es
08700                   mov     esi, VVC_ARGS(esp)      ! source
08701                   mov     edi, VVC_ARGS+4(esp)    ! destination
08702                   mov     edx, VVC_ARGS+4+4(esp)  ! count
08703                   mov     es, (_vid_seg)          ! use video segment
08704                   cmp     esi, edi                ! copy up or down?
08705                   jb      vvc_down
08706           vvc_up:
08707                   cld                             ! direction is up
08708           vvc_uploop:
08709                   and     esi, (_vid_mask)        ! wrap addresses
08710                   and     edi, (_vid_mask)
08711                   mov     ecx, edx                ! one chunk to copy
08712                   mov     eax, (_vid_size)
08713                   sub     eax, esi
08714                   cmp     ecx, eax
08715                   jbe     0f
08716                   mov     ecx, eax                ! ecx = min(ecx, vid_size - esi)
08717           0:      mov     eax, (_vid_size)
08718                   sub     eax, edi
08719                   cmp     ecx, eax
08720                   jbe     0f
08721                   mov     ecx, eax                ! ecx = min(ecx, vid_size - edi)
08722           0:      sub     edx, ecx                ! count -= ecx
08723                   shl     esi, 1
08724                   shl     edi, 1                  ! byte addresses
08725                   rep
08726           eseg o16 movs                           ! copy video words
08727                   shr     esi, 1
08728                   shr     edi, 1                  ! word addresses
08729                   test    edx, edx
08730                   jnz     vvc_uploop              ! again?
08731                   jmp     vvc_done
08732           vvc_down:
08733                   std                             ! direction is down
08734                   lea     esi, -1(esi)(edx*1)     ! start copying at the top
```

```
08735            lea      edi, -1(edi)(edx*1)
08736    vvc_downloop:
08737            and      esi, (_vid_mask)        ! wrap addresses
08738            and      edi, (_vid_mask)
08739            mov      ecx, edx                ! one chunk to copy
08740            lea      eax, 1(esi)
08741            cmp      ecx, eax
08742            jbe      0f
08743            mov      ecx, eax                ! ecx = min(ecx, esi + 1)
08744    0:      lea      eax, 1(edi)
08745            cmp      ecx, eax
08746            jbe      0f
08747            mov      ecx, eax                ! ecx = min(ecx, edi + 1)
08748    0:      sub      edx, ecx                ! count -= ecx
08749            shl      esi, 1
08750            shl      edi, 1                  ! byte addresses
08751            rep
08752    eseg o16 movs                            ! copy video words
08753            shr      esi, 1
08754            shr      edi, 1                  ! word addresses
08755            test     edx, edx
08756            jnz      vvc_downloop            ! again?
08757            cld                              ! C compiler expect up
08758            !jmp     vvc_done
08759    vvc_done:
08760            pop      es
08761            pop      edi
08762            pop      esi
08763            ret
08764
08765
08766    !*===========================================================================*
08767    !*                              level0                                       *
08768    !*===========================================================================*
08769    ! PUBLIC void level0(void (*func)(void))
08770    ! Call a function at permission level 0.  This allows kernel tasks to do
08771    ! things that are only possible at the most privileged CPU level.
08772    !
08773    _level0:
08774            mov      eax, 4(esp)
08775            mov      (_level0_func), eax
08776            int      LEVEL0_VECTOR
08777            ret
```

```
++++++++++++++++++++++++++++++++++++++++++++++++++++++++++++++++++++++++++++++++
                              src/kernel/misc.c
++++++++++++++++++++++++++++++++++++++++++++++++++++++++++++++++++++++++++++++++

08800    /* This file contains a collection of miscellaneous procedures:
08801     *      mem_init:       initialize memory tables.  Some memory is reported
08802     *                      by the BIOS, some is guesstimated and checked later
08803     *      env_parse       parse environment variable.
08804     *      bad_assertion   for debugging
08805     *      bad_compare     for debugging
08806     */
08807
08808    #include "kernel.h"
08809    #include "assert.h"
```

```
08810    #include <stdlib.h>
08811    #include <minix/com.h>
08812
08813    #define EM_BASE      0x100000L    /* base of extended memory on AT's */
08814    #define SHADOW_BASE 0xFA0000L    /* base of RAM shadowing ROM on some AT's */
08815    #define SHADOW_MAX  0x060000L    /* maximum usable shadow memory (16M limit) */
08816
08817    /*===========================================================================*
08818     *                              mem_init                                      *
08819     *===========================================================================*/
08820    PUBLIC void mem_init()
08821    {
08822    /* Initialize the memory size tables.  This is complicated by fragmentation
08823     * and different access strategies for protected mode.  There must be a
08824     * chunk at 0 big enough to hold Minix proper.  For 286 and 386 processors,
08825     * there can be extended memory (memory above 1MB).  This usually starts at
08826     * 1MB, but there may be another chunk just below 16MB, reserved under DOS
08827     * for shadowing ROM, but available to Minix if the hardware can be re-mapped.
08828     * In protected mode, extended memory is accessible assuming CLICK_SIZE is
08829     * large enough, and is treated as ordinary memory.
08830     */
08831
08832      u32_t ext_clicks;
08833      phys_clicks max_clicks;
08834
08835      /* Get the size of ordinary memory from the BIOS. */
08836      mem[0].size = k_to_click(low_memsize);        /* base = 0 */
08837
08838      if (pc_at && protected_mode) {
08839            /* Get the size of extended memory from the BIOS.  This is special
08840             * except in protected mode, but protected mode is now normal.
08841             * Note that no more than 16M can be addressed in 286 mode, so make
08842             * sure that the highest memory address fits in a short when counted
08843             * in clicks.
08844             */
08845            ext_clicks = k_to_click((u32_t) ext_memsize);
08846            max_clicks = USHRT_MAX - (EM_BASE >> CLICK_SHIFT);
08847            mem[1].size = MIN(ext_clicks, max_clicks);
08848            mem[1].base = EM_BASE >> CLICK_SHIFT;
08849
08850            if (ext_memsize <= (unsigned) ((SHADOW_BASE - EM_BASE) / 1024)
08851                        && check_mem(SHADOW_BASE, SHADOW_MAX) == SHADOW_MAX) {
08852                  /* Shadow ROM memory. */
08853                  mem[2].size = SHADOW_MAX >> CLICK_SHIFT;
08854                  mem[2].base = SHADOW_BASE >> CLICK_SHIFT;
08855            }
08856      }
08857
08858      /* Total system memory. */
08859      tot_mem_size = mem[0].size + mem[1].size + mem[2].size;
08860    }
08862    /*===========================================================================*
08863     *                              env_parse                                     *
08864     *===========================================================================*/
08865    PUBLIC int env_parse(env, fmt, field, param, min, max)
08866    char *env;                  /* environment variable to inspect */
08867    char *fmt;                  /* template to parse it with */
08868    int field;                  /* field number of value to return */
08869    long *param;                /* address of parameter to get */
```

```
08870  long min, max;              /* minimum and maximum values for the parameter */
08871  {
08872  /* Parse an environment variable setting, something like "DPETH0=300:3".
08873   * Panic if the parsing fails.  Return EP_UNSET if the environment variable
08874   * is not set, EP_OFF if it is set to "off", EP_ON if set to "on" or a
08875   * field is left blank, or EP_SET if a field is given (return value through
08876   * *param).  Commas and colons may be used in the environment and format
08877   * string, fields in the environment string may be empty, and punctuation
08878   * may be missing to skip fields.  The format string contains characters
08879   * 'd', 'o', 'x' and 'c' to indicate that 10, 8, 16, or 0 is used as the
08880   * last argument to strtol.
08881   */
08882
08883    char *val, *end;
08884    long newpar;
08885    int i = 0, radix, r;
08886
08887    if ((val = k_getenv(env)) == NIL_PTR) return(EP_UNSET);
08888    if (strcmp(val, "off") == 0) return(EP_OFF);
08889    if (strcmp(val, "on") == 0) return(EP_ON);
08890
08891    r = EP_ON;
08892    for (;;) {
08893        while (*val == ' ') val++;
08894
08895        if (*val == 0) return(r);        /* the proper exit point */
08896
08897        if (*fmt == 0) break;            /* too many values */
08898
08899        if (*val == ',' || *val == ':') {
08900            /* Time to go to the next field. */
08901            if (*fmt == ',' || *fmt == ':') i++;
08902            if (*fmt++ == *val) val++;
08903        } else {
08904            /* Environment contains a value, get it. */
08905            switch (*fmt) {
08906            case 'd':       radix =   10;   break;
08907            case 'o':       radix =  010;   break;
08908            case 'x':       radix = 0x10;   break;
08909            case 'c':       radix =    0;   break;
08910            default:        goto badenv;
08911            }
08912            newpar = strtol(val, &end, radix);
08913
08914            if (end == val) break;  /* not a number */
08915            val = end;
08916
08917            if (i == field) {
08918                /* The field requested. */
08919                if (newpar < min || newpar > max) break;
08920                *param = newpar;
08921                r = EP_SET;
08922            }
08923        }
08924    }
08925  badenv:
08926    printf("Bad environment setting: '%s = %s'\n", env, k_getenv(env));
08927    panic("", NO_NUM);
08928    /*NOTREACHED*/
08929  }
```

```
08931    #if DEBUG
08932    /*===========================================================================*
08933     *                              bad_assertion                                *
08934     *===========================================================================*/
08935    PUBLIC void bad_assertion(file, line, what)
08936    char *file;
08937    int line;
08938    char *what;
08939    {
08940      printf("panic at %s(%d): assertion \"%s\" failed\n", file, line, what);
08941      panic(NULL, NO_NUM);
08942    }

08944    /*===========================================================================*
08945     *                              bad_compare                                  *
08946     *===========================================================================*/
08947    PUBLIC void bad_compare(file, line, lhs, what, rhs)
08948    char *file;
08949    int line;
08950    int lhs;
08951    char *what;
08952    int rhs;
08953    {
08954      printf("panic at %s(%d): compare (%d) %s (%d) failed\n",
08955             file, line, lhs, what, rhs);
08956      panic(NULL, NO_NUM);
08957    }
08958    #endif /* DEBUG */


+++++++++++++++++++++++++++++++++++++++++++++++++++++++++++++++++++++++++++++++++
                             src/kernel/driver.h
+++++++++++++++++++++++++++++++++++++++++++++++++++++++++++++++++++++++++++++++++

09000    /* Types and constants shared between the generic and device dependent
09001     * device driver code.
09002     */
09003
09004    #include <minix/callnr.h>
09005    #include <minix/com.h>
09006    #include "proc.h"
09007    #include <minix/partition.h>
09008
09009    /* Info about and entry points into the device dependent code. */
09010    struct driver {
09011      _PROTOTYPE( char *(*dr_name), (void) );
09012      _PROTOTYPE( int (*dr_open), (struct driver *dp, message *m_ptr) );
09013      _PROTOTYPE( int (*dr_close), (struct driver *dp, message *m_ptr) );
09014      _PROTOTYPE( int (*dr_ioctl), (struct driver *dp, message *m_ptr) );
09015      _PROTOTYPE( struct device *(*dr_prepare), (int device) );
09016      _PROTOTYPE( int (*dr_schedule), (int proc_nr, struct iorequest_s *request) );
09017      _PROTOTYPE( int (*dr_finish), (void) );
09018      _PROTOTYPE( void (*dr_cleanup), (void) );
09019      _PROTOTYPE( void (*dr_geometry), (struct partition *entry) );
09020    };
09021
09022    #if (CHIP == INTEL)
09023
09024    /* Number of bytes you can DMA before hitting a 64K boundary: */
```

```
09025     #define dma_bytes_left(phys)      \
09026         ((unsigned) (sizeof(int) == 2 ? 0 : 0x10000) - (unsigned) ((phys) & 0xFFFF))
09027
09028     #endif /* CHIP == INTEL */
09029
09030     /* Base and size of a partition in bytes. */
09031     struct device {
09032       unsigned long dv_base;
09033       unsigned long dv_size;
09034     };
09035
09036     #define NIL_DEV          ((struct device *) 0)
09037
09038     /* Functions defined by driver.c: */
09039     _PROTOTYPE( void driver_task, (struct driver *dr) );
09040     _PROTOTYPE( int do_rdwt, (struct driver *dr, message *m_ptr) );
09041     _PROTOTYPE( int do_vrdwt, (struct driver *dr, message *m_ptr) );
09042     _PROTOTYPE( char *no_name, (void) );
09043     _PROTOTYPE( int do_nop, (struct driver *dp, message *m_ptr) );
09044     _PROTOTYPE( int nop_finish, (void) );
09045     _PROTOTYPE( void nop_cleanup, (void) );
09046     _PROTOTYPE( void clock_mess, (int ticks, watchdog_t func) );
09047     _PROTOTYPE( int do_diocntl, (struct driver *dr, message *m_ptr) );
09048
09049     /* Parameters for the disk drive. */
09050     #define SECTOR_SIZE      512     /* physical sector size in bytes */
09051     #define SECTOR_SHIFT       9     /* for division */
09052     #define SECTOR_MASK      511     /* and remainder */
09053
09054     /* Size of the DMA buffer buffer in bytes. */
09055     #define DMA_BUF_SIZE     (DMA_SECTORS * SECTOR_SIZE)
09056
09057     #if (CHIP == INTEL)
09058     extern u8_t *tmp_buf;                    /* the DMA buffer */
09059     #else
09060     extern u8_t tmp_buf[];                   /* the DMA buffer */
09061     #endif
09062     extern phys_bytes tmp_phys;              /* phys address of DMA buffer */


++++++++++++++++++++++++++++++++++++++++++++++++++++++++++++++++++++++++++++++++
                                src/kernel/driver.c
++++++++++++++++++++++++++++++++++++++++++++++++++++++++++++++++++++++++++++++++

09100     /* This file contains device independent device driver interface.
09101      *                                              Author: Kees J. Bot.
09102      *
09103      * The drivers support the following operations (using message format m2):
09104      *
09105      *    m_type    DEVICE    PROC_NR    COUNT    POSITION ADRRESS
09106      * ----------------------------------------------------------------
09107      * | DEV_OPEN  | device  | proc nr |         |         |         |
09108      * |-----------+---------+---------+---------+---------+---------|
09109      * | DEV_CLOSE | device  | proc nr |         |         |         |
09110      * |-----------+---------+---------+---------+---------+---------|
09111      * | DEV_READ  | device  | proc nr | bytes   | offset  | buf ptr |
09112      * |-----------+---------+---------+---------+---------+---------|
09113      * | DEV_WRITE | device  | proc nr | bytes   | offset  | buf ptr |
09114      * |-----------+---------+---------+---------+---------+---------|
```

```
09115    *  |SCATTERED_IO| device  | proc nr | requests|            | iov ptr |
09116    * --------------------------------------------------------------------
09117    *  |  DEV_IOCTL | device  | proc nr |func code|            | buf ptr |
09118    * --------------------------------------------------------------------
09119    *
09120    * The file contains one entry point:
09121    *
09122    *   driver_task:        called by the device dependent task entry
09123    *
09124    *
09125    * Constructed 92/04/02 by Kees J. Bot from the old AT wini and floppy driver.
09126    */
09127
09128    #include "kernel.h"
09129    #include <sys/ioctl.h>
09130    #include "driver.h"
09131
09132    #define BUF_EXTRA        0
09133
09134    /* Claim space for variables. */
09135    PRIVATE u8_t buffer[(unsigned) 2 * DMA_BUF_SIZE + BUF_EXTRA];
09136    u8_t *tmp_buf;                   /* the DMA buffer eventually */
09137    phys_bytes tmp_phys;            /* phys address of DMA buffer */
09138
09139    FORWARD _PROTOTYPE( void init_buffer, (void) );
09140
09141    /*=========================================================================*
09142    *                              driver_task                                *
09143    *=========================================================================*/
09144    PUBLIC void driver_task(dp)
09145    struct driver *dp;        /* Device dependent entry points. */
09146    {
09147    /* Main program of any device driver task. */
09148
09149      int r, caller, proc_nr;
09150      message mess;
09151
09152      init_buffer();            /* Get a DMA buffer. */
09153
09154      /* Here is the main loop of the disk task.  It waits for a message, carries
09155       * it out, and sends a reply.
09156       */
09157
09158      while (TRUE) {
09159            /* First wait for a request to read or write a disk block. */
09160            receive(ANY, &mess);
09161
09162            caller = mess.m_source;
09163            proc_nr = mess.PROC_NR;
09164
09165            switch (caller) {
09166            case HARDWARE:
09167                    /* Leftover interrupt. */
09168                    continue;
09169            case FS_PROC_NR:
09170                    /* The only legitimate caller. */
09171                    break;
09172            default:
09173                    printf("%s: got message from %d\n", (*dp->dr_name)(), caller);
09174                    continue;
```

```
09175            }
09176
09177            /* Now carry out the work. */
09178            switch(mess.m_type) {
09179                case DEV_OPEN:      r = (*dp->dr_open)(dp, &mess);  break;
09180                case DEV_CLOSE:     r = (*dp->dr_close)(dp, &mess); break;
09181                case DEV_IOCTL:     r = (*dp->dr_ioctl)(dp, &mess); break;
09182
09183                case DEV_READ:
09184                case DEV_WRITE:     r = do_rdwt(dp, &mess);         break;
09185
09186                case SCATTERED_IO:  r = do_vrdwt(dp, &mess);        break;
09187                default:            r = EINVAL;                     break;
09188            }
09189
09190            /* Clean up leftover state. */
09191            (*dp->dr_cleanup)();
09192
09193            /* Finally, prepare and send the reply message. */
09194            mess.m_type = TASK_REPLY;
09195            mess.REP_PROC_NR = proc_nr;
09196
09197            mess.REP_STATUS = r;        /* # of bytes transferred or error code */
09198            send(caller, &mess);        /* send reply to caller */
09199        }
09200    }

09202    /*===========================================================================*
09203     *                              init_buffer                                   *
09204     *===========================================================================*/
09205    PRIVATE void init_buffer()
09206    {
09207    /* Select a buffer that can safely be used for dma transfers.  It may also
09208     * be used to read partition tables and such.  Its absolute address is
09209     * 'tmp_phys', the normal address is 'tmp_buf'.
09210     */
09211
09212      tmp_buf = buffer;
09213      tmp_phys = vir2phys(buffer);
09214
09215      if (tmp_phys == 0) panic("no DMA buffer", NO_NUM);
09216
09217      if (dma_bytes_left(tmp_phys) < DMA_BUF_SIZE) {
09218            /* First half of buffer crosses a 64K boundary, can't DMA into that */
09219            tmp_buf += DMA_BUF_SIZE;
09220            tmp_phys += DMA_BUF_SIZE;
09221      }
09222    }

09224    /*===========================================================================*
09225     *                              do_rdwt                                       *
09226     *===========================================================================*/
09227    PUBLIC int do_rdwt(dp, m_ptr)
09228    struct driver *dp;              /* device dependent entry points */
09229    message *m_ptr;                 /* pointer to read or write message */
09230    {
09231    /* Carry out a single read or write request. */
09232      struct iorequest_s ioreq;
09233      int r;
09234
```

```
09235            if (m_ptr->COUNT <= 0) return(EINVAL);
09236
09237            if ((*dp->dr_prepare)(m_ptr->DEVICE) == NIL_DEV) return(ENXIO);
09238
09239            ioreq.io_request = m_ptr->m_type;
09240            ioreq.io_buf = m_ptr->ADDRESS;
09241            ioreq.io_position = m_ptr->POSITION;
09242            ioreq.io_nbytes = m_ptr->COUNT;
09243
09244            r = (*dp->dr_schedule)(m_ptr->PROC_NR, &ioreq);
09245
09246            if (r == OK) (void) (*dp->dr_finish)();
09247
09248            r = ioreq.io_nbytes;
09249            return(r < 0 ? r : m_ptr->COUNT - r);
09250    }

09252    /*===========================================================================*
09253     *                              do_vrdwt                                      *
09254     *===========================================================================*/
09255    PUBLIC int do_vrdwt(dp, m_ptr)
09256    struct driver *dp;          /* device dependent entry points */
09257    message *m_ptr;             /* pointer to read or write message */
09258    {
09259    /* Fetch a vector of i/o requests.  Handle requests one at a time.  Return
09260     * status in the vector.
09261     */
09262
09263            struct iorequest_s *iop;
09264            static struct iorequest_s iovec[NR_IOREQS];
09265            phys_bytes iovec_phys;
09266            unsigned nr_requests;
09267            int request;
09268            int r;
09269            phys_bytes user_iovec_phys;
09270
09271            nr_requests = m_ptr->COUNT;
09272
09273            if (nr_requests > sizeof iovec / sizeof iovec[0])
09274                    panic("FS passed too big an I/O vector", nr_requests);
09275
09276            iovec_phys = vir2phys(iovec);
09277            user_iovec_phys = numap(m_ptr->PROC_NR, (vir_bytes) m_ptr->ADDRESS,
09278                              (vir_bytes) (nr_requests * sizeof iovec[0]));
09279
09280            if (user_iovec_phys == 0)
09281                    panic("FS passed a bad I/O vector", (int) m_ptr->ADDRESS);
09282
09283            phys_copy(user_iovec_phys, iovec_phys,
09284                                (phys_bytes) nr_requests * sizeof iovec[0]);
09285
09286            if ((*dp->dr_prepare)(m_ptr->DEVICE) == NIL_DEV) return(ENXIO);
09287
09288            for (request = 0, iop = iovec; request < nr_requests; request++, iop++) {
09289                    if ((r = (*dp->dr_schedule)(m_ptr->PROC_NR, iop)) != OK) break;
09290            }
09291
09292            if (r == OK) (void) (*dp->dr_finish)();
09293
09294            phys_copy(iovec_phys, user_iovec_phys,
```

```
09295                                     (phys_bytes) nr_requests * sizeof iovec[0]);
09296        return(OK);
09297    }

09299    /*===========================================================================*
09300     *                              no_name                                      *
09301     *===========================================================================*/
09302    PUBLIC char *no_name()
09303    {
09304    /* If no specific name for the device. */
09305
09306       return(tasktab[proc_number(proc_ptr) + NR_TASKS].name);
09307    }

09309    /*===========================================================================*
09310     *                              do_nop                                       *
09311     *===========================================================================*/
09312    PUBLIC int do_nop(dp, m_ptr)
09313    struct driver *dp;
09314    message *m_ptr;
09315    {
09316    /* Nothing there, or nothing to do. */
09317
09318       switch (m_ptr->m_type) {
09319       case DEV_OPEN:       return(ENODEV);
09320       case DEV_CLOSE:      return(OK);
09321       case DEV_IOCTL:      return(ENOTTY);
09322       default:             return(EIO);
09323       }
09324    }

09326    /*===========================================================================*
09327     *                              nop_finish                                   *
09328     *===========================================================================*/
09329    PUBLIC int nop_finish()
09330    {
09331    /* Nothing to finish, all the work has been done by dp->dr_schedule. */
09332       return(OK);
09333    }

09335    /*===========================================================================*
09336     *                              nop_cleanup                                  *
09337     *===========================================================================*/
09338    PUBLIC void nop_cleanup()
09339    {
09340    /* Nothing to clean up. */
09341    }

09343    /*===========================================================================*
09344     *                              clock_mess                                   *
09345     *===========================================================================*/
09346    PUBLIC void clock_mess(ticks, func)
09347    int ticks;                          /* how many clock ticks to wait */
09348    watchdog_t func;                    /* function to call upon time out */
09349    {
09350    /* Send the clock task a message. */
09351
09352       message mess;
09353
09354       mess.m_type = SET_ALARM;
```

```
09355          mess.CLOCK_PROC_NR = proc_number(proc_ptr);
09356          mess.DELTA_TICKS = (long) ticks;
09357          mess.FUNC_TO_CALL = (sighandler_t) func;
09358          sendrec(CLOCK, &mess);
09359      }

09361      /*===========================================================================*
09362       *                              do_diocntl                                   *
09363       *===========================================================================*/
09364      PUBLIC int do_diocntl(dp, m_ptr)
09365      struct driver *dp;
09366      message *m_ptr;                    /* pointer to ioctl request */
09367      {
09368      /* Carry out a partition setting/getting request. */
09369        struct device *dv;
09370        phys_bytes user_phys, entry_phys;
09371        struct partition entry;
09372
09373        if (m_ptr->REQUEST != DIOCSETP && m_ptr->REQUEST != DIOCGETP) return(ENOTTY);
09374
09375        /* Decode the message parameters. */
09376        if ((dv = (*dp->dr_prepare)(m_ptr->DEVICE)) == NIL_DEV) return(ENXIO);
09377
09378        user_phys = numap(m_ptr->PROC_NR, (vir_bytes) m_ptr->ADDRESS, sizeof(entry));
09379        if (user_phys == 0) return(EFAULT);
09380
09381        entry_phys = vir2phys(&entry);
09382
09383        if (m_ptr->REQUEST == DIOCSETP) {
09384            /* Copy just this one partition table entry. */
09385            phys_copy(user_phys, entry_phys, (phys_bytes) sizeof(entry));
09386            dv->dv_base = entry.base;
09387            dv->dv_size = entry.size;
09388        } else {
09389            /* Return a partition table entry and the geometry of the drive. */
09390            entry.base = dv->dv_base;
09391            entry.size = dv->dv_size;
09392            (*dp->dr_geometry)(&entry);
09393            phys_copy(entry_phys, user_phys, (phys_bytes) sizeof(entry));
09394        }
09395        return(OK);
09396      }
```

```
++++++++++++++++++++++++++++++++++++++++++++++++++++++++++++++++++++++++++++++++
                              src/kernel/drvlib.h
++++++++++++++++++++++++++++++++++++++++++++++++++++++++++++++++++++++++++++++++
```

```
09400      /* IBM device driver definitions              Author: Kees J. Bot
09401       *                                                   7 Dec 1995
09402       */
09403
09404      #include <ibm/partition.h>
09405
09406      _PROTOTYPE( void partition, (struct driver *dr, int device, int style) );
09407
09408      /* BIOS parameter table layout. */
09409      #define bp_cylinders(t)          (* (u16_t *) (&(t)[0]))
```

```
09410     #define bp_heads(t)              (* (u8_t *)  (&(t)[2]))
09411     #define bp_reduced_wr(t)         (* (u16_t *) (&(t)[3]))
09412     #define bp_precomp(t)            (* (u16_t *) (&(t)[5]))
09413     #define bp_max_ecc(t)            (* (u8_t *)  (&(t)[7]))
09414     #define bp_ctlbyte(t)            (* (u8_t *)  (&(t)[8]))
09415     #define bp_landingzone(t)        (* (u16_t *) (&(t)[12]))
09416     #define bp_sectors(t)            (* (u8_t *)  (&(t)[14]))
09417
09418     /* Miscellaneous. */
09419     #define DEV_PER_DRIVE    (1 + NR_PARTITIONS)
09420     #define MINOR_hd1a       128
09421     #define MINOR_fd0a       (28<<2)
09422     #define P_FLOPPY         0
09423     #define P_PRIMARY        1
09424     #define P_SUB            2
```

```
+++++++++++++++++++++++++++++++++++++++++++++++++++++++++++++++++++++++++++++
                          src/kernel/drvlib.c
+++++++++++++++++++++++++++++++++++++++++++++++++++++++++++++++++++++++++++++
09500     /* IBM device driver utility functions.        Author: Kees J. Bot
09501      *                                                      7 Dec 1995
09502      * Entry point:
09503      *   partition: partition a disk to the partition table(s) on it.
09504      */
09505
09506     #include "kernel.h"
09507     #include "driver.h"
09508     #include "drvlib.h"
09509
09510
09511     FORWARD _PROTOTYPE( void extpartition, (struct driver *dp, int extdev,
09512                                                 unsigned long extbase) );
09513     FORWARD _PROTOTYPE( int get_part_table, (struct driver *dp, int device,
09514                         unsigned long offset, struct part_entry *table) );
09515     FORWARD _PROTOTYPE( void sort, (struct part_entry *table) );
09516
09517
09518     /*===========================================================================*
09519      *                              partition                                    *
09520      *===========================================================================*/
09521     PUBLIC void partition(dp, device, style)
09522     struct driver *dp;        /* device dependent entry points */
09523     int device;              /* device to partition */
09524     int style;               /* partitioning style: floppy, primary, sub. */
09525     {
09526     /* This routine is called on first open to initialize the partition tables
09527      * of a device.  It makes sure that each partition falls safely within the
09528      * device's limits.  Depending on the partition style we are either making
09529      * floppy partitions, primary partitions or subpartitions.  Only primary
09530      * partitions are sorted, because they are shared with other operating
09531      * systems that expect this.
09532      */
09533       struct part_entry table[NR_PARTITIONS], *pe;
09534       int disk, par;
```

```
09535          struct device *dv;
09536          unsigned long base, limit, part_limit;
09537
09538          /* Get the geometry of the device to partition */
09539          if ((dv = (*dp->dr_prepare)(device)) == NIL_DEV || dv->dv_size == 0) return;
09540          base = dv->dv_base >> SECTOR_SHIFT;
09541          limit = base + (dv->dv_size >> SECTOR_SHIFT);
09542
09543          /* Read the partition table for the device. */
09544          if (!get_part_table(dp, device, 0L, table)) return;
09545
09546          /* Compute the device number of the first partition. */
09547          switch (style) {
09548          case P_FLOPPY:
09549                  device += MINOR_fd0a;
09550                  break;
09551          case P_PRIMARY:
09552                  sort(table);                    /* sort a primary partition table */
09553                  device += 1;
09554                  break;
09555          case P_SUB:
09556                  disk = device / DEV_PER_DRIVE;
09557                  par = device % DEV_PER_DRIVE - 1;
09558                  device = MINOR_hd1a + (disk * NR_PARTITIONS + par) * NR_PARTITIONS;
09559          }
09560
09561          /* Find an array of devices. */
09562          if ((dv = (*dp->dr_prepare)(device)) == NIL_DEV) return;
09563
09564          /* Set the geometry of the partitions from the partition table. */
09565          for (par = 0; par < NR_PARTITIONS; par++, dv++) {
09566                  /* Shrink the partition to fit within the device. */
09567                  pe = &table[par];
09568                  part_limit = pe->lowsec + pe->size;
09569                  if (part_limit < pe->lowsec) part_limit = limit;
09570                  if (part_limit > limit) part_limit = limit;
09571                  if (pe->lowsec < base) pe->lowsec = base;
09572                  if (part_limit < pe->lowsec) part_limit = pe->lowsec;
09573
09574                  dv->dv_base = pe->lowsec << SECTOR_SHIFT;
09575                  dv->dv_size = (part_limit - pe->lowsec) << SECTOR_SHIFT;
09576
09577                  if (style == P_PRIMARY) {
09578                          /* Each Minix primary partition can be subpartitioned. */
09579                          if (pe->sysind == MINIX_PART)
09580                                  partition(dp, device + par, P_SUB);
09581
09582                          /* An extended partition has logical partitions. */
09583                          if (pe->sysind == EXT_PART)
09584                                  extpartition(dp, device + par, pe->lowsec);
09585                  }
09586          }
09587  }


09590  /*===========================================================================*
09591   *                              extpartition                                 *
09592   *===========================================================================*/
09593  PRIVATE void extpartition(dp, extdev, extbase)
09594  struct driver *dp;         /* device dependent entry points */
```

```
09595    int extdev;               /* extended partition to scan */
09596    unsigned long extbase;    /* sector offset of the base extended partition */
09597    {
09598    /* Extended partitions cannot be ignored alas, because people like to move
09599     * files to and from DOS partitions.  Avoid reading this code, it's no fun.
09600     */
09601      struct part_entry table[NR_PARTITIONS], *pe;
09602      int subdev, disk, par;
09603      struct device *dv;
09604      unsigned long offset, nextoffset;
09605
09606      disk = extdev / DEV_PER_DRIVE;
09607      par = extdev % DEV_PER_DRIVE - 1;
09608      subdev = MINOR_hd1a + (disk * NR_PARTITIONS + par) * NR_PARTITIONS;
09609
09610      offset = 0;
09611      do {
09612            if (!get_part_table(dp, extdev, offset, table)) return;
09613            sort(table);
09614
09615            /* The table should contain one logical partition and optionally
09616             * another extended partition.  (It's a linked list.)
09617             */
09618            nextoffset = 0;
09619            for (par = 0; par < NR_PARTITIONS; par++) {
09620                    pe = &table[par];
09621                    if (pe->sysind == EXT_PART) {
09622                            nextoffset = pe->lowsec;
09623                    } else
09624                    if (pe->sysind != NO_PART) {
09625                            if ((dv = (*dp->dr_prepare)(subdev)) == NIL_DEV) return;
09626
09627                            dv->dv_base = (extbase + offset
09628                                            + pe->lowsec) << SECTOR_SHIFT;
09629                            dv->dv_size = pe->size << SECTOR_SHIFT;
09630
09631                            /* Out of devices? */
09632                            if (++subdev % NR_PARTITIONS == 0) return;
09633                    }
09634            }
09635      } while ((offset = nextoffset) != 0);
09636    }


09639    /*===========================================================================*
09640     *                              get_part_table                               *
09641     *===========================================================================*/
09642    PRIVATE int get_part_table(dp, device, offset, table)
09643    struct driver *dp;
09644    int device;
09645    unsigned long offset;          /* sector offset to the table */
09646    struct part_entry *table;      /* four entries */
09647    {
09648    /* Read the partition table for the device, return true iff there were no
09649     * errors.
09650     */
09651      message mess;
09652
09653      mess.DEVICE = device;
09654      mess.POSITION = offset << SECTOR_SHIFT;
```

```
09655            mess.COUNT = SECTOR_SIZE;
09656            mess.ADDRESS = (char *) tmp_buf;
09657            mess.PROC_NR = proc_number(proc_ptr);
09658            mess.m_type = DEV_READ;
09659
09660            if (do_rdwt(dp, &mess) != SECTOR_SIZE) {
09661                    printf("%s: can't read partition table\n", (*dp->dr_name)());
09662                    return 0;
09663            }
09664            if (tmp_buf[510] != 0x55 || tmp_buf[511] != 0xAA) {
09665                    /* Invalid partition table. */
09666                    return 0;
09667            }
09668            memcpy(table, (tmp_buf + PART_TABLE_OFF), NR_PARTITIONS * sizeof(table[0]));
09669            return 1;
09670    }


09673    /*===========================================================================*
09674     *                                  sort                                      *
09675     *===========================================================================*/
09676    PRIVATE void sort(table)
09677    struct part_entry *table;
09678    {
09679    /* Sort a partition table. */
09680      struct part_entry *pe, tmp;
09681      int n = NR_PARTITIONS;
09682
09683      do {
09684            for (pe = table; pe < table + NR_PARTITIONS-1; pe++) {
09685                    if (pe[0].sysind == NO_PART
09686                            || (pe[0].lowsec > pe[1].lowsec
09687                                            && pe[1].sysind != NO_PART)) {
09688                            tmp = pe[0]; pe[0] = pe[1]; pe[1] = tmp;
09689                    }
09690            }
09691      } while (--n > 0);
09692    }


++++++++++++++++++++++++++++++++++++++++++++++++++++++++++++++++++++++++++++++
                             src/kernel/memory.c
++++++++++++++++++++++++++++++++++++++++++++++++++++++++++++++++++++++++++++++

09700    /* This file contains the device dependent part of the drivers for the
09701     * following special files:
09702     *      /dev/null        - null device (data sink)
09703     *      /dev/mem         - absolute memory
09704     *      /dev/kmem        - kernel virtual memory
09705     *      /dev/ram         - RAM disk
09706     *
09707     * The file contains one entry point:
09708     *
09709     *    mem_task:  main entry when system is brought up
09710     *
09711     *   Changes:
09712     *        20 Apr  1992 by Kees J. Bot: device dependent/independent split
09713     */
09714
```

```
09715  #include "kernel.h"
09716  #include "driver.h"
09717  #include <sys/ioctl.h>
09718
09719  #define NR_RAMS            4     /* number of RAM-type devices */
09720
09721  PRIVATE struct device m_geom[NR_RAMS];  /* Base and size of each RAM disk */
09722  PRIVATE int m_device;              /* current device */
09723
09724  FORWARD _PROTOTYPE( struct device *m_prepare, (int device) );
09725  FORWARD _PROTOTYPE( int m_schedule, (int proc_nr, struct iorequest_s *iop) );
09726  FORWARD _PROTOTYPE( int m_do_open, (struct driver *dp, message *m_ptr) );
09727  FORWARD _PROTOTYPE( void m_init, (void) );
09728  FORWARD _PROTOTYPE( int m_ioctl, (struct driver *dp, message *m_ptr) );
09729  FORWARD _PROTOTYPE( void m_geometry, (struct partition *entry) );
09730
09731
09732  /* Entry points to this driver. */
09733  PRIVATE struct driver m_dtab = {
09734    no_name,        /* current device's name */
09735    m_do_open,      /* open or mount */
09736    do_nop,         /* nothing on a close */
09737    m_ioctl,        /* specify ram disk geometry */
09738    m_prepare,      /* prepare for I/O on a given minor device */
09739    m_schedule,     /* do the I/O */
09740    nop_finish,     /* schedule does the work, no need to be smart */
09741    nop_cleanup,    /* nothing's dirty */
09742    m_geometry,     /* memory device "geometry" */
09743  };
09744
09745
09746  /*===========================================================================*
09747   *                              mem_task                                     *
09748   *===========================================================================*/
09749  PUBLIC void mem_task()
09750  {
09751    m_init();
09752    driver_task(&m_dtab);
09753  }
09754
09755
09756  /*===========================================================================*
09757   *                              m_prepare                                    *
09758   *===========================================================================*/
09759  PRIVATE struct device *m_prepare(device)
09760  int device;
09761  {
09762  /* Prepare for I/O on a device. */
09763
09764    if (device < 0 || device >= NR_RAMS) return(NIL_DEV);
09765    m_device = device;
09766
09767    return(&m_geom[device]);
09768  }
09769
09770
09771  /*===========================================================================*
09772   *                              m_schedule                                   *
09773   *===========================================================================*/
09774  PRIVATE int m_schedule(proc_nr, iop)
```

```
09775    int proc_nr;                        /* process doing the request */
09776    struct iorequest_s *iop;            /* pointer to read or write request */
09777    {
09778    /* Read or write /dev/null, /dev/mem, /dev/kmem, or /dev/ram. */
09779
09780      int device, count, opcode;
09781      phys_bytes mem_phys, user_phys;
09782      struct device *dv;
09783
09784      /* Type of request */
09785      opcode = iop->io_request & ~OPTIONAL_IO;
09786
09787      /* Get minor device number and check for /dev/null. */
09788      device = m_device;
09789      dv = &m_geom[device];
09790
09791      /* Determine address where data is to go or to come from. */
09792      user_phys = numap(proc_nr, (vir_bytes) iop->io_buf,
09793                                            (vir_bytes) iop->io_nbytes);
09794      if (user_phys == 0) return(iop->io_nbytes = EINVAL);
09795
09796      if (device == NULL_DEV) {
09797            /* /dev/null: Black hole. */
09798            if (opcode == DEV_WRITE) iop->io_nbytes = 0;
09799            count = 0;
09800      } else {
09801            /* /dev/mem, /dev/kmem, or /dev/ram: Check for EOF */
09802            if (iop->io_position >= dv->dv_size) return(OK);
09803            count = iop->io_nbytes;
09804            if (iop->io_position + count > dv->dv_size)
09805                    count = dv->dv_size - iop->io_position;
09806      }
09807
09808      /* Set up 'mem_phys' for /dev/mem, /dev/kmem, or /dev/ram */
09809      mem_phys = dv->dv_base + iop->io_position;
09810
09811      /* Book the number of bytes to be transferred in advance. */
09812      iop->io_nbytes -= count;
09813
09814      if (count == 0) return(OK);
09815
09816      /* Copy the data. */
09817      if (opcode == DEV_READ)
09818            phys_copy(mem_phys, user_phys, (phys_bytes) count);
09819      else
09820            phys_copy(user_phys, mem_phys, (phys_bytes) count);
09821
09822      return(OK);
09823    }


09826    /*===========================================================================*
09827     *                              m_do_open                                    *
09828     *===========================================================================*/
09829    PRIVATE int m_do_open(dp, m_ptr)
09830    struct driver *dp;
09831    message *m_ptr;
09832    {
09833    /* Check device number on open.  Give I/O privileges to a process opening
09834     * /dev/mem or /dev/kmem.
```

```
09835        */
09836
09837        if (m_prepare(m_ptr->DEVICE) == NIL_DEV) return(ENXIO);
09838
09839        if (m_device == MEM_DEV || m_device == KMEM_DEV)
09840             enable_iop(proc_addr(m_ptr->PROC_NR));
09841
09842        return(OK);
09843    }


09846    /*===========================================================================*
09847     *                               m_init                                      *
09848     *===========================================================================*/
09849    PRIVATE void m_init()
09850    {
09851      /* Initialize this task. */
09852      extern int _end;
09853
09854      m_geom[KMEM_DEV].dv_base = vir2phys(0);
09855      m_geom[KMEM_DEV].dv_size = vir2phys(&_end);
09856
09857    #if (CHIP == INTEL)
09858      if (!protected_mode) {
09859             m_geom[MEM_DEV].dv_size =   0x100000;    /* 1M for 8086 systems */
09860      } else {
09861    #if _WORD_SIZE == 2
09862             m_geom[MEM_DEV].dv_size =   0x1000000;   /* 16M for 286 systems */
09863    #else
09864             m_geom[MEM_DEV].dv_size = 0xFFFFFFFF;   /* 4G-1 for 386 systems */
09865    #endif
09866      }
09867    #endif
09868    }


09871    /*===========================================================================*
09872     *                               m_ioctl                                     *
09873     *===========================================================================*/
09874    PRIVATE int m_ioctl(dp, m_ptr)
09875    struct driver *dp;
09876    message *m_ptr;                    /* pointer to read or write message */
09877    {
09878    /* Set parameters for one of the RAM disks. */
09879
09880      unsigned long bytesize;
09881      unsigned base, size;
09882      struct memory *memp;
09883      static struct psinfo psinfo = { NR_TASKS, NR_PROCS, (vir_bytes) proc, 0, 0 };
09884      phys_bytes psinfo_phys;
09885
09886      switch (m_ptr->REQUEST) {
09887      case MIOCRAMSIZE:
09888             /* FS sets the RAM disk size. */
09889             if (m_ptr->PROC_NR != FS_PROC_NR) return(EPERM);
09890
09891             bytesize = m_ptr->POSITION * BLOCK_SIZE;
09892             size = (bytesize + CLICK_SHIFT-1) >> CLICK_SHIFT;
09893
09894             /* Find a memory chunk big enough for the RAM disk. */
```

```
09895                memp= &mem[NR_MEMS];
09896                while ((--memp)->size < size) {
09897                        if (memp == mem) panic("RAM disk is too big", NO_NUM);
09898                }
09899                base = memp->base;
09900                memp->base += size;
09901                memp->size -= size;
09902
09903                m_geom[RAM_DEV].dv_base = (unsigned long) base << CLICK_SHIFT;
09904                m_geom[RAM_DEV].dv_size = bytesize;
09905                break;
09906        case MIOCSPSINFO:
09907                /* MM or FS set the address of their process table. */
09908                if (m_ptr->PROC_NR == MM_PROC_NR) {
09909                        psinfo.mproc = (vir_bytes) m_ptr->ADDRESS;
09910                } else
09911                if (m_ptr->PROC_NR == FS_PROC_NR) {
09912                        psinfo.fproc = (vir_bytes) m_ptr->ADDRESS;
09913                } else {
09914                        return(EPERM);
09915                }
09916                break;
09917        case MIOCGPSINFO:
09918                /* The ps program wants the process table addresses. */
09919                psinfo_phys = numap(m_ptr->PROC_NR, (vir_bytes) m_ptr->ADDRESS,
09920                                                        sizeof(psinfo));
09921                if (psinfo_phys == 0) return(EFAULT);
09922                phys_copy(vir2phys(&psinfo), psinfo_phys, (phys_bytes) sizeof(psinfo));
09923                break;
09924        default:
09925                return(do_diocntl(&m_dtab, m_ptr));
09926        }
09927        return(OK);
09928     }


09931     /*===========================================================================*
09932      *                              m_geometry                                    *
09933      *===========================================================================*/
09934     PRIVATE void m_geometry(entry)
09935     struct partition *entry;
09936     {
09937        /* Memory devices don't have a geometry, but the outside world insists. */
09938        entry->cylinders = (m_geom[m_device].dv_size >> SECTOR_SHIFT) / (64 * 32);
09939        entry->heads = 64;
09940        entry->sectors = 32;
09941     }
```

```
++++++++++++++++++++++++++++++++++++++++++++++++++++++++++++++++++++++++++++++++
                               src/kernel/wini.c
++++++++++++++++++++++++++++++++++++++++++++++++++++++++++++++++++++++++++++++++
10000   /*      wini.c - choose a winchester driver.          Author: Kees J. Bot
10001    *                                                              28 May 1994
10002    * Several different winchester drivers may be compiled
10003    * into the kernel, but only one may run.  That one is chosen here using
10004    * the boot variable 'hd'.
10005    */
10006
10007   #include "kernel.h"
10008   #include "driver.h"
10009
10010   #if ENABLE_WINI
10011
10012   /* Map driver name to task function. */
10013   struct hdmap {
10014     char            *name;
10015     task_t          *task;
10016   } hdmap[] = {
10017
10018   #if ENABLE_AT_WINI
10019     { "at",         at_winchester_task      },
10020   #endif
10021
10022   #if ENABLE_BIOS_WINI
10023     { "bios",       bios_winchester_task    },
10024   #endif
10025
10026   #if ENABLE_ESDI_WINI
10027     { "esdi",       esdi_winchester_task    },
10028   #endif
10029
10030   #if ENABLE_XT_WINI
10031     { "xt",         xt_winchester_task      },
10032   #endif
10033
10034   };
10035
10036
10037   /*===========================================================================*
10038    *                              winchester_task                              *
10039    *===========================================================================*/
10040   PUBLIC void winchester_task()
10041   {
10042     /* Call the default or selected winchester task. */
10043     char *hd;
10044     struct hdmap *map;
10045
10046     hd = k_getenv("hd");
10047
10048     for (map = hdmap; map < hdmap + sizeof(hdmap)/sizeof(hdmap[0]); map++) {
10049           if (hd == NULL || strcmp(hd, map->name) == 0) {
10050                   /* Run the selected winchester task. */
10051                   (*map->task)();
10052           }
10053     }
10054     panic("no hd driver", NO_NUM);
```

```
10055      }
10056      #endif /* ENABLE_WINI */




++++++++++++++++++++++++++++++++++++++++++++++++++++++++++++++++++++++++++++++++++
                              src/kernel/at_wini.c
++++++++++++++++++++++++++++++++++++++++++++++++++++++++++++++++++++++++++++++++++

10100      /* This file contains the device dependent part of a driver for the IBM-AT
10101       * winchester controller.
10102       * It was written by Adri Koppes.
10103       *
10104       * The file contains one entry point:
10105       *
10106       *   at_winchester_task:         main entry when system is brought up
10107       *
10108       *
10109       * Changes:
10110       *        13 Apr 1992 by Kees J. Bot: device dependent/independent split.
10111       */
10112
10113      #include "kernel.h"
10114      #include "driver.h"
10115      #include "drvlib.h"
10116
10117      #if ENABLE_AT_WINI
10118
10119      /* I/O Ports used by winchester disk controllers. */
10120
10121      /* Read and write registers */
10122      #define REG_BASE0       0x1F0    /* base register of controller 0 */
10123      #define REG_BASE1       0x170    /* base register of controller 1 */
10124      #define REG_DATA        0        /* data register (offset from the base reg.) */
10125      #define REG_PRECOMP     1        /* start of write precompensation */
10126      #define REG_COUNT       2        /* sectors to transfer */
10127      #define REG_SECTOR      3        /* sector number */
10128      #define REG_CYL_LO      4        /* low byte of cylinder number */
10129      #define REG_CYL_HI      5        /* high byte of cylinder number */
10130      #define REG_LDH         6        /* lba, drive and head */
10131      #define    LDH_DEFAULT           0xA0    /* ECC enable, 512 bytes per sector */
10132      #define    LDH_LBA               0x40    /* Use LBA addressing */
10133      #define    ldh_init(drive)       (LDH_DEFAULT | ((drive) << 4))
10134
10135      /* Read only registers */
10136      #define REG_STATUS      7        /* status */
10137      #define    STATUS_BSY            0x80    /* controller busy */
10138      #define    STATUS_RDY            0x40    /* drive ready */
10139      #define    STATUS_WF             0x20    /* write fault */
10140      #define    STATUS_SC             0x10    /* seek complete (obsolete) */
10141      #define    STATUS_DRQ            0x08    /* data transfer request */
10142      #define    STATUS_CRD            0x04    /* corrected data */
10143      #define    STATUS_IDX            0x02    /* index pulse */
10144      #define    STATUS_ERR            0x01    /* error */
10145      #define REG_ERROR       1        /* error code */
10146      #define    ERROR_BB              0x80    /* bad block */
10147      #define    ERROR_ECC             0x40    /* bad ecc bytes */
10148      #define    ERROR_ID              0x10    /* id not found */
10149      #define    ERROR_AC              0x04    /* aborted command */
```

```
10150     #define     ERROR_TK          0x02    /* track zero error */
10151     #define     ERROR_DM          0x01    /* no data address mark */
10152
10153     /* Write only registers */
10154     #define REG_COMMAND           7       /* command */
10155     #define     CMD_IDLE          0x00    /* for w_command: drive idle */
10156     #define     CMD_RECALIBRATE   0x10    /* recalibrate drive */
10157     #define     CMD_READ          0x20    /* read data */
10158     #define     CMD_WRITE         0x30    /* write data */
10159     #define     CMD_READVERIFY    0x40    /* read verify */
10160     #define     CMD_FORMAT        0x50    /* format track */
10161     #define     CMD_SEEK          0x70    /* seek cylinder */
10162     #define     CMD_DIAG          0x90    /* execute device diagnostics */
10163     #define     CMD_SPECIFY       0x91    /* specify parameters */
10164     #define     ATA_IDENTIFY      0xEC    /* identify drive */
10165     #define REG_CTL       0x206          /* control register */
10166     #define     CTL_NORETRY       0x80    /* disable access retry */
10167     #define     CTL_NOECC         0x40    /* disable ecc retry */
10168     #define     CTL_EIGHTHEADS    0x08    /* more than eight heads */
10169     #define     CTL_RESET         0x04    /* reset controller */
10170     #define     CTL_INTDISABLE    0x02    /* disable interrupts */
10171
10172     /* Interrupt request lines. */
10173     #define AT_IRQ0           14        /* interrupt number for controller 0 */
10174     #define AT_IRQ1           15        /* interrupt number for controller 1 */
10175
10176     /* Common command block */
10177     struct command {
10178       u8_t  precomp;           /* REG_PRECOMP, etc. */
10179       u8_t  count;
10180       u8_t  sector;
10181       u8_t  cyl_lo;
10182       u8_t  cyl_hi;
10183       u8_t  ldh;
10184       u8_t  command;
10185     };
10186
10187
10188     /* Error codes */
10189     #define ERR               (-1)    /* general error */
10190     #define ERR_BAD_SECTOR    (-2)    /* block marked bad detected */
10191
10192     /* Some controllers don't interrupt, the clock will wake us up. */
10193     #define WAKEUP            (32*HZ) /* drive may be out for 31 seconds max */
10194
10195     /* Miscellaneous. */
10196     #define MAX_DRIVES        4       /* this driver supports 4 drives (hd0 - hd19) */
10197     #if _WORD_SIZE > 2
10198     #define MAX_SECS          256     /* controller can transfer this many sectors */
10199     #else
10200     #define MAX_SECS          127     /* but not to a 16 bit process */
10201     #endif
10202     #define MAX_ERRORS        4       /* how often to try rd/wt before quitting */
10203     #define NR_DEVICES        (MAX_DRIVES * DEV_PER_DRIVE)
10204     #define SUB_PER_DRIVE     (NR_PARTITIONS * NR_PARTITIONS)
10205     #define NR_SUBDEVS        (MAX_DRIVES * SUB_PER_DRIVE)
10206     #define TIMEOUT           32000   /* controller timeout in ms */
10207     #define RECOVERYTIME      500     /* controller recovery time in ms */
10208     #define INITIALIZED       0x01    /* drive is initialized */
10209     #define DEAF              0x02    /* controller must be reset */
```

```
10210   #define SMART            0x04      /* drive supports ATA commands */
10211
10212
10213   /* Variables. */
10214   PRIVATE struct wini {              /* main drive struct, one entry per drive */
10215     unsigned state;                 /* drive state: deaf, initialized, dead */
10216     unsigned base;                  /* base register of the register file */
10217     unsigned irq;                   /* interrupt request line */
10218     unsigned lcylinders;            /* logical number of cylinders (BIOS) */
10219     unsigned lheads;                /* logical number of heads */
10220     unsigned lsectors;              /* logical number of sectors per track */
10221     unsigned pcylinders;            /* physical number of cylinders (translated) */
10222     unsigned pheads;                /* physical number of heads */
10223     unsigned psectors;              /* physical number of sectors per track */
10224     unsigned ldhpref;               /* top four bytes of the LDH (head) register */
10225     unsigned precomp;               /* write precompensation cylinder / 4 */
10226     unsigned max_count;             /* max request for this drive */
10227     unsigned open_ct;               /* in-use count */
10228     struct device part[DEV_PER_DRIVE];    /* primary partitions: hd[0-4] */
10229     struct device subpart[SUB_PER_DRIVE]; /* subpartitions: hd[1-4][a-d] */
10230   } wini[MAX_DRIVES], *w_wn;
10231
10232   PRIVATE struct trans {
10233     struct iorequest_s *iop;        /* belongs to this I/O request */
10234     unsigned long block;            /* first sector to transfer */
10235     unsigned count;                 /* byte count */
10236     phys_bytes phys;                /* user physical address */
10237   } wtrans[NR_IOREQS];
10238
10239   PRIVATE struct trans *w_tp;              /* to add transfer requests */
10240   PRIVATE unsigned w_count;               /* number of bytes to transfer */
10241   PRIVATE unsigned long w_nextblock;      /* next block on disk to transfer */
10242   PRIVATE int w_opcode;                   /* DEV_READ or DEV_WRITE */
10243   PRIVATE int w_command;                  /* current command in execution */
10244   PRIVATE int w_status;                   /* status after interrupt */
10245   PRIVATE int w_drive;                    /* selected drive */
10246   PRIVATE struct device *w_dv;            /* device's base and size */
10247
10248   FORWARD _PROTOTYPE( void init_params, (void) );
10249   FORWARD _PROTOTYPE( int w_do_open, (struct driver *dp, message *m_ptr) );
10250   FORWARD _PROTOTYPE( struct device *w_prepare, (int device) );
10251   FORWARD _PROTOTYPE( int w_identify, (void) );
10252   FORWARD _PROTOTYPE( char *w_name, (void) );
10253   FORWARD _PROTOTYPE( int w_specify, (void) );
10254   FORWARD _PROTOTYPE( int w_schedule, (int proc_nr, struct iorequest_s *iop) );
10255   FORWARD _PROTOTYPE( int w_finish, (void) );
10256   FORWARD _PROTOTYPE( int com_out, (struct command *cmd) );
10257   FORWARD _PROTOTYPE( void w_need_reset, (void) );
10258   FORWARD _PROTOTYPE( int w_do_close, (struct driver *dp, message *m_ptr) );
10259   FORWARD _PROTOTYPE( int com_simple, (struct command *cmd) );
10260   FORWARD _PROTOTYPE( void w_timeout, (void) );
10261   FORWARD _PROTOTYPE( int w_reset, (void) );
10262   FORWARD _PROTOTYPE( int w_intr_wait, (void) );
10263   FORWARD _PROTOTYPE( int w_waitfor, (int mask, int value) );
10264   FORWARD _PROTOTYPE( int w_handler, (int irq) );
10265   FORWARD _PROTOTYPE( void w_geometry, (struct partition *entry) );
10266
10267   /* w_waitfor loop unrolled once for speed. */
10268   #define waitfor(mask, value)    \
10269           ((in_byte(w_wn->base + REG_STATUS) & mask) == value \
```

```
10270                    || w_waitfor(mask, value))
10271
10272
10273    /* Entry points to this driver. */
10274    PRIVATE struct driver w_dtab = {
10275      w_name,                /* current device's name */
10276      w_do_open,             /* open or mount request, initialize device */
10277      w_do_close,            /* release device */
10278      do_diocntl,            /* get or set a partition's geometry */
10279      w_prepare,             /* prepare for I/O on a given minor device */
10280      w_schedule,            /* precompute cylinder, head, sector, etc. */
10281      w_finish,              /* do the I/O */
10282      nop_cleanup,           /* nothing to clean up */
10283      w_geometry,            /* tell the geometry of the disk */
10284    };
10285
10286    #if ENABLE_ATAPI
10287    #include "atapi.c"       /* extra code for ATAPI CD-ROM */
10288    #endif
10289
10290
10291    /*===========================================================================*
10292     *                          at_winchester_task                               *
10293     *===========================================================================*/
10294    PUBLIC void at_winchester_task()
10295    {
10296    /* Set special disk parameters then call the generic main loop. */
10297
10298      init_params();
10299
10300      driver_task(&w_dtab);
10301    }
10304    /*===========================================================================*
10305     *                              init_params                                   *
10306     *===========================================================================*/
10307    PRIVATE void init_params()
10308    {
10309    /* This routine is called at startup to initialize the drive parameters. */
10310
10311      u16_t parv[2];
10312      unsigned int vector;
10313      int drive, nr_drives, i;
10314      struct wini *wn;
10315      u8_t params[16];
10316      phys_bytes param_phys = vir2phys(params);
10317
10318      /* Get the number of drives from the BIOS data area */
10319      phys_copy(0x475L, param_phys, 1L);
10320      if ((nr_drives = params[0]) > 2) nr_drives = 2;
10321
10322      for (drive = 0, wn = wini; drive < MAX_DRIVES; drive++, wn++) {
10323            if (drive < nr_drives) {
10324                    /* Copy the BIOS parameter vector */
10325                    vector = drive == 0 ? WINI_0_PARM_VEC : WINI_1_PARM_VEC;
10326                    phys_copy(vector * 4L, vir2phys(parv), 4L);
10327
10328                    /* Calculate the address of the parameters and copy them */
10329                    phys_copy(hclick_to_physb(parv[1]) + parv[0], param_phys, 16L);
```

```
10330
10331                              /* Copy the parameters to the structures of the drive */
10332                              wn->lcylinders = bp_cylinders(params);
10333                              wn->lheads = bp_heads(params);
10334                              wn->lsectors = bp_sectors(params);
10335                              wn->precomp = bp_precomp(params) >> 2;
10336                      }
10337                  wn->ldhpref = ldh_init(drive);
10338                  wn->max_count = MAX_SECS << SECTOR_SHIFT;
10339                  if (drive < 2) {
10340                          /* Controller 0. */
10341                          wn->base = REG_BASE0;
10342                          wn->irq = AT_IRQ0;
10343                  } else {
10344                          /* Controller 1. */
10345                          wn->base = REG_BASE1;
10346                          wn->irq = AT_IRQ1;
10347                  }
10348          }
10349      }


10352      /*===========================================================================*
10353       *                              w_do_open                                    *
10354       *===========================================================================*/
10355      PRIVATE int w_do_open(dp, m_ptr)
10356      struct driver *dp;
10357      message *m_ptr;
10358      {
10359      /* Device open: Initialize the controller and read the partition table. */
10360
10361        int r;
10362        struct wini *wn;
10363        struct command cmd;
10364
10365        if (w_prepare(m_ptr->DEVICE) == NIL_DEV) return(ENXIO);
10366        wn = w_wn;
10367
10368        if (wn->state == 0) {
10369              /* Try to identify the device. */
10370              if (w_identify() != OK) {
10371                      printf("%s: probe failed\n", w_name());
10372                      if (wn->state & DEAF) w_reset();
10373                      wn->state = 0;
10374                      return(ENXIO);
10375              }
10376        }
10377        if (wn->open_ct++ == 0) {
10378              /* Partition the disk. */
10379              partition(&w_dtab, w_drive * DEV_PER_DRIVE, P_PRIMARY);
10380        }
10381        return(OK);
10382      }


10385      /*===========================================================================*
10386       *                              w_prepare                                    *
10387       *===========================================================================*/
10388      PRIVATE struct device *w_prepare(device)
10389      int device;
```

```
10390   {
10391   /* Prepare for I/O on a device. */
10392
10393       /* Nothing to transfer as yet. */
10394       w_count = 0;
10395
10396       if (device < NR_DEVICES) {                          /* hd0, hd1, ... */
10397           w_drive = device / DEV_PER_DRIVE;        /* save drive number */
10398           w_wn = &wini[w_drive];
10399           w_dv = &w_wn->part[device % DEV_PER_DRIVE];
10400       } else
10401       if ((unsigned) (device -= MINOR_hd1a) < NR_SUBDEVS) { /* hd1a, hd1b, ... */
10402           w_drive = device / SUB_PER_DRIVE;
10403           w_wn = &wini[w_drive];
10404           w_dv = &w_wn->subpart[device % SUB_PER_DRIVE];
10405       } else {
10406           return(NIL_DEV);
10407       }
10408       return(w_dv);
10409   }


10412   /*===========================================================================*
10413    *                              w_identify                                   *
10414    *===========================================================================*/
10415   PRIVATE int w_identify()
10416   {
10417   /* Find out if a device exists, if it is an old AT disk, or a newer ATA
10418    * drive, a removable media device, etc.
10419    */
10420
10421       struct wini *wn = w_wn;
10422       struct command cmd;
10423       char id_string[40];
10424       int i, r;
10425       unsigned long size;
10426   #define id_byte(n)       (&tmp_buf[2 * (n)])
10427   #define id_word(n)       (((u16_t) id_byte(n)[0] <<  0) \
10428                            |((u16_t) id_byte(n)[1] <<  8))
10429   #define id_longword(n)   (((u32_t) id_byte(n)[0] <<  0) \
10430                            |((u32_t) id_byte(n)[1] <<  8) \
10431                            |((u32_t) id_byte(n)[2] << 16) \
10432                            |((u32_t) id_byte(n)[3] << 24))
10433
10434       /* Check if the one of the registers exists. */
10435       r = in_byte(wn->base + REG_CYL_LO);
10436       out_byte(wn->base + REG_CYL_LO, ~r);
10437       if (in_byte(wn->base + REG_CYL_LO) == r) return(ERR);
10438
10439       /* Looks OK; register IRQ and try an ATA identify command. */
10440       put_irq_handler(wn->irq, w_handler);
10441       enable_irq(wn->irq);
10442
10443       cmd.ldh     = wn->ldhpref;
10444       cmd.command = ATA_IDENTIFY;
10445       if (com_simple(&cmd) == OK) {
10446           /* This is an ATA device. */
10447           wn->state |= SMART;
10448
10449           /* Device information. */
```

```
10450                port_read(wn->base + REG_DATA, tmp_phys, SECTOR_SIZE);
10451
10452                /* Why are the strings byte swapped??? */
10453                for (i = 0; i < 40; i++) id_string[i] = id_byte(27)[i^1];
10454
10455                /* Preferred CHS translation mode. */
10456                wn->pcylinders = id_word(1);
10457                wn->pheads = id_word(3);
10458                wn->psectors = id_word(6);
10459                size = (u32_t) wn->pcylinders * wn->pheads * wn->psectors;
10460
10461                if ((id_byte(49)[1] & 0x02) && size > 512L*1024*2) {
10462                        /* Drive is LBA capable and is big enough to trust it to
10463                         * not make a mess of it.
10464                         */
10465                        wn->ldhpref |= LDH_LBA;
10466                        size = id_longword(60);
10467                }
10468
10469                if (wn->lcylinders == 0) {
10470                        /* No BIOS parameters?  Then make some up. */
10471                        wn->lcylinders = wn->pcylinders;
10472                        wn->lheads = wn->pheads;
10473                        wn->lsectors = wn->psectors;
10474                        while (wn->lcylinders > 1024) {
10475                                wn->lheads *= 2;
10476                                wn->lcylinders /= 2;
10477                        }
10478                }
10479        } else {
10480                /* Not an ATA device; no translations, no special features.  Don't
10481                 * touch it unless the BIOS knows about it.
10482                 */
10483                if (wn->lcylinders == 0) return(ERR);   /* no BIOS parameters */
10484                wn->pcylinders = wn->lcylinders;
10485                wn->pheads = wn->lheads;
10486                wn->psectors = wn->lsectors;
10487                size = (u32_t) wn->pcylinders * wn->pheads * wn->psectors;
10488        }
10489        /* The fun ends at 4 GB. */
10490        if (size > ((u32_t) -1) / SECTOR_SIZE) size = ((u32_t) -1) / SECTOR_SIZE;
10491
10492        /* Base and size of the whole drive */
10493        wn->part[0].dv_base = 0;
10494        wn->part[0].dv_size = size << SECTOR_SHIFT;
10495
10496        if (w_specify() != OK && w_specify() != OK) return(ERR);
10497
10498        printf("%s: ", w_name());
10499        if (wn->state & SMART) {
10500                printf("%.40s\n", id_string);
10501        } else {
10502                printf("%ux%ux%u\n", wn->pcylinders, wn->pheads, wn->psectors);
10503        }
10504        return(OK);
10505 }


10508 /*===========================================================================*
10509  *                              w_name                                       *
```

```
10510       *===========================================================================*/
10511   PRIVATE char *w_name()
10512   {
10513   /* Return a name for the current device. */
10514     static char name[] = "at-hd15";
10515     unsigned device = w_drive * DEV_PER_DRIVE;
10516
10517     if (device < 10) {
10518           name[5] = '0' + device;
10519           name[6] = 0;
10520     } else {
10521           name[5] = '0' + device / 10;
10522           name[6] = '0' + device % 10;
10523     }
10524     return name;
10525   }


10528   /*===========================================================================*
10529    *                              w_specify                                     *
10530    *===========================================================================*/
10531   PRIVATE int w_specify()
10532   {
10533   /* Routine to initialize the drive after boot or when a reset is needed. */
10534
10535     struct wini *wn = w_wn;
10536     struct command cmd;
10537
10538     if ((wn->state & DEAF) && w_reset() != OK) return(ERR);
10539
10540     /* Specify parameters: precompensation, number of heads and sectors. */
10541     cmd.precomp = wn->precomp;
10542     cmd.count   = wn->psectors;
10543     cmd.ldh     = w_wn->ldhpref | (wn->pheads - 1);
10544     cmd.command = CMD_SPECIFY;              /* Specify some parameters */
10545
10546     if (com_simple(&cmd) != OK) return(ERR);
10547
10548     if (!(wn->state & SMART)) {
10549           /* Calibrate an old disk. */
10550           cmd.sector  = 0;
10551           cmd.cyl_lo  = 0;
10552           cmd.cyl_hi  = 0;
10553           cmd.ldh     = w_wn->ldhpref;
10554           cmd.command = CMD_RECALIBRATE;
10555
10556           if (com_simple(&cmd) != OK) return(ERR);
10557     }
10558
10559     wn->state |= INITIALIZED;
10560     return(OK);
10561   }


10564   /*===========================================================================*
10565    *                              w_schedule                                    *
10566    *===========================================================================*/
10567   PRIVATE int w_schedule(proc_nr, iop)
10568   int proc_nr;                    /* process doing the request */
10569   struct iorequest_s *iop;        /* pointer to read or write request */
```

```
10570    {
10571    /* Gather I/O requests on consecutive blocks so they may be read/written
10572     * in one controller command.  (There is enough time to compute the next
10573     * consecutive request while an unwanted block passes by.)
10574     */
10575      struct wini *wn = w_wn;
10576      int r, opcode;
10577      unsigned long pos;
10578      unsigned nbytes, count;
10579      unsigned long block;
10580      phys_bytes user_phys;
10581
10582      /* This many bytes to read/write */
10583      nbytes = iop->io_nbytes;
10584      if ((nbytes & SECTOR_MASK) != 0) return(iop->io_nbytes = EINVAL);
10585
10586      /* From/to this position on the device */
10587      pos = iop->io_position;
10588      if ((pos & SECTOR_MASK) != 0) return(iop->io_nbytes = EINVAL);
10589
10590      /* To/from this user address */
10591      user_phys = numap(proc_nr, (vir_bytes) iop->io_buf, nbytes);
10592      if (user_phys == 0) return(iop->io_nbytes = EINVAL);
10593
10594      /* Read or write? */
10595      opcode = iop->io_request & ~OPTIONAL_IO;
10596
10597      /* Which block on disk and how close to EOF? */
10598      if (pos >= w_dv->dv_size) return(OK);            /* At EOF */
10599      if (pos + nbytes > w_dv->dv_size) nbytes = w_dv->dv_size - pos;
10600      block = (w_dv->dv_base + pos) >> SECTOR_SHIFT;
10601
10602      if (w_count > 0 && block != w_nextblock) {
10603            /* This new request can't be chained to the job being built */
10604            if ((r = w_finish()) != OK) return(r);
10605      }
10606
10607      /* The next consecutive block */
10608      w_nextblock = block + (nbytes >> SECTOR_SHIFT);
10609
10610      /* While there are "unscheduled" bytes in the request: */
10611      do {
10612            count = nbytes;
10613
10614            if (w_count == wn->max_count) {
10615                  /* The drive can't do more then max_count at once */
10616                  if ((r = w_finish()) != OK) return(r);
10617            }
10618
10619            if (w_count + count > wn->max_count)
10620                  count = wn->max_count - w_count;
10621
10622            if (w_count == 0) {
10623                  /* The first request in a row, initialize. */
10624                  w_opcode = opcode;
10625                  w_tp = wtrans;
10626            }
10627
10628            /* Store I/O parameters */
10629            w_tp->iop = iop;
```

```
10630                w_tp->block = block;
10631                w_tp->count = count;
10632                w_tp->phys = user_phys;
10633
10634                /* Update counters */
10635                w_tp++;
10636                w_count += count;
10637                block += count >> SECTOR_SHIFT;
10638                user_phys += count;
10639                nbytes -= count;
10640        } while (nbytes > 0);
10641
10642        return(OK);
10643     }


10646     /*===========================================================================*
10647      *                              w_finish                                     *
10648      *===========================================================================*/
10649     PRIVATE int w_finish()
10650     {
10651     /* Carry out the I/O requests gathered in wtrans[]. */
10652
10653        struct trans *tp = wtrans;
10654        struct wini *wn = w_wn;
10655        int r, errors;
10656        struct command cmd;
10657        unsigned cylinder, head, sector, secspcyl;
10658
10659        if (w_count == 0) return(OK); /* Spurious finish. */
10660
10661        r = ERR;        /* Trigger the first com_out */
10662        errors = 0;
10663
10664        do {
10665                if (r != OK) {
10666                        /* The controller must be (re)programmed. */
10667
10668                        /* First check to see if a reinitialization is needed. */
10669                        if (!(wn->state & INITIALIZED) && w_specify() != OK)
10670                                return(tp->iop->io_nbytes = EIO);
10671
10672                        /* Tell the controller to transfer w_count bytes */
10673                        cmd.precomp = wn->precomp;
10674                        cmd.count   = (w_count >> SECTOR_SHIFT) & BYTE;
10675                        if (wn->ldhpref & LDH_LBA) {
10676                                cmd.sector = (tp->block >>  0) & 0xFF;
10677                                cmd.cyl_lo = (tp->block >>  8) & 0xFF;
10678                                cmd.cyl_hi = (tp->block >> 16) & 0xFF;
10679                                cmd.ldh    = wn->ldhpref | ((tp->block >> 24) & 0xF);
10680                        } else {
10681                                secspcyl = wn->pheads * wn->psectors;
10682                                cylinder = tp->block / secspcyl;
10683                                head = (tp->block % secspcyl) / wn->psectors;
10684                                sector = tp->block % wn->psectors;
10685                                cmd.sector = sector + 1;
10686                                cmd.cyl_lo = cylinder & BYTE;
10687                                cmd.cyl_hi = (cylinder >> 8) & BYTE;
10688                                cmd.ldh    = wn->ldhpref | head;
10689                        }
```

```
10690                         cmd.command = w_opcode == DEV_WRITE ? CMD_WRITE : CMD_READ;
10691
10692                 if ((r = com_out(&cmd)) != OK) {
10693                         if (++errors == MAX_ERRORS) {
10694                                 w_command = CMD_IDLE;
10695                                 return(tp->iop->io_nbytes = EIO);
10696                         }
10697                         continue;        /* Retry */
10698                 }
10699         }
10700
10701         /* For each sector, wait for an interrupt and fetch the data (read),
10702          * or supply data to the controller and wait for an interrupt (write).
10703          */
10704
10705         if (w_opcode == DEV_READ) {
10706                 if ((r = w_intr_wait()) == OK) {
10707                         /* Copy data from the device's buffer to user space. */
10708
10709                         port_read(wn->base + REG_DATA, tp->phys, SECTOR_SIZE);
10710
10711                         tp->phys += SECTOR_SIZE;
10712                         tp->iop->io_nbytes -= SECTOR_SIZE;
10713                         w_count -= SECTOR_SIZE;
10714                         if ((tp->count -= SECTOR_SIZE) == 0) tp++;
10715                 } else {
10716                         /* Any faulty data? */
10717                         if (w_status & STATUS_DRQ) {
10718                                 port_read(wn->base + REG_DATA, tmp_phys,
10719                                                              SECTOR_SIZE);
10720                         }
10721                 }
10722         } else {
10723                 /* Wait for data requested. */
10724                 if (!waitfor(STATUS_DRQ, STATUS_DRQ)) {
10725                         r = ERR;
10726                 } else {
10727                         /* Fill the buffer of the drive. */
10728
10729                         port_write(wn->base + REG_DATA, tp->phys, SECTOR_SIZE);
10730                         r = w_intr_wait();
10731                 }
10732
10733                 if (r == OK) {
10734                         /* Book the bytes successfully written. */
10735
10736                         tp->phys += SECTOR_SIZE;
10737                         tp->iop->io_nbytes -= SECTOR_SIZE;
10738                         w_count -= SECTOR_SIZE;
10739                         if ((tp->count -= SECTOR_SIZE) == 0) tp++;
10740                 }
10741         }
10742
10743         if (r != OK) {
10744                 /* Don't retry if sector marked bad or too many errors */
10745                 if (r == ERR_BAD_SECTOR || ++errors == MAX_ERRORS) {
10746                         w_command = CMD_IDLE;
10747                         return(tp->iop->io_nbytes = EIO);
10748                 }
10749
```

```
10750                              /* Reset if halfway, but bail out if optional I/O. */
10751                              if (errors == MAX_ERRORS / 2) {
10752                                      w_need_reset();
10753                                      if (tp->iop->io_request & OPTIONAL_IO) {
10754                                              w_command = CMD_IDLE;
10755                                              return(tp->iop->io_nbytes = EIO);
10756                                      }
10757                              }
10758                              continue;          /* Retry */
10759                      }
10760                  errors = 0;
10761          } while (w_count > 0);
10762
10763          w_command = CMD_IDLE;
10764          return(OK);
10765  }


10768  /*===========================================================================*
10769   *                               com_out                                     *
10770   *===========================================================================*/
10771  PRIVATE int com_out(cmd)
10772  struct command *cmd;                  /* Command block */
10773  {
10774  /* Output the command block to the winchester controller and return status */
10775
10776          struct wini *wn = w_wn;
10777          unsigned base = wn->base;
10778
10779          if (!waitfor(STATUS_BSY, 0)) {
10780                  printf("%s: controller not ready\n", w_name());
10781                  return(ERR);
10782          }
10783
10784          /* Select drive. */
10785          out_byte(base + REG_LDH, cmd->ldh);
10786
10787          if (!waitfor(STATUS_BSY, 0)) {
10788                  printf("%s: drive not ready\n", w_name());
10789                  return(ERR);
10790          }
10791
10792          /* Schedule a wakeup call, some controllers are flaky. */
10793          clock_mess(WAKEUP, w_timeout);
10794
10795          out_byte(base + REG_CTL, wn->pheads >= 8 ? CTL_EIGHTHEADS : 0);
10796          out_byte(base + REG_PRECOMP, cmd->precomp);
10797          out_byte(base + REG_COUNT, cmd->count);
10798          out_byte(base + REG_SECTOR, cmd->sector);
10799          out_byte(base + REG_CYL_LO, cmd->cyl_lo);
10800          out_byte(base + REG_CYL_HI, cmd->cyl_hi);
10801          lock();
10802          out_byte(base + REG_COMMAND, cmd->command);
10803          w_command = cmd->command;
10804          w_status = STATUS_BSY;
10805          unlock();
10806          return(OK);
10807  }
```

```
10810    /*===========================================================================*
10811     *                          w_need_reset                                     *
10812     *===========================================================================*/
10813    PRIVATE void w_need_reset()
10814    {
10815    /* The controller needs to be reset. */
10816      struct wini *wn;
10817
10818      for (wn = wini; wn < &wini[MAX_DRIVES]; wn++) {
10819            wn->state |= DEAF;
10820            wn->state &= ~INITIALIZED;
10821      }
10822    }


10825    /*===========================================================================*
10826     *                          w_do_close                                       *
10827     *===========================================================================*/
10828    PRIVATE int w_do_close(dp, m_ptr)
10829    struct driver *dp;
10830    message *m_ptr;
10831    {
10832    /* Device close: Release a device. */
10833
10834      if (w_prepare(m_ptr->DEVICE) == NIL_DEV) return(ENXIO);
10835      w_wn->open_ct--;
10836      return(OK);
10837    }


10840    /*===========================================================================*
10841     *                          com_simple                                       *
10842     *===========================================================================*/
10843    PRIVATE int com_simple(cmd)
10844    struct command *cmd;           /* Command block */
10845    {
10846    /* A simple controller command, only one interrupt and no data-out phase. */
10847      int r;
10848
10849      if ((r = com_out(cmd)) == OK) r = w_intr_wait();
10850      w_command = CMD_IDLE;
10851      return(r);
10852    }


10855    /*===========================================================================*
10856     *                          w_timeout                                        *
10857     *===========================================================================*/
10858    PRIVATE void w_timeout()
10859    {
10860      struct wini *wn = w_wn;
10861
10862      switch (w_command) {
10863      case CMD_IDLE:
10864            break;          /* fine */
10865      case CMD_READ:
10866      case CMD_WRITE:
10867            /* Impossible, but not on PC's:  The controller does not respond. */
10868
10869            /* Limiting multisector I/O seems to help. */
```

```
10870                if (wn->max_count > 8 * SECTOR_SIZE) {
10871                        wn->max_count = 8 * SECTOR_SIZE;
10872                } else {
10873                        wn->max_count = SECTOR_SIZE;
10874                }
10875                /*FALL THROUGH*/
10876        default:
10877                /* Some other command. */
10878                printf("%s: timeout on command %02x\n", w_name(), w_command);
10879                w_need_reset();
10880                w_status = 0;
10881                interrupt(WINCHESTER);
10882        }
10883   }


10886   /*===========================================================================*
10887    *                              w_reset                                      *
10888    *===========================================================================*/
10889   PRIVATE int w_reset()
10890   {
10891   /* Issue a reset to the controller.  This is done after any catastrophe,
10892    * like the controller refusing to respond.
10893    */
10894
10895     struct wini *wn;
10896     int err;
10897
10898     /* Wait for any internal drive recovery. */
10899     milli_delay(RECOVERYTIME);
10900
10901     /* Strobe reset bit */
10902     out_byte(w_wn->base + REG_CTL, CTL_RESET);
10903     milli_delay(1);
10904     out_byte(w_wn->base + REG_CTL, 0);
10905     milli_delay(1);
10906
10907     /* Wait for controller ready */
10908     if (!w_waitfor(STATUS_BSY | STATUS_RDY, STATUS_RDY)) {
10909           printf("%s: reset failed, drive busy\n", w_name());
10910           return(ERR);
10911     }
10912
10913     /* The error register should be checked now, but some drives mess it up. */
10914
10915     for (wn = wini; wn < &wini[MAX_DRIVES]; wn++) {
10916           if (wn->base == w_wn->base) wn->state &= ~DEAF;
10917     }
10918     return(OK);
10919   }


10922   /*===========================================================================*
10923    *                              w_intr_wait                                  *
10924    *===========================================================================*/
10925   PRIVATE int w_intr_wait()
10926   {
10927   /* Wait for a task completion interrupt and return results. */
10928
10929     message mess;
```

```
10930        int r;
10931
10932        /* Wait for an interrupt that sets w_status to "not busy". */
10933        while (w_status & STATUS_BSY) receive(HARDWARE, &mess);
10934
10935        /* Check status. */
10936        lock();
10937        if ((w_status & (STATUS_BSY | STATUS_RDY | STATUS_WF | STATUS_ERR))
10938                                                        == STATUS_RDY) {
10939                r = OK;
10940                w_status |= STATUS_BSY; /* assume still busy with I/O */
10941        } else
10942        if ((w_status & STATUS_ERR) && (in_byte(w_wn->base + REG_ERROR) & ERROR_BB)) {
10943                r = ERR_BAD_SECTOR;      /* sector marked bad, retries won't help */
10944        } else {
10945                r = ERR;                /* any other error */
10946        }
10947        unlock();
10948        return(r);
10949    }


10952    /*===========================================================================*
10953     *                              w_waitfor                                     *
10954     *===========================================================================*/
10955    PRIVATE int w_waitfor(mask, value)
10956    int mask;                       /* status mask */
10957    int value;                      /* required status */
10958    {
10959    /* Wait until controller is in the required state.  Return zero on timeout. */
10960
10961        struct milli_state ms;
10962
10963        milli_start(&ms);
10964        do {
10965                if ((in_byte(w_wn->base + REG_STATUS) & mask) == value) return 1;
10966        } while (milli_elapsed(&ms) < TIMEOUT);
10967
10968        w_need_reset();         /* Controller gone deaf. */
10969        return(0);
10970    }


10973    /*===========================================================================*
10974     *                              w_handler                                     *
10975     *===========================================================================*/
10976    PRIVATE int w_handler(irq)
10977    int irq;
10978    {
10979    /* Disk interrupt, send message to winchester task and reenable interrupts. */
10980
10981        w_status = in_byte(w_wn->base + REG_STATUS);  /* acknowledge interrupt */
10982        interrupt(WINCHESTER);
10983        return 1;
10984    }


10987    /*===========================================================================*
10988     *                              w_geometry                                    *
10989     *===========================================================================*/
```

```
10990    PRIVATE void w_geometry(entry)
10991    struct partition *entry;
10992    {
10993      entry->cylinders = w_wn->lcylinders;
10994      entry->heads = w_wn->lheads;
10995      entry->sectors = w_wn->lsectors;
10996    }
10997    #endif /* ENABLE_AT_WINI */
```

```
++++++++++++++++++++++++++++++++++++++++++++++++++++++++++++++++++++++++++++++++
                              src/kernel/clock.c
++++++++++++++++++++++++++++++++++++++++++++++++++++++++++++++++++++++++++++++++
```

```
11000    /* This file contains the code and data for the clock task.  The clock task
11001     * accepts six message types:
11002     *
11003     *   HARD_INT:    a clock interrupt has occurred
11004     *   GET_UPTIME:  get the time since boot in ticks
11005     *   GET_TIME:    a process wants the real time in seconds
11006     *   SET_TIME:    a process wants to set the real time in seconds
11007     *   SET_ALARM:   a process wants to be alerted after a specified interval
11008     *   SET_SYN_AL:  set the sync alarm
11009     *
11010     *
11011     * The input message is format m6.  The parameters are as follows:
11012     *
11013     *     m_type    CLOCK_PROC   FUNC     NEW_TIME
11014     * -------------------------------------------
11015     * | HARD_INT   |          |         |         |
11016     * |------------+----------+---------+---------|
11017     * | GET_UPTIME |          |         |         |
11018     * |------------+----------+---------+---------|
11019     * | GET_TIME   |          |         |         |
11020     * |------------+----------+---------+---------|
11021     * | SET_TIME   |          |         | newtime |
11022     * |------------+----------+---------+---------|
11023     * | SET_ALARM  | proc_nr  |f to call| delta   |
11024     * |------------+----------+---------+---------|
11025     * | SET_SYN_AL | proc_nr  |         | delta   |
11026     * -------------------------------------------
11027     * NEW_TIME, DELTA_CLICKS, and SECONDS_LEFT all refer to the same field in
11028     * the message, depending upon the message type.
11029     *
11030     * Reply messages are of type OK, except in the case of a HARD_INT, to
11031     * which no reply is generated. For the GET_* messages the time is returned
11032     * in the NEW_TIME field, and for the SET_ALARM and SET_SYN_AL the time
11033     * in seconds remaining until the alarm is returned is returned in the same
11034     * field.
11035     *
11036     * When an alarm goes off, if the caller is a user process, a SIGALRM signal
11037     * is sent to it.  If it is a task, a function specified by the caller will
11038     * be invoked.  This function may, for example, send a message, but only if
11039     * it is certain that the task will be blocked when the timer goes off. A
11040     * synchronous alarm sends a message to the synchronous alarm task, which
11041     * in turn can dispatch a message to another server. This is the only way
11042     * to send an alarm to a server, since servers cannot use the function-call
11043     * mechanism available to tasks and servers cannot receive signals.
11044     */
```

```
11045
11046      #include "kernel.h"
11047      #include <signal.h>
11048      #include <minix/callnr.h>
11049      #include <minix/com.h>
11050      #include "proc.h"
11051
11052      /* Constant definitions. */
11053      #define MILLISEC          100     /* how often to call the scheduler (msec) */
11054      #define SCHED_RATE (MILLISEC*HZ/1000)    /* number of ticks per schedule */
11055
11056      /* Clock parameters. */
11057      #define COUNTER_FREQ (2*TIMER_FREQ)      /* counter frequency using sqare wave*/
11058      #define LATCH_COUNT      0x00     /* cc00xxxx, c = channel, x = any */
11059      #define SQUARE_WAVE      0x36     /* ccaammmb, a = access, m = mode, b = BCD */
11060                                       /*    11x11, 11 = LSB then MSB, x11 = sq wave */
11061      #define TIMER_COUNT ((unsigned) (TIMER_FREQ/HZ)) /* initial value for counter*/
11062      #define TIMER_FREQ  1193182L     /* clock frequency for timer in PC and AT */
11063
11064      #define CLOCK_ACK_BIT    0x80     /* PS/2 clock interrupt acknowledge bit */
11065
11066      /* Clock task variables. */
11067      PRIVATE clock_t realtime;           /* real time clock */
11068      PRIVATE time_t boot_time;           /* time in seconds of system boot */
11069      PRIVATE clock_t next_alarm;          /* probable time of next alarm */
11070      PRIVATE message mc;                  /* message buffer for both input and output */
11071      PRIVATE int watchdog_proc;           /* contains proc_nr at call of *watch_dog[]*/
11072      PRIVATE watchdog_t watch_dog[NR_TASKS+NR_PROCS];
11073
11074      /* Variables used by both clock task and synchronous alarm task */
11075      PRIVATE int syn_al_alive= TRUE; /* don't wake syn_alrm_task before inited*/
11076      PRIVATE int syn_table[NR_TASKS+NR_PROCS]; /* which tasks get CLOCK_INT*/
11077
11078      /* Variables changed by interrupt handler */
11079      PRIVATE clock_t pending_ticks;  /* ticks seen by low level only */
11080      PRIVATE int sched_ticks = SCHED_RATE;    /* counter: when 0, call scheduler */
11081      PRIVATE struct proc *prev_ptr;  /* last user process run by clock task */
11082
11083      FORWARD _PROTOTYPE( void common_setalarm, (int proc_nr,
11084                      long delta_ticks, watchdog_t fuction) );
11085      FORWARD _PROTOTYPE( void do_clocktick, (void) );
11086      FORWARD _PROTOTYPE( void do_get_time, (void) );
11087      FORWARD _PROTOTYPE( void do_getuptime, (void) );
11088      FORWARD _PROTOTYPE( void do_set_time, (message *m_ptr) );
11089      FORWARD _PROTOTYPE( void do_setalarm, (message *m_ptr) );
11090      FORWARD _PROTOTYPE( void init_clock, (void) );
11091      FORWARD _PROTOTYPE( void cause_alarm, (void) );
11092      FORWARD _PROTOTYPE( void do_setsyn_alrm, (message *m_ptr) );
11093      FORWARD _PROTOTYPE( int clock_handler, (int irq) );
11094
11095      /*===========================================================================*
11096       *                              clock_task                                   *
11097       *===========================================================================*/
11098      PUBLIC void clock_task()
11099      {
11100      /* Main program of clock task.  It corrects realtime by adding pending
11101       * ticks seen only by the interrupt service, then it determines which
11102       * of the 6 possible calls this is by looking at 'mc.m_type'.  Then
11103       * it dispatches.
11104       */
```

```
11105
11106      int opcode;
11107
11108      init_clock();                      /* initialize clock task */
11109
11110      /* Main loop of the clock task.  Get work, process it, sometimes reply. */
11111      while (TRUE) {
11112          receive(ANY, &mc);             /* go get a message */
11113          opcode = mc.m_type;           /* extract the function code */
11114
11115          lock();
11116          realtime += pending_ticks; /* transfer ticks from low level handler */
11117          pending_ticks = 0;            /* so we don't have to worry about them */
11118          unlock();
11119
11120          switch (opcode) {
11121              case HARD_INT:   do_clocktick();        break;
11122              case GET_UPTIME: do_getuptime();        break;
11123              case GET_TIME:   do_get_time();         break;
11124              case SET_TIME:   do_set_time(&mc);      break;
11125              case SET_ALARM:  do_setalarm(&mc);      break;
11126              case SET_SYNC_AL:do_setsyn_alrm(&mc);   break;
11127              default: panic("clock task got bad message", mc.m_type);
11128          }
11129
11130          /* Send reply, except for clock tick. */
11131          mc.m_type = OK;
11132          if (opcode != HARD_INT) send(mc.m_source, &mc);
11133      }
11134  }


11137  /*===========================================================================*
11138   *                              do_clocktick                                 *
11139   *===========================================================================*/
11140  PRIVATE void do_clocktick()
11141  {
11142  /* Despite its name, this routine is not called on every clock tick. It
11143   * is called on those clock ticks when a lot of work needs to be done.
11144   */
11145
11146    register struct proc *rp;
11147    register int proc_nr;
11148
11149    if (next_alarm <= realtime) {
11150          /* An alarm may have gone off, but proc may have exited, so check. */
11151          next_alarm = LONG_MAX;   /* start computing next alarm */
11152          for (rp = BEG_PROC_ADDR; rp < END_PROC_ADDR; rp++) {
11153                  if (rp->p_alarm != 0) {
11154                          /* See if this alarm time has been reached. */
11155                          if (rp->p_alarm <= realtime) {
11156                                  /* A timer has gone off.  If it is a user proc,
11157                                   * send it a signal.  If it is a task, call the
11158                                   * function previously specified by the task.
11159                                   */
11160                                  proc_nr = proc_number(rp);
11161                                  if (watch_dog[proc_nr+NR_TASKS]) {
11162                                          watchdog_proc= proc_nr;
11163                                          (*watch_dog[proc_nr+NR_TASKS])();
11164                                  }
```

```
11165                               else
11166                                       cause_sig(proc_nr, SIGALRM);
11167                               rp->p_alarm = 0;
11168                       }
11169
11170                       /* Work on determining which alarm is next. */
11171                       if (rp->p_alarm != 0 && rp->p_alarm < next_alarm)
11172                               next_alarm = rp->p_alarm;
11173               }
11174       }
11175   }
11176
11177   /* If a user process has been running too long, pick another one. */
11178   if (--sched_ticks == 0) {
11179       if (bill_ptr == prev_ptr) lock_sched(); /* process has run too long */
11180       sched_ticks = SCHED_RATE;               /* reset quantum */
11181       prev_ptr = bill_ptr;                    /* new previous process */
11182   }
11183 }


11186   /*===========================================================================*
11187    *                              do_getuptime                                 *
11188    *===========================================================================*/
11189   PRIVATE void do_getuptime()
11190   {
11191   /* Get and return the current clock uptime in ticks. */
11192
11193     mc.NEW_TIME = realtime;        /* current uptime */
11194   }


11197   /*===========================================================================*
11198    *                              get_uptime                                   *
11199    *===========================================================================*/
11200   PUBLIC clock_t get_uptime()
11201   {
11202   /* Get and return the current clock uptime in ticks.  This function is
11203    * designed to be called from other tasks, so they can get uptime without
11204    * the overhead of messages. It has to be careful about pending_ticks.
11205    */
11206
11207     clock_t uptime;
11208
11209     lock();
11210     uptime = realtime + pending_ticks;
11211     unlock();
11212     return(uptime);
11213   }


11216   /*===========================================================================*
11217    *                              do_get_time                                  *
11218    *===========================================================================*/
11219   PRIVATE void do_get_time()
11220   {
11221   /* Get and return the current clock time in seconds. */
11222
11223     mc.NEW_TIME = boot_time + realtime/HZ;       /* current real time */
11224   }
```

```
11227   /*===========================================================================*
11228    *                             do_set_time                                   *
11229    *===========================================================================*/
11230   PRIVATE void do_set_time(m_ptr)
11231   message *m_ptr;                 /* pointer to request message */
11232   {
11233   /* Set the real time clock.  Only the superuser can use this call. */
11234
11235      boot_time = m_ptr->NEW_TIME - realtime/HZ;
11236   }


11239   /*===========================================================================*
11240    *                             do_setalarm                                   *
11241    *===========================================================================*/
11242   PRIVATE void do_setalarm(m_ptr)
11243   message *m_ptr;                 /* pointer to request message */
11244   {
11245   /* A process wants an alarm signal or a task wants a given watch_dog function
11246    * called after a specified interval.
11247    */
11248
11249      register struct proc *rp;
11250      int proc_nr;                   /* which process wants the alarm */
11251      long delta_ticks;              /* in how many clock ticks does he want it? */
11252      watchdog_t function;           /* function to call (tasks only) */
11253
11254      /* Extract the parameters from the message. */
11255      proc_nr = m_ptr->CLOCK_PROC_NR;        /* process to interrupt later */
11256      delta_ticks = m_ptr->DELTA_TICKS;      /* how many ticks to wait */
11257      function = (watchdog_t) m_ptr->FUNC_TO_CALL;
11258                                             /* function to call (tasks only) */
11259      rp = proc_addr(proc_nr);
11260      mc.SECONDS_LEFT = (rp->p_alarm == 0 ? 0 : (rp->p_alarm - realtime)/HZ );
11261      if (!istaskp(rp)) function= 0;         /* user processes get signaled */
11262      common_setalarm(proc_nr, delta_ticks, function);
11263   }


11266   /*===========================================================================*
11267    *                             do_setsyn_alrm                                *
11268    *===========================================================================*/
11269   PRIVATE void do_setsyn_alrm(m_ptr)
11270   message *m_ptr;                 /* pointer to request message */
11271   {
11272   /* A process wants a synchronous alarm.
11273    */
11274
11275      register struct proc *rp;
11276      int proc_nr;                   /* which process wants the alarm */
11277      long delta_ticks;              /* in how many clock ticks does he want it? */
11278
11279      /* Extract the parameters from the message. */
11280      proc_nr = m_ptr->CLOCK_PROC_NR;        /* process to interrupt later */
11281      delta_ticks = m_ptr->DELTA_TICKS;      /* how many ticks to wait */
11282      rp = proc_addr(proc_nr);
11283      mc.SECONDS_LEFT = (rp->p_alarm == 0 ? 0 : (rp->p_alarm - realtime)/HZ );
11284      common_setalarm(proc_nr, delta_ticks, cause_alarm);
```

```
11285    }


11288    /*===========================================================================*
11289     *                              common_setalarm                              *
11290     *===========================================================================*/
11291    PRIVATE void common_setalarm(proc_nr, delta_ticks, function)
11292    int proc_nr;                        /* which process wants the alarm */
11293    long delta_ticks;                   /* in how many clock ticks does he want it? */
11294    watchdog_t function;                /* function to call (0 if cause_sig is
11295                                         * to be called */
11296    {
11297    /* Finish up work of do_set_alarm and do_setsyn_alrm.  Record an alarm
11298     * request and check to see if it is the next alarm needed.
11299     */
11300
11301      register struct proc *rp;
11302
11303      rp = proc_addr(proc_nr);
11304      rp->p_alarm = (delta_ticks == 0 ? 0 : realtime + delta_ticks);
11305      watch_dog[proc_nr+NR_TASKS] = function;
11306
11307      /* Which alarm is next? */
11308      next_alarm = LONG_MAX;
11309      for (rp = BEG_PROC_ADDR; rp < END_PROC_ADDR; rp++)
11310            if(rp->p_alarm != 0 && rp->p_alarm < next_alarm)next_alarm=rp->p_alarm;
11311
11312    }


11315    /*===========================================================================*
11316     *                              cause_alarm                                   *
11317     *===========================================================================*/
11318    PRIVATE void cause_alarm()
11319    {
11320    /* Routine called if a timer goes off and the process requested a synchronous
11321     * alarm. The process number is in the global variable watchdog_proc (HACK).
11322     */
11323      message mess;
11324
11325      syn_table[watchdog_proc + NR_TASKS]= TRUE;
11326      if (!syn_al_alive) send (SYN_ALRM_TASK, &mess);
11327    }


11330    /*===========================================================================*
11331     *                              syn_alrm_task                                 *
11332     *===========================================================================*/
11333    PUBLIC void syn_alrm_task()
11334    {
11335    /* Main program of the synchronous alarm task.
11336     * This task receives messages only from cause_alarm in the clock task.
11337     * It sends a CLOCK_INT message to a process that requested a syn_alrm.
11338     * Synchronous alarms are so called because, unlike a signals or the
11339     * activation of a watchdog, a synchronous alarm is received by a process
11340     * when it is in a known part of its code, that is, when it has issued
11341     * a call to receive a message.
11342     */
11343
11344      message mess;
```

```
11345        int work_done;          /* ready to sleep ? */
11346        int *al_ptr;            /* pointer in syn_table */
11347        int i;
11348
11349        syn_al_alive= TRUE;
11350        for (i= 0, al_ptr= syn_table; i<NR_TASKS+NR_PROCS; i++, al_ptr++)
11351              *al_ptr= FALSE;
11352
11353        while (TRUE) {
11354              work_done= TRUE;
11355              for (i= 0, al_ptr= syn_table; i<NR_TASKS+NR_PROCS; i++, al_ptr++)
11356                    if (*al_ptr) {
11357                          *al_ptr= FALSE;
11358                          mess.m_type= CLOCK_INT;
11359                          send (i-NR_TASKS, &mess);
11360                          work_done= FALSE;
11361                    }
11362              if (work_done) {
11363                    syn_al_alive= FALSE;
11364                    receive (CLOCK, &mess);
11365                    syn_al_alive= TRUE;
11366              }
11367        }
11368  }


11371  /*===========================================================================*
11372   *                              clock_handler                                *
11373   *===========================================================================*/
11374  PRIVATE int clock_handler(irq)
11375  int irq;
11376  {
11377  /* This executes on every clock tick (i.e., every time the timer chip
11378   * generates an interrupt). It does a little bit of work so the clock
11379   * task does not have to be called on every tick.
11380   *
11381   * Switch context to do_clocktick if an alarm has gone off.
11382   * Also switch there to reschedule if the reschedule will do something.
11383   * This happens when
11384   *      (1) quantum has expired
11385   *      (2) current process received full quantum (as clock sampled it!)
11386   *      (3) something else is ready to run.
11387   * Also call TTY and PRINTER and let them do whatever is necessary.
11388   *
11389   * Many global global and static variables are accessed here.  The safety
11390   * of this must be justified.  Most of them are not changed here:
11391   *      k_reenter:
11392   *            This safely tells if the clock interrupt is nested.
11393   *      proc_ptr, bill_ptr:
11394   *            These are used for accounting.  It does not matter if proc.c
11395   *            is changing them, provided they are always valid pointers,
11396   *            since at worst the previous process would be billed.
11397   *      next_alarm, realtime, sched_ticks, bill_ptr, prev_ptr,
11398   *      rdy_head[USER_Q]:
11399   *            These are tested to decide whether to call interrupt().  It
11400   *            does not matter if the test is sometimes (rarely) backwards
11401   *            due to a race, since this will only delay the high-level
11402   *            processing by one tick, or call the high level unnecessarily.
11403   * The variables which are changed require more care:
11404   *      rp->user_time, rp->sys_time:
```

```
11405       *              These are protected by explicit locks in system.c.  They are
11406       *              not properly protected in dmp.c (the increment here is not
11407       *              atomic) but that hardly matters.
11408       *      pending_ticks:
11409       *              This is protected by explicit locks in clock.c.  Don't
11410       *              update realtime directly, since there are too many
11411       *              references to it to guard conveniently.
11412       *      lost_ticks:
11413       *              Clock ticks counted outside the clock task.
11414       *      sched_ticks, prev_ptr:
11415       *              Updating these competes with similar code in do_clocktick().
11416       *              No lock is necessary, because if bad things happen here
11417       *              (like sched_ticks going negative), the code in do_clocktick()
11418       *              will restore the variables to reasonable values, and an
11419       *              occasional missed or extra sched() is harmless.
11420       *
11421       * Are these complications worth the trouble?  Well, they make the system 15%
11422       * faster on a 5MHz 8088, and make task debugging much easier since there are
11423       * no task switches on an inactive system.
11424       */
11425
11426       register struct proc *rp;
11427       register unsigned ticks;
11428       clock_t now;
11429
11430       if (ps_mca) {
11431              /* Acknowledge the PS/2 clock interrupt. */
11432              out_byte(PORT_B, in_byte(PORT_B) | CLOCK_ACK_BIT);
11433       }
11434
11435       /* Update user and system accounting times.
11436        * First charge the current process for user time.
11437        * If the current process is not the billable process (usually because it
11438        * is a task), charge the billable process for system time as well.
11439        * Thus the unbillable tasks' user time is the billable users' system time.
11440        */
11441       if (k_reenter != 0)
11442              rp = proc_addr(HARDWARE);
11443       else
11444              rp = proc_ptr;
11445       ticks = lost_ticks + 1;
11446       lost_ticks = 0;
11447       rp->user_time += ticks;
11448       if (rp != bill_ptr && rp != proc_addr(IDLE)) bill_ptr->sys_time += ticks;
11449
11450       pending_ticks += ticks;
11451       now = realtime + pending_ticks;
11452       if (tty_timeout <= now) tty_wakeup(now);       /* possibly wake up TTY */
11453       pr_restart();                                  /* possibly restart printer */
11454
11455       if (next_alarm <= now ||
11456           sched_ticks == 1 &&
11457           bill_ptr == prev_ptr &&
11458           rdy_head[USER_Q] != NIL_PROC) {
11459              interrupt(CLOCK);
11460              return 1;        /* Reenable interrupts */
11461       }
11462
11463       if (--sched_ticks == 0) {
11464              /* If bill_ptr == prev_ptr, no ready users so don't need sched(). */
```

```
11465                sched_ticks = SCHED_RATE;        /* reset quantum */
11466                prev_ptr = bill_ptr;            /* new previous process */
11467        }
11468    return 1;      /* Reenable clock interrupt */
11469  }

11471  /*==========================================================================*
11472   *                              init_clock                                  *
11473   *==========================================================================*/
11474  PRIVATE void init_clock()
11475  {
11476  /* Initialize channel 0 of the 8253A timer to e.g. 60 Hz. */
11477
11478    out_byte(TIMER_MODE, SQUARE_WAVE);     /* set timer to run continuously */
11479    out_byte(TIMER0, TIMER_COUNT);         /* load timer low byte */
11480    out_byte(TIMER0, TIMER_COUNT >> 8);    /* load timer high byte */
11481    put_irq_handler(CLOCK_IRQ, clock_handler);    /* set the interrupt handler */
11482    enable_irq(CLOCK_IRQ);                 /* ready for clock interrupts */
11483  }


11486  /*==========================================================================*
11487   *                              clock_stop                                  *
11488   *==========================================================================*/
11489  PUBLIC void clock_stop()
11490  {
11491  /* Reset the clock to the BIOS rate. (For rebooting) */
11492
11493    out_byte(TIMER_MODE, 0x36);
11494    out_byte(TIMER0, 0);
11495    out_byte(TIMER0, 0);
11496  }


11499  /*==========================================================================*
11500   *                              milli_delay                                *
11501   *==========================================================================*/
11502  PUBLIC void milli_delay(millisec)
11503  unsigned millisec;
11504  {
11505  /* Delay some milliseconds. */
11506
11507    struct milli_state ms;
11508
11509    milli_start(&ms);
11510    while (milli_elapsed(&ms) < millisec) {}
11511  }

11513  /*==========================================================================*
11514   *                              milli_start                                *
11515   *==========================================================================*/
11516  PUBLIC void milli_start(msp)
11517  struct milli_state *msp;
11518  {
11519  /* Prepare for calls to milli_elapsed(). */
11520
11521    msp->prev_count = 0;
11522    msp->accum_count = 0;
11523  }
```

```
11526    /*===========================================================================*
11527     *                              milli_elapsed                                *
11528     *===========================================================================*/
11529    PUBLIC unsigned milli_elapsed(msp)
11530    struct milli_state *msp;
11531    {
11532    /* Return the number of milliseconds since the call to milli_start().  Must be
11533     * polled rapidly.
11534     */
11535      unsigned count;
11536
11537      /* Read the counter for channel 0 of the 8253A timer.  The counter
11538       * decrements at twice the timer frequency (one full cycle for each
11539       * half of square wave).  The counter normally has a value between 0
11540       * and TIMER_COUNT, but before the clock task has been initialized,
11541       * its maximum value is 65535, as set by the BIOS.
11542       */
11543      out_byte(TIMER_MODE, LATCH_COUNT);    /* make chip copy count to latch */
11544      count = in_byte(TIMER0);         /* countdown continues during 2-step read */
11545      count |= in_byte(TIMER0) << 8;
11546
11547      /* Add difference between previous and new count unless the counter has
11548       * increased (restarted its cycle).  We may lose a tick now and then, but
11549       * microsecond precision is not needed.
11550       */
11551      msp->accum_count += count <= msp->prev_count ? (msp->prev_count - count) : 1;
11552      msp->prev_count = count;
11553
11554      return msp->accum_count / (TIMER_FREQ / 1000);
11555    }
```

```
++++++++++++++++++++++++++++++++++++++++++++++++++++++++++++++++++++++++++++++++
                                src/kernel/tty.h
++++++++++++++++++++++++++++++++++++++++++++++++++++++++++++++++++++++++++++++++
```

```
11600    /*      tty.h - Terminals       */
11601
11602    #define TTY_IN_BYTES       256     /* tty input queue size */
11603    #define TAB_SIZE             8     /* distance between tab stops */
11604    #define TAB_MASK             7     /* mask to compute a tab stop position */
11605
11606    #define ESC              '\33'     /* escape */
11607
11608    #define O_NOCTTY         00400     /* from <fcntl.h>, or cc will choke */
11609    #define O_NONBLOCK       04000
11610
11611    typedef _PROTOTYPE( void (*devfun_t), (struct tty *tp) );
11612    typedef _PROTOTYPE( void (*devfunarg_t), (struct tty *tp, int c) );
11613
11614    typedef struct tty {
11615      int tty_events;                  /* set when TTY should inspect this line */
11616
11617      /* Input queue.  Typed characters are stored here until read by a program. */
11618      u16_t *tty_inhead;               /* pointer to place where next char goes */
11619      u16_t *tty_intail;               /* pointer to next char to be given to prog */
```

```
11620      int tty_incount;              /* # chars in the input queue */
11621      int tty_eotct;                /* number of "line breaks" in input queue */
11622      devfun_t tty_devread;         /* routine to read from low level buffers */
11623      devfun_t tty_icancel;         /* cancel any device input */
11624      int tty_min;                  /* minimum requested #chars in input queue */
11625      clock_t tty_time;             /* time when the input is available */
11626      struct tty *tty_timenext;     /* for a list of ttys with active timers */
11627
11628      /* Output section. */
11629      devfun_t tty_devwrite;        /* routine to start actual device output */
11630      devfunarg_t tty_echo;         /* routine to echo characters input */
11631      devfun_t tty_ocancel;         /* cancel any ongoing device output */
11632      devfun_t tty_break;           /* let the device send a break */
11633
11634      /* Terminal parameters and status. */
11635      int tty_position;             /* current position on the screen for echoing */
11636      char tty_reprint;             /* 1 when echoed input messed up, else 0 */
11637      char tty_escaped;             /* 1 when LNEXT (^V) just seen, else 0 */
11638      char tty_inhibited;           /* 1 when STOP (^S) just seen (stops output) */
11639      char tty_pgrp;                /* slot number of controlling process */
11640      char tty_openct;              /* count of number of opens of this tty */
11641
11642      /* Information about incomplete I/O requests is stored here. */
11643      char tty_inrepcode;           /* reply code, TASK_REPLY or REVIVE */
11644      char tty_incaller;            /* process that made the call (usually FS) */
11645      char tty_inproc;              /* process that wants to read from tty */
11646      vir_bytes tty_in_vir;         /* virtual address where data is to go */
11647      int tty_inleft;               /* how many chars are still needed */
11648      int tty_incum;                /* # chars input so far */
11649      char tty_outrepcode;          /* reply code, TASK_REPLY or REVIVE */
11650      char tty_outcaller;           /* process that made the call (usually FS) */
11651      char tty_outproc;             /* process that wants to write to tty */
11652      vir_bytes tty_out_vir;        /* virtual address where data comes from */
11653      int tty_outleft;              /* # chars yet to be output */
11654      int tty_outcum;               /* # chars output so far */
11655      char tty_iocaller;            /* process that made the call (usually FS) */
11656      char tty_ioproc;              /* process that wants to do an ioctl */
11657      int tty_ioreq;                /* ioctl request code */
11658      vir_bytes tty_iovir;          /* virtual address of ioctl buffer */
11659
11660      /* Miscellaneous. */
11661      devfun_t tty_ioctl;           /* set line speed, etc. at the device level */
11662      devfun_t tty_close;           /* tell the device that the tty is closed */
11663      void *tty_priv;               /* pointer to per device private data */
11664      struct termios tty_termios;   /* terminal attributes */
11665      struct winsize tty_winsize;   /* window size (#lines and #columns) */
11666
11667      u16_t tty_inbuf[TTY_IN_BYTES];/* tty input buffer */
11668  } tty_t;
11669
11670  EXTERN tty_t tty_table[NR_CONS+NR_RS_LINES+NR_PTYS];
11671
11672  /* Values for the fields. */
11673  #define NOT_ESCAPED      0     /* previous character is not LNEXT (^V) */
11674  #define ESCAPED          1     /* previous character was LNEXT (^V) */
11675  #define RUNNING          0     /* no STOP (^S) has been typed to stop output */
11676  #define STOPPED          1     /* STOP (^S) has been typed to stop output */
11677
11678  /* Fields and flags on characters in the input queue. */
11679  #define IN_CHAR      0x00FF    /* low 8 bits are the character itself */
```

```
11680     #define IN_LEN          0x0F00     /* length of char if it has been echoed */
11681     #define IN_LSHIFT            8     /* length = (c & IN_LEN) >> IN_LSHIFT */
11682     #define IN_EOT          0x1000     /* char is a line break (^D, LF) */
11683     #define IN_EOF          0x2000     /* char is EOF (^D), do not return to user */
11684     #define IN_ESC          0x4000     /* escaped by LNEXT (^V), no interpretation */
11685
11686     /* Times and timeouts. */
11687     #define TIME_NEVER      ((clock_t) -1 < 0 ? (clock_t) LONG_MAX : (clock_t) -1)
11688     #define force_timeout() ((void) (tty_timeout = 0))
11689
11690     EXTERN tty_t *tty_timelist;      /* list of ttys with active timers */
11691
11692     /* Number of elements and limit of a buffer. */
11693     #define buflen(buf)     (sizeof(buf) / sizeof((buf)[0]))
11694     #define bufend(buf)     ((buf) + buflen(buf))
```

```
++++++++++++++++++++++++++++++++++++++++++++++++++++++++++++++++++++++++++++++++
                                 src/kernel/tty.c
++++++++++++++++++++++++++++++++++++++++++++++++++++++++++++++++++++++++++++++++
```

```
11700     /* This file contains the terminal driver, both for the IBM console and regular
11701      * ASCII terminals.  It handles only the device-independent part of a TTY, the
11702      * device dependent parts are in console.c, rs232.c, etc.  This file contains
11703      * two main entry points, tty_task() and tty_wakeup(), and several minor entry
11704      * points for use by the device-dependent code.
11705      *
11706      * The device-independent part accepts "keyboard" input from the device-
11707      * dependent part, performs input processing (special key interpretation),
11708      * and sends the input to a process reading from the TTY.  Output to a TTY
11709      * is sent to the device-dependent code for output processing and "screen"
11710      * display.  Input processing is done by the device by calling 'in_process'
11711      * on the input characters, output processing may be done by the device itself
11712      * or by calling 'out_process'.  The TTY takes care of input queuing, the
11713      * device does the output queuing.  If a device receives an external signal,
11714      * like an interrupt, then it causes tty_wakeup() to be run by the CLOCK task
11715      * to, you guessed it, wake up the TTY to check if input or output can
11716      * continue.
11717      *
11718      * The valid messages and their parameters are:
11719      *
11720      *   HARD_INT:      output has been completed or input has arrived
11721      *   DEV_READ:      a process wants to read from a terminal
11722      *   DEV_WRITE:     a process wants to write on a terminal
11723      *   DEV_IOCTL:     a process wants to change a terminal's parameters
11724      *   DEV_OPEN:      a tty line has been opened
11725      *   DEV_CLOSE:     a tty line has been closed
11726      *   CANCEL:        terminate a previous incomplete system call immediately
11727      *
11728      *   m_type        TTY_LINE   PROC_NR    COUNT    TTY_SPEK  TTY_FLAGS  ADDRESS
11729      * ---------------------------------------------------------------------------
11730      * | HARD_INT    |          |          |          |          |          |          |
11731      * |-------------+----------+----------+----------+----------+----------+----------|
11732      * | DEV_READ    |minor dev| proc nr  |  count   |          O_NONBLOCK| buf ptr  |
11733      * |-------------+----------+----------+----------+----------+----------+----------|
11734      * | DEV_WRITE   |minor dev| proc nr  |  count   |          |          | buf ptr  |
```

```
11735  *  |-------------+---------+---------+---------+---------+---------+---------|
11736  *  | DEV_IOCTL   |minor dev| proc nr |func code|erase etc|  flags  |         |
11737  *  |-------------+---------+---------+---------+---------+---------+---------|
11738  *  | DEV_OPEN    |minor dev| proc nr | O_NOCTTY|         |         |         |
11739  *  |-------------+---------+---------+---------+---------+---------+---------|
11740  *  | DEV_CLOSE   |minor dev| proc nr |         |         |         |         |
11741  *  |-------------+---------+---------+---------+---------+---------+---------|
11742  *  | CANCEL      |minor dev| proc nr |         |         |         |         |
11743  *  -------------------------------------------------------------------------
11744  */
11745
11746  #include "kernel.h"
11747  #include <termios.h>
11748  #include <sys/ioctl.h>
11749  #include <signal.h>
11750  #include <minix/callnr.h>
11751  #include <minix/com.h>
11752  #include <minix/keymap.h>
11753  #include "tty.h"
11754  #include "proc.h"
11755
11756  /* Address of a tty structure. */
11757  #define tty_addr(line)  (&tty_table[line])
11758
11759  /* First minor numbers for the various classes of TTY devices. */
11760  #define CONS_MINOR        0
11761  #define LOG_MINOR        15
11762  #define RS232_MINOR      16
11763  #define TTYPX_MINOR     128
11764  #define PTYPX_MINOR     192
11765
11766  /* Macros for magic tty types. */
11767  #define isconsole(tp)   ((tp) < tty_addr(NR_CONS))
11768
11769  /* Macros for magic tty structure pointers. */
11770  #define FIRST_TTY       tty_addr(0)
11771  #define END_TTY         tty_addr(sizeof(tty_table) / sizeof(tty_table[0]))
11772
11773  /* A device exists if at least its 'devread' function is defined. */
11774  #define tty_active(tp)  ((tp)->tty_devread != NULL)
11775
11776  /* RS232 lines or pseudo terminals can be completely configured out. */
11777  #if NR_RS_LINES == 0
11778  #define rs_init(tp)       ((void) 0)
11779  #endif
11780  #if NR_PTYS == 0
11781  #define pty_init(tp)      ((void) 0)
11782  #define do_pty(tp, mp)    ((void) 0)
11783  #endif
11784
11785  FORWARD _PROTOTYPE( void do_cancel, (tty_t *tp, message *m_ptr)       );
11786  FORWARD _PROTOTYPE( void do_ioctl, (tty_t *tp, message *m_ptr)        );
11787  FORWARD _PROTOTYPE( void do_open, (tty_t *tp, message *m_ptr)         );
11788  FORWARD _PROTOTYPE( void do_close, (tty_t *tp, message *m_ptr)        );
11789  FORWARD _PROTOTYPE( void do_read, (tty_t *tp, message *m_ptr)         );
11790  FORWARD _PROTOTYPE( void do_write, (tty_t *tp, message *m_ptr)        );
11791  FORWARD _PROTOTYPE( void in_transfer, (tty_t *tp)                     );
11792  FORWARD _PROTOTYPE( int echo, (tty_t *tp, int ch)                     );
11793  FORWARD _PROTOTYPE( void rawecho, (tty_t *tp, int ch)                 );
11794  FORWARD _PROTOTYPE( int back_over, (tty_t *tp)                        );
```

```
11795    FORWARD _PROTOTYPE( void reprint, (tty_t *tp)                    );
11796    FORWARD _PROTOTYPE( void dev_ioctl, (tty_t *tp)                  );
11797    FORWARD _PROTOTYPE( void setattr, (tty_t *tp)                    );
11798    FORWARD _PROTOTYPE( void tty_icancel, (tty_t *tp)                );
11799    FORWARD _PROTOTYPE( void tty_init, (tty_t *tp)                   );
11800    FORWARD _PROTOTYPE( void settimer, (tty_t *tp, int on)           );
11801
11802    /* Default attributes. */
11803    PRIVATE struct termios termios_defaults = {
11804      TINPUT_DEF, TOUTPUT_DEF, TCTRL_DEF, TLOCAL_DEF, TSPEED_DEF, TSPEED_DEF,
11805      {
11806            TEOF_DEF, TEOL_DEF, TERASE_DEF, TINTR_DEF, TKILL_DEF, TMIN_DEF,
11807            TQUIT_DEF, TTIME_DEF, TSUSP_DEF, TSTART_DEF, TSTOP_DEF,
11808            TREPRINT_DEF, TLNEXT_DEF, TDISCARD_DEF,
11809      },
11810    };
11811    PRIVATE struct winsize winsize_defaults;        /* = all zeroes */
11812
11813
11814    /*===========================================================================*
11815     *                              tty_task                                      *
11816     *===========================================================================*/
11817    PUBLIC void tty_task()
11818    {
11819    /* Main routine of the terminal task. */
11820
11821      message tty_mess;               /* buffer for all incoming messages */
11822      register tty_t *tp;
11823      unsigned line;
11824
11825      /* Initialize the terminal lines. */
11826      for (tp = FIRST_TTY; tp < END_TTY; tp++) tty_init(tp);
11827
11828      /* Display the Minix startup banner. */
11829      printf("Minix %s.%s  Copyright 1997 Prentice-Hall, Inc.\n\n",
11830                                              OS_RELEASE, OS_VERSION);
11831      printf("Executing in 32-bit protected mode\n\n");
11832
11833      while (TRUE) {
11834            /* Handle any events on any of the ttys. */
11835            for (tp = FIRST_TTY; tp < END_TTY; tp++) {
11836                    if (tp->tty_events) handle_events(tp);
11837            }
11838
11839            receive(ANY, &tty_mess);
11840
11841            /* A hardware interrupt is an invitation to check for events. */
11842            if (tty_mess.m_type == HARD_INT) continue;
11843
11844            /* Check the minor device number. */
11845            line = tty_mess.TTY_LINE;
11846            if ((line - CONS_MINOR) < NR_CONS) {
11847                    tp = tty_addr(line - CONS_MINOR);
11848            } else
11849            if (line == LOG_MINOR) {
11850                    tp = tty_addr(0);
11851            } else
11852            if ((line - RS232_MINOR) < NR_RS_LINES) {
11853                    tp = tty_addr(line - RS232_MINOR + NR_CONS);
11854            } else
```

```
11855                if ((line - TTYPX_MINOR) < NR_PTYS) {
11856                        tp = tty_addr(line - TTYPX_MINOR + NR_CONS + NR_RS_LINES);
11857                } else
11858                if ((line - PTYPX_MINOR) < NR_PTYS) {
11859                        tp = tty_addr(line - PTYPX_MINOR + NR_CONS + NR_RS_LINES);
11860                        do_pty(tp, &tty_mess);
11861                        continue;                               /* this is a pty, not a tty */
11862                } else {
11863                        tp = NULL;
11864                }
11865
11866                /* If the device doesn't exist or is not configured return ENXIO. */
11867                if (tp == NULL || !tty_active(tp)) {
11868                        tty_reply(TASK_REPLY, tty_mess.m_source,
11869                                                        tty_mess.PROC_NR, ENXIO);
11870                        continue;
11871                }
11872
11873                /* Execute the requested function. */
11874                switch (tty_mess.m_type) {
11875                    case DEV_READ:      do_read(tp, &tty_mess);             break;
11876                    case DEV_WRITE:     do_write(tp, &tty_mess);            break;
11877                    case DEV_IOCTL:     do_ioctl(tp, &tty_mess);            break;
11878                    case DEV_OPEN:      do_open(tp, &tty_mess);             break;
11879                    case DEV_CLOSE:     do_close(tp, &tty_mess);            break;
11880                    case CANCEL:        do_cancel(tp, &tty_mess);           break;
11881                    default:            tty_reply(TASK_REPLY, tty_mess.m_source,
11882                                                        tty_mess.PROC_NR, EINVAL);
11883                }
11884        }
11885    }


11888    /*===========================================================================*
11889     *                              do_read                                       *
11890     *===========================================================================*/
11891    PRIVATE void do_read(tp, m_ptr)
11892    register tty_t *tp;                     /* pointer to tty struct */
11893    message *m_ptr;                         /* pointer to message sent to the task */
11894    {
11895    /* A process wants to read from a terminal. */
11896      int r;
11897
11898      /* Check if there is already a process hanging in a read, check if the
11899       * parameters are correct, do I/O.
11900       */
11901      if (tp->tty_inleft > 0) {
11902            r = EIO;
11903      } else
11904      if (m_ptr->COUNT <= 0) {
11905            r = EINVAL;
11906      } else
11907      if (numap(m_ptr->PROC_NR, (vir_bytes) m_ptr->ADDRESS, m_ptr->COUNT) == 0) {
11908            r = EFAULT;
11909      } else {
11910            /* Copy information from the message to the tty struct. */
11911            tp->tty_inrepcode = TASK_REPLY;
11912            tp->tty_incaller = m_ptr->m_source;
11913            tp->tty_inproc = m_ptr->PROC_NR;
11914            tp->tty_in_vir = (vir_bytes) m_ptr->ADDRESS;
```

```
11915                    tp->tty_inleft = m_ptr->COUNT;
11916
11917                    if (!(tp->tty_termios.c_lflag & ICANON)
11918                                            && tp->tty_termios.c_cc[VTIME] > 0) {
11919                            if (tp->tty_termios.c_cc[VMIN] == 0) {
11920                                    /* MIN & TIME specify a read timer that finishes the
11921                                     * read in TIME/10 seconds if no bytes are available.
11922                                     */
11923                                    lock();
11924                                    settimer(tp, TRUE);
11925                                    tp->tty_min = 1;
11926                                    unlock();
11927                            } else {
11928                                    /* MIN & TIME specify an inter-byte timer that may
11929                                     * have to be cancelled if there are no bytes yet.
11930                                     */
11931                                    if (tp->tty_eotct == 0) {
11932                                            lock();
11933                                            settimer(tp, FALSE);
11934                                            unlock();
11935                                            tp->tty_min = tp->tty_termios.c_cc[VMIN];
11936                                    }
11937                            }
11938                    }
11939
11940                    /* Anything waiting in the input buffer? Clear it out... */
11941                    in_transfer(tp);
11942                    /* ...then go back for more */
11943                    handle_events(tp);
11944                    if (tp->tty_inleft == 0) return;                /* already done */
11945
11946                    /* There were no bytes in the input queue available, so either suspend
11947                     * the caller or break off the read if nonblocking.
11948                     */
11949                    if (m_ptr->TTY_FLAGS & O_NONBLOCK) {
11950                            r = EAGAIN;                             /* cancel the read */
11951                            tp->tty_inleft = tp->tty_incum = 0;
11952                    } else {
11953                            r = SUSPEND;                            /* suspend the caller */
11954                            tp->tty_inrepcode = REVIVE;
11955                    }
11956            }
11957            tty_reply(TASK_REPLY, m_ptr->m_source, m_ptr->PROC_NR, r);
11958    }


11961    /*===========================================================================*
11962     *                              do_write                                      *
11963     *===========================================================================*/
11964    PRIVATE void do_write(tp, m_ptr)
11965    register tty_t *tp;
11966    register message *m_ptr;          /* pointer to message sent to the task */
11967    {
11968    /* A process wants to write on a terminal. */
11969      int r;
11970
11971      /* Check if there is already a process hanging in a write, check if the
11972       * parameters are correct, do I/O.
11973       */
11974      if (tp->tty_outleft > 0) {
```

```
11975                 r = EIO;
11976         } else
11977         if (m_ptr->COUNT <= 0) {
11978                 r = EINVAL;
11979         } else
11980         if (numap(m_ptr->PROC_NR, (vir_bytes) m_ptr->ADDRESS, m_ptr->COUNT) == 0) {
11981                 r = EFAULT;
11982         } else {
11983                 /* Copy message parameters to the tty structure. */
11984                 tp->tty_outrepcode = TASK_REPLY;
11985                 tp->tty_outcaller = m_ptr->m_source;
11986                 tp->tty_outproc = m_ptr->PROC_NR;
11987                 tp->tty_out_vir = (vir_bytes) m_ptr->ADDRESS;
11988                 tp->tty_outleft = m_ptr->COUNT;
11989
11990                 /* Try to write. */
11991                 handle_events(tp);
11992                 if (tp->tty_outleft == 0) return;             /* already done */
11993
11994                 /* None or not all the bytes could be written, so either suspend the
11995                  * caller or break off the write if nonblocking.
11996                  */
11997                 if (m_ptr->TTY_FLAGS & O_NONBLOCK) {          /* cancel the write */
11998                         r = tp->tty_outcum > 0 ? tp->tty_outcum : EAGAIN;
11999                         tp->tty_outleft = tp->tty_outcum = 0;
12000                 } else {
12001                         r = SUSPEND;                         /* suspend the caller */
12002                         tp->tty_outrepcode = REVIVE;
12003                 }
12004         }
12005         tty_reply(TASK_REPLY, m_ptr->m_source, m_ptr->PROC_NR, r);
12006 }


12009 /*===========================================================================*
12010  *                              do_ioctl                                     *
12011  *===========================================================================*/
12012 PRIVATE void do_ioctl(tp, m_ptr)
12013 register tty_t *tp;
12014 message *m_ptr;                        /* pointer to message sent to task */
12015 {
12016 /* Perform an IOCTL on this terminal. Posix termios calls are handled
12017  * by the IOCTL system call
12018  */
12019
12020     int r;
12021     union {
12022         int i;
12023         /* these non-Posix params are not used now, but the union is retained
12024          * to minimize code differences with backward compatible version
12025          * struct sgttyb sg;
12026          * struct tchars tc;
12027          */
12028     } param;
12029     phys_bytes user_phys;
12030     size_t size;
12031
12032     /* Size of the ioctl parameter. */
12033     switch (m_ptr->TTY_REQUEST) {
12034       case TCGETS:          /* Posix tcgetattr function */
```

```
12035          case TCSETS:        /* Posix tcsetattr function, TCSANOW option */
12036          case TCSETSW:       /* Posix tcsetattr function, TCSADRAIN option */
12037          case TCSETSF:       /* Posix tcsetattr function, TCSAFLUSH option */
12038              size = sizeof(struct termios);
12039              break;
12040
12041          case TCSBRK:        /* Posix tcsendbreak function */
12042          case TCFLOW:        /* Posix tcflow function */
12043          case TCFLSH:        /* Posix tcflush function */
12044          case TIOCGPGRP:     /* Posix tcgetpgrp function */
12045          case TIOCSPGRP:     /* Posix tcsetpgrp function */
12046              size = sizeof(int);
12047              break;
12048
12049          case TIOCGWINSZ:    /* get window size (not Posix) */
12050          case TIOCSWINSZ:    /* set window size (not Posix) */
12051              size = sizeof(struct winsize);
12052              break;
12053
12054          case KIOCSMAP:      /* load keymap (Minix extension) */
12055              size = sizeof(keymap_t);
12056              break;
12057
12058          case TIOCSFON:      /* load font (Minix extension) */
12059              size = sizeof(u8_t [8192]);
12060              break;
12061
12062          case TCDRAIN:       /* Posix tcdrain function -- no parameter */
12063          default:            size = 0;
12064      }
12065
12066      if (size != 0) {
12067              user_phys = numap(m_ptr->PROC_NR, (vir_bytes) m_ptr->ADDRESS, size);
12068              if (user_phys == 0) {
12069                      tty_reply(TASK_REPLY, m_ptr->m_source, m_ptr->PROC_NR, EFAULT);
12070                      return;
12071              }
12072      }
12073
12074      r = OK;
12075      switch (m_ptr->TTY_REQUEST) {
12076        case TCGETS:
12077              /* Get the termios attributes. */
12078              phys_copy(vir2phys(&tp->tty_termios), user_phys, (phys_bytes) size);
12079              break;
12080
12081        case TCSETSW:
12082        case TCSETSF:
12083        case TCDRAIN:
12084              if (tp->tty_outleft > 0) {
12085                      /* Wait for all ongoing output processing to finish. */
12086                      tp->tty_iocaller = m_ptr->m_source;
12087                      tp->tty_ioproc = m_ptr->PROC_NR;
12088                      tp->tty_ioreq = m_ptr->REQUEST;
12089                      tp->tty_iovir = (vir_bytes) m_ptr->ADDRESS;
12090                      r = SUSPEND;
12091                      break;
12092              }
12093              if (m_ptr->TTY_REQUEST == TCDRAIN) break;
12094              if (m_ptr->TTY_REQUEST == TCSETSF) tty_icancel(tp);
```

```
12095                    /*FALL THROUGH*/
12096            case TCSETS:
12097                    /* Set the termios attributes. */
12098                    phys_copy(user_phys, vir2phys(&tp->tty_termios), (phys_bytes) size);
12099                    setattr(tp);
12100                    break;
12101
12102            case TCFLSH:
12103                    phys_copy(user_phys, vir2phys(&param.i), (phys_bytes) size);
12104                    switch (param.i) {
12105                        case TCIFLUSH:     tty_icancel(tp);                              break;
12106                        case TCOFLUSH:     (*tp->tty_ocancel)(tp);                       break;
12107                        case TCIOFLUSH:    tty_icancel(tp); (*tp->tty_ocancel)(tp);break;
12108                        default:           r = EINVAL;
12109                    }
12110                    break;
12111
12112            case TCFLOW:
12113                    phys_copy(user_phys, vir2phys(&param.i), (phys_bytes) size);
12114                    switch (param.i) {
12115                        case TCOOFF:
12116                        case TCOON:
12117                            tp->tty_inhibited = (param.i == TCOOFF);
12118                            tp->tty_events = 1;
12119                            break;
12120                        case TCIOFF:
12121                            (*tp->tty_echo)(tp, tp->tty_termios.c_cc[VSTOP]);
12122                            break;
12123                        case TCION:
12124                            (*tp->tty_echo)(tp, tp->tty_termios.c_cc[VSTART]);
12125                            break;
12126                        default:
12127                            r = EINVAL;
12128                    }
12129                    break;
12130
12131            case TCSBRK:
12132                    if (tp->tty_break != NULL) (*tp->tty_break)(tp);
12133                    break;
12134
12135            case TIOCGWINSZ:
12136                    phys_copy(vir2phys(&tp->tty_winsize), user_phys, (phys_bytes) size);
12137                    break;
12138
12139            case TIOCSWINSZ:
12140                    phys_copy(user_phys, vir2phys(&tp->tty_winsize), (phys_bytes) size);
12141                    /* SIGWINCH... */
12142                    break;
12143
12144            case KIOCSMAP:
12145                    /* Load a new keymap (only /dev/console). */
12146                    if (isconsole(tp)) r = kbd_loadmap(user_phys);
12147                    break;
12148
12149            case TIOCSFON:
12150                    /* Load a font into an EGA or VGA card (hs@hck.hr) */
12151                    if (isconsole(tp)) r = con_loadfont(user_phys);
12152                    break;
12153
12154    /* These Posix functions are allowed to fail if _POSIX_JOB_CONTROL is
```

```
12155      * not defined.
12156      */
12157        case TIOCGPGRP:
12158        case TIOCSPGRP:
12159        default:
12160            r = ENOTTY;
12161      }
12162
12163      /* Send the reply. */
12164      tty_reply(TASK_REPLY, m_ptr->m_source, m_ptr->PROC_NR, r);
12165    }


12168    /*===========================================================================*
12169     *                              do_open                                       *
12170     *===========================================================================*/
12171    PRIVATE void do_open(tp, m_ptr)
12172    register tty_t *tp;
12173    message *m_ptr;                          /* pointer to message sent to task */
12174    {
12175    /* A tty line has been opened.  Make it the callers controlling tty if
12176     * O_NOCTTY is *not* set and it is not the log device.  1 is returned if
12177     * the tty is made the controlling tty, otherwise OK or an error code.
12178     */
12179      int r = OK;
12180
12181      if (m_ptr->TTY_LINE == LOG_MINOR) {
12182            /* The log device is a write-only diagnostics device. */
12183            if (m_ptr->COUNT & R_BIT) r = EACCES;
12184      } else {
12185            if (!(m_ptr->COUNT & O_NOCTTY)) {
12186                  tp->tty_pgrp = m_ptr->PROC_NR;
12187                  r = 1;
12188            }
12189            tp->tty_openct++;
12190      }
12191      tty_reply(TASK_REPLY, m_ptr->m_source, m_ptr->PROC_NR, r);
12192    }


12195    /*===========================================================================*
12196     *                              do_close                                      *
12197     *===========================================================================*/
12198    PRIVATE void do_close(tp, m_ptr)
12199    register tty_t *tp;
12200    message *m_ptr;                          /* pointer to message sent to task */
12201    {
12202    /* A tty line has been closed.  Clean up the line if it is the last close. */
12203
12204      if (m_ptr->TTY_LINE != LOG_MINOR && --tp->tty_openct == 0) {
12205            tp->tty_pgrp = 0;
12206            tty_icancel(tp);
12207            (*tp->tty_ocancel)(tp);
12208            (*tp->tty_close)(tp);
12209            tp->tty_termios = termios_defaults;
12210            tp->tty_winsize = winsize_defaults;
12211            setattr(tp);
12212      }
12213      tty_reply(TASK_REPLY, m_ptr->m_source, m_ptr->PROC_NR, OK);
12214    }
```

```
12217  /*===========================================================================*
12218   *                              do_cancel                                    *
12219   *===========================================================================*/
12220  PRIVATE void do_cancel(tp, m_ptr)
12221  register tty_t *tp;
12222  message *m_ptr;                      /* pointer to message sent to task */
12223  {
12224  /* A signal has been sent to a process that is hanging trying to read or write.
12225   * The pending read or write must be finished off immediately.
12226   */
12227
12228    int proc_nr;
12229    int mode;
12230
12231    /* Check the parameters carefully, to avoid cancelling twice. */
12232    proc_nr = m_ptr->PROC_NR;
12233    mode = m_ptr->COUNT;
12234    if ((mode & R_BIT) && tp->tty_inleft != 0 && proc_nr == tp->tty_inproc) {
12235          /* Process was reading when killed.  Clean up input. */
12236          tty_icancel(tp);
12237          tp->tty_inleft = tp->tty_incum = 0;
12238    }
12239    if ((mode & W_BIT) && tp->tty_outleft != 0 && proc_nr == tp->tty_outproc) {
12240          /* Process was writing when killed.  Clean up output. */
12241          (*tp->tty_ocancel)(tp);
12242          tp->tty_outleft = tp->tty_outcum = 0;
12243    }
12244    if (tp->tty_ioreq != 0 && proc_nr == tp->tty_ioproc) {
12245          /* Process was waiting for output to drain. */
12246          tp->tty_ioreq = 0;
12247    }
12248    tp->tty_events = 1;
12249    tty_reply(TASK_REPLY, m_ptr->m_source, proc_nr, EINTR);
12250  }


12253  /*===========================================================================*
12254   *                              handle_events                                *
12255   *===========================================================================*/
12256  PUBLIC void handle_events(tp)
12257  tty_t *tp;                           /* TTY to check for events. */
12258  {
12259  /* Handle any events pending on a TTY.  These events are usually device
12260   * interrupts.
12261   *
12262   * Two kinds of events are prominent:
12263   *      - a character has been received from the console or an RS232 line.
12264   *      - an RS232 line has completed a write request (on behalf of a user).
12265   * The interrupt handler may delay the interrupt message at its discretion
12266   * to avoid swamping the TTY task.  Messages may be overwritten when the
12267   * lines are fast or when there are races between different lines, input
12268   * and output, because MINIX only provides single buffering for interrupt
12269   * messages (in proc.c).  This is handled by explicitly checking each line
12270   * for fresh input and completed output on each interrupt.
12271   */
12272    char *buf;
12273    unsigned count;
12274
```

```
12275        do {
12276                tp->tty_events = 0;
12277
12278                /* Read input and perform input processing. */
12279                (*tp->tty_devread)(tp);
12280
12281                /* Perform output processing and write output. */
12282                (*tp->tty_devwrite)(tp);
12283
12284                /* Ioctl waiting for some event? */
12285                if (tp->tty_ioreq != 0) dev_ioctl(tp);
12286        } while (tp->tty_events);
12287
12288        /* Transfer characters from the input queue to a waiting process. */
12289        in_transfer(tp);
12290
12291        /* Reply if enough bytes are available. */
12292        if (tp->tty_incum >= tp->tty_min && tp->tty_inleft > 0) {
12293                tty_reply(tp->tty_inrepcode, tp->tty_incaller, tp->tty_inproc,
12294                                                        tp->tty_incum);
12295                tp->tty_inleft = tp->tty_incum = 0;
12296        }
12297     }


12300     /*===========================================================================*
12301      *                              in_transfer                                  *
12302      *===========================================================================*/
12303     PRIVATE void in_transfer(tp)
12304     register tty_t *tp;              /* pointer to terminal to read from */
12305     {
12306     /* Transfer bytes from the input queue to a process reading from a terminal. */
12307
12308       int ch;
12309       int count;
12310       phys_bytes buf_phys, user_base;
12311       char buf[64], *bp;
12312
12313       /* Anything to do? */
12314       if (tp->tty_inleft == 0 || tp->tty_eotct < tp->tty_min) return;
12315
12316       buf_phys = vir2phys(buf);
12317       user_base = proc_vir2phys(proc_addr(tp->tty_inproc), 0);
12318       bp = buf;
12319       while (tp->tty_inleft > 0 && tp->tty_eotct > 0) {
12320                ch = *tp->tty_intail;
12321
12322                if (!(ch & IN_EOF)) {
12323                        /* One character to be delivered to the user. */
12324                        *bp = ch & IN_CHAR;
12325                        tp->tty_inleft--;
12326                        if (++bp == bufend(buf)) {
12327                                /* Temp buffer full, copy to user space. */
12328                                phys_copy(buf_phys, user_base + tp->tty_in_vir,
12329                                                        (phys_bytes) buflen(buf));
12330                                tp->tty_in_vir += buflen(buf);
12331                                tp->tty_incum += buflen(buf);
12332                                bp = buf;
12333                        }
12334                }
```

```
12335
12336                /* Remove the character from the input queue. */
12337                if (++tp->tty_intail == bufend(tp->tty_inbuf))
12338                        tp->tty_intail = tp->tty_inbuf;
12339            tp->tty_incount--;
12340            if (ch & IN_EOT) {
12341                    tp->tty_eotct--;
12342                    /* Don't read past a line break in canonical mode. */
12343                    if (tp->tty_termios.c_lflag & ICANON) tp->tty_inleft = 0;
12344            }
12345        }
12346
12347        if (bp > buf) {
12348            /* Leftover characters in the buffer. */
12349            count = bp - buf;
12350            phys_copy(buf_phys, user_base + tp->tty_in_vir, (phys_bytes) count);
12351            tp->tty_in_vir += count;
12352            tp->tty_incum += count;
12353        }
12354
12355        /* Usually reply to the reader, possibly even if incum == 0 (EOF). */
12356        if (tp->tty_inleft == 0) {
12357            tty_reply(tp->tty_inrepcode, tp->tty_incaller, tp->tty_inproc,
12358                                                        tp->tty_incum);
12359            tp->tty_inleft = tp->tty_incum = 0;
12360        }
12361    }


12364    /*===========================================================================*
12365     *                              in_process                                    *
12366     *===========================================================================*/
12367    PUBLIC int in_process(tp, buf, count)
12368    register tty_t *tp;             /* terminal on which character has arrived */
12369    char *buf;                      /* buffer with input characters */
12370    int count;                      /* number of input characters */
12371    {
12372    /* Characters have just been typed in.  Process, save, and echo them.  Return
12373     * the number of characters processed.
12374     */
12375
12376        int ch, sig, ct;
12377        int timeset = FALSE;
12378        static unsigned char csize_mask[] = { 0x1F, 0x3F, 0x7F, 0xFF };
12379
12380        for (ct = 0; ct < count; ct++) {
12381            /* Take one character. */
12382            ch = *buf++ & BYTE;
12383
12384            /* Strip to seven bits? */
12385            if (tp->tty_termios.c_iflag & ISTRIP) ch &= 0x7F;
12386
12387            /* Input extensions? */
12388            if (tp->tty_termios.c_lflag & IEXTEN) {
12389
12390                    /* Previous character was a character escape? */
12391                    if (tp->tty_escaped) {
12392                            tp->tty_escaped = NOT_ESCAPED;
12393                            ch |= IN_ESC;    /* protect character */
12394                    }
```

```
12395
12396                        /* LNEXT (^V) to escape the next character? */
12397                        if (ch == tp->tty_termios.c_cc[VLNEXT]) {
12398                                tp->tty_escaped = ESCAPED;
12399                                rawecho(tp, '^');
12400                                rawecho(tp, '\b');
12401                                continue;           /* do not store the escape */
12402                        }
12403
12404                        /* REPRINT (^R) to reprint echoed characters? */
12405                        if (ch == tp->tty_termios.c_cc[VREPRINT]) {
12406                                reprint(tp);
12407                                continue;
12408                        }
12409                }
12410
12411        /* _POSIX_VDISABLE is a normal character value, so better escape it. */
12412        if (ch == _POSIX_VDISABLE) ch |= IN_ESC;
12413
12414        /* Map CR to LF, ignore CR, or map LF to CR. */
12415        if (ch == '\r') {
12416                if (tp->tty_termios.c_iflag & IGNCR) continue;
12417                if (tp->tty_termios.c_iflag & ICRNL) ch = '\n';
12418        } else
12419        if (ch == '\n') {
12420                if (tp->tty_termios.c_iflag & INLCR) ch = '\r';
12421        }
12422
12423        /* Canonical mode? */
12424        if (tp->tty_termios.c_lflag & ICANON) {
12425
12426                /* Erase processing (rub out of last character). */
12427                if (ch == tp->tty_termios.c_cc[VERASE]) {
12428                        (void) back_over(tp);
12429                        if (!(tp->tty_termios.c_lflag & ECHOE)) {
12430                                (void) echo(tp, ch);
12431                        }
12432                        continue;
12433                }
12434
12435                /* Kill processing (remove current line). */
12436                if (ch == tp->tty_termios.c_cc[VKILL]) {
12437                        while (back_over(tp)) {}
12438                        if (!(tp->tty_termios.c_lflag & ECHOE)) {
12439                                (void) echo(tp, ch);
12440                                if (tp->tty_termios.c_lflag & ECHOK)
12441                                        rawecho(tp, '\n');
12442                        }
12443                        continue;
12444                }
12445
12446                /* EOF (^D) means end-of-file, an invisible "line break". */
12447                if (ch == tp->tty_termios.c_cc[VEOF]) ch |= IN_EOT | IN_EOF;
12448
12449                /* The line may be returned to the user after an LF. */
12450                if (ch == '\n') ch |= IN_EOT;
12451
12452                /* Same thing with EOL, whatever it may be. */
12453                if (ch == tp->tty_termios.c_cc[VEOL]) ch |= IN_EOT;
12454        }
```

```
12455
12456             /* Start/stop input control? */
12457             if (tp->tty_termios.c_iflag & IXON) {
12458
12459                     /* Output stops on STOP (^S). */
12460                     if (ch == tp->tty_termios.c_cc[VSTOP]) {
12461                             tp->tty_inhibited = STOPPED;
12462                             tp->tty_events = 1;
12463                             continue;
12464                     }
12465
12466                     /* Output restarts on START (^Q) or any character if IXANY. */
12467                     if (tp->tty_inhibited) {
12468                             if (ch == tp->tty_termios.c_cc[VSTART]
12469                                     || (tp->tty_termios.c_iflag & IXANY)) {
12470                                     tp->tty_inhibited = RUNNING;
12471                                     tp->tty_events = 1;
12472                                     if (ch == tp->tty_termios.c_cc[VSTART])
12473                                             continue;
12474                             }
12475                     }
12476             }
12477
12478             if (tp->tty_termios.c_lflag & ISIG) {
12479                     /* Check for INTR (^?) and QUIT (^\) characters. */
12480                     if (ch == tp->tty_termios.c_cc[VINTR]
12481                                             || ch == tp->tty_termios.c_cc[VQUIT]) {
12482                             sig = SIGINT;
12483                             if (ch == tp->tty_termios.c_cc[VQUIT]) sig = SIGQUIT;
12484                             sigchar(tp, sig);
12485                             (void) echo(tp, ch);
12486                             continue;
12487                     }
12488             }
12489
12490             /* Is there space in the input buffer? */
12491             if (tp->tty_incount == buflen(tp->tty_inbuf)) {
12492                     /* No space; discard in canonical mode, keep in raw mode. */
12493                     if (tp->tty_termios.c_lflag & ICANON) continue;
12494                     break;
12495             }
12496
12497             if (!(tp->tty_termios.c_lflag & ICANON)) {
12498                     /* In raw mode all characters are "line breaks". */
12499                     ch |= IN_EOT;
12500
12501                     /* Start an inter-byte timer? */
12502                     if (!timeset && tp->tty_termios.c_cc[VMIN] > 0
12503                                     && tp->tty_termios.c_cc[VTIME] > 0) {
12504                             lock();
12505                             settimer(tp, TRUE);
12506                             unlock();
12507                             timeset = TRUE;
12508                     }
12509             }
12510
12511             /* Perform the intricate function of echoing. */
12512             if (tp->tty_termios.c_lflag & (ECHO|ECHONL)) ch = echo(tp, ch);
12513
12514             /* Save the character in the input queue. */
```

```
12515                     *tp->tty_inhead++ = ch;
12516                     if (tp->tty_inhead == bufend(tp->tty_inbuf))
12517                             tp->tty_inhead = tp->tty_inbuf;
12518                     tp->tty_incount++;
12519                     if (ch & IN_EOT) tp->tty_eotct++;
12520
12521                     /* Try to finish input if the queue threatens to overflow. */
12522                     if (tp->tty_incount == buflen(tp->tty_inbuf)) in_transfer(tp);
12523             }
12524             return ct;
12525     }


12528     /*========================================================================*
12529      *                              echo                                      *
12530      *========================================================================*/
12531     PRIVATE int echo(tp, ch)
12532     register tty_t *tp;                    /* terminal on which to echo */
12533     register int ch;                       /* pointer to character to echo */
12534     {
12535     /* Echo the character if echoing is on.  Some control characters are echoed
12536      * with their normal effect, other control characters are echoed as "^X",
12537      * normal characters are echoed normally.  EOF (^D) is echoed, but immediately
12538      * backspaced over.  Return the character with the echoed length added to its
12539      * attributes.
12540      */
12541       int len, rp;
12542
12543       ch &= ~IN_LEN;
12544       if (!(tp->tty_termios.c_lflag & ECHO)) {
12545             if (ch == ('\n' | IN_EOT) && (tp->tty_termios.c_lflag
12546                                     & (ICANON|ECHONL)) == (ICANON|ECHONL))
12547                     (*tp->tty_echo)(tp, '\n');
12548             return(ch);
12549       }
12550
12551       /* "Reprint" tells if the echo output has been messed up by other output. */
12552       rp = tp->tty_incount == 0 ? FALSE : tp->tty_reprint;
12553
12554       if ((ch & IN_CHAR) < ' ') {
12555             switch (ch & (IN_ESC|IN_EOF|IN_EOT|IN_CHAR)) {
12556                 case '\t':
12557                     len = 0;
12558                     do {
12559                             (*tp->tty_echo)(tp, ' ');
12560                             len++;
12561                     } while (len < TAB_SIZE && (tp->tty_position & TAB_MASK) != 0);
12562                     break;
12563                 case '\r' | IN_EOT:
12564                 case '\n' | IN_EOT:
12565                     (*tp->tty_echo)(tp, ch & IN_CHAR);
12566                     len = 0;
12567                     break;
12568                 default:
12569                     (*tp->tty_echo)(tp, '^');
12570                     (*tp->tty_echo)(tp, '@' + (ch & IN_CHAR));
12571                     len = 2;
12572             }
12573       } else
12574       if ((ch & IN_CHAR) == '\177') {
```

```
12575                 /* A DEL prints as "^?". */
12576                 (*tp->tty_echo)(tp, '^');
12577                 (*tp->tty_echo)(tp, '?');
12578                 len = 2;
12579         } else {
12580                 (*tp->tty_echo)(tp, ch & IN_CHAR);
12581                 len = 1;
12582         }
12583         if (ch & IN_EOF) while (len > 0) { (*tp->tty_echo)(tp, '\b'); len--; }
12584
12585         tp->tty_reprint = rp;
12586         return(ch | (len << IN_LSHIFT));
12587   }


12590   /*===========================================================================*
12591    *                              rawecho                                       *
12592    *===========================================================================*/
12593   PRIVATE void rawecho(tp, ch)
12594   register tty_t *tp;
12595   int ch;
12596   {
12597   /* Echo without interpretation if ECHO is set. */
12598     int rp = tp->tty_reprint;
12599     if (tp->tty_termios.c_lflag & ECHO) (*tp->tty_echo)(tp, ch);
12600     tp->tty_reprint = rp;
12601   }


12604   /*===========================================================================*
12605    *                              back_over                                     *
12606    *===========================================================================*/
12607   PRIVATE int back_over(tp)
12608   register tty_t *tp;
12609   {
12610   /* Backspace to previous character on screen and erase it. */
12611     u16_t *head;
12612     int len;
12613
12614     if (tp->tty_incount == 0) return(0);  /* queue empty */
12615     head = tp->tty_inhead;
12616     if (head == tp->tty_inbuf) head = bufend(tp->tty_inbuf);
12617     if (*--head & IN_EOT) return(0);                /* can't erase "line breaks" */
12618     if (tp->tty_reprint) reprint(tp);               /* reprint if messed up */
12619     tp->tty_inhead = head;
12620     tp->tty_incount--;
12621     if (tp->tty_termios.c_lflag & ECHOE) {
12622         len = (*head & IN_LEN) >> IN_LSHIFT;
12623         while (len > 0) {
12624                 rawecho(tp, '\b');
12625                 rawecho(tp, ' ');
12626                 rawecho(tp, '\b');
12627                 len--;
12628         }
12629     }
12630     return(1);                              /* one character erased */
12631   }


12634   /*===========================================================================*
```

```
12635          *                          reprint                              *
12636          *===========================================================================*/
12637   PRIVATE void reprint(tp)
12638   register tty_t *tp;              /* pointer to tty struct */
12639   {
12640   /* Restore what has been echoed to screen before if the user input has been
12641    * messed up by output, or if REPRINT (^R) is typed.
12642    */
12643     int count;
12644     u16_t *head;
12645
12646     tp->tty_reprint = FALSE;
12647
12648     /* Find the last line break in the input. */
12649     head = tp->tty_inhead;
12650     count = tp->tty_incount;
12651     while (count > 0) {
12652          if (head == tp->tty_inbuf) head = bufend(tp->tty_inbuf);
12653          if (head[-1] & IN_EOT) break;
12654          head--;
12655          count--;
12656     }
12657     if (count == tp->tty_incount) return;           /* no reason to reprint */
12658
12659     /* Show REPRINT (^R) and move to a new line. */
12660     (void) echo(tp, tp->tty_termios.c_cc[VREPRINT] | IN_ESC);
12661     rawecho(tp, '\r');
12662     rawecho(tp, '\n');
12663
12664     /* Reprint from the last break onwards. */
12665     do {
12666          if (head == bufend(tp->tty_inbuf)) head = tp->tty_inbuf;
12667          *head = echo(tp, *head);
12668          head++;
12669          count++;
12670     } while (count < tp->tty_incount);
12671   }


12674   /*===========================================================================*
12675    *                          out_process                              *
12676    *===========================================================================*/
12677   PUBLIC void out_process(tp, bstart, bpos, bend, icount, ocount)
12678   tty_t *tp;
12679   char *bstart, *bpos, *bend;     /* start/pos/end of circular buffer */
12680   int *icount;                    /* # input chars / input chars used */
12681   int *ocount;                    /* max output chars / output chars used */
12682   {
12683   /* Perform output processing on a circular buffer. *icount is the number of
12684    * bytes to process, and the number of bytes actually processed on return.
12685    * *ocount is the space available on input and the space used on output.
12686    * (Naturally *icount < *ocount.)  The column position is updated modulo
12687    * the TAB size, because we really only need it for tabs.
12688    */
12689
12690     int tablen;
12691     int ict = *icount;
12692     int oct = *ocount;
12693     int pos = tp->tty_position;
12694
```

```
12695          while (ict > 0) {
12696                  switch (*bpos) {
12697                  case '\7':
12698                          break;
12699                  case '\b':
12700                          pos--;
12701                          break;
12702                  case '\r':
12703                          pos = 0;
12704                          break;
12705                  case '\n':
12706                          if ((tp->tty_termios.c_oflag & (OPOST|ONLCR))
12707                                                          == (OPOST|ONLCR)) {
12708                                  /* Map LF to CR+LF if there is space.  Note that the
12709                                   * next character in the buffer is overwritten, so
12710                                   * we stop at this point.
12711                                   */
12712                                  if (oct >= 2) {
12713                                          *bpos = '\r';
12714                                          if (++bpos == bend) bpos = bstart;
12715                                          *bpos = '\n';
12716                                          pos = 0;
12717                                          ict--;
12718                                          oct -= 2;
12719                                  }
12720                                  goto out_done;  /* no space or buffer got changed */
12721                          }
12722                          break;
12723                  case '\t':
12724                          /* Best guess for the tab length. */
12725                          tablen = TAB_SIZE - (pos & TAB_MASK);
12726
12727                          if ((tp->tty_termios.c_oflag & (OPOST|XTABS))
12728                                                          == (OPOST|XTABS)) {
12729                                  /* Tabs must be expanded. */
12730                                  if (oct >= tablen) {
12731                                          pos += tablen;
12732                                          ict--;
12733                                          oct -= tablen;
12734                                          do {
12735                                                  *bpos = ' ';
12736                                                  if (++bpos == bend) bpos = bstart;
12737                                          } while (--tablen != 0);
12738                                  }
12739                                  goto out_done;
12740                          }
12741                          /* Tabs are output directly. */
12742                          pos += tablen;
12743                          break;
12744                  default:
12745                          /* Assume any other character prints as one character. */
12746                          pos++;
12747                  }
12748                  if (++bpos == bend) bpos = bstart;
12749                  ict--;
12750                  oct--;
12751          }
12752  out_done:
12753    tp->tty_position = pos & TAB_MASK;
12754
```

```
12755        *icount -= ict;        /* [io]ct are the number of chars not used */
12756        *ocount -= oct;        /* *[io]count are the number of chars that are used */
12757      }


12760   /*===========================================================================*
12761    *                            dev_ioctl                                      *
12762    *===========================================================================*/
12763   PRIVATE void dev_ioctl(tp)
12764   tty_t *tp;
12765   {
12766   /* The ioctl's TCSETSW, TCSETSF and TCDRAIN wait for output to finish to make
12767    * sure that an attribute change doesn't affect the processing of current
12768    * output.  Once output finishes the ioctl is executed as in do_ioctl().
12769    */
12770     phys_bytes user_phys;
12771
12772     if (tp->tty_outleft > 0) return;                /* output not finished */
12773
12774     if (tp->tty_ioreq != TCDRAIN) {
12775           if (tp->tty_ioreq == TCSETSF) tty_icancel(tp);
12776           user_phys = proc_vir2phys(proc_addr(tp->tty_ioproc), tp->tty_iovir);
12777           phys_copy(user_phys, vir2phys(&tp->tty_termios),
12778                                      (phys_bytes) sizeof(tp->tty_termios));
12779           setattr(tp);
12780     }
12781     tp->tty_ioreq = 0;
12782     tty_reply(REVIVE, tp->tty_iocaller, tp->tty_ioproc, OK);
12783   }


12786   /*===========================================================================*
12787    *                            setattr                                        *
12788    *===========================================================================*/
12789   PRIVATE void setattr(tp)
12790   tty_t *tp;
12791   {
12792   /* Apply the new line attributes (raw/canonical, line speed, etc.) */
12793     u16_t *inp;
12794     int count;
12795
12796     if (!(tp->tty_termios.c_lflag & ICANON)) {
12797           /* Raw mode; put a "line break" on all characters in the input queue.
12798            * It is undefined what happens to the input queue when ICANON is
12799            * switched off, a process should use TCSAFLUSH to flush the queue.
12800            * Keeping the queue to preserve typeahead is the Right Thing, however
12801            * when a process does use TCSANOW to switch to raw mode.
12802            */
12803           count = tp->tty_eotct = tp->tty_incount;
12804           inp = tp->tty_intail;
12805           while (count > 0) {
12806                 *inp |= IN_EOT;
12807                 if (++inp == bufend(tp->tty_inbuf)) inp = tp->tty_inbuf;
12808                 --count;
12809           }
12810     }
12811
12812     /* Inspect MIN and TIME. */
12813     lock();
12814     settimer(tp, FALSE);
```

```
12815       unlock();
12816       if (tp->tty_termios.c_lflag & ICANON) {
12817             /* No MIN & TIME in canonical mode. */
12818             tp->tty_min = 1;
12819       } else {
12820             /* In raw mode MIN is the number of chars wanted, and TIME how long
12821              * to wait for them.  With interesting exceptions if either is zero.
12822              */
12823             tp->tty_min = tp->tty_termios.c_cc[VMIN];
12824             if (tp->tty_min == 0 && tp->tty_termios.c_cc[VTIME] > 0)
12825                     tp->tty_min = 1;
12826       }
12827
12828       if (!(tp->tty_termios.c_iflag & IXON)) {
12829             /* No start/stop output control, so don't leave output inhibited. */
12830             tp->tty_inhibited = RUNNING;
12831             tp->tty_events = 1;
12832       }
12833
12834       /* Setting the output speed to zero hangs up the phone. */
12835       if (tp->tty_termios.c_ospeed == B0) sigchar(tp, SIGHUP);
12836
12837       /* Set new line speed, character size, etc at the device level. */
12838       (*tp->tty_ioctl)(tp);
12839       }


12842       /*===========================================================================*
12843        *                            tty_reply                                      *
12844        *===========================================================================*/
12845       PUBLIC void tty_reply(code, replyee, proc_nr, status)
12846       int code;                       /* TASK_REPLY or REVIVE */
12847       int replyee;                    /* destination address for the reply */
12848       int proc_nr;                    /* to whom should the reply go? */
12849       int status;                     /* reply code */
12850       {
12851       /* Send a reply to a process that wanted to read or write data. */
12852
12853         message tty_mess;
12854
12855         tty_mess.m_type = code;
12856         tty_mess.REP_PROC_NR = proc_nr;
12857         tty_mess.REP_STATUS = status;
12858         if ((status = send(replyee, &tty_mess)) != OK)
12859               panic("tty_reply failed, status\n", status);
12860       }


12863       /*===========================================================================*
12864        *                            sigchar                                        *
12865        *===========================================================================*/
12866       PUBLIC void sigchar(tp, sig)
12867       register tty_t *tp;
12868       int sig;                        /* SIGINT, SIGQUIT, SIGKILL or SIGHUP */
12869       {
12870       /* Process a SIGINT, SIGQUIT or SIGKILL char from the keyboard or SIGHUP from
12871        * a tty close, "stty 0", or a real RS-232 hangup.  MM will send the signal to
12872        * the process group (INT, QUIT), all processes (KILL), or the session leader
12873        * * (HUP).
12874        */
```

```
12875
12876      if (tp->tty_pgrp != 0) cause_sig(tp->tty_pgrp, sig);
12877
12878      if (!(tp->tty_termios.c_lflag & NOFLSH)) {
12879            tp->tty_incount = tp->tty_eotct = 0;     /* kill earlier input */
12880            tp->tty_intail = tp->tty_inhead;
12881            (*tp->tty_ocancel)(tp);                  /* kill all output */
12882            tp->tty_inhibited = RUNNING;
12883            tp->tty_events = 1;
12884      }
12885  }


12888  /*===========================================================================*
12889   *                              tty_icancel                                  *
12890   *===========================================================================*/
12891  PRIVATE void tty_icancel(tp)
12892  register tty_t *tp;
12893  {
12894  /* Discard all pending input, tty buffer or device. */
12895
12896    tp->tty_incount = tp->tty_eotct = 0;
12897    tp->tty_intail = tp->tty_inhead;
12898    (*tp->tty_icancel)(tp);
12899  }


12902  /*===========================================================================*
12903   *                              tty_init                                     *
12904   *===========================================================================*/
12905  PRIVATE void tty_init(tp)
12906  tty_t *tp;                           /* TTY line to initialize. */
12907  {
12908  /* Initialize tty structure and call device initialization routines. */
12909
12910    tp->tty_intail = tp->tty_inhead = tp->tty_inbuf;
12911    tp->tty_min = 1;
12912    tp->tty_termios = termios_defaults;
12913    tp->tty_icancel = tp->tty_ocancel = tp->tty_ioctl = tp->tty_close =
12914                                                        tty_devnop;
12915    if (tp < tty_addr(NR_CONS)) {
12916          scr_init(tp);
12917    } else
12918    if (tp < tty_addr(NR_CONS+NR_RS_LINES)) {
12919          rs_init(tp);
12920    } else {
12921          pty_init(tp);
12922    }
12923  }


12926  /*===========================================================================*
12927   *                              tty_wakeup                                   *
12928   *===========================================================================*/
12929  PUBLIC void tty_wakeup(now)
12930  clock_t now;                           /* current time */
12931  {
12932  /* Wake up TTY when something interesting is happening on one of the terminal
12933   * lines, like a character arriving on an RS232 line, a key being typed, or
12934   * a timer on a line expiring by TIME.
```

```
12935    */
12936      tty_t *tp;
12937
12938      /* Scan the timerlist for expired timers and compute the next timeout time. */
12939      tty_timeout = TIME_NEVER;
12940      while ((tp = tty_timelist) != NULL) {
12941            if (tp->tty_time > now) {
12942                    tty_timeout = tp->tty_time;      /* this timer is next */
12943                    break;
12944            }
12945            tp->tty_min = 0;                        /* force read to succeed */
12946            tp->tty_events = 1;
12947            tty_timelist = tp->tty_timenext;
12948      }
12949
12950      /* Let TTY know there is something afoot. */
12951      interrupt(TTY);
12952    }


12955    /*===========================================================================*
12956     *                              settimer                                     *
12957     *===========================================================================*/
12958    PRIVATE void settimer(tp, on)
12959    tty_t *tp;                        /* line to set or unset a timer on */
12960    int on;                           /* set timer if true, otherwise unset */
12961    {
12962    /* Set or unset a TIME inspired timer.  This function is interrupt sensitive
12963     * due to tty_wakeup(), so it must be called from within lock()/unlock().
12964     */
12965      tty_t **ptp;
12966
12967      /* Take tp out of the timerlist if present. */
12968      for (ptp = &tty_timelist; *ptp != NULL; ptp = &(*ptp)->tty_timenext) {
12969            if (tp == *ptp) {
12970                    *ptp = tp->tty_timenext;         /* take tp out of the list */
12971                    break;
12972            }
12973      }
12974      if (!on) return;                              /* unsetting it is enough */
12975
12976      /* Timeout occurs TIME deciseconds from now. */
12977      tp->tty_time = get_uptime() + tp->tty_termios.c_cc[VTIME] * (HZ/10);
12978
12979      /* Find a new place in the list. */
12980      for (ptp = &tty_timelist; *ptp != NULL; ptp = &(*ptp)->tty_timenext) {
12981            if (tp->tty_time <= (*ptp)->tty_time) break;
12982      }
12983      tp->tty_timenext = *ptp;
12984      *ptp = tp;
12985      if (tp->tty_time < tty_timeout) tty_timeout = tp->tty_time;
12986    }


12989    /*===========================================================================*
12990     *                              tty_devnop                                   *
12991     *===========================================================================*/
12992    PUBLIC void tty_devnop(tp)
12993    tty_t *tp;
12994    {
```

```
12995     /* Some functions need not be implemented at the device level. */
12996     }




++++++++++++++++++++++++++++++++++++++++++++++++++++++++++++++++++++++++++++++
                              src/kernel/keyboard.c
++++++++++++++++++++++++++++++++++++++++++++++++++++++++++++++++++++++++++++++

13000     /* Keyboard driver for PC's and AT's.
13001      *
13002      * Changed by Marcus Hampel     (04/02/1994)
13003      *   - Loadable keymaps
13004      */
13005
13006     #include "kernel.h"
13007     #include <termios.h>
13008     #include <signal.h>
13009     #include <unistd.h>
13010     #include <minix/callnr.h>
13011     #include <minix/com.h>
13012     #include <minix/keymap.h>
13013     #include "tty.h"
13014     #include "keymaps/us-std.src"
13015
13016     /* Standard and AT keyboard.  (PS/2 MCA implies AT throughout.) */
13017     #define KEYBD            0x60    /* I/O port for keyboard data */
13018
13019     /* AT keyboard. */
13020     #define KB_COMMAND       0x64    /* I/O port for commands on AT */
13021     #define KB_GATE_A20      0x02    /* bit in output port to enable A20 line */
13022     #define KB_PULSE_OUTPUT  0xF0    /* base for commands to pulse output port */
13023     #define KB_RESET         0x01    /* bit in output port to reset CPU */
13024     #define KB_STATUS        0x64    /* I/O port for status on AT */
13025     #define KB_ACK           0xFA    /* keyboard ack response */
13026     #define KB_BUSY          0x02    /* status bit set when KEYBD port ready */
13027     #define LED_CODE         0xED    /* command to keyboard to set LEDs */
13028     #define MAX_KB_ACK_RETRIES 0x1000      /* max #times to wait for kb ack */
13029     #define MAX_KB_BUSY_RETRIES 0x1000     /* max #times to loop while kb busy */
13030     #define KBIT             0x80    /* bit used to ack characters to keyboard */
13031
13032     /* Miscellaneous. */
13033     #define ESC_SCAN           1     /* Reboot key when panicking */
13034     #define SLASH_SCAN        53     /* to recognize numeric slash */
13035     #define HOME_SCAN         71     /* first key on the numeric keypad */
13036     #define DEL_SCAN          83     /* DEL for use in CTRL-ALT-DEL reboot */
13037     #define CONSOLE            0     /* line number for console */
13038     #define MEMCHECK_ADR     0x472   /* address to stop memory check after reboot */
13039     #define MEMCHECK_MAG     0x1234  /* magic number to stop memory check */
13040
13041     #define kb_addr()        (&kb_lines[0])  /* there is only one keyboard */
13042     #define KB_IN_BYTES       32     /* size of keyboard input buffer */
13043
13044     PRIVATE int alt1;                /* left alt key state */
13045     PRIVATE int alt2;                /* right alt key state */
13046     PRIVATE int capslock;            /* caps lock key state */
13047     PRIVATE int esc;                 /* escape scan code detected? */
13048     PRIVATE int control;             /* control key state */
13049     PRIVATE int caps_off;            /* 1 = normal position, 0 = depressed */
```

```
13050   PRIVATE int numlock;              /* number lock key state */
13051   PRIVATE int num_off;              /* 1 = normal position, 0 = depressed */
13052   PRIVATE int slock;                /* scroll lock key state */
13053   PRIVATE int slock_off;            /* 1 = normal position, 0 = depressed */
13054   PRIVATE int shift;                /* shift key state */
13055
13056   PRIVATE char numpad_map[] =
13057                   {'H', 'Y', 'A', 'B', 'D', 'C', 'V', 'U', 'G', 'S', 'T', '@'};
13058
13059   /* Keyboard structure, 1 per console. */
13060   struct kb_s {
13061     char *ihead;                    /* next free spot in input buffer */
13062     char *itail;                    /* scan code to return to TTY */
13063     int icount;                     /* # codes in buffer */
13064     char ibuf[KB_IN_BYTES];         /* input buffer */
13065   };
13066
13067   PRIVATE struct kb_s kb_lines[NR_CONS];
13068
13069   FORWARD _PROTOTYPE( int kb_ack, (void) );
13070   FORWARD _PROTOTYPE( int kb_wait, (void) );
13071   FORWARD _PROTOTYPE( int func_key, (int scode) );
13072   FORWARD _PROTOTYPE( int scan_keyboard, (void) );
13073   FORWARD _PROTOTYPE( unsigned make_break, (int scode) );
13074   FORWARD _PROTOTYPE( void set_leds, (void) );
13075   FORWARD _PROTOTYPE( int kbd_hw_int, (int irq) );
13076   FORWARD _PROTOTYPE( void kb_read, (struct tty *tp) );
13077   FORWARD _PROTOTYPE( unsigned map_key, (int scode) );
13078
13079
13080   /*===========================================================================*
13081    *                              map_key0                                      *
13082    *===========================================================================*/
13083   /* Map a scan code to an ASCII code ignoring modifiers. */
13084   #define map_key0(scode)  \
13085           ((unsigned) keymap[(scode) * MAP_COLS])
13086
13087
13088   /*===========================================================================*
13089    *                              map_key                                       *
13090    *===========================================================================*/
13091   PRIVATE unsigned map_key(scode)
13092   int scode;
13093   {
13094   /* Map a scan code to an ASCII code. */
13095
13096     int caps, column;
13097     u16_t *keyrow;
13098
13099     if (scode == SLASH_SCAN && esc) return '/';    /* don't map numeric slash */
13100
13101     keyrow = &keymap[scode * MAP_COLS];
13102
13103     caps = shift;
13104     if (numlock && HOME_SCAN <= scode && scode <= DEL_SCAN) caps = !caps;
13105     if (capslock && (keyrow[0] & HASCAPS)) caps = !caps;
13106
13107     if (alt1 || alt2) {
13108          column = 2;
13109          if (control || alt2) column = 3;          /* Ctrl + Alt1 == Alt2 */
```

```
13110              if (caps) column = 4;
13111        } else {
13112              column = 0;
13113              if (caps) column = 1;
13114              if (control) column = 5;
13115        }
13116      return keyrow[column] & ~HASCAPS;
13117      }


13120      /*===========================================================================*
13121       *                              kbd_hw_int                                   *
13122       *===========================================================================*/
13123      PRIVATE int kbd_hw_int(irq)
13124      int irq;
13125      {
13126      /* A keyboard interrupt has occurred.  Process it. */
13127
13128        int code;
13129        unsigned km;
13130        register struct kb_s *kb;
13131
13132        /* Fetch the character from the keyboard hardware and acknowledge it. */
13133        code = scan_keyboard();
13134
13135        /* The IBM keyboard interrupts twice per key, once when depressed, once when
13136         * released.  Filter out the latter, ignoring all but the shift-type keys.
13137         * The shift-type keys 29, 42, 54, 56, 58, and 69 must be processed normally.
13138         */
13139
13140        if (code & 0200) {
13141              /* A key has been released (high bit is set). */
13142              km = map_key0(code & 0177);
13143              if (km != CTRL && km != SHIFT && km != ALT && km != CALOCK
13144                            && km != NLOCK && km != SLOCK && km != EXTKEY)
13145                    return 1;
13146        }
13147
13148        /* Store the character in memory so the task can get at it later. */
13149        kb = kb_addr();
13150        if (kb->icount < KB_IN_BYTES) {
13151              *kb->ihead++ = code;
13152              if (kb->ihead == kb->ibuf + KB_IN_BYTES) kb->ihead = kb->ibuf;
13153              kb->icount++;
13154              tty_table[current].tty_events = 1;
13155              force_timeout();
13156        }
13157        /* Else it doesn't fit - discard it. */
13158        return 1;          /* Reenable keyboard interrupt */
13159      }


13162      /*===========================================================================*
13163       *                              kb_read                                      *
13164       *===========================================================================*/
13165      PRIVATE void kb_read(tp)
13166      tty_t *tp;
13167      {
13168      /* Process characters from the circular keyboard buffer. */
13169
```

```
13170          struct kb_s *kb;
13171          char buf[3];
13172          int scode;
13173          unsigned ch;
13174
13175          kb = kb_addr();
13176          tp = &tty_table[current];              /* always use the current console */
13177
13178          while (kb->icount > 0) {
13179                  scode = *kb->itail++;                  /* take one key scan code */
13180                  if (kb->itail == kb->ibuf + KB_IN_BYTES) kb->itail = kb->ibuf;
13181                  lock();
13182                  kb->icount--;
13183                  unlock();
13184
13185                  /* Function keys are being used for debug dumps. */
13186                  if (func_key(scode)) continue;
13187
13188                  /* Perform make/break processing. */
13189                  ch = make_break(scode);
13190
13191                  if (ch <= 0xFF) {
13192                          /* A normal character. */
13193                          buf[0] = ch;
13194                          (void) in_process(tp, buf, 1);
13195                  } else
13196                  if (HOME <= ch && ch <= INSRT) {
13197                          /* An ASCII escape sequence generated by the numeric pad. */
13198                          buf[0] = ESC;
13199                          buf[1] = '[';
13200                          buf[2] = numpad_map[ch - HOME];
13201                          (void) in_process(tp, buf, 3);
13202                  } else
13203                  if (ch == ALEFT) {
13204                          /* Choose lower numbered console as current console. */
13205                          select_console(current - 1);
13206                  } else
13207                  if (ch == ARIGHT) {
13208                          /* Choose higher numbered console as current console. */
13209                          select_console(current + 1);
13210                  } else
13211                  if (AF1 <= ch && ch <= AF12) {
13212                          /* Alt-F1 is console, Alt-F2 is ttyc1, etc. */
13213                   '        select_console(ch - AF1);
13214                  }
13215          }
13216  }


13219  /*===========================================================================*
13220   *                              make_break                                   *
13221   *===========================================================================*/
13222  PRIVATE unsigned make_break(scode)
13223  int scode;                       /* scan code of key just struck or released */
13224  {
13225  /* This routine can handle keyboards that interrupt only on key depression,
13226   * as well as keyboards that interrupt on key depression and key release.
13227   * For efficiency, the interrupt routine filters out most key releases.
13228   */
13229    int ch, make;
```

```
13230          static int CAD_count = 0;
13231
13232          /* Check for CTRL-ALT-DEL, and if found, halt the computer. This would
13233           * be better done in keyboard() in case TTY is hung, except control and
13234           * alt are set in the high level code.
13235           */
13236          if (control && (alt1 || alt2) && scode == DEL_SCAN)
13237          {
13238                  if (++CAD_count == 3) wreboot(RBT_HALT);
13239                  cause_sig(INIT_PROC_NR, SIGABRT);
13240                  return -1;
13241          }
13242
13243          /* High-order bit set on key release. */
13244          make = (scode & 0200 ? 0 : 1);          /* 0 = release, 1 = press */
13245
13246          ch = map_key(scode & 0177);             /* map to ASCII */
13247
13248          switch (ch) {
13249              case CTRL:
13250                      control = make;
13251                      ch = -1;
13252                      break;
13253              case SHIFT:
13254                      shift = make;
13255                      ch = -1;
13256                      break;
13257              case ALT:
13258                      if (make) {
13259                              if (esc) alt2 = 1; else alt1 = 1;
13260                      } else {
13261                              alt1 = alt2 = 0;
13262                      }
13263                      ch = -1;
13264                      break;
13265              case CALOCK:
13266                      if (make && caps_off) {
13267                              capslock = 1 - capslock;
13268                              set_leds();
13269                      }
13270                      caps_off = 1 - make;
13271                      ch = -1;
13272                      break;
13273              case NLOCK:
13274                      if (make && num_off) {
13275                              numlock = 1 - numlock;
13276                              set_leds();
13277                      }
13278                      num_off = 1 - make;
13279                      ch = -1;
13280                      break;
13281              case SLOCK:
13282                      if (make & slock_off) {
13283                              slock = 1 - slock;
13284                              set_leds();
13285                      }
13286                      slock_off = 1 - make;
13287                      ch = -1;
13288                      break;
13289              case EXTKEY:
```

```
13290                          esc = 1;
13291                          return(-1);
13292                  default:
13293                          if (!make) ch = -1;
13294          }
13295      esc = 0;
13296      return(ch);
13297    }


13300    /*===========================================================================*
13301     *                              set_leds                                      *
13302     *===========================================================================*/
13303    PRIVATE void set_leds()
13304    {
13305    /* Set the LEDs on the caps lock and num lock keys */
13306
13307      unsigned leds;
13308
13309      if (!pc_at) return;      /* PC/XT doesn't have LEDs */
13310
13311      /* encode LED bits */
13312      leds = (slock << 0) | (numlock << 1) | (capslock << 2);
13313
13314      kb_wait();                        /* wait for buffer empty   */
13315      out_byte(KEYBD, LED_CODE);        /* prepare keyboard to accept LED values */
13316      kb_ack();                         /* wait for ack response   */
13317
13318      kb_wait();                        /* wait for buffer empty   */
13319      out_byte(KEYBD, leds);            /* give keyboard LED values */
13320      kb_ack();                         /* wait for ack response   */
13321    }


13324    /*===========================================================================*
13325     *                              kb_wait                                       *
13326     *===========================================================================*/
13327    PRIVATE int kb_wait()
13328    {
13329    /* Wait until the controller is ready; return zero if this times out. */
13330
13331      int retries;
13332
13333      retries = MAX_KB_BUSY_RETRIES + 1;
13334      while (--retries != 0 && in_byte(KB_STATUS) & KB_BUSY)
13335              ;                         /* wait until not busy */
13336      return(retries);                  /* nonzero if ready */
13337    }


13340    /*===========================================================================*
13341     *                              kb_ack                                        *
13342     *===========================================================================*/
13343    PRIVATE int kb_ack()
13344    {
13345    /* Wait until kbd acknowledges last command; return zero if this times out. */
13346
13347      int retries;
13348
13349      retries = MAX_KB_ACK_RETRIES + 1;
```

```
13350        while (--retries != 0 && in_byte(KEYBD) != KB_ACK)
13351            ;                          /* wait for ack */
13352        return(retries);              /* nonzero if ack received */
13353    }


13356    /*===========================================================================*
13357     *                              kb_init                                       *
13358     *===========================================================================*/
13359    PUBLIC void kb_init(tp)
13360    tty_t *tp;
13361    {
13362    /* Initialize the keyboard driver. */
13363
13364      register struct kb_s *kb;
13365
13366      /* Input function. */
13367      tp->tty_devread = kb_read;
13368
13369      kb = kb_addr();
13370
13371      /* Set up input queue. */
13372      kb->ihead = kb->itail = kb->ibuf;
13373
13374      /* Set initial values. */
13375      caps_off = 1;
13376      num_off = 1;
13377      slock_off = 1;
13378      esc = 0;
13379
13380      set_leds();                       /* turn off numlock led */
13381
13382      scan_keyboard();                  /* stop lockup from leftover keystroke */
13383
13384      put_irq_handler(KEYBOARD_IRQ, kbd_hw_int);    /* set the interrupt handler */
13385      enable_irq(KEYBOARD_IRQ);         /* safe now everything initialised! */
13386    }


13389    /*===========================================================================*
13390     *                              kbd_loadmap                                   *
13391     *===========================================================================*/
13392    PUBLIC int kbd_loadmap(user_phys)
13393    phys_bytes user_phys;
13394    {
13395    /* Load a new keymap. */
13396
13397      phys_copy(user_phys, vir2phys(keymap), (phys_bytes) sizeof(keymap));
13398      return(OK);
13399    }


13402    /*===========================================================================*
13403     *                              func_key                                      *
13404     *===========================================================================*/
13405    PRIVATE int func_key(scode)
13406    int scode;                          /* scan code for a function key */
13407    {
13408    /* This procedure traps function keys for debugging and control purposes. */
13409
```

```
13410       unsigned code;
13411
13412       code = map_key0(scode);                         /* first ignore modifiers */
13413       if (code < F1 || code > F12) return(FALSE);     /* not our job */
13414
13415       switch (map_key(scode)) {                        /* include modifiers */
13416
13417       case F1:      p_dmp(); break;            /* print process table */
13418       case F2:      map_dmp(); break;          /* print memory map */
13419       case F3:      toggle_scroll(); break; /* hardware vs. software scrolling */
13420       case CF7:     sigchar(&tty_table[CONSOLE], SIGQUIT); break;
13421       case CF8:     sigchar(&tty_table[CONSOLE], SIGINT); break;
13422       case CF9:     sigchar(&tty_table[CONSOLE], SIGKILL); break;
13423       default:      return(FALSE);
13424       }
13425       return(TRUE);
13426     }


13429     /*===========================================================================*
13430      *                           scan_keyboard                                   *
13431      *===========================================================================*/
13432     PRIVATE int scan_keyboard()
13433     {
13434     /* Fetch the character from the keyboard hardware and acknowledge it. */
13435
13436       int code;
13437       int val;
13438
13439       code = in_byte(KEYBD);        /* get the scan code for the key struck */
13440       val = in_byte(PORT_B);        /* strobe the keyboard to ack the char */
13441       out_byte(PORT_B, val | KBIT); /* strobe the bit high */
13442       out_byte(PORT_B, val);        /* now strobe it low */
13443       return code;
13444     }


13447     /*===========================================================================*
13448      *                           wreboot                                         *
13449      *===========================================================================*/
13450     PUBLIC void wreboot(how)
13451     int how;                  /* 0 = halt, 1 = reboot, 2 = panic!, ... */
13452     {
13453     /* Wait for keystrokes for printing debugging info and reboot. */
13454
13455       int quiet, code;
13456       static u16_t magic = MEMCHECK_MAG;
13457       struct tasktab *ttp;
13458
13459       /* Mask all interrupts. */
13460       out_byte(INT_CTLMASK, ~0);
13461
13462       /* Tell several tasks to stop. */
13463       cons_stop();
13464       floppy_stop();
13465       clock_stop();
13466
13467       if (how == RBT_HALT) {
13468           printf("System Halted\n");
13469           if (!mon_return) how = RBT_PANIC;
```

```
13470            }
13471
13472      if (how == RBT_PANIC) {
13473            /* A panic! */
13474            printf("Hit ESC to reboot, F-keys for debug dumps\n");
13475
13476            (void) scan_keyboard(); /* ack any old input */
13477            quiet = scan_keyboard();/* quiescent value (0 on PC, last code on AT)*/
13478            for (;;) {
13479                    milli_delay(100);        /* pause for a decisecond */
13480                    code = scan_keyboard();
13481                    if (code != quiet) {
13482                            /* A key has been pressed. */
13483                            if (code == ESC_SCAN) break; /* reboot if ESC typed */
13484                            (void) func_key(code);         /* process function key */
13485                            quiet = scan_keyboard();
13486                    }
13487            }
13488            how = RBT_REBOOT;
13489      }
13490
13491      if (how == RBT_REBOOT) printf("Rebooting\n");
13492
13493      if (mon_return && how != RBT_RESET) {
13494            /* Reinitialize the interrupt controllers to the BIOS defaults. */
13495            intr_init(0);
13496            out_byte(INT_CTLMASK, 0);
13497            out_byte(INT2_CTLMASK, 0);
13498
13499            /* Return to the boot monitor. */
13500            if (how == RBT_HALT) {
13501                    reboot_code = vir2phys("");
13502            } else
13503            if (how == RBT_REBOOT) {
13504                    reboot_code = vir2phys("delay;boot");
13505            }
13506            level0(monitor);
13507      }
13508
13509      /* Stop BIOS memory test. */
13510      phys_copy(vir2phys(&magic), (phys_bytes) MEMCHECK_ADR,
13511                                          (phys_bytes) sizeof(magic));
13512
13513      if (protected_mode) {
13514            /* Use the AT keyboard controller to reset the processor.
13515             * The A20 line is kept enabled in case this code is ever
13516             * run from extended memory, and because some machines
13517             * appear to drive the fake A20 high instead of low just
13518             * after reset, leading to an illegal opode trap.  This bug
13519             * is more of a problem if the fake A20 is in use, as it
13520             * would be if the keyboard reset were used for real mode.
13521             */
13522            kb_wait();
13523            out_byte(KB_COMMAND,
13524                    KB_PULSE_OUTPUT | (0x0F & ~(KB_GATE_A20 | KB_RESET)));
13525            milli_delay(10);
13526
13527            /* If the nice method fails then do a reset.  In protected
13528             * mode this means a processor shutdown.
13529             */
```

```
13530              printf("Hard reset...\n");
13531              milli_delay(250);
13532      }
13533      /* In real mode, jumping to the reset address is good enough. */
13534      level0(reset);
13535  }
```

```
++++++++++++++++++++++++++++++++++++++++++++++++++++++++++++++++++++++++++++++
                            src/kernel/console.c
++++++++++++++++++++++++++++++++++++++++++++++++++++++++++++++++++++++++++++++
```

```
13600  /* Code and data for the IBM console driver.
13601   *
13602   * The 6845 video controller used by the IBM PC shares its video memory with
13603   * the CPU somewhere in the 0xB0000 memory bank.  To the 6845 this memory
13604   * consists of 16-bit words.  Each word has a character code in the low byte
13605   * and a so-called attribute byte in the high byte.  The CPU directly modifies
13606   * video memory to display characters, and sets two registers on the 6845 that
13607   * specify the video origin and the cursor position.  The video origin is the
13608   * place in video memory where the first character (upper left corner) can
13609   * be found.  Moving the origin is a fast way to scroll the screen.  Some
13610   * video adapters wrap around the top of video memory, so the origin can
13611   * move without bounds.  For other adapters screen memory must sometimes be
13612   * moved to reset the origin.  All computations on video memory use character
13613   * (word) addresses for simplicity and assume there is no wrapping.  The
13614   * assembly support functions translate the word addresses to byte addresses
13615   * and the scrolling function worries about wrapping.
13616   */
13617
13618  #include "kernel.h"
13619  #include <termios.h>
13620  #include <minix/callnr.h>
13621  #include <minix/com.h>
13622  #include "protect.h"
13623  #include "tty.h"
13624  #include "proc.h"
13625
13626  /* Definitions used by the console driver. */
13627  #define MONO_BASE    0xB0000L    /* base of mono video memory */
13628  #define COLOR_BASE   0xB8000L    /* base of color video memory */
13629  #define MONO_SIZE    0x1000      /* 4K mono video memory */
13630  #define COLOR_SIZE   0x4000      /* 16K color video memory */
13631  #define EGA_SIZE     0x8000      /* EGA & VGA have at least 32K */
13632  #define BLANK_COLOR  0x0700      /* determines cursor color on blank screen */
13633  #define SCROLL_UP        0       /* scroll forward */
13634  #define SCROLL_DOWN      1       /* scroll backward */
13635  #define BLANK_MEM ((u16_t *) 0) /* tells mem_vid_copy() to blank the screen */
13636  #define CONS_RAM_WORDS   80      /* video ram buffer size */
13637  #define MAX_ESC_PARMS    2       /* number of escape sequence params allowed */
13638
13639  /* Constants relating to the controller chips. */
13640  #define M_6845       0x3B4       /* port for 6845 mono */
13641  #define C_6845       0x3D4       /* port for 6845 color */
13642  #define EGA          0x3C4       /* port for EGA or VGA card */
13643  #define INDEX            0       /* 6845's index register */
13644  #define DATA             1       /* 6845's data register */
```

```
13645      #define VID_ORG            12      /* 6845's origin register */
13646      #define CURSOR             14      /* 6845's cursor register */
13647
13648      /* Beeper. */
13649      #define BEEP_FREQ     0x0533     /* value to put into timer to set beep freq */
13650      #define B_TIME             3      /* length of CTRL-G beep is ticks */
13651
13652      /* definitions used for font management */
13653      #define GA_SEQUENCER_INDEX     0x3C4
13654      #define GA_SEQUENCER_DATA      0x3C5
13655      #define GA_GRAPHICS_INDEX      0x3CE
13656      #define GA_GRAPHICS_DATA       0x3CF
13657      #define GA_VIDEO_ADDRESS       0xA0000L
13658      #define GA_FONT_SIZE           8192
13659
13660      /* Global variables used by the console driver. */
13661      PUBLIC unsigned vid_seg;          /* video ram selector (0xB0000 or 0xB8000) */
13662      PUBLIC unsigned vid_size;         /* 0x2000 for color or 0x0800 for mono */
13663      PUBLIC unsigned vid_mask;         /* 0x1FFF for color or 0x07FF for mono */
13664      PUBLIC unsigned blank_color = BLANK_COLOR; /* display code for blank */
13665
13666      /* Private variables used by the console driver. */
13667      PRIVATE int vid_port;             /* I/O port for accessing 6845 */
13668      PRIVATE int wrap;                 /* hardware can wrap? */
13669      PRIVATE int softscroll;           /* 1 = software scrolling, 0 = hardware */
13670      PRIVATE unsigned vid_base;        /* base of video ram (0xB000 or 0xB800) */
13671      PRIVATE int beeping;              /* speaker is beeping? */
13672      #define scr_width          80     /* # characters on a line */
13673      #define scr_lines          25     /* # lines on the screen */
13674      #define scr_size      (80*25) /* # characters on the screen */
13675
13676      /* Per console data. */
13677      typedef struct console {
13678        tty_t *c_tty;                   /* associated TTY struct */
13679        int c_column;                   /* current column number (0-origin) */
13680        int c_row;                      /* current row (0 at top of screen) */
13681        int c_rwords;                   /* number of WORDS (not bytes) in outqueue */
13682        unsigned c_start;               /* start of video memory of this console */
13683        unsigned c_limit;               /* limit of this console's video memory */
13684        unsigned c_org;                 /* location in RAM where 6845 base points */
13685        unsigned c_cur;                 /* current position of cursor in video RAM */
13686        unsigned c_attr;                /* character attribute */
13687        unsigned c_blank;               /* blank attribute */
13688        char c_esc_state;               /* 0=normal, 1=ESC, 2=ESC[ */
13689        char c_esc_intro;               /* Distinguishing character following ESC */
13690        int *c_esc_parmp;               /* pointer to current escape parameter */
13691        int c_esc_parmv[MAX_ESC_PARMS];     /* list of escape parameters */
13692        u16_t c_ramqueue[CONS_RAM_WORDS];   /* buffer for video RAM */
13693      } console_t;
13694
13695      PRIVATE int nr_cons= 1;           /* actual number of consoles */
13696      PRIVATE console_t cons_table[NR_CONS];
13697      PRIVATE console_t *curcons;       /* currently visible */
13698
13699      /* Color if using a color controller. */
13700      #define color     (vid_port == C_6845)
13701
13702      /* Map from ANSI colors to the attributes used by the PC */
13703      PRIVATE int ansi_colors[8] = {0, 4, 2, 6, 1, 5, 3, 7};
13704
```

```
13705   /* Structure used for font management */
13706   struct sequence {
13707           unsigned short index;
13708           unsigned char port;
13709           unsigned char value;
13710   };
13711
13712   FORWARD _PROTOTYPE( void cons_write, (struct tty *tp)                  );
13713   FORWARD _PROTOTYPE( void cons_echo, (tty_t *tp, int c)                );
13714   FORWARD _PROTOTYPE( void out_char, (console_t *cons, int c)           );
13715   FORWARD _PROTOTYPE( void beep, (void)                                 );
13716   FORWARD _PROTOTYPE( void do_escape, (console_t *cons, int c)          );
13717   FORWARD _PROTOTYPE( void flush, (console_t *cons)                     );
13718   FORWARD _PROTOTYPE( void parse_escape, (console_t *cons, int c)       );
13719   FORWARD _PROTOTYPE( void scroll_screen, (console_t *cons, int dir)    );
13720   FORWARD _PROTOTYPE( void set_6845, (int reg, unsigned val)            );
13721   FORWARD _PROTOTYPE( void stop_beep, (void)                            );
13722   FORWARD _PROTOTYPE( void cons_org0, (void)                            );
13723   FORWARD _PROTOTYPE( void ga_program, (struct sequence *seq) );
13724
13725
13726   /*===========================================================================*
13727    *                              cons_write                                    *
13728    *===========================================================================*/
13729   PRIVATE void cons_write(tp)
13730   register struct tty *tp;          /* tells which terminal is to be used */
13731   {
13732   /* Copy as much data as possible to the output queue, then start I/O.  On
13733    * memory-mapped terminals, such as the IBM console, the I/O will also be
13734    * finished, and the counts updated.  Keep repeating until all I/O done.
13735    */
13736
13737     int count;
13738     register char *tbuf;
13739     char buf[64];
13740     phys_bytes user_phys;
13741     console_t *cons = tp->tty_priv;
13742
13743     /* Check quickly for nothing to do, so this can be called often without
13744      * unmodular tests elsewhere.
13745      */
13746     if ((count = tp->tty_outleft) == 0 || tp->tty_inhibited) return;
13747
13748     /* Copy the user bytes to buf[] for decent addressing. Loop over the
13749      * copies, since the user buffer may be much larger than buf[].
13750      */
13751     do {
13752             if (count > sizeof(buf)) count = sizeof(buf);
13753             user_phys = proc_vir2phys(proc_addr(tp->tty_outproc), tp->tty_out_vir);
13754             phys_copy(user_phys, vir2phys(buf), (phys_bytes) count);
13755             tbuf = buf;
13756
13757             /* Update terminal data structure. */
13758             tp->tty_out_vir += count;
13759             tp->tty_outcum += count;
13760             tp->tty_outleft -= count;
13761
13762             /* Output each byte of the copy to the screen.  Avoid calling
13763              * out_char() for the "easy" characters, put them into the buffer
13764              * directly.
```

```
13765                     */
13766             do {
13767                     if ((unsigned) *tbuf < ' ' || cons->c_esc_state > 0
13768                             || cons->c_column >= scr_width
13769                             || cons->c_rwords >= buflen(cons->c_ramqueue))
13770                     {
13771                             out_char(cons, *tbuf++);
13772                     } else {
13773                             cons->c_ramqueue[cons->c_rwords++] =
13774                                             cons->c_attr | (*tbuf++ & BYTE);
13775                             cons->c_column++;
13776                     }
13777             } while (--count != 0);
13778     } while ((count = tp->tty_outleft) != 0 && !tp->tty_inhibited);
13779
13780     flush(cons);                    /* transfer anything buffered to the screen */
13781
13782     /* Reply to the writer if all output is finished. */
13783     if (tp->tty_outleft == 0) {
13784             tty_reply(tp->tty_outrepcode, tp->tty_outcaller, tp->tty_outproc,
13785                                             tp->tty_outcum);
13786             tp->tty_outcum = 0;
13787     }
13788 }


13791 /*===========================================================================*
13792  *                              cons_echo                                    *
13793  *===========================================================================*/
13794 PRIVATE void cons_echo(tp, c)
13795 register tty_t *tp;            /* pointer to tty struct */
13796 int c;                        /* character to be echoed */
13797 {
13798 /* Echo keyboard input (print & flush). */
13799   console_t *cons = tp->tty_priv;
13800
13801   out_char(cons, c);
13802   flush(cons);
13803 }


13806 /*===========================================================================*
13807  *                              out_char                                     *
13808  *===========================================================================*/
13809 PRIVATE void out_char(cons, c)
13810 register console_t *cons;      /* pointer to console struct */
13811 int c;                        /* character to be output */
13812 {
13813 /* Output a character on the console.  Check for escape sequences first. */
13814   if (cons->c_esc_state > 0) {
13815           parse_escape(cons, c);
13816           return;
13817   }
13818
13819   switch(c) {
13820       case 000:                 /* null is typically used for padding */
13821               return;           /* better not do anything */
13822
13823       case 007:                 /* ring the bell */
13824               flush(cons);      /* print any chars queued for output */
```

```
13825                           beep();
13826                           return;
13827
13828           case '\b':                /* backspace */
13829                   if (--cons->c_column < 0) {
13830                           if (--cons->c_row >= 0) cons->c_column += scr_width;
13831                   }
13832                   flush(cons);
13833                   return;
13834
13835           case '\n':                /* line feed */
13836                   if ((cons->c_tty->tty_termios.c_oflag & (OPOST|ONLCR))
13837                                                   == (OPOST|ONLCR)) {
13838                           cons->c_column = 0;
13839                   }
13840                   /*FALL THROUGH*/
13841           case 013:                 /* CTRL-K */
13842           case 014:                 /* CTRL-L */
13843                   if (cons->c_row == scr_lines-1) {
13844                           scroll_screen(cons, SCROLL_UP);
13845                   } else {
13846                           cons->c_row++;
13847                   }
13848                   flush(cons);
13849                   return;
13850
13851           case '\r':                /* carriage return */
13852                   cons->c_column = 0;
13853                   flush(cons);
13854                   return;
13855
13856           case '\t':                /* tab */
13857                   cons->c_column = (cons->c_column + TAB_SIZE) & ~TAB_MASK;
13858                   if (cons->c_column > scr_width) {
13859                           cons->c_column -= scr_width;
13860                           if (cons->c_row == scr_lines-1) {
13861                                   scroll_screen(cons, SCROLL_UP);
13862                           } else {
13863                                   cons->c_row++;
13864                           }
13865                   }
13866                   flush(cons);
13867                   return;
13868
13869           case 033:                 /* ESC - start of an escape sequence */
13870                   flush(cons);      /* print any chars queued for output */
13871                   cons->c_esc_state = 1;   /* mark ESC as seen */
13872                   return;
13873
13874           default:                  /* printable chars are stored in ramqueue */
13875                   if (cons->c_column >= scr_width) {
13876                           if (!LINEWRAP) return;
13877                           if (cons->c_row == scr_lines-1) {
13878                                   scroll_screen(cons, SCROLL_UP);
13879                           } else {
13880                                   cons->c_row++;
13881                           }
13882                           cons->c_column = 0;
13883                           flush(cons);
13884                   }
```

```
13885                       if (cons->c_rwords == buflen(cons->c_ramqueue)) flush(cons);
13886                       cons->c_ramqueue[cons->c_rwords++] = cons->c_attr | (c & BYTE);
13887                       cons->c_column++;                         /* next column */
13888                       return;
13889          }
13890      }


13893      /*===========================================================================*
13894       *                              scroll_screen                                *
13895       *===========================================================================*/
13896      PRIVATE void scroll_screen(cons, dir)
13897      register console_t *cons;           /* pointer to console struct */
13898      int dir;                            /* SCROLL_UP or SCROLL_DOWN */
13899      {
13900        unsigned new_line, new_org, chars;
13901
13902        flush(cons);
13903        chars = scr_size - scr_width;             /* one screen minus one line */
13904
13905        /* Scrolling the screen is a real nuisance due to the various incompatible
13906         * video cards.  This driver supports software scrolling (Hercules?),
13907         * hardware scrolling (mono and CGA cards) and hardware scrolling without
13908         * wrapping (EGA and VGA cards).  In the latter case we must make sure that
13909         *              c_start <= c_org && c_org + scr_size <= c_limit
13910         * holds, because EGA and VGA don't wrap around the end of video memory.
13911         */
13912        if (dir == SCROLL_UP) {
13913              /* Scroll one line up in 3 ways: soft, avoid wrap, use origin. */
13914              if (softscroll) {
13915                      vid_vid_copy(cons->c_start + scr_width, cons->c_start, chars);
13916              } else
13917              if (!wrap && cons->c_org + scr_size + scr_width >= cons->c_limit) {
13918                      vid_vid_copy(cons->c_org + scr_width, cons->c_start, chars);
13919                      cons->c_org = cons->c_start;
13920              } else {
13921                      cons->c_org = (cons->c_org + scr_width) & vid_mask;
13922              }
13923              new_line = (cons->c_org + chars) & vid_mask;
13924        } else {
13925              /* Scroll one line down in 3 ways: soft, avoid wrap, use origin. */
13926              if (softscroll) {
13927                      vid_vid_copy(cons->c_start, cons->c_start + scr_width, chars);
13928              } else
13929              if (!wrap && cons->c_org < cons->c_start + scr_width) {
13930                      new_org = cons->c_limit - scr_size;
13931                      vid_vid_copy(cons->c_org, new_org + scr_width, chars);
13932                      cons->c_org = new_org;
13933              } else {
13934                      cons->c_org = (cons->c_org - scr_width) & vid_mask;
13935              }
13936              new_line = cons->c_org;
13937        }
13938        /* Blank the new line at top or bottom. */
13939        blank_color = cons->c_blank;
13940        mem_vid_copy(BLANK_MEM, new_line, scr_width);
13941
13942        /* Set the new video origin. */
13943        if (cons == curcons) set_6845(VID_ORG, cons->c_org);
13944        flush(cons);
```

```
13945      }


13948      /*===========================================================================*
13949       *                              flush                                         *
13950       *===========================================================================*/
13951      PRIVATE void flush(cons)
13952      register console_t *cons;          /* pointer to console struct */
13953      {
13954      /* Send characters buffered in 'ramqueue' to screen memory, check the new
13955       * cursor position, compute the new hardware cursor position and set it.
13956       */
13957        unsigned cur;
13958        tty_t *tp = cons->c_tty;

13960        /* Have the characters in 'ramqueue' transferred to the screen. */
13961        if (cons->c_rwords > 0) {
13962              mem_vid_copy(cons->c_ramqueue, cons->c_cur, cons->c_rwords);
13963              cons->c_rwords = 0;

13965              /* TTY likes to know the current column and if echoing messed up. */
13966              tp->tty_position = cons->c_column;
13967              tp->tty_reprint = TRUE;
13968        }

13970        /* Check and update the cursor position. */
13971        if (cons->c_column < 0) cons->c_column = 0;
13972        if (cons->c_column > scr_width) cons->c_column = scr_width;
13973        if (cons->c_row < 0) cons->c_row = 0;
13974        if (cons->c_row >= scr_lines) cons->c_row = scr_lines - 1;
13975        cur = cons->c_org + cons->c_row * scr_width + cons->c_column;
13976        if (cur != cons->c_cur) {
13977              if (cons == curcons) set_6845(CURSOR, cur);
13978              cons->c_cur = cur;
13979        }
13980      }


13983      /*===========================================================================*
13984       *                            parse_escape                                    *
13985       *===========================================================================*/
13986      PRIVATE void parse_escape(cons, c)
13987      register console_t *cons;          /* pointer to console struct */
13988      char c;                            /* next character in escape sequence */
13989      {
13990      /* The following ANSI escape sequences are currently supported.
13991       * If n and/or m are omitted, they default to 1. Omitted s defaults to 0.
13992       *    ESC [nA moves up n lines
13993       *    ESC [nB moves down n lines
13994       *    ESC [nC moves right n spaces
13995       *    ESC [nD moves left n spaces
13996       *    ESC [m;nH moves cursor to (m,n)
13997       *    ESC [sJ clears screen relative to cursor (0 to end, 1 from start, 2 all)
13998       *    ESC [sK clears line relative to cursor (0 to end, 1 from start, 2 all)
13999       *    ESC [nL inserts n lines at cursor
14000       *    ESC [nM deletes n lines at cursor
14001       *    ESC [nP deletes n chars at cursor
14002       *    ESC [n@ inserts n chars at cursor
14003       *    ESC [nm enables rendition n (0= normal, 1=bold, 4=underline, 5=blinking,
14004       *        7=reverse, 30..37 set foreground color, 40..47 set background color)
```

```
14005     *   ESC M scrolls the screen backwards if the cursor is on the top line
14006     */
14007
14008     switch (cons->c_esc_state) {
14009        case 1:                    /* ESC seen */
14010            cons->c_esc_intro = '\0';
14011            cons->c_esc_parmp = cons->c_esc_parmv;
14012            cons->c_esc_parmv[0] = cons->c_esc_parmv[1] = 0;
14013            switch (c) {
14014                case '[':   /* Control Sequence Introducer */
14015                    cons->c_esc_intro = c;
14016                    cons->c_esc_state = 2;
14017                    break;
14018                case 'M':   /* Reverse Index */
14019                    do_escape(cons, c);
14020                    break;
14021                default:
14022                    cons->c_esc_state = 0;
14023            }
14024            break;
14025
14026        case 2:                       /* ESC [ seen */
14027            if (c >= '0' && c <= '9') {
14028                if (cons->c_esc_parmp < bufend(cons->c_esc_parmv))
14029                    *cons->c_esc_parmp = *cons->c_esc_parmp * 10 + (c-'0');
14030            } else
14031            if (c == ';') {
14032                if (++cons->c_esc_parmp < bufend(cons->c_esc_parmv))
14033                    *cons->c_esc_parmp = 0;
14034            } else {
14035                do_escape(cons, c);
14036            }
14037            break;
14038     }
14039 }


14042 /*===========================================================================*
14043  *                              do_escape                                    *
14044  *===========================================================================*/
14045 PRIVATE void do_escape(cons, c)
14046 register console_t *cons;        /* pointer to console struct */
14047 char c;                          /* next character in escape sequence */
14048 {
14049   int value, n;
14050   unsigned src, dst, count;
14051
14052   /* Some of these things hack on screen RAM, so it had better be up to date */
14053   flush(cons);
14054
14055   if (cons->c_esc_intro == '\0') {
14056        /* Handle a sequence beginning with just ESC */
14057        switch (c) {
14058            case 'M':              /* Reverse Index */
14059                if (cons->c_row == 0) {
14060                    scroll_screen(cons, SCROLL_DOWN);
14061                } else {
14062                    cons->c_row--;
14063                }
14064                flush(cons);
```

```
14065                         break;
14066
14067                 default: break;
14068         }
14069     } else
14070     if (cons->c_esc_intro == '[') {
14071         /* Handle a sequence beginning with ESC [ and parameters */
14072         value = cons->c_esc_parmv[0];
14073         switch (c) {
14074             case 'A':              /* ESC [nA moves up n lines */
14075                 n = (value == 0 ? 1 : value);
14076                 cons->c_row -= n;
14077                 flush(cons);
14078                 break;
14079
14080             case 'B':              /* ESC [nB moves down n lines */
14081                 n = (value == 0 ? 1 : value);
14082                 cons->c_row += n;
14083                 flush(cons);
14084                 break;
14085
14086             case 'C':              /* ESC [nC moves right n spaces */
14087                 n = (value == 0 ? 1 : value);
14088                 cons->c_column += n;
14089                 flush(cons);
14090                 break;
14091
14092             case 'D':              /* ESC [nD moves left n spaces */
14093                 n = (value == 0 ? 1 : value);
14094                 cons->c_column -= n;
14095                 flush(cons);
14096                 break;
14097
14098             case 'H':              /* ESC [m;nH" moves cursor to (m,n) */
14099                 cons->c_row = cons->c_esc_parmv[0] - 1;
14100                 cons->c_column = cons->c_esc_parmv[1] - 1;
14101                 flush(cons);
14102                 break;
14103
14104             case 'J':              /* ESC [sJ clears in display */
14105                 switch (value) {
14106                     case 0:    /* Clear from cursor to end of screen */
14107                         count = scr_size - (cons->c_cur - cons->c_org);
14108                         dst = cons->c_cur;
14109                         break;
14110                     case 1:    /* Clear from start of screen to cursor */
14111                         count = cons->c_cur - cons->c_org;
14112                         dst = cons->c_org;
14113                         break;
14114                     case 2:    /* Clear entire screen */
14115                         count = scr_size;
14116                         dst = cons->c_org;
14117                         break;
14118                     default:   /* Do nothing */
14119                         count = 0;
14120                         dst = cons->c_org;
14121                 }
14122                 blank_color = cons->c_blank;
14123                 mem_vid_copy(BLANK_MEM, dst, count);
14124                 break;
```

```
14125
14126                case 'K':                /* ESC [sK clears line from cursor */
14127                    switch (value) {
14128                        case 0:      /* Clear from cursor to end of line */
14129                            count = scr_width - cons->c_column;
14130                            dst = cons->c_cur;
14131                            break;
14132                        case 1:      /* Clear from beginning of line to cursor */
14133                            count = cons->c_column;
14134                            dst = cons->c_cur - cons->c_column;
14135                            break;
14136                        case 2:      /* Clear entire line */
14137                            count = scr_width;
14138                            dst = cons->c_cur - cons->c_column;
14139                            break;
14140                        default:     /* Do nothing */
14141                            count = 0;
14142                            dst = cons->c_cur;
14143                    }
14144                    blank_color = cons->c_blank;
14145                    mem_vid_copy(BLANK_MEM, dst, count);
14146                    break;
14147
14148                case 'L':                /* ESC [nL inserts n lines at cursor */
14149                    n = value;
14150                    if (n < 1) n = 1;
14151                    if (n > (scr_lines - cons->c_row))
14152                            n = scr_lines - cons->c_row;
14153
14154                    src = cons->c_org + cons->c_row * scr_width;
14155                    dst = src + n * scr_width;
14156                    count = (scr_lines - cons->c_row - n) * scr_width;
14157                    vid_vid_copy(src, dst, count);
14158                    blank_color = cons->c_blank;
14159                    mem_vid_copy(BLANK_MEM, src, n * scr_width);
14160                    break;
14161
14162                case 'M':                /* ESC [nM deletes n lines at cursor */
14163                    n = value;
14164                    if (n < 1) n = 1;
14165                    if (n > (scr_lines - cons->c_row))
14166                            n = scr_lines - cons->c_row;
14167
14168                    dst = cons->c_org + cons->c_row * scr_width;
14169                    src = dst + n * scr_width;
14170                    count = (scr_lines - cons->c_row - n) * scr_width;
14171                    vid_vid_copy(src, dst, count);
14172                    blank_color = cons->c_blank;
14173                    mem_vid_copy(BLANK_MEM, dst + count, n * scr_width);
14174                    break;
14175
14176                case '@':                /* ESC [n@ inserts n chars at cursor */
14177                    n = value;
14178                    if (n < 1) n = 1;
14179                    if (n > (scr_width - cons->c_column))
14180                            n = scr_width - cons->c_column;
14181
14182                    src = cons->c_cur;
14183                    dst = src + n;
14184                    count = scr_width - cons->c_column - n;
```

```
14185                         vid_vid_copy(src, dst, count);
14186                         blank_color = cons->c_blank;
14187                         mem_vid_copy(BLANK_MEM, src, n);
14188                         break;
14189
14190             case 'P':            /* ESC [nP deletes n chars at cursor */
14191                     n = value;
14192                     if (n < 1) n = 1;
14193                     if (n > (scr_width - cons->c_column))
14194                             n = scr_width - cons->c_column;
14195
14196                     dst = cons->c_cur;
14197                     src = dst + n;
14198                     count = scr_width - cons->c_column - n;
14199                     vid_vid_copy(src, dst, count);
14200                     blank_color = cons->c_blank;
14201                     mem_vid_copy(BLANK_MEM, dst + count, n);
14202                     break;
14203
14204             case 'm':            /* ESC [nm enables rendition n */
14205                     switch (value) {
14206                         case 1:     /* BOLD  */
14207                             if (color) {
14208                                     /* Can't do bold, so use yellow */
14209                                     cons->c_attr = (cons->c_attr & 0xf0ff) | 0x0E00;
14210                             } else {
14211                                     /* Set intensity bit */
14212                                     cons->c_attr |= 0x0800;
14213                             }
14214                             break;
14215
14216                         case 4:     /* UNDERLINE */
14217                             if (color) {
14218                                     /* Use light green */
14219                                     cons->c_attr = (cons->c_attr & 0xf0ff) | 0x0A00;
14220                             } else {
14221                                     cons->c_attr = (cons->c_attr & 0x8900);
14222                             }
14223                             break;
14224
14225                         case 5:     /* BLINKING */
14226                             if (color) {
14227                                     /* Use magenta */
14228                                     cons->c_attr = (cons->c_attr & 0xf0ff) | 0x0500;
14229                             } else {
14230                                     /* Set the blink bit */
14231                                     cons->c_attr |= 0x8000;
14232                             }
14233                             break;
14234
14235                         case 7:     /* REVERSE */
14236                             if (color) {
14237                                     /* Swap fg and bg colors */
14238                                     cons->c_attr =
14239                                             ((cons->c_attr & 0xf000) >> 4) |
14240                                             ((cons->c_attr & 0x0f00) << 4);
14241                             } else
14242                             if ((cons->c_attr & 0x7000) == 0) {
14243                                     cons->c_attr = (cons->c_attr & 0x8800) | 0x7000;
14244                             } else {
```

```
14245                                              cons->c_attr = (cons->c_attr & 0x8800) | 0x0700;
14246                                      }
14247                                      break;
14248
14249                              default:     /* COLOR */
14250                                  if (30 <= value && value <= 37) {
14251                                      cons->c_attr =
14252                                              (cons->c_attr & 0xf0ff) |
14253                                              (ansi_colors[(value - 30)] << 8);
14254                                      cons->c_blank =
14255                                              (cons->c_blank & 0xf0ff) |
14256                                              (ansi_colors[(value - 30)] << 8);
14257                                  } else
14258                                  if (40 <= value && value <= 47) {
14259                                      cons->c_attr =
14260                                              (cons->c_attr & 0x0fff) |
14261                                              (ansi_colors[(value - 40)] << 12);
14262                                      cons->c_blank =
14263                                              (cons->c_blank & 0x0fff) |
14264                                              (ansi_colors[(value - 40)] << 12);
14265                                  } else {
14266                                      cons->c_attr = cons->c_blank;
14267                                  }
14268                                  break;
14269                          }
14270                      break;
14271              }
14272      }
14273      cons->c_esc_state = 0;
14274  }


14277  /*===========================================================================*
14278   *                              set_6845                                      *
14279   *===========================================================================*/
14280  PRIVATE void set_6845(reg, val)
14281  int reg;                        /* which register pair to set */
14282  unsigned val;                   /* 16-bit value to set it to */
14283  {
14284  /* Set a register pair inside the 6845.
14285   * Registers 12-13 tell the 6845 where in video ram to start
14286   * Registers 14-15 tell the 6845 where to put the cursor
14287   */
14288    lock();                               /* try to stop h/w loading in-between value */
14289    out_byte(vid_port + INDEX, reg);           /* set the index register */
14290    out_byte(vid_port + DATA, (val>>8) & BYTE);  /* output high byte */
14291    out_byte(vid_port + INDEX, reg + 1);       /* again */
14292    out_byte(vid_port + DATA, val&BYTE);       /* output low byte */
14293    unlock();
14294  }


14297  /*===========================================================================*
14298   *                              beep                                          *
14299   *===========================================================================*/
14300  PRIVATE void beep()
14301  {
14302  /* Making a beeping sound on the speaker (output for CRTL-G).
14303   * This routine works by turning on the bits 0 and 1 in port B of the 8255
14304   * chip that drives the speaker.
```

```
14305    */
14306
14307    message mess;
14308
14309    if (beeping) return;
14310    out_byte(TIMER_MODE, 0xB6);    /* set up timer channel 2 (square wave) */
14311    out_byte(TIMER2, BEEP_FREQ & BYTE);    /* load low-order bits of frequency */
14312    out_byte(TIMER2, (BEEP_FREQ >> 8) & BYTE);    /* now high-order bits */
14313    lock();                        /* guard PORT_B from keyboard intr handler */
14314    out_byte(PORT_B, in_byte(PORT_B) | 3);    /* turn on beep bits */
14315    unlock();
14316    beeping = TRUE;
14317
14318    mess.m_type = SET_ALARM;
14319    mess.CLOCK_PROC_NR = TTY;
14320    mess.DELTA_TICKS = B_TIME;
14321    mess.FUNC_TO_CALL = (sighandler_t) stop_beep;
14322    sendrec(CLOCK, &mess);
14323  }


14326  /*===========================================================================*
14327   *                              stop_beep                                    *
14328   *===========================================================================*/
14329  PRIVATE void stop_beep()
14330  {
14331  /* Turn off the beeper by turning off bits 0 and 1 in PORT_B. */
14332
14333    lock();                        /* guard PORT_B from keyboard intr handler */
14334    out_byte(PORT_B, in_byte(PORT_B) & ~3);
14335    beeping = FALSE;
14336    unlock();
14337  }


14340  /*===========================================================================*
14341   *                              scr_init                                     *
14342   *===========================================================================*/
14343  PUBLIC void scr_init(tp)
14344  tty_t *tp;
14345  {
14346  /* Initialize the screen driver. */
14347    console_t *cons;
14348    phys_bytes vid_base;
14349    u16_t bios_crtbase;
14350    int line;
14351    unsigned page_size;
14352
14353    /* Associate console and TTY. */
14354    line = tp - &tty_table[0];
14355    if (line >= nr_cons) return;
14356    cons = &cons_table[line];
14357    cons->c_tty = tp;
14358    tp->tty_priv = cons;
14359
14360    /* Initialize the keyboard driver. */
14361    kb_init(tp);
14362
14363    /* Output functions. */
14364    tp->tty_devwrite = cons_write;
```

```
14365          tp->tty_echo = cons_echo;
14366
14367          /* Get the BIOS parameters that tells the VDU I/O base register. */
14368          phys_copy(0x463L, vir2phys(&bios_crtbase), 2L);
14369
14370          vid_port = bios_crtbase;
14371
14372          if (color) {
14373                  vid_base = COLOR_BASE;
14374                  vid_size = COLOR_SIZE;
14375          } else {
14376                  vid_base = MONO_BASE;
14377                  vid_size = MONO_SIZE;
14378          }
14379          if (ega) vid_size = EGA_SIZE; /* for both EGA and VGA */
14380          wrap = !ega;
14381
14382          vid_seg = protected_mode ? VIDEO_SELECTOR : physb_to_hclick(vid_base);
14383          init_dataseg(&gdt[VIDEO_INDEX], vid_base, (phys_bytes) vid_size,
14384                                                      TASK_PRIVILEGE);
14385          vid_size >>= 1;                 /* word count */
14386          vid_mask = vid_size - 1;
14387
14388          /* There can be as many consoles as video memory allows. */
14389          nr_cons = vid_size / scr_size;
14390          if (nr_cons > NR_CONS) nr_cons = NR_CONS;
14391          if (nr_cons > 1) wrap = 0;
14392          page_size = vid_size / nr_cons;
14393          cons->c_start = line * page_size;
14394          cons->c_limit = cons->c_start + page_size;
14395          cons->c_org = cons->c_start;
14396          cons->c_attr = cons->c_blank = BLANK_COLOR;
14397
14398          /* Clear the screen. */
14399          blank_color = BLANK_COLOR;
14400          mem_vid_copy(BLANK_MEM, cons->c_start, scr_size);
14401          select_console(0);
14402  }


14405  /*===========================================================================*
14406   *                              putk                                         *
14407   *===========================================================================*/
14408  PUBLIC void putk(c)
14409  int c;                          /* character to print */
14410  {
14411  /* This procedure is used by the version of printf() that is linked with
14412   * the kernel itself.  The one in the library sends a message to FS, which is
14413   * not what is needed for printing within the kernel.  This version just queues
14414   * the character and starts the output.
14415   */
14416
14417          if (c != 0) {
14418                  if (c == '\n') putk('\r');
14419                  out_char(&cons_table[0], (int) c);
14420          } else {
14421                  flush(&cons_table[0]);
14422          }
14423  }
```

```
14426    /*===========================================================================*
14427     *                               toggle_scroll                               *
14428     *===========================================================================*/
14429    PUBLIC void toggle_scroll()
14430    {
14431    /* Toggle between hardware and software scroll. */
14432
14433      cons_org0();
14434      softscroll = !softscroll;
14435      printf("%sware scrolling enabled.\n", softscroll ? "Soft" : "Hard");
14436    }



14439    /*===========================================================================*
14440     *                               cons_stop                                   *
14441     *===========================================================================*/
14442    PUBLIC void cons_stop()
14443    {
14444    /* Prepare for halt or reboot. */
14445
14446      cons_org0();
14447      softscroll = 1;
14448      select_console(0);
14449      cons_table[0].c_attr = cons_table[0].c_blank = BLANK_COLOR;
14450    }



14453    /*===========================================================================*
14454     *                               cons_org0                                   *
14455     *===========================================================================*/
14456    PRIVATE void cons_org0()
14457    {
14458    /* Scroll video memory back to put the origin at 0. */
14459
14460      int cons_line;
14461      console_t *cons;
14462      unsigned n;
14463
14464      for (cons_line = 0; cons_line < nr_cons; cons_line++) {
14465            cons = &cons_table[cons_line];
14466            while (cons->c_org > cons->c_start) {
14467                    n = vid_size - scr_size;          /* amount of unused memory */
14468                    if (n > cons->c_org - cons->c_start)
14469                            n = cons->c_org - cons->c_start;
14470                    vid_vid_copy(cons->c_org, cons->c_org - n, scr_size);
14471                    cons->c_org -= n;
14472            }
14473            flush(cons);
14474      }
14475      select_console(current);
14476    }



14479    /*===========================================================================*
14480     *                               select_console                              *
14481     *===========================================================================*/
14482    PUBLIC void select_console(int cons_line)
14483    {
14484    /* Set the current console to console number 'cons_line'. */
```

```
14485
14486        if (cons_line < 0 || cons_line >= nr_cons) return;
14487        current = cons_line;
14488        curcons = &cons_table[cons_line];
14489        set_6845(VID_ORG, curcons->c_org);
14490        set_6845(CURSOR, curcons->c_cur);
14491    }


14494    /*===========================================================================*
14495     *                           con_loadfont                                    *
14496     *===========================================================================*/
14497    PUBLIC int con_loadfont(user_phys)
14498    phys_bytes user_phys;
14499    {
14500    /* Load a font into the EGA or VGA adapter. */
14501
14502        static struct sequence seq1[7] = {
14503               { GA_SEQUENCER_INDEX, 0x00, 0x01 },
14504               { GA_SEQUENCER_INDEX, 0x02, 0x04 },
14505               { GA_SEQUENCER_INDEX, 0x04, 0x07 },
14506               { GA_SEQUENCER_INDEX, 0x00, 0x03 },
14507               { GA_GRAPHICS_INDEX, 0x04, 0x02 },
14508               { GA_GRAPHICS_INDEX, 0x05, 0x00 },
14509               { GA_GRAPHICS_INDEX, 0x06, 0x00 },
14510        };
14511        static struct sequence seq2[7] = {
14512               { GA_SEQUENCER_INDEX, 0x00, 0x01 },
14513               { GA_SEQUENCER_INDEX, 0x02, 0x03 },
14514               { GA_SEQUENCER_INDEX, 0x04, 0x03 },
14515               { GA_SEQUENCER_INDEX, 0x00, 0x03 },
14516               { GA_GRAPHICS_INDEX, 0x04, 0x00 },
14517               { GA_GRAPHICS_INDEX, 0x05, 0x10 },
14518               { GA_GRAPHICS_INDEX, 0x06,    0 },
14519        };
14520
14521        seq2[6].value= color ? 0x0E : 0x0A;
14522
14523        if (!ega) return(ENOTTY);
14524
14525        lock();
14526        ga_program(seq1);       /* bring font memory into view */
14527
14528        phys_copy(user_phys, (phys_bytes)GA_VIDEO_ADDRESS, (phys_bytes)GA_FONT_SIZE);
14529
14530        ga_program(seq2);       /* restore */
14531        unlock();
14532
14533        return(OK);
14534    }


14537    /*===========================================================================*
14538     *                           ga_program                                      *
14539     *===========================================================================*/
14540    PRIVATE void ga_program(seq)
14541    struct sequence *seq;
14542    {
14543    /* support function for con_loadfont */
14544
```

```
14545        int len= 7;
14546        do {
14547                out_byte(seq->index, seq->port);
14548                out_byte(seq->index+1, seq->value);
14549                seq++;
14550        } while (--len > 0);
14551    }
```

```
++++++++++++++++++++++++++++++++++++++++++++++++++++++++++++++++++++++++++++++
                               src/kernel/dmp.c
++++++++++++++++++++++++++++++++++++++++++++++++++++++++++++++++++++++++++++++
```

```
14600    /* This file contains some dumping routines for debugging. */
14601
14602    #include "kernel.h"
14603    #include <minix/com.h>
14604    #include "proc.h"
14605
14606    char *vargv;
14607
14608    FORWARD _PROTOTYPE(char *proc_name, (int proc_nr));
14609
14610    /*===========================================================================*
14611     *                              p_dmp                                        *
14612     *===========================================================================*/
14613    PUBLIC void p_dmp()
14614    {
14615    /* Proc table dump */
14616
14617      register struct proc *rp;
14618      static struct proc *oldrp = BEG_PROC_ADDR;
14619      int n = 0;
14620      phys_clicks text, data, size;
14621      int proc_nr;
14622
14623      printf("\n--pid --pc- ---sp- flag -user --sys-- -text- -data- -size- -recv- command\n");
14624
14625      for (rp = oldrp; rp < END_PROC_ADDR; rp++) {
14626              proc_nr = proc_number(rp);
14627              if (rp->p_flags & P_SLOT_FREE) continue;
14628              if (++n > 20) break;
14629              text = rp->p_map[T].mem_phys;
14630              data = rp->p_map[D].mem_phys;
14631              size = rp->p_map[T].mem_len
14632                      + ((rp->p_map[S].mem_phys + rp->p_map[S].mem_len) - data);
14633              printf("%5d %5lx %6lx %2x %7U %7U %5uK %5uK %5uK ",
14634                      proc_nr < 0 ? proc_nr : rp->p_pid,
14635                      (unsigned long) rp->p_reg.pc,
14636                      (unsigned long) rp->p_reg.sp,
14637                      rp->p_flags,
14638                      rp->user_time, rp->sys_time,
14639                      click_to_round_k(text), click_to_round_k(data),
14640                      click_to_round_k(size));
14641              if (rp->p_flags & RECEIVING) {
14642                      printf("%-7.7s", proc_name(rp->p_getfrom));
14643              } else
14644              if (rp->p_flags & SENDING) {
```

```
14645                        printf("S:%-5.5s", proc_name(rp->p_sendto));
14646                } else
14647                if (rp->p_flags == 0) {
14648                        printf("         ");
14649                }
14650                printf("%s\n", rp->p_name);
14651        }
14652        if (rp == END_PROC_ADDR) rp = BEG_PROC_ADDR; else printf("--more--\r");
14653        oldrp = rp;
14654   }


14657   /*===========================================================================*
14658    *                              map_dmp                                       *
14659    *===========================================================================*/
14660   PUBLIC void map_dmp()
14661   {
14662     register struct proc *rp;
14663     static struct proc *oldrp = cproc_addr(HARDWARE);
14664     int n = 0;
14665     phys_clicks size;
14666
14667     printf("\nPROC NAME-  -----TEXT-----  -----DATA-----  ----STACK-----  -SIZE-\n");
14668     for (rp = oldrp; rp < END_PROC_ADDR; rp++) {
14669             if (rp->p_flags & P_SLOT_FREE) continue;
14670             if (++n > 20) break;
14671             size = rp->p_map[T].mem_len
14672                     + ((rp->p_map[S].mem_phys + rp->p_map[S].mem_len)
14673                                             - rp->p_map[D].mem_phys);
14674             printf("%3d %-6.6s  %4x %4x %4x  %4x %4x %4x  %4x %4x %4x  %5uK\n",
14675                     proc_number(rp),
14676                     rp->p_name,
14677                     rp->p_map[T].mem_vir, rp->p_map[T].mem_phys, rp->p_map[T].mem_len,
14678                     rp->p_map[D].mem_vir, rp->p_map[D].mem_phys, rp->p_map[D].mem_len,
14679                     rp->p_map[S].mem_vir, rp->p_map[S].mem_phys, rp->p_map[S].mem_len,
14680                     click_to_round_k(size));
14681     }
14682     if (rp == END_PROC_ADDR) rp = cproc_addr(HARDWARE); else printf("--more--\r");
14683     oldrp = rp;
14684   }


14687   /*===========================================================================*
14688    *                              proc_name                                     *
14689    *===========================================================================*/
14690   PRIVATE char *proc_name(proc_nr)
14691   int proc_nr;
14692   {
14693     if (proc_nr == ANY) return "ANY";
14694     return proc_addr(proc_nr)->p_name;
14695   }
```

```
++++++++++++++++++++++++++++++++++++++++++++++++++++++++++++++++++++++++++++++
                             src/kernel/system.c
++++++++++++++++++++++++++++++++++++++++++++++++++++++++++++++++++++++++++++++
14700   /* This task handles the interface between file system and kernel as well as
14701    * between memory manager and kernel.  System services are obtained by sending
14702    * sys_task() a message specifying what is needed.  To make life easier for
14703    * MM and FS, a library is provided with routines whose names are of the
14704    * form sys_xxx, e.g. sys_xit sends the SYS_XIT message to sys_task.  The
14705    * message types and parameters are:
14706    *
14707    *    SYS_FORK     informs kernel that a process has forked
14708    *    SYS_NEWMAP   allows MM to set up a process memory map
14709    *    SYS_GETMAP   allows MM to get a process' memory map
14710    *    SYS_EXEC     sets program counter and stack pointer after EXEC
14711    *    SYS_XIT      informs kernel that a process has exited
14712    *    SYS_GETSP    caller wants to read out some process' stack pointer
14713    *    SYS_TIMES    caller wants to get accounting times for a process
14714    *    SYS_ABORT    MM or FS cannot go on; abort MINIX
14715    *    SYS_FRESH    start with a fresh process image during EXEC (68000 only)
14716    *    SYS_SENDSIG  send a signal to a process (POSIX style)
14717    *    SYS_SIGRETURN complete POSIX-style signalling
14718    *    SYS_KILL     cause a signal to be sent via MM
14719    *    SYS_ENDSIG   finish up after SYS_KILL-type signal
14720    *    SYS_COPY     request a block of data to be copied between processes
14721    *    SYS_VCOPY    request a series of data blocks to be copied between procs
14722    *    SYS_GBOOT    copies the boot parameters to a process
14723    *    SYS_MEM      returns the next free chunk of physical memory
14724    *    SYS_UMAP     compute the physical address for a given virtual address
14725    *    SYS_TRACE    request a trace operation
14726    *
14727    * Message types and parameters:
14728    *
14729    *    m_type        PROC1       PROC2      PID       MEM_PTR
14730    * -------------------------------------------------------------
14731    * | SYS_FORK   | parent  | child   | pid     |         |
14732    * |------------+---------+---------+---------+---------|
14733    * | SYS_NEWMAP | proc nr |         |         | map ptr |
14734    * |------------+---------+---------+---------+---------|
14735    * | SYS_EXEC   | proc nr | traced  | new sp  |         |
14736    * |------------+---------+---------+---------+---------|
14737    * | SYS_XIT    | parent  | exitee  |         |         |
14738    * |------------+---------+---------+---------+---------|
14739    * | SYS_GETSP  | proc nr |         |         |         |
14740    * |------------+---------+---------+---------+---------|
14741    * | SYS_TIMES  | proc nr |         | buf ptr |         |
14742    * |------------+---------+---------+---------+---------|
14743    * | SYS_ABORT  |         |         |         |         |
14744    * |------------+---------+---------+---------+---------|
14745    * | SYS_FRESH  | proc nr | data_cl |         |         |
14746    * |------------+---------+---------+---------+---------|
14747    * | SYS_GBOOT  | proc nr |         |         | bootptr |
14748    * |------------+---------+---------+---------+---------|
14749    * | SYS_GETMAP | proc nr |         |         | map ptr |
14750    * -------------------------------------------------------------
14751    *
14752    *    m_type          m1_i1     m1_i2     m1_i3       m1_p1
14753    * ---------------+---------+---------+---------+--------------
14754    * | SYS_VCOPY     | src p   | dst p   | vec siz | vc addr     |
```

```
14755   * |----------------+---------+---------+---------+------------|
14756   * | SYS_SENDSIG    | proc nr |         |         | smp        |
14757   * |----------------+---------+---------+---------+------------|
14758   * | SYS_SIGRETURN  | proc nr |         |         | scp        |
14759   * |----------------+---------+---------+---------+------------|
14760   * | SYS_ENDSIG     | proc nr |         |         |            |
14761   * --------------------------------------------------------------
14762   *
14763   *    m_type        m2_i1     m2_i2     m2_l1     m2_l2
14764   * ----------------------------------------------------------
14765   * | SYS_TRACE   | proc_nr | request |  addr   |  data    |
14766   * ----------------------------------------------------------
14767   *
14768   *
14769   *    m_type        m6_i1     m6_i2     m6_i3     m6_f1
14770   * ----------------------------------------------------------
14771   * | SYS_KILL    | proc_nr |  sig    |         |          |
14772   * ----------------------------------------------------------
14773   *
14774   *
14775   *    m_type        m5_c1    m5_i1    m5_l1   m5_c2   m5_i2   m5_l2   m5_l3
14776   * --------------------------------------------------------------------------
14777   * | SYS_COPY    |src seg|src proc|src vir|dst seg|dst proc|dst vir| byte ct |
14778   * --------------------------------------------------------------------------
14779   * | SYS_UMAP    | seg   |proc nr |vir adr|       |        |       | byte ct |
14780   * --------------------------------------------------------------------------
14781   *
14782   *
14783   *    m_type        m1_i1     m1_i2     m1_i3
14784   * |------------+----------+----------+---------
14785   * | SYS_MEM    | mem base | mem size | tot mem |
14786   * ------------------------------------------
14787   *
14788   * In addition to the main sys_task() entry point, there are 5 other minor
14789   * entry points:
14790   *    cause_sig: take action to cause a signal to occur, sooner or later
14791   *    inform:    tell MM about pending signals
14792   *    numap:     umap D segment starting from process number instead of pointer
14793   *    umap:      compute the physical address for a given virtual address
14794   *    alloc_segments: allocate segments for 8088 or higher processor
14795   */
14796
14797   #include "kernel.h"
14798   #include <signal.h>
14799   #include <unistd.h>
14800   #include <sys/sigcontext.h>
14801   #include <sys/ptrace.h>
14802   #include <minix/boot.h>
14803   #include <minix/callnr.h>
14804   #include <minix/com.h>
14805   #include "proc.h"
14806   #include "protect.h"
14807
14808   /* PSW masks. */
14809   #define IF_MASK 0x00000200
14810   #define IOPL_MASK 0x003000
14811
14812   PRIVATE message m;
14813
14814   FORWARD _PROTOTYPE( int do_abort, (message *m_ptr) );
```

```
14815    FORWARD _PROTOTYPE( int do_copy, (message *m_ptr) );
14816    FORWARD _PROTOTYPE( int do_exec, (message *m_ptr) );
14817    FORWARD _PROTOTYPE( int do_fork, (message *m_ptr) );
14818    FORWARD _PROTOTYPE( int do_gboot, (message *m_ptr) );
14819    FORWARD _PROTOTYPE( int do_getsp, (message *m_ptr) );
14820    FORWARD _PROTOTYPE( int do_kill, (message *m_ptr) );
14821    FORWARD _PROTOTYPE( int do_mem, (message *m_ptr) );
14822    FORWARD _PROTOTYPE( int do_newmap, (message *m_ptr) );
14823    FORWARD _PROTOTYPE( int do_sendsig, (message *m_ptr) );
14824    FORWARD _PROTOTYPE( int do_sigreturn, (message *m_ptr) );
14825    FORWARD _PROTOTYPE( int do_endsig, (message *m_ptr) );
14826    FORWARD _PROTOTYPE( int do_times, (message *m_ptr) );
14827    FORWARD _PROTOTYPE( int do_trace, (message *m_ptr) );
14828    FORWARD _PROTOTYPE( int do_umap, (message *m_ptr) );
14829    FORWARD _PROTOTYPE( int do_xit, (message *m_ptr) );
14830    FORWARD _PROTOTYPE( int do_vcopy, (message *m_ptr) );
14831    FORWARD _PROTOTYPE( int do_getmap, (message *m_ptr) );
14832
14833
14834    /*===========================================================================*
14835     *                              sys_task                                     *
14836     *===========================================================================*/
14837    PUBLIC void sys_task()
14838    {
14839    /* Main entry point of sys_task.  Get the message and dispatch on type. */
14840
14841      register int r;
14842
14843      while (TRUE) {
14844            receive(ANY, &m);
14845
14846            switch (m.m_type) {        /* which system call */
14847                case SYS_FORK:      r = do_fork(&m);        break;
14848                case SYS_NEWMAP:    r = do_newmap(&m);      break;
14849                case SYS_GETMAP:    r = do_getmap(&m);      break;
14850                case SYS_EXEC:      r = do_exec(&m);        break;
14851                case SYS_XIT:       r = do_xit(&m);         break;
14852                case SYS_GETSP:     r = do_getsp(&m);       break;
14853                case SYS_TIMES:     r = do_times(&m);       break;
14854                case SYS_ABORT:     r = do_abort(&m);       break;
14855                case SYS_SENDSIG:   r = do_sendsig(&m);     break;
14856                case SYS_SIGRETURN: r = do_sigreturn(&m);   break;
14857                case SYS_KILL:      r = do_kill(&m);        break;
14858                case SYS_ENDSIG:    r = do_endsig(&m);      break;
14859                case SYS_COPY:      r = do_copy(&m);        break;
14860                case SYS_VCOPY:     r = do_vcopy(&m);       break;
14861                case SYS_GBOOT:     r = do_gboot(&m);       break;
14862                case SYS_MEM:       r = do_mem(&m);         break;
14863                case SYS_UMAP:      r = do_umap(&m);        break;
14864                case SYS_TRACE:     r = do_trace(&m);       break;
14865                default:            r = E_BAD_FCN;
14866            }
14867
14868            m.m_type = r;             /* 'r' reports status of call */
14869            send(m.m_source, &m);     /* send reply to caller */
14870      }
14871    }


14874    /*===========================================================================*
```

```
14875     *                            do_fork                                    *
14876     *===========================================================================*/
14877   PRIVATE int do_fork(m_ptr)
14878   register message *m_ptr;          /* pointer to request message */
14879   {
14880   /* Handle sys_fork().  m_ptr->PROC1 has forked.  The child is m_ptr->PROC2. */
14881
14882     reg_t old_ldt_sel;
14883     register struct proc *rpc;
14884     struct proc *rpp;
14885
14886     if (!isoksusern(m_ptr->PROC1) || !isoksusern(m_ptr->PROC2))
14887           return(E_BAD_PROC);
14888     rpp = proc_addr(m_ptr->PROC1);
14889     rpc = proc_addr(m_ptr->PROC2);
14890
14891     /* Copy parent 'proc' struct to child. */
14892     old_ldt_sel = rpc->p_ldt_sel; /* stop this being obliterated by copy */
14893
14894     *rpc = *rpp;                   /* copy 'proc' struct */
14895
14896     rpc->p_ldt_sel = old_ldt_sel;
14897     rpc->p_nr = m_ptr->PROC2;      /* this was obliterated by copy */
14898
14899     rpc->p_flags |= NO_MAP;        /* inhibit the process from running */
14900
14901     rpc->p_flags &= ~(PENDING | SIG_PENDING | P_STOP);
14902
14903     /* Only 1 in group should have PENDING, child does not inherit trace status*/
14904     sigemptyset(&rpc->p_pending);
14905     rpc->p_pendcount = 0;
14906     rpc->p_pid = m_ptr->PID;       /* install child's pid */
14907     rpc->p_reg.retreg = 0;         /* child sees pid = 0 to know it is child */
14908
14909     rpc->user_time = 0;            /* set all the accounting times to 0 */
14910     rpc->sys_time = 0;
14911     rpc->child_utime = 0;
14912     rpc->child_stime = 0;
14913
14914     return(OK);
14915   }


14918   /*===========================================================================*
14919    *                            do_newmap                                     *
14920    *===========================================================================*/
14921   PRIVATE int do_newmap(m_ptr)
14922   message *m_ptr;                    /* pointer to request message */
14923   {
14924   /* Handle sys_newmap().  Fetch the memory map from MM. */
14925
14926     register struct proc *rp;
14927     phys_bytes src_phys;
14928     int caller;                      /* whose space has the new map (usually MM) */
14929     int k;                           /* process whose map is to be loaded */
14930     int old_flags;                   /* value of flags before modification */
14931     struct mem_map *map_ptr;         /* virtual address of map inside caller (MM) */
14932
14933     /* Extract message parameters and copy new memory map from MM. */
14934     caller = m_ptr->m_source;
```

```
14935          k = m_ptr->PROC1;
14936          map_ptr = (struct mem_map *) m_ptr->MEM_PTR;
14937          if (!isokprocn(k)) return(E_BAD_PROC);
14938          rp = proc_addr(k);              /* ptr to entry of user getting new map */
14939
14940          /* Copy the map from MM. */
14941          src_phys = umap(proc_addr(caller), D, (vir_bytes) map_ptr, sizeof(rp->p_map));
14942          if (src_phys == 0) panic("bad call to sys_newmap", NO_NUM);
14943          phys_copy(src_phys, vir2phys(rp->p_map), (phys_bytes) sizeof(rp->p_map));
14944
14945          alloc_segments(rp);
14946          old_flags = rp->p_flags;        /* save the previous value of the flags */
14947          rp->p_flags &= ~NO_MAP;
14948          if (old_flags != 0 && rp->p_flags == 0) lock_ready(rp);
14949
14950          return(OK);
14951      }


14954      /*===========================================================================*
14955       *                              do_getmap                                     *
14956       *===========================================================================*/
14957      PRIVATE int do_getmap(m_ptr)
14958      message *m_ptr;                 /* pointer to request message */
14959      {
14960      /* Handle sys_getmap().  Report the memory map to MM. */
14961
14962        register struct proc *rp;
14963        phys_bytes dst_phys;
14964        int caller;                   /* where the map has to be stored */
14965        int k;                        /* process whose map is to be loaded */
14966        struct mem_map *map_ptr;      /* virtual address of map inside caller (MM) */
14967
14968          /* Extract message parameters and copy new memory map to MM. */
14969          caller = m_ptr->m_source;
14970          k = m_ptr->PROC1;
14971          map_ptr = (struct mem_map *) m_ptr->MEM_PTR;
14972
14973          if (!isokprocn(k))
14974              panic("do_getmap got bad proc: ", m_ptr->PROC1);
14975
14976          rp = proc_addr(k);              /* ptr to entry of the map */
14977
14978          /* Copy the map to MM. */
14979          dst_phys = umap(proc_addr(caller), D, (vir_bytes) map_ptr, sizeof(rp->p_map));
14980          if (dst_phys == 0) panic("bad call to sys_getmap", NO_NUM);
14981          phys_copy(vir2phys(rp->p_map), dst_phys, sizeof(rp->p_map));
14982
14983          return(OK);
14984      }


14987      /*===========================================================================*
14988       *                              do_exec                                       *
14989       *===========================================================================*/
14990      PRIVATE int do_exec(m_ptr)
14991      register message *m_ptr;        /* pointer to request message */
14992      {
14993      /* Handle sys_exec().  A process has done a successful EXEC. Patch it up. */
14994
```

```
14995        register struct proc *rp;
14996        reg_t sp;                       /* new sp */
14997        phys_bytes phys_name;
14998        char *np;
14999    #define NLEN (sizeof(rp->p_name)-1)
15000
15001        if (!isoksusern(m_ptr->PROC1)) return E_BAD_PROC;
15002        /* PROC2 field is used as flag to indicate process is being traced */
15003        if (m_ptr->PROC2) cause_sig(m_ptr->PROC1, SIGTRAP);
15004        sp = (reg_t) m_ptr->STACK_PTR;
15005        rp = proc_addr(m_ptr->PROC1);
15006        rp->p_reg.sp = sp;              /* set the stack pointer */
15007        rp->p_reg.pc = (reg_t) m_ptr->IP_PTR; /* set pc */
15008        rp->p_alarm = 0;               /* reset alarm timer */
15009        rp->p_flags &= ~RECEIVING;     /* MM does not reply to EXEC call */
15010        if (rp->p_flags == 0) lock_ready(rp);
15011
15012        /* Save command name for debugging, ps(1) output, etc. */
15013        phys_name = numap(m_ptr->m_source, (vir_bytes) m_ptr->NAME_PTR,
15014                                                    (vir_bytes) NLEN);
15015        if (phys_name != 0) {
15016            phys_copy(phys_name, vir2phys(rp->p_name), (phys_bytes) NLEN);
15017            for (np = rp->p_name; (*np & BYTE) >= ' '; np++) {}
15018            *np = 0;
15019        }
15020        return(OK);
15021    }


15024    /*===========================================================================*
15025     *                              do_xit                                       *
15026     *===========================================================================*/
15027    PRIVATE int do_xit(m_ptr)
15028    message *m_ptr;                     /* pointer to request message */
15029    {
15030    /* Handle sys_xit().  A process has exited. */
15031
15032        register struct proc *rp, *rc;
15033        struct proc *np, *xp;
15034        int parent;                     /* number of exiting proc's parent */
15035        int proc_nr;                    /* number of process doing the exit */
15036        phys_clicks base, size;
15037
15038        parent = m_ptr->PROC1;          /* slot number of parent process */
15039        proc_nr = m_ptr->PROC2;         /* slot number of exiting process */
15040        if (!isoksusern(parent) || !isoksusern(proc_nr)) return(E_BAD_PROC);
15041        rp = proc_addr(parent);
15042        rc = proc_addr(proc_nr);
15043        lock();
15044        rp->child_utime += rc->user_time + rc->child_utime;   /* accum child times */
15045        rp->child_stime += rc->sys_time + rc->child_stime;
15046        unlock();
15047        rc->p_alarm = 0;                /* turn off alarm timer */
15048        if (rc->p_flags == 0) lock_unready(rc);
15049
15050        strcpy(rc->p_name, "<noname>");          /* process no longer has a name */
15051
15052        /* If the process being terminated happens to be queued trying to send a
15053         * message (i.e., the process was killed by a signal, rather than it doing an
15054         * EXIT), then it must be removed from the message queues.
```

```
15055        */
15056      if (rc->p_flags & SENDING) {
15057          /* Check all proc slots to see if the exiting process is queued. */
15058          for (rp = BEG_PROC_ADDR; rp < END_PROC_ADDR; rp++) {
15059                  if (rp->p_callerq == NIL_PROC) continue;
15060                  if (rp->p_callerq == rc) {
15061                          /* Exiting process is on front of this queue. */
15062                          rp->p_callerq = rc->p_sendlink;
15063                          break;
15064                  } else {
15065                          /* See if exiting process is in middle of queue. */
15066                          np = rp->p_callerq;
15067                          while ( ( xp = np->p_sendlink) != NIL_PROC)
15068                                  if (xp == rc) {
15069                                          np->p_sendlink = xp->p_sendlink;
15070                                          break;
15071                                  } else {
15072                                          np = xp;
15073                                  }
15074                  }
15075          }
15076      }
15077
15078      if (rc->p_flags & PENDING) --sig_procs;
15079      sigemptyset(&rc->p_pending);
15080      rc->p_pendcount = 0;
15081      rc->p_flags = P_SLOT_FREE;
15082      return(OK);
15083    }


15086    /*===========================================================================*
15087     *                              do_getsp                                      *
15088     *===========================================================================*/
15089    PRIVATE int do_getsp(m_ptr)
15090    register message *m_ptr;          /* pointer to request message */
15091    {
15092    /* Handle sys_getsp().  MM wants to know what sp is. */
15093
15094      register struct proc *rp;
15095
15096      if (!isoksusern(m_ptr->PROC1)) return(E_BAD_PROC);
15097      rp = proc_addr(m_ptr->PROC1);
15098      m_ptr->STACK_PTR = (char *) rp->p_reg.sp;      /* return sp here (bad type) */
15099      return(OK);
15100    }


15103    /*===========================================================================*
15104     *                              do_times                                      *
15105     *===========================================================================*/
15106    PRIVATE int do_times(m_ptr)
15107    register message *m_ptr;          /* pointer to request message */
15108    {
15109    /* Handle sys_times().  Retrieve the accounting information. */
15110
15111      register struct proc *rp;
15112
15113      if (!isoksusern(m_ptr->PROC1)) return E_BAD_PROC;
15114      rp = proc_addr(m_ptr->PROC1);
```

```
15115
15116      /* Insert the times needed by the TIMES system call in the message. */
15117      lock();                          /* halt the volatile time counters in rp */
15118      m_ptr->USER_TIME   = rp->user_time;
15119      m_ptr->SYSTEM_TIME = rp->sys_time;
15120      unlock();
15121      m_ptr->CHILD_UTIME = rp->child_utime;
15122      m_ptr->CHILD_STIME = rp->child_stime;
15123      m_ptr->BOOT_TICKS  = get_uptime();
15124      return(OK);
15125    }


15128      /*===========================================================================*
15129       *                              do_abort                                      *
15130       *===========================================================================*/
15131      PRIVATE int do_abort(m_ptr)
15132      message *m_ptr;                  /* pointer to request message */
15133      {
15134      /* Handle sys_abort.  MINIX is unable to continue.  Terminate operation. */
15135        char monitor_code[64];
15136        phys_bytes src_phys;
15137
15138        if (m_ptr->m1_i1 == RBT_MONITOR) {
15139            /* The monitor is to run user specified instructions. */
15140            src_phys = numap(m_ptr->m_source, (vir_bytes) m_ptr->m1_p1,
15141                                        (vir_bytes) sizeof(monitor_code));
15142            if (src_phys == 0) panic("bad monitor code from", m_ptr->m_source);
15143            phys_copy(src_phys, vir2phys(monitor_code),
15144                                        (phys_bytes) sizeof(monitor_code));
15145            reboot_code = vir2phys(monitor_code);
15146        }
15147        wreboot(m_ptr->m1_i1);
15148        return(OK);                     /* pro-forma (really EDISASTER) */
15149    }


15154      /*===========================================================================*
15155       *                              do_sendsig                                    *
15156       *===========================================================================*/
15157      PRIVATE int do_sendsig(m_ptr)
15158      message *m_ptr;                  /* pointer to request message */
15159      {
15160      /* Handle sys_sendsig, POSIX-style signal */
15161
15162        struct sigmsg smsg;
15163        register struct proc *rp;
15164        phys_bytes src_phys, dst_phys;
15165        struct sigcontext sc, *scp;
15166        struct sigframe fr, *frp;
15167
15168        if (!isokusern(m_ptr->PROC1)) return(E_BAD_PROC);
15169        rp = proc_addr(m_ptr->PROC1);
15170
15171        /* Get the sigmsg structure into our address space.  */
15172        src_phys = umap(proc_addr(MM_PROC_NR), D, (vir_bytes) m_ptr->SIG_CTXT_PTR,
15173                        (vir_bytes) sizeof(struct sigmsg));
15174        if (src_phys == 0)
```

```
15175                 panic("do_sendsig can't signal: bad sigmsg address from MM", NO_NUM);
15176        phys_copy(src_phys, vir2phys(&smsg), (phys_bytes) sizeof(struct sigmsg));
15177
15178        /* Compute the usr stack pointer value where sigcontext will be stored. */
15179        scp = (struct sigcontext *) smsg.sm_stkptr - 1;
15180
15181        /* Copy the registers to the sigcontext structure. */
15182        memcpy(&sc.sc_regs, &rp->p_reg, sizeof(struct sigregs));
15183
15184        /* Finish the sigcontext initialization. */
15185        sc.sc_flags = SC_SIGCONTEXT;
15186
15187        sc.sc_mask = smsg.sm_mask;
15188
15189        /* Copy the sigcontext structure to the user's stack. */
15190        dst_phys = umap(rp, D, (vir_bytes) scp,
15191                        (vir_bytes) sizeof(struct sigcontext));
15192        if (dst_phys == 0) return(EFAULT);
15193        phys_copy(vir2phys(&sc), dst_phys, (phys_bytes) sizeof(struct sigcontext));
15194
15195        /* Initialize the sigframe structure. */
15196        frp = (struct sigframe *) scp - 1;
15197        fr.sf_scpcopy = scp;
15198        fr.sf_retadr2= (void (*)()) rp->p_reg.pc;
15199        fr.sf_fp = rp->p_reg.fp;
15200        rp->p_reg.fp = (reg_t) &frp->sf_fp;
15201        fr.sf_scp = scp;
15202        fr.sf_code = 0;          /* XXX - should be used for type of FP exception */
15203        fr.sf_signo = smsg.sm_signo;
15204        fr.sf_retadr = (void (*)()) smsg.sm_sigreturn;
15205
15206        /* Copy the sigframe structure to the user's stack. */
15207        dst_phys = umap(rp, D, (vir_bytes) frp, (vir_bytes) sizeof(struct sigframe));
15208        if (dst_phys == 0) return(EFAULT);
15209        phys_copy(vir2phys(&fr), dst_phys, (phys_bytes) sizeof(struct sigframe));
15210
15211        /* Reset user registers to execute the signal handler. */
15212        rp->p_reg.sp = (reg_t) frp;
15213        rp->p_reg.pc = (reg_t) smsg.sm_sighandler;
15214
15215        return(OK);
15216    }
15217
15218    /*===========================================================================*
15219     *                              do_sigreturn                                 *
15220     *===========================================================================*/
15221    PRIVATE int do_sigreturn(m_ptr)
15222    register message *m_ptr;
15223    {
15224    /* POSIX style signals require sys_sigreturn to put things in order before the
15225     * signalled process can resume execution
15226     */
15227
15228        struct sigcontext sc;
15229        register struct proc *rp;
15230        phys_bytes src_phys;
15231
15232        if (!isokusern(m_ptr->PROC1)) return(E_BAD_PROC);
15233        rp = proc_addr(m_ptr->PROC1);
15234
```

```
15235        /* Copy in the sigcontext structure. */
15236        src_phys = umap(rp, D, (vir_bytes) m_ptr->SIG_CTXT_PTR,
15237                        (vir_bytes) sizeof(struct sigcontext));
15238        if (src_phys == 0) return(EFAULT);
15239        phys_copy(src_phys, vir2phys(&sc), (phys_bytes) sizeof(struct sigcontext));
15240
15241        /* Make sure that this is not just a jmp_buf. */
15242        if ((sc.sc_flags & SC_SIGCONTEXT) == 0) return(EINVAL);
15243
15244        /* Fix up only certain key registers if the compiler doesn't use
15245         * register variables within functions containing setjmp.
15246         */
15247        if (sc.sc_flags & SC_NOREGLOCALS) {
15248            rp->p_reg.retreg = sc.sc_retreg;
15249            rp->p_reg.fp = sc.sc_fp;
15250            rp->p_reg.pc = sc.sc_pc;
15251            rp->p_reg.sp = sc.sc_sp;
15252            return (OK);
15253        }
15254        sc.sc_psw  = rp->p_reg.psw;
15255
15256  #if (CHIP == INTEL)
15257        /* Don't panic kernel if user gave bad selectors. */
15258        sc.sc_cs = rp->p_reg.cs;
15259        sc.sc_ds = rp->p_reg.ds;
15260        sc.sc_es = rp->p_reg.es;
15261  #if _WORD_SIZE == 4
15262        sc.sc_fs = rp->p_reg.fs;
15263        sc.sc_gs = rp->p_reg.gs;
15264  #endif
15265  #endif
15266
15267        /* Restore the registers. */
15268        memcpy(&rp->p_reg, (char *)&sc.sc_regs, sizeof(struct sigregs));
15269
15270        return(OK);
15271  }


15273  /*===========================================================================*
15274   *                              do_kill                                       *
15275   *===========================================================================*/
15276  PRIVATE int do_kill(m_ptr)
15277  register message *m_ptr;         /* pointer to request message */
15278  {
15279  /* Handle sys_kill(). Cause a signal to be sent to a process via MM.
15280   * Note that this has nothing to do with the kill (2) system call, this
15281   * is how the FS (and possibly other servers) get access to cause_sig to
15282   * send a KSIG message to MM
15283   */
15284
15285    if (!isokusern(m_ptr->PR)) return(E_BAD_PROC);
15286    cause_sig(m_ptr->PR, m_ptr->SIGNUM);
15287    return(OK);
15288  }


15291  /*===========================================================================*
15292   *                              do_endsig                                     *
15293   *===========================================================================*/
15294  PRIVATE int do_endsig(m_ptr)
```

```
15295  register message *m_ptr;         /* pointer to request message */
15296  {
15297  /* Finish up after a KSIG-type signal, caused by a SYS_KILL message or a call
15298   * to cause_sig by a task
15299   */
15300
15301    register struct proc *rp;
15302
15303    if (!isokusern(m_ptr->PROC1)) return(E_BAD_PROC);
15304    rp = proc_addr(m_ptr->PROC1);
15305
15306    /* MM has finished one KSIG. */
15307    if (rp->p_pendcount != 0 && --rp->p_pendcount == 0
15308        && (rp->p_flags &= ~SIG_PENDING) == 0)
15309        lock_ready(rp);
15310    return(OK);
15311  }


15313  /*===========================================================================*
15314   *                              do_copy                                       *
15315   *===========================================================================*/
15316  PRIVATE int do_copy(m_ptr)
15317  register message *m_ptr;         /* pointer to request message */
15318  {
15319  /* Handle sys_copy().  Copy data for MM or FS. */
15320
15321    int src_proc, dst_proc, src_space, dst_space;
15322    vir_bytes src_vir, dst_vir;
15323    phys_bytes src_phys, dst_phys, bytes;
15324
15325    /* Dismember the command message. */
15326    src_proc = m_ptr->SRC_PROC_NR;
15327    dst_proc = m_ptr->DST_PROC_NR;
15328    src_space = m_ptr->SRC_SPACE;
15329    dst_space = m_ptr->DST_SPACE;
15330    src_vir = (vir_bytes) m_ptr->SRC_BUFFER;
15331    dst_vir = (vir_bytes) m_ptr->DST_BUFFER;
15332    bytes = (phys_bytes) m_ptr->COPY_BYTES;
15333
15334    /* Compute the source and destination addresses and do the copy. */
15335    if (src_proc == ABS)
15336        src_phys = (phys_bytes) m_ptr->SRC_BUFFER;
15337    else {
15338        if (bytes != (vir_bytes) bytes)
15339                /* This would happen for 64K segments and 16-bit vir_bytes.
15340                 * It would happen a lot for do_fork except MM uses ABS
15341                 * copies for that case.
15342                 */
15343                panic("overflow in count in do_copy", NO_NUM);
15344
15345        src_phys = umap(proc_addr(src_proc), src_space, src_vir,
15346                        (vir_bytes) bytes);
15347    }
15348
15349    if (dst_proc == ABS)
15350        dst_phys = (phys_bytes) m_ptr->DST_BUFFER;
15351    else
15352        dst_phys = umap(proc_addr(dst_proc), dst_space, dst_vir,
15353                        (vir_bytes) bytes);
15354
```

```
15355        if (src_phys == 0 || dst_phys == 0) return(EFAULT);
15356        phys_copy(src_phys, dst_phys, bytes);
15357        return(OK);
15358    }


15361    /*===========================================================================*
15362     *                              do_vcopy                                      *
15363     *===========================================================================*/
15364    PRIVATE int do_vcopy(m_ptr)
15365    register message *m_ptr;          /* pointer to request message */
15366    {
15367    /* Handle sys_vcopy(). Copy multiple blocks of memory */
15368
15369      int src_proc, dst_proc, vect_s, i;
15370      vir_bytes src_vir, dst_vir, vect_addr;
15371      phys_bytes src_phys, dst_phys, bytes;
15372      cpvec_t cpvec_table[CPVEC_NR];
15373
15374      /* Dismember the command message. */
15375      src_proc = m_ptr->m1_i1;
15376      dst_proc = m_ptr->m1_i2;
15377      vect_s = m_ptr->m1_i3;
15378      vect_addr = (vir_bytes)m_ptr->m1_p1;
15379
15380      if (vect_s > CPVEC_NR) return EDOM;
15381
15382      src_phys= numap (m_ptr->m_source, vect_addr, vect_s * sizeof(cpvec_t));
15383      if (!src_phys) return EFAULT;
15384      phys_copy(src_phys, vir2phys(cpvec_table),
15385                                  (phys_bytes) (vect_s * sizeof(cpvec_t)));
15386
15387      for (i = 0; i < vect_s; i++) {
15388            src_vir= cpvec_table[i].cpv_src;
15389            dst_vir= cpvec_table[i].cpv_dst;
15390            bytes= cpvec_table[i].cpv_size;
15391            src_phys = numap(src_proc,src_vir,(vir_bytes)bytes);
15392            dst_phys = numap(dst_proc,dst_vir,(vir_bytes)bytes);
15393            if (src_phys == 0 || dst_phys == 0) return(EFAULT);
15394            phys_copy(src_phys, dst_phys, bytes);
15395      }
15396      return(OK);
15397    }


15400    /*===========================================================================*
15401     *                              do_gboot                                      *
15402     *===========================================================================*/
15403    PUBLIC struct bparam_s boot_parameters;
15404
15405    PRIVATE int do_gboot(m_ptr)
15406    message *m_ptr;                    /* pointer to request message */
15407    {
15408    /* Copy the boot parameters.  Normally only called during fs init. */
15409
15410      phys_bytes dst_phys;
15411
15412      dst_phys = umap(proc_addr(m_ptr->PROC1), D, (vir_bytes) m_ptr->MEM_PTR,
15413                                  (vir_bytes) sizeof(boot_parameters));
15414      if (dst_phys == 0) panic("bad call to SYS_GBOOT", NO_NUM);
```

```
15415        phys_copy(vir2phys(&boot_parameters), dst_phys,
15416                                (phys_bytes) sizeof(boot_parameters));
15417        return(OK);
15418    }


15421    /*===========================================================================*
15422     *                              do_mem                                        *
15423     *===========================================================================*/
15424    PRIVATE int do_mem(m_ptr)
15425    register message *m_ptr;          /* pointer to request message */
15426    {
15427    /* Return the base and size of the next chunk of memory. */
15428
15429        struct memory *memp;
15430
15431        for (memp = mem; memp < &mem[NR_MEMS]; ++memp) {
15432            m_ptr->m1_i1 = memp->base;
15433            m_ptr->m1_i2 = memp->size;
15434            m_ptr->m1_i3 = tot_mem_size;
15435            memp->size = 0;
15436            if (m_ptr->m1_i2 != 0) break;              /* found a chunk */
15437        }
15438        return(OK);
15439    }


15442    /*===========================================================================*
15443     *                              do_umap                                       *
15444     *===========================================================================*/
15445    PRIVATE int do_umap(m_ptr)
15446    register message *m_ptr;          /* pointer to request message */
15447    {
15448    /* Same as umap(), for non-kernel processes. */
15449
15450        m_ptr->SRC_BUFFER = umap(proc_addr((int) m_ptr->SRC_PROC_NR),
15451                            (int) m_ptr->SRC_SPACE,
15452                            (vir_bytes) m_ptr->SRC_BUFFER,
15453                            (vir_bytes) m_ptr->COPY_BYTES);
15454        return(OK);
15455    }


15458    /*===========================================================================*
15459     *                              do_trace                                      *
15460     *===========================================================================*/
15461    #define TR_PROCNR        (m_ptr->m2_i1)
15462    #define TR_REQUEST       (m_ptr->m2_i2)
15463    #define TR_ADDR          ((vir_bytes) m_ptr->m2_l1)
15464    #define TR_DATA          (m_ptr->m2_l2)
15465    #define TR_VLSIZE        ((vir_bytes) sizeof(long))
15466
15467    PRIVATE int do_trace(m_ptr)
15468    register message *m_ptr;
15469    {
15470    /* Handle the debugging commands supported by the ptrace system call
15471     * The commands are:
15472     * T_STOP       stop the process
15473     * T_OK         enable tracing by parent for this process
15474     * T_GETINS     return value from instruction space
```

```
15475    * T_GETDATA     return value from data space
15476    * T_GETUSER     return value from user process table
15477    * T_SETINS      set value from instruction space
15478    * T_SETDATA     set value from data space
15479    * T_SETUSER     set value in user process table
15480    * T_RESUME      resume execution
15481    * T_EXIT        exit
15482    * T_STEP        set trace bit
15483    *
15484    * The T_OK and T_EXIT commands are handled completely by the memory manager,
15485    * all others come here.
15486    */
15487
15488     register struct proc *rp;
15489     phys_bytes src, dst;
15490     int i;
15491
15492     rp = proc_addr(TR_PROCNR);
15493     if (rp->p_flags & P_SLOT_FREE) return(EIO);
15494     switch (TR_REQUEST) {
15495     case T_STOP:                     /* stop process */
15496             if (rp->p_flags == 0) lock_unready(rp);
15497             rp->p_flags |= P_STOP;
15498             rp->p_reg.psw &= ~TRACEBIT;     /* clear trace bit */
15499             return(OK);
15500
15501     case T_GETINS:                   /* return value from instruction space */
15502             if (rp->p_map[T].mem_len != 0) {
15503                     if ((src = umap(rp, T, TR_ADDR, TR_VLSIZE)) == 0) return(EIO);
15504                     phys_copy(src, vir2phys(&TR_DATA), (phys_bytes) sizeof(long));
15505                     break;
15506             }
15507             /* Text space is actually data space - fall through. */
15508
15509     case T_GETDATA:                  /* return value from data space */
15510             if ((src = umap(rp, D, TR_ADDR, TR_VLSIZE)) == 0) return(EIO);
15511             phys_copy(src, vir2phys(&TR_DATA), (phys_bytes) sizeof(long));
15512             break;
15513
15514     case T_GETUSER:                  /* return value from process table */
15515             if ((TR_ADDR & (sizeof(long) - 1)) != 0 ||
15516                 TR_ADDR > sizeof(struct proc) - sizeof(long))
15517                     return(EIO);
15518             TR_DATA = *(long *) ((char *) rp + (int) TR_ADDR);
15519             break;
15520
15521     case T_SETINS:                   /* set value in instruction space */
15522             if (rp->p_map[T].mem_len != 0) {
15523                     if ((dst = umap(rp, T, TR_ADDR, TR_VLSIZE)) == 0) return(EIO);
15524                     phys_copy(vir2phys(&TR_DATA), dst, (phys_bytes) sizeof(long));
15525                     TR_DATA = 0;
15526                     break;
15527             }
15528             /* Text space is actually data space - fall through. */
15529
15530     case T_SETDATA:                        /* set value in data space */
15531             if ((dst = umap(rp, D, TR_ADDR, TR_VLSIZE)) == 0) return(EIO);
15532             phys_copy(vir2phys(&TR_DATA), dst, (phys_bytes) sizeof(long));
15533             TR_DATA = 0;
15534             break;
```

```
15535
15536        case T_SETUSER:                          /* set value in process table */
15537            if ((TR_ADDR & (sizeof(reg_t) - 1)) != 0 ||
15538                    TR_ADDR > sizeof(struct stackframe_s) - sizeof(reg_t))
15539                    return(EIO);
15540            i = (int) TR_ADDR;
15541 #if (CHIP == INTEL)
15542            /* Altering segment registers might crash the kernel when it
15543             * tries to load them prior to restarting a process, so do
15544             * not allow it.
15545             */
15546            if (i == (int) &((struct proc *) 0)->p_reg.cs ||
15547                i == (int) &((struct proc *) 0)->p_reg.ds ||
15548                i == (int) &((struct proc *) 0)->p_reg.es ||
15549 #if _WORD_SIZE == 4
15550                i == (int) &((struct proc *) 0)->p_reg.gs ||
15551                i == (int) &((struct proc *) 0)->p_reg.fs ||
15552 #endif
15553                i == (int) &((struct proc *) 0)->p_reg.ss)
15554                    return(EIO);
15555 #endif
15556            if (i == (int) &((struct proc *) 0)->p_reg.psw)
15557                    /* only selected bits are changeable */
15558                    SETPSW(rp, TR_DATA);
15559            else
15560                    *(reg_t *) ((char *) &rp->p_reg + i) = (reg_t) TR_DATA;
15561            TR_DATA = 0;
15562            break;
15563
15564        case T_RESUME:                  /* resume execution */
15565            rp->p_flags &= ~P_STOP;
15566            if (rp->p_flags == 0) lock_ready(rp);
15567            TR_DATA = 0;
15568            break;
15569
15570        case T_STEP:                    /* set trace bit */
15571            rp->p_reg.psw |= TRACEBIT;
15572            rp->p_flags &= ~P_STOP;
15573            if (rp->p_flags == 0) lock_ready(rp);
15574            TR_DATA = 0;
15575            break;
15576
15577        default:
15578            return(EIO);
15579        }
15580      return(OK);
15581 }
15582
15583 /*===========================================================================*
15584  *                              cause_sig                                     *
15585  *===========================================================================*/
15586 PUBLIC void cause_sig(proc_nr, sig_nr)
15587 int proc_nr;                            /* process to be signalled */
15588 int sig_nr;                             /* signal to be sent, 1 to _NSIG */
15589 {
15590 /* A task wants to send a signal to a process.   Examples of such tasks are:
15591  *    TTY wanting to cause SIGINT upon getting a DEL
15592  *    CLOCK wanting to cause SIGALRM when timer expires
15593  * FS also uses this to send a signal, via the SYS_KILL message.
15594  * Signals are handled by sending a message to MM.  The tasks don't dare do
```

```
15595        * that directly, for fear of what would happen if MM were busy.  Instead they
15596        * call cause_sig, which sets bits in p_pending, and then carefully checks to
15597        * see if MM is free.  If so, a message is sent to it.  If not, when it becomes
15598        * free, a message is sent.  The process being signaled is blocked while MM
15599        * has not seen or finished with all signals for it.  These signals are
15600        * counted in p_pendcount, and the SIG_PENDING flag is kept nonzero while
15601        * there are some.  It is not sufficient to ready the process when MM is
15602        * informed, because MM can block waiting for FS to do a core dump.
15603        */
15604
15605          register struct proc *rp, *mmp;
15606
15607          rp = proc_addr(proc_nr);
15608          if (sigismember(&rp->p_pending, sig_nr))
15609                return;                    /* this signal already pending */
15610          sigaddset(&rp->p_pending, sig_nr);
15611          ++rp->p_pendcount;               /* count new signal pending */
15612          if (rp->p_flags & PENDING)
15613                return;                    /* another signal already pending */
15614          if (rp->p_flags == 0) lock_unready(rp);
15615          rp->p_flags |= PENDING | SIG_PENDING;
15616          ++sig_procs;                     /* count new process pending */
15617
15618          mmp = proc_addr(MM_PROC_NR);
15619          if ( ((mmp->p_flags & RECEIVING) == 0) || mmp->p_getfrom != ANY) return;
15620          inform();
15621        }


15624   /*===========================================================================*
15625    *                                inform                                      *
15626    *===========================================================================*/
15627   PUBLIC void inform()
15628   {
15629   /* When a signal is detected by the kernel (e.g., DEL), or generated by a task
15630    * (e.g. clock task for SIGALRM), cause_sig() is called to set a bit in the
15631    * p_pending field of the process to signal.  Then inform() is called to see
15632    * if MM is idle and can be told about it.  Whenever MM blocks, a check is
15633    * made to see if 'sig_procs' is nonzero; if so, inform() is called.
15634    */
15635
15636          register struct proc *rp;
15637
15638          /* MM is waiting for new input.  Find a process with pending signals. */
15639          for (rp = BEG_SERV_ADDR; rp < END_PROC_ADDR; rp++)
15640                if (rp->p_flags & PENDING) {
15641                        m.m_type = KSIG;
15642                        m.SIG_PROC = proc_number(rp);
15643                        m.SIG_MAP = rp->p_pending;
15644                        sig_procs--;
15645                        if (lock_mini_send(proc_addr(HARDWARE), MM_PROC_NR, &m) != OK)
15646                                panic("can't inform MM", NO_NUM);
15647                        sigemptyset(&rp->p_pending); /* the ball is now in MM's court */
15648                        rp->p_flags &= ~PENDING;/* remains inhibited by SIG_PENDING */
15649                        lock_pick_proc();       /* avoid delay in scheduling MM */
15650                        return;
15651                }
15652   }
```

```
15655   /*===========================================================================*
15656    *                              umap                                         *
15657    *===========================================================================*/
15658   PUBLIC phys_bytes umap(rp, seg, vir_addr, bytes)
15659   register struct proc *rp;         /* pointer to proc table entry for process */
15660   int seg;                          /* T, D, or S segment */
15661   vir_bytes vir_addr;               /* virtual address in bytes within the seg */
15662   vir_bytes bytes;                  /* # of bytes to be copied */
15663   {
15664   /* Calculate the physical memory address for a given virtual address. */
15665
15666     vir_clicks vc;                  /* the virtual address in clicks */
15667     phys_bytes pa;                  /* intermediate variables as phys_bytes */
15668     phys_bytes seg_base;
15669
15670     /* If 'seg' is D it could really be S and vice versa.  T really means T.
15671      * If the virtual address falls in the gap,  it causes a problem. On the
15672      * 8088 it is probably a legal stack reference, since "stackfaults" are
15673      * not detected by the hardware.  On 8088s, the gap is called S and
15674      * accepted, but on other machines it is called D and rejected.
15675      * The Atari ST behaves like the 8088 in this respect.
15676      */
15677
15678     if (bytes <= 0) return( (phys_bytes) 0);
15679     vc = (vir_addr + bytes - 1) >> CLICK_SHIFT;    /* last click of data */
15680
15681     if (seg != T)
15682           seg = (vc < rp->p_map[D].mem_vir + rp->p_map[D].mem_len ? D : S);
15683
15684     if((vir_addr>>CLICK_SHIFT) >= rp->p_map[seg].mem_vir+ rp->p_map[seg].mem_len)
15685           return( (phys_bytes) 0 );
15686     seg_base = (phys_bytes) rp->p_map[seg].mem_phys;
15687     seg_base = seg_base << CLICK_SHIFT;    /* segment origin in bytes */
15688     pa = (phys_bytes) vir_addr;
15689     pa -= rp->p_map[seg].mem_vir << CLICK_SHIFT;
15690     return(seg_base + pa);
15691   }


15694   /*===========================================================================*
15695    *                              numap                                        *
15696    *===========================================================================*/
15697   PUBLIC phys_bytes numap(proc_nr, vir_addr, bytes)
15698   int proc_nr;                      /* process number to be mapped */
15699   vir_bytes vir_addr;               /* virtual address in bytes within D seg */
15700   vir_bytes bytes;                  /* # of bytes required in segment   */
15701   {
15702   /* Do umap() starting from a process number instead of a pointer.  This
15703    * function is used by device drivers, so they need not know about the
15704    * process table.  To save time, there is no 'seg' parameter. The segment
15705    * is always D.
15706    */
15707
15708     return(umap(proc_addr(proc_nr), D, vir_addr, bytes));
15709   }

15711   #if (CHIP == INTEL)
15712   /*===========================================================================*
15713    *                              alloc_segments                               *
15714    *===========================================================================*/
```

```
15715    PUBLIC void alloc_segments(rp)
15716    register struct proc *rp;
15717    {
15718    /* This is called only by do_newmap, but is broken out as a separate function
15719     * because so much is hardware-dependent.
15720     */
15721
15722      phys_bytes code_bytes;
15723      phys_bytes data_bytes;
15724      int privilege;
15725
15726      if (protected_mode) {
15727            data_bytes = (phys_bytes) (rp->p_map[S].mem_vir + rp->p_map[S].mem_len)
15728                        << CLICK_SHIFT;
15729            if (rp->p_map[T].mem_len == 0)
15730                    code_bytes = data_bytes;           /* common I&D, poor protect */
15731            else
15732                    code_bytes = (phys_bytes) rp->p_map[T].mem_len << CLICK_SHIFT;
15733            privilege = istaskp(rp) ? TASK_PRIVILEGE : USER_PRIVILEGE;
15734            init_codeseg(&rp->p_ldt[CS_LDT_INDEX],
15735                        (phys_bytes) rp->p_map[T].mem_phys << CLICK_SHIFT,
15736                        code_bytes, privilege);
15737            init_dataseg(&rp->p_ldt[DS_LDT_INDEX],
15738                        (phys_bytes) rp->p_map[D].mem_phys << CLICK_SHIFT,
15739                        data_bytes, privilege);
15740            rp->p_reg.cs = (CS_LDT_INDEX * DESC_SIZE) | TI | privilege;
15741    #if _WORD_SIZE == 4
15742            rp->p_reg.gs =
15743            rp->p_reg.fs =
15744    #endif
15745            rp->p_reg.ss =
15746            rp->p_reg.es =
15747            rp->p_reg.ds = (DS_LDT_INDEX*DESC_SIZE) | TI | privilege;
15748      } else {
15749            rp->p_reg.cs = click_to_hclick(rp->p_map[T].mem_phys);
15750            rp->p_reg.ss =
15751            rp->p_reg.es =
15752            rp->p_reg.ds = click_to_hclick(rp->p_map[D].mem_phys);
15753      }
15754    }
15755    #endif /* (CHIP == INTEL) */
```

```
++++++++++++++++++++++++++++++++++++++++++++++++++++++++++++++++++++++++++++++++++
                                  src/mm/mm.h
++++++++++++++++++++++++++++++++++++++++++++++++++++++++++++++++++++++++++++++++++
15800    /* This is the master header for mm.  It includes some other files
15801     * and defines the principal constants.
15802     */
15803    #define _POSIX_SOURCE     1     /* tell headers to include POSIX stuff */
15804    #define _MINIX            1     /* tell headers to include MINIX stuff */
15805    #define _SYSTEM           1     /* tell headers that this is the kernel */
15806
15807    /* The following are so basic, all the *.c files get them automatically. */
15808    #include <minix/config.h>       /* MUST be first */
15809    #include <ansi.h>               /* MUST be second */
```

```
15810     #include <sys/types.h>
15811     #include <minix/const.h>
15812     #include <minix/type.h>
15813
15814     #include <fcntl.h>
15815     #include <unistd.h>
15816     #include <minix/syslib.h>
15817
15818     #include <limits.h>
15819     #include <errno.h>
15820
15821     #include "const.h"
15822     #include "type.h"
15823     #include "proto.h"
15824     #include "glo.h"
```

```
++++++++++++++++++++++++++++++++++++++++++++++++++++++++++++++++++++++++++++++++
                              src/mm/const.h
++++++++++++++++++++++++++++++++++++++++++++++++++++++++++++++++++++++++++++++++
```

```
15900     /* Constants used by the Memory Manager. */
15901
15902     #define NO_MEM ((phys_clicks) 0)  /* returned by alloc_mem() with mem is up */
15903
15904     #if (CHIP == INTEL && _WORD_SIZE == 2)
15905     /* These definitions are used in size_ok and are not needed for 386.
15906      * The 386 segment granularity is 1 for segments smaller than 1M and 4096
15907      * above that.
15908      */
15909     #define PAGE_SIZE          16       /* how many bytes in a page (s.b.HCLICK_SIZE)*/
15910     #define MAX_PAGES        4096       /* how many pages in the virtual addr space */
15911     #endif
15912
15913     #define printf          printk
15914
15915     #define INIT_PID          1       /* init's process id number */
```

```
++++++++++++++++++++++++++++++++++++++++++++++++++++++++++++++++++++++++++++++++
                              src/mm/type.h
++++++++++++++++++++++++++++++++++++++++++++++++++++++++++++++++++++++++++++++++
```

```
16000     /* If there were any type definitions local to the Memory Manager, they would
16001      * be here.  This file is included only for symmetry with the kernel and File
16002      * System, which do have some local type definitions.
16003      */
16004
```

```
++++++++++++++++++++++++++++++++++++++++++++++++++++++++++++++++++++++++++++++
                              src/mm/proto.h
++++++++++++++++++++++++++++++++++++++++++++++++++++++++++++++++++++++++++++++
16100    /* Function prototypes. */
16101
16102    struct mproc;            /* need types outside of parameter list --kub */
16103    struct stat;
16104
16105    /* alloc.c */
16106    _PROTOTYPE( phys_clicks alloc_mem, (phys_clicks clicks)                   );
16107    _PROTOTYPE( void free_mem, (phys_clicks base, phys_clicks clicks)        );
16108    _PROTOTYPE( phys_clicks max_hole, (void)                                 );
16109    _PROTOTYPE( void mem_init, (phys_clicks *total, phys_clicks *free)       );
16110    _PROTOTYPE( phys_clicks mem_left, (void)                                 );
16111    _PROTOTYPE( int do_brk3, (void)                                          );
16112
16113    /* break.c */
16114    _PROTOTYPE( int adjust, (struct mproc *rmp,
16115                            vir_clicks data_clicks, vir_bytes sp)            );
16116    _PROTOTYPE( int do_brk, (void)                                           );
16117    _PROTOTYPE( int size_ok, (int file_type, vir_clicks tc, vir_clicks dc,
16118                            vir_clicks sc, vir_clicks dvir, vir_clicks s_vir) );
16119
16120    /* exec.c */
16121    _PROTOTYPE( int do_exec, (void)                                          );
16122    _PROTOTYPE( struct mproc *find_share, (struct mproc *mp_ign, Ino_t ino,
16123                            Dev_t dev, time_t ctime)                         );
16124
16125    /* forkexit.c */
16126    _PROTOTYPE( int do_fork, (void)                                          );
16127    _PROTOTYPE( int do_mm_exit, (void)                                       );
16128    _PROTOTYPE( int do_waitpid, (void)                                       );
16129    _PROTOTYPE( void mm_exit, (struct mproc *rmp, int exit_status)           );
16130
16131    /* getset.c */
16132    _PROTOTYPE( int do_getset, (void)                                        );
16133
16134    /* main.c */
16135    _PROTOTYPE( void main, (void)                                            );
16136
16137    #if (MACHINE == MACINTOSH)
16138    _PROTOTYPE( phys_clicks start_click, (void)                             );
16139    #endif
16140
16141    _PROTOTYPE( void reply, (int proc_nr, int result, int res2, char *respt));
16142
16143    /* putk.c */
16144    _PROTOTYPE( void putk, (int c)                                           );
16145
16146    /* signal.c */
16147    _PROTOTYPE( int do_alarm, (void)                                         );
16148    _PROTOTYPE( int do_kill, (void)                                          );
16149    _PROTOTYPE( int do_ksig, (void)                                          );
16150    _PROTOTYPE( int do_pause, (void)                                         );
16151    _PROTOTYPE( int set_alarm, (int proc_nr, int sec)                        );
16152    _PROTOTYPE( int check_sig, (pid_t proc_id, int signo)                    );
16153    _PROTOTYPE( void sig_proc, (struct mproc *rmp, int sig_nr)               );
16154    _PROTOTYPE( int do_sigaction, (void)                                     );
```

```
16155     _PROTOTYPE( int do_sigpending, (void)                      );
16156     _PROTOTYPE( int do_sigprocmask, (void)                     );
16157     _PROTOTYPE( int do_sigreturn, (void)                       );
16158     _PROTOTYPE( int do_sigsuspend, (void)                      );
16159     _PROTOTYPE( int do_reboot, (void)                          );
16160
16161     /* trace.c */
16162     _PROTOTYPE( int do_trace, (void)                           );
16163     _PROTOTYPE( void stop_proc, (struct mproc *rmp, int sig_nr) );
16164
16165     /* utility.c */
16166     _PROTOTYPE( int allowed, (char *name_buf, struct stat *s_buf, int mask) );
16167     _PROTOTYPE( int no_sys, (void)                             );
16168     _PROTOTYPE( void panic, (char *format, int num)           );
16169     _PROTOTYPE( void tell_fs, (int what, int p1, int p2, int p3)  );
```

```
++++++++++++++++++++++++++++++++++++++++++++++++++++++++++++++++++++++++++++
                               src/mm/glo.h
++++++++++++++++++++++++++++++++++++++++++++++++++++++++++++++++++++++++++++
```

```
16200     /* EXTERN should be extern except in table.c */
16201     #ifdef _TABLE
16202     #undef EXTERN
16203     #define EXTERN
16204     #endif
16205
16206     /* Global variables. */
16207     EXTERN struct mproc *mp;      /* ptr to 'mproc' slot of current process */
16208     EXTERN int dont_reply;        /* normally 0; set to 1 to inhibit reply */
16209     EXTERN int procs_in_use;      /* how many processes are marked as IN_USE */
16210
16211     /* The parameters of the call are kept here. */
16212     EXTERN message mm_in;         /* the incoming message itself is kept here. */
16213     EXTERN message mm_out;        /* the reply message is built up here. */
16214     EXTERN int who;               /* caller's proc number */
16215     EXTERN int mm_call;           /* system call number */
16216
16217     /* The following variables are used for returning results to the caller. */
16218     EXTERN int err_code;          /* temporary storage for error number */
16219     EXTERN int result2;           /* secondary result */
16220     EXTERN char *res_ptr;         /* result, if pointer */
16221
16222     extern _PROTOTYPE (int (*call_vec[]), (void) ); /* system call handlers */
16223     extern char core_name[];      /* file name where core images are produced */
16224     EXTERN sigset_t core_sset;     /* which signals cause core images */
```

```
++++++++++++++++++++++++++++++++++++++++++++++++++++++++++++++++++++++++++++++++
                              src/mm/mproc.h
++++++++++++++++++++++++++++++++++++++++++++++++++++++++++++++++++++++++++++++++
16300    /* This table has one slot per process.  It contains all the memory management
16301     * information for each process.  Among other things, it defines the text, data
16302     * and stack segments, uids and gids, and various flags.  The kernel and file
16303     * systems have tables that are also indexed by process, with the contents
16304     * of corresponding slots referring to the same process in all three.
16305     */
16306
16307    EXTERN struct mproc {
16308      struct mem_map mp_seg[NR_SEGS];/* points to text, data, stack */
16309      char mp_exitstatus;               /* storage for status when process exits */
16310      char mp_sigstatus;                /* storage for signal # for killed procs */
16311      pid_t mp_pid;                     /* process id */
16312      pid_t mp_procgrp;                 /* pid of process group (used for signals) */
16313      pid_t mp_wpid;                    /* pid this process is waiting for */
16314      int mp_parent;                    /* index of parent process */
16315
16316      /* Real and effective uids and gids. */
16317      uid_t mp_realuid;                 /* process' real uid */
16318      uid_t mp_effuid;                  /* process' effective uid */
16319      gid_t mp_realgid;                 /* process' real gid */
16320      gid_t mp_effgid;                  /* process' effective gid */
16321
16322      /* File identification for sharing. */
16323      ino_t mp_ino;                     /* inode number of file */
16324      dev_t mp_dev;                     /* device number of file system */
16325      time_t mp_ctime;                  /* inode changed time */
16326
16327      /* Signal handling information. */
16328      sigset_t mp_ignore;               /* 1 means ignore the signal, 0 means don't */
16329      sigset_t mp_catch;                /* 1 means catch the signal, 0 means don't */
16330      sigset_t mp_sigmask;              /* signals to be blocked */
16331      sigset_t mp_sigmask2;             /* saved copy of mp_sigmask */
16332      sigset_t mp_sigpending;           /* signals being blocked */
16333      struct sigaction mp_sigact[_NSIG + 1]; /* as in sigaction(2) */
16334      vir_bytes mp_sigreturn;           /* address of C library __sigreturn function */
16335
16336      /* Backwards compatibility for signals. */
16337      sighandler_t mp_func;             /* all sigs vectored to a single user fcn */
16338
16339      unsigned mp_flags;                /* flag bits */
16340      vir_bytes mp_procargs;            /* ptr to proc's initial stack arguments */
16341    } mproc[NR_PROCS];
16342
16343    /* Flag values */
16344    #define IN_USE          001       /* set when 'mproc' slot in use */
16345    #define WAITING         002       /* set by WAIT system call */
16346    #define HANGING         004       /* set by EXIT system call */
16347    #define PAUSED          010       /* set by PAUSE system call */
16348    #define ALARM_ON        020       /* set when SIGALRM timer started */
16349    #define SEPARATE        040       /* set if file is separate I & D space */
16350    #define TRACED          0100      /* set if process is to be traced */
16351    #define STOPPED         0200      /* set if process stopped for tracing */
16352    #define SIGSUSPENDED    0400      /* set by SIGSUSPEND system call */
16353
16354    #define NIL_MPROC ((struct mproc *) 0)
```

```
++++++++++++++++++++++++++++++++++++++++++++++++++++++++++++++++++++++++++++++++
                              src/mm/param.h
++++++++++++++++++++++++++++++++++++++++++++++++++++++++++++++++++++++++++++++++

16400   /* The following names are synonyms for the variables in the input message. */
16401   #define addr           mm_in.m1_p1
16402   #define exec_name      mm_in.m1_p1
16403   #define exec_len       mm_in.m1_i1
16404   #define func           mm_in.m6_f1
16405   #define grpid          (gid_t) mm_in.m1_i1
16406   #define namelen        mm_in.m1_i1
16407   #define pid            mm_in.m1_i1
16408   #define seconds        mm_in.m1_i1
16409   #define sig            mm_in.m6_i1
16410   #define stack_bytes    mm_in.m1_i2
16411   #define stack_ptr      mm_in.m1_p2
16412   #define status         mm_in.m1_i1
16413   #define usr_id         (uid_t) mm_in.m1_i1
16414   #define request        mm_in.m2_i2
16415   #define taddr          mm_in.m2_l1
16416   #define data           mm_in.m2_l2
16417   #define sig_nr         mm_in.m1_i2
16418   #define sig_nsa        mm_in.m1_p1
16419   #define sig_osa        mm_in.m1_p2
16420   #define sig_ret        mm_in.m1_p3
16421   #define sig_set        mm_in.m2_l1
16422   #define sig_how        mm_in.m2_i1
16423   #define sig_flags      mm_in.m2_i2
16424   #define sig_context    mm_in.m2_p1
16425   #ifdef _SIGMESSAGE
16426   #define sig_msg        mm_in.m1_i1
16427   #endif
16428   #define reboot_flag    mm_in.m1_i1
16429   #define reboot_code    mm_in.m1_p1
16430   #define reboot_size    mm_in.m1_i2
16431
16432   /* The following names are synonyms for the variables in the output message. */
16433   #define reply_type     mm_out.m_type
16434   #define reply_i1       mm_out.m2_i1
16435   #define reply_p1       mm_out.m2_p1
16436   #define ret_mask       mm_out.m2_l1
16437


++++++++++++++++++++++++++++++++++++++++++++++++++++++++++++++++++++++++++++++++
                              src/mm/table.c
++++++++++++++++++++++++++++++++++++++++++++++++++++++++++++++++++++++++++++++++

16500   /* This file contains the table used to map system call numbers onto the
16501    * routines that perform them.
16502    */
16503
16504   #define _TABLE
16505
16506   #include "mm.h"
16507   #include <minix/callnr.h>
16508   #include <signal.h>
16509   #include "mproc.h"
```

```
16510        #include "param.h"
16511
16512        /* Miscellaneous */
16513        char core_name[] = "core";          /* file name where core images are produced */
16514
16515        _PROTOTYPE (int (*call_vec[NCALLS]), (void) ) = {
16516                no_sys,          /*  0 = unused  */
16517                do_mm_exit,      /*  1 = exit    */
16518                do_fork,         /*  2 = fork    */
16519                no_sys,          /*  3 = read    */
16520                no_sys,          /*  4 = write   */
16521                no_sys,          /*  5 = open    */
16522                no_sys,          /*  6 = close   */
16523                do_waitpid,      /*  7 = wait    */
16524                no_sys,          /*  8 = creat   */
16525                no_sys,          /*  9 = link    */
16526                no_sys,          /* 10 = unlink  */
16527                do_waitpid,      /* 11 = waitpid */
16528                no_sys,          /* 12 = chdir   */
16529                no_sys,          /* 13 = time    */
16530                no_sys,          /* 14 = mknod   */
16531                no_sys,          /* 15 = chmod   */
16532                no_sys,          /* 16 = chown   */
16533                do_brk,          /* 17 = break   */
16534                no_sys,          /* 18 = stat    */
16535                no_sys,          /* 19 = lseek   */
16536                do_getset,       /* 20 = getpid  */
16537                no_sys,          /* 21 = mount   */
16538                no_sys,          /* 22 = umount  */
16539                do_getset,       /* 23 = setuid  */
16540                do_getset,       /* 24 = getuid  */
16541                no_sys,          /* 25 = stime   */
16542                do_trace,        /* 26 = ptrace  */
16543                do_alarm,        /* 27 = alarm   */
16544                no_sys,          /* 28 = fstat   */
16545                do_pause,        /* 29 = pause   */
16546                no_sys,          /* 30 = utime   */
16547                no_sys,          /* 31 = (stty)  */
16548                no_sys,          /* 32 = (gtty)  */
16549                no_sys,          /* 33 = access  */
16550                no_sys,          /* 34 = (nice)  */
16551                no_sys,          /* 35 = (ftime) */
16552                no_sys,          /* 36 = sync    */
16553                do_kill,         /* 37 = kill    */
16554                no_sys,          /* 38 = rename  */
16555                no_sys,          /* 39 = mkdir   */
16556                no_sys,          /* 40 = rmdir   */
16557                no_sys,          /* 41 = dup     */
16558                no_sys,          /* 42 = pipe    */
16559                no_sys,          /* 43 = times   */
16560                no_sys,          /* 44 = (prof)  */
16561                no_sys,          /* 45 = unused  */
16562                do_getset,       /* 46 = setgid  */
16563                do_getset,       /* 47 = getgid  */
16564                no_sys,          /* 48 = (signal)*/
16565                no_sys,          /* 49 = unused  */
16566                no_sys,          /* 50 = unused  */
16567                no_sys,          /* 51 = (acct)  */
16568                no_sys,          /* 52 = (phys)  */
16569                no_sys,          /* 53 = (lock)  */
```

```
16570          no_sys,         /* 54 = ioctl    */
16571          no_sys,         /* 55 = fcntl    */
16572          no_sys,         /* 56 = (mpx)    */
16573          no_sys,         /* 57 = unused   */
16574          no_sys,         /* 58 = unused   */
16575          do_exec,        /* 59 = execve   */
16576          no_sys,         /* 60 = umask    */
16577          no_sys,         /* 61 = chroot   */
16578          do_getset,      /* 62 = setsid   */
16579          do_getset,      /* 63 = getpgrp  */
16580
16581          do_ksig,        /* 64 = KSIG: signals originating in the kernel */
16582          no_sys,         /* 65 = UNPAUSE  */
16583          no_sys,         /* 66 = unused   */
16584          no_sys,         /* 67 = REVIVE   */
16585          no_sys,         /* 68 = TASK_REPLY  */
16586          no_sys,         /* 69 = unused   */
16587          no_sys,         /* 70 = unused   */
16588          do_sigaction,   /* 71 = sigaction    */
16589          do_sigsuspend,  /* 72 = sigsuspend   */
16590          do_sigpending,  /* 73 = sigpending   */
16591          do_sigprocmask, /* 74 = sigprocmask  */
16592          do_sigreturn,   /* 75 = sigreturn    */
16593          do_reboot,      /* 76 = reboot   */
16594    };
```

```
+++++++++++++++++++++++++++++++++++++++++++++++++++++++++++++++++++++++++++++++++
                                src/mm/main.c
+++++++++++++++++++++++++++++++++++++++++++++++++++++++++++++++++++++++++++++++++
```

```
16600    /* This file contains the main program of the memory manager and some related
16601     * procedures.  When MINIX starts up, the kernel runs for a little while,
16602     * initializing itself and its tasks, and then it runs MM and FS.  Both MM
16603     * and FS initialize themselves as far as they can.  FS then makes a call to
16604     * MM, because MM has to wait for FS to acquire a RAM disk.  MM asks the
16605     * kernel for all free memory and starts serving requests.
16606     *
16607     * The entry points into this file are:
16608     *   main:       starts MM running
16609     *   reply:      reply to a process making an MM system call
16610     */
16611
16612    #include "mm.h"
16613    #include <minix/callnr.h>
16614    #include <minix/com.h>
16615    #include <signal.h>
16616    #include <fcntl.h>
16617    #include <sys/ioctl.h>
16618    #include "mproc.h"
16619    #include "param.h"
16620
16621    FORWARD _PROTOTYPE( void get_work, (void)                        );
16622    FORWARD _PROTOTYPE( void mm_init, (void)                         );
16623
16624    /*===========================================================================*
```

```
16625      *                            main                            *
16626      *===========================================================================*/
16627   PUBLIC void main()
16628   {
16629   /* Main routine of the memory manager. */
16630
16631     int error;
16632
16633     mm_init();                      /* initialize memory manager tables */
16634
16635     /* This is MM's main loop-  get work and do it, forever and forever. */
16636     while (TRUE) {
16637           /* Wait for message. */
16638           get_work();               /* wait for an MM system call */
16639           mp = &mproc[who];
16640
16641           /* Set some flags. */
16642           error = OK;
16643           dont_reply = FALSE;
16644           err_code = -999;
16645
16646           /* If the call number is valid, perform the call. */
16647           if (mm_call < 0 || mm_call >= NCALLS)
16648                   error = EBADCALL;
16649           else
16650                   error = (*call_vec[mm_call])();
16651
16652           /* Send the results back to the user to indicate completion. */
16653           if (dont_reply) continue;       /* no reply for EXIT and WAIT */
16654           if (mm_call == EXEC && error == OK) continue;
16655           reply(who, error, result2, res_ptr);
16656     }
16657   }


16660   /*===========================================================================*
16661    *                            get_work                            *
16662    *===========================================================================*/
16663   PRIVATE void get_work()
16664   {
16665   /* Wait for the next message and extract useful information from it. */
16666
16667     if (receive(ANY, &mm_in) != OK) panic("MM receive error", NO_NUM);
16668     who = mm_in.m_source;           /* who sent the message */
16669     mm_call = mm_in.m_type;         /* system call number */
16670   }


16673   /*===========================================================================*
16674    *                            reply                            *
16675    *===========================================================================*/
16676   PUBLIC void reply(proc_nr, result, res2, respt)
16677   int proc_nr;                      /* process to reply to */
16678   int result;                      /* result of the call (usually OK or error #)*/
16679   int res2;                        /* secondary result */
16680   char *respt;                     /* result if pointer */
16681   {
16682   /* Send a reply to a user process. */
16683
16684     register struct mproc *proc_ptr;
```

```
16685
16686        proc_ptr = &mproc[proc_nr];
16687        /*
16688         * To make MM robust, check to see if destination is still alive.  This
16689         * validy check must be skipped if the caller is a task.
16690         */
16691        if ((who >=0) && ((proc_ptr->mp_flags&IN_USE) == 0 ||
16692             (proc_ptr->mp_flags&HANGING))) return;
16693
16694        reply_type = result;
16695        reply_i1 = res2;
16696        reply_p1 = respt;
16697        if (send(proc_nr, &mm_out) != OK) panic("MM can't reply", NO_NUM);
16698      }


16701  /*===========================================================================*
16702   *                              mm_init                                      *
16703   *===========================================================================*/
16704  PRIVATE void mm_init()
16705  {
16706  /* Initialize the memory manager. */
16707
16708      static char core_sigs[] = {
16709             SIGQUIT, SIGILL, SIGTRAP, SIGABRT,
16710             SIGEMT, SIGFPE, SIGUSR1, SIGSEGV,
16711             SIGUSR2, 0 };
16712      register int proc_nr;
16713      register struct mproc *rmp;
16714      register char *sig_ptr;
16715      phys_clicks ram_clicks, total_clicks, minix_clicks, free_clicks, dummy;
16716      message mess;
16717      struct mem_map kernel_map[NR_SEGS];
16718      int mem;
16719
16720      /* Build the set of signals which cause core dumps. Do it the Posix
16721       * way, so no knowledge of bit positions is needed.
16722       */
16723      sigemptyset(&core_sset);
16724      for (sig_ptr = core_sigs; *sig_ptr != 0; sig_ptr++)
16725             sigaddset(&core_sset, *sig_ptr);
16726
16727      /* Get the memory map of the kernel to see how much memory it uses,
16728       * including the gap between address 0 and the start of the kernel.
16729       */
16730      sys_getmap(SYSTASK, kernel_map);
16731      minix_clicks = kernel_map[S].mem_phys + kernel_map[S].mem_len;
16732
16733      /* Initialize MM's tables. */
16734      for (proc_nr = 0; proc_nr <= INIT_PROC_NR; proc_nr++) {
16735             rmp = &mproc[proc_nr];
16736             rmp->mp_flags |= IN_USE;
16737             sys_getmap(proc_nr, rmp->mp_seg);
16738             if (rmp->mp_seg[T].mem_len != 0) rmp->mp_flags |= SEPARATE;
16739             minix_clicks += (rmp->mp_seg[S].mem_phys + rmp->mp_seg[S].mem_len)
16740                                    - rmp->mp_seg[T].mem_phys;
16741      }
16742      mproc[INIT_PROC_NR].mp_pid = INIT_PID;
16743      sigemptyset(&mproc[INIT_PROC_NR].mp_ignore);
16744      sigemptyset(&mproc[INIT_PROC_NR].mp_catch);
```

```
16745        procs_in_use = LOW_USER + 1;
16746
16747        /* Wait for FS to send a message telling the RAM disk size then go "on-line".
16748         */
16749        if (receive(FS_PROC_NR, &mess) != OK)
16750                panic("MM can't obtain RAM disk size from FS", NO_NUM);
16751
16752        ram_clicks = mess.m1_i1;
16753
16754        /* Initialize tables to all physical mem. */
16755        mem_init(&total_clicks, &free_clicks);
16756
16757        /* Print memory information. */
16758        printf("\nMemory size =%5dK   ", click_to_round_k(total_clicks));
16759        printf("MINIX =%4dK    ", click_to_round_k(minix_clicks));
16760        printf("RAM disk =%5dK   ", click_to_round_k(ram_clicks));
16761        printf("Available =%5dK\n\n", click_to_round_k(free_clicks));
16762
16763        /* Tell FS to continue. */
16764        if (send(FS_PROC_NR, &mess) != OK)
16765                panic("MM can't sync up with FS", NO_NUM);
16766
16767        /* Tell the memory task where my process table is for the sake of ps(1). */
16768        if ((mem = open("/dev/mem", O_RDWR)) != -1) {
16769                ioctl(mem, MIOCSPSINFO, (void *) mproc);
16770                close(mem);
16771        }
16772    }


++++++++++++++++++++++++++++++++++++++++++++++++++++++++++++++++++++++++++++++++++
                                src/mm/forkexit.c
++++++++++++++++++++++++++++++++++++++++++++++++++++++++++++++++++++++++++++++++++

16800    /* This file deals with creating processes (via FORK) and deleting them (via
16801     * EXIT/WAIT).  When a process forks, a new slot in the 'mproc' table is
16802     * allocated for it, and a copy of the parent's core image is made for the
16803     * child.  Then the kernel and file system are informed.  A process is removed
16804     * from the 'mproc' table when two events have occurred: (1) it has exited or
16805     * been killed by a signal, and (2) the parent has done a WAIT.  If the process
16806     * exits first, it continues to occupy a slot until the parent does a WAIT.
16807     *
16808     * The entry points into this file are:
16809     *   do_fork:     perform the FORK system call
16810     *   do_mm_exit:  perform the EXIT system call (by calling mm_exit())
16811     *   mm_exit:     actually do the exiting
16812     *   do_wait:     perform the WAITPID or WAIT system call
16813     */
16814
16815
16816    #include "mm.h"
16817    #include <sys/wait.h>
16818    #include <minix/callnr.h>
16819    #include <signal.h>
16820    #include "mproc.h"
16821    #include "param.h"
16822
16823    #define LAST_FEW            2   /* last few slots reserved for superuser */
16824
```

```
16825   PRIVATE pid_t next_pid = INIT_PID+1;     /* next pid to be assigned */
16826
16827   FORWARD _PROTOTYPE (void cleanup, (register struct mproc *child) );
16828
16829   /*===========================================================================*
16830    *                              do_fork                                       *
16831    *===========================================================================*/
16832   PUBLIC int do_fork()
16833   {
16834   /* The process pointed to by 'mp' has forked.  Create a child process. */
16835
16836     register struct mproc *rmp;    /* pointer to parent */
16837     register struct mproc *rmc;    /* pointer to child */
16838     int i, child_nr, t;
16839     phys_clicks prog_clicks, child_base = 0;
16840     phys_bytes prog_bytes, parent_abs, child_abs; /* Intel only */
16841
16842    /* If tables might fill up during FORK, don't even start since recovery half
16843     * way through is such a nuisance.
16844     */
16845     rmp = mp;
16846     if (procs_in_use == NR_PROCS) return(EAGAIN);
16847     if (procs_in_use >= NR_PROCS-LAST_FEW && rmp->mp_effuid != 0)return(EAGAIN);
16848
16849     /* Determine how much memory to allocate.  Only the data and stack need to
16850      * be copied, because the text segment is either shared or of zero length.
16851      */
16852     prog_clicks = (phys_clicks) rmp->mp_seg[S].mem_len;
16853     prog_clicks += (rmp->mp_seg[S].mem_vir - rmp->mp_seg[D].mem_vir);
16854     prog_bytes = (phys_bytes) prog_clicks << CLICK_SHIFT;
16855     if ( (child_base = alloc_mem(prog_clicks)) == NO_MEM) return(EAGAIN);
16856
16857     /* Create a copy of the parent's core image for the child. */
16858     child_abs = (phys_bytes) child_base << CLICK_SHIFT;
16859     parent_abs = (phys_bytes) rmp->mp_seg[D].mem_phys << CLICK_SHIFT;
16860     i = sys_copy(ABS, 0, parent_abs, ABS, 0, child_abs, prog_bytes);
16861     if (i < 0) panic("do_fork can't copy", i);
16862
16863     /* Find a slot in 'mproc' for the child process.  A slot must exist. */
16864     for (rmc = &mproc[0]; rmc < &mproc[NR_PROCS]; rmc++)
16865         if ( (rmc->mp_flags & IN_USE) == 0) break;
16866
16867     /* Set up the child and its memory map; copy its 'mproc' slot from parent. */
16868     child_nr = (int)(rmc - mproc);          /* slot number of the child */
16869     procs_in_use++;
16870     *rmc = *rmp;                    /* copy parent's process slot to child's */
16871
16872     rmc->mp_parent = who;          /* record child's parent */
16873     rmc->mp_flags &= ~TRACED;      /* child does not inherit trace status */
16874     /* A separate I&D child keeps the parents text segment.  The data and stack
16875      * segments must refer to the new copy.
16876      */
16877     if (!(rmc->mp_flags & SEPARATE)) rmc->mp_seg[T].mem_phys = child_base;
16878     rmc->mp_seg[D].mem_phys = child_base;
16879     rmc->mp_seg[S].mem_phys = rmc->mp_seg[D].mem_phys +
16880                         (rmp->mp_seg[S].mem_vir - rmp->mp_seg[D].mem_vir);
16881     rmc->mp_exitstatus = 0;
16882     rmc->mp_sigstatus = 0;
16883
16884     /* Find a free pid for the child and put it in the table. */
```

```
16885        do {
16886              t = 0;                          /* 't' = 0 means pid still free */
16887              next_pid = (next_pid < 30000 ? next_pid + 1 : INIT_PID + 1);
16888              for (rmp = &mproc[0]; rmp < &mproc[NR_PROCS]; rmp++)
16889                    if (rmp->mp_pid == next_pid || rmp->mp_procgrp == next_pid) {
16890                          t = 1;
16891                          break;
16892                    }
16893              rmc->mp_pid = next_pid; /* assign pid to child */
16894        } while (t);
16895
16896        /* Tell kernel and file system about the (now successful) FORK. */
16897        sys_fork(who, child_nr, rmc->mp_pid, child_base); /* child_base is 68K only*/
16898        tell_fs(FORK, who, child_nr, rmc->mp_pid);
16899
16900        /* Report child's memory map to kernel. */
16901        sys_newmap(child_nr, rmc->mp_seg);
16902
16903        /* Reply to child to wake it up. */
16904        reply(child_nr, 0, 0, NIL_PTR);
16905        return(next_pid);               /* child's pid */
16906   }


16909   /*===========================================================================*
16910    *                              do_mm_exit                                    *
16911    *===========================================================================*/
16912   PUBLIC int do_mm_exit()
16913   {
16914   /* Perform the exit(status) system call. The real work is done by mm_exit(),
16915    * which is also called when a process is killed by a signal.
16916    */
16917
16918        mm_exit(mp, status);
16919        dont_reply = TRUE;             /* don't reply to newly terminated process */
16920        return(OK);                    /* pro forma return code */
16921   }


16924   /*===========================================================================*
16925    *                              mm_exit                                       *
16926    *===========================================================================*/
16927   PUBLIC void mm_exit(rmp, exit_status)
16928   register struct mproc *rmp;      /* pointer to the process to be terminated */
16929   int exit_status;                 /* the process' exit status (for parent) */
16930   {
16931   /* A process is done.  Release most of the process' possessions.  If its
16932    * parent is waiting, release the rest, else hang.
16933    */
16934
16935        register int proc_nr;
16936        int parent_waiting, right_child;
16937        pid_t pidarg, procgrp;
16938        phys_clicks base, size, s;               /* base and size used on 68000 only */
16939
16940        proc_nr = (int) (rmp - mproc);           /* get process slot number */
16941
16942        /* Remember a session leader's process group. */
16943        procgrp = (rmp->mp_pid == mp->mp_procgrp) ? mp->mp_procgrp : 0;
16944
```

```
16945        /* If the exited process has a timer pending, kill it. */
16946        if (rmp->mp_flags & ALARM_ON) set_alarm(proc_nr, (unsigned) 0);
16947
16948        /* Tell the kernel and FS that the process is no longer runnable. */
16949        tell_fs(EXIT, proc_nr, 0, 0);  /* file system can free the proc slot */
16950        sys_xit(rmp->mp_parent, proc_nr, &base, &size);
16951
16952        /* Release the memory occupied by the child. */
16953        if (find_share(rmp, rmp->mp_ino, rmp->mp_dev, rmp->mp_ctime) == NULL) {
16954                /* No other process shares the text segment, so free it. */
16955                free_mem(rmp->mp_seg[T].mem_phys, rmp->mp_seg[T].mem_len);
16956        }
16957        /* Free the data and stack segments. */
16958        free_mem(rmp->mp_seg[D].mem_phys,
16959             rmp->mp_seg[S].mem_vir + rmp->mp_seg[S].mem_len - rmp->mp_seg[D].mem_vir);
16960
16961        /* The process slot can only be freed if the parent has done a WAIT. */
16962        rmp->mp_exitstatus = (char) exit_status;
16963        pidarg = mproc[rmp->mp_parent].mp_wpid;          /* who's being waited for? */
16964        parent_waiting = mproc[rmp->mp_parent].mp_flags & WAITING;
16965        if (pidarg == -1 || pidarg == rmp->mp_pid || -pidarg == rmp->mp_procgrp)
16966                right_child = TRUE;                 /* child meets one of the 3 tests */
16967        else
16968                right_child = FALSE;                /* child fails all 3 tests */
16969        if (parent_waiting && right_child)
16970                cleanup(rmp);                       /* tell parent and release child slot */
16971        else
16972                rmp->mp_flags |= HANGING;           /* parent not waiting, suspend child */
16973
16974        /* If the process has children, disinherit them.  INIT is the new parent. */
16975        for (rmp = &mproc[0]; rmp < &mproc[NR_PROCS]; rmp++) {
16976                if (rmp->mp_flags & IN_USE && rmp->mp_parent == proc_nr) {
16977                        /* 'rmp' now points to a child to be disinherited. */
16978                        rmp->mp_parent = INIT_PROC_NR;
16979                        parent_waiting = mproc[INIT_PROC_NR].mp_flags & WAITING;
16980                        if (parent_waiting && (rmp->mp_flags & HANGING)) cleanup(rmp);
16981                }
16982        }
16983
16984        /* Send a hangup to the process' process group if it was a session leader. */
16985        if (procgrp != 0) check_sig(-procgrp, SIGHUP);
16986 }


16989 /*===========================================================================*
16990  *                              do_waitpid                                   *
16991  *===========================================================================*/
16992 PUBLIC int do_waitpid()
16993 {
16994 /* A process wants to wait for a child to terminate. If one is already waiting,
16995  * go clean it up and let this WAIT call terminate.  Otherwise, really wait.
16996  * Both WAIT and WAITPID are handled by this code.
16997  */
16998
16999   register struct mproc *rp;
17000   int pidarg, options, children, res2;
17001
17002   /* A process calling WAIT never gets a reply in the usual way via the
17003    * reply() in the main loop (unless WNOHANG is set or no qualifying child
17004    * exists).  If a child has already exited, the routine cleanup() sends
```

```
17005        * the reply to awaken the caller.
17006        */
17007
17008       /* Set internal variables, depending on whether this is WAIT or WAITPID. */
17009       pidarg  = (mm_call == WAIT ? -1 : pid);        /* first param of waitpid */
17010       options = (mm_call == WAIT ?  0 : sig_nr);     /* third param of waitpid */
17011       if (pidarg == 0) pidarg = -mp->mp_procgrp;     /* pidarg < 0 ==> proc grp */
17012
17013       /* Is there a child waiting to be collected? At this point, pidarg != 0:
17014        *     pidarg  >  0 means pidarg is pid of a specific process to wait for
17015        *     pidarg == -1 means wait for any child
17016        *     pidarg  < -1 means wait for any child whose process group = -pidarg
17017        */
17018       children = 0;
17019       for (rp = &mproc[0]; rp < &mproc[NR_PROCS]; rp++) {
17020           if ( (rp->mp_flags & IN_USE) && rp->mp_parent == who) {
17021               /* The value of pidarg determines which children qualify. */
17022               if (pidarg  > 0 && pidarg != rp->mp_pid) continue;
17023               if (pidarg < -1 && -pidarg != rp->mp_procgrp) continue;
17024
17025               children++;              /* this child is acceptable */
17026               if (rp->mp_flags & HANGING) {
17027                   /* This child meets the pid test and has exited. */
17028                   cleanup(rp);     /* this child has already exited */
17029                   dont_reply = TRUE;
17030                   return(OK);
17031               }
17032               if ((rp->mp_flags & STOPPED) && rp->mp_sigstatus) {
17033                   /* This child meets the pid test and is being traced.*/
17034                   res2 =  0177 | (rp->mp_sigstatus << 8);
17035                   reply(who, rp->mp_pid, res2, NIL_PTR);
17036                   dont_reply = TRUE;
17037                   rp->mp_sigstatus = 0;
17038                   return(OK);
17039               }
17040           }
17041       }
17042
17043       /* No qualifying child has exited.  Wait for one, unless none exists. */
17044       if (children > 0) {
17045           /* At least 1 child meets the pid test exists, but has not exited. */
17046           if (options & WNOHANG) return(0);    /* parent does not want to wait */
17047           mp->mp_flags |= WAITING;             /* parent wants to wait */
17048           mp->mp_wpid = (pid_t) pidarg;        /* save pid for later */
17049           dont_reply = TRUE;                   /* do not reply now though */
17050           return(OK);                          /* yes - wait for one to exit */
17051       } else {
17052           /* No child even meets the pid test.  Return error immediately. */
17053           return(ECHILD);                      /* no - parent has no children */
17054       }
17055   }


17058   /*===========================================================================*
17059    *                              cleanup                                       *
17060    *===========================================================================*/
17061   PRIVATE void cleanup(child)
17062   register struct mproc *child;    /* tells which process is exiting */
17063   {
17064   /* Finish off the exit of a process.  The process has exited or been killed
```

```
17065       * by a signal, and its parent is waiting.
17066       */
17067
17068      int exitstatus;
17069
17070      /* Wake up the parent. */
17071      exitstatus = (child->mp_exitstatus << 8) | (child->mp_sigstatus & 0377);
17072      reply(child->mp_parent, child->mp_pid, exitstatus, NIL_PTR);
17073      mproc[child->mp_parent].mp_flags &= ~WAITING; /* parent no longer waiting */
17074
17075      /* Release the process table entry. */
17076      child->mp_flags = 0;
17077      procs_in_use--;
17078    }



++++++++++++++++++++++++++++++++++++++++++++++++++++++++++++++++++++++++++++++++
                                src/mm/exec.c
++++++++++++++++++++++++++++++++++++++++++++++++++++++++++++++++++++++++++++++++

17100    /* This file handles the EXEC system call.  It performs the work as follows:
17101     *    - see if the permissions allow the file to be executed
17102     *    - read the header and extract the sizes
17103     *    - fetch the initial args and environment from the user space
17104     *    - allocate the memory for the new process
17105     *    - copy the initial stack from MM to the process
17106     *    - read in the text and data segments and copy to the process
17107     *    - take care of setuid and setgid bits
17108     *    - fix up 'mproc' table
17109     *    - tell kernel about EXEC
17110     *    - save offset to initial argc (for ps)
17111     *
17112     * The entry points into this file are:
17113     *   do_exec:    perform the EXEC system call
17114     *   find_share: find a process whose text segment can be shared
17115     */
17116
17117    #include "mm.h"
17118    #include <sys/stat.h>
17119    #include <minix/callnr.h>
17120    #include <a.out.h>
17121    #include <signal.h>
17122    #include <string.h>
17123    #include "mproc.h"
17124    #include "param.h"
17125
17126    FORWARD _PROTOTYPE( void load_seg, (int fd, int seg, vir_bytes seg_bytes) );
17127    FORWARD _PROTOTYPE( int new_mem, (struct mproc *sh_mp, vir_bytes text_bytes,
17128                    vir_bytes data_bytes, vir_bytes bss_bytes,
17129                    vir_bytes stk_bytes, phys_bytes tot_bytes)            );
17130    FORWARD _PROTOTYPE( void patch_ptr, (char stack [ARG_MAX ], vir_bytes base) );
17131    FORWARD _PROTOTYPE( int read_header, (int fd, int *ft, vir_bytes *text_bytes,
17132                    vir_bytes *data_bytes, vir_bytes *bss_bytes,
17133                    phys_bytes *tot_bytes, long *sym_bytes, vir_clicks sc,
17134                    vir_bytes *pc)                                       );
17135
17136
17137    /*===========================================================================*
17138     *                              do_exec                                       *
17139     *===========================================================================*/
```

```
17140     PUBLIC int do_exec()
17141     {
17142     /* Perform the execve(name, argv, envp) call.  The user library builds a
17143      * complete stack image, including pointers, args, environ, etc.  The stack
17144      * is copied to a buffer inside MM, and then to the new core image.
17145      */
17146
17147       register struct mproc *rmp;
17148       struct mproc *sh_mp;
17149       int m, r, fd, ft, sn;
17150       static char mbuf[ARG_MAX];     /* buffer for stack and zeroes */
17151       static char name_buf[PATH_MAX]; /* the name of the file to exec */
17152       char *new_sp, *basename;
17153       vir_bytes src, dst, text_bytes, data_bytes, bss_bytes, stk_bytes, vsp;
17154       phys_bytes tot_bytes;          /* total space for program, including gap */
17155       long sym_bytes;
17156       vir_clicks sc;
17157       struct stat s_buf;
17158       vir_bytes pc;
17159
17160       /* Do some validity checks. */
17161       rmp = mp;
17162       stk_bytes = (vir_bytes) stack_bytes;
17163       if (stk_bytes > ARG_MAX) return(ENOMEM);        /* stack too big */
17164       if (exec_len <= 0 || exec_len > PATH_MAX) return(EINVAL);
17165
17166       /* Get the exec file name and see if the file is executable. */
17167       src = (vir_bytes) exec_name;
17168       dst = (vir_bytes) name_buf;
17169       r = sys_copy(who, D, (phys_bytes) src,
17170                   MM_PROC_NR, D, (phys_bytes) dst, (phys_bytes) exec_len);
17171       if (r != OK) return(r);        /* file name not in user data segment */
17172       tell_fs(CHDIR, who, FALSE, 0);        /* switch to the user's FS environ. */
17173       fd = allowed(name_buf, &s_buf, X_BIT);        /* is file executable? */
17174       if (fd < 0) return(fd);        /* file was not executable */
17175
17176       /* Read the file header and extract the segment sizes. */
17177       sc = (stk_bytes + CLICK_SIZE - 1) >> CLICK_SHIFT;
17178       m = read_header(fd, &ft, &text_bytes, &data_bytes, &bss_bytes,
17179                                       &tot_bytes, &sym_bytes, sc, &pc);
17180       if (m < 0) {
17181           close(fd);                 /* something wrong with header */
17182           return(ENOEXEC);
17183       }
17184
17185       /* Fetch the stack from the user before destroying the old core image. */
17186       src = (vir_bytes) stack_ptr;
17187       dst = (vir_bytes) mbuf;
17188       r = sys_copy(who, D, (phys_bytes) src,
17189                       MM_PROC_NR, D, (phys_bytes) dst, (phys_bytes)stk_bytes);
17190       if (r != OK) {
17191           close(fd);                 /* can't fetch stack (e.g. bad virtual addr) */
17192           return(EACCES);
17193       }
17194
17195       /* Can the process' text be shared with that of one already running? */
17196       sh_mp = find_share(rmp, s_buf.st_ino, s_buf.st_dev, s_buf.st_ctime);
17197
17198       /* Allocate new memory and release old memory.  Fix map and tell kernel. */
17199       r = new_mem(sh_mp, text_bytes, data_bytes, bss_bytes, stk_bytes, tot_bytes);
```

```
17200        if (r != OK) {
17201                close(fd);                 /* insufficient core or program too big */
17202                return(r);
17203        }
17204
17205        /* Save file identification to allow it to be shared. */
17206        rmp->mp_ino = s_buf.st_ino;
17207        rmp->mp_dev = s_buf.st_dev;
17208        rmp->mp_ctime = s_buf.st_ctime;
17209
17210        /* Patch up stack and copy it from MM to new core image. */
17211        vsp = (vir_bytes) rmp->mp_seg[S].mem_vir << CLICK_SHIFT;
17212        vsp += (vir_bytes) rmp->mp_seg[S].mem_len << CLICK_SHIFT;
17213        vsp -= stk_bytes;
17214        patch_ptr(mbuf, vsp);
17215        src = (vir_bytes) mbuf;
17216        r = sys_copy(MM_PROC_NR, D, (phys_bytes) src,
17217                            who, D, (phys_bytes) vsp, (phys_bytes)stk_bytes);
17218        if (r != OK) panic("do_exec stack copy err", NO_NUM);
17219
17220        /* Read in text and data segments. */
17221        if (sh_mp != NULL) {
17222                lseek(fd, (off_t) text_bytes, SEEK_CUR);   /* shared: skip text */
17223        } else {
17224                load_seg(fd, T, text_bytes);
17225        }
17226        load_seg(fd, D, data_bytes);
17227
17228
17229        close(fd);                 /* don't need exec file any more */
17230
17231        /* Take care of setuid/setgid bits. */
17232        if ((rmp->mp_flags & TRACED) == 0) { /* suppress if tracing */
17233                if (s_buf.st_mode & I_SET_UID_BIT) {
17234                        rmp->mp_effuid = s_buf.st_uid;
17235                        tell_fs(SETUID,who, (int)rmp->mp_realuid, (int)rmp->mp_effuid);
17236                }
17237                if (s_buf.st_mode & I_SET_GID_BIT) {
17238                        rmp->mp_effgid = s_buf.st_gid;
17239                        tell_fs(SETGID,who, (int)rmp->mp_realgid, (int)rmp->mp_effgid);
17240                }
17241        }
17242
17243        /* Save offset to initial argc (for ps) */
17244        rmp->mp_procargs = vsp;
17245
17246        /* Fix 'mproc' fields, tell kernel that exec is done,  reset caught sigs. */
17247        for (sn = 1; sn <= _NSIG; sn++) {
17248                if (sigismember(&rmp->mp_catch, sn)) {
17249                        sigdelset(&rmp->mp_catch, sn);
17250                        rmp->mp_sigact[sn].sa_handler = SIG_DFL;
17251                        sigemptyset(&rmp->mp_sigact[sn].sa_mask);
17252                }
17253        }
17254
17255        rmp->mp_flags &= ~SEPARATE;    /* turn off SEPARATE bit */
17256        rmp->mp_flags |= ft;           /* turn it on for separate I & D files */
17257        new_sp = (char *) vsp;
17258
17259        tell_fs(EXEC, who, 0, 0);      /* allow FS to handle FD_CLOEXEC files */
```

```
17260
17261     /* System will save command line for debugging, ps(1) output, etc. */
17262     basename = strrchr(name_buf, '/');
17263     if (basename == NULL) basename = name_buf; else basename++;
17264     sys_exec(who, new_sp, rmp->mp_flags & TRACED, basename, pc);
17265     return(OK);
17266   }


17269   /*===========================================================================*
17270    *                              read_header                                  *
17271    *===========================================================================*/
17272   PRIVATE int read_header(fd, ft, text_bytes, data_bytes, bss_bytes,
17273                                    tot_bytes, sym_bytes, sc, pc)
17274   int fd;                          /* file descriptor for reading exec file */
17275   int *ft;                         /* place to return ft number */
17276   vir_bytes *text_bytes;           /* place to return text size */
17277   vir_bytes *data_bytes;           /* place to return initialized data size */
17278   vir_bytes *bss_bytes;            /* place to return bss size */
17279   phys_bytes *tot_bytes;           /* place to return total size */
17280   long *sym_bytes;                 /* place to return symbol table size */
17281   vir_clicks sc;                   /* stack size in clicks */
17282   vir_bytes *pc;                   /* program entry point (initial PC) */
17283   {
17284   /* Read the header and extract the text, data, bss and total sizes from it. */
17285
17286     int m, ct;
17287     vir_clicks tc, dc, s_vir, dvir;
17288     phys_clicks totc;
17289     struct exec hdr;               /* a.out header is read in here */
17290
17291     /* Read the header and check the magic number.  The standard MINIX header
17292      * is defined in <a.out.h>.  It consists of 8 chars followed by 6 longs.
17293      * Then come 4 more longs that are not used here.
17294      *    Byte 0: magic number 0x01
17295      *    Byte 1: magic number 0x03
17296      *    Byte 2: normal = 0x10 (not checked, 0 is OK), separate I/D = 0x20
17297      *    Byte 3: CPU type, Intel 16 bit = 0x04, Intel 32 bit = 0x10,
17298      *            Motorola = 0x0B, Sun SPARC = 0x17
17299      *    Byte 4: Header length = 0x20
17300      *    Bytes 5-7 are not used.
17301      *
17302      *    Now come the 6 longs
17303      *    Bytes  8-11: size of text segments in bytes
17304      *    Bytes 12-15: size of initialized data segment in bytes
17305      *    Bytes 16-19: size of bss in bytes
17306      *    Bytes 20-23: program entry point
17307      *    Bytes 24-27: total memory allocated to program (text, data + stack)
17308      *    Bytes 28-31: size of symbol table in bytes
17309      * The longs are represented in a machine dependent order,
17310      * little-endian on the 8088, big-endian on the 68000.
17311      * The header is followed directly by the text and data segments, and the
17312      * symbol table (if any). The sizes are given in the header. Only the
17313      * text and data segments are copied into memory by exec. The header is
17314      * used here only. The symbol table is for the benefit of a debugger and
17315      * is ignored here.
17316      */
17317
17318     if (read(fd, (char *) &hdr, A_MINHDR) != A_MINHDR) return(ENOEXEC);
17319
```

```
17320        /* Check magic number, cpu type, and flags. */
17321        if (BADMAG(hdr)) return(ENOEXEC);
17322   #if (CHIP == INTEL && _WORD_SIZE == 2)
17323        if (hdr.a_cpu != A_I8086) return(ENOEXEC);
17324   #endif
17325   #if (CHIP == INTEL && _WORD_SIZE == 4)
17326        if (hdr.a_cpu != A_I80386) return(ENOEXEC);
17327   #endif
17328        if ((hdr.a_flags & ~(A_NSYM | A_EXEC | A_SEP)) != 0) return(ENOEXEC);
17329
17330        *ft = ( (hdr.a_flags & A_SEP) ? SEPARATE : 0);    /* separate I & D or not */
17331
17332        /* Get text and data sizes. */
17333        *text_bytes = (vir_bytes) hdr.a_text; /* text size in bytes */
17334        *data_bytes = (vir_bytes) hdr.a_data; /* data size in bytes */
17335        *bss_bytes  = (vir_bytes) hdr.a_bss;  /* bss size in bytes */
17336        *tot_bytes  = hdr.a_total;            /* total bytes to allocate for prog */
17337        *sym_bytes  = hdr.a_syms;             /* symbol table size in bytes */
17338        if (*tot_bytes == 0) return(ENOEXEC);
17339
17340        if (*ft != SEPARATE) {
17341
17342            /* If I & D space is not separated, it is all considered data. Text=0*/
17343            *data_bytes += *text_bytes;
17344            *text_bytes = 0;
17345
17346        }
17347        *pc = hdr.a_entry;    /* initial address to start execution */
17348
17349        /* Check to see if segment sizes are feasible. */
17350        tc = ((unsigned long) *text_bytes + CLICK_SIZE - 1) >> CLICK_SHIFT;
17351        dc = (*data_bytes + *bss_bytes + CLICK_SIZE - 1) >> CLICK_SHIFT;
17352        totc = (*tot_bytes + CLICK_SIZE - 1) >> CLICK_SHIFT;
17353        if (dc >= totc) return(ENOEXEC);       /* stack must be at least 1 click */
17354        dvir = (*ft == SEPARATE ? 0 : tc);
17355        s_vir = dvir + (totc - sc);
17356        m = size_ok(*ft, tc, dc, sc, dvir, s_vir);
17357        ct = hdr.a_hdrlen & BYTE;              /* header length */
17358        if (ct > A_MINHDR) lseek(fd, (off_t) ct, SEEK_SET); /* skip unused hdr */
17359        return(m);
17360   }


17363   /*===========================================================================*
17364    *                              new_mem                                       *
17365    *===========================================================================*/
17366   PRIVATE int new_mem(sh_mp, text_bytes, data_bytes,bss_bytes,stk_bytes,tot_bytes)
17367   struct mproc *sh_mp;            /* text can be shared with this process */
17368   vir_bytes text_bytes;          /* text segment size in bytes */
17369   vir_bytes data_bytes;          /* size of initialized data in bytes */
17370   vir_bytes bss_bytes;           /* size of bss in bytes */
17371   vir_bytes stk_bytes;           /* size of initial stack segment in bytes */
17372   phys_bytes tot_bytes;          /* total memory to allocate, including gap */
17373   {
17374   /* Allocate new memory and release the old memory.  Change the map and report
17375    * the new map to the kernel.  Zero the new core image's bss, gap and stack.
17376    */
17377
17378     register struct mproc *rmp;
17379     vir_clicks text_clicks, data_clicks, gap_clicks, stack_clicks, tot_clicks;
```

```
17380     phys_clicks new_base;
17381
17382     static char zero[1024];                    /* used to zero bss */
17383     phys_bytes bytes, base, count, bss_offset;
17384
17385     /* No need to allocate text if it can be shared. */
17386     if (sh_mp != NULL) text_bytes = 0;
17387
17388     /* Acquire the new memory.  Each of the 4 parts: text, (data+bss), gap,
17389      * and stack occupies an integral number of clicks, starting at click
17390      * boundary.  The data and bss parts are run together with no space.
17391      */
17392
17393     text_clicks = ((unsigned long) text_bytes + CLICK_SIZE - 1) >> CLICK_SHIFT;
17394     data_clicks = (data_bytes + bss_bytes + CLICK_SIZE - 1) >> CLICK_SHIFT;
17395     stack_clicks = (stk_bytes + CLICK_SIZE - 1) >> CLICK_SHIFT;
17396     tot_clicks = (tot_bytes + CLICK_SIZE - 1) >> CLICK_SHIFT;
17397     gap_clicks = tot_clicks - data_clicks - stack_clicks;
17398     if ( (int) gap_clicks < 0) return(ENOMEM);
17399
17400     /* Check to see if there is a hole big enough.  If so, we can risk first
17401      * releasing the old core image before allocating the new one, since we
17402      * know it will succeed.  If there is not enough, return failure.
17403      */
17404     if (text_clicks + tot_clicks > max_hole()) return(EAGAIN);
17405
17406     /* There is enough memory for the new core image.  Release the old one. */
17407     rmp = mp;
17408
17409     if (find_share(rmp, rmp->mp_ino, rmp->mp_dev, rmp->mp_ctime) == NULL) {
17410           /* No other process shares the text segment, so free it. */
17411           free_mem(rmp->mp_seg[T].mem_phys, rmp->mp_seg[T].mem_len);
17412     }
17413     /* Free the data and stack segments. */
17414     free_mem(rmp->mp_seg[D].mem_phys,
17415         rmp->mp_seg[S].mem_vir + rmp->mp_seg[S].mem_len - rmp->mp_seg[D].mem_vir);
17416
17417     /* We have now passed the point of no return.  The old core image has been
17418      * forever lost.  The call must go through now.  Set up and report new map.
17419      */
17420     new_base = alloc_mem(text_clicks + tot_clicks);      /* new core image */
17421     if (new_base == NO_MEM) panic("MM hole list is inconsistent", NO_NUM);
17422
17423     if (sh_mp != NULL) {
17424           /* Share the text segment. */
17425           rmp->mp_seg[T] = sh_mp->mp_seg[T];
17426     } else {
17427           rmp->mp_seg[T].mem_phys = new_base;
17428           rmp->mp_seg[T].mem_vir = 0;
17429           rmp->mp_seg[T].mem_len = text_clicks;
17430     }
17431     rmp->mp_seg[D].mem_phys = new_base + text_clicks;
17432     rmp->mp_seg[D].mem_vir = 0;
17433     rmp->mp_seg[D].mem_len = data_clicks;
17434     rmp->mp_seg[S].mem_phys = rmp->mp_seg[D].mem_phys + data_clicks + gap_clicks;
17435     rmp->mp_seg[S].mem_vir = rmp->mp_seg[D].mem_vir + data_clicks + gap_clicks;
17436     rmp->mp_seg[S].mem_len = stack_clicks;
17437
17438
17439     sys_newmap(who, rmp->mp_seg);    /* report new map to the kernel */
```

```
17440
17441     /* Zero the bss, gap, and stack segment. */
17442     bytes = (phys_bytes)(data_clicks + gap_clicks + stack_clicks) << CLICK_SHIFT;
17443     base = (phys_bytes) rmp->mp_seg[D].mem_phys << CLICK_SHIFT;
17444     bss_offset = (data_bytes >> CLICK_SHIFT) << CLICK_SHIFT;
17445     base += bss_offset;
17446     bytes -= bss_offset;
17447
17448     while (bytes > 0) {
17449             count = MIN(bytes, (phys_bytes) sizeof(zero));
17450             if (sys_copy(MM_PROC_NR, D, (phys_bytes) zero,
17451                                                 ABS, 0, base, count) != OK) {
17452                     panic("new_mem can't zero", NO_NUM);
17453             }
17454             base += count;
17455             bytes -= count;
17456     }
17457
17458     return(OK);
17459   }


17462   /*===========================================================================*
17463    *                              patch_ptr                                    *
17464    *===========================================================================*/
17465   PRIVATE void patch_ptr(stack, base)
17466   char stack[ARG_MAX];      /* pointer to stack image within MM */
17467   vir_bytes base;                   /* virtual address of stack base inside user */
17468   {
17469   /* When doing an exec(name, argv, envp) call, the user builds up a stack
17470    * image with arg and env pointers relative to the start of the stack.  Now
17471    * these pointers must be relocated, since the stack is not positioned at
17472    * address 0 in the user's address space.
17473    */
17474
17475     char **ap, flag;
17476     vir_bytes v;
17477
17478     flag = 0;                     /* counts number of 0-pointers seen */
17479     ap = (char **) stack;         /* points initially to 'nargs' */
17480     ap++;                         /* now points to argv[0] */
17481     while (flag < 2) {
17482             if (ap >= (char **) &stack[ARG_MAX]) return;     /* too bad */
17483             if (*ap != NIL_PTR) {
17484                     v = (vir_bytes) *ap;    /* v is relative pointer */
17485                     v += base;              /* relocate it */
17486                     *ap = (char *) v;        /* put it back */
17487             } else {
17488                     flag++;
17489             }
17490             ap++;
17491     }
17492   }


17495   /*===========================================================================*
17496    *                              load_seg                                     *
17497    *===========================================================================*/
17498   PRIVATE void load_seg(fd, seg, seg_bytes)
17499   int fd;                           /* file descriptor to read from */
```

```
17500     int seg;                          /* T or D */
17501     vir_bytes seg_bytes;              /* how big is the segment */
17502     {
17503     /* Read in text or data from the exec file and copy to the new core image.
17504      * This procedure is a little bit tricky.  The logical way to load a segment
17505      * would be to read it block by block and copy each block to the user space
17506      * one at a time.  This is too slow, so we do something dirty here, namely
17507      * send the user space and virtual address to the file system in the upper
17508      * 10 bits of the file descriptor, and pass it the user virtual address
17509      * instead of a MM address.  The file system extracts these parameters when
17510      * gets a read call from the memory manager, which is the only process that
17511      * is permitted to use this trick.  The file system then copies the whole
17512      * segment directly to user space, bypassing MM completely.
17513      */
17514
17515       int new_fd, bytes;
17516       char *ubuf_ptr;
17517
17518       new_fd = (who << 8) | (seg << 6) | fd;
17519       ubuf_ptr = (char *) ((vir_bytes)mp->mp_seg[seg].mem_vir << CLICK_SHIFT);
17520       while (seg_bytes != 0) {
17521             bytes = (INT_MAX / BLOCK_SIZE) * BLOCK_SIZE;
17522             if (seg_bytes < bytes)
17523                     bytes = (int)seg_bytes;
17524             if (read(new_fd, ubuf_ptr, bytes) != bytes)
17525                     break;          /* error */
17526             ubuf_ptr += bytes;
17527             seg_bytes -= bytes;
17528       }
17529     }


17532     /*===========================================================================*
17533      *                              find_share                                   *
17534      *===========================================================================*/
17535     PUBLIC struct mproc *find_share(mp_ign, ino, dev, ctime)
17536     struct mproc *mp_ign;            /* process that should not be looked at */
17537     ino_t ino;                       /* parameters that uniquely identify a file */
17538     dev_t dev;
17539     time_t ctime;
17540     {
17541     /* Look for a process that is the file <ino, dev, ctime> in execution.  Don't
17542      * accidentally "find" mp_ign, because it is the process on whose behalf this
17543      * call is made.
17544      */
17545       struct mproc *sh_mp;
17546
17547       for (sh_mp = &mproc[INIT_PROC_NR]; sh_mp < &mproc[NR_PROCS]; sh_mp++) {
17548             if ((sh_mp->mp_flags & (IN_USE | HANGING | SEPARATE))
17549                                         != (IN_USE | SEPARATE)) continue;
17550             if (sh_mp == mp_ign) continue;
17551             if (sh_mp->mp_ino != ino) continue;
17552             if (sh_mp->mp_dev != dev) continue;
17553             if (sh_mp->mp_ctime != ctime) continue;
17554             return sh_mp;
17555       }
17556       return(NULL);
17557     }
```

```
+++++++++++++++++++++++++++++++++++++++++++++++++++++++++++++++++++++++++++++
                              src/mm/break.c
+++++++++++++++++++++++++++++++++++++++++++++++++++++++++++++++++++++++++++++
17600   /* The MINIX model of memory allocation reserves a fixed amount of memory for
17601    * the combined text, data, and stack segments.  The amount used for a child
17602    * process created by FORK is the same as the parent had.  If the child does
17603    * an EXEC later, the new size is taken from the header of the file EXEC'ed.
17604    *
17605    * The layout in memory consists of the text segment, followed by the data
17606    * segment, followed by a gap (unused memory), followed by the stack segment.
17607    * The data segment grows upward and the stack grows downward, so each can
17608    * take memory from the gap.  If they meet, the process must be killed.  The
17609    * procedures in this file deal with the growth of the data and stack segments.
17610    *
17611    * The entry points into this file are:
17612    *   do_brk:      BRK/SBRK system calls to grow or shrink the data segment
17613    *   adjust:      see if a proposed segment adjustment is allowed
17614    *   size_ok:     see if the segment sizes are feasible
17615    */

17617   #include "mm.h"
17618   #include <signal.h>
17619   #include "mproc.h"
17620   #include "param.h"

17622   #define DATA_CHANGED       1    /* flag value when data segment size changed */
17623   #define STACK_CHANGED      2    /* flag value when stack size changed */

17625   /*===========================================================================*
17626    *                              do_brk                                       *
17627    *===========================================================================*/
17628   PUBLIC int do_brk()
17629   {
17630   /* Perform the brk(addr) system call.
17631    *
17632    * The call is complicated by the fact that on some machines (e.g., 8088),
17633    * the stack pointer can grow beyond the base of the stack segment without
17634    * anybody noticing it.
17635    * The parameter, 'addr' is the new virtual address in D space.
17636    */

17638     register struct mproc *rmp;
17639     int r;
17640     vir_bytes v, new_sp;
17641     vir_clicks new_clicks;

17643     rmp = mp;
17644     v = (vir_bytes) addr;
17645     new_clicks = (vir_clicks) ( ((long) v + CLICK_SIZE - 1) >> CLICK_SHIFT);
17646     if (new_clicks < rmp->mp_seg[D].mem_vir) {
17647           res_ptr = (char *) -1;
17648           return(ENOMEM);
17649     }
17650     new_clicks -= rmp->mp_seg[D].mem_vir;
17651     sys_getsp(who, &new_sp);        /* ask kernel for current sp value */
17652     r = adjust(rmp, new_clicks, new_sp);
17653     res_ptr = (r == OK ? addr : (char *) -1);
17654     return(r);                      /* return new address or -1 */
```

```
17655        }


17658        /*===========================================================================*
17659         *                                adjust                                     *
17660         *===========================================================================*/
17661        PUBLIC int adjust(rmp, data_clicks, sp)
17662        register struct mproc *rmp;          /* whose memory is being adjusted? */
17663        vir_clicks data_clicks;              /* how big is data segment to become? */
17664        vir_bytes sp;                        /* new value of sp */
17665        {
17666        /* See if data and stack segments can coexist, adjusting them if need be.
17667         * Memory is never allocated or freed.  Instead it is added or removed from the
17668         * gap between data segment and stack segment.  If the gap size becomes
17669         * negative, the adjustment of data or stack fails and ENOMEM is returned.
17670         */
17671
17672          register struct mem_map *mem_sp, *mem_dp;
17673          vir_clicks sp_click, gap_base, lower, old_clicks;
17674          int changed, r, ft;
17675          long base_of_stack, delta;     /* longs avoid certain problems */
17676
17677          mem_dp = &rmp->mp_seg[D];       /* pointer to data segment map */
17678          mem_sp = &rmp->mp_seg[S];       /* pointer to stack segment map */
17679          changed = 0;                   /* set when either segment changed */
17680
17681          if (mem_sp->mem_len == 0) return(OK); /* don't bother init */
17682
17683          /* See if stack size has gone negative (i.e., sp too close to 0xFFFF...) */
17684          base_of_stack = (long) mem_sp->mem_vir + (long) mem_sp->mem_len;
17685          sp_click = sp >> CLICK_SHIFT; /* click containing sp */
17686          if (sp_click >= base_of_stack) return(ENOMEM);          /* sp too high */
17687
17688          /* Compute size of gap between stack and data segments. */
17689          delta = (long) mem_sp->mem_vir - (long) sp_click;
17690          lower = (delta > 0 ? sp_click : mem_sp->mem_vir);
17691
17692          /* Add a safety margin for future stack growth. Impossible to do right. */
17693        #define SAFETY_BYTES   (384 * sizeof(char *))
17694        #define SAFETY_CLICKS ((SAFETY_BYTES + CLICK_SIZE - 1) / CLICK_SIZE)
17695          gap_base = mem_dp->mem_vir + data_clicks + SAFETY_CLICKS;
17696          if (lower < gap_base) return(ENOMEM); /* data and stack collided */
17697
17698          /* Update data length (but not data orgin) on behalf of brk() system call. */
17699          old_clicks = mem_dp->mem_len;
17700          if (data_clicks != mem_dp->mem_len) {
17701                mem_dp->mem_len = data_clicks;
17702                changed |= DATA_CHANGED;
17703          }
17704
17705          /* Update stack length and origin due to change in stack pointer. */
17706          if (delta > 0) {
17707                mem_sp->mem_vir -= delta;
17708                mem_sp->mem_phys -= delta;
17709                mem_sp->mem_len += delta;
17710                changed |= STACK_CHANGED;
17711          }
17712
17713          /* Do the new data and stack segment sizes fit in the address space? */
17714          ft = (rmp->mp_flags & SEPARATE);
```

```
17715      r = size_ok(ft, rmp->mp_seg[T].mem_len, rmp->mp_seg[D].mem_len,
17716           rmp->mp_seg[S].mem_len, rmp->mp_seg[D].mem_vir, rmp->mp_seg[S].mem_vir);
17717      if (r == OK) {
17718           if (changed) sys_newmap((int)(rmp - mproc), rmp->mp_seg);
17719           return(OK);
17720      }
17721
17722      /* New sizes don't fit or require too many page/segment registers. Restore.*/
17723      if (changed & DATA_CHANGED) mem_dp->mem_len = old_clicks;
17724      if (changed & STACK_CHANGED) {
17725           mem_sp->mem_vir += delta;
17726           mem_sp->mem_phys += delta;
17727           mem_sp->mem_len -= delta;
17728      }
17729      return(ENOMEM);
17730  }


17733  /*===========================================================================*
17734   *                              size_ok                                       *
17735   *===========================================================================*/
17736  PUBLIC int size_ok(file_type, tc, dc, sc, dvir, s_vir)
17737  int file_type;                  /* SEPARATE or 0 */
17738  vir_clicks tc;                  /* text size in clicks */
17739  vir_clicks dc;                  /* data size in clicks */
17740  vir_clicks sc;                  /* stack size in clicks */
17741  vir_clicks dvir;                /* virtual address for start of data seg */
17742  vir_clicks s_vir;               /* virtual address for start of stack seg */
17743  {
17744  /* Check to see if the sizes are feasible and enough segmentation registers
17745   * exist.  On a machine with eight 8K pages, text, data, stack sizes of
17746   * (32K, 16K, 16K) will fit, but (33K, 17K, 13K) will not, even though the
17747   * former is bigger (64K) than the latter (63K).  Even on the 8088 this test
17748   * is needed, since the data and stack may not exceed 4096 clicks.
17749   */
17750
17751  #if (CHIP == INTEL && _WORD_SIZE == 2)
17752    int pt, pd, ps;                /* segment sizes in pages */
17753
17754    pt = ( (tc << CLICK_SHIFT) + PAGE_SIZE - 1)/PAGE_SIZE;
17755    pd = ( (dc << CLICK_SHIFT) + PAGE_SIZE - 1)/PAGE_SIZE;
17756    ps = ( (sc << CLICK_SHIFT) + PAGE_SIZE - 1)/PAGE_SIZE;
17757
17758    if (file_type == SEPARATE) {
17759         if (pt > MAX_PAGES || pd + ps > MAX_PAGES) return(ENOMEM);
17760    } else {
17761         if (pt + pd + ps > MAX_PAGES) return(ENOMEM);
17762    }
17763  #endif
17764
17765    if (dvir + dc > s_vir) return(ENOMEM);
17766
17767    return(OK);
17768  }
```

```
++++++++++++++++++++++++++++++++++++++++++++++++++++++++++++++++++++++++++++++++
                              src/mm/signal.c
++++++++++++++++++++++++++++++++++++++++++++++++++++++++++++++++++++++++++++++++
17800   /* This file handles signals, which are asynchronous events and are generally
17801    * a messy and unpleasant business.  Signals can be generated by the KILL
17802    * system call, or from the keyboard (SIGINT) or from the clock (SIGALRM).
17803    * In all cases control eventually passes to check_sig() to see which processes
17804    * can be signaled.  The actual signaling is done by sig_proc().
17805    *
17806    * The entry points into this file are:
17807    *   do_sigaction:   perform the SIGACTION system call
17808    *   do_sigpending:  perform the SIGPENDING system call
17809    *   do_sigprocmask: perform the SIGPROCMASK system call
17810    *   do_sigreturn:   perform the SIGRETURN system call
17811    *   do_sigsuspend:  perform the SIGSUSPEND system call
17812    *   do_kill:  perform the KILL system call
17813    *   do_ksig:  accept a signal originating in the kernel (e.g., SIGINT)
17814    *   do_alarm:  perform the ALARM system call by calling set_alarm()
17815    *   set_alarm: tell the clock task to start or stop a timer
17816    *   do_pause:  perform the PAUSE system call
17817    *   do_reboot: kill all processes, then reboot system
17818    *   sig_proc:  interrupt or terminate a signaled process
17819    *   check_sig: check which processes to signal with sig_proc()
17820    */

17822   #include "mm.h"
17823   #include <sys/stat.h>
17824   #include <minix/callnr.h>
17825   #include <minix/com.h>
17826   #include <signal.h>
17827   #include <sys/sigcontext.h>
17828   #include <string.h>
17829   #include "mproc.h"
17830   #include "param.h"

17832   #define CORE_MODE      0777    /* mode to use on core image files */
17833   #define DUMPED         0200    /* bit set in status when core dumped */
17834   #define DUMP_SIZE      ((INT_MAX / BLOCK_SIZE) * BLOCK_SIZE)
17835                                  /* buffer size for core dumps */

17837   FORWARD _PROTOTYPE( void check_pending, (void)                       );
17838   FORWARD _PROTOTYPE( void dump_core, (struct mproc *rmp)              );
17839   FORWARD _PROTOTYPE( void unpause, (int pro)                          );


17842   /*===========================================================================*
17843    *                              do_sigaction                                 *
17844    *===========================================================================*/
17845   PUBLIC int do_sigaction()
17846   {
17847     int r;
17848     struct sigaction svec;
17849     struct sigaction *svp;

17851     if (sig_nr == SIGKILL) return(OK);
17852     if (sig_nr < 1 || sig_nr > _NSIG) return (EINVAL);
17853     svp = &mp->mp_sigact[sig_nr];
17854     if ((struct sigaction *) sig_osa != (struct sigaction *) NULL) {
```

```
17855            r = sys_copy(MM_PROC_NR,D, (phys_bytes) svp,
17856                    who, D, (phys_bytes) sig_osa, (phys_bytes) sizeof(svec));
17857            if (r != OK) return(r);
17858        }
17859
17860        if ((struct sigaction *) sig_nsa == (struct sigaction *) NULL) return(OK);
17861
17862        /* Read in the sigaction structure. */
17863        r = sys_copy(who, D, (phys_bytes) sig_nsa,
17864                    MM_PROC_NR, D, (phys_bytes) &svec, (phys_bytes) sizeof(svec));
17865        if (r != OK) return(r);
17866
17867        if (svec.sa_handler == SIG_IGN) {
17868            sigaddset(&mp->mp_ignore, sig_nr);
17869            sigdelset(&mp_sigpending, sig_nr);
17870            sigdelset(&mp->mp_catch, sig_nr);
17871        } else {
17872            sigdelset(&mp->mp_ignore, sig_nr);
17873            if (svec.sa_handler == SIG_DFL)
17874                    sigdelset(&mp->mp_catch, sig_nr);
17875            else
17876                    sigaddset(&mp->mp_catch, sig_nr);
17877        }
17878        mp->mp_sigact[sig_nr].sa_handler = svec.sa_handler;
17879        sigdelset(&svec.sa_mask, SIGKILL);
17880        mp->mp_sigact[sig_nr].sa_mask = svec.sa_mask;
17881        mp->mp_sigact[sig_nr].sa_flags = svec.sa_flags;
17882        mp->mp_sigreturn = (vir_bytes) sig_ret;
17883        return(OK);
17884    }

17886    /*===========================================================================*
17887     *                              do_sigpending                                *
17888     *===========================================================================*/
17889    PUBLIC int do_sigpending()
17890    {
17891      ret_mask = (long) mp->mp_sigpending;
17892      return OK;
17893    }

17895    /*===========================================================================*
17896     *                              do_sigprocmask                               *
17897     *===========================================================================*/
17898    PUBLIC int do_sigprocmask()
17899    {
17900    /* Note that the library interface passes the actual mask in sigmask_set,
17901     * not a pointer to the mask, in order to save a sys_copy.  Similarly,
17902     * the old mask is placed in the return message which the library
17903     * interface copies (if requested) to the user specified address.
17904     *
17905     * The library interface must set SIG_INQUIRE if the 'act' argument
17906     * is NULL.
17907     */
17908
17909      int i;
17910
17911      ret_mask = (long) mp->mp_sigmask;
17912
17913      switch (sig_how) {
17914          case SIG_BLOCK:
```

```
17915                    sigdelset((sigset_t *)&sig_set, SIGKILL);
17916                    for (i = 1; i < _NSIG; i++) {
17917                            if (sigismember((sigset_t *)&sig_set, i))
17918                                    sigaddset(&mp->mp_sigmask, i);
17919                    }
17920                  break;
17921
17922               case SIG_UNBLOCK:
17923                    for (i = 1; i < _NSIG; i++) {
17924                            if (sigismember((sigset_t *)&sig_set, i))
17925                                    sigdelset(&mp->mp_sigmask, i);
17926                    }
17927                  check_pending();
17928                  break;
17929
17930               case SIG_SETMASK:
17931                    sigdelset((sigset_t *)&sig_set, SIGKILL);
17932                    mp->mp_sigmask = (sigset_t)sig_set;
17933                  check_pending();
17934                  break;
17935
17936               case SIG_INQUIRE:
17937                  break;
17938
17939               default:
17940                  return(EINVAL);
17941                  break;
17942         }
17943       return OK;
17944       }
17945
17946       /*===========================================================================*
17947        *                              do_sigsuspend                                *
17948        *===========================================================================*/
17949       PUBLIC int do_sigsuspend()
17950       {
17951         mp->mp_sigmask2 = mp->mp_sigmask;      /* save the old mask */
17952         mp->mp_sigmask = (sigset_t) sig_set;
17953         sigdelset(&mp->mp_sigmask, SIGKILL);
17954         mp->mp_flags |= SIGSUSPENDED;
17955         dont_reply = TRUE;
17956         check_pending();
17957         return OK;
17958       }
17959
17960
17961       /*===========================================================================*
17962        *                              do_sigreturn                                 *
17963        *===========================================================================*/
17964       PUBLIC int do_sigreturn()
17965       {
17966       /* A user signal handler is done.  Restore context and check for
17967        * pending unblocked signals.
17968        */
17969
17970         int r;
17971
17972         mp->mp_sigmask = (sigset_t) sig_set;
17973         sigdelset(&mp->mp_sigmask, SIGKILL);
17974
```

```
17975        r = sys_sigreturn(who, (vir_bytes)sig_context, sig_flags);
17976        check_pending();
17977        return(r);
17978    }


17980    /*===========================================================================*
17981     *                                do_kill                                     *
17982     *===========================================================================*/
17983    PUBLIC int do_kill()
17984    {
17985    /* Perform the kill(pid, signo) system call. */

17987        return check_sig(pid, sig_nr);
17988    }



17991    /*===========================================================================*
17992     *                                do_ksig                                     *
17993     *===========================================================================*/
17994    PUBLIC int do_ksig()
17995    {
17996    /* Certain signals, such as segmentation violations and DEL, originate in the
17997     * kernel.  When the kernel detects such signals, it sets bits in a bit map.
17998     * As soon as MM is awaiting new work, the kernel sends MM a message containing
17999     * the process slot and bit map.  That message comes here.  The File System
18000     * also uses this mechanism to signal writing on broken pipes (SIGPIPE).
18001     */

18003        register struct mproc *rmp;
18004        int i, proc_nr;
18005        pid_t proc_id, id;
18006        sigset_t sig_map;

18008        /* Only kernel may make this call. */
18009        if (who != HARDWARE) return(EPERM);
18010        dont_reply = TRUE;              /* don't reply to the kernel */
18011        proc_nr = mm_in.SIG_PROC;
18012        rmp = &mproc[proc_nr];
18013        if ( (rmp->mp_flags & IN_USE) == 0 || (rmp->mp_flags & HANGING) ) return(OK);
18014        proc_id = rmp->mp_pid;
18015        sig_map = (sigset_t) mm_in.SIG_MAP;
18016        mp = &mproc[0];                 /* pretend kernel signals are from MM */
18017        mp->mp_procgrp = rmp->mp_procgrp;       /* get process group right */

18019        /* Check each bit in turn to see if a signal is to be sent.  Unlike
18020         * kill(), the kernel may collect several unrelated signals for a
18021         * process and pass them to MM in one blow.  Thus loop on the bit
18022         * map. For SIGINT and SIGQUIT, use proc_id 0 to indicate a broadcast
18023         * to the recipient's process group.  For SIGKILL, use proc_id -1 to
18024         * indicate a systemwide broadcast.
18025         */
18026        for (i = 1; i <= _NSIG; i++) {
18027            if (!sigismember(&sig_map, i)) continue;
18028            switch (i) {
18029                case SIGINT:
18030                case SIGQUIT:
18031                    id = 0; break;  /* broadcast to process group */
18032                case SIGKILL:
18033                    id = -1; break; /* broadcast to all except INIT */
18034                case SIGALRM:
```

```
18035                              /* Disregard SIGALRM when the target process has not
18036                               * requested an alarm.  This only applies for a KERNEL
18037                               * generated signal.
18038                               */
18039                              if ((rmp->mp_flags & ALARM_ON) == 0) continue;
18040                              rmp->mp_flags &= ~ALARM_ON;
18041                              /* fall through */
18042                      default:
18043                              id = proc_id;
18044                              break;
18045                  }
18046              check_sig(id, i);
18047              sys_endsig(proc_nr);     /* tell kernel it's done */
18048          }
18049      return(OK);
18050  }


18053      /*===========================================================================*
18054       *                              do_alarm                                     *
18055       *===========================================================================*/
18056  PUBLIC int do_alarm()
18057  {
18058  /* Perform the alarm(seconds) system call. */
18059
18060      return(set_alarm(who, seconds));
18061  }


18064      /*===========================================================================*
18065       *                              set_alarm                                    *
18066       *===========================================================================*/
18067  PUBLIC int set_alarm(proc_nr, sec)
18068  int proc_nr;                            /* process that wants the alarm */
18069  int sec;                                /* how many seconds delay before the signal */
18070  {
18071  /* This routine is used by do_alarm() to set the alarm timer.  It is also used
18072   * to turn the timer off when a process exits with the timer still on.
18073   */
18074
18075      message m_sig;
18076      int remaining;
18077
18078      if (sec != 0)
18079              mproc[proc_nr].mp_flags |= ALARM_ON;
18080      else
18081              mproc[proc_nr].mp_flags &= ~ALARM_ON;
18082
18083      /* Tell the clock task to provide a signal message when the time comes.
18084       *
18085       * Large delays cause a lot of problems.  First, the alarm system call
18086       * takes an unsigned seconds count and the library has cast it to an int.
18087       * That probably works, but on return the library will convert "negative"
18088       * unsigneds to errors.  Presumably no one checks for these errors, so
18089       * force this call through.  Second, If unsigned and long have the same
18090       * size, converting from seconds to ticks can easily overflow.  Finally,
18091       * the kernel has similar overflow bugs adding ticks.
18092       *
18093       * Fixing this requires a lot of ugly casts to fit the wrong interface
18094       * types and to avoid overflow traps.  DELTA_TICKS has the right type
```

```
18095        * (clock_t) although it is declared as long.  How can variables like
18096        * this be declared properly without combinatorial explosion of message
18097        * types?
18098        */
18099       m_sig.m_type = SET_ALARM;
18100       m_sig.CLOCK_PROC_NR = proc_nr;
18101       m_sig.DELTA_TICKS = (clock_t) (HZ * (unsigned long) (unsigned) sec);
18102       if ( (unsigned long) m_sig.DELTA_TICKS / HZ != (unsigned) sec)
18103            m_sig.DELTA_TICKS = LONG_MAX;    /* eternity (really CLOCK_T_MAX) */
18104       if (sendrec(CLOCK, &m_sig) != OK) panic("alarm er", NO_NUM);
18105       remaining = (int) m_sig.SECONDS_LEFT;
18106       if (remaining != m_sig.SECONDS_LEFT || remaining < 0)
18107            remaining = INT_MAX;     /* true value is not representable */
18108       return(remaining);
18109     }


18112     /*===========================================================================*
18113      *                            do_pause                                       *
18114      *===========================================================================*/
18115     PUBLIC int do_pause()
18116     {
18117     /* Perform the pause() system call. */
18118
18119       mp->mp_flags |= PAUSED;
18120       dont_reply = TRUE;
18121       return(OK);
18122     }


18125     /*===========================================================================*
18126      *                            do_reboot                                      *
18127      *===========================================================================*/
18128     PUBLIC int do_reboot()
18129     {
18130       register struct mproc *rmp = mp;
18131       char monitor_code[64];
18132
18133       if (rmp->mp_effuid != SUPER_USER)    return EPERM;
18134
18135       switch (reboot_flag) {
18136       case RBT_HALT:
18137       case RBT_REBOOT:
18138       case RBT_PANIC:
18139       case RBT_RESET:
18140            break;
18141       case RBT_MONITOR:
18142            if (reboot_size > sizeof(monitor_code)) return EINVAL;
18143            memset(monitor_code, 0, sizeof(monitor_code));
18144            if (sys_copy(who, D, (phys_bytes) reboot_code,
18145                 MM_PROC_NR, D, (phys_bytes) monitor_code,
18146                 (phys_bytes) reboot_size) != OK) return EFAULT;
18147            if (monitor_code[sizeof(monitor_code)-1] != 0) return EINVAL;
18148            break;
18149       default:
18150            return EINVAL;
18151       }
18152
18153       /* Kill all processes except init. */
18154       check_sig(-1, SIGKILL);
```

```
18155
18156        tell_fs(EXIT, INIT_PROC_NR, 0, 0);      /* cleanup init */
18157
18158        tell_fs(SYNC,0,0,0);
18159
18160        sys_abort(reboot_flag, monitor_code);
18161        /* NOTREACHED */
18162    }


18165    /*===========================================================================*
18166     *                                sig_proc                                    *
18167     *===========================================================================*/
18168    PUBLIC void sig_proc(rmp, signo)
18169    register struct mproc *rmp;        /* pointer to the process to be signaled */
18170    int signo;                         /* signal to send to process (1 to _NSIG) */
18171    {
18172    /* Send a signal to a process.  Check to see if the signal is to be caught,
18173     * ignored, or blocked.  If the signal is to be caught, coordinate with
18174     * KERNEL to push a sigcontext structure and a sigframe structure onto
18175     * the catcher's stack.  Also, KERNEL will reset the program counter and
18176     * stack pointer, so that when the process next runs, it will be executing
18177     * the signal handler.  When the signal handler returns,  sigreturn(2)
18178     * will be called.  Then KERNEL will restore the signal context from the
18179     * sigcontext structure.
18180     *
18181     * If there is insufficient stack space, kill the process.
18182     */
18183
18184      vir_bytes new_sp;
18185      int slot;
18186      int sigflags;
18187      struct sigmsg sm;
18188
18189      slot = (int) (rmp - mproc);
18190      if (!(rmp->mp_flags & IN_USE)) {
18191          printf("MM: signal %d sent to dead process %d\n", signo, slot);
18192          panic("", NO_NUM);
18193      }
18194      if (rmp->mp_flags & HANGING) {
18195          printf("MM: signal %d sent to HANGING process %d\n", signo, slot);
18196          panic("", NO_NUM);
18197      }
18198      if (rmp->mp_flags & TRACED && signo != SIGKILL) {
18199          /* A traced process has special handling. */
18200          unpause(slot);
18201          stop_proc(rmp, signo);  /* a signal causes it to stop */
18202          return;
18203      }
18204      /* Some signals are ignored by default. */
18205      if (sigismember(&rmp->mp_ignore, signo)) return;
18206
18207      if (sigismember(&rmp->mp_sigmask, signo)) {
18208          /* Signal should be blocked. */
18209          sigaddset(&rmp->mp_sigpending, signo);
18210          return;
18211      }
18212      sigflags = rmp->mp_sigact[signo].sa_flags;
18213      if (sigismember(&rmp->mp_catch, signo)) {
18214          if (rmp->mp_flags & SIGSUSPENDED)
```

```
18215                         sm.sm_mask = rmp->mp_sigmask2;
18216               else
18217                         sm.sm_mask = rmp->mp_sigmask;
18218             sm.sm_signo = signo;
18219             sm.sm_sighandler = (vir_bytes) rmp->mp_sigact[signo].sa_handler;
18220             sm.sm_sigreturn = rmp->mp_sigreturn;
18221             sys_getsp(slot, &new_sp);
18222             sm.sm_stkptr = new_sp;
18223
18224             /* Make room for the sigcontext and sigframe struct. */
18225             new_sp -= sizeof(struct sigcontext)
18226                                     + 3 * sizeof(char *) + 2 * sizeof(int);
18227
18228             if (adjust(rmp, rmp->mp_seg[D].mem_len, new_sp) != OK)
18229                     goto doterminate;
18230
18231             rmp->mp_sigmask |= rmp->mp_sigact[signo].sa_mask;
18232             if (sigflags & SA_NODEFER)
18233                     sigdelset(&rmp->mp_sigmask, signo);
18234             else
18235                     sigaddset(&rmp->mp_sigmask, signo);
18236
18237             if (sigflags & SA_RESETHAND) {
18238                     sigdelset(&rmp->mp_catch, signo);
18239                     rmp->mp_sigact[signo].sa_handler = SIG_DFL;
18240             }
18241
18242             sys_sendsig(slot, &sm);
18243             sigdelset(&rmp->mp_sigpending, signo);
18244             /* If process is hanging on PAUSE, WAIT, SIGSUSPEND, tty, pipe, etc.,
18245              * release it.
18246              */
18247             unpause(slot);
18248             return;
18249       }
18250   doterminate:
18251     /* Signal should not or cannot be caught.  Terminate the process. */
18252     rmp->mp_sigstatus = (char) signo;
18253     if (sigismember(&core_sset, signo)) {
18254             /* Switch to the user's FS environment and dump core. */
18255             tell_fs(CHDIR, slot, FALSE, 0);
18256             dump_core(rmp);
18257     }
18258     mm_exit(rmp, 0);                    /* terminate process */
18259   }


18262   /*===========================================================================*
18263    *                              check_sig                                     *
18264    *===========================================================================*/
18265   PUBLIC int check_sig(proc_id, signo)
18266   pid_t proc_id;                         /* pid of proc to sig, or 0 or -1, or -pgrp */
18267   int signo;                             /* signal to send to process (0 to _NSIG) */
18268   {
18269   /* Check to see if it is possible to send a signal.  The signal may have to be
18270    * sent to a group of processes.  This routine is invoked by the KILL system
18271    * call, and also when the kernel catches a DEL or other signal.
18272    */
18273
18274     register struct mproc *rmp;
```

```
18275          int count;                          /* count # of signals sent */
18276          int error_code;
18277
18278          if (signo < 0 || signo > _NSIG) return(EINVAL);
18279
18280          /* Return EINVAL for attempts to send SIGKILL to INIT alone. */
18281          if (proc_id == INIT_PID && signo == SIGKILL) return(EINVAL);
18282
18283          /* Search the proc table for processes to signal.  (See forkexit.c about
18284           * pid magic.)
18285           */
18286          count = 0;
18287          error_code = ESRCH;
18288          for (rmp = &mproc[INIT_PROC_NR]; rmp < &mproc[NR_PROCS]; rmp++) {
18289                  if ( (rmp->mp_flags & IN_USE) == 0) continue;
18290                  if (rmp->mp_flags & HANGING && signo != 0) continue;
18291
18292                  /* Check for selection. */
18293                  if (proc_id > 0 && proc_id != rmp->mp_pid) continue;
18294                  if (proc_id == 0 && mp->mp_procgrp != rmp->mp_procgrp) continue;
18295                  if (proc_id == -1 && rmp->mp_pid == INIT_PID) continue;
18296                  if (proc_id < -1 && rmp->mp_procgrp != -proc_id) continue;
18297
18298                  /* Check for permission. */
18299                  if (mp->mp_effuid != SUPER_USER
18300                      && mp->mp_realuid != rmp->mp_realuid
18301                      && mp->mp_effuid != rmp->mp_realuid
18302                      && mp->mp_realuid != rmp->mp_effuid
18303                      && mp->mp_effuid != rmp->mp_effuid) {
18304                          error_code = EPERM;
18305                          continue;
18306                  }
18307
18308                  count++;
18309                  if (signo == 0) continue;
18310
18311                  /* 'sig_proc' will handle the disposition of the signal.  The
18312                   * signal may be caught, blocked, ignored, or cause process
18313                   * termination, possibly with core dump.
18314                   */
18315                  sig_proc(rmp, signo);
18316
18317                  if (proc_id > 0) break; /* only one process being signaled */
18318          }
18319
18320          /* If the calling process has killed itself, don't reply. */
18321          if ((mp->mp_flags & IN_USE) == 0 || (mp->mp_flags & HANGING))
18322                  dont_reply = TRUE;
18323          return(count > 0 ? OK : error_code);
18324  }


18327  /*===========================================================================*
18328   *                              check_pending                                 *
18329   *===========================================================================*/
18330  PRIVATE void check_pending()
18331  {
18332    /* Check to see if any pending signals have been unblocked.  The
18333     * first such signal found is delivered.
18334     *
```

```
18335        * If multiple pending unmasked signals are found, they will be
18336        * delivered sequentially.
18337        *
18338        * There are several places in this file where the signal mask is
18339        * changed.  At each such place, check_pending() should be called to
18340        * check for newly unblocked signals.
18341        */

18343       int i;

18345       for (i = 1; i < _NSIG; i++) {
18346             if (sigismember(&mp->mp_sigpending, i) &&
18347                     !sigismember(&mp->mp_sigmask, i)) {
18348                     sigdelset(&mp->mp_sigpending, i);
18349                     sig_proc(mp, i);
18350                     break;
18351             }
18352       }
18353 }


18356 /*===========================================================================*
18357  *                              unpause                                       *
18358  *===========================================================================*/
18359 PRIVATE void unpause(pro)
18360 int pro;                        /* which process number */
18361 {
18362 /* A signal is to be sent to a process.  If that process is hanging on a
18363  * system call, the system call must be terminated with EINTR.  Possible
18364  * calls are PAUSE, WAIT, READ and WRITE, the latter two for pipes and ttys.
18365  * First check if the process is hanging on an MM call.  If not, tell FS,
18366  * so it can check for READs and WRITEs from pipes, ttys and the like.
18367  */

18369   register struct mproc *rmp;

18371   rmp = &mproc[pro];

18373   /* Check to see if process is hanging on a PAUSE call. */
18374   if ( (rmp->mp_flags & PAUSED) && (rmp->mp_flags & HANGING) == 0) {
18375         rmp->mp_flags &= ~PAUSED;
18376         reply(pro, EINTR, 0, NIL_PTR);
18377         return;
18378   }

18380   /* Check to see if process is hanging on a WAIT call. */
18381   if ( (rmp->mp_flags & WAITING) && (rmp->mp_flags & HANGING) == 0) {
18382         rmp->mp_flags &= ~WAITING;
18383         reply(pro, EINTR, 0, NIL_PTR);
18384         return;
18385   }

18387   /* Check to see if process is hanging on a SIGSUSPEND call. */
18388   if ((rmp->mp_flags & SIGSUSPENDED) && (rmp->mp_flags & HANGING) == 0) {
18389         rmp->mp_flags &= ~SIGSUSPENDED;
18390         reply(pro, EINTR, 0, NIL_PTR);
18391         return;
18392   }

18394   /* Process is not hanging on an MM call.  Ask FS to take a look. */
```

```
18395                   tell_fs(UNPAUSE, pro, 0, 0);
18396      }


18399      /*===========================================================================*
18400       *                                dump_core                                  *
18401       *===========================================================================*/
18402      PRIVATE void dump_core(rmp)
18403      register struct mproc *rmp;         /* whose core is to be dumped */
18404      {
18405      /* Make a core dump on the file "core", if possible. */
18406
18407        int fd, fake_fd, nr_written, seg, slot;
18408        char *buf;
18409        vir_bytes current_sp;
18410        phys_bytes left;                   /* careful; 64K might overflow vir_bytes */
18411        unsigned nr_to_write;              /* unsigned for arg to write() but < INT_MAX */
18412        long trace_data, trace_off;
18413
18414        slot = (int) (rmp - mproc);
18415
18416        /* Can core file be written?  We are operating in the user's FS environment,
18417         * so no special permission checks are needed.
18418         */
18419        if (rmp->mp_realuid != rmp->mp_effuid) return;
18420        if ( (fd = creat(core_name, CORE_MODE)) < 0) return;
18421        rmp->mp_sigstatus |= DUMPED;
18422
18423        /* Make sure the stack segment is up to date.
18424         * We don't want adjust() to fail unless current_sp is preposterous,
18425         * but it might fail due to safety checking.  Also, we don't really want
18426         * the adjust() for sending a signal to fail due to safety checking.
18427         * Maybe make SAFETY_BYTES a parameter.
18428         */
18429        sys_getsp(slot, &current_sp);
18430        adjust(rmp, rmp->mp_seg[D].mem_len, current_sp);
18431
18432        /* Write the memory map of all segments to begin the core file. */
18433        if (write(fd, (char *) rmp->mp_seg, (unsigned) sizeof rmp->mp_seg)
18434            != (unsigned) sizeof rmp->mp_seg) {
18435            close(fd);
18436            return;
18437        }
18438
18439        /* Write out the whole kernel process table entry to get the regs. */
18440        trace_off = 0;
18441        while (sys_trace(3, slot, trace_off, &trace_data) == OK) {
18442            if (write(fd, (char *) &trace_data, (unsigned) sizeof (long))
18443                != (unsigned) sizeof (long)) {
18444                    close(fd);
18445                    return;
18446            }
18447            trace_off += sizeof (long);
18448        }
18449
18450        /* Loop through segments and write the segments themselves out. */
18451        for (seg = 0; seg < NR_SEGS; seg++) {
18452            buf = (char *) ((vir_bytes) rmp->mp_seg[seg].mem_vir << CLICK_SHIFT);
18453            left = (phys_bytes) rmp->mp_seg[seg].mem_len << CLICK_SHIFT;
18454            fake_fd = (slot << 8) | (seg << 6) | fd;
```

```
18455
18456              /* Loop through a segment, dumping it. */
18457              while (left != 0) {
18458                      nr_to_write = (unsigned) MIN(left, DUMP_SIZE);
18459                      if ( (nr_written = write(fake_fd, buf, nr_to_write)) < 0) {
18460                              close(fd);
18461                              return;
18462                      }
18463                      buf += nr_written;
18464                      left -= nr_written;
18465              }
18466      }
18467      close(fd);
18468 }


++++++++++++++++++++++++++++++++++++++++++++++++++++++++++++++++++++++++++++++++++
                              src/mm/getset.c
++++++++++++++++++++++++++++++++++++++++++++++++++++++++++++++++++++++++++++++++++

18500  /* This file handles the 4 system calls that get and set uids and gids.
18501   * It also handles getpid(), setsid(), and getpgrp().  The code for each
18502   * one is so tiny that it hardly seemed worthwhile to make each a separate
18503   * function.
18504   */
18505
18506  #include "mm.h"
18507  #include <minix/callnr.h>
18508  #include <signal.h>
18509  #include "mproc.h"
18510  #include "param.h"
18511
18512  /*===========================================================================*
18513   *                              do_getset                                    *
18514   *===========================================================================*/
18515  PUBLIC int do_getset()
18516  {
18517  /* Handle GETUID, GETGID, GETPID, GETPGRP, SETUID, SETGID, SETSID.  The four
18518   * GETs and SETSID return their primary results in 'r'.  GETUID, GETGID, and
18519   * GETPID also return secondary results (the effective IDs, or the parent
18520   * process ID) in 'result2', which is returned to the user.
18521   */
18522
18523    register struct mproc *rmp = mp;
18524    register int r;
18525
18526    switch(mm_call) {
18527        case GETUID:
18528                r = rmp->mp_realuid;
18529                result2 = rmp->mp_effuid;
18530                break;
18531
18532        case GETGID:
18533                r = rmp->mp_realgid;
18534                result2 = rmp->mp_effgid;
18535                break;
18536
18537        case GETPID:
18538                r = mproc[who].mp_pid;
18539                result2 = mproc[rmp->mp_parent].mp_pid;
```

```
18540                           break;
18541
18542               case SETUID:
18543                       if (rmp->mp_realuid != usr_id && rmp->mp_effuid != SUPER_USER)
18544                               return(EPERM);
18545                       rmp->mp_realuid = usr_id;
18546                       rmp->mp_effuid = usr_id;
18547                       tell_fs(SETUID, who, usr_id, usr_id);
18548                       r = OK;
18549                       break;
18550
18551               case SETGID:
18552                       if (rmp->mp_realgid != grpid && rmp->mp_effuid != SUPER_USER)
18553                               return(EPERM);
18554                       rmp->mp_realgid = grpid;
18555                       rmp->mp_effgid = grpid;
18556                       tell_fs(SETGID, who, grpid, grpid);
18557                       r = OK;
18558                       break;
18559
18560               case SETSID:
18561                       if (rmp->mp_procgrp == rmp->mp_pid) return(EPERM);
18562                       rmp->mp_procgrp = rmp->mp_pid;
18563                       tell_fs(SETSID, who, 0, 0);
18564                       /*FALL THROUGH*/
18565
18566               case GETPGRP:
18567                       r = rmp->mp_procgrp;
18568                       break;
18569
18570               default:
18571                       r = EINVAL;
18572                       break;
18573        }
18574     return(r);
18575        }
```

```
++++++++++++++++++++++++++++++++++++++++++++++++++++++++++++++++++++++++++++++++++
                               src/mm/trace.c
++++++++++++++++++++++++++++++++++++++++++++++++++++++++++++++++++++++++++++++++++

18600     /* This file handles the memory manager's part of debugging, using the
18601      * ptrace system call. Most of the commands are passed on to the system
18602      * task for completion.
18603      *
18604      * The debugging commands available are:
18605      * T_STOP         stop the process
18606      * T_OK           enable tracing by parent for this process
18607      * T_GETINS       return value from instruction space
18608      * T_GETDATA      return value from data space
18609      * T_GETUSER      return value from user process table
18610      * T_SETINS       set value in instruction space
18611      * T_SETDATA      set value in data space
18612      * T_SETUSER      set value in user process table
18613      * T_RESUME       resume execution
18614      * T_EXIT         exit
```

```
18615    * T_STEP        set trace bit
18616    *
18617    * The T_OK and T_EXIT commands are handled here, and the T_RESUME and
18618    * T_STEP commands are partially handled here and completed by the system
18619    * task. The rest are handled entirely by the system task.
18620    */
18621
18622   #include "mm.h"
18623   #include <sys/ptrace.h>
18624   #include <signal.h>
18625   #include "mproc.h"
18626   #include "param.h"
18627
18628   #define NIL_MPROC       ((struct mproc *) 0)
18629
18630   FORWARD _PROTOTYPE( struct mproc *findproc, (pid_t lpid) );
18631
18632   /*===========================================================================*
18633    *                                 do_trace                                  *
18634    *===========================================================================*/
18635   PUBLIC int do_trace()
18636   {
18637     register struct mproc *child;
18638
18639     /* the T_OK call is made by the child fork of the debugger before it execs
18640      * the process to be traced
18641      */
18642     if (request == T_OK) {/* enable tracing by parent for this process */
18643           mp->mp_flags |= TRACED;
18644           mm_out.m2_l2 = 0;
18645           return(OK);
18646     }
18647     if ((child = findproc(pid)) == NIL_MPROC || !(child->mp_flags & STOPPED)) {
18648           return(ESRCH);
18649     }
18650     /* all the other calls are made by the parent fork of the debugger to
18651      * control execution of the child
18652      */
18653     switch (request) {
18654     case T_EXIT:          /* exit */
18655           mm_exit(child, (int)data);
18656           mm_out.m2_l2 = 0;
18657           return(OK);
18658     case T_RESUME:
18659     case T_STEP:          /* resume execution */
18660           if (data < 0 || data > _NSIG) return(EIO);
18661           if (data > 0) {          /* issue signal */
18662                 child->mp_flags &= ~TRACED;  /* so signal is not diverted */
18663                 sig_proc(child, (int) data);
18664                 child->mp_flags |= TRACED;
18665           }
18666           child->mp_flags &= ~STOPPED;
18667           break;
18668     }
18669     if (sys_trace(request, (int) (child - mproc), taddr, &data) != OK)
18670           return(-errno);
18671     mm_out.m2_l2 = data;
18672     return(OK);
18673   }
```

```
18675    /*===========================================================================*
18676     *                              findproc                                      *
18677     *===========================================================================*/
18678    PRIVATE struct mproc *findproc(lpid)
18679    pid_t lpid;
18680    {
18681      register struct mproc *rmp;
18682
18683      for (rmp = &mproc[INIT_PROC_NR + 1]; rmp < &mproc[NR_PROCS]; rmp++)
18684            if (rmp->mp_flags & IN_USE && rmp->mp_pid == lpid) return(rmp);
18685      return(NIL_MPROC);
18686    }


18688    /*===========================================================================*
18689     *                              stop_proc                                     *
18690     *===========================================================================*/
18691    PUBLIC void stop_proc(rmp, signo)
18692    register struct mproc *rmp;
18693    int signo;
18694    {
18695    /* A traced process got a signal so stop it. */
18696
18697      register struct mproc *rpmp = mproc + rmp->mp_parent;
18698
18699      if (sys_trace(-1, (int) (rmp - mproc), 0L, (long *) 0) != OK) return;
18700      rmp->mp_flags |= STOPPED;
18701      if (rpmp->mp_flags & WAITING) {
18702            rpmp->mp_flags &= ~WAITING;       /* parent is no longer waiting */
18703            reply(rmp->mp_parent, rmp->mp_pid, 0177 | (signo << 8), NIL_PTR);
18704      } else {
18705            rmp->mp_sigstatus = signo;
18706      }
18707      return;
18708    }



+++++++++++++++++++++++++++++++++++++++++++++++++++++++++++++++++++++++++++++++
                              src/mm/alloc.c
+++++++++++++++++++++++++++++++++++++++++++++++++++++++++++++++++++++++++++++++

18800    /* This file is concerned with allocating and freeing arbitrary-size blocks of
18801     * physical memory on behalf of the FORK and EXEC system calls.  The key data
18802     * structure used is the hole table, which maintains a list of holes in memory.
18803     * It is kept sorted in order of increasing memory address. The addresses
18804     * it contains refer to physical memory, starting at absolute address 0
18805     * (i.e., they are not relative to the start of MM).  During system
18806     * initialization, that part of memory containing the interrupt vectors,
18807     * kernel, and MM are "allocated" to mark them as not available and to
18808     * remove them from the hole list.
18809     *
18810     * The entry points into this file are:
18811     *   alloc_mem: allocate a given sized chunk of memory
18812     *   free_mem:  release a previously allocated chunk of memory
18813     *   mem_init:  initialize the tables when MM start up
18814     *   max_hole:  returns the largest hole currently available
18815     */
18816
18817    #include "mm.h"
18818    #include <minix/com.h>
18819
```

```
18820   #define NR_HOLES        128     /* max # entries in hole table */
18821   #define NIL_HOLE (struct hole *) 0
18822
18823   PRIVATE struct hole {
18824     phys_clicks h_base;           /* where does the hole begin? */
18825     phys_clicks h_len;            /* how big is the hole? */
18826     struct hole *h_next;          /* pointer to next entry on the list */
18827   } hole[NR_HOLES];
18828
18829
18830   PRIVATE struct hole *hole_head; /* pointer to first hole */
18831   PRIVATE struct hole *free_slots;        /* ptr to list of unused table slots */
18832
18833   FORWARD _PROTOTYPE( void del_slot, (struct hole *prev_ptr, struct hole *hp) );
18834   FORWARD _PROTOTYPE( void merge, (struct hole *hp)                         );
18835
18836
18837   /*===========================================================================*
18838    *                              alloc_mem                                     *
18839    *===========================================================================*/
18840   PUBLIC phys_clicks alloc_mem(clicks)
18841   phys_clicks clicks;             /* amount of memory requested */
18842   {
18843   /* Allocate a block of memory from the free list using first fit. The block
18844    * consists of a sequence of contiguous bytes, whose length in clicks is
18845    * given by 'clicks'.  A pointer to the block is returned.  The block is
18846    * always on a click boundary.  This procedure is called when memory is
18847    * needed for FORK or EXEC.
18848    */
18849
18850     register struct hole *hp, *prev_ptr;
18851     phys_clicks old_base;
18852
18853     hp = hole_head;
18854     while (hp != NIL_HOLE) {
18855         if (hp->h_len >= clicks) {
18856             /* We found a hole that is big enough.  Use it. */
18857             old_base = hp->h_base;  /* remember where it started */
18858             hp->h_base += clicks;   /* bite a piece off */
18859             hp->h_len -= clicks;    /* ditto */
18860
18861             /* If hole is only partly used, reduce size and return. */
18862             if (hp->h_len != 0) return(old_base);
18863
18864             /* The entire hole has been used up.  Manipulate free list. */
18865             del_slot(prev_ptr, hp);
18866             return(old_base);
18867         }
18868
18869         prev_ptr = hp;
18870         hp = hp->h_next;
18871     }
18872     return(NO_MEM);
18873   }
18876   /*===========================================================================*
18877    *                              free_mem                                      *
18878    *===========================================================================*/
18879   PUBLIC void free_mem(base, clicks)
```

```
18880    phys_clicks base;                    /* base address of block to free */
18881    phys_clicks clicks;                  /* number of clicks to free */
18882    {
18883    /* Return a block of free memory to the hole list.  The parameters tell where
18884     * the block starts in physical memory and how big it is.  The block is added
18885     * to the hole list.  If it is contiguous with an existing hole on either end,
18886     * it is merged with the hole or holes.
18887     */
18888
18889      register struct hole *hp, *new_ptr, *prev_ptr;
18890
18891      if (clicks == 0) return;
18892      if ( (new_ptr = free_slots) == NIL_HOLE) panic("Hole table full", NO_NUM);
18893      new_ptr->h_base = base;
18894      new_ptr->h_len = clicks;
18895      free_slots = new_ptr->h_next;
18896      hp = hole_head;
18897
18898      /* If this block's address is numerically less than the lowest hole currently
18899       * available, or if no holes are currently available, put this hole on the
18900       * front of the hole list.
18901       */
18902      if (hp == NIL_HOLE || base <= hp->h_base) {
18903            /* Block to be freed goes on front of the hole list. */
18904            new_ptr->h_next = hp;
18905            hole_head = new_ptr;
18906            merge(new_ptr);
18907            return;
18908      }
18909
18910      /* Block to be returned does not go on front of hole list. */
18911      while (hp != NIL_HOLE && base > hp->h_base) {
18912            prev_ptr = hp;
18913            hp = hp->h_next;
18914      }
18915
18916      /* We found where it goes.  Insert block after 'prev_ptr'. */
18917      new_ptr->h_next = prev_ptr->h_next;
18918      prev_ptr->h_next = new_ptr;
18919      merge(prev_ptr);                    /* sequence is 'prev_ptr', 'new_ptr', 'hp' */
18920    }


18923    /*===========================================================================*
18924     *                                del_slot                                   *
18925     *===========================================================================*/
18926    PRIVATE void del_slot(prev_ptr, hp)
18927    register struct hole *prev_ptr; /* pointer to hole entry just ahead of 'hp' */
18928    register struct hole *hp;       /* pointer to hole entry to be removed */
18929    {
18930    /* Remove an entry from the hole list.  This procedure is called when a
18931     * request to allocate memory removes a hole in its entirety, thus reducing
18932     * the numbers of holes in memory, and requiring the elimination of one
18933     * entry in the hole list.
18934     */
18935
18936      if (hp == hole_head)
18937            hole_head = hp->h_next;
18938      else
18939            prev_ptr->h_next = hp->h_next;
```

```
18940
18941      hp->h_next = free_slots;
18942      free_slots = hp;
18943    }


18946    /*===========================================================================*
18947     *                              merge                                         *
18948     *===========================================================================*/
18949    PRIVATE void merge(hp)
18950    register struct hole *hp;        /* ptr to hole to merge with its successors */
18951    {
18952    /* Check for contiguous holes and merge any found.  Contiguous holes can occur
18953     * when a block of memory is freed, and it happens to abut another hole on
18954     * either or both ends.  The pointer 'hp' points to the first of a series of
18955     * three holes that can potentially all be merged together.
18956     */
18957
18958      register struct hole *next_ptr;
18959
18960      /* If 'hp' points to the last hole, no merging is possible.  If it does not,
18961       * try to absorb its successor into it and free the successor's table entry.
18962       */
18963      if ( (next_ptr = hp->h_next) == NIL_HOLE) return;
18964      if (hp->h_base + hp->h_len == next_ptr->h_base) {
18965            hp->h_len += next_ptr->h_len;   /* first one gets second one's mem */
18966            del_slot(hp, next_ptr);
18967      } else {
18968            hp = next_ptr;
18969      }
18970
18971      /* If 'hp' now points to the last hole, return; otherwise, try to absorb its
18972       * successor into it.
18973       */
18974      if ( (next_ptr = hp->h_next) == NIL_HOLE) return;
18975      if (hp->h_base + hp->h_len == next_ptr->h_base) {
18976            hp->h_len += next_ptr->h_len;
18977            del_slot(hp, next_ptr);
18978      }
18979    }


18982    /*===========================================================================*
18983     *                              max_hole                                      *
18984     *===========================================================================*/
18985    PUBLIC phys_clicks max_hole()
18986    {
18987    /* Scan the hole list and return the largest hole. */
18988
18989      register struct hole *hp;
18990      register phys_clicks max;
18991
18992      hp = hole_head;
18993      max = 0;
18994      while (hp != NIL_HOLE) {
18995            if (hp->h_len > max) max = hp->h_len;
18996            hp = hp->h_next;
18997      }
18998      return(max);
18999    }
```

```
19002     /*===========================================================================*
19003      *                              mem_init                                      *
19004      *===========================================================================*/
19005     PUBLIC void mem_init(total, free)
19006     phys_clicks *total, *free;               /* memory size summaries */
19007     {
19008     /* Initialize hole lists.  There are two lists: 'hole_head' points to a linked
19009      * list of all the holes (unused memory) in the system; 'free_slots' points to
19010      * a linked list of table entries that are not in use.  Initially, the former
19011      * list has one entry for each chunk of physical memory, and the second
19012      * list links together the remaining table slots.  As memory becomes more
19013      * fragmented in the course of time (i.e., the initial big holes break up into
19014      * smaller holes), new table slots are needed to represent them.  These slots
19015      * are taken from the list headed by 'free_slots'.
19016      */
19017
19018       register struct hole *hp;
19019       phys_clicks base;                 /* base address of chunk */
19020       phys_clicks size;                 /* size of chunk */
19021       message mess;
19022
19023       /* Put all holes on the free list. */
19024       for (hp = &hole[0]; hp < &hole[NR_HOLES]; hp++) hp->h_next = hp + 1;
19025       hole[NR_HOLES-1].h_next = NIL_HOLE;
19026       hole_head = NIL_HOLE;
19027       free_slots = &hole[0];
19028
19029       /* Ask the kernel for chunks of physical memory and allocate a hole for
19030        * each of them.  The SYS_MEM call responds with the base and size of the
19031        * next chunk and the total amount of memory.
19032        */
19033       *free = 0;
19034       for (;;) {
19035             mess.m_type = SYS_MEM;
19036             if (sendrec(SYSTASK, &mess) != OK) panic("bad SYS_MEM?", NO_NUM);
19037             base = mess.m1_i1;
19038             size = mess.m1_i2;
19039             if (size == 0) break;              /* no more? */
19040
19041             free_mem(base, size);
19042             *total = mess.m1_i3;
19043             *free += size;
19044       }
19045     }
```

```
++++++++++++++++++++++++++++++++++++++++++++++++++++++++++++++++++++++++++++++++
                                src/mm/utility.c
++++++++++++++++++++++++++++++++++++++++++++++++++++++++++++++++++++++++++++++++

19100   /* This file contains some utility routines for MM.
19101    *
19102    * The entry points are:
19103    *   allowed:   see if an access is permitted
19104    *   no_sys:    this routine is called for invalid system call numbers
19105    *   panic:     MM has run aground of a fatal error and cannot continue
19106    *   tell_fs:   interface to FS
19107    */
19108
19109   #include "mm.h"
19110   #include <sys/stat.h>
19111   #include <minix/callnr.h>
19112   #include <minix/com.h>
19113   #include <fcntl.h>
19114   #include <signal.h>                /* needed only because mproc.h needs it */
19115   #include "mproc.h"
19116
19117   /*===========================================================================*
19118    *                              allowed                                       *
19119    *===========================================================================*/
19120   PUBLIC int allowed(name_buf, s_buf, mask)
19121   char *name_buf;                 /* pointer to file name to be EXECed */
19122   struct stat *s_buf;             /* buffer for doing and returning stat struct*/
19123   int mask;                       /* R_BIT, W_BIT, or X_BIT */
19124   {
19125   /* Check to see if file can be accessed.  Return EACCES or ENOENT if the access
19126    * is prohibited.  If it is legal open the file and return a file descriptor.
19127    */
19128
19129     int fd;
19130     int save_errno;
19131
19132     /* Use the fact that mask for access() is the same as the permissions mask.
19133      * E.g., X_BIT in <minix/const.h> is the same as X_OK in <unistd.h> and
19134      * S_IXOTH in <sys/stat.h>.  tell_fs(DO_CHDIR, ...) has set MM's real ids
19135      * to the user's effective ids, so access() works right for setuid programs.
19136      */
19137     if (access(name_buf, mask) < 0) return(-errno);
19138
19139     /* The file is accessible but might not be readable.  Make it readable. */
19140     tell_fs(SETUID, MM_PROC_NR, (int) SUPER_USER, (int) SUPER_USER);
19141
19142     /* Open the file and fstat it.  Restore the ids early to handle errors. */
19143     fd = open(name_buf, O_RDONLY);
19144     save_errno = errno;             /* open might fail, e.g. from ENFILE */
19145     tell_fs(SETUID, MM_PROC_NR, (int) mp->mp_effuid, (int) mp->mp_effuid);
19146     if (fd < 0) return(-save_errno);
19147     if (fstat(fd, s_buf) < 0) panic("allowed: fstat failed", NO_NUM);
19148
19149     /* Only regular files can be executed. */
19150     if (mask == X_BIT && (s_buf->st_mode & I_TYPE) != I_REGULAR) {
19151           close(fd);
19152           return(EACCES);
19153     }
19154     return(fd);
```

```
19155    }


19158    /*===========================================================================*
19159     *                              no_sys                                        *
19160     *===========================================================================*/
19161    PUBLIC int no_sys()
19162    {
19163    /* A system call number not implemented by MM has been requested. */
19164
19165      return(EINVAL);
19166    }


19169    /*===========================================================================*
19170     *                              panic                                         *
19171     *===========================================================================*/
19172    PUBLIC void panic(format, num)
19173    char *format;                    /* format string */
19174    int num;                         /* number to go with format string */
19175    {
19176    /* Something awful has happened.  Panics are caused when an internal
19177     * inconsistency is detected, e.g., a programming error or illegal value of a
19178     * defined constant.
19179     */
19180
19181      printf("Memory manager panic: %s ", format);
19182      if (num != NO_NUM) printf("%d",num);
19183      printf("\n");
19184      tell_fs(SYNC, 0, 0, 0);          /* flush the cache to the disk */
19185      sys_abort(RBT_PANIC);
19186    }


19189    /*===========================================================================*
19190     *                              tell_fs                                       *
19191     *===========================================================================*/
19192    PUBLIC void tell_fs(what, p1, p2, p3)
19193    int what, p1, p2, p3;
19194    {
19195    /* This routine is only used by MM to inform FS of certain events:
19196     *        tell_fs(CHDIR, slot, dir, 0)
19197     *        tell_fs(EXEC, proc, 0, 0)
19198     *        tell_fs(EXIT, proc, 0, 0)
19199     *        tell_fs(FORK, parent, child, pid)
19200     *        tell_fs(SETGID, proc, realgid, effgid)
19201     *        tell_fs(SETSID, proc, 0, 0)
19202     *        tell_fs(SETUID, proc, realuid, effuid)
19203     *        tell_fs(SYNC, 0, 0, 0)
19204     *        tell_fs(UNPAUSE, proc, signr, 0)
19205     */
19206
19207      message m;
19208
19209      m.m1_i1 = p1;
19210      m.m1_i2 = p2;
19211      m.m1_i3 = p3;
19212      _taskcall(FS_PROC_NR, what, &m);
19213    }
```

```
++++++++++++++++++++++++++++++++++++++++++++++++++++++++++++++++++++++++++++++++
                               src/mm/putk.c
++++++++++++++++++++++++++++++++++++++++++++++++++++++++++++++++++++++++++++++++
19300   /* MM must occasionally print some message.  It uses the standard library
19301    * routine printk().  (The name "printf" is really a macro defined as
19302    * "printk"). Printing is done by calling the TTY task directly, not going
19303    * through FS.
19304    */
19305
19306   #include "mm.h"
19307   #include <minix/com.h>
19308
19309   #define BUF_SIZE          100    /* print buffer size */
19310
19311   PRIVATE int buf_count;              /* # characters in the buffer */
19312   PRIVATE char print_buf[BUF_SIZE];       /* output is buffered here */
19313   PRIVATE message putch_msg;         /* used for message to TTY task */
19314
19315   _PROTOTYPE( FORWARD void flush, (void) );
19316
19317   /*===========================================================================*
19318    *                              putk                                         *
19319    *===========================================================================*/
19320   PUBLIC void putk(c)
19321   int c;
19322   {
19323   /* Accumulate another character.  If 0 or buffer full, print it. */
19324
19325     if (c == 0 || buf_count == BUF_SIZE) flush();
19326     if (c == '\n') putk('\r');
19327     if (c != 0) print_buf[buf_count++] = c;
19328   }


19331   /*===========================================================================*
19332    *                              flush                                        *
19333    *===========================================================================*/
19334   PRIVATE void flush()
19335   {
19336   /* Flush the print buffer by calling TTY task. */
19337
19338     if (buf_count == 0) return;
19339     putch_msg.m_type = DEV_WRITE;
19340     putch_msg.PROC_NR  = 0;
19341     putch_msg.TTY_LINE = 0;
19342     putch_msg.ADDRESS  = print_buf;
19343     putch_msg.COUNT = buf_count;
19344     sendrec(TTY, &putch_msg);
19345     buf_count = 0;
19346   }
```

```
++++++++++++++++++++++++++++++++++++++++++++++++++++++++++++++++++++++++++++++++
                                 src/fs/fs.h
++++++++++++++++++++++++++++++++++++++++++++++++++++++++++++++++++++++++++++++++
19400     /* This is the master header for fs.  It includes some other files
19401      * and defines the principal constants.
19402      */
19403     #define _POSIX_SOURCE      1     /* tell headers to include POSIX stuff */
19404     #define _MINIX             1     /* tell headers to include MINIX stuff */
19405     #define _SYSTEM            1     /* tell headers that this is the kernel */
19406
19407     /* The following are so basic, all the *.c files get them automatically. */
19408     #include <minix/config.h>        /* MUST be first */
19409     #include <ansi.h>                /* MUST be second */
19410     #include <sys/types.h>
19411     #include <minix/const.h>
19412     #include <minix/type.h>
19413
19414     #include <limits.h>
19415     #include <errno.h>
19416
19417     #include <minix/syslib.h>
19418
19419     #include "const.h"
19420     #include "type.h"
19421     #include "proto.h"
19422     #include "glo.h"




++++++++++++++++++++++++++++++++++++++++++++++++++++++++++++++++++++++++++++++++
                                src/fs/const.h
++++++++++++++++++++++++++++++++++++++++++++++++++++++++++++++++++++++++++++++++
19500     /* Tables sizes */
19501     #define V1_NR_DZONES       7     /* # direct zone numbers in a V1 inode */
19502     #define V1_NR_TZONES       9     /* total # zone numbers in a V1 inode */
19503     #define V2_NR_DZONES       7     /* # direct zone numbers in a V2 inode */
19504     #define V2_NR_TZONES      10     /* total # zone numbers in a V2 inode */
19505
19506     #define NR_FILPS         128     /* # slots in filp table */
19507     #define NR_INODES         64     /* # slots in "in core" inode table */
19508     #define NR_SUPERS          8     /* # slots in super block table */
19509     #define NR_LOCKS           8     /* # slots in the file locking table */
19510
19511     /* The type of sizeof may be (unsigned) long.  Use the following macro for
19512      * taking the sizes of small objects so that there are no surprises like
19513      * (small) long constants being passed to routines expecting an int.
19514      */
19515     #define usizeof(t) ((unsigned) sizeof(t))
19516
19517     /* File system types. */
19518     #define SUPER_MAGIC   0x137F     /* magic number contained in super-block */
19519     #define SUPER_REV     0x7F13     /* magic # when 68000 disk read on PC or vv */
19520     #define SUPER_V2      0x2468     /* magic # for V2 file systems */
19521     #define SUPER_V2_REV  0x6824     /* V2 magic written on PC, read on 68K or vv */
19522
19523     #define V1                 1     /* version number of V1 file systems */
19524     #define V2                 2     /* version number of V2 file systems */
```

```
19525
19526   /* Miscellaneous constants */
19527   #define SU_UID      ((uid_t) 0)     /* super_user's uid_t */
19528   #define SYS_UID     ((uid_t) 0)     /* uid_t for processes MM and INIT */
19529   #define SYS_GID     ((gid_t) 0)     /* gid_t for processes MM and INIT */
19530   #define NORMAL            0     /* forces get_block to do disk read */
19531   #define NO_READ           1     /* prevents get_block from doing disk read */
19532   #define PREFETCH          2     /* tells get_block not to read or mark dev */
19533
19534   #define XPIPE   (-NR_TASKS-1)     /* used in fp_task when susp'd on pipe */
19535   #define XOPEN   (-NR_TASKS-2)     /* used in fp_task when susp'd on open */
19536   #define XLOCK   (-NR_TASKS-3)     /* used in fp_task when susp'd on lock */
19537   #define XPOPEN  (-NR_TASKS-4)     /* used in fp_task when susp'd on pipe open */
19538
19539   #define NO_BIT    ((bit_t) 0)     /* returned by alloc_bit() to signal failure */
19540
19541   #define DUP_MASK         0100     /* mask to distinguish dup2 from dup */
19542
19543   #define LOOK_UP           0     /* tells search_dir to lookup string */
19544   #define ENTER             1     /* tells search_dir to make dir entry */
19545   #define DELETE            2     /* tells search_dir to delete entry */
19546   #define IS_EMPTY          3     /* tells search_dir to ret. OK or ENOTEMPTY */
19547
19548   #define CLEAN             0     /* disk and memory copies identical */
19549   #define DIRTY             1     /* disk and memory copies differ */
19550   #define ATIME           002     /* set if atime field needs updating */
19551   #define CTIME           004     /* set if ctime field needs updating */
19552   #define MTIME           010     /* set if mtime field needs updating */
19553
19554   #define BYTE_SWAP         0     /* tells conv2/conv4 to swap bytes */
19555   #define DONT_SWAP         1     /* tells conv2/conv4 not to swap bytes */
19556
19557   #define END_OF_FILE    (-104)     /* eof detected */
19558
19559   #define ROOT_INODE        1     /* inode number for root directory */
19560   #define BOOT_BLOCK  ((block_t) 0)     /* block number of boot block */
19561   #define SUPER_BLOCK ((block_t) 1)     /* block number of super block */
19562
19563   #define DIR_ENTRY_SIZE       usizeof (struct direct)  /* # bytes/dir entry   */
19564   #define NR_DIR_ENTRIES   (BLOCK_SIZE/DIR_ENTRY_SIZE)  /* # dir entries/blk   */
19565   #define SUPER_SIZE       usizeof (struct super_block) /* super_block size    */
19566   #define PIPE_SIZE         (V1_NR_DZONES*BLOCK_SIZE)   /* pipe size in bytes  */
19567   #define BITMAP_CHUNKS (BLOCK_SIZE/usizeof (bitchunk_t))/* # map chunks/blk   */
19568
19569   /* Derived sizes pertaining to the V1 file system. */
19570   #define V1_ZONE_NUM_SIZE          usizeof (zone1_t)   /* # bytes in V1 zone  */
19571   #define V1_INODE_SIZE             usizeof (d1_inode)  /* bytes in V1 dsk ino */
19572   #define V1_INDIRECTS   (BLOCK_SIZE/V1_ZONE_NUM_SIZE)  /* # zones/indir block */
19573   #define V1_INODES_PER_BLOCK (BLOCK_SIZE/V1_INODE_SIZE)/* # V1 dsk inodes/blk */
19574
19575   /* Derived sizes pertaining to the V2 file system. */
19576   #define V2_ZONE_NUM_SIZE          usizeof (zone_t)    /* # bytes in V2 zone  */
19577   #define V2_INODE_SIZE             usizeof (d2_inode)  /* bytes in V2 dsk ino */
19578   #define V2_INDIRECTS   (BLOCK_SIZE/V2_ZONE_NUM_SIZE)  /* # zones/indir block */
19579   #define V2_INODES_PER_BLOCK (BLOCK_SIZE/V2_INODE_SIZE)/* # V2 dsk inodes/blk */
19580
19581   #define printf printk
```

```
++++++++++++++++++++++++++++++++++++++++++++++++++++++++++++++++++++++++++++++
                              src/fs/type.h
++++++++++++++++++++++++++++++++++++++++++++++++++++++++++++++++++++++++++++++

19600    /* Declaration of the V1 inode as it is on the disk (not in core). */
19601    typedef struct {                  /* V1.x disk inode */
19602      mode_t d1_mode;                 /* file type, protection, etc. */
19603      uid_t d1_uid;                   /* user id of the file's owner */
19604      off_t d1_size;                  /* current file size in bytes */
19605      time_t d1_mtime;                /* when was file data last changed */
19606      gid_t d1_gid;                   /* group number */
19607      nlink_t d1_nlinks;              /* how many links to this file */
19608      u16_t d1_zone[V1_NR_TZONES];    /* block nums for direct, ind, and dbl ind */
19609    } d1_inode;
19610
19611    /* Declaration of the V2 inode as it is on the disk (not in core). */
19612    typedef struct {                  /* V2.x disk inode */
19613      mode_t d2_mode;                 /* file type, protection, etc. */
19614      u16_t d2_nlinks;                /* how many links to this file. HACK! */
19615      uid_t d2_uid;                   /* user id of the file's owner. */
19616      u16_t d2_gid;                   /* group number HACK! */
19617      off_t d2_size;                  /* current file size in bytes */
19618      time_t d2_atime;                /* when was file data last accessed */
19619      time_t d2_mtime;                /* when was file data last changed */
19620      time_t d2_ctime;                /* when was inode data last changed */
19621      zone_t d2_zone[V2_NR_TZONES];   /* block nums for direct, ind, and dbl ind */
19622    } d2_inode;



++++++++++++++++++++++++++++++++++++++++++++++++++++++++++++++++++++++++++++++
                              src/fs/proto.h
++++++++++++++++++++++++++++++++++++++++++++++++++++++++++++++++++++++++++++++

19700    /* Function prototypes. */
19701
19702    /* Structs used in prototypes must be declared as such first. */
19703    struct buf;
19704    struct filp;
19705    struct inode;
19706    struct super_block;
19707
19708    /* cache.c */
19709    _PROTOTYPE( zone_t alloc_zone, (Dev_t dev, zone_t z)              );
19710    _PROTOTYPE( void flushall, (Dev_t dev)                           );
19711    _PROTOTYPE( void free_zone, (Dev_t dev, zone_t numb)             );
19712    _PROTOTYPE( struct buf *get_block, (Dev_t dev, block_t block,int only_search));
19713    _PROTOTYPE( void invalidate, (Dev_t device)                     );
19714    _PROTOTYPE( void put_block, (struct buf *bp, int block_type)     );
19715    _PROTOTYPE( void rw_block, (struct buf *bp, int rw_flag)         );
19716    _PROTOTYPE( void rw_scattered, (Dev_t dev,
19717                      struct buf **bufq, int bufqsize, int rw_flag)  );
19718
19719    /* device.c */
19720    _PROTOTYPE( void call_task, (int task_nr, message *mess_ptr)     );
19721    _PROTOTYPE( void dev_opcl, (int task_nr, message *mess_ptr)      );
19722    _PROTOTYPE( int dev_io, (int rw_flag, int nonblock, Dev_t dev,
19723                      off_t pos, int bytes, int proc, char *buff)    );
19724    _PROTOTYPE( int do_ioctl, (void)                                 );
```

```
19725    _PROTOTYPE( void no_dev, (int task_nr, message *m_ptr)             );
19726    _PROTOTYPE( void call_ctty, (int task_nr, message *mess_ptr)       );
19727    _PROTOTYPE( void tty_open, (int task_nr, message *mess_ptr)        );
19728    _PROTOTYPE( void ctty_close, (int task_nr, message *mess_ptr)      );
19729    _PROTOTYPE( void ctty_open, (int task_nr, message *mess_ptr)       );
19730    _PROTOTYPE( int do_setsid, (void)                                  );
19731    #if ENABLE_NETWORKING
19732    _PROTOTYPE( void net_open, (int task_nr, message *mess_ptr)        );
19733    #else
19734    #define net_open  0
19735    #endif
19736
19737    /* filedes.c */
19738    _PROTOTYPE( struct filp *find_filp, (struct inode *rip, Mode_t bits)   );
19739    _PROTOTYPE( int get_fd, (int start, Mode_t bits, int *k, struct filp **fpt) );
19740    _PROTOTYPE( struct filp *get_filp, (int fild)                      );
19741
19742    /* inode.c */
19743    _PROTOTYPE( struct inode *alloc_inode, (Dev_t dev, Mode_t bits)    );
19744    _PROTOTYPE( void dup_inode, (struct inode *ip)                     );
19745    _PROTOTYPE( void free_inode, (Dev_t dev, Ino_t numb)              );
19746    _PROTOTYPE( struct inode *get_inode, (Dev_t dev, int numb)         );
19747    _PROTOTYPE( void put_inode, (struct inode *rip)                    );
19748    _PROTOTYPE( void update_times, (struct inode *rip)                 );
19749    _PROTOTYPE( void rw_inode, (struct inode *rip, int rw_flag)        );
19750    _PROTOTYPE( void wipe_inode, (struct inode *rip)                   );
19751
19752    /* link.c */
19753    _PROTOTYPE( int do_link, (void)                                    );
19754    _PROTOTYPE( int do_unlink, (void)                                  );
19755    _PROTOTYPE( int do_rename, (void)                                  );
19756    _PROTOTYPE( void truncate, (struct inode *rip)                     );
19757
19758    /* lock.c */
19759    _PROTOTYPE( int lock_op, (struct filp *f, int req)                 );
19760    _PROTOTYPE( void lock_revive, (void)                               );
19761
19762    /* main.c */
19763    _PROTOTYPE( void main, (void)                                      );
19764    _PROTOTYPE( void reply, (int whom, int result)                     );
19765
19766    /* misc.c */
19767    _PROTOTYPE( int do_dup, (void)                                     );
19768    _PROTOTYPE( int do_exit, (void)                                    );
19769    _PROTOTYPE( int do_fcntl, (void)                                   );
19770    _PROTOTYPE( int do_fork, (void)                                    );
19771    _PROTOTYPE( int do_exec, (void)                                    );
19772    _PROTOTYPE( int do_revive, (void)                                  );
19773    _PROTOTYPE( int do_set, (void)                                     );
19774    _PROTOTYPE( int do_sync, (void)                                    );
19775
19776    /* mount.c */
19777    _PROTOTYPE( int do_mount, (void)                                   );
19778    _PROTOTYPE( int do_umount, (void)                                  );
19779
19780    /* open.c */
19781    _PROTOTYPE( int do_close, (void)                                   );
19782    _PROTOTYPE( int do_creat, (void)                                   );
19783    _PROTOTYPE( int do_lseek, (void)                                   );
19784    _PROTOTYPE( int do_mknod, (void)                                   );
```

```
19785    _PROTOTYPE( int do_mkdir, (void)                                  );
19786    _PROTOTYPE( int do_open, (void)                                   );
19787
19788    /* path.c */
19789    _PROTOTYPE( struct inode *advance,(struct inode *dirp, char string[NAME_MAX]));
19790    _PROTOTYPE( int search_dir, (struct inode *ldir_ptr,
19791                       char string [NAME_MAX], ino_t *numb, int flag)  );
19792    _PROTOTYPE( struct inode *eat_path, (char *path)                  );
19793    _PROTOTYPE( struct inode *last_dir, (char *path, char string [NAME_MAX]));
19794
19795    /* pipe.c */
19796    _PROTOTYPE( int do_pipe, (void)                                   );
19797    _PROTOTYPE( int do_unpause, (void)                                );
19798    _PROTOTYPE( int pipe_check, (struct inode *rip, int rw_flag,
19799                        int oflags, int bytes, off_t position, int *canwrite));
19800    _PROTOTYPE( void release, (struct inode *ip, int call_nr, int count)   );
19801    _PROTOTYPE( void revive, (int proc_nr, int bytes)                 );
19802    _PROTOTYPE( void suspend, (int task)                              );
19803
19804    /* protect.c */
19805    _PROTOTYPE( int do_access, (void)                                 );
19806    _PROTOTYPE( int do_chmod, (void)                                  );
19807    _PROTOTYPE( int do_chown, (void)                                  );
19808    _PROTOTYPE( int do_umask, (void)                                  );
19809    _PROTOTYPE( int forbidden, (struct inode *rip, Mode_t access_desired)  );
19810    _PROTOTYPE( int read_only, (struct inode *ip)                     );
19811
19812    /* putk.c */
19813    _PROTOTYPE( void putk, (int c)                                    );
19814
19815    /* read.c */
19816    _PROTOTYPE( int do_read, (void)                                   );
19817    _PROTOTYPE( struct buf *rahead, (struct inode *rip, block_t baseblock,
19818                        off_t position, unsigned bytes_ahead)         );
19819    _PROTOTYPE( void read_ahead, (void)                               );
19820    _PROTOTYPE( block_t read_map, (struct inode *rip, off_t position)  );
19821    _PROTOTYPE( int read_write, (int rw_flag)                         );
19822    _PROTOTYPE( zone_t rd_indir, (struct buf *bp, int index)          );
19823
19824    /* stadir.c */
19825    _PROTOTYPE( int do_chdir, (void)                                  );
19826    _PROTOTYPE( int do_chroot, (void)                                 );
19827    _PROTOTYPE( int do_fstat, (void)                                  );
19828    _PROTOTYPE( int do_stat, (void)                                   );
19829
19830    /* super.c */
19831    _PROTOTYPE( bit_t alloc_bit, (struct super_block *sp, int map, bit_t origin));
19832    _PROTOTYPE( void free_bit, (struct super_block *sp, int map,
19833                                        bit_t bit_returned)           );
19834    _PROTOTYPE( struct super_block *get_super, (Dev_t dev)            );
19835    _PROTOTYPE( int mounted, (struct inode *rip)                      );
19836    _PROTOTYPE( int read_super, (struct super_block *sp)              );
19837
19838    /* time.c */
19839    _PROTOTYPE( int do_stime, (void)                                  );
19840    _PROTOTYPE( int do_time, (void)                                   );
19841    _PROTOTYPE( int do_tims, (void)                                   );
19842    _PROTOTYPE( int do_utime, (void)                                  );
19843
19844    /* utility.c */
```

```
19845     _PROTOTYPE( time_t clock_time, (void)                              );
19846     _PROTOTYPE( unsigned conv2, (int norm, int w)                      );
19847     _PROTOTYPE( long conv4, (int norm, long x)                         );
19848     _PROTOTYPE( int fetch_name, (char *path, int len, int flag)        );
19849     _PROTOTYPE( int no_sys, (void)                                     );
19850     _PROTOTYPE( void panic, (char *format, int num)                    );
19851
19852     /* write.c */
19853     _PROTOTYPE( void clear_zone, (struct inode *rip, off_t pos, int flag)  );
19854     _PROTOTYPE( int do_write, (void)                                   );
19855     _PROTOTYPE( struct buf *new_block, (struct inode *rip, off_t position)  );
19856     _PROTOTYPE( void zero_block, (struct buf *bp)                      );
```

```
++++++++++++++++++++++++++++++++++++++++++++++++++++++++++++++++++++++++++++++
                                src/fs/glo.h
++++++++++++++++++++++++++++++++++++++++++++++++++++++++++++++++++++++++++++++
```

```
19900     /* EXTERN should be extern except for the table file */
19901     #ifdef _TABLE
19902     #undef EXTERN
19903     #define EXTERN
19904     #endif
19905
19906     /* File System global variables */
19907     EXTERN struct fproc *fp;            /* pointer to caller's fproc struct */
19908     EXTERN int super_user;              /* 1 if caller is super_user, else 0 */
19909     EXTERN int dont_reply;              /* normally 0; set to 1 to inhibit reply */
19910     EXTERN int susp_count;              /* number of procs suspended on pipe */
19911     EXTERN int nr_locks;                /* number of locks currently in place */
19912     EXTERN int reviving;                /* number of pipe processes to be revived */
19913     EXTERN off_t rdahedpos;             /* position to read ahead */
19914     EXTERN struct inode *rdahed_inode;      /* pointer to inode to read ahead */
19915
19916     /* The parameters of the call are kept here. */
19917     EXTERN message m;                   /* the input message itself */
19918     EXTERN message m1;                  /* the output message used for reply */
19919     EXTERN int who;                     /* caller's proc number */
19920     EXTERN int fs_call;                 /* system call number */
19921     EXTERN char user_path[PATH_MAX];/* storage for user path name */
19922
19923     /* The following variables are used for returning results to the caller. */
19924     EXTERN int err_code;                /* temporary storage for error number */
19925     EXTERN int rdwt_err;                /* status of last disk i/o request */
19926
19927     /* Data which need initialization. */
19928     extern _PROTOTYPE (int (*call_vector[]), (void) ); /* sys call table */
19929     extern int max_major;   /* maximum major device (+ 1) */
19930     extern char dot1[2];    /* dot1 (&dot1[0]) and dot2 (&dot2[0]) have a special */
19931     extern char dot2[3];    /* meaning to search_dir: no access permission check. */
```

```
++++++++++++++++++++++++++++++++++++++++++++++++++++++++++++++++++++++++++++++++
                              src/fs/fproc.h
++++++++++++++++++++++++++++++++++++++++++++++++++++++++++++++++++++++++++++++++

20000    /* This is the per-process information.  A slot is reserved for each potential
20001     * process. Thus NR_PROCS must be the same as in the kernel. It is not possible
20002     * or even necessary to tell when a slot is free here.
20003     */
20004
20005
20006    EXTERN struct fproc {
20007       mode_t fp_umask;              /* mask set by umask system call */
20008       struct inode *fp_workdir;     /* pointer to working directory's inode */
20009       struct inode *fp_rootdir;     /* pointer to current root dir (see chroot) */
20010       struct filp *fp_filp[OPEN_MAX];/* the file descriptor table */
20011       uid_t fp_realuid;             /* real user id */
20012       uid_t fp_effuid;              /* effective user id */
20013       gid_t fp_realgid;             /* real group id */
20014       gid_t fp_effgid;              /* effective group id */
20015       dev_t fp_tty;                 /* major/minor of controlling tty */
20016       int fp_fd;                    /* place to save fd if rd/wr can't finish */
20017       char *fp_buffer;              /* place to save buffer if rd/wr can't finish*/
20018       int  fp_nbytes;               /* place to save bytes if rd/wr can't finish */
20019       int  fp_cum_io_partial;       /* partial byte count if rd/wr can't finish */
20020       char fp_suspended;            /* set to indicate process hanging */
20021       char fp_revived;              /* set to indicate process being revived */
20022       char fp_task;                 /* which task is proc suspended on */
20023       char fp_sesldr;               /* true if proc is a session leader */
20024       pid_t fp_pid;                 /* process id */
20025       long fp_cloexec;              /* bit map for POSIX Table 6-2 FD_CLOEXEC */
20026    } fproc[NR_PROCS];
20027
20028    /* Field values. */
20029    #define NOT_SUSPENDED     0   /* process is not suspended on pipe or task */
20030    #define SUSPENDED         1   /* process is suspended on pipe or task */
20031    #define NOT_REVIVING      0   /* process is not being revived */
20032    #define REVIVING          1   /* process is being revived from suspension */


++++++++++++++++++++++++++++++++++++++++++++++++++++++++++++++++++++++++++++++++
                              src/fs/buf.h
++++++++++++++++++++++++++++++++++++++++++++++++++++++++++++++++++++++++++++++++

20100    /* Buffer (block) cache.  To acquire a block, a routine calls get_block(),
20101     * telling which block it wants.  The block is then regarded as "in use"
20102     * and has its 'b_count' field incremented.  All the blocks that are not
20103     * in use are chained together in an LRU list, with 'front' pointing
20104     * to the least recently used block, and 'rear' to the most recently used
20105     * block.  A reverse chain, using the field b_prev is also maintained.
20106     * Usage for LRU is measured by the time the put_block() is done.  The second
20107     * parameter to put_block() can violate the LRU order and put a block on the
20108     * front of the list, if it will probably not be needed soon.  If a block
20109     * is modified, the modifying routine must set b_dirt to DIRTY, so the block
20110     * will eventually be rewritten to the disk.
20111     */
20112
20113    #include <sys/dir.h>                    /* need struct direct */
20114
```

```
20115   EXTERN struct buf {
20116     /* Data portion of the buffer. */
20117     union {
20118       char b__data[BLOCK_SIZE];                /* ordinary user data */
20119       struct direct b__dir[NR_DIR_ENTRIES];    /* directory block */
20120       zone1_t b__v1_ind[V1_INDIRECTS];         /* V1 indirect block */
20121       zone_t  b__v2_ind[V2_INDIRECTS];         /* V2 indirect block */
20122       d1_inode b__v1_ino[V1_INODES_PER_BLOCK]; /* V1 inode block */
20123       d2_inode b__v2_ino[V2_INODES_PER_BLOCK]; /* V2 inode block */
20124       bitchunk_t b__bitmap[BITMAP_CHUNKS];     /* bit map block */
20125     } b;
20126
20127     /* Header portion of the buffer. */
20128     struct buf *b_next;           /* used to link all free bufs in a chain */
20129     struct buf *b_prev;           /* used to link all free bufs the other way */
20130     struct buf *b_hash;           /* used to link bufs on hash chains */
20131     block_t b_blocknr;            /* block number of its (minor) device */
20132     dev_t b_dev;                  /* major | minor device where block resides */
20133     char b_dirt;                  /* CLEAN or DIRTY */
20134     char b_count;                 /* number of users of this buffer */
20135   } buf[NR_BUFS];
20136
20137   /* A block is free if b_dev == NO_DEV. */
20138
20139   #define NIL_BUF ((struct buf *) 0)       /* indicates absence of a buffer */
20140
20141   /* These defs make it possible to use to bp->b_data instead of bp->b.b__data */
20142   #define b_data    b.b__data
20143   #define b_dir     b.b__dir
20144   #define b_v1_ind b.b__v1_ind
20145   #define b_v2_ind b.b__v2_ind
20146   #define b_v1_ino b.b__v1_ino
20147   #define b_v2_ino b.b__v2_ino
20148   #define b_bitmap b.b__bitmap
20149
20150   EXTERN struct buf *buf_hash[NR_BUF_HASH];       /* the buffer hash table */
20151
20152   EXTERN struct buf *front;     /* points to least recently used free block */
20153   EXTERN struct buf *rear;      /* points to most recently used free block */
20154   EXTERN int bufs_in_use;       /* # bufs currently in use (not on free list)*/
20155
20156   /* When a block is released, the type of usage is passed to put_block(). */
20157   #define WRITE_IMMED       0100 /* block should be written to disk now */
20158   #define ONE_SHOT          0200 /* set if block not likely to be needed soon */
20159
20160   #define INODE_BLOCK        (0 + MAYBE_WRITE_IMMED)      /* inode block */
20161   #define DIRECTORY_BLOCK    (1 + MAYBE_WRITE_IMMED)      /* directory block */
20162   #define INDIRECT_BLOCK     (2 + MAYBE_WRITE_IMMED)      /* pointer block */
20163   #define MAP_BLOCK          (3 + MAYBE_WRITE_IMMED)      /* bit map */
20164   #define ZUPER_BLOCK        (4 + WRITE_IMMED + ONE_SHOT) /* super block */
20165   #define FULL_DATA_BLOCK    5                            /* data, fully used */
20166   #define PARTIAL_DATA_BLOCK 6                            /* data, partly used*/
20167
20168   #define HASH_MASK (NR_BUF_HASH - 1)      /* mask for hashing block numbers */
```

```
++++++++++++++++++++++++++++++++++++++++++++++++++++++++++++++++++++++++++++++++
                              src/fs/dev.h
++++++++++++++++++++++++++++++++++++++++++++++++++++++++++++++++++++++++++++++++

20200    /* Device table.  This table is indexed by major device number.  It provides
20201     * the link between major device numbers and the routines that process them.
20202     */
20203
20204    typedef _PROTOTYPE (void (*dmap_t), (int task, message *m_ptr) );
20205
20206    extern struct dmap {
20207      dmap_t dmap_open;
20208      dmap_t dmap_rw;
20209      dmap_t dmap_close;
20210      int dmap_task;
20211    } dmap[];
20212




++++++++++++++++++++++++++++++++++++++++++++++++++++++++++++++++++++++++++++++++
                              src/fs/file.h
++++++++++++++++++++++++++++++++++++++++++++++++++++++++++++++++++++++++++++++++

20300    /* This is the filp table.  It is an intermediary between file descriptors and
20301     * inodes.  A slot is free if filp_count == 0.
20302     */
20303
20304    EXTERN struct filp {
20305      mode_t filp_mode;              /* RW bits, telling how file is opened */
20306      int filp_flags;                /* flags from open and fcntl */
20307      int filp_count;                /* how many file descriptors share this slot?*/
20308      struct inode *filp_ino;        /* pointer to the inode */
20309      off_t filp_pos;                /* file position */
20310    } filp[NR_FILPS];
20311
20312    #define FILP_CLOSED    0          /* filp_mode: associated device closed */
20313
20314    #define NIL_FILP (struct filp *) 0     /* indicates absence of a filp slot */




++++++++++++++++++++++++++++++++++++++++++++++++++++++++++++++++++++++++++++++++
                              src/fs/lock.h
++++++++++++++++++++++++++++++++++++++++++++++++++++++++++++++++++++++++++++++++

20400    /* This is the file locking table.  Like the filp table, it points to the
20401     * inode table, however, in this case to achieve advisory locking.
20402     */
20403    EXTERN struct file_lock {
20404      short lock_type;               /* F_RDLOCK or F_WRLOCK; 0 means unused slot */
20405      pid_t lock_pid;                /* pid of the process holding the lock */
20406      struct inode *lock_inode;      /* pointer to the inode locked */
20407      off_t lock_first;              /* offset of first byte locked */
20408      off_t lock_last;               /* offset of last byte locked */
20409    } file_lock[NR_LOCKS];
```

```
++++++++++++++++++++++++++++++++++++++++++++++++++++++++++++++++++++++++++++
                              src/fs/inode.h
++++++++++++++++++++++++++++++++++++++++++++++++++++++++++++++++++++++++++++

20500   /* Inode table.  This table holds inodes that are currently in use.  In some
20501    * cases they have been opened by an open() or creat() system call, in other
20502    * cases the file system itself needs the inode for one reason or another,
20503    * such as to search a directory for a path name.
20504    * The first part of the struct holds fields that are present on the
20505    * disk; the second part holds fields not present on the disk.
20506    * The disk inode part is also declared in "type.h" as 'd1_inode' for V1
20507    * file systems and 'd2_inode' for V2 file systems.
20508    */
20509
20510   EXTERN struct inode {
20511     mode_t i_mode;                  /* file type, protection, etc. */
20512     nlink_t i_nlinks;               /* how many links to this file */
20513     uid_t i_uid;                    /* user id of the file's owner */
20514     gid_t i_gid;                    /* group number */
20515     off_t i_size;                   /* current file size in bytes */
20516     time_t i_atime;                 /* time of last access (V2 only) */
20517     time_t i_mtime;                 /* when was file data last changed */
20518     time_t i_ctime;                 /* when was inode itself changed (V2 only)*/
20519     zone_t i_zone[V2_NR_TZONES];    /* zone numbers for direct, ind, and dbl ind */
20520
20521     /* The following items are not present on the disk. */
20522     dev_t i_dev;                    /* which device is the inode on */
20523     ino_t i_num;                    /* inode number on its (minor) device */
20524     int i_count;                    /* # times inode used; 0 means slot is free */
20525     int i_ndzones;                  /* # direct zones (Vx_NR_DZONES) */
20526     int i_nindirs;                  /* # indirect zones per indirect block */
20527     struct super_block *i_sp;       /* pointer to super block for inode's device */
20528     char i_dirt;                    /* CLEAN or DIRTY */
20529     char i_pipe;                    /* set to I_PIPE if pipe */
20530     char i_mount;                   /* this bit is set if file mounted on */
20531     char i_seek;                    /* set on LSEEK, cleared on READ/WRITE */
20532     char i_update;                  /* the ATIME, CTIME, and MTIME bits are here */
20533   } inode[NR_INODES];
20534
20535
20536   #define NIL_INODE (struct inode *) 0    /* indicates absence of inode slot */
20537
20538   /* Field values.  Note that CLEAN and DIRTY are defined in "const.h" */
20539   #define NO_PIPE            0    /* i_pipe is NO_PIPE if inode is not a pipe */
20540   #define I_PIPE             1    /* i_pipe is I_PIPE if inode is a pipe */
20541   #define NO_MOUNT           0    /* i_mount is NO_MOUNT if file not mounted on*/
20542   #define I_MOUNT            1    /* i_mount is I_MOUNT if file mounted on */
20543   #define NO_SEEK            0    /* i_seek = NO_SEEK if last op was not SEEK */
20544   #define ISEEK              1    /* i_seek = ISEEK if last op was SEEK */
```

```
++++++++++++++++++++++++++++++++++++++++++++++++++++++++++++++++++++++++++++++
                              src/fs/param.h
++++++++++++++++++++++++++++++++++++++++++++++++++++++++++++++++++++++++++++++
20600    /* The following names are synonyms for the variables in the input message. */
20601    #define acc_time        m.m2_l1
20602    #define addr            m.m1_i3
20603    #define buffer          m.m1_p1
20604    #define child           m.m1_i2
20605    #define co_mode         m.m1_i1
20606    #define eff_grp_id      m.m1_i3
20607    #define eff_user_id     m.m1_i3
20608    #define erki            m.m1_p1
20609    #define fd              m.m1_i1
20610    #define fd2             m.m1_i2
20611    #define ioflags         m.m1_i3
20612    #define group           m.m1_i3
20613    #define real_grp_id     m.m1_i2
20614    #define ls_fd           m.m2_i1
20615    #define mk_mode         m.m1_i2
20616    #define mode            m.m3_i2
20617    #define c_mode          m.m1_i3
20618    #define c_name          m.m1_p1
20619    #define name            m.m3_p1
20620    #define name1           m.m1_p1
20621    #define name2           m.m1_p2
20622    #define name_length     m.m3_i1
20623    #define name1_length    m.m1_i1
20624    #define name2_length    m.m1_i2
20625    #define nbytes          m.m1_i2
20626    #define offset          m.m2_l1
20627    #define owner           m.m1_i2
20628    #define parent          m.m1_i1
20629    #define pathname        m.m3_ca1
20630    #define pid             m.m1_i3
20631    #define pro             m.m1_i1
20632    #define rd_only         m.m1_i3
20633    #define real_user_id    m.m1_i2
20634    #define request         m.m1_i2
20635    #define sig             m.m1_i2
20636    #define slot1           m.m1_i1
20637    #define tp              m.m2_l1
20638    #define utime_actime    m.m2_l1
20639    #define utime_modtime   m.m2_l2
20640    #define utime_file      m.m2_p1
20641    #define utime_length    m.m2_i1
20642    #define whence          m.m2_i2
20643
20644    /* The following names are synonyms for the variables in the output message. */
20645    #define reply_type      m1.m_type
20646    #define reply_l1        m1.m2_l1
20647    #define reply_i1        m1.m1_i1
20648    #define reply_i2        m1.m1_i2
20649    #define reply_t1        m1.m4_l1
20650    #define reply_t2        m1.m4_l2
20651    #define reply_t3        m1.m4_l3
20652    #define reply_t4        m1.m4_l4
20653    #define reply_t5        m1.m4_l5
```

```
++++++++++++++++++++++++++++++++++++++++++++++++++++++++++++++++++++++++++++
                            src/fs/super.h
++++++++++++++++++++++++++++++++++++++++++++++++++++++++++++++++++++++++++++
20700   /* Super block table.  The root file system and every mounted file system
20701    * has an entry here.  The entry holds information about the sizes of the bit
20702    * maps and inodes.  The s_ninodes field gives the number of inodes available
20703    * for files and directories, including the root directory.  Inode 0 is
20704    * on the disk, but not used.  Thus s_ninodes = 4 means that 5 bits will be
20705    * used in the bit map, bit 0, which is always 1 and not used, and bits 1-4
20706    * for files and directories.  The disk layout is:
20707    *
20708    *      Item          # blocks
20709    *     boot block       1
20710    *     super block      1
20711    *     inode map      s_imap_blocks
20712    *     zone map       s_zmap_blocks
20713    *     inodes         (s_ninodes + 'inodes per block' - 1)/'inodes per block'
20714    *     unused         whatever is needed to fill out the current zone
20715    *     data zones     (s_zones - s_firstdatazone) << s_log_zone_size
20716    *
20717    * A super_block slot is free if s_dev == NO_DEV.
20718    */
20719
20720
20721   EXTERN struct super_block {
20722     ino_t s_ninodes;                /* # usable inodes on the minor device */
20723     zone1_t  s_nzones;              /* total device size, including bit maps etc */
20724     short s_imap_blocks;            /* # of blocks used by inode bit map */
20725     short s_zmap_blocks;            /* # of blocks used by zone bit map */
20726     zone1_t s_firstdatazone;        /* number of first data zone */
20727     short s_log_zone_size;          /* log2 of blocks/zone */
20728     off_t s_max_size;               /* maximum file size on this device */
20729     short s_magic;                  /* magic number to recognize super-blocks */
20730     short s_pad;                    /* try to avoid compiler-dependent padding */
20731     zone_t s_zones;                 /* number of zones (replaces s_nzones in V2) */
20732
20733     /* The following items are only used when the super_block is in memory. */
20734     struct inode *s_isup;           /* inode for root dir of mounted file sys */
20735     struct inode *s_imount;         /* inode mounted on */
20736     unsigned s_inodes_per_block;    /* precalculated from magic number */
20737     dev_t s_dev;                    /* whose super block is this? */
20738     int s_rd_only;                  /* set to 1 iff file sys mounted read only */
20739     int s_native;                   /* set to 1 iff not byte swapped file system */
20740     int s_version;                  /* file system version, zero means bad magic */
20741     int s_ndzones;                  /* # direct zones in an inode */
20742     int s_nindirs;                  /* # indirect zones per indirect block */
20743     bit_t s_isearch;                /* inodes below this bit number are in use */
20744     bit_t s_zsearch;                /* all zones below this bit number are in use*/
20745   } super_block[NR_SUPERS];
20746
20747   #define NIL_SUPER (struct super_block *) 0
20748   #define IMAP            0       /* operating on the inode bit map */
20749   #define ZMAP            1       /* operating on the zone bit map */
```

```
++++++++++++++++++++++++++++++++++++++++++++++++++++++++++++++++++++++++++++++++
                                src/fs/table.c
++++++++++++++++++++++++++++++++++++++++++++++++++++++++++++++++++++++++++++++++
20800     /* This file contains the table used to map system call numbers onto the
20801      * routines that perform them.
20802      */
20803
20804     #define _TABLE
20805
20806     #include "fs.h"
20807     #include <minix/callnr.h>
20808     #include <minix/com.h>
20809     #include "buf.h"
20810     #include "dev.h"
20811     #include "file.h"
20812     #include "fproc.h"
20813     #include "inode.h"
20814     #include "lock.h"
20815     #include "super.h"
20816
20817     PUBLIC _PROTOTYPE (int (*call_vector[NCALLS]), (void) ) = {
20818             no_sys,         /*  0 = unused  */
20819             do_exit,        /*  1 = exit    */
20820             do_fork,        /*  2 = fork    */
20821             do_read,        /*  3 = read    */
20822             do_write,       /*  4 = write   */
20823             do_open,        /*  5 = open    */
20824             do_close,       /*  6 = close   */
20825             no_sys,         /*  7 = wait    */
20826             do_creat,       /*  8 = creat   */
20827             do_link,        /*  9 = link    */
20828             do_unlink,      /* 10 = unlink  */
20829             no_sys,         /* 11 = waitpid */
20830             do_chdir,       /* 12 = chdir   */
20831             do_time,        /* 13 = time    */
20832             do_mknod,       /* 14 = mknod   */
20833             do_chmod,       /* 15 = chmod   */
20834             do_chown,       /* 16 = chown   */
20835             no_sys,         /* 17 = break   */
20836             do_stat,        /* 18 = stat    */
20837             do_lseek,       /* 19 = lseek   */
20838             no_sys,         /* 20 = getpid  */
20839             do_mount,       /* 21 = mount   */
20840             do_umount,      /* 22 = umount  */
20841             do_set,         /* 23 = setuid  */
20842             no_sys,         /* 24 = getuid  */
20843             do_stime,       /* 25 = stime   */
20844             no_sys,         /* 26 = ptrace  */
20845             no_sys,         /* 27 = alarm   */
20846             do_fstat,       /* 28 = fstat   */
20847             no_sys,         /* 29 = pause   */
20848             do_utime,       /* 30 = utime   */
20849             no_sys,         /* 31 = (stty)  */
20850             no_sys,         /* 32 = (gtty)  */
20851             do_access,      /* 33 = access  */
20852             no_sys,         /* 34 = (nice)  */
20853             no_sys,         /* 35 = (ftime) */
20854             do_sync,        /* 36 = sync    */
```

```
20855          no_sys,        /* 37 = kill    */
20856          do_rename,     /* 38 = rename  */
20857          do_mkdir,      /* 39 = mkdir   */
20858          do_unlink,     /* 40 = rmdir   */
20859          do_dup,        /* 41 = dup     */
20860          do_pipe,       /* 42 = pipe    */
20861          do_tims,       /* 43 = times   */
20862          no_sys,        /* 44 = (prof)  */
20863          no_sys,        /* 45 = unused  */
20864          do_set,        /* 46 = setgid  */
20865          no_sys,        /* 47 = getgid  */
20866          no_sys,        /* 48 = (signal)*/
20867          no_sys,        /* 49 = unused  */
20868          no_sys,        /* 50 = unused  */
20869          no_sys,        /* 51 = (acct)  */
20870          no_sys,        /* 52 = (phys)  */
20871          no_sys,        /* 53 = (lock)  */
20872          do_ioctl,      /* 54 = ioctl   */
20873          do_fcntl,      /* 55 = fcntl   */
20874          no_sys,        /* 56 = (mpx)   */
20875          no_sys,        /* 57 = unused  */
20876          no_sys,        /* 58 = unused  */
20877          do_exec,       /* 59 = execve  */
20878          do_umask,      /* 60 = umask   */
20879          do_chroot,     /* 61 = chroot  */
20880          do_setsid,     /* 62 = setsid  */
20881          no_sys,        /* 63 = getpgrp */
20882
20883          no_sys,        /* 64 = KSIG: signals originating in the kernel */
20884          do_unpause,    /* 65 = UNPAUSE */
20885          no_sys,        /* 66 = unused  */
20886          do_revive,     /* 67 = REVIVE  */
20887          no_sys,        /* 68 = TASK_REPLY      */
20888          no_sys,        /* 69 = unused */
20889          no_sys,        /* 70 = unused */
20890          no_sys,        /* 71 = SIGACTION */
20891          no_sys,        /* 72 = SIGSUSPEND */
20892          no_sys,        /* 73 = SIGPENDING */
20893          no_sys,        /* 74 = SIGPROCMASK */
20894          no_sys,        /* 75 = SIGRETURN */
20895          no_sys,        /* 76 = REBOOT */
20896   };
20897
20898
20899   /* Some devices may or may not be there in the next table. */
20900   #define DT(enable, open, rw, close, task) \
20901           { (enable ? (open) : no_dev), (enable ? (rw) : no_dev), \
20902             (enable ? (close) : no_dev), (enable ? (task) : 0) },
20903
20904   /* The order of the entries here determines the mapping between major device
20905    * numbers and tasks.  The first entry (major device 0) is not used.  The
20906    * next entry is major device 1, etc.  Character and block devices can be
20907    * intermixed at random.  If this ordering is changed, the devices in
20908    * <include/minix/boot.h> must be changed to correspond to the new values.
20909    * Note that the major device numbers used in /dev are NOT the same as the
20910    * task numbers used inside the kernel (as defined in <include/minix/com.h>).
20911    * Also note that if /dev/mem is changed from 1, NULL_MAJOR must be changed
20912    * in <include/minix/com.h>.
20913    */
20914   PUBLIC struct dmap dmap[] = {
```

```
20915    /*  ?    Open         Read/Write   Close         Task #        Device  File
20916       -    ----         ----------   -----         -------       ------  ----       */
20917       DT(1, no_dev,      no_dev,      no_dev,       0)            /*  0 = not used   */
20918       DT(1, dev_opcl,    call_task,   dev_opcl,     MEM)          /*  1 = /dev/mem   */
20919       DT(1, dev_opcl,    call_task,   dev_opcl,     FLOPPY)       /*  2 = /dev/fd0   */
20920       DT(ENABLE_WINI,
20921             dev_opcl,    call_task,   dev_opcl,     WINCHESTER)   /*  3 = /dev/hd0   */
20922       DT(1, tty_open,    call_task,   dev_opcl,     TTY)          /*  4 = /dev/tty00 */
20923       DT(1, ctty_open,   call_ctty,   ctty_close,   TTY)          /*  5 = /dev/tty   */
20924       DT(1, dev_opcl,    call_task,   dev_opcl,     PRINTER)      /*  6 = /dev/lp    */
20925
20926    #if (MACHINE == IBM_PC)
20927       DT(ENABLE_NETWORKING,
20928             net_open,    call_task,   dev_opcl,     INET_PROC_NR)/*  7 = /dev/ip     */
20929       DT(ENABLE_CDROM,
20930             dev_opcl,    call_task,   dev_opcl,     CDROM)        /*  8 = /dev/cd0   */
20931       DT(0, 0,           0,           0,            0)            /*  9 = not used   */
20932       DT(ENABLE_SCSI,
20933             dev_opcl,    call_task,   dev_opcl,     SCSI)         /* 10 = /dev/sd0   */
20934       DT(0, 0,           0,           0,            0)            /* 11 = not used   */
20935       DT(0, 0,           0,           0,            0)            /* 12 = not used   */
20936       DT(ENABLE_AUDIO,
20937             dev_opcl,    call_task,   dev_opcl,     AUDIO)        /* 13 = /dev/audio */
20938       DT(ENABLE_AUDIO,
20939             dev_opcl,    call_task,   dev_opcl,     MIXER)        /* 14 = /dev/mixer */
20940    #endif /* IBM_PC */
20941
20942    #if (MACHINE == ATARI)
20943       DT(ENABLE_SCSI,
20944             dev_opcl,    call_task,   dev_opcl,     SCSI)         /*  7 = /dev/hdscsi0 */
20945    #endif
20946    };
20947
20948    PUBLIC int max_major = sizeof(dmap)/sizeof(struct dmap);


+++++++++++++++++++++++++++++++++++++++++++++++++++++++++++++++++++++++++++++++++++
                                 src/fs/cache.c
+++++++++++++++++++++++++++++++++++++++++++++++++++++++++++++++++++++++++++++++++++

21000    /* The file system maintains a buffer cache to reduce the number of disk
21001     * accesses needed.  Whenever a read or write to the disk is done, a check is
21002     * first made to see if the block is in the cache.  This file manages the
21003     * cache.
21004     *
21005     * The entry points into this file are:
21006     *   get_block:    request to fetch a block for reading or writing from cache
21007     *   put_block:    return a block previously requested with get_block
21008     *   alloc_zone:   allocate a new zone (to increase the length of a file)
21009     *   free_zone:    release a zone (when a file is removed)
21010     *   rw_block:     read or write a block from the disk itself
21011     *   invalidate:   remove all the cache blocks on some device
21012     */
21013
21014    #include "fs.h"
21015    #include <minix/com.h>
21016    #include <minix/boot.h>
21017    #include "buf.h"
21018    #include "file.h"
21019    #include "fproc.h"
```

```
21020    #include "super.h"
21021
21022    FORWARD _PROTOTYPE( void rm_lru, (struct buf *bp) );
21023
21024    /*===========================================================================*
21025     *                              get_block                                    *
21026     *===========================================================================*/
21027    PUBLIC struct buf *get_block(dev, block, only_search)
21028    register dev_t dev;              /* on which device is the block? */
21029    register block_t block;          /* which block is wanted? */
21030    int only_search;                 /* if NO_READ, don't read, else act normal */
21031    {
21032    /* Check to see if the requested block is in the block cache.  If so, return
21033     * a pointer to it.  If not, evict some other block and fetch it (unless
21034     * 'only_search' is 1).  All the blocks in the cache that are not in use
21035     * are linked together in a chain, with 'front' pointing to the least recently
21036     * used block and 'rear' to the most recently used block.  If 'only_search' is
21037     * 1, the block being requested will be overwritten in its entirety, so it is
21038     * only necessary to see if it is in the cache; if it is not, any free buffer
21039     * will do.  It is not necessary to actually read the block in from disk.
21040     * If 'only_search' is PREFETCH, the block need not be read from the disk,
21041     * and the device is not to be marked on the block, so callers can tell if
21042     * the block returned is valid.
21043     * In addition to the LRU chain, there is also a hash chain to link together
21044     * blocks whose block numbers end with the same bit strings, for fast lookup.
21045     */
21046
21047      int b;
21048      register struct buf *bp, *prev_ptr;
21049
21050      /* Search the hash chain for (dev, block). Do_read() can use
21051       * get_block(NO_DEV ...) to get an unnamed block to fill with zeros when
21052       * someone wants to read from a hole in a file, in which case this search
21053       * is skipped
21054       */
21055      if (dev != NO_DEV) {
21056            b = (int) block & HASH_MASK;
21057            bp = buf_hash[b];
21058            while (bp != NIL_BUF) {
21059                    if (bp->b_blocknr == block && bp->b_dev == dev) {
21060                            /* Block needed has been found. */
21061                            if (bp->b_count == 0) rm_lru(bp);
21062                            bp->b_count++;  /* record that block is in use */
21063                            return(bp);
21064                    } else {
21065                            /* This block is not the one sought. */
21066                            bp = bp->b_hash; /* move to next block on hash chain */
21067                    }
21068            }
21069      }
21070
21071      /* Desired block is not on available chain.  Take oldest block ('front'). */
21072      if ((bp = front) == NIL_BUF) panic("all buffers in use", NR_BUFS);
21073      rm_lru(bp);
21074
21075      /* Remove the block that was just taken from its hash chain. */
21076      b = (int) bp->b_blocknr & HASH_MASK;
21077      prev_ptr = buf_hash[b];
21078      if (prev_ptr == bp) {
21079            buf_hash[b] = bp->b_hash;
```

```
21080            } else {
21081                /* The block just taken is not on the front of its hash chain. */
21082                while (prev_ptr->b_hash != NIL_BUF)
21083                    if (prev_ptr->b_hash == bp) {
21084                        prev_ptr->b_hash = bp->b_hash;  /* found it */
21085                        break;
21086                    } else {
21087                        prev_ptr = prev_ptr->b_hash;    /* keep looking */
21088                    }
21089            }
21090
21091        /* If the block taken is dirty, make it clean by writing it to the disk.
21092         * Avoid hysteresis by flushing all other dirty blocks for the same device.
21093         */
21094        if (bp->b_dev != NO_DEV) {
21095                if (bp->b_dirt == DIRTY) flushall(bp->b_dev);
21096        }
21097
21098        /* Fill in block's parameters and add it to the hash chain where it goes. */
21099        bp->b_dev = dev;                  /* fill in device number */
21100        bp->b_blocknr = block;            /* fill in block number */
21101        bp->b_count++;                    /* record that block is being used */
21102        b = (int) bp->b_blocknr & HASH_MASK;
21103        bp->b_hash = buf_hash[b];
21104        buf_hash[b] = bp;                 /* add to hash list */
21105
21106        /* Go get the requested block unless searching or prefetching. */
21107        if (dev != NO_DEV) {
21108                if (only_search == PREFETCH) bp->b_dev = NO_DEV;
21109                else
21110                if (only_search == NORMAL) rw_block(bp, READING);
21111        }
21112        return(bp);                       /* return the newly acquired block */
21113    }


21116    /*===========================================================================*
21117     *                              put_block                                     *
21118     *===========================================================================*/
21119    PUBLIC void put_block(bp, block_type)
21120    register struct buf *bp;          /* pointer to the buffer to be released */
21121    int block_type;                   /* INODE_BLOCK, DIRECTORY_BLOCK, or whatever */
21122    {
21123    /* Return a block to the list of available blocks.   Depending on 'block_type'
21124     * it may be put on the front or rear of the LRU chain.  Blocks that are
21125     * expected to be needed again shortly (e.g., partially full data blocks)
21126     * go on the rear; blocks that are unlikely to be needed again shortly
21127     * (e.g., full data blocks) go on the front.  Blocks whose loss can hurt
21128     * the integrity of the file system (e.g., inode blocks) are written to
21129     * disk immediately if they are dirty.
21130     */
21131
21132        if (bp == NIL_BUF) return;    /* it is easier to check here than in caller */
21133
21134        bp->b_count--;                /* there is one use fewer now */
21135        if (bp->b_count != 0) return; /* block is still in use */
21136
21137        bufs_in_use--;                /* one fewer block buffers in use */
21138
21139        /* Put this block back on the LRU chain.  If the ONE_SHOT bit is set in
```

```
21140        * 'block_type', the block is not likely to be needed again shortly, so put
21141        * it on the front of the LRU chain where it will be the first one to be
21142        * taken when a free buffer is needed later.
21143        */
21144       if (block_type & ONE_SHOT) {
21145               /* Block probably won't be needed quickly. Put it on front of chain.
21146                * It will be the next block to be evicted from the cache.
21147                */
21148               bp->b_prev = NIL_BUF;
21149               bp->b_next = front;
21150               if (front == NIL_BUF)
21151                       rear = bp;       /* LRU chain was empty */
21152               else
21153                       front->b_prev = bp;
21154               front = bp;
21155       } else {
21156               /* Block probably will be needed quickly.  Put it on rear of chain.
21157                * It will not be evicted from the cache for a long time.
21158                */
21159               bp->b_prev = rear;
21160               bp->b_next = NIL_BUF;
21161               if (rear == NIL_BUF)
21162                       front = bp;
21163               else
21164                       rear->b_next = bp;
21165               rear = bp;
21166       }
21167
21168       /* Some blocks are so important (e.g., inodes, indirect blocks) that they
21169        * should be written to the disk immediately to avoid messing up the file
21170        * system in the event of a crash.
21171        */
21172       if ((block_type & WRITE_IMMED) && bp->b_dirt==DIRTY && bp->b_dev != NO_DEV)
21173               rw_block(bp, WRITING);
21174  }


21177  /*===========================================================================*
21178   *                              alloc_zone                                   *
21179   *===========================================================================*/
21180  PUBLIC zone_t alloc_zone(dev, z)
21181  dev_t dev;                            /* device where zone wanted */
21182  zone_t z;                             /* try to allocate new zone near this one */
21183  {
21184  /* Allocate a new zone on the indicated device and return its number. */
21185
21186    int major, minor;
21187    bit_t b, bit;
21188    struct super_block *sp;
21189
21190    /* Note that the routine alloc_bit() returns 1 for the lowest possible
21191     * zone, which corresponds to sp->s_firstdatazone.  To convert a value
21192     * between the bit number, 'b', used by alloc_bit() and the zone number, 'z',
21193     * stored in the inode, use the formula:
21194     *     z = b + sp->s_firstdatazone - 1
21195     * Alloc_bit() never returns 0, since this is used for NO_BIT (failure).
21196     */
21197    sp = get_super(dev);           /* find the super_block for this device */
21198
21199    /* If z is 0, skip initial part of the map known to be fully in use. */
```

```
21200        if (z == sp->s_firstdatazone) {
21201                bit = sp->s_zsearch;
21202        } else {
21203                bit = (bit_t) z - (sp->s_firstdatazone - 1);
21204        }
21205        b = alloc_bit(sp, ZMAP, bit);
21206        if (b == NO_BIT) {
21207                err_code = ENOSPC;
21208                major = (int) (sp->s_dev >> MAJOR) & BYTE;
21209                minor = (int) (sp->s_dev >> MINOR) & BYTE;
21210                printf("No space on %sdevice %d/%d\n",
21211                        sp->s_dev == ROOT_DEV ? "root " : "", major, minor);
21212                return(NO_ZONE);
21213        }
21214        if (z == sp->s_firstdatazone) sp->s_zsearch = b;        /* for next time */
21215        return(sp->s_firstdatazone - 1 + (zone_t) b);
21216  }


21219  /*===========================================================================*
21220   *                              free_zone                                    *
21221   *===========================================================================*/
21222  PUBLIC void free_zone(dev, numb)
21223  dev_t dev;                                      /* device where zone located */
21224  zone_t numb;                                    /* zone to be returned */
21225  {
21226  /* Return a zone. */
21227
21228    register struct super_block *sp;
21229    bit_t bit;
21230
21231    /* Locate the appropriate super_block and return bit. */
21232    sp = get_super(dev);
21233    if (numb < sp->s_firstdatazone || numb >= sp->s_zones) return;
21234    bit = (bit_t) (numb - (sp->s_firstdatazone - 1));
21235    free_bit(sp, ZMAP, bit);
21236    if (bit < sp->s_zsearch) sp->s_zsearch = bit;
21237  }


21240  /*===========================================================================*
21241   *                              rw_block                                     *
21242   *===========================================================================*/
21243  PUBLIC void rw_block(bp, rw_flag)
21244  register struct buf *bp;        /* buffer pointer */
21245  int rw_flag;                    /* READING or WRITING */
21246  {
21247  /* Read or write a disk block. This is the only routine in which actual disk
21248   * I/O is invoked. If an error occurs, a message is printed here, but the error
21249   * is not reported to the caller.  If the error occurred while purging a block
21250   * from the cache, it is not clear what the caller could do about it anyway.
21251   */
21252
21253    int r, op;
21254    off_t pos;
21255    dev_t dev;
21256
21257    if ( (dev = bp->b_dev) != NO_DEV) {
21258            pos = (off_t) bp->b_blocknr * BLOCK_SIZE;
21259            op = (rw_flag == READING ? DEV_READ : DEV_WRITE);
```

```
21260                 r = dev_io(op, FALSE, dev, pos, BLOCK_SIZE, FS_PROC_NR, bp->b_data);
21261             if (r != BLOCK_SIZE) {
21262                 if (r >= 0) r = END_OF_FILE;
21263                 if (r != END_OF_FILE)
21264                   printf("Unrecoverable disk error on device %d/%d, block %ld\n",
21265                         (dev>>MAJOR)&BYTE, (dev>>MINOR)&BYTE, bp->b_blocknr);
21266                     bp->b_dev = NO_DEV;      /* invalidate block */
21267
21268                     /* Report read errors to interested parties. */
21269                     if (rw_flag == READING) rdwt_err = r;
21270             }
21271       }
21272
21273       bp->b_dirt = CLEAN;
21274 }


21277   /*===========================================================================*
21278    *                              invalidate                                   *
21279    *===========================================================================*/
21280   PUBLIC void invalidate(device)
21281   dev_t device;                    /* device whose blocks are to be purged */
21282   {
21283   /* Remove all the blocks belonging to some device from the cache. */
21284
21285     register struct buf *bp;
21286
21287     for (bp = &buf[0]; bp < &buf[NR_BUFS]; bp++)
21288           if (bp->b_dev == device) bp->b_dev = NO_DEV;
21289   }


21292   /*===========================================================================*
21293    *                              flushall                                     *
21294    *===========================================================================*/
21295   PUBLIC void flushall(dev)
21296   dev_t dev;                       /* device to flush */
21297   {
21298   /* Flush all dirty blocks for one device. */
21299
21300     register struct buf *bp;
21301     static struct buf *dirty[NR_BUFS];     /* static so it isn't on stack */
21302     int ndirty;
21303
21304     for (bp = &buf[0], ndirty = 0; bp < &buf[NR_BUFS]; bp++)
21305           if (bp->b_dirt == DIRTY && bp->b_dev == dev) dirty[ndirty++] = bp;
21306     rw_scattered(dev, dirty, ndirty, WRITING);
21307   }


21310   /*===========================================================================*
21311    *                              rw_scattered                                 *
21312    *===========================================================================*/
21313   PUBLIC void rw_scattered(dev, bufq, bufqsize, rw_flag)
21314   dev_t dev;                             /* major-minor device number */
21315   struct buf **bufq;                     /* pointer to array of buffers */
21316   int bufqsize;                          /* number of buffers */
21317   int rw_flag;                           /* READING or WRITING */
21318   {
21319   /* Read or write scattered data from a device. */
```

```
21320
21321          register struct buf *bp;
21322          int gap;
21323          register int i;
21324          register struct iorequest_s *iop;
21325          static struct iorequest_s iovec[NR_IOREQS];  /* static so it isn't on stack */
21326          int j;
21327
21328          /* (Shell) sort buffers on b_blocknr. */
21329          gap = 1;
21330          do
21331                  gap = 3 * gap + 1;
21332          while (gap <= bufqsize);
21333          while (gap != 1) {
21334                  gap /= 3;
21335                  for (j = gap; j < bufqsize; j++) {
21336                          for (i = j - gap;
21337                               i >= 0 && bufq[i]->b_blocknr > bufq[i + gap]->b_blocknr;
21338                               i -= gap) {
21339                                  bp = bufq[i];
21340                                  bufq[i] = bufq[i + gap];
21341                                  bufq[i + gap] = bp;
21342                          }
21343                  }
21344          }
21345
21346          /* Set up i/o vector and do i/o.  The result of dev_io is discarded because
21347           * all results are returned in the vector.  If dev_io fails completely, the
21348           * vector is unchanged and all results are taken as errors.
21349           */
21350          while (bufqsize > 0) {
21351                  for (j = 0, iop = iovec; j < NR_IOREQS && j < bufqsize; j++, iop++) {
21352                          bp = bufq[j];
21353                          iop->io_position = (off_t) bp->b_blocknr * BLOCK_SIZE;
21354                          iop->io_buf = bp->b_data;
21355                          iop->io_nbytes = BLOCK_SIZE;
21356                          iop->io_request = rw_flag == WRITING ?
21357                                          DEV_WRITE : DEV_READ | OPTIONAL_IO;
21358                  }
21359                  (void) dev_io(SCATTERED_IO, 0, dev, (off_t) 0, j, FS_PROC_NR,
21360                                                          (char *) iovec);
21361
21362                  /* Harvest the results.  Leave read errors for rw_block() to complain. */
21363                  for (i = 0, iop = iovec; i < j; i++, iop++) {
21364                          bp = bufq[i];
21365                          if (rw_flag == READING) {
21366                              if (iop->io_nbytes == 0)
21367                                  bp->b_dev = dev;          /* validate block */
21368                              put_block(bp, PARTIAL_DATA_BLOCK);
21369                          } else {
21370                              if (iop->io_nbytes != 0) {
21371                                printf("Unrecoverable write error on device %d/%d, block %ld\n",
21372                                          (dev>>MAJOR)&BYTE, (dev>>MINOR)&BYTE, bp->b_blocknr);
21373                                  bp->b_dev = NO_DEV;     /* invalidate block */
21374                              }
21375                              bp->b_dirt = CLEAN;
21376                          }
21377                  }
21378                  bufq += j;
21379                  bufqsize -= j;
```

```
21380        }
21381    }


21384    /*===========================================================================*
21385     *                              rm_lru                                        *
21386     *===========================================================================*/
21387    PRIVATE void rm_lru(bp)
21388    struct buf *bp;
21389    {
21390    /* Remove a block from its LRU chain. */
21391
21392        struct buf *next_ptr, *prev_ptr;
21393
21394        bufs_in_use++;
21395        next_ptr = bp->b_next;            /* successor on LRU chain */
21396        prev_ptr = bp->b_prev;            /* predecessor on LRU chain */
21397        if (prev_ptr != NIL_BUF)
21398                prev_ptr->b_next = next_ptr;
21399        else
21400                front = next_ptr;         /* this block was at front of chain */
21401
21402        if (next_ptr != NIL_BUF)
21403                next_ptr->b_prev = prev_ptr;
21404        else
21405                rear = prev_ptr;          /* this block was at rear of chain */
21406    }



+++++++++++++++++++++++++++++++++++++++++++++++++++++++++++++++++++++++++++++++
                              src/fs/inode.c
+++++++++++++++++++++++++++++++++++++++++++++++++++++++++++++++++++++++++++++++

21500    /* This file manages the inode table.  There are procedures to allocate and
21501     * deallocate inodes, acquire, erase, and release them, and read and write
21502     * them from the disk.
21503     *
21504     * The entry points into this file are
21505     *   get_inode:    search inode table for a given inode; if not there, read it
21506     *   put_inode:    indicate that an inode is no longer needed in memory
21507     *   alloc_inode:  allocate a new, unused inode
21508     *   wipe_inode:   erase some fields of a newly allocated inode
21509     *   free_inode:   mark an inode as available for a new file
21510     *   update_times: update atime, ctime, and mtime
21511     *   rw_inode:     read a disk block and extract an inode, or corresp. write
21512     *   old_icopy:    copy to/from in-core inode struct and disk inode (V1.x)
21513     *   new_icopy:    copy to/from in-core inode struct and disk inode (V2.x)
21514     *   dup_inode:    indicate that someone else is using an inode table entry
21515     */
21516
21517    #include "fs.h"
21518    #include <minix/boot.h>
21519    #include "buf.h"
21520    #include "file.h"
21521    #include "fproc.h"
21522    #include "inode.h"
21523    #include "super.h"
21524
```

```
21525    FORWARD _PROTOTYPE( void old_icopy, (struct inode *rip, d1_inode *dip,
21526                                                int direction, int norm));
21527    FORWARD _PROTOTYPE( void new_icopy, (struct inode *rip, d2_inode *dip,
21528                                                int direction, int norm));
21529
21530
21531    /*===========================================================================*
21532     *                              get_inode                                     *
21533     *===========================================================================*/
21534    PUBLIC struct inode *get_inode(dev, numb)
21535    dev_t dev;                       /* device on which inode resides */
21536    int numb;                        /* inode number (ANSI: may not be unshort) */
21537    {
21538    /* Find a slot in the inode table, load the specified inode into it, and
21539     * return a pointer to the slot.  If 'dev' == NO_DEV, just return a free slot.
21540     */
21541
21542      register struct inode *rip, *xp;
21543
21544      /* Search the inode table both for (dev, numb) and a free slot. */
21545      xp = NIL_INODE;
21546      for (rip = &inode[0]; rip < &inode[NR_INODES]; rip++) {
21547            if (rip->i_count > 0) { /* only check used slots for (dev, numb) */
21548                    if (rip->i_dev == dev && rip->i_num == numb) {
21549                            /* This is the inode that we are looking for. */
21550                            rip->i_count++;
21551                            return(rip);    /* (dev, numb) found */
21552                    }
21553            } else {
21554                    xp = rip;         /* remember this free slot for later */
21555            }
21556      }
21557
21558      /* Inode we want is not currently in use.  Did we find a free slot? */
21559      if (xp == NIL_INODE) {          /* inode table completely full */
21560            err_code = ENFILE;
21561            return(NIL_INODE);
21562      }
21563
21564      /* A free inode slot has been located.  Load the inode into it. */
21565      xp->i_dev = dev;
21566      xp->i_num = numb;
21567      xp->i_count = 1;
21568      if (dev != NO_DEV) rw_inode(xp, READING);     /* get inode from disk */
21569      xp->i_update = 0;               /* all the times are initially up-to-date */
21570
21571      return(xp);
21572    }


21575    /*===========================================================================*
21576     *                              put_inode                                     *
21577     *===========================================================================*/
21578    PUBLIC void put_inode(rip)
21579    register struct inode *rip;     /* pointer to inode to be released */
21580    {
21581    /* The caller is no longer using this inode.  If no one else is using it either
21582     * write it back to the disk immediately.  If it has no links, truncate it and
21583     * return it to the pool of available inodes.
21584     */
```

```
21585
21586        if (rip == NIL_INODE) return; /* checking here is easier than in caller */
21587        if (--rip->i_count == 0) {     /* i_count == 0 means no one is using it now */
21588              if ((rip->i_nlinks & BYTE) == 0) {
21589                    /* i_nlinks == 0 means free the inode. */
21590                    truncate(rip);  /* return all the disk blocks */
21591                    rip->i_mode = I_NOT_ALLOC;       /* clear I_TYPE field */
21592                    rip->i_dirt = DIRTY;
21593                    free_inode(rip->i_dev, rip->i_num);
21594              } else {
21595                    if (rip->i_pipe == I_PIPE) truncate(rip);
21596              }
21597              rip->i_pipe = NO_PIPE;  /* should always be cleared */
21598              if (rip->i_dirt == DIRTY) rw_inode(rip, WRITING);
21599        }
21600  }


21602  /*===========================================================================*
21603   *                              alloc_inode                                  *
21604   *===========================================================================*/
21605  PUBLIC struct inode *alloc_inode(dev, bits)
21606  dev_t dev;                             /* device on which to allocate the inode */
21607  mode_t bits;                           /* mode of the inode */
21608  {
21609  /* Allocate a free inode on 'dev', and return a pointer to it. */
21610
21611    register struct inode *rip;
21612    register struct super_block *sp;
21613    int major, minor, inumb;
21614    bit_t b;
21615
21616    sp = get_super(dev);  /* get pointer to super_block */
21617    if (sp->s_rd_only) {  /* can't allocate an inode on a read only device. */
21618          err_code = EROFS;
21619          return(NIL_INODE);
21620    }
21621
21622    /* Acquire an inode from the bit map. */
21623    b = alloc_bit(sp, IMAP, sp->s_isearch);
21624    if (b == NO_BIT) {
21625          err_code = ENFILE;
21626          major = (int) (sp->s_dev >> MAJOR) & BYTE;
21627          minor = (int) (sp->s_dev >> MINOR) & BYTE;
21628          printf("Out of i-nodes on %sdevice %d/%d\n",
21629                sp->s_dev == ROOT_DEV ? "root " : "", major, minor);
21630          return(NIL_INODE);
21631    }
21632    sp->s_isearch = b;                    /* next time start here */
21633    inumb = (int) b;                      /* be careful not to pass unshort as param */
21634
21635    /* Try to acquire a slot in the inode table. */
21636    if ((rip = get_inode(NO_DEV, inumb)) == NIL_INODE) {
21637          /* No inode table slots available.  Free the inode just allocated. */
21638          free_bit(sp, IMAP, b);
21639    } else {
21640          /* An inode slot is available. Put the inode just allocated into it. */
21641          rip->i_mode = bits;             /* set up RWX bits */
21642          rip->i_nlinks = (nlink_t) 0;    /* initial no links */
21643          rip->i_uid = fp->fp_effuid;     /* file's uid is owner's */
21644          rip->i_gid = fp->fp_effgid;     /* ditto group id */
```

```
21645              rip->i_dev = dev;                    /* mark which device it is on */
21646              rip->i_ndzones = sp->s_ndzones;  /* number of direct zones */
21647              rip->i_nindirs = sp->s_nindirs;  /* number of indirect zones per blk*/
21648              rip->i_sp = sp;                      /* pointer to super block */
21649
21650              /* Fields not cleared already are cleared in wipe_inode().  They have
21651               * been put there because truncate() needs to clear the same fields if
21652               * the file happens to be open while being truncated.  It saves space
21653               * not to repeat the code twice.
21654               */
21655              wipe_inode(rip);
21656      }
21657
21658    return(rip);
21659  }
21660
21661  /*===========================================================================*
21662   *                              wipe_inode                                   *
21663   *===========================================================================*/
21664  PUBLIC void wipe_inode(rip)
21665  register struct inode *rip;      /* the inode to be erased */
21666  {
21667  /* Erase some fields in the inode.  This function is called from alloc_inode()
21668   * when a new inode is to be allocated, and from truncate(), when an existing
21669   * inode is to be truncated.
21670   */
21671
21672    register int i;
21673
21674    rip->i_size = 0;
21675    rip->i_update = ATIME | CTIME | MTIME;        /* update all times later */
21676    rip->i_dirt = DIRTY;
21677    for (i = 0; i < V2_NR_TZONES; i++) rip->i_zone[i] = NO_ZONE;
21678  }
21679
21680
21681  /*===========================================================================*
21682   *                              free_inode                                   *
21683   *===========================================================================*/
21684  PUBLIC void free_inode(dev, inumb)
21685  dev_t dev;                       /* on which device is the inode */
21686  ino_t inumb;                     /* number of inode to be freed */
21687  {
21688  /* Return an inode to the pool of unallocated inodes. */
21689
21690    register struct super_block *sp;
21691    bit_t b;
21692
21693    /* Locate the appropriate super_block. */
21694    sp = get_super(dev);
21695    if (inumb <= 0 || inumb > sp->s_ninodes) return;
21696    b = inumb;
21697    free_bit(sp, IMAP, b);
21698    if (b < sp->s_isearch) sp->s_isearch = b;
21699  }
21700
21701  /*===========================================================================*
21702   *                              update_times                                 *
21703   *===========================================================================*/
21704  PUBLIC void update_times(rip)
```

```
21705   register struct inode *rip;     /* pointer to inode to be read/written */
21706   {
21707   /* Various system calls are required by the standard to update atime, ctime,
21708    * or mtime.  Since updating a time requires sending a message to the clock
21709    * task--an expensive business--the times are marked for update by setting
21710    * bits in i_update.  When a stat, fstat, or sync is done, or an inode is
21711    * released, update_times() may be called to actually fill in the times.
21712    */
21713
21714     time_t cur_time;
21715     struct super_block *sp;
21716
21717     sp = rip->i_sp;                 /* get pointer to super block. */
21718     if (sp->s_rd_only) return;      /* no updates for read-only file systems */
21719
21720     cur_time = clock_time();
21721     if (rip->i_update & ATIME) rip->i_atime = cur_time;
21722     if (rip->i_update & CTIME) rip->i_ctime = cur_time;
21723     if (rip->i_update & MTIME) rip->i_mtime = cur_time;
21724     rip->i_update = 0;             /* they are all up-to-date now */
21725   }


21728   /*===========================================================================*
21729    *                              rw_inode                                      *
21730    *===========================================================================*/
21731   PUBLIC void rw_inode(rip, rw_flag)
21732   register struct inode *rip;     /* pointer to inode to be read/written */
21733   int rw_flag;                    /* READING or WRITING */
21734   {
21735   /* An entry in the inode table is to be copied to or from the disk. */
21736
21737     register struct buf *bp;
21738     register struct super_block *sp;
21739     d1_inode *dip;
21740     d2_inode *dip2;
21741     block_t b, offset;
21742
21743     /* Get the block where the inode resides. */
21744     sp = get_super(rip->i_dev);    /* get pointer to super block */
21745     rip->i_sp = sp;                /* inode must contain super block pointer */
21746     offset = sp->s_imap_blocks + sp->s_zmap_blocks + 2;
21747     b = (block_t) (rip->i_num - 1)/sp->s_inodes_per_block + offset;
21748     bp = get_block(rip->i_dev, b, NORMAL);
21749     dip  = bp->b_v1_ino + (rip->i_num - 1) % V1_INODES_PER_BLOCK;
21750     dip2 = bp->b_v2_ino + (rip->i_num - 1) % V2_INODES_PER_BLOCK;
21751
21752     /* Do the read or write. */
21753     if (rw_flag == WRITING) {
21754           if (rip->i_update) update_times(rip);   /* times need updating */
21755           if (sp->s_rd_only == FALSE) bp->b_dirt = DIRTY;
21756     }
21757
21758     /* Copy the inode from the disk block to the in-core table or vice versa.
21759      * If the fourth parameter below is FALSE, the bytes are swapped.
21760      */
21761     if (sp->s_version == V1)
21762           old_icopy(rip, dip,  rw_flag, sp->s_native);
21763     else
21764           new_icopy(rip, dip2, rw_flag, sp->s_native);
```

```
21765
21766        put_block(bp, INODE_BLOCK);
21767        rip->i_dirt = CLEAN;
21768    }


21771    /*===========================================================================*
21772     *                              old_icopy                                     *
21773     *===========================================================================*/
21774    PRIVATE void old_icopy(rip, dip, direction, norm)
21775    register struct inode *rip;      /* pointer to the in-core inode struct */
21776    register d1_inode *dip;          /* pointer to the d1_inode inode struct */
21777    int direction;                   /* READING (from disk) or WRITING (to disk) */
21778    int norm;                        /* TRUE = do not swap bytes; FALSE = swap */
21779
21780    {
21781    /* The V1.x IBM disk, the V1.x 68000 disk, and the V2 disk (same for IBM and
21782     * 68000) all have different inode layouts.  When an inode is read or written
21783     * this routine handles the conversions so that the information in the inode
21784     * table is independent of the disk structure from which the inode came.
21785     * The old_icopy routine copies to and from V1 disks.
21786     */
21787
21788      int i;
21789
21790      if (direction == READING) {
21791            /* Copy V1.x inode to the in-core table, swapping bytes if need be. */
21792            rip->i_mode   = conv2(norm, (int) dip->d1_mode);
21793            rip->i_uid    = conv2(norm, (int) dip->d1_uid );
21794            rip->i_size   = conv4(norm,       dip->d1_size);
21795            rip->i_mtime  = conv4(norm,       dip->d1_mtime);
21796            rip->i_atime  = rip->i_mtime;
21797            rip->i_ctime  = rip->i_mtime;
21798            rip->i_nlinks = (nlink_t) dip->d1_nlinks;      /* 1 char */
21799            rip->i_gid    = (gid_t) dip->d1_gid;           /* 1 char */
21800            rip->i_ndzones = V1_NR_DZONES;
21801            rip->i_nindirs = V1_INDIRECTS;
21802            for (i = 0; i < V1_NR_TZONES; i++)
21803                    rip->i_zone[i] = conv2(norm, (int) dip->d1_zone[i]);
21804      } else {
21805            /* Copying V1.x inode to disk from the in-core table. */
21806            dip->d1_mode   = conv2(norm, (int) rip->i_mode);
21807            dip->d1_uid    = conv2(norm, (int) rip->i_uid );
21808            dip->d1_size   = conv4(norm,       rip->i_size);
21809            dip->d1_mtime  = conv4(norm,       rip->i_mtime);
21810            dip->d1_nlinks = (nlink_t) rip->i_nlinks;      /* 1 char */
21811            dip->d1_gid    = (gid_t) rip->i_gid;           /* 1 char */
21812            for (i = 0; i < V1_NR_TZONES; i++)
21813                    dip->d1_zone[i] = conv2(norm, (int) rip->i_zone[i]);
21814      }
21815    }


21818    /*===========================================================================*
21819     *                              new_icopy                                     *
21820     *===========================================================================*/
21821    PRIVATE void new_icopy(rip, dip, direction, norm)
21822    register struct inode *rip;      /* pointer to the in-core inode struct */
21823    register d2_inode *dip; /* pointer to the d2_inode struct */
21824    int direction;                   /* READING (from disk) or WRITING (to disk) */
```

```
21825    int norm;                              /* TRUE = do not swap bytes; FALSE = swap */
21826
21827    {
21828    /* Same as old_icopy, but to/from V2 disk layout. */
21829
21830      int i;
21831
21832      if (direction == READING) {
21833            /* Copy V2.x inode to the in-core table, swapping bytes if need be. */
21834            rip->i_mode   = conv2(norm,dip->d2_mode);
21835            rip->i_uid    = conv2(norm,dip->d2_uid );
21836            rip->i_nlinks = conv2(norm,(int) dip->d2_nlinks);
21837            rip->i_gid    = conv2(norm,(int) dip->d2_gid );
21838            rip->i_size   = conv4(norm,dip->d2_size);
21839            rip->i_atime  = conv4(norm,dip->d2_atime);
21840            rip->i_ctime  = conv4(norm,dip->d2_ctime);
21841            rip->i_mtime  = conv4(norm,dip->d2_mtime);
21842            rip->i_ndzones = V2_NR_DZONES;
21843            rip->i_nindirs = V2_INDIRECTS;
21844            for (i = 0; i < V2_NR_TZONES; i++)
21845                    rip->i_zone[i] = conv4(norm, (long) dip->d2_zone[i]);
21846      } else {
21847            /* Copying V2.x inode to disk from the in-core table. */
21848            dip->d2_mode   = conv2(norm,rip->i_mode);
21849            dip->d2_uid    = conv2(norm,rip->i_uid );
21850            dip->d2_nlinks = conv2(norm,rip->i_nlinks);
21851            dip->d2_gid    = conv2(norm,rip->i_gid );
21852            dip->d2_size   = conv4(norm,rip->i_size);
21853            dip->d2_atime  = conv4(norm,rip->i_atime);
21854            dip->d2_ctime  = conv4(norm,rip->i_ctime);
21855            dip->d2_mtime  = conv4(norm,rip->i_mtime);
21856            for (i = 0; i < V2_NR_TZONES; i++)
21857                    dip->d2_zone[i] = conv4(norm, (long) rip->i_zone[i]);
21858      }
21859    }


21862    /*===========================================================================*
21863     *                              dup_inode                                     *
21864     *===========================================================================*/
21865    PUBLIC void dup_inode(ip)
21866    struct inode *ip;                 /* The inode to be duplicated. */
21867    {
21868    /* This routine is a simplified form of get_inode() for the case where
21869     * the inode pointer is already known.
21870     */
21871
21872      ip->i_count++;
21873    }
```

```
++++++++++++++++++++++++++++++++++++++++++++++++++++++++++++++++++++++++++++++++
                                src/fs/super.c
++++++++++++++++++++++++++++++++++++++++++++++++++++++++++++++++++++++++++++++++
21900   /* This file manages the super block table and the related data structures,
21901    * namely, the bit maps that keep track of which zones and which inodes are
21902    * allocated and which are free.  When a new inode or zone is needed, the
21903    * appropriate bit map is searched for a free entry.
21904    *
21905    * The entry points into this file are
21906    *   alloc_bit:      somebody wants to allocate a zone or inode; find one
21907    *   free_bit:       indicate that a zone or inode is available for allocation
21908    *   get_super:      search the 'superblock' table for a device
21909    *   mounted:        tells if file inode is on mounted (or ROOT) file system
21910    *   read_super:     read a superblock
21911    */
21912
21913   #include "fs.h"
21914   #include <string.h>
21915   #include <minix/boot.h>
21916   #include "buf.h"
21917   #include "inode.h"
21918   #include "super.h"
21919
21920   #define BITCHUNK_BITS   (usizeof(bitchunk_t) * CHAR_BIT)
21921   #define BITS_PER_BLOCK  (BITMAP_CHUNKS * BITCHUNK_BITS)
21922
21923   /*===========================================================================*
21924    *                              alloc_bit                                     *
21925    *===========================================================================*/
21926   PUBLIC bit_t alloc_bit(sp, map, origin)
21927   struct super_block *sp;          /* the filesystem to allocate from */
21928   int map;                         /* IMAP (inode map) or ZMAP (zone map) */
21929   bit_t origin;                    /* number of bit to start searching at */
21930   {
21931   /* Allocate a bit from a bit map and return its bit number. */
21932
21933     block_t start_block;           /* first bit block */
21934     bit_t map_bits;                /* how many bits are there in the bit map? */
21935     unsigned bit_blocks;           /* how many blocks are there in the bit map? */
21936     unsigned block, word, bcount, wcount;
21937     struct buf *bp;
21938     bitchunk_t *wptr, *wlim, k;
21939     bit_t i, b;
21940
21941     if (sp->s_rd_only)
21942         panic("can't allocate bit on read-only filesys.", NO_NUM);
21943
21944     if (map == IMAP) {
21945         start_block = SUPER_BLOCK + 1;
21946         map_bits = sp->s_ninodes + 1;
21947         bit_blocks = sp->s_imap_blocks;
21948     } else {
21949         start_block = SUPER_BLOCK + 1 + sp->s_imap_blocks;
21950         map_bits = sp->s_zones - (sp->s_firstdatazone - 1);
21951         bit_blocks = sp->s_zmap_blocks;
21952     }
21953
21954     /* Figure out where to start the bit search (depends on 'origin'). */
```

```
21955        if (origin >= map_bits) origin = 0;    /* for robustness */
21956
21957        /* Locate the starting place. */
21958        block = origin / BITS_PER_BLOCK;
21959        word = (origin % BITS_PER_BLOCK) / BITCHUNK_BITS;
21960
21961        /* Iterate over all blocks plus one, because we start in the middle. */
21962        bcount = bit_blocks + 1;
21963        do {
21964                bp = get_block(sp->s_dev, start_block + block, NORMAL);
21965                wlim = &bp->b_bitmap[BITMAP_CHUNKS];
21966
21967                /* Iterate over the words in block. */
21968                for (wptr = &bp->b_bitmap[word]; wptr < wlim; wptr++) {
21969
21970                        /* Does this word contain a free bit? */
21971                        if (*wptr == (bitchunk_t) ~0) continue;
21972
21973                        /* Find and allocate the free bit. */
21974                        k = conv2(sp->s_native, (int) *wptr);
21975                        for (i = 0; (k & (1 << i)) != 0; ++i) {}
21976
21977                        /* Bit number from the start of the bit map. */
21978                        b = ((bit_t) block * BITS_PER_BLOCK)
21979                            + (wptr - &bp->b_bitmap[0]) * BITCHUNK_BITS
21980                            + i;
21981
21982                        /* Don't allocate bits beyond the end of the map. */
21983                        if (b >= map_bits) break;
21984
21985                        /* Allocate and return bit number. */
21986                        k |= 1 << i;
21987                        *wptr = conv2(sp->s_native, (int) k);
21988                        bp->b_dirt = DIRTY;
21989                        put_block(bp, MAP_BLOCK);
21990                        return(b);
21991                }
21992                put_block(bp, MAP_BLOCK);
21993                if (++block >= bit_blocks) block = 0;   /* last block, wrap around */
21994                word = 0;
21995        } while (--bcount > 0);
21996        return(NO_BIT);                       /* no bit could be allocated */
21997 }


22000  /*===========================================================================*
22001   *                              free_bit                                     *
22002   *===========================================================================*/
22003  PUBLIC void free_bit(sp, map, bit_returned)
22004  struct super_block *sp;          /* the filesystem to operate on */
22005  int map;                         /* IMAP (inode map) or ZMAP (zone map) */
22006  bit_t bit_returned;              /* number of bit to insert into the map */
22007  {
22008  /* Return a zone or inode by turning off its bitmap bit. */
22009
22010    unsigned block, word, bit;
22011    struct buf *bp;
22012    bitchunk_t k, mask;
22013    block_t start_block;
22014
```

```
22015        if (sp->s_rd_only)
22016                panic("can't free bit on read-only filesys.", NO_NUM);
22017
22018        if (map == IMAP) {
22019                start_block = SUPER_BLOCK + 1;
22020        } else {
22021                start_block = SUPER_BLOCK + 1 + sp->s_imap_blocks;
22022        }
22023        block = bit_returned / BITS_PER_BLOCK;
22024        word = (bit_returned % BITS_PER_BLOCK) / BITCHUNK_BITS;
22025        bit = bit_returned % BITCHUNK_BITS;
22026        mask = 1 << bit;
22027
22028        bp = get_block(sp->s_dev, start_block + block, NORMAL);
22029
22030        k = conv2(sp->s_native, (int) bp->b_bitmap[word]);
22031        if (!(k & mask)) {
22032                panic(map == IMAP ? "tried to free unused inode" :
22033                        "tried to free unused block", NO_NUM);
22034        }
22035
22036        k &= ~mask;
22037        bp->b_bitmap[word] = conv2(sp->s_native, (int) k);
22038        bp->b_dirt = DIRTY;
22039
22040        put_block(bp, MAP_BLOCK);
22041  }


22044  /*===========================================================================*
22045   *                              get_super                                    *
22046   *===========================================================================*/
22047  PUBLIC struct super_block *get_super(dev)
22048  dev_t dev;                      /* device number whose super_block is sought */
22049  {
22050  /* Search the superblock table for this device.  It is supposed to be there. */
22051
22052    register struct super_block *sp;
22053
22054    for (sp = &super_block[0]; sp < &super_block[NR_SUPERS]; sp++)
22055            if (sp->s_dev == dev) return(sp);
22056
22057    /* Search failed.  Something wrong. */
22058    panic("can't find superblock for device (in decimal)", (int) dev);
22059
22060    return(NIL_SUPER);              /* to keep the compiler and lint quiet */
22061  }


22064  /*===========================================================================*
22065   *                              mounted                                      *
22066   *===========================================================================*/
22067  PUBLIC int mounted(rip)
22068  register struct inode *rip;     /* pointer to inode */
22069  {
22070  /* Report on whether the given inode is on a mounted (or ROOT) file system. */
22071
22072    register struct super_block *sp;
22073    register dev_t dev;
22074
```

```
22075        dev = (dev_t) rip->i_zone[0];
22076        if (dev == ROOT_DEV) return(TRUE);     /* inode is on root file system */
22077
22078        for (sp = &super_block[0]; sp < &super_block[NR_SUPERS]; sp++)
22079               if (sp->s_dev == dev) return(TRUE);
22080
22081        return(FALSE);
22082   }


22085   /*===========================================================================*
22086    *                               read_super                                  *
22087    *===========================================================================*/
22088   PUBLIC int read_super(sp)
22089   register struct super_block *sp; /* pointer to a superblock */
22090   {
22091   /* Read a superblock. */
22092
22093     register struct buf *bp;
22094     dev_t dev;
22095     int magic;
22096     int version, native;
22097
22098     dev = sp->s_dev;                      /* save device (will be overwritten by copy) */
22099     bp = get_block(sp->s_dev, SUPER_BLOCK, NORMAL);
22100     memcpy( (char *) sp, bp->b_data, (size_t) SUPER_SIZE);
22101     put_block(bp, ZUPER_BLOCK);
22102     sp->s_dev = NO_DEV;                   /* restore later */
22103     magic = sp->s_magic;                 /* determines file system type */
22104
22105     /* Get file system version and type. */
22106     if (magic == SUPER_MAGIC || magic == conv2(BYTE_SWAP, SUPER_MAGIC)) {
22107            version = V1;
22108            native  = (magic == SUPER_MAGIC);
22109     } else if (magic == SUPER_V2 || magic == conv2(BYTE_SWAP, SUPER_V2)) {
22110            version = V2;
22111            native  = (magic == SUPER_V2);
22112     } else {
22113            return(EINVAL);
22114     }
22115
22116     /* If the super block has the wrong byte order, swap the fields; the magic
22117      * number doesn't need conversion. */
22118     sp->s_ninodes =        conv2(native, (int) sp->s_ninodes);
22119     sp->s_nzones =         conv2(native, (int) sp->s_nzones);
22120     sp->s_imap_blocks =    conv2(native, (int) sp->s_imap_blocks);
22121     sp->s_zmap_blocks =    conv2(native, (int) sp->s_zmap_blocks);
22122     sp->s_firstdatazone = conv2(native, (int) sp->s_firstdatazone);
22123     sp->s_log_zone_size = conv2(native, (int) sp->s_log_zone_size);
22124     sp->s_max_size =       conv4(native, sp->s_max_size);
22125     sp->s_zones =          conv4(native, sp->s_zones);
22126
22127     /* In V1, the device size was kept in a short, s_nzones, which limited
22128      * devices to 32K zones.  For V2, it was decided to keep the size as a
22129      * long.  However, just changing s_nzones to a long would not work, since
22130      * then the position of s_magic in the super block would not be the same
22131      * in V1 and V2 file systems, and there would be no way to tell whether
22132      * a newly mounted file system was V1 or V2.  The solution was to introduce
22133      * a new variable, s_zones, and copy the size there.
22134      *
```

```
22135        * Calculate some other numbers that depend on the version here too, to
22136        * hide some of the differences.
22137        */
22138       if (version == V1) {
22139             sp->s_zones = sp->s_nzones;        /* only V1 needs this copy */
22140             sp->s_inodes_per_block = V1_INODES_PER_BLOCK;
22141             sp->s_ndzones = V1_NR_DZONES;
22142             sp->s_nindirs = V1_INDIRECTS;
22143       } else {
22144             sp->s_inodes_per_block = V2_INODES_PER_BLOCK;
22145             sp->s_ndzones = V2_NR_DZONES;
22146             sp->s_nindirs = V2_INDIRECTS;
22147       }
22148
22149       sp->s_isearch = 0;               /* inode searches initially start at 0 */
22150       sp->s_zsearch = 0;               /* zone searches initially start at 0 */
22151       sp->s_version = version;
22152       sp->s_native  = native;
22153
22154       /* Make a few basic checks to see if super block looks reasonable. */
22155       if (sp->s_imap_blocks < 1 || sp->s_zmap_blocks < 1
22156                                 || sp->s_ninodes < 1 || sp->s_zones < 1
22157                                 || (unsigned) sp->s_log_zone_size > 4) {
22158             return(EINVAL);
22159       }
22160       sp->s_dev = dev;                 /* restore device number */
22161       return(OK);
22162 }



++++++++++++++++++++++++++++++++++++++++++++++++++++++++++++++++++++++++++++++++
                               src/fs/filedes.c
++++++++++++++++++++++++++++++++++++++++++++++++++++++++++++++++++++++++++++++++

22200    /* This file contains the procedures that manipulate file descriptors.
22201     *
22202     * The entry points into this file are
22203     *   get_fd:    look for free file descriptor and free filp slots
22204     *   get_filp:  look up the filp entry for a given file descriptor
22205     *   find_filp: find a filp slot that points to a given inode
22206     */
22207
22208    #include "fs.h"
22209    #include "file.h"
22210    #include "fproc.h"
22211    #include "inode.h"
22212
22213    /*===========================================================================*
22214     *                              get_fd                                       *
22215     *===========================================================================*/
22216    PUBLIC int get_fd(start, bits, k, fpt)
22217    int start;                       /* start of search (used for F_DUPFD) */
22218    mode_t bits;                     /* mode of the file to be created (RWX bits) */
22219    int *k;                          /* place to return file descriptor */
22220    struct filp **fpt;               /* place to return filp slot */
22221    {
22222    /* Look for a free file descriptor and a free filp slot.  Fill in the mode word
22223     * in the latter, but don't claim either one yet, since the open() or creat()
22224     * may yet fail.
```

```
22225      */
22226
22227      register struct filp *f;
22228      register int i;
22229
22230      *k = -1;                          /* we need a way to tell if file desc found */
22231
22232      /* Search the fproc fp_filp table for a free file descriptor. */
22233      for (i = start; i < OPEN_MAX; i++) {
22234            if (fp->fp_filp[i] == NIL_FILP) {
22235                    /* A file descriptor has been located. */
22236                    *k = i;
22237                    break;
22238            }
22239      }
22240
22241      /* Check to see if a file descriptor has been found. */
22242      if (*k < 0) return(EMFILE);    /* this is why we initialized k to -1 */
22243
22244      /* Now that a file descriptor has been found, look for a free filp slot. */
22245      for (f = &filp[0]; f < &filp[NR_FILPS]; f++) {
22246            if (f->filp_count == 0) {
22247                    f->filp_mode = bits;
22248                    f->filp_pos = 0L;
22249                    f->filp_flags = 0;
22250                    *fpt = f;
22251                    return(OK);
22252            }
22253      }
22254
22255      /* If control passes here, the filp table must be full.  Report that back. */
22256      return(ENFILE);
22257    }


22260    /*===========================================================================*
22261     *                              get_filp                                     *
22262     *===========================================================================*/
22263    PUBLIC struct filp *get_filp(fild)
22264    int fild;                        /* file descriptor */
22265    {
22266    /* See if 'fild' refers to a valid file descr.  If so, return its filp ptr. */
22267
22268      err_code = EBADF;
22269      if (fild < 0 || fild >= OPEN_MAX ) return(NIL_FILP);
22270      return(fp->fp_filp[fild]);    /* may also be NIL_FILP */
22271    }


22274    /*===========================================================================*
22275     *                              find_filp                                    *
22276     *===========================================================================*/
22277    PUBLIC struct filp *find_filp(rip, bits)
22278    register struct inode *rip;      /* inode referred to by the filp to be found */
22279    Mode_t bits;                     /* mode of the filp to be found (RWX bits) */
22280    {
22281    /* Find a filp slot that refers to the inode 'rip' in a way as described
22282     * by the mode bit 'bits'. Used for determining whether somebody is still
22283     * interested in either end of a pipe.  Also used when opening a FIFO to
22284     * find partners to share a filp field with (to shared the file position).
```

```
22285        * Like 'get_fd' it performs its job by linear search through the filp table.
22286        */
22287
22288        register struct filp *f;
22289
22290        for (f = &filp[0]; f < &filp[NR_FILPS]; f++) {
22291              if (f->filp_count != 0 && f->filp_ino == rip && (f->filp_mode & bits)){
22292                    return(f);
22293              }
22294        }
22295
22296        /* If control passes here, the filp wasn't there.  Report that back. */
22297        return(NIL_FILP);
22298    }


+++++++++++++++++++++++++++++++++++++++++++++++++++++++++++++++++++++++++++++++++++
                              src/fs/lock.c
+++++++++++++++++++++++++++++++++++++++++++++++++++++++++++++++++++++++++++++++++++

22300    /* This file handles advisory file locking as required by POSIX.
22301     *
22302     * The entry points into this file are
22303     *   lock_op:    perform locking operations for FCNTL system call
22304     *   lock_revive: revive processes when a lock is released
22305     */
22306
22307    #include "fs.h"
22308    #include <fcntl.h>
22309    #include <unistd.h>      /* cc runs out of memory with unistd.h :-( */
22310    #include "file.h"
22311    #include "fproc.h"
22312    #include "inode.h"
22313    #include "lock.h"
22314    #include "param.h"
22315
22316    /*===========================================================================*
22317     *                              lock_op                                      *
22318     *===========================================================================*/
22319    PUBLIC int lock_op(f, req)
22320    struct filp *f;
22321    int req;                           /* either F_SETLK or F_SETLKW */
22322    {
22323    /* Perform the advisory locking required by POSIX. */
22324
22325        int r, ltype, i, conflict = 0, unlocking = 0;
22326        mode_t mo;
22327        off_t first, last;
22328        struct flock flock;
22329        vir_bytes user_flock;
22330        struct file_lock *flp, *flp2, *empty;
22331
22332        /* Fetch the flock structure from user space. */
22333        user_flock = (vir_bytes) name1;
22334        r = sys_copy(who, D, (phys_bytes) user_flock,
22335              FS_PROC_NR, D, (phys_bytes) &flock, (phys_bytes) sizeof(flock));
22336        if (r != OK) return(EINVAL);
22337
22338        /* Make some error checks. */
22339        ltype = flock.l_type;
```

```
22340          mo = f->filp_mode;
22341          if (ltype != F_UNLCK && ltype != F_RDLCK && ltype != F_WRLCK) return(EINVAL);
22342          if (req == F_GETLK && ltype == F_UNLCK) return(EINVAL);
22343          if ( (f->filp_ino->i_mode & I_TYPE) != I_REGULAR) return(EINVAL);
22344          if (req != F_GETLK && ltype == F_RDLCK && (mo & R_BIT) == 0) return(EBADF);
22345          if (req != F_GETLK && ltype == F_WRLCK && (mo & W_BIT) == 0) return(EBADF);
22346
22347          /* Compute the first and last bytes in the lock region. */
22348          switch (flock.l_whence) {
22349                case SEEK_SET:  first = 0; break;
22350                case SEEK_CUR:  first = f->filp_pos; break;
22351                case SEEK_END:  first = f->filp_ino->i_size; break;
22352                default:        return(EINVAL);
22353          }
22354          /* Check for overflow. */
22355          if (((long)flock.l_start > 0) && ((first + flock.l_start) < first))
22356                return(EINVAL);
22357          if (((long)flock.l_start < 0) && ((first + flock.l_start) > first))
22358                return(EINVAL);
22359          first = first + flock.l_start;
22360          last = first + flock.l_len - 1;
22361          if (flock.l_len == 0) last = MAX_FILE_POS;
22362          if (last < first) return(EINVAL);
22363
22364          /* Check if this region conflicts with any existing lock. */
22365          empty = (struct file_lock *) 0;
22366          for (flp = &file_lock[0]; flp < & file_lock[NR_LOCKS]; flp++) {
22367                if (flp->lock_type == 0) {
22368                      if (empty == (struct file_lock *) 0) empty = flp;
22369                      continue;        /* 0 means unused slot */
22370                }
22371                if (flp->lock_inode != f->filp_ino) continue;   /* different file */
22372                if (last < flp->lock_first) continue;   /* new one is in front */
22373                if (first > flp->lock_last) continue;   /* new one is afterwards */
22374                if (ltype == F_RDLCK && flp->lock_type == F_RDLCK) continue;
22375                if (ltype != F_UNLCK && flp->lock_pid == fp->fp_pid) continue;
22376
22377                /* There might be a conflict.  Process it. */
22378                conflict = 1;
22379                if (req == F_GETLK) break;
22380
22381                /* If we are trying to set a lock, it just failed. */
22382                if (ltype == F_RDLCK || ltype == F_WRLCK) {
22383                      if (req == F_SETLK) {
22384                            /* For F_SETLK, just report back failure. */
22385                            return(EAGAIN);
22386                      } else {
22387                            /* For F_SETLKW, suspend the process. */
22388                            suspend(XLOCK);
22389                            return(0);
22390                      }
22391                }
22392
22393                /* We are clearing a lock and we found something that overlaps. */
22394                unlocking = 1;
22395                if (first <= flp->lock_first && last >= flp->lock_last) {
22396                      flp->lock_type = 0;      /* mark slot as unused */
22397                      nr_locks--;              /* number of locks is now 1 less */
22398                      continue;
22399                }
```

```
22400
22401                    /* Part of a locked region has been unlocked. */
22402                    if (first <= flp->lock_first) {
22403                            flp->lock_first = last + 1;
22404                            continue;
22405                    }
22406
22407                    if (last >= flp->lock_last) {
22408                            flp->lock_last = first - 1;
22409                            continue;
22410                    }
22411
22412                    /* Bad luck. A lock has been split in two by unlocking the middle. */
22413                    if (nr_locks == NR_LOCKS) return(ENOLCK);
22414                    for (i = 0; i < NR_LOCKS; i++)
22415                            if (file_lock[i].lock_type == 0) break;
22416                    flp2 = &file_lock[i];
22417                    flp2->lock_type = flp->lock_type;
22418                    flp2->lock_pid = flp->lock_pid;
22419                    flp2->lock_inode = flp->lock_inode;
22420                    flp2->lock_first = last + 1;
22421                    flp2->lock_last = flp->lock_last;
22422                    flp->lock_last = first - 1;
22423                    nr_locks++;
22424          }
22425      if (unlocking) lock_revive();
22426
22427      if (req == F_GETLK) {
22428              if (conflict) {
22429                      /* GETLK and conflict. Report on the conflicting lock. */
22430                      flock.l_type = flp->lock_type;
22431                      flock.l_whence = SEEK_SET;
22432                      flock.l_start = flp->lock_first;
22433                      flock.l_len = flp->lock_last - flp->lock_first + 1;
22434                      flock.l_pid = flp->lock_pid;
22435
22436              } else {
22437                      /* It is GETLK and there is no conflict. */
22438                      flock.l_type = F_UNLCK;
22439              }
22440
22441              /* Copy the flock structure back to the caller. */
22442              r = sys_copy(FS_PROC_NR, D, (phys_bytes) &flock,
22443                      who, D, (phys_bytes) user_flock, (phys_bytes) sizeof(flock));
22444              return(r);
22445      }
22446
22447      if (ltype == F_UNLCK) return(OK);       /* unlocked a region with no locks */
22448
22449      /* There is no conflict.  If space exists, store new lock in the table. */
22450      if (empty == (struct file_lock *) 0) return(ENOLCK);  /* table full */
22451      empty->lock_type = ltype;
22452      empty->lock_pid = fp->fp_pid;
22453      empty->lock_inode = f->filp_ino;
22454      empty->lock_first = first;
22455      empty->lock_last = last;
22456      nr_locks++;
22457      return(OK);
22458  }
```

```
22460   /*===========================================================================*
22461    *                              lock_revive                                  *
22462    *===========================================================================*/
22463   PUBLIC void lock_revive()
22464   {
22465   /* Go find all the processes that are waiting for any kind of lock and
22466    * revive them all.  The ones that are still blocked will block again when
22467    * they run.  The others will complete.  This strategy is a space-time
22468    * tradeoff.  Figuring out exactly which ones to unblock now would take
22469    * extra code, and the only thing it would win would be some performance in
22470    * extremely rare circumstances (namely, that somebody actually used
22471    * locking).
22472    */
22473
22474     int task;
22475     struct fproc *fptr;
22476
22477     for (fptr = &fproc[INIT_PROC_NR + 1]; fptr < &fproc[NR_PROCS]; fptr++){
22478             task = -fptr->fp_task;
22479             if (fptr->fp_suspended == SUSPENDED && task == XLOCK) {
22480                     revive( (int) (fptr - fproc), 0);
22481             }
22482     }
22483   }
```

```
++++++++++++++++++++++++++++++++++++++++++++++++++++++++++++++++++++++++++++++
                                 src/fs/main.c
++++++++++++++++++++++++++++++++++++++++++++++++++++++++++++++++++++++++++++++
```

```
22500   /* This file contains the main program of the File System.  It consists of
22501    * a loop that gets messages requesting work, carries out the work, and sends
22502    * replies.
22503    *
22504    * The entry points into this file are
22505    *   main:      main program of the File System
22506    *   reply:     send a reply to a process after the requested work is done
22507    */
22508
22509   struct super_block;                   /* proto.h needs to know this */
22510
22511   #include "fs.h"
22512   #include <fcntl.h>
22513   #include <string.h>
22514   #include <sys/ioctl.h>
22515   #include <minix/callnr.h>
22516   #include <minix/com.h>
22517   #include <minix/boot.h>
22518   #include "buf.h"
22519   #include "dev.h"
22520   #include "file.h"
22521   #include "fproc.h"
22522   #include "inode.h"
22523   #include "param.h"
22524   #include "super.h"
22525
22526   FORWARD _PROTOTYPE( void buf_pool, (void)                           );
22527   FORWARD _PROTOTYPE( void fs_init, (void)                           );
22528   FORWARD _PROTOTYPE( void get_boot_parameters, (void)               );
22529   FORWARD _PROTOTYPE( void get_work, (void)                          );
```

```
22530   FORWARD _PROTOTYPE( void load_ram, (void)                        );
22531   FORWARD _PROTOTYPE( void load_super, (Dev_t super_dev)           );
22532
22533
22534   /*===========================================================================*
22535    *                               main                                        *
22536    *===========================================================================*/
22537   PUBLIC void main()
22538   {
22539   /* This is the main program of the file system.  The main loop consists of
22540    * three major activities: getting new work, processing the work, and sending
22541    * the reply.  This loop never terminates as long as the file system runs.
22542    */
22543     int error;
22544
22545     fs_init();
22546
22547     /* This is the main loop that gets work, processes it, and sends replies. */
22548     while (TRUE) {
22549           get_work();                   /* sets who and fs_call */
22550
22551           fp = &fproc[who];        /* pointer to proc table struct */
22552           super_user = (fp->fp_effuid == SU_UID ? TRUE : FALSE);   /* su? */
22553           dont_reply = FALSE;      /* in other words, do reply is default */
22554
22555           /* Call the internal function that does the work. */
22556           if (fs_call < 0 || fs_call >= NCALLS)
22557                   error = EBADCALL;
22558           else
22559                   error = (*call_vector[fs_call])();
22560
22561           /* Copy the results back to the user and send reply. */
22562           if (dont_reply) continue;
22563           reply(who, error);
22564           if (rdahed_inode != NIL_INODE) read_ahead(); /* do block read ahead */
22565     }
22566   }


22569   /*===========================================================================*
22570    *                               get_work                                    *
22571    *===========================================================================*/
22572   PRIVATE void get_work()
22573   {
22574     /* Normally wait for new input.  However, if 'reviving' is
22575      * nonzero, a suspended process must be awakened.
22576      */
22577
22578     register struct fproc *rp;
22579
22580     if (reviving != 0) {
22581           /* Revive a suspended process. */
22582           for (rp = &fproc[0]; rp < &fproc[NR_PROCS]; rp++)
22583                   if (rp->fp_revived == REVIVING) {
22584                           who = (int)(rp - fproc);
22585                           fs_call = rp->fp_fd & BYTE;
22586                           fd = (rp->fp_fd >>8) & BYTE;
22587                           buffer = rp->fp_buffer;
22588                           nbytes = rp->fp_nbytes;
22589                           rp->fp_suspended = NOT_SUSPENDED; /*no longer hanging*/
```

```
22590                        rp->fp_revived = NOT_REVIVING;
22591                        reviving--;
22592                        return;
22593                }
22594        panic("get_work couldn't revive anyone", NO_NUM);
22595    }
22596
22597    /* Normal case.  No one to revive. */
22598    if (receive(ANY, &m) != OK) panic("fs receive error", NO_NUM);
22599
22600    who = m.m_source;
22601    fs_call = m.m_type;
22602  }


22605  /*===========================================================================*
22606   *                              reply                                         *
22607   *===========================================================================*/
22608  PUBLIC void reply(whom, result)
22609  int whom;                      /* process to reply to */
22610  int result;                    /* result of the call (usually OK or error #) */
22611  {
22612  /* Send a reply to a user process. It may fail (if the process has just
22613   * been killed by a signal), so don't check the return code.  If the send
22614   * fails, just ignore it.
22615   */
22616
22617    reply_type = result;
22618    send(whom, &m1);
22619  }


22622  /*===========================================================================*
22623   *                              fs_init                                       *
22624   *===========================================================================*/
22625  PRIVATE void fs_init()
22626  {
22627  /* Initialize global variables, tables, etc. */
22628
22629    register struct inode *rip;
22630    int i;
22631    message mess;
22632
22633    /* The following initializations are needed to let dev_opcl succeed .*/
22634    fp = (struct fproc *) NULL;
22635    who = FS_PROC_NR;
22636
22637    buf_pool();                   /* initialize buffer pool */
22638    get_boot_parameters();        /* get the parameters from the menu */
22639    load_ram();                   /* init RAM disk, load if it is root */
22640    load_super(ROOT_DEV);         /* load super block for root device */
22641
22642    /* Initialize the 'fproc' fields for process 0 .. INIT. */
22643    for (i = 0; i <= LOW_USER; i+= 1) {
22644          if (i == FS_PROC_NR) continue;  /* do not initialize FS */
22645          fp = &fproc[i];
22646          rip = get_inode(ROOT_DEV, ROOT_INODE);
22647          fp->fp_rootdir = rip;
22648          dup_inode(rip);
22649          fp->fp_workdir = rip;
```

```
22650              fp->fp_realuid = (uid_t) SYS_UID;
22651              fp->fp_effuid = (uid_t) SYS_UID;
22652              fp->fp_realgid = (gid_t) SYS_GID;
22653              fp->fp_effgid = (gid_t) SYS_GID;
22654              fp->fp_umask = ~0;
22655          }
22656
22657      /* Certain relations must hold for the file system to work at all. */
22658      if (SUPER_SIZE > BLOCK_SIZE) panic("SUPER_SIZE > BLOCK_SIZE", NO_NUM);
22659      if (BLOCK_SIZE % V2_INODE_SIZE != 0)  /* this checks V1_INODE_SIZE too */
22660              panic("BLOCK_SIZE % V2_INODE_SIZE != 0", NO_NUM);
22661      if (OPEN_MAX > 127) panic("OPEN_MAX > 127", NO_NUM);
22662      if (NR_BUFS < 6) panic("NR_BUFS < 6", NO_NUM);
22663      if (V1_INODE_SIZE != 32) panic("V1 inode size != 32", NO_NUM);
22664      if (V2_INODE_SIZE != 64) panic("V2 inode size != 64", NO_NUM);
22665      if (OPEN_MAX > 8 * sizeof(long)) panic("Too few bits in fp_cloexec", NO_NUM);
22666
22667      /* Tell the memory task where my process table is for the sake of ps(1). */
22668      mess.m_type = DEV_IOCTL;
22669      mess.PROC_NR = FS_PROC_NR;
22670      mess.REQUEST = MIOCSPSINFO;
22671      mess.ADDRESS = (void *) fproc;
22672      (void) sendrec(MEM, &mess);
22673  }


22676  /*===========================================================================*
22677   *                              buf_pool                                     *
22678   *===========================================================================*/
22679  PRIVATE void buf_pool()
22680  {
22681  /* Initialize the buffer pool. */
22682
22683      register struct buf *bp;
22684
22685      bufs_in_use = 0;
22686      front = &buf[0];
22687      rear = &buf[NR_BUFS - 1];
22688
22689      for (bp = &buf[0]; bp < &buf[NR_BUFS]; bp++) {
22690              bp->b_blocknr = NO_BLOCK;
22691              bp->b_dev = NO_DEV;
22692              bp->b_next = bp + 1;
22693              bp->b_prev = bp - 1;
22694      }
22695      buf[0].b_prev = NIL_BUF;
22696      buf[NR_BUFS - 1].b_next = NIL_BUF;
22697
22698      for (bp = &buf[0]; bp < &buf[NR_BUFS]; bp++) bp->b_hash = bp->b_next;
22699      buf_hash[0] = front;
22700  }


22703  /*===========================================================================*
22704   *                          get_boot_parameters                              *
22705   *===========================================================================*/
22706  PUBLIC struct bparam_s boot_parameters;
22707
22708  PRIVATE void get_boot_parameters()
22709  {
```

```
22710   /* Ask kernel for boot parameters. */
22711
22712     m1.m_type = SYS_GBOOT;
22713     m1.PROC1 = FS_PROC_NR;
22714     m1.MEM_PTR = (char *) &boot_parameters;
22715     (void) sendrec(SYSTASK, &m1);
22716   }


22719   /*===========================================================================*
22720    *                              load_ram                                     *
22721    *===========================================================================*/
22722   PRIVATE void load_ram()
22723   {
22724   /* If the root device is the RAM disk, copy the entire root image device
22725    * block-by-block to a RAM disk with the same size as the image.
22726    * Otherwise, just allocate a RAM disk with size given in the boot parameters.
22727    */
22728
22729     register struct buf *bp, *bp1;
22730     long k_loaded, lcount;
22731     u32_t ram_size, fsmax;
22732     zone_t zones;
22733     struct super_block *sp, *dsp;
22734     block_t b;
22735     int major, task;
22736     message dev_mess;
22737
22738     ram_size = boot_parameters.bp_ramsize;
22739
22740     /* Open the root device. */
22741     major = (ROOT_DEV >> MAJOR) & BYTE;    /* major device nr */
22742     task = dmap[major].dmap_task;          /* device task nr */
22743     dev_mess.m_type = DEV_OPEN;            /* distinguish from close */
22744     dev_mess.DEVICE = ROOT_DEV;
22745     dev_mess.COUNT = R_BIT|W_BIT;
22746     (*dmap[major].dmap_open)(task, &dev_mess);
22747     if (dev_mess.REP_STATUS != OK) panic("Cannot open root device",NO_NUM);
22748
22749     /* If the root device is the ram disk then fill it from the image device. */
22750     if (ROOT_DEV == DEV_RAM) {
22751           major = (IMAGE_DEV >> MAJOR) & BYTE;    /* major device nr */
22752           task = dmap[major].dmap_task;          /* device task nr */
22753           dev_mess.m_type = DEV_OPEN;            /* distinguish from close */
22754           dev_mess.DEVICE = IMAGE_DEV;
22755           dev_mess.COUNT = R_BIT;
22756           (*dmap[major].dmap_open)(task, &dev_mess);
22757           if (dev_mess.REP_STATUS != OK) panic("Cannot open root device", NO_NUM);
22758
22759           /* Get size of RAM disk by reading root file system's super block. */
22760           sp = &super_block[0];
22761           sp->s_dev = IMAGE_DEV;
22762           if (read_super(sp) != OK) panic("Bad root file system", NO_NUM);
22763
22764           lcount = sp->s_zones << sp->s_log_zone_size;    /* # blks on root dev*/
22765
22766           /* Stretch the RAM disk file system to the boot parameters size, but
22767            * no further than the last zone bit map block allows.
22768            */
22769           if (ram_size < lcount) ram_size = lcount;
```

```
22770                    fsmax = (u32_t) sp->s_zmap_blocks * CHAR_BIT * BLOCK_SIZE;
22771                    fsmax = (fsmax + (sp->s_firstdatazone-1)) << sp->s_log_zone_size;
22772                    if (ram_size > fsmax) ram_size = fsmax;
22773            }
22774
22775            /* Tell RAM driver how big the RAM disk must be. */
22776            m1.m_type = DEV_IOCTL;
22777            m1.PROC_NR = FS_PROC_NR;
22778            m1.REQUEST = MIOCRAMSIZE;
22779            m1.POSITION = ram_size;
22780            if (sendrec(MEM, &m1) != OK || m1.REP_STATUS != OK)
22781                    panic("Can't set RAM disk size", NO_NUM);
22782
22783            /* Tell MM the RAM disk size, and wait for it to come "on-line". */
22784            m1.m1_i1 = ((long) ram_size * BLOCK_SIZE) >> CLICK_SHIFT;
22785            if (sendrec(MM_PROC_NR, &m1) != OK)
22786                    panic("FS can't sync up with MM", NO_NUM);
22787
22788            /* If the root device is not the RAM disk, it doesn't need loading. */
22789            if (ROOT_DEV != DEV_RAM) return;
22790
22791            /* Copy the blocks one at a time from the image to the RAM disk. */
22792            printf("Loading RAM disk.\33[23CLoaded:    OK ");
22793
22794            inode[0].i_mode = I_BLOCK_SPECIAL;      /* temp inode for rahead() */
22795            inode[0].i_size = LONG_MAX;
22796            inode[0].i_dev = IMAGE_DEV;
22797            inode[0].i_zone[0] = IMAGE_DEV;
22798
22799            for (b = 0; b < (block_t) lcount; b++) {
22800                    bp = rahead(&inode[0], b, (off_t)BLOCK_SIZE * b, BLOCK_SIZE);
22801                    bp1 = get_block(ROOT_DEV, b, NO_READ);
22802                    memcpy(bp1->b_data, bp->b_data, (size_t) BLOCK_SIZE);
22803                    bp1->b_dirt = DIRTY;
22804                    put_block(bp, FULL_DATA_BLOCK);
22805                    put_block(bp1, FULL_DATA_BLOCK);
22806                    k_loaded = ( (long) b * BLOCK_SIZE)/1024L;        /* K loaded so far */
22807                    if (k_loaded % 5 == 0) printf("\b\b\b\b\b\b%5ldK ", k_loaded);
22808            }
22809
22810            printf("\rRAM disk loaded.\33[K\n\n");
22811
22812            /* Close and invalidate image device. */
22813            dev_mess.m_type = DEV_CLOSE;
22814            dev_mess.DEVICE = IMAGE_DEV;
22815            (*dmap[major].dmap_close)(task, &dev_mess);
22816            invalidate(IMAGE_DEV);
22817
22818            /* Resize the RAM disk root file system. */
22819            bp = get_block(ROOT_DEV, SUPER_BLOCK, NORMAL);
22820            dsp = (struct super_block *) bp->b_data;
22821            zones = ram_size >> sp->s_log_zone_size;
22822            dsp->s_nzones = conv2(sp->s_native, (u16_t) zones);
22823            dsp->s_zones = conv4(sp->s_native, zones);
22824            bp->b_dirt = DIRTY;
22825            put_block(bp, ZUPER_BLOCK);
22826    }


22829    /*===========================================================================*
```

```
22830        *                          load_super                          *
22831        *===========================================================*/
22832    PRIVATE void load_super(super_dev)
22833    dev_t super_dev;                              /* place to get superblock from */
22834    {
22835      int bad;
22836      register struct super_block *sp;
22837      register struct inode *rip;
22838
22839      /* Initialize the super_block table. */
22840      for (sp = &super_block[0]; sp < &super_block[NR_SUPERS]; sp++)
22841            sp->s_dev = NO_DEV;
22842
22843      /* Read in super_block for the root file system. */
22844      sp = &super_block[0];
22845      sp->s_dev = super_dev;
22846
22847      /* Check super_block for consistency (is it the right diskette?). */
22848      bad = (read_super(sp) != OK);
22849      if (!bad) {
22850            rip = get_inode(super_dev, ROOT_INODE); /* inode for root dir */
22851            if ( (rip->i_mode & I_TYPE) != I_DIRECTORY || rip->i_nlinks < 3) bad++;
22852      }
22853      if (bad)panic("Invalid root file system.  Possibly wrong diskette.",NO_NUM);
22854
22855      sp->s_imount = rip;
22856      dup_inode(rip);
22857      sp->s_isup = rip;
22858      sp->s_rd_only = 0;
22859      return;
22860    }
```

```
++++++++++++++++++++++++++++++++++++++++++++++++++++++++++++++++++++++++++++++++
                              src/fs/open.c
++++++++++++++++++++++++++++++++++++++++++++++++++++++++++++++++++++++++++++++++
```

```
22900    /* This file contains the procedures for creating, opening, closing, and
22901     * seeking on files.
22902     *
22903     * The entry points into this file are
22904     *   do_creat:  perform the CREAT system call
22905     *   do_open:   perform the OPEN system call
22906     *   do_mknod:  perform the MKNOD system call
22907     *   do_mkdir:  perform the MKDIR system call
22908     *   do_close:  perform the CLOSE system call
22909     *   do_lseek:  perform the LSEEK system call
22910     */
22911
22912    #include "fs.h"
22913    #include <sys/stat.h>
22914    #include <fcntl.h>
22915    #include <minix/callnr.h>
22916    #include <minix/com.h>
22917    #include "buf.h"
22918    #include "dev.h"
22919    #include "file.h"
```

```
22920    #include "fproc.h"
22921    #include "inode.h"
22922    #include "lock.h"
22923    #include "param.h"
22924
22925    PRIVATE message dev_mess;
22926    PRIVATE char mode_map[] = {R_BIT, W_BIT, R_BIT|W_BIT, 0};
22927
22928    FORWARD _PROTOTYPE( int common_open, (int oflags, Mode_t omode)          );
22929    FORWARD _PROTOTYPE( int pipe_open, (struct inode *rip,Mode_t bits,int oflags));
22930    FORWARD _PROTOTYPE( struct inode *new_node, (char *path, Mode_t bits,
22931                                                             zone_t z0)         );
22932
22933
22934    /*===========================================================================*
22935     *                              do_creat                                      *
22936     *===========================================================================*/
22937    PUBLIC int do_creat()
22938    {
22939    /* Perform the creat(name, mode) system call. */
22940      int r;
22941
22942      if (fetch_name(name, name_length, M3) != OK) return(err_code);
22943      r = common_open(O_WRONLY | O_CREAT | O_TRUNC, (mode_t) mode);
22944      return(r);
22945    }


22948    /*===========================================================================*
22949     *                              do_open                                       *
22950     *===========================================================================*/
22951    PUBLIC int do_open()
22952    {
22953    /* Perform the open(name, flags,...) system call. */
22954
22955      int create_mode = 0;           /* is really mode_t but this gives problems */
22956      int r;
22957
22958      /* If O_CREAT is set, open has three parameters, otherwise two. */
22959      if (mode & O_CREAT) {
22960            create_mode = c_mode;
22961            r = fetch_name(c_name, name1_length, M1);
22962      } else {
22963            r = fetch_name(name, name_length, M3);
22964      }
22965
22966      if (r != OK) return(err_code); /* name was bad */
22967      r = common_open(mode, create_mode);
22968      return(r);
22969    }


22972    /*===========================================================================*
22973     *                              common_open                                   *
22974     *===========================================================================*/
22975    PRIVATE int common_open(oflags, omode)
22976    register int oflags;
22977    mode_t omode;
22978    {
22979    /* Common code from do_creat and do_open. */
```

```
22980
22981      register struct inode *rip;
22982      int r, b, major, task, exist = TRUE;
22983      dev_t dev;
22984      mode_t bits;
22985      off_t pos;
22986      struct filp *fil_ptr, *filp2;
22987
22988      /* Remap the bottom two bits of oflags. */
22989      bits = (mode_t) mode_map[oflags & O_ACCMODE];
22990
22991      /* See if file descriptor and filp slots are available. */
22992      if ( (r = get_fd(0, bits, &fd, &fil_ptr)) != OK) return(r);
22993
22994      /* If O_CREATE is set, try to make the file. */
22995      if (oflags & O_CREAT) {
22996            /* Create a new inode by calling new_node(). */
22997            omode = I_REGULAR | (omode & ALL_MODES & fp->fp_umask);
22998            rip = new_node(user_path, omode, NO_ZONE);
22999            r = err_code;
23000            if (r == OK) exist = FALSE;       /* we just created the file */
23001            else if (r != EEXIST) return(r); /* other error */
23002            else exist = !(oflags & O_EXCL); /* file exists, if the O_EXCL
23003                                               flag is set this is an error */
23004      } else {
23005             /* Scan path name. */
23006            if ( (rip = eat_path(user_path)) == NIL_INODE) return(err_code);
23007      }
23008
23009      /* Claim the file descriptor and filp slot and fill them in. */
23010      fp->fp_filp[fd] = fil_ptr;
23011      fil_ptr->filp_count = 1;
23012      fil_ptr->filp_ino = rip;
23013      fil_ptr->filp_flags = oflags;
23014
23015      /* Only do the normal open code if we didn't just create the file. */
23016      if (exist) {
23017            /* Check protections. */
23018            if ((r = forbidden(rip, bits)) == OK) {
23019                    /* Opening reg. files directories and special files differ. */
23020                    switch (rip->i_mode & I_TYPE) {
23021                        case I_REGULAR:
23022                            /* Truncate regular file if O_TRUNC. */
23023                            if (oflags & O_TRUNC) {
23024                                    if ((r = forbidden(rip, W_BIT)) !=OK) break;
23025                                    truncate(rip);
23026                                    wipe_inode(rip);
23027                                    /* Send the inode from the inode cache to the
23028                                     * block cache, so it gets written on the next
23029                                     * cache flush.
23030                                     */
23031                                    rw_inode(rip, WRITING);
23032                            }
23033                            break;
23034
23035                        case I_DIRECTORY:
23036                            /* Directories may be read but not written. */
23037                            r = (bits & W_BIT ? EISDIR : OK);
23038                            break;
23039
```

```
23040                         case I_CHAR_SPECIAL:
23041                         case I_BLOCK_SPECIAL:
23042                             /* Invoke the driver for special processing. */
23043                             dev_mess.m_type = DEV_OPEN;
23044                             dev = (dev_t) rip->i_zone[0];
23045                             dev_mess.DEVICE = dev;
23046                             dev_mess.COUNT = bits | (oflags & ~O_ACCMODE);
23047                             major = (dev >> MAJOR) & BYTE;  /* major device nr */
23048                             if (major <= 0 || major >= max_major) {
23049                                     r = ENODEV;
23050                                     break;
23051                             }
23052                             task = dmap[major].dmap_task;   /* device task nr */
23053                             (*dmap[major].dmap_open)(task, &dev_mess);
23054                             r = dev_mess.REP_STATUS;
23055                             break;
23056
23057                         case I_NAMED_PIPE:
23058                             oflags |= O_APPEND;      /* force append mode */
23059                             fil_ptr->filp_flags = oflags;
23060                             r = pipe_open(rip, bits, oflags);
23061                             if (r == OK) {
23062                                     /* See if someone else is doing a rd or wt on
23063                                      * the FIFO.  If so, use its filp entry so the
23064                                      * file position will be automatically shared.
23065                                      */
23066                                     b = (bits & R_BIT ? R_BIT : W_BIT);
23067                                     fil_ptr->filp_count = 0; /* don't find self */
23068                                     if ((filp2 = find_filp(rip, b)) != NIL_FILP) {
23069                                             /* Co-reader or writer found. Use it.*/
23070                                             fp->fp_filp[fd] = filp2;
23071                                             filp2->filp_count++;
23072                                             filp2->filp_ino = rip;
23073                                             filp2->filp_flags = oflags;
23074
23075                                             /* i_count was incremented incorrectly
23076                                              * by eatpath above, not knowing that
23077                                              * we were going to use an existing
23078                                              * filp entry.  Correct this error.
23079                                              */
23080                                             rip->i_count--;
23081                                     } else {
23082                                             /* Nobody else found.  Restore filp. */
23083                                             fil_ptr->filp_count = 1;
23084                                             if (b == R_BIT)
23085                                                 pos = rip->i_zone[V2_NR_DZONES+1];
23086                                             else
23087                                                 pos = rip->i_zone[V2_NR_DZONES+2];
23088                                             fil_ptr->filp_pos = pos;
23089                                     }
23090                             }
23091                             break;
23092                     }
23093             }
23094     }
23095
23096     /* If error, release inode. */
23097     if (r != OK) {
23098             fp->fp_filp[fd] = NIL_FILP;
23099             fil_ptr->filp_count= 0;
```

```
23100                   put_inode(rip);
23101                   return(r);
23102           }
23103
23104       return(fd);
23105   }


23108   /*===========================================================================*
23109    *                               new_node                                    *
23110    *===========================================================================*/
23111   PRIVATE struct inode *new_node(path, bits, z0)
23112   char *path;                        /* pointer to path name */
23113   mode_t bits;                       /* mode of the new inode */
23114   zone_t z0;                         /* zone number 0 for new inode */
23115   {
23116   /* New_node() is called by common_open(), do_mknod(), and do_mkdir().
23117    * In all cases it allocates a new inode, makes a directory entry for it on
23118    * the path 'path', and initializes it.  It returns a pointer to the inode if
23119    * it can do this; otherwise it returns NIL_INODE.  It always sets 'err_code'
23120    * to an appropriate value (OK or an error code).
23121    */
23122
23123       register struct inode *rlast_dir_ptr, *rip;
23124       register int r;
23125       char string[NAME_MAX];
23126
23127       /* See if the path can be opened down to the last directory. */
23128       if ((rlast_dir_ptr = last_dir(path, string)) == NIL_INODE) return(NIL_INODE);
23129
23130       /* The final directory is accessible. Get final component of the path. */
23131       rip = advance(rlast_dir_ptr, string);
23132       if ( rip == NIL_INODE && err_code == ENOENT) {
23133               /* Last path component does not exist.  Make new directory entry. */
23134               if ( (rip = alloc_inode(rlast_dir_ptr->i_dev, bits)) == NIL_INODE) {
23135                       /* Can't creat new inode: out of inodes. */
23136                       put_inode(rlast_dir_ptr);
23137                       return(NIL_INODE);
23138               }
23139
23140               /* Force inode to the disk before making directory entry to make
23141                * the system more robust in the face of a crash: an inode with
23142                * no directory entry is much better than the opposite.
23143                */
23144               rip->i_nlinks++;
23145               rip->i_zone[0] = z0;               /* major/minor device numbers */
23146               rw_inode(rip, WRITING);            /* force inode to disk now */
23147
23148               /* New inode acquired.  Try to make directory entry. */
23149               if ((r = search_dir(rlast_dir_ptr, string, &rip->i_num,ENTER)) != OK) {
23150                       put_inode(rlast_dir_ptr);
23151                       rip->i_nlinks--;           /* pity, have to free disk inode */
23152                       rip->i_dirt = DIRTY;       /* dirty inodes are written out */
23153                       put_inode(rip); /* this call frees the inode */
23154                       err_code = r;
23155                       return(NIL_INODE);
23156               }
23157
23158       } else {
23159               /* Either last component exists, or there is some problem. */
```

```
23160                    if (rip != NIL_INODE)
23161                            r = EEXIST;
23162                    else
23163                            r = err_code;
23164            }
23165
23166            /* Return the directory inode and exit. */
23167            put_inode(rlast_dir_ptr);
23168            err_code = r;
23169            return(rip);
23170    }


23173    /*===========================================================================*
23174     *                              pipe_open                                     *
23175     *===========================================================================*/
23176    PRIVATE int pipe_open(rip, bits, oflags)
23177    register struct inode *rip;
23178    register mode_t bits;
23179    register int oflags;
23180    {
23181    /*  This function is called from common_open. It checks if
23182     *  there is at least one reader/writer pair for the pipe, if not
23183     *  it suspends the caller, otherwise it revives all other blocked
23184     *  processes hanging on the pipe.
23185     */
23186
23187            if (find_filp(rip, bits & W_BIT ? R_BIT : W_BIT) == NIL_FILP) {
23188                    if (oflags & O_NONBLOCK) {
23189                            if (bits & W_BIT) return(ENXIO);
23190                    } else
23191                            suspend(XPOPEN);          /* suspend caller */
23192            } else if (susp_count > 0) {/* revive blocked processes */
23193                    release(rip, OPEN, susp_count);
23194                    release(rip, CREAT, susp_count);
23195            }
23196            rip->i_pipe = I_PIPE;
23197
23198            return(OK);
23199    }


23202    /*===========================================================================*
23203     *                              do_mknod                                      *
23204     *===========================================================================*/
23205    PUBLIC int do_mknod()
23206    {
23207    /* Perform the mknod(name, mode, addr) system call. */
23208
23209            register mode_t bits, mode_bits;
23210            struct inode *ip;
23211
23212            /* Only the super_user may make nodes other than fifos. */
23213            mode_bits = (mode_t) m.m1_i2; /* mode of the inode */
23214            if (!super_user && ((mode_bits & I_TYPE) != I_NAMED_PIPE)) return(EPERM);
23215            if (fetch_name(m.m1_p1, m.m1_i1, M1) != OK) return(err_code);
23216            bits = (mode_bits & I_TYPE) | (mode_bits & ALL_MODES & fp->fp_umask);
23217            ip = new_node(user_path, bits, (zone_t) m.m1_i3);
23218            put_inode(ip);
23219            return(err_code);
```

```
23220        }


23223    /*===========================================================================*
23224     *                               do_mkdir                                     *
23225     *===========================================================================*/
23226    PUBLIC int do_mkdir()
23227    {
23228    /* Perform the mkdir(name, mode) system call. */

23230      int r1, r2;                       /* status codes */
23231      ino_t dot, dotdot;                /* inode numbers for . and .. */
23232      mode_t bits;                      /* mode bits for the new inode */
23233      char string[NAME_MAX];            /* last component of the new dir's path name */
23234      register struct inode *rip, *ldirp;

23236      /* Check to see if it is possible to make another link in the parent dir. */
23237      if (fetch_name(name1, name1_length, M1) != OK) return(err_code);
23238      ldirp = last_dir(user_path, string);  /* pointer to new dir's parent */
23239      if (ldirp == NIL_INODE) return(err_code);
23240      if ( (ldirp->i_nlinks & BYTE) >= LINK_MAX) {
23241            put_inode(ldirp);         /* return parent */
23242            return(EMLINK);
23243      }

23245      /* Next make the inode. If that fails, return error code. */
23246      bits = I_DIRECTORY | (mode & RWX_MODES & fp->fp_umask);
23247      rip = new_node(user_path, bits, (zone_t) 0);
23248      if (rip == NIL_INODE || err_code == EEXIST) {
23249            put_inode(rip);           /* can't make dir: it already exists */
23250            put_inode(ldirp);         /* return parent too */
23251            return(err_code);
23252      }

23254      /* Get the inode numbers for . and .. to enter in the directory. */
23255      dotdot = ldirp->i_num;         /* parent's inode number */
23256      dot = rip->i_num;              /* inode number of the new dir itself */

23258      /* Now make dir entries for . and .. unless the disk is completely full. */
23259      /* Use dot1 and dot2, so the mode of the directory isn't important. */
23260      rip->i_mode = bits;   /* set mode */
23261      r1 = search_dir(rip, dot1, &dot, ENTER);       /* enter . in the new dir */
23262      r2 = search_dir(rip, dot2, &dotdot, ENTER);    /* enter .. in the new dir */

23264      /* If both . and .. were successfully entered, increment the link counts. */
23265      if (r1 == OK && r2 == OK) {
23266            /* Normal case.  It was possible to enter . and .. in the new dir. */
23267            rip->i_nlinks++;          /* this accounts for . */
23268            ldirp->i_nlinks++;        /* this accounts for .. */
23269            ldirp->i_dirt = DIRTY;    /* mark parent's inode as dirty */
23270      } else {
23271            /* It was not possible to enter . or .. probably disk was full. */
23272            (void) search_dir(ldirp, string, (ino_t *) 0, DELETE);
23273            rip->i_nlinks--;          /* undo the increment done in new_node() */
23274      }
23275      rip->i_dirt = DIRTY;           /* either way, i_nlinks has changed */

23277      put_inode(ldirp);              /* return the inode of the parent dir */
23278      put_inode(rip);                /* return the inode of the newly made dir */
23279      return(err_code);              /* new_node() always sets 'err_code' */
```

```
23280        }


23283    /*===========================================================================*
23284     *                              do_close                                      *
23285     *===========================================================================*/
23286    PUBLIC int do_close()
23287    {
23288    /* Perform the close(fd) system call. */
23289
23290       register struct filp *rfilp;
23291       register struct inode *rip;
23292       struct file_lock *flp;
23293       int rw, mode_word, major, task, lock_count;
23294       dev_t dev;
23295
23296       /* First locate the inode that belongs to the file descriptor. */
23297       if ( (rfilp = get_filp(fd)) == NIL_FILP) return(err_code);
23298       rip = rfilp->filp_ino;          /* 'rip' points to the inode */
23299
23300       if (rfilp->filp_count - 1 == 0 && rfilp->filp_mode != FILP_CLOSED) {
23301             /* Check to see if the file is special. */
23302             mode_word = rip->i_mode & I_TYPE;
23303             if (mode_word == I_CHAR_SPECIAL || mode_word == I_BLOCK_SPECIAL) {
23304                   dev = (dev_t) rip->i_zone[0];
23305                   if (mode_word == I_BLOCK_SPECIAL)  {
23306                         /* Invalidate cache entries unless special is mounted
23307                          * or ROOT
23308                          */
23309                         if (!mounted(rip)) {
23310                               (void) do_sync();          /* purge cache */
23311                               invalidate(dev);
23312                         }
23313                   }
23314                   /* Use the dmap_close entry to do any special processing
23315                    * required.
23316                    */
23317                   dev_mess.m_type = DEV_CLOSE;
23318                   dev_mess.DEVICE = dev;
23319                   major = (dev >> MAJOR) & BYTE;  /* major device nr */
23320                   task = dmap[major].dmap_task;    /* device task nr */
23321                   (*dmap[major].dmap_close)(task, &dev_mess);
23322             }
23323       }
23324
23325       /* If the inode being closed is a pipe, release everyone hanging on it. */
23326       if (rip->i_pipe == I_PIPE) {
23327             rw = (rfilp->filp_mode & R_BIT ? WRITE : READ);
23328             release(rip, rw, NR_PROCS);
23329       }
23330
23331       /* If a write has been done, the inode is already marked as DIRTY. */
23332       if (--rfilp->filp_count == 0) {
23333             if (rip->i_pipe == I_PIPE && rip->i_count > 1) {
23334                   /* Save the file position in the i-node in case needed later.
23335                    * The read and write positions are saved separately.  The
23336                    * last 3 zones in the i-node are not used for (named) pipes.
23337                    */
23338                   if (rfilp->filp_mode == R_BIT)
23339                         rip->i_zone[V2_NR_DZONES+1] = (zone_t) rfilp->filp_pos;
```

```
23340                   else
23341                           rip->i_zone[V2_NR_DZONES+2] = (zone_t) rfilp->filp_pos;
23342           }
23343           put_inode(rip);
23344     }
23345
23346     fp->fp_cloexec &= ~(1L << fd);          /* turn off close-on-exec bit */
23347     fp->fp_filp[fd] = NIL_FILP;
23348
23349     /* Check to see if the file is locked.  If so, release all locks. */
23350     if (nr_locks == 0) return(OK);
23351     lock_count = nr_locks;          /* save count of locks */
23352     for (flp = &file_lock[0]; flp < &file_lock[NR_LOCKS]; flp++) {
23353           if (flp->lock_type == 0) continue;        /* slot not in use */
23354           if (flp->lock_inode == rip && flp->lock_pid == fp->fp_pid) {
23355                   flp->lock_type = 0;
23356                   nr_locks--;
23357           }
23358     }
23359     if (nr_locks < lock_count) lock_revive();      /* lock released */
23360     return(OK);
23361 }


23364 /*===========================================================================*
23365  *                              do_lseek                                      *
23366  *===========================================================================*/
23367 PUBLIC int do_lseek()
23368 {
23369 /* Perform the lseek(ls_fd, offset, whence) system call. */
23370
23371   register struct filp *rfilp;
23372   register off_t pos;
23373
23374   /* Check to see if the file descriptor is valid. */
23375   if ( (rfilp = get_filp(ls_fd)) == NIL_FILP) return(err_code);
23376
23377   /* No lseek on pipes. */
23378   if (rfilp->filp_ino->i_pipe == I_PIPE) return(ESPIPE);
23379
23380   /* The value of 'whence' determines the start position to use. */
23381   switch(whence) {
23382         case 0: pos = 0;          break;
23383         case 1: pos = rfilp->filp_pos;  break;
23384         case 2: pos = rfilp->filp_ino->i_size;   break;
23385         default: return(EINVAL);
23386   }
23387
23388   /* Check for overflow. */
23389   if (((long)offset > 0) && ((long)(pos + offset) < (long)pos)) return(EINVAL);
23390   if (((long)offset < 0) && ((long)(pos + offset) > (long)pos)) return(EINVAL);
23391   pos = pos + offset;
23392
23393   if (pos != rfilp->filp_pos)
23394         rfilp->filp_ino->i_seek = ISEEK;          /* inhibit read ahead */
23395   rfilp->filp_pos = pos;
23396   reply_l1 = pos;                  /* insert the long into the output message */
23397   return(OK);
23398 }
```

```
          ++++++++++++++++++++++++++++++++++++++++++++++++++++++++++++++++++++++++++++++
                                        src/fs/read.c
          ++++++++++++++++++++++++++++++++++++++++++++++++++++++++++++++++++++++++++++++

23400     /* This file contains the heart of the mechanism used to read (and write)
23401      * files.  Read and write requests are split up into chunks that do not cross
23402      * block boundaries.  Each chunk is then processed in turn.  Reads on special
23403      * files are also detected and handled.
23404      *
23405      * The entry points into this file are
23406      *   do_read:    perform the READ system call by calling read_write
23407      *   read_write: actually do the work of READ and WRITE
23408      *   read_map:   given an inode and file position, look up its zone number
23409      *   rd_indir:   read an entry in an indirect block
23410      *   read_ahead: manage the block read ahead business
23411      */

23413     #include "fs.h"
23414     #include <fcntl.h>
23415     #include <minix/com.h>
23416     #include "buf.h"
23417     #include "file.h"
23418     #include "fproc.h"
23419     #include "inode.h"
23420     #include "param.h"
23421     #include "super.h"

23423     #define FD_MASK          077     /* max file descriptor is 63 */

23425     PRIVATE message umess;           /* message for asking SYSTASK for user copy */

23427     FORWARD _PROTOTYPE( int rw_chunk, (struct inode *rip, off_t position,
23428                         unsigned off, int chunk, unsigned left, int rw_flag,
23429                         char *buff, int seg, int usr)                  );

23431     /*===========================================================================*
23432      *                              do_read                                      *
23433      *===========================================================================*/
23434     PUBLIC int do_read()
23435     {
23436       return(read_write(READING));
23437     }


23440     /*===========================================================================*
23441      *                              read_write                                   *
23442      *===========================================================================*/
23443     PUBLIC int read_write(rw_flag)
23444     int rw_flag;                     /* READING or WRITING */
23445     {
23446     /* Perform read(fd, buffer, nbytes) or write(fd, buffer, nbytes) call. */

23448       register struct inode *rip;
23449       register struct filp *f;
23450       off_t bytes_left, f_size, position;
23451       unsigned int off, cum_io;
23452       int op, oflags, r, chunk, usr, seg, block_spec, char_spec;
23453       int regular, partial_pipe = 0, partial_cnt = 0;
23454       dev_t dev;
```

```
23455          mode_t mode_word;
23456          struct filp *wf;
23457
23458          /* MM loads segments by putting funny things in upper 10 bits of 'fd'. */
23459          if (who == MM_PROC_NR && (fd & (~BYTE)) ) {
23460                  usr = (fd >> 8) & BYTE;
23461                  seg = (fd >> 6) & 03;
23462                  fd &= FD_MASK;          /* get rid of user and segment bits */
23463          } else {
23464                  usr = who;              /* normal case */
23465                  seg = D;
23466          }
23467
23468          /* If the file descriptor is valid, get the inode, size and mode. */
23469          if (nbytes < 0) return(EINVAL);
23470          if ((f = get_filp(fd)) == NIL_FILP) return(err_code);
23471          if (((f->filp_mode) & (rw_flag == READING ? R_BIT : W_BIT)) == 0) {
23472                  return(f->filp_mode == FILP_CLOSED ? EIO : EBADF);
23473          }
23474          if (nbytes == 0) return(0);   /* so char special files need not check for 0*/
23475          position = f->filp_pos;
23476          if (position > MAX_FILE_POS) return(EINVAL);
23477          if (position + nbytes < position) return(EINVAL); /* unsigned overflow */
23478          oflags = f->filp_flags;
23479          rip = f->filp_ino;
23480          f_size = rip->i_size;
23481          r = OK;
23482          if (rip->i_pipe == I_PIPE) {
23483                  /* fp->fp_cum_io_partial is only nonzero when doing partial writes */
23484                  cum_io = fp->fp_cum_io_partial;
23485          } else {
23486                  cum_io = 0;
23487          }
23488          op = (rw_flag == READING ? DEV_READ : DEV_WRITE);
23489          mode_word = rip->i_mode & I_TYPE;
23490          regular = mode_word == I_REGULAR || mode_word == I_NAMED_PIPE;
23491
23492          char_spec = (mode_word == I_CHAR_SPECIAL ? 1 : 0);
23493          block_spec = (mode_word == I_BLOCK_SPECIAL ? 1 : 0);
23494          if (block_spec) f_size = LONG_MAX;
23495          rdwt_err = OK;                  /* set to EIO if disk error occurs */
23496
23497          /* Check for character special files. */
23498          if (char_spec) {
23499                  dev = (dev_t) rip->i_zone[0];
23500                  r = dev_io(op, oflags & O_NONBLOCK, dev, position, nbytes, who,buffer);
23501                  if (r >= 0) {
23502                          cum_io = r;
23503                          position += r;
23504                          r = OK;
23505                  }
23506          } else {
23507                  if (rw_flag == WRITING && block_spec == 0) {
23508                          /* Check in advance to see if file will grow too big. */
23509                          if (position > rip->i_sp->s_max_size - nbytes) return(EFBIG);
23510
23511                          /* Check for O_APPEND flag. */
23512                          if (oflags & O_APPEND) position = f_size;
23513
23514                          /* Clear the zone containing present EOF if hole about
```

```
23515                          * to be created.  This is necessary because all unwritten
23516                          * blocks prior to the EOF must read as zeros.
23517                          */
23518                         if (position > f_size) clear_zone(rip, f_size, 0);
23519                 }
23520
23521                 /* Pipes are a little different.  Check. */
23522                 if (rip->i_pipe == I_PIPE) {
23523                         r = pipe_check(rip,rw_flag,oflags,nbytes,position,&partial_cnt);
23524                         if (r <= 0) return(r);
23525                 }
23526
23527                 if (partial_cnt > 0) partial_pipe = 1;
23528
23529                 /* Split the transfer into chunks that don't span two blocks. */
23530                 while (nbytes != 0) {
23531                         off = (unsigned int) (position % BLOCK_SIZE);/* offset in blk*/
23532                         if (partial_pipe) {  /* pipes only */
23533                                 chunk = MIN(partial_cnt, BLOCK_SIZE - off);
23534                         } else
23535                                 chunk = MIN(nbytes, BLOCK_SIZE - off);
23536                         if (chunk < 0) chunk = BLOCK_SIZE - off;
23537
23538                         if (rw_flag == READING) {
23539                                 bytes_left = f_size - position;
23540                                 if (position >= f_size) break;  /* we are beyond EOF */
23541                                 if (chunk > bytes_left) chunk = (int) bytes_left;
23542                         }
23543
23544                         /* Read or write 'chunk' bytes. */
23545                         r = rw_chunk(rip, position, off, chunk, (unsigned) nbytes,
23546                                         rw_flag, buffer, seg, usr);
23547                         if (r != OK) break;       /* EOF reached */
23548                         if (rdwt_err < 0) break;
23549
23550                         /* Update counters and pointers. */
23551                         buffer += chunk;          /* user buffer address */
23552                         nbytes -= chunk;          /* bytes yet to be read */
23553                         cum_io += chunk;          /* bytes read so far */
23554                         position += chunk;        /* position within the file */
23555
23556                         if (partial_pipe) {
23557                                 partial_cnt -= chunk;
23558                                 if (partial_cnt <= 0)  break;
23559                         }
23560                 }
23561         }
23562
23563         /* On write, update file size and access time. */
23564         if (rw_flag == WRITING) {
23565                 if (regular || mode_word == I_DIRECTORY) {
23566                         if (position > f_size) rip->i_size = position;
23567                 }
23568         } else {
23569                 if (rip->i_pipe == I_PIPE && position >= rip->i_size) {
23570                         /* Reset pipe pointers. */
23571                         rip->i_size = 0;          /* no data left */
23572                         position = 0;             /* reset reader(s) */
23573                         if ( (wf = find_filp(rip, W_BIT)) != NIL_FILP) wf->filp_pos =0;
23574                 }
```

```
23575          }
23576          f->filp_pos = position;
23577
23578          /* Check to see if read-ahead is called for, and if so, set it up. */
23579          if (rw_flag == READING && rip->i_seek == NO_SEEK && position % BLOCK_SIZE== 0
23580                          && (regular || mode_word == I_DIRECTORY)) {
23581                  rdahed_inode = rip;
23582                  rdahedpos = position;
23583          }
23584          rip->i_seek = NO_SEEK;
23585
23586          if (rdwt_err != OK) r = rdwt_err;      /* check for disk error */
23587          if (rdwt_err == END_OF_FILE) r = OK;
23588          if (r == OK) {
23589                  if (rw_flag == READING) rip->i_update |= ATIME;
23590                  if (rw_flag == WRITING) rip->i_update |= CTIME | MTIME;
23591                  rip->i_dirt = DIRTY;            /* inode is thus now dirty */
23592                  if (partial_pipe) {
23593                          partial_pipe = 0;
23594                                  /* partial write on pipe with */
23595                                  /* O_NONBLOCK, return write count */
23596                          if (!(oflags & O_NONBLOCK)) {
23597                                  fp->fp_cum_io_partial = cum_io;
23598                                  suspend(XPIPE); /* partial write on pipe with */
23599                                  return(0);      /* nbyte > PIPE_SIZE - non-atomic */
23600                          }
23601                  }
23602                  fp->fp_cum_io_partial = 0;
23603                  return(cum_io);
23604          } else {
23605                  return(r);
23606          }
23607  }


23610  /*===========================================================================*
23611   *                              rw_chunk                                     *
23612   *===========================================================================*/
23613  PRIVATE int rw_chunk(rip, position, off, chunk, left, rw_flag, buff, seg, usr)
23614  register struct inode *rip;       /* pointer to inode for file to be rd/wr */
23615  off_t position;                   /* position within file to read or write */
23616  unsigned off;                     /* off within the current block */
23617  int chunk;                        /* number of bytes to read or write */
23618  unsigned left;                    /* max number of bytes wanted after position */
23619  int rw_flag;                      /* READING or WRITING */
23620  char *buff;                       /* virtual address of the user buffer */
23621  int seg;                          /* T or D segment in user space */
23622  int usr;                          /* which user process */
23623  {
23624  /* Read or write (part of) a block. */
23625
23626    register struct buf *bp;
23627    register int r;
23628    int n, block_spec;
23629    block_t b;
23630    dev_t dev;
23631
23632    block_spec = (rip->i_mode & I_TYPE) == I_BLOCK_SPECIAL;
23633    if (block_spec) {
23634          b = position/BLOCK_SIZE;
```

```
23635                        dev = (dev_t) rip->i_zone[0];
23636            } else {
23637                        b = read_map(rip, position);
23638                        dev = rip->i_dev;
23639            }
23640
23641            if (!block_spec && b == NO_BLOCK) {
23642                    if (rw_flag == READING) {
23643                                /* Reading from a nonexistent block.  Must read as all zeros.*/
23644                                bp = get_block(NO_DEV, NO_BLOCK, NORMAL);     /* get a buffer */
23645                                zero_block(bp);
23646                    } else {
23647                                /* Writing to a nonexistent block. Create and enter in inode.*/
23648                                if ((bp= new_block(rip, position)) == NIL_BUF)return(err_code);
23649                    }
23650            } else if (rw_flag == READING) {
23651                    /* Read and read ahead if convenient. */
23652                    bp = rahead(rip, b, position, left);
23653            } else {
23654                    /* Normally an existing block to be partially overwritten is first read
23655                     * in.  However, a full block need not be read in.  If it is already in
23656                     * the cache, acquire it, otherwise just acquire a free buffer.
23657                     */
23658                    n = (chunk == BLOCK_SIZE ? NO_READ : NORMAL);
23659                    if (!block_spec && off == 0 && position >= rip->i_size) n = NO_READ;
23660                    bp = get_block(dev, b, n);
23661            }
23662
23663            /* In all cases, bp now points to a valid buffer. */
23664            if (rw_flag == WRITING && chunk != BLOCK_SIZE && !block_spec &&
23665                                                position >= rip->i_size && off == 0) {
23666                    zero_block(bp);
23667            }
23668            if (rw_flag == READING) {
23669                    /* Copy a chunk from the block buffer to user space. */
23670                    r = sys_copy(FS_PROC_NR, D, (phys_bytes) (bp->b_data+off),
23671                                      usr, seg, (phys_bytes) buff,
23672                                      (phys_bytes) chunk);
23673            } else {
23674                    /* Copy a chunk from user space to the block buffer. */
23675                    r = sys_copy(usr, seg, (phys_bytes) buff,
23676                                    FS_PROC_NR, D, (phys_bytes) (bp->b_data+off),
23677                                    (phys_bytes) chunk);
23678                    bp->b_dirt = DIRTY;
23679            }
23680            n = (off + chunk == BLOCK_SIZE ? FULL_DATA_BLOCK : PARTIAL_DATA_BLOCK);
23681            put_block(bp, n);
23682            return(r);
23683    }


23686    /*===========================================================================*
23687     *                              read_map                                      *
23688     *===========================================================================*/
23689    PUBLIC block_t read_map(rip, position)
23690    register struct inode *rip;        /* ptr to inode to map from */
23691    off_t position;                    /* position in file whose blk wanted */
23692    {
23693    /* Given an inode and a position within the corresponding file, locate the
23694     * block (not zone) number in which that position is to be found and return it.
```

```
23695      */
23696
23697      register struct buf *bp;
23698      register zone_t z;
23699      int scale, boff, dzones, nr_indirects, index, zind, ex;
23700      block_t b;
23701      long excess, zone, block_pos;
23702
23703      scale = rip->i_sp->s_log_zone_size;    /* for block-zone conversion */
23704      block_pos = position/BLOCK_SIZE;       /* relative blk # in file */
23705      zone = block_pos >> scale;      /* position's zone */
23706      boff = (int) (block_pos - (zone << scale) ); /* relative blk # within zone */
23707      dzones = rip->i_ndzones;
23708      nr_indirects = rip->i_nindirs;
23709
23710      /* Is 'position' to be found in the inode itself? */
23711      if (zone < dzones) {
23712          zind = (int) zone;        /* index should be an int */
23713          z = rip->i_zone[zind];
23714          if (z == NO_ZONE) return(NO_BLOCK);
23715          b = ((block_t) z << scale) + boff;
23716          return(b);
23717      }
23718
23719      /* It is not in the inode, so it must be single or double indirect. */
23720      excess = zone - dzones;        /* first Vx_NR_DZONES don't count */
23721
23722      if (excess < nr_indirects) {
23723          /* 'position' can be located via the single indirect block. */
23724          z = rip->i_zone[dzones];
23725      } else {
23726          /* 'position' can be located via the double indirect block. */
23727          if ( (z = rip->i_zone[dzones+1]) == NO_ZONE) return(NO_BLOCK);
23728          excess -= nr_indirects;                 /* single indir doesn't count*/
23729          b = (block_t) z << scale;
23730          bp = get_block(rip->i_dev, b, NORMAL);  /* get double indirect block */
23731          index = (int) (excess/nr_indirects);
23732          z = rd_indir(bp, index);                /* z= zone for single*/
23733          put_block(bp, INDIRECT_BLOCK);          /* release double ind block */
23734          excess = excess % nr_indirects;         /* index into single ind blk */
23735      }
23736
23737      /* 'z' is zone num for single indirect block; 'excess' is index into it. */
23738      if (z == NO_ZONE) return(NO_BLOCK);
23739      b = (block_t) z << scale;                   /* b is blk # for single ind */
23740      bp = get_block(rip->i_dev, b, NORMAL);      /* get single indirect block */
23741      ex = (int) excess;                          /* need an integer */
23742      z = rd_indir(bp, ex);                       /* get block pointed to */
23743      put_block(bp, INDIRECT_BLOCK);              /* release single indir blk */
23744      if (z == NO_ZONE) return(NO_BLOCK);
23745      b = ((block_t) z << scale) + boff;
23746      return(b);
23747  }


23750  /*===========================================================================*
23751   *                              rd_indir                                     *
23752   *===========================================================================*/
23753  PUBLIC zone_t rd_indir(bp, index)
23754  struct buf *bp;                 /* pointer to indirect block */
```

```
23755    int index;                        /* index into *bp */
23756    {
23757    /* Given a pointer to an indirect block, read one entry.  The reason for
23758     * making a separate routine out of this is that there are four cases:
23759     * V1 (IBM and 68000), and V2 (IBM and 68000).
23760     */
23761
23762      struct super_block *sp;
23763      zone_t zone;                      /* V2 zones are longs (shorts in V1) */
23764
23765      sp = get_super(bp->b_dev);     /* need super block to find file sys type */
23766
23767      /* read a zone from an indirect block */
23768      if (sp->s_version == V1)
23769            zone = (zone_t) conv2(sp->s_native, (int)  bp->b_v1_ind[index]);
23770      else
23771            zone = (zone_t) conv4(sp->s_native, (long) bp->b_v2_ind[index]);
23772
23773      if (zone != NO_ZONE &&
23774                    (zone < (zone_t) sp->s_firstdatazone || zone >= sp->s_zones)) {
23775            printf("Illegal zone number %ld in indirect block, index %d\n",
23776                  (long) zone, index);
23777            panic("check file system", NO_NUM);
23778      }
23779      return(zone);
23780    }


23783    /*===========================================================================*
23784     *                              read_ahead                                   *
23785     *===========================================================================*/
23786    PUBLIC void read_ahead()
23787    {
23788    /* Read a block into the cache before it is needed. */
23789
23790      register struct inode *rip;
23791      struct buf *bp;
23792      block_t b;
23793
23794      rip = rdahed_inode;               /* pointer to inode to read ahead from */
23795      rdahed_inode = NIL_INODE;         /* turn off read ahead */
23796      if ( (b = read_map(rip, rdahedpos)) == NO_BLOCK) return;      /* at EOF */
23797      bp = rahead(rip, b, rdahedpos, BLOCK_SIZE);
23798      put_block(bp, PARTIAL_DATA_BLOCK);
23799    }


23802    /*===========================================================================*
23803     *                              rahead                                       *
23804     *===========================================================================*/
23805    PUBLIC struct buf *rahead(rip, baseblock, position, bytes_ahead)
23806    register struct inode *rip;       /* pointer to inode for file to be read */
23807    block_t baseblock;                /* block at current position */
23808    off_t position;                   /* position within file */
23809    unsigned bytes_ahead;             /* bytes beyond position for immediate use */
23810    {
23811    /* Fetch a block from the cache or the device.  If a physical read is
23812     * required, prefetch as many more blocks as convenient into the cache.
23813     * This usually covers bytes_ahead and is at least BLOCKS_MINIMUM.
23814     * The device driver may decide it knows better and stop reading at a
```

```
23815        * cylinder boundary (or after an error).  Rw_scattered() puts an optional
23816        * flag on all reads to allow this.
23817        */
23818
23819       /* Minimum number of blocks to prefetch. */
23820       # define BLOCKS_MINIMUM          (NR_BUFS < 50 ? 18 : 32)
23821
23822         int block_spec, scale, read_q_size;
23823         unsigned int blocks_ahead, fragment;
23824         block_t block, blocks_left;
23825         off_t ind1_pos;
23826         dev_t dev;
23827         struct buf *bp;
23828         static struct buf *read_q[NR_BUFS];
23829
23830         block_spec = (rip->i_mode & I_TYPE) == I_BLOCK_SPECIAL;
23831         if (block_spec) {
23832               dev = (dev_t) rip->i_zone[0];
23833         } else {
23834               dev = rip->i_dev;
23835         }
23836
23837         block = baseblock;
23838         bp = get_block(dev, block, PREFETCH);
23839         if (bp->b_dev != NO_DEV) return(bp);
23840
23841         /* The best guess for the number of blocks to prefetch:  A lot.
23842          * It is impossible to tell what the device looks like, so we don't even
23843          * try to guess the geometry, but leave it to the driver.
23844          *
23845          * The floppy driver can read a full track with no rotational delay, and it
23846          * avoids reading partial tracks if it can, so handing it enough buffers to
23847          * read two tracks is perfect.  (Two, because some diskette types have
23848          * an odd number of sectors per track, so a block may span tracks.)
23849          *
23850          * The disk drivers don't try to be smart.  With todays disks it is
23851          * impossible to tell what the real geometry looks like, so it is best to
23852          * read as much as you can.  With luck the caching on the drive allows
23853          * for a little time to start the next read.
23854          *
23855          * The current solution below is a bit of a hack, it just reads blocks from
23856          * the current file position hoping that more of the file can be found.  A
23857          * better solution must look at the already available zone pointers and
23858          * indirect blocks (but don't call read_map!).
23859          */
23860
23861         fragment = position % BLOCK_SIZE;
23862         position -= fragment;
23863         bytes_ahead += fragment;
23864
23865         blocks_ahead = (bytes_ahead + BLOCK_SIZE - 1) / BLOCK_SIZE;
23866
23867         if (block_spec && rip->i_size == 0) {
23868               blocks_left = NR_IOREQS;
23869         } else {
23870               blocks_left = (rip->i_size - position + BLOCK_SIZE - 1) / BLOCK_SIZE;
23871
23872               /* Go for the first indirect block if we are in its neighborhood. */
23873               if (!block_spec) {
23874                     scale = rip->i_sp->s_log_zone_size;
```

```
23875                         ind1_pos = (off_t) rip->i_ndzones * (BLOCK_SIZE << scale);
23876                         if (position <= ind1_pos && rip->i_size > ind1_pos) {
23877                                 blocks_ahead++;
23878                                 blocks_left++;
23879                         }
23880                 }
23881         }
23882
23883         /* No more than the maximum request. */
23884         if (blocks_ahead > NR_IOREQS) blocks_ahead = NR_IOREQS;
23885
23886         /* Read at least the minimum number of blocks, but not after a seek. */
23887         if (blocks_ahead < BLOCKS_MINIMUM && rip->i_seek == NO_SEEK)
23888                 blocks_ahead = BLOCKS_MINIMUM;
23889
23890         /* Can't go past end of file. */
23891         if (blocks_ahead > blocks_left) blocks_ahead = blocks_left;
23892
23893         read_q_size = 0;
23894
23895         /* Acquire block buffers. */
23896         for (;;) {
23897                 read_q[read_q_size++] = bp;
23898
23899                 if (--blocks_ahead == 0) break;
23900
23901                 /* Don't trash the cache, leave 4 free. */
23902                 if (bufs_in_use >= NR_BUFS - 4) break;
23903
23904                 block++;
23905
23906                 bp = get_block(dev, block, PREFETCH);
23907                 if (bp->b_dev != NO_DEV) {
23908                         /* Oops, block already in the cache, get out. */
23909                         put_block(bp, FULL_DATA_BLOCK);
23910                         break;
23911                 }
23912         }
23913         rw_scattered(dev, read_q, read_q_size, READING);
23914         return(get_block(dev, baseblock, NORMAL));
23915 }
```

```
++++++++++++++++++++++++++++++++++++++++++++++++++++++++++++++++++++++++++++++++++++
                               src/fs/write.c
++++++++++++++++++++++++++++++++++++++++++++++++++++++++++++++++++++++++++++++++++++

24000  /* This file is the counterpart of "read.c".  It contains the code for writing
24001   * insofar as this is not contained in read_write().
24002   *
24003   * The entry points into this file are
24004   *   do_write:     call read_write to perform the WRITE system call
24005   *   clear_zone:   erase a zone in the middle of a file
24006   *   new_block:    acquire a new block
24007   */
24008
24009  #include "fs.h"
```

```
24010   #include <string.h>
24011   #include "buf.h"
24012   #include "file.h"
24013   #include "fproc.h"
24014   #include "inode.h"
24015   #include "super.h"
24016
24017   FORWARD _PROTOTYPE( int write_map, (struct inode *rip, off_t position,
24018                           zone_t new_zone)                              );
24019
24020   FORWARD _PROTOTYPE( void wr_indir, (struct buf *bp, int index, zone_t zone) );
24021
24022   /*===========================================================================*
24023    *                              do_write                                      *
24024    *===========================================================================*/
24025   PUBLIC int do_write()
24026   {
24027   /* Perform the write(fd, buffer, nbytes) system call. */
24028
24029     return(read_write(WRITING));
24030   }
24031
24032
24033   /*===========================================================================*
24034    *                              write_map                                     *
24035    *===========================================================================*/
24036   PRIVATE int write_map(rip, position, new_zone)
24037   register struct inode *rip;     /* pointer to inode to be changed */
24038   off_t position;                 /* file address to be mapped */
24039   zone_t new_zone;                /* zone # to be inserted */
24040   {
24041   /* Write a new zone into an inode. */
24042     int scale, ind_ex, new_ind, new_dbl, zones, nr_indirects, single, zindex, ex;
24043     zone_t z, z1;
24044     register block_t b;
24045     long excess, zone;
24046     struct buf *bp;
24047
24048     rip->i_dirt = DIRTY;           /* inode will be changed */
24049     bp = NIL_BUF;
24050     scale = rip->i_sp->s_log_zone_size;          /* for zone-block conversion */
24051     zone = (position/BLOCK_SIZE) >> scale;       /* relative zone # to insert */
24052     zones = rip->i_ndzones;        /* # direct zones in the inode */
24053     nr_indirects = rip->i_nindirs;/* # indirect zones per indirect block */
24054
24055     /* Is 'position' to be found in the inode itself? */
24056     if (zone < zones) {
24057           zindex = (int) zone;     /* we need an integer here */
24058           rip->i_zone[zindex] = new_zone;
24059           return(OK);
24060     }
24061
24062     /* It is not in the inode, so it must be single or double indirect. */
24063     excess = zone - zones;         /* first Vx_NR_DZONES don't count */
24064     new_ind = FALSE;
24065     new_dbl = FALSE;
24066
24067     if (excess < nr_indirects) {
24068           /* 'position' can be located via the single indirect block. */
24069           z1 = rip->i_zone[zones];         /* single indirect zone */
```

```
24070                  single = TRUE;
24071          } else {
24072                  /* 'position' can be located via the double indirect block. */
24073                  if ( (z = rip->i_zone[zones+1]) == NO_ZONE) {
24074                          /* Create the double indirect block. */
24075                          if ( (z = alloc_zone(rip->i_dev, rip->i_zone[0])) == NO_ZONE)
24076                                  return(err_code);
24077                          rip->i_zone[zones+1] = z;
24078                          new_dbl = TRUE; /* set flag for later */
24079                  }
24080
24081                  /* Either way, 'z' is zone number for double indirect block. */
24082                  excess -= nr_indirects; /* single indirect doesn't count */
24083                  ind_ex = (int) (excess / nr_indirects);
24084                  excess = excess % nr_indirects;
24085                  if (ind_ex >= nr_indirects) return(EFBIG);
24086                  b = (block_t) z << scale;
24087                  bp = get_block(rip->i_dev, b, (new_dbl ? NO_READ : NORMAL));
24088                  if (new_dbl) zero_block(bp);
24089                  z1 = rd_indir(bp, ind_ex);
24090                  single = FALSE;
24091          }
24092
24093          /* z1 is now single indirect zone; 'excess' is index. */
24094          if (z1 == NO_ZONE) {
24095                  /* Create indirect block and store zone # in inode or dbl indir blk. */
24096                  z1 = alloc_zone(rip->i_dev, rip->i_zone[0]);
24097                  if (single)
24098                          rip->i_zone[zones] = z1;              /* update inode */
24099                  else
24100                          wr_indir(bp, ind_ex, z1);            /* update dbl indir */
24101
24102                  new_ind = TRUE;
24103                  if (bp != NIL_BUF) bp->b_dirt = DIRTY;  /* if double ind, it is dirty*/
24104                  if (z1 == NO_ZONE) {
24105                          put_block(bp, INDIRECT_BLOCK);  /* release dbl indirect blk */
24106                          return(err_code);           /* couldn't create single ind */
24107                  }
24108          }
24109          put_block(bp, INDIRECT_BLOCK);             /* release double indirect blk */
24110
24111          /* z1 is indirect block's zone number. */
24112          b = (block_t) z1 << scale;
24113          bp = get_block(rip->i_dev, b, (new_ind ? NO_READ : NORMAL) );
24114          if (new_ind) zero_block(bp);
24115          ex = (int) excess;                        /* we need an int here */
24116          wr_indir(bp, ex, new_zone);
24117          bp->b_dirt = DIRTY;
24118          put_block(bp, INDIRECT_BLOCK);
24119
24120          return(OK);
24121  }


24124  /*===========================================================================*
24125   *                              wr_indir                                     *
24126   *===========================================================================*/
24127  PRIVATE void wr_indir(bp, index, zone)
24128  struct buf *bp;                         /* pointer to indirect block */
24129  int index;                              /* index into *bp */
```

```
24130    zone_t zone;                        /* zone to write */
24131    {
24132    /* Given a pointer to an indirect block, write one entry. */
24133
24134      struct super_block *sp;
24135
24136      sp = get_super(bp->b_dev);     /* need super block to find file sys type */
24137
24138      /* write a zone into an indirect block */
24139      if (sp->s_version == V1)
24140            bp->b_v1_ind[index] = (zone1_t) conv2(sp->s_native, (int)  zone);
24141      else
24142            bp->b_v2_ind[index] = (zone_t)  conv4(sp->s_native, (long) zone);
24143    }


24146    /*===========================================================================*
24147     *                              clear_zone                                    *
24148     *===========================================================================*/
24149    PUBLIC void clear_zone(rip, pos, flag)
24150    register struct inode *rip;     /* inode to clear */
24151    off_t pos;                      /* points to block to clear */
24152    int flag;                       /* 0 if called by read_write, 1 by new_block */
24153    {
24154    /* Zero a zone, possibly starting in the middle.  The parameter 'pos' gives
24155     * a byte in the first block to be zeroed.  Clearzone() is called from
24156     * read_write and new_block().
24157     */
24158
24159      register struct buf *bp;
24160      register block_t b, blo, bhi;
24161      register off_t next;
24162      register int scale;
24163      register zone_t zone_size;
24164
24165      /* If the block size and zone size are the same, clear_zone() not needed. */
24166      scale = rip->i_sp->s_log_zone_size;
24167      if (scale == 0) return;
24168
24169      zone_size = (zone_t) BLOCK_SIZE << scale;
24170      if (flag == 1) pos = (pos/zone_size) * zone_size;
24171      next = pos + BLOCK_SIZE - 1;
24172
24173      /* If 'pos' is in the last block of a zone, do not clear the zone. */
24174      if (next/zone_size != pos/zone_size) return;
24175      if ( (blo = read_map(rip, next)) == NO_BLOCK) return;
24176      bhi = (  ((blo>>scale)+1) << scale)   - 1;
24177
24178      /* Clear all the blocks between 'blo' and 'bhi'. */
24179      for (b = blo; b <= bhi; b++) {
24180            bp = get_block(rip->i_dev, b, NO_READ);
24181            zero_block(bp);
24182            put_block(bp, FULL_DATA_BLOCK);
24183      }
24184    }


24187    /*===========================================================================*
24188     *                              new_block                                     *
24189     *===========================================================================*/
```

```
24190      PUBLIC struct buf *new_block(rip, position)
24191      register struct inode *rip;        /* pointer to inode */
24192      off_t position;                    /* file pointer */
24193      {
24194      /* Acquire a new block and return a pointer to it.  Doing so may require
24195       * allocating a complete zone, and then returning the initial block.
24196       * On the other hand, the current zone may still have some unused blocks.
24197       */
24198
24199        register struct buf *bp;
24200        block_t b, base_block;
24201        zone_t z;
24202        zone_t zone_size;
24203        int scale, r;
24204        struct super_block *sp;
24205
24206        /* Is another block available in the current zone? */
24207        if ( (b = read_map(rip, position)) == NO_BLOCK) {
24208              /* Choose first zone if possible. */
24209              /* Lose if the file is nonempty but the first zone number is NO_ZONE
24210               * corresponding to a zone full of zeros.  It would be better to
24211               * search near the last real zone.
24212               */
24213              if (rip->i_zone[0] == NO_ZONE) {
24214                      sp = rip->i_sp;
24215                      z = sp->s_firstdatazone;
24216              } else {
24217                      z = rip->i_zone[0];      /* hunt near first zone */
24218              }
24219              if ( (z = alloc_zone(rip->i_dev, z)) == NO_ZONE) return(NIL_BUF);
24220              if ( (r = write_map(rip, position, z)) != OK) {
24221                      free_zone(rip->i_dev, z);
24222                      err_code = r;
24223                      return(NIL_BUF);
24224              }
24225
24226              /* If we are not writing at EOF, clear the zone, just to be safe. */
24227              if ( position != rip->i_size) clear_zone(rip, position, 1);
24228              scale = rip->i_sp->s_log_zone_size;
24229              base_block = (block_t) z << scale;
24230              zone_size = (zone_t) BLOCK_SIZE << scale;
24231              b = base_block + (block_t)((position % zone_size)/BLOCK_SIZE);
24232        }
24233
24234        bp = get_block(rip->i_dev, b, NO_READ);
24235        zero_block(bp);
24236        return(bp);
24237      }


24240      /*===========================================================================*
24241       *                              zero_block                                   *
24242       *===========================================================================*/
24243      PUBLIC void zero_block(bp)
24244      register struct buf *bp;           /* pointer to buffer to zero */
24245      {
24246      /* Zero a block. */
24247
24248        memset(bp->b_data, 0, BLOCK_SIZE);
24249        bp->b_dirt = DIRTY;
```

```
24250        }




++++++++++++++++++++++++++++++++++++++++++++++++++++++++++++++++++++++++++++++++
                                    src/fs/pipe.c
++++++++++++++++++++++++++++++++++++++++++++++++++++++++++++++++++++++++++++++++


24300    /* This file deals with the suspension and revival of processes.  A process can
24301     * be suspended because it wants to read or write from a pipe and can't, or
24302     * because it wants to read or write from a special file and can't.  When a
24303     * process can't continue it is suspended, and revived later when it is able
24304     * to continue.
24305     *
24306     * The entry points into this file are
24307     *   do_pipe:     perform the PIPE system call
24308     *   pipe_check:  check to see that a read or write on a pipe is feasible now
24309     *   suspend:     suspend a process that cannot do a requested read or write
24310     *   release:     check to see if a suspended process can be released and do it
24311     *   revive:      mark a suspended process as able to run again
24312     *   do_unpause:  a signal has been sent to a process; see if it suspended
24313     */

24314
24315    #include "fs.h"
24316    #include <fcntl.h>
24317    #include <signal.h>
24318    #include <minix/boot.h>
24319    #include <minix/callnr.h>
24320    #include <minix/com.h>
24321    #include "dev.h"
24322    #include "file.h"
24323    #include "fproc.h"
24324    #include "inode.h"
24325    #include "param.h"
24326
24327    PRIVATE message mess;
24328
24329    /*===========================================================================*
24330     *                              do_pipe                                       *
24331     *===========================================================================*/
24332    PUBLIC int do_pipe()
24333    {
24334    /* Perform the pipe(fil_des) system call. */
24335
24336      register struct fproc *rfp;
24337      register struct inode *rip;
24338      int r;
24339      struct filp *fil_ptr0, *fil_ptr1;
24340      int fil_des[2];                  /* reply goes here */
24341
24342      /* Acquire two file descriptors. */
24343      rfp = fp;
24344      if ( (r = get_fd(0, R_BIT, &fil_des[0], &fil_ptr0)) != OK) return(r);
24345      rfp->fp_filp[fil_des[0]] = fil_ptr0;
24346      fil_ptr0->filp_count = 1;
24347      if ( (r = get_fd(0, W_BIT, &fil_des[1], &fil_ptr1)) != OK) {
24348            rfp->fp_filp[fil_des[0]] = NIL_FILP;
24349            fil_ptr0->filp_count = 0;
```

```
24350              return(r);
24351        }
24352        rfp->fp_filp[fil_des[1]] = fil_ptr1;
24353        fil_ptr1->filp_count = 1;
24354
24355        /* Make the inode on the pipe device. */
24356        if ( (rip = alloc_inode(PIPE_DEV, I_REGULAR) ) == NIL_INODE) {
24357              rfp->fp_filp[fil_des[0]] = NIL_FILP;
24358              fil_ptr0->filp_count = 0;
24359              rfp->fp_filp[fil_des[1]] = NIL_FILP;
24360              fil_ptr1->filp_count = 0;
24361              return(err_code);
24362        }
24363
24364        if (read_only(rip) != OK) panic("pipe device is read only", NO_NUM);
24365
24366        rip->i_pipe = I_PIPE;
24367        rip->i_mode &= ~I_REGULAR;
24368        rip->i_mode |= I_NAMED_PIPE;  /* pipes and FIFOs have this bit set */
24369        fil_ptr0->filp_ino = rip;
24370        fil_ptr0->filp_flags = O_RDONLY;
24371        dup_inode(rip);              /* for double usage */
24372        fil_ptr1->filp_ino = rip;
24373        fil_ptr1->filp_flags = O_WRONLY;
24374        rw_inode(rip, WRITING);      /* mark inode as allocated */
24375        reply_i1 = fil_des[0];
24376        reply_i2 = fil_des[1];
24377        rip->i_update = ATIME | CTIME | MTIME;
24378        return(OK);
24379  }


24382  /*===========================================================================*
24383   *                            pipe_check                                     *
24384   *===========================================================================*/
24385  PUBLIC int pipe_check(rip, rw_flag, oflags, bytes, position, canwrite)
24386  register struct inode *rip;       /* the inode of the pipe */
24387  int rw_flag;                      /* READING or WRITING */
24388  int oflags;                       /* flags set by open or fcntl */
24389  register int bytes;               /* bytes to be read or written (all chunks) */
24390  register off_t position;          /* current file position */
24391  int *canwrite;                    /* return: number of bytes we can write */
24392  {
24393  /* Pipes are a little different.  If a process reads from an empty pipe for
24394   * which a writer still exists, suspend the reader.  If the pipe is empty
24395   * and there is no writer, return 0 bytes.  If a process is writing to a
24396   * pipe and no one is reading from it, give a broken pipe error.
24397   */
24398
24399    int r = 0;
24400
24401    /* If reading, check for empty pipe. */
24402    if (rw_flag == READING) {
24403        if (position >= rip->i_size) {
24404              /* Process is reading from an empty pipe. */
24405              if (find_filp(rip, W_BIT) != NIL_FILP) {
24406                    /* Writer exists */
24407                    if (oflags & O_NONBLOCK)
24408                          r = EAGAIN;
24409                    else
```

```
24410                              suspend(XPIPE); /* block reader */
24411
24412                          /* If need be, activate sleeping writers. */
24413                          if (susp_count > 0) release(rip, WRITE, susp_count);
24414                  }
24415                  return(r);
24416          }
24417    } else {
24418          /* Process is writing to a pipe. */
24419    /*       if (bytes > PIPE_SIZE) return(EFBIG); */
24420          if (find_filp(rip, R_BIT) == NIL_FILP) {
24421                  /* Tell kernel to generate a SIGPIPE signal. */
24422                  sys_kill((int)(fp - fproc), SIGPIPE);
24423                  return(EPIPE);
24424          }
24425
24426          if (position + bytes > PIPE_SIZE) {
24427                  if ((oflags & O_NONBLOCK) && bytes < PIPE_SIZE)
24428                          return(EAGAIN);
24429                  else if ((oflags & O_NONBLOCK) && bytes > PIPE_SIZE) {
24430                          if ( (*canwrite = (PIPE_SIZE - position)) > 0)  {
24431                                  /* Do a partial write. Need to wakeup reader */
24432                                  release(rip, READ, susp_count);
24433                                  return(1);
24434                          } else {
24435                                  return(EAGAIN);
24436                          }
24437                  }
24438                  if (bytes > PIPE_SIZE) {
24439                          if ((*canwrite = PIPE_SIZE - position) > 0) {
24440                                  /* Do a partial write. Need to wakeup reader
24441                                   * since we'll suspend ourself in read_write()
24442                                   */
24443                                  release(rip, READ, susp_count);
24444                                  return(1);
24445                          }
24446                  }
24447                  suspend(XPIPE); /* stop writer -- pipe full */
24448                  return(0);
24449          }
24450
24451          /* Writing to an empty pipe.  Search for suspended reader. */
24452          if (position == 0) release(rip, READ, susp_count);
24453    }
24454
24455    *canwrite = 0;
24456    return(1);
24457 }


24460 /*===========================================================================*
24461  *                              suspend                                       *
24462  *===========================================================================*/
24463 PUBLIC void suspend(task)
24464 int task;                          /* who is proc waiting for? (PIPE = pipe) */
24465 {
24466 /* Take measures to suspend the processing of the present system call.
24467  * Store the parameters to be used upon resuming in the process table.
24468  * (Actually they are not used when a process is waiting for an I/O device,
24469  * but they are needed for pipes, and it is not worth making the distinction.)
```

```
24470          */
24471
24472          if (task == XPIPE || task == XPOPEN) susp_count++;/* #procs susp'ed on pipe*/
24473          fp->fp_suspended = SUSPENDED;
24474          fp->fp_fd = fd << 8 | fs_call;
24475          fp->fp_task = -task;
24476          if (task == XLOCK) {
24477                  fp->fp_buffer = (char *) name1;  /* third arg to fcntl() */
24478                  fp->fp_nbytes =request;         /* second arg to fcntl() */
24479          } else {
24480                  fp->fp_buffer = buffer;           /* for reads and writes */
24481                  fp->fp_nbytes = nbytes;
24482          }
24483          dont_reply = TRUE;                /* do not send caller a reply message now */
24484  }


24487  /*===========================================================================*
24488   *                              release                                     *
24489   *===========================================================================*/
24490  PUBLIC void release(ip, call_nr, count)
24491  register struct inode *ip;        /* inode of pipe */
24492  int call_nr;                      /* READ, WRITE, OPEN or CREAT */
24493  int count;                        /* max number of processes to release */
24494  {
24495  /* Check to see if any process is hanging on the pipe whose inode is in 'ip'.
24496   * If one is, and it was trying to perform the call indicated by 'call_nr',
24497   * release it.
24498   */
24499
24500    register struct fproc *rp;
24501
24502    /* Search the proc table. */
24503    for (rp = &fproc[0]; rp < &fproc[NR_PROCS]; rp++) {
24504          if (rp->fp_suspended == SUSPENDED &&
24505                          rp->fp_revived == NOT_REVIVING &&
24506                          (rp->fp_fd & BYTE) == call_nr &&
24507                          rp->fp_filp[rp->fp_fd>>8]->filp_ino == ip) {
24508                  revive((int)(rp - fproc), 0);
24509                  susp_count--;    /* keep track of who is suspended */
24510                  if (--count == 0) return;
24511          }
24512    }
24513  }


24516  /*===========================================================================*
24517   *                              revive                                      *
24518   *===========================================================================*/
24519  PUBLIC void revive(proc_nr, bytes)
24520  int proc_nr;                      /* process to revive */
24521  int bytes;                        /* if hanging on task, how many bytes read */
24522  {
24523  /* Revive a previously blocked process. When a process hangs on tty, this
24524   * is the way it is eventually released.
24525   */
24526
24527    register struct fproc *rfp;
24528    register int task;
24529
```

```
24530        if (proc_nr < 0 || proc_nr >= NR_PROCS) panic("revive err", proc_nr);
24531        rfp = &fproc[proc_nr];
24532        if (rfp->fp_suspended == NOT_SUSPENDED || rfp->fp_revived == REVIVING)return;
24533
24534        /* The 'reviving' flag only applies to pipes.  Processes waiting for TTY get
24535         * a message right away.  The revival process is different for TTY and pipes.
24536         * For TTY revival, the work is already done, for pipes it is not: the proc
24537         * must be restarted so it can try again.
24538         */
24539        task = -rfp->fp_task;
24540        if (task == XPIPE || task == XLOCK) {
24541                /* Revive a process suspended on a pipe or lock. */
24542                rfp->fp_revived = REVIVING;
24543                reviving++;                /* process was waiting on pipe or lock */
24544        } else {
24545                rfp->fp_suspended = NOT_SUSPENDED;
24546                if (task == XPOPEN) /* process blocked in open or create */
24547                        reply(proc_nr, rfp->fp_fd>>8);
24548                else {
24549                        /* Revive a process suspended on TTY or other device. */
24550                        rfp->fp_nbytes = bytes; /*pretend it wants only what there is*/
24551                        reply(proc_nr, bytes);  /* unblock the process */
24552                }
24553        }
24554 }


24557 /*===========================================================================*
24558  *                              do_unpause                                   *
24559  *===========================================================================*/
24560 PUBLIC int do_unpause()
24561 {
24562 /* A signal has been sent to a user who is paused on the file system.
24563  * Abort the system call with the EINTR error message.
24564  */
24565
24566   register struct fproc *rfp;
24567   int proc_nr, task, fild;
24568   struct filp *f;
24569   dev_t dev;
24570
24571   if (who > MM_PROC_NR) return(EPERM);
24572   proc_nr = pro;
24573   if (proc_nr < 0 || proc_nr >= NR_PROCS) panic("unpause err 1", proc_nr);
24574   rfp = &fproc[proc_nr];
24575   if (rfp->fp_suspended == NOT_SUSPENDED) return(OK);
24576   task = -rfp->fp_task;
24577
24578   switch(task) {
24579        case XPIPE:                     /* process trying to read or write a pipe */
24580                break;
24581
24582        case XOPEN:                     /* process trying to open a special file */
24583                panic ("fs/do_unpause called with XOPEN\n", NO_NUM);
24584
24585        case XLOCK:                     /* process trying to set a lock with FCNTL */
24586                break;
24587
24588        case XPOPEN:                    /* process trying to open a fifo */
24589                break;
```

```
24590
24591            default:                    /* process trying to do device I/O (e.g. tty)*/
24592                    fild = (rfp->fp_fd >> 8) & BYTE;/* extract file descriptor */
24593                    if (fild < 0 || fild >= OPEN_MAX)panic("unpause err 2",NO_NUM);
24594                    f = rfp->fp_filp[fild];
24595                    dev = (dev_t) f->filp_ino->i_zone[0];   /* device hung on */
24596                    mess.TTY_LINE = (dev >> MINOR) & BYTE;
24597                    mess.PROC_NR = proc_nr;
24598
24599                    /* Tell kernel R or W. Mode is from current call, not open. */
24600                    mess.COUNT = (rfp->fp_fd & BYTE) == READ ? R_BIT : W_BIT;
24601                    mess.m_type = CANCEL;
24602                    fp = rfp;          /* hack - call_ctty uses fp */
24603                    (*dmap[(dev >> MAJOR) & BYTE].dmap_rw)(task, &mess);
24604        }
24605
24606        rfp->fp_suspended = NOT_SUSPENDED;
24607        reply(proc_nr, EINTR);            /* signal interrupted call */
24608        return(OK);
24609    }
```

```
++++++++++++++++++++++++++++++++++++++++++++++++++++++++++++++++++++++++++++++++
                              src/fs/path.c
++++++++++++++++++++++++++++++++++++++++++++++++++++++++++++++++++++++++++++++++
```

```
24700    /* This file contains the procedures that look up path names in the directory
24701     * system and determine the inode number that goes with a given path name.
24702     *
24703     *  The entry points into this file are
24704     *    eat_path:   the 'main' routine of the path-to-inode conversion mechanism
24705     *    last_dir:   find the final directory on a given path
24706     *    advance:    parse one component of a path name
24707     *    search_dir: search a directory for a string and return its inode number
24708     */
24709
24710    #include "fs.h"
24711    #include <string.h>
24712    #include <minix/callnr.h>
24713    #include "buf.h"
24714    #include "file.h"
24715    #include "fproc.h"
24716    #include "inode.h"
24717    #include "super.h"
24718
24719    PUBLIC char dot1[2] = ".";       /* used for search_dir to bypass the access */
24720    PUBLIC char dot2[3] = "..";      /* permissions for . and ..                 */
24721
24722    FORWARD _PROTOTYPE( char *get_name, (char *old_name, char string [NAME_MAX]) );
24723
24724    /*===========================================================================*
24725     *                              eat_path                                      *
24726     *===========================================================================*/
24727    PUBLIC struct inode *eat_path(path)
24728    char *path;                      /* the path name to be parsed */
24729    {
```

```
24730    /* Parse the path 'path' and put its inode in the inode table. If not possible,
24731     * return NIL_INODE as function value and an error code in 'err_code'.
24732     */
24733
24734      register struct inode *ldip, *rip;
24735      char string[NAME_MAX];          /* hold 1 path component name here */
24736
24737      /* First open the path down to the final directory. */
24738      if ( (ldip = last_dir(path, string)) == NIL_INODE)
24739            return(NIL_INODE);          /* we couldn't open final directory */
24740
24741      /* The path consisting only of "/" is a special case, check for it. */
24742      if (string[0] == '\0') return(ldip);
24743
24744      /* Get final component of the path. */
24745      rip = advance(ldip, string);
24746      put_inode(ldip);
24747      return(rip);
24748    }


24751    /*===========================================================================*
24752     *                              last_dir                                      *
24753     *===========================================================================*/
24754    PUBLIC struct inode *last_dir(path, string)
24755    char *path;                     /* the path name to be parsed */
24756    char string[NAME_MAX];          /* the final component is returned here */
24757    {
24758    /* Given a path, 'path', located in the fs address space, parse it as
24759     * far as the last directory, fetch the inode for the last directory into
24760     * the inode table, and return a pointer to the inode.  In
24761     * addition, return the final component of the path in 'string'.
24762     * If the last directory can't be opened, return NIL_INODE and
24763     * the reason for failure in 'err_code'.
24764     */
24765
24766      register struct inode *rip;
24767      register char *new_name;
24768      register struct inode *new_ip;
24769
24770      /* Is the path absolute or relative?  Initialize 'rip' accordingly. */
24771      rip = (*path == '/' ? fp->fp_rootdir : fp->fp_workdir);
24772
24773      /* If dir has been removed or path is empty, return ENOENT. */
24774      if (rip->i_nlinks == 0 || *path == '\0') {
24775            err_code = ENOENT;
24776            return(NIL_INODE);
24777      }
24778
24779      dup_inode(rip);                 /* inode will be returned with put_inode */
24780
24781      /* Scan the path component by component. */
24782      while (TRUE) {
24783            /* Extract one component. */
24784            if ( (new_name = get_name(path, string)) == (char*) 0) {
24785                  put_inode(rip); /* bad path in user space */
24786                  return(NIL_INODE);
24787            }
24788            if (*new_name == '\0')
24789                  if ( (rip->i_mode & I_TYPE) == I_DIRECTORY)
```

```
24790                                    return(rip);     /* normal exit */
24791                           else {
24792                                    /* last file of path prefix is not a directory */
24793                                    put_inode(rip);
24794                                    err_code = ENOTDIR;
24795                                    return(NIL_INODE);
24796                           }
24797
24798                  /* There is more path.  Keep parsing. */
24799                  new_ip = advance(rip, string);
24800                  put_inode(rip);              /* rip either obsolete or irrelevant */
24801                  if (new_ip == NIL_INODE) return(NIL_INODE);
24802
24803                  /* The call to advance() succeeded.  Fetch next component. */
24804                  path = new_name;
24805                  rip = new_ip;
24806          }
24807  }


24810  /*===========================================================================*
24811   *                              get_name                                      *
24812   *===========================================================================*/
24813  PRIVATE char *get_name(old_name, string)
24814  char *old_name;                        /* path name to parse */
24815  char string[NAME_MAX];                 /* component extracted from 'old_name' */
24816  {
24817  /* Given a pointer to a path name in fs space, 'old_name', copy the next
24818   * component to 'string' and pad with zeros.  A pointer to that part of
24819   * the name as yet unparsed is returned.  Roughly speaking,
24820   * 'get_name' = 'old_name' - 'string'.
24821   *
24822   * This routine follows the standard convention that /usr/ast, /usr//ast,
24823   * //usr///ast and /usr/ast/ are all equivalent.
24824   */
24825
24826    register int c;
24827    register char *np, *rnp;
24828
24829    np = string;                       /* 'np' points to current position */
24830    rnp = old_name;                    /* 'rnp' points to unparsed string */
24831    while ( (c = *rnp) == '/') rnp++;     /* skip leading slashes */
24832
24833    /* Copy the unparsed path, 'old_name', to the array, 'string'. */
24834    while ( rnp < &old_name[PATH_MAX]  &&  c != '/'  &&  c != '\0') {
24835          if (np < &string[NAME_MAX]) *np++ = c;
24836          c = *++rnp;                 /* advance to next character */
24837    }
24838
24839    /* To make /usr/ast/ equivalent to /usr/ast, skip trailing slashes. */
24840    while (c == '/' && rnp < &old_name[PATH_MAX]) c = *++rnp;
24841
24842    if (np < &string[NAME_MAX]) *np = '\0';        /* Terminate string */
24843
24844    if (rnp >= &old_name[PATH_MAX]) {
24845          err_code = ENAMETOOLONG;
24846          return((char *) 0);
24847    }
24848    return(rnp);
24849  }
```

```
24852   /*===========================================================================*
24853    *                               advance                                     *
24854    *===========================================================================*/
24855   PUBLIC struct inode *advance(dirp, string)
24856   struct inode *dirp;              /* inode for directory to be searched */
24857   char string[NAME_MAX];           /* component name to look for */
24858   {
24859   /* Given a directory and a component of a path, look up the component in
24860    * the directory, find the inode, open it, and return a pointer to its inode
24861    * slot.  If it can't be done, return NIL_INODE.
24862    */
24863
24864     register struct inode *rip;
24865     struct inode *rip2;
24866     register struct super_block *sp;
24867     int r, inumb;
24868     dev_t mnt_dev;
24869     ino_t numb;
24870
24871     /* If 'string' is empty, yield same inode straight away. */
24872     if (string[0] == '\0') return(get_inode(dirp->i_dev, (int) dirp->i_num));
24873
24874     /* Check for NIL_INODE. */
24875     if (dirp == NIL_INODE) return(NIL_INODE);
24876
24877     /* If 'string' is not present in the directory, signal error. */
24878     if ( (r = search_dir(dirp, string, &numb, LOOK_UP)) != OK) {
24879           err_code = r;
24880           return(NIL_INODE);
24881     }
24882
24883     /* Don't go beyond the current root directory, unless the string is dot2. */
24884     if (dirp == fp->fp_rootdir && strcmp(string, "..") == 0 && string != dot2)
24885                 return(get_inode(dirp->i_dev, (int) dirp->i_num));
24886
24887     /* The component has been found in the directory.  Get inode. */
24888     if ( (rip = get_inode(dirp->i_dev, (int) numb)) == NIL_INODE)
24889           return(NIL_INODE);
24890
24891     if (rip->i_num == ROOT_INODE)
24892           if (dirp->i_num == ROOT_INODE) {
24893                 if (string[1] == '.') {
24894                     for (sp = &super_block[1]; sp < &super_block[NR_SUPERS]; sp++){
24895                             if (sp->s_dev == rip->i_dev) {
24896                                     /* Release the root inode.  Replace by the
24897                                      * inode mounted on.
24898                                      */
24899                                     put_inode(rip);
24900                                     mnt_dev = sp->s_imount->i_dev;
24901                                     inumb = (int) sp->s_imount->i_num;
24902                                     rip2 = get_inode(mnt_dev, inumb);
24903                                     rip = advance(rip2, string);
24904                                     put_inode(rip2);
24905                                     break;
24906                             }
24907                     }
24908                 }
24909           }
```

```
24910        if (rip == NIL_INODE) return(NIL_INODE);
24911
24912        /* See if the inode is mounted on.  If so, switch to root directory of the
24913         * mounted file system.  The super_block provides the linkage between the
24914         * inode mounted on and the root directory of the mounted file system.
24915         */
24916        while (rip != NIL_INODE && rip->i_mount == I_MOUNT) {
24917                /* The inode is indeed mounted on. */
24918                for (sp = &super_block[0]; sp < &super_block[NR_SUPERS]; sp++) {
24919                        if (sp->s_imount == rip) {
24920                                /* Release the inode mounted on.  Replace by the
24921                                 * inode of the root inode of the mounted device.
24922                                 */
24923                                put_inode(rip);
24924                                rip = get_inode(sp->s_dev, ROOT_INODE);
24925                                break;
24926                        }
24927                }
24928        }
24929        return(rip);            /* return pointer to inode's component */
24930 }


24933  /*===========================================================================*
24934   *                              search_dir                                   *
24935   *===========================================================================*/
24936  PUBLIC int search_dir(ldir_ptr, string, numb, flag)
24937  register struct inode *ldir_ptr;         /* ptr to inode for dir to search */
24938  char string[NAME_MAX];              /* component to search for */
24939  ino_t *numb;                        /* pointer to inode number */
24940  int flag;                           /* LOOK_UP, ENTER, DELETE or IS_EMPTY */
24941  {
24942  /* This function searches the directory whose inode is pointed to by 'ldip':
24943   * if (flag == ENTER)  enter 'string' in the directory with inode # '*numb';
24944   * if (flag == DELETE) delete 'string' from the directory;
24945   * if (flag == LOOK_UP) search for 'string' and return inode # in 'numb';
24946   * if (flag == IS_EMPTY) return OK if only . and .. in dir else ENOTEMPTY;
24947   *
24948   *    if 'string' is dot1 or dot2, no access permissions are checked.
24949   */
24950
24951    register struct direct *dp;
24952    register struct buf *bp;
24953    int i, r, e_hit, t, match;
24954    mode_t bits;
24955    off_t pos;
24956    unsigned new_slots, old_slots;
24957    block_t b;
24958    struct super_block *sp;
24959    int extended = 0;
24960
24961    /* If 'ldir_ptr' is not a pointer to a dir inode, error. */
24962    if ( (ldir_ptr->i_mode & I_TYPE) != I_DIRECTORY) return(ENOTDIR);
24963
24964    r = OK;
24965
24966    if (flag != IS_EMPTY) {
24967        bits = (flag == LOOK_UP ? X_BIT : W_BIT | X_BIT);
24968
24969        if (string == dot1 || string == dot2) {
```

```
24970                        if (flag != LOOK_UP) r = read_only(ldir_ptr);
24971                                        /* only a writable device is required. */
24972                }
24973            else r = forbidden(ldir_ptr, bits); /* check access permissions */
24974        }
24975        if (r != OK) return(r);
24976
24977        /* Step through the directory one block at a time. */
24978        old_slots = (unsigned) (ldir_ptr->i_size/DIR_ENTRY_SIZE);
24979        new_slots = 0;
24980        e_hit = FALSE;
24981        match = 0;                       /* set when a string match occurs */
24982
24983        for (pos = 0; pos < ldir_ptr->i_size; pos += BLOCK_SIZE) {
24984                b = read_map(ldir_ptr, pos);    /* get block number */
24985
24986                /* Since directories don't have holes, 'b' cannot be NO_BLOCK. */
24987                bp = get_block(ldir_ptr->i_dev, b, NORMAL);     /* get a dir block */
24988
24989                /* Search a directory block. */
24990                for (dp = &bp->b_dir[0]; dp < &bp->b_dir[NR_DIR_ENTRIES]; dp++) {
24991                        if (++new_slots > old_slots) { /* not found, but room left */
24992                                if (flag == ENTER) e_hit = TRUE;
24993                                break;
24994                        }
24995
24996                        /* Match occurs if string found. */
24997                        if (flag != ENTER && dp->d_ino != 0) {
24998                                if (flag == IS_EMPTY) {
24999                                        /* If this test succeeds, dir is not empty. */
25000                                        if (strcmp(dp->d_name, "." ) != 0 &&
25001                                            strcmp(dp->d_name, "..") != 0) match = 1;
25002                                } else {
25003                                        if (strncmp(dp->d_name, string, NAME_MAX) == 0)
25004                                                match = 1;
25005                                }
25006                        }
25007
25008                        if (match) {
25009                                /* LOOK_UP or DELETE found what it wanted. */
25010                                r = OK;
25011                                if (flag == IS_EMPTY) r = ENOTEMPTY;
25012                                else if (flag == DELETE) {
25013                                        /* Save d_ino for recovery. */
25014                                        t = NAME_MAX - sizeof(ino_t);
25015                                        *((ino_t *) &dp->d_name[t]) = dp->d_ino;
25016                                        dp->d_ino = 0;  /* erase entry */
25017                                        bp->b_dirt = DIRTY;
25018                                        ldir_ptr->i_update |= CTIME | MTIME;
25019                                        ldir_ptr->i_dirt = DIRTY;
25020                                } else {
25021                                        sp = ldir_ptr->i_sp;    /* 'flag' is LOOK_UP */
25022                                        *numb = conv2(sp->s_native, (int) dp->d_ino);
25023                                }
25024                                put_block(bp, DIRECTORY_BLOCK);
25025                                return(r);
25026                        }
25027
25028
25029                        /* Check for free slot for the benefit of ENTER. */
```

```
25030                         if (flag == ENTER && dp->d_ino == 0) {
25031                                 e_hit = TRUE;    /* we found a free slot */
25032                                 break;
25033                         }
25034                 }
25035
25036                 /* The whole block has been searched or ENTER has a free slot. */
25037                 if (e_hit) break;            /* e_hit set if ENTER can be performed now */
25038                 put_block(bp, DIRECTORY_BLOCK); /* otherwise, continue searching dir */
25039         }
25040
25041         /* The whole directory has now been searched. */
25042         if (flag != ENTER) return(flag == IS_EMPTY ? OK : ENOENT);
25043
25044         /* This call is for ENTER.  If no free slot has been found so far, try to
25045          * extend directory.
25046          */
25047         if (e_hit == FALSE) { /* directory is full and no room left in last block */
25048                 new_slots++;               /* increase directory size by 1 entry */
25049                 if (new_slots == 0) return(EFBIG); /* dir size limited by slot count */
25050                 if ( (bp = new_block(ldir_ptr, ldir_ptr->i_size)) == NIL_BUF)
25051                         return(err_code);
25052                 dp = &bp->b_dir[0];
25053                 extended = 1;
25054         }
25055
25056         /* 'bp' now points to a directory block with space. 'dp' points to slot. */
25057         (void) memset(dp->d_name, 0, (size_t) NAME_MAX); /* clear entry */
25058         for (i = 0; string[i] && i < NAME_MAX; i++) dp->d_name[i] = string[i];
25059         sp = ldir_ptr->i_sp;
25060         dp->d_ino = conv2(sp->s_native, (int) *numb);
25061         bp->b_dirt = DIRTY;
25062         put_block(bp, DIRECTORY_BLOCK);
25063         ldir_ptr->i_update |= CTIME | MTIME;   /* mark mtime for update later */
25064         ldir_ptr->i_dirt = DIRTY;
25065         if (new_slots > old_slots) {
25066                 ldir_ptr->i_size = (off_t) new_slots * DIR_ENTRY_SIZE;
25067                 /* Send the change to disk if the directory is extended. */
25068                 if (extended) rw_inode(ldir_ptr, WRITING);
25069         }
25070         return(OK);
25071 }
```

```
++++++++++++++++++++++++++++++++++++++++++++++++++++++++++++++++++++++++++++++++
                                src/fs/mount.c
++++++++++++++++++++++++++++++++++++++++++++++++++++++++++++++++++++++++++++++++

25100    /* This file performs the MOUNT and UMOUNT system calls.
25101     *
25102     * The entry points into this file are
25103     *   do_mount:  perform the MOUNT system call
25104     *   do_umount: perform the UMOUNT system call
25105     */
25106
25107    #include "fs.h"
25108    #include <fcntl.h>
25109    #include <minix/com.h>
```

```
25110    #include <sys/stat.h>
25111    #include "buf.h"
25112    #include "dev.h"
25113    #include "file.h"
25114    #include "fproc.h"
25115    #include "inode.h"
25116    #include "param.h"
25117    #include "super.h"
25118
25119    PRIVATE message dev_mess;
25120
25121    FORWARD _PROTOTYPE( dev_t name_to_dev, (char *path)                    );
25122
25123    /*===========================================================================*
25124     *                              do_mount                                     *
25125     *===========================================================================*/
25126    PUBLIC int do_mount()
25127    {
25128    /* Perform the mount(name, mfile, rd_only) system call. */
25129
25130      register struct inode *rip, *root_ip;
25131      struct super_block *xp, *sp;
25132      dev_t dev;
25133      mode_t bits;
25134      int rdir, mdir;                    /* TRUE iff {root|mount} file is dir */
25135      int r, found, major, task;
25136
25137        /* Only the super-user may do MOUNT. */
25138        if (!super_user) return(EPERM);
25139
25140        /* If 'name' is not for a block special file, return error. */
25141        if (fetch_name(name1, name1_length, M1) != OK) return(err_code);
25142        if ( (dev = name_to_dev(user_path)) == NO_DEV) return(err_code);
25143
25144        /* Scan super block table to see if dev already mounted & find a free slot.*/
25145        sp = NIL_SUPER;
25146        found = FALSE;
25147        for (xp = &super_block[0]; xp < &super_block[NR_SUPERS]; xp++) {
25148              if (xp->s_dev == dev) found = TRUE;     /* is it mounted already? */
25149              if (xp->s_dev == NO_DEV) sp = xp;       /* record free slot */
25150        }
25151        if (found) return(EBUSY);        /* already mounted */
25152        if (sp == NIL_SUPER) return(ENFILE);  /* no super block available */
25153
25154        dev_mess.m_type = DEV_OPEN;             /* distinguish from close */
25155        dev_mess.DEVICE = dev;                  /* Touch the device. */
25156        if (rd_only) dev_mess.COUNT = R_BIT;
25157        else  dev_mess.COUNT = R_BIT|W_BIT;
25158
25159        major = (dev >> MAJOR) & BYTE;
25160        if (major <= 0 || major >= max_major) return(ENODEV);
25161        task = dmap[major].dmap_task;           /* device task nr */
25162        (*dmap[major].dmap_open)(task, &dev_mess);
25163        if (dev_mess.REP_STATUS != OK) return(EINVAL);
25164
25165        /* Fill in the super block. */
25166        sp->s_dev = dev;                 /* read_super() needs to know which dev */
25167        r = read_super(sp);
25168
25169        /* Is it recognized as a Minix filesystem? */
```

```
25170          if (r != OK) {
25171                  dev_mess.m_type = DEV_CLOSE;
25172                  dev_mess.DEVICE = dev;
25173                  (*dmap[major].dmap_close)(task, &dev_mess);
25174                  return(r);
25175          }
25176
25177          /* Now get the inode of the file to be mounted on. */
25178          if (fetch_name(name2, name2_length, M1) != OK) {
25179                  sp->s_dev = NO_DEV;
25180                  dev_mess.m_type = DEV_CLOSE;
25181                  dev_mess.DEVICE = dev;
25182                  (*dmap[major].dmap_close)(task, &dev_mess);
25183                  return(err_code);
25184          }
25185          if ( (rip = eat_path(user_path)) == NIL_INODE) {
25186                  sp->s_dev = NO_DEV;
25187                  dev_mess.m_type = DEV_CLOSE;
25188                  dev_mess.DEVICE = dev;
25189                  (*dmap[major].dmap_close)(task, &dev_mess);
25190                  return(err_code);
25191          }
25192
25193          /* It may not be busy. */
25194          r = OK;
25195          if (rip->i_count > 1) r = EBUSY;
25196
25197          /* It may not be special. */
25198          bits = rip->i_mode & I_TYPE;
25199          if (bits == I_BLOCK_SPECIAL || bits == I_CHAR_SPECIAL) r = ENOTDIR;
25200
25201          /* Get the root inode of the mounted file system. */
25202          root_ip = NIL_INODE;            /* if 'r' not OK, make sure this is defined */
25203          if (r == OK) {
25204                  if ( (root_ip = get_inode(dev, ROOT_INODE)) == NIL_INODE) r = err_code;
25205          }
25206          if (root_ip != NIL_INODE && root_ip->i_mode == 0) r = EINVAL;
25207
25208          /* File types of 'rip' and 'root_ip' may not conflict. */
25209          if (r == OK) {
25210                  mdir = ((rip->i_mode & I_TYPE) == I_DIRECTORY);  /* TRUE iff dir */
25211                  rdir = ((root_ip->i_mode & I_TYPE) == I_DIRECTORY);
25212                  if (!mdir && rdir) r = EISDIR;
25213          }
25214
25215          /* If error, return the super block and both inodes; release the maps. */
25216          if (r != OK) {
25217                  put_inode(rip);
25218                  put_inode(root_ip);
25219                  (void) do_sync();
25220                  invalidate(dev);
25221
25222                  sp->s_dev = NO_DEV;
25223                  dev_mess.m_type = DEV_CLOSE;
25224                  dev_mess.DEVICE = dev;
25225                  (*dmap[major].dmap_close)(task, &dev_mess);
25226                  return(r);
25227          }
25228
25229          /* Nothing else can go wrong.  Perform the mount. */
```

```
25230          rip->i_mount = I_MOUNT;          /* this bit says the inode is mounted on */
25231          sp->s_imount = rip;
25232          sp->s_isup = root_ip;
25233          sp->s_rd_only = rd_only;
25234          return(OK);
25235     }


25238     /*===========================================================================*
25239      *                              do_umount                                    *
25240      *===========================================================================*/
25241     PUBLIC int do_umount()
25242     {
25243     /* Perform the umount(name) system call. */
25244
25245          register struct inode *rip;
25246          struct super_block *sp, *sp1;
25247          dev_t dev;
25248          int count;
25249          int major, task;
25250
25251          /* Only the super-user may do UMOUNT. */
25252          if (!super_user) return(EPERM);
25253
25254          /* If 'name' is not for a block special file, return error. */
25255          if (fetch_name(name, name_length, M3) != OK) return(err_code);
25256          if ( (dev = name_to_dev(user_path)) == NO_DEV) return(err_code);
25257
25258          /* See if the mounted device is busy.  Only 1 inode using it should be
25259           * open -- the root inode -- and that inode only 1 time.
25260           */
25261          count = 0;
25262          for (rip = &inode[0]; rip< &inode[NR_INODES]; rip++)
25263               if (rip->i_count > 0 && rip->i_dev == dev) count += rip->i_count;
25264          if (count > 1) return(EBUSY); /* can't umount a busy file system */
25265
25266          /* Find the super block. */
25267          sp = NIL_SUPER;
25268          for (sp1 = &super_block[0]; sp1 < &super_block[NR_SUPERS]; sp1++) {
25269               if (sp1->s_dev == dev) {
25270                    sp = sp1;
25271                    break;
25272               }
25273          }
25274
25275          /* Sync the disk, and invalidate cache. */
25276          (void) do_sync();               /* force any cached blocks out of memory */
25277          invalidate(dev);                /* invalidate cache entries for this dev */
25278          if (sp == NIL_SUPER) return(EINVAL);
25279
25280          major = (dev >> MAJOR) & BYTE;        /* major device nr */
25281          task = dmap[major].dmap_task; /* device task nr */
25282          dev_mess.m_type = DEV_CLOSE;         /* distinguish from open */
25283          dev_mess.DEVICE = dev;
25284          (*dmap[major].dmap_close)(task, &dev_mess);
25285
25286          /* Finish off the unmount. */
25287          sp->s_imount->i_mount = NO_MOUNT;    /* inode returns to normal */
25288          put_inode(sp->s_imount);        /* release the inode mounted on */
25289          put_inode(sp->s_isup);          /* release the root inode of the mounted fs */
```

```
25290          sp->s_imount = NIL_INODE;
25291          sp->s_dev = NO_DEV;
25292          return(OK);
25293      }


25296      /*===========================================================================*
25297       *                          name_to_dev                                      *
25298       *===========================================================================*/
25299      PRIVATE dev_t name_to_dev(path)
25300      char *path;                      /* pointer to path name */
25301      {
25302      /* Convert the block special file 'path' to a device number.  If 'path'
25303       * is not a block special file, return error code in 'err_code'.
25304       */
25305
25306        register struct inode *rip;
25307        register dev_t dev;
25308
25309        /* If 'path' can't be opened, give up immediately. */
25310        if ( (rip = eat_path(path)) == NIL_INODE) return(NO_DEV);
25311
25312        /* If 'path' is not a block special file, return error. */
25313        if ( (rip->i_mode & I_TYPE) != I_BLOCK_SPECIAL) {
25314              err_code = ENOTBLK;
25315              put_inode(rip);
25316              return(NO_DEV);
25317        }
25318
25319        /* Extract the device number. */
25320        dev = (dev_t) rip->i_zone[0];
25321        put_inode(rip);
25322        return(dev);
25323      }


++++++++++++++++++++++++++++++++++++++++++++++++++++++++++++++++++++++++++++++++++++
                                  src/fs/link.c
++++++++++++++++++++++++++++++++++++++++++++++++++++++++++++++++++++++++++++++++++++

25400      /* This file handles the LINK and UNLINK system calls.  It also deals with
25401       * deallocating the storage used by a file when the last UNLINK is done to a
25402       * file and the blocks must be returned to the free block pool.
25403       *
25404       * The entry points into this file are
25405       *   do_link:    perform the LINK system call
25406       *   do_unlink:  perform the UNLINK and RMDIR system calls
25407       *   do_rename:  perform the RENAME system call
25408       *   truncate:   release all the blocks associated with an inode
25409       */
25410
25411      #include "fs.h"
25412      #include <sys/stat.h>
25413      #include <string.h>
25414      #include <minix/callnr.h>
25415      #include "buf.h"
25416      #include "file.h"
25417      #include "fproc.h"
25418      #include "inode.h"
25419      #include "param.h"
```

```
25420     #include "super.h"
25421
25422     #define SAME 1000
25423
25424     FORWARD _PROTOTYPE( int remove_dir, (struct inode *rldirp, struct inode *rip,
25425                        char dir_name[NAME_MAX])                    );
25426
25427     FORWARD _PROTOTYPE( int unlink_file, (struct inode *dirp, struct inode *rip,
25428                        char file_name[NAME_MAX])                   );
25429
25430
25431     /*===========================================================================*
25432      *                              do_link                                      *
25433      *===========================================================================*/
25434     PUBLIC int do_link()
25435     {
25436     /* Perform the link(name1, name2) system call. */
25437
25438       register struct inode *ip, *rip;
25439       register int r;
25440       char string[NAME_MAX];
25441       struct inode *new_ip;
25442
25443       /* See if 'name' (file to be linked) exists. */
25444       if (fetch_name(name1, name1_length, M1) != OK) return(err_code);
25445       if ( (rip = eat_path(user_path)) == NIL_INODE) return(err_code);
25446
25447       /* Check to see if the file has maximum number of links already. */
25448       r = OK;
25449       if ( (rip->i_nlinks & BYTE) >= LINK_MAX) r = EMLINK;
25450
25451       /* Only super_user may link to directories. */
25452       if (r == OK)
25453             if ( (rip->i_mode & I_TYPE) == I_DIRECTORY && !super_user) r = EPERM;
25454
25455       /* If error with 'name', return the inode. */
25456       if (r != OK) {
25457             put_inode(rip);
25458             return(r);
25459       }
25460
25461       /* Does the final directory of 'name2' exist? */
25462       if (fetch_name(name2, name2_length, M1) != OK) {
25463             put_inode(rip);
25464             return(err_code);
25465       }
25466       if ( (ip = last_dir(user_path, string)) == NIL_INODE) r = err_code;
25467
25468       /* If 'name2' exists in full (even if no space) set 'r' to error. */
25469       if (r == OK) {
25470             if ( (new_ip = advance(ip, string)) == NIL_INODE) {
25471                     r = err_code;
25472                     if (r == ENOENT) r = OK;
25473             } else {
25474                     put_inode(new_ip);
25475                     r = EEXIST;
25476             }
25477       }
25478
25479       /* Check for links across devices. */
```

```
25480        if (r == OK)
25481                if (rip->i_dev != ip->i_dev) r = EXDEV;
25482
25483        /* Try to link. */
25484        if (r == OK)
25485                r = search_dir(ip, string, &rip->i_num, ENTER);
25486
25487        /* If success, register the linking. */
25488        if (r == OK) {
25489                rip->i_nlinks++;
25490                rip->i_update |= CTIME;
25491                rip->i_dirt = DIRTY;
25492        }
25493
25494        /* Done.  Release both inodes. */
25495        put_inode(rip);
25496        put_inode(ip);
25497        return(r);
25498    }


25501    /*===========================================================================*
25502     *                              do_unlink                                     *
25503     *===========================================================================*/
25504    PUBLIC int do_unlink()
25505    {
25506    /* Perform the unlink(name) or rmdir(name) system call. The code for these two
25507     * is almost the same.  They differ only in some condition testing.  Unlink()
25508     * may be used by the superuser to do dangerous things; rmdir() may not.
25509     */
25510
25511      register struct inode *rip;
25512      struct inode *rldirp;
25513      int r;
25514      char string[NAME_MAX];
25515
25516        /* Get the last directory in the path. */
25517        if (fetch_name(name, name_length, M3) != OK) return(err_code);
25518        if ( (rldirp = last_dir(user_path, string)) == NIL_INODE)
25519                return(err_code);
25520
25521        /* The last directory exists.  Does the file also exist? */
25522        r = OK;
25523        if ( (rip = advance(rldirp, string)) == NIL_INODE) r = err_code;
25524
25525        /* If error, return inode. */
25526        if (r != OK) {
25527                put_inode(rldirp);
25528                return(r);
25529        }
25530
25531        /* Do not remove a mount point. */
25532        if (rip->i_num == ROOT_INODE) {
25533                put_inode(rldirp);
25534                put_inode(rip);
25535                return(EBUSY);
25536        }
25537
25538        /* Now test if the call is allowed, separately for unlink() and rmdir(). */
25539        if (fs_call == UNLINK) {
```

```
25540                /* Only the su may unlink directories, but the su can unlink any dir.*/
25541                if ( (rip->i_mode & I_TYPE) == I_DIRECTORY && !super_user) r = EPERM;
25542
25543                /* Don't unlink a file if it is the root of a mounted file system. */
25544                if (rip->i_num == ROOT_INODE) r = EBUSY;
25545
25546                /* Actually try to unlink the file; fails if parent is mode 0 etc. */
25547                if (r == OK) r = unlink_file(rldirp, rip, string);
25548
25549        } else {
25550                r = remove_dir(rldirp, rip, string); /* call is RMDIR */
25551        }
25552
25553        /* If unlink was possible, it has been done, otherwise it has not. */
25554        put_inode(rip);
25555        put_inode(rldirp);
25556        return(r);
25557 }


25560      /*===========================================================================*
25561       *                              do_rename                                    *
25562       *===========================================================================*/
25563      PUBLIC int do_rename()
25564      {
25565      /* Perform the rename(name1, name2) system call. */
25566
25567        struct inode *old_dirp, *old_ip;        /* ptrs to old dir, file inodes */
25568        struct inode *new_dirp, *new_ip;        /* ptrs to new dir, file inodes */
25569        struct inode *new_superdirp, *next_new_superdirp;
25570        int r = OK;                             /* error flag; initially no error */
25571        int odir, ndir;                         /* TRUE iff {old|new} file is dir */
25572        int same_pdir;                          /* TRUE iff parent dirs are the same */
25573        char old_name[NAME_MAX], new_name[NAME_MAX];
25574        ino_t numb;
25575        int r1;
25576
25577        /* See if 'name1' (existing file) exists.  Get dir and file inodes. */
25578        if (fetch_name(name1, name1_length, M1) != OK) return(err_code);
25579        if ( (old_dirp = last_dir(user_path, old_name))==NIL_INODE) return(err_code);
25580
25581        if ( (old_ip = advance(old_dirp, old_name)) == NIL_INODE) r = err_code;
25582
25583        /* See if 'name2' (new name) exists.  Get dir and file inodes. */
25584        if (fetch_name(name2, name2_length, M1) != OK) r = err_code;
25585        if ( (new_dirp = last_dir(user_path, new_name)) == NIL_INODE) r = err_code;
25586        new_ip = advance(new_dirp, new_name); /* not required to exist */
25587
25588        if (old_ip != NIL_INODE)
25589                odir = ((old_ip->i_mode & I_TYPE) == I_DIRECTORY);  /* TRUE iff dir */
25590
25591        /* If it is ok, check for a variety of possible errors. */
25592        if (r == OK) {
25593                same_pdir = (old_dirp == new_dirp);
25594
25595                /* The old inode must not be a superdirectory of the new last dir. */
25596                if (odir && !same_pdir) {
25597                        dup_inode(new_superdirp = new_dirp);
25598                        while (TRUE) {          /* may hang in a file system loop */
25599                                if (new_superdirp == old_ip) {
```

```
25600                                        r = EINVAL;
25601                                        break;
25602                                }
25603                                next_new_superdirp = advance(new_superdirp, dot2);
25604                                put_inode(new_superdirp);
25605                                if (next_new_superdirp == new_superdirp)
25606                                        break;  /* back at system root directory */
25607                                new_superdirp = next_new_superdirp;
25608                                if (new_superdirp == NIL_INODE) {
25609                                        /* Missing ".." entry.  Assume the worst. */
25610                                        r = EINVAL;
25611                                        break;
25612                                }
25613                        }
25614                        put_inode(new_superdirp);
25615                }
25616
25617                /* The old or new name must not be . or .. */
25618                if (strcmp(old_name, ".")==0 || strcmp(old_name, "..")==0 ||
25619                    strcmp(new_name, ".")==0 || strcmp(new_name, "..")==0) r = EINVAL;
25620
25621                /* Both parent directories must be on the same device. */
25622                if (old_dirp->i_dev != new_dirp->i_dev) r = EXDEV;
25623
25624                /* Parent dirs must be writable, searchable and on a writable device */
25625                if ((r1 = forbidden(old_dirp, W_BIT | X_BIT)) != OK ||
25626                    (r1 = forbidden(new_dirp, W_BIT | X_BIT)) != OK) r = r1;
25627
25628                /* Some tests apply only if the new path exists. */
25629                if (new_ip == NIL_INODE) {
25630                        /* don't rename a file with a file system mounted on it. */
25631                        if (old_ip->i_dev != old_dirp->i_dev) r = EXDEV;
25632                        if (odir && (new_dirp->i_nlinks & BYTE) >= LINK_MAX &&
25633                            !same_pdir && r == OK) r = EMLINK;
25634                } else {
25635                        if (old_ip == new_ip) r = SAME; /* old=new */
25636
25637                        /* has the old file or new file a file system mounted on it? */
25638                        if (old_ip->i_dev != new_ip->i_dev) r = EXDEV;
25639
25640                        ndir = ((new_ip->i_mode & I_TYPE) == I_DIRECTORY); /* dir ? */
25641                        if (odir == TRUE && ndir == FALSE) r = ENOTDIR;
25642                        if (odir == FALSE && ndir == TRUE) r = EISDIR;
25643                }
25644        }
25645
25646        /* If a process has another root directory than the system root, we might
25647         * "accidently" be moving it's working directory to a place where it's
25648         * root directory isn't a super directory of it anymore. This can make
25649         * the function chroot useless. If chroot will be used often we should
25650         * probably check for it here.
25651         */
25652
25653        /* The rename will probably work. Only two things can go wrong now:
25654         * 1. being unable to remove the new file. (when new file already exists)
25655         * 2. being unable to make the new directory entry. (new file doesn't exists)
25656         *    [directory has to grow by one block and cannot because the disk
25657         *     is completely full].
25658         */
25659        if (r == OK) {
```

```
25660                  if (new_ip != NIL_INODE) {
25661                          /* There is already an entry for 'new'. Try to remove it. */
25662                      if (odir)
25663                              r = remove_dir(new_dirp, new_ip, new_name);
25664                      else
25665                              r = unlink_file(new_dirp, new_ip, new_name);
25666                  }
25667                  /* if r is OK, the rename will succeed, while there is now an
25668                   * unused entry in the new parent directory.
25669                   */
25670          }
25671
25672      if (r == OK) {
25673              /* If the new name will be in the same parent directory as the old one,
25674               * first remove the old name to free an entry for the new name,
25675               * otherwise first try to create the new name entry to make sure
25676               * the rename will succeed.
25677               */
25678              numb = old_ip->i_num;             /* inode number of old file */
25679
25680              if (same_pdir) {
25681                      r = search_dir(old_dirp, old_name, (ino_t *) 0, DELETE);
25682                                                  /* shouldn't go wrong. */
25683                      if (r==OK) (void) search_dir(old_dirp, new_name, &numb, ENTER);
25684              } else {
25685                      r = search_dir(new_dirp, new_name, &numb, ENTER);
25686                      if (r == OK)
25687                          (void) search_dir(old_dirp, old_name, (ino_t *) 0, DELETE);
25688              }
25689      }
25690      /* If r is OK, the ctime and mtime of old_dirp and new_dirp have been marked
25691       * for update in search_dir.
25692       */
25693
25694      if (r == OK && odir && !same_pdir) {
25695              /* Update the .. entry in the directory (still points to old_dirp). */
25696              numb = new_dirp->i_num;
25697              (void) unlink_file(old_ip, NIL_INODE, dot2);
25698              if (search_dir(old_ip, dot2, &numb, ENTER) == OK) {
25699                      /* New link created. */
25700                      new_dirp->i_nlinks++;
25701                      new_dirp->i_dirt = DIRTY;
25702              }
25703      }
25704
25705      /* Release the inodes. */
25706      put_inode(old_dirp);
25707      put_inode(old_ip);
25708      put_inode(new_dirp);
25709      put_inode(new_ip);
25710      return(r == SAME ? OK : r);
25711  }


25714  /*===========================================================================*
25715   *                              truncate                                     *
25716   *===========================================================================*/
25717  PUBLIC void truncate(rip)
25718  register struct inode *rip;        /* pointer to inode to be truncated */
25719  {
```

```
25720        /* Remove all the zones from the inode 'rip' and mark it dirty. */
25721
25722        register block_t b;
25723        zone_t z, zone_size, z1;
25724        off_t position;
25725        int i, scale, file_type, waspipe, single, nr_indirects;
25726        struct buf *bp;
25727        dev_t dev;
25728
25729        file_type = rip->i_mode & I_TYPE;      /* check to see if file is special */
25730        if (file_type == I_CHAR_SPECIAL || file_type == I_BLOCK_SPECIAL) return;
25731        dev = rip->i_dev;                 /* device on which inode resides */
25732        scale = rip->i_sp->s_log_zone_size;
25733        zone_size = (zone_t) BLOCK_SIZE << scale;
25734        nr_indirects = rip->i_nindirs;
25735
25736        /* Pipes can shrink, so adjust size to make sure all zones are removed. */
25737        waspipe = rip->i_pipe == I_PIPE;       /* TRUE is this was a pipe */
25738        if (waspipe) rip->i_size = PIPE_SIZE;
25739
25740        /* Step through the file a zone at a time, finding and freeing the zones. */
25741        for (position = 0; position < rip->i_size; position += zone_size) {
25742                if ( (b = read_map(rip, position)) != NO_BLOCK) {
25743                        z = (zone_t) b >> scale;
25744                        free_zone(dev, z);
25745                }
25746        }
25747
25748        /* All the data zones have been freed.  Now free the indirect zones. */
25749        rip->i_dirt = DIRTY;
25750        if (waspipe) {
25751                wipe_inode(rip);          /* clear out inode for pipes */
25752                return;                   /* indirect slots contain file positions */
25753        }
25754        single = rip->i_ndzones;
25755        free_zone(dev, rip->i_zone[single]);  /* single indirect zone */
25756        if ( (z = rip->i_zone[single+1]) != NO_ZONE) {
25757                /* Free all the single indirect zones pointed to by the double. */
25758                b = (block_t) z << scale;
25759                bp = get_block(dev, b, NORMAL); /* get double indirect zone */
25760                for (i = 0; i < nr_indirects; i++) {
25761                        z1 = rd_indir(bp, i);
25762                        free_zone(dev, z1);
25763                }
25764
25765                /* Now free the double indirect zone itself. */
25766                put_block(bp, INDIRECT_BLOCK);
25767                free_zone(dev, z);
25768        }
25769
25770        /* Leave zone numbers for de(1) to recover file after an unlink(2).  */
25771 }


25774 /*===========================================================================*
25775  *                              remove_dir                                    *
25776  *===========================================================================*/
25777 PRIVATE int remove_dir(rldirp, rip, dir_name)
25778 struct inode *rldirp;                  /* parent directory */
25779 struct inode *rip;                     /* directory to be removed */
```

```
25780        char dir_name[NAME_MAX];                      /* name of directory to be removed */
25781        {
25782          /* A directory file has to be removed. Five conditions have to met:
25783           *      - The file must be a directory
25784           *      - The directory must be empty (except for . and ..)
25785           *      - The final component of the path must not be . or ..
25786           *      - The directory must not be the root of a mounted file system
25787           *      - The directory must not be anybody's root/working directory
25788           */
25789
25790          int r;
25791          register struct fproc *rfp;
25792
25793          /* search_dir checks that rip is a directory too. */
25794          if ((r = search_dir(rip, "", (ino_t *) 0, IS_EMPTY)) != OK) return r;
25795
25796          if (strcmp(dir_name, ".") == 0 || strcmp(dir_name, "..") == 0)return(EINVAL);
25797          if (rip->i_num == ROOT_INODE) return(EBUSY); /* can't remove 'root' */
25798
25799          for (rfp = &fproc[INIT_PROC_NR + 1]; rfp < &fproc[NR_PROCS]; rfp++)
25800                if (rfp->fp_workdir == rip || rfp->fp_rootdir == rip) return(EBUSY);
25801                                            /* can't remove anybody's working dir */
25802
25803          /* Actually try to unlink the file; fails if parent is mode 0 etc. */
25804          if ((r = unlink_file(rldirp, rip, dir_name)) != OK) return r;
25805
25806          /* Unlink . and .. from the dir. The super user can link and unlink any dir,
25807           * so don't make too many assumptions about them.
25808           */
25809          (void) unlink_file(rip, NIL_INODE, dot1);
25810          (void) unlink_file(rip, NIL_INODE, dot2);
25811          return(OK);
25812        }


25815        /*===========================================================================*
25816         *                              unlink_file                                  *
25817         *===========================================================================*/
25818        PRIVATE int unlink_file(dirp, rip, file_name)
25819        struct inode *dirp;               /* parent directory of file */
25820        struct inode *rip;                /* inode of file, may be NIL_INODE too. */
25821        char file_name[NAME_MAX];         /* name of file to be removed */
25822        {
25823        /* Unlink 'file_name'; rip must be the inode of 'file_name' or NIL_INODE. */
25824
25825          ino_t numb;                     /* inode number */
25826          int   r;
25827
25828          /* If rip is not NIL_INODE, it is used to get faster access to the inode. */
25829          if (rip == NIL_INODE) {
25830                /* Search for file in directory and try to get its inode. */
25831                err_code = search_dir(dirp, file_name, &numb, LOOK_UP);
25832                if (err_code == OK) rip = get_inode(dirp->i_dev, (int) numb);
25833                if (err_code != OK || rip == NIL_INODE) return(err_code);
25834          } else {
25835                dup_inode(rip);           /* inode will be returned with put_inode */
25836          }
25837
25838          r = search_dir(dirp, file_name, (ino_t *) 0, DELETE);
25839
```

```
25840        if (r == OK) {
25841                rip->i_nlinks--;          /* entry deleted from parent's dir */
25842                rip->i_update |= CTIME;
25843                rip->i_dirt = DIRTY;
25844        }
25845
25846        put_inode(rip);
25847        return(r);
25848    }
```

```
++++++++++++++++++++++++++++++++++++++++++++++++++++++++++++++++++++++++++++++++
                                src/fs/stadir.c
++++++++++++++++++++++++++++++++++++++++++++++++++++++++++++++++++++++++++++++++
```

```
25900    /* This file contains the code for performing four system calls relating to
25901     * status and directories.
25902     *
25903     * The entry points into this file are
25904     *   do_chdir:   perform the CHDIR system call
25905     *   do_chroot:  perform the CHROOT system call
25906     *   do_stat:    perform the STAT system call
25907     *   do_fstat:   perform the FSTAT system call
25908     */
25909
25910    #include "fs.h"
25911    #include <sys/stat.h>
25912    #include "file.h"
25913    #include "fproc.h"
25914    #include "inode.h"
25915    #include "param.h"
25916
25917    FORWARD _PROTOTYPE( int change, (struct inode **iip, char *name_ptr, int len));
25918    FORWARD _PROTOTYPE( int stat_inode, (struct inode *rip, struct filp *fil_ptr,
25919                            char *user_addr)                         );
25920
25921    /*===========================================================================*
25922     *                              do_chdir                                      *
25923     *===========================================================================*/
25924    PUBLIC int do_chdir()
25925    {
25926    /* Change directory.  This function is  also called by MM to simulate a chdir
25927     * in order to do EXEC, etc.  It also changes the root directory, the uids and
25928     * gids, and the umask.
25929     */
25930
25931      int r;
25932      register struct fproc *rfp;
25933
25934      if (who == MM_PROC_NR) {
25935            rfp = &fproc[slot1];
25936            put_inode(fp->fp_rootdir);
25937            dup_inode(fp->fp_rootdir = rfp->fp_rootdir);
25938            put_inode(fp->fp_workdir);
25939            dup_inode(fp->fp_workdir = rfp->fp_workdir);
25940
25941            /* MM uses access() to check permissions.  To make this work, pretend
25942             * that the user's real ids are the same as the user's effective ids.
25943             * FS calls other than access() do not use the real ids, so are not
25944             * affected.
```

```
25945            */
25946            fp->fp_realuid =
25947            fp->fp_effuid = rfp->fp_effuid;
25948            fp->fp_realgid =
25949            fp->fp_effgid = rfp->fp_effgid;
25950            fp->fp_umask = rfp->fp_umask;
25951            return(OK);
25952      }
25953
25954      /* Perform the chdir(name) system call. */
25955      r = change(&fp->fp_workdir, name, name_length);
25956      return(r);
25957   }


25960   /*===========================================================================*
25961    *                              do_chroot                                    *
25962    *===========================================================================*/
25963   PUBLIC int do_chroot()
25964   {
25965   /* Perform the chroot(name) system call. */
25966
25967      register int r;
25968
25969      if (!super_user) return(EPERM);        /* only su may chroot() */
25970      r = change(&fp->fp_rootdir, name, name_length);
25971      return(r);
25972   }


25975   /*===========================================================================*
25976    *                              change                                       *
25977    *===========================================================================*/
25978   PRIVATE int change(iip, name_ptr, len)
25979   struct inode **iip;              /* pointer to the inode pointer for the dir */
25980   char *name_ptr;                 /* pointer to the directory name to change to */
25981   int len;                        /* length of the directory name string */
25982   {
25983   /* Do the actual work for chdir() and chroot(). */
25984
25985      struct inode *rip;
25986      register int r;
25987
25988      /* Try to open the new directory. */
25989      if (fetch_name(name_ptr, len, M3) != OK) return(err_code);
25990      if ( (rip = eat_path(user_path)) == NIL_INODE) return(err_code);
25991
25992      /* It must be a directory and also be searchable. */
25993      if ( (rip->i_mode & I_TYPE) != I_DIRECTORY)
25994            r = ENOTDIR;
25995      else
25996            r = forbidden(rip, X_BIT);       /* check if dir is searchable */
25997
25998      /* If error, return inode. */
25999      if (r != OK) {
26000            put_inode(rip);
26001            return(r);
26002      }
26003
26004      /* Everything is OK.  Make the change. */
```

```
26005      put_inode(*iip);                    /* release the old directory */
26006      *iip = rip;                         /* acquire the new one */
26007      return(OK);
26008    }


26011    /*===========================================================================*
26012     *                              do_stat                                       *
26013     *===========================================================================*/
26014    PUBLIC int do_stat()
26015    {
26016    /* Perform the stat(name, buf) system call. */
26017
26018      register struct inode *rip;
26019      register int r;
26020
26021      /* Both stat() and fstat() use the same routine to do the real work.  That
26022       * routine expects an inode, so acquire it temporarily.
26023       */
26024      if (fetch_name(name1, name1_length, M1) != OK) return(err_code);
26025      if ( (rip = eat_path(user_path)) == NIL_INODE) return(err_code);
26026      r = stat_inode(rip, NIL_FILP, name2); /* actually do the work.*/
26027      put_inode(rip);                     /* release the inode */
26028      return(r);
26029    }


26032    /*===========================================================================*
26033     *                              do_fstat                                      *
26034     *===========================================================================*/
26035    PUBLIC int do_fstat()
26036    {
26037    /* Perform the fstat(fd, buf) system call. */
26038
26039      register struct filp *rfilp;
26040
26041      /* Is the file descriptor valid? */
26042      if ( (rfilp = get_filp(fd)) == NIL_FILP) return(err_code);
26043
26044      return(stat_inode(rfilp->filp_ino, rfilp, buffer));
26045    }


26048    /*===========================================================================*
26049     *                              stat_inode                                    *
26050     *===========================================================================*/
26051    PRIVATE int stat_inode(rip, fil_ptr, user_addr)
26052    register struct inode *rip;      /* pointer to inode to stat */
26053    struct filp *fil_ptr;            /* filp pointer, supplied by 'fstat' */
26054    char *user_addr;                 /* user space address where stat buf goes */
26055    {
26056    /* Common code for stat and fstat system calls. */
26057
26058      struct stat statbuf;
26059      mode_t mo;
26060      int r, s;
26061
26062      /* Update the atime, ctime, and mtime fields in the inode, if need be. */
26063      if (rip->i_update) update_times(rip);
26064
```

```
26065        /* Fill in the statbuf struct. */
26066        mo = rip->i_mode & I_TYPE;
26067        s = (mo == I_CHAR_SPECIAL || mo == I_BLOCK_SPECIAL);  /* true iff special */
26068        statbuf.st_dev = rip->i_dev;
26069        statbuf.st_ino = rip->i_num;
26070        statbuf.st_mode = rip->i_mode;
26071        statbuf.st_nlink = rip->i_nlinks & BYTE;
26072        statbuf.st_uid = rip->i_uid;
26073        statbuf.st_gid = rip->i_gid & BYTE;
26074        statbuf.st_rdev = (dev_t) (s ? rip->i_zone[0] : NO_DEV);
26075        statbuf.st_size = rip->i_size;
26076
26077        if (rip->i_pipe == I_PIPE) {
26078                statbuf.st_mode &= ~I_REGULAR;  /* wipe out I_REGULAR bit for pipes */
26079                if (fil_ptr != NIL_FILP && fil_ptr->filp_mode & R_BIT)
26080                        statbuf.st_size -= fil_ptr->filp_pos;
26081        }
26082
26083        statbuf.st_atime = rip->i_atime;
26084        statbuf.st_mtime = rip->i_mtime;
26085        statbuf.st_ctime = rip->i_ctime;
26086
26087        /* Copy the struct to user space. */
26088        r = sys_copy(FS_PROC_NR, D, (phys_bytes) &statbuf,
26089                        who, D, (phys_bytes) user_addr, (phys_bytes) sizeof(statbuf));
26090        return(r);
26091 }
```

```
++++++++++++++++++++++++++++++++++++++++++++++++++++++++++++++++++++++++++++++++
                               src/fs/protect.c
++++++++++++++++++++++++++++++++++++++++++++++++++++++++++++++++++++++++++++++++
```

```
26100    /* This file deals with protection in the file system.  It contains the code
26101     * for four system calls that relate to protection.
26102     *
26103     * The entry points into this file are
26104     *   do_chmod:  perform the CHMOD system call
26105     *   do_chown:  perform the CHOWN system call
26106     *   do_umask:  perform the UMASK system call
26107     *   do_access: perform the ACCESS system call
26108     *   forbidden: check to see if a given access is allowed on a given inode
26109     */
26110
26111    #include "fs.h"
26112    #include <unistd.h>
26113    #include <minix/callnr.h>
26114    #include "buf.h"
26115    #include "file.h"
26116    #include "fproc.h"
26117    #include "inode.h"
26118    #include "param.h"
26119    #include "super.h"
26120
26121    /*===========================================================================*
26122     *                              do_chmod                                      *
26123     *===========================================================================*/
26124    PUBLIC int do_chmod()
```

```
26125      {
26126      /* Perform the chmod(name, mode) system call. */
26127
26128          register struct inode *rip;
26129          register int r;
26130
26131          /* Temporarily open the file. */
26132          if (fetch_name(name, name_length, M3) != OK) return(err_code);
26133          if ( (rip = eat_path(user_path)) == NIL_INODE) return(err_code);
26134
26135          /* Only the owner or the super_user may change the mode of a file.
26136           * No one may change the mode of a file on a read-only file system.
26137           */
26138          if (rip->i_uid != fp->fp_effuid && !super_user)
26139                  r = EPERM;
26140          else
26141                  r = read_only(rip);
26142
26143          /* If error, return inode. */
26144          if (r != OK)  {
26145                  put_inode(rip);
26146                  return(r);
26147          }
26148
26149          /* Now make the change. Clear setgid bit if file is not in caller's grp */
26150          rip->i_mode = (rip->i_mode & ~ALL_MODES) | (mode & ALL_MODES);
26151          if (!super_user && rip->i_gid != fp->fp_effgid)rip->i_mode &= ~I_SET_GID_BIT;
26152          rip->i_update |= CTIME;
26153          rip->i_dirt = DIRTY;
26154
26155          put_inode(rip);
26156          return(OK);
26157      }


26160      /*===========================================================================*
26161       *                              do_chown                                      *
26162       *===========================================================================*/
26163      PUBLIC int do_chown()
26164      {
26165      /* Perform the chown(name, owner, group) system call. */
26166
26167          register struct inode *rip;
26168          register int r;
26169
26170          /* Temporarily open the file. */
26171          if (fetch_name(name1, name1_length, M1) != OK) return(err_code);
26172          if ( (rip = eat_path(user_path)) == NIL_INODE) return(err_code);
26173
26174          /* Not permitted to change the owner of a file on a read-only file sys. */
26175          r = read_only(rip);
26176          if (r == OK) {
26177                  /* FS is R/W.  Whether call is allowed depends on ownership, etc. */
26178                  if (super_user) {
26179                          /* The super user can do anything. */
26180                          rip->i_uid = owner;     /* others later */
26181                  } else {
26182                          /* Regular users can only change groups of their own files. */
26183                          if (rip->i_uid != fp->fp_effuid) r = EPERM;
26184                          if (rip->i_uid != owner) r = EPERM;      /* no giving away */
```

```
26185                         if (fp->fp_effgid != group) r = EPERM;
26186                 }
26187         }
26188         if (r == OK) {
26189                 rip->i_gid = group;
26190                 rip->i_mode &= ~(I_SET_UID_BIT | I_SET_GID_BIT);
26191                 rip->i_update |= CTIME;
26192                 rip->i_dirt = DIRTY;
26193         }
26194
26195         put_inode(rip);
26196         return(r);
26197 }


26200 /*===========================================================================*
26201  *                              do_umask                                     *
26202  *===========================================================================*/
26203 PUBLIC int do_umask()
26204 {
26205 /* Perform the umask(co_mode) system call. */
26206   register mode_t r;
26207
26208   r = ~fp->fp_umask;                  /* set 'r' to complement of old mask */
26209   fp->fp_umask = ~(co_mode & RWX_MODES);
26210   return(r);                         /* return complement of old mask */
26211 }


26214 /*===========================================================================*
26215  *                              do_access                                    *
26216  *===========================================================================*/
26217 PUBLIC int do_access()
26218 {
26219 /* Perform the access(name, mode) system call. */
26220
26221   struct inode *rip;
26222   register int r;
26223
26224   /* First check to see if the mode is correct. */
26225   if ( (mode & ~(R_OK | W_OK | X_OK)) != 0 && mode != F_OK)
26226         return(EINVAL);
26227
26228   /* Temporarily open the file whose access is to be checked. */
26229   if (fetch_name(name, name_length, M3) != OK) return(err_code);
26230   if ( (rip = eat_path(user_path)) == NIL_INODE) return(err_code);
26231
26232   /* Now check the permissions. */
26233   r = forbidden(rip, (mode_t) mode);
26234   put_inode(rip);
26235   return(r);
26236 }


26239 /*===========================================================================*
26240  *                              forbidden                                    *
26241  *===========================================================================*/
26242 PUBLIC int forbidden(rip, access_desired)
26243 register struct inode *rip;      /* pointer to inode to be checked */
26244 mode_t access_desired;  /* RWX bits */
```

```
26245     {
26246     /* Given a pointer to an inode, 'rip', and the access desired, determine
26247      * if the access is allowed, and if not why not.  The routine looks up the
26248      * caller's uid in the 'fproc' table.  If access is allowed, OK is returned
26249      * if it is forbidden, EACCES is returned.
26250      */
26251
26252       register struct inode *old_rip = rip;
26253       register struct super_block *sp;
26254       register mode_t bits, perm_bits;
26255       int r, shift, test_uid, test_gid;
26256
26257       if (rip->i_mount == I_MOUNT)   /* The inode is mounted on. */
26258             for (sp = &super_block[1]; sp < &super_block[NR_SUPERS]; sp++)
26259                   if (sp->s_imount == rip) {
26260                         rip = get_inode(sp->s_dev, ROOT_INODE);
26261                         break;
26262                   } /* if */
26263
26264       /* Isolate the relevant rwx bits from the mode. */
26265       bits = rip->i_mode;
26266       test_uid = (fs_call == ACCESS ? fp->fp_realuid : fp->fp_effuid);
26267       test_gid = (fs_call == ACCESS ? fp->fp_realgid : fp->fp_effgid);
26268       if (test_uid == SU_UID) {
26269             /* Grant read and write permission.  Grant search permission for
26270              * directories.  Grant execute permission (for non-directories) if
26271              * and only if one of the 'X' bits is set.
26272              */
26273             if ( (bits & I_TYPE) == I_DIRECTORY ||
26274                 bits & ((X_BIT << 6) | (X_BIT << 3) | X_BIT))
26275                   perm_bits = R_BIT | W_BIT | X_BIT;
26276             else
26277                   perm_bits = R_BIT | W_BIT;
26278       } else {
26279             if (test_uid == rip->i_uid) shift = 6;         /* owner */
26280             else if (test_gid == rip->i_gid ) shift = 3;   /* group */
26281             else shift = 0;                                /* other */
26282             perm_bits = (bits >> shift) & (R_BIT | W_BIT | X_BIT);
26283       }
26284
26285       /* If access desired is not a subset of what is allowed, it is refused. */
26286       r = OK;
26287       if ((perm_bits | access_desired) != perm_bits) r = EACCES;
26288
26289       /* Check to see if someone is trying to write on a file system that is
26290        * mounted read-only.
26291        */
26292       if (r == OK)
26293             if (access_desired & W_BIT) r = read_only(rip);
26294
26295       if (rip != old_rip) put_inode(rip);
26296
26297       return(r);
26298     }


26301     /*===========================================================================*
26302      *                              read_only                                    *
26303      *===========================================================================*/
26304     PUBLIC int read_only(ip)
```

```
26305     struct inode *ip;                    /* ptr to inode whose file sys is to be cked */
26306     {
26307     /* Check to see if the file system on which the inode 'ip' resides is mounted
26308      * read only.  If so, return EROFS, else return OK.
26309      */
26310
26311       register struct super_block *sp;
26312
26313       sp = ip->i_sp;
26314       return(sp->s_rd_only ? EROFS : OK);
26315     }




++++++++++++++++++++++++++++++++++++++++++++++++++++++++++++++++++++++++++++++++
                              src/fs/time.c
++++++++++++++++++++++++++++++++++++++++++++++++++++++++++++++++++++++++++++++++

26400     /* This file takes care of those system calls that deal with time.
26401      *
26402      * The entry points into this file are
26403      *   do_utime:  perform the UTIME system call
26404      *   do_time:   perform the TIME system call
26405      *   do_stime:  perform the STIME system call
26406      *   do_tims:   perform the TIMES system call
26407      */
26408
26409     #include "fs.h"
26410     #include <minix/callnr.h>
26411     #include <minix/com.h>
26412     #include "file.h"
26413     #include "fproc.h"
26414     #include "inode.h"
26415     #include "param.h"
26416
26417     PRIVATE message clock_mess;
26418
26419     /*===========================================================================*
26420      *                              do_utime                                     *
26421      *===========================================================================*/
26422     PUBLIC int do_utime()
26423     {
26424     /* Perform the utime(name, timep) system call. */
26425
26426       register struct inode *rip;
26427       register int len, r;
26428
26429       /* Adjust for case of NULL 'timep'. */
26430       len = utime_length;
26431       if (len == 0) len = m.m2_i2;
26432
26433       /* Temporarily open the file. */
26434       if (fetch_name(utime_file, len, M1) != OK) return(err_code);
26435       if ( (rip = eat_path(user_path)) == NIL_INODE) return(err_code);
26436
26437       /* Only the owner of a file or the super_user can change its time. */
26438       r = OK;
26439       if (rip->i_uid != fp->fp_effuid && !super_user) r = EPERM;
```

```
26440        if (utime_length == 0 && r != OK) r = forbidden(rip, W_BIT);
26441        if (read_only(rip) != OK) r = EROFS;   /* not even su can touch if R/O */
26442        if (r == OK) {
26443                if (utime_length == 0) {
26444                        rip->i_atime = clock_time();
26445                        rip->i_mtime = rip->i_atime;
26446                } else {
26447                        rip->i_atime = utime_actime;
26448                        rip->i_mtime = utime_modtime;
26449                }
26450                rip->i_update = CTIME;   /* discard any stale ATIME and MTIME flags */
26451                rip->i_dirt = DIRTY;
26452        }
26453
26454    put_inode(rip);
26455    return(r);
26456  }


26459  /*===========================================================================*
26460   *                              do_time                                       *
26461   *===========================================================================*/
26462  PUBLIC int do_time()
26463
26464  {
26465  /* Perform the time(tp) system call. */
26466
26467    reply_l1 = clock_time();        /* return time in seconds */
26468    return(OK);
26469  }


26472  /*===========================================================================*
26473   *                              do_stime                                      *
26474   *===========================================================================*/
26475  PUBLIC int do_stime()
26476  {
26477  /* Perform the stime(tp) system call. */
26478
26479    register int k;
26480
26481    if (!super_user) return(EPERM);
26482    clock_mess.m_type = SET_TIME;
26483    clock_mess.NEW_TIME = (long) tp;
26484    if ( (k = sendrec(CLOCK, &clock_mess)) != OK) panic("do_stime error", k);
26485    return(OK);
26486  }


26489  /*===========================================================================*
26490   *                              do_tims                                       *
26491   *===========================================================================*/
26492  PUBLIC int do_tims()
26493  {
26494  /* Perform the times(buffer) system call. */
26495
26496    clock_t t[5];
26497
26498    sys_times(who, t);
26499    reply_t1 = t[0];
```

```
26500       reply_t2 = t[1];
26501       reply_t3 = t[2];
26502       reply_t4 = t[3];
26503       reply_t5 = t[4];
26504       return(OK);
26505     }
```

```
++++++++++++++++++++++++++++++++++++++++++++++++++++++++++++++++++++++++++++++++
                              src/fs/misc.c
++++++++++++++++++++++++++++++++++++++++++++++++++++++++++++++++++++++++++++++++
```

```
26600     /* This file contains a collection of miscellaneous procedures.  Some of them
26601      * perform simple system calls.  Some others do a little part of system calls
26602      * that are mostly performed by the Memory Manager.
26603      *
26604      * The entry points into this file are
26605      *   do_dup:     perform the DUP system call
26606      *   do_fcntl:   perform the FCNTL system call
26607      *   do_sync:    perform the SYNC system call
26608      *   do_fork:    adjust the tables after MM has performed a FORK system call
26609      *   do_exec:    handle files with FD_CLOEXEC on after MM has done an EXEC
26610      *   do_exit:    a process has exited; note that in the tables
26611      *   do_set:     set uid or gid for some process
26612      *   do_revive:  revive a process that was waiting for something (e.g. TTY)
26613      */
26614
26615     #include "fs.h"
26616     #include <fcntl.h>
26617     #include <unistd.h>      /* cc runs out of memory with unistd.h :-( */
26618     #include <minix/callnr.h>
26619     #include <minix/com.h>
26620     #include <minix/boot.h>
26621     #include "buf.h"
26622     #include "file.h"
26623     #include "fproc.h"
26624     #include "inode.h"
26625     #include "dev.h"
26626     #include "param.h"
26627
26628
26629     /*===========================================================================*
26630      *                              do_dup                                       *
26631      *===========================================================================*/
26632     PUBLIC int do_dup()
26633     {
26634     /* Perform the dup(fd) or dup2(fd,fd2) system call. These system calls are
26635      * obsolete.  In fact, it is not even possible to invoke them using the
26636      * current library because the library routines call fcntl().  They are
26637      * provided to permit old binary programs to continue to run.
26638      */
26639
26640       register int rfd;
26641       register struct filp *f;
26642       struct filp *dummy;
26643       int r;
26644
```

```
26645          /* Is the file descriptor valid? */
26646          rfd = fd & ~DUP_MASK;           /* kill off dup2 bit, if on */
26647          if ((f = get_filp(rfd)) == NIL_FILP) return(err_code);
26648
26649          /* Distinguish between dup and dup2. */
26650          if (fd == rfd) {                        /* bit not on */
26651                  /* dup(fd) */
26652                  if ( (r = get_fd(0, 0, &fd2, &dummy)) != OK) return(r);
26653          } else {
26654                  /* dup2(fd, fd2) */
26655                  if (fd2 < 0 || fd2 >= OPEN_MAX) return(EBADF);
26656                  if (rfd == fd2) return(fd2);    /* ignore the call: dup2(x, x) */
26657                  fd = fd2;                       /* prepare to close fd2 */
26658                  (void) do_close();        /* cannot fail */
26659          }
26660
26661          /* Success. Set up new file descriptors. */
26662          f->filp_count++;
26663          fp->fp_filp[fd2] = f;
26664          return(fd2);
26665  }
26666
26667  /*===========================================================================*
26668   *                              do_fcntl                                      *
26669   *===========================================================================*/
26670  PUBLIC int do_fcntl()
26671  {
26672  /* Perform the fcntl(fd, request, ...) system call. */
26673
26674    register struct filp *f;
26675    int new_fd, r, fl;
26676    long cloexec_mask;             /* bit map for the FD_CLOEXEC flag */
26677    long clo_value;                /* FD_CLOEXEC flag in proper position */
26678    struct filp *dummy;
26679
26680    /* Is the file descriptor valid? */
26681    if ((f = get_filp(fd)) == NIL_FILP) return(err_code);
26682
26683    switch (request) {
26684       case F_DUPFD:
26685          /* This replaces the old dup() system call. */
26686          if (addr < 0 || addr >= OPEN_MAX) return(EINVAL);
26687          if ((r = get_fd(addr, 0, &new_fd, &dummy)) != OK) return(r);
26688          f->filp_count++;
26689          fp->fp_filp[new_fd] = f;
26690          return(new_fd);
26691
26692       case F_GETFD:
26693          /* Get close-on-exec flag (FD_CLOEXEC in POSIX Table 6-2). */
26694          return( ((fp->fp_cloexec >> fd) & 01) ? FD_CLOEXEC : 0);
26695
26696       case F_SETFD:
26697          /* Set close-on-exec flag (FD_CLOEXEC in POSIX Table 6-2). */
26698          cloexec_mask = 1L << fd;        /* singleton set position ok */
26699          clo_value = (addr & FD_CLOEXEC ? cloexec_mask : 0L);
26700          fp->fp_cloexec = (fp->fp_cloexec & ~cloexec_mask) | clo_value;
26701          return(OK);
26702
26703       case F_GETFL:
26704          /* Get file status flags (O_NONBLOCK and O_APPEND). */
```

```
26705          fl = f->filp_flags & (O_NONBLOCK | O_APPEND | O_ACCMODE);
26706          return(fl);
26707
26708      case F_SETFL:
26709          /* Set file status flags (O_NONBLOCK and O_APPEND). */
26710          fl = O_NONBLOCK | O_APPEND;
26711          f->filp_flags = (f->filp_flags & ~fl) | (addr & fl);
26712          return(OK);
26713
26714      case F_GETLK:
26715      case F_SETLK:
26716      case F_SETLKW:
26717          /* Set or clear a file lock. */
26718          r = lock_op(f, request);
26719          return(r);
26720
26721      default:
26722          return(EINVAL);
26723      }
26724  }


26727  /*===========================================================================*
26728   *                              do_sync                                       *
26729   *===========================================================================*/
26730  PUBLIC int do_sync()
26731  {
26732  /* Perform the sync() system call.  Flush all the tables. */
26733
26734    register struct inode *rip;
26735    register struct buf *bp;
26736
26737    /* The order in which the various tables are flushed is critical.  The
26738     * blocks must be flushed last, since rw_inode() leaves its results in
26739     * the block cache.
26740     */
26741
26742    /* Write all the dirty inodes to the disk. */
26743    for (rip = &inode[0]; rip < &inode[NR_INODES]; rip++)
26744          if (rip->i_count > 0 && rip->i_dirt == DIRTY) rw_inode(rip, WRITING);
26745
26746    /* Write all the dirty blocks to the disk, one drive at a time. */
26747    for (bp = &buf[0]; bp < &buf[NR_BUFS]; bp++)
26748          if (bp->b_dev != NO_DEV && bp->b_dirt == DIRTY) flushall(bp->b_dev);
26749
26750    return(OK);                /* sync() can't fail */
26751  }


26754  /*===========================================================================*
26755   *                              do_fork                                       *
26756   *===========================================================================*/
26757  PUBLIC int do_fork()
26758  {
26759  /* Perform those aspects of the fork() system call that relate to files.
26760   * In particular, let the child inherit its parent's file descriptors.
26761   * The parent and child parameters tell who forked off whom. The file
26762   * system uses the same slot numbers as the kernel.  Only MM makes this call.
26763   */
26764
```

```
26765           register struct fproc *cp;
26766           int i;
26767
26768           /* Only MM may make this call directly. */
26769           if (who != MM_PROC_NR) return(EGENERIC);
26770
26771           /* Copy the parent's fproc struct to the child. */
26772           fproc[child] = fproc[parent];
26773
26774           /* Increase the counters in the 'filp' table. */
26775           cp = &fproc[child];
26776           for (i = 0; i < OPEN_MAX; i++)
26777                   if (cp->fp_filp[i] != NIL_FILP) cp->fp_filp[i]->filp_count++;
26778
26779           /* Fill in new process id. */
26780           cp->fp_pid = pid;
26781
26782           /* A child is not a process leader. */
26783           cp->fp_sesldr = 0;
26784
26785           /* Record the fact that both root and working dir have another user. */
26786           dup_inode(cp->fp_rootdir);
26787           dup_inode(cp->fp_workdir);
26788           return(OK);
26789   }


26792   /*===========================================================================*
26793    *                              do_exec                                       *
26794    *===========================================================================*/
26795   PUBLIC int do_exec()
26796   {
26797   /* Files can be marked with the FD_CLOEXEC bit (in fp->fp_cloexec).  When
26798    * MM does an EXEC, it calls FS to allow FS to find these files and close them.
26799    */
26800
26801     register int i;
26802     long bitmap;
26803
26804     /* Only MM may make this call directly. */
26805     if (who != MM_PROC_NR) return(EGENERIC);
26806
26807     /* The array of FD_CLOEXEC bits is in the fp_cloexec bit map. */
26808     fp = &fproc[slot1];             /* get_filp() needs 'fp' */
26809     bitmap = fp->fp_cloexec;
26810     if (bitmap == 0) return(OK);  /* normal case, no FD_CLOEXECs */
26811
26812     /* Check the file desriptors one by one for presence of FD_CLOEXEC. */
26813     for (i = 0; i < OPEN_MAX; i++) {
26814           fd = i;
26815           if ( (bitmap >> i) & 01) (void) do_close();
26816     }
26817
26818     return(OK);
26819   }


26822   /*===========================================================================*
26823    *                              do_exit                                       *
26824    *===========================================================================*/
```

```
26825   PUBLIC int do_exit()
26826   {
26827   /* Perform the file system portion of the exit(status) system call. */
26828
26829     register int i, exitee, task;
26830     register struct fproc *rfp;
26831     register struct filp *rfilp;
26832     register struct inode *rip;
26833     int major;
26834     dev_t dev;
26835     message dev_mess;
26836
26837     /* Only MM may do the EXIT call directly. */
26838     if (who != MM_PROC_NR) return(EGENERIC);
26839
26840     /* Nevertheless, pretend that the call came from the user. */
26841     fp = &fproc[slot1];              /* get_filp() needs 'fp' */
26842     exitee = slot1;
26843
26844     if (fp->fp_suspended == SUSPENDED) {
26845           task = -fp->fp_task;
26846           if (task == XPIPE || task == XPOPEN) susp_count--;
26847           pro = exitee;
26848           (void) do_unpause();     /* this always succeeds for MM */
26849           fp->fp_suspended = NOT_SUSPENDED;
26850     }
26851
26852     /* Loop on file descriptors, closing any that are open. */
26853     for (i = 0; i < OPEN_MAX; i++) {
26854           fd = i;
26855           (void) do_close();
26856     }
26857
26858     /* Release root and working directories. */
26859     put_inode(fp->fp_rootdir);
26860     put_inode(fp->fp_workdir);
26861     fp->fp_rootdir = NIL_INODE;
26862     fp->fp_workdir = NIL_INODE;
26863
26864     /* If a session leader exits then revoke access to its controlling tty from
26865      * all other processes using it.
26866      */
26867     if (!fp->fp_sesldr) return(OK);              /* not a session leader */
26868     fp->fp_sesldr = FALSE;
26869     if (fp->fp_tty == 0) return(OK);              /* no controlling tty */
26870     dev = fp->fp_tty;
26871
26872     for (rfp = &fproc[LOW_USER]; rfp < &fproc[NR_PROCS]; rfp++) {
26873           if (rfp->fp_tty == dev) rfp->fp_tty = 0;
26874
26875           for (i = 0; i < OPEN_MAX; i++) {
26876                 if ((rfilp = rfp->fp_filp[i]) == NIL_FILP) continue;
26877                 if (rfilp->filp_mode == FILP_CLOSED) continue;
26878                 rip = rfilp->filp_ino;
26879                 if ((rip->i_mode & I_TYPE) != I_CHAR_SPECIAL) continue;
26880                 if ((dev_t) rip->i_zone[0] != dev) continue;
26881                 dev_mess.m_type = DEV_CLOSE;
26882                 dev_mess.DEVICE = dev;
26883                 major = (dev >> MAJOR) & BYTE;  /* major device nr */
26884                 task = dmap[major].dmap_task;  /* device task nr */
```

```
26885                           (*dmap[major].dmap_close)(task, &dev_mess);
26886                           rfilp->filp_mode = FILP_CLOSED;
26887                   }
26888           }
26889           return(OK);
26890   }


26893   /*===========================================================================*
26894    *                              do_set                                       *
26895    *===========================================================================*/
26896   PUBLIC int do_set()
26897   {
26898   /* Set uid_t or gid_t field. */
26899
26900     register struct fproc *tfp;
26901
26902     /* Only MM may make this call directly. */
26903     if (who != MM_PROC_NR) return(EGENERIC);
26904
26905     tfp = &fproc[slot1];
26906     if (fs_call == SETUID) {
26907           tfp->fp_realuid = (uid_t) real_user_id;
26908           tfp->fp_effuid =  (uid_t) eff_user_id;
26909     }
26910     if (fs_call == SETGID) {
26911           tfp->fp_effgid =  (gid_t) eff_grp_id;
26912           tfp->fp_realgid = (gid_t) real_grp_id;
26913     }
26914     return(OK);
26915   }


26918   /*===========================================================================*
26919    *                              do_revive                                    *
26920    *===========================================================================*/
26921   PUBLIC int do_revive()
26922   {
26923   /* A task, typically TTY, has now gotten the characters that were needed for a
26924    * previous read.  The process did not get a reply when it made the call.
26925    * Instead it was suspended.  Now we can send the reply to wake it up.  This
26926    * business has to be done carefully, since the incoming message is from
26927    * a task (to which no reply can be sent), and the reply must go to a process
26928    * that blocked earlier.  The reply to the caller is inhibited by setting the
26929    * 'dont_reply' flag, and the reply to the blocked process is done explicitly
26930    * in revive().
26931    */
26932
26933   #if !ALLOW_USER_SEND
26934     if (who >= LOW_USER) return(EPERM);
26935   #endif
26936
26937     revive(m.REP_PROC_NR, m.REP_STATUS);
26938     dont_reply = TRUE;              /* don't reply to the TTY task */
26939     return(OK);
26940   }
```

```
+++++++++++++++++++++++++++++++++++++++++++++++++++++++++++++++++++++++++++++
                              src/fs/device.c
+++++++++++++++++++++++++++++++++++++++++++++++++++++++++++++++++++++++++++++
27000   /* When a needed block is not in the cache, it must be fetched from the disk.
27001    * Special character files also require I/O.  The routines for these are here.
27002    *
27003    * The entry points in this file are:
27004    *   dev_io:     perform a read or write on a block or character device
27005    *   dev_opcl:   perform generic device-specific processing for open & close
27006    *   tty_open:   perform tty-specific processing for open
27007    *   ctty_open:  perform controlling-tty-specific processing for open
27008    *   ctty_close: perform controlling-tty-specific processing for close
27009    *   do_setsid:  perform the SETSID system call (FS side)
27010    *   do_ioctl:   perform the IOCTL system call
27011    *   call_task:  procedure that actually calls the kernel tasks
27012    *   call_ctty:  procedure that actually calls task for /dev/tty
27013    */
27014
27015   #include "fs.h"
27016   #include <fcntl.h>
27017   #include <minix/callnr.h>
27018   #include <minix/com.h>
27019   #include "dev.h"
27020   #include "file.h"
27021   #include "fproc.h"
27022   #include "inode.h"
27023   #include "param.h"
27024
27025   PRIVATE message dev_mess;
27026   PRIVATE major, minor, task;
27027
27028   FORWARD _PROTOTYPE( void find_dev, (Dev_t dev)                         );
27029
27030   /*===========================================================================*
27031    *                              dev_io                                       *
27032    *===========================================================================*/
27033   PUBLIC int dev_io(op, nonblock, dev, pos, bytes, proc, buff)
27034   int op;                         /* DEV_READ, DEV_WRITE, DEV_IOCTL, etc. */
27035   int nonblock;                   /* TRUE if nonblocking op */
27036   dev_t dev;                      /* major-minor device number */
27037   off_t pos;                      /* byte position */
27038   int bytes;                      /* how many bytes to transfer */
27039   int proc;                       /* in whose address space is buff? */
27040   char *buff;                     /* virtual address of the buffer */
27041   {
27042   /* Read or write from a device.  The parameter 'dev' tells which one. */
27043
27044      find_dev(dev);               /* load the variables major, minor, and task */
27045
27046      /* Set up the message passed to task. */
27047      dev_mess.m_type    = op;
27048      dev_mess.DEVICE    = (dev >> MINOR) & BYTE;
27049      dev_mess.POSITION  = pos;
27050      dev_mess.PROC_NR   = proc;
27051      dev_mess.ADDRESS   = buff;
27052      dev_mess.COUNT     = bytes;
27053      dev_mess.TTY_FLAGS = nonblock; /* temporary kludge */
27054
```

```
27055        /* Call the task. */
27056        (*dmap[major].dmap_rw)(task, &dev_mess);
27057
27058        /* Task has completed.  See if call completed. */
27059        if (dev_mess.REP_STATUS == SUSPEND) {
27060                if (op == DEV_OPEN) task = XPOPEN;
27061                suspend(task);              /* suspend user */
27062        }
27063
27064        return(dev_mess.REP_STATUS);
27065   }


27068   /*===========================================================================*
27069    *                              dev_opcl                                      *
27070    *===========================================================================*/
27071   PUBLIC void dev_opcl(task_nr, mess_ptr)
27072   int task_nr;                            /* which task */
27073   message *mess_ptr;                      /* message pointer */
27074   {
27075   /* Called from the dmap struct in table.c on opens & closes of special files.*/
27076
27077      int op;
27078
27079      op = mess_ptr->m_type;               /* save DEV_OPEN or DEV_CLOSE for later */
27080      mess_ptr->DEVICE = (mess_ptr->DEVICE >> MINOR) & BYTE;
27081      mess_ptr->PROC_NR = fp - fproc;
27082
27083      call_task(task_nr, mess_ptr);
27084
27085      /* Task has completed.  See if call completed. */
27086      if (mess_ptr->REP_STATUS == SUSPEND) {
27087                if (op == DEV_OPEN) task_nr = XPOPEN;
27088                suspend(task_nr);           /* suspend user */
27089      }
27090   }

27092   /*===========================================================================*
27093    *                              tty_open                                      *
27094    *===========================================================================*/
27095   PUBLIC void tty_open(task_nr, mess_ptr)
27096   int task_nr;
27097   message *mess_ptr;
27098   {
27099   /* This procedure is called from the dmap struct in table.c on tty opens. */
27100
27101      int r;
27102      dev_t dev;
27103      int flags, proc;
27104      register struct fproc *rfp;
27105
27106      dev = (dev_t) mess_ptr->DEVICE;
27107      flags = mess_ptr->COUNT;
27108      proc = fp - fproc;
27109
27110      /* Add O_NOCTTY to the flags if this process is not a session leader, or
27111       * if it already has a controlling tty, or if it is someone elses
27112       * controlling tty.
27113       */
27114      if (!fp->fp_sesldr || fp->fp_tty != 0) {
```

```
27115                flags |= O_NOCTTY;
27116         } else {
27117                for (rfp = &fproc[LOW_USER]; rfp < &fproc[NR_PROCS]; rfp++) {
27118                      if (rfp->fp_tty == dev) flags |= O_NOCTTY;
27119                }
27120         }
27121
27122         r = dev_io(DEV_OPEN, mode, dev, (off_t) 0, flags, proc, NIL_PTR);
27123
27124         if (r == 1) {
27125                fp->fp_tty = dev;
27126                r = OK;
27127         }
27128
27129         mess_ptr->REP_STATUS = r;
27130    }


27133    /*===========================================================================*
27134     *                              ctty_open                                    *
27135     *===========================================================================*/
27136    PUBLIC void ctty_open(task_nr, mess_ptr)
27137    int task_nr;
27138    message *mess_ptr;
27139    {
27140    /* This procedure is called from the dmap struct in table.c on opening
27141     * /dev/tty, the magic device that translates to the controlling tty.
27142     */
27143
27144         mess_ptr->REP_STATUS = fp->fp_tty == 0 ? ENXIO : OK;
27145    }


27148    /*===========================================================================*
27149     *                              ctty_close                                   *
27150     *===========================================================================*/
27151    PUBLIC void ctty_close(task_nr, mess_ptr)
27152    int task_nr;
27153    message *mess_ptr;
27154    {
27155    /* Close /dev/tty. */
27156
27157         mess_ptr->REP_STATUS = OK;
27158    }


27161    /*===========================================================================*
27162     *                              do_setsid                                    *
27163     *===========================================================================*/
27164    PUBLIC int do_setsid()
27165    {
27166    /* Perform the FS side of the SETSID call, i.e. get rid of the controlling
27167     * terminal of a process, and make the process a session leader.
27168     */
27169      register struct fproc *rfp;
27170
27171      /* Only MM may do the SETSID call directly. */
27172      if (who != MM_PROC_NR) return(ENOSYS);
27173
27174      /* Make the process a session leader with no controlling tty. */
```

```
27175        rfp = &fproc[slot1];
27176        rfp->fp_sesldr = TRUE;
27177        rfp->fp_tty = 0;
27178    }


27181    /*===========================================================================*
27182     *                              do_ioctl                                      *
27183     *===========================================================================*/
27184    PUBLIC int do_ioctl()
27185    {
27186    /* Perform the ioctl(ls_fd, request, argx) system call (uses m2 fmt). */
27187
27188      struct filp *f;
27189      register struct inode *rip;
27190      dev_t dev;
27191
27192      if ( (f = get_filp(ls_fd)) == NIL_FILP) return(err_code);
27193      rip = f->filp_ino;              /* get inode pointer */
27194      if ( (rip->i_mode & I_TYPE) != I_CHAR_SPECIAL
27195          && (rip->i_mode & I_TYPE) != I_BLOCK_SPECIAL) return(ENOTTY);
27196      dev = (dev_t) rip->i_zone[0];
27197      find_dev(dev);
27198
27199      dev_mess= m;
27200
27201      dev_mess.m_type = DEV_IOCTL;
27202      dev_mess.PROC_NR = who;
27203      dev_mess.TTY_LINE = minor;
27204
27205      /* Call the task. */
27206      (*dmap[major].dmap_rw)(task, &dev_mess);
27207
27208      /* Task has completed.  See if call completed. */
27209      if (dev_mess.REP_STATUS == SUSPEND) {
27210          if (f->filp_flags & O_NONBLOCK) {
27211                  /* Not supposed to block. */
27212                  dev_mess.m_type = CANCEL;
27213                  dev_mess.PROC_NR = who;
27214                  dev_mess.TTY_LINE = minor;
27215                  (*dmap[major].dmap_rw)(task, &dev_mess);
27216                  if (dev_mess.REP_STATUS == EINTR) dev_mess.REP_STATUS = EAGAIN;
27217          } else {
27218                  suspend(task);              /* User must be suspended. */
27219          }
27220      }
27221      return(dev_mess.REP_STATUS);
27222    }


27225    /*===========================================================================*
27226     *                              find_dev                                      *
27227     *===========================================================================*/
27228    PRIVATE void find_dev(dev)
27229    dev_t dev;                        /* device */
27230    {
27231    /* Extract the major and minor device number from the parameter. */
27232
27233      major = (dev >> MAJOR) & BYTE;          /* major device number */
27234      minor = (dev >> MINOR) & BYTE;          /* minor device number */
```

```
27235        if (major >= max_major) {
27236                major = minor = 0;                /* will fail with ENODEV */
27237        }
27238        task = dmap[major].dmap_task; /* which task services the device */
27239      }


27242    /*===========================================================================*
27243     *                              call_task                                    *
27244     *===========================================================================*/
27245    PUBLIC void call_task(task_nr, mess_ptr)
27246    int task_nr;                       /* which task to call */
27247    message *mess_ptr;                 /* pointer to message for task */
27248    {
27249    /* All file system I/O ultimately comes down to I/O on major/minor device
27250     * pairs.  These lead to calls on the following routines via the dmap table.
27251     */
27252
27253      int r, proc_nr;
27254      message local_m;
27255
27256      proc_nr = mess_ptr->PROC_NR;
27257
27258      while ((r = sendrec(task_nr, mess_ptr)) == ELOCKED) {
27259            /* sendrec() failed to avoid deadlock. The task 'task_nr' is
27260             * trying to send a REVIVE message for an earlier request.
27261             * Handle it and go try again.
27262             */
27263            if ((r = receive(task_nr, &local_m)) != OK) break;
27264
27265            /* If we're trying to send a cancel message to a task which has just
27266             * sent a completion reply, ignore the reply and abort the cancel
27267             * request. The caller will do the revive for the process.
27268             */
27269            if (mess_ptr->m_type == CANCEL && local_m.REP_PROC_NR == proc_nr)
27270                   return;
27271
27272            /* Otherwise it should be a REVIVE. */
27273            if (local_m.m_type != REVIVE) {
27274                   printf(
27275                   "fs: strange device reply from %d, type = %d, proc = %d\n",
27276                           local_m.m_source,
27277                           local_m.m_type, local_m.REP_PROC_NR);
27278                   continue;
27279            }
27280
27281            revive(local_m.REP_PROC_NR, local_m.REP_STATUS);
27282      }
27283
27284      /* The message received may be a reply to this call, or a REVIVE for some
27285       * other process.
27286       */
27287      for (;;) {
27288            if (r != OK) panic("call_task: can't send/receive", NO_NUM);
27289
27290            /* Did the process we did the sendrec() for get a result? */
27291            if (mess_ptr->REP_PROC_NR == proc_nr) break;
27292
27293            /* Otherwise it should be a REVIVE. */
27294            if (mess_ptr->m_type != REVIVE) {
```

```
27295                      printf(
27296                      "fs: strange device reply from %d, type = %d, proc = %d\n",
27297                              mess_ptr->m_source,
27298                              mess_ptr->m_type, mess_ptr->REP_PROC_NR);
27299                      continue;
27300              }
27301          revive(mess_ptr->REP_PROC_NR, mess_ptr->REP_STATUS);
27302
27303          r = receive(task_nr, mess_ptr);
27304      }
27305  }


27308  /*===========================================================================*
27309   *                              call_ctty                                    *
27310   *===========================================================================*/
27311  PUBLIC void call_ctty(task_nr, mess_ptr)
27312  int task_nr;                       /* not used - for compatibility with dmap_t */
27313  message *mess_ptr;                 /* pointer to message for task */
27314  {
27315  /* This routine is only called for one device, namely /dev/tty.  Its job
27316   * is to change the message to use the controlling terminal, instead of the
27317   * major/minor pair for /dev/tty itself.
27318   */
27319
27320    int major_device;
27321
27322    if (fp->fp_tty == 0) {
27323          /* No controlling tty present anymore, return an I/O error. */
27324          mess_ptr->REP_STATUS = EIO;
27325          return;
27326    }
27327    major_device = (fp->fp_tty >> MAJOR) & BYTE;
27328    task_nr = dmap[major_device].dmap_task;          /* task for controlling tty */
27329    mess_ptr->DEVICE = (fp->fp_tty >> MINOR) & BYTE;
27330    call_task(task_nr, mess_ptr);
27331  }


27334  /*===========================================================================*
27335   *                              no_dev                                       *
27336   *===========================================================================*/
27337  PUBLIC void no_dev(task_nr, m_ptr)
27338  int task_nr;                       /* not used - for compatibility with dmap_t */
27339  message *m_ptr;                    /* message pointer */
27340  {
27341  /* No device there. */
27342
27343    m_ptr->REP_STATUS = ENODEV;
27344  }
```

```
++++++++++++++++++++++++++++++++++++++++++++++++++++++++++++++++++++++++++++++
                                src/fs/utility.c
++++++++++++++++++++++++++++++++++++++++++++++++++++++++++++++++++++++++++++++
27400    /* This file contains a few general purpose utility routines.
27401     *
27402     * The entry points into this file are
27403     *   clock_time:  ask the clock task for the real time
27404     *   copy:        copy a block of data
27405     *   fetch_name:  go get a path name from user space
27406     *   no_sys:      reject a system call that FS does not handle
27407     *   panic:       something awful has occurred;  MINIX cannot continue
27408     *   conv2:       do byte swapping on a 16-bit int
27409     *   conv4:       do byte swapping on a 32-bit long
27410     */
27411
27412    #include "fs.h"
27413    #include <minix/com.h>
27414    #include <minix/boot.h>
27415    #include <unistd.h>
27416    #include "buf.h"
27417    #include "file.h"
27418    #include "fproc.h"
27419    #include "inode.h"
27420    #include "param.h"
27421
27422    PRIVATE int panicking;              /* inhibits recursive panics during sync */
27423    PRIVATE message clock_mess;
27424
27425    /*===========================================================================*
27426     *                              clock_time                                    *
27427     *===========================================================================*/
27428    PUBLIC time_t clock_time()
27429    {
27430    /* This routine returns the time in seconds since 1.1.1970.  MINIX is an
27431     * astrophysically naive system that assumes the earth rotates at a constant
27432     * rate and that such things as leap seconds do not exist.
27433     */
27434
27435      register int k;
27436
27437      clock_mess.m_type = GET_TIME;
27438      if ( (k = sendrec(CLOCK, &clock_mess)) != OK) panic("clock_time err", k);
27439
27440      return( (time_t) clock_mess.NEW_TIME);
27441    }
27442
27443
27444    /*===========================================================================*
27445     *                              fetch_name                                    *
27446     *===========================================================================*/
27447    PUBLIC int fetch_name(path, len, flag)
27448    char *path;                         /* pointer to the path in user space */
27449    int len;                            /* path length, including 0 byte */
27450    int flag;                           /* M3 means path may be in message */
27451    {
27452    /* Go get path and put it in 'user_path'.
27453     * If 'flag' = M3 and 'len' <= M3_STRING, the path is present in 'message'.
27454     * If it is not, go copy it from user space.
```

```
27455      */
27456
27457      register char *rpu, *rpm;
27458      int r;
27459
27460      /* Check name length for validity. */
27461      if (len <= 0) {
27462            err_code = EINVAL;
27463            return(EGENERIC);
27464      }
27465
27466      if (len > PATH_MAX) {
27467            err_code = ENAMETOOLONG;
27468            return(EGENERIC);
27469      }
27470
27471      if (flag == M3 && len <= M3_STRING) {
27472            /* Just copy the path from the message to 'user_path'. */
27473            rpu = &user_path[0];
27474            rpm = pathname;          /* contained in input message */
27475            do { *rpu++ = *rpm++; } while (--len);
27476            r = OK;
27477      } else {
27478            /* String is not contained in the message.  Get it from user space. */
27479            r = sys_copy(who, D, (phys_bytes) path,
27480                  FS_PROC_NR, D, (phys_bytes) user_path, (phys_bytes) len);
27481      }
27482      return(r);
27483    }


27486    /*===========================================================================*
27487     *                              no_sys                                       *
27488     *===========================================================================*/
27489    PUBLIC int no_sys()
27490    {
27491    /* Somebody has used an illegal system call number */
27492
27493      return(EINVAL);
27494    }


27497    /*===========================================================================*
27498     *                              panic                                        *
27499     *===========================================================================*/
27500    PUBLIC void panic(format, num)
27501    char *format;                    /* format string */
27502    int num;                         /* number to go with format string */
27503    {
27504    /* Something awful has happened.  Panics are caused when an internal
27505     * inconsistency is detected, e.g., a programming error or illegal value of a
27506     * defined constant.
27507     */
27508
27509      if (panicking) return;         /* do not panic during a sync */
27510      panicking = TRUE;              /* prevent another panic during the sync */
27511      printf("File system panic: %s ", format);
27512      if (num != NO_NUM) printf("%d",num);
27513      printf("\n");
27514      (void) do_sync();              /* flush everything to the disk */
```

```
27515       sys_abort(RBT_PANIC);
27516   }


27519   /*===========================================================================*
27520    *                              conv2                                    *
27521    *===========================================================================*/
27522   PUBLIC unsigned conv2(norm, w)
27523   int norm;                       /* TRUE if no swap, FALSE for byte swap */
27524   int w;                          /* promotion of 16-bit word to be swapped */
27525   {
27526   /* Possibly swap a 16-bit word between 8086 and 68000 byte order. */
27527
27528       if (norm) return( (unsigned) w & 0xFFFF);
27529       return( ((w&BYTE) << 8) | ( (w>>8) & BYTE));
27530   }


27533   /*===========================================================================*
27534    *                              conv4                                    *
27535    *===========================================================================*/
27536   PUBLIC long conv4(norm, x)
27537   int norm;                       /* TRUE if no swap, FALSE for byte swap */
27538   long x;                         /* 32-bit long to be byte swapped */
27539   {
27540   /* Possibly swap a 32-bit long between 8086 and 68000 byte order. */
27541
27542       unsigned lo, hi;
27543       long l;
27544
27545       if (norm) return(x);                      /* byte order was already ok */
27546       lo = conv2(FALSE, (int) x & 0xFFFF); /* low-order half, byte swapped */
27547       hi = conv2(FALSE, (int) (x>>16) & 0xFFFF);   /* high-order half, swapped */
27548       l = ( (long) lo <<16) | hi;
27549       return(l);
27550   }




++++++++++++++++++++++++++++++++++++++++++++++++++++++++++++++++++++++++++++++++++++
                                  src/fs/putk.c
++++++++++++++++++++++++++++++++++++++++++++++++++++++++++++++++++++++++++++++++++++

27600   /* FS must occasionally print some message.  It uses the standard library
27601    * routine prink().  (The name "printf" is really a macro defined as "printk").
27602    * Printing is done by calling the TTY task directly, not going through FS.
27603    */
27604
27605   #include "fs.h"
27606   #include <minix/com.h>
27607
27608   #define BUF_SIZE        100   /* print buffer size */
27609
27610   PRIVATE int buf_count;              /* # characters in the buffer */
27611   PRIVATE char print_buf[BUF_SIZE];       /* output is buffered here */
27612   PRIVATE message putch_msg;       /* used for message to TTY task */
27613
27614   FORWARD _PROTOTYPE( void flush, (void)                               );
```

```
27615
27616     /*===========================================================================*
27617      *                              putk                                         *
27618      *===========================================================================*/
27619     PUBLIC void putk(c)
27620     int c;
27621     {
27622     /* Accumulate another character.  If 0 or buffer full, print it. */
27623
27624       if (c == 0 || buf_count == BUF_SIZE) flush();
27625       if (c == '\n') putk('\r');
27626       if (c != 0) print_buf[buf_count++] = c;
27627     }


27630     /*===========================================================================*
27631      *                              flush                                        *
27632      *===========================================================================*/
27633     PRIVATE void flush()
27634     {
27635     /* Flush the print buffer by calling TTY task. */
27636
27637
27638       if (buf_count == 0) return;
27639       putch_msg.m_type = DEV_WRITE;
27640       putch_msg.PROC_NR  = 1;
27641       putch_msg.TTY_LINE = 0;
27642       putch_msg.ADDRESS  = print_buf;
27643       putch_msg.COUNT = buf_count;
27644       call_task(TTY, &putch_msg);
27645       buf_count = 0;
27646     }
```

```
++++++++++++++++++++++++++++++++++++++++++++++++++++++++++++++++++++++++++++++++++
                              ./end_of_list
++++++++++++++++++++++++++++++++++++++++++++++++++++++++++++++++++++++++++++++++++
```

APPENDIX B

INDEX TO FILES

B

INDEX TO FILES

APPENDIX C

INDEX TO SYMBOLS

C

INDEX TO SYMBOLS

B110	1188	#define	CDIOPLAYTI	1903	#define	CNMIN	3855	#define
B115200	1266	#define	CDIOREADSUBCH	1907	#define	COLOR_BASE	13628	#define
B1200	1194	#define	CDIOREADTOC	1906	#define	COLOR_SIZE	13630	#define
B134	1189	#define	CDIOREADTOCHD	1905	#define	CONFORMING	5284	#define
B150	1190	#define	CDIORESUME	1910	#define	CONSOLE	13037	#define
B1800	1195	#define	CDIOSTOP	1908	#define	CONS_MINOR	11760	#define
B19200	1199	#define	CDOWN	3849	#define	CONS_RAM_WORD	13636	#define
B200	1191	#define	CDROM	3574	#define	COPROC_ERR_VE	5304	#define
B2400	1196	#define	CDROM_STACK	5666	#define	COPROC_NOT_VE	5252	#define
B300	1192	#define	CEND	3847	#define	COPROC_SEG_VE	5254	#define
B38400	1200	#define	CF1	3893	#define	COPY_BYTES	3677	#define
B4800	1197	#define	CF10	3902	#define	CORE_MODE	17832	#define
B50	1186	#define	CF11	3903	#define	COUNT	3650	#define
B57600	1265	#define	CF12	3904	#define	COUNTER_FREQ	11057	#define
B600	1193	#define	CF2	3894	#define	CPGDN	3853	#define
B75	1187	#define	CF3	3895	#define	CPGUP	3852	#define
B9600	1198	#define	CF4	3896	#define	CPLUS	3856	#define
BADMAG	1428	#define	CF5	3897	#define	CPVEC_NR	2922	#define
BASE_HIGH_SHI	5311	#define	CF6	3898	#define	CREAD	1141	#define
BASE_MIDDLE_S	5274	#define	CF7	3899	#define	CREAT	3409	#define
BEEP_FREQ	13649	#define	CF8	3900	#define	CRIGHT	3851	#define
BEG_PROC_ADDR	5163	#define	CF9	3901	#define	CS5	1143	#define
BEG_SERV_ADDR	5166	#define	CHAR_BIT	109	#define	CS6	1144	#define
BEG_USER_ADDR	5167	#define	CHAR_MAX	111	#define	CS7	1145	#define
BIG	5324	#define	CHAR_MIN	110	#define	CS8	1146	#define
BIOS_IRQ0_VEC	4349	#define	CHDIR	3413	#define	CSIZE	1142	#define
BIOS_IRQ8_VEC	4350	#define	CHILD_MAX	166	#define	CSTOPB	1147	#define
BIOS_VECTOR	4368	#define	CHILD_STIME	3683	#define	CS_INDEX	5213	#define
BITCHUNK_BITS	21920	#define	CHILD_UTIME	3682	#define	CS_LDT_INDEX	5239	#define
BITMAP_CHUNKS	19567	#define	CHIP	2778	#define	CS_SELECTOR	5229	#define
BITS_PER_BLOC	21921	#define	CHIP	2773	#define	CTIME	19551	#define
BLANK_COLOR	13632	#define	CHIP	2763	#define	CTL_EIGHTHEAD	10168	#define
BLANK_MEM	13635	#define	CHMOD	3416	#define	CTL_INTDISABL	10170	#define
BLOCKS_MINIMU	23820	#define	CHOME	3846	#define	CTL_NOECC	10167	#define
BLOCK_SIZE	2915	#define	CHOWN	3417	#define	CTL_NORETRY	10166	#define
BMS	2715	#define	CHROOT	3448	#define	CTL_RESET	10169	#define
BOOT_BLOCK	19560	#define	CINSRT	3857	#define	CTRL	3811	#define
BOOT_TICKS	3684	#define	CLEAN	19548	#define	CUP	3848	#define
BOTH	3503	#define	CLEFT	3850	#define	CURSOR	13646	#define
BOUNDS_VECTOR	5250	#define	CLICK_SHIFT	2959	#define	C_6845	13641	#define
BREAKPOINT_VE	4337	#define	CLICK_SHIFT	2964	#define	C_EXT	1506	#define
BRK	3418	#define	CLICK_SIZE	2963	#define	C_NULL	1505	#define
BRKINT	1124	#define	CLICK_SIZE	2958	#define	C_STAT	1507	#define
BUF_EXTRA	9132	#define	CLOCAL	1140	#define	CopyMess	6932	#define
BUF_SIZE	27608	#define	CLOCK	3602	#define	D	2928	#define
BUF_SIZE	19309	#define	CLOCK_ACK_BIT	11064	#define	DATA	13644	#define
BUSY_286_TSS	5294	#define	CLOCK_INT	3610	#define	DATA_CHANGED	17622	#define
BYTE	2941	#define	CLOCK_IRQ	4356	#define	DEAF	10209	#define
BYTE_GRAN_MAX	5312	#define	CLOCK_PROC_NR	3644	#define	DEBUG_VECTOR	4335	#define
BYTE_SWAP	19554	#define	CLOCK_STACK	5672	#define	DEFAULT	5323	#define
B_TIME	13650	#define	CLOSE	3407	#define	DELETE	19545	#define
C	3805	#define	CMD_DIAG	10162	#define	DELTA_TICKS	3641	#define
CA	3807	#define	CMD_FORMAT	10160	#define	DEL_SCAN	13036	#define
CALL_286_GATE	5295	#define	CMD_IDLE	10155	#define	DESC_386_BIT	5318	#define
CALOCK	3860	#define	CMD_READ	10157	#define	DESC_ACCESS	5267	#define
CANCEL	3519	#define	CMD_READVERIF	10159	#define	DESC_BASE	5265	#define
CASCADE_IRQ	4358	#define	CMD_RECALIBRA	10156	#define	DESC_BASE_HIG	5308	#define
CBHD	2717	#define	CMD_SEEK	10161	#define	DESC_BASE_MID	5266	#define
CDIOEJECT	1911	#define	CMD_SPECIFY	10163	#define	DESC_GRANULAR	5307	#define
CDIOPAUSE	1909	#define	CMD_WRITE	10158	#define	DESC_SIZE	5268	#define
CDIOPLAYMSS	1904	#define	CMID	3854	#define	DEVICE	3648	#define

INDEX

INDEX